A comprehensive economic history of the Netherlands during its rise to European economic leadership, Golden Age, and subsequent decline (1500–1815), which argues that the Dutch economy was the first modern economy. The authors defend their position with detailed analyses using simple economic theory of its major economic sectors: agriculture, fishing, trade, industry, and finance, as well as investigations of its social structure and macro-economic performance. The Dutch pioneered several aspects of economic modernization: a highly productive agriculture, a technically advanced industry, modern public finance, the capital market, and the modern corporation – the Dutch East India Company. Dutch economic history is placed in its European and world context. Comparisons are made with other European countries, and Dutch intercontinental and colonial trade are discussed fully. Special emphasis is placed on the environmental context of economic growth and later decline, as well as on demographic developments. The authors also argue that the Dutch model of development and stagnation is applicable to currently maturing economies.

The First Modern Economy

The First
Modern Economy

Success, failure, and perseverance
of the Dutch economy, 1500–1815

JAN DE VRIES
University of California, Berkeley

AD VAN DER WOUDE
Agricultural University, Wageningen

CAMBRIDGE
UNIVERSITY PRESS

PUBLISHED BY THE PRESS SYNDICATE OF THE UNIVERSITY OF CAMBRIDGE
The Pitt Building, Trumpington Street, Cambridge CB2 1RP, United Kingdom

CAMBRIDGE UNIVERSITY PRESS
The Edinburgh Building, Cambridge CB2 2RU, United Kingdom
40 West 20th Street, New York, NY 10011-4211, USA
10 Stamford Road, Oakleigh, Melbourne 3166, Australia

© Cambridge University Press 1997

Originally published in Dutch as *Nederland 1500–1815: De Eerste
Ronde van Moderne Economische Groei* by Uitgeverij Balans, 1995

First published in English by Cambridge University Press 1997

Printed in the United States of America

Typeset in Bembo

Library of Congress Cataloging-in-Publication Data
Vries, J. de (Jan)
The first modern economy : success, failure, and perseverance of
the Dutch economy, 1500–1815 / Jan de Vries, Ad van der Woude.
p.   cm.
Includes bibliographical references and index.
ISBN 0-521-57061-1 (hardcover). − ISBN 0-521-57825-6 (pbk.)
1. Netherlands − Economic conditions.   I. Woude, Ad van der.
HC324.V72   1996   96-3298
330.9492 − dc20   CIP

A catalog record for this book is available from the British Library.

ISBN 0 521 57061 1 hardback
ISBN 0 521 57825 6 paperback

Contents

Tables, figures, and maps

Tables

Figures

xvi

Maps

Preface

It is now many years ago that the two of us, sitting in Ad van der Woude's back yard on a pleasant summer evening, decided that the time was ripe to write a new economic history of the Dutch Republic. A compact survey of this dramatic history was what we professed to have in mind – an accessible interpretation of the Republic's economic rise and decline, useful to scholars, students, and lay persons alike.

What we now present to the reading public is a book that aspires to much more. In the course of preparing a survey of Dutch economic history, we came to realize more clearly than before that what is really needed is an interpretation – a study that synthesizes the accumulated mass of detailed research, provides a comprehensive account of this complex economy, and situates it firmly in its European historical context and in an economic theoretical framework. And only in the process of struggling with these challenges did we come to appreciate fully the modernity of the Dutch economy – that is, the necessity of interpreting its successes and failures in terms normally reserved for economies of today and the recent past. Researching and writing this book, then, has been a voyage of discovery – a longer voyage, but also a far more rewarding one than either of us expected at the time of embarkation.

Much of this book was written during our joint stays at the Netherlands Institute for Advanced Study (NIAS) in Wassenaar, the Netherlands, and at the Getty Center for the History of Art and the Humanities in Santa Monica, California. It is not too much to say that this book could never have taken its current form were it not for the time, the intellectual stimulation, and the logistical support provided by these research centers. To their directors and staffs we express our heartfelt thanks and our wish that they may long remain to support future scholarship.

Unfortunately, our work was not finished when we last left NIAS in June 1992. Electronic mail proved to be a godsend to authors separated by a distance of some 10,000 km as we finished the remaining chapters and translated each other's work, thereby producing a Dutch and an English text. This English version of the work differs in small ways from the Dutch version. A few matters are here explained in greater detail for the benefit of an international readership, and its later appearance permits the incorporation of a few newly published facts relevant to our arguments.

Even a completed manuscript does not bring to an end the labors of publishing a book. In Berkeley, Heath Pearson assisted in preparing the tables and bibliography and in improving the quality of the English text. Meanwhile, in Wageningen, Piet Holleman drafted the maps and graphs. Anonymous referees called to our attention important points deserving of clarification. We thank them all.

Jan de Vries, University of California at Berkeley
Ad van der Woude, Landbouwuniversitieit Wageningen
1 October 1995

The First Modern Economy

.

Chapter 1
By way of introduction

In its day – and long after – the world admired the Dutch Republic above all for its economic efficiency and social concord. In 1776, Adam Smith could find no more fitting example than the Republic as "a country that had acquired that full complement of riches which the nature of its soils and climate and its situation with respect to other countries allowed it to acquire."[1] Smith held that such a state of well-ordered efficiency – the goal of classical economics – had been most nearly achieved in Holland, and this gleaming vision of early prosperity has never since lost its hold on the public imagination.

But just what are the lessons to be learned from this celebrated "Dutch case"? Smith had no doubts, but since his time historical perspective has acted more to complicate than to clarify matters. Historians of varied plumage – Eric Hobsbawm, Fernand Braudel, Violet Barbor, and Immanuel Wallerstein come immediately to mind – felt certain that the Dutch achievement was essentially backward looking, the culmination of something with no future. "The emergence of Amsterdam prolonged the old pattern; took place, logically enough, according to the old rules . . ."[2] pronounced Braudel, while Hobsbawm warned against the temptation "to exaggerate the 'modernity' of the Dutch." Indeed, "to some extent [the Dutch] did a disservice to industrialization in the long run."[3]

Economists have been tempted to see something more positive, and more

---

[1] Adam Smith, *The Wealth of Nations* (Cannon ed., orig. published 1904, Chicago, 1976). Vol. I, p. 106; see, more generally, pp. 102–8.
[2] Fernand Braudel, *The Perspective of the World*, Vol. 3: *Civilization and Capitalism, 15th–18th Century* (New York, 1984), p. 175.
[3] E. J. Hobsbawm, "The Crisis of the 17th Century – II," *Past and Present 6* (1954), p. 54.

connected to the present, in the economic history of the Dutch Republic. Douglass North and Robert Paul Thomas did not mince words in *The Rise of the Western World*: "In point of fact the Netherlands was the first country to achieve sustained economic growth as we have defined it. . . ."[4] Nor was Angus Maddison in any doubt about the place of the Netherlands in modern history. "In the past four centuries there have been only three lead countries [defined as the country which operates nearest to the technical frontier, with the highest average labor productivity]. The Netherlands was the top performer until the Napoleonic Wars, when the UK took over. The British lead lasted till around 1890, and the USA has been the lead country since then."[5]

All of these scholars, and many more, found the "Dutch case" essential for their historical interpretations and social scientific analyses; but they all confronted an historical literature which, for all its richness and variety, had a notable weakness. There were few comprehensive interpretative studies.

A bit of historiography

There are, to be sure, a number of general histories of the economic development of the Netherlands between the late Middle Ages and the early nineteenth century produced by a collection of authors, with each assigned a specific chronological or thematic topic. An example of this approach is offered by *De economische geschiedenis van Nederland* (1977), edited by J. H. van Stuijvenberg. It covers the period in its first five chronologically organized chapters. The thematic approach is employed in *The Dutch Economy in the Golden Age* (1993), edited by Karl Davids and Leo Noordegraaf. Here, no fewer than ten authors treat specialized aspects of Dutch economic history up to 1650. Conceptually rather broader were the chapters devoted to economic history in the *Algemene Geschiedenis der Nederlanden* (1979–81). Here, too, a multitude of authors, in contributions distributed through volumes 4 through 10 of this 15-volume work, presented their understanding of special aspects of the period.

The strengths and weaknesses of such collective works need little elaboration. Alongside the advantage of having each period or topic handled by a specialist stands the considerable disadvantage that each author has his or her own approach and special interests. As the chapters are assembled, omissions and repetition arise, and it is an exceptional editor, indeed, who can harness the authors effectively to a detailed common agenda – let alone impose a coherent vision on the ensemble.

For this, one turns to the monograph written by one or at most two authors. In Dutch economic history, this genre has a much longer history than the collective work. The first such work appeared in 1890: the German Otto Pringsheim's *Beiträge zur wirtschaftlichen Entwicklungsgeschichte der Vereinigten Niederlande*

---

[4] Douglass North and Robert Paul Thomas, *The Rise of the Western World* (Cambridge, 1973), p. 145.
[5] Angus Maddison, *Dynamic Forces in Capitalist Development* (Oxford, 1991), p. 30.

im 17. und 18. Jahrhundert. It is really no accident that some forty years later it was once again a German who prepared the next monograph on this subject: Ernst Baasch, *Holländische Wirtschaftsgeschichte* (1927). This reflects both the rudimentary state of this field of study in the Netherlands and the great influence then enjoyed by German historical scholarship.

The leading position of German scholarship then exerted its influence throughout the western world, and it was especially apparent in economic history. But, its great authority in the Netherlands was not based simply on the high professional standards of the German scholars, or even on their superior numbers. To these factors must be added an ideological element. Of the generation of young Dutch historians who were attracted to economic issues, most were involved in the then still young social-democratic movement (the Social Democratic Workers' Party was founded in 1894). G. W. Kernkamp, N. W. Posthumus, and, most intensely, J. G. van Dillen, all of whom rank with Z. W. Sneller as the founding fathers of economic history in the Netherlands, felt themselves very strongly attracted to the ideals of this movement. In this period, Dutch social democracy maintained very close contact with its mighty German sister party. Thus, the young Dutch economic historians found themselves doubly attached to Germany: ideologically, via social democracy, and professionally, because of the great authority of their German academic colleagues. Through the work of Gustav Schmoller, Werner Sombart, and Max Weber, the Dutch scholars came under the influence of *Kathedersozialismus* and the German Historical School.

From the aforementioned works of Pringsheim and Baasch, a direct line runs to J. G. van Dillen, to whom fell the task of writing the first major synthetic study of the economic development of the Netherlands between 1500 and 1800 from a Dutch standpoint. This occurred first in his contributions to the original *Algemene Geschiedenis der Nederlanden*, published in the course of the 1950s, and then in a much fuller form in his posthumous *Van rijkdom en regenten* of 1970. Eighty years after Pringsheim, the first general work of Dutch economic history for the period 1500–1800 had appeared in the Dutch language.

Van Dillen's book was simultaneously a beginning and a conclusion. It provided an overview of his generation's research, inspired as it was by the German Historical School. But well before its publication, after the end of World War II, a new generation of scholars moved decisively in a different direction as Dutch economic history came to be influenced first by French, and later also by American, historical writing. The central figure in all this was B. H. Slicher van Bath. He had entered academic life in 1945 with a study that reflected the influence of his German dissertation director. But thereafter, in his pioneering works *Een samenleving onder spanning. Geschiedenis van het platteland van Overijssel* (1957) and *An Agrarian History of Western Europe, 500–1850* (1960, English trans. 1963), he moved in a direction that had much in common with the innovative French historians, known as the "Annales school," who sought closer contacts with the social sciences. And, again, it was Slicher van Bath who in 1967 brought the American

3

"New Economic History" to the attention of Dutch historians. None of these new developments in economic history left more than a faint trace in Van Dillen's standard reference work.

This book is the product of co-authors – one Dutch, one American – who have set as their goal the establishment of a new synthesis of Dutch economic history to replace the historical tradition that guided this field for nearly a century. With this work we accept the challenge of the modern historical schools; indeed, we even seek to integrate them.

The French historical school, or "Annales school," advocated a break with "event-centered history," and with the political and personal focus that necessarily attaches to it. It developed in its stead a more spacious conception of historical time capable of incorporating a broad range of economic, social, mental, and environmental processes. The American New Economic History, or "cliometrics," challenged the institutional and narrative economic history that found its inspiration and conceptual apparatus in the German historical school. Through its explicit application of economic theory, its systematic use of quantitative data, and its emphasis on hypothesis testing, cliometrics shifted the focus of the literature from politics and institutions to markets and rational decision makers.

In some respects these two movements of renewal complement each other. Where structural history is inclusive and integrative, the new economic history typically concerns itself with specific problems of market performance. Where the French school is conceptually rich but theoretically eclectic, the American school is narrower in focus but theoretically rigorous and formal. These complementary characteristics notwithstanding, the two schools are not commonly combined, and for good reason. The first emphasizes continuity and stability in human affairs while the second by design focuses on the dynamic – analyzing decision making and measuring growth. It is no accident that the French school has made its home in preindustrial European societies while the American school finds the industrializing world of the nineteenth century most congenial.

The authors state their purposes

Structure versus dynamism; broad vision versus analytical rigor. It is precisely these differences in the two schools that invite integration in this book, which presents a new interpretation of the economic history of the Netherlands in the period 1500–1815. The new research of the past generation which we here seek to interpret requires a conceptual framework that can do justice to an economy that was rooted in the early modern world (the special strength of the Annales school) but was pioneering the economic and social forms of behavior and achievement characteristic of the modern economies of the nineteenth and twentieth centuries (the special interest of the New Economic History).

This book, in short, presents the history of the first modern economy. In its first section we present the integrative structures of economic life – geographical, demographic, financial, and sociocultural. These structures reveal themselves to be far from static entities; even here the dynamic processes in Dutch economic life are evident. These become far more apparent in the book's second section, where economic change is analyzed sector by sector. The dynamics of this economy – indeed, its essential modernity – comes fully into view in the third, analytical, section, where theory and history come most directly into contact with each other. The organization of the book integrates structure and change but moves progressively from an emphasis on durable forms to processes of change and development.

The questions motivating this book include those of *structure* (how did the parts fit together; what durable features channeled and limited human action?) and of *context* (how did this Dutch economy function in its larger international setting; how did it exemplify or differ from, influence or become subject to, the European and intercontinental worlds with which it interacted?). But the chief questions of this book concern *growth and change*. How did the region that would become the Dutch Republic come to flourish so suddenly, so intensely, and with such great international effect? What can account for this economy's limitations, frustrations, and failures? These twinned questions bring Dutch history into direct confrontation with the major, overarching interpretive projects of western economic history. As we shall see, the experience of the Netherlands stands as a challenge to many historical conventions; with all this we grapple in the two last chapters.

Finally, a word about the beginning and ending dates of this study. The Republic of the United Netherlands, whose history is the focus of this book, took shape as an independent entity in the course of the 1580s. Its demise, in 1795, was more abrupt. But neither of these political dates is of much value for periodization in economic history. Our study begins in the late-fifteenth/early-sixteenth centuries, at the onset of an expansionary era for the European economy as a whole, the so-called *long sixteenth century*. It is in this larger chronological context that the rise of the Dutch economy should be placed.

The selection of an ending date is less clear-cut. Neither the economic trends of the Netherlands, much less those of Europe as a whole, recommend 1795 as a terminal date. The old Republic's successor states rattled and bent but could not break the bars that confined them to an economic regime which, in some respects, lingered on until the mid–nineteenth century. The Netherlands did not really enter its second epoch of modern economic development fully until after 1850, but we do not follow the story that far. The substantially altered institutional setting of the new Kingdom of the Netherlands established in 1815, the new demographic growth that set in after that date, and the break in international price trends (from inflationary to its reverse) that occurred in 1817, all reinforce the end of the "French Period" of Dutch history as a logical as well as practical terminal date for this book.

Structures

Chapter 2
Space and time,
structures and conjunctures

2.1. Structures

2.1.1. INTRODUCING GEOGRAPHY

A description of the Dutch Republic's territory – the physical container of the Dutch economy, if you will – is not a straightforward task. This is evident from the terminological confusion that frustrates discussion about the Netherlands as a political entity and from the continual alterations that must be made to the physical map of the northwestern corner of Europe.

At the beginning of the sixteenth century, the territories that would later comprise the United Provinces of the Netherlands (i.e., the Dutch Republic) were not yet all under the control of the Habsburg emperor, Charles V, who had inherited the Netherlands provinces accumulated by the Dukes of Burgundy over the course of two centuries of dynastic politics. Only after 1543, when the Duchy of Gelderland came under Habsburg control, can one speak of a "Burgundian Netherlands" that embraced all of the modern Dutch state plus, of course, Belgium and parts of present-day France.

This assemblage of provinces was by no means centrally governed. Indeed, steps in that direction taken by Philip II after 1555 provoked a particularist resistance of such vehemence that it must count as a major precipitant of the Dutch Revolt. Much remained to be achieved in the way of legal or fiscal unification – not to mention economic unification – before the outbreak of the Revolt rent the Netherlands asunder.

In the course of the Revolt against Spain, the Republic arose – unanticipated and in an ad hoc manner – as a union of seven provinces. We can say that it was

9

in existence by 1588, but the achievement of a definitive border dividing the northern Netherlands (the Republic) from the southern Netherlands (the Spanish, and after 1715 the Austrian Netherlands) required decades of further military activity. The fruits of those battles became known during the life of the Republic as the "Generality lands" and were acknowledged to form part of the Republic at the Peace of Westphalia in 1648. From then on, the political boundaries of the Republic remained unchanged until its demise in 1795.

The complex and changing political map of the Netherlands up to 1648 teaches us not to expect an economic history that turns on the directives of a central government, or that is neatly encompassed by the national frontiers. The excess of attention given by historians to the nation-state is often enough a source of error and distortion; in Dutch economic history we have no choice but to look elsewhere for unifying themes. Indeed, we cannot avoid questioning whether the Dutch Republic can be treated as a national economy at all.

In the early sixteenth century, the lands that were to form the Dutch Republic possessed small-scale local and regional economies. Such cohesion as they possessed emanated from towns and their particularist municipal economic policies. These miniature economic systems were, in turn, oriented to a larger, international economy, which had its most important northern European focal point at Antwerp and the other commercial and industrial centers of Brabant and Flanders.

During the Revolt of the Netherlands, this economic structure, already in retreat, came crashing down in ruins. These dramatic events will be given fuller attention in Chapter 9; for now it is important to note that the emergence of the Dutch Republic as a political entity occurred in parallel with a profound economic reorientation of these provinces. Economic links with the southern Netherlands were by no means broken, but they ceased to have either the importance or the character of earlier times. Meanwhile, the Republic's economic life came more and more to reach out in other directions: to the North Sea and Baltic, the White Sea and Davis Strait, Iberia and the Mediterranean, the East and West Indies.

An economic history of the Dutch Republic must emphasize its European and, indeed, its world setting, noting how both its political and economic orientation changed over time. But that is not all that was in motion. The physical features of the northern Netherlands also exhibited a dynamism that is both unusual and fascinating.

It is by now a commonplace of historical analysis to emphasize the role played by the geographical characteristics of a country as an "historical structure" – durable if not permanent features that constrain and channel human activity and thus help to determine the course of history by limiting human options. Yet in Dutch history, geography is a "structure" of unusual plasticity. The land visited by the Romans differed (in, among other things, its coastline, river courses, and soil elevation) from the birthplace of Erasmus, which, in turn, would have appeared unusual in many ways to the King-Stadhouder Willem III. Here the physical environment serves not only as a container of and restrainer of history but also as a dynamic element in and as a palimpsest of human activity.

This territory divided then, as it does today, into two distinctive geological zones. Penetrating westward from Germany and northward from Belgium are expanses of primarily sandy soils. These relatively infertile soils, lying at least several meters above sea level, are the product of glacial activity and form the more stable element of the Dutch landscape. These sandy protrusions—the "diluvial Netherlands" – are enveloped by the clays and peat soils of the "alluvial Netherlands" – soils that were deposited and developed by the actions of the rivers, seas, and winds in the most recent geological period, that is, during the last 10,000 years. The Rhine and Maas rivers disgorge in the northern Netherlands depositing rich river clays along the courses of their numerous distributaries. This low-lying delta was protected from inundation by a wall of sand dunes stretching in a great arc along the coast. Rising sea levels broke through this dune wall in places to inundate the land behind, laying down marine clay soils and transforming large tracts into peat bogs, as the silting and poor drainage of the lagoon behind the dunes starved the plant life of oxygen (see Map 2.1).

The growing peat bogs, veritable waterlogged cushions of decaying vegetable matter, contributed to the maintenance of an equilibrium by checking the invasive potential of the sea with the strong and constant outward pressure of water draining from the rivers and the bogs themselves. The disturbance of this equilibrium by human settlement beginning in the tenth century led in the period 1000 to 1300 to a sequence of natural and human interventions that transformed utterly the landscape of the alluvial Netherlands.

The clay and peat soils of the maritime Netherlands were penetrated by a tangle of small rivers and a profusion of sea arms and lakes, giving the region an amphibious character that was periodically intensified or relaxed by changes in the level of the sea and in the violence of storms.

The numerous, difficult-to-penetrate marshes and peat bogs long enforced an isolation on much of the northern Netherlands that kept it beyond the effective reach of both the Roman and Carolingian empires. But the region also possessed a potential for communication with a large area because of the presence of the rivers: the Schelde, which drains much of Flanders; the Maas, offering communication with Liège; and, most important, the Rhine, which allows navigation deep into Germany. These rivers formed numerous, ever-changing distributory channels as they sought outlet to the sea in the flat marshy lagoon behind the wall of dunes. The outlets formed navigable channels that offered sites for harbors.

In its natural state, the low-lying zones of the Netherlands offered few attractions to settlement and numerous dangers. A fascinating aspect of the Netherlands' geographical situation is that lands which pose dangers and are naturally resistant to human habitation also have the potential of richly rewarding efforts to alter these natural conditions. Much of the highly creative medieval development of what was then a rude and obscure land can be understood in the context of the

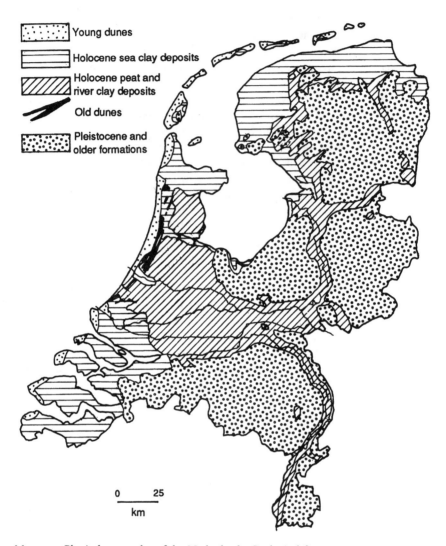

Map 2.1a. Physical geography of the Netherlands: Geological features.

tension between severe natural discomfort and a large potential for gain. By examining medieval efforts to alter and exploit the environment in these spheres of activity, we will set the stage for the study of Dutch economic life from the sixteenth century, the object of this book, and understand better how the Dutch natural environment could simultaneously function as a structure, channeling history, and as a catalyst of long-term developments.

Map 2.1b. Physical geography of the Netherlands: Elevations.

2.1.2. RIVERS AND WATERWAYS

The great rivers of the Netherlands and the numerous inlets, channels, and lakes spread throughout the alluvial zone did not naturally provide a ready-made network of internal communications. But through strategic improvements in the form of short connecting channels and sluices, medieval Netherlanders succeeded in creating a number of important inland water routes. The motivation was not so much to serve the modest needs of the local economy as to attract traffic passing between the more important economic centers of Brabant and Flanders (via the rivers Schelde and Zwin), the Rhineland, and the Hanseatic towns of the North Sea and Baltic coast. In the medieval era, when coastal shipping preferred to avoid the open seas and sought protected routes, inland waterways connecting the Zuider Zee (with coastal access to the Hanseatic cities) to the Rhineland and to Flanders promised to attract an important volume of traffic.

The routes developed to attract these traffic flows were competitive rather than complementary. The IJssel River (route I on Map 2.2) connects the Rhine and Zuider Zee naturally, and the cities along its banks – Kampen, Deventer, Zutphen – were among the largest and most important of the medieval Netherlands. A second route made use of the river Vecht, connected by an artificial channel to the Hollandse IJssel and Lek (route II). This route passed through the city and Bishopric of Utrecht. A third route (route III) passed through the County of Holland, making use of the IJ and a series of lakes, rivers, and channels connecting the cities of Haarlem and Gouda. Near both cities were sluices at which tolls were levied. Shipping proceeding south from Gouda had to reckon with Dordrecht, a city vested with toll and staple privileges that required all cargoes to be landed and offered for sale before further shipment up the Waal toward Germany or through the Delta channels to Flanders and Brabant.

Each of these routes enriched independent territories, all of which disputed violently with each other to secure economic and fiscal advantage from the interregional traffic. This competitive approach yielded a circuitous and incomplete network of waterways to which were attached numerous urban settlements that drew their sustenance from the levying of tolls and the provision of transport and commercial services.

Of less importance at this time, but also working toward decentralization and competition among cities, were the outlets to the open sea. By the early fourteenth century, they were, and remained until the nineteenth century, the following: ports on the Zuider Zee and Wadden Zee gained access to the North Sea via breaches in the dune wall at the islands of Texel (the Marsdiep, [B on Map 2.2] and Vlieland (A); most Rhine waters plus the river Maas flowed to the Delta, penetrating to the sea near Den Briel (the Brielse Gat-C) and near Hellevoetssluis (The Goereese Gat-D). The Schelde formed two arms in Zeeland, the Ooster- and Westerschelde (E and F). All harbors of consequence made use of these channels to communicate with the open sea, although the changing flows of river water and the action of the seas caused the navigability of these openings to vary continually. All of them suffered at times from shallow sand bars; moreover, all required ships departing Dutch harbors to sail against the prevailing winds.

Between the multiple channels offering access to the open sea and the multiple internal water routes through the region, the northern Netherlands raised and

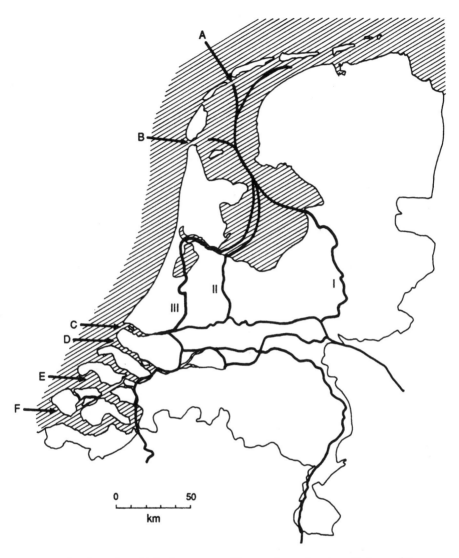

Map 2.2. Sea channels and inland waterways. (See text for explanation of letters and Roman numerals.)

maintained a large number of competitive trading cities in addition to the normal compliment of urban settlements performing the traditional administrative, religious, marketing, and distributional functions for their hinterlands. The decentralized urban pattern that emerged from these circumstances featured a deeply rooted particularism among the numerous cities and several territorial authorities.

This particularism long acted to check the overweening power of any single city and placed a distinctive impress on the political organization of the Dutch Republic.

2.1.3. SETTLEMENT PATTERNS

On the sandy soils of the east (in Drenthe, Overijssel, and the Veluwe and Achterhoek regions of Gelderland) and the south (North Limburg and North Brabant), settlement chiefly took the form of nucleated villages around which open fields had been cleared (called *essen*). These arable fields were divided among the farmers who together exercised a communal control of the wastelands (called the *marke*) surrounding the village. The soil quality in most areas was such that these villages were rather thinly scattered, separated by rough pasture and vast expanses of heath. These agricultural communities shared many common elements with villages found throughout northern Europe.

Very different was the settlement history of the alluvial Netherlands. The maritime clay soils of Friesland and Groningen, the clays that built up along the banks of the large rivers, and the sandy soils directly behind the coastal dunes attracted settlers at an early date, although occupation often required special measures. Occupation of the northern coastal area came to depend on the construction of refuge mounds, called *terpen*, allowing farms and even whole villages to keep dry during the frequent flooding of the surrounding land. By the Middle Ages, at least 1,200 of these mounds existed, many having been built up continuously since Roman times.

By the eleventh century, these communities achieved a degree of stability that allowed a more organized approach to the task of rendering the land safer and more productive: the construction of earthen dikes to prevent the penetration of flood tides and to close off coastal inlets and other lands exposed at low tides. These *bedijkingen* were mostly small, incremental extensions of the secured, cultivable land and were taken in hand by local interested parties. On the single Zeeland island of Zuid Beveland, the inhabitants extended their coastline outward through the construction of no less than 165 polders between the mid–thirteenth and mid–sixteenth centuries. In so doing they added 9,845 hectare to their island by 1500, although in the same period the onslaughts of the sea forced them to relinquish 1,455 hectare elsewhere on the island. *Bedijkingen*, or coastal polders, were generally opportunistic initiatives in the sense that currents, tides, and storm floods determined their timing and location at least as much as capital, technology, and prices.

Settlement patterns in these coastal districts tended to be highly decentralized: The incremental process of reclamation supported small villages and isolated farmsteads ensconced behind their dikes and hamlets nestled upon the *terpen*.

In the central zones, the provinces of Holland and Utrecht, the extension of settlement required different techniques, for there the challenge was to occupy

16

the extensive peat bogs. In the tenth and eleventh centuries, inhabitants of the villages on the bordering river clays and sandy soils encroached on the bogs, but large-scale colonization of these tracts required a systematic approach that was only forthcoming when the Counts of Holland and Bishops of Utrecht had achieved a position of sufficient authority to claim the empty lands and set in motion reclamation projects. These rulers appointed agents (such as religious chapters and noblemen) who constructed basic drainage facilities and roads and determined the pattern of field parcelization. Typically, after the construction of an earthen dike, drainage ditches were cut at right angles to the dike at regular intervals. These ditches formed the boundaries of the new farms, with their dwellings placed along the dike and their lands extending backward from the dike in a long, narrow strip. These measures brought about a lowering of the water table of the initially spongy peat bogs. After burning the surface peat, the land became well suited for both arable farming and animal husbandry.

The northern Netherlands, as with northern Europe more generally, experienced a great age of medieval colonization, but here it was paired with the evolution of distinctive techniques and institutions. Certainly the most conspicuous mark of exceptionality was the weakness of feudalism. The farming communities of the alluvial Netherlands were only lightly touched by manorial organization and serfdom. Roughly speaking, the strength of these institutions declined as one moved from the southern Netherlands, where they were fully developed along lines common to the rest of northern Europe, to the Friesian lands of the north, where they had never taken root. The colonization process, offering peasants the possibility of establishing themselves on "new land" as free settlers, further diluted the strength of these institutions. In most communities one finds free peasants, organized in *buurschappen*, in control of local affairs; their autonomy was modified, but not usually eliminated, by the authority of the ruler and his local representatives.

With large-scale settlement came new problems whose solution led to technical and institutional developments of central importance to the later history of the region. The threats of flooding from both the sea and the rivers and the increasing frequency of inundation and permanent loss of coastal areas galvanized the communities to band together in larger entities for the construction and maintenance of dikes and the damming of river mouths. In these drainage boards (*waterschappen*), a representative of the Count of Holland, a *schout*, shared power with representatives of the inhabitants of the area (*heemraden*), and these bodies often coalesced in larger, regional drainage authorities (*hoogheemraadschappen*). Despite the presence of a representative of the central authority, these drainage authorities exhibited a high degree of autonomy in both the setting of policy and their institutional development.

The new drainage organizations protected the settlers from the external threat of inundation, but soon after settlement, a new and steadily more insistent threat emerged from within in the form of soil subsidence. By lowering the water table of the peat soils, the colonists made settlement and arable farming possible, but the resulting aration caused the peat to oxidize, become more compact, and sink down. This subsidence process was most intense on land used for arable farming, and the rural dwellers on the peat soils found arable farming becoming more and more difficult. These problems reached crisis proportions in the fifteenth century as lands that had once stood several meters above sea level came to fall below the level of the rivers and channels that drained these lands. At that point residents faced the choice of innovation or emigration.

In response to these problems, local communities formed polders, areas encircled by dikes in which the water level could be artificially controlled. These local improvement districts differed from the coastal polders, the purpose of which was to gain new land from the sea. The new polders were intended to improve the drainage of existing cultivated land. They also differed from coastal polders in that drainage could not depend exclusively on releasing water during periods of low tide. The new polders required pumps to raise the polder water to the higher level of the surrounding drainage channels; this became technically feasible in the fifteenth century when the Dutch learned to build windmills that could be rotated to face into any wind – the *wipmolen*.

Another characteristic of these recently settled lands is that the peat soil served both as an agricultural resource and, when cut and dried, as a source of fuel. Moreover, in certain areas the peat could be burned to yield salt. Peat ranked as the only natural resource of importance, and Hollanders not only exploited it for local home and industrial use but also exported it in growing quantities to the large urban markets of Brabant.

In the early sixteenth century, the inhabitants of the low-lying zone of the northern Netherlands faced a physical environment that offered unique opportunities at the same time that it threatened them with physical and financial loss. The medieval occupation of the alluvial zone set in motion a treadmill of drainage, followed by land subsidence requiring new investments in improved drainage, and so forth. Compounding the problem was the digging of peat, often in locations near dikes (thus, close to navigable water for ease of transport) that weakened the defenses against inundation at the same time that it lowered the value of the cut-over land.

To the consequences of these human activities must be added the natural forces that appear to have become more menacing in the course of the fifteenth century. The frequent storms gnawed at the dune-covered coast shifting the coastline hundreds of meters inland and covering the once fertile lands behind the dunes with sand. Inundations enlarged the size of sea inlets, such as the Dollart and Zijpe, created a vast inland lake (the Haarlemmermeer), submerged vast stretches of the Zeeland islands (including the city of Reimerswaal), and, in the infamous St. Elizabeth's flood of 1421, inundated the Groot Zuidhollandse Waard, a district of 500 square kilometers including 34 villages, much of which remains unreclaimed to the present day. Meanwhile, on the subsiding soil of Holland, arable cultivation became steadily more problematic, a trend that even the introduction of windmills could not reverse. Much of this land stood registered in the tax survey of 1514, the *Informacie*, as *pro derelicto*. It supported fowlers and fishermen more readily than farmers.

This evidence of a deteriorating environment has as its counterweight the existence of a network of polders and regional drainage authorities that had developed over the centuries to provide effective instruments for investment in drainage works and the coordination and supervision of protective efforts. Similarly, the peat digging that added to the threat of land loss endowed the region with a fuel that, by the standards of the times, was cheap and abundant. But around 1500 the dangers must have seemed more impressive than the opportunities. The struggle against the sea was clearly a defensive one, one that neither the institutional nor technical resources then available seemed capable of winning. Moreover, much of the peat digging of that time produced a commodity for export beyond the immediate region to Antwerp in the southern Netherlands, leaving behind only exhausted lands prone to inundation.

The chief positive feature that we can observe in the physical environment of the early sixteenth century is the ability of the inhabitants to exploit their geographic location by developing routes to attract traffic to and from the North Sea region, the German Rhineland, and Flanders and Brabant through the waterways of the northern Netherlands. As we have seen, this encouraged the founding of a large number of cities intent on exploiting the commercial possibilities of their location.

The commercial cities were numerous, generally of modest size, and mostly very young. Only twelve urban charters in the northern Netherlands date from before 1200, and most date from after 1300. Still subordinate to the urban core of Flanders and Brabant, the northern cities of the late fifteenth century were in an anomalous position. Collectively they represented a high level of urbanization (see Chapter 3), but they held no commensurate or secure place in the urban hierarchy of northwestern Europe. Their fifteenth-century growth seems to have been related more to the growing crisis of the countryside than to any real urban prosperity. The decline of arable production, the shift to labor-saving livestock farming, and the rising costs of protecting the land led to a substantial migration to the towns. The fact that the urbanization of this era expressed itself more in the large *number* of cities than in their large *size* speaks to the importance of the "push" force of rural crisis relative to the "pull" of vigorous urban economies. In consequence, fifteenth-century Holland came to be characterized by a large, underemployed urban population available at low wages, and by rural villages with populations too large for their diminished agricultural potential.

The landscape that in 1500 was home to rather fewer than a million people scattered across some 1,500 villages and hamlets, and nearly 100 urban settlements showed important differences from 300 years earlier. Many of these differences revealed the still very limited ability of the inhabitants to control their environment and exploit it to their advantage. One cannot resist speculating that the Dutch rural scene that is now such a source of pleasure and contentment – a pasture landscape with windmills looming in the distance and a lake in the foreground – must have been a source of anxiety to the observer of 1500: The pasture reminded one that arable farming was becoming steadily less feasible; the windmill recalled the progressive soil subsidence that required costly investments to maintain drainage quality; the expanse of water was the sorry consequence of peat digging, which offered short-term income at the expense of long-term soil depletion. And that city whose walls and church steeple is visible at the horizon? Did it offer real opportunities to someone contemplating removal from this anxiety-inducing rural environment?

2.2. Conjunctures

2.2.1. INTRODUCING CONJUNCTURE

In the following three centuries, the physical setting of Dutch society was transformed, as generations of Netherlanders sought to exploit the opportunities it offered and struggled to limit their vulnerability to its threats – not to mention those threats provoked by their own actions. The geographical and institutional endowments of this region formed structures that channeled and constrained the feasible human initiatives, but relative to most other parts of the world, they were particularly pliable, capable of being altered in response to a changing economic and technical environment.

This changing environment is nothing less than history itself, as it is conventionally understood. But it is useful for both expositional and analytical purposes to distinguish historical phenomena that persist and endure for substantial periods – because of their extended gestation periods, their cumulative character, or their being the product of the habitual behavior of large numbers of people – from those phenomena that are more sudden or isolated. Likewise, it is useful to distinguish historical phenomena that are primarily endogenous to the social unit under investigation from those that are primarily exogenous. The ubiquity of feedback processes, of interaction between a society and the outside world, make *exogenous* and *endogenous* relative concepts in history. But there is value in identifying events that are external in the sense that the entity being studied must adjust to it and can only alter the external fact partially and with much time.

In economic life, a number of important historical phenomena can be categorized as external to a society and of long duration, being the product of mass behavior in an international setting. Price formation in market economies and population change are the two most prominent examples of such phenomena. Their general movement can much more easily be described than explained, for they are the products of innumerable small decisions which themselves are reactions to multiple stimuli and constraints. In what follows, we identify several long-term trends in the economic environment of the northern Netherlands to which behavior was adapted. Their treatment here as exogenous forces should be regarded as a "first approximation" of reality. In later chapters we explore in more detail the ways in which Dutch economic life itself influenced, and at times even shaped, the international economic environment.

2.2.2. THE "LITTLE ICE AGE"

Climate change is a long-term process that obviously must be regarded as exogenous to the economy of the Netherlands. This is a subject about which little can be said with certainty. It is widely held that the northern European climate became colder after the mid–sixteenth century, constituting a "Little Ice Age" that ended only in the nineteenth century. Detailed information about the sixteenth-century climate is scarce, although it is clear that the 1560s and '70s included an unusual number of weather extremes. In the seventeenth century, we are on firmer ground, and we know that severe winter weather occurred much more frequently than it has in recent decades, but also more frequently than in the very mild first six decades of the eighteenth century. From 1634 to 1698, a highly variable climate yielded an average winter temperature of 1.4°C, more than 1°C lower than in the succeeding sixty years and also well below twentieth-century averages. The period 1758–1839 was almost as severe as the seventeenth century.[1] The lasting agricultural consequences of such variation are difficult to trace but appear to have been marginal in character. In a diversified economy open to international markets, farmers, merchants, and other affected parties could usually adjust to such climatic changes as have been charted. Adjustment was not always possible in the very short run, of course, and crises arising from harvest failures were not unknown, but these, too, were usually both less severe and less frequent than in neighboring countries.

Of potentially far greater importance than the effect of climate on agriculture is the effect of climate change (via the size of glaciers and ice caps) on the sea levels and on the volume of Rhine and Maas river water entering the Netherlands. We have already noted the so-called "transgression" phases of rising sea level that physical geographers and geologists have held responsible for destructive inundations culminating in the fifteenth and early sixteenth centuries. The "regression" phase that followed, conveniently coextensive with the Little Ice Age, is thought to have created a more benign environment for land protection and reclamation. This seems to find its reflection in a decreasing incidence of dike failure and inundation. In the region of North Holland, important inundations since 1500 occurred as shown in Table 2.1.

Of course, the pattern of inundations does not reflect changes in sea levels exclusively; the available technology and the resources devoted to the mainte-

---

[1] Jan de Vries, "Histoire du climat et economie," *Annales: E. S. C. 32* (1977), 212.

Table 2.1. *Inundations in North Holland since 1500.*

Sixteenth century		Seventeenth century	Eighteenth century	Nineteenth century	Twentieth century
1502	1532	1601	1714	1825	1916
1508	1555	1610	1717		
1509	1570	1616	1775		
1512	1573	1625	1776		
1514	1575	1665			
1518	1580	1675			
1530	1597	1677			

Source: A. M. van der Woude, *Het Noorderkwartier* (Wageningen, 1972), p. 55.

nance of the dikes also played roles as important as they are impossible to isolate. To complicate matters, geologists have come to doubt the very existence of transgressions and regressions of the sea, preferring instead to emphasize movements in the level of the land. Whatever the ultimate explanation, it does seem safe to conclude that environmental conditions, after having been particularly destructive for some centuries, became measurably less threatening by the early seventeenth century. Only the sudden appearance of the *paal* worm (*Teredo limmoria*) in 1730 interrupted this more benign natural environment. It is thought that the warming coastal waters of that time provoked a population explosion of these mussel-like worms, which possessed a rasped head enabling them to bore through the wooden piles which, arrayed in palisades, formed the essential outer defenses of the sea dikes. The attack of the *paal* worm required that the sea dikes throughout the country be rebuilt with stone facing material to replace the traditional wooden piles. This was an exceedingly costly undertaking and was not completed until the next century.

Oceanic changes of another sort also directly affected the economic opportunities facing the Netherlanders. Changes in water temperature, by influencing everything from oceanic plant life to ice floes, affected the migratory behavior of fish and whales, both of which were important to the Dutch economy. The sixteenth-century cooling of the North Sea waters attracted herring from Scandinavian waters to fishing grounds near England, which made them more readily accessible to Dutch fishermen. Similarly, colder polar summers in the first half of the seventeenth century reduced the annual release of drift ice, thereby altering the migratory patterns of the Greenland whale, making it easier prey for European whalers, foremost among them the Dutch.

Another type of change in the natural environment, one common to all of northwestern Europe, was the disappearance of *pasturella pestis*, the bacilla that carries the bubonic plague. In the seventeenth century, plague outbreaks recurred with a frightening regularity, primarily in the cities of Europe. In the Dutch

Republic, we know of major outbreaks in 1601, 1616–17,* 1624–26, 1634–36,* 1655–57,* and 1664–66*; in each of the starred periods, mortality in Amsterdam carried away at least one-tenth of the population and was followed within one year by an epidemic in London.

The outbreak of 1664–66 was the last recorded in the Republic, as well as in surrounding countries. The spread of brick housing construction and the efforts of health authorities to quarantine infested areas are thought by some to help explain the disappearance. But it remains likely that the retreat of plague had as little to do with human agents as had its introduction. Other threats to life and health, particularly smallpox, expanded soon enough to take the place of the retreating plague, but none had the frightening severity of the seventeenth-century plague outbreaks.

Long-term trends in temperature, rainfall, sea level, and the microbiological environment are phenomena that have only recently been studied as autonomous historical agents. Their consequences are still difficult to distinguish from the human actions of response and adaptation that they precipitate. We can tentatively conclude that the Dutch Republic, along with the rest of Europe, stood powerless before epidemiological changes but possessed, by the sixteenth and seventeenth centuries, technical powers and a social organization that were sufficient to diffuse and dampen the adverse influence of climatological shocks. Moreover, it is possible that the longer-term manifestations of the Little Ice Age offered, on balance, more benefits to the Dutch than they imposed costs.

2.2.3. INTERNATIONAL POLITICAL ENVIRONMENT

Very much more consequential for the economic life of the region was the complex of long-term changes that brought about a permanent, structural shift of commercial and industrial leadership from the Mediterranean basin to Northwestern Europe. In any account of European economic history, the role of the Dutch in bringing about this dramatic historical discontinuity must be given a prominent place. That is, this structural shift is not wholly exogenous to Dutch history. Yet it would have been inconceivable apart from a series of long-term historical developments that *can* be seen as independent of the activities of the Dutch. In the first place, we must call attention to the gradual increase in the relative weight of northern European economic activity relative to the established Mediterranean centers. By 1500 this process was most evident in the rise of English woolen production, Baltic grain exports, and central European mining. These and other tokens of a more complex economic life in the north interacted with the sudden revolution in European trade with Asia and a specific constellation of political forces to endow northwestern European locations with a new potential for commercial and industrial development, a potential first realized by Antwerp, in the heart of the region's longest-established zone of advanced economic life.

The second major element in bringing about this shift is found in the Mediterranean lands themselves, where war, famine, and catastrophic epidemics brought about economic disorganization leading, by the end of the sixteenth century, to crises in agricultural production, urban economies, and, ultimately, political power.

These various events and processes endowed northwestern Europe with an augmented potential and created opportunities for a displacement of leadership. By no means did this necessitate the rise of the Dutch economy, let alone explain its rise. For this, initiatives within the Netherlands were necessary, initiatives that will receive attention in the chapters to follow. But neither can the economic behavior of the Dutch be understood in a vacuum: In the course of the sixteenth century, they faced new possibilities brought about by a structural shift of vast proportions, a process which they, in competition with others, could seek to modify and channel, but which they did not create single-handedly.

2.2.4. THE ECONOMIC ENVIRONMENT: THE SECULAR TREND

The third type of exogenous, long-term process that helped to shape the environment of Dutch economic life is more familiar: the long swings observable in many indicators of economic activity. The size of the labor force, the volume of agricultural production, and the money supply all are involved in these long-term movements, but the single most general indicator is the level of commodity prices. For our immediate purposes, it is less important to identify the relative influence of such forces as population change, coinage debasement, and money supply on price levels than to emphasize that long-term commodity price trends were a product of international market activities and reflect the behavior of numerous individuals in countless transactions. Many European regions were relatively isolated from the international market, feeling its impact through a thick filter of local price fixing, high transportation costs, tolls, tariffs, and trade disruptions. But the Netherlands always stood fully exposed to the price formation of international markets. To study Dutch prices is to study the international market.

Figure 12.4, a cost of living index, identifies the chief phases of the secular price trends, trends that the Netherlands shared with a much larger area. The most striking feature of any price index spanning the early modern period of European history is the irregular but persistent rise in the average price level that began in the third quarter of the fifteenth century and climaxed around the mid-seventeenth century. An inflationary epoch of such magnitude and duration was unprecedented until the twentieth century, and historians who had not yet experienced the intense inflation of recent decades were sufficiently impressed to call it a "price revolution." Not all prices rose at the same pace, but Dutch commodity price indices rose tenfold over the two centuries from 1450–74 to 1650–74, reflecting the important place held by the bread grains. When corrected for currency debasements (i.e., when prices are expressed in quantities of silver), the rise of the price level is about sixfold.

This "long sixteenth century" epoch of rising prices was not all of a piece. In the first place, it occurred in a context of great yearly fluctuations, such that contemporaries might easily lose sight of the secular trend. After all, the rate of price increase in the century of most rapid inflation amounted to only 1.4 percent per annum, a rate we today would hardly recognize as inflationary. Second, the underlying trend did not remain steady throughout this long period. The price rise was gradual until the 1540s; then began half a century of more intense inflation coupled with large annual fluctuations that peaked in 1598. Thereafter it is difficult to speak of a further increase in the general price level until after 1620. Through the duration of the Thirty Years' War, prices rose again, although not at the sixteenth century's pace, reaching a succession of roughly equal peaks in 1652, 1663, and again in 1675. But by this last peak, the underlying price trend had already begun to decline. Prices fell severely to the early 1680s only to rise again to a volatile series of peaks in 1693, 1699, and 1709. Thereafter deflation reassessed itself, driving prices to a low point in the 1730s. From this nadir the general price trend was upward: slowly until the 1770s, then at a higher rate until the period of the French Revolution and the Napoleonic Wars brought about severe inflation climaxing in 1812 and 1817.

The chronicle of prices is open to several types of interpretation. The numerous fluctuations reflect harvest conditions, financial machinations, and warfare. But the association of more extended periods of war with bouts of inflation (the Thirty Years' War, the War of the Spanish Succession, and the Revolutionary and Napoleonic Wars, among them) raises the possibility that the international political situation conditioned the course of prices. In what follows we embrace a third approach, treating these politically linked price changes as modifications of underlying, longer-term price trends that have their basis in slow-changing economic parameters as they affected supply and demand conditions. These determinants of production and consumption manifested themselves in *general* price trends but also, and often more significantly, in the trends of *relative* prices.

For the European economy as a whole, the long-term course of relative prices, including the "price" of labor, is commonly explained in the context of a Malthusian model. Assume that the supply of land is fixed and that the responsiveness of production to increased demand (the price elasticity of supply) is low, particularly for agricultural products. Assume further that the demand for basic foodstuffs (grains) is inelastic with respect to both price and income while demand is progressively more elastic for livestock products, industrial crops, and manufactured goods, in that order. This set of supply and demand characteristics suffices to explain the general course of prices in the preindustrial economy when one introduces (as a factor exogenous to the model) population growth or decline. Population growth increases the demand for grain more than for other products, but it has less impact on increasing the production of grain than that of other goods. This generates rising grain prices, which, other things remaining equal, diminishes the real income of consumers, reducing their demand for the less necessary products. Meanwhile the growing population increases the size of the labor force, whose employment in industry is rendered difficult by falling demand for manufactures and whose employment in agriculture drives downward the marginal productivity of labor. Labor's real wage tends to fall. Symmetrically opposite results are produced by this model if population should decline.

Thus, in Europe as a whole, the long periods of underlying inflation before the 1650s and after the 1740s witnessed a rise in the price of grain relative to livestock products, and of both of these relative to industrial products. It also witnessed falling real wages of labor. In the period between the 1660s and 1740s, when prices tended to fall, the opposite was the case.

At this point it is important to interject that the model just described presupposes a specific pattern of consumer behavior and a specific technology and investment pattern conditioning the possibilities of production. These can be valid for preindustrial Europe as a whole without being appropriate to the Dutch economy. Thus, within the general price trends described earlier which, so to speak, the Dutch received from the rest of Europe, there could arise, from sources internal to the Dutch economy, specific differences, affecting particularly the course of relative prices and wages, all of which testify to the existence of Dutch production and/or consumption patterns that deviate from the model. This, too, is explored in later chapters.

The history of prices plays a part at several levels in the analysis of the Dutch economy, among others as a transmitter of exogenous shocks, a reflector of internal supply and demand elasticities, a measure of the degree of market integration, and a determinant of the international terms of trade. Here we wish to emphasize the use of long-term price movements as an indicator of the secular trend. The turning points at the mid–seventeenth and mid–eighteenth centuries demarcate three periods: one to the 1660s; the second, 1660–1740; the third, 1740–1815. The first and third are often called eras of *expansion* and the second an era of *contraction* or *depression*. But these terms are likely to mislead. The eras of expansion – of increasing aggregate demand and rising prices – can bring either growth or impoverishment, and the depression eras – of contracting aggregate demand and falling prices – can occasion stagnation and collapse but also adjustment and growth. These epochs of secular trend do not by themselves determine the outcome; they help to shape the constraints and opportunities that face the economic actors.

The reader might well wonder what the Little Ice Age, the problems of Philip II, and relative price movements have to do with one another. We have introduced these factors here to emphasize that the historical phenomenon called "the rise of the Dutch Republic" should be approached in the broadest possible context, for what occurred in the sixteenth century was a conjuncture: the converging *in time* of several, not necessarily causally related, developments and their confrontation *in space* with a complex of physical, institutional, and technological structures. The new opportunities in the international economy faced the evolving structures of the northwestern corner of Europe, creating a context in which human action could convert liabilities into assets, as institutions intended for one purpose suddenly revealed their utility in the achievement of other goals, and what had been peripheral could aspire to become central.

The transformation of the northern Netherlands involved the perception of new opportunities and the integration of the elements necessary to exploit them. In the case of the Dutch physical and infrastructural setting, the institutions and practices that long had functioned defensively and reactively now faced in the sixteenth century a conjuncture that opened opportunities for offensive, constructive action.

2.3. A landscape in movement: constructing a "Golden Age" environment

A conjuncture of factors reshaping the economic environment created new possibilities for the locational and environmental structures of the northern Netherlands. But these could not be exploited without investment. In three very tangible ways, the Dutch acted to reshape their physical environment so they could take full advantage of new opportunities in trade, agriculture, and industry.

2.3.1. LAND RECLAMATION

The most enduring of Dutch achievements in this period is arguably the land reclamation that literally changed the face and shape of whole regions. Yet, as we have noted, the objective conditions around 1500 gave little reason for optimism that the defensive character of dike building and drainage efforts could soon be transformed into an offensive against the rivers and the sea. This defensive and often unsuccessful struggle continued until at least the mid–sixteenth century, as the floods of 1530, 1532, and 1555 imposed major losses, particularly on the Zeeland islands. The island of Zuid Beveland, which in the two centuries before 1500 had been painstakingly enlarged by 8,400 hectare (net), saw over 4,000 hectare swept away in the first seventy years of the sixteenth century; the island of Noord Beveland disappeared altogether.[2]

These decades of frequent and destructive inundations proved to be a turning point. The drainage authorities, with their dams and encircling dikes, and the windmill provided an arsenal of weapons that the Dutch gradually improved in

---

[2] C. Dekker, *Zuid-Beveland. De historische geografie en de instellingen van een Zeeuws eiland in de middeleeuwen* (Zaltbommel, 1970), pp. 310–19.

the face of adversity. When new economic incentives to create and improve land were coupled with a marginally less threatening physical environment, the response was immediate and intense.

By 1500 most drainage authorities were already institutions of long standing, and their defensive encircling dikes were mostly in place. The regional coordinating bodies and local polders alike depended on individual farmers, often only those whose lands actually abutted the dikes, to construct and maintain assigned stretches of the protective installations. Around the beginning of the sixteenth century, the drainage authorities began to replace this traditional system of personal labor service with one of centrally coordinated professional dike maintenance, requiring farmers to pay taxes in place of providing personal labor services. This monetization had far-reaching consequences, for it directly encouraged both the further commercialization of agriculture and the creation of a floating proletariat of dike and construction laborers. Of importance here, however, is the improved quality of dike maintenance as the new system reduced the potential for neglect and improved the technical competence of the drainage authorities. The new assessment system spread gradually: in 1477 and 1510 on several important North Holland dikes; in 1510–15 on the Spaarndammerdijk stretching from Haarlem to Amsterdam; in 1574 on the Vijfdelendijk in Friesland; gradually throughout the sixteenth century on the Zeeland islands. The transition took two centuries to be completed, but the critical steps were taken during the sixteenth century. Thereafter all new polders levied taxes to carry out their responsibilities rather than rely on the direct services of the inhabitants.

The existing windmills possessed inherent limits to their size, and hence their pumping capacity, which were dictated by the need to turn the entire body of the windmill into the wind. In the mid–sixteenth century, one begins to observe a new design, the *bovenkruier*, in which only the cap of the windmill, to which the sails are attached, needed to be turned. These more complex and costly mills escaped the size constraints of their predecessors and made possible not simply drainage of existing cultivated land but also the drainage of shallow lakes. With the successful drainage of the first small lakes around Alkmaar in the 1560s, investors and engineers were motivated to improve the windmills further. When they reached a pumping limit of approximately one meter, they placed the windmills one behind the other so that three or four windmills in concert could drain yet deeper lakes: the Wieringerwaard, in 1597, 2.0 meters deep; the Wogmeer, in 1608, 2.5 meters deep; the Beemster in 1612, 3.5 meters deep; the Wormer in 1624, 4.5 meters deep (see Figure 2.1). Nor was the pumping capacity of individual windmills ignored. The substitution of an Archimedes' screw for a paddle wheel increased the effectiveness of the windmill. Attributed to Symon Hulsebos of Leiden, thi. invention began to be adopted around 1630.

By these n ans the capacity to improve existing – and to win new – land developed rapidly in the second half of the sixteenth century, a process that the

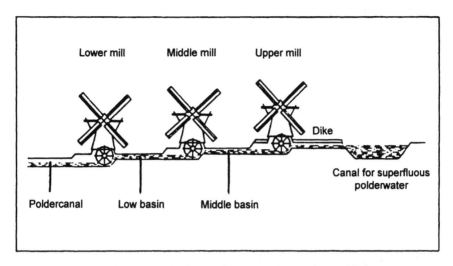

Figure 2.1. A row of three windmills (a *molengang*) to drain a deep polder.

years of the Revolt interrupted but could not halt. The increasing value of land, the related rise in the prices of agricultural commodities, and the accumulating capital of urban investors all directed attention to the profit possibilities in land reclamation and stimulated technical improvement.

The process of land reclamation in the northern Netherlands is often exemplified by the short period of intense lake drainage activity in North Holland from 1610 to 1640. Leading Amsterdam merchants and other urban interests then dared to plunge at least ten million guilders – far more than they and their contemporaries had invested to establish the Dutch East India Company in 1602 – into the application of new windmill pumping techniques to the drainage of a series of lakes covering in total 26,000 hectare. Their speculative investments changed the face of North Holland (see Map 2.3). The new polders removed the most dangerous threats to the Peninsula and augmented its land area by one-third, but, just as important, they altered the economic geography of the entire region, blocking access to the sea from many villages, and reducing inland fishing possibilities as they added a whole new class of large farmers and enlarged the marketing functions of the towns. But these justifiably celebrated initiatives formed only the "main event" of a vast pageant of activity.

In a less dramatic way, the traditional process of forming coastal polders added land along the Friesian and Groningen coast, on the islands of the Delta

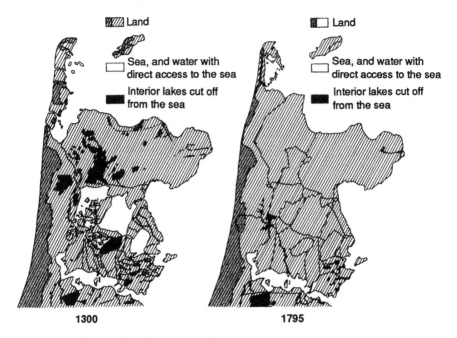

Map 2.3. Land area of North Holland before and after the reclamation projects.

region, and in western North Brabant. Moreover, most polder forming and windmill construction was taken in hand by local farmers and landowners for the prosaic purpose of improving the quality of the *existing* land surface of central Holland, and the Republic was well on its way to reaching the total of some 2,700 separate polders and drainage boards that were counted in the nineteenth century.

That number should make obvious the impossibility of summarizing in brief compass the multitude of land improvement and reclamation projects being carried out throughout the maritime provinces by everyone from urban speculators to the farmers themselves. Nevertheless, it is clear that one motivation dominated this multifaceted movement: profit.

Trends in agricultural prices and the threat of physical insecurity affected directly the pace of reclamation activities. In the twenty-five years after 1540, as prices rose rapidly, the scope of reclamation doubled its previous average level, only to be brought to a standstill during the Revolt against Spain. By the 1590s interest revived. Indeed, nearly half of all the land reclaimed in the period 1500–1815 was concentrated in the sixty years after 1590. After the 1650s the level of activity again receded. In the century after 1665, no more land was reclaimed than in the twenty-five years after 1615. Investors who had drawn up detailed plans and secured government permission in 1657 for the reclamation of the Koegras, an area of 9,000 hectare along the North Holland coast, set their plans aside after 1670; advocates of the drainage of the vast Haarlemmermeer, who produced numerous pamphlets in the 1640s, fell silent thereafter. Both of these projects waited until the nineteenth century to be carried out.

Not all of the land created in the two great waves of drainage activity was a net gain. Often new polders only restored land that had earlier been inundated or destroyed by peat digging. But we can acquire a rough idea of the scope of the achievement by comparing the chronicle of reclamation to the results of the first comprehensive cadastral survey of the Dutch land completed in 1833. The province of Holland then possessed 375,000 hectare of cultivated land, 68 percent of its land area. Lake drainage and new coastal polders in the period 1540–1815 accounted for 94,000 hectare of that area. In the *Informacie*, a tax survey of 1514, village respondents admitted to working a total of about 255,000 hectare, 120,000 hectare less than found in 1833. Neither their statements nor the surveying techniques of that time are wholly trustworthy, but it is probably safe to conclude that the farming land of Holland grew by some 100,000 hectare – by well over one-third – in the course of the sixteenth, seventeenth, and eighteenth centuries. In the provinces of Zeeland and Groningen, the gain was probably even larger, although for the former this was partially a restoration of earlier losses. Elsewhere the gains formed a more modest addition to the cultivable land, but all together the Dutch Republic reclaimed some 250,000 hectare in the period 1500–1815, increasing by one-third the cultivated land area of the alluvial zone of the Netherlands.

The higher-lying sandy soils of the eastern Netherlands shared none of the developments just described. But farmers there faced their own natural threats, primarily in the form of *zandverstuivingen*, drifting sand, which contributed to the abandonment of whole villages on the Veluwe in the late sixteenth century.

Little is known in detail about land reclamation in these areas, but topographical analysis suggests that nothing more than small-scale extensions of fields into the extensive waste lands was pursued until the nineteenth century, for only then did many villages give up their common control of the wastes (the *markegemeenschappen*). An exception to this rule is formed by those locations near the large cities of Holland. There the urban demand for sand (for construction purposes) encouraged investors to dig canals to carry away the sand and prepare cultivable fields (in one case settle a whole village ('s-Graveland in 1626) on the once sand-covered land. Far more important was the creation of new cultivable land on the *hoogveen*, the peat bogs in Friesland, Drenthe, and Groningen. This was closely associated with the market for peat, which is discussed later. Where urban economic interests did not penetrate, via the construction of new transportation routes, the process of reclamation remained linked to local demand for land and led to no drastic changes in the rural landscape.

Table 2.2. *Land reclamation in the Netherlands, 1540–1815 (in hectares).*

	Lake drainage			Coastal polders							Total lake and coastal reclamation
	North Holland	Other areas	Total	North Holland	South Holland	Zeeland	Friesland	Groningen	North Brabant	Total	
1540–65	1,710		1,710		5,723	3,535	1,188	13,873	5,758	30,077	31,787
1565–90	389	220	609		4,042	1,872	0	0	1,522	7,436	8,045
1590–1615	8,328	821	9,149	9,391	3,138	8,163	2,295	1,112	3,401	27,500	36,649
1615–40	15,371	4,689	20,060		4,539	12,478	556	7,139	916	25,628	45,688
1640–65	1,017	121	1,138		3,960	16,096		2,364	5,631	28,051	29,189
1665–90		2,008	2,008		2,184	5,504		910	1,774	10,372	12,380
1690–1715		641	641		1,259	7,982		1,093	1,560	11,894	12,535
1715–40		1,750	1,750		0	2,097	433	6,000	445	8,975	10,725
1740–65		3,724	3,724		3,063	1,579	437	436	1,083	6,598	10,322
1765–90		7,665	7,665		1,038	6,388		1,319	1,515	10,260	17,925
1790–1815		5,733	5,733		1,471	4,445		2,606	1,601	10,123	15,856
Total	26,815	27,372	54,187	9,391	30,417	70,139	4,909	36,852	25,206	176,914	231,101

Sources: R. H. A. Cools, *De strijd om den grond in het lage Nederland; het proces van bedijking, inpoldering en droogmaking sinds de vroegste tijden* (Rotterdam, 1948), pp. 131, 151, with corrections from A. M. van der Woude, *Het Noorderkwartier* (Wageningen, 1972) Vol. III, Bijlage 1, pp. 616–17.

2.3.2. COMMUNICATIONS

The medieval endowment of inland waterways consisted of the natural water-courses augmented and improved by strategic but mostly short canals. The resulting network was far from comprehensive, being confined to the alluvial zone and consisting of competitive rather than complimentary routes. Nor was it free, since the flow of interregional traffic had long since attracted dozens of princely and municipal tolls.

In the course of the sixteenth and early seventeenth centuries, the center of gravity of Dutch trade gradually shifted from the inland waterways to the ocean ports. The growing volume of trade at these ports focused attention on the need for harbor expansions and the improvement of lighthouses, buoys, and other channel markers. Table 2.3 presents a chronology of harbor expansions. The numerous projects varied enormously in size, of course, but the table demonstrates that these investments were broadly distributed geographically (sixteen ports increased their harbor capacity) and were substantially concentrated in time (most were taken in hand in the half century after 1570).

The growing importance of international trade placed new demands on inland transport, but surprisingly few changes were brought to the infrastructure of inland waterways. In this period the Dutch came to use their transport facilities differently, as we shall see later; but apart from the enlargement of sluices and incidental waterway improvements created by drainage projects, the physical facilities remained essentially unaltered.

In a society lacking a strong central authority, it should not surprise us that the cities enjoying local toll privileges opposed new canals that might divert traffic, nor that public funds tended to support only transport projects yielding local benefits. The new character of expansion certainly focused attention on the benefits to be gained from improvements in interregional transportation; yet one initiative after another intended to remove the costly barriers to such traffic foundered on the shoals of urban particularism. The jealous protection of longstanding toll privileges held by the cities of Dordrecht, Gouda, and Haarlem – and repeatedly confirmed by Holland's High Court – forced the other cities to abandon their hopes for improved interregional transportation.

Even before the Revolt, in 1536, Delft's effort to gain direct access to the Oude Rijn (and, hence, to Leiden, Haarlem, and Amsterdam) was stopped by Gouda and its allies. In 1589 Rotterdam's introduction of a new fast freight service to Amsterdam via the Hildam (a barrier between two drainage districts) met with the instant objection of the same three cities, protesting the circumvention of their tolls. In this case Rotterdam eventually gained a limited right to move goods across the Hildam barrier but not to remove the barrier. Even this minor victory cost decades of litigation.

In 1608 the city of Zaltbommel, suffering from the decline of the east–west traffic along the Waal and Maas, proposed to cut a new canal north to Culemborg

Table 2.3. *New harbor construction in the Dutch Republic, 1500–1800.*

	Zuiderzee	Maas	Zeeland
1536–42	Enkhuizen	Dordrecht (2x)	Middelburg (2x)
1560–5	Enkhuizen		
1572–7	Hoorn, Medemblik	Rotterdam (2x)	
1578–81	Amsterdam, Harlingen	Brielle	Middelburg, Vlissingen
1588–95	Enkhuizen (2x), Amsterdam	Rotterdam (2x)	Zierikzee, Arnemuiden
1597–1604	Medemblik, Harlingen	Rotterdam	Middelburg, Veere
1607–12	Amsterdam, Hoorn	Schiedam, Rotterdam (2x), Dordrecht, Brielle	Vlissingen
1613–19	Amsterdam, Hoorn, Enkhuizen	Rotterdam, Maassluis, Hellevoetsluis	
1630–6	Medemblik (2x)	Hellevoetsluis	
1643–9	Amsterdam, Hoorn	Dordrecht (2x)	
1655		Dordrecht	
1662–4	Amsterdam	Hellevoetsluis	
1694		Rotterdam	

Source: J. P. Sigmond, *Nederlandse zeehavens tussen 1500 en 1800* (Amsterdam, 1989), 59–60, 103–4, 156.

and thereby gain direct access to Amsterdam, bypassing Dordrecht. This, too, was stopped by the aggrieved cities' legal appeals.

Eventually, the compelling need for better intercity communications led to a breakthrough. Beginning in 1631 the cities began to cooperate with one another to finance the improvement of existing waterways and the construction of many new ones. They all received tow paths permitting horse-pulled barges to maintain frequent scheduled services between the cities. Yet the breakthrough was a limited one: The ancient rights of Dordrecht, Gouda, and Haarlem prevailed to forbid cargo vessels from navigating several of the new canals. As a consequence the new canals were dedicated to the improvement of passenger, parcel, and mail service. Nevertheless, the potential gains seemed so large that thirty cities spread across the alluvial Netherlands entered into thirty separate joint ventures to invest nearly five million guilders in the construction of 658 km of *trekvaart* (canals equipped with tow paths). This activity, begun in 1631, was concentrated in two distinct boom periods, the second ending in 1665 with the outbreak of the second Anglo-Dutch War. Shortly thereafter two gaps in the network of new canals – the product of squabbling among towns and of technical difficulties – were filled by the construction of paved roads, the only such roads of any length to be found in the Republic until the late eighteenth century.

Outside this zone of high mobility, canal construction and river navigation improvements were few and usually of limited impact. The essential condition for a major transportation improvement was an economic motive sufficiently strong to attract capital from the expansive cities of the west. Rising peat prices formed such a motive, directing the attention of investors to the *hoogveen* peat bogs of the northern provinces. The exploitation of these remote and desolate bogs required the digging of new canals, which then opened these districts to further economic development. These enterprises are discussed in more detail later, in conjunction with the production of peat.

In the sandy-soil zones of the Netherlands, the provincial cities – drained of their international commercial importance by the fortunes of war, the dictates of geography, and the competition of the maritime cities – sought compensation in the cultivation of commercial links with their hinterlands. Zwolle, Deventer, Zutphen, and Doesburg all invested in the improved navigability of the rivers – in truth, mere streams – that flowed toward them from the east (see Map 5.3). Deventer built sluices and cut channels throughout the first half of the seventeenth century in the hope of converting the Schipbeek into a dependable water route to Twente; in 1643 Zutphen's burgers invested 60,000 guilders in the Eerste Berkel Compagnie to make the Berkel navigable for flat-bottomed vessels of up to five tons. Zwolle extended the navigability of the Vecht as far as the German County of Bentheim. From the end of navigation at Nordhorn, goods were portaged to the river Ems, some 20 km distant, from where they could continue by water as far as Münster.

Finding the funds to maintain even the most elementary infrastructural improvements proved to be a constant struggle for these cities. Zutphen's civic-minded enterprise went bankrupt in 1670, and most of these rivers were, at best, marginally navigable a few months per year. Only Zwolle had more success, because the Vecht gave access to the stone quarries of Bentheim. The building boom in Holland's cities induced the organization of the Hollandse Steenhandel Compagnie to cut and ship sandstone, some 80,000 cubic feet per year in the mid-1640s, via the Vecht and the Zuider Zee to Holland. Emblematic of the

Map 2.4. The *trekvaart* network after 1665.

resistance offered by inland areas to economic transformation was a project to cut a canal from western Utrecht eastward through a sandy zone to the city of Amersfoort. It was abandoned just as the workers reached the sand – and just as economic prospects became more somber in the 1660s.

The 1631–65 boom in canal construction endowed the alluvial zone with a comprehensive network of intercity waterways that augmented the existing ensemble of rivers and canals. This had the effect of making even sharper the natural distinction between the ease of communications in the two zones of the Netherlands. In transportation facilities as in land reclamation, investors tended to concentrate their activities, building on initial strengths and experience.

2.3.3. PEAT SUPPLIES

We turn now to the physical changes brought to the peat bogs. The peat industry and its consequences for Dutch economic life will attract our attention more than once in the chapters to come, but it deserves attention here because of the special position that the production of peat held at the intersection of three important physical phenomena: the Netherlands' unique access to low-cost energy, the reclamation of land, and the development of the transportation network.

The Netherlands' peat deposits were extensive: Since 1600 some 275,000 hectare of land has been stripped of its peat. Historically, the exploitation of energy deposits has depended more on the cost of transportation than on the cost of gathering the resource itself, and this explains the early exploitation of the Dutch peat bogs. They are located at or very near the level of the water table, permitting waterborne transport to proceed from the point of production to the doorsteps of the consumer. The peat of the *laagveen* districts (the low bogs of the alluvial zone) was exploited first, since it was found in the very midst of the cities of Holland in a region well supplied with navigable waterways. No capital investment or organizational requirements hindered farmers and other rural dwellers from digging peat, whether for local use or more distant sale. On this small-scale, informal basis, peat production grew in importance in the fifteenth and early sixteenth century.

The first step toward intensification occurred around 1530. Until then peat diggers could do little more than strip away the top layer of peat; given the high water table, to do more would bring on almost immediate flooding. Since the bogs were actually several meters thick, this left the bulk of the peat untouched. The rising demand for peat, particularly that emanating from rapidly growing Antwerp, caused peat prices to rise rapidly, half again as fast as the general price level in the period 1480–1530.

In response, peat diggers developed a new tool, the *baggerbeugel*, permitting them to cut peat below the water level and haul it up to the surface. This at once permitted a more intensive exploitation of the bogs, required labor practiced in the special technique, called *slagturven*, and destroyed utterly the agricultural value of the affected peat bogs.

Peat digging became both a major pillar of the economy and a threat to the environment and the tax base as the exhausted bogs formed lakes that expanded to cover vast areas throughout central Holland and western Utrecht. The drainage authorities, seeing their tax base vanish before the onslaught of hordes of peat diggers, responded with export prohibitions, restrictions on *slagturven*, and, as these measures proved ineffective, taxes on the removal of peat to raise funds for later reclamation of the exhausted bogs.

Where the soil lying under the peat layer was suitable (i.e., clay instead of sand) the damage created by peat production could be undone by employing the

pumping techniques developed in the early seventeenth century to drain the natural lakes of north Holland. In fact, as the last of those lakes was drained, contractors who had been active in the north turned their attention to the deep peat
lakes (*veenplassen*) of south Holland. In 1646 and 1647, they successfully drained
two such exhausted and inundated peat bogs. But soon thereafter reclamation lost
its profitability, so that water covered more and more of the region until reclamation again became economically viable in the late eighteenth century. Until
then the area between Amsterdam, Rotterdam, and Utrecht took on the appearance of a veritable Swiss cheese, with dozens of water-filled, exhausted peat bogs
often separated from each other by nothing more than narrow, vulnerable strips
of land on which were scattered the structures of what once had been farms.

The exploitation of the second type of peat bog, the *hoogveen* of the diluvial
zone, proceeded very differently and with other consequences for the agricultural
economy. These bogs could not be penetrated for exploitation and settlement
until canals were dug, and this required a large initial capital investment. Thus,
in place of numerous individual peat diggers working parcels of a few hundred
square meters of *laagveen*, we encounter in the *hoogveen* consortia of investors who
judged market conditions sufficiently attractive to buy up vast tracts of uninhab-
ited bog, dig lengthy canals into the bogs, and hire armies of laborers to dig the
peat.

Once the peat was stripped away, these enterprises had a further interest in
making use of the newly exposed underlying soils. Since this soil lay above the
water table, the cost of converting it into productive agricultural land consisted
primarily of (1) taking the trouble to conserve the surface soil (which was in any
event poor-quality peat) so that it could be respread over the land, and (2) heavily
manuring the new soil. This occurred most systematically in Groningen, where
the capital city encouraged agricultural development of the *hoogveen* by subsidizing
the distribution of night soil. By 1800 some 23,000 hectare of *hoogveen* in Groningen alone had been brought under cultivation.

The expansion of peat production also affected the transportation system. In
the course of the seventeenth century, new canals opened up southeastern Friesland, the Veenkoloniën of eastern Groningen, and parts of Drenthe. Moreover,
the flow of peat throughout the canal network encouraged investment in larger
sluices, deeper channels, and new docks. These investments, justified by the high
volume of peat transport, served the rest of the economy as well, making available
a transport infrastructure that the other users, by themselves, could never have
financed.

The chronology of the peat industry's expansion and contraction, as it affects
the geographical conditions, follows a by now familiar pattern. The sixteenth
century growth in demand for peat, particularly from Brabant and Flanders, stimulated production on the *laagveen* of central Holland. During the Revolt this
market collapsed and peat prices plunged, but after 1580 the rapid growth of
Holland's cities and industries reoriented the peat industry to domestic markets,

markets growing at such a pace that peat prices once again began to outpace the general price level. This directed the attention of investors to the remote *hoogveen* bogs.

Before then, in 1546, the first peat consortium, or *veencompagnie*, organized the large-scale peat digging enterprise in the Gelderse Vallei, a desolate, low-lying district running along the border of Utrecht and Gelderland. Utrecht burgers invested in the area that would later become the town of Veenendaal, while in 1550 an Antwerp consortium led by the brewer and urban developer Gilbert van Schoonbeke set to work nearby. In the following year, local investors in Friesland organized the first *veencompagnie* in the north and set about digging the Schoter-landse Compagnonsvaart. By 1565 the richest noble family of Groningen, the Ewsums, embarked on a project to extract peat from their extensive lands. These northern ventures proved premature, and the capital of local investors was insufficient to bring the projects to fruition.

In 1595 Groningen's confiscation of monastic lands – which included vast tracts of *hoogveen* – set the stage for the entry of urban investors from Holland and Utrecht, who took over ventures begun earlier by local interests and started new ones. In Groningen these included the Stichtse Compagnie, formed in 1605, Pekelder Compagnie, formed in 1608, the Borger Compagnie of 1637, and the Muntendammer Compagnie and Trips Compagnie of 1648. In Friesland Mennonites began the exploitation of Surhuisterveen in 1600, and the Opsterlandse Compagnie was founded in 1645. In Drenthe the same sort of process got under way in 1612 when Holland investors, including the rich Amsterdammer Adriaan Pauw, financed the digging of the Smildervaart and in 1631 when similar interests, organized in the Compagnie van 5000 Morgen, canalized a stream from Meppel to what is now Hoogeveen.[3]

After 1650 further extension of the peat canals ceases. The investors exploited their existing facilities while the peat bog laborers began to form more permanent settlements in which agriculture assumed a growing importance. After a spectacular growth in the first half of the seventeenth century, output in the northern provinces fell by half in the second half. The peat industry held up better in the bogs of Holland and Utrecht; they were closer to the major markets, and the worsening agricultural depression forced many hard-pressed farmers to convert their lands to peat-digging operations. But here, too, production appears to have fallen. The revenue from Holland's excise tax on peat declined by nearly 20 percent between the 1660s and the 1680s. It later declined further to a low point

---

[3] Maria Hartgerink-Kooimans, *Het geslacht Ewsum* (Groningen, 1938), pp. 191–323, *passim*; F. J. de Voer, *Skiednis fan de lege feanterij yn Opsterlan en Smellingerlan* (Leeuwarden, 1954); W. H. Keikes, "Veenexploitatie in Drenthe met Amsterdamsch Regentenkapitaal in de 17e eeuw," *Jaarboek Amstelodamum 39* (1942), 11–20; M. A. W. Gerding, "Drentse turf in de zeventiende eeuw," *Nieuwe Drentse volksalmanak 10* (1984), 56–68; J. Stienstra and G. Groenhuis, "De Veenhuizer venen in de gouden Eeuw: een mislukte Hollandse investering," *Nieuwe Drentse volksalmanak 101* (1984), 69–83; M. A. W. Gerding, ed., *Geschiedenis van Meppel* (Meppel, 1991), pp. 114–19.

in the 1740s. This indicator may well exaggerate the decline, but the weakness of demand is revealed by the price of peat, which fell faster than the overall price level throughout this period.

After 1750 peat prices rose again, stimulating a renewal of investment to open fresh peat bogs. The peat excise taxes in Holland do not reflect this revival, but this may be the result of the changing composition of fuels consumed (different grades of peat had very different tax rates) and the exemptions from taxation given to fuel-intensive industries over the course of time. In the northern provinces, the physical evidence of a revival of peat production after 1750 is unmistakable. Migrants from exhausted bogs in Overijssel then opened up a new *laagveen* district in Friesland, while in the *hoogveen* the Stadskanaal in Groningen and the Meppelerdiep in Drenthe, plus extensions to the Opsterlandse Compagnonsvaart in Friesland were all taken in hand between 1765 and 1767. By 1774 the Drentse Hoofdvaart was completed, whereafter little was done again until the nineteenth century.

The long-term movements in the demand for peat, the prices of agricultural output, the value of land, and the demand for transportation services set in motion uncounted initiatives to alter the physical face of the Netherlands: to create land, to destroy it, to build canals, harbors, and sluices, even to redirect the flow of water though the rivers. They could also quickly put a halt to these activities, which were almost always either private undertakings or those of local governmental organs. What is more, these economic activities interacted with processes at work in the natural environment which, as we have seen, could aid or obstruct achievement of the intended result, sometimes in unforeseen ways.

2.4 The environment reacts

In the third quarter of the seventeenth century, the construction of the "Golden Age environment" was brought to a close. Much had been accomplished. The maritime Netherlands looked and functioned very differently than it had around 1500. The process of polder formation approached the saturation point, and a major addition had been made to the supply of high-quality agricultural land. The many small cities of the fifteenth century had been refashioned into an integrated urban system of major ports, industrial cities, specialist trade centers, and market towns. These were now connected by a system of inland waterways that overcame some, but by no means all, of the medieval obstacles to the efficient circulation of goods and persons. A highly capitalized peat digging and distribution sector replaced the informal and small-scale industry to supply urban industries with a level of per capita energy consumption unsurpassed until the British Industrial Revolution. By any standard known to the seventeenth century, the Dutch cityscapes and landscapes represented a triumph of human ingenuity, which had harnessed nature for the benefit of economic efficiency.

Notwithstanding the natural tendency to view this complex of mutually re-inforcing landscape elements as a completed whole, it was very much a work in progress when political and economic setbacks beginning in the 1660s suddenly cut short the process of infrastructural investment. We have noted the abandon-ment of plans to drain the Haarlemmermeer and the cessation of work in progress to reclaim the Koegras and extend a canal from western Utrecht to Amersfoort. Even more dramatic were the extensions of such cities as Haarlem, Groningen, and Amsterdam, which were finished in the 1670s and languished, only partially occupied, until the nineteenth century. Clearly, the Netherlands entered a new economic environment in the second half of the seventeenth century, one in-hospitable to the capital-intensive transformations of the landscape that had char-acterized the preceding century.

The cessation of investment produced, over time, a relative deterioration of Dutch infrastructure. But this economic and political failure was compounded by an absolute environmental deterioration that constituted a formidable challenge to even the best organized and economically most vigorous of societies. An en-vironment that had seemed so malleable and responsive to investment in im-provement now took its revenge, presenting the Dutch Republic with intractable problems that even costly expenditures could not overcome.

The flow of water in the rivers debouching in the Republic had long been a source of concern since it affected both the navigability of waterways and the security of the vast stretch of land extending from the German border to the sea. A natural process causing tidal action to become greater along the southern reaches of the Dutch coast than further north, plus the effects of a new, more direct route to the sea opened by the inundation of the Groot Zuidhollandse Waard in 1421, had the combined result of pulling ever more of the Rhine's water into the southernmost channels, which enjoyed a better discharge into the sea than the other routes. By the late sixteenth century, the northernmost Rhine distributary, the IJssel, was no longer regularly navigable by large vessels, and in the late seventeenth century, the Neder Rijn and Lek faced the same fate. Some 90 percent of all Rhine water then flowed via the Waal.

Provincial governments sought to improve the navigability of these rivers by redirecting the flow of water toward the northern channels with the placement of *kribben* (diversionary piers) in the river. But these efforts were neither successful nor unopposed; the Waal cities of Nijmegen and Dordrecht sent expeditions to destroy the offending piers.[4] It took until 1701 for the affected provinces to reach an agreement to create a new diversionary channel, the Pannerdens canal, in-tended to increase the flow of water to the northern arms of the Rhine. Its

---

[4] Geert Renting, " 'de Heeren van Doredrecht op het werck van Panderen.' Gelderse kaarten in het Dordtse gemeentearchief," *Holland, Regionaal-historisch tijdschrift* 22 (1990), 102–10.

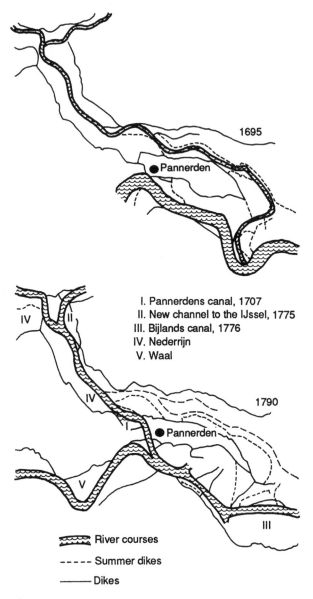

Map 2.5. The Rhine and its distributary channels. [*Source:* G. P. van de Ven, *Aan de wieg van Rijkswaterstaat* (Zutphen, 1976).]

completion in 1707, completion in 1773–6 of a new canal connecting the IJssel to the Neder Rijn, and the elimination of a meander in the Rhine by the cutting of a new channel, the Bijlands canal, were all intended to revise the distribution of Rhine water in favor of the northern branches (see Map 2.5). The goal was to divide Rhine water two-thirds to the Waal, two-ninths to the Neder Rijn, and one-ninth to the IJssel.

The Neder Rijn now received more water than before, but the silting process did not abate. Between 1700 and 1750, the bed of this river rose by one meter. The other stretches of the Rijn-Maas river system experienced much the same thing, and this, in turn, wrought havoc with the drainage of adjacent polders. Additional windmills were sometimes needed to pump water to the rising level of the silting rivers, locks had to be rebuilt, and, most seriously, mile after mile of river dike had to be raised. The changing distribution of Rhine water plus the always irregular flow of Maas water created problems for navigation and chronic flooding of the low-lying land extending from the German border to the Delta. Efforts to divert water to improve navigation in one area put new pressure on the dikes and stimulated the silting of river channels elsewhere in this complex web of waterways.

The increasing number of river-caused inundations in the eighteenth century concentrated the attention of surveyors and engineers on the hydrographic character of the rivers. The concept of a self-regulating river, one in which the proper channeling of river water would cause it to deepen its own channels, gained currency among these experts. But the decentralized institutional structure made it impossible to implement such concepts in the systematic way necessary for their success. Instead, the provinces and drainage boards relied on expedients such as reserving land for intentional flooding at designated points. This hydraulic equivalent to bloodletting did nothing to resist the progressive silting of the rivers. The phenomenal rise in river dike failures during the eighteenth century was reduced thereafter only by conceding defeat and permitting voluntary and, it was hoped, controlled flooding. Only after 1850 were truly effective river control measures implemented. In this case the theoretical understanding preceded by a century the institutional capacity for implementation.[5]

Another example of environmental deterioration is the effect of land protection and reclamation measures on the navigability of harbors. The polder forming and sluice building that spread throughout Holland reduced the speed at which surplus water discharged into the sea at the dammed river mouths. When, after 1544, the newly established *Hoogheemraadschap van de Uitwaterende Sluizen* pushed forward the completion of the defensive dikes and dams around North Holland, the shipbuilding center of Edam objected – and offered armed resistance. It feared that sluices in the harbor mouth would result in the silting of the harbor, which, indeed, is what happened in the seventeenth century. Edam's role as a center of shipbuilding dis-

---

[5] This is the assessment of Auke van der Woud, *Het lege land* (Amsterdam, 1987), pp. 95–107.

solved as the more accessible Zaandam rose to prominence. But here, too, a similar, if more gradual, process was at work. In 1736 Zaandam began dredging its harbor on the IJ, but neither there nor at Edam could the natural processes be stopped. By 1800 oceangoing vessels could reach the Zaan only during the highest tides.

Even the Republic's major ports were affected. The sand bank at the mouth of Amsterdam's harbor, the Pampus, grew during the eighteenth century. Naturally, a port of such size and wealth fought back. Amsterdam built large dredging vessels, each accommodating many horses to power the dredging buckets. By 1778 five of these elaborate contraptions worked steadily, filling 150 scows with mud at an annual cost to the city of 107,000 guilders. In 1691 Amsterdam built the first "ship's camels," floating drydocks that fit around the hull of large ships and raised them up to a height sufficient to clear the sand bars. Ever more lighters were employed to transfer cargoes to and from oceangoing vessels. But all of these measures added costs to the use of Amsterdam's harbor without stemming the silting process, which continued throughout the eighteenth century, threatening the very survival of Amsterdam as a port. The remedy, achieved only in the nineteenth century, involved abandoning the Zuider Zee entry altogether and digging canals (the North Holland Canal of 1824 and the North Sea Canal of 1876) to give the city entirely new access routes to the open sea.

In the Delta area, the port of Rotterdam spent steadily increasing sums on harbor dredging: 4,000 to 6,000 guilders annually in the 1680s; at least 25,000 in the 1740s; over 40,000 annually after 1760. But just as in the Zuider Zee, navigation problems extended beyond the harbor waters proper to the Delta's channels to the open sea. Already in the seventeenth century, the accretion of the sand bank island of Rozenburg had rendered the Brielse Gat steadily less navigable. The more southerly Goereese Gat and Brouwershavense Gat (see Map 2.2), while deeper, forced ships to follow circuitous routes (100 km versus 35 km via the Brielse Gat) and wait for the right winds and tides. Here, too, no relief came until entirely new channels were dug in the nineteenth century (the Voorne Canal of 1829 and the Nieuwe Waterweg of 1872 – a project first broached in 1732).

A particularly serious problem of the eighteenth century was the deterioration of the quality of the surface water in Holland. The reduced tidal action of the Zuider Zee (at Halfweg, in the IJ, ebb fell 79 inches in 1570, but only 36 inches in the eighteenth century), the slower discharge of drainage water to the sea, the reduction of the surface water area brought about by reclamation, the resulting penetration of salt water into formerly freshwater areas, and the growth of population, urbanization, and polluting industries, all conspired to intensify this problem. In the alluvial zone of the Netherlands, the main alternative to surface water for consumption and industry was rain water. Hence, the quality of surface water was a matter of grave importance. Its deterioration appears to have proceeded gradually, reaching truly dangerous dimensions in the eighteenth century.

Already in the early seventeenth century, brewers in the growing city of Leiden complained that the drainage of a nearby lake had slowed the circulation of water through the city. Within a few years, the brewers began to rely on water hauled in from outside. The city built windmills to speed water circulation through the city canals, but none of the steps taken made a measurable difference. Thus sensitized to the effect of land reclamation on the circulation of water, Leiden's city fathers became implacable opponents to all proposals to drain the Haarlemmermeer. Until the end of the Republic, "green" politics in Leiden took the form of an oath, required of every new regent, by which the aspiring officeholder abjured all cooperation with any proposal to drain that vast lake.[6]

In Amsterdam the city government built four windmills in 1681 to supplement tidal action in circulating water through its canals. Shortly thereafter the brewers of Amsterdam abandoned local water supplies and imported water via barges from the river Vecht. In 1761 the city built underground containers to store potable water for distribution in times of shortage – particularly during dry, hot summers. Private water haulers became more numerous. But these measures could do little to prevent waterborne diseases – malaria, typhus, and cholera among others – from becoming particularly virulent in the alluvial zone, especially where population density was also high.

The first detailed mortality statistics, available for the mid–nineteenth century, reveal this zone to have the highest mortality rates in the Netherlands.[7] Among the several factors that could help to account for the very high mortality levels in the alluvial zone, environment, particularly as it worked through the water quality, was of great importance. But it was not a constant. Although our knowledge of pre–nineteenth century mortality rates is not highly detailed, it appears likely that death rates in the alluvial zone had been lower in the seventeenth century, and less conspicuously at variance with other regions. Environmental deterioration appears to have driven mortality to unprecedented levels in the course of the eighteenth century.

Our knowledge of the timing of natural forces at work in the sixteenth through eighteenth centuries, and of the specific consequences of interaction between such forces and human intervention, is far from complete. But it is fascinating to observe how the natural environment at times permitted investments that improved the economic value of the territory, while at other times it undermined that value, setting in motion a process of deterioration that costly repair projects could not fully reverse. Superimposed on this is the economic environment which at times made drainage, reclamation, and navigation schemes profitable, and at other times discouraged even the maintenance of existing facilities. While it is by no means always possible to isolate the natural from the economic factors at work, it is clear that both are needed to account for the timing of improvement and retrogression of the physical infrastructure of the Dutch economy.

[6] Maarten Prak, *Gezeten burgers* (The Hague, 1985), p. 40.
[7] A. C. de Vooys, "De sterfte in Nederland in het midden der 19e eeuw," *Tijdschrift van het Koninklijk Nederlandsch Aardrijkskundig Genootschap 68* (1951), 233–71.

Chapter 3
The people

3.1. Introduction

The demographic characteristics of the population that lived between 1500 and 1800 on the land now known as the Netherlands differed little, if at all, from those of the rest of Europe. Everywhere one encountered high birth and death rates (between 30 to 40 per 1,000 population per annum), very high infant mortality rates (200 to 300 deaths before age one per 1,000 births), correspondingly high child mortality, and, as a consequence of all this, a low average life expectancy at birth (usually between 27 and 35 years). Mortality was dominated by exogenous causes, the most important being the consequence of infections, gastrointestinal illnesses, and respiratory problems. It remains a matter of debate whether the so-called "European Marriage Pattern" that prevailed throughout the seventeenth, eighteenth, and nineteenth centuries was fully developed by 1500. But once in place, marriage here as elsewhere in western and central Europe occurred late (usually between ages 23 and 30), and a substantial percentage of the population (10 to 20 percent) never married.

In all these dimensions, the Dutch did not differ much from other Europeans. But in several respects their demographic history revealed special characteristics and developments. These can be summarized in the following six points:

1. a long-sustained demographic growth, extending up to the turning point in the secular trend, in the third quarter of the seventeenth century;
2. a failure to participate in the general European revival of population growth in the second half of the eighteenth century;

46

3. large regional differences in demographic behavior over relatively short distances;
4. a high level of urbanization;
5. a large volume of interregional and international migration; and
6. a household structure of an apparently modern type.

The reader was introduced earlier to the terms *secular trend* and *long sixteenth century*. The latter refers to an era of expansion stretching from about 1460 to 1660 and can be thought of as a phase in the secular trend, which itself is a collective term embracing several outward signs of growth and contraction. In Chapter 2 (section 2.2.4), we described the secular trend chiefly on the basis of long-term price movements, trends in relative prices, and trends in purchasing power. It is clear that these long-term processes had their effects on numerous aspects of social and cultural life. Even geographical transformations could be linked to the secular trend (see Chapter 2, section 2.3.1). For the sake of simplicity, we regarded population change there as an exogenous variable.

But matters are not so simple. Given the present state of our knowledge, we cannot state unequivocally that population change was chiefly exogenous or endogenous to the performance of the economy. One thing is clear: The economic growth that first revealed itself in the late fifteenth century and persisted, with varying intensity, for some two centuries was intimately bound together with a dramatic growth of population.

Although our knowledge of fifteenth-century population developments in the northern Netherlands remains sketchy, it appears that the period from 1477 to about 1520 – the last period of widespread political and social unrest before the entire region fell, in 1543, under the administrative orbit of Charles V – most likely experienced some decline in population. Indeed, medievalists now hold that Holland's total population in 1514 did not much exceed its size on the eve of the Black Death.

By Charles V's reign (1515–55), the basis for expansion was definitely present, especially in the more populous western provinces. The struggle against the Duke of Alva (1572–76) temporarily renewed disorder to those provinces; otherwise, they were spared the scourge of war. The eastern and southern regions continued for several decades to experience the march of troops and the sound of battle, although military actions here never inflicted the devastation they did in the German lands during the Thirty Years' War (1618–48). The relative mildness – and in key regions the absence – of military action is an important reason for the long-sustained growth of population in the Northern Netherlands during the long sixteenth century.

Much the same can be said for the second great scourge that plagued preindustrial populations: hunger. With Amsterdam functioning as Europe's grain storage facility, the near absence of food crises after the 1570s cannot be altogether surprising. There were, to be sure, years of high prices resulting from harvest failures and warfare that disturbed the shipment of grain. But even then the Dutch population did not suffer the so-called *crise de subsistance*, where high prices and high mortality went hand in hand. At any rate, such social dramas are absent until the final decades of the eighteenth century. Then, as Chapter 12 describes in more detail, a persisting price inflation forced a structural deterioration of the working class diet. But in the two intervening centuries, reports of serious tensions arising from high grain prices come only in the years 1623, 1629–30, 1662, and 1698. For the great bulk of the population, the price of grain had only an incidental, and then a marginal, effect on mortality rates.

Before 1580 matters were quite different. On the basis of Utrecht price records, we can identify the following years of exceptionally high grain prices (with the percentage increase over the average of the preceding eleven years given in parentheses): 1480–82 (at their peak, prices rose 400%), 1519–22 (158%), 1555–7 (180%), 1570–3 (211%), 1592–8 (143%), 1620–4 (172%), and 1627–31 (116%). But even here the incidence of crisis years was not great by contemporary international standards, nor did these crises (except for the first) distinguish themselves by their severity. There were, to be sure, instances of extreme privation, such as during the sieges of Zutphen and Nijmegen in the 1580s (when prices tripled and quadrupled). But these isolated events could not influence the mortality levels of the Netherlands as a whole.

With respect to the third scourge, sickness, we cannot be so sanguine. By sickness we refer especially to recurring epidemics, among which the bubonic plague and smallpox were most feared. In a region so urbanized, and with the high density of rural population that existed in the western provinces already in the sixteenth century, only exceptionally favorable ecological circumstances could have prevented the regular recurrence of epidemic diseases. But the circumstances were anything but favorable.

Until bubonic plague disappeared from northwestern Europe between 1665 and 1670, it struck repeatedly in the Northern Netherlands. The form of its visitations changed over time. Until the mid–sixteenth century, it appears to have been endemic, causing a limited number of deaths every year. When natural conditions favored it, the plague took on an epidemic form, suddenly bringing death to thousands. After 1550 the plague ceased to be endemic in the Netherlands, whereupon the epidemic form became the norm. After 1606 serious plague years were 1624–25, 1635–6, 1654–6, and 1664–6. These epidemics alone appear to have accounted for about 10 percent of all deaths that occurred between 1620 and 1670.

We must not suppose, however, that the disappearance of plague after 1670 brought about a 10 percent reduction in the long-term death rate. Nature abhors a vacuum, and the conditions that had been so hospitable to the plague attracted other diseases, which quickly invaded the disease niches vacated by the plague. Besides dysentery the most important was smallpox, which grew in importance from the late seventeenth century. By the final third of the eighteenth century,

48

our evidence suggests that smallpox accounted for nearly 10 percent of total mortality in the Republic's larger cities. In years of epidemic, its impact could be much greater, of course, and epidemic years were frequent. Indeed, they were so common that medical opinion wrongly took smallpox to be a childhood illness, one that nearly all children would contract, and to which they would either succumb or develop a measure of immunity. In the eighteenth century, smallpox was probably the chief cause of death of children under age ten.

These newly potent diseases were joined, in large parts of the West and North, by yet another epidemiological novelty. In the course of the seventeenth century, a gradual but unstoppable process of ecological degradation occurred as a result of slowing circulation of surface water and the increased brackishness of the polders, all the result of processes described in Chapter 2 (sections 2.2.2 and 2.2.4). This combination created an excellent ecological niche for the anopheles mosquito, the carrier of the parasites causing malaria. Malaria is not, by itself, usually fatal, but the recurring bouts of fever that it induces weakens the patient, increasing the chance of succumbing to one or another opportunistic illness. We can document that malaria-spreading mosquitoes, breeding in the brackish polder waters, led to intense outbreaks of acute malaria in 1807 and 1826, resulting in massive mortality. It is likely that this disease had existed in an endemic form already for at least a century. We can furnish no direct evidence for this conclusion, but the indirect evidence is compelling. Especially important in this process was the increasing salinity of the Zuider Zee, which by the eighteenth century contained fresh water only in the direct vicinity of the mouth of the river IJssel. Against this background, we have a plausible explanation for the gradual increase in the annual number of deaths (while the number of births remains stable) throughout the region between Utrecht and Alkmaar. This increased mortality climaxed in the severe mortality crisis of 1726–8, although we cannot be certain whether this was the first true malaria epidemic or the result of other diseases.

An unfavorable balance of births and deaths, with little if any surplus of births in the countryside and a substantial surplus of deaths in the cities, persisted in the northwestern portion of the Netherlands into the nineteenth century. It fit neatly into the environment of economic contraction that took root in the late seventeenth century and, likewise, continued into the nineteenth century. In demographic terms, this tendency toward declining or, at best, stagnant, population was just compensated by the (generally modest) growth of population in the East and South of the Republic after 1650. Over the entire three-century period, there was first, during the long sixteenth century, a vigorous growth which turned, after the mid–seventeenth century, to stagnation or even decline. The absence of overall growth persisted into the early nineteenth century (see Table 3.1). Especially noteworthy is the absence of renewed population growth after 1750, when this became general everywhere else in Europe.

When we view the entire span of time from 1500 to the present, the population movements of the Netherlands appear to fit neatly with the major secular processes

Table 3.1. *The estimated population of the Netherlands (within modern borders), 1500–1800.*

1500	900,000	to	1,000,000
1550	1,200,000	to	1,300,000
1600	1,400,000	to	1,600,000
1650	1,850,000	to	1,900,000
1700	1,850,000	to	1,950,000
1750	1,900,000	to	1,950,000
1800	2,100,000		

Source: J. A. Faber et al., "Population Changes and Economic Development in the Netherlands: A Historical Survey," *A. A. G. Bijdragen 12* (1965), p. 110.

of economic change: two great phases of growth (the long sixteenth century and the nineteenth and twentieth centuries) separated by a phase of secular stagnation (and the most recent growth phase is possibly superseded now by a new era of stagnation). In these great cycles, the characteristics of Dutch population growth reveal at least three distinctive features. To begin with, nowhere else did the population growth of the long sixteenth century persist so far into the seventeenth century as in the Republic. Likewise, nowhere else did the contraction phase persist so long (to 1815 instead of 1740–50). And, true to tradition, the same seems to have occurred in the twentieth century, as Dutch population grew by some 50 percent between 1950 and 1980, while in nearby European countries, the long nineteenth century growth of population showed by then distinct signs of deceleration. In the five centuries since 1500, the population of the Netherlands has grown far more than in nearby countries: fifteenfold (see Figure 3.1) instead of France's fourfold increase and Belgium and Germany's sixfold increase.

3.2. Regional population growth to 1795

Our knowledge of the course of population change for several regions since the Middle Ages is poor to nonexistent. This is especially the case for the southwest (Zeeland and the South Holland islands), the center (Utrecht and the lands between the rivers), and Groningen in the far northeast. Moreover, when we confine ourselves to the districts that do provide sufficient information, substantial regional variation in the course of population growth reveals itself. Indeed, at times this variation seems to have assumed a pattern of opposites, and this pattern becomes most apparent when we pass over local variations to focus on the course of popu-

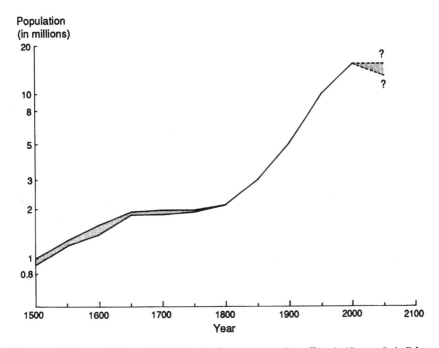

Figure 3.1. The population of the Netherlands, 1500–2050 (in millions). (*Sources:* J. A. Faber et al., "Population Changes," p. 110; Central Bureau of Statistics, Censuses, Demographic Projections.)

lation change in the two most basic regions of the Netherlands: the alluvial West and North and the diluvial East and South. This distinction is to some extent a product of the concentration of military activity in the East and, especially, the South during the Eighty Years' War. Indeed, the distinct status of the South as a bundle of territories (re)conquered by the Republic requires a separate discussion in what follows. But in general these regional demographic patterns appear to be well connected to the major phases of the secular trend discussed earlier. Thus we can maintain clarity in this discussion by treating the two large regions separately, in each case focusing in turn on the periods 1500–1650, 1650–1750, 1750–95.

3.2.1. THE WEST AND NORTH

Holland and Friesland (and probably adjacent parts of the alluvial zone) experienced a population explosion between 1500 and 1650. The number of inhabitants of these two provinces tripled (from 350,000 to 1,000,000), a growth unmatched in the Europe of this time. The English population, for example, just managed to double in the period 1520–1670, while that of the Southern Netherlands grew

Table 3.2. *The population of Holland, 1514–1795 (in thousands).*

	1514	1622	circa 1650	circa 1680	circa 1750	1795
Holland north of the IJ:						
Seven cities*	22	64	70	—	35	35
Zaan region	7	20	24	—	28	25
Rural population	52	106	117	—	65	68
Total	81	109	211	188	128	128
Holland south of the IJ:						
Twelve cities*	105	299	—	—	—	427
Rural population	89	183	—	—	—	228
Total	194	482	—	695	655	655
Grand total	275	672		883	783	783

*The 18 voting cities of Holland plus The Hague.
Source: A. M. van der Woude, *Het Noorderkwartier* (Wageningen, 1972), Vol. I, pp. 185–93.

by no more than 50–55 percent in the interval 1500–1665. Of course, this overall statement hides from view the dramatic growth, collapse, and recovery of the Southern Netherlands population. After growing at the same pace as the North up to 1565, the South suffered a loss of perhaps 25 percent of its population to death and migration in the following thirty years of Revolt and Reconquest. Antwerp alone lost half of the nearly 100,000 people living there in 1565. After 1600 the population of the South grew again, but by the time that this growth reached its apex in the 1660s, the position of a century earlier had been regained, but no more.

Not only did the total population of the North and West grow rapidly, but this growth persisted across the whole period (with the single exception of the 1570s, when warfare affected the region directly) and was shared by both the rural and urban sectors. Still, it is useful to divide this growth phase into two parts: Before 1580 the rate of rural population growth tended to exceed that of the cities; thereafter, the countryside continued its growth, but the urban pace accelerated. Indeed, a great wave of urbanization is the most striking feature of Dutch population history after 1580.

In the century of contraction after the 1650s, the demographic situation in this region exhibited less uniformity than before (see Table 3.2). Rural population ceased its growth soon after 1650, and not long thereafter, several important districts (especially North Holland and southwestern Friesland) experienced sharp demographic contraction. Elsewhere, we see a restless pattern of often contradictory local developments, but taken in the aggregate, they justify the conclusion that rural population growth in the alluvial zone ceased.

Table 3.3. *The population of Friesland, 1511–1796 (in thousands).*

	1511	1660	1689[a]	1714	1744	1796
Rural districts						
Clay pasture zone	—	—	20.5	19.5	19.5	21.5
Peat pasture zone	—	—	16.5	15	16.5	20
De Wouden	—	—	24.5	26.5	32	39
Clay arable zone	—	—	24.5	24	26	32
Total rural	60		86	85.5	94	112.5
Total cities	19		43	43.5	41	45
Total population	79	160	129	129	135	157.5

[a] The 1689 census is believed to suffer from a systematic underregistration of 5 to 10 percent. Thus, the total 1689 population probably stood between 135,000 and 142,000.
Source: J. A. Faber, *Drie eeuwen Friesland* (Wageningen, 1972), Vol. II, pp. 413–15.

As in the countryside, so in the cities; the century after 1650 was marked by local variation. No single trend shapes them all. In the cities of North Holland and most of those in Friesland, population decline set in soon after 1650; in Holland south of the IJ, urban growth seems to have persisted for another twenty years. After 1670 a few of them remained stable, but most suffered decline. We examine the experience of individual cities later on. Taken together, the population of Holland and Friesland, both urban and rural, fell between 1680 and 1750 by 100,000 to 125,000 – that is, by some 10 percent of its peak level.

After 1750 the demographic situation changed again. In Friesland (see Table 3.3), population growth returned as early as the 1730s; in rural West Friesland (a district of North Holland), modest growth set in after 1750. Simultaneously we see signs of population growth and recovery in the South Holland delta and adjacent districts. In between, in rural central Holland, it is hard to detect a pattern in the substantial local variation, and much the same may be said of the cities. Some continued to decline, while elsewhere the earlier declines were moderated or even reversed. Once again, the aggregate figures show little net change: Holland's population remained essentially constant at some 785,000, while Friesland's grew by 20,000 between 1750 and 1795.

3.2.2. THE EAST

The three contiguous territories for which demographic studies have been made (Veluwe, Overijssel, and Drenthe) provide quite accurate data concerning their populations in 1795 and around 1750. The claims to accuracy for population

Table 3.4. *The population of Overijssel, 1475–1795 (in thousands).*

	1475	1675	1748	1795
Rural districts				
Salland	16.5	23	35	41
Twente	11	18	49	53
Vollenhove	5	10	13.5	14
Subtotal	33	51	97	108
Three Cities	20	20	25	27
Total population	53	71	122	135

Source: B. H. Slicher van Bath, *Een samenleving onder spanning* (Assen, 1957).

estimates around 1650 must be tempered, and for 1500 matters are worse yet, since we have no information at all about sixteenth-century Drenthe (see Tables 3.4 and 3.5). We can observe an underlying peacetime growth rate of about 2 percent per annum on the sandy soils of these three territories after 1650. Before then, matters are complicated by the influence of military activities between 1580 and 1610. How much they are complicated is not known, so the best bases for an estimate of population in 1500 are documents suggesting the number of inhabitants in the Veluwe in 1526 and Overijssel in 1475. Adjusting these to 1500 (under the assumption of 2 percent annual growth), and assuming that Drenthe's (small) population followed the course traced out by its larger neighbors, yields the following total population estimates for the three territories together:

1500	105,000–110,000
1650	130,000
1750	215,000
1795	240,000

These estimates fashion something like a mirror image of the course of population change in the North and West. There we noted a tripling of population between 1500 and 1650, while in the East the means of subsistence allowed for little growth at all. Probably the only real expansion of employment occurred in districts where the digging and transport of peat were concentrated. But, we must also keep in mind the possibility that some sixteenth-century growth was undone by the military operations that plagued the region after 1580, causing temporary depopulation in various border zones.

Between 1650 and 1750, the Eastern region's population history reverses itself. While the West and North experienced a 10 percent decline in numbers, population growth in the East accelerated. This is consistent with what we know about the emergence of labor-intensive crops (especially tobacco), the spread of rural industrial employment (paper and textiles), the employment in the peat bogs,

Table 3.5. *The populations of the*
Veluwe and Drenthe, 1526–1795
(in thousands).

	Veluwe	Drenthe
1526	36.0	
1630		21.9
1650	40.7	
1672		25.2
1692		28.7
1742		34.1
1749	54.2	
1754		35.1
1764		36.1
1774		37.7
1784		38.3
1795	65.8	39.7

Source: H. K. Roessingh, "Het
Veluwse inwonertal, 1526–1947,"
A. A. G. Bijdragen 11 (1964), p.
108; Jan Bieleman, *Boeren op het*
Drentse zand (Wageningen, 1987),
p. 68.

and the market-driven transformation experienced by agriculture in Drenthe, all
of which are discussed in later chapters.

After 1750 there occurs yet another reversal of sorts, as population growth in
the East decelerates, while in the West and North the earlier decline shows signs
of giving way to slow growth. A definitive explanation for this development is
not yet at hand, but we are inclined to link deceleration in the East to the
weakening of the competitive position of its labor-intensive industrial and cash-
crop production.

3.2.3. THE SOUTH

In both Limburg and States-Brabant (i.e., the portion of the old Duchy of Brabant
under the control of the States General, the central organ of Republican government), the population in all their subregions grew between 1750 and 1795 by
about 20 percent. This performance corresponded closely with that of neighboring
Belgian districts to the south as well as the riverine zones directly to the north.
In absolute numbers the southern region grew from 295,000 to 340,000 inhabitants.

The century before 1750 should be seen as a period of revival after the depredations of the Eighty Years' War concluded with the treaty of Münster in 1648. In this period the population of Limburg varied between 110,000 and 120,000, but this can be decomposed into two distinct patterns, one for northern and another for the southern portions of the province. The experience in the northern portion corresponded to that of the neighboring eastern half of States-Brabant. Once peace came the population revived vigorously, but this revival came to a halt well before the region regained its pre-Revolt population level. For example, the area around 's-Hertogenbosch, the Meierij, could count only 100,000 inhabitants around 1750 yet had possessed some 120,000 in the 1560s. It is possible that uncertainties generated by new war dangers between 1672 and 1706 played some role in this new stagnation.

A conspicuous feature of the northern Limburg/eastern Brabant region was its strong deurbanization; between 1550 and 1750, the urban population fell from 25 to 15 percent of the total. In southern Limburg the revival of population growth was largely an eighteenth-century matter and was accompanied by pronounced urbanization, with city-dwellers reaching 35 percent of the total population by 1795. South Limburg was much more densely populated than the northern region (80 versus 40 inhabitants per square kilometer), a fact reflecting the greater fertility of the southern loess soils.

Over the entire period 1500–1795, no more than a minor net growth of population occurred in the southern region. A rapid growth in the first half of the sixteenth century was interrupted by the Revolt and the wars that followed, so that the pre-Revolt population level was not regained until two centuries later. In this long era of recovery, the urban–rural balance shifted decisively toward the countryside. Antwerp's altered function wreaked havoc with the economies of the towns that had been in its orbit, such as Roermond, Venlo, Weert, and, especially, 's-Hertogenbosch. They all suffered from the transfer of the economic center of gravity from south to north. The more successful eighteenth-century urbanization of South Limburg, focused on Maastricht, may be traced to stimuli that the region received from the metallurgical and textile industries of the nearby Liège region, and its intermediate position between that region and the Rhineland.

Before concluding this survey of regional population movements, some attention should be devoted to the exceptional character of two unusual subregions: the villages strung along the river Zaan in North Holland, and Twente, in easternmost Overijssel. The populations of both grew rapidly between 1650 and 1750. In the Zaan region, this growth flew directly in the face of the population collapse of the surrounding countryside; Twente's growth was simply much faster than that of adjacent districts. In both cases the same source fed this exceptional growth: the removal of industry from city to countryside. Both of these cases are considered in some detail in Chapter 8. Here we must emphasize that their growth was the pendant to the post-1650 deurbanization process, which affected industrial cities most severely.

3.3. The Batavian-French Era

The period 1795–1815 deserves a separate discussion, if only because for the first time we have at our disposal two comprehensive censuses separated by only twenty years. From Table 3.6, which shows the provincial totals for both 1795 and 1815, we can see that, just as before, contradictory forces characterized regional population movements: in the East, South, and now also the North, growth varied from 9 to 18 percent; in the West population fell absolutely, by 5.7 percent in Holland and 1.8 percent in Zeeland.

But these differences were not simply reflections of distinct regional economies. When we divide the population change into its urban and rural components, it becomes apparent that in all provinces (except Overijssel and Drenthe) the cities fell behind the growth of the rural populations. The period 1795–1815 is one of a pronounced deurbanization. In Holland and Zeeland, this resulted in a fall in urban population of some 51,000 inhabitants. In view of the great weight of Holland's cities in the total, this decline more than compensated for the modest growth of cities elsewhere to produce a net decline of 2.4 percent in the nation's urban population. The rural population grew in all provinces except Holland. But there, the total decline of rural population (less than 3,000) was more than accounted for by population decline in the Zaan region, the semi-urbanized industrial zone that lost 3,500 inhabitants during this period.

We can conclude that everywhere except in Holland the rural population experienced a substantial growth (averaging 12 percent), a growth that almost everywhere exceeded the growth of the cities. This rural population growth should be seen as an extension of the renewed growth that began in several subregions around 1750. This essentially rural and provincial growth is all but hidden from view by the great crisis being experienced by the urban economy, and most especially by the entirety of urbanized Holland. There, between 1795 and 1815, the semi-urban Zaan region declined by 14 percent, the cities of Holland and Zeeland declined by 10 percent, and even Holland's countryside, so symbiotically connected with its cities, could muster no growth at all.

3.4. Urbanization

We shall begin our investigation of urbanization near the end of our time period, with the first Dutch national census of 1795. This identifies ninety-eight places that qualify as urban. Table 3.7 groups these cities by size, from which it is quickly apparent that the urban population was by no means highly concentrated in one or a few cities. Every size category was well represented, with the numbers de-

Table 3.6. *Population in the Batavian-French period.*[a]

Province	1795	1815	Percentage growth
Urban population[b]			
Groningen	29,249	34,162	16.8
Friesland	44,824	47,137	5.2
Drenthe	9,646	11,594	20.2
Overijssel	46,954	52,415	11.6
Gelderland	58,365	64,207	10.0
Utrecht	47,835	50,945	6.5
Holland	483,078	439,780	-9.0
Zeeland	37,494	29,364	-21.7
North Brabant	41,037	42,798	9.2
Limburg	38,822	42,926	10.6
Netherlands	837,304	817,328	-2.4
Rural population			
Groningen	85,406	101,480	18.8
Friesland	116,689	129,417	10.9
Drenthe	30,026	34,885	16.2
Overijssel	88,421	95,238	7.7
Gelderland	164,851	190,483	15.5
Utrecht	49,307	56,762	15.1
Holland	311,068	308,788	-0.7
Zeeland	77,122	83,244	7.9
North Brabant	219,204	247,881	13.1
Limburg	99,293	112,390	13.2
Netherlands	1,241,387	1,360,568	9.6
Total population			
Groningen	114,655	135,642	18.3
Friesland	161,513	176,554	9.3
Drenthe	39,672	46,479	17.2
Overijssel	135,375	147,653	9.1
Gelderland	223,216	254,690	14.1
Utrecht	97,142	107,707	10.9
Holland	794,146	748,568	-5.7
Zeeland	114,616	112,608	-1.8
North Brabant	260,241	292,679	12.5
Limburg	138,115	155,316	12.5
Netherlands	2,078,691	2,177,896	4.8

[a]Modern provincial and national borders.
[b]98 cities, as listed in A. M. van der Woude, "Demografische ontwikkeling," p. 139.

Table 3.7. *Urban population in 1795.*

Size category	Number of cities	Urban population	Percentage
>100,000	1	217,024	25.9
25,000–100,000	4	154,894	18.5
10,000–25,000	11	181,208	21.6
5,000–10,000	18	130,691	11.3
2,500–5,000	27	94,367	11.3
<2,500	37	59,120	7.1
Total	98	837,304	100.0

Source: A. M. van der Woude, "Les villes," p. 238.

clining, of course, as their size increases. Table 3.8 organizes the cities of 1795 by province, demonstrating that a high urbanization rate was not confined to Holland alone. With the exception of North Brabant, every province was substantially urbanized. In Holland the urban percentage exceeded 60 percent, and in Utrecht it reached 50 percent. In the other provinces, it varied between 25 and 35 percent, yielding a national average of 40 percent. This level of urbanization had no equal in any other European country of the time, although the English urban population was fast moving toward it.

Cities held a substantial share of the population nearly everywhere, but already in the time of the Republic the urban pattern known in the twentieth century as the *Randstad* (literally, rim city) clearly was present. The territory enclosed by the great circle of cities Amsterdam–Haarlem–Leiden–The Hague–Delft–Rotterdam–Gouda–Utrecht–Amsterdam contained in 1795 a total of 625,000 inhabitants (about 30 percent of the total), of whom over 70 percent, or nearly 445,000, resided in the cities. In other words, of all the Republic's urban residents in 1795, 55 percent lived in the *Randstad*. To be sure, half of all *Randstad* residents were concentrated in one city: Amsterdam. Its standing as the leading city was undisputed; but it held no monopoly on urban functions. The distribution of functions among *Randstad* cities had been even more pronounced in the seventeenth century, leading the cultural historian Johan Huizinga to remark that "Truly, Dutch civilization in Rembrandt's day was concentrated in a region not much more than sixty miles square."[1] The vitality of this urban network helped to define the special character of economic, political, and cultural life in the Netherlands – then as now.

Nor should we forget what a bit of arithmetic reveals: outside the *Randstad* of 1795, there lived 1,350,000 persons, of whom some 415,000, or 30 percent, were

[1] Johan Huizinga, *Dutch Civilization in the Seventeenth Century* (London, 1968), p. 15.

Table 3.8. *Urbanization rate by province, and the share of each province in the urban, rural, and total population of the Netherlands in 1795.*

Province	Urbanization	Share of total		
		Urban pop.	Rural pop.	Total pop.
Groningen	26 %	3.5 %	6.9 %	5.5 %
Friesland	28	5.3	9.4	7.8
Drenthe	24	1.1	2.4	1.9
Overijssel	35	5.6	7.1	6.5
Gelderland	26	7.1	13.2	10.7
Utrecht	49	5.7	4.0	4.7
Holland	61	57.6	25.1	38.2
Zeeland	33	4.5	6.2	5.5
North Brabant	16	4.9	17.7	12.5
Limburg	28	4.6	8.0	6.6
Republic	40	100.0	100.0	100.0

urbanites. Thus, the Republic absent its urban heart was *still* the most urbanized country of Europe!

With Table 3.9 we turn to the development of Dutch urbanization since the early sixteenth century. In contrast to Tables 3.6 through 3.8, we now consider only those cities with at least 2,500 inhabitants. Note that in 1795 such a definition would reduce the urban percentage from 40 to 37 percent. There is no reason to believe that the population in cities of less than 2,500 would have been much more or less than 3 percent of the total in 1750 or even 1675. In the early sixteenth century, however, such little cities were relatively more prominent, accounting for 4 to 5 percent of the total population. When these adjustments are made to the data in Table 3.9, the total urbanization rate (including all cities, regardless of size) proceeds as follows:

1525	31–32%
1675	45%
1750	42%
1795	40%
1815	38%

These data reveal, first, the high level of urbanization obtaining already at the beginning of the sixteenth century; second, the great intensification of urbanization in the following 150 years; and third, the gradual deurbanization that persisted for the 140 years following 1675.

A further analysis of Table 3.9 reveals that the process of urbanization took a different form in Holland than in the other provinces taken together. Both of

Table 3.9. *The urbanization of the Northern Netherlands in 1525, 1675, 1750, 1795, and 1815 (cities of at least 2,500).*

	Holland	Other Provinces	Total
Number of Cities			
ca. 1525	17	21	38
ca. 1675	23	38	61
ca. 1750	21	39	60
1795	19	42	61
1815	20	43	63
Total Urban Population			
ca. 1525	120,000	180,000	300,000
ca. 1675	540,000	275,000	815,000
ca. 1750	475,000	280,000	755,000
1795	469,000	312,000	781,000
1815	429,000	332,000	761,000
Urbanization Rate (%)			
ca. 1525	44	22	27
ca. 1675	61	27	42
ca. 1750	61	25	39
1795	60	24	37
1815	57	23	35

these territorial units contained some 20 cities (of at least 2,500 inhabitants) in 1525, and their average size in both hovered around 7,000 to 8,000. In the following 150 years, Holland's cities grew very little in number, from 17 to 23, but they assumed a much higher average population, rising to 23,500. It is this growth in city size that pushed Holland's urbanization rate to 60 percent. In the rest of the country taken together, the number of cities with at least 2,500 inhabitants grew substantially, from 21 to 38, but the average size of these cities did not increase at all. As a consequence, the urbanization rate rose only modestly, from 22 to 27 percent. The increased density of the urban network in the outer provinces did not lead to a major advance in urbanization; this focuses our attention all the more on the special character of urbanization in Holland, where a fixed number of cities managed to grow enormously in size.

After 1675 both of these territorial units experienced a measure of deurbanization. But in Holland this took the form of a large decrease in the urban population (from 540,000 to 429,000), while in the other provinces the number of urban residents actually increased (from 275,000 to 332,000). These contrasting developments are consistent with the evidence presented earlier concerning regional population changes as a whole. In Holland the sharp decline in urban population did not result in a dramatic fall in its urbanization rate, because the rural population was also in decline. Outside Holland, the cities grew as they participated in the general population growth of their regions. But their growth did not keep pace with the underlying rural population growth, leading to a fall in the urbanization rate.

Let us return to the three special features of Dutch urbanization identified earlier – first, the high level of urbanization achieved already at the beginning of the sixteenth century. For a territory of this size, containing nearly one million inhabitants, an urbanization rate of 31–32 percent (rising to 45 percent in Holland) was highly unusual. It can be compared only with Venice and its Terrafirma, the Southern Netherlands, and, perhaps, Andalusia in southernmost Spain. But in contrast to these other highly urbanized zones of the early sixteenth century, the Northern Netherlands were no great focal point of international trade and industrial production. There were as yet no cities of great size such as Venice, Seville, Antwerp, and Ghent. To account for the strikingly high level of urbanization in the Northern Netherlands, we can point to its role in shipping and regional trade, to be sure, but even more to its intensive cultivation of a wide variety of small-scale nonagrarian activities.

Concerning the first of these, shipping and regional trade, we must recall the region's medieval endowment of internal shipping routes connecting Flanders and Brabant with the German Hanse trade systems of the north as well as the Rhineland with Flanders/Brabant and England to the west. As described in Chapter 2, section 2.1.2, the multiple inland water routes and channels to the sea provided numerous geographical niches for urban settlements devoted to shipping, commercial services, and toll collection.

The network of internal waterways also encouraged regional specialization and division of labor, which, in turn, gave opportunities to such industries as textiles and brewing. Moreover, the numerous waterways also gave access to fishing grounds of all sorts (freshwater, coastal, and ocean fishing). Around the transport and fishing sectors, there gathered a great tangle of support and processing activities, such as shipbuilding, timber sawing, cooperage, net and sail making, smoking and tanning works, anchor smiths, and so forth. In comparison to later times, all these activities functioned on a small scale, but they provided means of subsistence at many locations. The peculiar urbanization of Holland circa 1500 (based on many small cities) was largely the product of the preceding 150 years, when a substantial rural exodus sought refuge and employment in the towns.

Via this rural depopulation, the late-medieval economy of the Northern Netherlands had made a major commitment to nonagrarian activities. In the sixteenth century, two paths stood open for their continued development: further urbanization and the spread of nonagricultural functions in the countryside. As we shall see in more detail in Chapter 8, both roads were taken, albeit in varying degrees and with shifting accents over time. What is important here is that the widespread pursuit of these nonagrarian activities provided the institutional nucleus and social temperament on which the region's later growth would be based, and they provided it at many locations.

The second fact attracting our attention was the sharp acceleration in urban growth evident in the century beginning around 1580. By the end of this epoch of rapid urban growth, in the 1670s, the Republic reached the high point of its urbanization: 45 percent for all cities (42 percent in cities of over 2,500; 31 percent in cities over 10,000). Before 1580 the urban population also grew, to be sure, but this growth did not exceed that of the rural population. There was then no net urbanization, but one can detect shifts in the relative standing of individual cities pregnant with importance for the character of the later urban explosion. Amsterdam, no larger than a handful of other cities in 1500, experienced faster growth than most, while Leiden, a leading industrial town, stagnated. Outside Holland the two largest cities of the Northern Netherlands, 's-Hertogenbosch and Utrecht, saw their positions erode even before the outbreak of the Revolt, an event that toppled both from their privileged positions in the urban hierarchy. By 1600 they had both been far surpassed by the cities of Holland. 's-Hertogenbosch, Venlo, Bergen-op-Zoom, and Deventer all experienced major population losses, and all the cities south of the river delta became the victims of their orientation to a Southern Netherlands economy now in crisis. The numerous river towns (Heusden, Schoonhoven, Tiel, Gorinchem, Den Briel, Zaltbommel, Woudrichem) also suffered from the shift in the locus of economic activity and could count themselves fortunate if they avoided depopulation. Of all the cities in the river and delta region, only Dordrecht managed to hold its head above water.

With 45 percent of its population resident in cities (31 percent for cities of at least 10,000 inhabitants), the Northern Netherlands attained a level of urbanization that surpassed by a good margin the high point of urbanization in the Southern Netherlands (20 percent for cities of at least 10,000) attained in 1475 and again around 1550. Not until the Industrial Revolution would a third wave of urbanization, this time in England, replace the Republic's achievement with a new standard, as England's population moved from 20 percent urban in 1800 to 40 percent (in cities of at least 10,000) in 1850. Nearly a century later, a fourth, and probably final, wave of urbanization, this time in Germany's Rhine-Ruhr region, would surpass the English level. Four great waves of urbanization have taken place in northwestern Europe in the course of our era's second millennium. It is striking that (1) in each successive case the "saturation point" of urbanization reached a higher level than before; (2) the chief period of urban advance came to be briefer and more intense; and (3) the peak of urbanization was always followed by an unmistakable retrenchment. This last feature we noted earlier as the third of the striking characteristics of Dutch urban history. It is, of course, intimately associated with the economic setbacks and stagnation that afflicted the Dutch economy from

Table 3.10. *Population of the cities of Holland in 1622 and 1795, with index of population change in the interval.*

	1622	1795	Index (1622 = 100)
Dordrecht	18,270	18,014	98.6
Haarlem	39,455	21,227	53.8
Delft*	22,769	16,779	73.7
Leiden	44,745	30,955	69.2
Amsterdam	104,932	217,024	206.8
Gouda	14,627	11,715	80.1
Rotterdam	19,532	53,212	272.4
Gorinchem	5,913	4,969	84.0
Schiedam	5,997	9,111	151.9
Schoonhoven	2,891	2,489	86.1
Den Briel	3,632	3,170	87.3
Alkmaar	12,417	8,373	67.4
Hoorn	14,139	9,551	67.6
Enkhuizen	20,967	6,803	32.4
Edam	5,547	3,709	66.9
Monnikendam	3,990	2,058	51.6
Medemblik	3,983	2,008	50.4
Purmerend	2,556	2,499	97.8
The Hague	15,825	38,433	242.9
Total	362,187	462,099	127.6

*Includes the outport of Delfshaven and the jurisdiction beyond the walls in Overschie.

the third quarter of the seventeenth century, a subject to which we return repeatedly in later chapters. Here we focus on the actual course of urban population change.

Table 3.10 offers a good starting point for an analysis of deurbanization in Holland. A comparison of urban population totals for the two years in which headcounts were taken (1622 and 1795) reveals that Holland's total urban population grew by only 28 percent in the intervening 173 years. But it also reveals a large divergence in the experience of individual cities. Only four cities (Amsterdam, Rotterdam, The Hague, and Schiedam) had larger populations in 1795 than in 1622. Together they more than doubled in population. All the other cities of Holland possessed, in the best cases, the same population or, more commonly, but a fraction of their 1622 populations. Together, their populations fell by 28 percent, from 153,000 to 109,000. Here, too, the diversity of experience requires emphasis. Haarlem's population fell by nearly half, and most of the cities of North Holland declined by one-third to one-half in size. The collapse of Enkhuizen was worse still; in 1795 it possessed but one-third of its 1622 population. Only the small market center of Purmerend managed to buck the tide of urban decline in North Holland, as it benefited from the newly drained polders that enlarged and enriched its hinterland.

South of Haarlem and Amsterdam, the locus of urban decline resided in the industrial cities: Leiden, Delft, and Gouda. All three had from 20 to 30 percent fewer inhabitants in 1795 than in 1622. The cities of the rivers and delta (Dordrecht, Den Briel, Schoonhoven, and Gorinchem) also declined but rather less than the industrial cities.

These two censuses provide a useful starting point for an analysis of deurbanization. But it is only a start, for the year 1622 is an altogether arbitrary date in the history of Dutch urbanization. Thereafter, Holland's cities continued to grow rapidly. Thus, we know that Leiden's 45,000 inhabitants of 1622 grew to over 60,000 by the 1670s. Its decline to 31,000 in 1795 (and further to 28,500 in 1815) was therefore much more dramatic that is suggested by Table 3.10. In Delft the population grew further by a good 35 percent between 1622 and 1680. There, too, the decline that followed was more intense than Table 3.10 can reveal. Rotterdam achieved the largest percentage increase of any city in Holland between 1622 and 1795, growing from 20,000 to 53,000. But even Rotterdam experienced an intervening loss of some 5,000 inhabitants between 1690 and 1745. Haarlem also grew after 1622, becoming so overcrowded that the city fathers decided in 1671, after much dithering, to embark upon a major extension of the city. This costly enterprise could not have been more poorly timed. When completed in 1675, the population was already in decline, and the new space was not fully occupied until well into the nineteenth century.

Nowhere were new urban extensions executed after 1680, not even in Amsterdam, where the one consistent time series that broadly reflects the size of population, a count of marriages, shows a ceiling to have been reached by the 1670s. Thereafter, the annual numbers of marriages fluctuated but could never muster a renewal of sustained growth. The most careful effort to reconstruct Amsterdam's population history extends no further back than 1681, when comprehensive baptism and burial records are first available. By then the seventeenth-century crest of Amsterdam's population had been succeeded by the post-1672 setback. Estimated at 220,000 inhabitants in the 1680s, Amsterdam's population gradually recovered, reaching a peak of 240,000 in the 1720s. Thereafter, the city hovered in the 230,000–240,000 range until 1780, when a decline set in; that decline was not reversed until after 1815, by which date the city had lost some 20 percent of its population.

From all this only one conclusion is possible: The urbanization of Holland continued until the 1670s; thereafter, most cities suffered a sharp reduction of population, a reduction which various sources confirm was all but complete by the mid–eighteenth century. Yet this decline of urban population did not lead to true deurbanization since it was paced, more or less, by a decline of Holland's rural population. Indeed, these two developments were intimately connected, for Holland's rural decline was greatest where rural nonagricultural employments were concentrated (in fishing, seafaring, and industry). Thus, instead of the cities suffering while the countryside flourishes (a common occurrence elsewhere), we see in Holland between 1650 and 1750 a related process of structural change, affecting both city and countryside.

After 1750 the decline of Holland's industrial cities (Haarlem, Delft, and Leiden) slowed but did not stop. Since the rural population now showed signs of revival, a slight trend toward deurbanization asserted itself (see Table 3.10) becoming a major deurbanization during the crisis of the urban economies in 1795–1815. The most conspicuous case of urban decline in this period was Amsterdam. Her relative stability throughout the century 1680–1780 had moderated all tendencies to deurbanization. But now her population fell from 217,000 to 180,000, and she was joined in decline by the aforementioned industrial cities as well as fishing centers such as Enkhuizen (from 6,800 to 5,200), Hoorn (from 9,500 to 7,500), and Maassluis (from 4,900 to 4,400). The one major city to succeed in moving against the current was Rotterdam, which extended its post-1745 growth into the Batavian-French period, growing from 53,000 to 58,000 inhabitants.

One district in Holland followed a demographic course that was quite exceptional, and often at odds with the general trends just described: the rural industrial zone along the river Zaan. Before the mid–seventeenth century, this district's population growth was simply an extreme example of the dynamism characteristic of the entire province. But in contrast to the rest of rural Holland, the Zaan region's growth continued until 1735. Thereafter – that is, once the rest of rural Holland had reached a demographic low point and was beginning to revive – the Zaan region's population embarked on a decline that would be sharp and steady to 1815. The explanation for this exceptional pattern of growth and decline is most likely to be found in the region's success in combining low rural wages with high productivity in capital-intensive industries (described more fully in Chapter 8). The resulting low production costs allowed this major industrial zone to escape the structural decline of industry that affected Holland's cities and the rest of its countryside alike after the 1670s. But when the markets for the industries in which the region specialized (shipbuilding, lumber sawing, and sail-cloth weaving) fell into decline after 1730, not even its production-cost advantages could spare it from a long, painful contraction. In retrospect, the Zaan region appears to have experienced the same fate as the industrial cities, except that its decline was delayed while it could still benefit from the cost advantages that were denied to the cities.

Deurbanization in the eastern provinces is described in Tables 3.11 and 3.12. They reveal a striking similarity between the three large cities of Overijssel and the cities of the Veluwe between the mid–seventeenth and mid–eighteenth cen-

Table 3.11. *The urban and rural population of the Veluwe, 1659–1796.*

	Absolute numbers			Percentages	
	Cities	Countryside	Total	Urban	Rural
1650	13,100	27,600	40,700	32	68
1749	13,900	40,250	54,150	26	74
1795	17,769	48,032	65,801	26	74

Source: A. M. van der Woude, "Les Villes," p. 337.

turies. In both cases the urban share of total population made a decisive retreat (from 32 to 26 percent between 1650 and 1750 in the Veluwe; from 28 to 21 percent between 1675 and 1750 in Overijssel). Both cases also reveal no absolute decrease of urban population, for the deurbanization effect was entirely a product of a faster growing rural population. After 1750 the cities managed to keep pace with the growth of the rural population, bringing the deurbanization process to a close. But the truly spectacular deurbanization of the IJssel cities occurred earlier, from the fifteenth to the seventeenth centuries. Then, as the Hanse towns of Kampen and Deventer in particular lost their long-distance trading functions to Holland (discussed in Chapter 2, section 2.1.2), the cities of Overijssel fell from 38 to 28 percent of the total provincial population.

Our description of regional population trends noted the strong similarity of developments in Holland and Friesland. This is also true of their urban development. The Friesian censuses of 1689 and 1744 reveal a 15 percent fall in urban population, which stands in sharp contrast to the tripling of urban population that had been achieved in the expansive period 1511–1689. The Friesian cities grew in the second half of the eighteenth century, and even in the Batavian-French period, but this growth did not keep pace with that of the rural population. Table 3.13 shows with stark clarity how Friesland's population recovery after 1744 was concentrated in its many small agrarian villages. The larger places, whether official cities or *vlekken* (villages that had grown to become regional market centers), remained behind in this process. Thus, deurbanization in Friesland proceeded through two phases: First, the urban population fell faster than did the rural population; then, after 1744, the towns grew but failed to keep pace with the countryside. As a consequence, the urbanization level fell from 33 percent in 1689 to 30 percent in 1744 and 28 percent in 1795 and 1815.

Our discussion of population developments between 1500 and 1815 can be summarized with the following statements:

1. The chronological development of population is broadly consistent with that of the secular trend described in Chapter 2: vigorous growth until after the mid–seventeenth century, followed by stagnation until the mid–eighteenth

Table 3.12. *Urban population of Overijssel, 1475–1795.*

	Absolute numbers			Percentage of total		
	Total population	Three large cities	16 small cities	Three large cities	16 small cities	Total urban
1475	52,000	20,000	?	38	?	?
1675	70,700	19,700	10,300	28	15	43
1723	100,900	26,200	15,500	25	15	39
1748	122,400	25,100	17,600	21	14	35
1764	132,100	27,600	20,000	21	15	36
1795	134,100	26,700	17,200	20	13	33

Source: A. M. van der Woude, "Les villes," p. 336.

Table 3.13. *Population growth in Friesland by size of community, 1744-1795.*

	Number of towns and villages	1744 Total population	1795 Total population	1795 as percentage of 1744
Towns and villages with:				
0–299 inhabitants	247	31,134	39,969	128
300–699	71	31,678	36,575	115
700–1099	20	17,219	20,887	121
1100–1499	7	8,615	9,752	113
1500–1899	2	3,108	3,453	111
1900 and over	10	43,369	46,882	108
Total	357	135,123	157,518	117

Source: J. A. Faber, *Drie eeuwen Friesland*, Vol. II, p. 418.

century, followed by a renewal of growth which at the aggregate level is all but hidden from view by the situation in Holland, especially its cities.

2. The regional level revealed large differences in population trends, which sometimes moved in opposite directions.

3. Holland and Friesland experienced a major growth of population in the sixteenth and the first half of the seventeenth century. Although the evidence is weaker, we believe that a similar growth affected Zeeland and Groningen.

4. Between 1650 and 1750, the population of the lands surrounding the Zuider Zee was, at best, stagnant, while in Friesland and North Holland, it declined substantially.

5. In roughly the same period (1680–1750), the industrial cities of Holland (Haarlem, Leiden, Delft) experienced a major loss of population, while Rotterdam suffered a more modest decline.

6. After 1750 population growth returned to the North (Friesland and northernmost Holland) and to the southernmost parts of Holland. Central Holland (between Amsterdam and Rotterdam) remained stagnant, and its cities tended to decline further.

7. On the sandy-soil regions in the eastern Netherlands, a moderate growth of population was the rule. But military activities disturbed many areas profoundly during the Eighty Years' War, causing population growth to be greater after 1650 than before.

8. Two rural, industrial subregions followed a specific and exceptional course. In the west the Zaan region grew between 1650 and 1730 as every place around it suffered absolute decline. After 1730, when elsewhere the decline had nearly run its course, it began in earnest in the Zaan region. In the east the Twente region appears to have experienced a much more rapid population growth between 1675 and 1750 than any of the other eastern districts.

9. The South (States-Brabant and Limburg) experienced an overall population growth of about 20 percent in the second half of the eighteenth century, and a further 13 percent growth in the period 1795–1815.

10. Much greater uncertainty attaches to any generalizations about population change in the South before 1750. Between 1500 and 1565, the population of the region around 's-Hertogenbosch (the *Meierij*) grew rapidly. The war period that followed caused the loss of all the earlier gains, and then some. The cities of the region suffered especially as the trade flows on which they relied were diverted from Antwerp to the north. After 1648 the *Meierij* and northern Limburg enjoyed a measure of recovery, but this did not extend beyond 1700, when population growth ended once more. In South Limburg, on the other hand, population grew more after 1700 than before.

11. All of the aforementioned developments caused the regional distribution of population to shift. If we divide the Republic into three zones – the West and North, the East, and the South – then it appears that around 1500 just

under 50 percent lived in the West and North, 30 percent lived in the South, and 20 percent in the East. By 1650 the share of the West and North had grown to 65 percent, while the two remaining regions shared the remaining 35 percent in roughly equal portions. In 1800 the share of the West and North had receded to about 60 percent, and the East was now somewhat more populous than the South. The long-term deterioration of the South was a direct (in the case of the Generality lands) or an indirect (in the case of Zeeland) consequence of the division of the Netherlands, turning this zone into a theater of war and erecting trade-diverting barriers that forced a reorientation of economic life on both sides of the new boundary.

12. Around 1500 a surprisingly high level of urbanization – measured by the standards of the time – already existed in the northern Netherlands.

13. Between 1580 and 1675, the West experienced an explosive urbanization that caused the existing complement of cities to grow rapidly in size. Elsewhere in the Republic, urbanization tended to proceed via the growth in the number of small cities while several large cities of the periphery actually declined in size.

14. Between 1675 and 1815, the entire Republic (with the probable exception of South Limburg) experienced deurbanization. This long process assumed three forms:

   a. a long-term reduction of the urban population. This occurred primarily in the West and North. (Since Amsterdam's population resisted this trend until after 1780, this city became more dominant over time in the Republic's urban system.)

   b. a faster growth of the rural population than of the cities. This occurred from the outset in the East, which was joined after 1745 by the North.

   c. a sharp reduction of the urban population of Holland and Zeeland in the period 1795–1815, led by the decline of the port cities Amsterdam and Middelburg.

These conclusions raise important questions as to *why* and *how* the population developed as it did. Answering the *why* questions will occupy us through much of the rest of this book. How the population grew, declined, and changed its internal distribution requires that we address the demographic characteristics that determine the rate of natural increase and the role of migration. Here our attention is attracted first and foremost to Holland and immediately neighboring areas, where growth was most intense, urbanization reached unprecedented levels, and the later decline was most extreme. The demographic processes of this population remain a topic about which we still have many more questions than answers. We therefore abstain from a detailed analysis of historical demography and limit ourselves in the following section to several more general observations.

3.5. Migration and the composition of the population

With its relatively high standard of living, strong demand for labor, and religious toleration, the Republic long attracted immigrants from the rest of Europe. This well-known fact had profound implications for the Republic's culture, for its economy, and for its demographic characteristics.

The most thorough study of international migration to the Republic, by Lucassen, estimates that a total of about 500,000 migrants settled permanently in the Republic during the seventeenth and eighteenth centuries. A roughly equal number of migrants sojourned in the Republic while "in transit" to other destinations. The vast majority of these transmigrants made their way to the Republic's ports, where they signed on with the East and West India companies. Well over half of them never returned, having died (or, in a few cases, settled) in the tropics. Yet a third type of migration consisted of seasonal movements of workers attracted to the merchant marine, whaling, peat digging, linen bleaching, hay harvesting, and other agricultural work. These seasonal migrants worked in the Republic for several months, earning high wages by their standards, before returning to their small farms and cottages, mostly in Germany. This type of migration became important only after 1650, when it involved the annual movement of some 30,000 workers who spent up to three to four months working in the Republic. Both these seasonal workers and the transmigrants occupied important places in the Dutch labor market (see Chapter 12 for more on this), but their demographic impact was marginal.

But to return to the permanent migrants. The Republic attracted workers from all adjacent countries as well as those facing the shores of the North Sea. Over time, however, the German lands became the chief source of migrants. The inflow was not highly concentrated in a particular period, so it does no great violence to the historical record to think of it as an annual movement of some 2,500 men and women, mostly young adults. The significance of this annual augmentation of the adult population is suggested by comparing it to the annual number of, let us say, eighteen-year-olds produced annually by the Republic's own population. A population after 1650 of nearly two million, with a birth rate estimated conservatively at 32 per thousand, will have produced 64,000 births each year. Before those babies reached age eighteen, infant and child mortality will have taken its toll, reducing the birth cohort by 40 to 50 percent. Thus, the native-born eighteen-year-olds will have numbered each year something between 32,000 and 39,000. Immigrants, had they *all* been young adults, would have augmented this group by 6.5 to 7.8 percent. Since some were children (who might die before reaching adulthood), and others were beyond the childbearing years, this exercise overstates the demographic impact of immigrants to Dutch society. But, as we shall see in more detail later, the Republic's marriage market after 1650 tended to raise substantial obstacles to marriage, and these were most daunting for immigrant women. (Immigrant men married Dutch women with relative ease, but

72

their female counterparts had no comparable access to the scarcer Dutch male. In Amsterdam from 1601 to 1800, two German men married for every German woman, and these women were much more likely to marry immigrant men, and to do so at a late age – an average of four years later than native-born women who married in 1801–6.)

By no means did all immigrants to the Republic participate in demographic reproduction. But, even if we settled on 4 to 5 percent as the share of immigrants among child-raising young adults, the question remains: Did this make it a significant phenomenon? The answer must be that it *became* a significant phenomenon for the simple fact that this migration behavior persisted for so long, for 150 years. Moreover, it was always a *strategic* phenomenon, for these migrants were not randomly distributed across the face of the Republic; they settled overwhelmingly in the cities of Holland, affecting the urban age structure, sex ratio, and, as already noted, the behavior of the marriage markets.

The importance of migration to the growth and maintenance of urban populations – indeed, its indispensability – is a commonplace in the demographic history of preindustrial cities. In all of Europe no less than in the Republic, large cities usually experienced an excess of deaths over births, so that the maintenance of their populations depended on in-migration. What distinguished the Republic from the rest of Europe, of course, was the very high percentage of its population resident in cities, and, hence, subject to excess mortality. In highly urbanized Holland of the late seventeenth and eighteenth centuries, these urban deficits typically exceeded the size of rural surpluses, making her cities dependent on immigration from the outer provinces and abroad.

The widespread excess mortality of the cities usually is explained by their severe hygienic problems, but it may also be explained in part by their peculiar age structures and sex ratios. This is suggested by the example of The Hague, a city which, despite its substantial size, did not suffer an excess of deaths over births in the eighteenth century. This exception to the rule helps us to accept the possibility that urban excess mortality was not inevitable in the century before the 1670s when our view of demographic behavior is dimmed by scanty records, but when we know that the urban population grew rapidly. The volume of migration to the cities then would have had to be enormous in order to overcome a substantial excess urban mortality *and* to achieve a major increase in the level of urbanization. If the cities of Holland had suffered an average excess mortality of 5 percent throughout the period 1580–1800, then they would have suffered some 750,000 more deaths than births in these 220 years. In addition, we know that nearly 160,000 native residents of Holland's cities sailed with the East India Company to Asia, never to return. And there were certainly additional persons who set off for colonies in the New World and European and Mediterranean destinations. The total "drain" of Holland's urban population through death and departure in this period could easily have reached 950,000 to 1,000,000 persons. Besides the aforementioned 500,000 permanent immigrants, an equal number of domestic migrants must have established themselves permanently in Holland's cities in the course of the seventeenth and eighteenth centuries. This, at any rate, would appear necessary to achieve the observed urban growth under an assumed excess mortality of 5 per thousand per year. Our rough calculation implies an average net urban inflow of some 2,300 persons per year from the rest of the Republic. Such an internal migration flow would not have been impossible; but even if the true migration rate was something less than this, it is clear that migration, both international and internal, was very important for the growth and maintenance of the Republic's large urban population.

Unfortunately, the present state of our knowledge makes it impossible to be more specific about the undoubtedly large scope of migration in the post-1580 period. We do know, however, that the places of origin of migrants to the Republic shifted over time. In the first decades after 1580, the Southern Netherlands supplied the bulk of immigrants, and it is likely that much of this migration consisted of entire families. The importance of this migration to the economic development of the Republic was immense, since these migrants brought with them a wealth of commercial and technical know-how, not to mention a wealth of capital. By the early seventeenth century, this flow of migrants slowed, but it did not stop. Well into the seventeenth century, textile workers continued to make their way north, especially to Leiden. But this migration stream became not only quantitatively less important but also qualitatively different, consisting increasingly of poor workers from the region of Liège. The inflow of migrants from the South revived once again after 1685, when thousands of French Huguenot families made their way to the Republic, but it is striking that this dramatic product of religious intolerance left few marks on the demographic development of the Netherlands.

Through the first half of the seventeenth century, the dominant flow of migrants to Holland was from the North – from the countryside of North Holland and Friesland, the German North Sea coast, and Scandinavia. These migrants were especially prominent in everything having to do with shipbuilding and seafaring. After 1680 this migration flow diminished in both absolute and relative importance. In its place came a growing migration from the East – the eastern provinces of the Republic and the German lands beyond them. As the migration flows changed direction, so did their character. The migrants from the North were predominantly males, while females predominated among the migrants from the East. And in both cases single persons appear to have been numerically more important than families. These shifting characteristics of migration to the Republic were the joint product of developments in the demographic and economic situations in the "expulsion" regions and the changing character of the labor market in the maritime zone of the Republic.

Besides this massive inflow of persons to the Republic, there was, we must not forget, a certain outflow. It pales in comparison, but still there were in the early days some Catholics who moved South for religious reasons, and later, as the Republic's economic supremacy took shape, merchants who left to establish Dutch trading colonies (in France, the Mediterranean, and Russia, among others) and craftsmen attracted by high salaries to transfer their technical skills abroad.

Quantitatively far more important was the departure of men who signed on with the Dutch East India Company (the VOC). In the entire life of this company (1602–1795), nearly 975,000 persons boarded its ships to sail for Asia. About 485,000 of them eventually returned to the Netherlands, which means that some 490,000 men settled somewhere in Asia or Africa or, more likely, died. Now, of those 975,000 who set sail, only a half million were men born in the Netherlands. The rest had come to the Republic's port cities from abroad, and of those 475,000 immigrants, 255,000 never returned. Hence the German adage that "Holland is the graveyard of Germany." The Dutch recruits to the service of the VOC had slightly better survival chances (53 percent rather than 47 percent for the foreign-born). The native-born recruits came from all over the Republic, but a large majority came from Holland, and of those, in turn, the large majority came from Holland's cities. The share of VOC recruits from Holland varied over time (see Chapter 10, section 10.3.3, and Chapter 12, section 12.5.2), but always the company exerted its lugubrious influence on the demographic character of Holland and its cities.

Most of these mortality-prone seafarers were men of a marriageable age. Their removal must have skewed the sex-ratio of Holland's cities drastically. And as the migration *to* those cities shifted by 1700 from a male-dominated inflow from the North Sea coast to a female-dominated inflow from the East, the sex-ratios of the marriageable age categories must have become extremely imbalanced. In Amsterdam the census of 1795 counted 123 women for every 100 men. Yet when the children under age 14 and the Jewish population is set aside, the remaining adult population consisted of 132 women for every 100 men. One might suppose that Amsterdam, unusual in so many other ways, exhibited the nation's most skewed sex-ratio. But in Delft a population survey of 1749 reveals an even more extreme case. The population registration of that year did not always indicate the sex of children under age 14, but when we make the reasonable assumption that such children exhibited the typical sex-ratio at birth of 95 girls per 100 boys, then the entire city housed 135–140 women for every 100 men. And, when the children are set aside, the adult sex-ratio rises above 150!

This enormous shortage of adult men in Holland's cities had its consequences for these cities' ability to reproduce their populations. To begin with, a large portion of the women must have found it difficult to find a mate; they married late or, in many cases, not at all. The 1829 census, the first that permits us to relate marital status to age, reveals that 24 percent of Amsterdam women in the age category 40–55 had never been married. This figure may well have been even higher in the eighteenth century when the sex-ratio was even more skewed.

Among those who succeeded in marrying, the average age at marriage tended to rise. Table 3.14 shows that women who entered into their first marriages in

Table 3.14. *The average age at first marriage for brides in Amsterdam, and the distribution of their marriages by age categories, 1626–1810.*

Age	1626/27	1676/77	1726/27	1776/77	1809/10
<25	60.9 %	44.4 %	36.5 %	35.3 %	46.2 %
25–29	28.2	33.3	34.5	31.2	30.2
>29	10.9	22.3	29.0	33.5	23.6
Average age	24.5	26.5	27.2	27.8	26.3

Source: A. M. van der Woude, "Demografische ontwikkeling," p. 151.

Amsterdam in 1626 and 1627 did so at an average age of 24.5 years, and by age 30 nearly 90 percent of all women who would marry had done so. The population of Holland was then in the midst of its explosive growth, and the economy offered abundant possibilities for family formation. Fifty years later, in 1676 and 1677, matters had changed fundamentally (see Chapters 12, sections 12.4 and 12.5, and Chapter 13, section 13.1.3), and they left their mark on the marriage market. The average marriage age for women had risen by two years, and the percentage whose marriage was delayed beyond age 30 had doubled. The following century brought a further intensification of this trend. By 1776 and 1777, Amsterdam women married at an average age approaching 28, and fully a third of them did not marry until after their thirtieth birthdays.

An important factor underlying this long-term trend toward more restricted marriage is the changing gender-composition of immigration. To the extent that immigrants were single and married only after they arrived in Amsterdam, the data displayed in Figure 3.2 reveal the nature of this change. Overall (see line Z), Amsterdam's marriage market featured more men than women entering into first marriages in the period 1601–60, while thereafter the reverse was always true. This means that before 1660 many first-marrying grooms will have had widows at their sides, while after 1660 it was far more likely to be the first-marrying bride who resolved to go further through life with a widower. In its period of expansive growth, Amsterdam attracted more male migrants than female. The women being scarce, they married early, and probably few remained single. Moreover, widows found remarriage to be relatively easy. When the economic tide turned, it was the eligible bachelor who became scarce. It is hard to state with certitude whether the increased emigration of single men, the diminished immigration of such men, or the increased immigration of women contributed most to this shift. Some combination of these factors probably was at work, but it all signals the arrival of a less favorable economic climate.

A direct consequence of this pattern of women marrying late or never was to reduce the overall fertility of the population. We cannot observe this directly, but a fairly reliable reflection of the fertility level is the average number of children

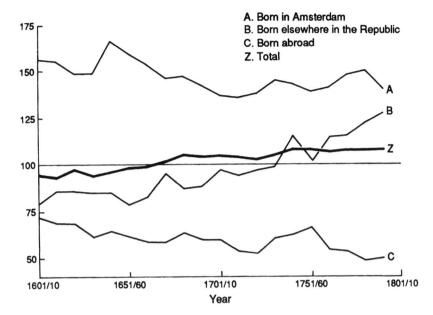

Figure 3.2. Sex ratio of persons marrying for the first time; Amsterdam, 1601–1800 (women per 100 men); ten-year periods. (*Source:* S. Hart, *Geschrift en getal.*)

per household. This tells us nothing about children born who had already died, of course, but we can be quite confident that the large decline in the average number of living children recorded between the period before 1650 and thereafter (on the order of 0.5 to 0.8 children per household) was chiefly the result of a lower fertility, which, in turn, was imposed by a later age at marriage and a lower marriage rate.

Resident children per household

Gouda, 1622	2.07	Gouda, 1674	1.71
Rijnland, 1622	2.52	Delft, 1740	1.27
		Leiden, 1749	1.42
Krimpenerwaard, 1622	2.72	Krimpenerwaard, 1680	2.08
		Noorderkwartier, 18th century	1.76

The fragmentary evidence available to us suggests strongly that structural deterioration of the urban marriage market drove down fertility in the course of the second half of the seventeenth century. In addition, we saw earlier that mortality may have risen in the first decades of the eighteenth century. At present we can make few general statements about demographic *processes* that are not provisional or hypothetical, but the population *trends* are much better established, and they feature (1) a sixteenth-century growth that led to a spectacular urbanization after 1580, and (2) a cessation and partial reversal of this growth that set in during the third quarter of the seventeenth century. The internal consistency of the changes that occurred then with respect to population totals, marriage age, children per household, and sex-ratios lead to the interpretation offered here, just as they fit seamlessly with the Republic's economic developments, to which we will turn in later chapters.

3.6. Conclusions

Around the beginning of the sixteenth century, the population of the Low Countries – both North and South – began to grow rapidly. The tempo varied regionally, to be sure, but the phenomenon was remarkably general. By the 1560s the population of the Habsburg Netherlands as a whole had grown by some 40 percent over the level of 1500. The political crisis that followed interrupted this upward trajectory and, more importantly, set in motion a sequence of pillages, sieges, exiles, and flights that set the populations of the North and South on fundamentally different paths of development. The population of what is now Belgium fell absolutely in the decades after the 1560s and did not much exceed that level again until the eighteenth century. The population growth of the new Republic, on the other hand, only paused during the Revolt and, stimulated by a large migration from the South, resumed its earlier growth path in the course of the 1580s. "Resumed" is not quite the right word, since the post-1580 growth was both more rapid – even explosive – than before, and it was more regionally concentrated in the maritime provinces of the West and North. In the Eastern provinces and, especially, the Southern Brabantine borderlands, population growth was slow and locally interrupted by stagnation and even decline. Military activity and its consequences were undoubtedly the chief cause of this deceleration. By the mid–seventeenth century, the population of the Low Countries as a whole had grown by some 65 percent since 1500, but the population of the Republic had doubled, and that of the coastal provinces had nearly tripled.

After the mid–seventeenth century, the pattern of population growth changed fundamentally from the preceding 150 years. A moderate growth prevailed in the South and East of the Republic, as long as new military dangers did not threaten these areas, but in the coastal provinces, the population growth came to a full stop. Population stagnated in many regions, but in North Holland and Southwest Friesland, not to mention many of the cities of Holland and Friesland, it fell absolutely.

It will be a task of later chapters to explain the new economic conditions that impinged on demographic behavior in the Republic. Here we can identify the path leading from the economic environment to demographic behavior. That path moved through the archway of marriage; changes in the average age at first marriage and the share of women who never married combined to influence the fertility rate. This mechanism, common to much of Europe in our period, was complicated in the Netherlands by the influence of migration. Changes in the scope of permanent immigration may have influenced the rate of population growth, but probably more important were shifts in the gender composition of the migrant stream. A complex interaction of supply and demand factors caused single women to predominate in this immigrant flow to the coastal cities after 1660. This combined with the growing exit of young men from these cities – the so-called "Indies drain" – to cause an intensification of the structural problems of the marriage market. In short, the characteristics of in- and out-migration reinforced those of the local, settled population to depress the marriage rate and press down on the level of fertility after the mid–seventeenth century.

This leaves the influence of mortality. Although much remains uncertain, it appears most likely that mortality levels declined in the last three decades of the seventeenth century, as plague epidemics, which had visited the Dutch cities frequently up to 1666, never reappeared after that date. The cessation of population growth in just the period when a major source of death was removed from the Netherlands places extra importance on the migration-marriage-fertility nexus discussed earlier. This is not to say that mortality played no special role in Dutch demographic history, for the deteriorating ecological situation of portions of the coastal provinces appears to have forced up death rates in the course of the eighteenth century. This must have reinforced and extended the duration of the population stagnation that set in, for other reasons, in the late seventeenth century.

After the mid–eighteenth century, the process of slow but persistent growth that had long characterized the East and South continued. In the West the signs of growth were much weaker but not altogether absent, while in the North they were actually quite strong. The causes of this new reversal in the West and North are not obvious. The renewal of rising prices in European commodity markets, however, with its consequences for profits and employment, may well have been influential, for it was especially in the agricultural districts where these first impulses to renewed population growth reveal themselves.

After 1780, and most dramatically in the Batavian-French era (1795–1815), these modest signs of demographic revival were overwhelmed by the roundhouse punches, one after another, that were dealt to the urban heart of the Republic, and that expressed themselves most obviously in a major deurbanization of Holland and Zeeland. The demographic performance of the rest of the nation was by no means unfavorable; one might even go so far as to say that it participated, at a lower rate of growth, to be sure, in the general European population expansion of this era. Once the era of French domination ended, the Netherlands were launched on a period of rapid and general population growth. Could it be that the stopping of the "Indies drain" in 1795, by restoring a normal sex-ratio in the cities, established by 1815 the conditions that made urban population growth possible once again?

Having reviewed the major trends of population change and explored the demographic mechanisms that stood behind them, there remains one other matter deserving emphasis here. The Republic of the United Netherlands was Europe's most urbanized society by far, an achievement made possible by a secure supply of food and energy. Any number of features specific to this state's political regime and to its social and cultural life must be understood in the context of its high level of urbanization. The structure of its economy, and the developments within each economic sector, must also be related to this large urban population and to trends in its urbanization and deurbanization. As we proceed to discussions of various aspects of economic life, this great urban presence must always be brought into the analysis. Were the Northern Netherlands not already highly urban before the Revolt, its rapid economic growth thereafter would be inexplicable; its industrial history is invariably implicated in the competitive relations between town and country; the high level of schooling made possible an advanced occupational specialization, but also introduced rigidities to the labor market that inhibited adjustment to changed international market conditions; the technological ferment in the industrial, commercial, and transport sectors depended on an urban environment; likewise, the urban preponderance ensured that agricultural interests would be subordinate in this society. These examples by no means exhaust the list of ways in which the high level of urbanization functioned as an essential structural feature that shaped, whether directly or indirectly, the behavior of the Dutch economy.

Chapter 4
Money and taxes,
borrowing and lending

4.1. The money supply

In the course of the sixteenth and early seventeenth centuries, the northern Netherlands became a highly monetized economy. Monetization did not spread uniformly to all areas, however, and even at the end of our period one could find rural areas in the eastern provinces where peasant's use of money was confined to the essentials of harvest markets and tax payments. But nowhere does one read of chronic "money famines" (i.e., of a systematic drainage of coin from regions or a structural shortage of money frustrating the development of a market economy).

The Netherlands were monetized, but they were not "systematically" monetized. The Republic inherited from the Habsburg regime a decentralized, uncoordinated minting establishment, and it did not gain effective control over internal coin production until the end of the seventeenth century. At no time during the life of the Republic can one speak of an effective "monetary policy." At best there were only monetary aspirations.

From 1487 onward, the Habsburg government sought to fashion a coherent monetary unit to help coordinate the financial and economic activity in the disparate provinces that had come under its control. In mint ordinances of 1496, 1521, and 1548, the central government introduced bimetalism (by issuing gold and silver coins at the fixed exchange rate of 10.77:1) and a circulating coinage with values equal to the money of account, the guilder (*gulden*): These were the gold *karolusgulden*, introduced in 1521, and the silver *karolusgulden* of 1544. These new coins not only united the money of account with the circulating currency but also linked the new currency to the older Flemish currency.

This coinage policy, admirable for its logic, did not long survive. The rapidly rising silver–gold price ratio drove the gold coin out of circulation, while monetary inflation forced the market value of the silver coin to diverge from the unit of account. What did survive from this initiative was the guilder as the unit of account, with each guilder divided into 20 *stuivers* (or 40 *groten* in the Flemish coinage), and each *stuiver* consisting of 16 *penningen*.

The circulating coinage consisted of a wide variety of foreign coins, particularly Rhenish and South German *Thalers*. Supplementing these were Netherlandic coins that sought to gain acceptance by imitating the popular German (and also Spanish) coins. The most important of these was the *Filipsdaalder*, introduced in 1559. Coin production increased substantially in the first two-thirds of the sixteenth century: The Netherlandic mints (concentrated in Flanders and Brabant) produced approximately 20 million guilders worth in the first decade of Philip II's reign, not much less than had been produced during the entire reign of Charles V.

Despite this the influence of foreign coins remained great, and without effective control over the weights and quality of the circulating coinage, the Habsburg government could do little to prevent the persistent revaluation of coins and, hence, the depreciation of the money of account in terms of silver and gold. The silver *gulden*, which began life in 1544 with a weight of 19.06 grams, contained but 12.7 grams of silver by 1581. To put it differently, the *karolusgulden*, valued at 20 *stuiver* (i.e., one guilder) in 1544, circulated as a 30-*stuiver* coin in 1581.

Foreign coins were not the only ones bringing debasement to the Netherlandic coinage, for several cities (and even some noblemen) minted coins, basing their claims to do so on privileges extended in the distant past by the Holy Roman Emperors. These small mints issued versions of German *Thalers* and masses of crude petty coins beyond the control of the central government.

The territories that freed themselves from Habsburg control possessed no less than fourteen active mints: two in Holland (one established in Dordrecht, the other circulating among the West Friesian cities), one in each of the six remaining provinces, and six in as many eastern cities. The Union of Utrecht of 1579 endowed the central government, in its *Generaliteits Muntkamer* (Generality Mint Chamber), with the authority to advance a unitary monetary policy, but in practice the mints pursued self-interested policies of maximizing seigniorage profits. All the while, foreign coinage was conspicuous in domestic circulation.

The monetary reform introduced in 1586 during the Earl of Leicester's brief sojourn in the rebel state, and consolidated in an ordinance of 1606, confirmed the silver *Rijksdaalder* and *Leeuwendaalder* as well as the gold *dukaat* as the Republic's heavy trade coins. The major mints now supplied a steady flow of these coins, each of which conformed to international usage in a major zone of Dutch trade. In contrast, the production of small coins for everyday use remained the domain of the numerous local mints. Diversity and debasement characterized the money supply; the state had little control over the effective value (in terms of the unit of account) of its heavy silver coins, nor could it influence either the volume or quality of the domestically circulating currency.

The *Rijksdaalder*'s value, originally set at 46 stuivers, rose to 48 stuivers by 1608 and 50 stuivers by 1619. The major force propelling this continuing revaluation was the monetary policy of the Habsburg government in the Southern Netherlands. The Brussels Government issued coins (the *Albertskruisdaalder* or *Patacon* and the *Ducaton*) with silver contents 4 percent lower than those of comparable Dutch coins. Since the Southern money of account was also devalued, these coins circulated with stuiver values equal to the heavier Dutch coins. The enormous trade deficit that the Southern Netherlands ran with the North throughout the first half of the seventeenth century resulted in a massive flow of these coins into the Republic. Between 1612 and 1675, the Habsburg mints produced some 200 million guilders worth of *patacon* and *ducaton*, a large part of which circulated in the North, where they became the dominant circulating currency.

The heavier coins of the Republic increasingly were reserved for use abroad, where traders accepted them for their actual metallic content, while the underweight South Netherlands coins and the output of the local mints circulated domestically at their face value. Thus a distinction arose between circulating coinage (*standpenningen*) and trade coins (*negotiepenningen*), and this distinction was reinforced by the practice of the Bank of Amsterdam.

The Bank of Amsterdam (*Wisselbank*), founded in 1609, was intended as a convenience to merchants (making payments from account to account like a modern giro bank) and for the purpose of reducing monetary confusion by supplying the mints with coin (supplied by depositors) for reminting as heavy trade coins. In time the Bank made a formal distinction between current money (influenced by the coinage of the Southern Netherlands) and bank money (the official, full-valued money in which the bank kept its accounts). The premium of bank money, or *agio*, generally hovered around 4 percent.

The coinage law of 1622 sought to accommodate this new reality, and that of 1659 completed the process by "domesticating" the circulating coinage. The Republic's mints now produced new coins, the *rijder* and *ducaat*, with 5 percent less silver than equivalent trade coins. These were direct competitors to the *patacon* and *ducaton* and, being overvalued, pushed the Southern Netherlands coins out of domestic circulation.

Toward the end of the seventeenth century, the declining volume of Southern Netherlands coins, the rising volume of domestic production, and the dominant position of Dutch trade gradually created the conditions in which the central government finally could exercise the control over coinage envisioned by the Union of Utrecht. The edicts of 1691 and 1694 established practices that continued beyond the end of the Republic. The six municipal mints were closed (bought off for an annual payment of 5,000 guilders). Of the eight remaining mints, two (Dordrecht and Utrecht) were supplied with the lion's share of metal, and these became European leaders in mechanized, precision minting.

Mint production now followed rules established in 1681, which provided for the minting of a new three-guilder piece and a guilder coin for domestic use, thereby reintroducing a coin equal to the money of account. It maintained the then world-renowned trade coins: the *leeuwendaalder* (for trade with the Levant), the *rijksdaalder* (for trade with the Baltic), the *dukaat* (for trade with Asia), and the golden *dukaat* (for trade with Russia). Finally, the reform stabilized the silver and gold content of the *gulden* (in fact, this had changed very little after 1622) at values that would be maintained until 1839, and, after a small adjustment, until September, 1936, when the Netherlands had the distinction of being the last country to leave the Gold Standard.

In the course of the seventeenth century, the Republic became, because of the character of its trade and the policies of the Bank of Amsterdam, a great reservoir of coin. Precious metals imported primarily from Spain, plus bullion and inferior coins deposited in the *Wisselbank,* were regularly sent to the mints for reminting into trade coins. From 1586 to 1795, the Republic's mints produced roughly 1,100 million guilders worth of coin (see Table 4.1). Production averaged 2.5 million per year through the first half of the seventeenth century and rose to three times that level by the first half of the eighteenth century. (By way of contrast, the Southern Netherlands' mint output in the same period totaled 420 million guilders, most of it produced before 1660.)

The supply of coinage issuing from the Dutch mints was supplemented, as we have noted, by foreign coin circulating in the Republic, by far the most important being the Southern Netherlands coinage that flooded the Republic in the period 1613–59). If just half the southern coinage of this period eventually circulated in the North, it nearly would have equaled the annual output of the northern mints.

The bulk of this coinage did not long remain in the Republic. Throughout its history the Republic – and Western Europe as a whole – ran persistent payment deficits with three major trade zones: the Baltic (including Russia), the Levant, and Asia. These deficits ultimately had to be settled by specie shipments, and we know that such transfers occurred regularly to all three "hard-currency" zones. Specie shipments to Asia are known in considerable detail, thanks to the records of the VOC. Altogether the company sent some 575 million guilders worth of specie, four-fifths of it in the eighteenth century. By no means was all of this Dutch minted coinage; Spanish *reals* and unminted bullion accounted for at least two-thirds of total shipments. On the other hand, the Dutch mints also supplied other Asian trading companies, particularly the English, with their widely accepted trade coins.

Since the amply documented Asian trade leaves some doubt about the amount of exported Dutch coin, it should not come as a surprise to hear that the estimates of such transfers to the Baltic and Levant vary enormously. One should acknowledge frankly that too little is known about the Levant trade to allow even the most general statement about the size of the Dutch trade deficit. The *Leeuwendaalder* was the Dutch trade coin most readily accepted in the Levant (and Russia),

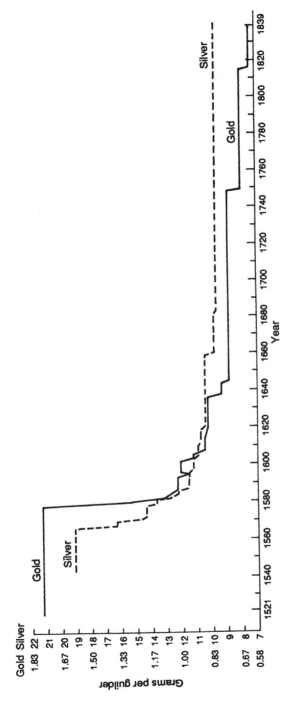

Figure 4.1. The silver and gold content of the guilder, 1521–1839. [*Source:* N. W. Posthumus, *Inquiry into the History of Prices in Holland* (Leiden, 1946), Tables IV and VIII. The silver content of the guilder was lowered from 9.61 grams to 9.41 grams in 1839, where it remained until the Netherlands adopted the Gold Standard in 1875. The gold content of the guilder remained at 0.605 gram from 1816 to 1936, when the Netherlands left the Gold Standard.]

Table 4.1. *Mint production in the Northern and Southern Netherlands, 1586–1802 (in millions).*

Period	Burgundian Netherlands	
	Total guilders	Annual average
1420–99	27 million	0.34 million

	Northern Netherlands			Southern Netherlands	
	Total guilders	Annual average		Total guilders	Annual average
1586–1659	185	2.5	1598–1612	28	1.9
			1613–1656	183	4.2
1659–1694	112	3.2	1657–1701	62	1.4
1690–1749	455	7.6	1702–1749	11	0.2
1750–1795	405	9.0	1750–1789	138	3.4
1797–1802	74	14.8			

	Dutch coin exported to Asia by the VOC		
	Total specie shipments	of which Dutch coin	Dutch coin export to Asia as % of mint output
1602–1659	54.7	10–20	5.4–10.8
1660–1689	42.6	22	19.6
1690–1749	255.3	90	19.8
1750–1795	221.5	50	12.4

Sources: J. R. Bruijn, F. S. Gaastra, and I. Schöffer, *Dutch-Asiatic Shipping in the Seventeenth and Eighteenth Centuries*, Rijksgeschiedkundigepublicatiën, Grote serie 165, pp. 223–45, Appendix iv; John H. Munro, "Monetary contractions and industrial change in the late-medieval Low Countries, 1335–1500" in N. J. Mayhew, ed., *Coinage in the Low Countries (880–1500)* (Oxford, 1979), pp. 138–61; John Day, *The Medieval Market Economy* (Oxford, 1987), pp. 55–71; Peter Spufford, *Money and Its Uses in Medieval Europe* (Cambridge, 1988); Michael Morineau, "Quelques remarques sur l'abondance monétaire aux Province Unies," *Annales E. S. C. 29* (1974), 767–76; H. Enno van Gelder and Marcel Hoc, *Les Monnaies des Pays-Bas Bourguignons et Espagnols, 1434–1713* (Amsterdam, 1960); R. van Uytven, "Sociaal-economische evoluties in de Nederlanden vóór de revoluties (veertiende-zestiende eeuw)," *Bijdragen en mededelingen betreffende de geschiedenis der Nederlanden 87* (1972), 60–93; *Nederlandsche Jaarboeken 4* (May 1750), 696–706.

but the entire production of this coin in the seventeenth century did not average 200,000 guilders per year. It is not impossible that the bulk of Dutch specie transfers, whatever their size, took the form of foreign coins and bullion.

Estimating the Dutch coinage transfer to the Baltic and Russia poses the greatest problem of all. The size of this transfer was always substantial, and Dutch trade coins played a dominant role in Baltic trade. Moreover, we know that Dutch banking houses handled payments for the English trade with the Baltic. In the eighteenth century, the English drew upon the large surpluses amassed in their trade with the Republic to make payment in the Baltic and Russia.

Artur Attman, in a comprehensive survey of European bullion flows, estimates annual Dutch bullion exports to the Baltic at 5 million guilders, and sometimes much higher. But one can doubt whether the flow to the Baltic of bullion, let alone of Dutch coins, regularly reached such a level. The large trade deficits were at least partly compensated by Dutch "invisible" earnings, especially from shipping and commercial services.

What then can we know about the domestic money supply in an economy through which the coinage of Europe flowed freely, and in which the mints functioned as an export industry? Obviously it is difficult to speak of a "monetary policy" apart from a general desire to maintain a plentiful supply of good coin with a stable silver or gold content. Actual control of the domestic stock of coin (high-powered money) always exceeded the power of the Generality. Estimates of the money stock in the Burgundian/Habsburg Netherlands (the seventeen provinces) are based on minting rates and assumptions about how long coins circulated before loss or reminting. In the 80 years ending in 1500, the mints produced an average of 340,000 guilders per year. If coins circulated for forty years, this would yield a money stock of 14 million; if we add foreign coins attracted to the Antwerp emporium, 20 million might not be a bad guess. Of course, much more of this circulated in Flanders and Brabant than in the northern provinces.

Just how much more is hinted at by a fiscal measure taken by Holland and Zeeland in 1573. In that difficult year, these rebel provinces resolved to raise desperately needed revenue by requiring all coins to be stamped. The owners were obliged to lend the Provincial States 15 percent of the value of the coins (a loan never paid back), while the stamped coins were henceforth to circulate at 15 percent above their face value. This effective devaluation yielded 250,000 guilders in immediate income to the two provinces, suggesting a money supply of 1.7 million guilders, or about 3.5 to 4 guilders per capita. These were not normal times (money was said to be exceptionally scarce), and surely not everyone came forth with all their cash.

If we jump ahead to the nineteenth century, we can exploit the knowledge that the 1845 recall of all Republican silver coinage yielded 86 million guilders (one-sixth of all silver coins minted between 1641 and 1808). How much could have circulated in the Republic's last decade? Michael Morineau's estimate of 150 to 200 million guilders hardly seems excessive; the upper figure represents only 20 to 25 years of mint production in the eighteenth century.[1]

At the end of the seventeenth century, the Englishman Gregory King estimated the Republic's money supply at 9 million pounds sterling, or about 100 million guilders. Annual mint output was then about half its eighteenth-century level, but we know that a large volume of Southern *patacon* and *ducaton* (200 million guilders worth had been produced in the period 1612–75) then circulated in the North. Moreover, we know that some 10 million guilders of coin lay in the vaults of the Bank of Amsterdam alone.

King's estimate (of unknown provenance) may understate the late seventeenth-century money stock somewhat. Consider the evidence provided by a source not often used in monetary history: probate inventories. The cash on hand in the homes of the deceased is certainly no exact reflection of average cash holdings of the population at large. The imminence of death may affect the demand for cash, and, of course, this source says nothing about the cash holdings of firms, banks, institutions, and the state. A stratified sample of inventories for the entire population of eighteenth-century Delft found cash balances in the period 1706–30 and again in 1738–62 that total 2.6 and 2.8 million guilders, respectively, or per capita cash holdings of 174 and 203 guilders. Smaller samples of farmers in Holland and Friesland around 1700 reveal cash balances of 300 guilders per household.

The P. J. Meertens Instituut's large samples of eighteenth-century probate inventories for the small towns of Medemblik, Weesp, and Maassluis revealed average cash holdings in excess of 1,500 guilders. By no means did every adult leave an estate warranting the drafting of an inventory. But even if these documents represented only one-third of all households, household size is assumed to average four persons, and all other households are assumed to have no cash at all, then these small places still would have maintained per capita cash holdings of 125 guilders. Matters may have been very different in the eastern and southern provinces. In Doesburg (in Gelderland) and Oirschot (in North Brabant), cash is recorded in only a small minority of probate inventories, and the sums are rarely large.

For the eighteenth century, we must keep in mind the very large cash holdings recorded in the probate inventories of urban regents, rentiers, and merchant families. These holdings usually accounted for 2 to 4 percent of total wealth (see Table 11.25). The study of such elites in eighteenth-century Leiden found average cash holdings of *f*.3,400 for regents, at least *f*.8,900 for rich burgers, and a breathtaking *f*.21,000 for rentiers. (*f*., standing for *florin*, is the symbol for the Dutch guilder.) In Hoorn rich burgers left *f*.4,100 in cash and regents *f*.7,700. Gouda's elites were both poorer and less flush with cash: Her regents left an average of *f*.838, while rich burgers died holding an average of *f*.2,740. But, if the household

---

[1] M. Morineau, "Quelques remarques sur l'abondance monétaire aux Province Unies," *Annales E. S. C. 29* (1974), 776.

heads listed as high government officials (mostly regents), merchants, and rentiers in Holland's 1742 income tax (the *Personeele Quotisatie* described in Chapter 11, section 11.5) held cash equal to the average of the regents and rich burgers of Leiden, Hoorn, and Gouda (we exclude the phenomenal holdings of the rentiers), the total would have exceeded 37 million guilders. And we have not yet considered the remaining 98 percent of Holland's population, the other provinces, or cash held by nonhousehold entities.

This evidence allows us to put forward *very tentative* estimates of the money stock circulating in the Dutch Republic. These estimates are highly uncertain, but if the level and trend revealed by the table are only generally correct, they call to our attention several important characteristics of the Republic's money supply. First, the Republic was better supplied with coin than other countries. In the early sixteenth century, we assume that the monetary circulation in the Northern provinces was less than that in Flanders and Brabant, where the main commercial centers and the chief mints were located. If the per capita northern money stock was two-thirds that of the south, one still finds a money supply, expressed in silver equivalents, exceeding the English supply and at least double that of France. By the end of the seventeenth century, the difference is even greater: The Republic's per capita money supply is nearly double that of England and triple that of France. In the late eighteenth century, the Republic's advantage is larger still.[2]

A second characteristic of Table 4.2 is the sharp increase in real per capita money stock in the late sixteenth and seventeenth centuries. At this same time, commercial and banking innovations (described later) certainly increased the velocity of circulation and expanded the use of credit instruments. The monetary equation ($MV = PT$) leaves us with little choice but to conclude that a massive expansion of the volume of transactions occurred in this period. [The quantity equation is an identity which holds that the stock of money (M) times the velocity of circulaton (V) equals the price level (P) times the volume of transactions (T). T is assumed to be linked closely to national income.]

The first and second characteristics are not really surprising; they fit well in the picture we have of a dynamic, growing economy. A third characteristic is both surprising *and* puzzling: In the course of the eighteenth century, the real per capita money stock grew further; by the end of the Republic, the money stock may have exceeded half of the gross national product. If our estimates are not grossly in error, the velocity of circulation must have fallen to a very low level

---

[2] Sources: These claims are based on money supply estimates found in: James C. Riley and John J. McCusker, "Money Supply, Economic Growth, and the Quantity Theory of Money: France, 1650–1788," *Explorations in Economic History 20* (1983), 274–93; Debra Glassman and Angela Redish, "New Estimates of the Money Stock in France, 1493–1680," *Journal of Economic History 45* (1985), 31–46; C. E. Challis, *The Tudor Coinage* (Manchester, 1978); Rondo E. Cameron, *Banking in the Early Stages of Industrialization* (Oxford, 1967), p. 42; N. J. Mayhew, "Population, Money Supply, and the Velocity of Circulation in England, 1300–1700," *Economic History Review 48* (1995), 238–57.

Table 4.2. *Rough estimates of Dutch money supply at selected dates.*

Year	Money stock (in millions)	Population (in millions)	Per capita money stock	Per capita grams silver	Price level index[b]	Per capita real money stock index
1540[a]	20	3	5–7.5	95	100	100
1690	120	2	60	576	440	273
1790	200	2	100	960	560	357

[a]The estimate for 1540 refers to the Habsburg Netherlands. We estimate per capita circulation in the North to be at the low end of the range, and that in the South to be at the upper end. The estimates for 1690 and 1790 refer to the Republic.

[b]The price level index: Cost of living index (see Figure 12.4).

while the demand for money rose. At the same time that the Amsterdam capital market emerged, Dutch households must have held cash balances so large as to suggest hoarding.

This analysis is preliminary and highly tentative. Very little is known about the monetary history of the Republic, but this initial reconnaissance reveals a terrain deserving of further exploration.

4.2. Public finance

4.2.1. UNDER THE HABSBURGS

The economic historian is attracted to the fiscal records of the state for both practical and theoretical reasons. As a practical matter, fiscal records provide information about an economy that is usually unavailable from other sources. Land taxes shed light on the agricultural economy, tariffs on foreign trade. Excise taxes reveal the contours of the standard of living, while distributional inequality is illuminated by taxes on income and wealth.

The theoretical interest of fiscal history derives from the intimate relationship of the tax system to the development of state power. The weak states typical of subsistence agricultural economies relied on the income from domain lands, tithes, and various levies in kind. More monetized economies could bear land taxes, tariffs, and, with urbanization, excises. Ultimately, the systematic taxation of wealth and income came to characterize the fiscal system of strong states. Broadening the tax base, more systematic penetration of the economy, and unification of tax administration are basic achievements of successful, centralized states. The reason is not far to seek. Such a tax system enabled the state to command the resources necessary for the pursuit of war, which, in turn, generated further pressures for the growth of taxation. This describes a positive feedback loop of fiscal development leading to state formation leading to warfare leading to fiscal development, and so on. This loop is a staple of Early Modern European History, oriented as that history is to the "rise of the nation-state."

In this theoretical context, the Dutch Republic stands as a great exception, for the advanced fiscal system of this highly monetized economy did not lead to state centralization. The pressure of war certainly led to fiscal innovations, but these innovations were by no means calculated to advance the cause of political unification. This fiscally powerful decentralized state is of considerable theoretical interest, but substantial practical problems stand in the way of understanding its historical development. We are frustrated especially by the decentralized character of taxation, by the reliance on tax farmers, and by the reluctance to tax commerce and foreign trade. As a consequence, the fiscal administration is confusing, has left few records, and sheds little light on key sectors of the economy.

The fiscal history of the Netherlands is exceptional in several respects, but it is also exemplary. This history is bracketed by the efforts of two administrators, both servitors of the centralizing state, to fashion unified fiscal systems: Lodewijk van Schoor in 1542 and Isaac Gogel in 1806. The failure of the first effort at centralization inaugurated a long era of Dutch fiscal exceptionality that was reinforced – indeed, raised to a principle of statecraft – by the new Republic. It was an era marked by notable triumphs in the management of public debt and the pioneering of new forms of taxation. It was marked as well by the long persistence of budgetary secrecy and by fiscal crises with far-reaching implications: the Tenth Penny (*Tiende Penning*) crisis of the 1560s, the "fiscal exhaustion" of the early eighteenth century, the revolt against the tax farmers (*Pachtersoproer*) of 1747–8, and the impending bankruptcy of the state at the end of the eighteenth century.

The fiscal system of the Netherlands under its Habsburg ruler, Charles V, was little changed from that left by his Burgundian predecessors. The central government in Brussels, headed in the Emperor's absence by his regent, disposed of income from two sources. The lesser of these flowed from the *domain*, the personal possessions of the Crown. Periodic efforts to raise money had caused the choicest parcels of the domain to be pledged as collateral for loans. Consequently, the Habsburg government depended for easily three-quarters of its revenues on subsidies granted by the States (*staten*), the representative bodies of the provinces that formed the Netherlands. These subsidies were of two kinds: the ordinary and the extraordinary *beden*. Since the reign of Philip the Good, the principle was established that the states owed an annual tax. The only issues left for negotiation between the regent and the representatives of the states were the amount to be paid and the duration of the agreement. In contrast, the states expected extraordinary *beden* to be requested only in cases of pressing need, and here the fundamental question of whether or not to grant at all was open for discussion.

Once the parties agreed on the amount to be paid, the *bede* was levied according to a multi-tiered quota system. The share of the *bede* to be paid by each province had been set after laborious and rancorous negotiation. Throughout the Habsburg period, Flanders paid the largest amount. Whatever Flanders paid, Brabant paid one-sixth less; Holland paid one-half of Brabant's sum, Zeeland one-quarter of Holland, and so forth. Then the provincial officers divided the amount for which they were responsible among the cities and villages according to another quota system. This was known in Holland as the *Schildtal* and was last revised in 1515 in light of a survey of property and general economic well-being taken the year before. Thus, whatever Holland's quota, Delft, the city with the largest *Schildtal* quota, paid 8.58 percent, and the six largest cities combined paid 41.96 percent. At the local level, the specific personal assessment was left to local officials.

Provincial Receivers of Subsidies, appointees of the central government, collected these taxes while appointees of the provincial states collected minor taxes based on the *Schildtal*, the *omslagen*, to raise funds to cover the administrative expenses of the provincial states. In addition to this, the cities levied their own taxes. Municipal finance, it has been said, floated as a cork on a great pool of beer, and since the fourteenth century, many cities in the Netherlands sold to their citizens bonds secured by excise tax revenue. According to their testimony in the *Informacie*, the fiscal survey of 1514, Holland's cities then had some two million guilders of outstanding debt. The central government had no such ready access to credit markets since its direct access to tax revenue was limited and the personal credit of the sovereign was suspect. The need to augment the fiscal strength of the central government was obvious to the Habsburg rulers and their advisors. In the course of the frequent Habsburg-Valois wars, the budgets of the Netherlands registered enormous deficits. Subsidies from Spain were no permanent solution since the debts of the Castilian Crown rose from 5 million to 81 million ducats in the course of Charles V's reign. Even in years of peace, the budgets of the Brussels government did not balance, a fact that Spain found difficult to reconcile with the Netherlands' reputation for being particularly rich. Clearly, the central government needed a broadened tax base to increase revenue and to form a secure foundation for raising money through the issuance of bonds.

We cannot here rehearse in detail the hectic history of Habsburg initiatives and expedients that stretched across the reigns of Charles V and Philip II. When the demands of warfare became pressing, the provincial states agreed to anticipate future revenue – to pay a large *bede* by issuing bonds that would be funded by future *bede* revenues. This expedient solved the immediate financial difficulties of the central government, but at the cost of future income that was pledged to bondholders. This only guaranteed that the next financial crisis would be both larger and harder to overcome.

The alternative, that the central government borrow directly, was effectively closed as long as it possessed no substantial direct tax revenue. The only creditors willing to deal with such a weak borrower were Antwerp bankers, who lent short term at interest rates of 12 to 22 percent.

A serious effort to set government finances on a firmer footing got under way in 1542. The president of the Council of State (*Raad van State*), Lodewijk van Schoor, with the support of the Habsburg Regentess, Maria of Hungary, proposed the introduction of "new expedients" (the *nieuwe middelen*) to be levied throughout the Habsburg Netherlands: a Tenth Penny (10 percent tax) on the income of real property and private loans and excise taxes on beer, wine, and woolen cloth. On the basis of these ongoing taxes, the provinces would pay enlarged subsidies to Brussels and, by issuing bonds secured by these revenues, be able to supply ample extraordinary *beden* as the need arose.

This initiative of the central government – greatly modified by the resistant provinces – was introduced in the years that followed, raising substantial revenues. But instead of strengthening the position of the central government, it strengthened the position of the provincial states, most notably the States of Holland. The research of James Tracy shows how Holland secured modifications of the new taxes to suit the needs of its economy. This province, dominated by trading and industrial cities, always sheltered commerce from heavy taxation and therefore proved particularly resistant to accepting the "new expedients." Holland used a portion of the new tax revenues to issue bonds, as Van Schoor envisioned. "But as a condition for raising unprecedented sums, the *Staten* demanded and got nearly total control over the collection and disbursement of tax revenues."[3] In Holland the collection of the new taxes was now in the hands of the Receiver for the Common Territory – an appointment recommended by the States – instead of the central government's official, the Receiver of the *Beden*. This change gave the province greater potential autonomy, a potential that was realized after 1553 when the States demonstrated their ability to fund and retire bonds issued in earlier decades. The holders of those bonds had purchased them under compulsion, as was common at the time; a truly voluntary credit market did not yet exist. But as Holland succeeded in retiring debt and lightening its debt service burden, it "demonstrated to wealthy individuals that *renten* backed by the *Staten* of Holland were worthy of trust."[4] The province now began to enjoy a confidence that city governments had gained for themselves in earlier times. In the years that followed, Holland and the other provinces found that they could borrow at reasonable rates of interest (6.25 percent) from a large pool of private, voluntary investors. At the same time, the central government found that the (enlarged) *beden* supplied by the provincial States never sufficed to cover its rising, war-inflated expenses.

The growing deficits of the central government and the resulting subsidies from Spain rose astronomically as the religious and political crisis of the 1560s gave way to open revolt. The maintenance of an army of occupation under the Duke of Alva gave rise, in 1569, to yet another attempt to strengthen the central government's grip on taxation: the infamous *Tiende Penning*, a plan to impose a uniform, "nationwide" sales tax of 10 percent on all commercial transactions, and 5 percent on real property transactions. Its intention was clear immediately: to sidestep the *bede* and its associated quota system, and to give the central government direct access to taxpayers. The *Tiende Penning* was never successfully enforced. The fiscal achievements of the previous 25 years not only gave the provinces reason to resist the central government but also gave them the power to raise the funds necessary to resist in fact. Some of them, notably Holland and Zeeland, made use of this new power.

The Revolt drew upon several sources for the wherewithal to carry on an armed struggle against the Habsburg Empire. The personal resources of the Prince of Orange and other nobles plus English and French subsidies appear to

[3] James D. Tracy, *A Financial Revolution in the Habsburg Netherlands* (Los Angeles and Berkeley, 1985), p. 75.

[4] Tracy, *Financial Revolution*, p. 107.

have played important roles. In the later years of the conflict, from 1585 to 1610, these foreign subsidies totaled 25 million guilders. On the other side, the stream of Spanish subsidies to the Brussels government became a gusher: From 1566 to 1654, Spain supplied its Army of Flanders with 218 million *ducats*, or an annual average of 5.5 million guilders, a sum nearly twice as large as the Spanish Crown's share of New World silver shipments in the period, and the chief cause of the rise of Castile's public debt from 36 million *ducats* in 1557 to 180 million in 1667.

The rebel provinces simply continued to make use of the tax system that had been put in place in the preceding decades – without, of course, paying the *bede* to Brussels. In the early years of the Revolt, the uncertain outcome of the rebel cause denied Holland and Zeeland access to the long-term credit market. More-over, the cessation of all interest payments on Holland's outstanding debt in the years 1572–5 and a temporary suspension of payments in 1581 must have given even the most fervent patriot pause. Repudiation of this debt of about 1.3 million guilders was never at issue, and for good reason. The debt was locally held for the most part, and the States would have understood that they would need the cooperation of these bondholders in the future. Restoration of a free credit market for provincial bonds did not come quickly, however, and in the meantime, the rebel cause had to resort to forced lending. After 1572 fund raising devolved to the cities, which prevailed upon citizens, outlying villages, and charitable insti-tutions to buy bonds in accordance with assessments of their wealth. This was formalized with the *capitale imposities* beginning in 1585. Beginning in 1587 the States of Holland again assumed responsibility for the bonds sold on their behalf by the individual cities.

Under these difficult circumstances, a large share of military expenditures had to be paid from current income, and Holland and Zeeland emerged from the first phase of the Revolt with a level of taxation vastly increased from pre–Revolt levels. The States proved willing to tax for their independence in ways they never tolerated for purposes of Habsburg policy. From 1572 on, provincial excise taxes (which had grudgingly been introduced in the cities in the 1540s) became a fixed element of the tax system. Pre– and post–Revolt taxation re-cords are not easily compared, but the direction of change is indisputable. Hol-land's average annual *bede* payments in 1552–60 (a period of peak demands occasioned by the Habsburg-Valois wars) reached ƒ.338,000. In 1588 the prov-ince raised ten times that amount in tax revenue, 3.4 million guilders; in 1608 the excise taxes alone yielded 4.3 million. By 1635 total tax revenues stood at 10.2 million guilders. This thirtyfold increase in tax revenues between the 1550s and 1630s needs to be deflated by the rising price level (which rose more than threefold) and by the growth of population (which doubled). The crude esti-mate of Holland's real per capita tax burden that results from this information reveals an increase of more than fourfold, most of it occurring quite suddenly between 1572 and 1588.

The institutions

It was one thing for a province to resist the taxing claims of the Brussels government; it was another to join hands with other provinces to fashion a new central governing and taxing authority. The Republic of the United Netherlands that emerged from the Revolt had no "moment of creation" defined by the introduction of a new constitution. For purposes of taxation, the closest approximation to such a moment was the Union of Utrecht, a mutual defense pact that served, for want of an alternative, as the United Provinces' basic document throughout its existence. Its provisions for financing a common defense included the establishment of a Council of State (*Raad van State*, to advise the central organs of government) that would be responsible for financial administration, including the drafting of a periodic *Staat van Oorlog* (war budget), a specification of central government expenditures (assumed to be chiefly military expenditures) to be shouldered in common by the United Provinces. This was put to the seven provinces in a General Petition, which required unanimous consent to be adopted.

The Union of Utrecht further provided that the tax revenues to cover these expenditures would be levied "equally in all the United Provinces, and at the same rate."[5] Finally, it forbade any province from introducing taxes, transit fees, or other tariffs to prejudice the commerce of any of the other provinces. In short, there were to be no internal tariffs.

These last two provisions remained dead letters. Indeed, in view of the long and successful history of resistance to central government taxation, the provision for common taxation is surprising. It has been suggested that these provisions reflect the idealism of Jan van Nassau and Floris Thin, leaders in the struggle against Spain. It is also possible that Holland, the dominant member of the union, sought hereby to spread the burden of ever-increasing military expenditures among the other allied provinces, whose tax rates had been much lower than Holland's.

Political reality soon asserted itself. In renouncing allegiance to their king, the provinces became sovereign. In fact, the fifty-seven cities with voting rights in the seven provinces often functioned as the "building blocks" of sovereignty. This was not an environment in which uniform national taxation had a chance of arising.

The unitary taxation provision of the Union of Utrecht soon had to be acknowledged as wishful thinking, and another, practical formula had to be found to provide for the expenditures of the central government. That formula was none other than the quota system long used by the Burgundian and Habsburg

---

[5] "in alle die geunieerde provincien eenpaerlick ende op eenen voet"

Table 4.3. *Tax revenue and tax burden indicators for Holland (1552–1792) and the Republic (1716–1815).*

[a] Year(s)	[b] Total tax revenue (millions)	[c] Approx. Population (thousands)	[d] Per cap. tax burden (guilders)	[e] Tax as % of income of unskilled laborer	[f] Tax burden deflated by cost of living index (1624 = 100)
		Holland			
1552–60	0.34	360	0.94	7.7	26
1588	3.40	495	6.87	21.8	102
1599	4.60	550	8.36	21.2	88
1624	7.20	672	10.71	21.5	100
1635	10.50	718	14.62	22.0	119
1653	10.50	800	13.13	19.1	92
1669–71	11.40	880	12.95	19.8	108
1672–8	16.50	880	18.75	28.2	151
1679–87	13.20	880	15.00	23.2	142
1688–97	21.70	860	25.23	39.3	196
1701–13	19.40	845	22.96	36.6	195
1720–8	19.30	821	23.51	37.5	208
1740–5	20.80	790	26.33	43.5	217
1746–8	25.80	783	32.95	54.5	249
1749–54	22.00	783	28.10	44.8	240
1761–5	22.30	783	28.48	47.1	230
1788–92	24.90	783	31.80	53.0	221
		Republic (1716 = 100)			
1716	31.0	1900	17.10		100
1790	39.0	2100	19.30		96
1795–1803	34.5	2100	16.40		61
1807–8	46.6	2150	21.70		80
1815	38.5	2200	17.50		63

governments. Indeed, a quota system had not ceased to be used in the early years of the alliance, but in the absence of an acceptable formula, the issue provoked ceaseless rancor until the Advocate of the States of Holland (the *Landsadvocaat*, an office later known as "Grand Pensionary"), Johan van Oldenbarnevelt, pushed through a quota structure that found favor, probably, because of its familiarity: It featured the same division of the Generality's General Petition as had been used by the Brussels government in collecting the *Bede* since the early sixteenth, and in some cases, the fifteenth century. Whatever Holland paid, Zeeland paid one-quarter as much, Friesland one-fifth, and Utrecht and Groningen (from 1595) one-tenth each. Gelderland and Overijssel, which had not participated directly in the old quotas, were fitted in after 1600.

These relationships, with origins dating back more than a century, remained in force, with one significant exception, until the last years of the Republic. The exception is Zeeland's quota. The truce with Spain negotiated in 1609 brought Overijssel and Gelderland fully into the Republican tax system, and the need to revise the quota system provided the opportunity for Zeeland to press its case for tax relief. That same truce, which it bitterly opposed, reinforced the decline in Zeeland's commercial activity, and justified, by its argument, a reduction of its quota. The reduction agreed to in 1612 did not settle the matter: Zeeland soon pressed for a further reduction. The quota of 1616, which carefully preserved the ancient formulas for the other provinces, offered Zeeland a further concession. It remained in force until 1792, when the old Burgundian interprovincial relationships were abandoned in a final, short-lived revision of the quota system.

The request for funds fell considerably short of being a true budget, while the unanimity principle and quota system fell far short of establishing a powerful central government. But that had not been the aim of the "allies." The Republic provided for central government expenditures much as had the Habsburg regime before it. The *bede* that had once been requested by the crown was now the General Petition (with the *Staat van Oorlog* specifying expenditures) requested by the Council of State. With the unanimous consent of the provinces assembled in the States General, the sum established in the General Petition was raised according to the quota system.

Unlike the pre–revolt central government, the Generality under the Republic did not enjoy most of the revenues of the *domain*. These rights and properties fell under provincial control. The Generality did tax directly the territories conquered by the Republic in the course of its wars with Spain. These "generality lands" (Zeeland Flanders, North Brabant, and parts of Limburg) never became politically equal to the original seven united provinces. They remained outside the quota system, paying taxes levied directly from The Hague.

The only other fiscal right of the Generality, and the only tax to apply uniformly to the entire Republic, was the tariffs levied on foreign trade beginning in 1582, the *Convooien en Licenten*. The Republic dedicated all revenues from this source to the support of the Admiralties, since it was thought appropriate that maritime commerce should support the naval power that protected merchant vessels with convoys, did battle with pirates, and upheld the freedom of the seas.

Unfortunately, the administrative structure given to the Republic's naval establishment undermined the principle of uniformity. From 1597, when it attained its permanent form, the Republic possessed five admiralties: three in Holland (centered in Amsterdam, Rotterdam, and the West Friesian cities), and one each in Zeeland and Friesland. Each admiralty collected the *Convooien en Licenten* in its own territory (which included the land borders in adjacent provinces) and

Table 4.4. *Quota systems, 1462–1792.*

Quotas under the Burgundian/Habsburg Regime		
Province	1462	1515
Brabant	1/4 of total *Bede*	1/4 of total *Bede*
Vlaanderen	1/3 more than Brabant	1/6 more than Brabant
Holland	1/2 of Brabant	1/2 of Brabant
Zeeland	1/4 of Holland	1/4 of Holland
Utrecht		1/10 of Holland
Friesland		1/5 of Holland
Groningen		1/2 of Friesland

	Quotas under the Republic				
	1586	1595	1612	1616	1792
	Percentage of total budget				
Holland	66.45	59.77	57.14	58.31	62.05
	Percentage of Holland's quota				
Zeeland	24.6	24.6	19.25	15.75	6.12
Utrecht	10.0	10.3	10.0	10.0	7.25
Friesland	20.0	20.7	20.0	20.0	15.07
Groningen		11.7	10.0	10.0	8.68
Gelderland		*a*	9.625	9.625	9.74
Overijssel		*a*	6.125	6.124	5.60
Drenthe			[From 1610 until 1792, it paid 1% of the total amount paid by the seven provinces]		1.60

*a*Gelderland and Overijssel made contributions before 1612, but these were separately negotiated and varied according to the war conditions in these provinces. From 1622 to 1634, their quotas were lowered to 7.3 and 3.9 percent of Holland's quota, respectively.

The Generality lands stood outside the quota system, being taxed directly by the central government. In the revision of 1792, the Generality lands contribution was set at 4.406 percent of the total budget, or 7.1 percent of Holland's quota.

Sources: Burgundian/Habsburg period: F. H. M. Grapperhaus, *Alva en de Tiende Penning* (Zutphen, 1982), pp. 25–9, 114. Republican period: Robert Fruin, *Geschiedenis der staatsinstellingen in Nederland tot den val der Republiek* (1922; rev. ed., The Hague, 1980), p. 50; H. L. Zwitzer, *'De militie van den staat' Het leger van de Republiek van de Republiek der Verenigde Nederlanden* (Amsterdam, 1991), pp. 62–73.

asserted an autonomy that left considerable scope for a selective enforcement of theoretically uniform tariffs. The financial health of the Admiralties required the suppression of wholesale smuggling, but the interests of local commerce encouraged widespread connivance at selective underreporting. For this reason (quite apart from the interpretive difficulties arising from periodic alterations in the basis of assessment), the records of *Convooien en Licenten* revenue are a highly imperfect mirror of the volume of Dutch trade (see Chapter 10, section 10.7).

The Generality began to issue bonds in 1596. Given its very limited direct taxing power, the bonds were far from fully funded, and it soon became necessary to secure guarantees from the provinces, usually Holland, in order to reassure creditors. After 1618 Holland's involvement in the Generality debt became even more direct, confirming that the fiscal potency achieved by Holland in the 1550s remained, after the formation of the Republic, a provincial monopoly.

Whatever coherence and flexibility the Republic's fiscal system ever displayed depended on the policy of Holland. This province's population was less than half of the total of the contributing provinces, but it provided 58 percent of Generality revenues. In practice, the other provinces often failed to honor fully their quota obligations (the inland provinces, for instance, felt little obligation to support the Admiralties), so that the Generality regularly turned to Holland to make good the shortfalls. Holland, in turn, could assume this added burden because although its quota for the Generality stood at 58 percent, it collected two-thirds of the tax revenue of all the contributing provinces combined. On this basis Holland could borrow more extensively than the other provinces: In 1795 it was responsible for three-quarters of the total debt of all the provinces and had guaranteed much of the debt of the Admiralties and the East and West India Companies (see Table 4.5).

The decentralized form of the fiscal system makes it impossible today – just as it was impossible for contemporaries – to acquire a comprehensive overview of all incomes and expenditures and all borrowing and redemption. In what follows we are often forced to restrict ourselves to an examination of taxation in Holland. This is not the whole story, but in view of Holland's fiscal weight and political leadership, this restriction is not disabling.

Expenditures and income

Military expenditures formed by far the largest category of expenses of the young Republic. It was no accident that what passed for a budget was called the *Staat van Oorlog*. The costs of maintaining the army rose from 3 million guilders per year in 1586–90 to an astonishing 9 million per year in 1602–7, when the Republic fielded an army of 60,000 men. Even during the Twelve Years' Truce, military expenditures remained around 7 million guilders per year, and with the resumption of hostilities in 1621, they immediately doubled, exceeding 20 million per year in the mid-1630s. In these decades the naval forces frequently needed financial support above and beyond the revenues raised by the *Convooien en Li-*

Table 4.5. *Provincial distribution of population, generality quotas, taxation, and public debt.*

	Holland	Utrecht Zeeland Friesland[a]	Groningen	Gelderland Overijssel Drenthe
As percentage of Republic total				
Population in 1795	48.0	21.0	7.0	24.0
Quota, 1616–1792	57.7	26.4	5.8	10.1
Total tax revenue in 1716 and 1785–94	66.5	20.5	4.5	8.5
Public debt in 1795	75.0	21.0	1.6	3.3
Quota, 1792–1806	64.9	18.5	5.6	11.0
Unified tax revenue,1807–8	60.5	24.2	5.3	10.0
Per capita, relative to the average for the Republic (Republic = 100)				
Quota, 1616–1792	120	126	83	42
Tax revenue, 1716, 1785–92	138	98	64	35
Public Debt, 1795	156	100	23	14

Note: In order to render all distributions comparable, the Generality lands and successor territories are excluded.

centen. Increasing government revenue was the United Republic's constant pre-occupation during the Eighty Years' War, but the power to do so resided with the provinces, and none of the exigencies faced in those turbulent years dislodged that power from its dispersed locations. This is not to say that each province stubbornly held fast to its old habits. On the contrary, it was only through fiscal innovation that provincial autonomy could be preserved.

We noted earlier that the unitary system of excise taxes envisioned by the Union of Utrecht was never realized. But each province, as it entered into the quota system, found itself under strong practical pressure – reinforced by the browbeating of the States General – to approve new taxes sufficient to meet its new obligations, and to construct central organs of provincial administration adequate to the tasks of the new polity. The tax systems of the seven provinces soon evinced a strong family resemblance, and while the central government remained dependent on the provinces, the provinces themselves, through the introduction of executive councils (*gecommitteerde raden*) and fiscal offices (*rekenkamers*), became effective administrative units, often for the first time.

In all of this, the example of Holland was of great influence. In 1583 the States of Holland introduced under its own authority the *gemene middelen*, a set of excise taxes that the Union of Utrecht had envisioned as a Generality tax. No other provinces followed Holland's lead precisely. They all introduced excise taxes, but the rates of taxation and the goods burdened with excise varied considerably. Moreover, few provinces, least of all Holland, resisted the temptation to discriminate between "foreign" (i.e., nonprovincial) and domestic goods, thereby doubly violating the intentions of the Union.

Holland's *gemene middelen* levied excises on the sale of wine, beer, meat, peat, salt, soap, grain (levied at the point of milling), woolen cloth, spirits, and on the use of market scales. It also levied annual charges on the possession of cattle and arable land.

The *gemene middelen* immediately became the cornerstone of Holland's system of taxation. By adjustments of the rates and extension of the excise to new goods and services, this complex of indirect taxes proved to be very flexible. The war effort of 1605–7 motivated the introduction of new taxes on luxury textiles, candles, and peat; in response to the rising expenditures of the 1620s, Holland imposed new taxes on salted fish, cheese, and butter, and increased the rates of most existing excises. The crisis of 1672 launched yet another round of excise intensification, while in 1683 all these taxes were raised by 10 percent. The States occasionally abolished an excise when the yield proved disappointing, but by the early eighteenth century the number of excise taxes exceeded forty, including excises on tobacco, coffee, tea, and chocolate, plus annual levies on the possession of household servants, luxury coaches, and private yachts. The States offered prizes for those who could think of new objects for taxation, which may account for the introduction in 1674 of a tax on the consumption of food and drink in taverns. This *recreatiegeld* varied according to the time of day and the substance consumed.

To the eternal disappointment of social historians, this tax was abandoned as unenforceable in 1676.

The *gemene middelen* extracted annually just under 3 guilders per inhabitant of Holland when introduced in 1584. This rose steadily to 10 guilders per head by the 1630s, when these taxes accounted for two-thirds of Holland's total tax revenue. Most of these excises were fixed amounts of money per unit of sale (rather than *ad valorem* taxes) levied on the seller (usually the retailer) rather than on the consumer. Government officials did not collect these taxes; rather, collection rested with private tax farmers who bid at auction for the right to collect a particular excise tax in one of Holland's tax districts (usually a city plus its hinterland).

Such a tax system could have had little appeal to a state striving for centralized, bureaucratic power, nor could it have worked in an economy only partially monetized with a major element of nonmarket production and consumption. However, Holland's governing elite, the regents, found the *gemene middelen* to be full of virtues. As we have seen, it was flexible, being capable of expansion and intensification literally at the stroke of a pen. It was predictable, the net tax revenue being known and collectable as soon as the auctions had been held. It deflected public anger from the regents and their government, for the tax farms were, as Professor van Deursen puts it, "the singularly cherished hunting ground of small-time operators and speculators of modest means;" what a government document called "geringe en vile [petty and contemptible] personen."[6]

In France the vast tax farms, controlled by a handful of great financiers, were a symbol of the state's fiscal impotence and dependence on creditors. In Holland the tax farms were small and numerous. Around 1700 the forty separate excise taxes divided into seventeen districts produced 680 separate tax farms, each auctioned for a six-month period. Moreover, the practice of holding all auctions on the same day discouraged multiple ownership. Consequently, the tax farmers were small fry, unambiguously subordinate to and socially distinct from government officials. They acted as a political buffer, absorbing the dissatisfactions and suspicions of the taxpayers.

One is tempted to add that excise taxes appealed to the governing circles because they touched the rich but lightly. No social group in Holland enjoyed legal exception from any taxes; what better way to shift the tax burden to the common man than by relying on flat-rate excises on basic articles of consumption? Historians have long criticized the Republic's heavy reliance on excise taxes for its regressive incidence and its tendency to drive up the cost of living. The retailers who paid most of these taxes presumably "passed them on" to the consumer, increasing the cost of everything from bread, beer, and fuel to coffee, tea, and tobacco. This, it is argued, forced up wages, undermining the competitiveness of

---

[6] "bij uitstek geliefkoosd jachtveld van kleine scharrelaars en speculanten zonder vermogen," A. Th. van Deursen, *Het kopergeld van de Gouden Eeuw* (Assen, 1979), Vol. III, p. 27.

Table 4.6. *Revenues from the* Gemene Middelen *(excise taxes) in Holland, 1584–1794.*

[a] Year	[b] Revenue (3-year average) (000s guilders)	[c] Revenue per capita (guilders)	[d] As % of maximum annual earnings of unskilled laborer[a]
1584	1,440	2.9	11.2
1599–1600	2,200	4.0	10.5
1608	4,344	7.2	17.2
1624–6	5,990	8.9	17.9
1630	6,983	10.0	17.7
1635	7,272	10.1	15.2
1640	7,953	10.7	15.7
1645	9,146	12.0	17.5
1650	8,363	10.6	15.4
1655	7,710	9.5	14.1
1660	8,040	9.7	14.7
1665	7,730	9.0	13.3
1670	7,950	9.0	13.7
1675	8,330	9.5	14.3
1680	8,450	9.6	14.4
1685	9,740	11.1	17.7
1690	10,140	11.7	17.4
1695	10,250	11.9	19.5
1700	9,360	11.0	17.5
1705	9,320	11.0	17.5
1710	9,390	11.2	17.8
1715	8,790	10.6	16.9
1720	9,080	11.1	17.7
1725	9,430	11.6	18.5
1730	9,270	11.5	17.1
1735	9,050	11.3	16.9
1740	8,930	11.3	18.7
1745	8,460	10.8	17.9
1750–1759	9,990	12.8	21.1
1790–1794	11,035	14.1	23.5

[a]Assuming household size of four persons.
Sources: M. 't Hart, *In quest of funds* (Leiden, 1989), Appendix VII; A. R. A. The Hague, Financie van Holland no. 826–8.

industrial production among other things. We will return to this issue in Chapter 12, but here it can be noted that the level of excise taxes, when expressed as a percentage of the wages of an unskilled worker (see Table 4.6) rose sharply in the twenty-five years after their introduction to become a very considerable burden. Table 4.6 actually understates the overall burden of the excise taxes, since until 1750 the figures refer to *net* revenue (the payment made by tax farmers) rather than the gross revenue, the amounts actually collected. Moreover, cities imposed their own excises. These usually took the form of supplements to the provincial tax and, if the levies of Leiden and Amsterdam can serve as a guide, added 1.5 to 3 guilders to the per capita tax burden of urban residents. In these early years of the Republic, the provincial and municipal excises most certainly pressed heavily upon the purse of the common worker.

It is striking that the real burden of the excise taxes in later years rarely exceeded the level reached by 1608 and 1625, and was often lower. This is surprising in view of the many additions and rate increases discussed earlier. The explanation is to be found in three factors: First, the tax burden is related here to maximum earnings of unskilled laborers; our calculations assume full employment. In periods when this was unattainable, the tax burden would have weighed more heavily. Second, the single most important excise until 1650, the tax on beer, declined steadily as beer consumption fell. It accounted for 29 percent of excise revenues in 1650, 13 percent in 1700, and only 3 percent by 1790. In many cases the new and increased taxes could do no more than compensate for this loss.

Finally, there is the difficult matter of enforcement. In theory, the excise taxes applied equally throughout Holland; in practice, the effective levies varied from city to city, since enforcement was in the hands of the urban magistrates. Just as the Generality could not enforce uniform administration on the Admiralties, so the States of Holland had no bureaucratic machinery to enforce uniform application of the excise laws among the cities.

Indirect taxes on necessities are a classical "regressive" tax, weighing on the poor more heavily than on the rich. But many of Holland's *gemene middelen*, especially those introduced after 1670, incorporated provisions – exemptions or sliding scales – that we associate with direct taxation. They were related to the income or wealth of the taxpayer rather than simply to the consumption of the taxed commodity. From the beginning the provincial excise on beer varied with its cost and quality from 20 percent for cheap beer to over 100 percent for the most expensive. Moreover, the cheapest "thin beer" was exempt from taxation altogether. In 1680 the grain-milling tax in rural areas was converted to a per capita tax. To avoid evasion, each taxpayer was taxed on an assumed level of consumption, rising with the occupation or assessed wealth of the taxpayer. This principle had been introduced earlier in a revision of the salt tax, and in later years this conversion of excises to progressive head taxes found other applications wherever collection and enforcement costs were particularly high. In addition the States introduced a tax on household servants in 1680 that was doubly progressive, the tax levied on an employer with property valued at over 2,000 guilders was twice that of his less wealthy neighbor, and the taxes on additional servants were large multiples of the tax on the first one. In 1695 yet another set of taxes was introduced – on marriages and burials. These head taxes were sharply progressive, ranging from *pro deo* (i.e., free) for the majority of persons, or corpses, of modest wealth (under 300 guilders), to 30 guilders for those in the fifth, and highest, category, whose taxable wealth exceeded 12,000 guilders.

Another group of taxes, while not precisely excise taxes, can be mentioned here. The *kleine zegel*, a stamp tax required for a wide variety of legal and official documents, was introduced in 1624. It was followed by the "40th penny," a 2.5 percent tax levied at the point of sale on the value of real estate, ships, bonds, and goods sold at auction. Both of these counted among the *gemene middelen*.

We do not know enough about the social incidence of most of these taxes to come to a firm conclusion about their net regressivity. But it is evident that after 1670 a declining percentage of the *gemene middelen* revenue was drawn from flat rate levies on the necessities of life. In her analysis of Republican taxation, Wantje Fritschy showed that the typically regressive excises accounted for 83 percent of all such revenue in 1650, but only 66 percent by the 1790s. The intrinsic regressivity of the excise tax was moderated over time. But the *gemene middelen* were not the only taxes levied by Holland. As we survey the others, this provisional statement will require further modification.

Next in importance to the *gemene middelen* were the taxes on land and other real property. This had been the basis of the old *schildtal* of Holland, and most other provinces possessed its equivalent: the *floreen* in Friesland, the *jaartax* in Groningen, the *oudschildgeld* in Utrecht. From 1584 Holland's land tax, now called *verponding*, amounted to 8.5 percent of the rental value of all real property. As time passed the old land registers ceased to bear much relation to reality. Finally, in 1632, the States introduced new registers and took the occasion to revise the real property tax. Henceforth, Holland collected 20 percent of land rents and 8.5 percent of house rental values as they stood in 1632. These taxes raised approximately 2.4 million guilders per year.

Every other province possessed or eventually introduced a comparable tax, although the antiquity of the property registers and the levies per unit of land varied greatly. Groningen introduced a *verponding* in 1600 on 25 percent of assessed value; Friesland continued to charge varying amounts on land registers dating from 1511; Gelderland levied the "9th penny" (11.1 percent) on land, while Zeeland's *verponding* was a flat levy nearly double the effective rate in Holland. These taxes were levied annually, but when the quota demanded more revenue, additional levies of the *verponding* might be decreed; in Holland this happened occasionally after 1653 and regularly after 1680. In 1694–7, 1704–12, and finally in 1731, Holland's property owners paid *verponding* three times per year. Otherwise they paid one or one-half "extraordinary" *verponding* besides the "ordinary" levy. During these decades of frequent extraordinary taxation, property owners also suffered from the fact that assessed valuation of their property had been set in 1632, which happened to have been near the peak of property prices. As rents and commodity prices plunged after the 1660s, the real burden of the *verponding* rose sharply.

Pressure to revise the *verponding* registers was long resisted by the state, but finally resulted in new assessments in 1732, after the old registers had served for a century. Even then, to ensure that the total tax yield would not fall, only house rents were revised. Relief for farmers only came with the rise of prices after the 1740s (see Chapter 6).

The third major component of taxation in the Republic consisted of direct taxes on wealth and income. All provinces levied an inheritance tax, the *collaterale successie*. At first only legacies passing to collateral heirs were taxed (hence its name), but in Holland, Zeeland, Utrecht, and Groningen, direct heirs also became subject to the tax, which in Holland amounted to 5 percent of the estate, and from 1743, 10 percent for indirect inheritance.

Direct capital levies began soon after the formation of the Republic, although they long remained occasional taxes, activated in times of extraordinary need. In 1585 the States of Holland introduced an assessment on the net worth of well-to-do citizens. Called the *capitale impositie*, it was actually a forced loan. The success of any such levy depended on the accuracy of registers recording the taxable assets or income of those subject to the tax, and this long proved to be beyond the capacity of Holland's decentralized administration. In 1622 the States decided to collect an income tax, the *hoofdgeld*, for which we have to thank the only census taken in Holland until 1795. This effort did not result in a workable tax. A century later, in 1715, registers were drawn up to collect another income tax, the *familiegeld*. It, too, was abandoned in 1723 as unsuccessful. In 1742 Holland tried again with the *personeele quotisatie*, which lasted eleven years before being abandoned. It taxed households with incomes above 600 guilders (thereby exempting about four-fifths of all households) with a progressive income tax, ranging from 1.0 to 2.5 percent. These taxes have left the historian with important documents (see Chapter 11, section 11.5), but they yielded the state too little in relation to the collection effort.

Wealth taxes proved to be more feasible. Levies ranging from the 100th to the 1,000th Penny (i.e., 1.0 to 0.1 percent) were levied on real and personal property beginning in 1625. The taxes were always called "extraordinary," being levied as the need arose, but in time they became a fixed element of Holland's tax system. From 1653 the registers incorporated a graduated scale, distinguishing between *capitalisten* (persons possessing taxable wealth of at least 2,000 guilders) and *halve capitalisten* (those with 1,000 to 2,000).

Wealth taxes became much more frequent from the time of Louis XIV's invasion in 1672. Indeed, between 1671 and 1678, Holland levied the 200th Penny twenty-eight times, claiming for the state (in theory) 14 percent of the value of all real property, financial instruments, seigniorial rights, tithes, and personal objects of value. (Technically, half of these levies were forced loans.)

In 1674 Holland assembled a new register fixing the assessed taxable wealth of its inhabitants (the *personele kohier*). On this basis the 100th and 200th Penny wealth taxes could be collected with relative ease, and they were, indeed, frequently imposed. But the very regularity of the tax made revision and updating of the register a sensitive issue. The cities whose inhabitants' wealth increased – Amsterdam above all – resisted updating, which resulted in a steadily falling revenue as the tax registers, still in use over forty years after they were assembled, bore steadily less relation to reality. The problem was finally resolved in 1722, when the effort to tax a broad range of personal wealth was abandoned in exchange for the agreement to levy every year the 100th and 200th Penny taxes on provincial bonds.

In the eighteenth century, these taxes laid hold of a substantial portion of the income of the wealthy. The frequent surcharges on the *verponding* could reduce net rental incomes of landowners to half of gross receipts, while holders of Holland's bonds, then paying 4 percent interest, actually received only 2.5 percent. The 100th and 200th Penny subtracted 1.5 percent (a 37.5 percent tax on bond income), an amount withheld directly by the tax offices that paid this interest to bondholders.

Holland's total tax revenues were composed of a broad array of excises (*gemene middelen*), property taxes (*verponding*), "extraordinary" taxes on wealth and income, plus a miscellany of other taxes, fees, and tolls. The other provinces all imposed their own mix of these same elements. In addition, the cities levied excises, market fees, street and lantern taxes, and so on, while the drainage boards levied land taxes for dike, windmill, and sluice maintenance. The level of these drainage charges varied from polder to polder but could be as high as the *verponding* itself. Finally, we must mention the ubiquitous tolls for the use of roads, canals, locks, bridges, and harbors.

Municipal and drainage board charges are significant, for these levies financed nearly all infrastructural investment and social and educational expenditure. Taken together, Dutch taxation was both broadly based and deeply penetrating. Feudal and clerical exemptions from taxation were all but nonexistent, exposing the entire society to taxation, and the young Republic possessed the political authority to impose substantial burdens on its citizens. In this context the pressure to increase revenue did not lead to bureaucratic centralization but rather to the reverse, for local institutions possessed more taxing legitimacy than did distant ones, and the broad and varied tax base allowed the provinces and cities to tailor their specific taxes to local conditions.

What all these impositions yielded annually in tax revenue cannot now be known, for contemporaries themselves had no way of knowing. In the absence of comprehensive budgets and uniform taxation, the fiscal situation was always difficult to assess, and the suspicions that some provinces shirked their responsibilities, and that tax farmers collected vastly more than the States received, could never convincingly be dispelled.

In the case of Holland, enough is known about its tax revenues to reconstruct a reasonably complete picture. We already noted the tenfold increase in revenues across the decades of the Revolt. In this moment of creation, the States of Holland displayed a resolve and an ability to draw far more revenue from the taxpayer than it had ever dared or wished to previously. In real terms the tax burden suddenly increased by threefold to fourfold (see Table 4.3).

Powered by the expansion of the *gemene middelen*, Holland's tax revenues continued to grow after 1588, tripling in the next forty years. But, from 1588 to 1671, while the Republic waged effective war against first Spain and then England, the real per capita tax burden showed no signs of rising. During this "Golden Age," the tax base probably expanded more rapidly than taxes rose.

After 1671 everything changed. Taxes rose, doubling by the 1690s, but wages did not rise, and commodity prices fell. The tax base almost certainly shrank, causing the per capita tax burden during the first decade of the eighteenth century to be *at least* double what it had been a generation earlier. In this difficult period, an English traveler famously observed of the Hollanders: "Though the people boast of their Free State, I am confident no subjects in the world are more burdened with taxes then they. . . . [T]here comes not a joint of meat to their tables but what has paid excise at least 18 or 20 times."[7]

After the Peace of Utrecht, substantial further increases in tax revenue were limited to the war conditions of the 1740s, and the Republic's terminal crisis after 1787. Most of that long era was one of peace for the Republic, but neither of the measures of real tax burden displayed in Table 4.3 reveals any significant reduction. The accelerating price inflation after 1770 reduced the real tax burden for some, but in the economic crisis of those years, it is likely that the shrinking tax base made the tax innovations of the "French era" more burdensome than ever.

Our limited knowledge of the fiscal histories of Holland's direct neighbors – Zeeland, Utrecht, and Friesland – does not permit a detailed account of the tax burden over time. But there is no reason to think that the experience of these provinces differed substantially from Holland's. The Generality's quotas were even higher than Holland's on a per capita basis, the excises were nearly as high, and the per capita tax revenues in the late eighteenth century stood at about 80 percent of Holland's level. Taxes in Groningen stood not far below this level.

In the inland provinces – Drenthe, Overijssel, Gelderland, and the Generality lands – the fiscal situation was rather different. In these territories the excises were levied on fewer goods, and the charges were substantially lower. Instead of the 9 to 11 guilders per head paid in Holland, inhabitants of Drenthe paid on average from 2.5 to 3.5 guilders, those of Overijssel paid 4.5 (1680–1710) to 3.0 (after 1750), and the rural inhabitants of Brabant usually paid less than 1.5 guilders (1650–1795). In these more rural territories, the land taxes figured more prominently in the fiscal system, and here, too, the combination of falling commodity prices and rising taxes in the period 1670–1730 imposed an extraordinary burden

---

[7] Ellis Verryard, *An Account of Divers Choice Remarks Taken in a Journey through the Low Countries, France, Italy and Part of Spain* (London, 1682), p. 121.

on the rural economy. In Drenthe, land and other taxes especially burdensome on agriculture stood at an equivalent of 800 lasts of rye (Drenthe's main crop) from 1610 to 1670. (A last equals 2,000 kg., or 2 tons.) The pressure then rose steadily to a peak in 1700–4, when 3,400 lasts of rye needed to be sold to pay provincial taxes, and over 2,000 lasts per year continued to be needed until 1745, when rising prices gradually lightened the tax burden.

In general it appears that the inland provinces experienced each of the first three phases of fiscal pressure charted in Holland, with the important difference that the general level of taxation was rather less than half as high. Given the lower level of economic development in those regions, the real tax burden *may* not have been lower than in Holland. It is difficult to be sure. But we can be more confident in asserting that in the fourth period, after 1715, the per capita tax burden fell substantially in most inland regions. Population grew in these regions, and after the 1740s, commodity prices rose; but tax revenues remained stable at best. By the 1790s per capita tax revenues were little more than one-third of the level in Holland. One gets the impression that an established fiscal regime, enforced with few changes over many decades, proved ever less capable of capturing a constant share of regional product. It stands to reason that over time an economy will grow away from a fixed tax structure.

The tax revenue of the entire Republic is first known for 1716, when all the provinces and the Generality (including Admiralties) collected a total of 32.5 million guilders. It is known again for the years around 1790, when a commission gathered information for the 1792 revision of the quota system. Then revenues totaled 40.5 million. Total revenues are also available for the years after 1795, when the Batavian Republic and its successors worked to reform the fiscal regime (see Table 4.3).

Several observations can be made about these total figures:

1. Table 4.3 does not represent total "public sector" revenue. The cities levied excises and other taxes that probably exceeded 2 to 3 guilders per urban resident, while the drainage boards levied charges on land that sometimes rivaled the *verponding* in severity.
2. The total revenue is a composite of two very different levels of taxation, some three times in the maritime provinces what it was in the inland provinces.
3. In 1790 the *national* per capita tax revenue of the Republic stood at the same level as that of Great Britain; in both countries the per capita tax burden was double that of France in the years immediately preceding the Revolution.[8] Both French and British tax revenues rose rapidly throughout the eighteenth century (between 1715 and 1789 by 50 percent in France and 65 percent in

---

[8] P. O'Brien and P. Mathias, "Taxation in Britain and France, 1715–1810. A comparison of the social and economic incidence of taxes collected for the central governments," *Journal of European Economic History* 5 (1976), 601–50; J. M. F. Fritschy, *De patriotten en de financiën van de Bataafse Republiek* (The Hague, 1988), pp. 57–70; John Brewer, *The Sinews of Power* (New York, 1988), Chapter 4.

Britain, in real per capita terms). Indeed, by 1790 Britain's excise taxes, first introduced in 1689, raised at least as much per capita as did the Republic's.

4. It follows that taxation in the Republic in 1716–20, and in fact much earlier, stood at a far higher level than in surrounding countries; it was then nearly twice as high as in Britain.

5. It is striking that Britain – but also France and other European states – acted to raise tax revenues (by among other measures introducing Dutch fiscal "inventions" such as excises and stamp taxes) from about 1690–1700, by which time Dutch tax revenue was approaching a ceiling. The expansion of the Republic's revenue, which took place in the century after the 1580s, was followed with a century's delay by its great rival across the North Sea.

The term "tax ceiling" deserves some further elaboration. The Republic's decentralized political system isolated and expelled every suggestion of or tendency toward fiscal centralization or bureaucratization. Reform and timely decision making never characterized the fiscal regime. But the fiscal regime was also broadly based, and its decentralization allowed for a flexible exploitation of the many taxing opportunities of a diversified, highly monetized economy. The Republic's fiscal policies succeeded in defining a broad tax base and taxing it heavily. In this sense, the charge that the Republic suffered from an "institutional impotence" in the fiscal sphere is very far from the mark, as Wantje Fritschy convincingly has demonstrated.

However, in the eighteenth century, the Republic displayed no ability or willingness to increase taxes further. While other European states gradually developed tax structures that moved their revenues toward the position earlier achieved by the Republic, the Republic itself appears to have been "impotent" to increase its own revenue further. Had it exhausted the economy's taxing possibilities, or even exceeded that point, undermining the economy through excessive taxation? Or was the cessation of major taxing initiatives more a sign of the State's political vulnerability, its inability to overcome the endless political compromises that had given the fiscal regime its peculiar shape?

It is, of course, possible that both factors – the economic ceiling and the political will – are essential to a fully satisfactory explanation. The growing economic obstacles to increasing tax revenues could stiffen resistance to institutional reform, a theme to which we shall return presently. Here we wish to call attention to the way in which Holland's overall tax structure became less regressive as the tax burden was increased (for the last time until the 1790s) to finance Willem III's wars against France. One of the most telling bits of evidence in support of the thesis that taxes on the common man had reached a limit in the late seventeenth century is the knowledge that almost all post-1672 tax initiatives avoided direct attacks on his purse.

We have already examined the measures taken to reduce the regressivity of the *gemene middelen*. Other measures included increases in the collateral succession,

Table 4.7. *Analysis of the "regressivity" of taxation in Holland.*

Taxes (in millions)	1624	1650	1720–9	1750–65	1790–4
Progressive	0.9	1.4	8.0	10.3	10.2
Indeterminate	.5	2.4	4.6	5.4	6.0
Regressive	4.6	7.1	6.5	6.9	7.6
Total tax revenue	7.0	11.0	19.1	22.6	23.8
Progressive as % of total revenue	13%	13	42	45	43

Definitions:
• "Progressive": *Gemene middelen* on luxuries and those levied as capitation (i.e., direct) taxes, the *collaterale successie* (inheritance tax), the 100th and 200th pennies (wealth taxes), marriage and burial taxes, and withholdings on public salaries.
• "Indeterminate": the *verponding* (property tax).
• "Regressive": *Gemene middelen* levied *ad valorem* on nonluxuries.

Rough estimate of the per capita tax burden of "richer" and "poorer" households. Assumptions: that progressive taxes are paid exclusively by the richest 30 percent of households; that regressive taxes are distributed on an equal per capita basis among all households; that indeterminate taxes are paid for 50 percent by the richer, and 50 percent by the poorer groups.

	1624	1650	1720–9	1750–65	1790–4
"Richer 30 %"	15.01	20.03	49.79	64.13	65.88
"Poorer 70 %"	8.45	11.20	11.92	13.74	15.18

Sources: M. 't Hart, "Staatsvorming, sociale relaties en oorlogsfinanciering in de Nederlandse republiek," *Tijdschrift voor sociale geschiedenis 16* (1990), 61–85; J. M. F. Fritschy, *Patriotten en de financiën van de Bataafse Republiek* (The Hague, 1988), Appendix A.

and stamp taxes, introduction of the 100th and 200th penny on bonds, the marriage and burial taxes, and taxes on public office holders. All were distinctly progressive in their incidence.

The frequent levying of extraordinary land taxes, the *verponding*, had a less obviously progressive character, but since *verponding* in Holland was paid by the property owner rather than the tenant, its impact on the propertyless was indirect at worst. The course of rents shows that in periods of weak rental markets, these extra costs often had to be absorbed by the owner. Table 4.7 presents a rough division of Holland's taxes by their progressive or regressive character and a much more speculative allocation of these taxes among the "richer" and "poorer" social groups. If these allocations are only generally correct, they uncover several important characteristics of Holland's taxes.

First, through at least the 1650s, the regressive character of the *gemene middelen* governed the entire tax regime. The higher per capita taxes of the "rich" in no way corresponded to their much higher incomes. The Golden Age was definitely one of low taxation for those with higher than average incomes.

Second, the doubling of tax revenue between 1670 and 1710 touched the per capita tax burden of working people but lightly. To the extent that the tax burden became more onerous for them – which is suggested by increasingly violent resistance to tax collectors – this must have been the consequence of falling incomes.

Third, throughout the eighteenth century, the richer group paid far higher taxes than the poorer. Did this suffice to remove the earlier pronounced regressivity of the tax structure? We know too little about income distribution to answer this question with any confidence (see Chapter 11, section 11.5). But more important than the size of one's income in Holland's tax system was the *source* of one's income. A person – whether rich or not – owning real property and Holland's bonds was very heavily taxed. A rich person investing in commercial ventures and foreign bonds was not. Moreover, such a person in the prosperous city of Amsterdam enjoyed shelter from the full rigor of the tax law because of the continued use of obsolete assessments of real property (until 1732) and personal wealth (until 1722). A rich person in a declining city, and persons in possession of "old wealth," did not enjoy this *de facto* protection.

The Republic's tax regime had its peculiarities, but not all of its provisions were flagrantly biased against the working population. This was the conclusion reluctantly reached by the Patriots who gained power in 1795, determined to sweep away what they held to be a self-serving jerry-built structure of taxation. Their labors to replace this fiscal relic with a new enlightened, unified, and fair system gave rise to a new tax system remarkably similar to the old one. Given the state's heavy defense costs and vulnerable economic base, the margins for a new fiscal policy were small indeed.[9]

The public debt

The history of Republican taxation is intimately tied to the history of its public borrowing. We have noted how Holland in the mid–sixteenth century acquired a capacity long enjoyed only by municipal authorities: to borrow funds for long terms and against favorable interest rates in a free capital market. The outbreak of the Revolt sharply reduced Holland's ability to attract voluntary lenders, and, as we have seen, the rebel cause depended primarily on foreign subsidies, sharply increased taxation, and forced lending.

Even after the rebel provinces were out of imminent danger, voluntary lenders were not numerous. In fact, most lenders possessed close ties to the state, such as noble families and holders of public office. Of special importance were the assets confiscated by the new Protestant state from the Catholic church. The rebels

[9] Fritschy, *De patriotten*, p. 119.

placed these assets, mainly real property, in the hands of an Office of Ecclesiastical Property and charged it with the duty to support "pious purposes" such as education, payment of salaries to Protestant clergy, pensions to their widows, and pensions to the dispossessed Catholic clergy. Year by year this office sold off its real property – thereby responding to a demand for these often choice properties – and invested the proceeds in public bonds – thereby responding to a pressing need of the state.

Holland's public debt in 1574 is thought to have stood at about 1.4 million guilders. As late as 1600, it appears not to have exceeded 5 million guilders, and voluntary lenders were scarce despite the continued offer of bonds at 8.33 percent interest. By the 1590s the reason for this scarcity of capital had less to do with fear than with hope: Investments in the commercial sector offered much better prospects. This, at any rate, is the impression given by two characteristics of Holland's borrowing in these years. The first is the commitment of some cities, Amsterdam among them, to buy bonds from its citizens on whom bond purchases had been imposed by assessment. This commitment to maintaining a secondary market, in James Tracy's view, helped to reconcile urban merchants to forced lending by allowing them to reclaim (most of) their capital for private investment as opportunities presented themselves. The second piece of evidence, also uncovered by Tracy, is the conspicuous role of female and institutional investors. In 1600–8 such buyers were far more numerous, and their purchases larger, than had been the case under the last free market for public bonds in 1553–65. As late as 1608, an 8.33 percent interest rate had appeal principally as a fund for widows and orphans.[10]

Provincial (and urban) borrowers then issued three types of debt instrument. *Obligatien* were promissory notes intended to be short-term and, as bearer bonds, readily negotiable. More important were the longer-term debt instruments known as *losrenten* and *lijfrenten*. *Losrenten* were, strictly speaking, redeemable bonds, although they tended to become perpetual. Until the issuer redeemed them, the holder, whose name was recorded in a debt ledger, enjoyed an annual interest payment. *Lijfrenten* were life annuities, self-amortizing loans in which the issuer contracts to make annual payments to the buyer, or nominee, during his or her life. At death the principal of the loan is extinguished. In the 1570s *losrenten* paid the 12th Penny (i.e., 8.33 percent), while *lijfrenten* paid the 6th Penny (16.67 percent); by 1609 the interest rates were the 16th Penny (6.25 percent) and the 8th Penny (12.5 percent), respectively.

The Twelve Years' Truce begun in 1609 reduced to zero Holland's need to issue new bonds. Then, as in 1621, its debt stood at 23 million guilders (in addition, the Generality's debt was nearly 5 million). When war resumed in 1621, so did Holland's issuance of new bonds. By then the reluctance of investors to

---

[10] James D. Tracy, "Redeemable Bonds (*Losrenten*) in the Early Dutch Republic," unpublished paper, University of Minnesota, 1988.

tie up capital in public debt had diminished substantially. From 1621 to the end of hostilities with Spain in 1647, Holland and the Generality borrowed 115 million guilders, over 4 million per year. This level of borrowing supplemented Holland's tax revenues by some 40 percent, which goes a long way to accounting for the generally stable tax burden of these decades. Of course, with a growing debt came steadily increasing interest payments. By 1640 the debt of some 95 million guilders required 6.5 million per year in debt service – itself about 60 percent of Holland's tax revenue.

In that year confidence in Holland's public debt was such that the *losrenten* portion of the debt could be converted (i.e., the old bonds redeemed and new ones issued) to a 5 percent rate of interest. A second conversion in 1655 succeeded in reducing credit costs to 4 percent.

Lijfrenten, the life annuities, also received careful attention, and from no less than Johan de Witt, Holland's Grand Pensionary and effective head of government. He wrote the first treatise applying probability theory to compare the costs to the issuer of *lijfrenten* (where the age and life expectancy of the nominee determines the real interest rate) versus *losrenten* [Johan de Witt, *Waerdije van lijfrenten naer proportie van losrenten* (The Hague, 1671)]. His findings exposed the high cost of *lijfrenten* issued without regard to the age of the nominee. Henceforth, when Holland issued *lijfrenten*, it should do so, de Witt argued, only at rates that varied with the nominee's age. In fact, the Republic made steadily diminishing use of *lijfrenten* as Dutch governments found that they "were able to borrow by means of long-term redeemable (but in practice perpetual) annuities at rates equal to the lowest interest returns demanded in the private sector. The United Provinces had shifted to a program of credit exploitation that gave investors guarantees sufficient to convince them to accept interest-only lending formats."[11] This exploitation of the credit markets endowed the Republic with an ability to spend that greatly exceeded its short-term ability to tax.

By converting bonds to lower interest rates and by reducing the issue of expensive life annuities, Holland succeeded in reducing its annual debt service considerably. In 1668 Johan de Witt took satisfaction in the fact that annual debt service charges had fallen by 1.1 million guilders since he took office (in 1652) even though Holland's public debt had increased. In comparison with 1640, we can note that the debt had increased by 30 million guilders, but debt service had fallen from 60 to 50 percent of annual tax revenue, and the tax burden had become lighter relative to both wages and commodity prices.

A well-managed public debt offers timely increases in purchasing power to the state, as well as short-term tax moderation to taxpayers. But in the long run, it has a substantial redistributive effect, channeling money from hundreds of thousands of taxpayers to a much smaller number of bondholders. In the first

---

[11] James C. Riley, *International Government Finance and the Amsterdam Capital Market, 1740–1815* (Cambridge, 1980), p. 104.

century of Republican government, this tendency was moderated by the relatively broad distribution of the debt across the population. Until 1620 most bonds had been acquired in the context of forced lending measures, and among the voluntary lenders, charitable institutions and persons in need of financial security were prominently represented. For later years the observations of contemporaries plus probate inventories confirm the view that a broad spectrum of society held public bonds.

The purchase of public bonds was readily arranged even by the unsophisticated or occasional investor. Every "voting" city in Holland possessed a revenue office (*gemenelandscomptoir*), an office that arranged both the collection of taxes and the placement of bonds. The Receiver in charge of each office was free to tailor his bond offerings to the needs of the local market. Thus, especially outside Amsterdam and The Hague, the Receivers issued many bonds of small coupon, and everywhere the lists of buyers were larded with humble craftsmen, the residents of villages, and, always, many women (they were 40 percent of all private buyers in 1628 and 1650). It is this broad market for government bonds that impressed contemporaries, for in most other countries, such lending was a monopoly of powerful office holders (France), bankers (the London goldsmiths), or privileged, usually foreign, merchants (Sweden). Sir William Temple, England's ambassador to the Republic in the 1660s, claimed that Holland's debt was held by no less than 65,500 persons (the province then possessed perhaps 220,000 households).

We cannot check the accuracy of Temple's observation, and it must at any rate be remembered that widespread bond ownership is not the same thing as a wide distribution of the value of the public debt, any more than the astonished observations of seventeenth century visitors that Dutch peasants owned paintings implies that farmhouse walls were graced by Rembrandts and Vermeers.

Ownership of these financial assets surely was highly concentrated, but what distinguished seventeenth-century Dutch society from its neighbors was a numerous middle-income group capable of owning (modest) paintings and (a few) government bonds.

Until the final decade of the Eighty Years' War, Holland and the Generality usually had to place new bonds substantially in excess of the annual interest payments made to existing bondholders. This fact by itself stimulated the spread of bond ownership, for even if existing bondholders invested 40 percent of their interest income in the purchase of new bonds – which would seem high in view of the many small and institutional owners and the numerous alternative investment possibilities – the Republic's provinces still had to attract new funds at the rate of nearly 3 million guilders per year throughout the period 1620–47. The fact that this was done at declining interest rates testifies to the growing capital abundance of these decades.

In the following twenty-five years, net public borrowing was negligible, while bondholders received interest payment of some 9 million guilders per year. Since hardly any of this money could have been reinvested in bonds, the question of

Millions of guilders

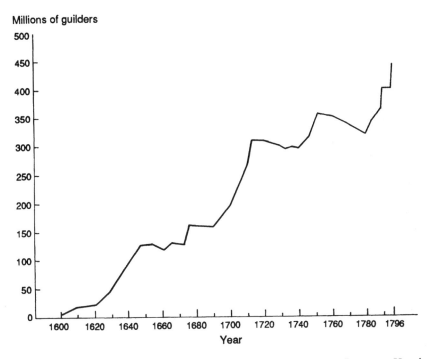

Figure 4.2. The public debt of Holland, 1599–1796. [*Source:* E. H. M. Dormans, *Het tekort. Staatsschuld in de tijd der Republiek* (Amsterdam, 1991).]

how it was used in this prosperous and turbulent era is of special interest. It is possible that the term "embarrassment of riches" then had a rather literal meaning for Holland's bondholders. Their accumulations of cash may have fueled the real estate boom of the 1650s and '60s, which featured hectic urban construction (including much of Amsterdam's famous concentric belt of canals) and the rapid rise of property values.

From 1672 to 1713, the Republic, hitherto so resourceful in gathering the fiscal means to defend itself and its interests, was plunged into a fiscal nightmare. As the economic environment shifted to one of contraction, with falling prices putting a squeeze on profits and discouraging investment, the Republic faced life-threatening military dangers, and its new leader, Stadhouder Willem III, embarked on a political course that required vast expenditures. Holland's tax revenues were nearly doubled, with the economic consequences already discussed, but they still fell far short of the expenses incurred in the wars against France and England, the War of the League of Augsburg, and the War of the Spanish Succession. The Republic turned, as never before, to the full exploitation of its formidable public credit.

The combined French land invasion and British sea blockade of 1672 brought Holland back into the bond market on a large scale. For each of six consecutive years, it issued nearly 7 million guilders in bonds. In the face of this sudden and intense demand for funds, interest rates remained low; indeed, investors lent to both the state and the VOC in these years with an eagerness suggesting gratitude for the opportunity.

After 1677 followed another period in which bondholders received some 10 million guilders per year, without the option of placing their savings in new bonds. Unlike the 1650s and '60s, no rising real property market now stood ready to absorb this capital, but the outbreak of war in 1689 changed the bond market once again. For the next twenty-four years, Holland and the Generality together borrowed an average of over 8 million guilders per year. Just as in the 1670s, the state's borrowing needs exceeded by far what existing bondholders could have made available from reinvested interest earnings. But in this period, the new investments did not come effortlessly. A glance at Table 4.8 suggests why.

The current state of our knowledge of the Republic's bond market does not allow us to do more than speculate about the practices of holders of the public debt. But if we assume that bondholders, as a group, saved between 25 and 40 percent of annual interest payments, and if we assume further that existing bondholders were prime candidates to purchase new issues (both domestic and foreign), then the arithmetic exercise in Table 4.8 reveals that bondholders accumulated tens of millions of guilders after 1646, which even the crisis of 1672–7 could not absorb. In the period 1646–89, the owners of the Republic's public debt were awash in cash. How did they invest these funds? As we shall later see, investors bought VOC bonds eagerly, and several minor public borrowers – cities and drainage boards – must also have absorbed a bit. But most of the 33 to 99 million guilders that might theoretically have accumulated in the hands of bondholders by 1689 must have been placed in much riskier sectors, such as shipping, whaling, marine insurance, and acceptance credit. How much lay idle in cash balances?

Even if this total accumulation had been readily available after 1689 for new bond purchases, the persisting government demand, stretching across twenty-four years of almost continuous warfare, was such that these and many tens of millions of guilders in addition had to be disinvested from the commercial, industrial, and agricultural sectors.

Holland's good credit, which had long been a source of strength, began to be called into question. To attract funds during the War of the Spanish Succession, Holland reactivated the sale of *lijfrenten* on the unfavorable terms that de Witt had argued against a generation earlier. By 1710 Holland's credit was strained to the breaking point. Finding it impossible to attract lenders with the customary credit instruments, Holland embarked on the issue of lottery bonds, hoping to attract investors by adding a gambling element to its traditional *losrenten*. The purchaser of a bond gambled that his would be among the 15 percent of each issue to which would be awarded, by drawing, a life annuity. Even with this expensive feature, the investor of 1710–13 had to be offered 6 percent interest.

By 1713 Holland's debt had reached 310 million guilders, that of the Generality 68 million, and that of other provinces, the cities, and the admiralties many tens of millions more. In that year Holland's debt service required 14 million guilders, a sum exceeding its ordinary tax revenue (i.e., regular tax revenue, excluding the proceeds of "extraordinary" levies).

Then, as earlier, charitable institutions, guilds, and many persons of modest means relied upon the annual interest payments, and many more well-to-do persons possessed bonds because of the frequent forced lending campaigns. But by 1713 a long era of bond purchases by wealthy families, whether for the diversification of their portfolios or in order to withdraw from active commerce, plus many years of reinvesting bond interest earnings, had led to a much higher degree of concentration of public debt ownership than had been the case before 1672. It is likely that a higher percentage of interest earnings now sought placement in comparable assets than had been the case earlier, both because of the very high incomes – and, hence, high savings rates – of the bondholders and because of the relative paucity of alternatives.

Throughout the eighteenth century, the regent and rich merchant families of Leiden, Gouda, and Hoorn left estates in which provincial bonds regularly accounted for over half of all their assets (see Table 11.25). In contrast, the Leiden regents who died before 1674 left estates in which public bondholdings accounted for no more than a quarter of total value. D. J. Noordam's study showed that private loans and company stock then still rivaled bonds as regental assets, while real property dominated most estates. In Delft the richest 5 percent of households in 1706–30 held nearly 60 percent of their assets in bonds of all types. Moreover, these 200-odd families appear to have owned 85 percent of all bonds held by Delft private owners (i.e., excluding institutions), and by 1770–94, their share had risen to 91 percent. By no means did these cities house the greatest of the Republic's rentiers; these were concentrated in Amsterdam and the Hague, which between them accounted for 56 percent of all Holland's taxable wealth in 1742 (see Chapter 11, section 11.5).

The existence of a gigantic public debt concentrated in the hands of families of great wealth, and the direct access of many of those families to political office, established the basic framework in which the "oligarchization" of political life – always implicit in the Republic's urban institutions – became intensified. This hallmark of the "Periwig Age" was consolidated by the fiscal dynamic of the decades of war against Louis XIV's France. But as the Treaty of Utrecht brought an end to these wars, both the state and its creditors faced grave problems.

In 1713 the secretary of the Council of State, Simon van Slingelandt, took stock of the financial situation and despaired. Holland, he sighed, was "tot zinken toe bezwaard" [burdened to the point of sinking]. As though to confirm his

Table 4.8. *The bond market: the demand for funds and the supply of capital, 1600–1811 (in millions of guilders).*

Period	No. of years	Holland and Generality	Other provinces	Foreign govts.	West Indies plantations	Total annual borrowing
		Average annual borrowing by				
1600–19	20	1.09	1.00			2.09
1620–46	27	4.26	1.00			5.26
1647–71	25	0.20	1.00			1.20
1672–77	6	6.79	1.00			7.79
1678–89	12	0.07	0.00			0.07
1690–1713	24	8.34	2.50			10.84
1714–39	26	-0.95	0.00	4.00		3.05
1740–51	12	5.60	0.00	4.00		9.60
1752–62	11	-2.84	0.00	4.00	2.80	3.96
1763–79	17	-2.84	0.00	8.30	2.80	8.26
1780–94	15	15.32	1.50	20.00		36.82
1795–1804	10	40.00		10.00		50.00
1805–11	7	12.40		10.00		22.40

Period	No. of years	Assumed saving rates: 40%	25%	Additional financing required (-) surplus savings At 40%	At 25%
		reinvestment			
1600–19	20	0.85	0.53	1.24	1.56
1620–46	27	2.63	1.64	2.63	3.62
1647–71	25	3.75	2.35	-2.55	-1.15
1672–77	6	4.33	2.71	3.46	5.09
1678–89	12	4.76	2.98	-4.69	-2.91
1690–1713	24	5.49	3.43	5.35	7.41
1714–39	26	7.53	4.71	-4.48	-1.66
1740–51	12	8.12	5.08	1.48	4.52
1752–62	11	8.92	5.58	-4.96	-1.62
1763–79	17	10.41	6.50	-2.15	1.76
1780–94	15	15.66	9.79	21.16	27.03
1795–1804	10	20.04	12.53	29.96	37.48
1805–11	7	20.48	12.80	1.92	9.60

Domestic: Holland	Generality	Other prov.	Foreign govts.	Total interest income	VOC dividends	Total div. and interest income after taxes
0.85	0.13	0.50		1.48	0.64	2.12
3.85	0.43	1.00		5.28	1.29	6.57
6.05	0.54	1.80		8.39	0.99	9.38
6.40	0.56	2.50		9.46	1.36	10.82
7.00	0.70	2.70		10.40	1.51	11.91
10.90	1.76	3.50		16.16	1.65	13.72
13.75	2.60	4.10	2.00	22.45	1.53	18.82
14.00	2.32	4.10	4.00	24.42	1.14	20.31
14.80	1.90	4.10	6.00	26.80	1.05	22.30
13.70	1.30	4.10	11.00	30.10	1.05	26.01
17.50	0.77	4.40	22.50	45.17	0.54	39.15
	28.60		21.50	50.10		50.10
	34.00		17.20	51.20		51.20

Total additional financing needed or investment capital available (-) in the period

40%	25%
24.84	31.20
71.06	97.67
-63.80	-28.63
20.77	30.51
-56.33	-34.89
128.42	177.83
-116.47	-43.05
17.71	54.27
-54.56	-17.77
-36.47	29.87
317.42	405.50
299.60	374.75
13.44	67.20

Explanation: All figures are averages for the period, except for the final two columns, which are totals for the period. All estimates of borrowing needs are net; they do not include refinanced or extended debt. All estimates of interest payments refer to interest only, not the return of the principal component of life annuities. The deducation for taxes refers only to the 37.5 percent tax on Holland bonds.

Interest payments: The sources below indicate the interest rates paid on domestic and foreign government debt. No effort is made to estimate actual interest paid on the Plantation loans, which results in an underestimate of total interest earnings, especially in the 1763–79 period. VOC dividends: from Tables 9.4 and 10.6. Interest on VOC long-term bonds is not included.

Sources: BORROWING: For Holland the Generality, Dormans, *Het tekort, passim.*; Fritschy, *De patriotten en financiën van de Bataafse Republiek*, p. 156. OTHER PROVINCES: The first comprehensive data are available for 1795 (Fritschy, p. 156). Their borrowing is assumed generally to follow the path of Holland, except that after 1713 these provinces borrowed little. We know Friesland's debt as of 1748, and we know that Zeeland, the other major borrower, was no longer able to borrow on a large scale. FOREIGN GOVERNMENTS: James Riley, *International Government Finance*, p. 221. WEST INDIES PLANTATION LOANS: The overall scope of this form of lending is described in J. P. Van de Voort, *De Westindische plantages*, pp. 102–3.

pessimism, the Generality suspended interest payments for nine months. Payments were resumed only after a state-imposed reduction of the interest rate from 4 to 3 percent.

This forced reduction in the interest rate payable on bonds already in the hands of the public should not be confused with a bond conversion. It constituted a partial default and was made possible by the policy of the States of Holland to levy extraordinary taxes on wealth. By 1715 these taxes, occasional in theory, had become very predictable in fact. In 1722 they were recognized as an annual 1.5 percent levy on the nominal value of stocks and provincial bonds. The paper issued by the Generality – as well as by foreign issuers – was now exempt. The eighteenth-century investor could effectively choose between untaxed Generality obligations at 3 percent and Holland's obligations, which paid a nominal 4 percent but in reality yielded an after-tax return of 2.5 percent.

In 1716 Van Slingelandt urged reform of the Republic's decentralized fiscal system, observing that: "It must be counted as a miracle of Divine Providence that a Republic which has no firmer foundation than that of the United Netherlands, a Republic which is undermined from within by the extravagances of the Union and without by shock after shock, is still standing."[12] He initiated the convening of a Great Council in 1716–17 to consider his proposals for a strengthened central authority, including taxing authority. Without a state bureaucracy to enforce the tax laws, the five admiralties obstructed uniform enforcement of *convooien en licenten*; the seven provinces fell into arrears in the payment of their quota obligations, thereby bringing the Generality into the financial embarrassment of 1715; and the eighteen voting cities of Holland wrangled over needed reform of the *verponding* and the wealth tax registers, scheming endlessly to underpay the excise taxes. As long as specific taxes could not be earmarked to fund the public debt, the shaken creditworthiness of the state would remain unaddressed. No serious effort to address the Republic's fiscal impasse could sidestep these issues – but the Great Council rejected all reform proposals. They had not been rid of the Duke of Alva for nothing.

Ten years later, as Grand Pensionary Van Slingelandt restated the need for reform: "For the salvation of finances and the conservation of this country, the maintenance of a national authority over a unified system of finance is *indispensable*." But by then his proposal to abolish the ancient provincial quota system was a dead letter; he had been appointed to his high office only after promising not to press for constitutional reforms.

The Republic's political elites were by no means indifferent to the state's fiscal exhaustion. They were, after all, themselves the largest holders of the public debt. In rejecting constitutional reform, and confirming the unwisdom of further tax increases, they were left with the "muddling through" option, the most important

---

[12] Quoted in Simon Schama, *Patriots and Liberators* (New York, 1977), p. 495.

element of which was the adoption of a foreign policy of neutrality. This was in frank recognition of the Republic's inability to maintain the level of land and naval forces needed to play an active role in European diplomacy – a bitter lesson of the Treaty of Utrecht. By drastically reducing military expenditures, the government hoped to gain room for maneuver that would permit a gradual redemption of bonds, a reduction of the annual debt service costs, and the removal of the most oppressive taxes.

Such a policy would have been assisted enormously by an expanding economy. When economic growth enlarges the tax base and/or inflation reduces the real value of the public debt, it is possible for a government to work itself out of the fiscal bind imposed by massive indebtedness. Governments have done this repeatedly in the twentieth century. But in the first three decades after 1713, the Republic faced a contracting tax base and a deflationary price trend. In this inauspicious environment, the burden of taxation only rose, despite the reduction of government to virtual inaction.

The austerity measures introduced after 1713 accomplished very little. Even the sale of state property – the domain lands of Holland and Utrecht, the church property of Groningen, and, later, the Bildt in Friesland – made little difference. Moreover, just as Van Slingelandt foresaw, external shocks could prove disastrous to a state so fiscally malnourished. The *paal* worm problem (see Chapter 2, section 2.2.2) presented the affected provinces with no choice but to subsidize the hard-pressed drainage boards beginning in 1730, and an even greater fiscal shock struck in 1740 with the outbreak of the War of the Austrian Succession. As an indecisive government found itself pushed by foreign and domestic pressures to rearm and finally to declare war, expenditures began to mount once again.

The introduction in 1742 of a graduated income tax could cover only a fraction of the increased costs. Holland turned to forced loans from public officeholders (the *Ambtsgeldlening*) in 1744 and another large-scale issue of lottery bonds in 1746–52. In the twelve years ending in 1752, Holland borrowed 67 million guilders; in the preceding twenty-six years of painful austerity, it had managed to retire bonds worth only 25 million guilders.

The rising real tax burden had provoked taxpayers to public disorders at intervals ever since the 1690s. These riots took the form of attacks on tax farmers, on their houses, and on symbols of their activities. Widespread riots in 1748 (the *Pachtersoproer*) took on a deeper meaning in the context of the Republic's undisguisable military impotence and led to the greatest political and fiscal changes in the Republic's history. In most provinces the excise taxes ceased to be farmed. Henceforth, direct collection would be the rule.

Critics had long claimed that the tax farmers collected far more in taxes than the state received. Those expecting direct collection to yield a much increased revenue must have been disappointed by the results. Holland's *gemene middelen*, when collected directly beginning in 1750, raised on average 10 percent more than had been paid by tax farmers in the 1740s. But the state's direct collections were "gross" receipts, while the tax farmers' payments were "net" (i.e., after deduction of collection costs).

With the end of the war and internal disorder, the state once again embarked upon a policy of austerity and neutrality with the aim of reducing the public debt. In the three decades after 1750, this policy met with a measure of success. Gently rising prices and a selective economic expansion established an environment in which Holland's debt was reduced by 40 million guilders. In the same period, the Generality's debt fell by nearly 30 million. Holland hereby reduced its annual debt servicing costs by over 2 million guilders and succeeded in reducing the frequency with which it levied extraordinary taxes on wealth and income.

Every year from 1714 to 1780, some 15 million guilders (post-fiscal) flowed into the hands of the Republic's bondholders while the gradual redemption policy returned, after 1752, nearly 3 million per year to these same investors. They acquired the reputation for being great savers; the banker Henry Hope, who knew the richest of them well, estimated their savings rate to have been between 37.5 and 25 percent of their income, and modern studies of elite portfolios do not contradict this estimate (see Chapter 11, section 11.5). This high propensity to save may have derived from inherited Calvinist norms that militated against extravagance; however, the high income levels of many bondholders made it perfectly possible to wallow in luxury *and* reserve large sums for investment. A more important stimulus to saving, even in the face of low interest rates, would have been the fact that so much of elite wealth consisted of domestic public debt. Such bonds are, in fact, a sort of interest-bearing money that holds the promise of future taxation needed to honor the claims represented by those very bonds. The classical economist David Ricardo explained (in his "equivalence theorem") why such assetholders should save in anticipation of future taxation; eighteenth-century Dutch elites appear to have possessed an intuitive understanding of this insight (and, indeed, after 1795 the bill began to come due). Whatever its cause, this savings phenomenon is the essential backdrop for the major new economic initiative of the period: the emergence of Amsterdam as an international capital market. Rentiers with large holdings of domestic government bonds sought to place their interest earnings and redemptions in comparable debt instruments abroad, a subject to which we return later in this chapter.

Holland's eighteenth-century tax regime was far less regressive than it had been a century earlier, but state expenditures were, if anything, more strongly redistributive in favor of rentiers. Such employment stimulus as emanated from military expenditures at shipyards, in garrison towns, and in fortifications diminished after 1713 (and was partly displaced to the barrier towns in the Austrian Netherlands); what remained was the enormous flow of funds to a narrowed population of bondholders.

Table 4.8 presents a sketch of how the Dutch international capital market may have developed from the domestic government bond market in the course of the eighteenth century. We say "may have" because the table reflects assumptions which, however plausible, await confirmation by further research – that bond-holders tended to save a large fraction of their interest income and were inclined to reinvest their savings in comparable debt instruments. The purpose of this exercise is to discover the extent to which the capital market *could have been* financed on this "self-contained" basis.

Table 4.8 makes clear that the rentiers of 1714 could easily have financed the entire growth of foreign lending until 1780, as well as the extensive plantation loans to the West Indies, by reinvesting their bond redemptions plus about 25 percent of the after-tax interest earnings. In fact, it is likely that the spectacular growth of foreign lending fell considerably short of absorbing the supply of available capital after 1752.

The substantial redemptions of domestic debt that took place after 1752 seemed essential to the restoration of Holland's fiscal health, but among large bondholders, they created a personal discomfort to which a Gouda burgemeester gave voice in 1770 when he observed that "the ongoing redemptions pursued by the tax office place many rentiers in a predicament concerning how to invest their ready cash."[13]

This discomfort gave rise to a theoretical critique of the Republic's austerity policy. In 1771 the rich Amsterdam investor Isaac de Pinto wrote his *Traité de la Circulation et du Credit*, in which he argued for the beneficial consequences of a growing public debt. His was a proto-Keynesian argument: Larger government expenditures, funded by fresh borrowing, would stimulate economic activity. He sensed, correctly, that the owners of the public debt stood before the choice of consuming their interest income or saving it. If their savings went to purchase new bonds, this too would increase consumption – public consumption. But when the state ceased borrowing, the owners of the public debt tended to hoard or invest abroad. In either case, domestic consumption fell. De Pinto's treatise was highly influential; it spoke directly to the problem of a rich but stagnant economy, and of the great rentiers whose vast pools of capital, so it seemed, had only one possible taker. This "investors' dilemma" helps to account for the ease with which the Republic usually was able to borrow large sums at low interest rates. Certainly after 1700 this was not so much a sign of its solidity and credit-worthiness as it was a consequence of its privileged position as one of the only eligible borrowers of a colossal stream of income. To whom besides the states of Europe could one lend such large sums at acceptable levels of risk?

By the 1770s the Republic's austerity program had its critics, who decried the effects of a slowing circulation of money. But practical alternatives to this policy were few, and optimists among the Republic's governing families could congratulate themselves on having salvaged their fortunes while at the same time

---

[13] "de continueelen aflossing van weegens 't gemeeneland bij veele rentenieren groote verleegenheijd baarde, omtrent het beleggen hunner gereden gelden." Quoted in: J. J. de Jong, *Met goed fatsoen* (The Hague, 1985), p. 117.

preserving the particularistic, oligarchic system of government that offered them so many opportunities for personal advantage. "Muddling through" seemed to have its advantages. In actuality, the slightly increased room for fiscal maneuver was far from sufficient to accommodate major shocks.

In 1780 England declared war on the Republic (the Fourth Anglo-Dutch War), claiming that the Republic's support of the American Revolution was inconsistent with its neutral status. The costs of defense, the funds needed to cover the losses inflicted by British attacks on the VOC (see Chapter 10, section 10.3.3), and the public revenues lost as a consequence of the nearly complete cessation of trade enforced by British blockades, all plunged the Republic into a fiscal crisis – one from which she would never recover, as additional external and internal shocks succeeded one another until the fall of the Republic in 1795 and, indeed, for many years thereafter.

From 1780 to 1794, Holland placed 120 million guilders of new bonds, more than undoing all the hard-won gains of the previous decades. The rising costs of debt service once again made unavoidable the frequent resort to extraordinary capital levies. In this way Holland forced its tax revenues up to approximately 25 million guilders in the last years of the Republic, but even then debt service alone absorbed 70 percent of total revenues.

The collapse of the old United Republic and the establishment of the Batavian Republic did not bring the fiscal crisis to an end. On the contrary, it was intensified, not least by the 100-million-guilder indemnity demanded by France as the price for its assistance in establishing the new regime. The Batavian revolutionaries gave no more thought to repudiating the debts of the predecessor state than had the provincial States that rebelled against Habsburg rule. Consequently, among the new Republic's first acts was a survey of all the inherited debt, a subject about which even high officials of the old Republic knew very little.

Holland's debt in 1795 stood at 455 million guilders, that of all the other provinces together amounted to 155 million, and the bonds issued by the Admiralties, the WIC (West India Company), and the VOC totaled 150 million. The grand total, 760 million, imposed an annual service cost of 25 million guilders. Once again, the issue before the Dutch state was unification of the fiscal system. It took over a decade of deliberation to finally pull the ancient, jerry-built structure of Republican fiscalism down and replace it with a unitary system of taxation. All the while, government expenditures vastly exceeded revenues, causing the new state's debt burden to balloon to the incredible sum of 1,126 million – and growing – in 1804.

In the twenty-five years after 1780, rentiers faced a sharp rise in demand for their funds; they also faced an unprecedented (and not immediately recognized) increase in risk. Over this period the stream of interest income from both foreign and domestic bonds rose from over 30 to 50 million guilders per year, but the new demands were such that reinvested savings from this income stream surely failed to cover the enormous new issues of domestic bonds – some 15 million per year until 1795 – plus the even larger placements abroad. With the establishment of the Batavian Republic in 1795, the pressure intensified further, as domestic funding requirements alone skyrocketed to 40 million guilders per year. By the assumptions used in calculating the final columns of Table 4.8, somewhere between 600 and 775 million guilders of "new money" – disinvested from other sectors or drawn from current earned income – flowed into the foreign and domestic bond markets between 1780 and 1804.

It did not all come voluntarily. Once again, forced loans and capital levies pressed on the Dutch taxpayer. Between 1787 and 1804, extraordinary wealth taxes amounted to a total of 36 percent of the assessed value of taxable property (the tax base of real and financial assets was valued at nearly 1,000 million guilders); the income tax levied from 1797 on claimed an annual average of 6.5 percent of taxable income (limited to the relatively well-to-do citizens subject to this tax). The enormous liquidation of assets forced by these measures called into being in 1795 a General Lending Bank (*Generale Beleenbank*) to grant advances on collateral for the purpose of paying taxes.

The unification of debts, achieved in 1798, was followed with a long delay by the unification of taxation. A decade of persistent labor by Isaac Jan Alexander Gogel finally achieved in 1806 what Dutch statecraft had persistently resisted from the reign of Charles V. The surrender finally came when all means of resistance had been utterly and unambiguously spent, when the financial exhaustion of the institutions, cities, and provinces was total. Only when every sort of tax-levying institution stared bankruptcy in the face could Gogel's plans be carried out.

The resulting rationalization of administration, imposition of uniform tax rates, and shift from a reliance on indirect to direct taxation, all had the immediate effect of increasing total tax revenues by nearly one-third, notwithstanding the somber economic conditions of the times. The newly centralized tax system swept the old quotas aside. These quotas had been an abiding concern of municipal and provincial politicians ever since the sixteenth century. In every quarter the belief was fervently held that the quotas were unjust: Some thought that their provinces benefited from this injustice and resisted revision; others were certain that they were harmed and excused their arrears in quota payments with complaints of overtaxation. These beliefs long immobilized reform.

Only in the Republic's final years did the States General finally agree to a revision of the quota system that had been in force since 1616 (and the chief characteristics of which dated from much earlier). The geographical maldistribution of tax liabilities proved, in fact, to be much less significant than either side had anticipated. Zeeland and Utrecht, the loudest complainers of overtaxation, received substantial quota reductions in 1792. But the same two provinces saw their share of total tax revenue rise most sharply in 1807, when for the first time taxes were raised on the basis of a unitary fiscal system (see Table 4.5).

The year 1806 marks the end of an era of Dutch fiscal exceptionalism. For nearly three centuries, the provincial States had successfully resisted a trend toward centralization experienced by almost every other European state. It took prolonged fiscal exhaustion and a decade of political domination by France to overcome the resistance to a unitary tax system. That system offered immediate advantages, but in the political and economic environment of the time, it could not restore solvency. In 1808–9 the Kingdom of Holland (succeeding the Batavian Republic) fell into arrears in interest payments on its debt, and in 1810, after the incorporation of the Netherlands into the French Empire, a disguised repudiation was imposed. This arbitrary reduction of the state's liabilities, known as the *tiërcering*, was modeled on the 1797 debt repudiation of Revolutionary France. It involved reducing all interest payments to one-third of the previous amount.

This single act touched directly like few others the day-to-day life of the nation. It reduced the income of schools, orphanages, poorhouses, churches, and other institutions as well as of families that had long been accustomed to a secure and easy prosperity. It knocked the foundation stone of the Amsterdam capital market out from under it. But the unpopularity of the *tiërcering* did nothing to diminish its necessity.

When in 1814 independence was restored to a new Kingdom of the Netherlands, the new government confirmed the effective bankruptcy of the state by reformulating the *tiërcering* as follows: The 1.7 billion guilders of debt inherited from the predecessor regimes was divided into two types of paper, real and deferred. One-third was real debt, paying 2.5 percent interest, and two-thirds was deferred debt, small amounts of which periodically would be selected by lottery for activation as real debt. Projections prepared in 1814 indicated that nearly three centuries would have to pass before the principal could be extinguished. The financial markets showed little confidence in the state's ability to honor even its scaled-down commitments. In 1816 the "real" bonds traded on the *Beurs* at 42 percent of par, the deferred bonds at 4 percent.

From the 1550s, when Holland acquired the fiscal strength and built the investor confidence to embark on a course of long-term public borrowing, to the 1810s, and the *de facto* acknowledgment of bankruptcy, the Northern Netherlands passed through a great cycle of public debt. In the sixteenth century, the ability to borrow on favorable terms gave the separate provinces the means to defend their autonomy; in the seventeenth century, this experience, coupled to a growing tax base and a rapid accumulation of capital, supported a program of borrowing at steadily diminishing costs that permitted the Republic to play a great-power role disproportionate to its taxable resources. This role was played too long: The borrowing that had leveraged the Republic's power up to the 1670s became by the eighteenth century a millstone tied around the "neck of state."

Without either substantial economic growth or inflation, and in the absence of the political will to introduce significant fiscal reforms, the weight of the debt burden could not be reduced quickly enough to endow the state with the means to survive the shocks that came, one after another, beginning in 1780. Even then there was, to paraphrase Smith, "a great deal of ruin in it," for it look thirty years, including fifteen years functioning as a financial milch cow for France, before the ruin was complete.

This lengthy cycle of public borrowing was tied to a structure of taxation and a set of institutions and customs that changed only in details from the Habsburg era to 1806. Indeed, the debt restructured in 1806 included bonds issued as early as 1515, on which interest had been paid annually (except for 1572–5) for 290 years. The key characteristic of that fiscal regime, the reservation of decision making to the provincial level and of enforcement and administration to the municipal level, gave maximum scope for the protection of favored economic interests. The States of Holland repeatedly acted to shelter commercial capital from taxation, the enforcement of the *Convooien en Licenten* varied among the Admiralties, and the regressive *gemene middelen* quickly became the chief source of public revenue. This fiscal regime reflected the interests of the urban elites. But what began as a structure of preferences for urban and trading capital shifted by degrees to become a machine for the maintenance of a colossal public debt which, in turn, nurtured a state-rentier complex that evolved into an international capital market. The study of taxation quickly becomes the study of the whole society.

4.3. Commercial finance

4.3.1. BANKING PRACTICES

In our discussions of agriculture, industrial production, international trade, and government finance, we observe time and again the need for financing investment in fixed capital stock and inventory formation and financing commercial credit and government borrowing. Credit stands at the intersection of changes in the money supply, the accumulation of capital, physical production, and governmental activity. In the view of Joseph Schumpeter, credit creation is the very essence of the capitalist economy, and many economic historians of an earlier generation regarded the unraveling of the legal and institutional developments that gave rise to modern banking as akin to searching for the holy grail of capitalism.

Another view regards money as a more passive factor, accommodating the needs of the real economy. To this view we incline; but one must be blinded by dogma not to see the autonomous importance of financial institutions and investor behavior in giving shape to the Dutch economy. As it developed, the Republic fashioned institutions and adopted commercial practices designed to manage effectively the rapidly accumulating stocks of capital. As it matured, the Republic became Europe's foremost supplier of short-and long-term credit and the central depository of precious metals. Financial activity became an important sector of the economy in its own right. How did this happen?

It is hard to know where to start the discussion of Dutch financial practice, for it forms an integral part of Europe's banking and commercial history, which originates in Medieval Italy and is brought forward with contributions in Iberia, the South German cities, and Antwerp.

Arguably, the central issue is the development of the bill of exchange. A product of fourteenth-century Italian communes, the bill of exchange became the principal and most flexible vehicle for creating credit, effecting exchanges between currencies, and transferring payment internationally. The bill of exchange was drawn by a creditor on his debtor – typically, by the seller of goods on his customer. It required the debtor to pay a stated amount (in another currency than that in which the debt is reckoned), at a stated time (usually, some months after the date of the transaction), and at a stated location (usually that of the creditor). In contrast to a simple promissory note, the drawer did not ordinarily hold the bill of exchange to maturity but rather sold it or placed it with a correspondent (a banker responsible for collecting the money owed), who used it to pay debts owed by other customers in the place of residence of the original debtor named in the bill. In this way two debts might be canceled out with a minimal use of actual cash and an avoidance of the danger and expense of transporting cash over long distances.

As late as the mid–sixteenth century, this backbone of international commerce was little used in northern Europe, and especially not in trade with the Baltic. In the following half century, it became general, replacing the "letter obligatory" as the dominant credit instrument in northwestern Europe.

In the commercial world of sixteenth-century Antwerp, the bill of exchange acquired a flexibility that made it the nearly universal short-term credit instrument of international trade in the following 200 years. This new flexibility was conferred by the legal and institutional consolidation of the practices of "assignment," "endorsement," and "discount."

By the seventeenth century (as codified in the *Antwerpse Costuymen*, which were published and applied in Amsterdam in 1597 and 1613), the bill could be *assigned* by the drawer to others, the successive bearers possessing the same legal rights vis-à-vis the debtor as the original drawer. To add to the protection of the bearer (in effect, the purchaser of the bill), the assignment of bills required *endorsement* – that is, the signature of each successive bearer – thereby implicating them in responsibility for the bill in the event of the debtor's default. These practices gave the bill a high degree of transferability, permitting it to act as a form of payment. In a final step, the bill acquired negotiability when the bearer could have it *discounted* – that is, when a third party agreed to purchase a bill before its due date, paying a cash sum which, of course, was less than the nominal value of the bill at maturity.

It is notoriously difficult to determine when particular practices become widespread (as opposed to when they are first mentioned), but Herman van der Wee, the authority on sixteenth-century Antwerp, is convinced that "the great financial progress [of sixteenth-century northern Europe] was clearly visible in all the growing commercial centers of the North, but nowhere was renovation so intense as at Antwerp." In that city there arose the "crucial innovations in the field of financial instruments which, backed by the success of the Antwerp Exchange, pointed directly toward further institutional progress in following centuries."[14]

These practices spread, with the post-1585 diaspora of Antwerp merchants to the northern centers, but their "further institutional progress" referred to by Van der Wee did not occur in a linear fashion. Amsterdam's government prohibited the assignment of bills and restricted the activities of *kassiers*, who held and managed merchant's cash balances, discounted and handled bills, and changed money. We should not suppose that these restrictions actually limited the use of bills of exchange, for the *kassiers'* business flourished in Amsterdam, but their imposition reveals a definite skepticism about the recent innovations – specifically, a concern that the *kassiers'* activities intensified coinage instability. In an effort to assert control over money-changing and to limit lengthy chains of payment in bills of exchange, the city of Amsterdam drew upon a banking tradition that arose and flourished in Italy but which had no precedent in Antwerp or anywhere else in Northern Europe at the time, the municipal deposit and clearing bank.

The Bank of Amsterdam, or Amsterdam *Wisselbank* was established in 1609 to take deposits, effect transfers between accounts (the giro function), and accept (i.e., pay) bills of exchange. Indeed, merchants were required to make all bills of 600 guilders or more payable via the Bank, a provision that effectively forced all substantial merchants to open an account. In all of these provisions, the Bank modeled itself after the Venetian *Banco della Piassa di Rialto*, established in 1587. The Bank obviated the need for *kassiers* by replacing chain assignments with a single assignment to the *Wisselbank*; indeed, simultaneous with the establishment of the *Wisselbank*, the city prohibited the activities of *kassiers*. The great concern of the city fathers was to protect and enlarge the supply of good, full-valued coin. This they regarded as far more important to the prosperity of a commercial economy than the proliferation of circulating bills. We noted earlier the limited success of the Bank in achieving its monetary objectives. Here we should pause to consider how the establishment of the *Wisselbank* influenced the financial history of the Republic. The Bank of Amsterdam succeeded instantly in attracting depositors, who became the envy of Europe for their access to deposit, transfer, and payment services that were trustworthy, safe, efficient, and virtually costless. It grew with the expansion of Amsterdam's commerce to become the clearinghouse of world trade, settling international debts and effecting transfers of capital. Moreover, it did this on a continuous basis rather than at long intervals, as had been the practice of the old fairs.

These achievements notwithstanding, the character of Dutch banking (banks modeled on Amsterdam functioned in Middelburg [established in 1616], Delft

---

[14] Herman van der Wee, "Monetary, Credit and Banking Systems," in E. E. Rich and C. H. Wilson, eds., *Cambridge Economic History of Europe*, Vol. V (Cambridge, 1977), p. 332.

[1621], and Rotterdam [1635]) raises an important question, one put by Van der Wee when he asks, "Why . . . did the Dutch commercial towns turn their back on the more modern financial techniques which had come into being in Antwerp in the sixteenth century? . . . Why did [Amsterdam and the other cities] opt for the more conservative banking system originating in Italy?"[15] Van der Wee sees Amsterdam perfecting the Italian tradition of the deposit and clearing bank while neglecting the innovations of Antwerp, which – in the hands of the English a century later – would usher forth into the modern discount and issuing bank, a bank that maintains fractional reserves and is therefore able to extend credit and issue circulating notes.

The leap-frog pattern of banking development identified by Van der Wee invites nuancing. The sophisticated practices of the Antwerp *kassiers* had not enjoyed a long or trouble-free life before 1585, and the more cautious principles of the *Wisselbank* did not, in fact, abort the innovations of the *kassiers*. On the contrary, they became an integral part of Dutch commercial finance. *Kassiers* operated openly again by 1621, holding merchants' cash balances for which they issued circulating receipts, discounting bills, and lending on collateral. In fact, a certain division of labor emerged: As the premium for the *Wisselbank's bankgeld* relative to the circulating *courantgeld* solidified (the *agio* became official in 1659), the *kassiers'* receipts (which were expressed in *courantgeld*) came to be used as promissory notes in domestic transactions among merchants. The *Wisselbank* tended to specialize in foreign bills. The regulations governing the *kassiers* required that promissory notes be cashed within ten days of issuance. Older notes lost all legal standing. But in practice they often circulated much longer, effectively augmenting the supply of money.

In 1742 there were at least sixty-one *kassiers* active in Amsterdam, but the absence of records leaves us in the dark about many aspects of this informal sector of Dutch banking. What remains valid of Van der Wee's sharp distinction is the fact that these banking practices never became consolidated in large, well-capitalized banking institutions. In that arena the *Wisselbank* reigned alone to the end of the Republic.

The original functions of the Bank of Amsterdam were by no means of negligible importance to the functioning of a large commercial economy, but over time the Bank added others that bordered on credit creation and money issue. Shortly after the founding of the *Wisselbank*, the city established the *Bank van Lening*, or Lombard (in 1614). The same occurred in other cities (there were eighty-four such banks scattered across the Republic by the 1790s), all with the purpose of lending small sums on collateral to necessitous consumers, small merchants, and artisans. The Amsterdam *Bank van Lening* seems to have drawn very little of its capital from the *Wisselbank*, raising most of its capitalization of 1 to 2

[15] Van der Wee, "Monetary, Credit and Banking Systems," p. 347.

million guilders directly through the sale of bonds. However, similar banks in Rotterdam and Middelburg did borrow heavily from their *Wisselbanken*.

The provincial *Wisselbanken* differed from the Amsterdam bank in their active lending of deposited funds to local businesses and to city treasuries, a practice that forced them to suspend payments during runs on the banks in 1672, as depositors panicked in the face of the advancing French army. The Middelburg *Wisselbank*, with deposits that usually ranged between 1 and 2 million guilders, frequently held reserves amounting to less than half of its deposits.

The much larger Amsterdam *Wisselbank* weathered the storm of 1672 nicely, since it held in its vaults a metal stock sufficient to cover 90 percent of total deposits. It too lent money, but to only two borrowers, the Dutch East India Company and the city treasury. This was in violation of the Bank's charter, although loans to the city often were technically nothing more than advances of balances that the city held in its capacity as owner of the Bank and beneficiary of its profits. The East India Company borrowed *anticipatie penningen*, short-term loans to cover a yearly recurring cash-flow problem arising from the company's need to equip its outgoing fleet before the goods of the incoming fleet could be sold. These secure loans caused no problems. But ultimately, surreptitious lending proved to be the *Wisselbank*'s undoing when, in the course of the Fourth Anglo-Dutch War, both the East India Company and the city borrowed on a vast scale in a desperate effort to recover financial viability.

The Bank of Amsterdam never revealed any information about its deposits, reserves, and so on. This led to extravagant rumors about its condition, which, for most of its history, worked to the Bank's advantage. Since it withstood the run of 1672, the world was prepared to believe that its deposits were vast multiples of reality and that the metal coverage was 100 percent. But in the 1780s, the rumors swung in the other direction, giving rise to massive withdrawals. The *agio*, which normally stood at about 4 percent (reflecting the higher metal content of full-weight bank money), could deviate from that norm depending on supply and demand conditions. There had been times when traders had placed great premiums on the safety and convenience of bank money, raising the *agio* to 10 percent. In 1790 the unprecedented situation arose where *agio* fell to a discount, suggesting that deposits were seen as an unadulterated liability, and with good reason: In 1791 the Bank suspended payments. Financial rescue measures soon allowed the Bank to reopen, but in 1795, when the Republic fell, zealous reformers lifted for the first time the veil of secrecy that had obscured the Bank's dealings since its founding. They found that the metal stock in the cellars of the Town Hall (the location of the Bank's offices) sufficed to cover only 21 percent of its liabilities. The Bank continued to exist until 1820, but it no longer figured in the commercial life of the city, let alone of Europe.

The final, and by far the most important, way in which the *Wisselbank* contributed to credit creation dates from 1683, when the Bank began to accommodate traders in silver and gold by accepting specie deposits. The depositors paid a premium to the Bank (for gold, 0.5 percent; for silver, 0.25 percent every six months), but they received in return bank receipts (*recepissen*) that were readily transferable and tradeable as money.

The new policy of accepting specie deposits, coupled with the removal of the last legal restrictions on the export of precious metals, made Amsterdam Europe's reservoir of gold and silver coin and bullion. Later, we shall see how this step was related to the VOC's sudden need for exportable coin at this same time (see Chapter 10, section 10.3.2). For the first time, decisions taken at the other end of Eurasia (Japan's trade policy) have direct repercussions in Europe. The steady demand for specie emanating from the VOC and other purchasers could now be accommodated to the highly irregular inflow of specie from the New World by the creation of the Amsterdam stockpiles.

With this specie policy, the *Wisselbank* entered a new era of its operations. Its attractiveness to specie traders brought about a sudden jump in the number of depositors and a vast increase in the average level of deposits (from about 6 million guilders before 1683 to about 20 million after 1720; see Figure 4.3). But while deposits before 1683 were frequently transferred from account to account, or withdrawn and redeposited, the new specie deposits generally remained in the Bank for extended periods. In the eighteenth century, the *bankgeld* of the *Wisselbank* took on the character of a reservoir of funds infrequently withdrawn, which backed the circulation of the Bank's specie receipts and the dealings of the private *kassiers*, who all held accounts with the *Wisselbank*.

4.3.2. COMMERCIAL CREDIT, PRIVATE LOANS, AND INSURANCE

Short-term lending in the Republic began in close association with the needs of commodity trade. This, of course, is where the bill of exchange found its origins, usually in the seller extending credit to his customer, with the goods themselves as surety. Dutch traders often extended credit to suppliers, thereby binding commodity producers to the Republic's entrepôt and securing steady supplies at agreed upon prices. This suppliers' and purchasers' credit (*leveranciers en afnemers-crediet*), usually provided as a bill of exchange, was the backbone of the entrepôt, reinforcing low transport and transactions costs with cheap credit. Moreover, by continually prolonging these credits, short-term loans acquired a structural character, further binding suppliers and customers to the entrepôt.

The low interest rates prevailing in the Republic also made possible the maintenance of larger inventories in the warehouses of the port cities, which further strengthened the Republic's reputation as a place where everything was always available.

The credit dealings that insured the Republic's abundant supplies of every traded commodity also laid the basis for a trade in money, for here one could find bills of exchange to make payment in all the places with which the Dutch

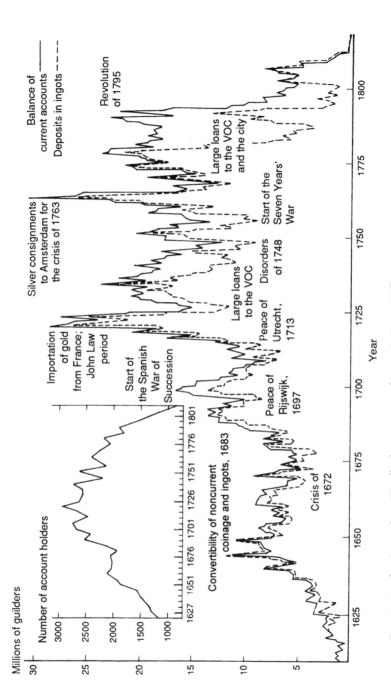

Figure 4.3. Deposits in the Amsterdam *Wisselbank*, 1609–1820. [*Source:* J. G. van Dillen, "De Amsterdamsche Wisselbank," *Economisch Historisch Jaarboek 11* (1925), 245–8.]

merchants traded. In the sixteenth century, one had to go to Antwerp to secure most bills of exchange, but by 1600 Amsterdam's commerce already sufficed to generate regular exchange rate quotations with ten locations: Antwerp, Danzig, Frankfurt, Hamburg, Cologne, London, Nuremberg, Paris, Rouen, and Venice. The *Price Courants* of the early eighteenth century regularly quoted exchange rates on twenty-five locations, but there were in fact many more. The freedom to export monetary metals from the Republic tended to stabilize exchange rates, the easy movement of coin dampening deviations of the market rate from the "official" rates set by the metallic content of the various currencies.

For these reasons Amsterdam attracted a business in bills that exceeded by far the needs of its own trade. French, Spanish, Portuguese, and Italian cities could rarely provide direct exchange quotations for cities in northern and Baltic Europe, and vice versa. Merchants in these places bought bills on Amsterdam, where other bills on the intended destination could be acquired. Even London long relied on the Amsterdam financial market. As late as the Seven Years' War (1756–63), English subsidies to German states proceeded via bills on Amsterdam, and until the financial crisis that arose in the aftermath of that war, England's substantial trade with Russia relied on the Amsterdam money market, since Russia's only regular exchange quotations until 1763 were on Amsterdam. Thereafter, both London and Hamburg became important competitors to Amsterdam in the bills market. Until then, however, the statement of an observer of 1701 remained true: "Amsterdam is the place where very nearly all the bills payable within Europe are drawn, remitted or otherwise discounted and traded."[16]

The bills of exchange originally served Dutch trade, but the vast scope attained by the Dutch entrepôt inevitably created opportunities for the bills business to acquire a life of its own, serving third parties with no direct trade to the Republic. By the early eighteenth century, the international importance of the Amsterdam business in bills of exchange and the relative decline of commodity trade set the stage for two related developments: the rise of commission trade (*commissiehandel*) and of acceptance houses (extenders of *acceptkrediet*). The commission trade is discussed more fully in Chapter 10. Here it can be noted that it involved agents who did not assume the full risk of trade involved in buying and selling goods. Rather, the *commissionair* carried out the orders of a merchant, finding buyers and arranging transactions, and for this service he received a commission as payment. The expansion of commission trading tended to reduce the scope for loans to suppliers and purchasers (*leveranciers en afnemerscrediet*), and this, in turn, stimulated the redirection of commercial capital toward the acceptance business.

Acceptance houses were financial firms specializing in the acceptance and dis-

---

[16] "Amsterdam [is] de plaetze, alwaer genoegzaem alle de wisselbrieven, die binnen Europa te betaelen staen, werde getrokken, remitteert of anders disconteert en verhandelt." Quoted in: J. G. van Dillen, *Bronnen tot de geschiedenis der Wisselbanken*, Rijksgeschiedkundige publicatiën 59 (The Hague, 1925), document 373, p. 333.

counting of foreign bills of exchange. By "acceptance" is meant the granting of permission to a client to issue bills of exchange with a guarantee that the acceptance house will pay the bill, if necessary. Until the client covers the bill, presumably by its expiration date, the acceptance house had provided credit (*acceptkrediet*).

This placed Dutch commercial capital at the service of international trade, including trade with no physical connection to the Dutch entrepôt. The disintegration of the unified trading and financing functions of the seventeenth-century merchant house into the separate commission and acceptance businesses has been decried as the means by which increasingly risk-averse, passive businessmen stripped the Dutch entrepôt of its dynamism and freed foreigners from dependence on it. An alternative view sees these innovations as unavoidable adjustments to a more competitive international economy, innovations that succeeded in defending a portion of Dutch trade and in finding profitable placement for the large accumulation of trading capital. We suspect that the second interpretation is closer to the truth, but it cannot be denied that the growth of acceptance credit, which was thought by contemporaries to have involved at least 200 million guilders at any given time up to the crisis of 1773, exposed Dutch commercial life to a large measure of instability.

Another financial transaction of importance to the Republic's trade was maritime insurance. In 1598 the municipal ordinances of Amsterdam required the establishment of a Chamber of Marine Insurance (*Kamer van Assuratie en Avarij*). The insurance regulations established at that date drew heavily on Antwerp practice, and the Chamber's purpose was to register policies and adjudicate disputes. From the time it was established (in fact, not until 1612), *Heeren Assuradeurs*, sworn dealers in insurance, could be found at fixed places at the *Beurs* to arrange insurance on hulls and cargoes to a steadily lengthening list of destinations. In 1626 the Price Courant listed regular insurance quotations for ten groups of destinations. A century later quotes existed for twenty-one groups of destinations throughout Europe, the Mediterranean, and the West Indies.

Many local shipping ventures self-insured by dividing ownership among many partners – for which the common ownership form, the *partenrederij*, was well suited. The long-distance trade of the VOC was also self-insured, in this case by maintaining its own armed forces (i.e., by internalizing protection costs). But the demand for maritime insurance appears to have grown over a long period of time. In the seventeenth century, insurance generally remained a secondary function of certain merchant houses, although a partnership dedicated to insuring ships is known to have been formed in Amsterdam in 1614. In 1635 a contemporary estimated the annual total of insurance premiums registered in the Amsterdam Chamber at 434,700 guilders. We know little about the insurance premiums charged in those years. If, hypothetically, the average premium stood at 3 percent of the value of ship and cargo, the value insured would have approached 15 million guilders.

One hundred thirty years later, we know that insurance rates had reached a historic nadir, reflecting the combined influences of the peaceful conditions in European waters, low interest rates in a land of abundant capital, and competitive pressure from London and Hamburg insurers. Then, the premium on ships destined for London stood at 0.75 percent. Destinations stretching from Copenhagen to the Bay of Biscay paid 1 percent; Norway, the Baltic, Ireland, and Iberia paid 1.5 percent; Italy and the Mediterranean paid 1.75 to 2.0 percent; and West Indian destinations paid 2.5 percent.

By then, insurance had evolved into a specialized enterprise. The speculative frenzy of 1720 had given birth to several joint stock companies specialized in insurance, one of which, the *Maatschappij van Assuratie, Discontering en Beleening der Stad Rotterdam*, not only survived the 1720 Bubble but functions to this day. This sort of firm remained exceptional, but a multitude of private firms insured domestic and foreign ships alike, making Amsterdam Europe's foremost center for maritime insurance until the third quarter of the eighteenth century. In the late eighteenth century, these firms pioneered fire insurance (to compensate for a decline in sea insurance) and even dabbled in life insurance. But for this the time was not yet ripe. Private insurers could not compete with the naively generous life annuities available from the state.

When, after 1670, Holland turned away from the issuance of *lijfrenten* (see "The public debt" in section 4.2.2), middle-class persons seeking income security for dependents and for old age began to form group investment pools. These survivorship contracts (*contracten van overleving*) varied enormously in their details, but they usually involved regular contributions by the members, investment of the proceeds in bonds and VOC shares, and payment of pensions to nominees. Many pools incorporated a tontine format, whereby "a lucky few surviving nominees in a group would reap windfall returns in the distant future."[17]

Several thousand persons joined such private income security associations after 1670, before the market dwindled during the 1690s. The renewal of generous *lijfrenten* issuance by a hard-pressed government caused income-security–seeking investors to revert to custom. But after the 1710s, *lijfrenten* issues dried up once again, and there began a second, much larger and longer wave of investment pools. By the mid–eighteenth century, these pools were controlled and marketed by brokers. They became larger, involving hundreds of participants per unit, and often invested in riskier assets than their seventeenth-century predecessors. The market for these more professionally organized "income security pools" dwindled after 1780, as the French government's life annuity borrowing emerged to dominate the market. As long as necessitous governments offered lavishly generous life annuities, no private insurance business could survive.

These investment pools offer a glimpse into a vast arena of credit and debt that is still largely *terra incognita* to the historian. We have called attention to the

---

[17] Riley, *International Government Finance*, p. 107.

fact that the holders of the public debt often saved millions of guilders per year, which could not be reinvested in new debt issues. We know that the many hundreds of *partenrederijen*, the partnerships that operated merchant ships and industrial windmills, usually had one member, the *commisaris*, who invested idle funds pending the periodic distribution of profits to the partners. Furthermore, we know that the income stream of many ordinary people was highly irregular. How did all these people handle their idle balances, or cover episodic cash shortfalls?

Consider the case of the skippers who operated the intercity passenger barges: These men were united in guilds, and their incomes consisted of fixed wages, which were paid for each trip they made, plus their share in the profits, if any, of their joint enterprise. The records of the guild operating the Haarlem-Leiden route between 1780 and 1815 show that the skippers' incomes varied enormously; in some years they earned no more than the income of an unskilled laborer, in others they earned over three times this amount. Their guild sometimes invested accumulated reserves in public bonds and at other times contracted loans to maintain the basic income of its members. But how did the skippers themselves deal with their highly variable income? What did they regard as their "permanent income"? What did they do with windfalls? What credit instruments were available to them to help smooth out these stark fluctuations?

Notaries functioned as financial intermediaries, literally bringing lenders and borrowers together, and their handiwork is evident in probate inventories, itemizations of the possessions, assets, and liabilities of deceased persons leaving minor children. A tangle of debt and credit linked the Republic's households, but we know very little about how this financial market functioned; and the possibility uncovered at the beginning of this chapter, that many people sat on vast cash hoards, hints that financial intermediation left much to be desired.

4.4.3. THE MERCHANT BANKERS AND THE INTERNATIONAL CAPITAL MARKET

Besides the *Wisselbanken,* the *kassiers,* and the notaries, the Republic spawned yet another type of financial institution, the merchant banking house. These firms emerged from merchant families, and they long combined commodity trade and the trade in money. The growing competitive pressure facing trading firms in the second quarter of the eighteenth century provoked some, particularly those active in England, to redeploy their working capital from direct trade to the provision of acceptance credit. Few merchant bankers took deposits; their capital consisted of private wealth supplemented by borrowing, usually via collateral loans from private parties.

The oldest of these houses, Weduwe Jean Deutz en Co., had cultivated a special relationship with the Austrian Emperor as early as 1659. Other merchant houses, settled in Amsterdam from the 1650s, were R. en Th. de Smeth and

Clifford en Zoonen, which cultivated relations in the Southern Netherlands and England, respectively, to deal in financial transactions.

In the first quarter of the eighteenth century, a spate of firms joined this group: Andries Pels en Zoonen (1707), Muilman en Meulenaar (1712), Horneca en Hogguer (1720), and, what would become the greatest of them all, the firm of Hope en Co.

Archibald Hope, born in Rotterdam of English parents in 1664, pursued trade with England and Ireland. By 1720 he owned malting houses in East Anglia, two ships dedicated to the transport of malt to the jenever (gin) distilleries of Schiedam, and at least two other ships.[18] Around this time the family shifted its activities to Amsterdam. Archibald's eight sons struck off in several directions, but two, Thomas and Adrian, established a firm in 1734, bearing their names, that combined acceptance banking with a variety of trading interests.

In 1751 the firm's commitment to trade was still great. Indeed, Thomas Hope, then a trusted adviser of Stadhouder Willem IV, authored the *Propositie van 1751*, a radical proposal to revive the Republic's trade by establishing a type of free trade zone. But ten years later, the transition to banking was all but complete. As cousins joined the firm in 1763, enlarging its capital, and as a major competitor, Andries Pels en Zoonen, was liquidated in the aftermath of the 1773 crisis, Hope and Co. emerged as Amsterdam's – and Europe's – leading banking house. By then the firm's capital exceeded 8 million guilders, and it distributed profits to the family partners of at least 500,000 guilders annually for the next twenty-five years. By 1800 the firm's capital exceeded 15 million guilders.

Hope and the other banking houses dealt in bills of exchange and other commercial credit instruments, but they became increasingly committed to a new activity, the issuance of loans on behalf of foreign governments (the *emmissiebedrijf*). In contrast to the forms of credit discussed so far, this new activity involved long-term investments.

The issue and sale of foreign government bonds is obviously closely related to the sale of domestic government bonds (which were sold not by banks but directly at the regional tax offices). In the second half of the eighteenth century, both types of bonds appealed to similar investors, and for similar reasons. But lending to foreign governments did not begin then, and in earlier decades it had, in fact, almost nothing in common with the domestic bond market that had arisen gradually from the mid–sixteenth century.

In the seventeenth century, the political dimension and the high risk associated with lending to foreign governments made it a business reserved to the largest, most daring merchant firms, usually those who could secure guarantees from the Generality and/or use the loan to gain access to valuable commodities in the debtor country. At the time of the Revolt, Holland's funding needs attracted subsidies and loans from other governments, but soon thereafter the first in a long

---

[18] Marten G. Buist, *At Spes non Fracta: Hope & Co., 1770–1815* (The Hague, 1974), pp. 10–18.

line of financially strapped princes sought to raise funds in Holland. In 1616 the Elector of Brandenburg raised 248,000 guilders at 7 percent interest from the Admiralty of Amsterdam – a clear indication of the state's interest in the loan. At this same time, the States General lent 400,000 Reichtalers to Gustavus Adolphus, but when the Swedish king could not meet his payments, the merchant Louis de Geer agreed to assume the payments in return for Swedish commercial concessions. This gambit opened a "long intricate chapter of financial commitments which were to continue throughout his life and into the lives of his heirs. [De Geer] made repeated loans, advanced credit for long or short periods, made payments for the Swedish government both in Sweden and abroad, armed and equipped Swedish armies, and . . . carried out a variety of commissions for the court."[19] De Geer's investments (and those of associates who entrusted their funds with him) posed a complex problem of repayment. The claims were settled not in cash but by consignments of copper, leases of Crown lands, allocations of customs duties, and other privileges, not least of which was entry into the Swedish nobility.

Beginning in 1659 the merchant Johan Deutz lent money to the Emperor in Vienna, in exchange for a trading concession in the mercury produced in Imperial mines. The States General guaranteed these loans (it was no accident that Johan de Witt was Deutz's brother-in-law), laying the basis for a trading and lending operation later expanded to Hungarian copper that was carried out by the Deutz firm for nearly a century.

Less impressive from an entrepreneurial perspective were loans to the English monarchs. In 1642 Queen Henrietta Maria pawned the Crown Jewels to raise money for the Royalist cause.

Given the dubious creditworthiness of seventeenth-century governments, foreign lending depended on guarantees from the States General and tangible economic concessions. These concessions usually proved sufficient to shelter Dutch merchants from the fate of earlier generations of court financiers, and they built important economic interests, particularly in Sweden and Central Europe.

The first step in the transition to a modern form of international lending can be dated easily: 1688. The Glorious Revolution brought the Dutch Stadhouder Willem III to the English throne and set in motion constitutional changes that made England the first country to achieve a creditworthiness capable of attracting voluntary, long-term Dutch investment in its public debt and in the English joint stock companies. The key innovation, England's "financial revolution," consisted of the introduction of excise taxes to fund a public debt that simultaneously became the responsibility of Parliament rather than the personal obligation of the monarch. In this, England followed in Holland's footsteps; with the establishment in 1694 of the Bank of England to manage this debt, among other things, the English took a long step further.

---

[19] Violet Barbour, *Amsterdam Capitalism in the Seventeenth Century* (Baltimore, 1950), p. 111.

The convergence of Dutch and English public debt institutions, the relatively high return on English bonds, and the appeal of investment in the English joint stock companies (the Bank, the East India Company, and, from 1711, the South Sea Company), all drew Dutch investors toward the English market. Indeed, by 1723 the English joint stock companies and certain government bonds were traded jointly on the London Stock Exchange and the Amsterdam *Beurs*.

English public opinion expressed anxiety about foreign ownership of such important instruments of public policy, and this gave rise to extravagantly exaggerated estimates of the size of Dutch participation. No wholly convincing study has since been made to correct these eighteenth-century rumors, but Dutch investments could never have been as great as British xenophobes feared: Dutch holdings of Bank of England, South Sea Company, and East India Company assets were good for only 6.4 percent of the total in 1723–4. By 1750 the Dutch share had more than doubled to 15.3 percent, and during the Seven Years' War, funds from neutral Holland poured into belligerent England, financing at "peacetime" interest rates the war that would decide the politico-economic struggle between England or France. By the 1770s Dutch holdings of English bonds totaled some 200 million guilders, although the estimates of contemporary observers were all at least twice this amount. These English securities long remained the province of the very richest Dutch investors. English records show that in 1750, eighty-nine Dutchmen controlled nearly 30 percent of the entire Dutch share of the English funds. The average holding of each of these investors approached 200,000 guilders. Another 2,617 Dutch accounts (held by a smaller number of individuals) controlled the remaining amount; the average size of these accounts was 17,000 guilders.

A second important date in the emergence of a modern capital market was 1713. Until then, foreign government loans carried guarantees from the States General. That is, foreign lending depended largely on foreign policy and had the character of subsidies to allies. In 1713 the Republic embarked upon a policy of neutrality; there was no further justification for loan guarantees. "The divorce of international finance from diplomatic consideration . . . was a progressive step for the Amsterdam capital market, and especially for firms involved in negotiating and managing foreign loans."[20] As an immediate consequence, a 1714 loan floated for Austria offered an 8 percent return while the previous Austrian loan, guaranteed by the States General, had been sold at 5 percent.

The groundwork for the rise of an international capital market was laid in the first half of the eighteenth century, as foreign governments beginning with England arranged their fiscal policies to appeal to Dutch investors, and as the Dutch investor was freed of political constraints. However, no massive flow of Dutch funds abroad emerged until the 1740s and '50s, at which time numerous Amsterdam banking houses began to cultivate their contacts with foreign govern-

[20] Riley, *International Government Finance*, p. 58.

ments with a view to issuing bonds, and brokers and commission agents began to cultivate private investors to encourage the purchase of these bonds.

Until the end of the Seven Years' War, Dutch foreign lending focused almost exclusively on the bonds of two states: England, the first foreign government to establish a modern public debt, and Austria, where the banking house of Deutz had longstanding ties. But in the 1750s, the flow of funds abroad was substantially redirected by the sudden appeal of loans to finance the expansion of West Indies plantations, the *plantageleningen*. Amsterdam banking houses (led by Willem Gideon Deutz) succeeded in extracting some 80 million guilders from investors between 1750 until the widespread default of these loans in 1773 (see Chapter 10, section 10.4.2). As of 1763 Dutch investment in foreign government bonds stood at about 200 million guilders (by James Riley's estimate), well over half of that total being tied up in English bonds.

After 1763 the Republic's era as the capital market for all of Europe began in earnest. Several new governments applied to Amsterdam banking houses to issue bonds (Denmark, Sweden, Russia, and various German states), while the investing public became particularly receptive as a consequence of the substantial redemptions of domestic debt discussed earlier. Bringing supply and demand together was the task of the banking houses; their *emmissiebedrijf* consisted of floating guilder-denominated bonds and creating an attractive market for the new issues. For this they called upon specialist brokers, called "entrepreneurs," who steered their clients to the new issues. Hope and Co.'s great strength in this business is said to have resided in its network of some forty of these bond brokerage houses, which allowed it to float successfully the largest bond issues.

Table 4.8 provides an overview of the levels of net foreign and domestic lending. Until the financial crisis of 1773, foreign lending was probably financed primarily by domestic redemption and interest earnings. Thereafter, the scope of capital exports grew further, fueled now by a withdrawal of capital from the acceptance credit business. The collapse of the plantation loans in 1773 and waning confidence in the VOC (share prices fell from 373 in 1777 to 229 in 1782) also stimulated interest in foreign government issues.

The market in foreign government bonds always remained the preserve for investors of substantial wealth. Small savers and institutions generally confined their investments to provincial and local bonds. But one Amsterdam banker, Abraham van Ketwich, sought to broaden the market for foreign bonds in the aftermath of the 1773 crisis by packaging them in mutual funds, probably the first ever formed. In 1774 he floated "*Eendracht maakt macht*" [In unity there is power], promising low risk and high return to the purchasers of the two thousand 500-guilder shares. Van Ketwich invested the million guilders thus raised in a portfolio of Danish, Austrian, and Spanish bonds, plus various plantation loans. He hoped to reduce the risk of foreign loans via this broad geographic distribution of the fund's investments. The following year a second fund was launched in Utrecht with the name "*Voordeeling en voorsigtig*" [advantageous and cautious], and shortly thereafter a third. Brokers floated a total of 5,000 shares representing a 2.5-million-guilder investment in the foreign bond market. As a risk-reduction strategy, these mutual funds failed miserably. By 1815 the funds traded at no more than a quarter of their initial value.

By 1780 the net value of Dutch foreign government lending probably exceeded 350 million guilders, and interest earnings from abroad – then some 16 million guilders per annum – far exceeded capital exports. At least two-thirds of this total foreign investment had been placed in the British public debt – in a country, that is, whose financial markets were closely integrated with the Dutch.

The Fourth Anglo-Dutch War and its aftermath changed drastically the character of foreign lending. From 1780 until the fall of the Republic, an explosive growth of investment in foreign government debt coincided with unprecedented increases in the taxation of capital, forced lending, and voluntary lending to Holland and other Republican governmental agencies desperately seeking to raise a credible military defense and bail out institutions facing bankruptcy.

The precise amount of foreign investment after 1780 remains in dispute. Well-placed contemporaries were prepared to believe that foreign holdings exceeded a billion guilders at the time the old Republic fell, a figure that French authorities, as they readied their 100-million-guilder bill for services rendered in 1795, were only too eager to believe. Marten Buist estimates the outstanding investment in foreign loans at 700 to 800 million in 1795, while James Riley offers the range of 500 to 650 million for 1790.[21] Even this conservative estimate implies a doubling of the net foreign investment rate after 1780 to a level of at least 20 million guilders per year. Simultaneously, investors added 15 million per year to the domestic public debt (including guaranteed loans to the VOC, WIC, and Admiralties). One cannot escape the conclusion that the fifteen years after the outbreak of the Fourth Anglo-Dutch War witnessed a major liquidation of real assets and withdrawal of capital from commercial circulation.

This rapid growth of foreign lending also coincided with a major redirection of capital among borrowing governments. The new, unwelcome political situation in which the Republic found itself provoked many rentiers to withdraw from English bonds (which registered immediately on British interest rates) and invest more heavily in those of France. Poland, Spain, and the newly independent United States also captured large shares of the Amsterdam capital market in this period (indeed, Dutch support of the American cause had provoked the British declaration of war). By 1803 the Dutch had bought over 30 million guilders' worth of United States government bonds, one-quarter of the total U.S. federal debt.

The establishment of the Batavian Republic did not halt the liquidation of

[21] Riley, *International Government Finance*, p. 221; Martin Buist, "Geld, bankwezen en handel in de Noordelijke Nederlanden, 1795–1844," *Algemene geschiedenis der Nederlanden* (Haarlem, 1981), Vol. 10, p. 296.

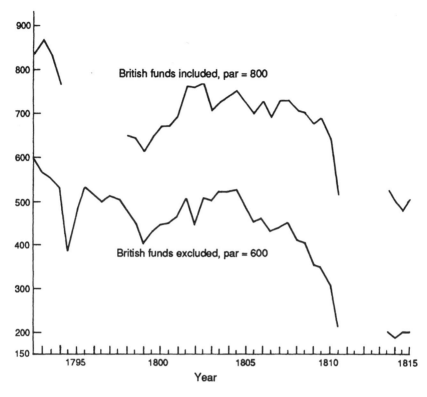

Figure 4.4. Index of the *Beurs* value of foreign government bonds, 1793–1815. [*Source:* James C. Riley, *International Finance and the Amsterdam Capital Market* (Cambridge, 1980), p. 242.]

assets and further investment in government bonds. Total net placements in public debt issues rose from an average of 37 million guilders per year in 1780–95 to some 50 million per year in 1795–1804; but the place of foreign investment, still dominant until 1793, now diminished. The insistent, insatiable credit demands of the Batavian regime absorbed the bulk of all loanable funds. Foreign government default and deferrals (beginning with Revolutionary France in 1793) unnerved investors, and the growing inflation and currency instability only compounded the aversion to foreign investment. Figure 4.4 shows how the Amsterdam Beurs valued the foreign bonds held in Dutch portfolios as of 1793.

Despite all these discouragements, foreign placements did not cease, and there was certainly no massive liquidation of foreign bondholdings. Dutch investors continued to add something under 10 million guilders per year to their holdings throughout the revolutionary era, which helps to explain why the Amsterdam Price Courant listed seventy foreign issues from fourteen countries in 1800 and eighty-nine issues from nineteen countries in 1815. Before 1795 investors placed two-fifths of their new investments abroad; thereafter only one-fifth left the Netherlands.

The low interest rates prevailing in the capital-abundant Dutch Republic of the eighteenth century obviously motivated the owners of "proprietary wealth" to seek opportunities abroad. The ability to tap that large pool of capital by establishing a funded public debt (i.e., by assigning specific revenues to the payment of specific bond issues) appealed to governments eager to gain command of revenues far in excess of their immediate taxing power. In this classic example of supply and demand, the capital markets do not appear to have functioned with great efficiency. The Dutch bankers who floated the loans protected the interests of the borrowing states far more effectively than they protected the investors, who remained largely ignorant of information relevant to the assessment of a government's creditworthiness. The credulity of investors reinforced this institutional bias, causing interest rates on government bonds to hover in a range far too narrow, and far too close to the rates enjoyed by the most creditworthy borrowers, to reflect accurately the riskiness of most of these bonds. In the 1780s all foreign bonds paid interest rates in the 4.5 to 5.0 percent range, while the bonds of Holland paid 4 percent (before taxes). Riley, mindful as the investors apparently were not of the price inflation of the era, and with the hindsight that many states ultimately defaulted or deferred payment, concludes that the governments (including the Republic) succeeded in borrowing on such advantageous terms that they effectively converted their creditors into "voluntary taxpayers." This, of course, was not the last time that the holders of government bonds traded the appearance of security for the reality of capital loss. But in this case, the losses proved to be large indeed.

The combined holdings of domestic and foreign government debt in the first years of the nineteenth century exceeded 1.5 billion guilders, yielding Dutch investors in excess of 50 million guilders annually. At that time the Republic's commitment to foreign investment reached a level that probably has never since been exceeded by any other nation. Foreign investments stood at over twice the level of our "guesstimate" of Dutch GNP (see Chapter 13). The nineteenth-century's greatest foreign investor, Great Britain, held assets abroad at the peak of its imperialist career in 1914 estimated at no more than 1.5 times per capita GNP. The absolute level was then vastly larger, of course, but the relative commitment was less.

What did the Republic and its inhabitants gain from this outflow of capital? The simple, short-term answer is that the investors (a numerically tiny group) earned by the 1790s at least 30 million guilders per year in interest payments from abroad, a sum with important consequences for domestic income distribution, consumer demand, the balance of payments, and the exchange rate. These factors influenced, in turn, the character of the economy as a whole, a subject steeped in controversy from the end of the eighteenth century to the present day. We defer an assessment of this issue to Chapter 13.

That assessment must take into account one final fact, that a large portion of the capital invested in government bonds, foreign and domestic, was ultimately lost. The Dutch bonds, as the French bonds before them, were subjected to the *tiërcering*, an effective annulment of over half their nominal value. Other foreign governments repudiated their debts or suspended payment for a period of time. Even bondholders fortunate enough to avoid these losses had to contend with the inflation of the period 1780–1817, which eroded the real value of their assets. Riley has assessed the total loss of real capital from all these causes over the period 1793 to 1840 at between one-third and one-half of the total.

Remarkably, neither the losses of this period nor the lessons presumably taught to Dutch investors prevented the reemergence of the Netherlands as a major capital exporter. In 1895 Dutch foreign investment had again reached 1.75 times GNP (i.e., higher than the contemporary British figure). Many of these investments (especially those in colonial enterprises) were later lost, too, but a century later, at the end of the twentieth century, the Netherlands is for a third time a major holder of foreign assets, now chiefly in the hands of multinational enterprises.

4.4. Greed, fear, and efficient markets

We have observed the growth of the Republic's commodity trade and the elaboration of a broad range of shipping, insurance, and financing services. These functions came together at the highest level at the Amsterdam *Beurs*, arguably the nerve center of the entire international economy. Built in 1611, this building of arcades around a central courtyard gathered merchants and brokers who traded in literally everything known to that society. Together with the nearby *Wisselbank* (established in 1609) and the specialized *Korenbeurs* (built in 1617), Amsterdam offered the merchant an unparalleled range of business opportunities: One could trade commodities as well as financial instruments such as company shares and government bonds; one could buy sea insurance, arrange for freight, and get foreign exchange quotations. (Map 4.1 shows how close to each other all these institutions were clustered.) Moreover, at Amsterdam these services were available to the international economy on a continuous basis, in contrast to their availability only at periodic fairs in the commercial centers of the sixteenth century. This new characteristic was symbolized by the appearance of the price courant, a listing of price quotations that first appeared, as far as we know, in 1583 and appeared on a regular, twice-weekly, basis from 1613 onward.

The efficient provision of these commercial services, the sum total of which constitute what are sometimes known as "transaction costs," required the presence of one additional commodity: information. Information flowed to the Republic

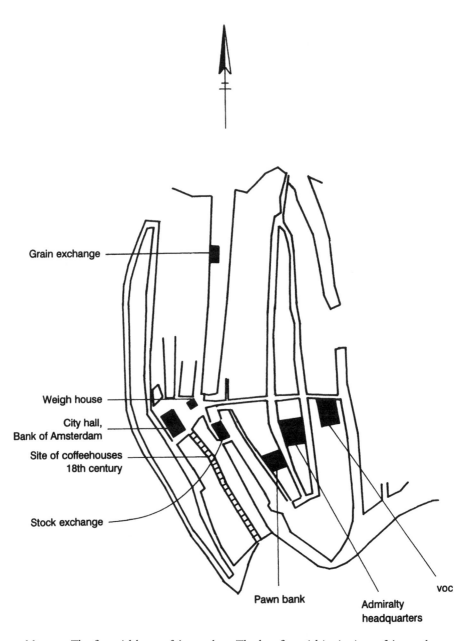

Map 4.1. The financial heart of Amsterdam. The key financial institutions of Amsterdam were all located within a few minutes walk from one another.

and ultimately to the Dam and neighboring streets of Amsterdam by many channels: by merchant ships, by the correspondence from branches of Amsterdam merchant and banking houses, via the bureaucracies of the VOC and WIC, via consuls and foreign agents of the city government, the Generality, and the Directorate of the Levant Trade.

The flow of information impresses the twentieth-century observer chiefly by its slowness and incompleteness. The VOC needed to wait two years to receive an answer to a question put to its agents in Batavia. But by the standards of the time, Amsterdam and all of Holland overflowed with information: a fact reflected by the early establishment there of newspapers – the *Amsterdamsche Courant* in 1618, the *Tydinghen* of 1619, and the *Oprechte Haarlemsche Courant* in 1667 – and by the publication in the Republic of French-language newspapers with international readerships – the *Gazette d'Amsterdam*, the *Gazette de Leyde*, and many others.

The early presence of newspapers and the price courant notwithstanding, information did not flow freely. Just as today, the incentive to monopolize information was great; and unlike today, major institutions such as the State, the *Wisselbank*, and the VOC were under no obligation to provide basic information about public finance, bank deposits, or company operations.

Information was not free, far from it. But it was obtainable more cheaply in the Republic, and especially Amsterdam, than in other places. Just as the trading world of early modern Europe tended to concentrate commodity flows at a single entrepôt in order to reduce costs and dampen supply irregularities, so was the process of information gathering concentrated. In the pre-telegraphic world, the dissemination of information took time, and news could not reach all places at the same moment. The single location that received the most fresh news from the largest number of separate locations enjoyed a major advantage over its competitors, one that powerfully reinforced the concentration of trade (and laid the basis for the rise of the financial sector). The natural geographical advantage of the Republic was reinforced by intelligence networks of merchants, further strengthened by the commercial institutions and, finally, solidified by the Republic's toleration of religious minorities (with their intelligence networks) and uncensored publishing.

The aggregation and analysis of information can take two basic forms: (1) the dispassionate analysis of data, assembled in archives and processed by bureaucracies; and (2) rumor mongering and "mood creation" at the stock exchange, in coffee houses, and so on. Not surprisingly, the second, more ancient, of these forms predominated in the Republic. It is worth noting, however, that the "modern" form of information analysis, representing an internalization of information gathering, was not entirely absent. The VOC in particular expended much effort on market analysis in order to prepare the annual *eis*, the orders sent to Batavia for execution.

The "informal" use of information found two general applications: (1) information about the creditworthiness of firms and governments determined the risk premium of bonds and the willingness of merchants to accept and discount bills; (2) information about future supplies, changes in demand, rumors of war or plague, and suspicion about the size of warehoused inventories or the content of arriving ships found immediate application in price speculation.

Speculation in prices, with associated hoarding, was a constant source of concern to medieval municipal authorities, and it gave rise to mountains of legislation intended to guarantee supplies, prevent hoarding, and restrict the role of middlemen and nonmarket transactions. The Netherlands, under both Habsburg and Republican governments, had its share of such restrictive ordinances, but the reality of the entrepôt repeatedly undermined the feasibility of traditional municipal market regulation, certainly in the major commercial centers.

Because of the *de facto* character of the new commercial practices, documentation is incomplete. But already in the 1550s, Amsterdam merchants practiced an early form of futures trading, when they wrote contracts for future delivery of Baltic grain and North Sea herring before the grain had been harvested or the herring caught.

The enlargement of the range of goods traded in the Republic and the establishment of continuous markets at the Amsterdam *Beurs* created an environment in which speculative practices could spread and mature. In the seventeenth century, futures contracts came to be written for a large range of products, including pepper, coffee, cacao, saltpeter, brandywine, whale oil, and whale bone. Moreover, purchasers of these contracts increasingly had no intention of taking delivery, just as sellers did not possess and did not intend to acquire the promised goods.

This form of speculative trading found its most dramatic – and notorious – expression in the tulip mania of 1636–7, which combined the practices just described with a relatively new commodity enjoying great popularity and possessing a natural characteristic that lent itself to gambling. Tulip bulbs can propagate through the formation of outgrowths on the mother bulb, and when they are invaded by a mosaic virus, an effect, called "breaking," produces multicolored patterns in the flowers that were highly desired. These developments could be verified only between June, when the bulbs can be removed from the ground, and September, when they must be replanted. Connoisseurs regularly speculated on these developments, but in 1634 they were joined by large numbers of "nonprofessionals." Prices rose. By the summer of 1636, this activity spread far beyond the circle of tulip fanciers, the flames of speculation being fanned (or so say commentators) by severe outbreaks of Bubonic Plague, which released inhibitions. The trade shifted from the offices of notaries to taverns, where futures contracts were struck informally and on a very large scale. By then the speculation had expanded beyond the precious bulbs, which were sold individually (a single Semper Augustus bulb sold for 5,500 guilders), to ordinary "pound goods." In early 1637 the mania reached its climax, as hundreds of ordinary citizens gathered at taverns to buy and sell bulbs they could not deliver and did not want to receive.

They were betting on the future price of bulbs. This *windhandel*, as futures trading came to be called, collapsed suddenly in the second week of February 1637. The specific catalyst remains in dispute, but once prices declined, there was no incentive to honor the futures contracts since they were unenforceable in the courts, and petitions to clarify the legal standing of these contracts were turned down by the States of Holland. Public officials viewed this democratized speculation with both fear and loathing, and once the mania collapsed (but not before), pamphlets appeared denouncing the irrational and immoral conduct of the speculators.[22] These pamphlets continue to speak to the preconceptions of modern historians, and the bizarre object of speculation will always attract the puzzled attention of posterity, but the trading techniques of the tulip speculators were by then common to the *Beurs* and its specialist traders.

As early as 1609, futures trading emerged in the shares of the VOC (established only seven years earlier) as a disgruntled former participant in the company, Isaac le Maire, organized the first known conspiracy of "bears" to drive down share prices. The following year the States General prohibited short-selling and other *windhandel*, a prohibition that would be repeated many times in later decades. But speculation in the prices of VOC and other joint-stock company shares continued (to be joined after 1723 by trade in English company shares). In time, it became the specialty of Portuguese Jewish traders.

The States General softened its position in 1689, when regulation and taxation appeared to offer better prospects than unenforceable prohibitions. Perhaps this change of policy was encouraged by the publication a year earlier of *Confusion de Confusiones*, a book describing speculative trading techniques in detail, and written by one of the foremost speculators at the *Beurs*, Joseph Penso de la Vega. Among the techniques that he described were futures contracts, options (puts and calls), margin buying, bull and bear *cabalas*, and a form of stock index purchase known as *ducat-actions*, where small speculators could follow the market, winning or losing a ducat for every point of rise or fall in the price of shares.

VOC share speculation must have been encouraged by the difficulty of actually buying shares. Although the original subscription in 1602 allowed investors to place any amount of money, later trading usually took the form of single "shares" of 3,000 guilders in nominal value, the stake required for "*hoofd participanten*" – shareholders eligible for appointment as company directors (*bewindhebber*). This meant that the purchase of a single share after 1650, when *Beurs* quotations usually stood above 500, involved at least 15,000 guilders – a small fortune. Much of the interest in futures trading came from persons whose modest means precluded the actual purchase of shares.

---

[22] Simon Schama, *Embarrassment of Riches* (New York, 1988), pp. 350–66; N. W. Posthumus, "The Tulip Mania in Holland in the years 1636 and 1637," *Journal of Economic and Business History* I (1929); E. H. Krelage, *Bloemenspeculatie in Nederland* (Amsterdam, 1942); Peter M. Garber, "Tulipmania," *Journal of Political Economy* 97 (1989), 535–60.

A further encouragement to futures trading was the VOC's practice of making legal transfer of share ownership only when the books were opened for the payment of dividends – twice per year at most. In time the *Beurs* established *rescounter* dates, quarterly deadlines for the settlement of mutually contingent financial contracts (monthly in the case of *ducat-actions*).

When the *Beurs* began trading in the English funds, futures trading again predominated, in marked contrast to the London Stock Exchange where the House of Commons continued to do battle against the practice throughout the eighteenth century. English shares were then traded continuously on two exchanges: in London, which was closed on Sundays, and in Amsterdam, where the predominance of Jewish traders made Saturday the day of rest. Communications between the two markets relied on the packet boats, sailing biweekly between Hellevoetsluis and Harwich. Larry Neal's study of these markets reveals a very strong correlation between quotations on the two markets (the correlation coefficient between first differences of natural logs for Bank and EIC stock was .99) and also a persistent tendency for Amsterdam prices to be higher than London prices by 1 to 3 percent, which is persuasive evidence that the London quotes were spot prices while the Amsterdam quotes were more commonly for future delivery. This may also help to explain part of a much larger difference between prices of VOC shares traded in Amsterdam and those traded in the seats of the other VOC chambers. In the provincial cities, where less sophisticated trading occurred, share prices were always lower than at Amsterdam.

The growing sophistication and internationalism of financial activity spawned the first real international speculative mania, or bubble, in 1720. The War of the Spanish Succession had strained the finances of every participant. We have already noted the desperate state of Dutch public finance in this period. In England the government experimented with what today would be called "debt-for-equity swaps," in which it granted charters to new joint-stock companies, and the holders of public debt could exchange their bonds for shares in the new companies. This benefited the government, which reduced its debt; the companies, in return, received trading or commercial monopolies. The Bank of England had been created in such a conversion, and in 1711 a more ambitious conversion created the South Sea Company. Inspired by these innovations, the Scotsman John Law persuaded the French government to allow him to engineer an even grander debt-for-equity swap. In 1719 a newly formed Mississippi Company (*Compagnie des Indes*) was to assume the royal debt, using an enormous issue of bank notes by the *Banque Royale* to finance the conversion.

The example of these seemingly successful joint-stock companies, whose share prices soared on the hope for profit from government-guaranteed monopolies, captured the public imagination. Promoters exploited this favorable atmosphere by floating new companies, attracting subscribers with promises of great profits. This enthusiasm spread to the Republic, where promoters established, on paper, over twenty joint-stock companies in 1720 and set about finding subscribers who would be granted negotiable shares on the deposit of 5 percent, or even less, of the projected capitalization. It was, of course, the subscriber's hope to sell these shares for a higher price before full payment was required. Enthusiasm pushed prices up until the realization dawned that the companies could never achieve the profits needed to justify their lofty share prices and, indeed, that the promoters often had no intention of conducting any ongoing business at all.

This *windhandel* never assumed in the Netherlands the scale of England and France, and consequently it did far less damage. The Republic's debt-issuing governments felt no urge to convert public debt into company shares; indeed, many public authorities, including several provinces and such important cities as Amsterdam, Haarlem, and Leiden, forbade the establishment of new joint-stock companies in their jurisdictions. The 1720 bubble remained a provincial phenomenon, flourishing in secondary cities where boosterism appealed as a means of combating the growing predominance of Amsterdam.

Three of the companies founded in 1720 actually survived to carry out sustained business activities. The *Utrechtsche Geoctroyeerde Provinciale Compagnie* (with a nominal capitalization of 10 million guilders, but requiring a deposit of only 5 percent of this amount) had grand plans to dig a long canal that would make Utrecht a seaport. It attracted the particular interest of Jewish subscribers, and it survived until 1750 as an organizer of lotteries.

The *Middelburgsche Commercie Compagnie* attracted 587 shareholders prepared to deposit a speculation-discouraging 25 percent of the company's nominal capitalization of 12 million guilders. It embarked on shipping ventures and after 1734 became active in the Atlantic triangle trade of slaves and sugar (see Chapter 10, section 10.4.2). The company survived into the nineteenth century.

The *Rotterdamsche Maatschappij van Assurautie* eventually attracted over 1 million guilders in two issues of shares to establish a commercial company specialized in sea insurance. It is unique among all the dubious products of 1720 in operating continuously to the present day.

The marginal character of the 1720 bubble in the Netherlands bespeaks its more mature financial system and less adventure-prone government. In contrast to the havoc wreaked by the collapse of Law's System in France, the bubble had no lasting impact on domestic Dutch credit markets. However, the international consequences of the bubble were not negligible. For the first time, short-term international capital flowed in large volumes between Paris (where Law's System created enormous liquidity), London, and Amsterdam. As the bubble burst, this capital moved toward the safe haven of Amsterdam (see the sharp rise of Bank of Amsterdam deposits, Figure 4.3). In the wake of this crisis, Paris was revealed as an unstable financial center while London recovered on the strength of its banking system. From then on short-term, or "spot," bills (bills intended purely for financial transfers) joined the traditional longer-term commercial bills of exchange to internationalize the European investment community, around a durable London–Amsterdam axis, giving London privileged access to Dutch investment funds.

In the decades that followed, the Amsterdam capital market expanded, exposing the financial sector to different sources of instability. Two crises occurring in rapid succession – in 1763 and 1772–3 – sufficiently disrupted credit operations to erode international confidence in Amsterdam merchant bankers, giving rival centers, particularly Hamburg and London, new competitive opportunities.

The crisis of 1763 occurred in the wake of the Seven Years' War, which had created the closest thing to boom conditions that the Republic's commercial sector was to experience in the eighteenth century. The demands of belligerent powers buoyed the commodity trade of the neutral Republic, while the need to transfer funds from England and France to Central European allies gorged Amsterdam's banking houses with acceptance business and flooded the Republic with bullion to cover these transactions. After the war, commodity prices plummeted, and monetary debasements in Central Europe disrupted the bullion trade. In response, some banking houses expanded their acceptance of bills of exchange that were not covered by corresponding shipments of goods or bullion. These "finance bills" (or accommodation paper) depended on the drawing of further bills to prolong the extension of credit until, it was hoped, real assets could be liquidated to cover finally the chain of bills. Contemporaries called this extended chain of uncovered bills *wisselruiterij*.

In the summer of 1763, two major Amsterdam houses (A. Joseph en Co. and Gebr. de Neufville) suspended payments; others were caught in the resulting liquidity crisis. In all, thirty-eight bankruptcies, including seven large merchant bankers, caused nearly 27 million guilders of debt to be dishonored. To prevent the total evaporation of credit, some bankers proposed the establishment of a *Bank van Krediet*, or *Bank Courant ter Beleening*, an emergency reserve bank to restore liquidity by discounting bills bearing good names and to grant loans backed by collateral. This is just the sort of institution that the modern economist recognizes as missing in Amsterdam's financial system, which revolved around merchant banking houses that did not take deposits, were not as a rule highly capitalized, and tended to be highly individualistic in their business dealings. The *Wisselbank* served primarily a transfer function; it did not (legally) practice fractional reserve banking and could not function as a central credit institution. The new reserve bank did not come to pass. Many bankers took private satisfaction in the collapse of Leendert de Neufville, who had acquired many enemies in his aggressive business dealings, and it did not take long for the revival of trade and credit to dissipate the sense of urgency.

Ten years later acceptance credit faced another liquidity crisis. It was triggered by speculation in English East India stock stimulated by shady practices in Scotland and London. This scheme also had Dutch participants, of course, since the shares were also traded in Amsterdam. In 1772 optimism about future EIC profits turned into its opposite as the company's problems became evident. Simultaneously, but independently, Surinam planters confronted falling prices and slave revolts, forcing them to suspend interest payments and default on the many millions of guilders of plantation loans negotiated since 1750. The simultaneous fall of stock and commodity prices forced banking firms to liquidate, and the consequent drying up of acceptance credit affected trade, causing Amsterdam warehouses to fill with unsaleable goods.

The first firm to fail was Clifford en Zoonen, a firm of hitherto unimpeachable reputation. This time the merchant community rallied to the support of the stricken firms, petitioning the city to establish a new reserve bank, this time called the *Fonds tot maintien van het publiek crediet*. With 2 million guilders supplied by the city (possibly borrowed from the *Wisselbank*), the *Fonds* strove to restore liquidity by providing short-term credit on collateral of commodities and government bonds.

This primitive central bank was dissolved within the year of its establishment, even though the commercial revival from the crisis was slow in coming. In fact, acceptance credit and stock speculation never returned to their former levels, as investors shied away from an unstable short-term credit market and committed larger sums to long-term foreign government lending. This, as we have seen, posed dangers of its own, but it would take twenty years before they began to reveal themselves.

The *Fonds* so quickly dissolved in 1773 was revived in 1782, in the wake of the trade depression occasioned by the Fourth Anglo-Dutch War. Now called the *Stads Beleeningkamer*, it never possessed the resources (again supplied by *Wisselbank* loans) to compensate for the instability inherent in a credit structure based on atomistic firms periodically exposed to risks that far exceeded their assets.

Yet another credit bank, the *Generale Beleenbank*, took shape in 1795 for the purpose of providing liquidity to taxpayers who were being called upon to raise unprecedented amounts of cash for the payment of taxes. None of these institutions lasted for long or, it seems, played a large role during their short lives. Even in times of crisis, people could draw on large reserves of cash, and among commercial leaders, the opinion remained firmly rooted that a supplementary paper currency would undermine international confidence in the Amsterdam capital market.

A central bank modeled after the Bank of England was first proposed by Gogel in 1798, but the attachment to hard cash was such that it became a reality only in 1814, with the establishment of the *Nederlandsche Bank*. By then the Amsterdam capital market had lost its international importance.

The banking families saw Amsterdam's eclipse coming long before the fact, and they gradually transferred at least some of their activities and assets to other centers. This "rootless cosmopolitanism" is hardly surprising, since many of these families had earlier moved their offices from Swiss, French, and German cities to Amsterdam as its leadership became apparent in the course of the eighteenth century. The circulation of these families and of their capital is a fascinating, but imperfectly documented, spectacle. We see the Portuguese Jew Manuel Teixeira moving his operations from Hamburg to Amsterdam in 1698, followed by Johannes Goll from Frankfurt and then by a constellation of French and Swiss Protestant bankers: Jacques and Daniel Hogguer from Lyon, Jean-Jacques Horneca from Geneva, and George Grand from Lausanne. Meanwhile, Dutch firms with branches in London began to shift their activities more fully across the North Sea: Gerard van Neck and the Barings early on, Huguenots and Portuguese Jews in the course of the century (Abraham Ricardo – father of David Ricardo – made the move in 1760), and Henry Hope, the greatest of them all, in 1794 as the Republic lay *in extremis*.

The growth of the Republic's financial activity has had few defenders, either among contemporary observers or among later historians. The eighteenth-century periodical (spectator) literature linked finance to a perceived increase in ostentatious display and extravagant luxury. The cosmopolitan character of Amsterdam's financial world, in particular the conspicuous role of Jews, certainly encouraged this effort to link the rise of finance with defects of character, and with the abandonment of those traditional values that had made the earlier growth of the economy possible.

Modern historians have offered interpretations of the rise of finance that are not identical to, but also not incompatible with, the prejudices of contemporaries. Thus, Violet Barbour introduced her discussion of speculation in Amsterdam by observing, as the seventeenth century progressed, "a tendency on the part of capital . . . to prefer speculative trading . . . and investment in money lending and insurance, to the toil and hazards of foreign trade."[23] In short, finance was (is?) a lazy man's way to make money.

The eighteenth-century shift from active trade toward both acceptance credit and commission trade has long been assessed as imposing far greater costs (in enabling commercial trade to dispense with the Dutch entrepôt) than it garnered benefits. It seemed to represent a trade-off that could appeal only to the sedentary and risk-averse. To many nineteenth-century observers, the diminished energy and initiative of the eighteenth-century elite – satiated, rendered effete, and bloated by their great wealth – could hardly be better demonstrated than by pointing to the transition from seafaring to money-changing, from buying and selling goods to buying and selling paper.

The late eighteenth-century rush to invest in government bonds, particularly those of foreign governments, has also met with bitter criticisms. Bitter, because the issue of patriotism is injected into the argument. The *Patriot* finance minister Gogel denounced foreign investment in 1796, and modern historians have elaborated on his critique. The objections take two general forms. One, a universally

---

[23] Barbour, *Amsterdam Capitalism*, p. 74.

applicable objection to foreign lending, was enunciated by John Maynard Keynes when he observed that after the default of foreign borrowers, the lending country has nothing, while after the default of domestic borrowers, the structures, machines, inventories, and so forth financed by the loan remain available for further use. After 1793, as losses on foreign lending mounted, this argument gained in appeal. A second objection addresses shortcomings of rentier investment policy. The flow of funds into government bonds, it is argued, resulted from tariff and tax policies of a government dominated by commercial and financial interests that made domestic industrial production unprofitable. Self-serving public policy discouraged investment in industrial production, "so [that] Dutch economic development [i.e., industrialization] was postponed by a leakage of capital into international finance."[24] The historian just quoted, Charles Wilson, may well have had in mind the identical critique made of public policy and investor behavior in his native Britain in the twentieth century.

Speculation reflected weakness of character; acceptance credit undermined the staple market; foreign investment denied the domestic economy the capital needed to industrialize; and, as a final indictment, the very success of the financial sector worked to intensify income inequality, as rentiers effortlessly collected dividends from taxpayers (at home and abroad), while domestic labor was reduced to idleness and poverty by the withdrawal of capital from the productive sectors of the economy.

There are reasons to be skeptical of all these indictments of the Republic's financial sector. Speculation on future events is an integral part of commodity and financial markets, and it need not be a source of instability greater than the external shocks it seeks to anticipate. The growth of the Republic's market activity increased the scope for speculative activity, but that should not be confused with an abandonment of real trade in favor of the "easy profits" of speculation. The appeal of gambling in the eighteenth century seems to have been particularly strong, but this was a general European phenomenon rather than unique to the Republic, and it was by no means confined to financial markets.

The growth of acceptance banking and the later interest in foreign government lending cannot be understood as resulting simply from the sovereign choices of Dutch merchants and rentiers. The evolving international economy confronted these agents with new circumstances that constrained their behavior. In Chapter 10 we document structural changes reducing the Republic's hold over its trading partners, and forcing it into a subordinate position vis-à-vis customers whose options had grown more numerous. Simultaneously, the internal decline of industrial production increased the commercial sector's reliance on footloose reexport trades. In combination, increased foreign competition and diminished

---

[24] Charles Wilson, *Anglo-Dutch Commerce and Finance in the Eighteenth Century* (Cambridge, 1941), p. 201.

domestically oriented trade made the disintegration of shipping, merchant, and financial functions into separate specialties an unavoidable second-best strategy. Not to adapt in this way meant to speed the decline of all three functions.

A similar argument can be made concerning the rise of foreign government lending. The contrast between interventionist Dutch investors in seventeenth-century Sweden, who could force concessions from the debtor state, and the passive Dutch investors of the eighteenth century, who let themselves be exploited by both their debtors and their bankers, cannot adequately be explained as the product of diminished energy. In the eighteenth century, the better organization of state fiscal systems and the elaboration of effective mercantilist policies made the behavior of a Louis de Geer impossible. Moreover, the vast accumulations of capital in the hands of the eighteenth-century capitalists placed them (ironically) in a position of dependence vis-à-vis national states. Only the states, with their taxing power, could hope to absorb such sums and make regular interest payments. The fact that governments sought to borrow almost exclusively to wage war guaranteed that Dutch capital would do little to stimulate economic growth directly; but neither the immediate economic possibilities nor the grandiose development projects that we, in retrospect, may be capable of imagining could have absorbed a large portion of the late eighteenth-century stock of financial capital. In the circumstances of the times, governments held a monopsonistic position in the capital markets.

We find the periwigged rentiers largely innocent of the charges discussed so far. There were good reasons for the growth of that sector, and there were objective circumstances to account for its relative passivity. But there remains one valid criticism that can be leveled against the Republic's financial sector. One cannot easily explain away its instability and vulnerability. The absence of institutional modifications to accommodate the growth of credit, the absence of a bank of issue, and the systematic bias of banking houses against the interests of investors, all contributed to the ultimate failure of Amsterdam as a major financial center. The problem is not that the Republic developed a large financial sector but that it failed to develop institutions capable of giving that sector strength and stability.

Chapter 5
Three questions

5.1. What was the influence of the medieval legacy?

Both the suddenness and the intensity of the Republic's economic prosperity provoke amazement and compel us to search for factors that might help to account for such an achievement. In this first section, we address the historical background factors that distinguished the Northern Netherlands from its neighbors, and we then turn in the second section to an examination of the claims made for the most striking and profound alterations in sixteenth-century social life. In this chapter's third section, we confront the basic issue of the coherence of the phenomenon to which this study is dedicated: In what sense was there a unified Dutch economy?

In the preceding chapters, we explored three mutually related background factors: the geographic situation and all that attaches to it, the high level of urbanization, and the economy's high level of monetization. One might properly ask whether these conditions – so different from those of most of Europe, and in place well before 1500 – contributed to the development of mentalities and social structures that were especially suited to the rapid emergence and intense prosperity of a modern economy. Such a question requires that we enter a terrain where quantification is useless, convincing demonstrations are difficult, and tentative and suggestive treatments are as much as one can hope for. Yet this should be no reason peremptorily to dismiss an issue that invites us to an appreciation of mentalities and an evaluation of the influence of institutions and structural conditions as brakes on, or catalysts of, social processes.

If one asks what appears around 1500 as the most characteristic difference between society in the Northern Netherlands and that of the rest of western

Europe, the answer would have to be the absence of a truly feudal past. The reasons for this divergent development in the alluvial zone along the North Sea coast and north of the Delta were considered in Chapter 2. Here we consider its consequences for the structure and character of society.

The absence of firmly anchored feudal relations meant, in the first place, the absence of a society of orders, where each member held a legally fixed position assigned by birth. In a society where the traditional orders did not exist as judicial categories, or existed only in a weak form, barriers against social mobility rooted in the legal system and its power relationships were absent as well. Elsewhere such barriers lingered for centuries and persisted even longer in the mental habits of society. The judicial – and often the geographical and social – place in society that the feudal system imposed for generations on the bulk of the European population could hardly have encouraged innovation and initiative. This is not to say that creative initiatives never took place. Rather, our point is that the changes sought in a society of orders rarely took the form of breaking down or extending traditional boundaries. The tendency to think in terms of adjustments and adaptations was far more characteristic than was inventiveness and exploration. Consistent with this situation was the tendency for the feudal system to concentrate nearly all power in the hands of persons with no interest in innovation.

The absence of significant feudal traditions also had the consequence of diminishing the influence of communal institutions and collective behavior. Where the collectivity is weak, the individual and individualistic behavior necessarily become more prominent. This creates situations in which personal initiative, innovation, and responsibility can develop, and where political, economic, and personal freedom is valued more highly.

We can translate these abstract concepts about how feudal and nonfeudal societies differed into specific Dutch historical realities, especially in its alluvial zone, by surveying a number of phenomena that help to demonstrate its special social character. These include: the diversified character of landownership and land use; the weakness or absence of collective institutions such as open fields and guilds; the open relations between town and country; the strongly nuclear household structure of the population and its implications for the character of family life; the occupational flexibility that made possible, for instance, the integrating of farming, fishing, and seafaring; the pluriform religious life made possible by a relatively high degree of toleration and space for personal freedom; the strong attachment to local autonomy; and the jealous protection of vested rights and privileges. What ties these phenomena together is their appearance to us as early expressions of something with which we are familiar: an open, bourgeois society. This "proto-modernity" was directly related to the high level of urbanization that had been attained already in the late Middle Ages and to the high degree of geographical – and an incipient social – mobility. Internally, this society possessed relatively few formal barriers; the individual could aspire to prevail over the collective. Externally, this society could project a powerful will to protect this situation.

In Chapter 2, where the process of rural settlement in the alluvial zone was discussed (section 2.1.3), we called attention to the existence, or emergence, of a free peasantry. In contrast to most of the rest of Europe, the peasants here possessed full personal freedom and faced no institutional limitations in the conduct of their occupations. Apart from the communal institutions erected to manage the struggle against the water, no communal obligations – emanating from manor lord or village collectivity – limited the farmers in the individual management of their properties. We do not exaggerate much in asserting that the only factors they had to take into account were nature and the market. And these two forces directed agriculture, ultimately, toward a concentration on livestock and dependence on a monetized economy. Freedom, individualism, and market orientation characterized this agrarian society long before the end of the Middle Ages.

It bears emphasizing that the independence of the cultivators was no reflection of an autonomy stemming from ownership of their own land – of control over the means of production and the defense of "arm's-length" relations with the market. On the contrary, it was precisely in those regions of greatest personal and economic freedom that peasant proprietorship tended to be particularly low. In Friesland in 1511, it was the monasteries that owned a large amount of agricultural land, while in Holland the economic survey of 1514 reveals a situation in which nobles, clergy, monasteries, burgers, and urban institutions together owned a great deal. But here as elsewhere in the alluvial zone, formal commercial contracts governed the relationship between landowners and their tenants. Little is known about the terms of tenancy before the fifteenth century, but by then leases usually ran for a reasonably long period (at least five years) and were primarily concerned to protect the property from permanent changes that would reduce its intrinsic quality. Contracts sometimes forbade the plowing of pasture and its conversion to arable, or restricted the planting of especially soil-exhausting crops. Also common was the requirement that land lie fallow at the end of the lease, that specified amounts of manure be spread on the fields, and that the property's fencing be left in good repair. But these stipulations generally did not constitute a direct intervention in farm decision making by the owner. Moreover, the boundaries they set on the tenant's management tended over time to become progressively more standardized and general.

One also observes that farm leases tended to be renewed, so that the same tenant remained on a farm for decades on end. Even his death did not necessarily bring change, as his widow, children, and other family members continued as tenants thereafter. This tenant continuity was supported by the concept of property rights prevailing in the Netherlands. In contrast to Roman law, the region's customary Old Dutch law (*Oudvaderlands recht*) did not define the owner's property rights as absolute; it acknowledged explicitly the rights of tenants. Thus, the death of a tenant did not extinguish a lease (*sterfdag breekt geen huur*), nor did the sale of a property to a new owner (*verkoop breekt geen huur*). In addition, the rights of a tenant to what in practice amounted to preferential treatment in the renewal of a lease came to be quite generally acknowledged. The strength of the tenant's legal position was increased further by the common requirement that an owner desiring to replace his tenant compensate the departing tenant for permanent improvements made to the property. Among such improvements were buildings erected by the tenant. There had been a time when even the farmhouse hardly counted as a *permanent* improvement, but as structures became larger and built of brick, they came to represent substantial investments and stood as a real obstacle to an owner desiring to replace a tenant. In some areas, and most famously in Groningen, this compensation requirement gave tenants a protection that resulted in a transfer of effective ownership rights: The tenants acquired *de facto* permanent possession while the owners held nothing more than an old right to collect a fixed money rental (see Chapter 11, section 11.4).

To be sure, these characteristics of Old Dutch law did not rule unopposed. From the fifteenth century on, the precepts of Roman law gained ground in questions of property rights, but this process was gradual and generally did not undo the tenant protections just described. Only in the nineteenth century did the systematic application of the new concepts of private property attack frontally the position of farm tenants – a development that so weakened the tenants as to require in the twentieth century new laws to protect them.

The market orientation of Dutch rural society and the entrepreneurial freedom that was made possible by voluntary, commercially based leases and contracts give a distinctly modern impression. The mental and social spirit associated with hierarchical feudal relationships and collective production decisions is weakly developed in the alluvial provinces. This medieval achievement must stand as the most distinctive feature of the region's economy.

Of course, it will not do to exaggerate: Hierarchical and collective forces were not altogether absent. The burgers of the Dutch towns invested great importance in their guilds and militias (*schutterij*), local corporate bodies that they saw as securing their economic and political rights, respectively. However, almost everywhere these institutions were far more potent as symbols of civic politics than as actual policy-making agencies.[1] The Dutch guilds rarely possessed the influence that they had elsewhere in Europe. Rather, their role typically was to implement municipal economic policies – policies about which they could submit requests, but which were decided in their absence. Internally, the guilds' importance to their members resided in their protective functions. The appeal of guild membership resided chiefly in matters of safety and security, such as the suppression of competition, preferential treatment for children of members in gaining admission (usually via the submission of a "masterpiece") and discounts on their entry

[1] Maarten Prak, "Civil disturbances and Urban Middle Class in the Dutch Republic," *Tijdschrift voor sociale geschiedenis* 15 (1989), 165–73.

fees, improving the position of daughters of guild members in the marriage market, preferential treatment in securing work, economic assistance during illness or invalidity, old age assistance, and widows' pensions. In addition, some guilds appear to have provided other economic services, such as the extension of credit in poor years, an example of which is offered in Chapter 4, section 4.3.2.

The patrician urban magistracies always kept their thumb on the guilds. They controlled the appointment of guild managers and orchestrated their very establishment, fission, and dissolution. In this way, guild independence vis-à-vis city government could not arise; and, as a result, many of the regulations imposed upon the guilds were intended more to serve the economic and financial interests of the city as a whole rather than to protect the specific interests of the guild itself. In this context it seems fitting that only in the most "medieval" of the cities of the Northern Netherlands, Utrecht, did the guilds make serious, though never successful, efforts to acquire political power. The guilds were a prominent feature of municipal economic life in the Republic, but almost always as a vehicle whereby the government sought to advance its vision of an urban general interest. This vision tolerated a measure of particularism relative to the outside world, but it did not usually tolerate the maintenance of unequal market access within the city.

Family life in the Republic is another area in which relatively modern characteristics present themselves. We know very little about the early development of Dutch family structure, but it is highly significant that when documents first allow a glimpse, we are already dealing with a family structure that conforms better than any other in Europe to the features associated with the modern nuclear family. The predominance of the nuclear family, a household shorn of a coresident older generation or coresident siblings and other relations of the married couple, had established itself in much of western Europe, certainly by the late sixteenth century. But in the western and northern provinces of the Republic, this individualization of the household had proceeded further than elsewhere. Not only had the nuclear family here rid itself of resident kin other than parents and their children, but it also made relatively little use of live-in servants. In neighboring countries such resident nonkin generally amounted to from 12 to 16 percent of the total population in the seventeenth and eighteenth centuries; in the alluvial provinces of the Republic, their presence ranged between 4 and 8 percent. In the cities these percentages often stood at even lower levels. What we observe, then, is the modern, individualized family, living as a self-contained social unit. The household was unusually small (averaging 3.5 to 4.0 persons), while in other countries (and also in the eastern provinces of the Republic) household size averaged in excess of 5 persons and first shrank to the standard of the western provinces in the late nineteenth century.

The modernity of the household is not limited to these quantitative and structural dimensions. The affective relations among family members also present us with relationships that strike us as especially characteristic of the twentieth century.

The ties binding parents with children and siblings with each other were not absent, to be sure, but they assumed a voluntaristic character. The ability of the community and neighborhood to exercise their social control over the family was correspondingly limited. The choice of marriage partners tended to become a matter of individual preference, whereby affection could make its influence felt.

This freedom of choice had its limits, of course, the most obvious being religious identity. Here boundaries existed that rarely were crossed – and would not be on any scale until after 1950. Likewise, divorce always remained a rarity, but legal separation (*scheiding van tafel en bed*) occurred more often, a phenomenon that is undoubtedly related to the relatively independent position that women were able to hold in Dutch civil society.

We can summarize this all with the double claim that within society the (nuclear) family held a substantially autonomous place, and within the family the individuals maintained positions of relative equality. Independence and individuality predominated, while ties binding the individual to large collectivities (the extended family and neighborhood over the nuclear family, and the family over the individual) tended to be weak.

Independence, individuality, and rationality were characteristics imparting a special flavor to life in Holland under the Republic. Instead of pursuing further the many ways in which these characteristics expressed themselves, we turn now to the task of accounting for the very existence of these characteristics. To begin with we can recall the argument made earlier concerning the weakness of feudalism (and related collective and juridically enforced social relations). A second explanatory terrain, closely associated with the first, can be sought in the important role of the cities and the urban cultural patterns emanating from them. A precocious bourgeois culture took form, one that did not stop at the gates of the numerous cities. For this the contacts between city and country were too intensive, the similarity in juridical position and social relations too great. City and country did not form opposite and conflicting spheres, a fact easing the passage of urban patterns of life and culture to the countryside. The city gates did not give access to another world, a point demonstrated not only by the personal judicial freedom, economic freedom, and market-orientation of rural society discussed earlier but also by the early presence in rural communities of schools and a wide variety of service occupations (see Chapter 11, section 11.1) that elsewhere tended to remain confined to urban locations.

The prominence assumed already in the late Middle Ages by cities and urban cultural patterns received a powerful reinforcement during the struggle for independence in the last quarter of the sixteenth century. We have noted already how the growth of cities accelerated after 1580. Highly significant for our argument here is the simultaneous ascent of their political power. In Holland and Zeeland, the cities achieved unchallenged supremacy in the political decision-making structure, and together with their enhanced influence in the other provinces, the cities of the Republic became not only *a* major factor in the social and political regime – they became *the* dominant center of political power, a fact that could not fail to have important consequences for the character of the entire society. It resulted in a transformation of political representation in the provincial states from one where before the Revolt the cities had to share power with the nobles and (usually) the clergy, to a situation in which the Revolt had removed the clergy from formal political power and the nobles (many of whom remained loyal to Crown and Church) had lost much of their influence. The States of Holland, for example, consisted before the Revolt of seven representatives, one for each of the six large cities (Dordrecht, Haarlem, Delft, Leiden, Amsterdam, and Gouda) and one for the college of nobles, which was regarded as the representative of the countryside and the small cities. During the Revolt the small cities managed to secure for themselves direct representation in the provincial States, a step that inflated the number of urban votes to eighteen, while it limited the lone noble voice to the representation of rural society. Further examples of provincial voting arrangements are provided in Chapter 11; here it is sufficient to observe that in all provinces except Friesland, the cities managed to secure for themselves about half or more of all political representation.

The strong urban representation in the outer provinces combined with the urban preponderance in Holland and Zeeland to impart to the cities of the Republic a position of dominance – a dominance that allowed the burger populations to stamp the cultural patterns of the Republic as a whole with their urban values and way of life. To be sure, the political structure favored by this urban ascendancy was patrician and oligarchic, but this did not prevent the establishment of a large measure of freedom in economic activity. The central government of this union had little authority over domestic economic life, and the cities that dominated the provinces tended to favor freedom in the economic sphere as long as this did not threaten to disturb the social order. In these arrangements the countryside was generally treated as something between a hinterland for the city and a direct extension of the urban economy, but the opportunities for independent economic activity were rarely limited. With the exception of the relationship of the city of Groningen to its countryside, nowhere did these relationships approach that of an exploited, subordinated rural economy beholden to a monopolistic city – this despite the earnest desire of many cities to tie their hinterlands to them. The countryside generally possessed sufficient legal rights and a loud enough political voice to resist such efforts.

5.2. Was this a Calvinist economy?

A second question that deserves our attention concerns the role of Calvinism in the development of the Dutch economy. Ever since 1904–5, when Max Weber formulated his thesis linking a "Protestant Ethic" to a new "Spirit of Capitalism," the influence of Reformed teachings on economic life has attracted the unending attention of scholars. This fascination stems in part from Weber's rich and nuanced discussion, which has lent itself to many reformulations. It has also led to a lack of clarity about the Protestant Ethic itself. Surely, Weber's chief interest was in Protestantism's new conception of the secular life. This was to be, in the words of Kemper Fullerton, "a life of strict discipline (an idea borrowed from Catholic monasticism) lived in the secular sphere (an idea borrowed from Luther) with the sole intent of glorifying God and with the blessed sense of assurance of election as its reward (the special contribution of Calvinism)."[2] All this gave rise to a rationalized theory of life, a dedication to one's secular calling, and an ascetic discipline which together, in Weber's view, infused secular life with the moral energy that could convert ordinary commerce (with its connotation of baseness) into modern capitalism (dynamic and liberated from its corrupted origins).

Some Marxists have stood the thesis on its head, arguing that it was the spread of capitalism that made Calvinism appealing, not the other way around. More recently, Simon Schama's interpretation of seventeenth-century Dutch culture turned the thesis on its side, so to speak, by shifting the focus from the believer as capitalist accumulator to the believer as anguished consumer. He argued that economic success did not function as much to reassure the anxious believer of his election (as Weber had argued) as it "acted on contemporary consciences as a moral agitator" generating anxieties about the corrupting consequences of accumulated riches. To him the terrible dilemma facing the Dutch Calvinist was that "without [wealth] the Republic would collapse; with it, the Dutch could fall prey to false gods, Mammon and Baal, and engineer their own downfall."[3]

If we return to the Weber thesis in its original form, it is a curious fact that even though Dutch society is invoked often enough as an obvious confirmation of the thesis, very few scholars have actually applied it specifically to the situation in the Republic – and the few detailed investigations that exist express serious doubts. One such study, by P. J. Meertens, examined the published views of Calvinist theologians up to 1650 concerning the Work Ethic. These later Calvinist writings seemed to be the appropriate place to search since Weber had argued that it was Calvin's followers, not the great reformer himself, who stressed the importance of worldly asceticism and success in one's secular calling as a reassuring sign of election. Unfortunately, precious little evidence could be found to suggest that Dutch theologians developed Calvin's teachings in this way. A later study by J. C. Riemersma concentrated on the positions taken by Calvinist authors on ethical questions concerning economic behavior and policy. It concluded that these authors were always mindful to distinguish sharply between spiritual and profane concerns. In such questions as overseas expansion, missionary activities, monetary policy, the toleration of monopolies, lending and usury, the clerical

---

[2] Kemper Fullerton, "Calvinism and Capitalism. An Explanation of the Weber Thesis," in Robert W. Green, ed., *Protestantism, Capitalism, and Social Science: The Weber Thesis Controversy* (Lexington, MA, 1973), p. 23.

[3] Simon Schama, *The Embarrassment of Riches* (New York, 1987), p. 124.

writers sought to avoid crossing an invisible line that would land them in the sphere of the secular authority.

The Reformed Church's caution in this regard sometimes led to policies that give the appearance of a double standard. Consider the classic issue of usury as it applied to consumer loans and pawnbroking. The Church did not object to the establishment of municipal lending banks and lombards (as long as their profits were put to a charitable use), but it upheld a traditional condemnation of *private* lending of this type. Such lenders acted unrighteously and could not be admitted to the communion table, yet the Church stopped short of insisting that consumer lending at interest be made illegal. It was prepared to tolerate a matter that the secular authority saw fit to allow, presumably for reasons of state. Indeed, reasons of state led the Church to tolerate quite a number of morally dubious activities that seemed necessary in the Republic's long war against Catholic Spain.

In view of the Reformed Church's generally passive posture with respect to questions of economic practice and policy, this seems an unpromising area in which to search for the origins of a capitalist spirit in the Netherlands. Weber, to be sure, sought insights about the capitalist spirit in Calvinism's theology, not in its social politics. Yet we cannot ignore the fact that the region's medieval legacy – a monetized, market economy with substantial individual autonomy – offered real advantages to the spread of both capitalism and Calvinism.

It makes more sense to argue that the spread of Calvinism drew advantages from the already existing social structure of the Netherlands than to maintain that a capitalist society emerged from the ascetic discipline of Calvinism. Indeed, this latter causal argument hardly seems plausible in view of the still highly incomplete spread of Calvinism in the very period of the new Republic's most explosive economic growth and institutional development. The key city of Amsterdam remained under the control of committed Catholics until 1578, when it was the last major city to join the side of the Prince of Orange and Calvinism (see Chapter 9). Until then, the controlling faction continued to see the struggle to leave the Habsburg world-empire as a particularly risky gamble. Thereafter, committed Calvinists returned from exile to assume political leadership in Amsterdam, and five years later, measures to restrict Catholic worship and exclude Catholics from public office came into effect. But even then Catholics remained numerous, and many who embraced the Reformed faith, especially among the urban elites, had both principled and practical reasons to resist a rigorous suppression of other forms of religious belief.

For its part the Reformed Church aspired to monopolize religious life just as had the Catholic Church before it. But this goal would remain ever elusive. It remained out of reach in part because of a second goal of the Calvinists – to establish high confessional standards for all those wishing to be communicant members. By placing heavy demands on those seeking to partake of the Lord's Supper, the Calvinists effectively denied themselves the possibility of becoming a broad spiritual home for all Christians. Moreover, this demanding policy set many urban magistrates in opposition to the Reformed Church. Their practical interest in securing for their towns a commercially beneficial social peace caused them to insist upon a measure of religious toleration and subordination of the religious to the secular authority.

Besides this practical interest, the urban elites had principled motives to resist the monopoly claims of the Reformed Church. It is, of course, not difficult to identify fervent Calvinists among the merchants and town regents of the early Republic. But they may well have been outnumbered in the upper reaches of urban society by persons whose religious convictions were infused by the moderate Christian humanism advocated by Erasmus. This, in any event, is the view of the Netherlands' foremost cultural historian, Johan Huizinga, who argued in his famous essay "Dutch Civilization in the Seventeenth Century": "Despite all its touches of Protestant orthodoxy, the basis of Dutch life continued to be set by Erasmus rather than by the Genevan reformer."[4] It is an irony of Dutch historiography that the influence of Calvinism is minimized in the seventeenth century, an age of rigorous confessionalization throughout Europe, while its influence is invoked incessantly in interpretations of the twentieth century, an age of secularization. Thus, Huizinga had no difficulty in seeing the Republic's economic and political flowering as a direct consequence of her medieval heritage, while the sudden emergence of its unique Golden Age culture he linked directly to "a specifically northern form" of humanism.

Must we conclude then that the Reformation was of no special importance to the economic history of the Netherlands? Huizinga's great authority notwithstanding, we regard such a position to be untenable. To begin with, we cannot sidestep the hard historical fact that an independent Republic could never have been secured without the Reformation. In the absence of the religious struggle of the Calvinists, the political struggle against Habsburg Spain would have sputtered to an ignominious end. Moreover, without the Reformation political relationships would not have shifted so strongly in favor of the cities. And this shift in political constitution undergirded a state in which dynastic goals would ordinarily be subordinated to those of an urban regental elite, which never lost entirely its sensitivity to economic interests. In this regard the contrast between the cautious foreign policy of Johan de Witt and the dynastically motivated initiatives of stadhouders Willem II and Willem III speak volumes. The fact that the Republic's sovereignty came to be lodged effectively in the regent class was a direct result of the Revolt and, therefore, an indirect result of the Calvinist struggle against Habsburg oppression.

But Calvinism's influence certainly was not limited to the Republic's political point of origin. It extended to the manner in which even the humanists among the urban elite understood themselves and their social legitimacy. The Genevan reformer had no special message for economic policy makers, but he and his

---

[4] Johan Huizinga, *Dutch Civilization in the Seventeenth Century* (London, 1968), p. 53.

followers did present a new conception of the secular life, one whose appeal and influence extended well beyond the often tightly drawn circle of the devout. At its core is the joint injunction to serve God through one's calling and to avoid the destructive temptations of the secular life through an ascetic discipline. This bold conception certainly was not intended to advance a specific form of economic behavior, but it furnished the merchant, the artisan, and, indeed, all commercial people a basis upon which to claim a legitimate place in the Christian polity – not through the conspicuous performance of pious acts, nor through dramatic renunciations of one's wealth, but precisely through the diligent exercise of one's secular calling.

Early in the Republic's history, it became apparent that the ideal of the *corpus christianum* – the unity of the secular and spiritual life – could never be achieved, not in the state, nor the province, nor even in a city. The ideologies and symbols developed to fill the void in this unstable situation were not strictly religious but relied heavily on the Reformed vision of society. In this way Calvinism undergirded the legitimacy of the Republic. Without the inner-psychological and outer-political "fixing agent" of Calvinism, the claims of merchants to govern in a Republic would have been difficult to justify – to themselves as much as to others.

The influence of Calvinism in rationalizing personal life remains a matter of debate, for however plausible the theoretical argument might be, the direct evidence remains scarce and contradictory and will probably always remain so. Its influence in rationalizing public life is rather more apparent. The Reformation transferred control of clerical property (primarily monastic possessions) to the cities and provinces. Some long remained in public ownership, the income dedicated to educational, charitable, and religious purposes. But much appears (for systematic studies remain scarce) to have been sold in the late sixteenth century to raise funds for hard-pressed governments. In addition, the disorder of local life brought about by the Revolt caused the extinction or modification of some property rights. The result of all this turmoil was especially great in the old bishops' see of Utrecht where before the Reformation some 31 percent of all land within the city walls had been in the hands of churches, monasteries, brotherhoods, immunities, and the like. The Reformation transferred most of it to the city and to secular owners, thereby setting in motion a rigorous restructuring of urban land use. The newly "liberated" properties absorbed a substantial growth of population, permitting Utrecht to avoid investment in a costly extension of the city walls, and several evacuated monastic structures proved highly attractive as industrial sites for space-intensive enterprise. As we see in Chapter 8, the recycling of old religious structures played a prominent role in the industrial development policies of several Dutch cities.

Not only did the Reformation invest *physical capital* with a higher market value, it also acted to increase the investment in *human capital*. Calvinism's interest in education does not mark the beginning of public investment in general education;

this is apparent from the fact that in Amsterdam in 1583 (just five years after the city's abandonment of Catholicism and the Habsburg dynasty), 55 percent of bridegrooms and 38 percent of brides could sign their marriage certificates. Such high literacy rates could only have existed if schooling had been valued already before the Reformation. And this is precisely what the Italian observer Ludovico Guicciardini found so remarkable in his *Descrittione de Tutti i Paesi-Bassi* of 1567.

The Reformed Church saw education as an integral part of its project of confessionalization and took up with great energy the extension of elementary education to every nook and cranny of the country. The first synod of Dordt, in 1574, urged the establishment of schools in every village, and later conclaves addressed the need to provide free access to the schools for the children of paupers. The task was taken up most systematically in the remote territory of Drenthe, where an ordinance of 1630 directed the provincial treasury to pay school tuition for every child from the age of seven until he or she had learned to read and write. This policy seems to have had the desired effect, for around 1800 this most rural of Dutch provinces had the highest literacy rates in the nation, as measured by the ability of men and women to sign their marriage certificates: 86 percent of grooms and 75 percent of brides.

As for the Republic as a whole, its basic educational level stood high by international standards, when comparisons can first be made toward the end of the eighteenth century. Then about 75 percent of all grooms and 60 percent of brides could sign their names, a literacy level that will not have been much lower a century earlier. In the 1670s some 70 percent of Amsterdam grooms signed their marriage certificates, and since the men marrying in Amsterdam came from all over the Republic – and all over northern Europe – their literacy levels illustrate conditions in many other places. In some twelve Dutch cities, migrants to Amsterdam were sufficiently numerous to track literacy in those places on the basis of their ability to sign their names in the Amsterdam marriage rolls. In this way we find that the literacy level attained by Brussels by 1845 (55 percent of grooms able to sign) had existed in eleven of the twelve Dutch cities already before 1600. As for the brides, the Brussels level of 1845 (45 percent able to sign) had been attained before 1700 in three northern towns (Zwolle, Deventer, and The Hague), before 1750 in three more (Haarlem, Leiden, and Dordrecht), and before 1775 in another five (Delft, Rotterdam, Arnhem, Nijmegen, and Leeuwarden).

The interest of the Reformed Church did not limit itself to elementary education; over 70 Latin schools and Gymnasia offering secondary education also benefited from its intervention. These enrolled only boys. In this the Republic was not unique, of course, but what did distinguish it was the large enrollment: In the seventeenth century, between 100 and 150 of every 1,000 boys beyond age ten attended such a school, at least for a while.

Higher education also attracted the attention of the Reformed Church, given its need to train its clergy. No fewer than five universities were established in the Republic (where none had existed before the Revolt): Leiden (founded in 1575),

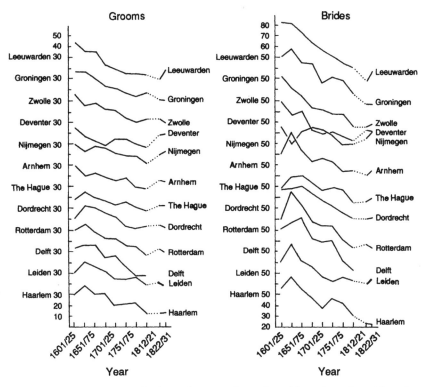

Figure 5.1. Illiteracy among brides and grooms in twelve cities, 1601–1831. After 1800, based on local records; before 1800, based on migrants from these cities who married in Amsterdam. [*Source:* A. M. van der Woude, "De alfabetisering," *Algemene Geschiedenis der Nederlanden 7* (Haarlem, 1980), 257–64.]

Franeker (1585), Groningen (1612), Utrecht (1636), and Harderwijk (1648). In addition, no fewer than seven *Illustere* schools (university-level institutions without degree-granting rights) were founded in this time. By the late seventeenth century, no other country of Europe could claim such a density of institutions of higher education. Not all of these institutions flourished, but together they educated a large number of students. The incomplete figures suggest that about 25 of every 1,000 young men who attained age eighteen attended university in the seventeenth century. In the eighteenth century, this level fell by half. By modern standards even the Golden Age participation rates appear anemic, but they sufficed then to place the Republic's dedication to education at the highest level in Europe. In fact, these rates were not exceeded again until after World War I.

The Reformed Church infused the Republic with an unusual commitment to human capital formation, and its benefits spilled over far beyond the confines of theology and biblical knowledge. It benefited tangibly and directly any number of seaborne occupations (to mention but one important category), where the need to keep records, make toll and tariff declarations, provision ships, and act independently on behalf of distant shipowners effectively disqualified the illiterate from any position of responsibility.

Whether the Republic possessed a "Calvinist economy" in the sense proposed by Max Weber may be doubted – not so much because it exhibited none of the characteristics whose origins Weber sought to uncover, but because those characteristics did not follow *uniquely* from a belief in Reformed theology. What cannot be doubted is the important impress left by Calvinism on the structure of the state, the cultural claims of urban elites, the productive use of real property, and the dedication to education. The Reformation removed from its hinges the door leading to a rationalized, commercial society. But, in truth, that door was already open.

5.3. Did the Dutch Republic form a single economy?

5.3.1. "NATIONAL" ECONOMIES IN EARLY MODERN EUROPE

In this survey of structural characteristics, we have called attention to many ways in which the Northern Netherlands differed from the rest of Europe. But just as often, we have emphasized the pronounced regional differences *within* the territory that would form the United Republic. In view of these differences, can we treat the Republic as constituting a single integrated economy?

A major theme of European history in the early modern period is the emergence of national economies – economies given coherence and direction by the power of territorial states. From this perspective the experience of the Northern Netherlands is deviant to the point of being puzzling. Its undeniably influential economy functioned in a physical "body" of modest size, while its central organs of state, long capable of functioning as a great power abroad, were neither centralizing nor expansionist at home.

Traditionally, economies are defined by the boundaries of national states, and on that basis the Dutch economy was certainly not large. But, in fact, few large nation-states before the nineteenth century really succeeded in fashioning integrated economies. France, for example, was carved up by formidable tariff barriers right up to its Revolution; and quite apart from these formal subdivisions, the large territory of the French state faced in too many different directions to share a single economic fate. The economic lives of its Atlantic coast, the Mediterranean region, Alsace, and the vast, agrarian center, all marched to the beat of different drummers. Before the transportation and communications revolutions of the mid–nineteenth century, the effective maximum size of an integrated economy fell substantially short of the size of the largest political units. When this is kept in mind, a seventeenth- and eighteenth-century Dutch economy of some 2 million inhabitants was hardly Lilliputian. It was clearly of a wholly different order of magnitude than the Mediterranean and Hanseatic city states with which some seek to compare it.

If the Dutch Republic formed one economy, it would not be too small. But did it, in fact, achieve a sufficient internal coherence and integration to be analyzed as a national economy? We have already seen that the Habsburg provinces of the sixteenth century maintained a substantial political autonomy. Such interprovincial economic integration as existed derived from the enormous market power of Antwerp, which attracted Holland, Zeeland, and Flanders to its Brabantine core. The formation of the United Republic tore asunder that embryonic integration, throwing a formidable new barrier across Brabant and Flanders. At the same time, the new Republic ratified the "medieval" autonomy of the seven member provinces insofar as it affirmed their success in preserving a sovereignty that the "modernizing" policies of Philip II had threatened. Not only did the new Republic's provinces claim sovereign powers, but within the provinces the politically empowered cities – some fifty-seven all told – cultivated their autonomy and exerted important, often dominant, influence in the provincial political structures.

In this decentralized system, the scope for a national economic policy always remained severely restricted. The States General, just like the central government of the Habsburgs before it, never succeeded in levying taxes directly on the entire population. As Chapter 4 made clear, it depended on provincial contributions, the quotas, just as the Habsburgs had depended on the *beden*. The Generality did exercise more far-reaching controls over the lands won from Habsburg control after the foundation of the Republic. It governed these "Generality lands" as conquered territories, taxing them directly for as long as the Republic existed.

The separate status of the Generality lands only previews the distinct and independent policies that each of the seven provinces of the United Republic aspired to follow. The Union of Utrecht (which functioned, by default, as the Republic's constitution) contained an article forbidding the provinces from discriminating against each other in economic matters, but this soon was ignored universally. The provinces habitually taxed "foreign" goods differently from home-produced goods, and restricted the export of some commodities to other provinces. In this they only followed the historical practices of the cities. Throughout the life of the Republic, the cities levied their own excise taxes and tolls and sought, through a combination of their own authority and influence on higher levels of government, to subordinate their hinterlands to the benefit of town employment and tax revenue, and to the detriment of rival towns.

Several cities claimed staple privileges. For example, Brielle and Naarden required local farmers to bring commodities to their city markets and nowhere else. The city of Groningen managed to extinguish the market privileges of all potential rivals in its province, thereby exerting a market monopoly over a large territory. Other towns claimed staple rights on trade, requiring commodities being transported past the city to be landed there and offered for sale. Venlo claimed this right on the river Maas into the sixteenth century. Dordrecht, the most important staple market, claimed this right on all trade on the rivers Waal and Maas and on the channels connecting Holland with the south.

Toll privileges formed another dimension of urban economic power. The cities of Gouda and Haarlem sought to secure their municipal well-being by insisting that commerce destined to certain points could not use routes that bypassed their established tolls. They used every means at their disposal to prohibit the construction of new waterways having that effect, and if they failed in this, they acted to prohibit the use of such waterways by large freight-carrying vessels. Alkmaar, which could not invoke old legal privileges, did this differently: by withholding its cooperation from new polder drainage projects unless the developers agreed to arrange the placement of roads and canals on the new land so that they led to Alkmaar, and by obstructing waterways that bypassed the city.

The cities also dominated what we would call industrial policy. As Chapter 8 demonstrates, they sought to attract industries away from each other by offering advantages to entrepreneurs (such as the low-cost use of former monastic buildings), they protected their established industries by prohibiting the removal from their towns of strategic raw materials (such as wool from Leiden and Delft), they bought up the seigneurial rights of neighboring villages to limit rural competition in retail trade, and they solicited the support of higher levels of government in a long struggle to limit rural industrial production.

The economic power of the cities was considerable, but this, too, had its limits. The very particularism that motivated these numerous efforts of urban-monopoly creation tended also to undermine their long-run efficacy. The cities were many, and few of them enjoyed large natural hinterlands. In Holland and Friesland especially, rural dwellers often had access to more than one urban market, and everywhere merchants could be found to buy farm produce outside the official markets (forestalling). Competitive conditions placed limits on the self-serving character of both urban and provincial economic policy, but this did nothing to lend real unity to those policies.

One might conclude that the Republic was a flimsy political umbrella of a number of municipal and regional economies divided from each other by tolls, provincial trade restrictions, differing tax structures, independent mints (until 1694), and even independent tariff-enforcement policies (since this was in the hands of five separate Admiralties). There were, indeed, many contemporaries who saw things just this way. Political leaders in Holland, the most important of the provinces, frequently betrayed their view that the other provinces, the "outer provinces," were simply a buffer zone, a protective and ultimately expendable skirt around Holland. The dominant position of Holland is clear enough: It contained some 40 percent of the Republic's population, furnished the Generality with 57 percent of its revenue, supported 75 percent of the public debt, and supplied the navy with nearly all of its funds. This strategic position made Holland enormously influential, but it did not generally translate into a desire to extend

its formal control over more territory. While other European states pursued expansionary foreign policies, the Republic, especially when led by Holland's merchant oligarchy, pursued "contractionary" strategies. This inclination motivated
the dismissal of seventeenth-century opportunities to add territory in the Rhineland and the Spanish Netherlands and is displayed with classic clarity by the
Republic's provisions for military defense, which depended on a "water line," a
floodable zone protecting Holland, but none of the other provinces, from invasion.

At least one prominent seventeenth-century political thinker, the Leiden textile
magnate Pieter de la Court, pushed this Hollando-centric ideal to its logical conclusion: Holland should become a true island by cutting a permanent canal from
the Zuider Zee to the great rivers. At a cost of about 1.5 million guilders, Holland
could become a sort of Venice, with the other provinces taking on the role of
the "Terraferma."[5] Given Holland's ambivalent posture toward the extension of
its territorial authority – and, hence, of its commitments – the scope for pursuit
of autonomous policies by the other provinces long remained considerable. One
of them, Zeeland, even claimed its own portion of the Republic's colonial possessions (the South American plantations of Berbice and Essequebo), and Zeeland's chamber of the VOC threatened, as late as 1783, to leave the Dutch
company and join the English East India Company.

Political unity and centralization of policy making are not the only criteria for
economic unity. In preindustrial Europe the state, even where it was strong and
aspired to centralization, could not always achieve its goals. In this light an ironic
quality of the Republic is that economic integration was in several respects far-
reaching and intense *in practice* despite persistently decentralized economic policy
formation. When pressed, the cities proved themselves capable of acknowledging
a need for cooperation. This was especially the case in Holland, where an appreciation of the broader view may have emerged from the fact that so much of
Holland's sixteenth-century economic expansion occurred outside the six great
cities that held voting powers in the provincial States. Except for Amsterdam, all
of those cities suffered substantial economic setbacks while smaller cities, especially
the Zuider Zee and Maas towns, flourished. The very dispersion of economic
activity militated in favor of a territorial rather than simply a municipal approach
to the formation of policy. In the view of Jonathan Israel, "this tempering of
civic particularism with a much greater measure of provincial collaboration than
pertained in any of the South Netherlands provinces was to prove an abiding
pillar of strength to the future Dutch world entrepôt."[6]

Civic particularism could also be tempered by the enlightened self-interest

---

[5] M. van der Bijl, "Pieter de la Court en de politieke werkelijkheid," in H. W. Blom and I. W.
Wildenberg, *Pieter de la Court in zijn tijd. Aspecten van een veelzijdig publicist (1618–1685)* (Amsterdam,
1986), pp. 86–8.
[6] J. I. Israel, *Dutch Primacy in World Trade, 1585–1740* (Oxford, 1989), p. 24.

expressed most fully in Peter de la Court's 't Welvaren der stad Leiden [Prosperity of the city of Leiden] (1659), where he proposed that the ideal of a "closed" city, whose economy was protected by a vast chain of regulations and prohibitions, should be replaced by the ideal of an "open" city, whose economy could flourish thanks to minimal regulation, low taxes, the abolition of monopolistic guilds, and the free entry of newcomers.[7] The open city, he argued, could secure the wealth and political power of the regents better than could the restrictive measures to which they habitually turned.

It cannot be said that de la Court's open-city ideal was everywhere embraced. The economic and fiscal crises that emerged soon after he wrote encouraged no small number of short-sighted measures designed to protect local interests. But the municipal economies remained sufficiently open to reach a high level of integration. Commodity prices set at the internationally important Amsterdam market were quickly transmitted to the other cities and provincial centers. The low cost of waterborne transportation contributed to this, of course, but so did the pronounced specialization of regional economies, which ensured continual flows of goods among the various markets.

In most of Europe, one could speak in this period only of "crisis market integration." That is, the relatively autonomous subregions went their own way except when harvests failed and prices shot upward. Such an event activated the intermarket transport links and secured a measure of uniformity in prices among regions, but it did so sporadically and then only for short periods.

In contrast, the market system of the Republic showed consistently high correlations in price fluctuations. For example, in the first half of the seventeenth century, Amsterdam and Utrecht rye prices exhibited a coefficient of correlation of 0.953 (1.0 would signify exact correspondence in the fluctuations of prices in two places), while the correlation of Amsterdam's prices with those of the more distant Arnhem stood at 0.866. Similarly high coefficients are observable among provincial centers in the eastern provinces (such as Arnhem-Deventer) as well as between two widely separated provincial markets that had little direct trade with each other (Arnhem-Dordrecht).[8]

The correlations become a bit weaker at or near the eastern borders of the Republic, for there one begins to perceive the influence of independent agricultural regions. On the Rhine connecting the Republic and Germany, and on the Maas between the Republic and Liège, small flows of grain moving upstream alternated with small flows moving in the opposite direction. Substantial tolls, tariffs, and not infrequent military interruptions frustrated trade on these routes;

---

[7] M. Prak, "Sociale geschiedschriving van Nederlands Ancien Régime," Tijdschrift voor sociale geschiedenis 14 (1988), p. 154.
[8] B. H. Slicher van Bath, Een samenleving onder spanning (Assen, 1957), p. 592; C. Baars, De geschiedenis van de landbouw in de Beijerlanden (Wageningen, 1973), p. 184.

but even so, the correlation between rye prices in Amsterdam and Liège in the period 1620–1749 was a respectable 0.790.

Further testimony to economic coherence is the fact that integrated markets existed not only for commodities but also for the factors of production. The circulation of capital through interprovincial investment and public lending should not surprise us, for that is readily achieved in an urbanized society. Indeed, capital circulated beyond the borders of the Republic as easily as within them. More impressive were the legal institutions that reduced to routine the alienation and transfer of real property and the physical and social mobility that helped to achieve integrated labor markets. More is said about the labor markets in Chapter 12. There we see that a substantial wage gap always distinguished the inland provinces from the alluvial zone, with its persistently higher productivity of agricultural labor. But *within* the alluvial zone, wage levels by the early seventeenth century hardly differed among cities (i.e., Amsterdam's wages were comparable to those of, say, Medemblik or Middelburg), nor did they differ much between urban and rural locations.

From the perspective of policy, the economic life of the northern Netherlands appears fragmented: The relevant units are smaller than the Republic as a whole. But from the perspective of market integration – as reflected in prices, flows of labor, capital, raw materials, and information – the Dutch economy seems quite tangibly integrated. When Pieter de la Court first proposed that Holland be turned into an island, the Grand Pensionary of Holland, Johan de Witt, who was closely associated with de la Court's writings, had the impolitic suggestion suppressed from the published version of *Interest van Holland.* (It re-emerged in a later edition.) De Witt argued quite differently that the many provinces and cities of the Republic formed a durable unity despite the absence of strong central political leadership. De Witt, of course, advocated being rid of the only unifying political leadership that the Republic possessed, the stadhoudership of the House of Orange. The Republic's unity, he argued, was based on something else, on the fact that "through commonalities, association, and consultation in commercial and other matters, [through] discussion, the reciprocal possession of property, customs, and other things, they [the provinces] are so fastened to and interwoven with each other that it is almost impossible, except by great violence, to tear them apart."[9]

One of the ties that bound all of these regions together was the commonality of outlook – particular differences notwithstanding – of the urban patriciates that

---

[9] "[door] gemeenschappen, compagnieën, cofreriën, zo van commercie als van andere interessen conversatiën reciproque possessiën van goederen, gewoonten ende anderzints zodanig aan de anderen gehecht, ja door malkanderen geknoopt ende gevlochten [zijn] dat het bijnaar onmogelijk is dezelve buiten excessieve violentie van den anderen te scheuren." Quoted in P. Geyl, *Kernproblemen van onze geschiedenis* (Utrecht, 1937), p. 11.

dominated the political life of the dozens of cities and that of most provinces. Another more active unifying force was the enormous influence exerted by Holland and its cities over the rest of the Republic. The core of the Dutch economy was not so much a single city as it was the larger urbanized region of the maritime zone. The commercial and industrial functions and the agricultural specialization of this "heartland" quickly assumed such a scope that the economic life of the other regions came to be oriented more and more to this polycentric core.

But it was not only the outer regions of the Republic that became so oriented. This brings us to the final difficulty in deciding how to evaluate the character of the Dutch economy. That which was administratively and politically fragmented possessed an informal unity based on economic relations. But in many cases, those strong ties extended far beyond the borders of the Republic. The high correlation of grain prices between regional markets extended to the grain ports of the Baltic Sea. The correlation of Danzig rye prices with those of Amsterdam, which had been only 0.686 in the period 1551–1600 (an era full of war-related disruptions), rose to 0.881 in the period 1601–50 and to 0.917 in the following fifty-year period.[10] Similarly, the urban labor markets of Holland attracted workers not only from the outer provinces but from Westphalia (for servants and seasonal laborers), from the North Sea coast as far as Norway (for maritime employment), and from Flanders and Liège (for textile workers). Holland's intensive livestock husbandry imported cattle for fattening and dairy production not only from the outer provinces but also from northern Germany and Denmark.

In following these ties of interdependence, we are frequently led beyond the borders of the Republic, and we have not yet touched upon the international entrepôt functions of Amsterdam or the colonial activities of the East and West India Companies. Clearly, the Dutch economy became much larger than its land area and native population could support. But if this is so, where does one draw the line between the Dutch economy and the European, indeed, the world economy? At least one historian, Robert Brenner, denied that such a line could be drawn: "Dutch production hardly constituted an economy in its own right; it grew up as an integral part of the overall European economy and naturally shared its fate."[11] This is a convenient position for those wishing to dismiss an inconvenient historical phenomenon (and emphasize the achievements of England). But it does justice neither to the history of the Netherlands nor of the Europe in which it was so firmly implanted.

The problem before us is clear. The Dutch Republic exhibited often striking regional differences and held fast to a decentralized political structure at the same time that it performed economic functions on an international stage. In describing and analyzing these phenomena, we cannot fall back on the conventional but

---

[10] W. Achilles, "Getreidepreise und Getreidehandelsbeziehungen europäischner Räume im 16. und 17. Jahrhundert," *Zeitschrift für Agrargeschichte und Agrarsoziologie 7* (1959), 32–55.
[11] Robert Brenner, "The Agrarian Roots of European Capitalism," *Past and Present 97* (1982), 112.

anachronistic concept of the "national" economy as defined by tariff walls and the taxing policies of the state. But we *can* appeal to the tightly interwoven economic relations emphasized by Johan de Witt. His statement was self-serving but not wrong. The farmers, traders, and industrial producers of the Northern Netherlands could marshal resources on a scale sufficient to create an economy whose innovations exerted influence on, and attracted people, capital, and goods from, distant places. Markets, more than politics or culture, articulated the common space of the Dutch people. The international leadership of this economy was neither an accident of geography nor of history. We argue here that it should be approached in the context of interaction between the often unique structures described in this section and the international opportunities to which it came to be so directly exposed.

5.3.2. INTERNAL TRADE AND DISTRIBUTION

It is an irony of the history of a nation whose economy was defined more by the reality of its market integration than by policy, ideology, or coercion, that the internal trade of the Republic has been little studied. It is as though the misguided views of the eighteenth-century political arithmeticians, who believed industry and commerce for domestic use added no value to the economy (see Chapter 13), continue to live in the minds of modern historians. In fact, the chief avenue of productivity growth in the preindustrial era (and still an important one today) followed Adam Smith's famous maxim: "The division of labor is limited by the extent of the market." Regional specialization and urbanization enabled the Northern Netherlands to push the productivity of existing technologies to the outer limits of their potential, and this "Smithian growth" depended in its turn on the efficient distribution of goods, people, capital, and information.

In Chapter 2 we called attention to the fragmented character of Dutch economic life in the fifteenth century: a multitude of mostly small cities competing for shares of the interregional trade that flowed through the rivers, inlets, and channels of the region. Three major routes competed for north–south traffic to and from Brabant and Flanders (see Map 2.2), and any number of towns and even large villages maintained an independent trade with foreign markets. By 1500 it was clear that one city in the Zuider Zee region, Amsterdam, had achieved a dominance in the Baltic trade sufficient to force the subordination of its erstwhile rivals, such as Kampen and Hoorn. In the Maas delta, Dordrecht enjoyed preeminence based on its staple privileges and its hold on the river traffic, while among the Zeeland ports serving the great trade of Antwerp, Middelburg had emerged as the dominant center.

This sorting-out process placed new demands on internal trade. The growth of a commercial center depended on the reduction of transactions costs, and in the sixteenth century, this required the replacement of thin, irregular markets with a commercial system that secured predictable concentrations of supply and a regular flow of buyers at the major centers. An important innovation to secure this new commercial system was the *beurtveer*, a regulated transportation service between two points. Amsterdam and Hoorn were the first cities to establish a *beurtveer*, in 1529. The cities licensed skippers who were committed to depart on a regular schedule, from a set place to a set destination, and to provide their services at tariffs established by the cities. The skipper on duty stood waiting to receive freight, parcels, and passengers until departure time and was required to depart whether his vessel was fully loaded or not. The fixed rotation (*beurt*) among the skippers was the key to the system's viability and gave it its name.

This municipally sanctioned "common carrier" service spread gradually after 1529. At first only the most active ports and industrial cities possessed the volume of trade to warrant these services. By 1589 Amsterdam and Rotterdam agreed to operate fast rowing vessels over a direct route to enable merchants to transfer goods between these ports, the one oriented to the Baltic, the other to England and France. As noted in Chapter 2, this service, by challenging the monopoly rights of Gouda, encountered stiff opposition, but in the decades that followed, *beurtveer* services spread quickly. By the mid–seventeenth century, a complex web of scheduled services knit together nearly every town that could be reached by water – and wagon services reached many of those that could not. In the eighteenth century, Amsterdam saw 800 *beurtveer* vessels depart each week for 121 specified destinations. Haarlem and Leiden each maintained regularly scheduled services with 26 separate destinations; Breda, in 1721, sent out 16 scheduled vessels per week to 11 destinations, mostly in Zeeland and Holland. Its ten teamsters set out on regular rotations for destinations in Limburg, Liège, and Brabant. One could go on in this vein, but Maps 5.1 and 5.2 make the essential point: The Republic came to be blanketed by a complex structure of bilateral transportation routes connecting small places to regional centers, and regional centers (such as those shown on Map 5.2) to major cities (Map 5.1), offering a predictable, regulated service for the domestic distribution of goods.

This common-carrier transport system offered regular and dependable service to nearly every city and most large villages in the Republic, but it did not suit all the transportation needs of the economy. High-volume shippers and those moving bulk cargoes bypassed the high costs of the *beurtveer* by chartering private vessels. Shipments using less than the full capacity of a vessel were required to make use of the *beurtveer*, but larger shipments (such as peat, agricultural products, lumber, stone, and sand) made use of vessels sailing "outside the *beurt*" – outside the rotation system. The skippers' guilds usually handled both the scheduled and the unscheduled demand for transport service, but in the larger places, these guilds split into large and small guilds – the larger vessels performing the *beurtveer* services, the smaller the private service. Major distribution centers such as Gouda and Dordrecht had guilds of 200 to 400 members, while regional centers such as Gorinchem and Meppel supported 80 to 150.

The latter town, Meppel, offers a good example of the importance of peat in

Map 5.1. Scheduled *beurtveer* services from Amsterdam, 1700. [*Source:* Clé Lesger, "Intra-regional Trade," *Economic and Social History in the Netherlands 4* (1993), p. 200.]

the Republic's transportation system. Meppel's function as a market town for the agricultural villages of Drenthe supported scheduled *beurtveren* with Amsterdam and the chief cities of nearby Overijssel. In the eighteenth century, other destinations in Holland were added. But this occupied only a fraction of the town's

Map 5.2. Scheduled *beurtveer* services from six regional centers: Middelburg, Dordrecht, Utrecht, Nijmegen, Sneek, and Groningen, 1700. [*Source:* Clé Lesger, "Intraregional Trade," *Economic and Social History in the Netherlands 4* (1993), p. 200.]

120 to 150 skippers, who supported themselves chiefly by moving peat from the region's bogs to Holland. Already in 1636 8,314 boat loads of peat arrived in Amsterdam (from all points of origin), and from 1645 to 1800, we know that 7,000 to 8,000 vessels left Meppel and ports of northwest Overijssel (Blokzijl,

Zwartesluis, Zwolle, and Kampen) each year to cross the Zuider Zee with food-stuffs, cattle, and hay, but principally with peat.[12]

The *beurtveer* services carried passengers and parcels besides freight, and on some routes this was the principal business. The Zwolle skippers' guild supported forty-two members, primarily by operating daily sailings to Amsterdam. Nearby Hasselt catered to the streams of migrant laborers tramping in from Westphalia; in season its guild operated day and night boats to Holland. The Zuider Zee formed a giant traffic interchange, with boats moving passengers and freight among all the ports of its littoral. The island-rich delta region was similarly endowed with *beurtveer* services linking the southern Holland towns to Zeeland, Brabant, and Flanders.

But the growing economy's need for regular communication pressed against the technological limits of sailing vessels, particularly when they operated on rivers and narrow channels. The vagaries of wind and tide limited the ability of these services to satisfy demands that intensified with the increased interaction of cities becoming part of a tightly organized urban system of specialized ports and industrial cities. Cities all over Holland advanced plans to build canals equipped with tow paths and establish regular passenger barge (*trekschuit*) services. These barges, pulled by horses, could achieve year-round regularity and dependability and offer a frequency and carrying capacity unmatched by sailing vessels. By 1632 the new *trekschuit* service was available to travelers between Amsterdam and Haarlem, offering hourly departures and a fixed trip duration of two hours and fifteen minutes. With the striking of the church bells, the barges departed, and the ordinances required the skipper to turn an hourglass designed to run out when the barge was due at its destination. In the following thirty-three years, the entire maritime zone was effectively covered with *trekschuit* services. The process of canal construction, always financed by the cities connected, was described in Chapter 2. Here our concern is the frequent, interconnected transportation service established on these canals. Tables 5.1 and 5.2 display the schedules for most routes in Holland as they existed through most of the late seventeenth century, while Table 5.3 displays the routes that spanned Friesland and Groningen. The only force capable of interrupting the clockwork regularity of this service was winter frost, when ice closed the canals. But even this was not taken with philosophic resignation: ice sleds on the frozen canals and wagons on the tow paths were then pressed into service.

At an average speed of seven kilometers per hour, the *trekschuit* cannot impress us today by its speed, but it struck contemporaries differently. Thus, Sir William Temple, the acutely observant English ambassador of the early 1670s, enthused that "by this easie way of travelling an industrious man loses no time from his

---

[12] E. Vroom, "Het Ensser-geld," *Verslagen en mededelingen, Vereniging tot Beoefening van Overijsselsch Regt en Geschiedenis 63* (1948), 168–81.

Table 5.1. *Passenger barge schedules in Holland, second half of seventeenth century.*

Route	Schedule times
Rotterdam	5.00 6.00 7.00 8.00 9.00 10.00 11.00 12.00 13.00 14.00 15.00 16.00 17.00 18.00 19.00 20.30
Delft	6.45 7.45 8.45 9.45 10.45 11.45 12.45 13.45 14.45 15.45 16.45 17.45 18.45 19.45 20.45 22.15
Maassluis	5.30 6.00 — 8.00 — — 11.30 — — 14.00 16.00 18.00
Delft	6.45 8.00 — 10.00 — — 13.30 — — 16.00 18.00 20.00
Delft	6.30 and every half hour to — 19.00
The Hague	7.45 and every half hour to — 20.15
Delft (also The Hague)	6.30 7.30 9.00 10.30 13.30 15.00 16.30 17.00 18.00 18.30 22.00 5.00
Leiden (also The Hague)	9.30 10.30 12.00 13.30 16.00 16.30 18.00 18.30 20.00 21.30 1.00 8.00
Leiden	13.00 13.00 21.00 5.00
Utrecht	21.00 21.00 5.00
Leiden	10.00 11.00 13.00 14.00 17.00 20.00 23.00 4.00 6.30 9.00
Haarlem	14.00 15.00 17.00 18.00 21.00 — 3.00 8.00 10.30 13.00
Haarlem	9.00 9.00
Alkmaar	14.00 13.00
Haarlem	15.00 16.00 17.00 18.00 20.00 *via Alphen* → 5.00 6.00 7.00 8.00 9.00 10.00 11.00 12.00 13.00 14.00
Amsterdam	17.15 18.15 19.15 20.15 21.15 22.15 6.00 7.15 8.15 9.15 10.15 11.15 12.15 13.15 14.15 15.15 16.15
Amsterdam	*Every hour a ferry*
Buiksloot	*Every hour a ferry*
Buiksloot	19.00 16.00 23.00 → 7.00 8.00 → 6.00 → 9.00 11.00 → 11.00 → 13.00 14.00 → 16.00 → 15.00 14.00 16.00 17.00 18.00
Monnikendam	21.00 18.15 → 9.00 7.00 8.00 9.00 9.00 11.00 13.30 15.00 16.30 17.00 19.00
Pumerend	→ → 8.30 → 10.30 → 18.30 → 20.00 20.30
Edam	5.00 8.00 10.00 10.00 12.00 16.00 18.00 20.00
Hoorn	5.00 8.00 10.00 11.00 12.00 14.00 16.00 18.00 19.00 21.00
Hoorn	5.00 8.00 13.00 16.00
Alkmaar	9.00 12.00 17.00 20.00
Hoorn	6.00 8.00 10.00 14.00 16.00 16.00 18.00
Enkhuizen (coach route)	8.00 12.00 16.00 18.00

Source: Jan de Vries, *Barges and Capitalism* (Utrecht, 1981), pp. 64–5.

Table 5.2. *Passenger barge and coach schedules via Gouda, second half of seventeenth century.*

Dordrecht	—	—	6.30 →	—	—	12.30 →	—	—	—	—
Rotterdam	6.00	8.00	—	10.00	12.00	—	15.00	16.00	17.00	18.00
Gouda (arr.)	8.00	10.00	11.00	12.00	14.00	14.00	17.00	18.00	19.00	20.00
Gouda (lv.)	9.00 →	11.00	11.00	13.00 →			20.00	21.00 →		
Leiden	16.00	16.00								
Utrecht[a]	17.00 →	19.00	21.00				4.00 →	4.00		
Amsterdam		19.00						—		

[a] Passengers traveling from Gouda to Utrecht boarded barges to Bodegraven, where connections were made with the barges from Leiden to Utrecht.

Source: J. de Vries, *Barges and Capitalism* (Utrecht), p. 66.

Table 5.3. *Passenger barge schedules in Friesland and Groningen, seventeenth and eighteenth centuries.*

Nieuwe Schans	—	—	6.00	—	10.00	—
Winschoten	—	—	9.00	—	13.00	—
Winschoten	—	5.00	10.00	—	14.00	2.00
Noordbroek	6.00	↓	↓	15.00	↓	↓
Groningen	10.30	12.30	17.30	19.30	21.30	9.30
Delfzijl	5.00	8.00	13.00	16.00	—	—
Groningen	11.00	12.00	17.00	20.00	—	—
Groningen	—	13.00	—	—	4.00	9.00
Dokkum	—	20.00	—	—	11.00	16.00
Dokkum	—	—	5.00	9.00	12.00	16.00
Leeuwarden	—	—	8.00	12.00	15.00	19.00
Leeuwarden	—	4.00	9.00	13.00	16.00	—
Sneek	—	7.00ᵃ	12.30	16.30	19.30	—
Leeuwarden	—	4.00	9.00	13.00	16.00	—
Bolsward	—	8.00	13.00	17.00	20.00	—
Bolsward	6.00	9.00	14.00	18.00	—	—
Workum	8.00ᵇ	11.00ᶜ	16.00	20.00	—	—
Leeuwarden	—	4.00	9.00	13.00	16.00	20.00
Harlingen	—	8.00	13.00	17.00	20.00	4.00ᵈ

ᵃSneek to Amsterdam, daily at 9.00.
ᵇWorkum to Amsterdam, daily at 9.00. In the 17th century, a second boat departed at 11.00.
ᶜWorkum to Enkhuizen, daily at 12.00.
ᵈHarlingen to Amsterdam, daily at 6.00.
The 20.00 departure is often mentioned in the 18th century. It was not in the official schedule, but the Harlingen skippers' guild (operator of the *beurtschip* to Amsterdam) subsidized the *trekschuit* skippers to ensure that this night barge service was provided.
Source: Jan de Vries, *Barges and Capitalism* (Utrecht, 1981), p. 66.

business, for he writes or eats, or sleeps while he goes; whereas the time of labouring or industrious men is the greatest native commodity of any country."[13]

One of the time-saving features of the *trekschuit* that particularly impressed Temple was the night barge, offered on several routes, where the ordinances required that "the benches [be] turned down and covered with straw for the comfort of the passengers."

[13] Sir William Temple, *Observations upon the United Provinces of the Netherlands* (London, 1673), p. 152.

In the 1660s nearly 300,000 *trekschuit* passengers traveled annually on the Amsterdam-Haarlem route, 140,000 glided between Haarlem and Leiden, and some 200,000 traveled between Leiden and the joint destinations of The Hague and Delft. Another 120,000 passengers per year traveled north from Amsterdam on the routes to Hoorn. The overall course of passenger travel on the entire system is charted in Figure 13.2. It reveals that the economic forces pressing for the establishment of this high-capacity system abated after the 1670s, whereafter the volume of intercity travel declined on almost every route. But the system continued to form the backbone of public transportation in the Netherlands' maritime zone until the coming of the railway. By the late eighteenth century, as road improvements and innovations in coach design permitted a considerable increase in the speed and comfort of land transportation, the Dutch passenger barges lost their allure. By any international comparison, the volume of travel remained very high, but the "industrious man" was no longer impressed. The English traveler James Mitchell put it this way around 1800: "This mode of travelling seems to afford a fair example of Dutch arrangements generally; it is economical of money, but expensive of time. . . . While a Dutchman travels three miles in an hour, an Englishman travels six or eight, and this is nearly the difference between the spirit and energy of the two nations."[14]

Road transport in the Republic always remained subordinate to the overlapping networks of *beurtveren* and *trekschuiten*. A few short paved roads connected cities where canals could not be dug, but where the need for good roads was greatest, in the canal-less, rural inland zones, most overland transport had to make do with meandering sand tracks and rutted dirt roads. To prevent the rutting from making the roads altogether impassable, the provinces agreed to a common axle width (the *Hollandse spoor* of 1.28 meters), but this was very nearly the only measure one can cite that addressed overland transport in the seventeenth century. One of its consequences was that the broad-gauged German freight wagons, especially the large *Hessenwagens* pulled by four to six horses, had to make use of alternative routes, called *Hessenwegen*, which wandered over the sandy heaths of the eastern provinces.

The one major project to build a paved road in the eighteenth century aimed to connect 's-Hertogenbosch with Liège. Begun in 1741, 's-Hertogenbosch managed to build south a distance of 25 kilometers before funding dried up. At the fall of the old Republic, the entire country had but 165 kilometers of paved road, and most of that was in the maritime region already well served by waterways. Beyond the maritime zone, travel remained costly, undependable, and subject to seasonal shutdowns well into the nineteenth century. By then even the Germans were unimpressed with Dutch road transport: "The stage coaches in the Dutch provinces are, as all wheeled vehicles in Holland, veritable *Rumpelkasten*. . . .

---

[14] Quoted in Benjamin Silliman, *Journal of Travels in England, Holland and Scotland*, 3 vols. (New Haven, 1820), II: 291, 293.

Coach construction in Holland seems to be at least 150 years behind the times. Country wagons are still covered with canvas or oilcloth, looking literally like the coaches one sees in the kermis paintings of Breugel and Teniers."[15]

The organization of domestic transportation featured a comprehensive system of common-carrier *beurtveren* serving nearly every place of importance by means of an integrated intercity *trekvaart* system, connecting thirty cities with frequent, scheduled passenger services, and a large supply of privately chartered vessels carrying bulk cargoes and large shipments. The supplementary road transport services offered advantages in neither capacity nor quality, and this reinforced the sharp contrast between the precocious mobility of the maritime zone and the typical rural isolation of the inland regions. But wherever a vessel could be floated (and this was done on some unlikely little streams), the local economy was integrated into an impressive system of internal distribution.

The internal freight transportation system had three chief purposes. One was to serve the ports by distributing goods among them for re-export and for use in the processing industries (the *trafieken*). This function seems to have motivated the first of the *beurtveer* services. As cities like Hoorn and Enkhuizen came to specialize in timber, salt, and fish, they needed more than before to maintain regular contact with the central market of Amsterdam. Clé Lesger has shown that seventeenth-century Hoorn was primarily an importing port while the Friesian port of Harlingen was primarily an exporter. They both cultivated specializations in the context of the Amsterdam entrepôt, and this required systematic recourse to internal redistribution. Likewise, we have seen that the specialties of Rotterdam and Amsterdam were such that there arose a regular need to move goods intended for re-export from one port to the other. The decentralization of the East India Company, whereby ships returning from Asia put in at six different ports, generated a constant need for the redistribution of colonial commodities for sale and re-export. This function appears to have brought congestion to the bottlenecks in the transport system, for a 1637 ordinance governing the sluices at Spaarndam allowed any ship with East Indies, West Indies, or Admiralty goods to be given priority in passing through the sluices for a supplemental fee.

A second mission of inland transport was to provision the urbanized West with foodstuffs, building materials, fuel, and everything else demanded by one of Europe's largest concentrations of urban population – and by the enormous fleet of oceangoing ships in need of construction, repairs, and provisions. We have already

---

[15] "In den holländischen Provinzen sind die Diligencen so wie alles Räderwerk in Holland wahre Rumpelkasten . . . Der Kutschenbau scheint in Holland wenigstens um anderhalb Jaharhunderte zurück zu seyn Die Landkutschen haben daselbst noch verdeckte von Pappendeckel oder Wachsleinwan, und se ıen buchstäblich noch so aus, wie die kutschen in den Jahrmärkten von Breugel und Tenniers." Anon. "Bemerkungen über das Niederländische Postwesen," *Archiv der Postwissenschaft* 1 (1830), 17.

noted the veritable armada of little vessels that supplied the region with peat. In Chapter 10 we encounter the giant timber floats that came down the Rhine from Germany, and in Chapter 6, the thousands of head of cattle that were ferried across the Zuider Zee and down the rivers to fatten near the urban markets. We should also note that the Republic's dependence on Baltic grain imports did not mean that there was no domestic production. The cities of Holland looked to the Amsterdam market to supply them with rye, whether shipped from Danzig or from Kampen; but they looked to Rotterdam to set the price of wheat, much of which flowed north from Zeeland and adjacent regions.

The third major function of internal transportation was the distribution of manufactures and imported goods from the ports to the markets of the Republic and its hinterlands. The volume of these shipments paled in comparison with the bulk commodities flowing toward Holland's cities, but their value usually exceeded that of the inbound raw materials, even though the vessels and wagons pressing east- and southbound often traveled only partially laden.

The cities of the Republic's outer provinces formed a great arc, from Breda in the southwest, via 's-Hertogenbosch, Nijmegen, Zutphen, and Deventer to Zwolle in the northeast, each marking a point where regular waterborne shipments broke bulk to be distributed further inland either by smaller vessels or wagons (see Map 5.3). The Republic's boundaries did not define the effective economic hinterlands of these towns, but the chronic lack of investment in transportation infrastructure (see Chapter 2, section 2.3.2) placed limits on their ability to penetrate and dominate these large rural zones.

For most of these regional distribution centers, the Golden Age was a period of depression. The wars with Spain, the Thirty Years' War, and the 1672 French-Münster invasion reduced the purchasing power of these markets as they increased the risks of commerce. They fared much better in the eighteenth century as their hinterlands stabilized and the growing demand for colonial products propelled steady growth in the volume of trade. The predominantly coastal orientation of inland trade – oriented to the north–south routes connecting the maritime provinces – gradually gave way, in the course of the eighteenth century, to an east–west orientation that increased the importance of the Rhine and Maas rivers and put new pressures on the inadequate hinterland connections of the regional cities. This slow reorientation of inland trade was directly linked to the changing character of Holland's entrepôt function (see Chapter 10), which offers testimony on behalf of our thesis that the decentralized Republic truly functioned, in practice, as a single economy.

Domestic commerce is a neglected topic, the history of which remains to be written. But the scraps of available evidence suggest that it played an important role in the establishment of the Republic's advanced economic life. The high-volume passenger barge system was a phenomenon without equal in Europe until the coming of the railways. Domestic commodity trade may also have reached

Map 5.3. Routes of inland distribution.

Table 5.4. *Number and size of inland commercial vessels, 1808.*[a]

Capacity	Number	Assumed average capacity	Total lasts
Under 5 lasts	11,605	3	34,815
5–10	2,714	7	18,998
10–20	1,857	14	25,998
20–30	1,150	24	27,600
Over 30	187	35	6,545
Paid by trip[b]	516	24	12,384
Trekschuiten	392	—	
Total	18,421		126,340

[a]These vessels belonged to *beroepsvervoerders* (professional transporters); the tax assessors expected to tax an additional 7,000 *vaartuigen van plaisier* (pleasure craft).
[b]Vessels falling under this provision appear to be *beurtschepen*, which would have been larger than average.
Source: I. Gogel, *Memoriën*, p. 506.

uncommonly high levels. Consider the sheer size of the inland shipping fleet. An 1808 tax document listed some 18,000 inland vessels, large and small, with a total carrying capacity of 126,000 lasts (1 last = 2 tons). The nation's fleet of ocean vessels probably did not much exceed 200,000 lasts at its peak (see Table 5.4).

How many loads could these thousands of vessels carry in a year, and over what distances? We are not in a position to answer, but we do know that they did not always lie still in the water. The many tolls levied on passing shipping offer the historian an archival basis to investigate inland commerce, and they reveal impressive flows of traffic. We have already noted that some 7,000 to 8,000 vessels sailed annually from, and a comparable number to, the ports of Overijssel between 1645 and 1800. The Rhine tolls at Emmerich, at the Republic's border with Prussia, recorded the annual downstream movement of some 1,200 vessels in the 1780s. At the same time, a similar number of vessels left the river Lek at Vreeswijk, passing through the locks there to enter the waterways leading to Utrecht and Amsterdam. Yet this flow pales by comparison with the 8,500 vessels, large and small, that annually moved from the IJ into the waterways of central Holland at Spaarndam, and the 4,000 to 5,000 vessels that entered central Holland through the locks at Gouda – and the equal numbers passing in the opposite directions (see Map 5.3 for locations). The inland fleet of 1808 certainly would have been capable of moving annually the 3.5 to 5.0 million tons of commodities that the recent study of Filarski estimated for the early nineteenth century. If such freight volumes were moved over any considerable average distance (about this we know little, but 100 km would certainly not have taxed the shipping technology of the time), then we can conclude that the domestic circulation of goods in the Republic stood at a level distinctly above any other European country before the Railway Age.

The domestic economy suffered, as long as the old Republic lasted, from the obstructionist policies of the cities with ancient toll privileges and from the institutional inability to invest in infrastructural improvements in the inland provinces. (In the Republic the direct beneficiaries were expected to pay for long-term improvements; if short-term profit prospect were in doubt, few projects could hope to attract central government subsidies with appeals to *raison d'etat*.) Despite this, the achievements of the internal transportation system remained considerable, supporting an intensive movement of persons and goods that laid the foundations for an advanced market economy that penetrated (almost) every corner of the country. The economy was a practical reality before it became a political reality.

Sectors

Chapter 6
Agriculture

6.1. Introduction

In most preindustrial societies, agriculture dominated economic life by its sheer size, and functioned as a limiting and constraining force – as a great weight immobilizing the society. The central problem of the rural economy is sometimes cast in a Malthusian framework, where technical limitations set a ceiling beyond which production cannot rise, and sometimes in an institutional or political framework, where "feudal" social relations limit the economic options of cultivators and waste potentially productive resources. Either way, economic development is thought to require a revolution in the agricultural sector.

Dutch historical writing long placed agriculture in a subordinate position. This reflected the belief that the urban, trading economy of the Dutch Republic functioned independently from the agriculture of its hinterland and, hence, was unconstrained by the limitations of the rural economy.

This is not our view. Agriculture is first among the component sectors of the Dutch economy reviewed in this book, because of the integral part it played through interaction with commercial and industrial activity in creating the dynamic qualities of the seventeenth-century economy and the unique texture of social and economic relations in good times and bad. Even though we insist that agriculture should be granted its traditional place of priority, we cannot also rely on the traditional concepts and assumptions used in the study of agricultural development. Agriculture in the northern Netherlands was the largest single sector in the economy, but it never absorbed more than about half of the labor force, and in the seventeenth century much less. Its development cannot be placed in the context of a "transition from feudalism to capitalism" since, as we have already seen, in most regions feudal institutions had never developed fully. We have already emphasized the distinctiveness of the geographical and institutional structures in which Dutch agricultural life was rooted. The development of agricultural production is the story of the interaction of those durable features with changes in international markets, relative prices, and domestic demographic and market conditions, to achieve lasting technical and organizational improvements.

6.2. The early sixteenth century

With few exceptions, the three-quarters of a million rural dwellers of the early sixteenth century supported themselves through land-extensive farming on soils that responded to their labor with great recalcitrance. In the eastern provinces, vast stretches of common wastes surrounded the arable open fields (*essen*) of the villages. The farmers had earlier organized themselves (in what were called *markegenootschappen*) to control communally their access to and use of these wastes, which, despite their name, were a crucial element in the farming system. The fertility of the arable fields depended on the manure of the livestock herds that were grazed on the wastes and on the humus-rich soil that was dug from the wastes and deposited on the arable. The large area of waste needed to fertilize the weak sandy soils acted as an obstacle to the expansion of the arable beyond the open fields of the nucleated villages.

Rye was by far the most important crop. Barley and oats could alternate with winter rye, but in the course of the sixteenth century, a two-course rotation of winter rye and summer rye became dominant. In Drenthe, this rotation was generally uninterrupted by fallow and was complemented by stubble grazing of the numerous livestock after the harvest. In the sandy-soil districts less remote from markets than Drenthe, the communal controls on the use of open fields and common wastes were less rigid. On the Veluwe and in Salland, buckwheat spread as a new crop, often cultivated outside the open fields; in more densely populated North Brabant, catch crops of fodder were inserted in the grain rotations to help support livestock, which, in this area of limited wastes, were often stalled.

Everywhere in this large zone, grain crops served first and foremost to support the farm households. Yields were low and the marketable surpluses small and irregular. Grain shipments out of the immediate locale, especially in Overijssel and Gelderland, depended on the surpluses gathered by the landowning petty nobility, the church, and the tithe collectors. Payment of rent in kind, often in the context of sharecropping agreements, long remained characteristic of these districts. Moreover, some farmers, especially in Overijssel, continued to be subject to feudal dues and would remain so until 1795.

Rural life in the maritime zones functioned in an institutional and physical setting utterly distinct from that of the sandy-soil regions, but at the beginning of the sixteenth century, the two had one thing in common: poor soil quality. Travelers to Holland were often impressed by the signs of rural abundance encountered along their routes. The Florentine observer Ludovico Guicciardini wrote in his *Descrittione di tutti i Paesi-Bassi* (1567) that "the fields have mainly a very favorable appearance . . . with rich green pastures full of all sorts of grazing cattle. . . ." Portions of Zeeland, particularly the island of Walcheren, the lands behind the dunes in coastal Holland, and the sea-clay soils of Friesland certainly answered to such a ·description. But few travelers then penetrated the extensive peat bogs and marshy pastures. A large part of the region lay, remote and ill-drained, as virtually uninhabitable and unfertilized haylands; inundation was in many ways a more immediate threat than ever before, and the long-term process of soil subsidence was undermining the region's ability to produce arable crops.

As agriculture shifted away from arable crops, it became less labor intensive. The dynamic process of hydrographic change described in Chapter 2 is the essential context for the economic crisis, faced with special force by Holland, in which rural dwellers were forced to migrate to towns or to find new, or supplementary, employments on the land. Cattle raising offered new opportunities, to be sure, as the fattening of oxen and dairy production was stimulated by growing markets, particularly in the Southern Netherlands. But in most areas the amount of land needed to support a cow was so great that even peasants with substantial farms could not maintain large herds (a herd of 10 to 12 cows was unusual), and those cattle were of small size and low milk yields.

Even though arable production was of declining importance, the two main sources at our disposal about early sixteenth-century agriculture (the *Informacie* of 1514 and the *Aanbreng* of 1511, tax surveys in Holland and Friesland, respectively) refer to arable fields in places where today they can hardly be imagined. With great effort and risk, peasants dredged mud from the drainage ditches to build up small arable fields that often had more the character of gardens. Here and on other relatively well-drained fields, the peasants sought to supply themselves with the necessary bread grains.

Farming in the maritime zone stood to benefit from the proximity of urban markets and the presence of inland waterways, but the low productivity of the agricultural factors of production set limits on production and forced even those peasants with access to full-sized farms to supplement husbandry with a broad range of other activities, among them peat digging, boat and wagon transport, reed gathering, freshwater fishing, fowling, spinning, dike and drainage labor, and a wide variety of household handicrafts.

This unspecialized, indeed improvised, peasant household economy must not be confused with a striving for self-sufficiency. On the contrary, the rural population was already deeply involved in a monetized market economy that featured interregional trade in grain, livestock, dairy products, fibers for the textile industry, and peat. As far as we can tell from the few extant records, the volume of this trade did not exceed modest dimensions. This was a rural economy with widespread market relations, placed in a modern social and institutional setting. But it was a simple, relatively poor rural economy because of low agricultural productivity. This, in turn, forced most peasant households to distribute their labor among numerous by-employments in order to make ends meet. Finally, the absence of occupational specialization and the low productivity of capital necessarily restricted the level of output, limiting the role that agriculture could play in the supply of home and foreign markets.

6.3. 1500–1650

Beginning in the late fifteenth century, three factors began to act on the Dutch rural economy, creating an economic environment that offered new opportunities for agricultural development. Two of these were common to nearly all of Europe: the rise of prices and the growth of the population. The third, while by no means internal to the Dutch economy, exerted its greatest impact there, to the point of altering fundamentally the role of the first two mentioned factors. This third factor, the growth of grain production in and export from the lands east of the river Elbe, affected the maritime zone of the Northern Netherlands with particular force. This was because the region already displayed a chronic need for grain imports to feed its urban population, and, partly for this reason, the merchants of Amsterdam had in the fifteenth century succeeded in establishing themselves as import traders in Baltic grain (see Chapter 9).

The bulk of the late fifteenth-century demand for grain in the Northern Netherlands continued to be supplied locally. But, as we have seen, physical conditions were such as to make the maritime provinces in particular a region of high-cost production. Wheat and rye prices throughout the maritime Low Countries, when expressed in silver equivalents, were then higher than anywhere else in Europe. This attracted grain imports from nearby regions, such as Walloon Brabant, the territories drained by the river Maas and Picardy, and the Cambresis in Northern France. In comparison to these export regions, Baltic grain exports, which varied between 2,000 and 3,000 lasts per year in the 1470s, probably played a marginal role.

In the last two decades of the fifteenth century, when crop failures repeatedly interrupted the supply of French grain, the domestic situation in the East Elbian lands was such as to encourage increased production for export, and the commercial contacts of Amsterdam stood ready to convey that grain to the Dutch market. By 1500 grain exports from the Baltic had reached some 10,000 lasts per year, and by the 1560s shipments reached 50,000 lasts, enough to feed perhaps 15–20 percent of the population of the entire Burgundian Netherlands, and a far greater proportion of the coastal and urban populations to which it was principally destined. By the first half of the seventeenth century, an annual average of 53,000 lasts of grain passed westbound through the Danish sound in Dutch bottoms alone. More will be said about the Baltic grain trade later; here we restrict our attention to the profound impact of this invasion of imported wheat and rye on the Dutch rural economy. The word *invasion* is not idly chosen, for the grain imports were now far more than a supplement to domestic production. The rise of Amsterdam as the central grain market and storage center for Europe brought the Dutch rural economy under the direct influence of an international market price which, in turn, was highly correlated to prices in the Baltic ports (see Chapter 10, section 10.2.1). As a direct consequence, the Dutch grain price *level*, which in 1460–1500 was among the very highest in Europe, came under the influence of the low-cost production centers. Thus, in this era of price inflation, Dutch grain prices rose less rapidly than elsewhere.

The integration of distant markets in an era filled with political, climatological, and monetary shocks did not proceed without interruption, but the long-term trend is unmistakable. The correlation of grain prices in the two markets rose substantially across the sixteenth century. Lübeck and Utrecht rye prices showed no more than a moderate tendency to rise and fall together in the first half of the sixteenth century ($r = .52$), while Danzig and Utrecht rye prices moved in much greater sympathy during the politically volatile second half of the sixteenth century ($r = .69$). By the first half of the seventeenth century, the correlation had become very strong (Danzig-Amsterdam: $r = .88$), indeed, uniquely strong in all of Europe. Correlation in annual fluctuations is not the same as reduction of the absolute difference between prices, and the latter is more difficult to measure with accuracy because of the monetary conversion that must be made. When expressed in grams of silver, the price of grain in the Netherlands stood at nearly twice the Danzig level in 1511–20 and 1531–40. Thereafter it usually stood no more than 50 percent above the Danzig prices, and in the half century after 1610, the gap diminished still further.

As a consequence of all this, when wheat and rye prices in various parts of Europe are compared (by converting prices at all locations to silver equivalents and setting them equal to 100 in the period 1460–1500), the Dutch prices rise less than those of the other places listed in Table 6.1 – in all except the cases indicated in the table. In this way the region with prices among the highest in Europe in the late fifteenth and early sixteenth centuries experienced a relative reduction of its grain prices to levels that often were lower than in other West European markets. This long-term process had important consequences for Dutch foreign trade and consumer demand; here our concern is the influence of this "invasion" of the Dutch market on the agricultural economy.

The most widely felt consequence of cheap grain was communicated via changes in relative prices. Almost everywhere in Europe, the growing demand for foodstuffs, emanating from a growing population, exceeded the technical capabilities of agriculture to satisfy that demand. The result was that food prices tended to rise more rapidly than those of industrial products, and the prices of the most basic necessities – the bread grains – tended to rise more than relative luxuries such as meat and dairy products. The Northern Netherlands did not fully conform to this pattern. Here the products of livestock husbandry rose more than arable production. This suggests a greater purchasing power among Dutch con-

Table 6.1. *Index of grain prices, expressed in grams of silver per 100 kg. (1460–1500 = 100).*

Period	Netherlands rye	Belgium wheat	England wheat	France wheat	Germany rye
1460–1500	100	100	100	100	100
Grams of silver	24.38	28.15	21.83	19.65	18.65
1550–70	175	202	160	346	191
1590–1600	269	329	419	954	282
1600–20	210	268	399	478	263
1650–70	287	345	476	567	218[a]
1700–20	225	293	436	402	255
1720–40	183	212	399	333	235
1770–90	277	276[a]	536	458	322
1800–20	454		973	661	457

[a]Indicates exceptions to the rule that grain prices rose more rapidly in the listed countries than they did in the Netherlands. See text.
Source: Data drawn from Wilhelm Abel, *Agricultural Fluctuations in Europe from the Thirteenth to the Twentieth Centuries,* third ed. (London, 1978), pp. 304–7.

sumers (discussed later), and this character of local demand (via its effects on relative prices) exerted, in turn, a direct influence on the development of agriculture. The specialist farmer who sold butter and bought rye received 30 percent more rye for every pound of butter he sold in the fourth quarter of the sixteenth century than in the first or second quarters. By the first quarter of the seventeenth century, he received over 80 percent more rye, and after a brief period in the second quarter of the century when rye prices rose steeply, that margin of advantage returned and actually increased further in the final quarter of the seventeenth century. A comparison of rye with beef and cowhide prices shows a similar pattern.

These unique trends in the internal terms of trade induced responses among the cultivators. Most obviously, grain disappeared from marginal areas of both high cost and high risk. The small arable plots of Holland often became rededicated to garden and industrial crops; others, particularly in Friesland, were converted to pasture. Evidence for this is offered by probate inventories drawn up upon the death of farmers. In low-lying districts of Friesland now devoted to livestock husbandry, the percentage of farmers owning arable plots fell by half between 1550–74 and 1640–86.

If farmers had limited their responses to marginal adjustments of their output mix, the rural economy would have realized little in the way of lasting improvements, for the poor soils and low physical productivity of labor would have remained. An effective response to the opportunities created by the process of international market integration and the resulting pattern of relative prices depended on investment to improve the quality of the factors of production. Such investment laid the basis for greater specialization in production, allowing the rural economy to benefit from higher productivity and organizational efficiency as well as favorable terms of trade.

Given the existence of opportunities for profit, investment in agriculture depended on the existence of an appropriate legal and institutional context. Here the "medieval legacy" of the maritime provinces offered specific advantages. The polders and drainage boards, the individual right to own, mortgage, and sell land, the absence of feudal bonds, and security of tenure, all contributed to the creation of a setting in which landowners possessed the motivation to invest, and investors could confidently extend credit in the rural economy.

In the first two-thirds of the sixteenth century – up to the outbreak of the Revolt – the investment process was principally in the hands of the farmers themselves and consisted of small-scale projects designed to gain new cultivable land from tidal marshes, to improve the drainage of existing land, and to substitute personal labor services on dike maintenance with monetary payments. In this way a measure of specialization could be achieved that found its chief expression in the increased import of oxen for fattening and the increase in butter and cheese production. In both cases, as well as in the rise of peat production in rural Holland, the principal markets were outside the region, notably in Antwerp. Eventually, Antwerp merchants and Brussels courtiers took a financial interest in northern reclamation projects. As for the cities of Holland itself, most of them failed to keep pace with the population growth of the countryside in this period. Indeed, the rise of new rural markets for agricultural commodities and the growing diversity of crafts and services available in the villages became an object of grave concern to the cities (see Chapter 8, section 8.2).

The first decade of the Eighty Years' War called a halt to this process of agricultural development. Sieges, inundations, and the depredations of marching troops interrupted production and trade, while the fear of such calamities dried up the sources of capital for land reclamation and improvement. The impact of the Revolt can be read directly from the financial records. Rents, which had been rising steadily from the beginning of the century, stagnated or fell in the 1570s, while the pressure of taxation, including polder taxes, caused arrears in rent payment to become widespread.

However dramatic were the events of those years, still we must not exaggerate their consequences for the rural economy of the maritime provinces. The Revolt was an interruption, not a turning point. The creation of an independent state did not alter fundamentally the legal and institutional framework of rural society, although it certainly intensified the ongoing redistribution of landownership (see Chapter 11). In most of the maritime zones, the factors that had been encouraging agricultural improvement already for several decades continued to do so. Consequently, the removal of imminent military danger sufficed to permit the rural economy to resume its development, only now with the significant additional element of an explosive urban growth, which opened up new markets at the same time that it made available new sources of capital for investment in the rural economy.

The growing wealth of urban merchants, the development of windmill technology, and the opportunities for profit in a period of sharply rising agricultural prices, all combined in the first years of the seventeenth century to set in motion one of the most impressive and lasting achievements of the Golden Age: the explosion of speculative investment in projects to drain the lakes of North Holland. Primarily urban investors sank at least 10 million guilders in those projects by 1640; the six largest of these schemes added over 1,400 large new farms (average size: 16.5 ha.) to the peninsula, transforming permanently its agrarian character. At the same time, many additional millions were being invested in the peat-digging enterprises of Friesland and Groningen and in canal building throughout the maritime zone (see Chapter 2, section 2.3.2). The *hoogveen* moors of east Groningen attracted Amsterdam capital because of the demand for peat, but the interest of the city of Groningen fastened on the possibility of transforming these barren moors into permanent agricultural settlements. By insisting that the topsoil (which was not suitable as fuel) be saved and mixed with the sandy undersoil (after the peat layer was stripped away), and by offering municipal night soil at no cost to the new farmers, the city of Groningen encouraged the systematic creation of agricultural colonies, the *Veenkoloniën*. These large-scale projects, all financed principally by urban investors, enabled agricultural production to increase and rural commercial services to improve.

In this context, investment by the farmers themselves tended to focus (1) on the further improvement of soil quality, (2) on augmenting the physical capital on the farms, and (3) on augmenting the enterprises' "human capital" via education. The first of these had begun much earlier but neared a point of saturation by the mid–seventeenth century, when virtually all the land in the central Holland drainage districts of Rijnland and Amstelland had been organized into polders and many hundreds of windmills (still uncommon at the outbreak of the Revolt) drained the new polders.

The investment in land, which was necessary for more intensive land use, led in turn to investment in new buildings and equipment. Old, small farmhouses, with little storage space or room for livestock, were gradually replaced by new farm types. For example, in Friesland the probate inventories up to the 1580s invariably referred to the medieval *Oude Friese huis*, a low narrow structure, originally of wattle and daub construction and with no separation of living quarters from the stalls. Thereafter, farmers in the maritime provinces embarked on a veritable "rebuilding of the rural Netherlands," introducing new farm types – the *Stolp* of North Holland, the Friesian *Boerenhuis*, the Groningen *Schuur*, and the *Vlaamse Schuur* in South Holland and Zeeland – all of which possessed lofty barns, separate and more elaborate living quarters, brick construction, and often dairies and cooling cellars. In Friesland two-thirds of the probate inventories drawn up in the district of Leeuwarderadeel between 1634 and 1641 recorded the presence of a separate barn (a *schuur*). In nearby Hennaarderadeel all the inventories mention it by the 1650s.

Probate inventories also allow us to observe the accumulation of more farm equipment, such as wagons, boats, and utensils for the dairy. In the Friesian district of Leeuwarderadeel in the 1580s, all such equipment accounted for under 10 percent of the total value of the farms; a century later it accounted for 17 percent of a much higher total.

Directly related to this process of investment in the quality of land and the quantity of capital goods were the introduction of new farming practices and alterations in the output mix of Dutch agriculture. Technological and organizational change together made possible an increase in the volume and, even more, in the value of production.

Given the emphasis on livestock husbandry in the maritime zones, farmers had access to relatively large supplies of manure. The rising level of urbanization added to this bounty by supplying night soil and industrial wastes, and their efficient use was encouraged by the developing transport infrastructure, which allowed a lively trade in manure to arise. We have already noted the shipment of Groningen night soil to the Veenkoloniën.

In order to attract additional manure for this region, Groningen offered a bounty of 10 guilders per boatload to encourage shippers of agricultural commodities to Holland to return with manure. Sheep and pigeon dung moved across the Zuider Zee to the tobacco fields near Amersfoort, while various wastes from the cities of Holland made their way to the hemp fields of the Krimpenerwaard and surrounding districts.

Farmers with access to such a market could benefit from an extra degree of freedom when compared to the conditions then typical of western Europe. Consequently, arable fields lay fallow less frequently, crop rotation systems exhibited greater flexibility, and industrial and horticultural crops, which called for large applications of fertilizer, were introduced on a large scale.

Friesian probate inventories of around 1600 give little evidence that farmers regularly let their arable fields lie fallow. In fact, it is difficult to establish the existence of any regular crop rotation systems. However, we can observe that (1) bread-grain crops tended to alternate with crops of peas, beans, and oil seeds, and (2) the latter crops slowly but surely increased in relative importance. Before 1600 they were grown on about 10 percent of the arable, after 1650 about 20 percent.

In Zeeland and the South Holland islands, where arable farming was of great importance, farmers are said to have followed a seven-year rotation, including one year of fallow. After a year of coleseed and one or two harvests of grain, the fields were to be given over to pulses or flax. A detailed study of the Beijerlanden, a district of South Holland, has demonstrated that such a rotation might have existed as an ideal but certainly not as a rule. Farmers who began with the first steps of this rotation changed course midway, or stopped and began again from the beginning, always in apparent reaction to changing market conditions, the weather, or the available supply of fertilizer.

The classical rotation systems thought to have stood at the heart of the agricultural revolution in Flanders and later in England (the alternate husbandry, which alternated bread grains with fodder and pulse crops; and the convertible husbandry, which rotated crop production with artificial grasses) appear not to have played a role of importance in the development of agriculture of the maritime provinces. Dutch farmers faced the same physical challenges and limitations as others when it came to disease, weather, and soil. But their greater market orientation offered an additional flexibility in the organization of production. Two margins of adaptation deserve emphasis in this regard: the market for *outputs* and the market for farm *inputs* and intermediate outputs. What distinguished maritime-zone agriculture was in part the large share of final output that was marketed. The account books of the Friesian farmer Rienck Hemmema show that in the 1570s he sold nearly all his wheat crop (his only bread grain) and purchased rye to feed his household. In the seventeenth century, observers claimed that Holland butter was exported while inferior Irish and Brabant butter was imported for domestic use. Low transaction costs (and a Spartan lifestyle) made such extreme market dependence feasible.

But the market orientation of Dutch agriculture went beyond the marketing of most final outputs. The technology of European agriculture until the late nineteenth century depended on the production on the farm of a wide variety of intermediate outputs required as inputs in the production of the final outputs – those marketed or consumed by the household. These intermediate outputs – fodder, fertilizer, breeding stock, equipment, transport services – were usually not obtainable via the market, or available only in limited quantities, at the wrong time of year, on an undependable basis, and so on. Well-organized markets in farm inputs are a late development in agricultural history, one which makes possible advanced forms of specialization that, one might argue, distinguish the "farmer" from the "peasant." As long as the cultivator must produce inputs on his farm, production can hardly become highly specialized. The peasant can respond at the margins to market developments, but a large amount of his land, labor, and capital remains unavoidably committed to the production of intermediate, nonmarketed, products and services.

A combination of low transport costs, large urban markets, and international horizons permitted agriculture in the maritime zone to develop markets in farm inputs. The scale of this development was modest in comparison with the nineteenth century, with its chemical fertilizers, factory-produced farm implements, and imported fodder; but the fertilizer trade, the industrial wastes such as distillers' mash and oilseed cakes, and the development of specialist services, all made possible a substantial specialization in production and overall diversification of agricultural output.

The rapid growth of the urban sector created markets for both foodstuffs and industrial raw materials. Crops such as hemp, hops, flax, and madder long had been grown on small intensively fertilized plots, but from the end of the sixteenth century, growing demand encouraged an increase of the scale of production: hemp (for rope and sails) was combined with livestock raising in western Utrecht and the Krimpenerwaard; hops (for beer) spread through the Land van Heusden and Altena, flax was concentrated in the South Holland islands and madder (a dyestuff) further south on the Zeeland islands. Oilseeds did well on the newly drained polders of North Holland. Horticulture, which had been limited to the outskirts of the cities in which the produce was to be sold, could now benefit from the improved transportation system to expand in areas of optimal soil and labor-market conditions. The Langedijk (north of Alkmaar), the Streek (between Hoorn and Enkhuizen), and Menaldumadeel in Friesland specialized in crops such as carrots, onions, beets, and cabbage; Midden Kennemerland (north of Haarlem), Aalsmeer, and Boskoop, all in Holland, found niches in flower bulbs and arboriculture. The produce of these districts was shipped to the urban centers, as well as abroad.

Livestock husbandry also shows evidence of growing specialization in this period. For example, Friesian probate inventories show by the changing nature of farm equipment that the coastal heavy clay soil region was becoming more specialized in arable production, while elsewhere the arable was disappearing in favor of livestock husbandry. Moreover, the composition of the herds reveals that farmers on the light clay soils devoted themselves increasingly to dairying, while on the wetter peat soils and in more remote locations generally, farmers emphasized cattle breeding.

In Holland one can distinguish districts that specialized in fresh milk production (nearest the large cities) with herds consisting almost entirely of milk cows, districts specializing in cheese or butter, and fattening zones. Map 6.1 displays the zones of concentrations of dairying (and fresh milk) specialists and of breeding specialists as of 1807. The seventeenth-century pattern will not have been the same in all respects (we know, for example, that Drenthe then specialized in cattle breeding), but the principle of specialization and large-scale trade in young cattle was by then firmly established.

Agriculture on the sandy soils of the diluvial Netherlands experienced almost none of the vigorous development just described for the alluvial zones. Here the century and a half up to 1650 brought to the rural economy only modest population growth and very little investment, technical change, or increased market orientation. The reasons for this have little to do with the absence of markets. The numerous provincial cities and the rapid growth of the nearby cities of Holland endowed the region with market possibilities that most European regions would have envied, although the decline of the IJssel towns must have dampened market incentives in their immediate environs. Certain districts in the east and south lay isolated from the main trade routes and had no effective access to cheap

0 ⊢——⊣——⊣ 50
km

▨ Districts where cows two years and older make up at least 73 percent of total number of cattle. Dairying and fattening specialists.

▨ Districts where cows two years and older make up under 62 percent of total number of cattle. Breeding specialists.

☐ Districts where cows two years and older make up between 62 and 73 percent of total number of cattle. "Mixed" regions.

⟵ Arrows indicate the general routes of trade in young cattle.

Map 6.1. Regional specialization in cattle raising, 1807. (*Source:* Gogel, *Memoriën*, p. 503.

waterborne transportation, but in general these disadvantages are striking only in comparison to the unique maritime provinces, certainly not in comparison to the norms prevailing generally in western Europe. Nevertheless, the markets of Holland seem to have stirred the agriculture of Poland more profoundly than they did the agriculture of North Limburg or the "Achterhoek" of Gelderland.

The inland provinces, which the Hollanders often saw as a protective buffer zone skirting their province, experienced the disadvantages of their situation during the Eighty Years' War. The military operations, which had been pushed out of Holland after 1576, continued in the border regions until the Twelve Years' Truce (1609–21), and in the south it resumed thereafter. The annual military campaigns in Brabant and Limburg, as well as the long Spanish occupation of parts of Overijssel, undermined the profitability of agriculture both through physical destruction and through the repeated disruption of normal trade routes.

The mixed farming systems of the region, the communal controls over the arable fields, and the extensive wastes, all acted to limit the potential response to changing market conditions. Still, inflexibility was not ossification. Specialized production as in Holland hardly existed, but many more modest adjustments testify to the basic market orientation of agriculture even in the most remote of villages.

As noted earlier large, regular grain exports to the urban markets of the maritime zone never characterized the sandy-soil districts. But this may have been more a reflection of market forces than market failure. The growing importation of Baltic grain to the maritime provinces could have removed incentives to increase arable production in the east. The downward pressure that this trade placed on grain prices in Dutch markets (and Amsterdam rye prices were strongly correlated with prices in the market towns of the eastern provinces by 1600 at the latest) probably discouraged investment on the relatively infertile soils of the diluvial zone. Thus, a force stimulating investment in agriculture in the west may have had the opposite impact in the inland zones. A partial exception to this generalization was the spread of buckwheat cultivation – often outside the normal rotation of the open fields – on the Veluwe and in Overijssel in the course of the sixteenth century. This cheap substitute for the bread grains, consumed as porridge and pancakes, grew well on poor soils and enjoyed a growing demand in this inflationary era.

Arable production in the inland zones failed to develop a strong market orientation, but this was generally compensated for by the livestock-raising side of the mixed farming regime. Early sixteenth-century tax documents reveal the presence of extraordinarily large numbers of cattle and horses. On large Drenthe farms where two horses and 10–12 head of cattle were the norm in the eighteenth century, 4 horses and 24 head of cattle were typical as of 1605. On the Veluwe, when 6,000 horses and 40,000 sheep were counted in 1824, a livestock tax registered 13,000 horses and 111,100 sheep in 1526. The large sixteenth-century livestock counts testify to the strategic role of manure for the small, intensively exploited arable fields, but they also reveal that farms in the east were oriented to urban markets chiefly via the sale of livestock.

The large number of horses testifies to the importance of breeding; Drenthe farmers bred cattle – just as did farms from Groningen, via northwestern Germany into Jutland – for sale to fatteners in the coastal pasture districts near the urban markets; the Veluwe sheep were raised for wool to supply the textile industries that still flourished in many small cities throughout the Netherlands. In any case, the relative isolation and low population density of the sandy-soil districts caused farmers to reach the market via the sale of livestock. Market avoidance was hardly the governing factor in the agriculture of the inland zones.

The underlying factors encouraging the transformation of the rural economy – population growth, rising prices, growing grain imports, and urbanization – persisted until the decades before and after 1650. In taking the measure of the agricultural sector around that date, the characteristic that stands out most strikingly is the apparently high level of labor productivity. We say *apparently* because no direct aggregative evidence on this subject is available; the statement must be defended with circumstantial evidence, but this is often compelling.

In most of Europe during the long sixteenth century, the persistent growth of population so increased the size of the labor force in agriculture that the marginal productivity of labor fell sharply, a phenomenon reflected in the drastic reduction in the purchasing power of wages. In the Northern Netherlands, where the population doubled between the early sixteenth and mid–seventeenth century, the rural labor force, despite its initial rapid growth, grew by no more than about one-third. At the same time, investment in land reclamation so increased the quantity of cultivable land that the man–land ratio (in the maritime provinces) rose very little. When adjusted for quality improvements, the ratio may have fallen.

Yet the growth of agricultural production was not limited to the 33 percent increase implied by the foregoing. Investment in transport facilities and farm equipment, together with the new market opportunities created by foreign trade and domestic urban growth, set in motion a process of household specialization that increased the proportion of a farm household's labor devoted to agricultural production at the same time that it increased the physical productivity of that labor.

This process of specialization is most readily observed in the rural social stratification apparent by the mid–seventeenth century. A farm of 15 to 20 hectares – which could not wholly absorb a family's labor in 1500 – could, when well drained, absorb that same family's full energies, plus one or two servants and perhaps some seasonal workers as well. The many by-employments which had been so important for the farm household in 1500, now tended to be carried out by specialist traders, craftsmen, contractors, and day laborers. As a consequence, the larger villages throughout the maritime zone grew thick with a diversified nonfarmer population. These many laborers, with no land at their disposal to

208

speak of, were not primarily dependent on rural industrial employment organized and financed by urban merchants. By the mid–seventeenth century, the removal of industrial production from the high-cost cities to rural locations was well under way (see Chapter 8, sections 8.3 and 8.4), but this search for low-cost labor sent manufacturers to the sandy soils of the east and south. The landless rural dwellers of the maritime zone formed a "proletariat" of another sort, for rural wage levels were not appreciably lower than in the cities. The rural wage level reflected the high productivity of maritime agriculture, and the chief employers of the rural nonfarming population remained – directly or indirectly – the agricultural producers. A portion worked as farm servants and day laborers, while many others provided services to agriculture as traders and transporters, dike maintenance workers, windmill operators, barge and wagon makers, smiths and implement makers, and so on. The rural occupational structure became highly diverse, a point discussed further in Chapter 11.

The village social structure of the inland provinces developed very differently. Here, where the vast majority of the rural population depended on the land for its livelihood, the existence of open fields and common wastes controlled by the larger farmers created a situation where even at low population densities, a social class of cotters arose. Cotters were farmers with very small parcels of land who depended for survival on labor-intensive crops, industrial by-employments, and/ or agricultural labor on the large farms. The larger farmers, in contrast to their counterparts in the maritime provinces, generated little employment for the cotters outside of harvest time. As a consequence these cotters were forced to develop their own household economy, one substantially independent of the community of large farmers. Early in the seventeenth century, trade and industry in the cities of Holland began to take an interest in this pool of underutilized labor. Around the mid–seventeenth century, Leiden textile manufacturers began to transfer a portion of their wool-weaving activity to the region around Tilburg, in North Brabant. Haarlem merchants set poor rural folk in the Meierij, the district around 's-Hertogenbosch, to work spinning linen yarn. Even earlier, around 1620, Amsterdam merchants became interested in developing a domestic supply of tobacco in order to gain some control over the price of foreign leaf on the Amsterdam market. They began to encourage production among poor cottagers in eastern Utrecht and Gelderland.

We have already noted that urban investors exhibited little interest in the agriculture of the inland provinces, and that the market contact of the larger farmers mainly took the form of livestock sales. Ironically, it was the poor cotter population that provided a more intensive economic integration through their contacts with urban merchants interested in cheap labor. This relationship, begun in the first half of the seventeenth century, was to become much more important later as the cotter population grew in size.

The related processes of labor-force specialization and investment in more and improved inputs secured an increase in agricultural production in the maritime zones. The absence of direct aggregative evidence makes it impossible to quantify the increase, but, once again, indirect and local evidence is unambiguous in arguing for a major increase in output.

The opening of new weekly markets in the larger villages of Holland and Friesland, the physical enlargement of the major market facilities for butter and cheese, the increase in average herd size in the Friesian probate inventories, and the increasingly frequent mention of cheese as an export commodity, all are suggestive of a growth of output that is demonstrated most comprehensively by the course of agricultural land rents. The rental value of land in Friesland and Holland rose about fourfold between 1511–14 and the 1570s and another three to fourfold between the 1570s and 1650s (see Table 6.2). This increase exceeded, particularly in the second period, the price rise of the principal dairy products, and these prices, in turn, exceeded the price rise of the bread grains. In short, agricultural rents outstripped the price increases of the goods whose sale had to pay those rents. Production costs in agriculture (land and drainage taxes, labor costs, fodder and livestock prices) also outstripped the price rise of the principal farm products.

The levies imposed by the Hoogheemraadschap van Rijnland on the land in its jurisdiction rose from 2 to 3 stuivers per morgen in 1537–75 to 6 stuivers in 1590, 20 stuivers in 1625–35, and 30 stuivers in 1655–65; the prices of inputs (milk cows, hay, and oilcakes) rose from an index of 100 in 1550–74 to 360–75 in 1600–24, while outputs (butter and cheese) rose only to 248–52 in the same interval (see Figure 6.1). In view of the continued willingness to invest in land and agricultural improvements, this pattern of prices suggests strongly that productivity must have risen substantially.

6.4. 1650–1750

The era of rising prices, population growth, and expanding production lasted longer in the Northern Netherlands than in most of Europe, but here too it ended. Rye prices, after peaking in 1662, plunged to a far lower level by 1669, and after rising during the war with France and England, they fell back to very low levels throughout the 1680s. War and crop failure again brought episodes of higher prices to Europe and the Republic, but the underlying trend was downward: Most agricultural prices reached a low point in the 1730s. In general, the pattern of relative price changes was a mirror image of what the Low Countries and all Europe had experienced in the previous century: Grain prices were again most unstable, falling furthest; livestock prices fell less; and the prices of industrial products fell least.

This "agricultural depression" affected farmers throughout Europe, encouraging marginal substitutions in output to cushion the fall in revenues and, sometimes, substitutions in production methods to reduce costs. In the Republic the effects of the agricultural depression differed radically between the inland and maritime zones. In the latter, which we treat first, farmers faced special constraints

210

Table 6.2. *Index of rye and butter prices,*
and rent on agricultural land, 1500–1674.

Period	Rye	Butter	Rent
1500–24	100	100	100
1525–49	132	133	157
1550–74	177	233	385
1575–99	309	397	399
1600–24	333	608	842
1625–49	467	741	1,141
1650–74	421	758	1,306[a]

[a]Period = the year 1650.
Sources: Rye and butter prices from N.
W. Posthumus, *History of Prices in*
Holland (Leiden, 1964), Vol. 2; Rent
index from J. Kuys and J. T.
Schoenmakers, *Landpachten in Holland*
(Amsterdam, 1981), table 7.

limiting their ability to make these adjustments, which caused the agricultural depression to assume the form of a genuine rural crisis.

The impressive achievements of the previous century had been based on a thoroughgoing commercialization of rural society and specialization of production. These past decisions now constrained producers in their choices of responses to changing structures of price and cost. Farmers who for generations had invested to improve the productivity of their assets for dairy production had little latitude to alter radically their output mix. Even worse, the cost structure of farming proved to be very unresponsive to a decline in the prices of agricultural commodities.

The cost of farm inputs and the level of taxation had, from all we can tell, more than kept pace with commodity prices in the century before 1650. As long as growing markets encouraged investments that improved productivity, farmers could nevertheless prosper. In the century after 1650, demand for most agricultural commodities was no longer increasing. In order to prosper, farmers now had to find ways to reduce costs. Neither the labor market nor the state, neither the drainage authorities nor luck assisted in achieving that goal.

The cost of agricultural labor, whether day laborers or live-in servants, remained constant at best in the century after 1650. This phenomenon was general to all sectors of the economy and is discussed in more detail in Chapter 12, section 12.4. The rigidity of this important cost for commercial farmers in the maritime provinces was reinforced by the levies of polders and drainage boards. The "professionalization" of their functions had added a taxlike burden on land that did

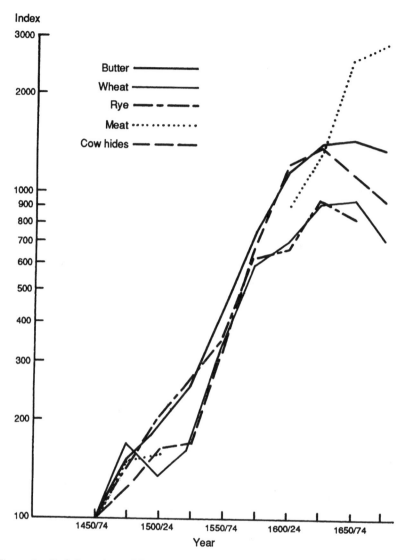

Figure 6.1. Relative prices of five commodities in twenty-five-year averages, 1450–1699. (1450–74 = 100) (*Source:* Posthumus, *Inquiry into the History of Prices in Holland.*)

not decline with the fall in prices. Indeed, in all coastal locations, these levies rose sharply after 1730 in order to do battle against the threat of the *paal* worm to the integrity of the dikes.

Even worse than the burden of drainage charges was that of provincial land and excise taxes, for these rose sharply just as agricultural prices were falling. In

Holland the land tax (*verponding*) had last been revised in 1632, when it was set equal to 20 percent of the net rental value (rent minus polder and other maintenance costs) prevailing at that time. As prices fell after 1660, the real burden of this tax rose steadily, a problem compounded as the government levied periodic surcharges beginning in 1653. These extraordinary *verpondingen* of 50 percent of the normal tax became an annual visitation after 1680. By 1690 the *verponding* was regularly levied twice per year, and in many years (1694–7, 1704–12, and finally in 1731) the tax bill stood at three times the normal *verponding*. Not until 1733 did this tax again subside to 150 percent of the amount set in 1632.

The difficult position in which this placed farmers is made clear when the *verponding* (ordinary and extraordinary, due on agricultural land, thus excluding houses and urban property) is expressed in quantities of cheese. Cheese was certainly not Holland's only marketed farm product, but it was probably the single most important one. In 1632, when the *verponding* was reassessed, the sale of 12.5 million pounds of cheese was needed to pay the land tax. In the 1650s and '60s, higher cheese prices made the *verponding* somewhat easier to bear: 11.5 million pounds would have sufficed. But thereafter, the extraordinary levies combined with falling commodity prices changed completely the fiscal pressure on Holland's rural economy. Needed to pay the *verponding* in the 1680s were 21 million pounds of cheese per year, by 1694–7, 37 million pounds per year, and in 1704–12, a peak of 44 million pounds per year. The burden became lighter in later years, but still stood at 26 million pounds in 1725–30. Relief came only in the form of rising prices after the 1740s. By the 1780s the real tax burden once again approached the pre-1680s level: 14 million pounds of cheese. Farmers in Holland also had excise taxes to pay. In 1683 all of these, including one on cattle, rose by 10 percent.

In Friesland the land tax, called *floreen*, was based on the rental value of land as set in 1511. In contrast to the *verponding* of Holland, the Friesian levy varied year by year. It rose explosively between 1580 and 1600 but actually fell in the first thirty years of the seventeenth century. Thereafter, as prices fell, the *floreen* rose, reaching its highest level in 1695. When this tax is expressed in terms of quantities of butter, the burden doubles between 1655–64 and 1675–84. The following decade brought some respite, but throughout the first half of the eighteenth century, the burden hovered around the high level reached in 1675–84.

This was not the only tax weighing upon Friesian agriculture. Besides the *floreen* the government introduced in 1637 the *Vijf Speciën*, a group of direct taxes, and in 1711 the *Reële Goedschatting*, a tax on real property. The revenue generated by the three taxes together nearly doubled between 1660 and 1730–50; expressed in amounts of agricultural produce that had to be sold to pay them, they approximately tripled.

In the inland provinces, the tax levels stood rather lower than in Holland and Friesland, but the pattern of development was the same. In Drenthe, for example, a land tax similar to the *verponding* was introduced in 1640; the *Haardstedegeld*, based principally on the ownership of houses, was levied periodically from 1672, annually from 1691, and doubled from 1703 to 1741. The year 1691 also witnessed the introduction of a head tax. All in all, the real burden of these taxes, when expressed in amounts of rye (Drenthe's principal product), rose fourfold between the 1640s and 1700s.

Another major financial burden that weighed heavily on Dutch agriculture in this period was caused by the periodic outbreaks of cattle virus that all but destroyed the dairy herds of the coastal provinces in 1714–20, 1744–54, and again in 1769–84. The Friesian losses in 1714 alone exceeded 61,000 head; in 1744–5 they reached 110,000; and in 1769 nearly 100,000. Moreover, during the 1770s the cattle plague claimed another 100,000 head. Quantitative information about the first outbreak is not available for Holland, but for the second outbreak, beginning in 1744, it is known that of the 78,000 head of cattle aged at least two years in North Holland, 62,000 (80 percent) became infected and 54,000 (87 percent of the infected beasts) died by April 1745. In the entire province of Holland, 407,000 head perished in the repeated outbreaks between 1769 and 1784; another 182,000 contracted the virus but recovered.

Only inoculation could control this virus illness, which spread by direct contact between smitten and healthy beasts. During the third epizootic (animal epidemic), inoculations had some success, but until then only one measure was adequate to limit the spread of the epidemic: the immediate slaughter of all affected cattle. In England, where the scourge also appeared in 1714, this was done with success; in the decentralized Republic, no organ of government was adequate to the task of forcing all farmers to take this drastic step – a step whose effect is vitiated by less than full compliance. When a fourth epizootic broke out in 1798, the new Batavian Republic's Agricultural Commissioner, Jan Kops, introduced an insurance scheme, the *Veefonds*, to overcome the reluctance of farmers to slaughter without delay their infected beasts. All farmers paid two stuivers per cow (age two years and over) every six months and received monetary compensation for their lost cattle. The plan worked well, stopping later epizootics at an early stage.

Farmers succeeded in rebuilding their herds quickly, usually within a few years of a catastrophe. Little is known about just how this was done (i.e., whether breeding from surviving stock or import from abroad dominated the process). It is clear that the temporary loss of production and the cost of new cattle weighed particularly heavily in the first two periods, when multiple economic problems afflicted Dutch agriculture.

In the face of falling prices, farmers had to contend with rigid production costs, rising taxes, and a series of costly natural disasters. The long-term squeeze on agricultural profits set in motion a series of responses. The rising relative cost of labor reoriented such investments as were made from the goal of production expansion to the saving of labor. In the 1680s the probate inventories of large dairy farmers begin to reveal the presence of *karnmolens* – large, horse-powered butter churns that reduced the need for milkmaids. Where grain production was important, primarily on the heavy clays of northern Friesland, Groningen, and the Zeeland and South Holland islands, farmers partially "mechanized" the labor-intensive threshing process by introducing the *dorsblok*, a 500–1,000-kg. threshing cone pulled round a central point by one or two horses, and the *kaf-* or *wanmolen*, a device with a fan to blow the chaff away from the grain.

These labor-saving devices could not strike at the root of the problem. Dairy producers, whose substitution possibilities were very limited, had little recourse but to cut expenses by farming more extensively: by manuring the pastures and maintaining drainage ditches less frequently, by reducing herd size and devoting more land to hay production for sale in the cities, by reducing dairy production in favor of fattening cattle and raising sheep, and, when pressed to the wall, by bringing in the peat diggers.

Holland's milk production – and, hence, the number of milk cows pastured in the province – fell substantially. Apart from the fresh milk supplied to the cities, milk was marketed in the form of butter and cheese. Butter production served primarily domestic markets. In fact, the amount exported was probably exceeded by imports of cheaper butter, especially from North Brabant. The excise tax on marketed butter shows that per capita consumption remained roughly constant throughout the period 1650–1805, at around 10 kg. per person. Butter production declined sharply in North Holland (from 17 percent of the total in the 1650s to only 6 percent by the 1730s), as South Holland, especially the region around Leiden, became more specialized in this product (and its byproduct, de-creamed cheese).

Cheese production had emerged as the major export product of the dairy industry, having captured markets in France, Iberia, and the Southern Nether-lands. Commercial production concentrated in North and Southeast Holland, focusing on the markets of Alkmaar and Gouda (plus many subsidiary markets in both regions). The weigh-house taxes collected in those principal cheese markets reflect the broad movement of the commerce in cheese, since all other products, mainly for local use, represented a small and relatively stable element in total tax receipts. Between the 1650s and 1730s, both Gouda's and Alkmaar's weigh-house taxes fell by half (see Table 6.3). After the 1670s cheese prices proved weaker than butter prices, so the decline in dairy production came to be concentrated in the cheese sector.

The decline in dairy production testifies to the diminished appeal of such labor-intensive activities. In Holland the search for less labor-intensive production led to an increase in cattle raising for meat production. The earlier specialization of Drenthe and neighboring German territories in breeding and of Holland in fattening gave way to a concentration of both steps in the maritime zone, a move made feasible by sharply diminished land prices and encouraged by the protective tariffs of 1686, which limited cattle imports.

In Friesland a similar decline in dairy production took place; here farmers turned from butter production to the even more labor-saving alternative of pro-

Table 6.3. *Marketed butter and cheese production,*
1650–1805 (1650–9 and 1750–9 = 100).

Period	Taxed butter Holland	Taxed cheese Gouda	Alkmaar
1650–9	100	100	100
1660–9	108	105	96
1670–9	104	83	89
1680–9	103	84	92
1690–9	104	71	85
1700–9	101	71	76
1710–19	92	52	62
1720–9	96	55	62
1730–9	111	53	55
1740–7	109	45	32
1750–9	100	100	100
1760–9	107	111	117
1770–9	101	113	119
1780–9	98	117	111
1790–9	93	112	129
1800–5	87	139	174

Sources: J. L. van Zanden, "De economische
groei van Holland in de periode 1650–1805:
groei of achteruitgang?" *Bijdragen en*
Mededelingen Betreffende de Geschiedenis der
Nederlanden 102 (1987), table 13; A. M. van der
Woude, "De contractiefase van de seculaire
trend in het Noorderkwartier," *Bijdragen en*
Mededelingen Betreffende de Geschiedenis der
Nederlanden 103 (1988), 373–98.

ducing hay for shipment to the cities of Holland. Around 1740 some fifty specialized hay transporters shipped enough hay (according to later "reformers" who wished to forbid the export of hay) to feed 7,000 milk cows – equivalent to at least 10 percent of the province's dairy herd.

The shift toward more land-extensive farming reduced labor costs, but it also reduced revenues while the other costs pressing on the farm remained – and in the case of taxes, increased. The agricultural depression forced many farmers into the painful decision to abandon their farm, or at least their least productive fields.

By the symbolic act of *spasteken*, plunging a spade into the soil, a farmer could abandon a field (and absolve himself of the obligation to pay the land taxes). In this way hundreds of parcels fell into the hands of the state, which often had great difficulty in finding people willing to take them over. For similar reasons several polders drained earlier in the century were allowed to reflood (discussed in Chapter 2, section 2.2.2).

It cannot surprise us that farmers who took these often desperate measures to lower their production costs also had difficulty paying their rent. Arrears became frequent from the 1670s on, in part because landowners became lenient, realizing that it would be difficult to replace their nonpaying tenants. In spite of this, the eviction of tenants increased. In the Beijerlanden, a district of arable farms south of Rotterdam, there had been only 5 cases of eviction in the first half of the seventeenth century, but in the second half, 41 were recorded, while in the first half of the eighteenth century the, number reached 75. Thereafter, as commodity prices rose again, the number of evictions fell. In the five decades after 1750, there were only 14, none of them after 1770.

The pressure on agricultural profits could not wholly be absorbed by the accumulation and write-off of arrears. Landowners had no recourse but to accept lower rents: In Friesland rents on a sample of nine farms dropped to under 70 percent of their mid-century levels by the early 1680s, and they fell a further 20 percent by the 1690s. By the 1740s rents on another sample of five farms had risen by 11 percent from the low level of 1675–85, but they remained below the peak levels of the 1650s. In North Holland, probably the region hardest hit, rents plunged. Between 1660 and 1690, they fell to 60 percent of their initial level and, after a respite around 1700, they fell again, particularly after 1725, to reach by the mid-eighteenth century a level no higher than between 30 and 40 percent of what had prevailed a century earlier (see Figure 11.6). Figure 11.6 also shows clearly how the epizootic forced already hard-pressed farmers into arrears: Rental receipts plunged around 1714 and again around 1745.

In this environment many investors who a generation earlier had been prepared to speculate in daring projects of land reclamation now viewed their landholdings as too risky to justify continued ownership. Our knowledge of the distribution of landownership in the Republic is fragmentary, but it appears that by the mid–seventeenth century, urban interests – both individuals and institutions – had come into possession of a large amount of land: the land sold by distressed nobles in the sixteenth century, the confiscated monastic lands sold by the provinces to raise revenues after the Revolt, and the land created by reclamation investments between 1610 and 1640. Farmers often figured prominently as landowners, too, but evidence from both Friesland and Holland shows that they owned most of the land in districts with the poorest soils – soils unattractive as investment vehicles because of their poor drainage or infertility. Similarly, in the eastern provinces, it was the poor cotter who typically owned his loose parcel of land while the large farmer with rights to the common waste more often leased his land from a noble or institutional owner. Ironically, it was among these large farmers that feudal tenancy lingered on, while their poor neighbors had long stood face-to-face with the commercial economy. Large amounts of land changed hands during the agricultural crisis, as soil lost its attraction to urban investors. The municipal orphanage of Amsterdam, a large institutional landowner, bought farms regularly as late as 1655 for prices of over 1,000 guilders per morgen (0.85 ha.), with initial rents that offered a gross return of no more than 3 to 4 percent. As long as rents continued to increase (the orphanage's average rent receipts rose by 226 percent between 1627 and 1667), this practice remained attractive. But between 1667 and 1694, rents fell by 30 percent. The regents of the orphanage resolved to sell all their land that did not yield at least a 3 percent return. In fact, buyers were now so scarce that the market for land was worse than the rental market. A farm near Weesp purchased by the regents in 1655 for 1,350 guilders per morgen could be sold in 1700 for only 570 guilders per morgen; another farm near Egmond in North Holland, purchased for 721 guilders per morgen in 1638, could be sold for only 188 guilders per morgen. At those low prices, the rent far exceeded a 3 percent return, but the risk of further losses in the future apparently weighed heavily on the minds of the regents: They preferred the more certain 3 percent return of provincial government bonds.

In this the regents showed themselves to be rather more alert than the burgemeesters of Haarlem, who resolved to sell off their North Holland farm properties only in 1725. The sales proceeded slowly; ten years later, the last properties had yet to be sold. Realizing that the hour was late, the city fathers urged immediate action, noting that "it is to be feared that further delay will reveal a further descent of both the sale value and the rental value of [the farms]."[1] Haarlem's burgemeesters disposed of their lands in a very depressed market, for by then every institutional landowner was doing the same. In the village of Uitgeest between 1713 and 1736, the following institutions sold all the property they owned: the poor commissioners of Limmen and Westzaan; the cities of Alkmaar, Monnekendam, and Beverwijk; the orphanage of Jisp; two Haarlem hospitals; and the custodian of Haarlem's church properties.

This process of disinvestment was common to all the maritime provinces except one. In Friesland the ownership of certain farms (called *Schotschietende huizen*) brought with it voting rights and, hence, political power at the local and provincial level. Here the retreat of agricultural prosperity occasioned a new interest in landownership among the elites, in the hope that what the economy had taken away, political office might restore.

[1] "het te dugten was, dat [de landerijen] by langen toeven nog meer in waarde so wel in huur sullen komen te desceseren." Quoted in A. Groen, "Het Uitgeester verpondingskohier van 1731 bezien in het licht van de sociaal – economische veranderingen binnen dit dorp tijdens de 18e eeuw," *Holland. Regionaal-historisch tijdschrift* 18 (1986), 101.

This interest is revealed with particular clarity by the farms to which voting rights were attached that had been in the ownership of the provincial government since the confiscation of the monastic lands. In 1640 the government owned 253 such farms, which were later sold to raise revenue. In 1698 the ownership of 49 percent of these farms had fallen into the hands of aristocratic and urban regent families, while an additional 30 percent was owned by other merchant and urban families. Only 5 percent were owned by the farm occupants.

Elsewhere the personal benefits of political power were no less sought after than in Friesland, but they could be acquired through the outright purchase of seigneurial rights and offices; there was no need to buy up otherwise unprofitable agricultural lands. It appears that a growing portion of the land was coming to be owned by farmers and others close to the rural economy, and less by urban and institutional owners (see Chapter 11, section 11.3 and 11.4).

The agrarian crisis also introduced changes to land tenure. In many regions the customary law (*Oud-Vaderlandse recht*) protected the tenant from eviction (and encouraged improvement) by requiring the landowner to pay compensation in the event of termination for the value of physical structures owned or improved by the tenant. During the agricultural crisis, tenants were often forced to relinquish their ownership of the structures in order to reduce their debts to the landowners. Tenants then found themselves less secure in the control of their leased land, a vulnerability that was increased by the growing disposition of the courts to regard the customary rights of tenants to the renewal of their leases as in conflict with the precepts of Roman Law. These changes occurred very gradually, but over the course of the eighteenth century, they amounted to a significant weakening of the position of tenants.

Once again, there was one major exception to this rule, this time in the province of Groningen. There the rights of tenants based on their ownership and improvement of farm structures (*recht van beklemming*) became more secure, so that what had been simple short-term leases in 1600 became, by the late eighteenth century, virtually hereditary leases at fixed rentals.

The century after 1650 created a situation in which the relatively strong could take advantage of the widespread distress to add to their landholdings. Except where horticulture, industrial crops, or peat digging expanded, multiplying the number of very small holdings, average farm size tended to increase in the maritime zones. Here, again, no comprehensive indicators stand at our disposal, but village studies show repeatedly that the larger farms grew in size after 1650, absorbing more of the available land and increasing the social distinction between farmers and others in the rural communities.

Farmers in mixed farming areas enjoyed more options than did dairy farmers in responding to the new market pressures. The manipulation of their flexible rotation patterns to increase the emphasis on industrial crops such as coleseed (for soap, lighting, cooking oil, and fodder cakes), madder, hemp, and flax offered relief in certain districts. In addition, the reduction in the frequency of fallow years, often through the introduction of alternate husbandry, permitted farmers to squeeze in an occasional extra crop to improve their revenue. But the general problem was the same and was overcome by a long, painful process of reducing the value of agricultural assets, farming more extensively, and (among the survivors) fashioning larger holdings.

On the sandy soils of the eastern provinces, the crisis struck with less severity. The pincers movement of falling prices and rising costs squeezed less hard since farmers who were less dependent on the market for their inputs had more control over their costs, and since the continued payment of rents in kind, often in sharecropping terms, defused some of the pressure of falling prices.

The response to the agricultural depression took the general form of intensification: applying more (household) labor to increase the output per unit of land – but at the expense of lowered labor productivity. Among the larger farmers, intensification involved a shift of emphasis from livestock raising to arable crop production. This shift was not so much a reflection of relatively favorable grain prices as it was a means to increase total output (and, hence, stem the decline in income), by choosing more labor-intensive forms of production. The annual number of cattle driven from Drenthe to markets outside the province stood at 4,000 to 5,000 in the first half of the seventeenth century but fell by more than a third in the second half of the century.

Correspondingly, the open fields, which had been divided between arable and pasture, became more exclusively dedicated to arable production. (This was part of a process whereby cattle raising shifted from common grazing on the wastes and the arable stubble to controlled, fenced grazing of the smaller post–1650 herds.) As a consequence the communal controls of the open fields were weakened, permitting more individualized production.

The net result was a substantial increase in rye production making its way to regional markets. No sources allow us to quantify this growing supply in Drenthe, but in neighboring Overijssel, tithe records suggest a 30 percent rise in output between the 1660s and 1730s, while in Limburg a substantial growth of output in the period 1680–1720 has been charted.

This intensification of grain production in the sandy-soil regions occurred as farmers redirected their household labor in the context of the mixed farming system. But this does not mean that no influence was felt by workers beyond the farm gates. Farm intensification increased the demand for specialist goods and services, much as farm specialization a century earlier in Holland had stimulated occupational diversification among the rural nonfarm population (see Chapter 11, sections 11.1 and 11.2). It also increased the demand for harvest labor, to which a growing cotter population could respond. But this growing demand for seasonal labor did not, in most areas, change the fact that cotters and small holders depended much more on extraregional commodity markets for their livelihood than on the local labor market. It is among the poor families with little if any land that the most dramatic initiatives in the rural economy were taken in the century after 1650.

The production of tobacco, which Amsterdam merchants had introduced to eastern Utrecht in the 1610s, became particularly attractive to small farmers after 1650, as grain prices fell relative to those for tobacco. Tobacco production in the Netherlands took an extremely labor-intensive form, featuring the adoption of horticultural practices and the heavy application of manure on small plots of land.

In the half century after 1650, thousands of (mostly small) farmers, who saw their money income falling below their basic needs, began to produce tobacco. With this crop the family labor could be wholly absorbed on a small plot of land. The need for manure could be met by entering into share-cropping arrangements with landowners or investors. The farmer typically paid half the crop to the owner, who, in turn, paid for the required fertilizer, advanced the farmer cash, and arranged for the sale of the crop. In this way many cotters and landless laborers could become self-supporting but at the price of an intense self-exploitation of their families' labor, and with the substantial risk associated with the production of an internationally traded commodity.

The demand for the Dutch leaf was directly related to tastes and market conditions in the Baltic countries (the major importers of Dutch tobacco) and the price of the competing Virginia tobacco exported by the British. Tobacco production spread from eastern Utrecht eastward through Gelderland into Germany. At its peak, at the beginning of the eighteenth century, tobacco production on some 5,000 hectares of land (and many thousands of workers) approached the total production of the entire Chesapeake region: 15 to 17 million pounds, with a market value of at least 2 million guilders. The product was mixed with other types of tobacco leaf at Amsterdam and Rotterdam processing works. As New World supplies (and other European supplies) grew further, tobacco prices fell, and the Dutch processing industry lost market share. Since tobacco production required little specialized capital, producers responded sensitively to relative price changes (see Figure 6.2). Production declined after 1720, stabilized at a lower level, and then fell sharply after 1760. Thereafter, whenever international market conditions caused prices to rise (during the American War of Independence and the Napoleonic Wars), Dutch tobacco production enjoyed a revival, but it never again assumed the importance it had around 1700.

Similar forces encouraged the expansion of production of other labor–intensive crops among small farmers and landless laborers. Hops production spread in northern Drenthe, flax spread in Overijssel, and potato production was begun on a small scale in several districts, particularly in Gelderland, in the early eighteenth century. In the maritime districts, too, farmers devoted small plots of land to hemp, flax, coleseed, rapeseed, and madder. There, the labor–intensive crops often were contracted out to specialists, who engaged laborers, often migrants, to prepare the fields and later harvest the crops, usually for a share of the harvest. The expansion of fruit orchards in the Betuwe occurred under the same conditions, with the picking in the hands of contract labor groups that moved from farm to farm.

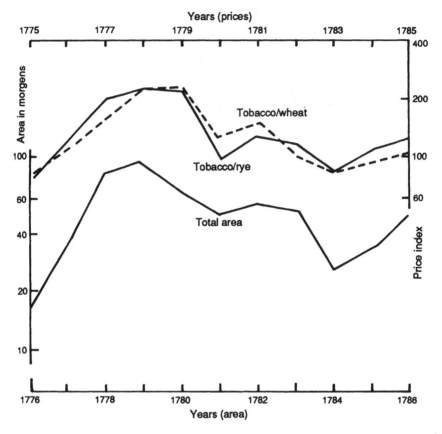

Figure 6.2. Relative prices of tobacco, wheat, and rye, and their effect on the amount of land cultivated with tobacco in the village of Wamel. *Note:* Prices (upper scales) refer to the year preceding the data on cultivated area (lower scales). [*Source:* H. K. Roessingh, "Landbouw in de Noordelijke Nederlanden," *Algemene Geschiedenis der Nederlanden 8* (Haarlem, 1980), 65.]

The economic conditions that encouraged all these labor-intensive crops among small farmers, while large farmers in the maritime zone struggled to reduce labor inputs and farm more extensively, also encouraged the growth of industrial production among rural dwellers. Production of linen in Twente, woolens in North Brabant, and paper on the Veluwe all expanded after 1650, creating the ironic situation that the larger farmers of the sandy-soil regions lived in the relatively stable economic environment of the regional grain market while the growing cotter and landless population produced specialized industrial and agricultural commodities for distant markets and stood exposed to international economic forces.

The importance of these industrial crops is apparent from the scraps of evidence we have regarding their volume and value. In assessing these data, keep in mind that the market value of all grain shipped from the Baltic to the Republic hovered between 4 and 5 million guilders per year during the first half of the eighteenth century. An estimate of 1726 set hemp production in the Krimpenerwaard (the center of a larger hemp-producing region) at 1.3 million kg., implying a market value of *f.*500,000. The madder production of Zeeland and the South Holland islands approached 5 million kg. at the beginning of the eighteenth century, when it was worth *f.*2.5 million. The annual value of tobacco production in the first decade of the eighteenth century stood at around *f.*2 million, which was about equal to the value of the cheese brought to all the markets of North Holland at that time.

Responses to the fall of agricultural prices after 1660, and to the persistently depressed price levels of the early eighteenth century, took several, seemingly contradictory forms: from more extensive, labor-saving farming in the maritime zones to more intensive, family labor-absorbing farming among cotters in the inland provinces; from the less market-oriented farming emphasizing payment in kind on the large farms in the inland provinces, to a desperate struggle to exploit both the commodity markets and the market for land in order to restore viability to large dairy farms and small cotter holdings alike.

This century of chronic unprofitability, punctuated by costly disasters, did not undo all of the previous achievements of the rural economy. As noted earlier, that development had been not simply a response to shifts in relative prices; correspondingly, the reversal of those price relationships was not sufficient to remove the modern characteristics of Dutch agriculture. It did encourage disinvestment, particularly by urban and institutional landowners, and that had the painful but ultimately beneficial effect of lowering one element in production costs, land rents. The government contributed to the restoration of agricultural profitability with tariff measures protecting domestic cattle raising, the removal of heavy export duties on dairy products, and, most significantly, by ceasing after 1750 to make a rule of double and triple levies of the land taxes. In these ways commercial agriculture gradually achieved a new equilibrium of costs and prices. But it remains remarkable that this adjustment process was so slow, taking nearly a century to reach balance.

6.5. 1750–1815

The domestic factors ameliorating the long agricultural crisis were joined by an external phenomenon after the 1750s: the international rise of commodity prices. The rise of agricultural prices began slowly but accelerated after 1780 to reach unprecedented levels during the Napoleonic wars. This era of rising prices in the Netherlands differed from the sixteenth-century inflation (but was similar to the experience common to Europe as a whole) in that grain prices rose much more rapidly than dairy prices. Rye doubled in price between 1735–44 and 1805–14, while cheese rose by 57 percent and butter by only 40 percent. Nevertheless, all of these commodities offered profits to the producers, because labor costs and tax levels remained constant while rents in the maritime zone, which had fallen to a fraction of their seventeenth-century peak, recovered only slowly and partially, never regaining the levels of the Golden Age.

In North Holland the rents on pasture land, when expressed in volume of cheese, had fallen by 30 percent between the 1650s and 1730s. Yet they fell by another 40 percent (while rising in money terms) from the 1730s to the first decade of the nineteenth century. In Groningen the average sale price of agricultural land rose by 58 percent between 1740–9 and 1788–1802, but this was only about half the rate of increase of prices for the bread grains that were the province's chief products. This puzzling phenomenon appears to have been quite general and is certainly difficult to reconcile with the stronger judicial position of landowners in the late eighteenth century. However, two factors can be suggested that might play a role in explaining the sluggish reaction of rents to rising agricultural profitability. Despite the low level of mid–eighteenth-century land values, urban capital did not return to the agricultural sector in force. The speculative element that helped to drive up land values before 1650 was less in evidence after 1750. The demand for land among potential farmers was also different than before 1650, for rural population growth in most maritime zones was extremely modest after 1750. This, plus the financial exhaustion of many farmers and the need for investment to restore depreciated capital, gave landowners an interest in stability and, hence, moderate rents.

In this setting commercial farmers (re)adopted intensive production methods to increase dairy production and, in Zeeland and Groningen, grain production. Polder drainage and land reclamation activities resumed, and toward the end of the century, the farmers of the open fields in the eastern provinces began to take in hand the enclosure and improvement of the extensive common wastes. This led to legislation in the Napoleonic period (1810) that set up procedures designed to stimulate enclosure.

The last-mentioned development was an expression of a general change in European elite opinion in the late eighteenth century. Agricultural development began to be viewed as a key to economic and cultural advance, and in order to secure such progress, landowners, scholars, and other worthies published periodicals and formed societies, such as the *Maatschappij ter Bevordering van den Landbouw* (Society for the Advancement of Agriculture), founded in 1776.

This fashion was particularly conspicuous in the Netherlands, where it contrasted so sharply with a past characterized by minimal government involvement in, or elite awareness of, the agricultural economy. In the Dutch case, the new appreciation was related to the fact that agriculture after 1795 was the only major sector of the economy that was obviously prospering and expanding. At a time of urban crisis and general impoverishment, the luxuries that large farmers could allow themselves stood out and attracted comment.

In fact, agriculture after 1750 was in the process of assuming a different place in the Dutch economy than it had held before. The growth of output and the increased prosperity of the late eighteenth century was not a replay of the sixteenth and early seventeenth centuries, the single most important difference being that agricultural expansion was now occurring in compensation for urban decline rather than as a complement to urban growth.

Several industrial crops that had formed a bright spot during the agricultural depression fell into obscurity as their domestic markets shrank: Hops suffered from both the decline of beer production and the importation of Flemish hops; hemp suffered from the decline of the domestic sail-cloth industry and the importation of Russian hemp; tobacco production shrank after 1765 as domestic processing retreated and the supply of Virginia leaf soared.

The decline of these crops may have provided the opening in local land-use practices to permit the growth of potato cultivation, a major new departure in eighteenth-century agriculture. Potato cultivation in the Netherlands is first registered in districts near its borders around 1700–Zeeland-Flanders and the Overbetuwe. By the 1730s it had attained a certain importance on the clay soils of Zeeland and Friesland and in the *Veenkoloniën* of Groningen. But it became a significant factor only later, probably because rising food prices stimulated the demand for this cheaper source of calories and carbohydrates.

It remains curious that potato cultivation then spread rapidly where hops and tobacco cultivation were in retreat, and in the Groningen *Veenkoloniën*, where German export markets stimulated production. It appears to have been less a crop for home consumption and more a new commercial crop than was the case in other European countries.

The spread of potato production had the additional effect of stimulating the further development of horticulture. Alongside the long-established coarse garden products (carrots, turnips, onions, beets, and cabbage), there now arose a demand for more refined vegetables – to be eaten together with potatoes – such as string beans, peas, lettuce, cauliflower, cucumbers, and even strawberries. Production of these crops expanded in the Westland near the Hague, near Leiden, and around Beverwijk, as well as in the polderlands of central Holland.

These new food-consumption patterns, to which the substitution of coffee, tea, and gin for beer should be added, reduced the aggregate demand for grain. Between the reduced demand and the increase of domestic grain production induced by the rising prices, the traditional Dutch dependence on grain imports eroded noticeably.

As late as 1768, an Englishman could describe the importance of the Dutch market for agricultural products as follows: "We look upon ourselves to rival the Polanders in their employment as ploughmen to the Dutch. . . . And at the same time we likewise allowed our brethren the Irish to rival the Danes in the office of being cowkeepers to them."[2] Yet, even as he wrote, England was ceasing to export foodstuffs and beginning to become Europe's largest food importer. At the same time, the Dutch Republic's urban markets ceased to absorb imported agricultural commodities in the volumes of earlier decades, while the stimulus of foreign, chiefly English, markets now played a major role in determining the course of Dutch agriculture.

A fundamental shift in the locus of demand in the international economy was taking place. To begin with, the intensification of grain production in the Republic – in the eastern provinces but also on the clay soils of Zeeland and Groningen – diminished the domestic role of Baltic grain. In the isolated seventeenth-century years for which we have data (1649, 1667, and 1680), retained grain imports at Amsterdam averaged some 60,000 lasts. Thereafter, the (still isolated) observations are highly variable but always much lower. By the 1770s imports to Zuider Zee ports from all foreign sources averaged 35,000 lasts per year, and in 1803–9, when national figures are first available, the annual average stood at only 27,000 lasts of rye and wheat. Amsterdam still functioned as a grain entrepôt for northwestern Europe in the late eighteenth century, but its role in domestic supply was now more modest than it had been. Most cities in Holland continued to look to the Amsterdam market price for rye (much of it imported) in setting their local bread prices, but they followed the Rotterdam price for wheat, and that market got its supplies from Zeeland and adjacent districts, which together supplied the great bulk of the wheat consumed in the Republic's urban centers.

As the import of bread grains diminished, the export of a wide variety of commodities grew. Madder, long a specialty of the South Holland and Zeeland islands, flourished with the rise of foreign textile production. The exports of this dyestuff to England alone were valued at 2 million guilders around 1800, while another million guilders' worth went to France. Groningen oat production was stimulated by a growing English demand. Direct exports date from 1780, and by 1803–9 over 18,000 lasts per year were shipped to England. The export of dairy products was nothing new, of course, but as we have noted, production and exports contracted significantly until the 1740s. Thereafter, production revived, led by a vigorous export demand. Friesian butter production rose by over 60 percent between 1762–3 and 1807 (from 3.3 to 5.4 million pounds), and the Alkmaar cheese market revived similarly after 1750. Much of the latter was a recovery from the epizootic of 1744, but marketed cheese output continued thereafter to drift upward. All the markets of North Holland received 16–17 million pounds in 1767–70 and 19–20 million pounds in the 1790s. Butter output also rose, and by 1800 the 3.5 million kilograms shipped to London constituted

[2] Joseph Marshall, *Travels through Holland, Flanders* . . . *in the years 1768, 1769 and 1770* (3 vols., London, 1772), Vol. II, p. 35.

a quarter of that metropolis's total supply. In 1803–9 butter and cheese exports brought in 6.3 million guilders annually. In this period some 20 percent of Dutch milk production was exported, and dairy products accounted for half of total agricultural exports. When the exported grains, industrial crops, and livestock are added, agricultural exports stood at some 12–13 million guilders in 1803–9. The value of imports (bread grains and industrial crops) was slightly less, despite the extraordinarily high level of grain prices in these years. As the term of trade for Dutch agriculture improved in later years, the net export surplus grew. Structurally, the Netherlands had embarked on its modern career as an important net exporter of agricultural commodities in the late eighteenth century.

From the initial era of large-scale investment in the improvement of agricultural capital, certain features have remained characteristic of agriculture in the maritime zones through good times and bad. Among them are specialized production, a free market for land and labor, price-elastic supply, and an efficient use of resources. But the specific relationships of agriculture to the rest of the economy experienced several changes. The mid–seventeenth-century prosperity was based on an international division of labor and the production of foodstuffs and inputs for the urban economy; the late eighteenth-century prosperity was based on "import substitution" and increased devotion of resources, including labor, to direct production for export markets. From an integral link in a trading and manufacturing economy, agriculture came to be an autonomous growth sector on the strength of its position in the international market.

6.6. Measuring agricultural production

In the period 1750–1815, Dutch agriculture grew, probably absorbing a larger share of the labor force around 1800 than it had since the first half of the seventeenth century. The new export orientation enlivened the commerce of regional ports such as Groningen (oats), Harlingen (butter), and Zierikzee (madder), connecting the maritime regions to the English market without the intermediation of the Amsterdam entrepôt.

The agricultural sector functioned as an autonomous center of growth in the second half of the eighteenth century, but no comprehensive data exist to sketch the contours of this development until the first decade of the nineteenth century. Then a battalion of French and French-inspired officials plagued the hapless mayors of the rural municipalities (themselves recent creations of the new administrative ideas) with questionnaires asking for information about every detail of local economic life. In the absence of local administrations with the expertise to respond to the flood of inquiries, the information sent to the central government was not always accurate, and sometimes there was reason for the local worthies to be less than truthful. But these early efforts at systematic, nationwide economic data-gathering offer, their imperfections notwithstanding, the first quantitative overview of the Dutch rural economy. When checked against later information

Table 6.4. *Arable and pasture land, by region, circa 1810.*[a]

Region	Arable	Pasture	Total
Maritime region	347,000 ha.	657,000 ha.	1,004,000 ha.
Inland region	410,000	426,000	836,000
Total	757,000	1,083,000	1,840,000

[a]N.B. The Maritime region refers to the provinces of Holland (North and South), Zeeland, Utrecht, Friesland, and Groningen. The Inland region refers to Drenthe, Overijssel, Gelderland, North Brabant, and Limburg.
Source: J. L. van Zanden, *De economische ontwikkeling van de Nederlandse landbouw in de negentiende eeuw, 1800–1914* (Wageningen, 1985), p. 86, table 5.1.

Table 6.5. *Rural and agricultural population, 1795 (in thousands).*

	Maritime		Inland		
	West	North	East	South	Total
Rural Pop.	437.4	202.1	283.3	318.5	
		639.5		601.8	1,241.3
Ag. pop.	221	136	226	250	
		357		476	833
Ag. pop as % of rural pop.	50.6	67.3	79.8	78.5	67.0
Ag. pop as % of total pop.	22.0	49.2	56.8	63.2	40.0

and corrected for internal inconsistencies (as J. L. van Zanden has done for much of what follows), they can be accepted as providing a reasonably accurate basis for the calculation of production and productivity levels. Upon this basis we may hope to identify the chief contours of the growth of the agricultural sector in the early modern era.

We begin with the amount of cultivated land. Working backward from the first cadastral survey of the Netherlands' land area (1833), the agricultural land area around 1810 can be estimated as shown in Table 6.4.

This land was worked by an agricultural labor force of farm families, live-in servants, hired laborers, and seasonal workers. It is difficult to sum these labor inputs in a single figure, but the available data on occupational distribution (discussed in greater detail in Chapter 11, section 11.2) permit us to venture the estimate shown in Table 6.5. The figure for "agricultural population" represents

AGRICULTURE

Table 6.6. *Value of gross agricultural output, imports, and exports, circa 1810 (in millions of guilders, prices of 1845/54–1875/84).*

Product	Output	Imports	Exports
Grains and other field crops	74.7	7.2	2.6
Dairy products	51.5		11.0
Meat, livestock	38.2		1.4
Potatoes	18.3		
Industrial crops	13.9	2.0	2.7
Other (fibers, leather, etc.)	8.1	2.1	
Total	204.7	11.3	17.7

Value of gross agricultural production by region
Maritime
  West   82.5 (Holland, Utrecht, Zeeland)
  North   47.3 (Friesland, Groningen)
Inland
  East   38.8 (Drenthe, Overijssel, Gelderland)
  South   40.4 (North Brabant, Limburg)
Total   209.0

Source: Van Zanden, *Nederlandse landbouw in de negentiende eeuw*, pp. 42 (table 3.2), 111 (table 5.18), 140 (table 7.8).

workers in agriculture and their dependents. The effective labor force was some subset of this population, but for current purposes, it is not necessary to estimate the precise labor force participation rates of women and children.

The final step in this survey of agriculture in the first decade of the nineteenth century is to estimate the volume and value of output. We rely here on a study by J. L. van Zanden, who supplemented the fiscal and questionnaire data referred to earlier with backward applications of data from later periods to achieve something approaching complete coverage. His estimates of gross agricultural product make use of mid–nineteenth-century prices. Prices around 1810 were lower on average, but more importantly, relative prices differed substantially from later decades, chiefly as a result of the very high prices of bread grains in the Napoleonic period. Our chief interest in the estimates summarized in Table 6.6 resides not so much in the guilder totals as in its description of the structure of production, by commodity type and by region.

With land area, agricultural population, and gross agricultural product known, it is a simple matter to calculate productivity, as shown in Table 6.7. The results of this exercise can be summarized as follows:

1. The output per hectare of land varied according to the input of labor, but there was a systematic productivity difference between the maritime and the

229

Table 6.7. *Output per hectare and per unit of labor, by region, circa 1810 (in 1845–84 guilders).*

	Maritime		Inland		
	West	North	East	South	Total
Output per ha.	140	114	82	115	114
Output per "ag. pop."	329	359	178	168	249
		340		172	
Avg. ag. wage 1819		ƒ.0.81		ƒ.0.53	
Avg. rent per ha. 1820		ƒ.27.80		ƒ.18.50	

Note: The productivity estimates follow Van Zanden but are cast in slightly different terms. Van Zanden, *Nederlandse landbouw in de negentiende eeuw*, 1800–1914, pp. 42, 114–22, 132–3.

inland provinces. The same labor input yielded a higher output in the maritime provinces (see Figure 6.3), which reflected the higher soil quality in the coastal regions, itself to a substantial degree the product of the large capital investments made to improve soil quality in these regions. The average difference in land rents is broadly consistent with this difference.

2. The labor productivity of the maritime zone was double that of the inland zone. In the south it was low primarily because of population pressure on the land, but in the east, where agricultural population densities were comparable to Holland and Zeeland, the difference is chiefly a reflection of the smaller complement of capital per farm worker.

3. When placed in a broader European perspective, this gap in labor productivity between the maritime and inland zones is revealed to be the result not of unusually low productivity in the latter but of unusually high productivity in the former. The inland zone's crop yields, labor costs, and so forth were typical of western European experience; the maritime zone was exceptional.

4. The total agricultural production of an economy with but 40 percent of its labor force active in agriculture – the second lowest percentage yet attained in European agriculture in 1800 – sufficed to produce a net export surplus as well as a more than adequate level of nutrition to the population (on this point, see Chapter 12), although there is compelling evidence that nutrition was substantially worse around 1810 than it had been a generation earlier, especially for the urban poor.

We now turn to the question of how agricultural production developed across the three centuries preceding 1810. With respect to the quantity of agricultural land, we established in Chapter 2 that drainage projects added approximately 250,000 hectare to the agricultural land area of the maritime provinces in the

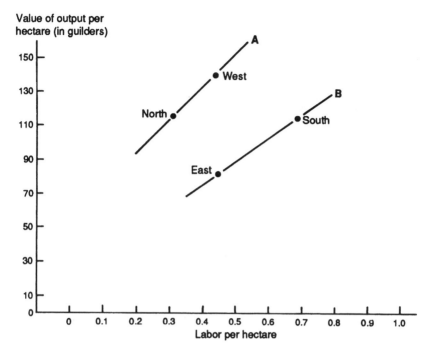

Figure 6.3. An indicator of the greater capital intensity of agriculture in the maritime zone of the Netherlands, circa 1810. (*Source:* van Zanden, *Nederlandse landbouw in de negentiende eeuw, 1800–1914*, pp. 42, 114–22, 132–3.)

three centuries ending in 1810. Most of this new land was in use by the 1650s. Besides this quantitative improvement, there was also a qualitative improvement brought about by polder forming, improved drainage, and increased fertilizer use. While this cannot be measured directly, it is likely that a substantial portion of the improvement in output per unit of land is revealed in the vertical difference in lines A and B of Figure 6.3. In the inland provinces, the augmentation of the cultivated land area took a different form than in the coastal regions. The extensive wastes of the sixteenth century were not altogether un-utilized. Agricultural development more commonly involved intensification of farming than it did the addition of previously unused land to cultivation.

The agricultural labor force before 1810 can be estimated on the basis of what we know of the size of the rural population. This was, of course, no more synonymous with the agricultural population in 1510 than it was in 1810. We have emphasized the unspecialized character of the rural population in sixteenth-century Holland as well as the partial involvement in industrial production of many eighteenth-century cotters in the inland zones. Nevertheless, a tentative division of the rural population into its agricultural and nonagricultural components is ventured here in Table 6.8 on the basis of evidence discussed more fully in Chapter 11. The overall development of the agricultural labor force can be summarized as follows: The total population of the Netherlands doubled between 1510 and 1795; because of the vigorous urbanization, the rural population grew less, by 72 percent. The occupational diversification of the rural economy – through the rise of services, industry, and fuel production – limited the growth of the effective agricultural labor force to 50 percent over the period.

The final step required for this reconstruction of the Dutch agricultural economy is the estimation of total output before 1810. This is a task still far beyond our reach, but two indirect estimation methods can give some idea of the order of magnitude that probably is involved.

The first exploits the knowledge that the Northern Netherlands were substantial net importers of foodstuffs in the first half of the sixteenth century, and net exporters at the beginning of the nineteenth. The sixteenth-century import of grain and cattle must have exceeded by far the value of exported dairy products and beer; for the years around 1810, Table 6.6 reveals the country's net export position. On the face of it, then, domestic agricultural output rose from *less* than was consumed by about 1 million persons to rather *more* than was consumed by the 2.1 million population of 1795. If per capita food consumption rose over the three centuries surveyed here (for which evidence discussed in Chapter 12 offers some support), and if the production of "industrial" commodities (flax, hemp, madder, wool, tobacco, etc.) rose more rapidly than food production (also likely since such commodities accounted for 10 percent of total agricultural output in 1810), then total agricultural production may have tripled in the period 1510–1810, with the great bulk of the increase concentrated before the mid–seventeenth century; see Table 6.9.

The second approach is based on the rental value of land, and assumes the existence of competitive markets for agricultural land. We will restrict our estimate here to the maritime zone, where we have already established that land rents in Holland and Friesland rose twelve- to fourteenfold over the period 1511–14 to the 1650s. Since land reclamation increased the amount of cultivated land in this region from approximately 750,000 hectare to 950,000 hectare (and to just over 1 million hectare by 1810), it follows that the total rental value rose by fifteen to eighteen times, or at an average annual rate of 1.96 to 2.07 percent. When adjusted for the rising price level, these estimates suggest a rising level of physical output of between 0.7 and 0.8 percent per year, or a total increase of 260 to 300 percent.

Neither of these methods can boast of great accuracy. The first is sensitive to our assumptions about changes in per capita consumption, while the second is sensitive to the inflation rate used to convert nominal into real prices. However, both approaches offer compatible results: Output tripled, while the agricultural labor force grew by only 50 percent, an achievement concentrated in the maritime zone, where labor productivity more than doubled, and in the period 1510–1650, when output rose at a rate of some 0.6–0.7 percent per year.

Table 6.8. *The rural and agricultural populations, by region, 1510–1795.*

Year	Maritime		Inland		Total		
Rural population[a]							
1510	300	60%	420	80%	720	70%	
1675	585	46	550	80	1135	58	
1795	639	50	602	76	1241	60	
Agricultural population[b]							
1510	225	75%	330	79	555	77	54
1675	320	55	420	76	740	65	38
1795	357	56	476	79	833	67	40

[a] In thousands, percent of total population.
[b] In thousands, percent of rural population; last column, percent of total population.

Table 6.9. *Sketch of possible growth of agricultural output, 1510–1810.*[a]

Year	Population	Per capita consumption	Domestic production	Industrial crops	Total	Index
1510	950	1.00	0.90	.05	898	100
1650	1900	1.10	0.95	.10	2300	243
1810	2080	1.10	1.10	.10	2768	308

[a] Per capita consumption: in units of 1510 per capita consumption. Domestic production: percentage of domestic consumption. Industrial crops: value as percentage of domestic food production. Total: output expressed as "consumption units of 1510."

In the maritime zone, the amount of land available per agricultural worker declined but little, as the region's total population rose by 150 percent. The agricultural labor force grew by 58 percent, while the land area rose by 33 percent. A capital-intensive agricultural strategy succeeded in increasing output while its share in the total labor force fell to historically unprecedented levels. After 1750 agriculture probably reabsorbed some labor, as a result of its relatively strong performance during an era of rising international demand. It does not appear that there was then a large gap between labor productivity in the agricultural and nonagricultural sectors. At any rate, there was no consistent difference between rural and urban wage rates in the maritime zone.

In the inland regions, the deterioration of the labor–land ratio was also modest, in this case because of the limited overall population growth. Limited though it was (44 percent over 300 years), almost all of the increase inserted itself in the rural economy as cotters. With little capital investment, there was little scope for increased labor productivity in this region. Output grew principally through intensification of effort.

Chapter 7
Fishing

In the Northwest European delta region, brimming with water, fishing had always assumed an important place in supplying the inhabitants with the necessities of life. The time came, however, when an informal, local activity became organized, specialized, and market oriented. This transition might be compared to the development of shipping. In Chapter 2, section 2.1, we noted how the lands behind the dunes made use of the many waterways and of a strategic location to develop an important position as a shipping intermediary over long distances. When later technical developments caused this shipping to move from protected inland waters increasingly to the open sea, the shippers of the Northern Netherlands did not relinquish their hold on this traffic. They adapted. The early emergence of the region's many small cities can also be accounted for in the context of this long-distance shipping activity.

The fisheries, which owed their initial existence to the geographical character of the region, received an important stimulus toward more formal organization and specialization from the growth of urban demand, which was, in turn, related to the rise of interregional shipping. In parallel with the developments occurring in shipping, the fisheries began pushing beyond the inland waters toward the open sea, and they encountered challenges and opportunities that led to important innovations which made possible the supply of distant markets. In this way the fisheries grew to become an important sector of the regional economy, producing a commodity that maintained for some two centuries a leading place among the exports of the Northern Netherlands and exerted a major influence on its balance of payments.

In time it became a set piece of foreign mercantilist propaganda to exaggerate wildly the size and profitability of the Dutch ocean fisheries, the better to lend credibility to the claim that it formed the very cornerstone of the Republic's seventeenth-century economic supremacy. This obsessive fascination that the fisheries held for contemporaries was rooted in a fundamentally correct appreciation of their strategic place in the overall economy. This sector not only employed many workers but possessed strong forward and backward linkages to shipbuilding, ropeworks, net and sail makers, the timber trade and sawing mills, ships provisioning, salt refining, cooperage and packing, smoking houses, and long-distance trade and shipping. It is not altogether surprising that jealous foreigners saw the fisheries as the secret weapon of Dutch merchants and shipowners.

The process whereby the fisheries were converted from local to export markets encouraged not only specialization within this sector but also a growing separation between fishing and agriculture, giving rise to distinctive communities of fishermen. It appears that flexibility lasted longest in the old connection between fishing and shipping. As late as the eighteenth century, one still encounters evidence that freight vessels worked as whalers in slack periods, and vice versa. The flexibility that still worked with vessels worked less well with labor, it appears, for already in the seventeenth century, the captains of warships complained mightily when the Admiralties sent them fishermen instead of proper sailors.

Within the fishing industry, the patterns of flexibility and rigidity worked rather differently. Every sort of fish has its special season, which made it possible for fishermen to move, in the course of the year, from coastal fishing to ocean fishing to Zuider Zee fishing. Here it was capital goods that suffered from inflexibility, for every branch of the fishing industry refined its own special ship designs and equipage. The equipage alone could make jumping from one type of fishing to another a costly proposition: In both the early seventeenth and the mid–eighteenth century, fishermen valued the nets of a herring buss at a third of the value of the vessel itself. Consequently, it seems best to begin this chapter by examining each branch of fishing separately before turning to several more general considerations concerning the place of the fisheries in the economy of the Republic.

The most basic distinction is between saltwater and freshwater fishing. Within the first of these, we need to distinguish further between coastal fishing and deep-sea fishing. Freshwater fishing can also be divided into river fishery on the one hand, and fishing in lakes, polders, and other interior waters on the other, but this is a distinction not always honored by the organization of inland fishing in the period that concerns us.

What affected the organization of inland fishing more were the characteristics of the various sorts of fish. Here we can begin by distinguishing migratory fish (those moving annually between fresh and salt water) from those that remain in marine or freshwater environments. The migratory fish divide, in turn, into the anadromous sorts, which dwell normally in the sea but seek out the oxygen-rich river waters to spawn (salmon, sturgeon, and allis shad dominated in Dutch waters), and the catadromous sorts, whose migratory patterns are just the opposite (most important being eel, a freshwater fish that spawns at sea). River fishermen focused above all on migratory fish, but they also caught freshwater fish such as carp, perch, pike, bream, and tench. Lake and polder fishermen focused primarily on these freshwater varieties, but they also involved themselves in the hunt for the migrating sorts, especially eel. Much depended, of course, on the seasons. A typical pattern for river fishermen was: December–April, winter salmon; April–mid May, allis shad; May–June, twaite shad; July–September, summer salmon; October–November, whitefish and lamprey.

7.1 Inland fishing

Inland fishing has never captured the imagination of historians as have the ocean fisheries. Consequently, this prosaic activity remains little studied, despite the high probability that in the fifteenth and most of the sixteenth centuries, inland fishing was at least as important as saltwater fishing for the supply of the domestic market. In edicts of 1592 and 1600, inland fishing is linked explicitly to "the lesser sort of folk [de schamele gemeente], who customarily sustain and feed themselves with fish," and shortly thereafter in Friesland, anyone found exporting freshwater fish out of the province faced heavy fines, while the construction of vessels designed to transport such fish was forbidden. We have very little on which to base an estimate of employment in inland fishing or of the size of the catch, but the frequency with which fishing is mentioned should prepare us to consider it capable of employing, often part-time, several thousand persons at its peak in the late sixteenth and early seventeenth centuries.

Freshwater fishing was especially concentrated in two regions. The first consisted of the major rivers and the Zeeland delta at their mouths, where such brackish water fish as flounder and smelt were found. The second was focused on the Zuider Zee and the IJ and extended via a complex of connecting watercourses to the numerous lakes of North Holland. The hydrographic character of this second zone changed fundamentally in the course of our period. On the one hand, a transgression phase of rising sea levels caused salt water to penetrate ever further into the Zuider Zee, whereby it ultimately became largely a saline basin; on the other hand, the interior waters were systematically cut off from the Zuider Zee by dikes, locks, and dams, and in the seventeenth century, most of these lakes were drained to form farm land. All of this had far-reaching consequences for the sorts of fish found in this region, as well as their numbers.

The two economic surveys upon which so much of our knowledge of early sixteenth-century Holland depends (the *Enqueste* of 1494 and the *Informacie* of 1514) describe "fishing and fowling" as significant activities in village after village. These references definitely refer to freshwater fishing, for where ocean fishing is practiced, these documents speak of "ten harinck gaan" – fishing for herring. Those active, often on a part-time basis, in inland fishing caught such fish as bream, roach, pike, perch, eel, carp, and ruffe on a scale that must have far

Table 7.1. *The number of market stalls rented by sellers of different sorts of fish in Amsterdam in 1662.*

Fish type	Markets		
	Damsluis	Korte Singel	Total
River fish	106	29	135
Eel	46	—	46
Waterschip (freshwater fish)	36	—	36
Sea fish	152	72	224
Total	340	101	441

Source: Y. N. Ypma, *Zuiderzeevisserij*, p. 75.

exceeded the needs of local consumption, for the cities were well supplied with freshwater fish stalls. These scraps of evidence give the impression that fish held a more important place in the diet of the sixteenth and early seventeenth centuries than was later the case, and the common man's fish was not salted herring – a luxury product at the time – but primarily the many varieties of freshwater fish.

The substantial importance of freshwater fish is suggested by occasional references to the number of fishing vessels and freshwater fish stalls in the cities, and by the scale of conflicts that arose in the sixteenth century among fishermen on the overfished Zuider Zee. It is not hard to believe that the rapidly growing and urbanizing population of this era, in conjunction with the rising price of most other foodstuffs, caused demand for the relatively cheap inland fish to grow vigorously.

The development around 1500 of an entirely new type of fishing boat, the *waterschip*, certainly points in the direction of rapidly growing markets. This vessel was as long as a herring buss and rather broader. In comparison to the other types of inland fishing vessels, the *waterschip* was a veritable castle. From two or three dozen in the early sixteenth century, the number in operation a century later rose to approximately 130, which then amounted to half the size of the entire Dutch herring-buss fleet. Not only were they large, but they made possible the application of new fishing techniques making use of tightly woven nets that literally vacuumed the waters of their fish. Yet these juggernauts formed no more than the core of the freshwater fishing fleet.

Indicative of the importance of inland fishing is the provision for fish sales in Rotterdam in 1620. The city then operated one market for saltwater fish; one mixed market for saltwater fish, river fish, and salted cod; and two "farmers' fish markets," where Dordrecht and Gorinchem river fishermen and farmers from the peat bogs sold fish three days each week. In 1662 a specification of Amsterdam's market stalls at each of its markets offers some insight into the relative position of the various types of fish (see Table 7.1). Half of the market space was then controlled by sellers of saltwater fish, but this is likely to reflect a recent development, for at the *Damsluis* fish market, which was the older of the two then operating in the city, a clear majority of the stalls sold freshwater fish.

By the mid–seventeenth century, the great days of freshwater fishing had passed. The supply of such fish was then in full retreat due to the aforementioned changes in the Zuider Zee, overfishing, and the decimation of freshwater fish stocks by damming and draining.

The diminishing importance of inland fishing as a whole after the mid–seventeenth century is displayed graphically in Figure 7.1, which gathers together quantitative data from locations throughout Holland. It shows the income from leased fishing rights in North Holland (the sluices at Westgraftdijk), in central Holland (at Lange and Korte Aar, Reeuwijk, and the Kromme Gouwe), and in the Biesbosch of southern Holland (Bergse Veld). Added to these data are the provincial revenues from the leased excise tax on the sale of salmon and sturgeon, and the revenues from the lease of the so-called *ingeld* of Geertruidenberg, a 5 percent tax on the sale of all fish landed at that place. From the 1650s or '60s, declining revenues characterize all the indicators of freshwater fishing, and the declines were far from trivial: Within 30 years the indicators fell to as little as a third of their initial levels.

The river fishing industry shared in this retreat. Revenue from the leasing of fishing rights in the Bergse Veld, an important domainal income of the House of Nassau, fell from some 30,000 guilders per year in the 1650s to under 9,000 in the period 1700–10. This conforms almost exactly to the record of Holland's excise tax on salmon and sturgeon, which, in turn, is certainly not contradicted by the only slightly less dramatic decline of revenue from fish sales at the river town of Geertruidenberg.

After 1700 we can follow only the course of events in the river fishery. Until mid-century the three available indicators are quite stable, showing at best a slight recovery. Thereafter, the revival is more pronounced but without approaching even remotely the levels of the mid–seventeenth century. Even this modest recovery appears to have been interrupted by a collapse in the 1780s (in the two indicators remaining after 1777).

The overall course of inland fishing between 1650 and 1805 follows the general course of long-term price trends for agricultural products (see Chapter 6, section 6.3) and for land rents (see Figures 11.4 through 11.6) in the same period. The fishing indicators differ in certain particulars (a steeper decline after 1650, an earlier turning point, a more modest eighteenth-century recovery), but before drawing conclusions, it might be best to consider first just what the fishing indicators brought together in Figure 7.1 actually show.

Most of the lines are the product of the combined effect of the size of the catch and of prices – or of expectations about these two variables. Since the total revenues generated by these levies on fish declined by 1700 to only 30 percent of their 1650 level, we can entertain two extreme interpretations: that prices fell

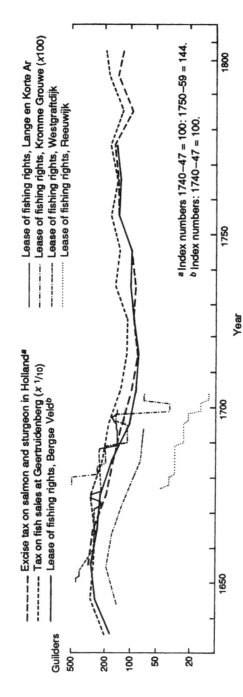

Figure 7.1. Trends in inland fishing, 1630–1805 (semi-logarithmic scale). (*Sources:* A. M. van der Woude, *De contractiefase*, 383; P. J. M. Martens, *De zalmvissers*, 485–500; A. Th. van Deursen, *Bronnen*, 58; A. R. A. 3.19.57, Heerlijkheid Voshol 1543–1835, inv. nr. 10, Memorien en notitiën van Voshol.)

by 70 percent while the volume of fish catches remained constant, or that prices held steady while the catches fell by 70 percent. In view of the general tendency for nearly all commodity prices to fall in this period, the second hypothesis seems unreasonable. But such a severe price decline within 50 years is also without precedent, so that the only reasonable interpretation is that some combination of price and quantity declines generated the observed results.

We may never be in a position to establish the relative contributions of these two variables to this decline, but it will remain difficult to avoid the conclusion that the inland fishery suffered setbacks between 1650 and 1700 of such severity that it lost permanently much of its economic importance. Its diminishing significance is tellingly revealed in van Deursen's detailed study of the social position of the persons who leased the fishing rights in the village of Westgraftdijk. The village notables of 1650 gradually made way for persons of a much lower social position, as what had been an important and lucrative activity became a marginal factor in the village economy.

Little is known about the prices of freshwater fish, but here too there may be an interesting story, for if, as we have argued, supplies were diminishing after 1650, a substantial fall of prices would point toward an even faster diminution of demand. A likely cause of such diminished demand for fish can be found in a growing competitiveness of the chief alternative source of protein: meat. The agricultural depression that gained momentum through the second half of the seventeenth century depressed meat prices, but it also caused a substantial reallocation of agricultural resources from the production of grains (the prices of which fell most of all) toward meat and other relative luxuries. If the fishing industry faced falling prices and falling profit margins because of this new competition, its survival would have hinged upon its ability to reduce production costs (through the introduction of new fishing techniques and improved equipment) or on the providential appearance in Dutch waters of much larger fish stocks. There is no evidence for the former, and concerning the freshwater fish stocks, all the evidence points in the opposite direction. Since most production costs (wages, vessels, nets, etc.) did not fall with declining commodity prices after 1650, the freshwater fishery found itself in an increasingly untenable position.

The present state of our knowledge about inland fishing precludes an explanation of its development in other than hypothetical terms. It does not appear possible, however, to treat it as a casual activity of noncommercial amateurs. By the sixteenth century, it played an important part in the feeding of Holland's towns, and it later faced the typical problems – production costs, resource exhaustion, competition – of a modern fishing industry.

7.2. Coastal fishing

Very little is known about the coastal fishery. In the Middle Ages, the Flemish coast, together with the adjacent Zeeland estuary and delta waters, formed its center of gravity. It owed its considerable importance to the large urban markets of Flanders and Brabant, which it supplied with fresh fish, but nothing is known of its historical development; the coastal fishery has yet to find its historian.

We do know that during the Twelve Years' Truce (1609–21), when the markets of the Southern Netherlands once again were readily accessible, the Zeeland fishery revived with vigor. This suggests that it had also been of importance before the closing of the Schelde in 1585. But by then the coastal fishery's chief focus had drifted north of the delta to villages along Holland's dune coast and even further to the islands of Texel and Vlieland. The explanation for this northward drift in the course of the fifteenth and sixteenth centuries appears to lie in a search for safety, as the Flemish coast was repeatedly threatened by hostilities, especially during the wars between Charles V and Francis I.

The growth of population in the North, and hence of markets for fish, may also have encouraged this displacement. But we know that distant markets also played an important role in this fishery. In the fifteenth century, large quantities of fish were shipped up the river IJssel to Cologne, and from there further up the Rhine as far as Basel. The sorts of fish mentioned in this trade point to the importance of the coastal fishery as a source of supply. In the first half of the sixteenth century, fishermen from Holland's coastal villages supplied the Pentecost market in Antwerp (Pentecost marked the end of the coastal fishing season) with such large quantities of dried plaice as to attract wholesale buyers from Cologne, Metz, and Strasbourg.

In the third quarter of the fifteenth century, the fishing communities along Holland's dune coast were sufficiently prosperous to finance their own participation in the rapidly emerging – and very capital-intensive – salted herring industry. Prosperity did not bless these communities for long, however, as the political disorders that began after 1477 hit the coastal fishing villages with such force that they never recovered fully. Nor, since they possessed no harbors (they beached their small craft along the coast), could they long continue direct participation in the new herring fishery. They had to use harbors in the river mouths to dock the large herring busses, and this necessarily involved them with cities such as Den Briel. By the early sixteenth century, this new industry was very largely in the hands of well-capitalized urban entrepreneurs.

Nor was nature kind to the sixteenth-century coastal fishery. The transgression phase of rising sea levels (see Chapter 2, section 2.1.3), which pushed salt water ever further into the Zuider Zee basin, also increased the frequency of violent storm tides that afflicted the coastal villages with erosion and drifting sand. Travel to the markets behind the dunes became more difficult, and on the islands of Texel and Vlieland, coastal locations became all but untenable. Many island fishermen redirected their attention from the ocean to the shrimp-rich tidal waters of the Wadden Zee; the rest sought work in the expanding shipping industry. It was especially on the northern half of Holland's coast that the fishing villages suffered a gradual depopulation, whereby they form a conspicuous exception to the rapid growth of the population as a whole. The explanation for this phenomenon can only be sought in the condition of the coastal fishery, the only source of livelihood in these villages. This process of deterioration continued in the seventeenth and eighteenth centuries, during which time these coastal places acquired the distinction of becoming among the poorest communities of Holland.

7.3. The herring fishery

The herring fishery, which came to be known as the "great fishery," refers to the catching of herring on the open sea – at the Dogger Bank and before the English coast – and the gutting and salting of those herring on board the fishing vessels. This "great fishery" was always distinguished from coastal fishing for lesser sorts of herring, unsuitable for the international commerce in salted herring, which were intended for local sale, whether fresh (pan herring), lightly salted (*korf* herring), or smoked (*bokking*).

The development of the herring buss, a veritable factory ship on which the herring were not only caught but processed on board, is undoubtedly one of the seminal innovations of the fifteenth century, and it played a leading role in the economic rise of the new Republic at the end of the sixteenth century. The herring fishery was actually a variant of a *trafiek* industry: An unfinished product (the salted herring) was brought to port, where it received further processing and packing, and then became an important export article. Alongside products such as wine, cloth, and salt, the salted herring took its place as one of the premier trade goods to the Baltic region and the German lands. It weighed heavily in the Republic's overall balance of trade with these markets, and the decline of this export article after the mid–seventeenth century had an impact that ramified widely through the economy of the Republic. Here, too, we are dealing with a branch of economic life that tracks the secular trend.

In contrast to fresh fish, which had to find consumers in reasonable proximity to port, fish preserved via drying, smoking, or pickling had already become important internationally traded goods in the thirteenth and fourteenth centuries. Hanseatic merchants regularly supplied Flanders with dried cod (*stokvis*) from Norway and salted herring caught off the coast of Schonen (southern Sweden). The Schonen herring fishery was a form of coastal fishing, whereby fresh herring was brought to port to be cleaned and salted. Fishermen along the Flemish coast and in the Zeeland delta also began fishing for herring, which was sold fresh or lightly salted. But such herring as could be caught near the coast was not suitable to become a quality salted product that could compete with the Schonen herring. For that purpose fishermen would have to venture farther from shore, to the Dogger Bank and the English coast near Yarmouth. As early as the first half of the fourteenth century, Zeeland and Holland fishermen took this step, but they operated with small vessels that supplied only the Netherlandish markets with fresh or lightly salted herring.

The breakthrough came after 1400, at a time when the herring schools off the Schonen coast became less numerous and the fishery there declined. As the supply of Schonen herring to the Netherlands contracted, an opportunity emerged for anyone who could catch these herring on the North Sea and thereby fill the place being vacated by the Hanse merchants. The problem faced by the would-be supplier was this: The further one sailed into the North Sea to catch the high-quality herring, the shorter the amount of time one could fish before having to return to port with the fresh catch. The economic success of this enterprise depended on innovations that made it possible to prolong one's time at sea – to spend more time fishing and to reach more distant fishing grounds – while maintaining the quality of the herring.

The essential breakthrough was the development of a technique to preserve the quality of the herring by quickly gutting and salting the fish while at sea. To both catch and process the fish on board, and to remain at sea for five to eight weeks at a time, required a second innovation: the herring buss, a large vessel which, by the mid–sixteenth century, carried a crew of eighteen to thirty men. In comparison to the other types of fishing vessels of the time, this was a floating factory, and it is not difficult to understand how a fleet of 400 to 500 of these gigantic fishing vessels – was this the world's first great fishing fleet? – captured the imagination of contemporaries.

The processing technique and the herring buss, as well as rigging and on-board organization, underwent a long-term process of experimentation and refinement throughout the fifteenth and sixteenth centuries. By 1600 these innovations had attained their classic forms, to which the industry remained steadfastly loyal for the next 200 years.

Besides these technical innovations, the herring fishery also experienced institutional innovations. In its early stages, the ownership of the herring busses was in the hands of partnerships, the *partenrederij* prevalent also in ocean shipping, which usually included as partners the skippers of the vessels. Even the fishermen sometimes invested in the partnership, typically by supplying a portion of the nets, which their wives and children, or they themselves during the off-season, had made. However, already in the fifteenth century, many fishermen worked for wages (one reads then of "ten harinc om een huyere"), and over time wage labor so grew in importance that first the fishermen and later even the skipper disappeared as participants in the partnerships, leaving a *partenrederij* composed primarily of urban investors. In the mid–sixteenth century, when the herring buss fleet of Holland alone already numbered some 400 vessels and other economic activities were yet of a rather modest scope, these *partenrederijen* must have formed one of Holland's most important fields of investment. Here, too, we can appreciate how jealous observers of the Republic's later commercial prowess saw the herring fishery as the veritable taproot of her economic strength.

Still, a plausible argument can be made that the herring fishery's profitability was, when compared with newly developing commercial activities, decidedly modest. A model account of revenues and expenses in this fishery made by van Gelder and Kranenburg for the beginning of the seventeenth century points in this direction. The revenue derived from the sale of the average annual catch of a herring buss then amounted to about 6,850 guilders. Net of expenses, this left investors a profit of only about 500 guilders. Better investment opportunities existed at that time, it would appear, and one of them may well have been the trade in herring. According to Unger, the trade in herring between Amsterdam and Danzig in the period 1630–49 generated a net profit of 27 percent on the invested capital. The *trade* in herring appears to have offered profit opportunities superior to those available in the *production* of herring.

Profit calculations for this period are invariably speculative, contingent as they are on several assumptions. But the presence of superior profit possibilities elsewhere is certainly suggested by the decline after 1600 of the *partenrederij* as the typical form of investment in the herring fishery. In its place one begins to observe traders in herring emerging as owners of the busses. Numerous shipping firms (*rederijen*) functioned over the years side by side with the *partenrederijen*, which by no means disappeared from the scene. Most of these firms owned only a few vessels, but some controlled as many as ten herring busses at a time.

For the herring fishery, this meant a radical change of structure, featuring vertical integration of production, processing, and trade. It is known that herring traders dominated the labor-intensive herring-packing sector, and it takes no great leap of faith to presume their active participation in the trade and refining of salt, the crucial agent in herring preservation. In this way a sequence of seasonal activities was knit together, whereby funds invested in the busses, which were most active from May or June to September, shifted to the herring trade to the Baltic in October and November. With the revenues generated from the sale of herring, the traders bought up grain in the Baltic ports through the winter months, which they shipped to Amsterdam or other Western European markets with the opening of navigation in the spring. These revenues, in turn, could be used to purchase unrefined salt for shipment to the Republic or invested, once again, in the equipping of herring busses for the new season. Thus was the annual investment cycle completed.

The herring fishery's achievements, legendary already in their own time, rested on a foundation of fifteenth- and sixteenth-century technological innovations and were advanced powerfully by new forms of organization and investment toward the end of the sixteenth century. But we must not neglect a third essential element in this success story: the development of a purposeful public policy in support of the industry. Already in the fifteenth century, the fishing towns drafted regulations concerning the sorting, salting, and packing of herring. These measures, designed to assure a uniform quality in what was becoming an internationally traded commodity, often were taken in response to complaints from foreign customers, such as the city of Cologne, whence the German hinterland was supplied. A second object of regulation concerned the convoying of the herring busses, to secure their protection from attacks at sea. In this matter the fishermen themselves often took the initiative.

As the number of cities and villages active in the deep-sea herring fishery increased, the quest for coordination intensified, and the central government began to intervene in its affairs. In 1495 the central government ordered that representatives of this fishery from Holland and Zeeland should meet yearly with spokesmen for the city of Cologne to discuss outstanding issues. By 1519 Charles V promulgated the first general laws intended to regulate the herring fishery. But the highly technical character of the industry rendered impossible the promulgation and enforcement of regulations without the involvement of the parties directly involved. In recognition of this fact, we see beginning around the 1550s representatives from various of the herring centers gathering to advance their interests. After passing through several permutations, this body took a permanent form in the third quarter of the sixteenth century, under the name *College van Commissarissen van de Groote Visscherij* (College of Commissioners of the Great Fishery). It may have begun as an advisory body, but it became in fact a regulatory one. With its superior command of the technical details of the trade, the college set about drafting regulations that the state had little option but to adopt as its own. The college also administered its own regulations, and in Holland after 1600, it acquired enforcement powers as well. In addition it organized the convoys to protect the herring fleet and levied a *lastgeld*, a tax to defray the costs of this service.

The *College van de Groote Visscherij* did not involve itself with the price of herring, and it left each firm and partnership free to operate on its own. But its numerous regulations forced the producers to function as a sort of consortium, one producing a standardized product, in their dealings with customers. The regulations touched nearly every aspect of the industry except the actual sale of the product: the beginning and ending dates of the fishing season; the speed with which the gutting and salting of herring was to occur on board the busses; the type, quality, and quantity of salt used; the size and construction of the barrels; the procedures to be followed in the transfer of fish at port from the vessels to the packers; the manner of packing; the trademarking of the barrels; the sorting of the herring by quality; the appointment of inspectors; and so on.

The combination of technical innovation with a high measure of integration of financing, production, and trade plus the careful regulation of all aspects of the industry secured for the Dutch salted herring a monopoly position on western European markets for some two centuries after 1500. Each of these factors contributed to the industry's success, but the pivotal factor was surely the fishing technology. The use of large busses pushed up the size of the herring catches for three reasons: (1) the busses were much heavier than the vessels customarily used in coastal fishing, and this required that they deploy many more nets, since fishing boats and their nets must keep each other in equilibrium during fishing operations; (2) once the gutting and salting of the herring could take place on board, the need to return to port at frequent intervals was removed, permitting long, uninterrupted fishing campaigns; and (3) since the large busses could operate on the high seas, it was possible to seek out and follow the schools of herring, which made the industry less dependent on the vagaries of nature than was the coastal fishery.

Besides this quantitative factor, the qualitative factor was not of less importance. Since the herring caught in each night of fishing were gutted and salted immediately the following morning, the quality of the product lay far above that of the coastal fishery, where the fish could not be processed until the boats returned to port, by which time the fish were invariably less fresh. The quality of the herring also depended on the properties of the salt used, which made Dutch domination of the salt trade so important to the success of the herring fishery. The rise of the two went hand in hand.

Implementing these technical developments called for a much larger investment of capital than had been needed in the coastal fishery. Before 1600 the *partenrederij*, a device to bundle the investments of many people and reduce the risk to which any individual was exposed, sufficed to supply the funds needed. But as we have seen, after 1600 the continued expansion of the industry drew the merchants who traded in herring back into the production sphere in order to assure themselves the supplies they needed. Their more concentrated commitments of capital exposed them to a greater risk than that faced by the participants in *partenrederijen*. Small wonder, then, that these large investors supported and advanced policies to coordinate the industry, protect their ships by convoying, and protect their markets with quality controls. The need for the College of Commissioners was felt more intensely than ever before, and its rise fixed the definitive form that the industry would exhibit until its collapse around 1800.

The final innovation in the herring fishery occurred as a response to the development, also toward the end of the sixteenth century, of the *fluitschip*, an economical, specialized cargo carrier. The herring buss could then no longer compete as a freight carrier outside the fishing season, which loosened and finally broke the connection between fishing and shipping that had long characterized the industry. In reaction, the busses became somewhat smaller – manned by crews of 12 to 14 instead of 18 to 30. This adaptation made them more specifically suited to the needs of fishing but at the expense of a dual use that earlier had helped to reduce the investors' overall level of risk.

Simultaneous with the herring fishery's technical and organizational consolidation, there occurred its geographical consolidation. Originally, when herring was still a coastal fishery, its locus was along the Flemish coast. As we noted earlier, in the course of the fourteenth and fifteenth centuries, the locus of herring fishery moved gradually northward toward Zeeland and then to the coast of Holland. The rise of the herring buss forced the fishery to places with suitable harbors, most of which were found in the delta of South Holland. Den Briel long reigned as the chief center of the herring fishery, to be superseded over time by

Rotterdam, Schiedam, Vlaardingen, and Delfshaven. Dordrecht remained until the mid–sixteenth century the center of herring packing. In 1476 contemporary estimates put the entire herring fleet – in Flanders, Zeeland, and Holland together – at some 250 vessels. By 1560 there were said to be about 100 in Flanders, 200 in Zeeland, and 400 in Holland, where the busses were larger than elsewhere. The delta region was well situated to receive the returning fleets: It offered the harbor facilities needed by the large busses, and it afforded direct access to major markets in the Southern Netherlands, the Rhineland, and other parts of Germany.

The first decades of the Revolt (1570–90) created a fundamentally new situation for the herring fishery, undermining the locational advantages long enjoyed by the delta region. To begin with, military activities made the waters of Zeeland and even the mouth of the Maas river unsafe. This, together with the closing of the Southern Netherlands market, proved to be the death knell for the Zeeland herring fishery. Representatives of the Zeeland fishing towns Goedereede, Bommenee, Zierikzee, Veere, Westkapelle, and Zoutelande had attended meetings of the deputies and commissioners of the fishery right through the third quarter of the sixteenth century. But in 1576 the Zeelanders stayed home because of a conflict with the Hollanders about the level of the *lastgeld* to be charged, and thereafter next to nothing is heard from them. Their fishery apparently collapsed in the years that followed.

In the Maas estuary, where most of Holland's industry was concentrated, the fleet also suffered much damage. This encouraged the fishermen and buss owners from North Holland, who had stationed their vessels in the South Holland river towns, to remove their operations to the more peaceful waters of the Zuider Zee. There the herring fishery focused on but one town, Enkhuizen. Enkhuizen's moment in the sun would have been fleeting were it not for simultaneous changes in both the fishing grounds and the markets for herring. The prime fishing grounds at the Dogger Bank and off the East Anglian coast were joined by a third zone when large herring schools suddenly appeared in the northwestern portion of the North Sea, between the Shetland Islands and the Norwegian coast. This new fishing ground, called *Hitland*, was far more accessible from Enkhuizen than from the delta region. Even more important was the emergence of the Baltic region and Northwest Germany as the largest foreign market for salted herring. On this matter the eastbound trade data gathered at the Danish Sound (Table 7.2) offer unambiguous evidence. Trustworthy estimates establish that of the 20,000 lasts of salted herring caught in an average year of the first half of the seventeenth century, about 40 percent was sent to the Baltic and another 20 percent to Northwest Germany.

Explanation of this market development must be sought in the unfathomable capriciousness of nature, which beginning in 1589 removed the herring schools from the Swedish coast. The Scandinavian fishery that earlier had supplied the Netherlands now could not satisfy local markets. The rapidly expanding com-

Table 7.2. *Lasts of herring shipped from the Netherlands through the Danish Sound, 1562–1780 (in annual averages).*

1562–69	2,619	1671–80	1,954
1574–79	456	1681–90	2,959
1580–89	852	1691–00	1,879
1590–99	5,044	1701–10	329
1600–09	8,495	1711–20	1,114
1610–19	8,658	1721–30	1,748
1620–29	7,593	1731–40	1,764
1630–39	7,512	1741–50	585
1640–49	8,089	1751–60	663
1650–57	3,383	1761–70	610
1661–70	2,607	1771–80	1,389

Source: W. S. Unger, "De Sonttabellen," p. 114; "De Sonttabellen voltooid," p. 190.

modity trade between the Netherlands and the Baltic moved with special eagerness to fill the breach, for the Baltic trade as a whole had been highly unbalanced, with far more westbound cargoes than eastbound. Sending herring on the ships sailing in ballast to the Baltic substantially improved the profitability of this trade. The Zuider Zee (Amsterdam and Enkhuizen) was far better situated than the established delta ports, both to reach the new fishing grounds and to supply what suddenly emerged as the largest export market for herring. From the 1590s the herring fishery was permanently divided between the delta and the Zuider Zee.

The number of active herring busses can be followed with high accuracy beginning in 1736, and in the case of Enkhuizen's fishery, annual data are available from 1688, with an isolated observation for 1669. In addition, estimates can be made for several years scattered through the sixteenth and seventeenth centuries. These various sources are brought together in Figure 7.2, which exhibits several notable developments.

1. The number of herring busses active in Holland in the second half of the sixteenth century was smaller than in the first half of the seventeenth, but not by much. When one recalls that there had been a substantial Zeeland fleet in the sixteenth century (some 200 vessels, by contemporary estimate) that later disappeared, the total fleet in, say, 1560 will not have been smaller than in the seventeenth century. When one recalls further that the sixteenth-century busses in Holland were on average bigger, using a larger crew, than after 1600, then the only possible conclusion is that the herring fishery employed more labor in the sixteenth century than in the early seventeenth.

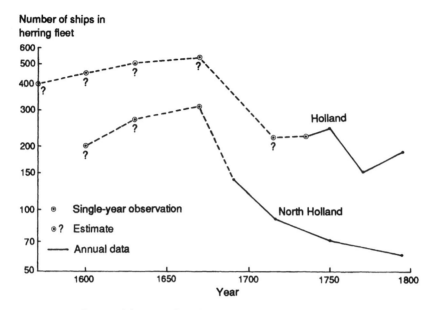

Figure 7.2. Evolution of the size of the herring fleet in North Holland and Holland as a whole, 1570–1795 (semi-logarithmic scale). (*Sources:* Kranenburg, *De zeevisscherij*, 32–41; Willemsen, *Enkhuizen*, 164–6.)

2. The high point of Holland's herring fishery, when measured by the number of ships (and also the size of the catch?), must be located in the early seventeenth century. The leading scholar of this industry, Kranenburg, locates the absolute peak around 1630. Then some 500 busses sailed into the North Sea each year. With crews averaging twelve to fourteen men, these vessels together employed some 6,000 to 7,000 fishermen. When we recall the observations made earlier concerning the larger number of vessels and the larger crews around 1560, it appears that at this earlier date some 9,000 to 10,000 fishermen earned their living in the herring fishery.

3. After the mid–seventeenth century, the herring fishery began its retreat. This is clear from the often detailed quantitative data available for the fishing ports in the delta, but the less informative North Holland data point in the same direction. Kranenburg's study proposes that Enkhuizen's fleet declined from 270 busses around 1630 to about 200 in 1700. A more recent study by Willemsen establishes that 315 herring busses counted Enkhuizen as their home port in 1669. This figure could vary considerably year by year. In the period 1688–92, and again in 1696–1700, the average number of vessels sailing from Enkhuizen was 181, but the short-term fluctuations were substantial since ves-

sels from the delta might shift their operations to Enkhuizen in response to war with France. Consequently, we regard 140 Enkhuizen vessels around 1690 as better reflecting the permanent fleet of that city.

4. The first decade of the eighteenth century witnessed a sudden collapse of the herring fishery. The French inflicted enormous losses on the herring fleet during the War of the Spanish Succession. Of course, such military disruptions were not exactly new. The Eighty Years' War had also inflicted great damage. In the single year 1625, the Dunkirk pirates are said to have taken 100 Enkhuizen busses as prizes. What distinguishes the disruptions at the beginning of the eighteenth century is that the fishery did not recover from its setbacks. When peace came, the Enkhuizen fleet stabilized at about half its pre-1700 size.

5. A second sharp contraction of the herring fleet (from about 225 vessels to 140) occurred in the years 1756–61. This time it was the delta region that suffered most. From 1761 to the 1790s, a gradual recovery is observable, but this did not regain more than a fraction of the lost ground.

6. A comparison of the fortunes of the delta ports with Enkhuizen reveals that the decline of the herring fishery was much more severe in Enkhuizen: from some 270 to 55 vessels as against a decline from about 220 to 95 in the delta. Enkhuizen's share in the industry declined from 55 to 35 percent.

An explanation for these various developments can be inferred from trends in the size of the herring catches and from shifts in the international markets for herring. The catches varied enormously year by year, of course, but the average annual catch around 1640 is reliably set at some 20,000 lasts. By the second half of the eighteenth century, the average catch had diminished to about 5,500 lasts. Throughout this period domestic demand accounted for about 20 percent of the supply (4,000 lasts around 1640 to 1,000 lasts after 1750). The chief export market until 1650 was the Baltic, and Table 7.2 indicates that some 8,000 lasts (40 percent of the Dutch catch) passed eastbound through the Sound. The largest single market for herring was actually Hamburg, which then took about 4,000 lasts per year (20 percent of the catch). The remaining 20 percent then found its way to consumers in the Rhineland (via Cologne), in northern France and Paris (via Rouen), and in Brabant and Flanders.

After 1650 the Baltic market quickly lost much of its earlier importance, declining to the mid–sixteenth-century level of 2,000 to 3,000 lasts. The difference of some 5,000 lasts constituted a serious loss of demand that could have been compensated for only very partially by the direct access to the Southern Netherlands' market secured by the Peace of Münster of 1648. The decline of Baltic demand was felt most severely by Enkhuizen's fishermen and the Amsterdam herring trade, which helps to account for the early contraction of the Enkhuizen fleet. After 1700 Baltic demand plunged once again, this time to an average of only 1,000 lasts per year. In this context the failure of the Enkhuizen fleet to recover the losses inflicted by the French in 1703 is no longer so strange.

The herring trade with the Baltic is uniquely well documented, but its decline is not really unique. All markets, domestic and foreign, declined in this period, some more severely than others. We already noted that the home market took no more than 1,000 lasts per year after 1750, a quarter of its consumption a century earlier; the North German market only absorbed about 1,500 lasts after 1750. This leaves about 2,000 lasts for all markets south and east of the Republic, or about half of their pre-1650 consumption.

After 1650 Holland's herring fishery lost ground in all its markets. Did new competitors divert her customers or did consumer preferences shift toward other products? In the case of the Baltic market, the emergence of competitive suppliers had a big impact. The many months of the year in which the waters of this region were frozen forced the inhabitants to lay on supplies of salted or dried fish, and between 1590 and 1650, the Hollanders were the only significant suppliers. In this period they enjoyed true monopoly power in this vast region, making the herring trade highly profitable. But after 1650 the Scandinavian fishery gradually began to recover, and new supplies pressed down the price of fish in Baltic markets. The price differences between Holland and the Baltic became smaller, and after 1690 fish prices were often lower in the Baltic, robbing this trade of profitability. Massive supplies of Scottish herring began to penetrate the Baltic markets after 1700, making matters even worse for the Hollanders. Their share of the total supply of herring passing through the Sound retreated steadily from 80–90 percent in the 1600–1650 period, to about 30 percent in 1710–1740, and to 10–15 percent after 1760.

If Holland's herring catches had remained at their old level, the drastic shrinkage of Baltic demand would have placed a pronounced downward pressure on prices in the remaining markets. But Kranenburg has demonstrated convincingly that the average eighteenth-century catch was much smaller than a century earlier (30 lasts per ship versus 40; see Figure 7.3). Perhaps overfishing reduced the catches; perhaps a change in herring migration patterns made them less numerous in the fishing grounds. At any rate the catches diminished while the costs of outfitting and operating the herring busses tended, if anything, to rise. The nets for one buss rose in price from 1,300 to 1,750 guilders between 1600 and 1750; the buss itself rose from about 3,500 to 4,700 guilders; the barrels used in herring packing rose from 6 to 15 guilders per 14 barrels. The consequence of all this was a tendency for Dutch herring prices to rise, but not enough to prevent a sharply diminished profitability of the industry.

The average catch per ship recovered its old level for a time after the War of the Spanish Succession (1702–13) (see Figure 7.3), but thereafter the catches declined again to much lower levels. Rising herring prices prevented an absolute decline in the value of the catches until the 1750s. The reduction of revenue that

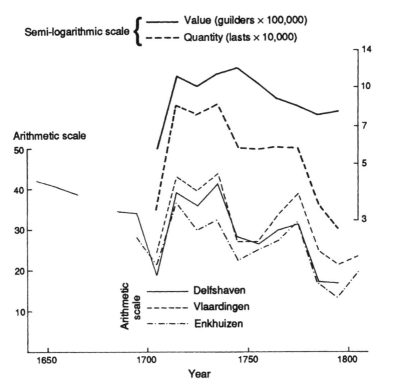

Figure 7.3. The average annual catch per herring buss by home port in lasts (arithmetic scale), and the total catch of the herring fishery of Holland in lasts and monetary value (semi-logarithmic scale), ten-year averages. (*Source:* Willemsen, *Enkhuizen*, p. 168.)

then set in makes the sharp decline in the number of active herring busses in the 1760s easier to understand. Moreover, the remaining fleet appears to have spent more time in freight service, since the number of fishing expeditions made per vessel was distinctly lower after 1750 than before. Beginning in 1780 war and political tension repeatedly brought the remnant of this industry to a standstill, leading to its complete collapse in the Batavian-French era.

During this long period of decline, foreign rivals managed to copy the old secrets of the Dutch herring fishery, and they proved to be strong competitors because of better access to the fishing grounds (in the case of the Scandinavians), lower wages (true of both the Scots and the Scandinavians), and protected markets (the salvation of the English). Moreover, these competitors were not bound, as were the Hollanders, by the myriad regulations enforced by the College of Commissioners. These regulations guaranteed the integrity of the Dutch product, to be sure, but they were predicated on an ability to fetch a premium price for that product. It is worth noting that the herring fishery responded to its market challenges by moving "up market" – by improving product quality yet further. That response might reflect a mental predisposition, but it is certainly possible that persons active in this sector understood that their cost structure doomed from the start any effort to compete with others in supplying a cheaper product.

7.4. The lesser fishery

A second branch of ocean fishing specialized in cod (and also shellfish), which were first sought at the Dogger Bank, but after the mid–seventeenth century also in waters off Iceland. The name given by contemporaries, *kleine visserij* (lesser fishery), should not mislead us; this was not a sector of trivial importance. It involved, just as the herring fishery, the delivery of fish already salted on board the fishing boat, especially salted cod, known as *labberdaan*. However, its fishing technique was utterly different. The fishermen used no nets but deployed hooks and bait, the latter supplied by the river fishery. Originally, the vessels used were smaller than the herring buss, but when the industry proceeded beyond the Dogger Bank to Iceland, it had to adopt a larger type, the *hoeker*. These fishing boats approached the buss in size.

Another difference with the herring fishery derives from the export markets. Salted herring found markets in two great regions: the Baltic and Hamburg to the north and the region between the Rhine and Seine to the south. Only the second of these generated a demand for salted cod. As a direct consequence, this fishery functioned only out of the delta region. Nor did the Dutch cod fishery ever exercise monopoly power over its market as the herring fishery long did. Throughout its history, Dutch cod had to compete with the French and English fisheries off the coast of Newfoundland.

Since it did without the protective ministrations of a College of Commissioners, quantitative information about the size of the fleet, the number of crew members, and the size of the catch is scarce. But we know enough to state that the lesser fishery experienced a much more stable development than did the herring fishery. The century after 1650, so full of travail for the herring fishery, brought continued expansion to the cod fishery, so that around 1765 it was of the same size as the herring fishery in the delta region. In 1768 a Dutch fleet of 160 ships fished for cod in Icelandic waters alone. The general position of this fishery is illustrated by the export data that happen to have been preserved for 1753. The delta ports then exported 2,186 lasts of herring versus 1,589 lasts of salted fish (primarily cod).

In 1780 a fleet of 150 vessels departed from delta ports to fish for cod, a number equal to all Holland's remaining herring busses. But this fishery, too, had fallen onto hard times. It was said to be quite profitable in the first half of the eighteenth century, but thereafter its performance faltered. There is insufficient evidence to sustain any interpretation of this reversal of fortune. More effective foreign competition is certainly a plausible cause, as is the impact of new protectionist measures limiting access to the Southern Netherlands. At any rate, by 1775 the cod fishery and the herring fishery alike required a public subsidy of 500 guilders per ship per year to continue operations. The ocean fisheries – once regarded as the principal gold mine of the Republic – had become another depressed industry.

7.5. Whaling

The organized and systematic pursuit of whales, which first appears in North European waters around 1600, must be understood in the context of the market for oils and fats. This seaborne hunt's most important commercial product, whale oil, competed with vegetable products such as rape, linseed, and hemp oils for the same final uses: soap production, lighting, and leather working. Consumers had good reason to prefer vegetable oils (because of the unpleasant smell of whale oil), which tended to force the price of whale oil under that of equal units of vegetable oils. But since they were close substitutes, whale oil prices were highly sensitive to harvest conditions and other factors determining the supply of vegetable oils. In addition, whaling, as with all fisheries, was highly dependent on the vagaries of nature and chance. Finally, whaling was directly influenced by political factors that determined access to, and safety at, sea. The combination of all these elements generated sharp annual fluctuations in the number of participating ships, the size of the catch, and the financial returns to whaling.

The great interest in whale oil that appeared suddenly and unexpectedly among English, Dutch, French, Basque, and Danish entrepreneurs between 1610 and 1615, and the stubborn persistence that they all exhibited in the face of setbacks inflicted by unskilled crews, disappointing catches, and mutually hostile conduct, can only be explained by the expectation of large profits borne by high oil prices. In view of the large measure of substitutability between vegetable and animal oils, we should pause a bit longer on the nature of the market for these products before continuing with a discussion of the whaling industry.

Oil was consumed directly (for lighting and cooking) and indirectly (as a raw material in soap production). Other uses for oil (such as paint production, lubrication, and leather working) were of minor importance. The three-pronged household demand for oil could be satisfied as follows: The demand for lighting and soap could be supplied by (1) rape, linseed, and hemp oil; (2) imported "sweet" oils (chiefly olive oil); and (3) whale oil. A comparison of prices suggests that the oils imported from the Mediterranean played no important role in these markets; they cost twice as much as domestically pressed vegetable oils. The price of whale oil was lower, but this did not drive out vegetable oils altogether because the smell and taste of whale oil reduced its appeal in cooking and soap production. We must also keep in mind that the production of these two types of oil generated by-products: Vegetable oils left a pulp suitable as animal fodder; the slaughtered whales left bones. Both by-products were sometimes significant for the viability of their industries as a whole.

The growth of demand for oil depended, in the long run, on population growth, increased per capita consumption, and growing export markets. Population growth certainly must have been an important factor in increasing the consumption of oil, but it is quite powerless to account for the sudden increase in demand observed after 1610. This increased demand, signaled by rising prices, is all the more noteworthy because of the substantial growth of vegetable oil supplies around this date. Horse-powered presses accounted for nearly all the production of rape and linseed oil in the sixteenth century. Then the development of the large *bovenkruier* windmill (see Chapter 2, section 2.3) as a source of industrial power caused a sudden enlargement of production capacity, and this capacity could be used even more effectively once a method was developed to introduce stone rollers in place of hammers to press the oil. These technical innovations made increased production possible by about 1600, but it is a curious fact that the new wind-powered, oil-pressing mills did not enter production until 1610 – the year that Hollanders launched their participation in the hunt for whales. From that date the number of oil-pressing windmills grew rapidly: In 1630 Holland possessed 72; in 1648 contemporaries believed there to be about 200; in 1768 about 220. Other provinces also possessed several, and, of course, the horse-powered mills did not all disappear. This industry was heavily concentrated in the Zaan region, which possessed some 60 percent of all oil mills. Its expansion seems to have proceeded into the third quarter of the seventeenth century, which corresponds broadly with the expansion of Dutch whaling itself, whose catches peaked in size around 1680. Between 1610 and 1680, oil production (both vegetable and animal) multiplied manyfold, far exceeding the growth of population. Growth of per capita domestic consumption, and/or strong export growth, must have stood behind this phenomenon.

Oil exports moved in all directions. In the second half of the eighteenth century, export volume varied around the 40,000 *amen* level (nearly 6 million liters). The production capacity of the pressing mills then in operation suggests a long-term annual production of between 22 and 33 million liters of vegetable oil. This is the equivalent of 150,000 to 225,000 *amen*. Exports of *all* oils in the late eighteenth century accounted for about one-fifth of Dutch *vegetable oil* production. The domestic market was clearly dominant in this period, but it is likely that exports had been rather larger at an earlier date. Early in the eighteenth century, complaints of growing competition in export markets became more frequent. The German market, for example, was said to be supplied increasingly by oil from Northern France and the Southern Netherlands. In the vicinity of Lille, some 200 oil-pressing windmills were then said to be active. Russian hemp oil also emerged as a factor in northern markets. The increasingly defensive position of the Republic in this trade is revealed in its tariff policy, which established a prohibitive tariff on oil imports already in 1725 and removed all export levies on oil in 1770. The export of oil may well have receded as early as 1700. This did not necessarily lead to a reduction of vegetable oil production but may rather have pushed whale oil out of the domestic market. This scenario is rendered plausible by the stability observed in the number of oil-pressing windmills throughout the eighteenth century. Only after 1795 did the number of these mills begin to decline, which is consistent with the sharp decline in oil exports during the Batavian-French period. After 1815 this industry managed to revive.

If we assume for a moment that per capita domestic oil use held constant through the course of the eighteenth century, then the vegetable oil output of about 28 million liters per year, one-fifth of which was exported, would leave 22 million kilograms for domestic use, or about 11 liters per capita. When we introduce to this exercise the fact that whale oil production at its peak around 1680 amounted to some 15 million liters, the unavoidable conclusion is either a vastly greater domestic consumption (which is implausible), or a vastly greater export of oil. A bit more than half of total oil production was then consumed domestically, and a nearly equal amount, some 20 million liters, was exported annually. Contrast this with the situation at the beginning of the seventeenth century, when, before the introduction of the oil-pressing windmill and before the advent of whaling, domestic use could not have been more than a fraction of what it later would become. The explosive growth of oil consumption in the first three quarters of the seventeenth century is powerful evidence of an improved standard of living, a process in which the whaling industry played a significant role.

The pioneers in Arctic whaling were the English (beginning in 1611), followed directly by the Dutch (1612) and others. During the early years of this chase after blubber, two contradictory features stand out: on the one hand, the sharp, often violent competition among the various participating nationalities; on the other, the diffusion of technical knowledge among the participants via the enticement, back and forth, of one another's more or less experienced labor force. In special demand were Basques, the first experienced harpooners.

The first of these features persuaded the States General to accede in 1614 to the establishment of the *Noordsche Compagnie* (The Northern Company), which acquired the Dutch monopoly to engage in whaling in the entire zone stretching from the coasts of Nova Zembla to the Davis Strait. This launched the first phase of Dutch whaling, which focused on the capture of whales near the coasts of Spitsbergen and Jan Mayen island. In the delicate Arctic ecological system, small, periodic fluctuations in climate can cause drastic shifts in the zones affected by drifting ice floes, which, in turn, affect the amount of plankton on which whales feed, and the *Noordsche Compagnie* experienced sharp fluctuations of fortune.

A combination of large catches and high prices was a great boon to the company's fortunes in the years between 1625 and 1635, creating a prosperity that induced many entrepreneurs to violate the company's monopoly by hunting for whales on the open sea. The many interlopers could point to the fact that England's whaling-enterprise monopoly, the Muscovy Company, had ceased to be a competitor of significance, removing the chief reason for the *Noordsche Compagnie*'s existence. Indeed, in 1642 the company's privileges were allowed to expire.

With this began the second phase of Dutch whaling, where dozens of firms set out to catch whales both near the coasts and on the open sea. The number of ships active in whaling grew especially fast after 1650, an expansion encouraged by the flexible movement of ships – depending on economic conditions – in or out of whaling, merchant shipping on the Archangel route, or salt haulage from the Bay of Biscay, among others. The type of ships used in whaling still permitted this flexible deployment.

All this changed when whaling entered its third phase, shifting from a concentration on coastal hunting grounds to hunting among the ice floes of the far north. Beginning in the 1660s, the whales began to change their customary movements, now dwelling mostly in the vicinity of the ice floes. Whether this retreat to the north was a symptom of overfishing or of climate change remains an open question. But its consequences for Dutch whaling were profound, requiring both technical and organizational changes in the industry. Technically, the whaling vessels now needed to be much sturdier, which was achieved by double-planking the hulls and by adding braces and beams at the bow. Such specialized vessels, which acquired the name *Groenlandvaarders* (sailors to Greenland), could no longer function economically as ordinary merchant ships, as a result of which the old connection between whaling and shipping was broken. Outside the whaling season, the *Groenlandvaarders* were typically laid up; whaling had become a highly specialized undertaking.

Around 1720 a fourth, and final, phase in the Dutch whaling industry began with the introduction of a new whaling zone in the Davis Straits, west of Greenland. Whaling at this distant location arose as a response to measures taken by Denmark to stop contacts between whalers and the Inuit people of Greenland. But it would be incorrect to suppose that the firms that had hunted whales in the drift ice between Spitsbergen and Greenland now simply shifted their activities to the Davis Strait. In fact, the fourth phase of Dutch whaling represents another major discontinuity. It is probable that the Davis Strait whalers were mostly new firms with no experience in the old hunting waters. These new firms did not use the heavy *Groenlandvaarders* (which were not required in the waters of the Davis Strait). The lighter, smaller vessels that they preferred restored the old connection between whaling and shipping, and especially between whaling and the shipbuilders of the Zaan region. Once again, the shipbuilders could hope to employ temporarily their unsold inventory of ships in the hunt for whales (see Chapter 8, section 8.3.2).

Each of the four phases imposed changes on the organization of the Dutch whaling industry, and each successive structure featured its own specific economic advantages and disadvantages. The *Noordsche Compagnie*, which structured the industry's first phase, was not really a single firm after the manner of the VOC. Rather, it was a cartel of substantially autonomous operators. These whalers cooperated not only in the suppression of competition but also in the establishment of settlements in the far north (most notably Smeerenburg, on Spitzbergen), where they could cut and refine the blubber. This required major investments in the construction and maintenance of ovens, barracks, storage buildings, and even a church. Besides large capital investments, the industry also appears to have faced substantial labor costs, for the ships employed by the participants in the *Noordsche Compagnie* sailed with large crews of up to eighty or ninety men. Against these high costs, the company's participants had the advantage of being able to use standard vessels that could be leased to merchant shippers outside the whaling season. Moreover, the average catch in this early period was very large, and the quality of the oil was high, since the blubber could be boiled at nearby locations directly after the whales were caught.

To guard against glutting the market (and perhaps also against overfishing), the company set limits to the allowable size of the total catch (before 1622 up to 19,000 *kwartelen* of oil; in 1622, 1630, and 1636, 21,000, 17,500, and 16,000 *kwartelen*, respectively; 1 *kwarteel* = 232.8 liters). These maxima appear to have been reached (and exceeded) often, for we know that additional ships were sometimes dispatched to Smeerenburg to carry home the entire season's production. Indeed, there were years when it was decided to abandon the whale bones in order to secure sufficient storage space for the more valuable oil.

Bruijn's calculations of the industry's revenues and expenses around 1650 reveal a situation of exorbitant profit: The value of the whale products then stood near 1 million guilders, while expenditures amounted to about 400,000. With such profit margins, it is not surprising that aspiring entrants to the whaling industry objected strenuously to the renewal of the *Noordsche Compagnie*'s monopoly charter. As we have seen, the company's charter was allowed to lapse in 1642. Low oil prices temporarily discouraged new investments, but the revival of prices after 1650 triggered a massive expansion of the Dutch whaling industry. Between the first and second Anglo-Dutch wars, the number of ships setting out for the whale hunt rose from 75 to nearly 200.

In these years the continuing retreat of drift ice to the Artic's far north drew the whalers ever farther away from their whaling stations, which forced them to strip the carcasses of their blubber while at sea, pack the blubber in barrels, and delay refining the blubber until the return of the ships to port at the end of the whaling campaign.

This new operating procedure reduced the quality of the whale oil, reducing in turn its value relative to the competing rapeseed and linseed oils. In 1625–34, when all whale oil was still processed on Spitzbergen, the prices of rapeseed, linseed, and whale oil stood in the ratio of 100:92:78. Between 1635 and 1680, as the transition was completed to processing in the Republic at the end of the hunting season, these prices hovered in the ratio of 100:92:circa 60. Compensating for this loss of revenue was the reduction of cost achieved by a smaller average crew size and the less frequent use of the costly Spitzbergen whaling station. In addition, the replacement of the old monopoly company by flexible, risk-spreading *partenrederijen* (marine partnerships) tended to reduce the cost of capital.

The explosive growth of the free whaling industry after 1650 focused a sudden and intense pressure on the labor market; seasonal demand jumped from about 2,500 men around 1650 to some 8,000 in 1663 and 1664. Where were these men to be found? The Dutch fishing communities could offer little labor since the herring fishery then stood at its peak, and whaling's pronounced seasonality (operations were confined to the period April–August) made it difficult to integrate with other branches of port employment. The industry's expansion came to depend on the attraction of a labor force willing and able to combine whaling with other activities in the off-season. This seasonal labor force was recruited among the rural population of the German coastal zone.

From the 1660s on, Holland's whaling fleets sailed each year with crews two-thirds of which came from northern Germany. As a consequence, expertise in the heavy and difficult work of whaling – knowledge of weather conditions and the movement of the ice floes, the behavior of sea mammals, and the techniques of harpooning and stripping the blubber at sea – became widespread along Germany's North Sea coast. This certainly helps to explain why North German whaling firms managed to emerge as effective competitors to the Dutch whalers, while the English and the Danes failed to make the transition to whaling among the ice floes and suspended their activities altogether for many years. In this period the only other participants in the whaling hunt were the Basques. But given the large distance to their home ports, they were forced to boil their blubber on board their ships, which limited severely the scale of their operations.

The potential profitability of whaling in the high Arctic must have been distinctly less than that of whaling near the island coasts. The whaling firms lost the flexibility that they had enjoyed in being able to transfer their vessels to freight service in the off-season. The Arctic waters required specially constructed ships unsuitable for ordinary freight service, and the high cost of these vessels forced the whaling firms to insure themselves against loss. Moreover, hunting whales among the ice floes proved to be inherently riskier, causing the catches to be more variable, while overfishing tended to reduce the catches in the long run. All these factors in combination gave whaling the aspect of a lottery. When all went well, a ship could make an enormous profit; when circumstances turned unfavorable (which could simply mean that the whales were on the wrong side of an ice floe!), enormous losses resulted.

Even when the annual whaling results are expressed in ten-year averages, as in Tables 7.3 and 7.4, a highly irregular pattern of profit and loss is revealed. The

Table 7.3. *Performances of the whaling industry east of Greenland (annual averages).*[a]

Period	Number of ships	Whales captured	Total vats of blubber	Estimated total revenue (oil and bones) in guilders	Estimated equipage and production costs in guilders	Estimated total profit or loss in guilders	Estimated profit or loss per ship in guilders
1662–9	167	872	42,198	3,074,000	2,400,000	674,000	4,036
1670–9	141	903	39,329	2,505,000	1,988,000	517,000	3,666
1680–9	198	953	37,019	2,195,000	2,537,000	-342,000	-1,727
1690–9	95	608	23,331	1,993,000	1,322,000	671,000	7,063
1700–9	163	798	27,944	2,345,000	2,228,000	117,000	718
1710–19	141	482	17,385	2,068,000	1,833,000	235,000	1,666
1720–9	141	330	12,720	1,445,000	1,774,000	-329,000	-2,333
1730–9	91	277	11,259	1,931,000	1,181,000	750,000	8,242
1740–9	136	599	19,622	2,178,000	1,834,000	344,000	2,529
1750–9	136	479	13,586	1,685,000	1,826,000	-141,000	-1,037
1760–9	130	356	10,305	1,558,000	1,807,000	-249,000	-1,915
1770–9	85	265	7,538	1,041,000	1,243,000	-202,000	-2,376
1780–9	57	308	6,708	1,097,000	860,000	237,000	4,158
1790–9	39	96	2,623	453,000	568,000	-115,000	-2,949
1800–9	13	38	621	224,000	244,000	- 20,000	-1,538

[a]Number of years profits were made: 62. Number of years losses were suffered: 64.
Source: C. de Jong, *Geschiedenis van de oude Nederlandse walvisvaart* (Pretoria-Johannesburg, 1972–8), Vol. 3, pp. 145–213.

Table 7.4. *Performance of the whaling industry in the Davis Strait (annual averages).*[a]

Period	Number of ships	Whales captured	Total vats of blubber	Estimated total revenue (oil & bones) in guilders	Estimated equipage and production costs in guilders	Estimated total profit or loss in guilders	Estimated profit or loss per ship in guilders
1720–9	82	144	8,024	1,034,000	1,276,000	-242,000	-2,951
1730–9	94	186	10,424	1,484,000	1,490,000	-6,000	-64
1740–9	35	146	6,737	656,000	599,000	57,000	1,629
1750–9	32	55	2,505	318,000	513,000	-195,000	-6,094
1760–9	32	94	4,145	640,000	561,000	79,000	2,469
1770–9	44	122	5,439	764,000	797,000	-33,000	-750
1780–9	11	29	1,264	193,000	195,000	-2,000	-182
1790–9	8	9	312	49,000	126,000	-77,000	-9,625

[a]Number of years profits were made: 32. Number of years losses were suffered: 43.

Source: C. de Jong, *Geschiedenis van de oude Nederlandse walvisvaart* (Pretoria-Johannesburg, 1972–8), Vol. 3, pp. 145–213.

Greenland whaling grounds (the zone between Greenland and Iceland) remained profitable in the long run until 1750, but this "long run" included entire decades of red ink in the 1680s and 1720s, and unceasing year-to-year volatility. This volatility was the joint product of highly variable annual catches and instability in the prices of whale oil and bones.

The size of the catches varied from year to year, but it also fell to a distinctly lower long-run level between the 1680s and 1720s. Until the 1680s whalers could count on catches of between 200 and 300 vats of blubber per ship, and after a sharp decline in the 1690s, catches of 200 or more vats per ship continued to be achieved into the 1710s. Thereafter, the average catch plunged: In the 1720s and '30s, and again after 1755, the whaling vessels were lucky to sail home with 100 vats of blubber.

Results that were judged poor in the seventeenth century came to be thought of as normal or even good in the eighteenth. It is very likely that overfishing contributed to this phenomenon, for not only did the number of vats per ship decline, but so did the number of vats per slaughtered whale. If the estimates of marine biologists are correct, and some 22,000 Greenland whales populated the hunting zone, then the annual catch could not exceed 500 if the whale population was to maintain itself. As long as the *Noordsche Compagnie* existed, the annual catch never came near to that limit. The total catch of the Dutch, English, Danish, and Basque whalers together probably did not exceed 300 whales per year, so the maintenance of the whale population was not yet threatened. But after 1660 matters quickly changed. The Dutch whalers alone then sent 150 to 250 ships a year in search of whales, and to that number must be added the growing presence of German ships. Together these whalers managed to kill and stow an average of 1,287 whales per year in the period 1670–1710 (more were killed, since only 80 percent of harpooned whales were successfully landed). This excessive harvesting sent the whale population into decline, which resulted in a reduction of the average number of captured whales to 635 per year in the period 1750–90, and these whales each yielded less blubber than those captured earlier, since many of them were smaller, not yet having reached maturity.

The collapse of the whaling catch did not necessarily spell financial ruin for the industry. Indeed, the 1730s – a decade of very small catches – proved to be highly profitable, since prices then rose sharply. The demand for whale bone was then especially strong, so that this product accounted for over half of the industry's total revenue. Both fifty years before and after the 1730s, whale bone did not account for more than 20 to 35 percent of total revenue.

After 1750 the Greenland whaling industry managed to eke out a profit only in one decade, the 1780s. The Davis Strait hunting waters west of Greenland, which were opened in 1719, failed to compensate for this deteriorating performance. From a long-run perspective, Davis Strait whaling was never a profitable activity (see Table 7.4). Being so much further away, the cost of outfitting ships for the Davis Strait was consistently higher than for the Greenland waters (14,000 to 16,000 guilders per ship versus 11,000 to 13,000 guilders), and the catches were not sufficiently larger to compensate for this difference. Davis Strait whaling persisted for so long, if contemporary discussions are to be believed, because of the profit that could be made from (illegal) trade along the west coast of Greenland.

Dutch whaling as a whole was an industry in distress in the second half of the eighteenth century. It came to depend, just as did the herring fishery, on government subsidies to stave off complete collapse. Already in 1751 the whaling firms secured exemption from the excise taxes on provisions; after 1777 they received a premium of 30 guilders per crew member; and beginning in 1788, the government effectively guaranteed a minimum income to every ship by paying 50 guilders per *kwarteel* of whale oil for any shortfall in its catch below a floor of 100 *kwarteel*. All to no avail. Operating costs climbed steadily after 1760 (especially for shipbuilding costs) while the average catch diminished. After 1770 the whaling fleet shrank steadily in size, as investors, ships, and crews abandoned whaling for the then more profitable shipping industry. The military situation into which the Netherlands was plunged at the time of the Batavian Revolution put an end to the Dutch whaling industry. When the wars ended, every effort at revival had to confront the hard fact that years of subsidized English overhunting had made it hopelessly unprofitable.

Falling incomes and rising costs made Dutch whaling structurally unviable during a good portion of the eighteenth century. A key element in this story of deterioration was the persistent reduction in the number of whales caught, a result of some combination of overhunting and climatic change. Rising oil prices could not fully compensate for the smaller catches, because the price of whale bone, apart from a brief final rise during the Fourth Anglo-Dutch War (when whaling was suspended!), was subject to persistent downward pressure. Whale oil prices could not rise enough to save the industry, since they were limited by the price level of the competing vegetable oils. We described the market weakness faced by these oils earlier in this section: The eighteenth-century Dutch market faced a chronic oversupply of oil products.

In view of this structural unprofitability, the industry's ability to extend its life over several decades of senescence attracts our attention. Why did investors remain attached to this moribund activity? The financing of each year's whaling fleet occurred in the context of broadly based partnerships, the *partenrederijen*. This secured a wide distribution of the enormous risk at the same time that it offered many investors a speculative investment – a gamble, really – with the potential for a large payout. Investment in Dutch and North German whaling always had a lotterylike character. Of course, not all investors were speculators. Many were directly involved in the industry, and some of them were prepared to invest, even when the results were disappointing, in order to secure the continued flow of orders to their shipbuilding, provisioning, and equipping businesses. What they lost in their investments they could hope to gain back as suppliers to the whaling partnerships. Their investments were, so to speak, a gamble with a limited down-side risk. Finally, the industry's life was extended by government subsidy. After 1777 this support amounted to some 1,200 guilders per ship, and by 1788 it had risen to cover a major part of the losses experienced in bad years.

One puzzling question remains: In the face of a structural problem that brought the ruin of Dutch whaling and all but the ruin of the North German industry, how did the English manage to build up a large whaling fleet in the late eighteenth century? The puzzle is less daunting than at first glance it might appear. A prohibitive English tariff on imported whale oil effectively separated the Dutch and English markets for this product. The American colonies supplied whale oil to this protected English market, but the Seven Years' War and later the American War of Independence disrupted their supplies. A domestic English whaling industry took root in this context of protected markets and blocked supplies; and, of course, once the colonies achieved independence, they too stood on the wrong side of the English tariff wall. English (and Scottish) whalers now had the market to themselves, and unlike the stagnant, chronically oversupplied Dutch market, the English demand for oil grew as a result of rapid population growth and rising private and public prosperity, which increased the use of oil for home and street lighting and industrial purposes.

English whale oil also faced competition from vegetable oils, to be sure, and this might well have stymied the expansion of English whaling, the favorable market conditions notwithstanding, were it not for the rescuing hand of British mercantilism. The same public policy that prohibited the import of foreign whale oil stood ready to extend direct cash subsidies to the industry for nearly half a century after 1750, seeing this industry through its prolonged "infant industry" phase. The justification for this largesse was that the whaling and fishing industries were "nurseries of seamen," maintaining the reserves of trained sailors that would be needed in time of war. Between 1733 and 1800, the government disbursed no less than £1,975,089 (about 20 million guilders) to the whaling firms. Until after 1780 these subsidies exceeded the market value of whale oil itself! A typical 150-ton English whaler enjoyed an annual subsidy of £600 (about 6,500 guilders), while its Dutch competitor got only about 1,200 guilders, and that only after 1777. The English subsidy amounted to about half the operating costs of a whaling vessel. Such a level of generosity, sustained for decades, was simply beyond the financial means of the Republic's treasuries. In England the subsidies did not end until Dutch and North German competition had been driven from the seas. Around 1800 the English had the whales to themselves. They then pursued a profitable, highly intensive whaling strategy that resulted, after several decades, in the destruction of the whale populations throughout the northern waters from Iceland to Baffin Island. Thereafter, the hunt for whales turned to the waters of the Southern Hemisphere.

7.6. Some conclusions

The conventional wisdom of well-informed Europeans at the beginning of the seventeenth century held that the herring fishery was the secret ingredient of Holland's prosperity. This was an exaggeration, but an understandable one in the context of the times. If some 400 herring busses left Holland's harbors for the open sea each year after 1550, with crews of eighteen to thirty men each, then even a cautious estimate must set the number of herring fishermen at 8,000. When the 200 herring vessels of Zeeland, rather smaller than Holland's busses, are added, a total employment of 10,000 men at sea from the mid–sixteenth century on cannot be an exaggerated estimate. In terms of both employment and capital investment, no other branch of economic activity then maintained such a high profile. Moreover, the herring fishery held strong linkages to other, related activities.

After 1600 the number of herring busses in Holland rose further, toward a peak of 500 around 1630. By then the Zeeland herring fishery had shrunk to insignificance, and Holland's busses were rather smaller than their sixteenth-century predecessors. With crews of 12 to 14 men, the fleet of 1630 could not have employed more than 6,000 or 7,000 men. This smaller total employment (which did not necessarily imply a smaller annual herring catch) would have been advantageous in dealing with the problem of the seasonal character of the herring fishery. It is likely that many workers in the June to November herring season found before- and after-season work in the still important freshwater, coastal, and gradually expanding cod fisheries. Earlier, in the sixteenth century, this problem could be dealt with by combining the herring fishery with merchant shipping and agriculture. But productivity growth in each of these sectors brought greater asset specificity and occupational differentiation, whereby the bonds connecting these activities were loosened and, by the early seventeenth century, broken altogether (see Chapter 12, section 12.5.1).

As an object of capital investment, the herring fishery must also have appeared unusual in the context of the sixteenth-century economy. Even Holland's pre–Revolt merchant fleet, which used essentially the same type of vessel, would not have absorbed more capital than the herring fishery, which employed as many ships and had higher equipage costs than the merchant marine. It should be kept in mind, however, that it is precisely the lack of full differentiation between the fishing and shipping sectors in the years before the development of the *fluitschip* that leads to double-counting and confusion as to the true size of each sector.

The herring fishery was certainly large and strategically placed. Whether it was a fabulous generator of profit is another matter. Here our knowledge is very incomplete, but the highly competitive nature of the herring fishery must stand as a cautionary signal. Organized in *partenrederijen*, this industry possessed nearly as many partnerships as there were herring busses. The emergence of more attractive investment possibilities toward the end of the sixteenth century probably reduced the incentive for investors to participate in the fishery's many hundreds of marine partnerships. At this point merchants active in the lucrative herring trade reached back toward the fishery itself, organizing firms that controlled fleets of busses.

After 1600 the flexible *partenrederij*, with its numerous investors, lost ground in the herring fishery without actually disappearing. But after 1660 this form of ownership expanded to dominate the whaling industry. It suited well the high-risk character of whaling, distributing that risk among many investors at the same time that it offered a chance of windfall profits to the investor willing to add a speculative asset to his portfolio. And, in the decades after 1660, there was an embarrassing abundance of capital in search of such an investment. The accumulations of the previous decades now faced a shortage of profitable investments, which increased interest in the lotterylike whaling partnerships.

It bears repeating that participation in a whaling venture only claimed a minor part of most investment portfolios. The total amount of capital invested in these *partenrederijen* in any given year stood at about 4 million guilders; only in a few peak years, such as 1685, 1701, and 1720 might the invested funds have reached 5 million. When compared to the vast sums then invested in public debt and the VOC, the bets placed with whaling partnerships appear quite modest. The capital invested in the herring fishery around 1600 can be estimated at 2.5 million guilders, a substantial sum at the time. But thereafter, as the economy became larger and wealthier, the capital invested in the fisheries no more than held its own. Around 1750, when the great (herring) and lesser fisheries together required a capital investment of about 2.5 million guilders, this sector of the economy no longer carried the weight that it once had.

The total value of the herring catch in the period 1630–40, when some 20,000 lasts were landed each year, stood at about 3 million guilders. Around 1755 the value of the herring catch had shrunk to 1 million guilders, to which can be added a half million guilders' worth of cod and a whaling industry that returned about 2 million guilders. These figures can be put in some perspective by comparing them to the 2-million-guilder value of the domestic tobacco crop around 1700 or the value of North Holland's marketed cheese around 1705 of 1.8 to 2 million guilders.

These scraps of quantitative evidence hint at a long-term tendency for the chief branches of the fisheries to decline both in terms of total revenue and of profitability, and the decline of profitability is abundantly confirmed by the knowledge that neither the whaling nor the herring industries would have survived as long as they did without public subsidies. Both of these industries experienced long-term reductions of output, as their catches declined in size. But both also faced serious reductions in the demand for their products. Whaling suffered most from restrictions faced by Dutch oil products in foreign markets. This sharpened the competition between whale and vegetable oils in the domestic market. In addition, the vicissitudes of fashion, which had allowed whale bone to make a substantial contribution to total revenue in the second quarter of the eighteenth century, moved against the industry later in the century. The herring trade faced new competition in its important Baltic markets after 1650. The Dutch product remained qualitatively superior, but its high price forced it to give up market share to the herring supplied by Scandinavian and English fishermen. Meanwhile, the domestic market experienced a major shift in consumer behavior: the 4,000 lasts of herring sold at home each year around 1650 fell to no more than 1,000 lasts by 1750. This trend was not limited to herring, for the consumption of freshwater and coastal fish also plummeted. Fresh and dried cod and shellfish appear to have resisted this trend, but they could compensate only partially for the general collapse of fish consumption in the Republic. Further research may find that shifts in relative prices account for much of this change in consumer behavior. Herring (and apparently other fish except cod) did not follow agricultural products in the long-term price decline that set in after 1660. Consumers therefore gave fish – especially the costly herring – a smaller place in their diet.

The early claims for the pivotal role of fishing in the Dutch economy always stressed the strong linkages extending to other branches of the economy, and, indeed, this long remained an important feature of both fishing and whaling. Around 1670 some 700 vessels were active in whaling and in the great and lesser fisheries. Even at this late date, these ships constituted a quarter of the total Dutch fleet of seagoing vessels operating in European waters. Moreover, the equipage of the fishing and whaling vessels (for nets, cutters, etc.) tended to be much costlier than for simple merchant ships. Processing and shipping herring formed a major source of port employment. Since every last of herring was packed in port into twelve large barrels, the enormous labor of processing 20,000 lasts is evident. It was not for nothing that Rotterdam used all its political power to prevent Maassluis from developing its own herring packing industry. Indeed, the spectacular collapse of Enkhuizen's population, from 21,000 in 1622 to 9,000 in 1795, was almost entirely the result of a loss of employment caused by the contraction of the herring fleet from 270 to about 60 busses.

Besides shipbuilding, sailcloth weaving, food provisioning, net making, herring packing, and blubber refining, the trades most closely connected to the fishing industry were cooperage and salt refining. We have just noted that the mid–seventeenth-century demand for herring barrels reached a quarter of a million per year. But additional barrels were needed for use on board the fishing vessels. The herring fleet needed some 100,000 barrels (200 per buss), the whalers used about 50,000 up to 1710, and the lesser fisheries would add to these figures. All in all, it appears that in the third quarter of the seventeenth century, all branches of fishing needed the use of about a half million barrels and vats. Given their typical diameter of 50 cm., if they had all been assembled side by side, the resulting wall of barrels would have extended for 250 kilometers, from Groningen to Rotterdam. Unfortunately, we know next to nothing about the average life span of a barrel or the productivity of labor in the cooper's trade. But surely, this was an important source of employment in every fishing center (see Chapter 11, section 11.1).

The production and transport of salt has already been discussed. Here we call attention only to the close connection between the herring fishery and the demand for salt. This connection is implied by the concentration of salt pans in the vicinity of the herring fleets of Enkhuizen and the Maas river towns. In 1674 the Republic possessed nearly 300 salt pans, most of which were concentrated in four zones: 73 in Zeeland, 55 in the South Holland delta, 77 in North Holland, and 40 around Amsterdam and Muiden. Contemporaries reckoned that an average salt pan yielded 70 lasts of salt per season (April 15 to November 15), and we know that each packed herring barrel needed 35 kilograms of salt. Thus, 20,000 lasts (240,000 barrels) would have required 4,200 lasts of salt, or the annual production of 60 of the Republic's 300 salt pans.

In the second half of the eighteenth century, when annual herring production had fallen to only 5,000 lasts, the output of a mere 15 salt pans sufficed to sustain the industry. In other words, the decline of the herring fishery between 1650 and 1750 made redundant 15 percent of the Republic's salt pans. Nor is this the end of the story of linkages working in reverse, for the salt pans of Holland did not rely on a hot tropical sun. They were fueled by peat, each salt pan consuming some 10,000 *manden* (baskets, with a volume of roughly 190 liters) per year. When the herring fishery stood at its high point, it alone accounted for the use of 6 million *manden* of peat; a century later its requirements had fallen to 1.5 million *manden*.

This exploration of the herring fishery's linkages offers but one additional illustration of the highly interconnected character of the Republic's economy. This was an important source of strength and dynamism for the economy as it grew; it also proved to be a force undermining sector after sector when the old "engines of growth" reached their limits and faced new competition.

Chapter 8
Industry

8.1. Introduction

The new appreciation for the importance of agriculture in historical research, combined with the traditional interest in trade, shipping, and fishing, accounts for the past generation's neglect of the industrial sector in the economic history of the Republic. With precious few exceptions, the major studies of Dutch industry date from before 1940. This state of affairs is to be regretted, for the crafts and industrial sector formed, certainly in the cities, the Republic's single most important source of employment. This is evident in the occupational data for the city of Amsterdam, best known as a center of shipping, foreign trade, and commerce. These specializations notwithstanding, 54 percent of the city's bridegrooms in the period 1676–1700 declared an occupation with an industrial or artisanal character. While Amsterdam held no place of special importance in the textile industry, this sector claimed 26 percent of all the grooms with an industrial occupation, which would suggest that some 14 percent of Amsterdam's married men were active in textile production!

These are surprising figures, to which we return later when discussing occupational structure. Our purpose here is to call attention to the important place held by the industrial sector in the cities of the Republic. Moreover, industry's importance in the countryside frequently was also very great. This is obviously the case in a unique district such as the Zaan region, where as late as 1811 industry claimed a strikingly large 60 percent of the male labor force. But industrial labor was prominent in other rural areas as well, such as the adjacent Schermereiland, the rope-making districts around Gouda, the paper-making villages in the Veluwe, and the brickworks spread along the rivers and in rural Friesland and Groningen.

Yet it was the textile industry that employed the largest numbers. Twente in the east and the region around Tilburg in Brabant harbored the largest concentrations, but important textile-producing regions existed elsewhere as well, in the Achterhoek of Gelderland, the Veluwe, het Gooi, and Friesland. When we set aside both the major industrial concentrations of Twente and the Zaan region, and the markedly agrarian regions of Drenthe and parts of Brabant and Limburg, the industrial and craft sectors accounted for between 15 and 25 percent of the male labor force in the rural districts of the eighteenth-century Republic.

The deurbanization that set in after 1650 and the expansion of proto-industrial activities certainly contributed to these high percentages. Indeed, these trends allow one to infer the importance of industry in the Republic's economic structure. In Chapter 3 we noted that the level of urbanization fell from 45 to 38 percent in the period 1675 to 1815. Between 1675 and 1750, the greatest population losses were suffered by Holland's industrial cities (Leiden, Haarlem, and Delft) and this retreat continued after 1750, albeit more slowly. The setbacks in the trade and shipping centers of Amsterdam and Rotterdam were much smaller, and here one can actually speak of a certain revival after 1750. When one adds to these developments the gradual decline of the fisheries and the deep agricultural depression of the first half of the eighteenth century, it becomes evident that developments in the industrial sector contributed significantly to the secular trend of expansion and contraction that was such a prominent feature of the Republic's economic history.

A second important feature of the industrial sector is its close association with the commercial sector, especially in the context of the entrepôt function which the Republic long performed in European trade. Commodity trade secured the movement of raw materials and semifinished products to the Republic, where they underwent (further) industrial processing before being distributed domestically and abroad as finished products. Among the important processing industries, known in the Republic as *trafieken,* were: salt refining, sugar refining, lumber sawing, and distilling. Alongside these *trafieken* were industries that received their raw materials from both domestic and foreign sources. The relative importance of these sources could vary over time, as the tobacco industry, which drew on both American and Dutch leaf, well demonstrates. Likewise, sail-cloth weavers and rope twiners drew upon both domestic and Baltic sources of hemp. It is evident that such processing industries were vulnerable to the protectionist policies of supplier nations and depended on the continued functioning of the entrepôt. Whenever direct trade relations emerged between a raw-materials–producing country and an importer of finished products, the danger existed that a processing industry would arise in one of the two economies. Indeed, this is the process by which certain industries had first arisen in the Republic itself.

When toward the end of the sixteenth century manufacturing expanded rapidly, a third feature of Dutch industry took shape, one that had previously been of minor importance. The towns now pursued active policies of industrial stimulation, which in some cases took the form of attracting a variety of industries, while in others the focus was on stimulating a single industrial specialty. Amsterdam and Rotterdam are the prime examples of cities encouraging industrial diversity. The specialization model is exemplified by Leiden (concentrating on woolen textiles), Haarlem (linen textiles), Delft (pottery), Gouda (clay pipes), and Schiedam (distilleries). This second group – Holland's true industrial cities – performed other industrial activities within their walls, of course, but these always remained of a distinctly secondary importance. On the other hand, their extreme specialization fell well short of establishing monopoly positions, for in each case there were other cities producing the same goods, although these competing cities never removed the dominant centers from their positions of leadership (something that rural producers eventually did succeed in doing).

8.2. Industry until 1585

The sixteenth century experienced a vigorous expansion of trade within Europe. The Europe-wide growth of population, increasing the demand for foodstuffs and other commodities, contributed mightily to this growth of trade, and a prime beneficiary, until the 1550s, proved to be the numerous industries, both urban and rural, of the Southern Netherlands. The substantial declines in purchasing power suffered by wage earners in this period of rising food prices is thought to have acted to limit their demand for industrial products, but other social groups learned to profit from this situation and buoyed the demand for the luxury products that were the specialties of the southern cities. The various export-oriented industries, such as the rapidly expanding rural textile industry, also prospered. A result of this industrial expansion was very likely the transformation of a large portion of this economy's hidden unemployment into wage labor, a process working to counteract the shrinking purchasing power of individual workers. This, too, stimulated the demand for industrial goods.

The Northern Netherlands, which played "periphery" to the Burgundian State's Flemish-Brabantine "core," experienced the general economic expansion emanating from the south in a variety of ways. The growing demand for foodstuffs encouraged a process of intensification and specialization in the agrarian sector, as a result of which dairy products and meat flowed to southern markets in growing volume. The fisheries also benefited in this way. The expansion of international trade acted to stimulate the north's important shipping sector, which succeeded in establishing for itself a central place in Europe's commercial system. This position would become stronger still in later decades, but already around 1550 the north, and especially Amsterdam, had learned to benefit enormously from Europe's burgeoning trade flows.

Developments in the industrial sector were rather less impressive. In order to clarify the diverse trends of the period, we must first make two sets of distinctions: (1) between production for domestic and for export markets, and (2) between industries whose growth depended on a demand derived from the growth of other sectors, such as shipping and fishing, and those whose growth was more autonomous. Thus, although useful quantitative data are all but nonexistent, we can be confident of the flourishing state of industries such as salt refining, ship-building, lumber milling, sail-cloth making, fishing net making, soap boiling, and the brickworks. These sectors were direct beneficiaries of either the expansion of shipping and the fisheries or of the growth of population and the shift toward brick construction. The salt refiners, for example, made the transition from (small-scale) salt extraction from peat to the (larger-scale) refining of raw salt imported from France and, later, Spain, Portugal, and South America. Refined salt became an important export product, first to the Southern Netherlands and the Rhineland, and later to the Baltic, where the Dutch shifted from the shipment of raw salt to the sale of the refined product in competition with the region's local suppliers (Lüneburg, Halle, Wieliczka, and Bochnia).

Shipbuilding and related suppliers must also have experienced prosperous times. The number of ships in both inland and ocean navigation grew rapidly, and their average life span, especially of oceangoing ships, remained quite short. Of the 88 ships that were registered in 1569 as lying at anchor in Zeeland, 63 appear to have been less than ten years old. Dordrecht, Haarlem, Alkmaar, Hoorn, Edam, and Amsterdam were, as far as we can tell, the foremost centers, but the shipbuilding industry in the early sixteenth century was still highly dispersed and modest in scale. Even rural builders competed for orders, especially for the smaller vessels. This is evident from an inquiry into rural industry commissioned by the city of Leiden in 1541, which identified 14 persons (out of a total rural adult labor force of 127 persons) involved in this industry in the city's immediate vicinity.

But over the course of the century, this industry came to exhibit distinct tendencies toward concentration. The most important shipbuilding centers became Dordrecht, Amsterdam, Edam, and Hoorn. Already in 1514 a fiscal survey described Edam as employing many "foreign" craftsmen at its ship wharves, and in 1561 the number of wharves was placed at forty-five, employing at least 100 workers. In Amsterdam, where the trade and sawing of timber had long been important, the number of shipbuilding workers must have been larger than in Edam.

The sawing of timber was an important source of employment in all these cities. This industry benefited not only from the growing production of ships but also from the growing urban population, which increased the demand for residential construction. To be sure, the increased use of brick reduced the wood content of new buildings, but this did not prevent a rise of the absolute demand for wood in the sixteenth century. As for the brickworks, their growth was all the more rapid. These facilities invariably sought rural locations, both because of their need for raw materials (clay deposits located along riverbanks) and because the smoke and smell required a measure of isolation. The most important concentrations of brickworks stretched along the major rivers of Holland and Utrecht, where the needed peat could easily be supplied. Later, rural Friesland and Groningen joined this region as important centers for brick and ceramic production.

To the extent that industrial production served domestic markets or a demand derived from expanding economic sectors, the sixteenth century was an era of prosperity. A very different situation confronted those industries that catered to markets for which they had to compete directly with producers in the Southern Netherlands and foreign locations. Such industries, the breweries and the many branches of the textile industry foremost among them, were not at the forefront of the technological and commercial advances of the sixteenth century, and they consequently suffered a growing competitive disadvantage. Unfortunately, beer and cloth production held important positions in the economies of most of the small cities of the Northern Netherlands, so that the benefits of growing trade, shipping, and associated industries were largely undone by the contraction of these traditional export industries.

This fact helps to explain the surprisingly slow rate of urbanization during the first three-quarters of the sixteenth century. In contrast to the steady growth of cities dependent on trade and shipping (such as Amsterdam), the other cities stagnated. At the same time, the rural population experienced substantial growth, spurred by the growth of agricultural output and the growing demand for fishermen and seafarers. In view of these developments, it is hardly surprising that the cities vigorously resisted the rise of rural industry. They feared, not without reason, that their economic position would further be undermined if they could not reserve as urban monopolies such industries as brewing, leather tanning, shipbuilding, and textile production. Nor were they inclined to tolerate the establishment of service occupations such as baking, tavern keeping, shoemaking, and so forth in their immediate vicinity. To protect their interests, the cities of Holland united in 1531 to secure from the central government a prohibition on the establishment of new industrial activities outside the cities (called the *Order op de buitennering*).

In practice this prohibition had little effect, since it prohibited only *new* rural industries; and even these could not always be suppressed because of the unwillingness of local noblemen to cooperate in enforcement. During the boom period toward the end of the century, the 1531 prohibition fell into utter desuetude. In 1641, as the first symptoms of decelerating urban growth were felt, the memory of this old anti-rural policy returned, but it proved too late to reinstate such a measure. Efforts in this direction came to nought, so that the cities could do no more than promulgate local edicts designed to protect their markets from rural competition. In this way the cities of Holland were able to beat back rural peddlers, brewers, biscuit bakers, and the like; but they could not choke off rural industry in general.

In the other provinces, measures against rural industry ran aground even before they could begin. Such was the case in Friesland, where the government always treated urban and rural industry equally. The most that these provincial cities could hope for was a prohibition on taverns in the immediate vicinity of urban jurisdictions.

The brewing of beer was the foremost industrial activity in several cities of the Northern Netherlands, some of which produced not only for regional consumption but also for more distant markets. From the time that hopped beer emerged to produce a tradeable commodity, a lively interregional trade in beer took root in northwestern Europe: North German beer from Bremen, Hamburg, Wismar, Stralsund, Rostock, and Lübeck flowed in large quantities to Dutch markets, as did English beer. In the Southern Netherlands, noteworthy exporters included Leuven, Brugge, Brussels, Antwerp, Liège, Lier, Mechelen, Tienen, Menen, Zoutleeuw, and Hoegaarden. In the Northern Netherlands, the great exporters of the sixteenth century were Haarlem, Delft, Gouda, and Amersfoort, whose export markets were found chiefly in Flanders and Brabant. They also catered to the needs of ocean shipping, where the maintenance of potable water supplies was an ongoing concern. These cities benefited not only from access to markets but also from easy access to fuel (peat) and pure water.

Recent estimates of Holland's annual beer production made by Yntema set output at about 1.3 million vats around 1475. The final quarter of the fifteenth century experienced a painful contraction, explained in no small measure by the disorders that followed the death of Charles the Bold (the last Burgundian Duke) in 1477. A recovery after 1500 restored the old production levels by 1515, when Gouda, Delft, and Haarlem (in that order of importance) together accounted for fully 900,000 vats annually. Over 90 percent of this output found markets outside the producing cities. Haarlem's markets were located primarily in North Holland, a district nearly devoid of breweries. Delft, and above all Gouda, sought their markets beyond Holland in the numerous cities of the Southern Netherlands.

Brewing was of extraordinary importance to Gouda, a city especially well placed to serve southern markets. In the 1470s annual production hovered around 400,000 vats, a level never reached again, except perhaps fleetingly in the next century, when the number of breweries totaled 148 in 1514, and 126 around 1550. Then, annual production was no more than half the level of the 1470s, a level that would shrink further to 100,000 vats by 1564 and to little more than 20,000 vats in the political crisis of the 1570s. In the course of a century, Gouda's beer production was more than decimated. The loss of markets in the Southern Netherlands explains much of this decline but not all of it. Gouda's hold over domestic markets also weakened.

In the first half of the sixteenth century, Gouda held fast to regulations designed to limit competition among its numerous brewers. In other cities, notably Delft, Leiden, and Haarlem, a more flexible regime allowed brewers to experiment with new production techniques, especially the use of two kettles instead of one. With two kettles, brewers could produce several grades of beer from a single grist. With a variety of beers to sell, these brewers could respond to changing market developments with an alacrity impossible for Gouda to follow. Gouda succeeded in 1550 in inducing the Emperor Charles V to forbid these innovations, but two years later he had to retract his edict.

The chief beneficiaries of Gouda's loss were Haarlem and Delft. The number of Delft brewers fell, but their volume of production managed to buck the trend of declining beer demand, rising from 300,000 vats in 1475 to 350,000 by the 1550s, which was then good for first place among Dutch brewing centers. In this same interval, Haarlem's production declined by 10 to 20 percent, to 180,000 to 200,000 vats per year, but when placed beside Gouda's collapse, this was by no means a disaster. Overall, Holland's brewing sector exhibited a shift of production away from Gouda and toward Delft, and a decline of total production of over 25 percent. This absolute decline occurred in a context of population growth, and at a time when no evidence exists to suggest a decline in per capita consumption. The most plausible conclusion is that Holland's brewers lost their hold on foreign markets.

The cause of this diminution in export sales must be sought in developments in the Southern Netherlands. There the brewing industry grew with vigor: Leuven's brewers increased output by 43 percent between the late fifteenth century and the 1560s; output in Brugge doubled in the century after 1482; Brussels' production rose by 70 percent between 1500 and 1617; and Antwerp produced 182 percent more beer in 1575 than in 1530. The growth of population, the rise of wine prices, and the shift toward the production of hopped beer (with its longer shelf life) stood behind this local expansion, an expansion that eroded the market share of North Netherlands brewers. The reasons for the competitive failure of northern brewers are not obvious but may well be located in the declining purchasing power of consumers. The steady rise of grain – and thus malt – prices forced the brewers to reduce gradually the malt content of their beer. Imported beers, which had to bear a large transportation cost, could not so easily follow this path toward reduced costs. They depended on a contracting market for high-quality beers, a market whose contraction was speeded by import duties. The two-kettle brewing process allowed them to diversify production, but it did not save the luxury beer export market.

The decline of the textile industry exceeded in importance that of brewing. The production of cloth, especially of woolens, provided employment in many locations. In the fifteenth century, hardly a city in Holland could not boast of one or another sort of textile production. Little is known of the situation in the towns outside Holland, but we do know that Maastricht was an important woolen cloth producer to the end of the sixteenth century. This city seems to have looked to the east (the German Rhineland and beyond) for its markets, as did the drapers of Roermond. The town of Weert joined with Maaseik and Helmond plus many nearby villages to form a zone of woolens production specializing in cheap, simple fabrics. Closely linked to the markets of Brabant and Flanders, this textile zone functioned into the 1570s, when war conditions led to its destruction. The textile village of Tilburg also suffered from military disruptions but managed to recover later on, probably because its textile workers had sought refuge in Rotterdam. By orienting its production to this growing and Republican center, Tilburg not only survived the unsettled times but emerged with new commercial possibilities.

Even less is known about the role of cloth production in other provinces. In view of its broad distribution in Holland, Brabant, and Limburg, it seems highly likely that textile producers of at least local importance functioned in these provinces. There, just as in such small cities of Holland as Naarden, Weesp, Oudewater, Woerden, and Heusden, we can expect to find evidence of modest production, oriented to local markets.

A larger-scale, export-oriented cloth production characterized late fifteenth-century Leiden, The Hague, Amsterdam, and, perhaps, Alkmaar, Hoorn, and Gouda. But before the next century could begin, the textile industries of these cities began to fall into serious decay. Alkmaar's cloth industry spiraled downward (between 1500 and 1514, production here fell by half), while in Hoorn the city fathers claimed that production in 1494 was but one-tenth of what it had been in 1477. By 1514 production had revived slightly, but in neither Hoorn nor Alkmaar did woolen cloth production then exceed 1,000 pieces (*halve lakens*). The Hague was a much larger production center. Specializing in processing of low-quality Scottish wool, it stood second only to Leiden in the fifteenth century; but output fell from 14,000–15,000 pieces in 1477 to 6,000 pieces in 1504, and to no more than 2,000 pieces in 1514. From this collapse there was no recovery.

The fate of the industry in Amsterdam and Naarden was less disastrous. In Amsterdam 80 to 90 looms were kept in operation in the later fifteenth century, and in 1514 there were still 45, capable of producing 5,000 to 6,000 pieces of cloth annually. Thereafter, textile production revived a bit (see Figure 8.1), fluctuating between 7,000 and 8,000 pieces per year between 1530 and 1557. But then Amsterdam followed the other cities into industrial decline: By 1570 annual production stood at less than 2,000 pieces; by 1572 Amsterdam's looms were idle. In Naarden and the villages of Het Gooi, much less is known, but it appears that the district's 1514 production of 9,000 pieces of woolen cloth suffered a gradual but inexorable erosion in the following decades.

Although none of these textile centers could, by itself, rank as a large producer, together they accounted for a substantial output. Yet one city, Leiden, towered above them all, not only in the quantity of its textile production but also in the quality. While the lesser centers concentrated on the cheaper sorts of cloth, Leiden's drapers focused on the highest-quality cloth, produced of English wool. The expansive years of textile production in the Burgundian era also benefited

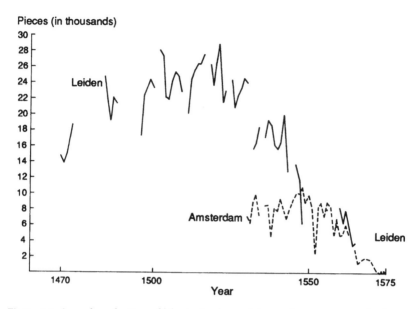

Pieces (in thousands)

Figure 8.1. Annual production of *laken* in Leiden and Amsterdam, 1470–1575 (in thousands of pieces). (*Sources:* N. W. Posthumus, *Leidsche lakenindustrie*, I, 370–1; J. G. van Dillen, *Bronnen bedrijfsleven Amsterdam*, XIV.)

Leiden, which found markets in the Baltic region, the German lands, and even in Russia. The general political and military disquiet that followed upon the death of Charles the Bold in 1477 affected Leiden less than Holland's other textile centers; the growth of output slowed, to be sure, but Leiden escaped the sharp declines that befell the other cities. The first thirty years of the sixteenth century formed a period of instability, marked by episodes of war (with the Hanse and France) that disrupted the flow of English wool. Annual production, which stood at 29,000 pieces in 1521, fell to 21,000 in the war year of 1526 but revived to 24,500 in 1529. Thereafter, Leiden's textile industry entered into a structural decline that persisted for decades: In 1532 output stood at under 16,000 pieces, in 1563 it was only 5,000 pieces, by 1573 barely 1,000 pieces (see Figure 8.1). Leiden had all but ceased to be a producer of woolen cloth.

The collapse of Leiden as a textile center only repeated a process pioneered by the lesser production centers. Consequently, Holland's total annual output of woolen cloth, which stood at over 50,000 pieces around 1500, could not have totaled more than a few thousand pieces in the 1560s. What was responsible for this phenomenon?

Military operations and related social tension can be held responsible for some of this collapse. For example, The Hague, an unwalled, "open" city, suffered severely from billeting and plunder in the last quarter of the fifteenth century, which destroyed or chased away the town's industrial capital. Alkmaar was forced to pay large fines and destroy its town walls as punishment for its part in the "Cheese and Bread" rebellion of 1492, circumstances that did its industrial sector no good. The severe social tensions of Hoorn led in 1470 to the abandonment of the city by most of its fullers, which pulled the rug out from under its textile industry as a whole.

Still, the fundamental cause of the textile industry's contraction lay deeper than this. As with the brewers, textile producers faced major structural changes brought on by their foreign competitors. Holland's cloth producers competed with the far larger textile centers of England and the Southern Netherlands. Around the mid-sixteenth century, the total annual cloth production of the Northern Netherlands stood at about 1 million *el* (circa 50,000 pieces), while production in the Southern Netherlands was about 5.5 million *el*, and another 3.5 million *el* of unfinished English cloth was imported. Northern production was thus only a small part – roughly one-tenth – of the total supply available in the Low Countries.

The large production of the Southern Netherlands fell into two general categories: the traditional heavy cloth of medieval origins (produced also in Leiden), and the so-called "new draperies," or light cloth, which by 1500 had taken root among rural producers around Hondschoote and in the Walloon cities around Lille. Production of heavy cloth rose in the first decades of the sixteenth century, in the Southern cities just as in Leiden, but gradually the emphasis shifted toward the new, light cloth, fabricated with Spanish and domestic rather than English wool, and in demand especially in Mediterranean and Spanish American markets. Around 1550 these two types of woolen cloth were of roughly equal importance in the Southern Netherlands, but no more than ten years later, production of light cloth stood some two to three times higher than that of heavy cloth.

Decline in the old, heavy cloth industry turned to collapse as its traditional markets were usurped by the emerging English production centers, which grew rapidly on the basis of high export duties on raw wool, as a result of which English costs fell (given the abundance of retained raw wool) while costs in the Netherlands rose. Most of the English heavy woolen cloth that came to dominate Continental markets continued to be dyed and finished in the Netherlands, but there was no longer a future for the "old drapery" in the towns of the Netherlands, north or south. This is amply demonstrated by the production data described earlier.

8.3. Industry after 1585

8.3.1. TEXTILES

The new drapery

Just as the textile industry reached the point of total collapse, there appeared the means for its rescue, indeed, for a new era of extraordinary growth. The religious

Table 8.1. *Persons admitted to the rights of municipal citizenship* (Poorters) *in Leiden, Amsterdam, Middelburg, Delft, and Gouda, 1575–1619 (five-year totals).*

Period	Leiden	Amsterdam	Middelburg	Delft	Gouda
1575–79	193	334	437	146	69
1580–84	328	440	426	165	108
1585–89	400	724	939	191	126
1590–94	580	853	998	205	72
1595–99	353	973	676	158	51
1600–04	314	1,481	382	138	95
1605–09	424	1,822	396	142	110
1610–14	485	2,605	340	176	115
1615–19	577	2,768	334	124	173
Total	3,654	12,010	4,928	1,445	919

Source: N. W. Posthumus, *Leidsche lakenindustrie*, Vol. II, p. 70.

persecution of Protestants had set in motion an emigration of textile workers from the Southern Netherlands beginning in the 1560s. This stream of emigrants became a flood as persecution was joined by open warfare, such as the plundering of Hondschoote in 1582. The initial destinations were primarily England and German border districts, but the search for suitable locations to re-establish the new drapery that had been the specialty of many of the refugees brought one such group, which had originally settled in England, to Leiden in 1577. Beginning in 1582 migrants from southern Flanders and from Artois began to move directly to Leiden, and with their arrival the center of light cloth production was relocated, setting in motion the emergence of Leiden as the most important industrial center of Europe (a claim that throughout the seventeenth century could only be challenged by Lyon).

This migration of cloth producers was, of course, but one aspect of the massive movement of people from the Southern to the Northern provinces (described in Chapter 3, section 3.4). The exact size of this migration remains uncertain, but its importance for the economy of the North is difficult to overestimate; it endowed the North with commercial and technical know-how, financial resources, and the intellectual and cultural capital of a long-established center of European civilization. We return to this phenomenon repeatedly in later chapters (especially sections 8.4 and 9.2).

Tables 8.1 through 8.3 reveal the overall pattern of immigration: the places of origin and the destinations in the Northern provinces. Since these data refer exclusively to those migrants who purchased formal citizenship rights (*poorterschap*) in their new locations, they cannot measure the total scope of the phenomenon, but they do reflect the chief characteristics of migration behavior. Among the

Table 8.2. *New urban citizens (Poorters) in Leiden, Amsterdam, and Middelburg 1590–4, by place of origin.*

Place of origin	Total number of persons			In percentages		
	Leiden	Amsterdam	Middelburg	Leiden	Amsterdam	Middelburg
Republic	85	422	179	15.5	50.9	18.0
Belgium	296	285	720	53.3	34.3	72.1
France	149	15	58	26.8	1.8	5.8
Germany	17	93	19	3.0	11.2	1.9
England	8	8	19	1.4	1.0	1.9
Other	—	7	3	—	0.8	0.3
Total	555	830	998	100.0	100.0	100.0

Source: N. W. Posthumus, *Leidsche lakenindustrie,* Vol. II, p. 75.

Table 8.3. *New urban citizens (Poorters) in Leiden and Amsterdam, 1575–1604, by place of origin (in five-year periods, expressed in percentages of total new citizens).*

Place of origin[a]	1575–9 L	1575–9 A	1580–4 L	1580–4 A	1585–9 L	1585–9 A	1590–4 L	1590–4 A	1595–9 L	1595–9 A	1600–4 L	1600–4 A	1575–1604 L	1575–1604 A
South Holland	35.3	8.3	11.5	9.0	8.0	4.4	7.6	6.0	8.2	7.0	10.6	3.8	10.7	5.7
North Holland	2.3	27.4	2.6	32.2	0.3	9.4	2.2	13.3	2.3	13.8	0.7	15.5	1.7	16.2
Other Provinces	6.7	37.9	7.0	36.9	5.5	31.6	5.7	31.6	8.5	33.4	9.2	34.7	7.0	33.8
Total Netherlands	44.3	73.6	21.1	78.1	13.8	45.4	15.5	50.9	19.0	54.2	20.5	54.0	19.4	55.7
Belgium	40.6	13.8	30.0	13.0	52.1	44.2	53.3	34.3	49.3	26.2	38.6	21.3	45.8	26.8
France	11.3	1.2	45.0	1.4	31.6	3.4	26.8	1.8	22.0	2.0	27.7	1.1	28.8	1.8
Germany	1.5	10.8	2.2	7.3	2.2	5.9	3.0	11.2	6.5	14.7	8.3	21.2	4.0	13.8
Other countries	2.3	0.6	1.4	0.2	3.0	1.1	1.4	1.8	3.2	2.9	4.9	2.4	2.0	1.9
Total abroad	55.7	26.4	78.9	21.9	86.2	54.6	84.5	49.1	81.0	45.8	79.5	46.0	80.6	44.3

[a] L = Leiden; A = Amsterdam.

Source: N. W. Posthumus, *Leidsche lakenindustrie*, Vol. II, p. 72.

destinations of the immigrants, Middelburg at first attracted the largest numbers, with Amsterdam in second place. By 1595 Amsterdam had emerged as the prime destination, and ten years later Leiden surpassed the rapidly fading Middelburg to take hold of second place as a destination for migrants. Delft and Gouda stood a distant fourth and fifth behind these three cities. Table 8.2, which describes migration in the period 1590–4, shows that Middelburg drew a large majority of its new burgers from modern Belgium, while Amsterdam drew its new burgers from a variety of destinations – half from the Republic itself, 34 percent from Belgium, and 11 percent from German territories. The origins of Leiden's new burgers were altogether more concentrated than those of the other cities: fully 80 percent came from Belgium and France, but even this understates the homogeneity of the migrants, which was actually one stream from a single textile zone through which the modern French-Belgian border runs.

Table 8.3 shows how Leiden gradually drew immigrants from other areas, including Germany. But these new supply zones were also overwhelmingly centers of textile production. Altogether, 48.4 percent of all Leiden's new burgers in the period 1575–1619 declared an occupation in the textile industry, and more than half of these specialized in the production of *says,* the foundation of the new drapery, which already in 1586 was acknowledged as the chief industry of the city.

It took only a few years for this newly imported textile industry to assume a durable organizational form. By 1596 Leiden's cloth masters recognized four types of light cloth: *says* (made of combed or carded wool), *bays* (using coarse wool), *fustian* (a wool-cotton blend), and *rashes* (made of twined wool). After 1630 the *laken,* Leiden's traditional heavy, high-quality wool cloth, re-emerged as an important product, but it was actually a refashioned, lighter cloth than the old *laken.* Production of this new-version *laken* was not restricted to Leiden; in Haarlem, Amsterdam, Delft, Gouda, Amersfoort, and Utrecht, *laken* production (re)emerged, although Leiden always remained by far the largest production center. Another new development of the 1630s was the establishment in Leiden of two new blended fabrics: the costly *camlets* (wool mixed with silk, camel hair, and angora), and the cheap *warps* (wool mixed with linen). These seven fabric types defined the Leiden textile industry for some two centuries, although the relative importance of each fluctuated enormously.

Initially, the says dominated Leiden's textile economy: In little more than ten years, annual output rose from nothing to over 35,000 pieces; after 1610 production stood at between 45,000 and 50,000 pieces (Figure 8.2). Fustians nestled in a secure second place after 1600, as production rose from over 10,000 in 1600 to 30,000 after 1623. The production of bays rose from 10,000 pieces per year around 1600 to a peak of about 20,000 pieces around 1635 – good for third place. The rashes never approached these three in importance; production peaked at about 10,000 pieces in the 1630s. When all these sectors are bundled together, we see Leiden's total production rising from some 40,000 pieces per year around 1590

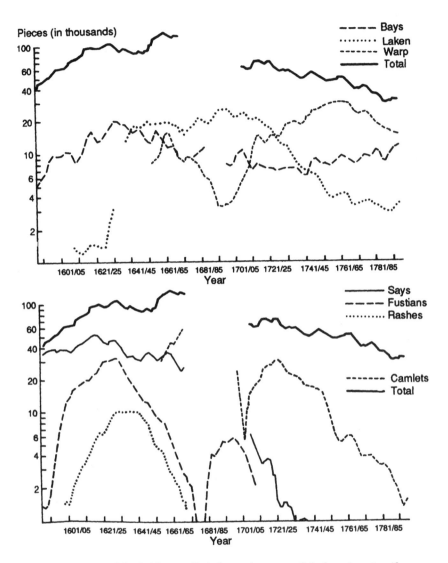

Figure 8.2. Output of the Leiden textile industry, by types of cloth, 1581–1800 (five-year moving averages, in thousands of pieces; semi-logarithmic scale). (*Source:* N. W. Posthumus, *Leidsche lakenindustrie*, II, 129; III, 930–1, 1098–9.)

to 100,000 pieces around 1630. In view of the moribund state of this industry around 1580, this constitutes a half-century of truly fabulous growth.

Leiden's cloth production appears to have fallen off somewhat in the period 1635–55, as total output remained below the 100,000 mark, sometimes substantially below. But, this conclusion is very likely misleading. Production data for the rapidly growing *laken* are missing in 1636 and 1637, and camlets and warp production emerged in these years but were not yet counted. The first available production data for these new fabrics appear in 1653, when Leiden produced nearly 8,000 pieces of warp, and 1655, when it turned out some 30,000 pieces of camlet. Thus, from 1655, when comprehensive production data are once again available, annual output stood at over 110,000 pieces, and over 130,000 pieces in the 1660s. Leiden's textile industry reached its all-time production peaks in this decade, with 1664 (144,723 pieces) the top year.

The further overall growth of the textile industry in the period 1635–65 was associated with dramatic internal shifts in the several subcategories. Against the emergence of the camlet, *laken*, and warp sectors (in this order of importance), we must place the rapid decline of the rashes, fustian, and say sectors (also in this order of importance). The once pre-eminent says offered a stubborn resistance to absolute decline, but the rashes all but disappeared by 1670, and the fustians appeared headed for the same fate before a modest revival extended the life of this sector until the 1720s. Of the four original new draperies upon which Leiden's modern industry was based, the bays fared best, although this sector too had to give some ground to the new fabrics that emerged in the 1630s.

Between 1670 and 1700, Leiden production data are fragmentary, but it is clear enough that the *laken* sector continued to grow, reaching a level of some 25,000 pieces per year, while warp production fell sharply. Camlets also declined from a high point around 1670 of nearly 60,000 pieces to less than half that amount at the end of the War of the Spanish Succession. After 1690 the by then venerable says production wasted away, so that by 1720, production barely reached a thousand pieces per year. Once again, it was the bays that fared best, although even here production was halved between 1660 and 1715 (from 15,000 to 7,500 pieces). But, in the rest of the eighteenth century, bays production held steady, even rose a bit. One can summarize Leiden's textile production between 1660 and 1720 by stating that of the four original branches, the says, fustians, and rashes all but disappeared, that production of bays and the newer camlets fell by half, that the warp sector contracted even more, and that only *laken* production managed to swim against this strong tide of contraction.

Shifts in the relative importance of the various Leiden fabrics continued throughout the eighteenth century. As noted already, production of bays experienced a modest revival. Of the three remaining sectors, warp experienced so great a comeback after the War of the Spanish Succession that this specialty accounted for half of Leiden's total output by 1750. It follows that the *laken* and

Table 8.4. *Estimated value of Leiden woolen cloth production, by type, in guilders, selected dates 1630– 1701.*

Cloth type	1630	1642	1654	1665	1679	1701
Says	1,630,000	1,380,000	960,000	770,000	410,000	150,000
Rashes	300,000	340,000	140,000	60,000	3,000	—
Fustians	570,000	310,000	150,000	45,000	10,000	70,000
Camlets	110,000	330,000	3,000,000	3,060,000	1,190,000	1,200,000
Warps	180,000	200,000	225,000	310,000	165,000	70,000
Bays	1,000,000	1,170,000	635,000	550,000	250,000	200,000
Lakens	110,000	3,000,000	4,000,000	2,960,000	2,720,000	4,200,000
Other	100,000	100,000	50,000	5,000	25,000	20,000
Total	4,000,000	6,830,000	9,160,000	7,805,000	4,773,000	5,910,000

Source: N. W. Posthumus, *Leidsche lakenindustrie*, Vol. III, p. 941.

the camlets lost ground in the eighteenth century: The decline of *laken* production was concentrated in the period 1715–50, camlets in the period 1725–55. After the latter date, only the warp, followed at a considerable distance by the bays, was of any real importance.

These internal shifts in textile production were also reflected in the total output of Leiden's industry. Total output data are not available for the period 1670–1700, but from eighteenth-century data, it is clear that the earlier production level of 130,000 pieces was definitively a thing of the past. By 1700 output was but half of the peak years. After the end of the War of the Spanish Succession, output recovered a bit, reaching an annual level of 70,000 to 75,000 pieces, but the downward trend quickly reasserted itself, so that total output fell to 50,000 pieces by 1750, 40,000 after 1775, and no more than 30,000 pieces toward the end of the century. Thus, the secular trend, which we have documented in the Netherlands' population history, the inland and herring fisheries, salt refining, and other sectors, reveals itself again in history of Leiden's textile production: rapid growth until the third quarter of the seventeenth century, followed by a sharp reversal to the early eighteenth century, followed finally by a long period of gradual decline mixed with periods of partial recovery.

The turning point in Leiden's textile industry came toward the end of the 1660s. Signs of diminished profitability in this industry were apparent even earlier. The course of prices for the various woolens has allowed N. W. Posthumus to calculate that Leiden's production had reached its maximum value of 9.2 million guilders already in 1654 (see Table 8.4). The accuracy of his calculations might be questioned, but the overall pattern is not in dispute. While output continued to rise after 1650, prices began to decline. As profit margins melted away, production growth slowed, then stopped, and finally turned to retreat. Producers sought escape from the profit squeeze by shifting production toward those fabrics whose prices held up better, but their efforts did no more than delay the day of reckoning.

Production of *laken*, the most expensive of Leiden's products, escaped the crisis of profitability that afflicted all other specialties. For the rest, it soon became clear that price reductions that squeezed profits to zero were still not sufficient to match the prices of new competitors. By 1700 Leiden's textile industry was in full retreat.

Useful price series for Leiden textiles are available only for certain combed wool fabrics (says and fustians) and not at all for the carded wool fabrics (*laken*, bays, and warp) that remained important the longest. Table 8.5 shows the price trends for several important fabrics. Here one can observe a break in prices already after 1645. The prices of says fell faster than those of fustians (mixed with cotton yarn), but for both the decline was concentrated between 1645 and 1665, while a low point was reached around 1710. Thereafter, prices revived a bit, and after 1725, prices for the remaining, now very small, output became strikingly rigid. After 1670 it was the newer carded wool fabrics to which the Leiden industry entrusted its destiny, and among these fabrics the luxury *laken* acquired primacy because of both the volume of production and premium price it commanded.

The downward course of cloth prices was partly caused by the decline of raw wool prices. But the factor primarily responsible was the lower cost of competing centers of production. After 1650 reports multiplied of competitors who could undercut the Leiden drapers even after these had cut their profits to the bone. After the price reductions of the 1650s, the *54-bays* were sold for 16 to 18 stuivers per *el*, while the similar English product sold for 13 to 15 stuivers. The various says fell in price by a quarter, but English and Liège substitutes usually remained cheaper. The price of fine warp fell from 32 stuivers to 20–21 stuivers, but the competing Liège product cost only 17 or 18 stuivers. This indicates the existence of structural features that kept Leiden's costs above those of its competitors, and most students of this problem, contemporaries and later historians alike, have located it primarily in the industry's wage bills.

Leiden's competitors included several cities within the Republic. *Laken* production took place in Amsterdam, Haarlem, Gouda, Utrecht, and Delft; the production of says and camlets was concentrated in Gouda, Delft, and Breda, and camlets were also produced in Amsterdam and Haarlem. But none of these cities really challenged Leiden as a producer of woolen textiles. An exception, perhaps, was Kampen, which proved very competitive as a producer of bays for the West Indies market. Otherwise, Leiden's real competitors were to be found not in other cities but in the countryside. We can see here the repetition of a competitive relationship that the Flemish cities had experienced earlier.

Driving the process of industrial rural relocation was foreign competition, especially that emanating from England and the Bishopric of Liège. This competition began to bite after 1620, and as we have already seen, by the 1650s Leiden producers found it increasingly difficult to match the prices set in England and

Table 8.5. *Price indices for five important types of woolen cloth, selected years between 1628 and 1783 (1628 = 100).*

	Hondschooten says 3-lood unbleached	Heren says 3-lood vervallen	Heren says double overkijkers	Double lion	Bombazijnen overkijkers	Average
1628	100	100	100	100	100	100
1645	111	108	100	108	86	103
1653	93	91	84	97	85	90
1665	78	73	72	72	—	74
1679	65	65	58	71	59	64
1682	80	75	63	77	63	72
1710	56	60	52	73	46	58
1718	67	64	55	94	69	70
1740	65	64	52	111	84	75
1757	69	60	49	111	84	75
1783	78	—	49	—	—	—

Source: N. W. Posthumus, *Leidsche lakenindustrie*, Vol. III, p. 860.

Liège, where the industry was in full expansion. Leiden's entrepreneurs then faced the choice of cutting output of uncompetitive lines or removing production to locations with lower wage rates. In fact, they did both. The overall volume of the Republic's woolen cloth production contracted, while a growing portion of what remained migrated from Leiden to the North Brabant countryside. Beginning in 1635, Leiden drapers were especially active in organizing production in and around Tilburg. In 1638 we read of 300 looms active in this district; by 1663 there were 600 to 700. Initially, rural production was restricted to combing, spinning and weaving; the more skill- and capital-intensive steps in the production process (dyeing, shearing, and fulling) continued to take place in Leiden. In this way the Brabant industry continued to be dependent on the Leiden drapers, a situation that persisted throughout the seventeenth century. But in the eighteenth century, as Leiden shrank as a production center, the finishing and fulling processes began to relocate to Brabant, making inevitable the emergence there of an independent industry.

The decline of Leiden's industry occurred in stages, as one specialty after another collapsed (Figure 8.2). The first to go, in the third quarter of the seventeenth century, was the rashes, followed shortly thereafter by the fustians. Says faded gradually from the scene between 1670 and 1730, while the camlets, which also experienced a considerable decline after 1670, went to the wall only after 1725.

Only the *laken* sector resisted the general trend, growing in importance after 1650, and reviving again after 1690. In this period Leiden experienced something like a reversal of the process by which the city's textile industry had been resuscitated in the decades after 1580. Then the industry had switched from the old drapery to the lighter fabrics of the new drapery, a shift that released Leiden from its dependence on high-quality English and Spanish wool and permitted greater use of the long-fiber combing wool of domestic sheep. The reputation of Leiden's cloth thus came to depend not on the quality of the raw material but on the quality of the finishing and dyeing. This industry faced growing problems between 1620 and 1650, as the English gradually achieved technical parity with Leiden while continuing to enjoy lower production costs.

In the face of these binds, the Leiden drapers managed to hold their own with two strategies: by developing a new high-quality, skill-intensive camlet known as the "Leidse Turken," and by returning to production of an old heavy cloth, the luxury *laken*. In both cases Leiden's access to specific raw materials played a decisive role. The Leiden camlet constituted an innovation, mixing camel and goat hair with wool and silk. This produced a new, light cloth much in demand for men's clothing – and it was an initiative to which the English could not immediately respond. The renewal of Leiden's production of high-quality woolen cloth, *laken*, depended on Holland's commercial prowess: its domination of the Spanish wool supply and its penetration of a new market for this product in the Levant, which before the close of the Eighty Years' War had never been dependably accessible.

Both of these strategies represented a kind of orderly retreat. Both camlets and *laken* were expensive fabrics for which labor costs weighed relatively lightly in total costs. But this step could only postpone the inevitable day of reckoning. Eventually, someone would produce a fabric of comparable quality at a lower price. This occurred first with the camlets, which began to lose ground after the 1670s. The good fortune of the *laken* sector, which even enjoyed a revival between 1690 and 1715, is puzzling but may be related to military orders, especially for officers' uniforms in this era of nearly continuous warfare. Both the English Parliament and the States of Holland required the troops in their pay to be supplied exclusively with domestically produced clothing. Leiden's drapers, favored by this protective legislation, may also have found customers among the armies of Bavaria, Saxony, Denmark, Russia, Prussia, and Poland. In this context, the "outbreak" of a peace of long duration (1715/21 to 1740) may have been the final blow for the Leiden textile industry. From 1725 onward camlet and *laken* production followed a parallel course of uninterrupted decline until the end of the century, when the only signs of life in Leiden's textile industry emanated from the warp and bays sectors, both of which saved themselves by specializing in the production of coarse, cheap fabrics. By the late eighteenth century, next to nothing remained of the the high-quality products of the Leiden textile industry, and what remained of the the domestic woolen textile industry as a whole had long since drifted to rural locations.

Linen, cotton, and silk

The fate of the woolens industry was no isolated phenomenon, for the same forces were at work on the linen and the cotton industries: That which could be transferred to low-wage rural districts departed, sooner or later, from the cities; what remained in the cities died off. The story of the linen industry revolves around the city of Haarlem, where linen production emerged after 1580 to make it the Republic's second greatest textile center. The key to Haarlem's strength in this industry was linen bleaching, which benefited from the abundant supplies of pure dune water in districts around the city, from the availability of buttermilk from nearby dairying districts, from its easy access to peat supplies, and from the extensive grasslands suitable as bleaching fields.

The local abundance and high quality of all the inputs necessary to linen bleaching gave Haarlem an advantage that drew the industry to it early in the sixteenth century; but the sector grew with special vigor after 1580, as linen yarn and unbleached cloth was shipped from as far afield as Silesia and northern France for further processing in Haarlem. The city's strength in bleaching drew to it many Southern Netherlands' immigrants with skills and experience as linen weavers. On this basis Haarlem developed a weaving sector that employed thousands at the same time that Leiden developed its immigrant-based new draperies.

Despite the large size that Haarlem's linen-weaving sector maintained for at least two generations (in 1610 and 1643, we find references to the incredible totals of 4,000 and 3,350 active looms, respectively), our knowledge of this activity is sketchy in the extreme. We do know that linen weaving in Haarlem began to face reversals in the 1640s, for then Haarlem entrepreneurs commenced the process of removing looms from the city to rural Brabant, around the towns of Helmond and Eindhoven. By 1700 very little linen weaving remained in Haarlem, a decline compensated for only in part by the persistence of such textile specialties as yarn twining, ribbon weaving, and silk production. The finishing and bleaching of linen remained concentrated in Haarlem much longer. Haarlem's locational advantages together with the use of seasonal labor from Brabant and Westphalia, kept most of the bleaching fields in operation until deep in the eighteenth century. But even these advantages could not stay the general reorientation of linen production in Western Europe. After 1740, as the German production centers achieved direct access to overseas markets and British subsidies stimulated the rise of Irish and Scottish production, the volume of linen sent to Haarlem for bleaching fell steadily. Around 1650 annual output exceeded 100,000 pieces and kept occupied some twenty bleaching works employing about 1,000 workers. In 1789 only eight bleaching works remained in operation, and annual output was less than half the mid–seventeenth century peak.

A third case of an urban industry pushed to the margins by rural competition is cotton textiles. Before the nineteenth century, cotton was always mixed with another fiber: with wool to make fustians, or with linen to make *bombazijn*. The city of Amersfoort enjoyed an ideal location for the production of the linen-cotton mixtures. It stood at the western end of overland routes reaching into Twente, Westphalia, and further to Silesia – the sources for linen yarn. It also stood in easy waterborne communication with Amsterdam, from which it could cheaply be supplied with imported cotton. On this basis *bombazijn* production took root early in the seventeenth century and quickly came to dominate the economy of this small city, completely overshadowing the more ancient specialty of woolens weaving. Around 1660 Amersfoort's *bombazijn* production reached a peak of nearly 50,000 pieces, employing 388 looms.

Of course, the temptation was great to transport the imported cotton further to the east and to intercept the westward flow of linen at locations of lower-cost labor. The costs of such a move continued to outweigh the benefits until the turn of the eighteenth century, when the emergence in Twente of a powerful linen-weaving industry fed by a rapidly growing labor force made the introduction there of *bombazijn* production the logical next step – a step taken by 1728. It can hardly be a coincidence that at the same time, around 1730, the weaving of *bonten*, another linen-cotton mixture, shifted from Haarlem to the linen districts around Helmond. Once the cotton industry took root in the countryside, urban production was reduced to a marginal existence, where it survived at all.

These three examples display common patterns that provide insights into the dynamics of industrial development in the preindustrial era. After the outbreak of hostilities during the Revolt and the shift of the economic center of gravity from the Southern to the Northern Netherlands, it was the urban economies that received the sharpest stimulation. Seen from the vantage point of an industry seeking a new location, two factors appear to have been decisive in encouraging the choice of urban centers. The first is economic in nature: To nurture a new industry, one must be able to draw upon existing traditions of production or, at least, upon productive inputs. The necessary combination of worksites, capital, skilled labor, and commercial facilities could be found in the North after 1580 only in the cities. Moreover, one notes in this period the persistent efforts of every city, without exception, to attract to itself both labor (immigrants) and capital (entrepreneurs) with the offer of bonuses, free or low-cost workplaces (often confiscated Church properties), tax exceptions, and other subsidies. In this phase of migration and the re-establishment of livelihoods in distant places, workers and their families were prepared to work under relatively unfavorable terms with respect to housing and pay.

A second factor encouraging urban locations in this early phase of development is military in nature – namely, the need for physical security. For decades on end, the ongoing military operations disqualified large stretches of the countryside as a reliable location for industrial production. For this reason we observe many textile activities relocating from the rural Southern Netherlands to *urban* locations in the North. Suddenly, the decades of urban hand-wringing about the growth of rural industries and efforts to suppress such activities (as in Holland's *Order op de buitennering* of 1531) disappeared from the political stage. For both economic and military reasons, even novel industrial activities sought urban locations unless there existed compelling reasons to prefer rural locations, and these were safe from military threat (as were industrial windmills, shipyards, and brickworks).

These forces encouraging urban industrial location lasted but a few generations. The economic motive weakened first, as the spread of commercial facilities during the Twelve Years' Truce loosened the locational constraint considerably. The "pioneer mentality" also disappeared in this period, as there emerged a new generation eager to take advantage of the newly won prosperity. The second motive for urban location lessened in importance gradually during the 1630s and '40s, as military activities touched fewer and fewer rural regions and disappeared altogether by 1648. Then a characteristic tendency of preindustrial society, to settle labor-intensive industries whenever possible in zones of cheap rural labor, could reassert itself.

With this the economy returned to the situation of the mid–sixteenth century, when the lower production costs of the countryside gave many rural producers a strong competitive advantage over the cities. The simpler the production methods, and the more those production methods were compatible with the rural traditions of home handicrafts, the sooner and the faster would be the removal of industrial production from the city to a rural location. For just these reasons, the "ruralization of the textile industry" began with linens and was followed by wool and, finally, by cotton.

The economic climate in which this industrial displacement occurred differed profoundly from that of the sixteenth century, most obviously in the new secular trend prevailing after the mid–seventeenth century, when the previous upward trend of prices reversed to usher in a deflationary epoch. For this reason the locational shifts after 1650 did not usher in a new round of vigorous expansion, as they had a century earlier. Contraction of total output was the likelier consequence, for the new search for low rural production costs was more an expression of economic defensiveness and caution than of growth and optimism. The leaders of the old urban industries typically continued to exercise commercial leadership and financial control in the new rural industrial districts. But just as typically, their hold over the rural industries weakened with time, so that ultimately all that remained to the city was its function as the distributor of rural industrial products to foreign markets.

The urban economies gradually lost all these "footloose" industries, but there remained many others which, for technical, commercial, or other reasons, remained effectively tied to urban locations. These include silk production, cotton printing, book publishing, sugar refining, and industries with artistic components such as ceramics and glass blowing. But these industries, too, functioned in a distinctly different atmosphere after the mid–seventeenth century: Some wasted away while the more fortunate could muster no more than their self-preservation. New industries capable of dynamic growth were all but absent. The best candidate for such an industry would be the gin distilleries, but even this success story must be set alongside the collapse of the breweries. All things considered, there is no escaping the conclusion that the Republic's cities experienced a long-term deindustrialization. Their economies came to depend more and more on their regional service functions and on commerce and finance.

The rapid urbanization that was altogether exceptional in the preindustrial world drew quickly to a close after 1660, not only in demographic terms but also in its economic and cultural dimensions. This is not to say that all the achievements of the period 1580–1660 were undone; rather, we wish to stress the fundamentally new situation after mid-century in which growth could no longer be taken for granted and new initiatives and energies were expended on the removal or repair of undesired developments. Thus, around 1640 and again in 1680, the cities of Holland sought to breathe new life into the old *Order op de buitennering* by initiating a new effort to suppress rural industry and transport. Plans to couple poor relief to one or another form of forced labor at low wages attracted increasing attention and ongoing refinements of guild regulations aimed at the more effective protection of local industries. None of these defensive measures met with much success.

Silk was one of those industries that always remained tied to urban locations, but which faced mounting challenges from foreign competition. Silk is yet another of those branches of textile production whose modern history in the Northern Netherlands was based on late sixteenth-century migration from the South. Amsterdam, Utrecht, and Haarlem became the most important centers for this industry, which benefited greatly from the Republic's emerging entrepôt function. This gave the industry access to raw silk from several sources: first, from the Mediterranean, later via VOC shipments from Persia, and sometimes also from Russia.

No quantitative production data are known for this industry, but it appears that its early growth focused on the production of the simpler, cheaper grades of cloth, while from the 1640s on, the costlier luxury grades, such as the renowned "velours d'Utrecht," became more important. Two factors bound the industry to the cities: the complicated production processes, requiring skilled and specialized labor, and the need to supervise production closely in order to limit fraud in the handling of such an expensive raw material.

The course of output is not known, but a telling indication of the industry's development is provided by the knowledge that Amsterdam, a major production center, issued only one set of regulations governing silk production before 1648. In the half-century in which this industry prospered, it could develop in almost total freedom. In the second half of the seventeenth century, matters were very different: The city promulgated no less than twenty-six ordinances, a sure sign that sharpened competition was giving rise to cost-reducing measures that raised concerns about quality and fraud, which the city felt compelled to address. The growing need to reduce costs is also indicated by the fact that – beginning in Haarlem in 1678, followed by Amsterdam and Utrecht in 1682 – the cities established or subsidized new institutions to set impoverished girls and women to work spinning silk. Amsterdam's municipal silk-spinning facility absorbed the labor of hundreds of such girls between eight and sixteen years of age. Also suggestive of the industry's mounting problems is the fact that the various efforts after 1685 to establish the many French Huguenot refugees in this industry all met with failure. Abroad, in Prussia and also directly across the Dutch border in Krefeld, similar efforts were often successful, a contrast which only highlights the fact that production conditions in the Republic no longer supported growth of the industry's market share.

The decline of this industry began later, after 1713, when the end of decades of warfare removed an important disability from the large French silk industry. Its growth could now proceed without impediment. This, combined with the development of new, more refined products, presented the Dutch industry with a challenge to which it could not adequately respond. After 1730 the complaints, calls for new regulations, and pleas for subsidy came with increasing frequency; by the end of the century, this industry had all but disappeared from the Republic's cities.

Cotton printing

This same fate befell cotton printing, an activity that emerged after 1680 and was concentrated primarily in Amsterdam. The cotton printers sought to imitate the Indian product imported to Europe in large volume by the VOC. In fact, the VOC imported much unprinted cotton cloth as well, and the printing of this cloth (plus the cloth entering Holland via London and the English East India Company) became one of Amsterdam's largest industries. Actually, the cotton printers were concentrated just outside the city, along the river Amstel and the Overtoom, which supplied water of sufficient purity to nurture the industry. The workers came from the city to labor at printing works – at least thirty-four in number by 1735 – that required large investments of capital and employed, many of them, over 100 people. Contemporaries did not exaggerate when they claimed that cotton printing put bread on the tables of thousands of Amsterdam's inhabitants. Moreover, the industry offered business to many suppliers – of dyestuffs (madder), peat, and transportation services.

The industry seems to have reached its peak of production around 1750, when some eighty cotton printers were active. Thereafter, the complaints of an uncompetitively high wage level and the news of firm closings grew in frequency. Some firms added the printing of wallpaper as a source of additional income, but this did not stem the recessionary tide. By 1780 hardly anything was left. Competitors in Switzerland, followed by Germany and, after 1750, France, swept the Amsterdam industry from the world markets.

Sail cloth

Yet another branch of the textile industry, one that at its peak surely employed over 2,000 persons, was sail cloth (canvas) weaving. It was wholly concentrated in the countryside, specifically in the Zaan region and several adjacent villages. This location gave sail-cloth producers immediate access to their largest customers, the shipbuilders and marine services of the Zaan region and Amsterdam; but Dutch sail cloth served export markets as well. This is another industry for which few quantitative indicators are available. The sail cloth of Brittany is said to have held a major share of the Dutch market until deep into the seventeenth century. It was, in fact, the aggressive commercial policies of Colbert and war with France in 1672–8 which are usually regarded as having spurred the Dutch to avoid dependence on this hostile supplier by developing a domestic substitute. If this is so, the industry must have grown rapidly after the 1670s, for we know that it had reached its peak by 1725. The 60,000 rolls then produced annually fell to no more than 35,000 rolls by 1751, to 28,000 in 1769, and to even less in later years. A combination of Russian competition and protectionist restriction on export to countries such as England and Sweden are thought to have speeded its decline.

8.3.2. WOODWORKING INDUSTRIES

Shipbuilding

Another industrial sector that could claim to join textiles among the Republic's most important, and that was also torn between rural and urban locations, was shipbuilding and the closely related activity of lumber sawing. From the early sixteenth century – certainly after the 1531 *Order op de buitennering* – shipbuilding was overwhelmingly an urban and guild-organized craft. The same was true of sawed lumber, then an entirely hand-produced commodity. As noted earlier, the main sixteenth-century shipbuilding centers of Dordrecht, Haarlem, Amsterdam, Edam, Hoorn, and Alkmaar flourished thanks to strong demand for additional ships.

In Chapter 9 we shall learn how the Dutch shipbuilders overcame the inferior position they held vis-à-vis their French and Spanish counterparts in the course of the sixteenth century. This learning process yielded two innovations that proved to be of critical importance to the expansion of Dutch shipping. The first was the development of the herring buss. This specialized fishing vessel, described in Chapter 7, was the first ship on which fish were not only caught but also processed and preserved – while remaining at sea for a month or two – by its crew of ten to thirty men.

The second innovation involved the merchant marine, which sought to adapt to local needs the dominant ship type, the caravel. This vessel, inspired by Iberian prototypes, possessed a three-mast rigging and could reach a very large carrying capacity of over 1,000 tons. The caravel was not well suited to the often shallow Dutch coastal waters, requiring frequent transfer of cargoes to lighters (other vessels) some distance from the harbor of destination. This restriction helps to explain the early sixteenth-century rise of the Zeeland outports serving Antwerp, such as Vlissingen, Arnemuiden, and Middelburg. After 1550 the awkward caravel came to be replaced by the smaller, more maneuverable *boeier* and *vlieboot*, ship types with one deck and but one mast, with a carrying capacity of from 100 to 200 tons. The explosive growth of Dutch trade in the final decades of the sixteenth century generated a need for a larger, faster, economical ship – and one with the shallow draught required by so many northern harbors. With the encouragement and, most probably, the financial support of a regent and merchant of Hoorn, Pieter Jansz. Liorne, a ship design took shape that featured a great lengthening of the existing types. Its hull was given a pronounced tumbledown form and a pear-shaped stern. Its three masts were rigged with small, easily handled square sails. The advantages of this new design quickly became apparent: enlarged carrying capacity, enhanced stability at sea due to its low center of gravity, a smaller crew in relation to payload, and, as a direct consequence of the steep stem and stern, an improved ability to tack against the wind. Above all, this new vessel – the *fluitschip* – sailed faster than its predecessors: Instead of two trips to the Baltic per season, a skipper could now make three, perhaps four, round trips. This combination of advantages constituted a technological breakthrough of the greatest importance. In the following century, the *fluit* reigned supreme in both the Dutch merchant marine and in its shipbuilding industry.

Thanks to the *fluit*, Holland functioned throughout the seventeenth century as the ship wharf of Europe. Although the total size of the Republic's fleet of seaworthy vessels is not known with precision, enough information is available to permit an estimate. At the time of its greatest extent in the second and third quarters of the seventeenth century, the combined naval, merchant, and fishing fleets may well have attained a total volume of 450,000 to 550,000 tons. We should think in terms of 3,000 to 4,000 vessels, half exceeding 100 tons in capacity. The typical life span of such vessels was such that the Republic's own demand for replacement vessels alone would have required the construction of over 300 ships per year. But ships were also built for foreign customers. Such orders account for the fact that seven of the ten large ships whose home port was Christiania (modern Oslo) had been built in the Republic. Under Richelieu, France even placed orders in the Republic for naval vessels. Besides these direct orders, the ship wharves also worked to replace the many ships lost to piracy and warfare. The low cost of Dutch shipping depended to a large extent on the light construction and sparse weaponry of its merchant ships, features that made them vulnerable to capture and loss. The estimated losses to the Dunkirk pirates and to English hostile action ran in the thousands (see Chapter 9, section 9.8) between 1628 and 1674, a fact that represented even greater orders for replacement vessels at Dutch wharves.

All told, we will not be far wrong to estimate average annual production at 400 to 500 seagoing vessels in the period 1625 to 1700. When one takes into account the time required to build one ship (averaging four months), and the average employment at a wharf, it is likely that some 10,000 persons found regular work in this industry, which made shipbuilding one of the Republic's largest industries. In Holland, where it was largely concentrated, it could claim close to 5 percent of the entire industrial labor force.

An industry so oriented to mass production ceased to fit within the organizational structures of the guilds, which had served well enough in the sixteenth century. Seventeenth-century shipbuilding came to possess a dual structure, one in which the large port cities of Amsterdam and Rotterdam specialized in repair work, while new construction took place in rural wharves, especially those concentrated along the banks of the river Zaan. In addition, there were the smaller port towns, such as Dordrecht, which performed repair functions and the construction of smaller vessels, and those cities endowed with wharves of the VOC and the Admiralties. In a city such as Middelburg, these wharves, specializing in the construction of the largest vessels of their day, stood as formidable pillars of the local economy.

The rapid rise of the Zaan region to dominance in shipbuilding after 1600 created an industrial phenomenon without precedent. A capital-intensive industry that had always been located in port cities now took root in the countryside and quickly succeeded in pushing most urban competitors out of the market. The ship wharves of nearby Edam and Hoorn disappeared under the competitive pressure, while those of Rotterdam declined sharply in number (from 23 in 1630 to 11 in 1650, and to 5 around 1700). The explanation for the rise of Zaan region shipbuilding is to be found in a combination of locational and cost advantages, the latter based in part on the more flexible social and institutional structures of a place without guilds. The presence in the region of wind-powered lumber sawing mills gave the Zaan shipbuilders ready access to a large and varied assortment of lumber inventories that they did not have to stock themselves. In this way they could work faster and cheaper than their competitors in, say, Rotterdam, where such suppliers did not exist.

But why did the mechanized lumber mill prosper in the Zaan region in the first place? The Zaan region's location gave it ready access to imported timber, cheap land on which to store this bulky material, and many sites with unobstructed access to the wind. These competitive advantages were real, but they might not have sufficed were it not for the fact that Amsterdam's guild of sawyers managed to obstruct the introduction of mechanized sawing to the city for several decades. That which benefited the Amsterdam sawyers' guild in the short term, stimulated both the mechanized sawing and the shipbuilding industry of the rural Zaan region in the long run. And this long-run advantage was reinforced by the lower wage rates paid in the Zaan region, which reflected both the absence of guilds and the lower cost of living in the countryside.

With all these advantages, the concentration of ship construction in this rural industrial zone can hardly come as a surprise. Contemporaries noted that a ship costing 27,500 guilders in the Zaan would have cost 28,500 in Amsterdam and 32,500 in Rotterdam. Another observer claimed that what cost 50,000 guilders in the Zaan would cost 56,000 in Rotterdam. The economies of scale incorporated in these price quotations weighed far less heavily in the provision of ship repair services, which helps to account for the persistence of this activity in the chief port cities.

The Zaan industry built a variety of ship types, including vessels for both inland and ocean shipping. The *fluitschip* dominated the seagoing vessels, accounting for some 80 percent of all those built in the seventeenth century and 70 percent in the following century. These vessels tended to become larger over time: Ships of under 100 feet in length dominated before 1650, while those of 100 to 150 feet became dominant after that date.

Just as striking as the Zaan region's low costs was its technical conservatism. Once the designs of the *fluitschip* and the herring buss had attained a certain stability, an era of mass production followed for which the Zaan region was ideally suited. But this constant repetition did not yield, as it had in the previous century, further innovations. This may have had something to do with the absence of guilds, for these institutions had sometimes functioned as clearinghouses for technical improvements. The Dutch shipbuilder of the seventeenth and eighteenth centuries was very much a private operator, who sought to keep his technical knowledge to himself as much as possible, revealing it only to his successor. Perhaps this characteristic of the industry's organization helps to explain the otherwise puzzling slowing of theoretical and technical development after the early seventeenth century.

Whatever its cause, this feature of Dutch shipbuilding made inevitable the gradual erosion of its technological edge over foreign competitors and ultimately the surrender of its industrial leadership. Toward the end of the seventeenth century, complaints of inferior Dutch shipbuilding techniques become frequent, especially with respect to English and French products. The protectionist policies of the governments of these two countries sought especially to foster domestic shipbuilding and met eventually with real success. England began as early as 1615 with measures to stimulate its domestic wharves, and the Navigation Acts of 1651 nurtured the industry even more. By 1662 England forbade altogether the purchase or commissioning of ships abroad, and by 1676 the last loopholes in these laws were closed. The French placed their faith in the systematic scientific study of shipbuilding methods. In this they became very proficient, although they long remained economically uncompetitive as shipbuilders.

English shipbuilding techniques came more and more to emphasize the use of iron, while the Dutch wharves held fast to methods using only wood. The steady relative rise in wood prices eventually yielded important cost advantages to the English methods while, at the same time, those methods allowed the English to pioneer in techniques that would lead to the innovations of the nineteenth century.

While the English and French were mastering advanced shipbuilding techniques, the Scandinavian nations, long important markets for Dutch ships, gradually developed the capacity to supply their own needs. Even Russia developed its own shipbuilding industry in the eighteenth century.

Still, it appears that Zaan shipbuilding did not wait for the force of foreign competition to precipitate its decline. While research has yet to remove all uncertainty on this issue, it now appears likely that the Zaan region reached its peak output before 1680. The number of wharves rose from 13 in 1608, to 20–25 in 1630, to a peak of 60–65 around 1670. By 1730 only 26 or 27 remained, and in 1792 there were only 2 or 3. The wharves that closed after 1670 tended to be the smaller ones, reflecting a process of concentration that was directly related to the increased average size of ships and to the growing practice among wharf owners to form consortia – *sociëteiten* and *compagnieschappen* – to attract large orders.

A second measure of the industry's size is based on counting the names of shipbuilders and traders mentioned in the notarial archives of the Zaan region. By ten-year periods the numbers rise from 27 in 1610–19, to 54 in 1630–9, 74 in 1650–9, and 112 in 1670–9. Thereafter, the numbers fall: to 86 in 1680–9, and thereafter in a regular regression to 53 in 1710–19. The decline of production after the 1670s was, in view of the tendency toward concentration, certainly slower than the rate of diminution of shipbuilders, but the sparse and often vague production figures confirm the general pattern sketched earlier. Annual production of seagoing vessels stood at about 40 around 1630, and at between 120 and 150 in the decades after 1650. By 1730 production had fallen to 100, and by the 1770s no more than 20 to 25 ships per year slid from the Zaan region wharves.

The decline of Zaan shipbuilding seems to have been intensified by the simultaneous decline of the whaling fleet, which was also concentrated in the region. Shipbuilders unable to sell new ships immediately often turned to the whaling industry, putting their ships to a (hopefully) profitable use while waiting for a buyer. Whaling played a useful role for shipbuilders in financing the maintenance of inventories of ships, available on short notice to potential buyers. Such a strategy reflects the intense competition and slim profit margins that the shipbuilders faced by the late seventeenth century. These shipbuilders sought to keep their heads above water by cultivating both backward and forward linkages: backward to the timber trade and milling, forward to the whaling industry. The sharp decline of whaling may well have speeded the collapse of the ship wharves by removing a means of financing inventories.

Even if whaling had not declined, the Zaan shipbuilding industry would still have had to face the serious consequences of the silting of the river and harbor channels leading to the wharves, a process discussed in Chapter 2, section 2.4. The reduced accessibility of the river Zaan to oceangoing vessels not only sped the industry's decay but also stimulated its partial displacement to other locations. The timber trade, and probably also shipbuilding, tended in the course of the eighteenth century to grow in the Delta region. Dordrecht and Rotterdam emerged as more than simply regional centers of the timber trade, thereby setting the stage for their later, nineteenth-century careers as shipbuilding centers. Amsterdam also benefited from this process, for in 1816 this severely depressed city still possessed some forty wharves, by which date the Zaan industry had become history.

Sawmilling

At intervals in the preceding discussion, we have had occasion to emphasize the links that existed between the timber trade, lumber milling, and shipbuilding. Indeed, so close were these links that many individuals were simultaneously involved in all three activities. The current state of research leaves unanswered several important questions concerning the course of timber imports to the Republic (an issue pursued further in Chapter 10, section 10.2.4). But from what we have just learned of the shipbuilding industry, we can be quite certain that timber imports grew up to the third quarter of the seventeenth century. The needs of residential and urban construction and of drainage installations joined with shipbuilding to strengthen this claim: The economy of the Republic became very wood-intensive, and this gave rise to a large and growing demand for sawed timber.

Timber sawing took place in both urban and rural locations. The urban sawyers were organized in guilds, but regardless of location, the technology consisted of hand sawing, usually by pairs of sawyers. This craft was challenged in 1594, with the construction of the first wind-powered saw mill, an invention that ranks with the development of the herring buss and the *fluitschip* as the most important technological achievements of the late sixteenth-century Netherlands. The inventor, Cornelis Cornelisz. van Uitgeest, built the first prototype in Alkmaar and introduced it to Zaandam the following year. With this the first step was taken in the development of a vast complex of industrial windmills in the Zaan region, a complex that would flourish for 150 years and that would, besides sawing wood, press oilseeds, pulp paper, cut tobacco, prepare paint, and process hemp. But the sawing windmills always remained numerically dominant: In 1630 the Zaan region contained 53 sawing windmills (of 86 in all of Holland), and in 1730 there were 256 (of Holland's total of 448). No other place possessed anything remotely comparable to this industrial concentration. Hoorn, with 11 sawing windmills in 1630, was the closest competitor.

Of the cities that possessed, or would possess, important positions in the trade and milling of timber – Amsterdam, Rotterdam, and Dordrecht – only the last-mentioned had any mechanized sawmills at all, two as of 1630. We can explain the surprising absence of these mills in Amsterdam and assume that a similar story can be told for Rotterdam and Dordrecht. In Amsterdam the opposition of the hand sawyers prevented the construction of sawing windmills, and the city government supported the sawyers' guild in its opposition by prohibiting the importation to the city of the (cheaper) mechanically sawn lumber from the rural areas (i.e., from the Zaan region). We know that Leiden and Enkhuizen struck a similarly protectionist posture, a posture that long postponed the introduction of mechanized sawing to the cities. Not until 1630 did Amsterdam's lumber traders succeed in establishing a company dedicated to the operation of sawing windmills. With this breakthrough the days of the hand sawyers' guild were numbered, but it could not undo the commanding lead that the Zaan region had developed in the preceding thirty-five years, for this industrial zone then combined the advantage of long experience with formidable locational advantages. The Zaan villages' location on a broad navigable river with numerous side channels proved to be ideally suited for low-cost transportation and storage. No less optimal was the way these villages became strung out as a long, thin ribbon on a north–south axis that faced directly into the prevailing west winds. Here, unlike a built-up urban setting, room could be found for a nearly unlimited number of windmills. In the Zaan region, numerous, cheap industrial sites and low labor costs could be combined, via direct water access to Amsterdam, with the Republic's foremost timber markets, and it enjoyed at its very doorstep the colossal local demand for sawn lumber emanating from the shipbuilding industry.

Powerful self-reinforcing processes led to industrial concentration in the Zaan region, but the limits to expansion of mechanized sawing in the cities that specialized in the import of foreign timber also worked to the region's advantage. Amsterdam's development offers a clear demonstration of this fact. Once the guild of hand sawyers lost its monopoly in 1630, the construction of sawing windmills proceeded rapidly: By 1645 there were about 34, by 1661, 61, and in 1678 a total of 80. But by then the possible locations had all been taken. Around the perimeter of Dordrecht, 27 sawing windmills eventually were erected, and around Rotterdam, 25. In both cases these totals represented the maximum of suitable locations.

As long as the total demand for sawn lumber did not decline, the Zaan region's inordinate share of this industry's productive capacity could not be threatened, for the urban timber centers faced binding constraints on expansion and depended on the Zaan to meet their excess demand. But, conversely, the Zaan region's hold over this industry could not last long once total demand began to decline. Once the demand for lumber sawing declined to match the production capacity of the urban sawmills, the cities could reassert their rights to protect municipal economic interests. And this is precisely what began to happen at the end of the 1730s. Actually, Amsterdam had declared a prohibition on the import of sawn lumber as early as 1631 and renewed its intentions in 1694. But the ordinance also provided for a large loophole, which suspended the prohibition as needed. In 1739 the flexible use of these provisions came to an end. From then on the city enforced with vigilance the prohibition on the use of "foreign" lumber, a practice in which it was followed by Rotterdam, which revived in 1741 an old prohibition that had long fallen into disuse.

The consequences of this protective strategy of the cities appeared dramatically in 1745, when no less than eight Zaan-region sawing windmills were torn down in a single year. By the end of the century, the number of sawmills in the Zaan region had fallen from 256 (in 1731) to 144, with the most intense contraction occurring between 1745 and 1765. In this same interval, the number of urban sawmills remained stable. The collapse of the Zaan shipbuilding industry and the multiplying mercantilist obstacles to the export of sawn lumber (see Chapter 10, section 10.2.4) constituted the structural causes of the retreat of mechanized sawing in the region. The crisis into which the rural economy plunged with the onset of the cattle plague of 1744 surely delivered another sharp setback, for the agricultural sector normally formed a large market for timber.

Looking back at the economic complex of timber trade, mechanized sawing, and shipbuilding, we can see how the technological innovations of the 1590s – the *fluitschip* and wind-powered sawing – established the conditions for a long era of increased production. Both domestic and foreign demand for wood and ships grew enormously. But further technological improvements of consequence did not occur, and in this situation foreign producers, assisted by protectionist measures, could gradually close the technological gap that had opened before 1600. In both timber-exporting lands and sawn-lumber–importing countries, domestic sawing industries arose during the first half of the eighteenth century. At the same time, foreign nations achieved total independence from the Republic's ship wharves: By then England, France, and the Scandinavian countries built their own ships, and often built them better. Meanwhile at home, the cessation of population growth and urbanization and the collapse of land reclamation activity undercut two important components of the domestic demand for lumber.

In a cycle of growth and decline that lasted two centuries, the sawing industry evolved continually as it adjusted to changes in the supply of timber, changes in the composition of demand, and changes in the competitive positions of city and countryside. At its peak between 1680 and 1730, the Zaan region appeared to hold an unchallengeable sway in this industry. But the swiftness of its demise teaches that its great size depended acutely on Dutch domination of international markets in timber and timber products. As the Republic lost its grip on these markets while the cities retained their hold on their local markets, the Zaan region stood exposed to the full force of the declining demand.

8.3.3. CERAMIC INDUSTRIES

Brickworks

Another industrial sector with both urban and rural branches was the potteries. But in contrast to the textile and wood-based industries already discussed, urban–rural competition was scarcely a factor here. Rather, there existed a stable division of labor: At rural locations we find the production of bricks, roof tiles, and floor tiles; in the cities we find the production of ceramics, decorative tiles, and clay (smoking) pipes.

The pottery sector as a whole formed a large and ancient industry, one intimately connected to the qualities and colors associated with the local clays of the Dutch riverbanks. The history of this industry goes back to the early Middle Ages, and its ongoing importance is suggested by the fact that as late as 1806, forty-six brickworks employing nearly 1,000 workers functioned in South Holland alone, together with 19 roof tile works with an unknown number of workers. Along the rivers in Gelderland, there were another 34 brick and tile works, while Friesland counted 26 brickworks and 21 roof tile works, employing together 839 workers. Friesland also possessed 38 pottery, pipe, and *plateel* (decorative tile) works that employed 295 persons. Groningen (including East Friesland) counted 70 brickworks in 1811. Their average size was small, since they employed all told only 577 workers and produced some 12 million bricks and tiles per year, compared with the 65.5 million units produced by the 49 South Holland installations. With this review we have covered the leading production centers; around 1810 the industry as a whole employed some 3,000 workers, mostly on a seasonal basis, who could turn out an annual total of some 150 million bricks and tiles.

The present state of our knowledge does not permit many firm statements about the evolution of this multifaceted industry before the nineteenth century. It seems highly likely, however, that brick making experienced a tremendous boom in the course of the long sixteenth century. The following circumstances stand in support of this view: (1) the transition to brick construction, especially in the cities where it became a legal requirement, (2) population growth and the numerous extensions to the cities, (3) the increased importance of brick exports (as ballast in ocean shipping), (4) the renewal and improvement of fortifications around the cities, which came to incorporate ever more brick, (5) the paving of city streets, and (6) the increased use of brick in the growing number of sluices, dams, docks, and related hydraulic and navigational installations.

Among these six factors, the role of brick (and tile) exports is the least certain. We know that either brick or sand served as the necessary ballast of empty or partially loaded ships departing Dutch harbors, and that bricks transported in this way played a role in the German and Baltic port cities sufficient to influence their architecture and outward appearance. The Sound Toll Registers generally failed to register the passage of ballast material. But we know from the Republic's own *Convooi* and *Licenten* charges that the ports of the Amsterdam Admiralty exported 100,000 guilders' worth of bricks and related products in 1668, which represented a value equal to some 30 million bricks. The shallow channels leading from Amsterdam caused many ships to take on their ballast only after arriving at the outports near the open sea (such as Harlingen and the Wadden Islands), and the surviving port books of Harlingen suggest that this town exported the equivalent of 5 million bricks in 1654–5.

Bricks also made their way, as ballast, to more distant destinations, such as Asia and Brazil. In the case of Asia, we must keep in mind that the cumulative total over some 200 years could be quite impressive, serving to build and maintain the trading stations, forts, churches, and much else at the East India Company's numerous posts. The shipments to Brazil lasted no more than fifteen years, but the export of bricks to build Recife and Mauritsstad (Pernambuco) was nothing less than prodigious: The value in Brazil of the bricks sent to Mauritsstad in the two years beginning June 1641 totaled 1,154,550 guilders. Even if Brazilian prices were triple the Dutch prices, this sum would have represented the shipment of 50 million bricks per year.

Of the remaining five factors listed as generating an increased demand for brick, we can be confident that they all ceased to generate much growth after the mid-seventeenth century. May we conclude from this that brick production stagnated after this date, or that the volume of production in 1625 stood well above that of 1675? A firm answer cannot be given, but an intriguing glimpse into the production of brick in the Rijnland district of Holland gives a clue. This region's brick producers formed a cartel in 1633, committing themselves to limit the annual number of times they fired their kilns to an agreed-upon figure. The number varied from year to year, but the average number of firings stood at 4.00 in the period 1633–51, and only 2.07 in the period 1652–67. Since the kilns in use in Holland typically produced 500,000 to 600,000 bricks per firing, this suggests that annual production averaged some 60 to 70 million bricks before 1652 and about half that amount in 1652–67.

The detailed information is too brief and too partial to permit the drawing of far-reaching conclusions, but it fits comfortably in the long-term development sketched in an account published in 1804 of the brickworks located along the Holland IJssel river. There, production was said to have fallen from 126 million in 1672 to 43 million in 1700. The number of brick kilns fell, according to this account, from 45 in 1672 to 31 in 1700, and further to 20 in 1802. There existed, of course, many other districts with numerous brickworks, and local conditions (especially the extent of clay deposits) could vary greatly, but the overall trend must have been downward. Receipts of Holland's excise tax on building materials, which included brick and every manner of construction tile (but also many other sorts of material), fell by half between the 1660s and the decade 1700–9. Surely, this says a lot about the fate of the brickworks in this period, just as it must about the overall course of the economy, in which construction always played a leading role. The first unambiguous signs of revival in this sector became evident only in the late eighteenth century, as a major new center of brick production arose along the rivers of Gelderland.

Pottery

The production of earthenware pots, tableware, and wall tiles, both utilitarian and decorative, always remained an urban industry. Although a few cities achieved a certain reputation as centers of ceramics production (Bergen op Zoom possessed no less than twenty-two pottery works in 1669), this industry was chiefly characterized by dispersion: Many cities possessed potteries that produced for local or regional markets (Groningen counted 12 firms in 1662 and 6 in 1700; Delft possessed 4 firms in 1600 and 9 in 1625, 5 in 1650, and 2 in 1670). Much like coopers, the potters often depended on derived demand from other industries. A 1662 description of Amsterdam's sugar refineries relates that such a firm annually purchased 50,000 to 60,000 guilders' worth of pots. It was said that four pottery works operated exclusively to supply this demand. Later in 1776 a group of these refiners formed a jointly held company for the operation of a pottery works, one that continued in existence until 1879.

Of much greater importance was the production of decorative ceramics, with which the city of Delft has long been associated, but which was also active in Haarlem, Rotterdam, Amsterdam, and Arnhem. In Friesland this craft flourished in Makkum, a coastal village that grew to acquire urban characteristics. The growth of this industry in Delft is instructive.

In the Middle Ages, the economy of Delft depended, like that of many other cities of Holland, on two major industries: brewing and textiles. Sooner or later most cities had to choose between these industries, for the one (textiles) polluted the water, the purity of which was critical to the viability of the other (brewing). In Delft the two industries managed to live side by side longer than elsewhere, but eventually brewing emerged as the city's dominant industry. As discussed earlier in this chapter, both textiles and brewing suffered serious reversals in the course of the sixteenth century, a phenomenon that did not leave Delft untouched. Moreover, when toward that century's end the demand for beer revived, the chief beneficiary was not Delft but the nearby port city of Rotterdam, which was better situated to cater to the growing demand for ships' beer.

Delft's magistrates sought to attract new industries to the city in these years – as did most other cities – by offering favorable relocation terms to would-be entrepreneurs and, especially, to immigrants from the Southern Netherlands. They even attempted to lure drapers and workers from Leiden and succeeded sufficiently to boast of 96 looms and 14 drapers active in Delft in 1597. The ferocious reaction of Leiden to these efforts forced Delft to back off, but as late as 1642, 14 *laken* drapers continued to function (compared to 217 in Leiden), and in 1660 there were 126 drapers with 325 workers producing says.

Delft also sought to stimulate tapestry weaving. In 1591 the magistrates attracted to the city François Spierinck, a prominent Antwerp tapestry producer. His firm became the most important tapestry works in the Northern Netherlands, acquiring important commissions from the central government, Henri IV of France, the Danish, Swedish, and English crowns, town governments, and wealthy individuals. Spiering's firm disappeared after 1634, but by then competing tapestry works had settled in Delft, among them those of Van der Gucht and of Karel van Mander, Jr., formerly a cartoon drawer for Spiering. Until around 1675 this labor-intensive and artistic industry prospered in Delft, yet it did not become the chief center of Dutch tapestry production. This honor went to Gouda, which had succeeded in attracting many more tapestry weavers, especially from the region of Oudenaarde. Between 1581 and 1620, no fewer than 506 persons from this Flemish district appear in Gouda's marriage registers, and other archival documents establish that at least 450 of them worked in the tapestry trade. Gouda's industry also fell into decay in the late seventeenth century, disappearing altogether by 1700.

Delft's magistrates launched yet another effort to breathe new life into the city's industrial economy in 1621, when they contracted with the Merchant Adventurers to remove their staple for undyed English woolen cloth from Middelburg to Delft. Since this merchant guild held monopoly rights to the export of English woolens to the Continent, the agreement promised to stimulate Delft's finishing industries as well as its trade; but Delft satisfied the English no more than Middelburg had, and in 1634 they moved again, this time to Rotterdam.

Delft made a fourth effort to stimulate its textile industry in 1631, by contracting with six Amsterdam *laken* merchants to supply buildings, equipment, and 150 orphans who were to produce 3,000 *lakens* in the course of six years. With the failure of this scheme, Delft's city fathers finally abandoned their efforts to rejuvenate the textile sector. They could do so because by then there had emerged, without municipal subsidies or concessions of any sort, an industry the expansion of which could compensate for the slow but sure decay of the city's breweries: the ceramics industry.

Here, once again, we are dealing with production techniques that appear to have been given an important boost by Southern Netherlands immigration. The tin-glazing methods that form the foundation of the majolica and *plateel* products which flourished in Delft were not altogether unknown in the North. We know that several ceramics works in Haarlem used these methods as early as the 1560s, and by 1600 specialist firms were active in several cities, of which Delft was but one. Haarlem long set the pace in this industry, and Rotterdam also cut an imposing figure with 11 tin glazing works producing *majolica* in 1642. But by 1650 Delft possessed 15 majolica works, and it quickly became the major production center.

Why did Delft emerge to become the dominant producer while elsewhere production stagnated (as in Rotterdam) or collapsed (as in Haarlem and Amsterdam)? Historians have proposed ready access to potting clay and peat as an answer, but in this, Delft can hardly be distinguished from nearly every other city of South Holland. Delft's achievement is closely connected to the successful transformation of the old *majolica* into the more refined, artistic product that came to characterize Delft faience after 1650. External factors stimulated this transformation. From the early seventeenth century, the VOC imported substantial quantities of Chinese porcelain to the Republic. Until about 1630 the annual import fluctuated between 50,000 and 100,000 pieces; thereafter, the volume jumped to 200,000. Consumers' preferences for this imported product were so strong that the existing *majolica* producers had no choice but to respond. They could (1) abandon *majolica* production and retreat to the production of the simpler lead-glazed articles intended for everyday use, (2) concentrate on such *majolica* products as escaped direct Chinese competition, notably decorative tiles, (3) reduce the quality, and thereby the cost and price, of *majolica* so as to attract consumers for whom the popular Chinese article was beyond reach, or (4) increase the quality of the domestic product to make it comparable to the imported porcelain.

The Dutch producers followed all four of these paths, of course. In the 1620s and '30s, cheap ceramics, with sketchy and sloppy decoration, made their entrée to the market. The second option also attracted many firms, especially to the production of wall tiles, but after 1650 demand ebbed.

It was the fourth option that led to the rise of the famed Delft ceramics industry. Soon after the introduction of Chinese porcelain, Dutch potters tried to imitate the Chinese designs on white domestic *majolica*. It long proved impossible to produce these domestic imitations at a competitive cost, but the domestic industry got its chance in 1644–7, when civil war in China interrupted the flow of porcelain to Europe. As the imported quantities fell from the 200,000-piece level to 115,000 in 1647, and no more than 15,000 pieces in 1652, the Dutch industry took energetic steps to supply the markets and, simultaneously, to refine its techniques.

Three Delft firms and one from Haarlem led the way. The death of the Haarlem firm's owner brought that city's participation in this industrial offensive to an untimely end, concentrating all further technological developments in Delft. There, the technical advances were paired with large investments of capital, and together they fueled an explosive industrial development. Between 1650 and 1661, 14 new firms emerged, and 2 more in the course of the 1660s brought the total to its high-point of 30 by 1670. And these firms became larger: from a handful of workers in the early days, to an average of about 15 in 1650 to an average of between 40 and 50 at the industry's peak, in 1670–1720. Between 1650 and 1680, the fixed capital of each firm rose from 3,000 to 10,000 guilders, while the average inventory of industrial materials stood at a considerable multiple of the fixed capital. During the industry's feverish expansion, there are numerous signs that demand far outstripped production capacity: Goods were sold long before they could be delivered, and complaints multiplied about paint mills that failed to deliver the contracted supplies or favored one customer over another.

As the production of delftware took flight, the decorative pottery sector experienced a process of concentration and specialization. The cessation of population growth after 1650 was soon followed by the collapse of the Republic's building boom, and this, in turn, reduced sharply the demand for tiles. Changing fashions further reduced this demand, as the practice of building separate kitchens caused decorative tiles to disappear from what became sitting rooms and parlors. Only in the countryside did the old tile-intensive fashions persist, providing a steady demand for the *majolica* industries of Rotterdam (which catered to the South Holland and Zeeland island markets) and those of Harlingen and Makkum (which served the northeastern Netherlands and northern Germany). The industry in Leiden, Haarlem, Amsterdam, and Gouda, which catered primarily to urban markets, fell into steep decline. Only Delft remained as a major ceramics center, producing both refined delftware and a wide variety of tiles and crockery for everyday use.

Delft's industry got its chance to develop thanks to the collapse of the Ming dynasty at the other end of the world. Eventually, the VOC found a substitute for Chinese porcelain in Japan, at which point shipments to Europe rebounded. This actually proved beneficial to Delft, as it popularized polychromatic designs which the Delft faienciers were quick to master, developing toward the end of the seventeenth century new techniques and introducing purple dyes made of manganese. Around 1700 the industry introduced in its highest-quality work decorations on dark backgrounds of black, brown, olive, and blue. Here one discerns the influence of Asian lacquer work. Later, the industry produced ceramics in imitation of Saxon and English porcelain.

These developments suggest a weakness of the Delft faience industry: its inability to build upon its own artistic strengths and its increasing reliance on foreign design fashions. As the industry's artistic and technical development stagnated, decline inevitably followed. Around 1750 some 20 firms continued to operate in Delft, in 1780 there were 16, in 1798 but 11. And these remaining firms now typically stoked one kiln in place of two and stoked them less frequently than before. In the face of this decline, qualified faience painters became increasingly scarce. In time, delftware not only lost its foreign markets but also a large part of the domestic market. An important industry, which in its day must have produced hundreds of millions of pieces, fell into ruin.

What can explain the untimely failure of this industry, so promising and innovative in the decades after 1650, and for whose product European demand grew throughout the eighteenth century? The cessation of Delft's technical and artistic development stands as a proximate cause of its decline, but standing behind this important source of vulnerability was the rise after 1710 of a European porcelain industry, and, once again (it is a recurring refrain), the protectionistic support given to those foreign competitors. Already in the 1670s, England forbade the importation of Dutch ceramics, a prohibition lifted after William III assumed the English crown. The Southern Netherlands placed a draconian tariff on Dutch ceramics imports in 1758, which effectively closed a major market. This measure elicited loud Dutch complaints, but it remained in place. Foreign competitors also attracted Delft craftsmen to assist in the development of their industries. As early as 1677, Delft's city government sought to legislate against such emigration, and the issue arose again in 1755, when the city threatened such "industrial traitors" with permanent banishment from the industry and a withdrawal of all future rights to poor relief. All to no avail. The international diffusion of the porcelain industry changed permanently Delft's competitive position in European markets. These new products, most spectacularly England's Wedgwood crockery, proved to be both stronger and more attuned to fashion than delftware. After 1750 the industry declined without relief, as firm after firm closed its doors.

Pipe makers

There was yet a third major branch of the clay-processing sector: the production of the clay pipes that became such an icon of everyday Dutch life. Little is known about this industry, perhaps because it involved a cheap, simple article of mass consumption. The clay pipe was the quintessential throwaway product – the Bic lighter of the seventeenth and eighteenth century. Of the hundreds of millions of pipes made in these centuries, there remain today, apart from numerous shards, only a handful of more or less intact examples.

The origins of this industry date back to the early seventeenth century, when English pipe makers entered the Republic as religious refugees. After service in the Republic's army, so the story goes, they settled in Dutch towns, married local women, and began to produce clay pipes. Gouda quickly emerged as the dominant center, but lesser concentrations of pipe makers were active in Schoonhoven, Gorinchem, Alphen aan de Rijn, and Utrecht; evidence of this industry also exists in Amsterdam, Rotterdam, and Leiden. The industry's chief raw material was nonferrous potting clay, which when baked yields a white product. The chief sources for this clay were located in the Southern Netherlands and the Rhineland around Cologne. The industry required cheap access to this clay as well as access to baking ovens. An important reason for Gouda's early prominence was said to be the existence of several underutilized ovens belonging to potters suffering from diminished trade. They were prepared to rent oven space to the pipe makers, and this joint use of potters' ovens remained characteristic of the pipe-making industry throughout its life in the Republic.

The daily output of a pipe maker seems to have varied in the range of 1,000 to 1,500 pipes. In this he was assisted by apprentices who rolled the stems, among other tasks. The labor of his wife and daughters often figured in the smoothing and finishing of pipes. Forming the bowl was the special task of the pipe maker. The productivity of such an enterprise varied, of course, according to the type of pipe: basically, whether the stem was long or short.

Gouda possessed a pipe-makers' guild after 1660, and in 1686 city regulations governed the operations of a weekly pipe market where all pipes had to be presented for sale. An important feature of this market was a special municipal pawn bank, where pipe makers could pawn unsold pipes at the prevailing market price. Traders, and pipe makers who produced insufficient pipes, could also turn to the bank, buying the pawned goods as needed. The city forbade direct trade among the pipe makers. This municipally sponsored financial arrangement bespeaks the pipe makers' lack of capital: Unable to finance production more than a day at a time, many producers would have been at the mercy of the merchants were it not for the intermediation of the pawn bank. The "firms" had little capital and, in most cases, few employees, relying primarily on the labor of family members. This image is consistent with the knowledge that Schoonhoven's 24 masters in 1718 employed a total of 40 assistants.

In Gouda, by far the largest center of pipe production, the pipe-makers' guild totaled 80 members in 1665. This number rose rapidly to 161 in 1679 and 223 in 1686, after which the industry must have grown further, for in 1730 the number of separate pipe marks (each firm possessed its own identifying mark) suggest the existence of no less than 611 producers. Thereafter, the demand for pipes began to soften, as the growing popularity of snuff gradually reduced the use of smoking tobacco. In 1750 the number of Gouda pipe makers still stood at about 500, but then the decline gathered momentum – to 349 in 1759 and but 130 in 1806. While 29 ovens were constantly being fired for the pipe makers in 1749, only 17 remained active in 1789, and 11 in 1806. Altogether, the number of workers involved in this industry at its peak, around 1730, can be estimated at between 3,000 and 4,000. Around 1760 total employment may have retreated to about 2,000, while in 1800 it may have stood at about 1,000.

This development is consistent with what little we know of Gouda's demographic evolution. In 1622 Gouda's population stood a bit under 15,000. The annual number of baptisms in the city in the 1690s (about 500) suggests a somewhat larger population of 16,000 to 17,000. Between 1700 and 1740, the number of baptisms varied between 550 and 600 per year, suggesting a population of 17,000 to 18,000, which jibes with the count of just under 4,000 houses in 1732. Thereafter, the population declined steadily to just under 12,000 in 1795.

The sketchy evidence shows Gouda developing countercyclically to Holland's other industrial cities – Leiden, Haarlem, and Delft. Gouda grew by some 3,000 inhabitants in the sixty years after 1680, precisely the period in which the other cities decayed most dramatically. The collapse of Gouda's industrial sector after 1740 came at a time when the other cities had already experienced their most rapid decline. As becomes apparent when the tobacco industry is discussed later, the Gouda pipe-making industry's expansion occurred simultaneously with that of Amsterdam's tobacco-processing industry. The growing popularity of snuff reduced the demand for Gouda pipes after 1740, but protectionist measures also harmed the industry. Prussia introduced a protective tariff in 1754 and later prohibited altogether the importation of smoking pipes. When a new center of pipe production arose in the vicinity of Cologne, where wage levels were far lower than in Holland, the Gouda pipe makers lost not only their German but also Scandinavian and Russian markets. In time, these new producers even penetrated the domestic market: The industry that remained in the Republic around 1800 was but a shadow of its former self.

8.3.4. PAPER MAKING AND PRINTING

While the pottery industry, with its many branches, could be found in both city and country, the production of paper was concentrated almost entirely in the countryside. This locational pattern was not obvious at the outset, for the first efforts to introduce paper making in the Northern Netherlands took place in Dordrecht, Alkmaar, Arnhem, and possibly Amsterdam. The young Republic faced a paper shortage as it found itself cut off from the traditional sources of supply in Antwerp – the center of the paper trade – and the production centers in Germany and Liège. This shortage motivated the establishment of the first northern paper-making enterprises, most of them founded by southern immigrants, in Arnhem and the delta region (Dordrecht, Zwijndrecht, Hendrik-Ido-Ambacht, Den Briel, Oud-Beijerland, Middelburg, and Domburg). Further north, short-lived enterprises were established in Alkmaar and the Zaan region. Everywhere the migration of skilled labor was critical, for paper making was a technically complex process where the transfer of knowledge depended on the physical presence of experienced workers.

As with pottery, paper making was initially attempted in many places. But the majority of these Revolt-era initiatives failed quickly, so that when we again survey the situation early in the seventeenth century, we observe an industry almost entirely concentrated in two rural districts: the Veluwe and the Zaan region. In the delta region and the cities, the industry quickly ran aground, probably because of its need for abundant supplies of pure water.

The sandy-soil Veluwe region possessed naturally pure water, but the same was not true of the Zaan region. There formidable ingenuity was necessary to overcome the handicap of low-quality water. Evidently, the proximity to Amsterdam, the new center of international trade, including paper, offered enough of an incentive to compensate for this disadvantage. The two centers of paper making differed in more than water quality alone. The Veluwe paper mills, driven by water power, were small operations, usually run by five or six workers, primarily family members. The Zaan region mills, driven by wind power, ranked among the largest industrial installations of the time, often employing forty to fifty workers. The large capital investment required for these paper mills caused investors to reduce their exposure to risk by forming *partenrederijen*, a form of limited partnership originally confined to ocean shipping and fishing. On the Veluwe, on the other hand, the mill owners were often the landlords, who leased them to the paper makers. The number of large Zaan paper mills reached about 40 by the eighteenth century, while the smaller Veluwe paper mills totaled about 160 at the peak, in 1720–40.

The Zaan region's first wind-driven paper mill dates from shortly after 1600, and by 1630 there were 5 of them. All of Holland then counted 14 or 15. However, after 1650 this dispersion gave way to concentration, as the number of mills in the Zaan region grew to 12 in 1660, 21 in 1680, and 36 in 1700. By this last date, the rest of Holland could count but 10 paper mills, 6 of which were concentrated in Waddinxveen, which constituted a third center of paper production in the eighteenth-century Republic. The peak of the Republic's wind-powered paper-making capacity came only after 1775, when some 60 mills were in operation: nearly 40 in the Zaan region, 16 in Waddinxveen, and 7 others scattered among six separate locations.

Two major technological innovations stood behind the rapid expansion of the paper industry after 1650. Until then the wind-powered mills were restricted almost exclusively to the production of the crudest types, gray paper and cardboard. Technical improvements then made possible the production of blue paper, used to wrap sugar and finished linens. Of even greater significance was the introduction of the so-called "Hollander," a pulping process that produced a much finer and more even distribution of the fibers. This innovation, introduced in 1674, allowed the wind-driven mills to produce white paper, the standard for writing and printing. The "Hollander" stands as the most important innovation in paper making between the Middle Ages and the nineteenth-century introduction of mechanized paper forming. It accounts for the rapid expansion of the Zaan region's white paper-producing capacity to some 80,000 reams per year between 1675 and 1700. Simultaneously, gray and blue paper production rose from not much more than 10,000 reams per year in 1650, to about 30,000 reams in 1670, 50,000 reams in 1700, and 65,000 to 75,000 reams between 1740 and 1790. A substantial expansion of production capacity per mill, especially in the innovative second half of the seventeenth century, allowed total production to grow rather faster than the increase in the number of mills would suggest.

These innovations effectively exempted the paper industry from the general secular trend that we have charted now for so many industries. In the short run, to be sure, the paper makers faced periodically soft markets. But the industry's long-run fortunes remained highly favorable right into the French era. Then the paper makers were plagued by chronic shortages of rag, the essential "raw material" that had previously been imported from a vast German hinterland. Permanent decline occurred only later in the nineteenth century, when the Dutch industry found itself incapable of adopting the new mechanized technologies then diffusing among other European countries.

We have already noted that Waddinxveen emerged in the eighteenth century as a third center of Dutch paper production, growing from 6 mills in 1700 to 14 in 1750, and 16 in 1775. All these mills produced gray and blue paper. They employed only about ten workers each, but together they accounted for a substantial production – perhaps 15,000 reams per year. When this production is added to that of the Zaan region, where output of gray and blue paper expanded more than writing and printing paper in the course of the eighteenth century, we are presented with an historical puzzle. After all, one would expect the demand for white paper to grow in this era (with the expansion of bureaucratic practices, increased literacy, and the growth of book and newspaper production) while the market for packing paper, used in industry and trade, should have been stagnant at best. The solution to this puzzle is probably to be found in Amsterdam's trade in paper, about which we know little except that the Republic supplied export markets in England, Norway, Russia, North America, Southern Europe, and even France, itself a major producer of paper.

Thanks to the monumental studies of H. Voorn, it is now possible to relate the overall development of paper production on the Veluwe. One might say that this region was foreordained to become a center of paper production, given its natural endowments of pure water and the numerous locations for water mills. Yet the military threats that continued to hang over the region until the Twelve Years' Truce (1609–21) discouraged investment. Once the truce was signed, the industry embarked on more than a century of expansion. Around 1625 the region possessed 25 paper mills, and around 1650 there were 50. A total of 75 was reached by 1670, and in 1700 there were over 125. The industry reached its peak in the 1730s, with no fewer than 160 active paper mills. This high point in production capacity led directly to an initiative of the Amsterdam traders and factors in paper to suspend paper production for the month of January 1740 in the hope of thereby reducing inventories and improving prices. This collusive measure only involved the producers of white writing and printing paper, and the participants were to be found exclusively in the Veluwe region. Overproduction of white paper remained a recurring problem, however, and after 1740 the number of Veluwe paper mills declined, slowly but steadily, until by 1815 but 135 remained in operation.

An official survey of 1812 reveals that nearly all the Veluwe paper mills operated but a single forming vat. The production capacity of a mill depended, thus, on the type of paper being produced (white, blue, gray, tobacco paper, etc.). The most plausible estimate of Veluwe production capacity places it at 125,000 to 150,000 reams per annum in the mid–eighteenth century. This assumes that some five of every eight mills specialized in the production of white paper, which implies that the production of writing and printing paper rose from 75,000 to 95,000 reams in the first forty years of the eighteenth century, only to fall back to about 75,000 reams by 1800.

When we add this information to what we know of the industry in Holland, it then appears that the eighteenth-century production of writing and printing paper in the Republic as a whole probably declined a bit (Zaan region production of 80,000 to 85,000 reams, plus the Veluwe production just described). Eighteenth-century production of gray and blue paper, on the other hand, rose substantially, from about 50,000 to 75,000 reams per year in the Zaan region, and from about 6,000 to 15,000 in Waddinxveen. This net increase of over 30,000 reams must have more than compensated for any slight decline registered in the Veluwe region. The total labor force active in the Republic's paper industry can be estimated at about 2,500 in most of the eighteenth century, with a peak around 1740 of perhaps 2,800.

The evolution of white paper production runs contrary to our expectations. After all, the paper intensity of public administration grew unrelentingly (a phenomenon apparent to every historian of the period), and the literacy of the general population rose substantially as well. We have noted how the percentage of Amsterdam grooms who could not sign their names at marriage declined from 43 percent in 1630 to but 15 percent in 1780; illiterate brides declined from 68 to 36 percent over the same interval. Much the same long-term trend was experienced in the rest of the Republic, both rural and urban, so that around 1810 the percentage of illiterate grooms in the Netherlands as a whole stood at only 25 percent, and for brides 40 percent. This long-term trend toward greater literacy must have caused the demand for writing paper and the size of print runs to increase.

The extension of the reading public must also have increased the number and variety of published works. Moreover, the Republic functioned as a major exporter of books to the rest of Europe. And then there was the emergence of newspapers and scientific and cultural publications. The last mentioned were often written in French, which facilitated their broad distribution through Europe, a custom that also applied to newspapers. It is said that 2,500 of the *Gazette de Leyde*'s total run of 4,200 copies were sold in France. But there were many other newspapers and periodicals in the eighteenth century: The *Oprecht Haarlemse Courant*, for instance, came out in runs of 6,000 copies. We are inclined to deduce from all this that expanding domestic demand for white paper more than compensated the loss of export markets for Dutch writing paper. But before we settle on this conclusion, it may be useful to examine the Republic's publishing industry more closely. Was this, in fact, an industry whose growth was fed by structural changes that exempted it from the secular trends that shaped so much of the rest of the Dutch economy?

Quantitative investigations of book and newspaper production in the Netherlands are still rare. We know that Amsterdam, Leiden, and in the eighteenth century also The Hague were publishing centers of international importance, but the scope of their output cannot now be expressed in figures. It is possible to reconstruct the number of book printing firms active in the Republic (firms that typically combined bookselling with printing), and this exercise reveals a surprising result (Figures 8.3 and 8.4). From about 1500, but with great force after 1570, the number of book printers and sellers grew explosively. With the sole exception of a hiatus in the 1620s, this growth continued into the 1660s, a decade in which no fewer than 781 firms were at some point active as publishers. This number may be compared to the 264 active in the 1630s, or the 102 active in the 1590s. After 1670 the number of printing firms fell steadily until the 1720s, when there were only 448 firms – just 58 percent of the peak level. Between 1670 and 1730, the Republic's publishing industry was caught in the same depression phase of the secular trend that we have charted for, among other things, grain shipments through the Sound, land reclamation, and textile production. From the 1730s the number of book printing and selling firms again began to grow. This growth was most intense in the periods 1730–49 and 1770–89. By the 1780s a second high point was reached, slightly exceeding that of the 1660s, as 828 firms were active at some point in this decade. The period 1750–69 witnessed a minor interruption in the upward trend, while the last decade of the century experienced a major setback. In general, the three centuries covered by our study reveal a course of publishing "activity" that is wholly consistent with the course of so many other sectors of the economy, and it holds out the possibility that the trends in the production of writing and printing paper may not be so puzzling after all.

Still, a few qualifications need to be made concerning the interpretation of our counts of book printers and sellers. To begin with, the total of active firms includes some double-counting (i.e., some firms were undoubtedly sold, inherited, or merely changed their names in the course of each decade). The true number of firms will be somewhat smaller, but this should not affect greatly the trends. Indeed, these trends are powerfully reinforced by the number of book

315

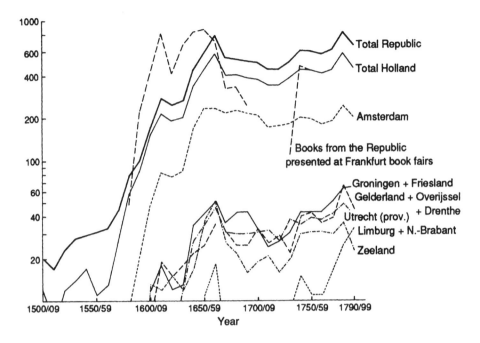

Figure 8.3. Number of active book publishers and sellers in the Netherlands, 1500–1800; number of books published in the Republic that were offered at the Frankfurt book fairs. (*Source:* Gruys en de Wolf, *Thesaurus 1473–1800*; A. H. Leaven, *The Frankfurt and Leipzig Book Fairs*, 190.)

titles of new Dutch language publications presented at the Frankfurt and Leipzig book fairs, decade by decade between 1560 and 1700, and again after 1730. There, too, we observe the sharp reversal of the 1660s and '70s, as well as the post–1730 revival.

The skeptical reader might also voice reservations about the adequacy of a count of firms selling and printing books as a reflection of the course of Dutch publishing as a whole. After all, these firms ranged from small shops, printing but a handful of pamphlets, to large establishments with an international clientele. Moreover, in the course of time, technological change may fundamentally have altered the average size of firms in this industry. Over the course of three centuries, technical improvements certainly must have occurred (and more than once). Until 1670 any such innovations can only serve to accentuate the upward course of the Dutch publishing industry. It is, however, rather doubtful that a major concen, ration of production in fewer, larger firms can undo the observed post–1670 dec.ine. The sharp collapse in the decade of the 1670s may signal a technological shake-up in the industry, but this seems an unlikely explanation for the gradual wasting away of the number of printers that characterized the follow-

316

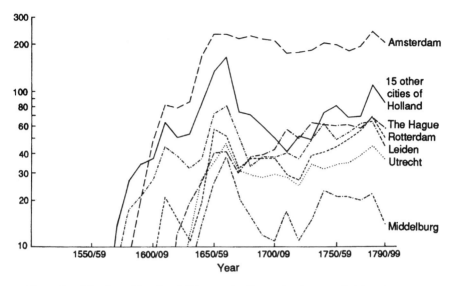

Figure 8.4. Number of book publishers and sellers active in several cities. (*Source:* Gruys en de Wolf, *Thesaurus 1473–1800.*)

ing fifty years. Such a long-term decline is more typically a symptom of chronic commercial weakness.

A closer examination of the curves in Figures 8.3 and 8.4 reinforce this interpretation. If a technological factor stood behind the sharp decline of the 1670s, we might expect it to have struck everywhere in a similar fashion. A major decline in the number of firms did take place everywhere (leaving aside the quantitatively insignificant eastern regions) with the striking exception of Amsterdam. Table 8.6 reveals a decline of 31 percent in the Republic as a whole, but no more than 7 percent in Amsterdam. Apart from a few aberrant provincial cities, the rest of the country's printing centers declined by a third or more. Rather than a change induced by technological developments, we are probably dealing here with a phenomenon observed in other sectors of the economy: a concentration of activity in Amsterdam, the largest market, as a survival strategy in the face of general contraction.

A striking characteristic of the book trades is their high sensitivity to general business conditions. What also deserves comment, however, is the exceptional size of the Dutch publishing industry throughout the seventeenth and eighteenth centuries. Even in its decrepitude after the Republic's fall, this industry's size remained unique in Europe, a fact revealed by the *Direction générale de l'impremerie et la librairie*, the Napoleonic Empire's organ of control over the book trades. In 1810–12 the French inspectors counted 582 booksellers in their new Dutch departments, or 28 for every 100,000 inhabitants. In Belgium there were then 7 booksellers per 100,000

Table 8.6. *Book printers and sellers active in the decades 1660–9 and 1670–9, with percentage increase or decrease.*

City	1660–9	1670–9	Percentage increase or decrease
Amsterdam	233	217	-7
The Hague	41	30	-27
Leiden	81	52	-36
Rotterdam	51	32	-37
Alkmaar	13	6	-54
Hoorn	14	8	-43
Enkhuizen	16	7	-56
Delft	31	10	-68
Dordrecht	28	14	-50
Gouda	9	6	-33
Haarlem	24	12	-50
Schiedam	9	1	-89
Middelburg	38	21	-45
Vlissingen	7	4	-43
Utrecht	46	31	-33
Groningen	15	13	-13
Leeuwarden	20	16	-20
Franeker	9	4	-56
Arnhem	6	4	-33
Zutphen	4	1	-75
Nijmegen	3	3	0
Deventer	3	10	+233
's-Hertogenbosch	5	3	-40
Total in the Republic	781	541	-31

Source: J. A. Gruys and C. de Wolf, *Thesaurus 1473–1800.*

inhabitants; in France itself only 6, and in the German and Italian territories (the Empire then stretched from Hamburg to Rome), fewer still.[1]

8.3.5. FOOD PROCESSING AND BEVERAGE PRODUCTION

Brewing

The production of beer took place in every part of the Netherlands. In Holland the cities claimed the exclusive right to brew beer, but elsewhere one could

[1] Jeremy D. Popkin, "The Book Trades in Western Europe during the Revolutionary Era," *The Papers of the Bibliographical Society of America 78* (1984), p. 413.

expect to find brewing kettles in nearly every city and village. The cheap beers in everyday use were perishable products, and where water transportation was not available, their movement over any considerable distance was costly. For these reasons, brewing took place in close proximity to its consumers. And since beer was the foremost popular beverage before the wide acceptance of tea and coffee, the large demand ensured that breweries would be thickly seeded across the landscape.

A well-equipped brewery required a considerable investment of capital, and their owners tended to number among the wealthiest individuals of rural society. In eighteenth-century Overijssel, for example, we know that burgemeesters owned many urban breweries while sheriffs and judges were prominent among the owners of rural breweries. Merchants and notables predominated among the owners of Amsterdam's twenty-three breweries in 1585. The brewers' guild of Dokkum supplied that Friesian town with burgemeesters – some in the possession of university degrees – throughout the eighteenth century. The 1742 survey of personal incomes preparatory to the introduction of an income tax in Holland revealed brewers as ranking with regents, merchants, and soap boilers in enjoying some of the province's highest average incomes (see Table 11.27).

The prominence of brewing as a local industry before the rise of coffee and tea drinking is easily demonstrated. A 1703 registration of beer kettles in Overijssel showed there to be three or four such kettles in every substantial village (*kerkdorp*), with as many as 16 in Oldenzaal and 12 in Ootmarsum. Yet by 1703 the decline of brewing was already under way, for the province then possessed 36 fewer than in 1675. Much worse was yet to come, however, for the entire province possessed but 18 functioning breweries in 1811.

This dismantling of brewing capacity was common to the nation as a whole. Friesland still possessed nearly 100 breweries in 1750 but no more than 30 by 1800. In its capital city of Leeuwarden, some 50 breweries functioned in 1700, only 21 in 1750, and a mere 4 in 1816. In Dokkum the number of breweries fell from 19 in 1711, to 17 in 1730, 14 in 1750, 12 in 1770, and 9 in 1790. Nor were the surviving breweries larger than their more numerous predecessors: The quantity of grain processed per brewery declined from about 15 lasts in 1711 to 5 lasts in 1790.

Only in Holland (and the nearby city of Amersfoort) did breweries serve more than their local markets. The reason for this concentration is evident: Only here could one find the combination of a high level of local demand, nearby export markets, and low transportation costs. This last was provided by the numerous waterways of Holland, while the Southern Netherlands long functioned as a market for export beer. At the beginning of this chapter, we noted that cities such as Haarlem, Gouda, Delft, and Amersfoort emerged in the fifteenth century as important centers of beer production, but we also noted that they all faced serious problems during the first half of the sixteenth century. The brewing centers of Holland lost ground in the Flemish market, a loss which the Revolt confirmed by the 1570s to be permanent. Indeed, Dutch brewers never again served significant export markets, with the minor exception of its West Indies colonies, until after World War II.

But after the 1570s the domestic market showed new signs of life. The growth of population caused the demand for beer to grow, while the expansion of ocean shipping and fishing generated a major market for ships' beer. Moreover, the brewing cities, which had already sought to suppress rural beer production in 1531 with the *Order op de buitennering*, managed to persuade the provincial government that fiscal oversight of this important object of taxation could best be performed if brewing remained the privilege of the cities. In this way, the scale of production in Holland's brewing centers remained fundamentally different from the numerous local breweries in the other provinces.

Yet even with these advantages, Holland's brewing industry passed through a severe crisis. Data assembled by Yntema reveal that even before the Revolt, the breweries of Gouda and Haarlem were in full retreat, a retreat not much mitigated by the growing production of Delft. And the Revolt itself made matters much worse, as production in all three major brewing centers collapsed.

Eventually the industry turned around, and by 1600 brewery capacity was rising in a large number of cities. In the first half of the seventeenth century, Rotterdam and Haarlem emerged as the leading centers, with Amsterdam, Dordrecht, and Weesp participating as strong secondary centers. All these brewing centers were well positioned to serve markets in the two large zones where breweries remained all but absent, North Holland and the province of Zeeland. In both regions the poor quality of local water supplies limited the industry. In this new pattern of regional brewing markets, Delft proved to be the chief loser, as Rotterdam's strength in serving both the Zeeland market and the demand for ships' beer proved insuperable. The maritime market also buoyed Amsterdam's breweries, and by 1650 Holland's major brewing centers had become Haarlem, Rotterdam, and Amsterdam, which together accounted for over 60 percent of the provincial excise tax levied on beer. The brewers of Delft, Dordrecht, and Leiden then each accounted for a bit under 10 percent of excise revenues, while the remaining 10 to 15 percent was divided among a long list of other cities.

In fact, among the major brewing centers, only Amsterdam managed to achieve a significant increase in output in the second and third quarters of the seventeenth century. The beer output of Haarlem and Rotterdam was already tending to decline – especially that of Haarlem. Thus around 1670 the two major port cities, Amsterdam and Rotterdam, stood out as the chief brewing centers, followed at some distance by Haarlem, Delft, and Dordrecht. Despite the substantial growth of Holland's population (plus that of Zeeland, which depended on Holland for most of its beer), Holland's total annual beer production around 1670 stood below the 1.3 million vats that seems to have been achieved two centuries earlier, in 1475, and again in 1515. This comparison makes clear how

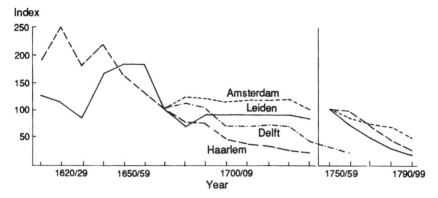

Figure 8.5. Beer production in Haarlem, Leiden, Amsterdam, and Delft, 1610–1799. (Index numbers: Haarlem, Leiden, and Amsterdam, 1670–9 and 1750–9 = 100; Delft, 1671 plus 1676–9 = 100). (*Source:* J. L. van Zanden, "De economie van Holland," 591; Th. Wijsenbeek-Olthuis, *Achter de gevels*, 418.)

important the loss of the Southern Netherlands' market was for Holland's brewing industry.

After 1675 the breweries once again faced a long-term contraction of demand, this time domestic in origin, that would end in the virtual destruction of the industry. The experience of Delft serves to illustrate the general trend. Delft's brewers still produced some 46,000 vats per year in 1685, a level that fell to 35,000 vats ten years later. At this level production stabilized for nearly fifty years, but after 1740 the downward slide resumed with a vengeance. By 1784 no more than 14,400 vats were brewed in Delft, one-third the level of a century earlier. Everywhere – in Overijssel and Friesland (as shown earlier) and in the other cities of Holland (see Figure 8.5) – the same decline was under way.

The explanation for this phenomenon must be sought in the increasing consumption of coffee and tea. Beer, all except for the poorest small beer, was burdened by heavy excise taxes. Taxes on coffee and tea were relatively light, and the prices of these beverages fell sharply through much of the eighteenth century: coffee by a good 50 percent, and tea by 75 percent. These prices fell most rapidly in the period 1720–50, just when Delft's brewing industry sank into industrial insignificance. After 1750 the decline of coffee and tea prices slowed, but brewers now faced sharply rising prices for grain and peat, the two chief inputs to the brewing process. Thus, the process of substitution continued until beer consumption (which may have exceeded 300 liters per capita around 1500, and near 200 liters around 1675) all but disappeared (perhaps 40 liters in 1800) while that of coffee and tea skyrocketed. The excise tax revenues of Friesland allow us to calculate a twentyfold increase in the consumption of the new beverages between

SECTORS

the beginning and end of the eighteenth century. This pattern must have repeated itself throughout the Republic.

Only the port cities, especially Rotterdam and Amsterdam, managed to preserve a brewing industry of any size, thanks to the continuing demand for ships' beer. Consumers on dry land increasingly satisfied their need for liquids with the ever more affordable coffee, chocolate, and especially tea. Until late in the eighteenth century, coffee remained an indulgence for the well-to-do. But it is also possible that the need for liquids from whatever source diminished somewhat, as a result of changing food consumption patterns. A decline in the consumption of salted meat and fish would have reduced the need to quaff the prodigious quantities of liquid that had characterized earlier centuries. We have already discussed the diminished importance of fish and, especially, salted herring. Much the same thing may have characterized the consumption of salted meat. This is suggested by a 1765 petition of the distillers of Weesp (who fattened hogs with byproducts of the distilling process) requesting that the tax exemption long enjoyed on salted pork sold to the VOC now be extended to smoked pork, since this was now preferred by the company. Since the VOC was definitely no trend setter in matters of consumption, it is very likely that a shift from salting to smoking as a means of meat conservation had taken place rather earlier in society at large.

Distilleries

Traditionally, the brewers had not only satisfied the Dutch consumers daily need for liquids; they also satisfied their need, or desire, for alcohol. For a large majority of the population, wine – all of which was imported – was far too expensive to serve as an alternative source of alcohol. Brandy, a wine distillate, found a growing market in the Republic and, after 1650, a grain distillate, sometimes flavored with juniper berries, found increasing favor. This *koornbrandewijn*, or jenever, supplied alcohol at a lower unit price than did beer. A mixture of jenever and tea was still much costlier than beer, but it offered the advantage that alcohol consumption could be adjusted to suit individual needs: a different "dosage" for adults than for children, for men than for women, different consumption by the day and the season. Given this flexibility, it is certainly possible that a family's total expenditure on beverages could be reduced by shifting away from beer.

Distillers were active in many cities already in the sixteenth century, but their number grew enormously in the course of the seventeenth century, a growth concentrated in periods of war with France. When the supply of French brandy stagnated or dried up altogether, the demand for domestic spirits grew explosively, leading to a feverish expansion of the number of stills. But the cessation of hostilities with France inevitably brought reversals, as the supply of brandy returned to normal. In this period Weesp was the largest production center, although each boom in demand brought efforts to develop distilleries in Amsterdam. Moreover, brewers in several cities sought to compensate for the declining demand for their beer by diversifying into distilling.

Toward the end of the seventeenth century, the towns of the Maas region emerged as major distilling centers. First Rotterdam, then Schiedam, followed by Delfshaven, and even Den Briel ventured to compete in the production of je-never. Schiedam emerged as the dominant producer, perhaps because the simul-taneous decline of its fishing industry freed warehouse and other industrial space at a crucial juncture in the distilleries' development. At any rate, the industry grew rapidly, from 30 distilleries in 1700 to 68 in 1711, 96 in 1721, and 124 in 1736. During the following thirty years, the industry stabilized at just under 100 distilleries, but after 1770 a second boom period ensued, bringing the number of distilleries from 111 in 1771 to 188 in 1795.

Schiedam left the competing centers in the dust. Delfshaven followed at a great distance, with 11 distilleries in 1738, 22 in 1771, and 32 in 1795. But nearby Rotterdam, where at least 57 distilleries functioned in 1674, could count but 43 in 1752, and about 40 in 1795. Weesp, which had once given every indication of dominating this industry, receded toward the third rank of distilling cities. Its impressive total of 33 distilleries in 1698 fell to 19 in 1748, and only 5 in 1795. Weesp's firms were larger than those in the Maas region, but its decline was unambiguous.

A survey of 1816 provides an overview of the number of distilleries and their employment totals:

	Distilleries	Employees
Schiedam	171	513
Rotterdam	29	120
Delfshaven	34	120
Dordrecht	2	8
Delft	3	25
Den Briel	2	4
Leiden	2	12
Weesp	4	28

Holland's distilleries probably never employed directly much more than 1,000 workers. Indirectly, this industry required transporters of raw material (grain, malt, peat, and coal) and of the finished product. The malting mills (concentrated around Schiedam and Weesp) must also be taken into account, as well as the hog-fattening activities clustered around the Weesp distilleries that made use of the spent mash. The Weesp distillers regarded hog fattening as crucial to their survival in competition with the Maas region distillers. Schiedam prohibited hog fattening in the immediate vicinity of the distilleries because of the intolerable stench. For this reason the distillers here sold their byproducts to the region's farmers, who used it to intensify cattle raising. Even without hogs, the distilleries made life in Schiedam miserable enough; from a considerable distance, the approaching visitor could see how this industrial center was continually enveloped in a cloud of vapor and smoke.

The reason for the concentration of the distilleries in the Maas region and the decline of Weesp is not in doubt. The industry's growth depended on foreign trade, and the Maas ports gave the easiest access to the most important sources of raw materials and to markets for the finished product. The malted barley came increasingly from eastern England, where the government subsidized heavily the export of barley throughout the first seven decades of the eighteenth century. The distillers also shifted from peat to coal in stoking their stills, and this, too, came from England. The markets for jenever were originally domestic, but the second growth phase of the industry was propelled by the rise of foreign markets, which were found in the East and West Indies as well as in France, Spain, and their colonies. After the War of Independence, the United States emerged as a major market. Jenever, a type of gin, stood out as one of the very few success stories of the eighteenth-century Dutch economy, but both its inputs and most of its markets were found abroad.

Tobacco processing

From the perspective of employment, another consumer industry exceeded distilling in importance for a considerable period. Tobacco processing, an industry concentrated in Amsterdam, employed at its late seventeenth-and early eighteenth-century peak some 3,000 persons. Besides the 30 to 40 tobacco-spinning works then in operation, there were also about 10 cutting works (*kerverijen*), and some 40 stem-crushing operations (*stelenpletterijen*). The two last were, on average, much smaller than the spinning works, but all these firms together employed at their peak something like 3 percent of Amsterdam's total labor force.

Tobacco processing had this in common with the distilling industry: They both enjoyed access to domestic as well as imported raw materials. The output of domestic malting mills was supplemented by cheap imported malt, which gave the Dutch distillers an important advantage in international competition; likewise, the special advantage of Dutch tobacco processors rested on their access to both (cheap) domestic leaf and (higher-quality) tobacco from the Chesapeake. It is, indeed, difficult to be certain whether Amsterdam became an international trading center of tobacco because of the presence of its processing industry or whether the lines of causation ran the other way – the industry arose because the world's tobacco was traded in Amsterdam. The fact remains that the great strength of Amsterdam's tobacco-processing industry was its ability to develop products that blended the New World, domestic, and other European tobaccos. With these mixtures by 1700 the Amsterdam firms dominated European markets wherever state monopolies (such as the French) did not obstruct their access.

The rise of this industry obviously acted as a great stimulus to the further expansion of domestic tobacco production, which spread through the provinces of Utrecht and Gelderland and parts of Overijssel (see Chapter 6, section 6.3). As long as Chesapeake tobacco remained relatively expensive, it offered the small farmers of these provinces an attractive alternative to their traditional grain crops, the prices of which were low and falling through much of the period 1670–1740.

Nor is it surprising to observe the tobacco-processing sector migrate to these eastern regions of tobacco production as the price of American leaf began to decline after 1720. This price development deprived the Dutch processing industry of an important advantage in foreign trade, for which it sought compensation by economizing on labor costs. Until 1720 Amsterdam virtually monopolized tobacco processing, but thereafter the search for lower costs sent the producers outside Holland to the regions of tobacco cultivation. Tobacco spinning and crushing could not become true rural industries, for these processes required a certain concentration of labor. But market towns such as Amersfoort and, especially, Nijkerk, both of which had direct access to the Zuider Zee, proved capable of attracting much of Amsterdam's industry. Between 1715 and 1732, no fewer than eleven Amsterdam firms shut their doors, while yet others moved their operations to the East. According to the (self-interested) testimony of the remaining producers, the tobacco-processing industry in Holland had paid some 400,000 guilders in annual wages around 1700, but only 270,000 guilders in 1713 and no more than 135,000 guilders by 1732. In 1751 only ten tobacco-spinning works remained in Amsterdam, and of these the largest produced no more than a small firm would have during the industry's prime. The truth may have been less dramatic, but not by much, for we know that the industry regularly processed some 8 to 10 million pounds of tobacco annually around 1700, and in peak years as much as 12 million pounds. Amsterdam's output fell to 6 million pounds around 1715 and further to 3 million by 1732. By that date, total production – including Utrecht and Gelderland spinners – stood at 4.6 million pounds of processed tobacco. Increasingly in these years, the Republic exported its tobacco as unprocessed leaf.

The reasons for this industrial devolution are to be sought in two areas. As noted, the falling price of American leaf struck at the heart of the Dutch industry's practice of mixing tobacco of different qualities. This ceased to offer price advantages. The second factor is located in the trade policies of the importing countries, which sought to encourage domestic tobacco processing by levying heavy tariffs on the importation of the processed product. In a manner analogous to the squeeze faced by Dutch lumber milling, tobacco processors saw their profits undermined by factors at work with both their raw material suppliers and their final markets.

Standing behind the great increase in the supply and the falling price of American tobacco, was the growing demand of the French market. The French used relatively little tobacco in the seventeenth century, but the new fashion of consuming it in the form of snuff found a ready response in France, and consumption grew tenfold in the century after 1675. The entire French market was controlled by a state-run tobacco monopoly. This enterprise, one of the largest of eighteenth-century Europe, became by far the largest purchaser of tobacco in international markets. Its influence in these markets worked to the disadvantage of intermediary traders and processors such as the Dutch. And what began as pressure on the processors soon spread to the tobacco growers. The falling price of competing tobacco reduced their export markets, and after 1750 the gradually rising price of grain caused ever more farmers to abandon tobacco growing in favor of the bread grains. Apart from a brief revival during the American war of independence, when the supplies of Chesapeake tobacco were interrupted, the Amsterdam processing industry and domestic tobacco cultivation declined together.

A domestic market for tobacco continued to exist, of course, as did the German markets served by the Republic's ports. American leaf played an increasingly important role in these markets, and Rotterdam emerged as the chief port for its importation (via the British colonial entrepôts) and distribution up the Rhine to Germany. Especially after 1750, Rotterdam's trade in tobacco grew rapidly, and it proved possible to re-establish here a small version of the processing industry that Amsterdam had already lost. This and the construction of several new industrial windmills to prepare snuff are the positive signs emanating from this industry in the late eighteenth century; but the Republic's tobacco-processing industry as a whole must have been much larger a century earlier.

Sugar refining

Sugar refining showed certain similarities to tobacco processing. Both processed colonial products, both were highly concentrated in Amsterdam, and both were of major importance to the city's economy because of the large investments of capital, the value of output, the important links to foreign trade, and the number of persons employed.

By the standards of its time, sugar refining was highly capital intensive. Therefore, this industry contributed rather less to employment than the labor-intensive tobacco industry. The growth of investment is indicated roughly by the number of refineries, which grew from 3 in 1607 to 40 in 1650, at which time the industry was experiencing a feverish expansion. By 1661 Amsterdam possessed 50; the Republic as a whole, 66. A dramatic decline in sugar prices stood behind this explosive growth of production capacity. In 1650–4 the Beurs quotations for refined sugar hovered around 80 cents per pound, but in the period 1664–7, the price level had fallen to just under 50 cents, and in the course of the 1670s, it fluctuated around 35 cents per pound. In this brief period, sugar came within reach of a much broader consuming public, a situation warranting major investments in refining capacity.

But this era of expansion was followed immediately by a severe crisis. The tariff policies of Colbert and the war begun in 1672 severely disrupted the trade in sugar. Only after the Peace of Nijmegen of 1678 were reasonable trade relations with France (and her colonies) restored. But by then Hamburg had emerged as a formidable competitor, thanks partly to a more favorable excise tax structure for its sugar refiners. Moreover, the Southern Netherlands' market was now protected by a high sugar tariff (introduced in 1669). It took until 1687 for the States General to come to the assistance of the refiners by reducing by two-thirds the Republic's export duties in refined sugar. Much remains to be learned about the Republic's sugar-refining industry in these years, but its depressed situation is suggested by the claims that the number of functioning refineries had fallen to 34 by 1668 and further to only 20 in 1680 (see Chapter 10, section 10.4.1).

Thereafter, the industry revived. Once again details are few, but the absence of petitions and memorials for relief to government bodies may be taken as silent evidence of prosperity in this sector. At any rate in 1752, when we once again can take the measure of the industry, it had grown enormously. The entire Republic possessed 145 refineries, of which 139 were in Holland. All but four of Holland's refineries were concentrated in three cities: Amsterdam with 90; Rotterdam with 30; and Dordrecht with 15. We have this information, of course, because the industry was once again in trouble. Competing industries were now functioning in Denmark, Sweden, and Prussia, and Hamburg's competitive prowess had reasserted itself. The refiners requested, and received, the lifting of all export duties on domestically refined sugar. They were also granted a reduced tax on coal, which earlier had been granted to distillers, brewers, and cloth dyers. The 1752 memorial of the sugar refineries also observed that the emergence of sugar refineries in the Southern Netherlands had recently forced the closure of 20 refineries: 15 in Rotterdam, 2 in Middelburg, 2 in Gouda, and 1 in 's-Hertogenbosch. These are, indeed, places that would have served southern markets. It suggests, moreover, that the Republic possessed about 165 sugar refineries around 1740.

After the setbacks of the 1740s, the sugar refiners' fortunes revived, especially as Dutch neutrality during the Seven Years' War (1756–63) restored access to markets previously lost. Holland's 139 refineries of 1752 grew to 152 by 1776. But this expansion, however gratifying to an economy with such bleak industrial prospects, was not nearly enough to maintain the Republic's relative standing among Europe's sugar refiners. An Amsterdam municipal commission estimated annual raw sugar imports from all sources at some 55 million pounds, of which 50 million was refined in the Republic. This yielded about 45 million pounds of refined sugar, some two-thirds of which was destined for foreign consumers. This constituted a major trading and industrial activity, but it is one that grew little in an era of rapidly growing European sugar consumption. In the international struggle for this market, England – where the domestic demand was much more important than re-exports – introduced generous export premiums. In 1776 the States of Holland followed suit. At the strenuous urging of the refiners, they set the export premium equal to their estimate of all fiscal levies attaching to the import and refining of sugar. But in 1781, in the context of renewed war with England, this subsidy (of some 224,000 guilders per year) was deemed no longer necessary and was abolished.

Not long thereafter, when the English waged war against the French (who had come to the assistance of the Americans in their war of independence), they confiscated large quantities of French raw sugar. When the English sold this booty after the war, sugar prices collapsed under the weight of excess supply. Once again, an export premium was granted Holland's sugar refiners, this time a generous one of 15 guilders per thousand pounds of exported refined sugar. The refiners knew a good thing when they saw it, and they managed to find foreign buyers for nearly 100 million pounds in a single year. In this way they pocketed nearly 1.6 million guilders in public subsidy. Little wonder that the States of Holland, which had expected to spend about one-third this sum, quickly abolished the program. In this golden year, the refiners of Amsterdam accounted for 78 percent of total Dutch sugar exports, Rotterdam 14 percent, and Dordrecht 8 percent, a distribution that corresponds reasonably well with the number of firms in 1796: 103 in Amsterdam (of which 80 were said to be functioning), 12 in Rotterdam, and 12 in Dordrecht. In the Batavian period, this industry – much like the jenever distillers and the tobacco spinners – managed to maintain its production levels more or less at former levels. Total collapse faced the industry only when the imposition of the Continental System provoked a blockade of the Dutch harbors.

Sugar loomed large in the eighteenth-century Republic's economic life. The production of some 45 million pounds of refined sugar entailed the importation of over 50 million pounds of feedstock and the re-export of about 30 million pounds of refined output. The gusto with which refiners and traders exploited the subsidy of 1786–7 reflected not only their greed but also the critical role that sugar played in European trade. The viability of Dutch trade on the Rhine depended especially on this commodity to load the ships sailing upstream to German destinations (see Chapter 10, section 10.6).

The total value of refined sugar output, expressed in average Beurs prices of 1770–5, stood at some 13.5 million guilders (about one-third refined sugar for domestic use, two-thirds loaf sugar for export, plus several hundred thousand guilders' worth of syrup). The significance of this sum will be apparent when it is placed beside the 2-million-guilder value of all the cheese marketed in North Holland, or the similar total value of all domestically produced tobacco around 1700. Of course, unlike these wholly domestic products, the gross value of refined sugar includes the cost of the imported raw material. The 55 million pounds of imported raw sugar consisted of some 25 million pounds from the colonies, for which Surinam prices are representative, and 30 million pounds imported chiefly via France, reckoned at what were called "Moscavedos" prices. In the period 1770–5, these imports will have cost some 9.25 million guilders. Since a portion of the imports consisted of the more expensive raw sugar from Brazil and Saint

Domingue, the total cost of imports will probably have exceeded 10 million guilders. The total process of refining sugar thus represented a "value added" equal to some 35 percent of the cost of raw materials. From this sum wages, fuel, and depreciation of capital had to be deducted in order to arrive at the profit. In view of the subsidy measures already discussed, it appears likely that sugar refining was no honeypot of profit, even though – or perhaps because – the industry tied up very large sums of money.

The capital invested in sugar refining was substantial. Illustrations and extant structures demonstrate that the buildings were of an extraordinary size for their time. A description of 1662 claims that the refineries were often of five or six stories. These are among the few industrial facilities that can be compared with the factories of the nineteenth century. Beginning in 1652, when their number was increasing yearly, Amsterdam restricted the refineries to two districts of the city. As their number grew after that date from about 40 to 100, they must have dominated completely the urban life of these two districts, and not of these districts alone, for their chimneys emitted soot and stench over a much larger zone. As early as 1614, the city sought to reduce this disamenity by forbidding the use of coal as the heating fuel at the refineries. In 1643 the city relented, allowing the use of coal in the four winter months, but by 1645 they returned to total prohibition because of the "insufferably great sorrow, vexation, and discomfort of the residents." The persistence of the refiners moved the city fathers once again to allow winter use of coal – and now for six months of the year – beginning in 1655; and in 1674, a year of industrial depression, the burgemeesters caved in altogether before the refiners' threats of closing down their operations, and gave permission for the burning of coal on a year-round basis. And so it remained, for the sugar refineries now loomed too large in the urban economy to suffer this sort of restriction. In retrospect one might wonder whether the city's government was not excessively solicitous of the industry's desires, for it is a striking fact that of the 31 refining firms known by name before 1670, no fewer than 21 survived under that name into the nineteenth century, emerging intact even from the disasters of the French era.

8.3.6. THE CONSTRUCTION TRADES

With this discussion of the development of sugar refining, we have reached the end of our survey of the various branches of industry whose importance is evident from their employment of labor. We have not discussed a number of industries of interest for one or another reason but of distinctly secondary quantitative importance. Examples include glass production, biscuit baking, leather tanning, whale oil refining, soap boiling (see Figure 8.6), rope making, and the oilseed industry. Besides their minor individual importance in the economy, there is in most cases too little known about them to construct a coherent sketch of their development. This is especially regrettable in the cases of the tanning of hides

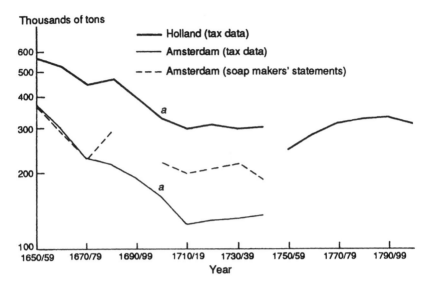

Figure 8.6. Soap production in Holland (1650–1805) and in the Amsterdam tax district (1650–1747). (Semi-logarithmic scale; in thousands of tons.) Lines marked *a* denote tax receipts converted to an estimate of tons produced under the assumption that tax farmers collected 20 percent in excess of their payments to the state (1650–1747). (*Source:* J. L. van Zanden, "De economie van Holland," 594.)

and the processing of hemp, two sectors that must at some point have achieved substantial importance.

The industry that remains conspicuously absent, for its weight in the economy was often very large, is construction. This sector's critical role in the production of capital goods makes the absence of direct information about its historical course especially regrettable. Yet one source does stand at our disposal to offer some insight into the evolution of levels of activity: the tax revenues generated by Holland's excises on building materials such as stone, brick, roofing tiles, floor tiles, and the like. Unfortunately, lumber was not subject to this levy, a gap in coverage that is particularly serious in North Holland, where wood construction remained important into the nineteenth century. This source permits no distinction between new construction and repair, nor between residential and commercial construction. And, of course, it tells us nothing about construction activity beyond the borders of Holland. Despite these shortcomings the record of this excise tax, the *grove waren*, remains a unique source.

Figure 8.7 presents the record of *grove waren* excise revenues. Immediately apparent is the high level attained in the period 1650–70 and the sharp fall in the demand for building materials in the early 1670s. After 1690 the level of building activity sank yet further, so that the revenues generated by this tax were little

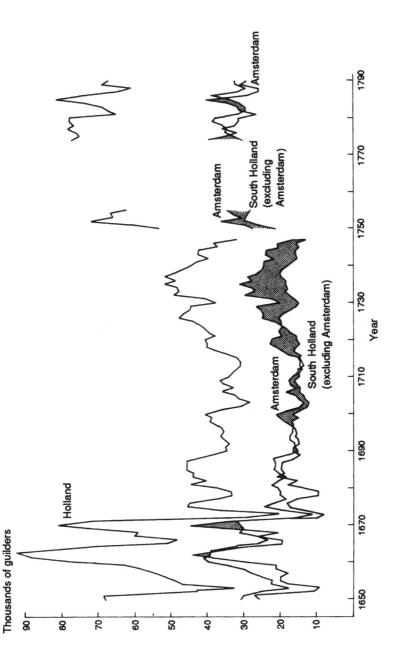

Figure 8.7. Annual tax revenue of the *grove waren*, the tax on building materials, in Holland as a whole, South Holland excluding Amsterdam, and the tax district of Amsterdam, 1650–1790. *Note:* The tax was leased to tax farmers until 1747 and collected directly from 1750. (In thousands of guilders.) (*Source:* A. R. A., Financie van Holland, inv. nrs. 826–8.)

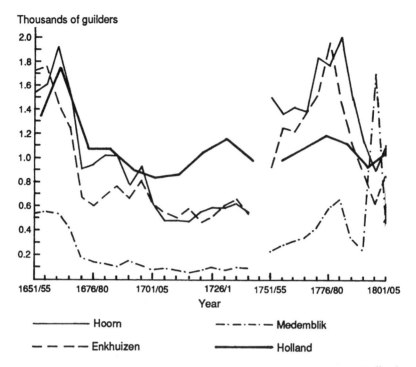

Figure 8.8. Tax revenue of the *grove waren*, 1651–1805, in ten-year averages (Holland as a whole; index numbers 1.0 = 1740–7, 1750–9) and five-year averages (the tax districts of Hoorn, Enkhuizen, and Medemblik; in thousands of guilders). (*Source:* C. M. Lesger, *Hoorn*, 158; A. R. A., Financie van Holland, inv. nrs. 826–8.)

more than half what they had been before 1670. After 1715 the demand for construction materials shows signs of revival, only to relapse again after 1735. The post-1750 data charts another construction revival, but this, too, sinks back after the late '70s. These cycles (shown most clearly in Figure 8.8) reveal variations of at most 20 percent above and below the long-term level. They are certainly of interest, but they are of a distinctly secondary order of magnitude compared to the abrupt and decisive break of the 1670s. This pattern is fully consistent with the demographic development described in Chapter 3, which would lead us to expect a sudden diminution of demand for residential construction as population growth ceased. The demand for nonresidential construction (farm, factory, harbor, commercial, government, and military structures) may have followed a different course than that for residential and repair construction. But the fact is we do not know what occurred. An inventory of public and commercial construction, city by city, could yield insights into this important component of investment, but no such research has yet been undertaken.

332

Just how residential and nonresidential construction may have been related remains to be studied, but it is clear that cities and regions that experienced the greatest demographic reversals also reveal the sharpest declines in construction activity. Figure 8.8 shows that the demand for construction materials in three North Holland tax districts (Hoorn, Enkhuizen, and Medemblik), while following the general trend of Holland as a whole, sank away much further than average after 1670. Figure 8.7 also offers a demonstration of the relationship between demography and construction activity. In Holland as a whole, each of the Anglo-Dutch wars (1652–4, 1665–7, and 1672–4) dealt severe blows to the construction sector. But after 1674 the revival that had set in after the first two wars failed to materialize. Nor did it take place after the Peace of Nijmegen with the French, in 1678. Gradually, tax revenue on building materials diminished further, reaching a low point after 1700. After 1715 revenues again begin to rise, but this is almost entirely the result of rising construction activity in and around Amsterdam. Construction in Amsterdam then bulked larger, sometimes much larger, than that of all the rest of South Holland (Holland excepting the North Holland peninsula). In the period 1672–89, the opposite had been the case; then, the weakness of Amsterdam's construction sector undermined such recovery as took place elsewhere in the province.

The severity of Amsterdam's construction crisis in the 1670s can also be read from the record of residential rental values. These already began to decline in the late 1660s (see Figure 8.9) but plunged after 1670. Such a large decline suggests the presence of a structural oversupply of housing. Yet Amsterdam was certainly not the only location placed in this situation, and it did at least manage gradually to restore some semblance of equilibrium to the housing market. Elsewhere, and especially in North Holland, this depression in the housing market became permanent. The average rental value of the 1,000-odd houses existing in Edam fell by 15 percent (from 22.00 to 18.50 guilders) between 1632 and 1734, when property tax registers were drawn up. Since prices probably rose for another 30 years after 1632, the decline was almost certainly more severe than this. Here, as in Amsterdam, the more expensive buildings fell most in value (see Figure 8.10).

The significance of these indicators to the construction industry can be demonstrated with a few additional figures. In 1811, when the Dutch economy was at its lowest ebb, the construction trades in North Holland still claimed somewhere between 20 and 26 percent of the male labor force, thereby constituting the largest industrial sector of this region. In Overijssel the construction trades accounted for 18 percent of all industrial operatives in Zwolle and Deventer in 1795, while in the rural district of Salland, this figure stood at 22 percent. In earlier times these figures are unlikely to have been smaller. It is probable, therefore, that the textile and construction industries were the most important branches of industry, and that their fortunes determined to a large extent the general economic situation. Their fortunes, and especially that of the construction trades, seem to have been closely bound up with the demographic situation.

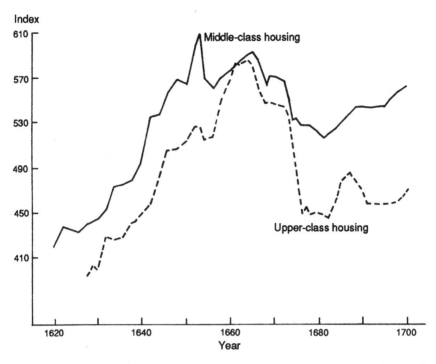

Figure 8.9. House rentals in Amsterdam, 1620–1700 (index: 1575 = 100). (*Source:* C. Lesger, *Huur en conjunctuur.*)

8.4. Conclusions

It is clear from this overview of the major branches of Dutch industry that a comprehensive evaluation of industry as a whole over the entire three-century period remains fraught with uncertainty. Let us begin by enumerating those features of which we can be confident:

1. The sixteenth century was not a period of vigorous industrial expansion. The most prominent urban industries, brewing and textiles, faced daunting setbacks, and the most conspicuous strategy whereby the cities sought to protect their industries was the suppression of rural industry. This was a defensive strategy that did little to stimulate industrial growth.

2. Beginning in the 1580s, many industries experienced vigorous growth. Critical to this growth was the migration of persons, knowledge, and capital from the Southern Netherlands to the new Republic, as a direct or indirect result of the fall of Antwerp, the ongoing military operations and destruction in the South, the suppression of religious freedom there, and the considerable social

334

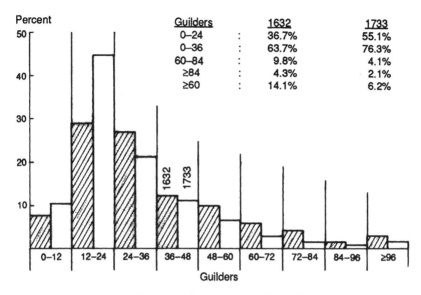

Figure 8.10. Frequency distribution of the rental value (in guilders per year) of structures in Edam in 1632 and 1733. (*Source:* G. A. Edam, inv. nr. 266.)

disorganization that persisted there for several decades as a result of the afore-mentioned developments.

3. From about 1585 until the mid–seventeenth century, vigorous expansion was punctuated by periodic downturns, but the grumbling and complaints tended to be muted and quickly allayed. It is, in fact, difficult to identify any branch of Dutch industry that faced structural problems in this era, or that failed to expand significantly its volume of production. The only sector that might qualify is brewing. The decline that set in after the late fifteenth century, as a result of the loss of export markets, had certainly come to a stop before 1600. What remains unclear, however, is whether the revival of production that followed amounted to much or lasted very long. It is not impossible that such growth of output as accompanied the population-based expansion of the market for beer reached its limit and even turned into decline well before 1650. In any event, declining per capita production set in long before the shift toward coffee and tea became a mass phenomenon, and this remains a puzzle. Between about 1700 and 1740, the available data on brewery output suggest that the decline of per capita beer consumption had been brought to a standstill, yet the receipts from taxes on beer continued to decline. This discrepancy may well be explained by a marked shift by consumers toward cheaper, and thus less heavily taxed, beer. But this too spelled decline for the brewers.

4. After 1650, and certainly by the 1660s, cries of distress and calls for all manner

of government protection emanate from a wide variety of industries. The complaints focused on the protective measures that limited, or even denied altogether, access to foreign markets, and also on the high wage levels within the Republic. The petitions for relief generally sought higher import duties on foreign products, the removal of import duties on raw materials, the removal of export duties on finished and semifinished products, exemption from taxation on commercial property, peat, coal, and other production inputs, diplomatic efforts to undo the new obstacles to free trade abroad, and measures to stop the transfer of technological knowledge and advanced equipment.

5. Between the mid–seventeenth and the mid–eighteenth centuries, the industrial sector as a whole presents a confusing image. Some branches of industry found themselves enmeshed throughout this century in a steady or a stepwise decline (for example, the various types of light woolen cloth, tapestry weaving, the breweries, soap boiling, salt refining, cooperage, the potteries). Others declined more rapidly to settle at a decidedly lower level of output (the building trades, the brick and tile works). Yet others maintained all or most of their mid–seventeenth-century production levels, often for many decades, before decline set in (*laken* weaving, to circa 1715; shipbuilding, lumber milling, and sailcloth weaving, all to about 1725). Then there are the newly developed branches of industry that grew in importance in the course of this century (tobacco, sugar, cotton printing, decorative tile baking, pipe making, distilling). Among these, tobacco processing appears to have flourished for only a brief period (1700–20), while the sugar refiners passed through a crisis in the late seventeenth century; but they all possessed a dynamic very different from the industries that had flourished a century earlier.

6. After the mid–eighteenth century, nearly all the Republic's industrial branches faced mounting problems. Only distilling and paper making (plus printing and publishing, a minor factor from the point of view of employment) escaped this fate. Even the long-nurtured *trafieken*, where imported raw materials (timber, tobacco, salt, diamonds) or semifinished commodities (malt, unrefined sugar, lead, linen yarn) were processed and, to a large extent, re-exported, faced serious problems. Thus, the growth of Rotterdam's snuff tobacco industry could not fully compensate for the collapse of Amsterdam's smoking tobacco processors. The sugar refiners did not decline by much in either number or production volume, but they saw their profit margins squeezed by competitors, especially those in Hamburg, a threat sufficiently great to bring the government to their assistance with subsidies. Even worse was the fate of the old domestic industries such as the various branches of textiles, shipbuilding and its suppliers, and the breweries. Of this type of industrial activity, precious little survived to the end of the eighteenth century.

7. The overall course of industrial production in the second half of the eighteenth century was much more uniform than in earlier periods. The era that followed,

the Batavian and French period (1795–1813), initially showed a continuation of the developments begun well before 1795. As the military situation increasingly restricted the flow of raw materials, the volume of industrial production contracted of necessity. But in several industries, such as textiles, the restriction or even complete cessation of competing imports created an economic environment in which domestic industrial production could once again operate profitably. The most important reason why the damage caused to industry by war and by the Continental System remained limited is that the deindustrialization of the Dutch economy had largely been accomplished before 1795. The remaining small-scale, artisanal industries, mostly supplying local or regional markets, survived this unsettled era because their modest scope sheltered them from the disrupting effects of warfare and politics.

This summary of almost three centuries of industrial development calls for a number of cautionary remarks. To begin with, we must not forget that a portion of the decline registered sooner or later by most industries was the result of a displacement of production to the low-wage countryside. Urban industrial decline was, thus, more serious than total industrial decline. The search for lower production costs could result in stronger production volume and a consequent rise in employment. The removal of shipbuilding to the Zaan region fits this scenario. But the removal of Haarlem's linen weaving to rural Brabant, where fewer workers earned much lower wages, cannot be evaluated so positively. Yet this second scenario was much more common than the first, as the gradual transfer of Leiden's textile production to rural Brabant testifies. Here, it is important to keep in mind that Leiden was not the only urban center of woolen cloth production to decline. It was by far the largest center, and the only one of international importance; but in 1643, when the *laken* producers formed a provincial organization, the participating guilds hailed from Amsterdam, Delft, Dordrecht, Gouda, Haarlem, and Rotterdam, as well as Leiden. And not long after, guilds in Hoorn, Enkhuizen, and Alkmaar joined as well. Clearly, Leiden was not the Republic's only producer of *lakens*, and the existence of this organization to the end of the Republic makes clear that production outside Leiden was not altogether insignificant. Leiden's production statistics, discussed earlier, reveal the overall trend of the textile industry but not the aggregate volume. This must have been substantially larger in the mid–seventeenth century, yet none of the cities listed earlier escaped the decline charted for Leiden.

The transfer of tobacco spinning from Amsterdam to Nijkerk and Amersfoort offers yet another illustration of this general principle. The new centers offered lower costs, but lower costs did not enlarge the market. They succeeded only in holding on, for a time, to a portion of the market that otherwise would have been lost earlier.

Nor were efforts to prohibit rural industry ever of much effect. Cities in Holland, Friesland, and Utrecht sought such prohibitions in the sixteenth century, and in Holland again in the seventeenth, but these restrictions on rural industry never offered the urban economies effective protection, for their reach never extended far enough to suppress all competition. The most that could be achieved was a slowing of the process of decline, or the support of a locally distributed product, such as small beer and bread.

A second observation must call attention to the important interrelation of trade and industry. This connection offered advantages in two directions. To be sure, not all industry was directly coupled to long-distance trade, nor did all the Republic's trade consist of domestically produced exports. Yet it is difficult to imagine how in isolation either of the two could have achieved the prosperity that they did together. An international commodity market wholly unconnected to domestic industry could never have maintained a position of prominence for as long as the Republic's did. The concern expressed in 1780 by Amsterdam merchants for the well-being of the sugar refineries illustrates this point, for the viability of their trade to the Rhineland depended on the availability of this bulky product to load vessels that otherwise would sail to Germany in ballast. The converse also held true, of course, for in most industries the producers could not hope to serve distant markets without the intermediation of the merchant. These sectors needed each other, and the decline of the one compromised, sooner or later, the viability of the other.

The presence of numerous merchants was certainly not the only precondition for a flourishing industrial sector. Abundant capital and consistently low interest rates after the first quarter of the seventeenth century proved to be of great benefit not only for trade but also for many industrial activities. Similarly beneficial was the development of risk-distributing forms of business organization, particularly the *partenrederij*, a form of passive partnership that spread from its origins in shipping to the ownership and operation of industrial windmills, breweries, tile works, and the like. By allowing participation to take the form of very small shares of an enterprise – as low as ¹⁄₆₄th – the risk of loss could be limited. Only in the eighteenth century did insurance as we now know it begin to become available for industrial property.

Often of decisive importance for the emergence of industry was access to what for the standards of the time was a sublime transport infrastructure. The natural waterways that criss-crossed especially the north and west made available both a raw material – water – essential to no small number of industries (beer, paper, salt, sugar, textiles) and low-cost access to other inputs and to markets. The cheap distribution of energy (peat and later coal) for home and industrial use is a key fact in accounting for the high level of urbanization already attained in the fifteenth century. It also goes far toward explaining the concentration in the northern cities of export-oriented breweries in this period. And in the seventeenth century, numerous export-oriented industries (bricks, tile and ceramics, pipes, beer, spirits, sugar, salt, soap, whale oil, glass – the list is a long one) shared a pronounced energy intensity, which suggest their common debt to the Repub-

338

lic's uniquely low-cost energy supplies. It appears that energy use in the Republic, both household and industrial, stood far above the levels common to the rest of Europe until the end of the eighteenth century.

Between 1510 and 1528, when Haarlem's breweries were still a major factor in the municipal economy, this industry consumed twice as much peat as all the city's households combined. A 1680 probate inventory of the estate of an Amsterdam textile printer recorded the presence of some 1,000 baskets of peat. During the war with France of 1672–8, when numerous distilleries sprang into operation in Amsterdam, some of these firms were said to use annually 4 to 6 thousand guilders' worth of fuel. In 1674 the average use of peat in salt refining was estimated at some 10,000 baskets per salt pan. Since the Republic then had 293 salt pans in operation, the total demand from that one industry must have reached nearly 3 million baskets. Even if these estimates are on the high side, it should be apparent that the Republic's substantial industrial concentrations depended on access to low-cost energy supplies.

Nearly all the rest of Europe depended on wood for heating, which resulted in deforestation and typically costly transportation over long distances. A concentration of energy-intensive industries such as arose in Holland was simply not possible elsewhere before the eighteenth century. And to this special advantage, we must add the extraordinary supply of kinetic energy produced by windmills at a time when elsewhere only water power was in general use. Moreover, windmills could be located with considerable flexibility at the same places that enjoyed access to abundant heat energy and cheap transportation; watermills, in contrast, were generally constrained by geography to locations of fast-moving water where no alternative to costly overland transportation existed.

To these economic factors stimulating industrial expansion in the Northern Netherlands must be added the still poorly understood role of government. We have already noted the active role of municipal governments, especially in attracting entrepreneurs and craftsmen from the Southern Netherlands toward the end of the sixteenth century. By offering concessions and privileges, urban regents sought to plant new industries, businesses, and workers in their cities. Besides the several examples of urban industrial development policy (concerning the textile and tapestry industries) already presented, many more can be added, for every city took active steps to attract industries, and industries of every sort. Consider the case of Utrecht, whose city fathers entered into negotiations in 1679 with an Italian glassblower who had most recently lived in Liège and Emmerich. They offered him exemption from taxation and from service in the civic guard if he would establish a glass works in their city. This he did until five years later, when the city of Deventer made him a better offer. Another five years after the Italian's departure, a new opportunity presented itself in the form of a Huguenot glassblower. Acting fast, the Utrecht magistrates assembled within eight days an attractive package of benefits: They offered an empty church as a factory; for the equipment of this work space, they offered 700 guilders, which the city had on hand from the sale of yet another church; the States of the province of Utrecht chipped in with an interest-free loan of 4,000 guilders. And yet these energetic steps to blow new life into Utrecht's industrial economy yielded little benefit: Within two years, this lavishly subsidized enterprise had ceased operations. The new firm suffered particularly from the shortage of skilled laborers: Efforts to attract a needed oven builder came to naught when the "head hunter" sent by Utrecht to recruit skilled personnel was arrested by Haarlem. The intense inter-urban competition for such labor is evident from the continual reappearance of the same persons' names in association with ventures in Deventer, then Zwolle, then Amersfoort, followed by Haarlem.

Municipal authorities everywhere were continually active in attracting new industrial enterprises and holding onto the ones they had. A whole arsenal of inducements was deployed to this end: building concessions, tax exemptions, interest-free loans, free housing, release from civic guard duty, subsidies, bonuses, and restitution of relocation costs.

These efforts to attract industry could degenerate into open conflict between competing cities. We noted earlier (see "Pottery" in section 8.3.2) how Delft was forced to abandon its efforts to attract Flemish textile workers in the face of Leiden's hostility. A related although less consequential dispute brought Amsterdam into conflict with Haarlem over the use of special looms for ribbon weaving. Amsterdam assumed the same posture in this matter that it had earlier in its efforts to protect its hand sawyers from the competition of the Zaan sawing windmills. In neither case did Amsterdam's obstructionist position long endure.

These economic tugs of war involved not only the Republic's numerous cities; the provinces also fought continually with each other in the defense of their economic interests. The Union of Utrecht's prohibition on internal tariffs not-withstanding, interprovincial trade was constantly hindered by such barriers. Holland, for example, protected its brick and tile makers by charging duties on imports from Friesland on the pretext that Friesland exempted its brick and tile producers from the tax on fuel. In time, Utrecht and Groningen introduced similar measures against Friesian brick and tile. More dramatic was the threat of a tobacco war on the Zuider Zee between Holland and Utrecht in 1689. Holland, intent on protecting Amsterdam's tobacco-processing industry, introduced export duties on leaf tobacco and pressured Gelderland and Utrecht (tobacco-growing provinces) to do the same. Their refusal led to the spectacle of armed ships arrayed against each other. The confrontation ended anticlimactically, without a shot fired, but it illustrates the aggressive role played by the local and provincial governments in nurturing their economic interests.

These few examples, which could easily be multiplied, allow us to conclude that in periods of expansion, economic policy focused on the attraction of new-comers. Once an industry successfully had sunk roots, public policy became no-ticeably more restrictive. This restriction often was effected via guild regulations, which generally required municipal confirmation. Guild provisions tended to raise obstacles to the entry of newcomers, certainly to the circle of masters. In their concern for protecting the quality of production and securing stability in the labor market, the guilds habitually turned to protectionism; and this reflex was more readily accommodated by the cities the more business conditions were depressed. Then, the quality controls were more strictly enforced, the departure of skilled workers resisted, and the export of technology forbidden.

More far-reaching than these ubiquitous local efforts to guide the economy was international trade policy, which took a decisively interventionist turn with the promulgation of England's Navigation Acts in 1651, and escalated dangerously with Colbert's highly protectionist tariffs of 1664 and 1667. We have already encountered these mercantilist measures in discussion of the distilleries, the sugar refineries, the lumber mills, the pipe makers, shipbuilding, and other industries, and in nearly every case they posed, sooner or later, very serious problems for Dutch industrial production. An industrial economy that was large relative to the size of its home market and dependent on imported raw materials was, of course, the ideal target for the mercantilist measures of its trading partners, for against these the Republic could deploy few effective countermeasures. This topic is discussed further in the chapters on trade, but here it is useful to emphasize that these commercial struggles always involved tariffs and (*de facto*) prohibitions on the import of specific products. And these measures were, in turn, intended to augment the might of the state. In this struggle the Republic could exercise but few levers of power.

During the first half of the seventeenth century, the Republic had been the conspicuous beneficiary of the unrest and internal difficulties that preoccupied the surrounding states. The Thirty Years' War not only brought disorder to the German market, it also diminished the strength of potential competitors in Central and Baltic Europe. As long as domestic religious and social conflicts kept France tied up in knots, the large French market lay relatively open to Dutch merchants. The English also had their hands full at home, as domestic tensions prevented the state from pursuing a consistent commercial policy. Once both England and France had secured domestic political stability, it could not be long before they turned their attention to reducing the economic preponderance of the Republic in their economies. Their eventual success in achieving this objective inevitably induced other states, such as Prussia, Sweden, and Denmark, to follow suit.

Yet it is by no means sufficient to ascribe the Republic's industrial advance up to 1650 to a fortuitous constellation of political events. It is evident that even without these specific political circumstances, a very powerful industrial expansion would have taken place. Geopolitics operated in conjuncture with commercial, technological, ecological, geographical, and other forces. In Chapter 12 we see that the Republic was apparently the only region that escaped the erosion of purchasing power that was general to Europe in the period 1580–1650. The "middling sort" accounted then for a growing demand, as both their numbers and their incomes grew. Unfortunately, we do not yet possess the evidence needed to distinguish quantitatively the growth of the domestic market from that of export markets. But there is every reason to believe that until the period 1650–70, the domestic market, buoyed by growing population and individual purchasing power, was of great importance to industrial producers. Two very different industries, construction and publishing, both highly dependent on the domestic market, demonstrate the far-reaching consequences for domestic demand when the number of consumers and their incomes both began to stagnate in the 1660s and '70s. "Stagnation" is, in fact, too soft a term. From the agricultural sector, which remained the Republic's largest, an earnings crisis in this period worked a long drawn-out depressive effect over the entire economy. Demand fell while social polarity intensified.

When foreign mercantilist measures began placing Dutch exports under growing pressure, it became painfully obvious that the domestic market could offer no real compensation. It was too small at the best of times, and by now it was in recession. Obviously, a retreat into autarky was not an option for the Republic's industries. Nor did the Republic enjoy much success in cultivating a protected colonial market of any size. It did enjoy an advantage conferred by geography, a privileged access to the markets of the German hinterland, and these markets could only grow after the end of the Thirty Years' War. Still, the domestic market plus that portion of the German market tied to it was in no sense the equal of the French, or the English–North American markets. Thus, the protectionist trade policies of the century after 1650 unavoidably hit the Republic harder than any countermeasures could affect England or France. This led to the Republic's assumption of a defensive posture after its great expansion earlier in the seventeenth century, while the other economic powers could only gain. Inevitably, this structural situation had its effect on the Republic's entrepreneurial climate.

The more cautious entrepreneurial climate was reinforced by a contemporaneous cultural shift that had unfavorable consequences for such industries as were sensitive to fashion and style in the broadest sense of the word. The Republic flourished in the era of Counter-Reformation and baroque. These were religious and cultural movements that sought to influence the broad base of society, and they left a deep mark on the design of everyday articles, interior decoration, and clothing. The Republic's cultural forms differed from these movements in detail, but not in general spirit, and her industries exemplified that spirit in both artistic products (ceramics, paintings, prints, maps, books, furniture, glass) and in the fashioning, dyeing, and printing of textiles. The "middle-class" character of this culture – its *burgerlijk* character – fit comfortably into the larger stylistic aspirations of Counter-Reformation Europe.

This connection of style to "industrial" production can most readily be grasped by a consideration of Dutch paintings. The celebrated works of the seventeenth-century painters are immediately recognizable because of their fascinating depictions of everyday bourgeois life, the material world, the prosaic. Even paintings treating the great religious and classical themes often contain elements that bring the great and the holy "down to earth." And what was true of the paintings also applied to the painters. The great majority of them earned their (generally modest) living not from the patronage of princes and bishops but from the sale of their products on the market. Dutch artists constituted a true industry, producing tens of thousands of paintings per year, many intended for specific export markets, and nearly all of them catering to the tastes of a broad middle-class public.

As the number of painters rose – from no more than 100 around 1590 to a peak of 700 to 800 masters in the 1650s – they (re)established their guilds, formalized apprenticeship practices, and pursued a far-reaching specialization. Thus organized, Dutch painters could achieve what the economist calls "product and process innovations." *Product innovation* refers to the development of genre, still life, and landscape paintings – all products responding to the new "private" nature of the art market. *Process innovation* induced technical developments that permitted the rapid creation of cheap landscapes, on the one hand, and the exquisite impressions of surfaces and textures characteristic of the *fijnschilders*, on the other.

This celebrated artistic phenomenon, which flourished thoughout the first half of the seventeenth century, faded from the scene with startling speed in the 1660s and '70s as the art market collapsed under the weight of oversupply (the total output of Golden Age artists must be counted in the *millions* of paintings) and a sharp fall in disposable incomes. The Utrecht painter Adriannus van Ysselsteyn complained in 1676 that "the business cycle [de conjunctuijre van tyden] has for some years been so poor that there has been nothing to earn as a painter."[2] His experience was not unique, for the number of active painters quickly fell to a quarter of its mid-century level.

This collapse in demand had an economic source, to be sure, but it also went hand in hand with a transformation in taste and style, one that had its (perhaps less dramatic) effects on a broad range of other products. From the late-seventeenth century on, a new cultural style gained ground associated with aristocracy and featuring classical and rococo forms, idealizing gallantry and refinement, and eventually giving birth to Enlightenment culture. In neither mentality nor lifestyle was Republican society equipped to offer much that was original to this cultural project. Nor was the social structure of the Republic well suited to play a leading role in fashioning a courtly and aristocratic material culture. Versailles, Paris, London, Vienna, Potsdam, and Berlin proved far better suited to play this role, whether it concerned music composition, painting, porcelain, wall decoration, or furniture making.

The fate of porcelain production in the Republic is revealing in this respect. Once Europeans first mastered the techniques for producing porcelain – in Saxony at the beginning of the eighteenth century – nearly every country followed with the establishment of porcelain works of their own (Meissen, Vienna, Doccia,

---

[2] Quoted in Marten Jan Bok, *Vraag en aanbod op de Nederlandse kunstmarkt, 1580–1700* (Utrecht, 1994), p. 101.

Buen Retiro, Copenhagen, St. Petersburg, Moscow, Sèvres, Worcester). In the Republic enterprises sprang up to participate in this new market, first in Weesp, then in Loosdrecht, The Hague, and Amstelveen. But notwithstanding the financial support of the state and access to the rich commercial experience of the Delft ceramics industry, all of these initiatives flopped.

The Republic's technological advantage over its rivals also diminished after the mid–seventeenth century. The foundation of that technological superiority was its effective utilization of energy supplies (peat, wind, and water), which took expression in the development of numerous specific applications of the available energy sources to the needs of the economy. The first major advances occurred, as one might expect, in the use of kinetic energy and heat. By the early seventeenth century, nautical techniques and windmill technology stood at a high level, and we can reasonably assume that the same was true of the industrial uses of heat. The Republic's position in the vanguard of these technologies created a favorable environment for further advances, advances derived from both indigenous invention and the early adaptation of advances pioneered elsewhere. The indigenous improvements focused primarily on shipping and windmills; the imported advances focused more on the applications of heat in industrial processes. Among the former, the development of the herring buss and the *fluitschip* have already been discussed. In fact, these two innovations are but the most conspicuous of a broad range of innovations, stretching from the perfection of gutting herring to the creation of an accurate nautical cartography.

A second indigenous advance in physical motion technology was the windmill, used for both industrial purposes and drainage. For the latter purpose, the application of the Archimedes' screw to pump water represented the highest stage of development. This innovation received a patent in 1634, although its diffusion was no more than gradual until after 1750. The agricultural depression that set in after the 1660s slowed to a near standstill not only the increase in the number of pumping mills but also the replacement of old ones. Industrial windmill technology experienced a veritable explosion of innovation, chiefly concentrated between 1591 (with the construction of the first mechanical lumber-sawing windmill, by Cornelis Cornelisz. van Uitgeest) and 1674 (with the introduction of the "Hollander" to the paper-making windmills, whereby high-quality "white" paper could be produced by the Zaan paper industry). In between these dates, craftsmen applied the principles of the windmill to the specific motion and striking action needed in pressing oilseeds, shelling kernels, beating hemp, crushing shells, fulling cloth, mixing mustard and paint, grinding tobacco for snuff, and other industrial processes. The production of these windmills sometimes required a high degree of specialized craftsmanship, as in the sawing blades of the lumber mills.

Contrasting with these "home-grown" technological traditions were the heat-based technologies that took root in the Republic via the importation of technical knowledge, usually via the migration of skilled workers. Most of these came from the Southern Netherlands. Their industrial experience lent sophistication to northern tile making and textile dyeing. Individual experts played crucial roles in transferring the technologies on which were based cotton printing, pipe making (English), and glass blowing (Italians, French, and Liègeois). Sephardic Jews introduced the techniques for chocolate production, diamond cutting, and silk production.

Yet it would be wrong to think that the Republic played no independent role in the development of these technologies. Technology transfer played a large role in the initial emergence of these industries, but later this role grew more incidental. In time, most technical advances emanated from the Republic's own creative talents, many of whom could almost be called professional inventors, such as: Simon Stevin (1548–1621), Cornelis Drebbel (1572–1631), Andries Vierlingh (1507–79), Jan Leeghwater (1575–circa 1650), Cornelis Cornelis. van Uitgeest (late sixteenth–early seventeenth century), Willem Meester (1643–1701), and Cornelis Vermuyden (1590–1656). Most inventions remained anonymous or arose as the cumulative result of many minor improvements devised by artisans. Examples of such advances include the "Hollander" in paper making, the development of a clay mill for the mixing of raw materials in brick making, the development of the ribbon loom in the silk industry, the development of methods to apply stone facing in dike construction (a pressing need when the *paal* worm attacked the wooden facing on which the Republic had relied), and many others.

Since so many of these gradual and anonymous innovations never acquired patent protection, the number of patents extended year by year can certainly not be regarded as representative of the overall development of Dutch technology. But the trends of patent activity (Figure 8.11) are too pronounced to dismiss this evidence as wholly uninformative. From 1590 until 1670, the number of technical patents issued by the States of Holland and the States General almost always exceeded 50 per decade; in the 1610s, '20s, and '30s, the decadal averages exceeded 75. After 1670 activity fell off quickly, so that in later decades the number of new patents often stood well below 25 per decade. Not every sector of technological development followed the same course of rise and decline, to be sure, but these data leave the distinct impression that technological innovation was much more intense before 1650 than thereafter.

Perhaps the single most telling demonstration of what had been accomplished in this area is the Republic's transition from the status of net beneficiary of imported technical knowledge to net exporter of technology and craftsmanship. Reports of this phenomenon arose hard on the heels of the great industrial expansion. Already in 1621 the operator of a Zaan-region timber-sawing windmill contracted to erect such a mill in Brittany. In 1629 the efforts of a Scottish merchant to recruit ships' carpenters in the Zaan villages elicited a ban on such practices. In 1635 a saw-mill operator contracted to practice his trade and introduce his knowledge to Göteborg in Sweden, and windmill builders were observed constructing saw mills in Antwerp (in 1665), in Saxen Gotha (in 1672),

Table 8.7. Industrial windmills in the Zaan region in 1630, 1731, and 1795.

	Oostzaan	Oostzaandam	Westzaandam	Westzaan	Koog	Zaandijk	Wormerveer	Wormer	Jisp	Assendelft	Krommenie	Total
1630												
Sawing	3	14	20	—	16	—	—	—	—	—	—	53
Oil pressing	1	4	5	—	13	—	—	10	8	3	1	45
Paper making	—	1	—	—	3	—	—	—	—	1	—	5
Milling	1	—	2	—	2	—	—	8	4	1	1	19
Hemp	—	—	—	—	2	—	—	—	—	1	1	4
Paint	—	—	—	—	1	—	—	—	—	—	—	1
Shell/sand crushing	—	—	1	—	—	—	—	—	—	—	—	1
Total	5	19	28	—	37	—	—	18	12	6	3	128
1731												
Sawing	—	46	159	33	14	2	—	1	—	—	1	256
Oil pressing	1	51	13	7	10	6	20	23	4	4	1	140
Shelling	6	40	4	2	7	2	1	1	—	—	—	62
Paper making	—	3	6	5	6	13	6	—	—	2	1	42
Tobacco	—	1	6	6	2	3	1	—	—	—	—	19
Paint	—	6	4	1	3	2	1	—	1	—	1	20
Milling	1	2	—	—	—	1	—	3	—	1	1	13
Fulling	1	5	—	—	—	—	—	3	—	1	1	7
Snuff	—	—	1	—	1	—	—	—	—	2	—	6
Shell/sand	1	—	—	—	—	—	—	—	—	1	—	2
Tannin	—	1	1	—	—	—	—	—	—	—	—	2
Mustard	—	1	—	—	—	—	—	—	—	—	—	1
Powder	—	—	—	—	—	—	—	—	—	—	—	1
Hemp	—	—	—	1	—	—	—	3	—	—	9	13
Total	9	156	194	58	43	29	31	34	5	19	15	584

1795

												Total
Sawing	—	22	91	20	8	2	—	1	—	—	—	144
Oil pressing	1	47	13	8	10	6	21	23	4	4	2	139
Shelling	3	44	13	2	6	2	7	1	—	—	1	62
Paper making	—	2	3	4	5	11	1	1	—	3	—	37
Tobacco	—	3	8	6	—	1	1	—	—	—	1	19
Paint	—	5	3	—	3	2	1	4	—	1	1	19
Milling	1	2	1	1	1	1	1	1	—	1	1	10
Fulling	1	4	—	—	—	—	—	—	—	—	—	6
Snuff	1	—	1	3	1	—	1	1	5	—	2	13
Shell/sand	—	1	—	—	—	—	1	—	—	—	—	2
Tannin	—	—	1	—	—	—	1	—	—	1	—	2
Mustard	—	—	2	2	—	—	1	—	—	—	—	5
Powder	—	1	—	1	—	—	—	—	—	—	—	1
Hemp	—	—	—	—	—	—	—	3	—	—	7	11
Loodwit	—	1	—	1	—	—	—	—	—	—	—	1
Bleach	—	—	—	—	—	—	—	—	—	—	—	1
Cement	—	—	—	1	—	—	—	—	—	1	1	1
Unknown	—	1	4	—	—	1	1	1	—	1	—	9
Total	7	133	132	48	33	26	35	34	4	15	15	482

Figure 8.11. Ten-year totals of technical patents issued by the States General and the States of Holland, 1590–1780. (*Source:* P. C. Jansen, "Nijverheid," 115.)

and even in South Carolina (in 1686). When the French sought to establish a tobacco-processing works in Dieppe in 1664, they attracted workmen from Holland. The first contract committing Dutch tobacco workers to work abroad, in Scandinavia, dates from 1652. Later, especially after 1700, a veritable flood of such specialists took work abroad. In general it appears that around 1680 the export of specialized talent began to lose its incidental character and assumed systematic characteristics. By then the export of technological expertise was reinforced by the publication of manuals, often in translation, on such topics as shipbuilding, windmill construction, and navigational techniques.

Dutch craftsmen were prepared to commit themselves to foreign service in return for good pay. These were mostly craftsmen of the highest level, who made their way throughout the Baltic region as well as deep into Russia. But besides this individual migration, one also encounters group migrations of craftsmen, such as the colony of Leiden textile workers who settled in Guadalajara in Spain, in 1719. Together with family members, they formed a colony of some 300 persons, attracted to Spain to form the skilled nucleus of a royal woolens factory. This was not the only such factory, and we know of a second such group colonization in Guadalajara organized in 1728, even though no small number of the first had straggled back to Leiden by then, disappointed in their Spanish adventure.

Not until 1751 did the States General respond to this development by prohibiting the export of machinery and the recruitment of skilled workers for foreign employment. The provocation triggering these measures was an attempt by the Southern Netherlands to develop its own mechanized timber-sawing industry, an effort that was accompanied by the introduction of a prohibitive tariff on imported sawn lumber. The Republic responded by prohibiting the export of every type of windmill part and tool. This was followed quickly by prohibitions that affected lead pigment production, pipe making, and distilling. Soon thereafter edicts forbade the recruitment and emigration of workmen in sawmills, oil presses, rope works, sail-cloth weaving, and twine production.

All to no avail. The structural problems faced by most industries in the Republic were not to be overcome by measures such as these. As technological expertise flowed out, neither new imported innovations nor domestically produced innovations rejuvenated adequately the Republic's stock of industrial knowledge. This obsolescence occurred as the incentives to innovate were diminished by the lasting depression that affected construction and most of the textile industries after 1670. With shipbuilding, these sectors employed far more labor than any others. Among the other, lesser industrial activities, many continued at their old levels of production, or even grew in the decades after 1670. But after about 1750, precious few industries escaped the malaise. The Batavian and French eras administered the coup de grace to many of these industries, but their decline had in most cases been of much longer duration. In 1813, as the new Kingdom was called into being, the (Northern) Netherlands was all but deindustrialized, and a fundamental change in this situation would not come until the last decades of the century.

Chapter 9
Foreign trade until the mid–seventeenth century

9.1. Early Dutch trade

Understanding the dynamic process by which the Northern Netherlands came to dominate the shipping, commerce, and, later, the finance of the European economy has long eluded the historian. The preference shown by economic historians in the last two decades, to shift attention from the often dramatic story of Dutch foreign trade to such prosaic dimensions of economic life as agriculture, energy supplies, and demography, has been motivated in part by the perception that the surprising emergence of Dutch trade can only be understood when placed in a broader and deeper context – broader in its internationalism, deeper in its domestic wellsprings.

In the absence of analysis, descriptions and celebrations of Dutch trade abound. And, indeed, there is much to admire and cause wonder. The first quantitative data at our disposal, dating from the very beginning of the sixteenth century, reveal the trade of Holland and Zeeland – the provinces in which almost the entire story of Dutch maritime trade is played out – as but a modest foreshadowing of what it would later become and yet at the same time as full-grown. In the early sixteenth century, no Dutch port city was of a size to be mentioned in the same breath with the long-established trade centers of Europe, yet fully half of Holland's population lived in cities.

The geographical range of Dutch merchants, and the variety of products in which they traded, were both sharply limited, and yet the first extant Danish Sound Toll Registers of 1497 and 1503 reveal Dutch shipping to be dominant in the Baltic trade. Seventy percent of all ships paying tolls upon entering the Baltic in those years were Dutch, and of those, 78 percent were from Holland.

Clearly, the early sixteenth century is not a satisfactory starting date for a study of the emergence of Dutch foreign trade. The commercial life of Holland and Zeeland's numerous little ports was already vigorous and impressive in 1500; this had not been the case a century earlier, so it is to the fifteenth century that we must first direct our attention.

The many towns scattered along the coasts and inland water routes of the Northern Netherlands had long sought to benefit from trade emanating from the industrial centers and commercial metropolises of the Southern Netherlands, the Rhine valley, England, and the vast North Sea–Baltic zone that then was dominated by the Hanseatic League. This geographical setting, which has endowed the Netherlands with a natural commercial potential to the present day, witnessed the emergence of a vigorous and expansive shipping industry in the fifteenth century because of the convergence of specific economic, political, technical, and environmental factors.

To begin with the last of these, we must recall the discussion in Chapter 2, section 2.1, where the worsening hydrological conditions of the coastal regions were described. The resulting diminution of agricultural opportunities encouraged the peculiar small-scale yet ubiquitous urban growth of the age. This structural transformation stands behind the elastic supply of labor available for industrial, fishing, and shipping employment in dozens of little cities. The growth of fishing, in turn, owes a great deal to the migration of herring schools from Scandinavian waters westward into the North Sea (see Chapter 2).

While this structural transformation was certainly not without its desperate aspects, the growing urban labor supply came into contact with external phenomena that provided unique opportunities. Flanders and Brabant, with their advanced industrial and commercial economies, had long formed the core around which the northern provinces of the Burgundian Netherlands, as well as much of northern Europe, oriented itself. The fourteenth-century crisis of the Flemish textile towns had undermined the strength of this core zone, but in the fifteenth century, Brabant, led by the commercial center of Antwerp, grew with vigor, and this growth spilled over into surrounding areas. The towns of Zeeland profited as outports of Antwerp, whose largely passive merchants made use of the shipping services available in Middelburg, Zierikzee, and Vlissingen. The towns of northern Brabant – Bergen op Zoom and 's-Hertogenbosch – participated in the overland trade and in the organization of the fairs around which Antwerp's commercial life revolved.

The North Sea and Baltic ports also exerted a magnetic attraction on Dutch traders. There they bought breadgrains and a variety of raw materials in demand both at home and at Antwerp, and they found markets for the industrial goods produced in the Low Countries and the exotic commodities available in increasing quantities in Antwerp.

These northern ports were attractive, but access to them was not gained without a struggle. The north German ports were organized in a mercantile confederation, the Hanseatic League, or Hanse, which also dominated the trade of Russia and Scandinavia and which exerted considerable influence at Brugge and London, its western trading outposts.

Dutch skippers succeeded as interlopers in the Baltic preserves of the Hanse thanks to a conjuncture of factors. They came with products in demand in the Baltic: herring (to compete with the diminishing supplies of Schonen herring), salt (imported from France and Portugal for, among other things, herring preservation), and English woolen cloth. This last product was new on the market (for England had traditionally exported raw wool), and it was generally unavailable in Flemish ports. Flanders, with a textile industry of its own, sought to prohibit the importation of English cloth; the new trading centers of Holland had no qualms in this regard.

While the skippers of Holland had several commodities to offer merchants in the Baltic, this was not their only weapon in breaking the domination of the Hanseatic League. They could offer a large shipping capacity at lower cost than the Hanse merchants through their use of off-season herring busses and their access to low-cost labor from the half-agrarian, half-maritime villages of North Holland. This proved to be an important advantage, for from the mid–fifteenth century onward, grain produced on the large estates that blanketed the vast German and Polish lands east of the river Elbe could be sold in ever growing quantities in the cities of the Low Countries. The low acquisition price of this Baltic grain made it attractive. It could drive out the traditional grain supplies from northern France *provided* that transport costs were pared to a minimum. The movement of a bulky commodity such as rye over a distance of 1,500 km (Danzig–Amsterdam) more than doubled its price. No wonder, then, that the shipper who could reduce costs even by 10 or 15 percent not only got the trade from his competitor, but at the same time opened up new markets and thereby enlarged the volume of trade in Baltic grain.

As the western demand for Baltic grain grew, exporters in the several Hanse cities found themselves depending increasingly on the Hollanders to provide low-cost shipping capacity. Consequently, these merchants evaded and ignored the official policies of the Hanse and of its leading center, Lübeck.

But Lübeck and its Hanse confederates did not give up without a struggle, and the resulting conflict was one in which the trading towns of Holland could not rely on the Habsburg government to intervene on their behalf. One of the North Holland trading towns, Amsterdam, led in this protracted commercial struggle and emerged by the mid–sixteenth century, on the strength of its domination of the Baltic trade, as the leading commercial center of the Northern Netherlands.

Holland first gained a toehold in the Baltic by supporting the King of Denmark in his war with Lübeck in 1438–41. Thereafter the piracy, boycotts, and warfare that flared up intermittently sometimes damaged Holland's trade, as when Lübeck exerted its influence over Denmark to close the Sound to Dutch ships (in 1510–

12, 1533–4, 1542–4), and sometimes stimulated it, as when a Hanse trade boycott of Flanders and its staple port of Brugge in 1451–6 diverted business to Holland. Lübeck later sought to elevate Brugge to a "forced entrepôt," requiring trade in most high-valued goods to be concentrated there. If strictly enforced, this would have made it difficult for Amsterdam to carry on its Baltic trade. But, in fact, the Hanseatic League's attachment to regulations and staple markets proved to offer the Hollanders their greatest advantage. In a trade where small differences in cost meant so much, the Hollanders were free to trade wherever and with whomever they could. They were also free to use whatever ships seemed most advantageous, a matter of no small consequence.

With the failure of Lübeck's staple policy and the perseverance of Amsterdam in undermining the Hanseatic League's dominance in the Baltic, the time came, in 1544, when the Dutch could secure from the Baltic powers in the Peace of Speyer the permanent right to pass through Danish waters and trade in all Baltic ports. Thereafter, the kings of Denmark continued periodically to restrict Dutch access to the Baltic, most notably in 1563–70, but increasingly the Dutch role in the Baltic changed from that of an interloper to that of a regional power, even a great power, acting to maintain a balance between Denmark and Sweden.

The 300 to 400 Dutch ships entering the Sound annually in the first years of the sixteenth century represented some 70 percent of all ships paying the Danish toll; but in view of the fact that Wendish and Scandinavian ships were then exempt from these tolls, and that many Lübeck ships bypassed the toll station, the Dutch share of total Baltic shipping probably did not exceed 50 percent. In the period 1537–60, the Dutch share continued to stand at about 50 percent, although the number of ships rose, peaking in the period 1562–8 at the annual average of 1,357 eastbound passages. The shipping records of Danzig, the chief Baltic grain port, probably offer more insight into what was happening. In 1475–85 Lübeck controlled 49 percent of Danzig's trade while the other Wendish and Pomeranian ports controlled an additional 12 percent. Western – almost all Dutch – traders controlled 39 percent. By 1550–5 Lübeck's share had fallen to 18 percent, and that of the western traders had risen to 53 percent.[1] In this same period, the annual volume of Danzig's grain exports tripled.

In these first six decades of the sixteenth century, the skippers of the Dutch ships entering the Baltic came from a large number of port towns and villages in North Holland. Amsterdam was easily the largest single home port, but it was overshadowed by the cumulative totals of the Waterland villages and the harbor towns of West Friesland.

Historians have long puzzled over the extent to which these competing shipping centers were autonomous. Towns such as Hoorn and Enkhuizen certainly were, and they remained so into the second quarter of the seventeenth century,

---

[1] Michael North, *Geldumlauf und Wirtschaftskonjunktur im südlichen Ostseeraum an der Wende zur Neuzeit* (Sigmaringen, 1990), p. 140

but the numerous smaller places increasingly became subordinated to Amsterdam. That city, having benefited from the reservoir of cheap labor in the villages of North Holland, sought in the 1540s and '50s to concentrate regional shipping interests within its boundaries by prohibiting Amsterdam shipowners from employing captains domiciled in the Waterland villages. Thus, we see Amsterdam at the mid–sixteenth century having secured its position as the dominant Baltic trader, actively working to further strengthen its position as the dominant commercial center on the Zuider Zee.

Very different from the free and rapidly growing trade of Amsterdam and the North Holland ports was the trade of Dordrecht, of old the most important merchant town of Holland and the leading port at the mouth of the Rhine and Maas rivers. Dordrecht's trade revolved around the city's staple privileges. Goods coming down the Rhine (wine and timber) and down the Maas (ironwares from Liège) had to be landed at Dordrecht and offered for sale. The city also required the produce of the surrounding countryside to be brought to market there and nowhere else. The city's merchants, relying on these legal privileges, were primarily passive traders, and they could not resist forever the initiatives of other cities to evade the Dordrecht staple and to challenge the legality of her privileges. Emperor Charles V, in response to one such challenge posed by a coalition of fifteen cities, pared Dordrecht's staple privileges down to a limited number of commodities. Later, this right was transformed into a simple tax. Passing goods no longer had to be physically landed and offered for sale.

Several small fishing and trading towns lay nearby Dordrecht in the delta region: Rotterdam, Schiedam, Delfshaven, and Den Briel. None of them as yet cut much of a figure in ocean transport, although some shipping to England supplemented the fishing on which most of these harbors relied.

The major center of merchants and skippers active in the *Westvaart* – the routes to England, France, and Iberia – was farther south, in Zeeland. On the island of Walcheren, which commands the entrance to the Schelde, Middelburg and its harbor extension of Arnemuiden enjoyed growing prosperity in the fifteenth and early sixteenth centuries as an outport for Brugge and, especially, for Antwerp. Other Zeeland harbors, notably Zierikzee, Veere (the seat of the Scottish staple thanks to a stroke of genealogical good fortune), and Vlissingen, also shared in this bounty to some extent.

Middelburg's shipping grew with the commerce of Antwerp and the fairs at Bergen op Zoom, but the Zeeland capital also benefited from the political struggle in which Flanders and England were involved. England had long supplied Flanders with raw wool. In the fifteenth century, this trade diminished as the English began exporting woolen cloth instead of raw wool. The Flemings struck back at this English development by forbidding the importation of English cloth. In the complex history of this struggle, Middelburg generally benefited as a nearby location that had no objection to the import of English woolen cloth. In time the English rewarded Middelburg by designating it (in 1558) as the seat of the Merchant Adventurers, the London merchant guild in possession of the monopoly right to export English cloth to the continent.

By then this trade no longer amounted to a great deal, but Middelburg had added to its English custom an important trade with France. The rise of Holland's herring fishery generated a growing demand for salt, for which ships sailed to the Bay of Bourgneuf and the Brouage. The raw salt was refined using local peat, especially near Zierikzee and around Dordrecht. French grain and wine also entered Middelburg to supply the Antwerp market; indeed, the Brussels government declared Middelburg the French wine staple in 1523, the obligatory entry point for that eminently taxable commodity. In the fifteenth century, the French trade was in the hands of Breton shippers, but their hold was weakened as skippers from Zeeland and Holland alike came to benefit from technical and organizational changes in shipping that allowed the Dutch to integrate the *Oostvaart* (Baltic trade) and *Westvaart* (trade to France and Iberia) into a single commercial network.

9.2. The merchant ship

European shipbuilding and navigation techniques booked impressive advances in the fifteenth and sixteenth centuries, advances that laid the groundwork for the age of discovery, European naval superiority, and commercial expansion. The Iberian powers pioneered most of these achievements; in the mid–fifteenth century, Dutch shipbuilding can only be described as technically backward and organizationally primitive. Indeed, the Hanseatic League then felt that it could nip the Hollanders' commercial challenge in the bud by barring them from purchasing Hanse-built vessels.

Dutch traders of the fifteenth century made use of a variety of ship types, many of which were built elsewhere. Simple cargo haulers such as the *kogge* and the *hulk*, and the herring buss were probably the most common. Dutch-built ships, like most northern European ships of the age, were square-rigged and hulled with the overlapping planking method. Merchants in need of ships usually sought out foreign builders or brought in master shipbuilders from abroad.

From these inauspicious origins, the Dutch shipbuilding industry developed, in the century and a half following 1460, into the largest and most technically advanced in Europe. Through the export of ships, the industry became a major economic factor in its own right, but, of course, its chief importance lay in the advantage conferred by this premier capital-goods industry upon Dutch shipping and commerce.

The full-rigged ship, first developed by the Iberians and later mastered by the French, reached the Low Countries in the second half of the fifteenth century. A Breton master shipwright instructed Zeeland shipbuilders in the construction of a *carveel* type ship in 1460. This foreign expertise was required to familiarize Dutch shipwrights with the edge-to-edge, or carveel-planking method of hull construction (whereby the hull is formed by a "skeleton" of staves and a covering of boards, rather than as a "shell" of weight- and pressure-bearing boards). It was also needed to introduce them to full-rigging, where three masts combine square sails (on the fore- and main masts) and lateen sails (on the mizzenmast).

By the beginning of the sixteenth century, Dutch shipbuilders had become the equal of their Iberian and Breton brethren and had modified the *carveel* type for the shallow waters characteristic of the Dutch and Baltic coasts. The new ship type permitted skippers to exploit a broader range of wind directions and velocities, which allowed them to reduce the time spent in port awaiting favorable winds. The net effect of this new advantage was to reduce average voyage time.

Obviously, this advantage was available to all users of full-rigged ships, but the Dutch could benefit in a second, critical way. The *carveel* made possible the completion in one sailing season of a triangular circuit (*deurgaande vaart*) from Holland to the Bay of Biscay (to load salt and wine), to the Baltic (to load grain and timber), and back to Holland. For the more northerly Hanse merchants, the shipping season usually began too late to complete such a voyage, requiring them to winter in southern Europe. For the Iberians and the French, the problems were different: The Portuguese were hampered by the fact that their spice-laden fleets from the Indies arrived in Lisbon too late to be shipped all the way to the Baltic in the same season. More generally, south European merchants and Baltic merchants alike were too far apart from each other to calculate their commercial strategies with the benefit of recent information about prices and supplies at the "other end" of the trade route.

The intermediate location of the Low Countries gave it natural advantages that allowed Antwerp to act as the northern terminus for Portuguese spices, Amsterdam to become the western distribution center for Baltic grain, and Dutch merchants generally to act as intermediaries in the exchange of northern and southern commodities. Geography does not explain everything, of course. After all, the Hollanders and Zeelanders were not the only seafaring peoples situated between Iberia and the Baltic. In the fifteenth century, Breton seafarers were active all along the Atlantic coast, as were the Normans. In the sixteenth century, the English became a factor in the North Sea and the Baltic.

The advantage of the Northern Netherlanders lay in a combination of factors: Their activity in the *Westvaart* was strengthened by the needs of Antwerp, the metropolis of the North, whose population rose from some 45,000 in 1500 to about 100,000 at its peak in the 1560s. The incorporation of the Burgundian Netherlands into the Habsburg empire also aided Dutch merchants – as it harmed the French – in granting them access to the growing Iberian market in the mid-sixteenth century. On the other hand, Amsterdam's dominance of the *Oostvaart* owed little to Habsburg power and much to commercial flexibility and shipping economy. In the fifteenth century, the source of economy had been cheap labor and the use of fishing busses; in the sixteenth century, its source became the technical adaptation of the full-rigged ship to the requirements of the bulk goods trades of the northern seas.

Once speed had been increased to make possible the single-season triangle route, further advances in this direction offered little in the way of commercial advantage. Now the primary goal became to increase cargo space. A long chain of minor refinements carried out by shipbuilders relatively free of guild restrictions or government intervention gave Dutch ship design a decisive edge in economy. In the mid–sixteenth century, when the Hanse reckoned that ships needed one crew member for every 5 lasts of payload, the ships of Holland averaged 7 lasts per crew member.

These refinements culminated at the end of the sixteenth century in the development of the *fluitschip*. The construction of the first *fluit* is conventionally attributed to Pieter Jansz. Liorne of Hoorn in 1595. His new ship can be seen as an adaptation of the *hulk* to the needs of the Baltic trade. By extending the length of the ship and adding a pronounced tumbledown form to the sides, he formed a rather tubelike hull that maximized loading space given the physical constraints on depth and breadth enforced by northern harbors and the fiscal constraints enforced by the Danish toll collectors at Helsingor, whose fees were based on the length and breadth of the vessel as measured at the deck.

The inventiveness of the shipwrights of Holland stands behind much of Dutch commercial expansion in the sixteenth century. But these largely anonymous innovators were spurred to their efforts by the vigorous growth in the demand for ships, a growth that had three chief sources. First, Amsterdam's hold on the Baltic trade, secured in the course of the fifteenth century, allowed it to ride the sixteenth-century boom in the grain trade. Second, Antwerp's commercial functions transmitted growth impulses to Zeeland and Holland skippers in 1493–1520 (on the strength of Genoese and Portuguese activity) and again in 1536–66 (on the strength of English cloth exports and the growing Iberian markets). Third, shipping volume grew as Dutch merchants fashioned a niche for themselves as intermediaries by knitting the *Westvaart* and *Oostvaart* into a single network of shipping services: French and Iberian salt could compete in Baltic markets against salt from German and Polish mines; Baltic grain could gain access to coastal markets in Atlantic Europe.

9.3. Foreign trade at the mid–sixteenth century

By the mid–sixteenth century, much had been accomplished. Domestic production of herring and woolen cloth provided export articles, while domestic demand for grain, salt, and timber filled the holds of returning vessels. A shipbuilding industry of growing expertise supplied merchants with efficient vessels that reinforced other, partly geographical, advantages to buoy the fortunes of Amsterdam, Middelburg, and the numerous lesser ports of the Zuider Zee and Delta regions.

Related to this growth in maritime commerce was a diminution in overland and river trade. From the 1540s onward, the flow of grain down the Maas from northern France dried up in the face of cheaper Baltic imports. Later in the century, political disturbances further reduced the use of these routes, bringing about the decay of the many small river towns of Gelderland and Limburg, not to mention the bypassed old Hanse cities on the river IJssel and the ports on the eastern shore of the Zuider Zee that had succumbed to Amsterdam's competition, to the deteriorating navigability of the IJssel, and to the stagnation of the German markets that formed their hinterland.

Estimating the size of the Dutch merchant marine was long a favorite activity of economic historians. Their estimates were not often based on extensive evidence or confidence-inspiring methods. The German scholar Vogel reckoned that Holland's merchant fleet in 1477 (the year of a tax survey) numbered 230–40 large seagoing vessels, plus some 60 vessels active in the coastal trade between northern France, England, and Hamburg. He guessed that once Zeeland's fleet was included, a total carrying capacity of some 30,000 lasts must have been at the disposal of Dutch merchants – most of this in the Baltic.

For 1532 another German, Häpke, estimates that Hollanders possessed some 400 seagoing vessels. The Danish Sound Toll Registers recorded the entry into the Baltic of nearly 400 ships captained by Northern Netherlanders in the years around 1532. In view of the fact that each Dutch skipper (and, presumably, each ship) is recorded in the Sound Toll Registers as entering an average of 1.5 times in 1565 (the earliest figures), it appears that at least 270 Dutch ships were more or less dedicated to the Baltic trade alone in 1532. By 1565 that figure must have risen to about 700.

These vessels were operated by skippers resident in scores of towns and villages throughout Holland and Zeeland, but by the early years of the sixteenth century, there was no question but that Amsterdam merchants controlled by far the largest single portion of the capital invested in seagoing voyages. The city's population, little larger in 1540 than the 11,000 there in 1514, still cut but a modest figure by international standards; it was probably not even the largest city in the Northern Netherlands until after the 1570s. But its concentration of trading capital was unparalleled.

In 1543 the Habsburg government imposed a tax on all individuals possessing a trading capital in excess of 1,000 Flemish pounds (equal to 6,000 guilders). The records for some cities have been lost, but what remains reveals Amsterdam, where 92 persons admitted to possessing 194,125 Flemish pounds, standing head and shoulders above the rest of the Northern Netherlands. Delft, an industrial city, possessed 29 persons liable to the tax who owned a total of 34,900 Flemish pounds, while in the entire province of Zeeland, 60 persons controlled 70,554 Flemish pounds.

Habsburg efforts to increase government revenue through levies on trade allow us a glimpse of the value of goods exported from the major ports in 1543–5. In the thirty-two–month period covered, the records show Amsterdam carrying on an export trade with twice the value of the second largest port of what would become the Dutch Republic. But it is here that the aggressive expansion of the city on the IJ and its Zuider Zee companions is put into a broader, and sobering, perspective: The value of Amsterdam's export trade was but 4 percent of that of the entire Habsburg Netherlands; over 80 percent of the total (19.9 million Flemish pounds) was accounted for by Antwerp.

The merchants and sailors of mid–sixteenth century Holland and Zeeland had established a secure place for themselves in the Baltic and were competing successfully with other seafarers along the Atlantic coast, but they remained in the shadow of, and in many respects dependent upon, the southern provinces, which functioned as the industrial and commercial heartland of northern Europe.

These trade statistics may exaggerate the predominance of Antwerp, but there can be no question of that city's leadership in the economic life of the Low Countries. Still, hers was not an economy of active traders, and this is where the Zeeland and Holland towns found their opportunities as shippers and commodity specialists. Antwerp's commerce was organized around fairs, which attracted merchants from all over Europe. Bands of merchants, organized in "nations," often with their own buildings, came to buy and sell in Antwerp. The English Merchant Adventurers, the Hanseatic League, and the Italians, particularly the Genoese, were all represented, but pride of place went to the south German financiers (the Fuggers, Welsers, Imhofs, Tuchers, and Hochstetters) and the Portuguese. The Germans sent their European copper and silver to Antwerp, and the Portuguese came to sell their Asian spices and buy the German metals. By the mid–sixteenth century, the influx of New World silver had reduced the importance of the central European mines, but now the Spaniards, too, were attracted to the Antwerp market.

From the perspective of Antwerp's commercial economy and the industrial centers of Brabant and Flanders, the Zeeland towns were little more than outports serving the needs of Antwerp. Amsterdam and North Holland could boast of greater autonomy, but they, too, served Antwerp with raw materials and foodstuffs in competition with the "nations" of Breton, Hanze, English, and Castilian merchants.

The Belgian historian W. Brulez has ventured to reconstruct the Habsburg Netherlands' balance of trade for the 1560s. His estimates are based on government documents and a remarkable survey of the Netherlands and its economy, *Descrittione di tutti i Paesi Bassi,* written by Ludovico Guicciardini, an Italian resident of Antwerp and first published in 1567. For the entire Habsburg Netherlands, Brulez settled on the estimates summarized in Table 9.1. They present a striking picture of a foreign trade very much dominated by the diverse, export-oriented textile industries of the southern provinces and oriented to Italy and Iberia both for raw materials and for export markets. Of all imports, 40 percent were foodstuffs, 30 percent were raw materials (nearly all textile inputs), and

Table 9.1. *Estimated balance of trade of the Habsburg Netherlands, circa 1567 (in guilders).*

Country of origin	Goods	Value	Total per country	% of total	Estimated total import
		Imports			
Germany	fustians	240,000			
	Rhine wine	720,000			
	copper	160,000	1,120,000	>50%	2,000,000
England	wool	500,000			
	cloth	3,240,000	3,740,000	>90%	4,155,000
Baltic countries	grain	3,000,000	3,000,000	>67%	4,500,000
France	wine	1,150,000			
	woad	400,000			
	salt	250,000	1,800,000	>67%	2,700,000
Spain	wool	1,250,000			
	cocineal	225,000			
	alum	100,000			
Portugal	spices	2,000,000			
	sugar	250,000			
Iberia	oil	200,000			
	salt	175,000			
	wine	250,000	4,450,000	>95%	4,700,000
Italy	silk and other mfgr.	4,000,000			
	alum	140,000			
	wine	250,000	4,390,000	>90%	4,500,000
Total imports					22,500,000

	Exports	
Type	Subtotals	Totals
Linen exports		
to Iberia	1,116,000	
England	600,000	
Italy	?	
Germany	?	
France	290,000	
Total		2,500,000
Serge exports		2,500,000
Woolen exports		1,400,000
Other textiles		600,000
Tapestry		700,000
Re-export of German textiles		240,000
Re-export of English finished textiles		3,120,000
Re-export of silk		500,000
Total textile exports		11,500,000
Nontextile exports		
overland to Italy	6 % of total value	
to Iberia	30 % of total value	
to France	54 % of total value	
Total exports		16,000,000

Source: W. Brulez, "The Balance of Trade in the Netherlands in the Middle of the Sixteenth Century," *Acta Historiae Neerlandica* vol. 4 (1970), 20–48.

another 30 percent were manufactured products (nearly all finished textiles). The textile industry accounted for over half of all imports and for much more than half of all exports.

If we now turn to the export records for Amsterdam for 1543–5, we find the dominant goods and trading regions to be very different. Four commodity groups dominated Amsterdam's exports: grain, herring, salt, and textiles. Together they accounted for nearly three-quarters of all exports. The destinations of these goods are also easily enumerated: 14 percent of all exports (by value) were sent to Lisbon, 14 percent to the Baltic, 20 percent to Hamburg and Bremen, and 7 percent to Norway. A final quarter of all exports went to destinations no further than the other side of the Zuider Zee.

In comparing these figures to those of Brulez for the Netherlands as a whole, we must not forget that 1544 was a war year and that twenty years of further growth would show Amsterdam's trade to be larger and more diverse, but not much altered in its basic orientation and character.

The Amsterdam *Waag* (weigh house) doubled its volume between 1531 and 1566, while the *Paalgeld*, a tax on incoming shipping volume, rose nearly threefold between 1540–4 and 1563–8. The Sound Toll Registers never record over 500 ships from North Netherlands home ports in any single year up to 1550, but thereafter the numbers rise sharply, to peak at an annual average of 1,357 east-bound sailings in 1562–8. In those years Dutch vessels accounted for 66 percent of all salt entering the Baltic, 74 percent of all Rhine wine, 64 percent of all other wine, and 76 percent of all herring. The Southern Netherlands imported fibers and dyestuffs for their textile industry; finished cloth was by far their largest export commodity. The Northern Netherlands also possessed an export-oriented textile industry, now in decline, but the primary imports for domestic use were grain and salt, while the chief exports were cloth, herring, and dairy products. Grain and salt figured as important re-exports, the salt often being refined (in Zeeland or around Dordrecht) before re-export.

A glimpse into the workings of the Northern Netherlands' trade with the Baltic is afforded by the activities of the Delft merchant Claes Adriaensz. van Adrichem. Born in 1538, he took over his father's grain trade – principally concerned with grain produced in the region – in the 1560s. He invested surplus funds in real property, short-term government bonds (*losrenten*), life annuities (*lijfrenten*), and short-term loans to farmers (*schulden van coren*). He also began investing in the fishery of Delfshaven, buying shares in herring busses. This became his entry route to the Baltic trade, for the new herring busses were capable of adaptation for use as merchant vessels in the off-season. By 1569 we know he was shipping salt and herring to Danzig and returning with grain. To be more accurate, Claes Adriaensz. invested in partnerships that financed ships for these purposes. For instance, in 1579 he owned shares in six separate ships, all of which sailed to the Baltic. In 1583 he again participated in six separate ventures. He owned ⅛th of four ships, ³⁄₁₆th of one, and ½ of yet another. The other owners of shares were the shipmasters, relatives, and a circle of nonrelatives whose names appear with regularity in the partnerships and who were, presumably, well known to Claes Adriaensz. After each voyage, sometimes after two voyages, an account-ing was made, and the partners decided how much was to remain *"bij de beurs"* (i.e., as working capital in the hands of the shipmasters) and how much was to be distributed as profit or added to the working capital via new investments by the partners. Claes Adriaensz.' distribution of capital among several partnerships was typical of merchants in the Baltic trade. This risk-reducing strategy substituted for maritime insurance, which long remained unusual in this trade. Gradually becoming less typical was his partnerships' reliance on shipmasters who carried cash and personally conducted trade at Baltic ports. Resident factors, correspond-ing with merchants via business letters and financing transactions with bills of exchange, were making their appearance and would soon become the rule rather than the exception.

9.4. The crisis and Dutch foreign trade

The political and economic structures in which Dutch trade had grown and developed for more than a century came apart in the 1560s and '70s; at the same time, the powerful wave of trade expansion begun around 1540 came suddenly to an end. These structural and conjunctural phenomena combined with political and religious factors to plunge the Habsburg Netherlands into a crisis that would result in its division into two states, in the transfer of commercial activity from Flanders and Brabant to Holland and Zeeland, and ultimately in the emergence of Amsterdam as the dominant trading center of all Europe.

The structural crisis was tied up with the economic malfunction of the Habs-burg Empire and manifested itself first in that empire's economic nerve center, Antwerp. This great marketplace suffered blow upon blow from the 1550s on-ward, finally succumbing in 1585 to the political crisis which rent the Low Coun-tries beginning in 1568.

The Portuguese had already removed their spice staple from Antwerp in 1548, while the south German merchant houses saw their prosperity eroded by the diminution of Italy's overland trade with the north and the reduced demand for central European copper and silver. Even worse was the Spanish Habsburg sus-pension of debt payment in 1557, the first of many, which ruined the major Augsburg financiers and dried up credit at Antwerp.

These events were but the opening salvos of the crisis, but they serve to remind us that Antwerp's demise as the metropole of northern Europe was not simply a consequence of the Revolt. Her prosperity was founded on the commercial and financial needs of the Habsburg Empire. As this empire's economic problems mounted, Antwerp was bound to feel the effects.

The traders and skippers of Holland and Zeeland had depended on the Ant-

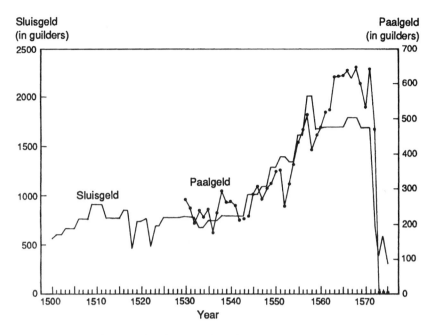

Figure 9.1. Two indicators of Holland's trade in the sixteenth century: *paalgeld* and *sluisgeld*. *Paalgeld:* A levy on ships entering the Zuider Zee to defray the cost of maintaining navigation aids (buoys and lighthouses). [W. G. Heeres, "De heffing van het Paalgeld door Kampen en Amsterdam," *Economisch- en sociaal-historisch jaarboek 46* (1983), 128–41.] *Sluisgeld:* A toll collected at the locks at Gouda, a strategic point in the inland waterways connecting the Southern Netherlands with North Holland. The toll collection rights were leased for several years at a time. [V. C. C. J. Pinkse, "Het Goudse kuitbier," in *Gouda zeven eeuwen stad* (Gouda, 1972), p. 117.] [*Source:* J. L. van Zanden, "Holland en de Zuidelijke Nederlanden in de periode 1500–1700: devergerende ontwikkelingen of voortgaande economische integratie?," in E. Aerts, ed., *Studia Historica Oeconomica* (Leuven, 1993), p. 361.]

werp market for much of their prosperity. What would be their fate if that market diminished in size and influence? If other trade connections could grow in compensation, all might not be lost; but the problems that engulfed Antwerp also threatened the other trading cities of the Netherlands. Figure 9.1 provides a glimpse into the nature of the impending crisis. The *paalgeld* receipts, which offer a comprehensive measure of the foreign trade of the Zuider Zee ports are here compared to the *sluisgeld*, the receipts from the toll on shipping passing the strategic sluices at Gouda. Nearly all inland freight en route from Antwerp and other southern points to the Zuider Zee ports, passed the Gouda sluices. The two trade indicators rise in sympathy during the boom years of the 1540s and '50s, indicative of the strong orientation of the specialized northern trades to the Antwerp metropole. But the crisis in Antwerp brought the growth of inland trade to a standstill, while the Baltic trade of the north continued to rise to 1565–8. Amsterdam's trade was hardly autonomous, but it now possessed growth impulses of its own.

The conjunctural crisis struck in 1565. Access to the Baltic, always a sensitive factor for the Netherlands' economy, became undependable during the Swedish-Danish-Polish wars of 1563–70. Just as the Dutch-Baltic trade stood at the highest levels thus far attained, a sudden disruption in 1565 brought famine to the Netherlands. This was followed in 1569 by a sharp trade contraction that inaugurated nearly a decade of depression. The number of Dutch ships entering the Sound fell from 1,294 in 1568 to 516 in 1569 and remained below normal thereafter as shipping was diverted to north German ports.

Access to England, indispensable for the production of and trade in textiles, was repeatedly disrupted by an English embargo on foreign shipping (in 1563–4), a Netherlands counter-embargo, piracy, and English reprisals associated with the campaign of the sea beggars (aided and abetted by letters of marque issued by William the Silent, in whose name they fought) to liberate the Netherlands from Philip II and from Catholicism. In addition to all this, trade suffered from the recurring decisions of the Merchant Adventurers (the monopoly exporters of English cloth) to remove their operations to (safer) German cities in 1564–5 and again in 1569–72.

As resistance turned into open revolt, the problems mounted. Access to Spain was made dangerous, and sometimes denied, beginning in 1574 when Philip II stepped up the pressure on his rebellious subjects in the Netherlands by confiscating their ships in Spanish harbors. Access to the Portuguese salt supplies on which the Dutch fishing industry depended was also periodically denied, beginning in 1571; in 1580, when Philip took possession of the Portuguese crown, his interdict extended to that realm also. Finally, as Protestantism spread among merchant communities, the danger of repression and confiscation of property encouraged merchants to remove themselves to safer locations. Ultimately, this factor would redound to the benefit of Holland and Zeeland, but until the safety of these provinces from Spain was clear, the political and religious forces unleashed during the Dutch Revolt encouraged a veritable merchant diaspora to such centers as Emden, Hamburg, Frankfurt, and Rouen, and to several cities in England, where for centuries thereafter the English sang of the year 1568:

> Bays, says and hopped beer
> came to England all in one year.

The struggle for religious and political freedom from the Habsburg crown cannot be discussed here in any detail, but we must pause briefly at certain features of the Revolt that are important to the development of Dutch trade.

The Habsburg central government had long sought to raise the level of taxation in the Netherlands and to borrow funds there. Much of this revenue was needed to honor obligations elsewhere in the vast Habsburg empire, where Charles V and his son Philip II did battle against Protestantism and Islam on several fronts. It was Philips II's tragedy that he managed the perverse feat of uniting against himself both conservatives, who mistrusted his centralizing innovations and feared for their privileges, and "progressives" who were alienated from what seemed to them antiquated Habsburg political and religious policies.

In Amsterdam, where two factions had long battled each other for political ascendency, the ruling faction instinctively chose the cautious path of loyalty to Catholicism and the Habsburg regime when the Iconoclasm and the first signs of revolt in 1566–8 put them to the test. The leaders of this faction were mainly brewers, manufacturers, and retail merchants, men with strong local economic interests. Their opponents included most of the city's international merchants. These were early attracted to Protestantism, fled Amsterdam as the Inquisition approached, and carried on their trade from German ports. Yet even if all merchants had shared the "progressive" criticism of Habsburg policy, we should not expect to observe many of them acting as leaders of the Revolt. The uncertain long-run advantages of a successful insurgency had to be weighed against the very real immediate disadvantages. For those whose religious conviction was not a decisive factor, the choice was difficult, and for those whose faith was decisive, as the Amsterdam merchants, the choice was more often flight than resistance.

Events in 1572 narrowed the range of options for many ambivalent merchants. The success of the sea beggars in capturing control of Den Briel, Vlissingen, and Enkhuizen gave these Calvinist partisans of William the Silent control of the navigation channels leading to Antwerp, the Maas harbors, and Amsterdam. After 1574, when Spanish troops left Holland and Zeeland and further military action moved beyond the coastal zones, the rebels could exploit their strong maritime position. They could deny Antwerp access to the sea (once the city was in Spanish hands) and could put pressure on the magistrates of Amsterdam (who remained loyal to Catholicism and Philip II) to choose the side of William the Silent. Until this happened, the other North Holland harbors – particularly Hoorn and Enkhuizen – leapt at the chance to expand their seaborne trade.

When in 1578 a new Amsterdam city council finally threw that city's lot in with the Prince of Orange, a new chapter in the history of Dutch foreign trade can be said to have begun. Among the merchants returning from as much as a decade of exile were Renier Pauw, Gerrit Bicker, Jonas Witsen, Nicolaas Hudde, and Jan Huydecoper. They and several generations of their descendants would long dominate the city. Seaborne trade, especially with the Baltic, began to revive, but the problems of the Netherlands were not over. The division of the briefly reunited Netherlands in 1579 and the reentry of the Spanish army under the Duke of Parma made it clear to everyone that peace was still not at hand. Warfare and the threat of armed conflict severely depressed overland and river trades; the sea lanes remained open to the rebels, but for how long?

When Parma's epic siege of Antwerp ended in 1585 with the reconquest of that city, the curtain was drawn on what remained of Antwerp's role as the great international metropole. The flight of its merchants, just as the earlier waves of departures since 1568, did not immediately redound to the exclusive benefit of the northern provinces. Fleeing to the north would seem foolhardy, since it was obviously not Philip II's intention to stop his armies at Antwerp. They pressed on to reconquer the rest of Brabant and much of the eastern provinces. Meanwhile, Philip II imposed a general embargo on all Dutch ships and goods in Spain and Portugal.

Thus pressured from without by land and sea, and lacking effective political leadership within, the free provinces could hardly hope to attract many of the richest and most cosmopolitan of Antwerp's merchants. But within this beleaguered citadel of the Revolt, several developments helped to turn the tide. The Baltic trade and herring fishery expanded; the urban textile industries – most spectacularly in Leiden and Haarlem – revived from their decayed state and grew rapidly thanks to the immigration of many thousands of Flemish textile workers (who had fewer migration options than the great merchants); the abundant shipping resources of Holland and Zeeland helped to thwart the plans of the Spanish Armada; and the vessels deployed along the Flemish coast to foil the Armada stayed thereafter to fortify the Dutch blockade of Flanders, ensuring the subordination of the Spanish Netherlands to trade routes controlled by the North. Finally, Dutch domination of the Baltic trade (as early as 1583, Holland's traders controlled 84 percent of Danzig's exports and 73 percent of her imports)[2] forced Philip II to repeal in 1590 his fitfully enforced embargo, as famine and new military problems placed Spain in acute need of grain and naval stores.

This recitation of events in the brief period 1585–90 calls attention to the traditional pillars of the maritime economy – herring, Baltic trade, shipping capacity, and urban textiles – that supported and strengthened the young Republic in its hour of need. Of course, external factors – England's own role in defeating the Armada and the events in France that distracted Philips II's attention and his army of Flanders in 1590 – also played a large role in this story.

A combination of internal dynamism and external developments brought about a large expansion of foreign trade and a vigorous competition among the Republic's several ports. Two cities, Middelburg and Amsterdam, quickly emerged as the ones best equipped to carry on the diverse functions of a general entrepôt. Middelburg drew upon its historic role as Antwerp's outport to attract many refugees. Amsterdam, with a more independent commercial base, attracted merchants from various places. Already by the late 1590s, Amsterdam's superiority had become evident, and many of the merchants who had made their way to Middelburg (or Dordrecht or Hoorn) pushed on once more to resettle in the city on the IJ (as shown by Figure 9.2). The long-settled merchant communities of Holland's cities were also supplemented by traders from the inland river cities, such as Elias Trip, who followed, as it were, the reorientation of trade from

---

[2] North, p. 141.

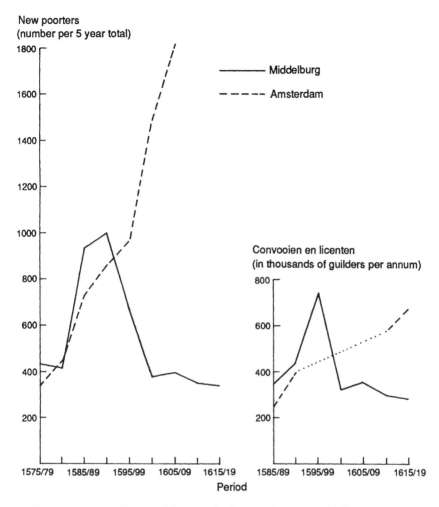

Figure 9.2. Two indicators of the growth of Amsterdam and Middelburg, 1575–1619. New burgers (*poorters*) enrolled in Amsterdam and Middelburg – an indicator of the attractive power of the cities to relatively well-off migrants. [J. G. van Dillen, *Bronnen tot de geschiedenis van het bedrijfsleven en het gildwezen van Amsterdam, 1512–1611*, R. P. G., Grote serie 69 (The Hague, 1929), p. xxiv. *Convooien en licenten* revenue – a rough measure of the foreign trade of these port cities. [Marjolein 't Hart, *In Quest of Funds* (Leiden, 1989), Appendix III.]

Zaltbommel to Dordrecht to Amsterdam. Others were "returnees," Holland and Zeeland merchants who had earlier been attracted to Antwerp but now returned to their "home towns," such as Balthasar de Moucheron, whose father, born in France, had long traded in Middelburg. Then there were the South Netherlanders, many of whom had earlier moved to German cities (Balthasar Coymans, Jan van der Straeten, Marcus de Vogelaer), and foreign merchants, especially those who had served the Habsburg Empire's commercial needs in Spain, Genoa, Augsburg, and Antwerp. Conspicuous in this last heterogeneous category were Portuguese "New Christians" and "Antwerp Italians" such as Guillielmo Bartholotti, Jaspar Quingetti, and the Calandrini clan. The Republic also attracted the humble but ambitious – often Germans such as Jan Poppen. In the course of the 1590s, the Republic's merchant communities benefited from major injections of capital and, at least as important, commercial contacts and expertise that gave Amsterdam especially a new cosmopolitan flavor.

In the short, heady period of 1585–1621, the ports of the Dutch Republic moved decisively to occupy center stage in the European trading world. The groundwork for this achievement had been laid in the century running up to the 1560s, when the integrated *Oost-* and *Westvaart* network was put in place. The new trading system of the seventeenth century continued to be based on this *moedernegotie,* or "mother commerce" as it was known to contemporaries, but what emerged with startling speed after 1585 was a new network of trade routes that very nearly spanned the globe.

In this period two transformations occurred simultaneously, interacting to bring into being a unique, world-embracing commercial system centered in the Republic. On the one hand, Amsterdam marshaled its shipping and trading resources as a specialist in the Baltic trade, initially subordinated to an Antwerp-focused commercial system, to replace the city on the Schelde as the emporium of northwestern Europe. On the other hand, the struggle in the Low Countries that worked to Holland's regional benefit was part of a much larger crisis that weakened the financial and military strength of the Habsburg Empire, the economic vitality of the Mediterranean region, and the commercial power of several leading cities of sixteenth-century Europe. In these decades Europe experienced what Fernand Braudel called a "decentering and recentering" of the world economy. The passing of the torch of commercial leadership in northwestern Europe from Antwerp to Amsterdam (as it had earlier passed from Brugge to Antwerp) took place at a time in which the organization of the entire international economy was in disarray and ripe for "recentering."

This brings us to the crux of the matter. Amsterdam took its turn in a succession of dominant trading centers, and it was the direct beneficiary of Antwerp's fall. But its own specific trading practices, political organization, and objective opportunities caused it to function very differently than its predecessor. To put it baldly, the merchants who flocked to Amsterdam brought capital, expertise, and contacts with them, but they now *used* these assets differently than before, as they came into contact with new resources, institutions, and opportunities.

In comparing Amsterdam with Antwerp the following points of difference deserve emphasis: (1) Amsterdam was overwhelmingly maritime in orientation, while Antwerp had leaned heavily on its continental relationships in overland trade with Italy and the south German cities; (2) Amsterdam's trade was continuous and atomistic, while Antwerp had never shed completely the older institutional forms of periodic fairs and the organization of merchants into privileged "nations"; (3) Amsterdam's merchants were "active," combining shipping, trade, and distribution, while Antwerp's were mainly "passive," trading in goods brought to them by others. Finally, and perhaps most significant, (4) Amsterdam did not hitch its fortunes to the star of a great imperial power, as Antwerp had with the Habsburgs. Amsterdam, or rather the Dutch Republic, struck out on its own, an act that exposed its merchants to different risks and different opportunities than had been faced by merchants in Antwerp, or in cities like Augsburg and Genoa.

The new state that emerged from the crisis was, and remained to its end, a bundle of contradictions: at once a precocious forerunner of liberal democracy and an atavism, preserving medieval political forms into the age of absolutism. The one objective of the opponents to Philip II that spoke with particular force to urban elites was the retention of municipal autonomy; and as we have seen, the Republic not only preserved, it strengthened the political power of the cities – and not just one or two but no less than fifty-seven cities that exercised direct political influence in the seven provinces.

The potential for municipal rivalry, provincialism, and political obstructionism was great, and that potential was not infrequently realized. But these cities, when pressed, also acknowledged a need for cooperation. This was especially the case in Holland, where a broader view may have emerged from the fact that so much of Holland's sixteenth-century economic growth occurred outside the six great cities that held voting powers in the pre–Revolt States of Holland. Except for Amsterdam, all of those cities suffered substantial economic setbacks while smaller cities, especially the Zuider Zee and Maas towns, flourished. The very dispersion of economic activity imposed the necessity of developing a territorial rather than simply a municipal approach to the formation of policy. In the view of Jonathan Israel, "this tempering of civic particularism with a much greater measure of provincial collaboration than pertained in any of the South Netherlands provinces was to prove an abiding pillar of strength to the future Dutch world entrepôt."[3]

In short, urban economic interests ultimately believed it advantageous to escape the Habsburg imperial framework, a political and economic structure that seemed to impose more liabilities than it offered advantages. But the opposition to centralization did not result in the erection of so many city-states thanks to the prior existence of a substantial economic interdependence and to acquired habits of consultation and, sometimes, cooperation.

The endless compromises and persisting conflicts between cities and provinces

---

[3] J. I. Israel, *Dutch Primacy in World Trade, 1585–1740* (Oxford, 1989), p. 24.

never allowed for the construction of a strong central authority, but neither did it produce an impotent shell. The United Republic was capable, under favorable conditions, of advancing its economic interests in the international arena with a consistency that surpassed a powerful empire, and with a power that surpassed a self-interested city-state.

In order to disengage themselves from the Habsburg imperium, the Dutch had to engage in eighty years of intermittent warfare with Spain. It is one of the great ironies of an historical phenomenon full of the unexpected that the Dutch trading economy flourished as the new nation was enmeshed in war, and that its prosperity depended very much on trade with its enemy. Just as the Dutch sought to rid themselves of Habsburg political control, they strove, through thick and thin, to nurture the economic ties with Iberia that were essential to the viability of their trade with the Baltic as well as to their many new ventures of the seventeenth century.

Habsburg Spain was, of course, the great economic prize of the age. Before the end of the sixteenth century, its economy had already lost much of its vitality, but it continued to hold a key place in the economic life of Europe because of the vast purchasing power with which it was endowed by the annual shipments of silver from the New World. The integrated *Oost-* and *Westvaart* also depended on trade with Iberia for strategic commodities, especially raw wool and salt. But why did Spain trade with a republic of heretics and rebels that she was actively spending her substance to crush? The answer, of course, is that Spain *did* act to sever its trade with the Netherlands: in 1574, 1584, 1598, and 1621. But when the embargoes were strictly enforced, they were brief, and when the embargoes endured for long, they could not be enforced. To understand this we must look first to the other end of the Netherlands' sixteenth-century trade routes, the Baltic. The Dutch hold on the grain trade made them indispensable in the frequent years of Mediterranean dearth from 1590 onward. In addition, the supply of Baltic naval stores and Swedish copper (the latter essential to Spain's domestic currency) came to be concentrated in Dutch hands. The Dutch also proved to be indispensable – or rather, unavoidable – because of the sheer size of their merchant fleet and the cheapness of their freight rates. Potential rivals often proved undependable, while the Dutch could add to their abundant facilities the advantage of insider knowledge, derived from contacts in the southern, Spanish Netherlands and from the Portuguese "New Christians" who settled in Amsterdam in growing numbers from 1595 onward.

Both parties had reason to continue trading with each other, for the deep-seated animosity that drove them apart was closely linked to an historically developed economic complementarity that did not cease with the breaking of political ties. This ironic situation pertained not only to trade between the Republic and Iberia but also to trade between the Republic and the Spanish Netherlands. The war was largely played out along the shifting boundaries between North and South, but here, too, an important trade was carried on, a trade on which the Spaniards depended in order to prosecute the war, and on which the Dutch – or some of the Dutch, at least – depended for their prosperity. Here, much as in the trade with Iberia, the Dutch supplied commodities, mainly food-stuffs and Baltic goods, in exchange for silver – very large amounts of silver.

The first steps toward open revolt may have been provoked by Habsburg measures to make the Netherlands a net contributor to the imperial finances, but from 1568 onward, Philip II found that he had no choice but to subsidize massively his Brussels government. The maintenance of Spain's Army of Flanders – a force that usually numbered over 60,000 men and innumerable camp followers – required in 1572–6 the annual transfer of over 4 million guilders per year; the flow usually exceeded 15 million per year after 1600. These payments buoyed the otherwise depressed economy of the reconquered provinces, but they buoyed the Republic even more, for much of the specie arriving in the Spanish Netherlands flowed directly to the North to balance the South's massive trade deficit. As early as 1588 (with the lifting of a Dutch embargo on trade with Spain), the specie shipments to the Southern Netherlands were often in Dutch, later Sephardic Jewish, hands. So large was Dutch trade with the "enemy" across the border that by the 1630s the coinage in circulation within the Republic was primarily minted in the South.

This trade went on despite the "closing of the Schelde," which drew the curtain on Antwerp's role as a seaport in 1585 and was not lifted until 1795. The purpose of this policy was not to stop Antwerp's trade entirely but to control it and tax it. All except Dutch vessels had to break bulk in Zeeland, transferring their cargoes to river vessels and paying Dutch license fees, or *licenten*. However, in time of war, the Spanish authorities in the South required a *second* transfer of cargoes, and at all times they imposed their own tariffs and fees. Amsterdam's regents liked to speak of the closing of the Schelde as the very linchpin of their prosperity, but like so many fossilized principles of statecraft, the real impact of this policy was not at all what it appeared to be. Its harm to Antwerp was certainly not greater than the harm imposed by the South's own tax policies and its efforts to divert trade to coastal ports. Moreover, Holland's interpretation of this policy brought it into a long conflict with Zeeland, which wished to blockade the Flemish coast for the purpose of funnelling as much of the South's trade to the Schelde as possible, so that it might profit from carrying and taxing that trade, as it had of old.

The vigorous expansion of the European trades experienced by Holland and Zeeland between the 1580s and the 1650s was closely linked to the dependence of a waning Habsburg Empire upon the economy of its enemy. But as noted earlier, this dependence was not always acknowledged and submitted to without protest. The confiscation of Dutch ships in Spanish harbors (in 1574, 1580, and repeatedly thereafter), the embargoes on all Dutch traffic with Spain declared by Philip II in 1585 and 1598, and the new restrictions after the expiration of the Twelve Years' Truce in 1621, sometimes brought trade to a standstill and always added to its risks. For its part, the Republic regulated trade with enemy territories by issuing licenses. When trade was permitted, the sale of these licenses generated revenue with which to prosecute the war; when political circumstances required some strategic interruption of trade, the provinces ceased issuing licenses, as was done several times after 1621.

The available information about the course of the Republic's trade volume within Europe demonstrates the sensitivity of the "mother trade" to the state of relations between the Republic and Spain. Detailed information exists only for the Baltic trade, which surged ahead from the mid-1570s to 1597, a period when Dutch access to Iberian salt and silver was generally unrestricted. In that last year, nearly 2,000 Dutch ships entered the Baltic, nearly double the (depressed) level of the 1574–80 period.

Dutch-Baltic shipping levels plunged in the decade that followed, partly because of the Habsburg ban on Dutch vessels in Iberian ports introduced in 1598. With the signing of a truce between the two governments, coastal trades stretching from Seville and Cadiz to the Baltic enjoyed their greatest era of expansion. The annual average of 1,708 Dutch ships entering the Baltic in the decade 1611–20 exceeded the average of 1562–4 (the high point of pre–Revolt trade to the Baltic) by 37 percent, while the capacity of those ships exceeded the 1562–4 level by at least 50 percent. We can be confident that the value of the cargoes rose by even more since textiles, spices, and other costly cargoes now weighted more heavily in Dutch trade with the Baltic. Of Dutch ships entering the Baltic, those loaded (i.e., not entering in ballast) rose from 30 percent in 1562–9 to 43 percent in 1611–20. Dutch merchants were exporting much more to this region, and it was not all salt, for this bulky commodity continued throughout this period to account for about 40 percent of eastbound loaded ships.

This vigorous expansion did not continue forever. The expiration in 1621 of the truce with Spain suddenly denied the Dutch legal access to Iberian ports and unleashed the Dunkirk privateers on Dutch shipping along the Atlantic coast. The entire *Oost-* and *Westvaart* suffered disruption, a fact well illustrated by the sharp decline in Dutch sailings eastbound through the Danish Sound – from over 2,020 in 1618 to under 1,000 by 1624.

The onset of decline in 1618 hints that Spanish policy was not the only factor at work in this crisis. The outbreak of war in Central Europe (what would become the Thirty Years' War) and monetary instability in the Baltic ushered in a serious contraction of trade that affected all of Europe. Correspondingly, the diversion of trade from the Dutch to their competitors played only a minor role in this crisis: The Dutch share of traffic through the Sound (measured in shipping capacity) fell only from 90 percent in 1618–21 to 83 percent in 1622–4.

After 1630 this sharp decline of 1618–24 was gradually made good, and throughout these decades, the percentage of Dutch ships entering the Sound with cargoes rather than in ballast continued to drift upward. The westbound traffic, dominated by the grain trade, was always subject to sharp fluctuations, but the eastbound goods traffic displayed much greater stability and grew in importance. The crisis of 1618–21 had harmed the English more than the Dutch, who now became the major exporters of cloth to the Baltic. Much of that cloth was the luxury *laken* produced from Spanish merino wool, evidence that the Spanish embargoes on Dutch trade were far from watertight. In fact, Spain became more dependent than before on Dutch trade and financial services.

When the Republic and Spain finally signed a treaty ending their war (the Peace of Westphalia) in 1648, Dutch dominance of trade with both Iberia and the Baltic was complete. Potential competitors – namely, England and France – were held in check by a combination of Dutch shipping superiority, internal weaknesses, and diplomatic obstacles.

The *Oost-* and *Westvaart*, connecting Iberia and the Baltic, absorbed the lion's share of Dutch shipping capacity. Since bulk goods loomed so large in this trade, it is sometimes thought that these many hundreds of vessels could not have made anything like a corresponding contribution to the trading profits of Dutch merchants. We know very little about the profitability of the various strands of trade, but such information as we have suggests that even the prosaic grain trade could be very lucrative. By 1600 the chief Baltic grain markets were highly integrated with those of the Republic: Wheat and rye price correlations usually stood above 0.9. But this sensitive mutual interaction between such distant markets did not preclude the maintenance of a substantial absolute difference in price level. Up to 1610, Amsterdam rye prices stood at least 45 percent higher than Danzig prices (measured in silver equivalents). The size of the price gap, over 40 guilders per last of grain in 1590–9, implies a revenue, after subtracting the acquisition cost of the grain in the Baltic, of 2 million guilders. The division of this revenue between trading expenses (freight, taxes, handling, information gathering, etc.) and profit can only be guessed at. If we follow Pierre Jeannin's analysis of freight charges in this period, nearly half of that 2 million guilders per year may have ended up as merchants' profit in 1590–9.

The depressed trade of the 1620s shows a very different picture. Then the Baltic-Dutch price gap had shrunk to less than 30 percent of the Danzig rye price, and trading expenses are likely to have absorbed nearly all of the revenue. After 1630 the price differences grew once more, and the 1640s are likely to have been a golden age of profit for the grain trade as Dutch traders imported some 74,000 lasts of rye and wheat per year against an average price differential of 42 guilders per last. In the resulting 3.1 million guilders of revenue, there must have been a very large amount of profit. In later sections, as we review the profitability of such proverbial fountains of lucre as the East India and the Levant trades, it will be useful to keep in mind that just one strand of the Baltic trade (admittedly, the thickest strand) may have generated over a million guilders of profit per year in the best decades of the era 1580–1650.

When contemporaries spoke of the Baltic trade as the "mother trade," they did not simply mean to convey that it was the original, or basic, trade of the Hollanders. They were often quite specific in justifying their belief "that (the Baltic trade) is substantially the soul of our commerce as a whole, upon which all other trades and processing industries depend."[4]

At the foundation of this "mother trade" lay cost advantages and institutional efficiencies, the product of geography, low wages, and technological advances in ship design and building. But upon that foundation, the Hollanders and Zeelanders had to erect a political power sufficient to guarantee access to the Baltic and to Iberia, the fulcrum of the European economy. The Dutch achieved the first task well before the outbreak of the Revolt; the second was obviously rendered more difficult by the Revolt itself, but this both required and made possible the creation of an independent commercial system, one no longer operating in the shadow of Antwerp and subject to a capricious dynasticism.

The new political status of the Northern Netherlands also influenced the evolution of trade with other traditional trading partners in Europe, generally for the better. The trade with France, which had long revolved around an exchange of manufactures and northern staples for salt and wine, continued along these lines after the Revolt. As the French economy recovered from the effects of the wars of religion, the volume of its foreign trade grew, and the shipping efficiency of the Netherlanders allowed them to replace the Bretons and other French subjects in the carrying trade. In addition, Dutch merchants invested in French production in order to increase the available supplies of export articles. This occurred at the salt pans of Brouage and most notably in the Bordeaux wine region. There, credits to wine growers and distillers stimulated the transformation of cheap wines into brandy, which the Dutch merchants knew would find eager markets in northern Europe.

Contemporary reports tell of the Dutch dominating trade in all the Atlantic ports of France. The French monk Jean Eon went so far as to claim (in a treatise on trade published in 1647) that the character of the merchant communities in these ports was more Dutch than French. He probably exaggerated, but the Dutch ascendancy was real and unquestionably abetted by the protection offered by central government policy. Both Henry IV and Cardinal Richelieu, advisor to Louis XIII, encouraged Dutch investments and services and even tolerated the purchase of Dutch-built ships – all in the name of economic revival.

Comprehensive trade statistics are lacking, but there can be little doubt that this trade – in which salt, wine, linen, paper, and sometimes grain was bought in exchange for Asian spices, Baltic timber and naval stores, Swedish copper and weapons, and Dutch dairy products, herring, and textiles – grew substantially until the 1640s. Jean Eon's estimates of French trade show France running large deficits

---

[4] "dat [Den Oosterschen handel] genoechsaem is de siele van de gehele negotie, waernaer alle ander commercien ende traffiqeren dependeren." From: *Nootwendig vertoog over den Oosterschen handel (1646).*

with the Republic. This view is shared by the modern historian Frank Spooner, who writes of a "hémorragie de métal blanc au détriment de la France, surtout en direction de la Hollande."[5]

In trading relations with England, the new Republic did not have such an easy time of it. Struggles over two major components, the English export of woolen cloth and the English import of Baltic commodities, shaped the contours of Anglo-Dutch trade up to the mid–seventeenth century.

Woolen cloth had dominated English exports since the fifteenth century and would continue to do so throughout the seventeenth century. The English had long relied on Antwerp to function as the distribution point for sales on the Continent. The crisis that overcame Antwerp inevitably disrupted this arrangement. In response, the English became more active traders, seeking out Baltic, Russian, and Mediterranean markets on their own. However, most cloth continued to cross the North Sea, now to Middelburg, where the Merchant Adventurers re-established their staple. The Republic attracted English cloth primarily because of the existence of firms skilled in fulling and dyeing. Unfinished English cloth was ordinarily sent to Holland for finishing before being dispatched to final markets.

This state of affairs irritated the English, who sought to establish domestic finishing industries just as in the fifteenth century they had replaced the export of raw wool with the export of woven cloth. The Dutch, for their part, resisted this, both to protect their fulling and dyeing firms and to preserve their role as traders in finished English cloth.

A group of London merchants secured parliamentary support in 1614–16 for what became known as the "Alderman Cokayne" project, a scheme to force the growth of a domestic finishing industry by forbidding the export of undressed cloth. (The new regulations had the added attraction to their supporters of breaking the hold of the Merchant Adventurers over cloth exports). The States General responded to this by forbidding the importation of finished English cloth. The English bluff was called; they were not yet in a position to do without Dutch skills in industry and commerce, and the Cokayne project collapsed. But the continual development of the English textile industry gradually reduced the volume of unfinished cloth crossing the North Sea in the course of the 1630s and '40s. Dutch laws forbidding the importation of finished English cloth, renewed in 1643, 1650, 1653, and 1663, became unenforceable, as their repeated promulgation suggests.

In the competitive struggle of the Dutch and English woolen textile industries, the English gradually gained the upper hand, and the once intense flow of cloth to Holland diminished. On the other hand, Holland's own woolen textile industry flourished in these decades, in part because of the growth of new specialties that

---

[5] F. Spooner, *The International Economy and Monetary Movements in France, 1493–1725* (Cambridge, MA., 1972), p. 173.

depended on imported wool from Spain and Turkey. Conflict was displaced from who would control the export of English cloth to who would control markets in which both competed.

Most English trade was bilateral, involving the exchange of English products, chiefly cloth, for the goods desired in a foreign market. Where the demand for English goods did not equal the English demand for the foreign goods, this system tended to break down. The Dutch, by way of contrast, could send specie and bills of exchange to such areas to purchase goods in the quantities desired. Particularly after 1618, when currency depreciation in central Europe raised the cost of English goods and brought about the collapse of their markets in the Baltic, the English could acquire sufficient Baltic products only indirectly, from the Dutch, whose ability to purchase in the Baltic had not been adversely affected.

The Hollanders supplied the English not only with Baltic products but also with wine, salt, spices, and domestically produced herring, linen, and merchant ships, thereby generating a strongly positive trade balance in the decades after 1620. After 1640, as England plunged into civil war while the Dutch enjoyed unfettered access to the markets of its old enemy, Spain, the Dutch advantage became greater still. It is in this context that England lashed out against the Republic. Pressed by a merchant community with aspirations to compete with the Dutch rather than merely occupy a niche in their trading system, the English government acted to curb the Dutch advance, first with the protectionist Navigation Acts of 1651, then with a declaration of war in 1652.

9.5. Expansion of the trading system

Dutch merchants faced both challenges and opportunities in trade relations with their neighbors in the decades following the Revolt. Surprisingly often, they were able to exploit the opportunities and deflect the challenges. But the emergence of the Republic to a position of European leadership in this period depended on something more than success in their traditional "mother trade" from Seville to Danzig: It sprang from the expansion of Dutch trade beyond these limits to new regions, both within and beyond Europe.

International conditions were not long propitious for expansion into new trading areas. Yet in a remarkable period of intense activity, lasting from the late 1570s to the early 1620s, merchants brought about a veritable explosion of their trade routes, extending the *Oostvaart* to Russia and the North Atlantic whaling grounds, and the *Westvaart* through the Straits of Gibraltar to Italy and the Levant (called the *Straatvaart* – straits trade), beyond Lisbon to the East Indies, and beyond Seville to the New World.

The following two generations would consolidate and elaborate on this new international trading system, so that once the dust settled on this era of aggressive expansion, the harbors of the Republic were in direct and continuous contact with Dutch settlements stretching from New Amsterdam and Curaçao in the west to Formosa and Deshima (Nagasaki) in the East, and from Smeerenburg on Spitzbergen in the North to Capetown at the southern tip of Africa.

9.5.1. RUSSIA

Sixteenth-century Dutch traders did not cut a figure in Riga, Revel, or Narva comparable to their role in Königsberg or Danzig, but after Muscovy conquered Narva in 1559, Dutch ships visited this gateway to the Russian market more frequently than did those of other western nations. With the backing of Antwerp merchants, they traded an assortment of luxury products for Russian tallow, wax, hides, furs, flax, and hemp. Sweden's conquest of Narva in 1581 denied Russia this access route to the Baltic. In response, Czar Ivan the Terrible in 1584 established Archangel, on the White Sea, as his empire's chief trading post with the West.

The White Sea area was not entirely unknown to the Netherlanders. Jan van de Walle, a merchant representing the Antwerp firm of Della Faille had actually established a modest factory (trading post) there in 1578, but the English had come earlier and had organized themselves in the Muscovy Company, a monopoly trading firm. Their established position notwithstanding, the English could offer little resistance to the Dutch traders who entered the White Sea with a handful of ships each year through the 1580s. With the founding of Archangel (and the fall of Antwerp), several Amsterdam merchants of Antwerp origin established partnerships dedicated to the Muscovy trade, hoping to build upon the pioneering work of van de Walle's enterprise.

While the English sought out the Russians to sell their textiles, and could at most barter cloth for Russian hides, fur, potash, and talc, the better-capitalized Netherlanders arrived at Archangel with a wide variety of metalwares, weapons, jewelry, and, most important, specie. Western trade with Russia, even more than with the Baltic, depended on silver in order to acquire the northern raw materials. As the Dutch traders' assortment of luxury commodities and supply of specie grew, they became the dominant merchants in Archangel, a position that they would maintain until well into the eighteenth century. And until the founding of St. Petersburg in 1703, domination at Archangel meant paramountcy in the Russia trade as a whole.

The fleets that left Amsterdam for Archangel each April averaged only 16 (albeit richly laden) ships per year until 1625. Then warfare in the Baltic seriously reduced the volume of grain shipped to Amsterdam and sent prices to record heights. For the first time, Russian grain could profitably be sent to western Europe via Archangel; by 1631–5 the Archangel fleets swelled to over 200 ships per year. Such emergency conditions arose again in 1658–63 and 1675–7, but otherwise grain was not among Archangel's exports, and fleets of 30 to 50 vessels sufficed to handle the trade throughout the rest of the seventeenth century. The ships, which grew to an average capacity of 150 lasts by the 1640s, usually sailed in two annual fleets and were controlled by a limited number of merchant consortia, whose freedom was very much dependent on internal Russian politics and on the diplomatic support that the States General was prepared to lend to the Russian czar.[6]

9.5.2. NORWAY

The ships setting sail for the White Sea traveled along the coast of Norway, and here, too, the Dutch began a major new trade in the 1580s. It was a trade that differed in important respects from that at Archangel. Russian products were not particularly voluminous, so that a handful of ships sufficed to handle the trade. But in Norway the Dutch were attracted to only one product: timber. This, the most voluminous per unit value of all major commodities, was needed in the Republic to satisfy the explosively growing demand for residential and urban construction and shipbuilding. From small beginnings in the sixteenth century, this trade grew rapidly, the more so since inland German timber supplies were often cut off by intervening Spanish armies. By 1648 nearly 400 ships, many of them *Noordvaarders*, vessels specially designed to haul timber, plied this route. Each year they completed at least two, and as many as four, round trips to south Norway harbors, where the captains bought up local timber supplies in exchange for salt, textiles, herrings, and, above all, silver. Once again, the willingness of the Dutch to pay with cash, indeed to extend credit to Norwegian merchants, and to buy in large quantities, made them the preferred customers and gave the Republic, itself nearly bereft of forests, access to timber at lower prices than many nations with abundant local supplies.

The Norway trade did not require a particularly sophisticated form of commercial organization. It was one of the last trade zones in which the ship captains continued to play a major role both as shipowners and as traders, and it was a trade in which the smaller ports, especially Hoorn and Medemblik, long continued to play an important role.[7]

9.5.3. SWEDEN

Sweden, until the founding of Göteborg in 1611, was accessible from the West only via the Danish Sound; geographically it belongs to the Baltic trade, but it was not an exporter of grain and hardly figured in sixteenth-century Dutch trade. The Hanse cities long dominated at Swedish ports. Sweden's importance as a

---

[6] E. H. Wijnroks, "Anglo-Dutch Rivalry in Russian Trade in the latter half of the sixteenth century," in J. Ph. S. Lemmink et al., eds., *Baltic Affairs* (Nijmegen, 1990), pp. 413–32.

[7] C. Lesger, *Hoorn als stedelijke knooppunt* (Hilversum, 1990), pp. 98–99.

trading zone emerged with the rise of its metallurgical industries. The Dutch share of Swedish foreign trade tripled, from a very low level, between 1600 and 1620, but it assumed an altogether more important role as Dutch merchant-industrialists settled in Sweden to exploit mining and other concessions granted by the king in consideration of loans and financial services: Louis de Geer (of Liègeois origin) expanded Swedish iron production; Elias (brother-in-law of De Geer) and Jacob Trip remained in the Republic, organizing Swedish armament sales; Marcus Kock became head of the Swedish mint; and the brothers Momma developed copper and iron mines in Lapland. These and other Dutch-based entrepreneurs flocked to the Sweden of Gustavus Adolphus, expanding the export of iron, copper, and armaments, for which the Thirty Years' War generated a strong demand, and orienting Swedish trade toward the Amsterdam entrepôt.

9.5.4. ITALY

At the southern end of the trading system, Holland's merchants were no less active than in the North. In 1586 a group of Hoorn merchants ventured their capital by loading a ship with codfish and sending it to Genoa. The Spanish crown confiscated the ship on its return voyage, and of the several other ships sent to the Mediterranean Sea, misfortune kept most investors from earning high profits. Dutch ships in the Mediterranean faced dangers from Spain and from English and Barbary pirates, as well as the competition of English merchants, who were already well established and organized in the Levant Company.

Despite these obstacles, Dutch merchants, and particularly refugee Antwerp capitalists who were experienced in the Italian trade, were prepared to commit large sums when ships returned in 1590 with little profit but with news of harvest failure and high grain prices in the Italian ports. Immediately, twenty-six ships laden with wheat set sail from Hoorn and Amsterdam. This venture also ended unhappily, as Spain captured the entire fleet on its return voyage (in spite of promises of safe passage in view of the famine conditions). Nevertheless, in the following year, Amsterdam merchants dared send some 100 grain ships to Italy, over the objections of more sober-minded colleagues in Zeeland and the North Holland cities who feared the large risks involved.

Almost every year through 1598, large Dutch fleets carried grain through the Straits of Gibraltar, establishing for the Hollanders a foothold in the Italian trade at what proved to be an opportune time. Although Spain's control of much of Italy exposed the Dutch to great danger, the independent Grand Duchy of Tuscany then embarked on a policy designed to raise its port of Livorno (Leghorn) into a major center of commerce. The Grand Duke Ferdinand I made the city a free port and offered foreign merchants extensive privileges. From this outpost the Dutch (but also the English and others) diversified their Mediterranean trade after 1600, adding to grain the export of textiles, fish, Asian pepper and spices, and Russian furs, leather, and caviar.

9.5.5. THE LEVANT

In the first decade of the seventeenth century, Dutch ships began to push into the eastern Mediterranean, trading at Constantinople and Aleppo in the Levant. The chief merchants were native Hollanders who, having developed the grain trade to Italy, now sought new commercial opportunities in the Ottoman Empire. Until 1612, when a trade treaty could be concluded between the Republic and the Sublime Porte, Dutch vessels sailed under foreign flags, particularly that of France under the accommodating Henry IV. These regions sometimes required northern grain and regularly bought Leiden woolens, although never in the quantities of English cloth, which ousted Italian textiles to dominate Levantine markets by the 1620s.

Under these circumstances the Dutch trade in the Levant was chiefly an import trade, in which merchants exchanged specie for silk, cotton, angora wool, camel hair (mohair), currants, and many other exotic commodities. The peculiarly unbalanced character of Dutch trade in southern waters gave rise to surplus cargo space that could be utilized by competing with the Genoese and the Venetians in the intra–Mediterranean carrying trade. Once Dutch ships had exchanged northern manufactures for silver at Seville or Cádiz, the empty hulls could be filled with Spanish salt and wool for sale in Italy and with Mediterranean grain (from Sicily, Greece, and Egypt) for sale in Constantinople and Spanish and Italian cities. Then the specie acquired in Spain could be used in the Levant for purchases destined for the Amsterdam market. In the Mediterranean, Dutch vessels enjoyed not only low operating costs but also low opportunity costs, permitting penetration of the regional carrying trade.

The years of truce with Spain were particularly propitious for the growth of a carrying trade that so obviously depended on Spanish suffrance. In these years the Dutch drew ahead of their English rivals in Mediterranean commerce, and the two together undermined decisively the age-old predominance of the Italians and the French.[8]

Trade in the Mediterranean waters had a very different character than trade in the North. This was partly because of the difference in commodities, which in the North tended to be more uniform and bulky, but it was even more because of the distinct political environment. The dangers of piracy and of Spanish economic warfare are evident, adding a risk factor that had largely disappeared in northern waters. In addition, the defense of the interests of Dutch merchants in the ports of the Ottoman Empire required an active diplomacy, the negotiation of extraterritorial rights, and habitual resort to bribery that no longer typified trade practices in Western Europe. To deal with all these problems, the city government of Amsterdam (with the endorsement of the States General) established in 1625 a college of merchants with the title *Directie van de Levantse Handel*

---

[8] Israel, *Dutch Primacy*, p. 101.

Table 9.2. *Dutch shipping to the Mediterranean Sea, 1591–1790.*

Period	Ships average per year	Ton	Average tons per ship
1591–1600	19.1	4,129	216
1601–10	66.2	15,789	238
1611–20	56.6	15,121	267
1645–8	97.5	22,142	227
1697–1700	123.0	28,200	230
1701–10	48.9	9,298	190
1711–20	109.6	13,952	122
1721–30	70.5	14,036	198
1731–40	72.9		
1741–43	58.7		
1778–90	59.0ᵃ		

*Ships from the Mediterranean to Amsterdam only.
Sources: 1591-1620: Simon Hart, "De Italië-vaart, 1590–1620," *Jaarboek Amstelodamum 70* (1978), p. 46; 1645–8: J. I. Israel, "The Phases of the Dutch *Straatvaart* (1590–1713). A chapter in the economic history of the Mediterranean," *Tijdschrift voor geschiedenis 99* (1986), p. 28; 1697–1725: K. Heeringa, *Bronnen tot de geschiedenis van den Levantschen handel,* Vol. 2, R.G.P. 34 (1917), pp. 30, 112, Vol. 3, R.G.P. 35 (1952), pp. 574–81, 1601–12; 1727–43: G. R. Bosscha Erdbrink, *On the Threshold of Felicity* (Ankara, 1975); 1778–90: W. F. H. Oldewelt, "De scheepvaartstatistiek van Amsterdam in de 17e en 18e eeuw," *Jaarboek Amstelodamum 45* (1953), 114–51.

en de Navigatie op de Middellandse Zee. Its mission was to enforce rules governing the safety of ships sailing to the Mediterranean (with respect to the number of cannon, crew size, and convoys) and to maintain (using revenues collected from ships active in the Mediterranean) a network of consuls in the region.

The creation of this body has also been interpreted as an effort to nurture a trade suffering from renewed hostilities with Spain. Unquestionably, the risks of trade rose sharply, and the closure of Iberian ports to Dutch shipping struck at the heart of its complex Mediterranean trade patterns. Moreover, the Republic's chief rival, England, largely escaped these problems. The severity of the post-1621 decline of the Dutch "Straits trade" is hard to gauge. Table 9.2 summarizes the available quantitative data. The dominance of grain in the early years gave way, after 1600, to a much more diversified trade in which grain from the Baltic flowed only in years of abnormally high grain prices. After 1620 no data are available until 1645–8, when the volume of Dutch trade was substantially greater than it had been in its pre-1621 era of dominance. Did the intervening period consist of a "disastrous slump and contraction" relieved only after 1645 by a revival "just as abrupt as the . . . collapse in the early twenties"?[9]

The immediate setbacks must have been severe; the lamentations of the merchants testify to this. But a part of the setback was a consequence of competition from other Dutch merchants, who supplied the Amsterdam entrepôt with silk acquired at Archangel and Persia, reducing the viability of the Levantine silk trade.

By the 1630s the "Straits trade" must have recovered a goodly part of its lost ground, although the dream of paramountcy in those distant and contested waters certainly had to be abandoned. In 1636 the States of Holland estimated that 200 large ships – 20 percent of the carrying capacity of the Dutch merchant fleet – were active in trade with Iberia and the Mediterranean. Between 1625 and 1645, Leiden's *laken* production grew to maturity, an industry requiring Spanish raw wool and finding its largest export markets in the Levant. After 1630 Leiden's clothiers initiated the production of camlet, a fabric made of Turkish mohair.

Dutch trade with the Mediterranean certainly did not lie dormant through the 1630s and '40s. A 1646–7 document describes the imports and exports of fifty-one Amsterdam ships that had sailed to the Mediterranean. This partial listing of that year's trade set the value of exports at 2,453,000 guilders (textiles, pepper, and spices were the most important commodities), while imports were valued at 2,350,000 guilders (the most important commodities being olive oil, rice, Spanish wine, all manner of dried fruits – especially currants – and raw silk). This may describe not the first year of revival but something approaching a culmination of the Dutch "Straits trade."

The Republic's trade with the Mediterranean in the 1650s had an altogether different character than had Antwerp's trade with that region a century earlier. In the course of that intervening century, the Mediterranean, particularly Italy, had ceased exporting finished manufactures (primarily textiles) and depended increasingly on the export of agricultural products and raw materials (wine, citrus fruits, olive oil, currants, alum, marble, wool, and raw silk). Synchronized with this shift in the composition of trade was a shift in the routes of trade. The predominantly overland trade connecting Italy and Antwerp had been, from the latter's perspective, a passive trade. Under Amsterdam's leadership the sea route came to dominate, and commerce was in the hands of "Dutch" merchants. Instead of an "Italian nation" in Antwerp, there were now colonies of Dutch merchants in Livorno, Smyrna, and Aleppo.

9.5.6. The rise of the VOC

As Dutch skippers and merchants made their way to ports throughout Europe, and as they found themselves capable of competing with established merchant

---

[9] J. I. Israel, "Phases of the Dutch *Straatvaart*," *Tijdschrift voor geschiedenis* 99 (1986), pp. 12, 16.

communities wherever they went, it is not surprising that they became impatient with their dependent status with respect to Spain, for access to New World commodities, and to Portugal, for access to Asian pepper and spices. The two Iberian empires were then united under the Habsburg crown, with whom the Dutch were fighting for their independence. All the more reason, thus, to ignore their assertions to monopoly rights in the New World and in Asia.

In the case of the Asian trade, two specific factors encouraged Dutch merchants to bypass Lisbon. The Portuguese colonial system functioned with diminishing efficiency. A Dutchman who had served the Portuguese in Asia for many years, Jan van Linschoten, documented this in his *Reys-Gheschrift* of 1595 and his famous *Itinerario*, published in 1596. In these travel journals, he provided detailed information on sailing routes, winds, ports, and the Portuguese empire in Asia. This invitation to interlope appealed to Dutch merchants all the more because of their exclusion from direct participation in the distribution of Asian commodities in northern Europe. The Portuguese sold their Asian goods in Europe via a system of contracts with "insider" merchants' houses. In 1591 the contract came into the hands of an international syndicate of the South German Fugger and Welser firms, Spanish and Italian merchants, and the Portuguese-Antwerp firm of Ximenes. This syndicate supplied the Dutch market via its agents in Amsterdam and Middelburg, but it preferred to use Hamburg as its northern staple.

The second factor of importance was the price of pepper. Through the inefficacy of the Portuguese colonial system, pepper supplies failed to keep pace with European demand, thereby creating an opportunity that the competing Venetians and overland caravan traders could not exploit fully.

In summary, in the early 1590s, the Dutch faced high pepper prices, exclusion from the European trade in pepper, and a Portuguese colonial system that was a manifestly weak, economically tempting, and politically appropriate target. And, finally, a number of Dutchmen had first-hand knowledge of Portuguese practices either through service in Asia (such as Van Linschoten) or through presence in Lisbon (such as Cornelis de Houtman).

By 1595 the stage was set for direct Dutch sailings to Asia. And yet the first effort to do so, organized by the Zeeland merchant Balthasar de Moucheron, sailed not south but north. De Moucheron had been a leader in the Archangel trade and sought an Arctic route to Asia, placing his money on the authority of the Amsterdam *predikant* (clergyman) Petrus Plancius rather than on the comprehensive cartographic data then available from Van Linschoten. Three successive expeditions sought a northeast passage. De Moucheron bailed out after the failure of the second, but the city of Amsterdam sponsored a third voyage, which resulted in the disastrous and remarkable landing at Nova Zembla, where the captain Willem Barentsz. and his crew were forced to endure the Arctic winter of 1596-7 before attempting a return.

In 1595 another expedition to Asia, organized by Cornelius de Houtman, sailed south. Of the four ships and 240 men that departed, only three ships and 87 men returned 30 months later, with goods that apparently yielded only enough to cover the 290,000-guilder investment.

The summer of 1597 must have been a somber one for merchants who had placed their hopes in trade with Asia, as the survivors of Nova Zembla and Java limped back to Amsterdam. But, just as with initial disappointment in the Italy trade, nothing seemed capable of dissuading Dutch merchants from making further investments in these years. In 1598 no less than five competing merchant consortia outfitted a total of twenty-two vessels to sail (south) to Asia. Of these, an Amsterdam group led by Jacob van Neck committed 768,000 guilders to their fleet of eight vessels, and this level of investment was sustained in the following years, until there were merchant groups in six cities. Their sometimes profitable ventures had several immediate ramifications: They exposed Portugal as a rather toothless power; they drove the English, who were also active in Asia, into such a marginal position that they bundled their remaining forces in 1600 into a monopoly enterprise, the (English) East India Company; and they so expanded the supply of pepper as to send the price plummeting, threatening the competing Dutch investors with ruin.

At this point the government of the Republic, in the person of the Grand Pensionary Johan van Oldenbarnevelt, intervened to secure a union of the rival merchant organizations. The immediate motive was to avoid the financial ruin that continued competition seemed destined to bring. However, it certainly did not escape the minds of the political leaders that a single, "united" Dutch presence in Asia could pursue military objectives in the struggle against Spain and Portugal, something that the competing merchant groups could never contemplate.

The form given the new monopoly company, the *Verenigde Oostindische Compagnie* (United East India Company, henceforth VOC), illustrates with perfect clarity the municipal autonomy and competition that characterized the Republic, not only in its first years but throughout its life. It illustrates as well the new capacity of this peculiar polity to hammer out compromises that made cooperation among rivals possible.

The charter (*octrooi*) issued by the States General provided for a single company consisting of six chambers, one for each of the cities where predecessor firms (called the *voorcompagnieën*) had participated in the Asia trade. Moreover, the smaller cities' fear of Amsterdam's overweening economic power could be overcome only by agreeing, before the capital of the new enterprise was actually raised, on a formula for the division of the Company's activities: Amsterdam was limited to one-half, Zeeland to one-quarter, and the four other participating cities (Rotterdam, Delft, Hoorn, and Enkhuizen) to one-sixteenth participation each. This did not end the discord. To further satisfy the smaller participants, Van Oldenbarneveldt arranged that the central administration of the VOC should be in the hands of seventeen representatives of the investors (the *Heren XVII*): eight from Amsterdam, eight from the five smaller chambers, and one rotating chair to circulate only among the smaller chambers.

Besides the interurban distribution of activity and power, the new Company had to address the distribution of power among the investors. A total of over 1,800 individuals contributed to the initial capitalization of 6,424,588 guilders. However, fewer than 200 investors together accounted for half this sum. Reflecting this reality as well as the practices of the predecessor companies, the charter distinguished between mere *participanten* and *bewindhebbers*. The latter, 76 in total (later reduced to 60), possessed sole authority in the management of the VOC. From their number, the seventeen active directors, the *Heren XVII*, were selected.

In the predecessor companies, the position of the *participanten* was equivalent to that of limited partners. They placed their money in the hands of the active partners (i.e., *bewindhebbers*) who alone bore an unlimited liability for the debts of the enterprise. When the voyage in which the limited and active partners had pooled their investments was over, the profits, if any, were distributed. *Participanten* unhappy with the performance of the *bewindhebbers* could decline to invest in later voyages.

The charter of the VOC envisioned a rather different sort of trading venture: The States General empowered the new Company to build forts, maintain armies, and conclude treaties with Asian rulers. With this in mind, the charter provided for a venture that would continue for twenty-one years, with a financial accounting only at the end of each decade. Moreover, in view of the enormous amount of capital involved, the charter provided that all investors, not simply the *participanten*, would be responsible for the Company's debts only to the extent of their investment. The VOC was what we now call a limited liability company, but the full implications of that fact were far from clear at the time of founding. Ad hoc decisions, made particularly in the first decade of the Company's life, established the principle that the capital invested would be permanent (not subject to liquidation and distribution among the investors) and that investors who wished to liquidate their interest in the VOC could sell their share to a buyer at the stock exchange, the *Beurs*, in the same manner as the owner of a physical commodity. A large number of shareholders, mainly small ones, exercised this option: The 1,143 founding shareholders in the Amsterdam chamber had shrunk to 830 ten years later. By the second decade of the seventeenth century, these practices were established, and the VOC had become Europe's first effective joint-stock company.

The Company's first two decades were also eventful with regard to the evolution of its organization in Asia. The new Company's first expeditions set out to attack the Portuguese frontally and to purchase spices at their points of production, which were in the Moluccan islands in the eastern Indonesian archipelago. In its first years, the VOC's commercial interest focused almost exclusively on the acquisition of spices (particularly cloves, nutmeg, and mace) and pepper.

After a decade of operation with mixed success, the *Heren XVII* felt the need to establish a permanent physical presence in Asia, which would be the residence of a governor-general who could coordinate on the spot both the economic and military activities of the Company. After modest beginnings in 1613, the VOC's Asian headquarters was firmly and ambitiously planted in 1619, when Jan Pietersz. Coen became governor-general.

Coen proved to be a man with a vision of the VOC as an Asian power, both political and economic, that went far beyond the rather cautious plans of the directors at home. He founded Batavia, on western Java, as the VOC's Asian headquarters and went on to tighten the Company's grip on the small but strategic spice islands in order to monopolize production more effectively. When they rose up in rebellion in 1621, Coen did not shirk from killing or expelling the entire native population of the clove-producing Banda islands and establishing plantations run by Dutchmen (the *perkeniers*) and worked by slaves. He overlooked no opportunity to push the VOC in the direction of becoming a territorial power, since he hoped to see large numbers of Dutch colonists in the East Indies. This never happened, and the *Heren XVII* at home were often skeptical toward his policies since they involved large, open-ended financial commitments.

A second of Coen's visions met with more ready acceptance. He urged the directors to send ships, supplies, and personnel in excess of the needs of direct commerce with the Republic, so that the VOC could become a major power in inter–Asian commerce. By buying and selling goods within Asia, Coen argued, "I am of the opinion that matters can be brought to a point that you [the *Heren XVII*] will not be obliged to send any money whatever from Holland." That is, Coen envisioned that the profits earned from trade within Asia would finance the purchase of the pepper and spices that filled the holds of the ships returning to the Republic, or as these empire-builders liked to say, to Patria.

The Company directors in Patria could not expect to receive replies to their correspondence with Batavia in less than twenty months. This fact, whose rough equivalent today would arise only with the establishment of regular trade with the nearest star in our galaxy, is of the first importance in understanding the VOC's behavior. It undermined the maintenance of financial control, since no single set of accounts could comprehend and summarize all the Company's activities. It also gave the governor-general in Batavia scope to undertake initiatives that often went far beyond the intentions of the directors in the Republic.

The directors were interested in commercial monopoly; an expenditure on military power sufficient to drive the Portuguese and English out of the chief spice-producing areas would allow the Company to buy cheap in Asia and sell dear in Europe. The Company officials in Asia often seemed more interested in political empire. In fairness to them, this was partly because the pursuit of monopoly was not as simple as the *Heren XVII* in Holland thought it would be. Rival European companies, smuggling, the commerce of indigenous traders, and the existence of independent Asian trading centers open to all merchants, all led the VOC into military ventures that seemed to have no end. In addition, the Company's commitment to the inter–Asian trade entailed the establishment of trading factories and the negotiation of commercial treaties with Asian rulers even in places where there were few products to buy for shipment to Europe.

The Company's early success depended on its speedy construction of a remarkably comprehensive network of trading stations stretching from Persia to Japan. The VOC's control of the Moluccan islands was still far from complete when it acted to deploy a growing proportion of its resources to the expansion of its trading empire in three large theaters that spanned most of Asia.

From the beginning the Company sought trading privileges on the Coromandel Coast of India, for success in the spice island trade depended on possessing Indian cotton textiles. By 1612 the Dutch had wrested Pulicat from the Portuguese, which later became their fortified center of trade in the region. This trade later expanded up the coast to Bengal, which became important for the Company after 1630. The next step, begun in 1637, was to secure the cinnamon trade of Ceylon by ousting the Portuguese from their coastal strongholds. The second trade zone encompassed the Far East. The Company established trading contacts with Japan as early as 1609. However, this trade could not flourish without simultaneous access to China, the source of goods most in demand in Japan. Jan Pietersz. Coen's bellicose efforts to penetrate this trading zone met with Chinese, Portuguese, and Spanish resistance. Denied direct access, the VOC in 1624 ravaged coastal Chinese shipping until it was granted permission to establish a fortified trading post on Taiwan, Fort Zeelandia. From this position of strength, the VOC received the Chinese junk trade, acted to isolate the Spaniards at Manila, and built up its trade with Japan.

The last trading zone entered by the VOC was the Malabar Coast of India, Persia, and Arabia. The great commercial center of this vast littoral was Surat, where the VOC established a permanent settlement in 1616. From there it extended its trade to Persia, and to Mocha at the entrance to the Red Sea.

As established by the charter of 1602, the VOC at home was highly decentralized, but the Company in Asia, as shaped by Coen, was highly centralized: The vast trading system stretching from the Persian Gulf to Japan was focused exclusively on Batavia, where the governor-general and his High Council (The *Hoge Regering*) made decisions for all Asian commerce, and their clerks kept the accounts of "the Asian business," known as *het Indisch Bedrijf*.

In the Company's first decade, the outbound fleets, averaging nearly ten ships annually, were supplied with a combination of military force and trading capital intended to secure access to the Moluccan (spice) islands. One year's *equipage* (the full cost of equipping and operating the yearly fleets) averaged nearly half the total capital stock of the new Company. Since a second fleet departed before the first return fleet could be expected, the VOC's initial capitalization quickly became fully committed. A great deal hinged on the profitability of the first return fleets.

The early return fleets benefited from high prices for pepper and spices, and the *Heren XVII* reinvested the proceeds in the expansion of the fleets and the shipment of a large trading capital (the *cargazoen*) to Asia. By 1610 the Company's original trading capital had been enlarged by some 40 percent, but the shareholders had yet to receive a penny.

As the VOC approached the end of its first decade of operation, the *bewindhebbers* felt considerable pressure to declare a dividend. Many smaller investors were disposing of their shares out of disappointment, while complaining of the directors' blatant refusal to honor a stipulation in the Company's charter to declare dividends when profits reached a certain size. The *bewindhebbers*, perhaps because they received substantial honoraria for their work on behalf of the Company (they shared 1 percent of the equipage costs), insisted on reinvesting the profits. Their aim was to expand the operations of the VOC sufficiently to secure its place vis-à-vis its Portuguese and English rivals.

The first dividend, paid in 1610, took the form of a distribution of pepper and mace. This was but the first of many dividends paid in kind rather than in cash. By the Company's calculation, the value of the distributed spices amounted to a 125 percent dividend, but many shareholders doubted that they could actually realize that return.

Dividends in kind were sometimes a device by which the Company transferred to the shareholders a portion of its problem of maintaining commodity prices when large inventories built up in its warehouses. Of course, payment in this form was not as bizarre as it might appear, since many shareholders (especially the large ones) were also merchants in Asian products. Nevertheless, many shareholders refused to take delivery of their dividends in 1610 and 1611. Under pressure, the *Heren XVII* agreed to pay cash dividends to these obdurate shareholders, but they made them wait several years. Thereafter, the payment of dividends in kind (now usually cloves) occurred repeatedly until 1644. Altogether some 40 percent of the declared value of all VOC dividends in the first fifty years took the form of cloves, mace, and pepper.

The decisions to establish an Asian headquarters in 1613, and to finance Jan Pietersz. Coen's expansive vision, required a major increase of the Company's capital stock. From 1613 to 1630, the annual shipments of specie to Asia rose to double the earlier level. The construction and equipping of ships rose steeply as well, for the VOC was now committed to supplying Batavia with a fleet of vessels to be permanently stationed in Asian waters.

Raising all this capital internally proved impossible, in part because of the competitive strength of the Portuguese and the English. Until 1620 the Portuguese continued to land roughly as many tons of Asian commodities in Europe as did the Dutch, which tended to depress prices. Moreover, the Twelve Year's Truce with Spain – and hence, with Portugal – extended to Asia, inhibiting after 1609 Dutch efforts to reduce the trade of their rival by force. The English, too, acted to build their trade in the Indonesian archipelago, and although the VOC generally succeeded in pushing them aside, the anticipated need for English friendship in Europe induced the Company directors in 1620 to concede to the English a one-third share of the spice trade. True monopoly power remained out of reach.

Between 1613 and 1620, the VOC borrowed 5.6 million guilders in order to finance *equipages* that exceeded considerably the revenues generated by the sale of return goods. The Company incurred further debts thereafter (see Table 9.3, column h). By 1630 a policy of limiting dividends in favor of the internal reinvestment of profits and the contraction of short-term debt succeeded in endowing the new Batavian headquarters with a capital stock (consisting of specie, European merchandise, and an inventory of Asian return goods) of 6.8 million guilders. Meanwhile, the fleet had been expanded sufficiently to sustain the departure of 50 percent more ships from Patria than in the period before 1620. The VOC's economic power now vastly overshadowed that of its European rivals in Asia.

The growth of the VOC had involved a risky policy of investment that depended on borrowing, the subordination of shareholders interests, and a strong measure of faith in the future. But beginning around 1630, the Company's growth proceeded, much as Coen had envisioned, on a much more agreeable basis. A golden age of profit had dawned.

A major investment in Asia was about to bear fruit, but the Company's organization, and particularly its bookkeeping practices, never were altered to reflect the multilateral character that was becoming the basis of its strength. The VOC's organization in Patria was that of a decentralized bilateral trading company, and it never ceased to reflect its origins out of six separate trading partnerships. The directors sent annually a list of the goods that they wished to have sent back – the *Eis der Retouren* – and accompanied this list with ships, men, supplies, precious metals, and goods in quantities that they deemed adequate to accomplish the task set in that list.

Corresponding to this annual process was a bookkeeping system that recorded all the costs incurred in Patria (i.e., the *equipage*) and all the revenues received in Patria (the *retouren*: the proceeds of the sale of goods returned by the Company in Asia). This bookkeeping system revealed nothing about the acquisition costs of the various goods or anything else about the business conducted within Asia.

The *Heren XVII* composed their list of requested goods in the early spring of each year. It arrived in Batavia, 13,500 nautical miles away, some nine months later, at the end of the year. At that time, between November and March of the following year, the return fleet set sail for Europe, but these ships were laden with goods requested in the *previous* year's list. In the course of the following year, ships set out from Batavia to various Asian destinations and returned within a year (on a schedule dictated by the monsoons) to assemble the cargoes for the returning fleet, which would sail between November and March and arrive in the Republic in September, two and one-half years after the dispatch of the list. With a commercial cycle of this length, careful coordination of the European and Asian branches of the Company was impossible. The high degree of autonomy exercised by the governor-general in Batavia, and by lesser personages at factories

Table 9.3. *Financial results of the VOC in Patria, 1602–50 (in thousands of guilders per year, unless noted otherwise).*

Year	A Revenues	B Equipage	C Patria surplus (A – B)	D Dividends	E Cash dividends
1602–10	[3,400]	[2,850]	550	0	0
1610–20	[3,400]	[3,800]	–400	1,288	765
1620–30	[4,750]	[4,000]	750	531	370
1630–40	[6,600]	[4,500]	2100	1,433	612
1640–50	7,922	5,594	2,328	1,195	1,401

F	G	H	I	J	K
Retained surplus (C – E)	Internal capital formation (years × f cumulative)	Debt: anticipatie penningen	Average price share (in guilders)	Current yield: total (D/I)	Current yield: cash (E/I)
550	4,400		134	0	0
-1,165	-7,250	5,600	160	12.50%	7.40%
380	-3,450	8,500	175	4.70%	3.30%
1,488	11,430	11,300	256	8.70%	3.70%
927	20,700	10,200	459	6.50%	4.80%

Sources: COL. A: REVENUES. The income from sale of Asia goods in Europe: From 1640, F. Gaastra, *Geschiedenis van de VOC* (Haarlem, 1982), p. 135. Before 1640 the revenue is estimated at a declining "gross margin" of the invoice value of goods shipped to Europe. COL. B: EQUIPAGE. The total costs of building, outfitting, and operating VOC ships incurred by the Chambers in Patria plus trading and other operating costs. Before 1640 these costs are estimated as an average of (1) 430 guilders per ton departing Patria, (2) 180,000 guilders per ship departing Patria, and (3) 1,000 guilders per crew member departing Patria. Added to this sum is the cargazoen, the value of specie and commodities shipped to Asia for trade purposes. COLS. D AND E: DIVIDENDS. G. C. de Klerk de Reus, *Geschichtliche Ueberblick der administrativen, rechlichen, und finanziellen Entwicklung der Niederländischen Ostindischen Compagnie* (The Hague, 1894), Beilage VI. Column E records the value of cash dividend minus the imported value of dividends paid in kind. In 1610–20 payments in kind were protested by shareholders, and the Company eventually agreed to give the dissatisfied shareholders the option of receiving cash. We do not know how many shareholders exercised this right. We assume here that half of these dividends were paid in cash. COL. H: DEBT. In this period the Company's only sizable debt took the form of short-term borrowing from the Bank.of Amsterdam. The figures shown are the total debt at the end of the period. Niels Steensgaard, "The Dutch East India Company as an Institutional Innovation," in M. Aymard, ed., *Dutch Capitalism and World Capitalism* (Cambridge and Paris, 1982), p. 249. COL. I: AVERAGE PRICE OF VOC SHARES ON AMSTERDAM BEURS. The prices given are averages of available quotations. J. G. van Dillen, "Effectenkoersen aan de Amsterdamse beurs, 1723–94," *Economisch historisch jaarboek* 17 (1931), 1–46; Jonathan Israel, Dutch Primacy in World Trade, 1585–1740 (Oxford, 1989), Tables 5.19 and 6.13. COLS. J AND K: CURRENT YIELD. The dividend as a percentage of the average share price (i.e., the yield that a new buyer of VOC shares could expect to receive).

throughout Asia, was clearly only partially the result of willful insubordination and corruption.

Seen from the perspective of Batavia, the VOC was a multilateral but highly centralized trading company with a sales office in Europe. Its centralization in Batavia was deemed necessary in order to gather the information on which the success of the multilateral trading activities depended. There the decisions were made concerning the deployment of the trading capital maintained in Asia, a capital stock (rising to over 20 million guilders during the 1660s) that had been built up over the years by infusions from the Republic before 1630, and thereafter by the retention of profits earned in the inter–Asian trade (see Table 9.4). While the directors in the Republic regarded this capital as liquid assets waiting to be turned into goods for shipment to Europe, the administrators in Batavia saw it as capital stock to be used to earn a profit within Asia which then might or might not be repatriated to the Republic, depending on where the greatest return could be achieved.

At the risk of oversimplification, the inter–Asian trade can be reduced to two principal activities: first, the sale of textiles and other, mainly Asian, merchandise in markets where it could be exchanged for precious metals or goods required for shipment to Europe; and second, the disposal of pepper and spices in Asian markets in such a way as to control the flow of these commodities to Europe and achieve a rough global optimization of revenue. Obviously, both of these activities had a direct impact on the Asia–Europe trade. The first could reduce expenses in Patria for goods and specie to be shipped to Asia (the *cargazoen*), while the second could increase the gross margins at which the Company's goods were sold in Europe. The separate accounts kept in Batavia and the Republic did nothing to facilitate an integrated approach to the inter–Asian and Europe–Asia trades, but we should not be misled by bookkeeping conventions into believing that the inter–Asian trade was an autonomous business, separate from the financial results of the chambers in Patria.

By the mid–seventeenth century, commercial reality corresponded closely to the multilateral trading company envisioned by the administrators in Asia. Commodities acquired in Asia were sold where they were expected to yield the largest profit, whether that was elsewhere in Asia or in the Netherlands. The Batavian headquarters' chastisement in 1645 of one of its merchants stationed in Japan illustrates both the multilateral character of the Company's operations, and the difficulty that some employees had in understanding its implications. The *Opperkoopman* (Chief Merchant) Pieter Overwater had exercised poor commercial judgment, declared the High Council, because he had shipped Persian silk from Japan, where it could not be sold above its purchase price, to Batavia for transshipment to Patria. This, the report insisted, had been a great mistake. Overwater should have realized that the sale of the silk in Japan, even at a low price, could enable him to acquire Japanese silver which, in turn, could be exchanged on the Coromandel coast (of India) for cloth, which would realize at least a 100 percent profit at Batavia. This chain of transac-

Table 9.4. *Financial results of the VOC in Asia, 1613–50: "Het Indisch Bedrijf" (in thousands of guilders per year, unless noted otherwise).*

	A	B	C	D	E	F	G	H
Year	Total revenue	Trade revenue	Trade as % of total revenue [b/c]	Total expenses	Asian surplus (B – D)	From (+) or to (–) Patria	Change in "Indisch Kapitaal" (E + F)	"Indisch Kapitaal" (years × G cumulative)
1613–20	635	383	60.30%	735	-100	700	600	4,800
1620–30	1,820	1,419	78.00%	1,720	100	105	205	6,850
1630–40	2,835	2,497	88.10%	1,645	1,190	-613	577	12,620
1640–50	3,743	3,336	89.10%	2,700	1,043	-669	374	16,360

Sources: See sources to Table 10.7.

tions would yield a superior total return than the simple sale in Patria and would achieve a quicker turnover of capital to boot.[10]

The Company in Asia was no longer simply filling the orders placed by the *Heren XVII* in their annual list of required goods, although, of course, these orders could not be ignored. VOC merchants had to remain informed about market conditions throughout Asia.

The trade with Surat and Persia illustrates the difficult decisions faced by the Company's merchants, and the importance to them of accurate information about conditions in multiple markets. The diversion of pepper and spices to these markets could serve both to limit supply and raise prices in Europe, and to acquire Persian silks and specie and Gujarati cloth, all of which were in demand in other Asian markets. But if the pepper and spices were sold too cheaply, they could be re-exported overland to Europe, undermining the Company's profitability there.

The VOC's chief interest at the Coromandel Coast, Bengal, and China (via Formosa) was the acquisition of silks, cotton textiles, and porcelain for shipment to Japan. The Company acquired some of these goods in exchange for other commodities, including Ceylonese elephants, which were highly prized in India and became a VOC monopoly after 1658. But at least three-quarters of the Company's purchases in these markets always had to be paid for in cash.

In the inter–Asian trade, Japan played a strategic role, for here, on a much larger scale than in Persia, the VOC traded goods for precious metals. Here it realized its inter–Asian trading profits in a form that could be used in the most flexible possible way to acquire textiles, spices, and pepper and to pay operating expenses and accumulate trading capital. Japan's key role in supplementing specie shipments from Europe is revealed in Table 9.5. In the period 1630–80, the Company in Asia received annually more than 3 million guilders of silver and gold. This represented more than a doubling of the specie flow available to Batavia before 1630, when Japan emerged to become by far the single largest source of the VOC's specie supply.

The Japan trade flourished in part because Jan Pietersz. Coen strong-armed his way into the China trade; but of greater importance were policies pursued, for its own reasons, by the Japanese Shogunate. By prohibiting Japanese merchants from traveling abroad in 1635, by expelling the last remaining Portuguese in 1637, and more generally by embarking on a policy of seclusion, Japan became highly dependent on Chinese traders for its imports. Chaotic conditions in China in these years (the Manchu invasion), and a natural desire not to rely entirely on a single supplier, caused the Shogunate to turn to the VOC, which proved to be a politically acceptable and economically capable alternative supplier. What was expedient for Japan given its seclusion policy became a bonanza for the VOC. First at Hirado and after 1641 at Deshima (a tiny island in Nagasaki harbor to which the Japanese confined the Dutch throughout the seclusion era), the VOC realized the lion's share of its inter–Asian trade profits.

[10] F. Gaastra, *Geschiedenis van de VOC* (Haarlem, 1982), pp. 58–59.

Table 9.5. *Sources of specie at Batavia, 1613–1730 (in thousands of guilders per year).*

Period	Specie supplied from Patria	Specie acquired via *Assignaties*	From Japan	From Persia	Total
1613–20	1,437				1,437
1620–30	1,236		c. 400		1,636
1630–40	850		2,338		3,188
1640–50	920	377	1,519	427	3,243
1650–60	840	451	1,315	c. 600	3,206
1660–70	1,210	249	1,048	400–700	2,900–3,200
1670–80	1,130	430	1,154	400–700	3,100–3,400
1680–90	1,972	802	298	400–700	3,500–3,800
1690–1700	2,861	756	0	400–700	4,000–4,300
1700–10	3,928	640	0	c. 600	5,100–5,200
1710–20	3,883	1120	0	>300	5,300–5,400
1720–30	6,600	800	0	>300	7,700–7,800

Sources: Netherlands: J. R. Bruijn, F. S. Gaastra, and I. Schöffer, *Dutch-Asiatic Shipping in the 17th and 18th Centuries*, Vol. I, Rijksgeschiedkundige publicatiën, grote serie 165 (The Hague, 1987). Japan: Oskar Nachod, *Die Beziehungen der Niederländischen Ostindischen Kompagnie zu Japan im siebzehnten Jahrhundert* (Leipzig, 1897), Appendix E; Eiichi Kato, "Unification and Adaptation. The Early Shogunate and Dutch Trade Policies," in L. Blussé and F. S. Gaastra, eds., *Companies and Trade* (Leiden, 1981), pp. 207–9. Persia: W. Ph. Coolhaas, ed., *Generale Missiven*, Rijksgeschied-kundige publicatiën, grote serie 112 and 125 (The Hague, 1964, 1968), Vol. II, pp. 205, 247, 274, 294, 317, 377, 418, 550–1, 735; Vol. III, pp. 39, 173, 228, 334.

The period 1630–50 was exceptionally profitable for the VOC. The reason for this is directly related to the strategy of building the inter–Asian trade. The transfer to Batavia of scores of ships and 6.8 million guilders of working capital in the period 1613–30 now bore fruit in the form of large Asian profits (see Table 9.4, column e). These profits were sufficient to finance the continued expansion of the Asian capital stock and to "repatriate" a portion to Patria in the form of Asian commodities (Table 9.5, column f). The six chambers in the Republic now found themselves receiving year by year a growing number of ships laden with goods for which they had not been obliged to pay the full acquisition costs.

These goods (pepper and spices continued to account for 68 percent by value in 1648–50) generated steadily rising revenues in the Republic, but the expenses of the chambers grew more slowly since the *cargazoen* (the shipments of specie and trade goods intended for the purchase of return goods) was now, in effect, being subsidized by Batavia. Consequently the surplus of revenue over *equipage* costs, what the *Heren XVII* treated as the profit (Table 9.3, column c), rose to exceed 2 million guilders per year. Large dividends could now regularly be distributed, amounting in the 1630s to annual returns of 22 percent of the original investment, and 30 percent in the 1640s. But until 1644 over half of these distributions continued to be paid in kind. The *Heren XVII* retained over half of their cash surplus in these decades for reinvestment in the further expansion of the business. They added over 20 million guilders to the capital stock of the firm in Patria in these years (Table 9.3, columns f and g).

The VOC's profitability and its high dividend payments found a ready response among traders at the *Beurs*. In 1630, despite the recent payment of several dividends, share prices remained below 200. The investor who had noted that Dutch commodity prices were then 77 percent higher than in 1602 could not have been overly impressed with his VOC shares. The dividends, averaging 10 percent per annum, would have pleased him more, but even then, approximately half that amount had been paid in kind.

The original investor, or more likely his heirs, who continued to hold VOC shares in 1650 (and who found a way to sell the dividends paid in kind at something near their declared value) numbered among the most fortunate investors of that or any age. Total dividend payments by 1650 exceeded eight times the initial investment, and this outward sign of the Company's profitability drove share prices to a high of 539 in 1648, and an average level of 450 in the years around 1650. The total return for an original investor who sold in 1648 averaged to 27 percent per annum.

9.5.7. Trade with Africa and the New World

In the 1590s, at the same time that Dutch ships first penetrated to the Mediterranean Sea and Indian Ocean, they also began trading in Equatorial West Africa, South America, and the Caribbean. Adventurous freebooters with stories of lucrative trade opportunities probably motivated the first of the expeditions to Africa. Soon thereafter, Portuguese (Sephardic) Jews (who could no longer carry on their trade in Portuguese colonial products at Antwerp because of the Dutch blockade of the Flemish coast begun in 1595) settled in Amsterdam and Middelburg, establishing merchant colonies with direct connections to Portugal and her empire in Brazil. Then, in 1598, the new Spanish king, Philip III, demonstrated his determination to crush the rebel Netherlanders by banning Dutch vessels from all Iberian harbors. Denied access to the salt of Setúbal, Dutch merchants cast about for alternative suppliers, a search that led them the following year to the salt lagoons of Punta de Araya, on the Venezuelan coast of South America.

The opportunities exposed by these varied events met with a vigorous response on the part of the Republic's merchants. Numerous sailings to West Africa led by 1600 to the formation by Amsterdam merchants of a *Guinea Compagnie*, a step soon imitated in Rotterdam, Delft, Dordrecht, and Zeeland. According to a petition made by these merchants in 1607, over 200 Dutch ships had sailed for Africa since 1592. In the 1610s some 20 ships per year sailed for West Africa laden with trade goods (textiles, copper, and ironwares) that were bartered at numerous coastal locations for ivory, hides, gum, and, most important, gold.

The Portuguese Jews newly resident in the Republic lost no time in cultivating their commercial contacts with Brazil. By 1609 it appears that at least half of Portugal's trade with its New World colony was ultimately destined for the Republic. The Dutch ships, usually under the Portuguese flag, brought rapidly increasing quantities of sugar to the Republic, such that the number of sugar refineries rose from 3 or 4 in 1594, to 29 by 1622, 25 of them in Amsterdam. During the Twelve Years' Truce, this trade grew with particular vigor, even though a Spanish motive for the truce had been the reduction of aggressive Dutch interloping in its colonial empire (which then included Portugal's empire as well).

The Venezuelan salt pans, according to a contemporary assessment, attracted no fewer than 768 Dutch vessels in the six years beginning in 1599. This overwhelming Dutch presence led to further exploration of the weak points in Spain's defenses of its monopoly over its colonial trades. In this reconnaissance, attention soon focused on South America's "Wild Coast," the region between the mouths of the Amazon and Orinoco rivers. Zeeland merchants had built small forts here already in the 1590s, and by 1613 they tried to plant settlements at the Essequibo and Corantine rivers with an eye to developing the region for plantation agriculture. From these little outposts, ships set out for the Spanish Caribbean islands of Española, Puerto Rico, and Cuba to trade in hides.

Yet another area of Dutch activity was North America, where in 1609 the Englishman Henry Hudson, while on a mission for the VOC to find a northeast passage to Asia, stumbled upon a splendid harbor and the majestic river that now bears his name. This expedition bore the intellectual imprint of the Amsterdam *predikant* Petrus Plancius, whose theory of an open polar sea had led to the disastrous voyage of Willem Barentsz. a decade earlier. In Hudson's case the results were far more satisfactory, but this had less to do with the worth of Plancius's geographical theories than with the fact that Hudson was 5,000 miles off course.[11] News of the discovery of what he now hoped would be a north*west* passage galvanized merchants eager for an alternative source of furs to Archangel and the French-controlled Saint Lawrence River. The chief investors, mostly Lutherans, merged their rival activities in 1614 to form the New Netherlands Company, which proceeded to build a fort near the confluence of the Mohawk and Hudson rivers (Fort Nassau), from where it traded with the Iroquois Indians for beaver pelts.

These varied trading ventures, in Africa, Brazil, Venezuela, the Wild Coast, and New Netherlands, had little in common except that they infringed on the exclusive claims of others and were all sensitively affected by the political situation in Europe. This common condition suggested to some the desirability of bundling these mercantile energies in a single chartered company capable of projecting a political and military power sufficient to defend Dutch trade and, more to the point, attack more directly the Spanish-Portuguese enemy than was possible with the marginal toeholds thus far acquired.

As early as 1600, the transplanted South Netherlander Willem Usselincx urged the formation of such a company. He had gained firsthand experience in the Atlantic trades and combined this commercial knowledge with a Calvinist social vision to advocate a joint-stock company that would pursue trade, organize Dutch colonization, and support a program of Christian education of the indigenous peoples. He envisioned the replacement of the Iberian empires based on slavery and the sword by a Dutch empire "rest[ing] on the foundation of goodwill and the irresistible example of Christian virtue."[12]

A draft charter for a West India Company – shorn of Usselincx's more visionary proposals – reached the States General in 1606 but soon fell victim to the diplomatic negotiations leading to the conclusion of a truce in the war between the Republic and Spain. Scrapping these plans to charter a West India Company became a concession made in negotiating the Twelve Years' Truce; and as long as the truce lasted, the States General could not allow the launching of an organization so obviously intent on dismembering Spain's New World empire.

This concession was bitterly resented in the more militant anti–Spanish and anti–Catholic circles that formed as the turbulent politico-religious disputes raged during the years of the truce. Jonathan Israel, the leading authority on Dutch-Iberian economic relations, affirms the validity of the grievances of these would-be empire-builders. Their hostility did not flow simply from a regrettable lack of patience; rather, it arose from their correct assessment that a "window of oppor-

---

[11] Oliver A. Rink, *Holland on the Hudson: An Economic and Social History of Dutch New York* (Ithaca, New York, 1986), pp. 24–7.

[12] Rink, *Holland on the Hudson*, p. 52.

tunity" was closing. In many ways the malleable world of the first decade of the century was to be an unyielding and resistant one by the third decade.

In 1621, as the truce lapsed, the "war party" was supreme in the Republic, and the States General granted a charter modeled on that of the VOC for the founding of a *Verenigde West Indische Compagnie* (henceforth, WIC). Usselincx had continued to campaign for a chartered company throughout the truce, so his influence over the WIC was considerable. Since his vision, rather like that of his contemporary Jan Pietersz. Coen at Batavia, went beyond the simple conduct of trade to advocate colonization and the acquisition of territorial possessions, Usselincx could play effectively upon religious and patriotic sentiments in soliciting supporters and investors. However, an abiding suspicion that the WIC's military expenses would undermine its profitability caused many others, especially experienced Amsterdam investors, to keep their distance.

The political and religious arguments played best in the provinces: The inland provinces generated 20 percent of the WIC's privately subscribed capital, and a similar proportion was raised in cities not active in oceanic trade. But these "innocent" enthusiasts could hardly compensate for the reluctance of Amsterdam's merchants. Ultimately, government concessions and direct government investment proved necessary to raise the initial capitalization of 7.1 million guilders, and even then it took three years.

The WIC was governed by nineteen directors (the *Heren XIX*) drawn from the Company's five chambers: Amsterdam with eight directors, Zeeland with four, Rotterdam, West Friesland (Hoorn and Enkhuizen), Friesland plus Stad en Lande (Groningen), with two each. In this case the odd (nineteenth) director represented the States General (which had invested 500,000 guilders and supplied a direct subsidy of the same size). The Company enjoyed a monopoly on trade for a territory embracing the west coast of Africa (below the Tropic of Cancer) and the entire New World.

In its first years, the new Company found it difficult to set a clear course. Its first military ventures, attacks on Bahia (in Brazil) and São Jorge da Mina (on the Gold Coast of Africa), both failed. In the absence of a new, profitable activity, the WIC was sustained only by privateering and the existing trades of its predecessor firms. Indeed, the various chambers acted to monopolize the pre–1621 trades of their local merchants: Zeeland claimed exclusive privileges on the Wild Coast of South America, the North Holland ports fought bitterly to keep the Venezuela salt trade under their control, and the Amsterdam chamber monopolized the New Netherlands enterprise.

So it remained until 1628, when the WIC suddenly achieved the greatest financial success of its history. Admiral Piet Heyn captured the entire Spanish silver fleet with its cargo of at least 11.5 million guilders' worth of silver. That great prize allowed the Company to pay a 75 percent dividend. It turned out to be the only large dividend that the WIC would ever pay, but for a fleeting moment, a verse used in the Company's promotional pamphlets rang true:

Westindjen Kan syn Nederlands groot gewin
Verkleynt 'svyands Macht brengt silver platen in.
[West India can become the Netherlands' great source of gain
Diminishing the enemy's power as it garners silver plate.]

Share prices immediately rose (to 206 in 1629), permitting the Company to attract additional capital to finance a large fleet of sixty-seven ships manned by some 7,000 sailors and soldiers. With this fleet the WIC relaunched in 1630 the one great venture expected to secure its future profitability, the conquest of Brazil from the Portuguese.

The conquest of Pernambuco (Recife) was followed by further territorial gains, putting the WIC in control of most of the settled, sugar-producing northeast by 1634. In that year the WIC also secured a permanent base of operations in the Caribbean by wresting Curaçao, with its excellent harbor, from the Spanish. In later years it added St. Eustatius, Saba, and (half of) St. Maarten to its possessions.

In 1636 Stadhouder Frederick Hendrik appointed his cousin, Prince Johan Maurits, as governor of New Holland, as Brazil came to be called, and the Company set about encouraging the expansion of sugar production. The Sephardic Jews of the Netherlands played a leading role in this enterprise. By 1644 they accounted for at least one-third of the white civilian population of Dutch Brazil, and they dominated the sugar trade.

Labor proved to be the weak link in the economic system being developed in Brazil. The plantations depended on slaves, the supply of which was inadequate to achieve increased production. Dutch merchants in West Africa had not been active in the slave trade in the pre–WIC era. They had concentrated on gold and ivory. The first Dutch slave shipments reached the New World in 1625, but in the absence of slave stations in West Africa, the trade remained episodic and difficult. The conquest of the Portuguese strongholds of São Jorge da Mina (renamed Elmina) in 1637 and of Luanda in Angola (1641) first put this trade on a secure footing. Up to 1636 it appears that the WIC landed no more than 2,800 slaves in the New World. In the following decade, the Dutch shipped 30,000 slaves, almost all to Brazil, and throughout the next three decades, now in possession of some twenty West African trading lodges, they had the dubious honor of being second only to the Portuguese as Atlantic slave traders.

Step by step the WIC had put together the elements needed for a triangular trade of Dutch merchandise to Africa (and South America), slave sales to the New World, and sugar exports to the Republic. There, the number of sugar refineries grew from 29 in 1622 to 54 in 1660. Refined sugar began to become a significant re-export commodity in northern European trade. The Company itself operated over 100 ships, and its employees reached the 10,000 level by 1644. The hope that New Netherlands could be integrated into this system as a supplier of foodstuffs completed the vision of an Atlantic trading system capable of contributing to the WIC's profitability just as the inter–Asian trade nourished the VOC.

The creation of this empire presupposed an investment that vastly exceeded the Company's original capital. Fortunately, the silver fleet windfall and the early success in Brazil in the 1630s eroded much of the reluctance that investors had shown a decade earlier. By 1639 the WIC succeeded in issuing 10 million guilders of new shares, 70 percent of which were purchased in Amsterdam, the former bastion of skepticism. Besides this new capital, the WIC's trade generated an average annual revenue between 1623 and 1636 of 2.6 million guilders. But the expenses incurred by the Company to 1636 averaged 3.2 million guilders per year; the cumulative losses by 1636 reached 7.8 million guilders, and they only grew thereafter.

One important reason for the WIC's later financial weakness was its inability to capture the full commercial benefits of its political and economic investments. The competitive and relatively accessible world of Atlantic trade could not be constrained to fit the WIC's structure, modeled so closely after the VOC, an Asian trading firm. In 1638 the WIC, under pressure from its now dominant Amsterdam shareholders, was forced to loosen its monopoly control of trade with Brazil and the Caribbean. Henceforth, these trades – but not others, such as the Africa trades, the slave trade, and all trade in ammunition – were open to all Company shareholders upon payment of a recognition fee. Consequently, the WIC handled only about one-third of the 6 to 7 million pounds of sugar (yielding nearly 4 million guilders in the Republic) exported annually from Brazil between 1637 and 1645. By 1648 the Atlantic trade was further liberalized: Then, any Dutchman, not only WIC shareholders, could participate upon payment of fees to the Company. Until then the WIC's loss was the private gain of its shareholders, and into the 1640s investors remained willing, despite the Company's many liabilities and poor dividend record, to buy its shares at or above par (as high as 134 in May 1640), a reflection of their abiding hopes for future Brazilian profits.

But this was not to be. The Portuguese planter class (*Moradores*) remained an important factor in New Holland, and with the restoration of Portuguese independence in 1640, their willingness to cooperate with the Dutch evaporated. They had not been badly treated under the enlightened administration of Prince Johan Maurits, but by shaking off Dutch rule, they could also shake off the 5-million-guilder debt that they had incurred in the purchase of slaves on credit extended by the WIC and Sephardic private traders. This was a loss that the WIC could ill afford, since it was already saddled by debt. Indeed, its penury had persuaded the Company to dismiss most of its troops (and the extravagant Prince Johan Maurits) as a cost-reducing measure in 1641, when the Republic signed a treaty with the newly independent Portugal. This proved to be a fatal misstep, for when the *Moradores* rose in revolt in 1645, the defenseless WIC found it difficult to persuade the States General to come to its rescue. Eventually, a squadron was sent to put pressure on the Portuguese, and the VOC contributed 1.5 million guilders to avoid being forced to merge with the hapless WIC, but the prevailing opinion in the Republic, and certainly in Amsterdam, was that good relations with Portugal (the premier source of salt) and free trade with New World sugar producers was preferable to investing millions in the recovery of New Holland. By 1654 the last areas under Dutch control (Recife and Paraiba) were relinquished, and the Brazilian adventure was brought to an end. Were the Dutch too rational to be good imperialists?

In retrospect this setback was decisive for the prospects of a Dutch Atlantic empire, and contemporaries understood immediately that it was decisive for the WIC: Its shares traded at 37 percent of par in 1646, fell to a dispirited 14 in 1650, and fell to practically zero by 1654. The WIC's shareholders suffered massive losses, yet the Dutch merchants active in this Atlantic economy responded with considerable resourcefulness to salvage what they could and to secure new areas for growth – now as ordinary traders rather than as belligerent crusaders.

The Dutch Caribbean island of Curaçao emerged as the major slave market for the West Indies. Instead of sending captive Africans to Brazil, the WIC (whose activities after 1648 were largely confined to the slave trade, the African gold trade, and the administration of its territorial possessions) sent them to Curaçao for sale to English, French, and Spanish buyers. The West Indian demand for slaves rose as the Jewish planters left Brazil to establish new sugar plantations elsewhere. Some colonized the Wild Coast; others settled on the English island of Barbados and, later, French Martinique. With Dutch encouragement and assistance, these Caribbean islands switched from growing tobacco and foodstuffs with European settlers to growing sugar with slave labor. The Dutch now functioned again primarily as traders: as the chief source of slaves, the low-cost suppliers of European manufactured goods, and the main transporter of sugar to Europe.

Meanwhile, in New Netherlands, the WIC sought to stimulate farming by granting large tracts of land to private partnerships. Between the colonizing activities of these investors, called *patroons*, and the founding of New Amsterdam on Manhattan Island (in 1623), a growing colony supported a modest trade, mainly with Amsterdam. The 9,000 inhabitants of New Netherlands in 1664 made it the third largest settler society in North America, after Massachusetts and the Chesapeake, but the beaver pelts, grain, and timber of this colony could not excite Dutch merchants as could the sugar of Brazil, or even Barbados. It remained, at best, in the peripheral vision of the Republic's New World traders.

9.5.8. Merchant shipping at mid-seventeenth century

The foreign trade of the Northern Netherlands had already been very large – when reckoned on a per capita basis – on the eve of the Revolt. Brulez's calculations for the 1560s yield a level of per capita imports some 4.5 times that of England or France. His estimates refer to the entire Habsburg Netherlands, and they should be accepted only as a rough indicator of the difference between the Low Countries and neighboring lands. But there can be no doubt that the products of the *Oost-* and *Westvaart* passing through the harbors of Holland and Zeeland had profoundly affected the structure of the regional economy.

From the time that the northern provinces were securely out of reach of Spanish troops until the middle of the seventeenth century, both the volume and the value of Dutch foreign trade rose enormously. No comprehensive quantitative data stand at our disposal to buttress this claim, but the foregoing survey of trade development allows for no other conclusion.

The growth pattern of foreign trade up to the mid–seventeenth century divides into two distinct periods. The first, from the 1580s until 1621, coupled a very rapid pace of growth with an explosive expansion into new trading areas. The second period, after 1621, brought further growth and expansion, but it now occurred in a general European environment of contracting trade and in the face of a determined resistance by neighboring countries to Dutch ascendency. Consequently, the overall rate of growth slowed, and the short-term fluctuations became more pronounced.

The size of the Dutch merchant fleet grew rapidly in this period, giving rise to a major shipbuilding industry and a market of such size as to induce numerous innovations in ship design and construction techniques. We have already reviewed the sixteenth-century estimates of the number of seagoing vessels. The 400 such ships thought to be operating from Holland in 1532 surely had grown to a larger number by the eve of the Revolt, for the Baltic trade alone then made use of over 400 Dutch vessels.

The resumed growth after the Revolt raised the total number of Dutch seagoing merchant vessels active in European waters to an estimated 1,750 by 1636. This, at any rate, is the figure presented by a government report prepared to forecast the revenue that could be expected from a planned tax on shipping capacity, the *lastgeld*. Excluded from this figure are the 600-odd busses of the herring fleet and the ships sailing for the VOC and WIC. The former's fleet in 1659 numbered 119, most of which were sailing permanently in Asian waters. These East Indiamen were some three or four times larger than the *fluits* sailing in Europe. The WIC operated over 100 ships in the 1630s.

The government estimate provided for 450 smallish vessels of 40 to 80 tons that handled the *kleine vaart*, the coastal trades stretching between Hamburg and Rouen, including the British Isles. Around the turn of the seventeenth century, regularly scheduled sailings between two points accepting cargo at fixed and published rates (*beurtveren*), sprang up to connect many of these nearby destinations with Dutch ports. The intensity of traffic in this region appears to have risen. At mid-century, English observers complained that Dutch ships made up from one-quarter to one-half of all ships calling at London and other east coast ports. Hamburg recorded the arrival of 994 Dutch ships in 1633; by comparison, only 22

French and 61 English vessels called in that year. It seems likely that far more than 450 Dutch vessels were active in the *kleine vaart*, but most of those vessels were very small.

Obviously, any estimate of the size of the merchant fleet is sensitive to the lower size limit employed. It is perhaps for this reason that foreigners often estimated the mid–seventeenth century Dutch fleet as exceeding the seemingly fantastic level of 10,000 vessels.

Keeping in mind the uncertainty of these estimates, and the presence of many unenumerated small coastal vessels, it is probably safe to conclude that the Dutch fleet rose to a peak level of some 2,000 seagoing merchant ships by the mid–seventeenth century. From the several score East Indiamen of 450 lasts through the many hundreds of *fluits* of 90 to 120 lasts, to the larger coastal vessels of 40 lasts, this fleet possessed a total carrying capacity of some 400,000 tons (2 tons = 1 last). At this time it stood head and shoulders above any other national fleet in Europe. England's merchant fleet probably failed to reach one-quarter the size of the Dutch fleet then, and it was generally thought that the Dutch fleet alone exceeded the combined size of the fleets of England, France, and Spain.

In this connection a word should be said about the impact of piracy and wartime confiscations. Dutch privateers – this was long a Zeeland specialty – had a considerable reputation; the WIC claimed to have taken 547 Iberian ships as prizes between 1623 and 1636. But generally the sheer size of the Dutch fleet exposed the Republic more than other nations to a large risk of loss. The notorious Dunkirk privateers posed a danger to Dutch shipping in the English Channel all the while war with Spain raged (until France captured Dunkirk in 1646). In the period 1626–34, Dunkirk piracy was responsible for sinking 336 ships, capturing 1,499, and raising though the sale of prizes over 11 million guilders. Eighty percent of this booty represented Dutch vessels and their cargoes. In the entire period 1626–46, their depredations netted ships valued in excess of 22 million guilders. Total Dutch losses in the 25-year period after 1621 are said to have reached 3,000 vessels (many of them fishing boats and small coastal craft), or an average of 125 per year.

No sooner did these heavy losses end, but the wars with Britain posed a new danger. Charles Wilson claims that the English captured at least 1,000 ships (against 351 English vessels captured by the Dutch) during the First Anglo-Dutch War (1652–4) and that these prizes "turned the English fleet into a well-balanced one."[13] During the Second Anglo-Dutch War (1655–7), the English captured some 500 Dutch vessels, but this time the Dutch captured a roughly equal number of English vessels. If these claims are anywhere near the truth, the rapid growth of the Dutch fleet – doubling or tripling in size between the 1580s and 1630s – is all the more extraordinary.

[13] C. H. Wilson, *Profit and Power: A Study of England and the Dutch Wars* (London, 1957), p. 13.

Associated with the growth of the merchant marine was the expansion of harbor facilities and the growth of port cities. The record of physical construction (see Table 2.3) tracks closely the chronology of trade growth presented earlier: 35 separate harbor expansion projects in the period 1578–1621, 7 more in 1621–50, and only 4 in the remaining life of the Republic.

Naturally, the growth of the merchant marine brought about an increased demand for sailors. Little can be said about employment levels in shipping during the sixteenth century, except that early on it had a pronounced seasonal character, reinforced by the use of fishing vessels in the Baltic trade. Later, the technical improvements in ship design that reduced the crew required per ton of shipping capacity ensured that the number of sailors did not grow as fast as the growth of the merchant marine itself.

Modern estimates of the number of seamen go back to 1610, when the European trades employed nearly 20,000 men while the fledgling East and West India trades employed an additional 4,000. Once the ocean fishing industry and the naval forces are added, a total of 33,000 men, or roughly 8 percent of all the Republic's males above fifteen years of age, earned their livelihood at sea. By the 1630s the numbers had grown to 46,000, and by the 1680s to a peak of 50,000. Table 9.6 summarizes the employment estimates and shows clearly that the growth after the early decades of the century depended almost entirely on the intercontinental trades and, after mid-century, on whaling.

The dynamism of oceanic trade in the sixteenth and early seventeenth centuries is revealed by the reorientation of urban population toward the port cities. As nearly as we can tell, all the port cities of Zeeland and Holland together housed no more than 70,000 inhabitants in the first quarter of the sixteenth century, or about 7 or 8 percent of the population of the Northern Netherlands. By the mid–seventeenth century, these same cities had grown sixfold, housing at least 400,000 inhabitants, or 20 percent of the Republic's total.

Almost every port grew substantially, but some grew more than others. Dordrecht ceased to be a major factor in ocean trade and oriented its commerce toward the river trades on the Maas and Rhine. Its population barely doubled between the early sixteenth and mid–seventeenth centuries. At the same time, the nearby city of Rotterdam emerged to play a major role in foreign trade, particularly with England and France. It grew from 5,000 to 30,000 inhabitants. The other Maas cities also grew, mainly on the strength of the herring fishery.

About the Zeeland ports, little is known. They grew in the sixteenth century as Antwerp's outports, and after the closure of the Schelde, Middelburg boomed as Flemings shifted their activities to that city. Its population grew, reaching 30,000 by 1650 and fueling aspirations to rival Amsterdam as a great trading city. But as we have seen, Middelburg's competitive position weakened at an early stage, and many of her recently arrived merchants drifted north to Amsterdam.

The cities of the Zuider Zee all grew rapidly until the mid–seventeenth cen-

Table 9.6. *Approximate employment levels in Dutch shipping, 1610–1825.*

Zone	1610	1630–40	1680	1725	1770	1825
Europe						
Baltic	4,000	4,000	2,000			
North Sea	500	800	800			
Iberia and Med.	5,000	6,000	6,000			
England	1,000	1,000	500			
France	4,500	4,500	4,000			
Archangel	500	1,000	1,200			
Norway	4,000	4,200	4,000			
West India & W. Africa	2000	4,000	2,000			
Total Merchant Marine	21,500	25,500	22,500	22,000	21,000	17,000
VOC	2,000	4,000	8,500	11,000	11,500	—
Ocean fishing	6,500	7,000	6,500	4,000	4,000	2,000
Whaling	0	1,500	9,000	9,000	6,000	—
Admiralties	3,000	8,000	3,500	3,500	2,000	5,000
Total	33,000	46,000	50,000	49,500	44,500	24,000

Sources: J. Lucassen, "Zeevarenden," in L. M. Alveld, S. Hart, and W. J. van Hoboken, eds., *Maritieme geschiedenis der Nederlanden*, Vol. 2 (Bussum, 1977), pp. 131–2; J. R. Bruijn, "Zeevarenden," in F. J. A. Broeze, J. R. Bruijn, and F. S. Gaastra, eds., *Maritieme geschiedenis der Nederlanden*, Vol. 3 (Bussum, 1977), p. 147; J. R. Bruijn and J. Lucassen, eds., *Op de schepen der Oost-Indische Compagnie* (Groningen, 1980), p. 14.

tury, but here, too, the rise of Amsterdam undermined their position, forcing them to specialize in particular activities: the herring fishery for Enkhuizen, the timber and salt trades for Hoorn.

The big winner in the competitive struggle among these numerous ports was Amsterdam. Its growth from some 30,000 inhabitants during the Revolt to 104,000 by 1622 and 200,000 by the 1660s outstripped all of its rivals. One might add to these numbers the growing population of the nearby Zaan villages, whose shipbuilding and industrial economy was closely tied to the Amsterdam harbor.

The revenue generated by the *Convooien en licenten*, a tax on imports and exports, is not a flawless indicator of commercial activity, but it can serve to reveal the changing relative importance of the various ports. In the period 1589–96, the Zeeland ports accounted for 39 percent of total revenue, while Rotterdam and other south Holland ports raised 25 percent, and Amsterdam and the other Zuider Zee ports brought in 36 percent. By the 1620s the proportions had shifted radically in favor of Amsterdam. It and the other Zuider Zee ports regularly collected about 58 percent of the *Convooien en licenten* revenues, while Zeeland's share had plummeted by half to 20 percent. Rotterdam's share, by contrast, had held roughly constant at about 21 percent.

The competition among the numerous ports was far from over, but by the mid–seventeenth century, no port could challenge Amsterdam's leading position. The continued prosperity of the other ports depended on their finding specialized niches in the Republic's trading system. This was a particular problem for Middelburg, which more than the others had sought to function as a full-fledged commercial center with interests in Europe, Asia, and the New World, and yet whose own hinterland had become a backwater with the closing of the Schelde and the gradual reorientation of the Flemish and Brabant economies away from maritime commerce.

In an international setting in which Amsterdam's merchants achieved the upper hand in competition with such considerable rivals as Hamburg, London, Rouen, and even Lisbon and Seville, it can come as no surprise that they also came to dominate domestic rivals such as Enkhuizen, Rotterdam, and Middelburg. In this context what is worth emphasizing, both because it is so unexpected and so important to understanding the Republic's economy, is the relative success of these secondary centers in preserving a measure of autonomy, either as rivals (Middelburg) or as complementary trading centers (Rotterdam and Hoorn). The organizational structures of the VOC and WIC, not to mention the political organization of the Republic itself, sought to achieve this result, of course. Not for nothing had these cities led the fight (while Amsterdam stood aside) for independence from a centralizing political authority.

Nevertheless, by the 1620s Amsterdam's international leadership could be denied by no one. Her metamorphosis had been the result of initiatives in several interrelated areas; the aggressive extension of new trade routes to the Arctic, the Mediterranean, Asia, and the West Indies have already been described. What is particularly noteworthy about this expansion is the degree to which merchants were prepared to assume risks on so many fronts at once, and to raise the stakes, committing ever larger sums, even in the face of mounting losses and uncertainties.

The institutional renovation of Amsterdam capitalism also occurred in the first two decades of the seventeenth century, as shown in Chapter 4. What deserves repetition here is that Amsterdam's commercial leadership was not simply an inheritance, a torch passed from Antwerp. The young northern city on the IJ unquestionably benefited from Antwerp's misfortunes: She received a large share of Antwerp's capital and also was much influenced by Antwerp's commercial practices and institutions. However, Amsterdam became a different sort of commercial center than Antwerp had been in its day. Just as Antwerp's vitality was being undermined long before it succumbed to the Duke of Parma's army in 1585 and by factors unrelated to Amsterdam's competition, so Amsterdam's growth began long before the fall of Antwerp and had many sources besides those transferred to the north during and after the Revolt. The essential difference between the two cities in their eras of hegemony was this: Antwerp had united European commerce as a meeting point of merchants from north and south; Amsterdam united European commerce by going out and knitting it together. Through the activities of its merchants, supported by effective state power, it became the mustering point for the goods of the world, or, as one contemporary said, it was "the warehouse of the world, the seat of opulence, the rendezvous of riches, and the darling of the gods."[14]

---

[14] Fernand Braudel, *Civilization and Capitalism*, Vol. 3, *The Perspective of the World* (New York, 1984), p. 189.

Chapter 10
Foreign trade after
the mid–seventeenth century

10.1. Hegemony and crisis

A description of the Dutch trading system at its peak is rendered difficult by the fleeting nature of that "hegemonic moment." If we follow tradition to regard the signing of the Peace of Westphalia in 1648 as the symbolic high point of both Dutch political stature and economic preponderance, then we must conclude that the Republic's offensive economic posture shifted to a defensive one before ink on the treaty signed at Münster had dried. The First Anglo-Dutch War, which began in 1652, ushered in a twenty-five-year period of repeated attacks – both military and economic – on Dutch commercial hegemony; and while none of these efforts could undo the Republic's economic leadership, they placed it in a new environment of instability and defensiveness. Grand Pensionary Pauw captured the situation perfectly when he observed ruefully as the First Anglo-Dutch War began: "The English are about to attack a mountain of gold; we are about to attack a mountain of iron."

The contractionary pressures working on the Dutch in this period were numerous. Besides the trade-inspired wars waged by the English and French (1652–4, 1664–7, 1672–6), there were the protectionist measures designed to limit the scope of Dutch trade. Most famous are the English Navigation Acts, introduced in 1651 and revised in 1660 and at intervals thereafter. Its chief provisions sought to limit the Republic's trade with England to direct trade between the two countries. That is, the Acts sought to end Dutch trade in goods originating in or destined for third countries – the heart and soul of the Dutch entrepôt function.

The Dutch Republic remained Europe's dominant trading nation through the second half of the seventeenth century, and this chapter describes the nature of her commercial leadership. But, simultaneously, Dutch trade had to respond to new constraints, more numerous and more unyielding than before, which gradually transformed the character of the Dutch entrepôt, altering its relationship to the domestic economy as well as its functions in the international economy.

A second purpose of the Navigation Acts was to wean England from dependence on Dutch industry, particularly in shipbuilding and its ancillary trades, with tariffs and trade restrictions. Finally, the Acts placed new restrictions on the trade of English colonists, forcing them to deal directly with the mother country and to make exclusive use of English or colonial ships. In other words, the colonies could no longer legally make use of Dutch shipping and commercial services.

The continued dependence of England on Dutch commerce caused these laws to be evaded on a large scale. Some were eventually withdrawn or redefined. But there can be little doubt as to the long-run effect of England's new mercantilist policy: It systematically restricted the scope of Dutch trade with England and its colonies, by protecting English merchants and shippers and by nurturing import-substituting industries, thereby reducing the demand for goods supplied by the Dutch entrepôt.

English mercantilism posed its greatest danger in raising up, in the fullness of time, a competitor for the leadership of the international economy. French mercantilism posed a greater immediate danger, for it threatened to deny the Dutch access to their largest single market. The French economy differed from the English in being more complementary to that of the Dutch, rather than directly competitive with it. In this way it was more like Spain, where the complementarity was such that the two nations had continued to trade with each other even when at war. However, France differed from Spain in its dissatisfaction with this state of affairs. Under Louis XIV France took active measures to end its dependence on the Dutch entrepôt.

Already in 1659 the French introduced high, discriminatory fees on Dutch vessels calling at and departing from French ports. These were no sooner moderated, in 1662, than the new *Controleur-General des Finances*, J. B. Colbert, struck out in two directions at once. He introduced new, higher tariffs in 1664 and raised them to prohibitory levels in 1667. In addition he pushed through the establishment of state-subsidized French East and West India Companies in 1664, plus a *Compagnie du Nord* (established in 1669) to compete with the Dutch in the Baltic.

When these ambitious plans did not quickly yield their desired result, Louis XIV decided that a war of conquest might achieve what commercial policy could not. In 1672 he led 120,000 troops plus those of the Bishops of Cologne and Münster down the Rhine valley while, in alliance with England, a fleet of 146 warships prepared to blockade the Dutch coasts.

The Republic withstood this massive two-pronged attack, as it had fended off the seaborne attacks of England in 1652-4 and 1665-7. But these wars, motivated by overtly economic issues, inflicted substantial damage on the Republic's economy in the form of higher taxes, interrupted trade, captured ships, and the further spread of protectionist measures.

For where the English and French led, other nations soon followed with protectionist legislation of their own. In the decade after 1674, the Republic's diplomats were kept busy negotiating trade pacts with France (to revoke the intolerable 1667 tariff list), Portugal, Sweden, Denmark, and Spain. In each case their aim was to support the Republic's entrepôt function by preserving access to the markets of these countries in the face of new protectionist policies.

This patchwork of treaties did not long stand; in 1687 the most important of them, with France, came unraveled as Louis XIV effectively banned the import of Dutch herring and then, a few months later, reinstated the draconian tariff of 1667. Within the next year, the Republic's cautious diplomacy was abandoned in favor of Willem III's English adventure and what inevitably followed, renewed war with France.

Active resistance to Dutch trading primacy did not limit itself to Europe. As later sections of this chapter show, restrictive forces were at work in Asia and the New World as well. These many efforts to throttle Dutch commercial expansion were not simply jealous reactions to her success; they should also be understood in the context of the international economic stagnation and declining commodity prices that characterized much of the second half of the seventeenth century. In the new economic and political environment after 1650, the continuation of rapid economic growth for an already dominant economic power could hardly be expected. What surprises, in this context, is the very temporary nature of the setbacks and the continued Dutch mastery of international trade throughout the 1650s and '60s. With unrestricted access to Iberia and the Mediterranean, the engine of Dutch trade could fire with all cylinders, and contractionary forces were not yet at full strength.

The Republic's primacy in foreign trade withstood all challengers in these decades; but after the crisis of 1672, the contractionary forces became much stronger and more persistent. The volume of Dutch trade within Europe declined sharply, while that of its chief rival, England, experienced unprecedented growth in 1675–88, precisely the period of adversity for the Republic. (English shipping tonnage rose from 200,000 to 340,000 tons between the 1660s and 1680s.) As early as 1673, the British ambassador to the Republic, Sir William Temple, reported to his government that in well-informed circles the Republic's trade was thought to be over its top and in decay. Most historians have discounted Temple's remarkably early diagnosis of economic decline as wishful thinking. The contraction of the 1670s was followed, after all, by periods of revival in the 1690s, again in the 1720s, and most notably during the Seven Years' War of 1756–63. This fluctuating pattern of decline and revival as charted by the trade levies, the *convooien en licenten,* and the annual number of arriving ships, has led most students of Dutch foreign trade to assume that the overall volume of that trade remained roughly constant until deep into the eighteenth century, and to conclude that the eighteenth-century history of Dutch trade is one of stagnation. That stagnation is often seen as the net result of ongoing defensive efforts to preserve as much of the Republic's seventeenth-century prosperity as possible, for as long as possible. In this view Dutch commerce was gradually overshadowed by the growing economies of England and France, but it did not decline absolutely until confronted by the successive shocks of 1780 (outbreak of the Fourth Anglo-Dutch War), 1795 (collapse of the old Republic), and 1806–13 (imposition of the Continental System and incorporation into Napoleon's French Empire).

Without question, the Republic's trade and shipping remained, long after 1672, the single greatest concentration of international economic activity in Europe, and its entrepôt function long dominated international markets. But in our view, it is fundamentally misleading to describe Dutch trade after 1670 in terms of long-term stability, maturity, conservation, and other terms suggesting continuity and a gradual fading of the vitality of a commercial complex – the *stapelmarkt* – that had attained its fullest expression in the mid-seventeenth century.

In what follows we interpret the decades after 1672, especially the first two, as an era posing major challenges to Dutch foreign trade. Sir William Temple's tidings of Dutch distress may have been what his government in London wanted to hear, but they were not just a product of wishful thinking. This era of distress gave rise to a number of responses and initiatives which, over a longer period stretching well into the next century, had the effect of restructuring Dutch foreign trade in several fundamental respects. In the eighteenth century, Dutch foreign trade played a different role in the international economy than it had in the seventeenth.

The external political and military pressures that arose to threaten Dutch trade after 1650 were not without their effects; but deep-seated, structural factors inflicted greater and more lasting damage to the Dutch trading system as it existed at the mid–seventeenth century. These long-term forces brought about a permanent reduction in the volume of trade in the chief commodities upon which Dutch trade depended.

We begin by examining what became of the foundation stones of Dutch trade in its "Golden Age." This is followed by a more detailed examination of new departures in the foreign trade sector, especially the East and West Indies trades. Finally, via a region-by-region study of trade after 1650, an overall assessment is offered of the evolving structure of Dutch foreign trade.

10.2. The main traded commodities

The enormous number of goods traded in the seventeenth-century Republic appears to present us with a daunting task. Yet, as is so often the case, a small number of goods accounted for a very large portion of the Republic's total foreign trade. Around the middle of the seventeenth century, six commodities held an

Table 10.1. *The volume of wine traded at Amsterdam, 1661–1808.*

| Period | Wine handled at Amsterdam | | Exported to the Baltic Hogsheads |
	Hogsheads	Liters (in millions)	
1661–70			5281
1671–80	135,535	31.2	5908
1681–90	160,645	37.0	6183
1691–1700	115,857	26.7	3451
1701–10	159,886	36.8	1515
1711–20	166,569	38.4	5786
1721–30	190,475	43.9	5475
1731–40	155,801	35.9	3955
1741–50	142,010	32.7	4084
1751–60	133,296	30.7	2817
1761–70	156,032	35.9	2266
1771–80	139,760	32.2	1955
1781–90	135,970	31.3	941[a]
1791–95	116,960	26.9	
1799–1808	89,066	20.5	

[a]1781–83

Sources: BALTIC SHIPMENTS: W. S. Unger, "De Sonttabellen voltooid," *Tijdschrift voor geschiedenis* 71 (1958), 158, 191; SHIPMENTS TO AMSTERDAM: G. A. Amsterdam, Part. Archief 343 [Aalmoezeniersweeshuis Archief]. The orphanage collected one stuiver per hogshead (230.4 liters) of wine (plus brandy and vinegar) handled at the port.

importance that deserves our special attention: grain, wine, salt, herring, textiles, and timber.

Wine, if the scraps of evidence at our disposal are any guide, ranked among the most important trade goods of the seventeenth and eighteenth centuries. Regretably, nearly nothing is known about the organization and development of the wine trade in the Republic. Such evidence as we have, summarized in Table 10.1, allows us to do little more than confirm a point made by Jacques Le Moine de l'Espine in his merchants' handbook of 1694, when he ranked wine with the "chief trades of Amsterdam."

Table 10.1 does suggest that little of the Republic's imported wine was re-exported. Not even 5 percent of Amsterdam's supply continued on toward the Baltic, which would have been its chief foreign destination. Thus, via Amsterdam alone, somewhere between 20 and 30 million liters of wine entered the domestic market annually. This unexpected relation between re-export and domestic consumption is confirmed by the foreign trade statistics of Amsterdam in 1667–8, the only year in the seventeenth century for which they have been preserved. Against an import of some 23,300 vats of French wine, only 2,700 vats were re-exported; against an import of 2,000 vats of Spanish wine, re-exports amounted to no more than 550.

These scraps of information, together with what is discussed in Chapter 11, convince us of the important place that wine held in the Repubic's foreign trade, but much more research is necessary before one can hope to write its history. We turn, therefore, to the five remaining chief articles of trade.

10.2.1. THE GRAIN TRADE

Grain was the commodity upon which Amsterdam built its trading preponderance in the Baltic in the sixteenth century, and grain was the commodity that gave Dutch merchants entrée to the Iberian and Mediterranean ports from the 1590s on. As the Dutch trading system expanded to new regions and handled a growing variety of goods, it never abandoned its primary commitment to the grain trade. Contemporaries no less than later historians were well aware of the central importance of this trade, this "source ende wortel van de notabelste commercie ende navigatie deser landen" [source and root of the most notable commerce and navigation of these lands] as Johan de Witt described it in the *Deductie* of 1671.

This prosaic trade stamped through its sheer bulk an indelible imprint on the commerce of the Republic. It influenced the design of the vessels that sailed each year by the hundreds to Baltic ports; it influenced commercial law and practice, as the thousands of notarial contracts and innumerable agreements to buy and sell at the *Beurs* encouraged uniformity, purchase by sample, and transparency in the distribution of information. It influenced the physical form of the port of Amsterdam, as storage facilities were created for tens of thousands of lasts of grain. In 1680, contemporaries claimed that 80 percent of all the city's warehouse space was devoted to the grain trade.

This bulky trade was a major source of employment. Lighters effected the transfer of grain between the ships and the warehouses; a *Korenlichtermansgilde* represented the hundreds of men who worked the 250 lighters known to have been in use in 1641. The grain was shipped in sacks and carried to and from the warehouses by the members of the *Korendragersgilde*, strong-backed men (required to be between the ages of eighteen and thirty-six) who numbered in the hundreds. Then there were those responsible for measuring the grain, the *Korenmeters* and *Korenzetters*. They, too, formed a guild already numbering eighty men in 1556.

Once in the warehouses, the stored grain required periodic turning to prevent spoilage. This heavy work, *verschieten*, came to be reserved for women, an unknown number of whom (unknown because they had no guild) worked in the warehouses of the port. Finally, the grain brokers functioned as "middlemen" in buying and selling at the *Korenbeurs* (Grain Exchange). The city regulated their fees and their numbers. In 1720, Amsterdam counted 395 official brokers. It is, thus, no exaggeration to say that several thousand Amsterdammers were directly involved in the transport, measurement, storage, regulation, purchase, and sale of grain.

After the mid–seventeenth century, the Republic's dominance of the Baltic grain trade did not diminish. Indeed, as late as the 1730s, Dutch shippers continued to carry over 70 percent of all wheat and rye passing westward through the Sound. But the volume of this trade did diminish. In global terms the Baltic exported an annual average of 68,500 lasts in the first half of the seventeenth century, 76 percent of it in Dutch bottoms. In the second half of the century, the average annual volume fell to 55,800 lasts, 78 percent carried in Dutch bottoms. In the first half of the eighteenth century, the decline took a more dramatic form. Then the average volume stood at less than half the level of a century earlier, at 31,800 lasts, 74 percent of which was handled by Dutch ships.

The highly irregular character of the year-to-year fluctuations makes it difficult to identify a clear turning point in the size of the Baltic grain trade. After the 1640s, when several years of 100,000-last shipments followed in rapid succession, such high levels were reached only in isolated years, while the mean levels of the period 1650–80 drifted steadily lower, to no more than 60 percent of the average for the 1640s.

What caused this shrinkage, so pregnant with implications for the Dutch trading system, not to mention for employment at the port of Amsterdam? The grain that entered Amsterdam from Danzig, Königsberg, and other Baltic ports in the seventeenth century was distributed to a large number of ultimate destinations, some of which were regular, dependable purchasers, some of which entered the market only in times of local dearth. A large portion of the grain – in some years nearly all of it – never left the Republic, where the bread and beer supply of the urban population depended on imports. The extent to which the grain laid up in Amsterdam warehouses made its way upstream to inland destinations and south and west along the coast of France, Iberia, and Italy depended on the price levels and, hence, on demand conditions in those markets.

Usually, the largest single influence on the Amsterdam price level for wheat and rye was the size of the Baltic shipments (i.e., the supply), which, in turn, reflected the success of the Polish and east German harvests. But after the 1660s, this relationship became weaker, and by the beginning of the eighteenth century, the statistical influence of Baltic supply on the Amsterdam price disappeared altogether. This occurred because Baltic supply lost its dominance in western European grain markets, as new sources of supply and new consumption habits eroded the market position of Baltic grain – and, hence, the position of Dutch merchants who ruled the trade in Baltic grain.

The cessation of population growth reduced the demand pressure, while regional agricultural improvements increased local food supplies. Grain prices, which had followed a highly irregular but persistently upward course for over a century, turned downward after 1663 and began to chart an irregular but persistently downward course into the eighteenth century. Contemporaries were by no means oblivious to this turning point. By 1680, when wheat and rye prices stood at little more than half their level in the 1650s, domestic producers, led by Zeeland, urged higher import tariffs to protect them from the falling price levels. At the same time, grain traders demanded a reduction of tariffs, warning that otherwise, cheaper ports would attract the international grain trade. The Republic's tariffs, the *Convooien en licenten*, were fixed amounts per last of imported *and* exported grain. When grain prices had been higher, these tariffs usually added no more than 4 percent to the price of re-exported grain. By 1680, these levies exceeded 9 percent of the market price of rye.

This classic confrontation between the interests of domestic producers and international traders was resolved, as always in the Republic, in favor of the latter, but not without offering a concession to the producers. Import duties were raised, as Zeeland wished, but the levy on exported grain was abolished, reducing the total tariff charge on re-exported grain, as the merchants wished. The net effect of these revisions was minimal; after a brief revival in the 1680s, the volume of imported Baltic grain continued to drift lower to reach its nadir in the 1710s – an era of warfare in the Baltic.

The character of the international grain trade was altered most forcefully by the emergence of England as a large-scale exporter, which occurred in the first quarter of the eighteenth century (see Table 10.2). For forty years after 1730, the volume of English exports of bread grains (chiefly wheat) rivaled the total of all shipments westbound through the Danish Sound. Even earlier, Britain had become a major exporter of barley and malt, which were chiefly used in brewing and distilling.

This new source of grain on the international market enforced a substantial contraction of the Amsterdam grain entrepôt. Dutch merchants and shippers participated in this trade, but it was largely in English hands, including the substantial shipments to the Republic itself. The low levels to which these abundant supplementary supplies pushed grain prices rarely left much room for the long-distance shipments in which the Amsterdam merchants had specialized.

By the 1720s the Amsterdam market usually functioned primarily as a supplier of the domestic market. Of course, this had always been an important dimension of Amsterdam's grain trade, but now only extraordinary circumstances (such as the harvest failure of 1740) could reactivate the broader functions of the old *graanschuur* (grain warehouse) of Europe. This situation is illustrated by Figure 10.1, which shows that the volume of rye shipped to Western Europe fluctuated greatly, and that these fluctuations moved in sympathy with rising and declining differentials between the Amsterdam and Danzig price levels. In this era of multiple sources of grain and stagnant total demand, the Baltic became a marginal supplier, and the Dutch merchants were no longer in a strong position to profit as middlemen; theirs had become a rather fickle business.

Table 10.2. *Indicators of the international grain trade, 1660–1799 (in lasts).*

Period	Grain westbound through the Danish Sound (total)	To the Netherlands	English exports of:		Total grain arrivals at Amsterdam
			Bread grains	Malt & barley	
1660–9	41,689	—	—	—	—
1670–9	46,432	37,650	—	—	—
1680–9	88,466	77,825	1,600	100	62,000ᵃ
1690–9	53,589	43,591	400	4,400	80,000
1700–9	28,285	25,391	14,300	12,000	54,000
1710–19	25,950	22,096	12,800	21,500	63,000
1720–9	43,547	33,765	12,100	26,600	46,000
1730–9	36,297	26,775	29,100	20,600	50,000
1740–9	36,147	16,616	33,600	28,300	47,000
1750–9	36,102	25,349	34,600	26,500	46,000
1760–9	60,930	32,293	24,100	17,400	52,000
1770–9	67,818	38,289	8,100ᵇ	—	62,000
1780–9	77,446ᶜ	20,212	—	—	46,000
1790–9	88,958ᵈ	44,533 ᵈ	—	—	60,000

ᵃ1683–9.
ᵇGross exports totaled 8,100 lasts. But imports stood at 12,100 lasts. Britain had again become a net importer of bread grains, which it would remain in later decades.
ᶜ1780–3, 1786–9.
ᵈ1790–3, wheat and rye only.
Sources: W. S. Unger, "De Sonttabellen voltooid," *Tijdschrift voor geschiedenis* 71 (1958), 196–8. The volume of wheat and rye shipped to Dutch ports is given; the volume of barley and oats is inferred from the data presented. David Ormrod, *English Grain Exports and the Structure of Agrarian Capitalism* (Hull, 1985), p. 46; G. A. Amsterdam, Part. Arch. 343 [Aalmoezeniersweeshuis archief] heffing op de inkomende granen. The orphanage collected 1.5 stuivers per last of wheat, 1.0 stuivers per last of rye, 0.75 stuivers per last of barley, and 0.5 stuivers per last of oats. Only the total annual revenue is known, not the breakdown among the various sorts of grain. We know from other sources, however, that rye dominated the imports, while the volume of wheat imports exceeded that of barley and oats combined. The estimates listed here assume a constant average revenue of 1.1 stuivers per last of grain. Post-1783 Sound Toll Register data are from J. A. Faber, "Scheepvaart op Nederland in een woelige periode: 1784–1810," *Economisch- en sociaal-historisch jaarboek* 47 (1984), 67–78.

After 1750 the west European population began to grow again, England's exportable grain surpluses shrank to nothing, and prices began to rise. The international demand for Baltic grain also rose. The Dutch, who had dominated this trade for over two centuries, did not fail to benefit from the new circumstances. The volume of grain shipments to Amsterdam rose, a larger percentage of Dutch Baltic shipping space was used for grain shipments, and re-exports from Amsterdam revived. But this expansion in the *absolute* volume of shipments was coupled with a *relative* decline as, for the first time, the Dutch share of the Baltic grain trade shrank. By the 1770s, Dutch bottoms carried only half of Baltic grain exports, and after the Fourth Anglo-Dutch War, the rise of direct shipment to ultimate destinations, as well as the competition of Hamburg as a rival (and neutral) grain entrepôt, enforced a further contraction of the Dutch role. Amsterdam enjoyed a brief, and final, revival as a grain re-exporter when the French harvest

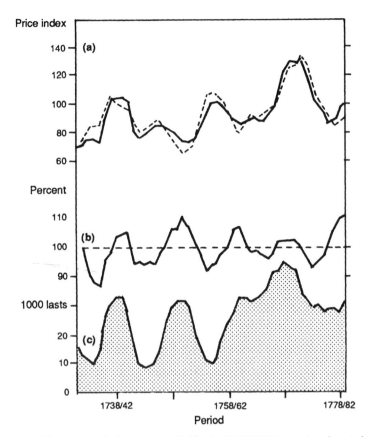

(*a*) Quotations of Prussian rye in Amsterdam (Gulden/last) 1731/83 (———) and quotations of rye in Danzig (gr. silver/last) 1732/83 (– – –). Index average 1761/80 = 100).
(*b*) Price index of Amsterdam (———) in percent of price index in Danzig (– – –).
(*c*) Rye shipped ,through the Sound 1731/83 (1000 lasts). Moving five-year average.

Figure 10.1. The impact of rye prices in Amsterdam and the Baltic on the volume of rye shipments westbound through the Sound, 1731–83. [*Source:* Staffan Högberg, "Baltic Grain Trade in the 18th Century," in J. Ph. S. Lemmink et al., eds., *Baltic Affairs* (Nijmegen, 1990), p. 124.]

failed in 1788 and in several succeeding years. The 5,000 to 10,000 lasts of Baltic wheat and rye that had entered Dutch ports annually in the mid-1780s jumped to the 40,000- to 50,000-last level between 1789 and 1793. But this proved to be a "last hurrah." Amsterdam's centuries-long specialization as Europe's grain warehouse had ended.

Analysis of the early modern international grain trade is a study in slow motion, for that which had been built up over more than a century after 1450 was undermined and lost only gradually in the course of the eighteenth century. It was lost, clearly, because of structural factors. The Dutch traders held fast to a formula throughout this long epoch. Ultimately, the world economy evolved – in the development of new consumption habits, new production centers, and new commercial practices – so that the Dutch formula gradually lost its relevance.

10.2.2. HERRING AND SALT

Herring was a pillar of Dutch trade in the sixteenth and seventeenth centuries. The herring fishery, whose economic benefits assumed legendary proportions in the eyes of contemporaries and jealous foreigners, is discussed in Chapter 7, section 7.4. Here we are concerned with exports, for this was always an export-oriented industry. Throughout the seventeenth and eighteenth centuries, no more than about one-quarter of the catch was consumed domestically.

As with so many articles of international trade, abundant quantitative information is available only for the Baltic market. In the case of herring, this was generally the most important market, although France could rival it. The Sound Toll Registers show the Dutch controlling over 80 percent of all herring shipped into the Baltic during the first half of the seventeenth century, with shipments averaging 7,100 lasts per annum.

Salt was a complementary product to herring, given its key role in preservation. Raw salt flowed to the Republic from the salt pans of southwestern France and Portugal (the only salt thought suitable for herring preservation). When the Dutch were denied access to Iberia, they sought out new sources along the coast of Venezuela. In 1621, Spain closed this source by building a great fort at the entrance to the salt lagoons; so the question of access to high-quality salt was one that gnawed at the minds of the political elites as they pondered how to respond to Portugal's efforts to regain Brazil in 1645. Was Brazilian sugar worth the alienation of Portugal and possible denial of access to the salt of Setúbal? Through the 1680s over 100 Dutch ships annually loaded salt at Setúbal, some 40 from the city of Hoorn, which specialized in this trade.

Salt refining was concentrated around Dordrecht and Zierikzee. The refined salt then had two principal destinations: the domestic market, which absorbed large amounts because of the salt-intensive herring trade, and the Baltic export markets. In the first half of the seventeenth century, the Dutch provided Baltic markets with 78 percent of the 25,900 lasts of salt that passed eastbound through the Sound in an average year. Together, salt and herring accounted for 45 percent of the value of all goods entering the Baltic in 1621.

The complementarity of these two commodity trades imparts a special importance to the precipitous decline in the Dutch herring catches after the 1650s. This decline did not at first bring about an appreciable reduction in the Dutch *share* of the remaining trade in herring, but after 1700 this, too, declined – from

80 percent before 1650 to a long-term average in the eighteenth century of no more than 20 percent.

Rival fisheries in Norway and Scotland had little use for the Amsterdam entrepôt, preferring Hamburg as a focal point for their activities. Later, protectionist measures in France (1751), the Southern Netherlands (1766), Denmark (1774), and Prussia (1775) restricted the export of Dutch herring yet further.

More important than the trade policies of other nations in the decline of Dutch herring exports were shifts in the location of the fishing grounds and the altered consumption habits of the north European peoples. These fundamental changes, discussed more fully in Chapter 7, could not be reversed by tariffs, subsidies, or stricter quality controls. By the 1780s Dutch herring shipments to the Baltic rarely exceeded 1,000 lasts per year. The river trade to Germany, then so expansive in most respects, did not take much more than 1,000 lasts either.

The salt trade might have benefited from these changes, since the northern and Baltic lands would demand more salt as their own fish preservation industries expanded. Indeed, the Sound Toll Registers show that salt shipments to the Baltic in the century after 1650 remained at least as large as before. Moreover, the Republic's position in this trade benefited from a treaty concluded with Portugal that granted the Dutch privileged access to the salt of Setúbal, a concession granted in recognition of the Dutch departure from Brazil. Despite all of this, the Dutch salt trade declined. It seems likely that the diminution of the Republic's own domestic demand for salt gradually loosened its grip on the international trade in this simple but essential commodity. Moreover, the remaining trade increasingly took the form of direct shipments of raw salt to its final destinations. The amount shipped through the Sound from Dutch ports – presumably salt refined in the Republic – fell by nearly half after 1680. Dutch shipments had averaged 20,000 lasts per year in 1600–50; by 1690–1740, they had slipped to 11,000 lasts per year.

10.2.3. TEXTILES

The character of the Dutch trade in textiles changed gradually but nonetheless decisively in the course of the century after 1670. Before then, the two major sectors, woolens and linens, were firmly anchored to major production centers in Leiden and Haarlem, respectively. Raw wool from domestic, German, and Spanish sources fueled the urban woolens industry, and this was supplemented by the importation of English unfinished woolen cloth, which was dyed and finished in Holland. The finished cloth, whether woven in England or Holland, then continued on its way to final markets, primarily in the Levant, the Baltic, and the German hinterland.

Linen production involved trade flows that were the mirror image of those traced out by wool. Linen yarn from the eastern provinces and Germany supplied the weaving industry of Haarlem, and, on a much larger scale, unbleached linen cloth from Flanders (the highest-quality producer), Westphalia, and Silesia was sent to the bleaching fields in the dunes near Haarlem. The bleached linen, whether woven in Holland or elsewhere, was then placed in the hands of merchants who found their markets primarily in England, Spain, and Spain's New World possessions.

The Dutch position as major traders of textiles weakened as Holland's urban textile industries lost their grip on production. Early in the seventeenth century, linen weaving left Haarlem for cheaper rural locations, including the Twente region of eastern Overijssel; then in the last third of the century, the transfer of the cheaper grades of woolen cloth weaving to Brabant and Liège restricted the range of the Leiden industry. Dyeing, finishing, and bleaching persisted as important activities until well into the eighteenth century, but here, too, competing installations located in new production regions beyond the Republic's borders gradually reduced the flow of unfinished cloth into Holland.

In the case of woolens, the Dutch position changed radically. By the 1670s England could bypass the Dutch entrepôt entirely, carrying its finished cloth directly to final markets. Into the eighteenth century, English "white" cloth continued to flow to Holland for dyeing and finishing, to satisfy certain markets, particularly the British military during the wars against France; but the Dutch role became progressively more marginal. The Republic's own production of woolen cloth shifted to high-quality *laken* and camlets, which depended on raw material imports from Spain and Anatolia. Both the production and export of these luxury textiles were especially sensitive to political conditions, and neither one enjoyed the expanding markets available for the cheaper grades of woolen cloth. In time, the Republic became a significant importer of woolens. By the end of the eighteenth century, the domestic market was estimated to require 2 million *el* of woolen cloth, only 20 percent of which was produced domestically. The transformation of the linen trade proceeded more gradually, as Amsterdam merchants came into increasing competition with those of Hamburg and Bremen for the supply of linen produced in Westphalia, the Rhineland, Silesia, Bohemia, and Russia. The one remaining card that Amsterdam could play in this new environment was its abundant credit. An eighteenth-century observer noted that Silesian linens were ordinarily sent to Hamburg, except when the manufacturers "have not been able to sell them in nearby regions and centers." Then the merchants forwarded their linen to Amsterdam, because "they can easily find [there] people who will advance them three-quarters of the value of the goods at a modest rate of interest, while waiting for a favorable opportunity to sell."[1]

By assuming the financing costs and the selling risks, Amsterdam merchants remained active in the linen trade, but these facilities appealed to manufacturers most in periods of slow trade, confirming the increased marginality of Dutch participation in the textile trades.

[1] Fernand Braudel, *Civilization and Capitalism, 15th–18th century* (New York, 1984), Vol. III, *The Perspective on the World*, p. 242.

It was not only the "escape" of production centers from the orbit of the Amsterdam entrepôt that eroded the Dutch position. Changes in the centers of demand also played a major role. Two great markets absorbed nearly all Dutch linen exports: England and Spain (including its colonies). In the 1680s and '90s, the nearly 2 million guilders' worth of linen shipped annually to England accounted for about a quarter of all Dutch exports to that country. English trade statistics also reveal that the demand for linen was rising strongly in the first half of the eighteenth century, and they show with brutal clarity that Dutch exports failed utterly to participate in this growth.

At first the Dutch lost market share to German producers newly capable of trading directly with England. Then around 1740, a new factor emerged in the English market, making the Dutch position even more precarious and bringing about an absolute decline in the volume of the Anglo-Dutch linen trade. The new factor was the rise of the Irish and Scottish linen industries, which British government policy encouraged with bounties and subsidies and placed in a privileged position by exempting them from the duties that became increasingly burdensome in the course of the century.

The well-documented experience of a prominent Amsterdam linen merchant, Jan Isaac de Neufville and Co., permits us to observe the diminution of trading opportunities. De Neufville, whose family had long been active linen merchants, established his own Amsterdam firm in 1730. In those early years, he bought raw linen cloth from the eastern provinces and Germany, had it bleached to his specifications near Haarlem, and exported nearly all of the finished product to England. Linen was then the only commodity in which he dealt.

The diminishing opportunities in the English market encouraged him to cultivate other markets (primarily in the Republic itself) and to add to his business the trade in certain raw materials. By 1745 only 65 percent of his linen was sent to England, and 20 percent of his revenue came from altogether different sources.

By the end of Jan Isaac's career as an active merchant, linen accounted for under 40 percent of his revenue, and England absorbed only 44 percent of that. Unfortunately, his new ventures, embarked upon for the sake of diversification, were not profitable, nor were his efforts to find new markets for his high-quality linen crowned with lasting success. In the face of these intractable difficulties, Jan Isaac de Neufville wound up his affairs in 1764, at the age of 58, preferring to retire on his remaining capital rather than expose it to further risk in a contracting trade.

The second major linen market, Spain, emerged as the most important destination by far for Dutch linen in the late eighteenth century. Contemporary estimates of the Spanish market imply a tripling of the value of its linen imports over the course of the eighteenth century. The growth of colonial demand for simple fabrics to clothe slaves stands behind this growth. Indeed, direct linen exports to the Caribbean smuggling centers of Curaçao and St. Eustatius must also have been substantial, for the exchange of linen and other manufactures for sugar was the basis for their illicit trade. After 1780 the complaint was raised that Dutch participation in illicit Caribbean trade was being held in check by insufficient supplies of linen.

The history of Dutch trade in woolens and linens after the mid–seventeenth century is one of marginalization, which in turn was rooted in the shifts of production away from the urban centers of Holland and, in time, beyond the borders of the Republic altogether. As Dutch merchants lost their hold on production, they had to fall back on specialization in steadily shrinking segments of the textile market: first dyeing and finishing, then cloth of the highest quality, and finally the financing of inventories. Ultimately, the Republic became a net importer of textiles.

10.2.4. TIMBER

Timber imports were indispensable to the seventeenth-century growth of the Dutch economy. The Republic's urbanization, its numerous hydraulic improvements and, of course, its shipbuilding industry, all called for ever larger quantities of wood. Yet domestic supplies of structural timber were next to nonexistent. Securing a dependable, inexpensive supply of this bulkiest of all major commodities stands alongside the control of the grain trade as a key accomplishment of the Republic's merchants.

We have already taken note of the practices by which the Dutch established an intensive trade relationship with Norway, using credit to buy standing timber, contracting for large quantities, and acquiring specially designed lumber-carrying *fluits* to reduce the cost on delivery in Dutch ports. Nonetheless, transport costs always exceeded initial purchase costs in Norway, and this bulky commodity absorbed a very large proportion of total Dutch shipping capacity. We know that in 1647, 387 ships specialized in the Norway timber trade, trundling back and forth several times per year. This is consistent with the record kept of seagoing vessels departing Amsterdam in 1652, the first year of the First Anglo-Dutch War. No fewer than 1,000 of the 3,000 ships departing in eight months of that atypical year were destined for Norwegian ports. The mid-century timber fleet possessed the capacity to carry annually some 375,000 cubic meters (m^3) of timber to the Republic, although it seems doubtful that the trade reached that level with regularity. The North Holland cities of Hoorn and Medemblik specialized in this trade, although most of the timber made its way to Amsterdam and, later, Dordrecht, where it was sold at auction.

Timber purchasers in the Republic were, for the most part, domestic users. The large, technically advanced sawing industry, however, which arose to cater to the demands of domestic industry, soon found export markets for sawn lumber to supplement their home markets in construction and shipbuilding.

Until the 1650s, Norway was the largest timber supplier by far. Thereafter, two new supply regions emerged to become effective competitors with Norway.

Landowners in the vast watershed of the Rhine and its tributaries turned with a special eagerness to the harvesting of their woodlands. In the aftermath of the Thirty Years' War, this was one of their few ways of raising cash, and as a result, the volume of timber floated down the Rhine grew explosively to form a major supplement to Norwegian supplies, reaching a peak in 1660 and during the Second Anglo-Dutch War. But the Rhine timber trade declined as quickly as it had grown when the lower Rhineland became a theater of war during the French invasion of 1672–3.

More durable foundations were laid for the German timber trade after 1691, when navigational improvements on the upper Rhine permitted timber traders to lash their log floats together to form enormous rafts. These giant timber floats could achieve a length of 320 meters, a breadth of 50 meters, and a thickness of 2.2 meters. Such a floating mass of up to 28,000 m³ of wood required a crew that could exceed 500 men to guide it down the river. Veritable villages, including cooks, butchers, and livestock, lived atop these rafts until they were broken up in the Republic for distribution to the auction centers at Dordrecht and Zaandam. This innovation made German timber competitive with Norse supplies.

The abundant timber supplies available along the shores of the eastern Baltic also began to figure in Western European timber markets in the second half of the seventeenth century. Beginning in 1683 the Danish crown's policy of restricting Norwegian exports of raw timber in order to encourage a domestic sawing industry involved the Republic in a conflict with Denmark-Norway and acted as a catalyst to shift trade to the eastern Baltic. The Northern Wars (1700–21) greatly reduced the trade of the Baltic, but in its aftermath (and with Swedish mercantilism now confined to a smaller territory), the Baltic emerged to become a major timber supplier throughout the rest of the eighteenth century. Government policy in Finland and Russia encouraged exports, and buyers found shipping space available at low rates as the volume of the grain trade declined. Baltic shipping periodically experienced excess capacity, and in such years low-value timber filled the holds that were intended for grain. In such years timber absorbed over half of all westbound Baltic shipping volume (see Figure 10.2). In this way transport costs were held to a minimum. This strategy did force merchants to incur substantial inventory costs, however, since they had to maintain timber inventories over several years to smooth out the irregularities in supply.

With three major supply zones to choose from and low-cost transport available in the form of specially designed *fluits*, residual Baltic shipping capacity, and giant timber floats, the Republic – as a large buyer of timber – would appear to have been in an ideal position to benefit from the competition. The Dutch could call upon Baltic supplies to counter Danish mercantilism, turn to the Rhineland during the Great Northern War, and return to the Norse and Baltic suppliers when Rhine river tolls, attracted by the growing traffic, became too burdensome. Indeed, the long success of the timber-intensive shipbuilding industry suggests that these benefits were real.

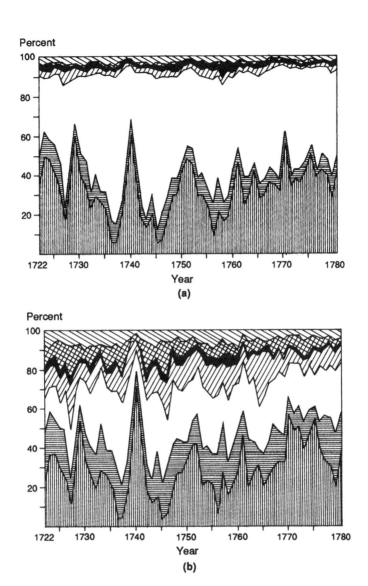

Percent

(a)

Percent

(b)

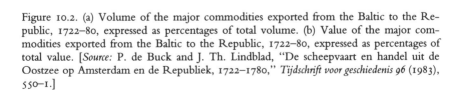

Grain	Ash and potash	Iron
Hemp and flax	Tar and pitch	
Timber	Hides and leather	

Figure 10.2. (a) Volume of the major commodities exported from the Baltic to the Republic, 1722–80, expressed as percentages of total volume. (b) Value of the major commodities exported from the Baltic to the Republic, 1722–80, expressed as percentages of total value. [*Source:* P. de Buck and J. Th. Lindblad, "De scheepvaart en handel uit de Oostzee op Amsterdam en de Republiek, 1722–1780," *Tijdschrift voor geschiedenis 96* (1983), 550–1.]

Despite these advantages, the conditions that enabled the Republic to dominate the European timber trade disappeared step by step. To begin with, the sheer volume of the trade appears to have declined substantially between the 1670s and 1700. This is a matter over which historians have long disputed. Until the 1680s, Norway remained by far the largest supplier, and little is known with certainty about the volume of the Norwegian timber trade except that her exports to all destinations fell and that the British share in the remainder grew larger. It follows that the Dutch imported substantially less Norwegian timber in 1700 than before 1670, but how much less? Some evidence suggests that Norwegian timber exports to the Republic fell to only one-third its mid-century level. Baltic and Rhineland timber supplies grew from nearly nothing after 1650, but, taken together, they hardly grew at all in the period 1670–1710, the period in which the decline of Norwegian supplies was concentrated (see Figure 10.3). After 1710, Baltic and Rhineland supplies grew substantially, but apart from the conspicuous peak in the 1730s, the eighteenth-century level of timber imports remained well below the mid–seventeenth century level.

The cause of the sharp decline of the late seventeenth century must be sought within the Netherlands, where the demand for urban construction and infrastructure collapsed. In this period the Norway trade ceased to be an exclusive preserve of Dutch merchants. Thereafter, Dutch domestic timber demand stabilized, but its share of international markets for sawn lumber stood under constant pressure.

Governments all over Europe sought to foster lumber sawing by either restricting the export of unmilled timber (in the case of exporters such as Denmark-Norway and Sweden) or restricting the import of milled lumber (in the case of importers such as England, which imposed high tariffs, and the Southern Netherlands, which prohibited altogether the import of sawn lumber in 1752).

In the tug of war between suppliers and consumers, the former had an advantage, since the reduction of bulk at the source of production offers clear cost advantages. But this inconsistent application of mercantilist theory jeopardized the Republic more than other countries, since it alone was both a major importer of raw timber *and* exporter of milled lumber. In the course of the eighteenth century, Dutch timber ships from Norway and the Baltic carried ever more sawn lumber, which undermined the domestic sawing industry, and these vessels sailed in growing numbers directly to their final markets, bypassing the Dutch entrepôt in order to satisfy the restrictive policies of both seller and buyer. The Sound Toll Registers provide a glimpse into the growth of this "bypass trade" (*voorbijlandvaart*). These documents reveal that 95 percent of the timber carried in Dutch vessels in the first half of the eighteenth century was declared to be destined for Dutch harbors; in the period 1751–80, that percentage fell to about 70 percent.

The weakening Dutch position in the international timber trade, as well as the diminished international competitiveness of Dutch lumber milling and shipbuilding, brought about both a relative and, probably, an absolute decline in the volume of Dutch timber imports after the 1740s. The case for absolute decline

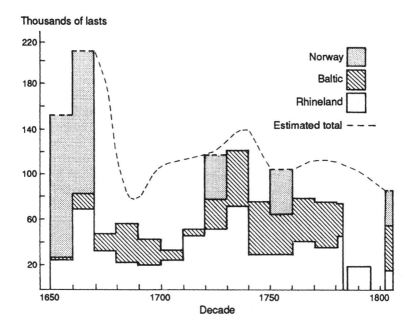

Figure 10.3. Estimated volume of timber imports to the Republic from Norway, the Rhineland, and the Baltic, 1650–1805. [*Sources:* FROM THE RHINELAND: L. A. van Prooije, "De invoer van Rijns hout per vlot, 1650–1795," *Economisch- en sociaal-historisch jaarboek 53* (1990), 30–79; W. F. Leemans, *De grote Gelderse tollen en hun tollenaars in de 18e en het begin der 19e eeuw* (Arnhem, 1981). FROM THE BALTIC: P. de Buck and J. T. Lindblad, "De scheepvaart en handel uit de Oostzee op Amsterdam en de Republiek, 1722–1780," *Tijdschrift voor geschiedenis 96* (1983), 536–62; W. S. Unger, "De publicatie der Sonttabellen voltooid," *Tijdschrift voor geschiedenis 71* (1958), Bijlage XIII; H. C. Johansen, "Ships and cargoes in the traffic between the Baltic and Amsterdam in the late eighteenth century," in *The Interaction of Amsterdam and Antwerp with the Baltic Region, 1400–1800* (Leiden, 1983), pp. 161–70. FROM NORWAY: J. R. Bruijn, "The timber trade. The case of Dutch-Norwegian relations in the 17th century," in Arne Bang-Andersen et al., eds., *The North Sea. A highway of economic and cultural exchange* (Stavanger, 1985), pp. 123–35; S. Kjaerheim, "The Norwegian timber trade in the seventeenth century," *Scandinavian Economic History Review 2* (1957), 188–201; J. Schreiner, *Nederland og Norge, 1625–1650. Trelastforsel og handelspolitikk* (Oslo, 1933), pp. 107–8; H. S. K. Kent, "The Anglo-Norwegian timber trade in the eighteenth century," *Economic History Review 7*, second series (1955), 66–7. OVERVIEWS OF THE TOTAL TRADE: J. Buis, *Historia Forestis. Nederlandse bosgeschiedenis*, 2 vols. (Wageningen, 1985), II: 512–18; C. Lesger, "Lange-termijn processen en de betekenis van politieke factoren in de Nederlandse houthandel ten tijde van de Republiek," *Economisch- en sociaal-historisch jaarboek 55* (1992), 105–42. In each supply region, the measurement conventions differed, and the accuracy of observations varied. The timber rafts floating down the Rhine were measured in *doorgangen*, the timber shipments through the Danish Sound were usually measured in "pieces," while the Norway trade is known chiefly from ship movements and estimates of their carrying capacity. The estimates presented here must be regarded as tentative. See Lesger, "Lange-termijn processen," pp. 130–4, for a discussion of the interpretive issues.]

hinges on the volume of shipments from Norway, for which we have few data. It appears that some 500 ships entered the Zuider Zee with Norse timber in the 1740s and again in the 1770s – about half of the mid–seventeenth century number. What *is* clear is that the *coup de grâce* to the Dutch timber trade was inflicted after 1780 when the American War of Independence redirected England's growing appetite for timber from North America to Norway and the Baltic. In the resulting competition, the English could more readily pay the higher timber prices, all but forcing the Dutch out of Norway. In the Baltic, where the Dutch had bought two-thirds of all exported timber until the 1740s, their market share fell to one-third in the 1770s and to a mere 9 percent in 1781–3. By the early nineteenth century, the timber trade had been reduced to a purely domestic function, supplying the limited needs of a stagnant Dutch economy.

The timing and extent of the decline of Dutch trade in grain, herring and salt, textiles, and timber varied, but its consequences for the overall volume of trade in Europe, most notably the Baltic trade, are palpable from the mid–seventeenth century on. The annual average of 2,322 Dutch ships passing the Danish Sound in both directions in the 1650s shrank decade by decade, with the single exception of the 1680s, to its nadir in the early eighteenth century, when annual averages of 728 and 880 Dutch ships passed the Sound in the 1700s and 1710s, respectively.

But this is only half the story of Dutch trade in the late seventeenth and early eighteenth centuries. Beside the decline of the "traditional" trades must be placed the growth of trades in new or previously minor commodities. Far and away the most important of these were the "colonial goods": sugar, coffee, and tobacco from the New World, and spices, cotton cloth, porcelain, silk, coffee, and tea from Asia. We have already discussed the founding and early expansion of the VOC and WIC. Indeed, the dramatic early years of exploration, conquest, and conflict with other colonial powers have always attracted the lion's share of attention. In the middle decades of the seventeenth century, as the VOC's trade stabilized after its rapid early growth, and the WIC faced grave financial problems and the need to reorient its activities away from Brazil, it cannot be said that either Asia or the New World bulked large in terms of either volume or value in the total trade of the Republic. Regarding both theaters one must speak of supplements to the European trades that continued to dominate the Amsterdam entrepôt.

This relationship of "colonial" to "European" trade changed in the century after 1650 and most radically in the period 1680–1720. As trade in European commodities could absorb less and less of the trading capital of Dutch merchants, they sought new investment opportunities. In many cases they found these outside the commercial sector, but investors committed a large amount of capital to the expansion of the volume of trade in both the East and West Indies. The growth of the colonial trades appears to have occurred in compensation for the more limited opportunities within Europe, and it led, ultimately, to a new Dutch trading system at the heart of which stood the trade in colonial products.

In the review of the East and West Indies trades that follows, no effort is made to offer a complete analysis of the colonial economies, which is a subject in its own right. The present account restricts itself to the relationship of the colonial economies to the economy of the Republic.

10.3. Trade with Asia

10.3.1. 1650–80

In the course of the 1640s, the United East India Company, after four decades of vigorous expansion and daring innovation, entered a period of relative stability in which it stood at the height of its powers as, without question, the paramount European commercial and political force in Asia. It was now no longer possible to grow rapidly, but the foundations on which the VOC's profitability rested remained in place into the 1670s, when the Dutch in Asia – just as the Dutch in Europe – encountered new constraints on their activities that threatened the Company's profitability.

The Company's return shipping capacity, which had grown at a long-term rate of 3 percent per annum from the 1610s to the 1650s, grew in the three following decades at only 0.5 percent per annum. In this environment the *Heren XVII* acted to strengthen their monopoly control of the spice trade in Asia and to perfect their exploitation of that power in European markets.

The founding in 1652 of the Cape Colony can serve as a beginning point, for it established an operating routine that continued unchanged throughout the remaining life of the VOC. The purpose of this station at the southern tip of Africa was to replenish the supplies of passing ships. The Cape Colony possessed no trading importance of its own for the Company, although it was originally hoped that the supplies needed for its provisioning function could be acquired via trade with native peoples in the interior. From the outset this proved to be an idle hope, and European farmers had to be attracted to the Cape to produce foodstuffs. By 1686 the colony, then being augmented by Huguenot refugees, had expanded eastward some 40 km. from Capetown to found the Stellenbosch settlement. In the following century, the colony grew steadily, chiefly by natural increase, to number some 15,000 European inhabitants spread out over a vast territory, producing goods sold at Capetown to the passing ships of the VOC (as well as to those of other nations).

The VOC used the conclusion of peace in Europe (in 1648) to build up its military strength in Asia by hiring thousands of decommissioned soldiers. The governor-general, Rycklof van Goens, deployed his new resources aggressively. He completed the conquest of coastal Ceylon (begun in 1637), allowing the VOC to replace the Portuguese as monopoly suppliers of cinnamon, and captured Portuguese forts on the Coromandel and Malabar coasts of India. A decade later the VOC closed down the independent Celebes trading port of Makassar (1667), and a decade after that, the Sultan of Ternate submitted to Company direction, removing a final uncertainty to the spice monopoly.

One might suppose that an aspiring monopolist's problems end once all supplies are secured. But the next step, the sale of goods in such a way that the monopoly benefits accrue to the seller, is by no means automatic. Until 1642 the Company sold all commodities by contract to merchant consortia (including directors of the VOC). Here the main question was whether the Company or the merchants were to receive the chief benefit. Beginning in 1642 the VOC adopted a policy of selling its goods at auction, although spices sometimes were exempted, as the Company sought to sell them at a fixed price. Now the Company's chief concern was to dominate the market through the control of information and the maintenance of sufficient inventories to frighten away private speculation and to discourage smuggling by interlopers and Company servants alike.

The Company sought to regulate the flow of spices to Europe, of course, since it understood demand to be inelastic; but in its capacity as monopsonist (sole buyer) in the production region, it either had to buy the crops or else arrange for the destruction of production capacity. Neither was without cost. To be sure, supplies in excess of European demand could be sold in Asia; indeed, the Company's rule of thumb generally was to give priority to Asian spice markets. But the oversupply of these markets ran risks as well, not the least of which was re-export to Europe. In 1653 the concern of the *Heren XVII* was such that they would no longer leave the Asian marketing of spices to Batavia, and they set minimum prices.[2]

The strategy employed in the sale of pepper, long the Company's single most important import, differed from that of the fine spices in one respect. The VOC was substantially the largest importer but never a monopoly supplier. Thus, the marketing of pepper involved the *Heren XVII* in the interplay of two price elasticities, an inelastic European demand and a highly elastic supply of pepper from rival merchants. The directors reckoned the size of the market for pepper at about 7 million pounds in the 1620s and essentially the same amount in 1688. In view of this stable demand, oversupply would send the price plummeting, while shortages would result in sharply higher prices. Normal mercantile practice in this period was to strive for maximum profit per unit of sale, but the VOC saw early in its history that such a policy would not maximize total returns. The VOC became the low-cost supplier of pepper but never a true monopoly supplier. Consequently, it became the aim of the *Heren XVII* to slightly oversupply the market, so as to keep the price low enough to discourage rivals while compensating through high volume for the low profit per unit of sale.

---

[2] K. Glamann, *Dutch-Asiatic Trade, 1640–1740* (The Hague–Copenhagen, 1958), pp. 97, 103.

In general, the Company's policy was to use its dominant position in both the pepper and spice markets to achieve a stable, medium-term optimum rather than short-term profit maximization. The sophistication of this policy has a great deal of appeal to the modern economist, who would like to report that it succeeded. But it often did not. Monopolist marketing practices in Europe never permanently brought to heel the unruly behavior of prices.

Time and again the attention of the Company's directors was directed back to Asia, to the goal of securing greater control over the sources of supply. The directors knew that this policy would be costly, but they renewed it with vigor, as we have seen in the 1650s. As a consequence the Company's profits came under pressure. By any standard except that of the immediately preceding decades, the VOC remained a very profitable enterprise. Accountants in both the Republic's six chambers and in Batavia booked surpluses throughout the period 1650–80, but they were smaller than before because *equipage* costs now grew more rapidly than revenues. In Asia, the inter–Asian trade profits continued to subsidize the acquisition of return goods, but the VOC's growing territorial possessions and frequent military interventions increased the "overhead costs" – the general costs of operating the Company, including its internalized protection costs.

A direct indicator of the shifting deployment of resources is provided in Table 10.3, which summarizes the size of the VOC's labor force (apart from those permanently employed in the Republic). The ratio of employees at stations in Asia relative to the number on board ships sailing to or from Europe doubled from 1.4:1 in 1625 to 2.7:1 in 1688. The rising employment level in Asia is related, of course, to the growth of the inter–Asian trade, a profit-making activity. But a portion of this increase was required by the Company's growing military and political commitments, a fact reflected in the rise of soldiers from 30 percent of all employees in 1625 to 47 percent in 1688.

Throughout this period, noncommercial revenues (taxes, tolls, tribute) never exceeded 10 percent of all Asian revenues. The VOC was still very much a commercial enterprise; its princely bearing was supported by its earnings as a merchant, and many *bewindhebbers* harbored reservations about the empire-building policies so expansively pursued by the High Council at Batavia. In 1662 Pieter van Dam, then secretary of the Amsterdam Chamber, argued vigorously against these policies. It would be preferable, he argued, to forego the heavy costs of conquest and seek enhanced profitability via greater commercial efficiency. He argued that free Dutch merchant ships could provide inter–Asian transport services more cheaply than the heavily armored VOC vessels.

The costs of which Van Dam complained could be absorbed as long as the gross margins at which Asian goods were sold in Europe – the ratio of sales price in Europe to acquisition cost in Asia – remained high. And his critics could point to the fact that it was the monopoly goods that enjoyed the highest gross margins, and that those high margins depended on the VOC's political power. In this statelike firm seeking monopoly power in a competitive environment, the correct

Table 10.3. *VOC personnel in Asia and en route, 1625–1780.*

						of which:	
	Seamen	Military	Other	Total		in Asia	en route
1625	3,420	3,030	1,250	7,700		4,500	3,200
1688	8,440	10,270	3,190	21,900		16,000	5,900
1700	8,920	12,310	3,570	24,800		18,100	6,700
1753	12,720	16,860	6,520	36,100		24,900	11,200
1780	9,750	13,125	5,375	28,250		18,500	9,750

In Asia

	1625	1688	1700	1753	1780
Batavia	665	2,651	3,853	4,860	3,283
Java (excluding Batavia)		427	1,391	3,377	2,135
Spice Islands	1,440	1,904	2,267	2,269	2,398
Makassar		467	834	995	902
Sumatra		492	319	651	436
Malakka		430	468	471	477
Ceylon		2,774	2,966	4,652	3,784
Coromandel	120	683	514	789	775
Bengal		72	162	440	205
Malabar		619	690	1,395	949
Surat		78	106	385	56
Nagasaki		27	10	12	12
Cape of Good Hope		500	544	1,439	1,687
All other locations[a]	134	1,050	63	111	116
On board ships in Asian waters	2,141	3,826	3,913	3,054	1,285
Total	4,500	16,000	18,100	24,900	18,500

[a] At various periods these included Formosa, Timor, Persia, Siam, and Tonkin.
Sources: F. S. Gaastra, *De geschiedenis van de VOC* (Bussum, 1982), pp. 79, 82; J. R. Bruijn and J. Lucassen, *Op de schepen der Oost-Indische Compagnie* (Groningen, 1980), pp. 134–7.

mix of the political and the commercial, of centralization and flexibility, was never obvious.

During the VOC's first seven decades, the overall gross margins never fell far below three; that is, sale prices in Europe exceeded purchase prices in Asia by at least a multiple of three. All the trading, shipping, and military costs, not to mention the profits, had to come from that margin. After 1670 the Company's gross margins came under increasing pressure. As they slid inexorably to lower levels, the Company's financial strength ebbed, and it stood before fundamental decisions. As befits a firm of the VOC's scope, the new forces working against it had their loci at either end of Eurasia: in England and Japan.

The English East India Company (EIC) had long been a thorn in the side of the VOC, but this thorn had usually been more of a nuisance than a threat. However, the English-French coalition war against the Dutch Republic, launched in 1672, presented the EIC with new commercial opportunities in Asia, which it exploited with vigor. The war interrupted the VOC's shipments of specie to Asia, reduced its sales in Europe, and forced a repatriation of resources from Asia to the Republic. The EIC could now expand its trade in India (where specie was essential to trade) and penetrate more deeply than before the pepper trade that the VOC had long dominated. In the decade of the 1670s, the EIC sold 38 million pounds of pepper in Europe, to the VOC's 48 million, giving the English a 44 percent market share, where as late as the 1650s, they had to be content with 25 percent. In the process, European pepper markets became glutted as the total sales of the two firms rose from 6.0 to 8.6 million pounds per year. Prices plummeted.

The *Heren XVII* surmised that the EIC was dumping pepper with a view to enlarging its market share and, ultimately, forcing Dutch recognition of the EIC's equality as a commercial power in Asia. To combat this the VOC's directors might have played a waiting game; their financial resources were much superior to those of the English company. Indeed, by 1683 the EIC's aggressive expansion ended in the collapse of its credit: Bankruptcy threatened, its shares price plunged from over 600 to 250, and its pugnacious president Josiah Child was forced to resign.

But the *Heren XVII* were not inclined simply to ride out the storm. The inroads of the English were being followed by the French (the *Compagnie des Indes Orientales*, founded in 1664) and the Danes (the Second Danish East India Company, founded in 1672). A decisive reassertion of the VOC's power seemed to be called for. The first step was to close down the flourishing pepper emporium of Bantam. This trade center had long been a source of irritation, and even before the 1682 directive to act reached the High Council, Batavia inserted itself in a dispute between the Sultan of Bantam and his son, securing by the treaty of 1684 the closure of Bantam to all competitors of the VOC.

From there the Company acted to exercise greater control over the west coast of Sumatra, another independent source of pepper. Finally, in 1689 on

433

the Coromandel coast, it moved its chief fortified stronghold from Pulicat to Negapatnam, the better to squeeze the nearby trading centers of the French and the Danes.

With these exertions the VOC by 1689 had secured for itself as much monopoly power as it was ever to possess over the trade in pepper and spices. But true monopoly power is an elusive goal. The importance of these traditional exports in Asian-European trade was diminishing rapidly; pepper and spices had accounted for 57 percent of the Company's revenue in 1668–70 but only 37 percent in 1698–1700. Were the profits of this trade worth the expense to which the VOC was repeatedly prepared to go to protect them? And was the redeployment of VOC power on the Coromandel coast, the better to limit the pepper trade of its rivals, not shortsighted in view of the growing commercial opportunities in "nontraditional" products? Historians have asked these questions repeatedly,[3] but in the absence of financial accounts capable of isolating the costs and benefits of specific branches of trade, it is as difficult for the historian to transcend convictions based on hindsight as it was for the bewindhebbers to doubt the inherent desirability of securing monopoly power.

The second force disturbing the VOC's prosperity after 1670 emanated from Japan. The spectacular growth of the Japan trade in the 1630s had depended on Dutch access to Chinese goods, especially silk, via its Taiwan trading station and on Japanese willingness to buy these goods in exchange for silver and gold.

The VOC's China connection crumbled in the course of the 1660s. Internal upheavals in China, as the Ch'ing dynasty consolidated its power, brought a change in policy with respect to the VOC. Chinese forces overran Fort Zeelandia, the Company's position on Taiwan, in 1662. Thereafter, Peking tolerated Dutch trade in selected Chinese ports, but in 1666 even this was prohibited.

The VOC substituted Bengali for Chinese silk in order to carry on with its Japan trade, but from Japan, too, a steady stream of measures intent on controlling and restricting foreign trade took their toll. The Shogunate was sensitive to the effects of foreign trade on the domestic money supply (since Japan financed her imports chiefly with precious metals) and enacted a succession of measures that either banned the export of gold (1641–64) or silver (from 1668) or forced a deterioration in the VOC's terms of trade with Japan. This was achieved by unilaterally raising the gold-silver exchange rate (1664–8, and again in 1672) and by introducing the taxatie handel (assessed price system), whereby Japanese officials fixed the prices of imported goods.

Upon hearing of this manipulation, the VOC's astonished Raad van Indië (Asian Council) protested to the governor of Nagasaki, noting that the Company traded with "all corners of the globe" but had "never yet found a single other place

[3] Glamann, Dutch-Asiatic Trade; K. N. Chaudhuri, The Trading World of Asia and the English East India Company, 1660–1760 (Cambridge, 1978); J. I. Israel, Dutch Primacy in World Trade, 1585–1740 (Oxford, 1989).

where the purchaser fixed the price."[4] Here the council members conveniently forgot their own policy of fixing the purchase price of spices in the Moluccan islands, but it would have been painful to acknowledge that Japan was placing the VOC in the same subordinate position as the VOC had placed the spice producers.

The "assessed price system" sharply reduced the volume of Dutch trade with Japan until it was replaced in 1685 with an even more restrictive policy, the "limited trade system," which placed a fixed ceiling on the total value of VOC imports to Japan, specifically restricted the importation of silk, and added a (temporary) ban on the export of gold to the existing ban on silver exports.

Japan now ceased to function as the linchpin of the inter–Asian trade. The annual value of VOC imports, which still stood at 1.02 million guilders in 1672–85, fell to 0.62 million in 1682–1700, and continued on its downward course into the eighteenth century.

The progressively more severe restrictions imposed by Japan on the VOC's trade had far-reaching consequences for both the inter–Asian trade and the VOC in Patria. In Asia the Company lost its flexibility in financing trade and in redirecting the flow of goods to their most advantageous markets. Since Japan no longer served as a source of specie, the Company immediately became wholly dependent upon Patria for access to specie and, within a decade, found itself unable to conduct its Asian operations at a profit. The small surpluses of the 1670s and '80s turned into losses of over 1 million guilders per year in the 1690s, and so it would remain throughout the eighteenth century.

In Patria the *Heren XVII* suddenly faced the need vastly to increase their shipments of specie to Batavia (see Table 9.5). It can hardly be a coincidence that the Bank of Amsterdam began to attract bullion traders in 1683 by issuing transferable bank receipts in exchange for bullion deposits. Deposits grew rapidly in the following years, as did the activity of Holland's mints.

The multilateral foundations of the VOC's sophisticated and profitable Asian trade began to crumble in the course of the 1670s and '80s, a process well illustrated by the VOC's large trade with Bengal. Until at least 1675, the VOC had directed half of all its purchases in Bengal – especially raw silk – to Japan. The other half was divided among several markets in both Europe and Asia. By 1693, when we can first observe the post–Japanese restriction situation, the VOC shipped only 10 percent of its Bengali exports to Japan. Now 75 to 80 percent of these goods were directed to Europe. The Company acquired these goods almost exclusively in exchange for silver and gold. Until 1676 the bulk of the specie was of Japanese provenance. Thereafter, Japanese specie disappears, replaced by European silver.[5]

---

[4] P. van Dam, *Beschrijvinge van de Oostindische Compagnie*, Vol II. p. 454.
[5] Om Prakash, *The Dutch East India Company and the Economy of Bengal, 1630–1720* (Princeton, 1985), pp. 66–72.

An era of great prosperity for the VOC came to an end in the 1670s and '80s as forces in both Europe and Asia undermined the viability of the inter–Asian trade as it had been organized for over half a century, and reduced the Company's profitability in Europe by forcing down prices. At first the *Heren XVII* responded defensively; they repatriated Asian capital in the 1670s to cover the financial crisis at home and then launched, as we have seen, a military campaign to shore up their hold over their traditional trades. The expenses incurred were largely financed by extensive borrowing in Asia, where the Company's debts rose from 4.1 million guilders in 1670 to 12.1 million in 1690.[6] The *Heren XVII* expressed considerable anxiety over the Company's future in these years, a feeling shared by the public at large. VOC share prices, after plummeting in the crisis of 1672 from 570 to 250, recovered only partially in the years that followed. Shares rarely sold for much over 400; as late as 1683, they traded at 397.

10.3.2. 1680–1730

These same volatile years that closed an era also formed the beginning of a new era. Step by step, the *Heren XVII* acted to increase the volume and adjust the commodity composition of the Company's trade. The proximate cause of their new confidence was probably the (temporary) collapse of the rival EIC's expansion drive. But their ongoing policy of investing in the growth of the Company rested on two structural features of the new era.

The first is well known: the revolutionary changes in tastes affecting the European demand for Asian textiles (especially cottons) and, after 1700, for coffee and tea. This fundamental characteristic of demand was complemented by the second new structural feature, an abundant supply of capital at low interest rates. The Company had sought to convert its short-term borrowing into long-term bonds as early as 1665 and had financed an obligation to the hard-pressed States General in 1672 by distributing state bonds as dividends. None of this had gone without resistance. But after 1672 investors quickly revealed themselves to be more than willing to accept bonds; from 1679 to 1699, the *Heren XVII* raised 8.9 million guilders by issuing nonredeemable bonds at 4 percent – 3.5 percent after 1696 – as dividend payments. The shareholders received something approximating preferred shares, while the directors gained access to undistributed profits for investment in the Company's expansion.

The directors found a second source of capital in the enormous inventories, mainly of pepper and spices, that had accumulated during the Company's price war with the EIC. To prevent further price decline and/or sale at a loss, the Company accumulated inventories valued at 14.6 million guilders by 1682. Thereafter, it reduced spice shipments to Europe, using the freed-up capital to increase shipments of other goods. The capital thus redirected was no trivial sum:

---

[6] F. Gaastra, *Bewind en beleid bij de VOC, 1672–1702* (Zutphen, 1989), pp. 206–7.

In 1699 the book value of inventories stood at 3.15 million guilders, 10.45 million less than in 1682.

The Company also increased greatly the size of its labor force. From the 1650s to the 1680s, the fleets of East Indiamen had departed with about 4,000 men per year; by the 1720s the chambers in Patria were recruiting 7,200 men per year. This extraordinary intensification of the VOC's labor recruitment was not unrelated to changing labor market conditions in the Dutch economy. Just as falling interest rates – and vanishing alternative investment opportunities – made large-scale borrowing possible, so did shrinking domestic demand for labor ease the VOC's labor recruitment problems. In the period 1655–65, Dutchmen comprised only half of the 4,000 annual recruits to the Company's service. The rest were drawn to the Dutch port cities from Germany and Scandinavia. But after 1680 increased recruitment levels were matched by an increased willingness of Netherlanders to accept the low pay and high risks of work for the VOC. By 1700, Dutchmen accounted for 75 percent of the 5,000 annual recruits, and around 1720 they comprised 61 percent of the 7,200 annual recruits. In other words, in a period of declining total population from 1650–70 to 1700–20, the number of Dutchmen annually setting sail for Asia doubled, from 2,000 to 4,000.

Between the 1680s and 1720s, the VOC raised the capital and recruited the labor force to build and equip additional ships, acquire vastly larger amounts of silver and gold, and, therewith, buy a wide range of Asian commodities for shipment to Europe. The overall effect was approximately to double the size of the Company. The number of ships sent to Asia rose from 20 per year in the 1680s to 38 in the 1720s; the ships became larger, so the tonnage sent doubled from 14,000 tons per year to 28,000. Fewer vessels were now retained in Asia – the inter–Asian fleet declined from 107 ships in the 1670s to 52 in the 1720s – so the annual returning tonnage increased even more, from 9,800 tons in the 1680s to 22,000 in the 1720s.

Thus, between the 1680s and 1720s, the returning tonnage rose by 125 percent. But the Company's revenues from the sale of goods landed in Patria rose only by 78 percent (while revenues within Asia appear to have declined). This basic feature of the VOC's expansion reflects both the changing character of its trade and the new problems that it faced as a commercial enterprise with major political functions.

When in the 1680s the VOC's directors embarked on a course of expansion, they had few illusions that the extraordinary profitability of earlier decades would return.[7] They regarded the monopoly spices as a "profit center" that was worth protecting with an expanded military presence, but they also recognized that this trade could not grow. The decision to invest in increasing the volume of return cargoes was a decision to diversify into the textiles, tea, coffee, porcelain, saltpeter, and other goods for which an elastic European demand was beginning to manifest

---

[7] Gaastra, *Bewind en beleid*, pp. 110–11.

Table 10.4. *VOC shipping production, 1602–1795.*

(A)	(B)	(C)	(D)	(E)	(F)	(G)
Period	Ships departing Patria	Ships arriving Asia	Ships departing Asia	Ships arriving Patria	Ships retained in Asia	Ships lost or captured en route
	Average per year				Totals per decade	
1602–10	9.5	8.6	5	4.4	29	12
1610–20	11.7	11.4	5	4.6	64	7
1620–30	14.1	13	7.1	6.8	59	14
1630–40	15.7	15.2	7.5	7.4	77	6
1640–50	16.5	16.3	9.3	9.2	70	3
1650–60	20.5	19.4	10.3	10.2	91	12
1660–70	23.8	22.8	12.7	11.5	101	22
1670–80	23.2	21.9	13.3	12.9	86	17
1680–90	20.4	19.3	14.1	13.3	52	19
1690–1700	23.5	21.9	15.6	14.7	63	25
1700–10	28.1	26.1	19.3	18.8	68	25
1710–20	31	29.5	24.5	24.1	50	19
1720–30	38.2	35.6	31.9	30.8	37	37
1730–40	37.5	36	31.1	29.1	49	35
1740–50	31.4	30.5	23.4	21.4	71	29
1750–60	29	28.5	24.5	23.5	40	15
1760–70	29.2	28.5	23.3	22.3	52	17
1770–80	29	26.9	24.5	23.1	24	35
1780–90	28.8	27.3	22.7	19.9	46	43
1790–5	23.8	19.4	22.6	17.2	-19	59

(H)	(I)	(J)	(K)	(O)	(P)
Tonnage departed to Asia	Tonnage arrived in Patria	Tonnage returned/ tonnage departed	Tonnage retained in Asia	Persons departing	Ton-miles per year, Europe–Asia shipping (in millions)
Average per year		(I/H)	Per decade	Average per year	
4,371	2,513	0.57	9,944	1,060	92,934
5,628	2,659	0.47	28,813	1,900	111,875
5,472	3,528	0.64	15,696	2,370	121,500
6,397	3,889	0.61	23,741	2,890	138,861
10,095	7,374	0.73	27,257	3,310	235,832
12,399	8,420	0.68	34,082	4,020	281,057
12,935	7,931	0.61	45,818	4,090	281,691
14,765	9,198	0.62	50,228	4,270	323,501
13,085	9,817	0.75	28,489	3,780	309,177
14,330	10,070	0.70	38,117	4,300	329,400
18,636	13,344	0.72	45,213	4,960	431,730
22,807	18,216	0.80	34,800	5,990	553,811
28,923	24,331	0.84	20,433	7,170	718,929
28,004	22,121	0.79	33,455	7,430	676,688
25,272	17,016	0.67	60,960	7,310	570,888
27,885	22,765	0.82	38,535	8,050	683,776
29,161	22,245	0.76	56,125	8,550	693,981
29,034	23,067	0.79	41,690	7,550	703,364
24,342	14,409	0.59	62,927	6,190	523,139
18,893	13,274	0.70	-7,577	4,580	434,255

Sources: J. R. Bruijn, F. S. Gaastra, and I. Schöffer, *Dutch-Asiatic Shipping in the 17th and 18th Centuries*, Vol. I, Rijksgeschiedkundige publicatiën, grote serie 165 (The Hague, 1987), Tables 27 and 35. Ton-miles calculated by multiplying Column H plus I by 13,500 nautical miles, the sailing distance from The Netherlands to Batavia. The distance to Colombo, another common destination, was nearly the same. These figures refer only to Europe–Asia sailings; inter–Asian shipping is not included. The chief shipping routes among Asian ports as described by Rijckloff van Goens for 1686 required 136,000 ton-miles of shipping, over 40 percent of the Europe–Asia shipping then produced. Calculated from data in Gaastra, *Bewind en beleid*, pp. 168–9.

itself. It was also – unavoidably – a decision to trade in a highly competitive environment for goods that were, as a rule, both acquired and sold in competitive markets.

Historians have often criticized the directors for entering these new markets hesitantly; the pioneering work was performed by the English and French East India Companies. But the large capital available to the VOC quickly made it a major importer of the new commodities.

The enormous growth of shipping capacity noted earlier was wholly devoted to the trade in new or previously minor commodities, and these commodities were almost all much bulkier per unit of value than the pepper and spices that had dominated before 1680. As a direct consequence, the Company's efficiency as a shipping business came to loom larger as a determinant of its profitability.

The need to increase the physical productivity of the firm might not have been so pressing if the newly important commodities had fetched very high prices in Patria – that is, if the gross margins at which these goods were sold had been as high as those for the quasi-monopolized pepper and spices. We already noted that the *Heren XVII* did not expect this to be the case, and in this they were correct. The Company's expansion increased its exposure to competitive markets, and this caused gross margins to deteriorate. Through the 1660s average sale prices in the Republic (for all commodities taken together) were at least three times the prices at which the Company acquired the goods in Asia. Thereafter, the margins fell to 2.5 in the period 1700–20 and to 2.3 in the half century after 1720.

The financial records of the VOC do not make it easy to reconstruct the margins per commodity, for the purchase prices were recorded only in the accounts kept in Batavia while the sale prices were the concern of the bookkeepers in the Republic. No single set of financial statements bring these two bodies of information together – not for us and not for the Company's directors at the time. Despite this, the historian K. Glamann argued that these gross margins, or *rendementen*, were the key data – "the alpha and omega" – governing the policies of the *Heren XVII* as formulated in the list of return goods that they sent annually to Batavia.

The routine bookkeeping of the VOC did not supply this critical information, but it appears that the directors commissioned special studies from time to time, and from these we can hope to reconstruct their view of the "profitability" of several major groups of commodities. Table 10.5 represents such an effort. Each number is a ratio of the sales revenue produced by the commodity to the purchase cost of that commodity, expressed as a percentage of the total revenue and total acquisition cost, respectively. A value in excess of 1.0 indicates that the commodity contributed more to revenue than to acquisition costs; a value below 1.0 means that the commodity contributed more to acquisition costs than to revenue.

By this measure spices always appeared to be highly profitable, and pepper became steadily more so over time. However, the relative importance of both fell; indeed, this was the chief condition allowing the margins for these goods to improve. Textiles, once their volume became significant, showed very poor *rendementen*, while tea, the chief item in the China trade, confronted the same fate as textiles as its volume rose in the course of the eighteenth century. As the composition of its commodity trade shifted in the direction of competitive goods, the VOC's margins inevitably fell.

Technically, a low score in Table 10.5 does not necessarily mean that trade in that commodity was unprofitable, or even that it was less profitable than other commodities. That would only be true under the assumption that the trading and shipping costs incurred by the Company were the same for all commodities. This was almost certainly far from the case. Conceivably, the *total costs* incurred in buying, shipping, and selling, say, tea were sufficiently low that it was profitable to the Company despite the low gross margin at which tea could be sold in Europe. Likewise, the high margin of certain spices *may* barely have compensated the extraordinary costs of military protection and administration.

A fundamental criticism of the VOC's bookkeeping – and, hence, of the quality of the directors' business decisions – is that no answer could be given to the question of the profitability of any particular branch of the Company's business. This charge, first leveled by the historian W. M. F. Mansfelt, can only be refuted by the argument that the *Heren XVII* had internal documents at their disposal, and/or possessed a *Fingerspitzengefühl* acquired by intimate knowledge of all aspects of this many-sided business, that compensated for the opacity of the Company's accounting practices.

The latter hypothesis is vitiated by the growing tendency for the *bewindhebbers* to be recruited from regent families that had turned from active commercial life to government service, while the former hypothesis is supported chiefly by occasional reports and other documents produced at the behest of unusually industrious and/or reform-minded *bewindhebbers*. Some of these men were, indeed, accomplished business managers, and the most recent student of the quality of the VOC's management has developed a high regard for their business acumen:

> Whatever the shortcomings of the Company's books, we find nonetheless that the *bewindhebbers* were prepared to take the time and trouble to check the figures and calculate the costs and revenues of individual branches of the business. In the period of reform from about 1680 to 1700 the *bewindhebbers* showed great expertise in these analyses. The directors of the VOC in these years were characterized by a great awareness of costs, by commercial insight, and by attentiveness.[8]

One thing is clear. The traditional term applied by Dutch historians to this period of the VOC's long history, an era of *nabloei* (afterglow), is entirely inappropriate. This term suggests an organization resting on its laurels, enjoying the fruits of its earlier exertions. What we see instead is a company growing, changing

[8] Gaastra, *Bewind en beleid*, p. 246.

Table 10.5A. *Gross margins of the VOC:*
The ratio of sale prices in Europe to purchase
prices in Asia, 1640–1795.

Period	Gross margins	
	Total	China trade
1640–50	3.97	
1650–60	3.43	
1660–70	3.32	
1670–80	2.89	
1680–90	2.59	
1690–1700	2.77	
1700–10	2.63	
1710–20	2.66	
1720–30	2.25	
1730–40	2.44	
1740–50	2.46	2.07
1750–60	2.19	1.88
1760–70	2.37	1.51
1770–80	2.71	1.90
1780–90	2.62	1.78
1790–95	3.27	1.29

Sources: See source note to Table 10.5B.

its structure, and thereby confronting new problems. In so doing the baggage of tradition and old routine weighed heavily, to be sure, but this is the case with most mature organizations.

For those periods, and they are the vast majority, where detailed studies of the decision-making processes are not available, we must base our assessments of *bewindhebber* quality on the results of their labors, always keeping in mind the special constraints under which they acted. One of the most important of these was the VOC's semipublic character; as an eighteenth-century contemporary expressed it, the VOC conducted itself as a prince in Asia, but its princely head was carried by the body of a merchant.

The VOC in Asia administered territories on Java, in the "Spice Islands," and on Ceylon. It maintained fortified trading posts all over Asia and patrolled strategic waters to enforce its treaty rights and monopoly aspirations. Its aggressive extension of these political claims in the 1680s – at Bantam, along Sumatra's west coast, and at the Coromandel coast of India – proved to be its last such show of force; but the continued maintenance of this political establishment remained a costly burden. One way to lighten that burden was to levy taxes and tolls (i.e., to supplement its commercial earnings with territorial administration). Since the early

Table 10.5B. *An index of the profitability of major commodities, 1648–1780 (% of total revenue / % of total cost).*[a]

	Total Asian trade				
	1648–50	1668–70	1698–1700	1738–40	1778–80
Spices	1.48	2.36	2.12	3.87	7.87
Pepper	0.65	0.95	1.19	1.41	1.22
Tea and coffee			0.97	0.77	0.84
Textiles	1.24	0.65	0.79	0.69	0.66
Sugar	1.38	0.48	0.83	0.81	1.00
Drugs and dyestuffs	0.86	1.00	0.79	0.96	1.28

	China trade					
	1730–40	1740–50	1750–60	1760–70	1770–80	1780–90
All goods	0.87	0.82	0.70	0.83	0.68	0.42

[a]For each commodity, its share of total revenue in Europe is divided by its share of total purchase costs in Asia. If the ratio exceeds one, trade in the commodity contributes relatively more to total revenue than to total costs; if less than one, it contributes more to total costs than to total revenue.
Sources: GROSS MARGINS: Revenues divided by invoice values of goods received in Patria, adjusted for changes in inventories. De Korte, *De financiële verantwoording in de VOC* (Leiden, 1984), Bijlagen 9A–9E. INDEX OF PROFITABILITY: Kristof Glamann, *Dutch-Asiatic Trade, 1640–1740* (Copenhagen, 1958), pp. 13–14; J. R. Bruijn, F. S. Gaastra, and I. Schöffer, *Dutch-Asiatic Schipping*, Rijksgeschiedkundige publicatiën no. 165, Vol. I, p. 192. CHINA TRADE: C. J. A. Jörg, *Porselein als handelswaar. De porseleinhandel als onderdeel van de Chinahandel van de V.O.C., 1729–1794* (Groningen, 1978).

years, when naval prizes added substantially to the Company's revenue, governmental income had never exceeded 10 percent of the revenue of the Asian enterprise (the *Indisch Bedrijf*). After 1690 this changed as the VOC sought to increase tax and toll revenue. By 1720 some 30 percent of Asian revenue came from this source, but it seems not to have lightened substantially the burden of "political overhead." The *Indisch Bedrijf* plunged into the red in the 1690s, after Japan restricted its external trade. Taxation never succeeded in compensating for this blow to the Batavian accounts.

Consequently, from 1690 on, the Company in Patria had to "subsidize" the Asian branch of the business, the *Indisch Bedrijf*. Subsidy may not be the correct word here, since Batavia paid at least part of many expenses that directly benefited the chambers in the Republic – the maintenance of employees while in Asia, the operation of trading stations, the administration of territory. We cannot be certain exactly how unprofitable the inter–Asian trade, strictly defined, really was.

What *is* clear is that the VOC's trading income had to support large fixed

Table 10.6. *Financial results of the VOC in Patria (in thousands of guilders, annual averages, except where noted).*

Year	A Revenues	B Equipage	C Other expenses	D Patria surplus [A –(B+C)]	E Dividends	F Cash dividends
1650–60	8,425	7,107	175	1,143	1,030	1,030
1660–70	9,226	8,037	435	754	950	950
1670–80	9,127	7,699	68	1,360	1,358	902
1680–90	10,446	8,757	60	1,629	1,513	1,154
1690–1700	12,736	10,643	1,097	996	1,320	1,030
1700–10	13,950	12,256	137	1,557	1,707	1,707
1710–20	16,370	13,518	-85	2,937	2,211	2,211
1720–30	18,555	17,286	-85	1,354	1,422	1,422
1730–40	16,704	15,886	210	608	1,304	1,304
1740–50	15,973	14,868	254	851	1,143	1,143
1750–60	18,796	18,492	391	-87	1,256	1,256
1760–70	21,360	19,895	-41	1,506	1,111	1,111
1770–80	19,951	18,645	85	1,221	805	805
1780–90	14,587	21,229	-203	-6,439	403	403
1790–5	10,230	15,778	0	-5.548	805	805

G	H	I	J	K	L
Retained surplus (D − F)	Internal capital formation (years × G cumulative)	Total debt	Average price share (in guilders)	Current yield: total (E/J)	Current yield: cash (F/J)
	Total at end of period				
113	21,830	10,800	400	4.00%	4.00%
-196	19,870	13,900	450	3.30%	3.20%
458	24,450	13,400	433	4.90%	3.30%
475	29,200	13,200	468	5.00%	3.80%
-34	28,860	11,900	500	4.10%	3.20%
-150	27,360	12,600	500	5.30%	5.30%
726	34,620	8,600	600	5.70%	5.70%
-68	33,940	9,800	642	3.40%	3.40%
-696	26,980	14,900	646	3.10%	3.10%
-292	24,060	18,400	435	4.10%	4.10%
-1,343	10,630	28,900	438	4.50%	4.50%
395	14,580	28,800	440	3.90%	3.90%
416	18,740	22,100	346	3.60%	3.60%
-6,842	-49,680	91,400	229	2.70%	2.70%
-6,353	-87,798	121,400	159	7.90%	7.90%

Sources: COLS. A–D: J. P. de Korte, *De jaarlijkse financiële verantwoording in de VOC*, Table 32. COLS. E AND F: G. C. Klerk de Reus, *Geschichtliche Ueberblick*, Beilage VI. The dividends paid in 1674 took the form of government bonds purchased by the Company the previous year. They were registered as a company expense. The dividends paid in 1679 through 1683, and again in 1697, 1698, and half paid in 1699, all were issued in nonredeemable bonds. These payments did not reduce the cash surplus of the Company; they increased its long-term debt. Consequently, they did not diminish the retained surplus. COL. I: Total debt outstanding at the end of the period. Steensgaard, "Institutional Innovation," p. 249; de Korte, *Financiële verantwoording*, bijlage 1; J. J. Steur, *Herstel of ondergang. De voorstellen tot redres van de VOC, 1740–1795*, bijlage VII, pp. 299–300. COL. J: J. G. van Dillen, "Effectenkoersen," *Economisch historisch jaarboek* 17 (1931), 1–46; Jonathan Israel, *Dutch Primacy in World Trade, 1585–1740*, Tables 6.13 and 7.12; Israel, "The Amsterdam Stock Exchange and the English Revolution of 1688," *Tijdschrift voor geschiedenis* 103 (1990), appendix; Larry Neal, "The Dutch and English East India Companies Compared: Evidence from the Stock and Foreign Exchange Markets," in James Tracy, ed., *The Rise of Merchant Empires* (Cambridge, 1990), 195–223.

Table 10.7. Financial results of the VOC in Asia, 1650–1795: "Het Indisch Bedrijf" (in thousands of guilders, annual averages, except where noted).

	A	B	C	D	E	F	G	H	I
								"Indisch Kapitaal" (years × G) cumulative	
								Total at end of period	
Period	Total revenue	Trade revenue	Trade as % of total revenue (B/C)	Total expenses	Asian surplus (A - D)	From (+) or to (-) Patria	Change in "Indisch Kapitaal" (E + F)	"Indisch Kapitaal" (years × G) cumulative	Debt in Asia
1650–60	4,068	3,716	91.30%	3,838	230	-276	-46	15,900	2,700
1660–70	5,780	5,483	94.90%	4,187	1,593	-607	986	25,760	4,100
1670–80	5,897	5,403	91.60%	5,608	289	-1,010	-721	18,550	8,600
1680–90	4,834	4,381	90.60%	4,462	372	-110	262	21,170	12,100
1690–1700	5,870	4,505	76.70%	6,905	-1,035	1,466	431	25,480	8,000
1700–10	4,428	3,354	75.70%	5,584	-1,156	1,625	469	30,170	5,000
1710–20	5,411	3,948	73.00%	6,338	-927	699	-228	27,890	7,000
1720–30	4,119	2,823	68.50%	5,346	-1,127	1,822	595	33,840	9,100
1730–40	4,532	3,020	66.60%	6,621	-1,729	1,532	-197	31,870	13,000
1740–50	6,561	4,787	73.00%	7,623	-1,062	846	-216	29,710	13,000
1750–60	7,260	5,239	72.20%	8,047	-787	1,454	667	36,380	12,000
1760–68	5,972	3,692	61.80%	8,142	-2,170	2,265	95	37,140	12,000
1768–80	4,870	2,577	52.90%	7,375	-2,505	1,911	-594	30,012	10,000
1780–90	4,998	2,768	55.40%	10,036	-5,038	4,384	-654	23,472	10,000
1790–5					-1,521	2,549	1,028	29,640	10,000

Sources: COLS. A–E: TO 1700: Gaastra, *Bewind en beleid*, bijlage 2b. AFTER 1700: de Korte, *Financiële verantwoording*, bijlagen 8 and 11. Until 1690, values are expressed in *zwaargeld* (i.e., currency of the same value as in Europe). Thereafter, the stated amounts are converted to *zwaargeld* as follows: multiplied by 0.8 to 1700, 0.646 to 1743, and 0.808 to 1743–68, after which the Asian bookkeeping reverts wholly to *zwaargeld*. COL. F: Gaastra, *Bewind en beleid*, bijlage 2b; de Korte, *Financiële verantwoording*, bijlage II. COL. G: See explanation for col. G, Table 9.5. COL. H: Gaastra, *Bewind en beleid*, bijlage 2b; de Korte, *Financiële verantwoording*, bijlage a–d. Values are reduced to *zwaargeld* as explained for cols. A–E. COL. I: TO 1700: A. R. A. Den Haag, VOC Archieven, Collectie Hudde, no. 4, 10; Gaastra, *Bewind en beleid*, pp. 206–7. AFTER 1700: Gaastra, "The shifting balance of trade of the Dutch East India Company," in L. Blussé and F. Gaastra, eds., *Companies and Trade* (The Hague, 1981), pp. 47–69.

costs, ranging from the shipbuilding wharves and warehouses in Patria, to the resupply station at the Cape, to the forts and possessions in Asia. All these overhead expenses had to be met from the Company's trading profits, which were based on the gross margins (the difference between the purchase price of commodities in Asia and their sale price in Europe) times the volume of commodities traded. We have already noted that the nature of the VOC's expansion brought about a deterioration of its gross margins. Profits might still be maintained, even improved, if an increase in the scale of trading operations could reduce the burden of overhead expenses by spreading them over a larger total turnover.

This possibility must have appealed to the *Heren XVII*, but it could not come effortlessly, for, as we have already observed, the changing composition of the VOC's trade brought with it an increase in shipping costs, since return goods became bulkier per unit of value. If expansion was to lighten the burden of the Company's overhead expenses, the directors would have to capture economies of scale or otherwise increase the productivity of the labor and capital employed in their shipping operations.

VOC records do not permit any precision in the measurement of productivity, and the global estimates that we can make do not speak with a single voice. For example, departing tonnage per departing employee rose gradually throughout the seventeenth and early eighteenth centuries, but the ton-miles of European–Asian shipping per employee showed an opposite trend. Nor does the picture become clearer if productivity is measured in financial terms. The most global measure, revenue per employee in both Europe and Asia, does not budge from the 722 to 746 guilder range from 1688 to 1753. The only conclusion one can venture at present is that larger ships and growing trade volume did not increase labor productivity or reduce the capital costs of providing shipping services.

In general, the Company's overhead costs rose in step with the growth in the volume of its trade. Since no economies of scale could be achieved, declining gross margins translated directly into a decline in the profitability of the invested capital. The least ambiguous expression of this is the fact that the absolute amount of profit did not rise in pace with the doubling of the Company's size and, after 1720, fell sharply. The era of expansion was one of "profitless growth": The VOC in the 1720s worked twice as hard as in the 1660s and '70s to earn the same absolute amount of profit.

The long-term average annual profit in the VOC's 1630–70 "Golden Age" was 2.1 million guilders, of which just under half was distributed as dividends and the remainder reinvested. The long-term average annual profit in the "Expansion Age" (1680–1730) was 2.0 million guilders, of which three-quarters was distributed as dividend and one-quarter reinvested. In the earlier period, profits averaged 18 percent of total revenues; in the latter period, 10 percent. The annual return on invested capital in the earlier period stood at approximately 6 percent; in the latter period, 3.4 percent.

The *bewindhebbers'* policies did not succeed in developing new money-makers comparable to those of the pre–1680 era. In this sense, the Company became less successful. But the absolute level of profit remained substantial, and dividends occasionally reached unprecedented heights (see Table 10.6). In an era when alternative investments yielded less and less, the shares of the VOC came to look ever more appealing. As a consequence, investors drove share prices upward, in an irregular pattern, to an all-time peak in the 1720s. Then, at an average price of 642, VOC shares offered investors a current return of 3.5 percent, slightly less than the yield on government bonds!

In this era investment in the VOC was not the path to riches it had been for the original investors of 1602. When Coenraad van Beuningen, a *burgemeester* of Amsterdam, became a VOC *bewindhebber* in 1681, he initiated a major drive to reform Company operations, stamp out corruption, and so raise the dividends. By his own calculations, the implementation of his policy recommendations should have driven the price of shares to 1,000. He put his money where his mouth was; contemporaries estimated that he had invested 550,000 guilders in VOC shares. We do not know the precise dates of his purchases, but in the early 1680s – his reform effort was launched in 1683 – shares stood at around 400. In the years that followed, share prices indeed rose, to a peak of 582 in August 1688. But the international tensions accompanying Stadhouder Willem III's invasion of England unleashed a frenzy of selling. Shares plunged to a low of 365 in September, and Van Beuningen, always a man of high emotion, suffered a complete mental collapse.

In any event, the market crash proved short-lived; the patient (and long-lived) investor who bought, as Van Beuningen apparently did, in the early 1680s at about 400, who kept his senses in 1688–9, and held on to the shares until the 1720s as share prices approached their all-time peak, would have enjoyed a total return of 7.6 percent per annum (about half dividend and half capital gain). This pales before the 27 percent total annual return garnered by the patient investors of 1602–48, but it compares very favorably indeed to the alternatives available in this era of falling prices, diminishing European trade, and industrial contraction.

10.3.3. 1730–95

The vise in which the VOC's expansion course placed it – with unbudgeable costs on the one side, and on the other, narrowing gross margins at home and falling trade revenue in Asia – showed signs of closing already in the 1720s, and it did so with a vengeance in the following decade. In the fifty years from 1730 to 1780, the Company's profits fell to a fraction of earlier levels in every decade but one (the 1760s, a period of high prices occasioned by war among the European powers, in which the Republic preserved its neutrality). Excepting the 1760s, profit hovered between 2 and 3 percent of total revenues, and they were more than exhausted by dividend payments. This forced the liquidation of much of the VOC's trading capital in both Asia and the Republic, which brought on, in turn, a cash-flow problem and forced increasing resort to short-term borrowing.

In this environment the VOC's path of long-term expansion came to an abrupt halt. The Company's volume of trade, measured in returning tons of shipping, was no greater in the 1770s than in the 1730s. The era of profitless growth had given way to the era of the unprofitable giant.

In this period of squeezed profits, the weaknesses in the Company's internal organization, as well as in its political position in Asia, became increasingly apparent. These problems did not fail to attract the attention of the *Heren XVII* at home and of the High Council in Batavia. The appointment of the reform-minded governors-general in Batavia – Gustav Willem Baron van Imhoff (1743–50), followed by Jacob Mossel (1750–61) – resulted in several initiatives intended to improve bookkeeping, reduce costs, and reassert VOC power in Asia, but few of them succeeded; meanwhile, the chronic differences between the insights of the *Heren XVII* and the aspirations of Batavia continued to hobble the management of the Company.

In contrast to the expert and energetic policy making chronicled by Gaastra for the period 1680–1700, the reform efforts of 1740–60 have impressed their most recent student, J. J. Steur, with their half-heartedness and lack of commercial insight.

> The *bewindhebbers* approached the unmistakable problems of the Company with a certain arrogance. . . . No one investigated the potential profitability of any of the Company's product lines. . . . One gets the distinct impression that commercial thinking had departed from the [*bewindhebbers* in] the Netherlands.[9]

Five major problems plagued the mid–eighteenth century VOC. The first was the steady erosion of the inter–Asian trade by changes in an environment that the VOC no longer had the power to affect. Dynastic changes in Persia and India, together with heightened competition from European traders, particularly the English and French, gradually squeezed the VOC out of Persia, Surat, the Malabar Coast, and Bengal. More and more the Company confined its operations to the areas that it physically controlled, stretching from Ceylon through the Indonesian archipelago, and relied on its command of the Straits of Sunda and Malakka.

In this environment the inter–Asian trade, which had long ceased to be a direct source of profit, began to shrink in volume. Paired with this contraction was a run-down of the Asian capital stock by nearly 10 million guilders in the fifteen years after 1763. To compensate for this contraction of trade, the Company worked to increase its tax revenues. These had jumped from under 10 percent of total Asian revenues before 1640 to 24–30 percent of Asian revenues after 1690, and now jumped again, from 28 percent to 44 percent of total Asian revenues in

---

[9] J. J. Steur, *Herstel of ondergang. De voorstellen tot redres van de VOC, 1740–1795* (Utrecht, 1984), p. 70.

the course of the 1760s. But in the 1760s, no less than in the 1690s, the growth of revenue generated by civil administration – chiefly on Java and Ceylon – did not offset the extra costs associated with the Company's role as a colonial power. The *Indisch Bedrijf* remained massively unprofitable, requiring in the period 1740–80 28 guilders of "subsidy" from Patria for every 100 guilders of Asian revenue in order to cover its expenses.

A second problem facing the Company was created by its organization in Asia. From 1613 on, the Company had centralized its Asian activities on Batavia. The advantages that this offered in the gathering of information was more than outweighed in the eighteenth century by the disadvantages of shipping goods first to Batavia before they could be sent on to Europe. The Company felt this problem most acutely in the rapidly growing tea trade. While English and Oostend Company ships purchased tea in Canton and sailed directly to Europe, the VOC relied on the Chinese junk trade to supply Batavia with tea. In a trade where quality and freshness counted for much, this traditional practice was a liability, yet it took direct action by dissatisfied directors in Amsterdam and Middelburg to force the High Council in Batavia in 1733 to allow direct Canton–Europe sailings, and then only by way of experiment. Not until 1756 did such sailings become customary. Similar resistance slowed the development of direct sailings to and from Bengal.

If centralization of the *Indisch Bedrijf* at Batavia had made possible an accurate and useful financial accounting that could guide future business decisions, the resulting transport inefficiencies may have been judged a fair price to pay. But this was far from the case. The knowledge that precious metals, always in heavy demand in Asia, possessed a greater purchasing power there than in Europe, led the High Council at Batavia to draw the erroneous conclusion that their cash holdings should be recorded in their accounts at a higher exchange rate (of silver to the unit of account) than prevailed in Europe. As early as 1655, we can observe a distinction between *zwaargeld* (the heavy money of Europe) and *lichtgeld* (the light money of Asia). This monetary misconception, whereby money sent to Asia suddenly became 25 percent more valuable, gradually infected the Asian bookkeeping, creating a monetary confusion that misled contemporaries (the Asian balances seemed stronger than they really were) and has bedeviled historians ever since.

The Company's third major problem revolved around its personnel policies. Complaints about the faithlessness and inefficiency of employees cannot always be taken at face value, but the VOC does appear to have suffered from both corruption and inadequate performance of duties on a scale that exceeded that of its competitors.

In the course of the eighteenth century, the VOC faced increasing difficulties in recruiting the thousands of sailors and soldiers needed each year. The Company had never been an appealing employer; its salaries were below the level paid in the merchant marine, and no better than the navy's. Among seafaring families it was often considered scandalous for a member to sign on with VOC. Nevertheless, as we have seen, around 1700 the Company managed to recruit nearly three-quarters of all its personnel from among Netherlanders (and half of these from the six port cities that hosted VOC chambers). This share declined steadily to under 40 percent by 1770 (see Figure 12.12). As the Company's demand for labor rose and the local supply shrank, it recruited more and more foreigners, chiefly Germans with no maritime experience.

In recruiting skilled and executive personnel, the Company neither paid high salaries nor allowed private-account trading (as the English company did). Among such personnel, private trading at the expense of the Company's well being is said to have proliferated, giving rise to demoralization and a deterioration of the Company's performance.

Upon the renewal of the VOC's charter in 1740, the States General commented specifically on this problem, and the *Heren XVII*, while downplaying the problem in its discussions with the government, were, in fact, boundlessly suspicious of their servants in Asia. The inter–Asian trade had ceased being profitable to the Company, but it continued to afford lucrative opportunities to the Company's officials.

Of necessity, little factual information exists concerning unofficial trading. But we know that ordinary seamen enjoyed the customary right to conduct such private trade as could be stowed in a seaman's chest of prescribed dimensions. Just as airplane passengers today shamelessly interpret the size limitations on carry-on luggage in their own favor, so the VOC employees pressed against the limits of toleration as periodically recodified by the Company.

Of greater consequence, surely, was the private trading and corruption of officers and high officials. Eventually, they would seek to repatriate their profits to Europe, and we can hope to catch a glimpse of their private gain via the *assignatie* transactions. The *assignatie* was a form of bill of exchange issued by the Company in Batavia to persons, mainly its own employees, who deposited precious metals on the Company's promise to repay them, with interest, upon their return to the Republic. Thus, the *assignatie* represents an addition to the stock of specie available in Asia and an addition to the liability of the Company in Patria. It was a means of supplying the Asian operation with capital without incurring the risk and expense of actually sending silver from Amsterdam to Batavia.

The Company encouraged the use of *assignaties* by paying a high implicit interest rate. The depositor of a *ducaton*, the most common trade coin, was credited with 78 stuivers upon return to Patria, even though the *ducaton* there was valued at 63 stuivers. This 24 percent difference (based on the *lichtgeld–zwaargeld* distinction discussed earlier) encouraged the smuggling of coin *to* Asia so that 63 stuivers might be converted into 78 – albeit with a lag of at least two years.

Such bills of exchange had been used since at least the 1640s, and, of course, they served many completely legitimate purposes. But after 1730 they grew in volume from under 1 million to some 4 million guilders per year. How did the

Company's employees and private persons acquire the money that they transferred to the Republic via the *assignaties*? The smuggling of coin to Asia to profit from the 24 percent premium became much less attractive after 1738, when the value assigned to deposited *ducatons* fell to 72 stuivers. On the other hand, Company servants who privately established the *Amfioen-Societeit* to sell opium to the Chinese communities earned dividends totaling some 12 million guilders during the second half of the eighteenth century. None of this profit accrued to the VOC, however, and as officials with annual salaries of no more than 1,200 guilders transferred home over 200,000 guilders at the end of their tours of duty, the *bewindhebbers* faced the inescapable conclusion that the VOC's official accounts no longer registered anything like the full extent of the commercial activities of their servants.[10] In this case, little was done. The *assignatie* was too useful to the Company to be restricted, and its users were too important to be punished.

Doubts about the quality and faithfulness of VOC personnel go right to the top. The *bewindhebbers* at the time of founding were simply the "active partners" of the predecessor companies; they were all merchants in Asian commodities, among other things. Later generations of *bewindhebbers*, selected from the pool of *hoofdparticipanten* (holders of at least 3,000 guilders, at par value, of VOC shares) were not necessarily active merchants, but their number was well larded with qualified administrators and sharp, experienced investors. As long as VOC shares offered the possibility of substantial profit, one could expect such figures to be well represented among the large shareholders.

After 1730 (admittedly, this is clearer in retrospect than it could have been to contemporaries), VOC shares functioned more like a bond than an equity for the long-term investor. Short-term speculation remained very active, and share prices were often highly volatile, but professional speculators, trading in a type of option rather than actual shares, accounted for much of this activity. Since VOC shares paid a 3 to 4 percent dividend with little hope of long-term capital gain, the major shareholders tended to become persons who aspired to the function of *bewindhebber*, with its appealing secondary benefits. Regents of the cities possessing VOC chambers, if they were also *bewindhebbers*, could enjoy patronage powers (appointing favorites to positions at the wharves and warehouses), direct contracts to favorites, and earn the honoraria attached to their office. In 1770 all but nine of the sixty-seven *bewindhebbers* were also regents; in 1780 all but six were also regents.[11]

The regent families of the eighteenth-century Republic had little if any direct involvement in commerce. They concerned themselves primarily with the performance of public functions. Unfortunately, the office of *bewindhebber*, which involved responsibility for the world's largest commercial enterprise (about which

[10] Gaastra, *Bewind en beleid*, pp. 236–7.
[11] Steur, *Herstel of ondergang*, p. 75.

452

they knew little), was often treated as a parochial benefit to the municipal economy (about which they knew much).

Related to the ineffective personnel policy of the Company was the problem of mortality and illness among its employees. This was not a problem unique to the mid–eighteenth century; it was inherent to the VOC as a business enterprise. From its beginning to its end, the physical danger of the long sea voyage (2 percent of all outbound and 4 percent of all return voyages ended in wreckage) and the insalubrity of the crowded life on board vessels that could take on no fresh food for months at a time, caused the death of about one-quarter of all the men embarking on the Company's ships. Besides this continual wastage, the Company's servants faced the special hazards of tropical diseases once they arrived in Asia. Batavia's location was especially dangerous, it seems, and the efforts of the Company's medical personnel to address these problems proved wholly ineffectual. Mortality on shore cannot be tracked with accuracy, but the net result of all forms of mortality (plus small amounts of emigration and desertion) is revealed by comparing the number of persons embarking for Asia to those disembarking in the Republic from the returning vessels.

For the entire 193-year history of the VOC, one person returned for every three departing. The return ratios were particularly low in the earliest decades and again after 1780, for reasons that may well have to do with inaccurate records and larger than normal emigration. In the remaining decades, the period 1680–1740 stands out for its high return rate of 41 percent, while in the immediately following period, 1740–80, the rate plummeted to 30 percent. These decades of extraordinary mortality in Asia, probably the results of malaria, decimated the Company's ranks and enervated many of the survivors. The Company's enlarged muster rolls on the outward voyage were intended to ensure that enough men would survive their three- to five-year tours of duty to man the returning vessels. As it was, Asian personnel were sometimes taken on board to round out the returning crews, and some ships reached Dutch shores seriously undermanned.

The fifth and final problem that will be considered here is the Company's dividend policy. The dividends distributed by the *Heren XVII* had exceeded the surplus garnered by the Company in Patria in every decade but one (1710–20) from 1690 to 1760. However, for many years the directors shipped resources to Asia to build up the trading capital there, so that a consolidated bookkeeping would show total profits to have exceeded the dividends and permitted an expansion of the capital stock until 1730. In addition, between 1700 and 1740, the *bewindhebbers* had retired 5.4 million guilders of the Company's long-term debt. Profits may not have grown as one could hope, but no one can accuse the *bewindhebbers* of financial imprudence in those years.

The situation changes after 1730. Then, as profits plummeted, the *bewindhebbers* reduced the level of dividends only slightly from the earlier level. From 1730 until its demise in 1795, the Company distributed dividends in excess of its earnings in every decade but one (1760–70). To accomplish this the directors drew down the Asian capital stock by 4 million guilders between 1730 and 1780 and reduced the liquid capital available to the chambers in Patria by 20 million guilders between 1730 and 1760. The dividend policy stripped the *bewindhebbers* of the liquid assets needed to carry on their business, forcing them to reactivate the practice of contracting short-term loans, usually from the Bank of Amsterdam. These "anticipation loans" *(anticipatiepenningen)* were contracted to finance the equipage of the outbound fleets *in anticipation of* revenues to be earned from the sale of goods from the inbound fleet underway but yet to arrive. The VOC had used *anticipatiepenningen* before 1660 in order to increase the size of the outbound fleets and thereby to finance the growth of the Company. The *anticipatiepenningen*, which grew from 2.3 million guilders in 1730 to 10.9 million in 1750 and 21.4 million in 1760, reflected a chronic cash-flow problem created by excessive dividend payments. Moreover, renewal of these short-term loans became critical, for by 1760 they exceeded the total value of the incoming goods that they "anticipated."

After 1760, an interlude of high sale prices in Patria (related to the Seven Years' War) and a revision of the dividend policy brought a partial restoration of the Company's finances. Its debt was reduced while the trade capital was built up, albeit partially by drawing down the Asian capital stock.

The VOC in 1780 remained an enormous operation, sending goods valued at 20 million guilders to the Republic annually. It was not a profitable enterprise – and had not been for some time. The Company's bookkeeping practices kept this fact disguised for a long time, but gradually its inadequate performance came to be recognized. In searching for effective reform measures, the directors suffered from insufficient information about specific costs. Consequently, many reform suggestions were highly unrealistic, a fact that only reduced further their limited ability to effect changes in distant Asia.

The VOC in 1780 no longer functioned efficiently. Its centralized decision-making structure in Asia required change, and the liquid assets available to initiate new activities had been eroded by years of losses. Nevertheless, its total capital stock remained large. Its capital in the Republic, consisting of the ships and the goods in inventory, totaled 28 million guilders while its capital in Asia, consisting of the liquid trading fund and the goods en route to Europe, totaled 46 million guilders. The total capital stock net of outstanding debt stood at 62 million guilders. Compare this to the result of a similar exercise for 1620, which yielded 17.1 million guilders, or the initial capitalization of 1602 of 6.4 million. While the Company was weakened, it was not without resources with which to restore itself to a profitable existence.

This, in any event, is the assessment of the most recent student of the VOC's late eighteenth-century reform efforts, J. J. Steur.[12] The Company's resources remained impressive, but they were committed to an unprofitable commercial sys-

---

[12] Steur, *Herstel of ondergang*, p. 160.

tem, and in order to become profitable, would-be reformers had to challenge strong rival firms and strong entrenched interests within the Company. Because it was marginalized in Bengal and the Coromandel Coast by the English and French, the VOC could not trade at Canton for tea as profitably as her rivals – she had to enter with bullion, while the English could trade cotton cloth and opium. Held on a close leash by the Japanese government at Deshima, her exclusive franchise there was of only symbolic value. On Ceylon, the VOC's former ally, the Prince of Kandy, sought to emancipate himself from the Company's embrace. In this more hostile environment, the costs of maintaining the VOC's coastal possessions after 1760 far exceeded the revenues from a diminishing trade. Even in the Indonesian archipelago, the invasions of rival trading powers became more frequent. At home the Company's growing liquidity problems limited its ability to adjust inventories in response to conditions at the auction markets. Auction prices fell steadily further below the *Beurs* prices for VOC–imported goods as cartels of traders gained leverage over the auction market. In 1740–50, VOC auction prices stood 7.9 percent below the prices of the same goods when traded at the *Beurs*. By 1780–85 the gap had grown to 15.4 percent.[13]

Contemporary investors were generally unimpressed with the Company's future prospects. Apart from brief episodes of optimism spurred by dividend increases, the long-term trend of VOC share prices was gently, but inexorably, downward. Investors did not usually demand a risk premium to hold VOC shares. The market priced them so as to yield returns about equal to government bonds, but that may have been because investors felt that the VOC could be treated as an arm of the state. The ensuing crisis would reveal the truth of that assumption. Unfortunately for those investors, the state itself would succumb to the crisis.

The Fourth Anglo-Dutch War, beginning in December 1780 and ending in 1784, extinguished any remaining hope of salvaging the Company in anything like its existing form. English attacks in Asia and Europe reduced by half the number of ships still at the disposal of the VOC in 1784, removed valuable cargo from its control, and gnawed away at its remaining political power in Asia. Altogether the VOC's direct losses can be calculated at 43 million guilders. Loans to keep the Company operating reduced its net assets to zero in 1784. Its creditworthiness destroyed, it became a ward of the state.

As the war drew to a close, the *Heren XVII* regarded the re-establishment of navigation at the prewar level as their highest priority. Once the goods then piled up at Batavia could be shipped to the Republic and sold, they argued, the Company could act to restore its finances. Given the loss of ships and goods in Europe, and the deterioration of ships and the serious depletion of manpower in Asia, the restoration of normal shipping activities urged by the directors re-

---

[13] Steur, *Herstel of ondergang*, p. 93

quired major injections of capital. Since the Company's net assets now stood at zero and its creditworthiness was destroyed, it had no choice but to turn to the state.

The States General and the States of Holland supplied the Company, via direct subsidy and loan guarantees, 58 million guilders in the period 1784–90, and as much again after 1790. The VOC's new dependency was confirmed by the establishment of a government board appointed by the States General, the *Hollands-Zeeuwse Staatscommissie*, to oversee the work of the *Heren XVII*.

None of these measures did anything to reinvigorate the VOC. The Company and the state had long been nearly identical, and the leaders of both simply hoped against hope that a massive injection of capital would restore the Company's fortunes. Yet as we have seen, the pre–1780 VOC had long ceased being a profitable enterprise. The overly cautious plan for revival did not stand a chance of succeeding.

This fact did not escape the attention of everyone, and reform plans far more radical than had ever before been entertained now surfaced – to remove the Company's monopoly, close trading stations, allow private shipping, and so on. But the combination of political instability and massive losses seemed to immobilize all decision makers. No serious reform efforts got off the ground; indeed, they were probably weighed down by the state's willingness to finance the ballooning losses with loan guarantees and subsidies. It did not even seem strange to the new creditor that the Company should resume the payment of dividends. It paid 12.5 percent on the original capital in almost every one of its last ten years despite being *in extremis*.

At the end, with the collapse of the Republic in 1795 and the nationalization of the VOC's assets and possessions by the new Batavian Republic, the VOC's debt stood at 120 million guilders. This debt was merged with that of the various provinces and assumed by the new government. A *Comité tot de Zaken van de Oostindische Handel en Bezittingen* (Committee for the Affairs of the East Indies Trade and Possessions) sought to continue the operations of the old VOC, but during the Napoleonic Wars, it usually found itself cut off from contact with Asia by the British fleet. This Committee was replaced in 1800 by the *Raad van Aziatische Bezittingen en Etablissementen*, which sought to reopen trade with Batavia after the Treaty of Amiens in 1802. It sent 65 ships to Asia, but by the time the return fleet set sail, war had resumed. Only 16 of these ships returned to the Netherlands; the rest were either captured by the British or sought safe haven at the Cape and other ports. Finally in 1806, all former VOC properties fell under the jurisdiction of a new *Ministerie van Koophandel en Koloniën*. For the first time since 1602, a Dutch government permitted free trade with Asia. It would be another eight years before many merchants would dare to take advantage of this opportunity. By then renewed Dutch trade focused exclusively on the Indonesian archipelago, as the old VOC's possessions outside that realm, most notably Ceylon and the Cape Colony, remained in British hands.

10.3.4. THE VOC AND THE DOMESTIC ECONOMY OF THE REPUBLIC

How important was the East Indies trade to the economy of the Dutch Republic? Opinions vary on this question. To some, the establishment of the first joint-stock company and its emergence as the dominant European trading enterprise in Asia is the capstone of the Republic's commercial system and the highest attainment of its merchant capitalism. To others, the construction of a gargantuan monopoly, its trade in precious nonessentials, and its gradual transformation into a *de facto* organ of state, all constitute a colossal aberration, something far removed from the flexible, competitive commercial environment that had made Amsterdam the entrepôt of Europe.

Of course, an enterprise of its physical size and geographical scope could never typify the commercial life of its age; the problems and opportunities it faced could not avoid being unique. Our concern here is with the integration of the VOC with the domestic economy of the Republic. Was this a substantially autonomous statelike entity whose fate was decided largely in Asia, or did it form an integral part of the Dutch economy, even assuming a key role in the development of the Republic's trading system?

The VOC's contribution to the volume and value of Dutch trade is superficially easy to measure and yet elusive. The handful of East Indiamen setting sail from the Republic's ports is easily lost among the 4,000 or so vessels making for the open sea each year. Even when the size of the East Indiamen is taken into account (400–500 lasts), the shipping volume of the VOC is unprepossessing. However, once the enormous distances traveled by these vessels is added to the calculation (13,500 nautical miles to Batavia), it becomes apparent that the VOC constituted a major shipping enterprise. Measured in ton-miles, the VOC in the 1770s (near the peak of its physical size) probably accounted for nearly a quarter of all the sea transport produced by the entire Dutch fleet, and when the Company's inter–Asian shipping activity is added, this percentage rises further.

But the VOC was not simply a long-distance shipping organization. It was a trading company (in both Asia and Europe), and the most direct measure of its importance is its contribution to the value of the Republic's foreign trade. The value of the goods landed annually at the docks of the six chambers and sold at auction hovered around 8 to 9 million guilders per year in the 1640–80 period. The ensuing expansion raised this figure to an annual average of 18 to 21 million guilders in the period 1750–80. In those years the value of Dutch imports from all Baltic ports combined did not reach the level of VOC shipments.

But even such a comparison does not do justice to the eighteenth-century importance of the East India trade, for the majority of these goods were not consumed in the Republic but rather were re-exported – mainly to Germany and the Baltic. Estimates of this re-export share range from 60 percent (based on Amsterdam's import and export statistics for 1774) to the statement of a well-informed *bewindhebber*, Cornelis van der Oudermeulen, that three-quarters to seven-eighths of all goods excepting tea and coffee were re-exported. (He thought that the inhabitants of Friesland and Groningen had developed such a taste for tea and coffee that there was little left for re-export!)

Van der Oudermeulen estimated the foreign trade turnover (imports plus re-exports) accounted for by the VOC in the 1770s at 35 million guilders, which amounted to 13 percent of the total value of the Republic's foreign trade. More recent studies have accepted Van der Oudermeulen's estimates as reasonable and interpreted the VOC's 13-percent share in foreign trade as a sign of its relatively modest place in the total trade of the Republic.

Neither Van der Oudermeulen's estimate that Asian goods accounted for 13 percent of Dutch trade, nor our estimate that the VOC produced 25 percent of Dutch ocean shipping volume in the years of its greatest physical size, really answers the question of the VOC's importance. Even if we could be confident of their accuracy, these calculations stop short of providing a penetrating insight into the VOC's interaction with the Dutch economy as a whole.

As we argue in the final section of this chapter, the place of colonial re-exports changed in the period 1680–1730 from being a sometimes lucrative supplement to the Republic's core European trades to assuming the key position in the Dutch entrepôt. In the eighteenth century, the intercontinental trades became (1) the generator of trade surpluses when other trades fell into deficit, and (2) a strategic factor in the maintenance of the position of Dutch merchants in European markets. As suppliers of colonial commodities, they could continue to engage in other trades that they otherwise would have lost. In other words, if the Asian trade had disappeared, the total value of Dutch foreign trade would have declined by more than the 13 percent (Van der Oudermeulen's estimate) of the Asian trade itself. The entrepôt of the eighteenth century became increasingly an emporium of colonial products.

The VOC's strategic position emerged in the course of the great expansion begun in the 1680s. This expansion compensated for the contraction of inter–European trade and the new Asian commodities substituted for the European commodities over which the grip of the Dutch entrepôt was weakening.

The Asian trade was known as an import trade: Europeans sailed to the East with bullion and sailed back with commodities. As such, this trade had a bad name with mercantilist officials and publicists, who complained that their merchants acquired luxuries and curiosities at the expense of a continual drain of specie – the sinews of domestic commerce and of war. In the Republic, with its open economy, the outflow of silver and gold never excited the protests and gnashing of teeth that it did in England and France. Bullion usually flowed in and out unrestricted, just as other commodities, and the re-export of Asian goods secured for the Republic (in a roundabout way) more than enough bullion to cover the bullion export requirements of the VOC (see Table 10.8).

But Dutch exports to Asia, the conventional image notwithstanding, did not consist exclusively of gold and silver coins. Commodity exports also played a role, and while their value rarely approached that of specie exports, the sheer size of the VOC made its commodity exports a significant factor in the Dutch economy. The value (purchase cost in Patria) of all commodities arriving in Batavia exceeded 1 million guilders per year in the 1660s and gradually rose to nearly 2 million guilders in the eighteenth century. Books kept in the Republic record the shipment of goods to Asia usually in excess of 2 million guilders per year from the 1720s on. The VOC's accounting practices did not systematically distinguish goods intended for sale in Asia (*koopmanschappen*) from those intended for Company use, but from the perspective of the Dutch economy, the distinction is not of great importance.

Not all goods sent to Asia were products of the Dutch economy, of course, but for certain Dutch industries, this trade was of great importance. The woolen textile industry of Leiden could count on regular orders for high-quality *lakens* to be sold in Japan and China. In the 1780s the VOC sold annually over 100,000 guilders' worth of this product at Canton. At the peak of the Leiden textile industry's prosperity, in the mid–seventeenth century, such orders would have counted for little, but in its decayed state a century later, the VOC's orders functioned to prop up the remains of Leiden's industrial sector.

In summary, the VOC's involvement, direct and indirect, in the Republic's foreign trade affected not only the import and re-export of Asian products but also the import of European commodities needed for the operation of the Company's shipping and the conduct of its trade, plus the export of commodities to Asia for these purposes. Table 10.8A displays our estimates of these trade volumes, the trades in European commodities being based on the details of eighteenth-century expenditures preserved for the Amsterdam Chamber, and a series of assumptions specified in the table.

The Republic retained Asian goods for domestic consumption, and the VOC imported from European suppliers most of its requirements for shipbuilding materials, about half its trade goods, and a smaller proportion of the ships' provisions. This import bill can be set against the export earnings attributable to the Asian trade, which was dominated, of course, by the re-export of Asian commodities. Apart from silk thread, an Asian import that functioned as a raw material in Dutch industry, most Asian products were only sorted, cleaned, and packaged before re-export. The value added to these goods by the Dutch entrepôt was modest, but export prices were probably substantially higher than VOC auction prices, or even than the Amsterdam *Beurs* prices that guide the estimation of re-export value in Table 10.8. Re-exports were supplemented by the export of trade goods and Company supplies to Asia (not to mention the "undocumented" exports stashed in the sea chests of employees).

The net balance of VOC-related trade – exports and re-exports minus retained imports – was always strongly positive at some 5 million guilders per year. Since the Asian balances were wholly comprehended by the financial structure of the

Table 10.8A. *The impact of the VOC on Dutch foreign trade in the 1660s, 1720s, and 1770s (in millions of guilders per year).*

	1660s	1720s	1770s
Total imports from Asia	9.2	18.2	20.0
Retained imports[a]	2.3	7.4	8.0
European imports for VOC use[b]	1.5	2.4	2.4
Total imports	3.8	9.8	10.4
Re-export of Asian goods[c]	7.6	12.3	13.2
VOC commodity exports to Asia[d]	1.8	2.4	2.3
Total exports	9.4	14.7	15.5
Trade balance (total ex. - total im.)	5.6	4.9	5.1
Specie export	1.2	6.6	4.8
Total trade turnover			
Asian imports and exports	16.8	30.5	33.2
European imports and exports	3.3	4.8	4.7
Total	20.1	35.3	37.9
Trade balance in Europe			
Exports	7.6	12.3	13.2
Imports	1.5	2.4	2.4
Net exports	6.1	9.9	10.8

[a]Following Amsterdam foreign trade statistics, we assume that 40 percent of Asian imports were retained in the eighteenth century; in the 1660s, when pepper and spices still predominated, we assume that only 25 percent were retained.
[b]Trade goods, shipbuilding materials, and provisions: We assume that 20 percent of provisions were imported, 80 percent of shipbuilding materials were imported, and 50 percent of trade goods were imported. Among the trade goods, wine and lead were both imported, and most other goods were domestically provided. Raw materials for shipbuilding were overwhelmingly imported, but the domestic value added of sail-cloth and rope production account for about 15 percent of the cost of raw materials.
[c]The value of re-exports are set at 110 percent of the VOC auction prices that define their import value. Prices of these commodities at the Beurs were higher than auction prices by 7 to 15 percent in the eighteenth century. Actual sale prices in foreign markets were surely substantially higher than the estimates presented here.
[d]Trade goods and company supplies.

Table 10.8B. *Domestic expenditures of the VOC (in millions of guilders per year).*

	1660s	1720s	1770s
Domestic commodity purchases[a]	1.2	1.8	1.8
Employee payroll:			
Domestic employees	0.8	1.2	1.4
Employees at sea and abroad	2.3	2.8	3.3
Total	3.1	4.0	4.7
Financial expenditures:			
Dividends and interest	1.9	1.9	1.9
Assignaties	0.25	0.8	3.6
Taxes	0.35	0.5	0.5
Total	2.5	3.2	6.0
Grand total	6.8	9.0	12.5
Percentage of total equipage expense disbursed within the Republic	85%	52%	67%

[a]That portion of expenditures for trade goods, shipbuilding materials, and provisions not imported. Note *b* in Table 10.8A specifies how imports are estimated; the remainder is supplied from domestic sources.

VOC itself, it is useful to isolate the European balances of VOC-related trade. These were also highly positive and tended to grow over time. It was these balances that constituted the claims on foreign specie which, as noted earlier, far exceeded Dutch exports of gold and silver to Asia.

From the VOC's impact on the Republic's external balances, we now turn to its impact on the domestic economy (see Table 10.8B). As the VOC grew and the Republic's industrial base shrank, the orders placed by the Company for goods and supplies, plus its own shipbuilding activity, became steadily more important to the cities that controlled the six chambers. Each chamber operated warehouses and a wharf, and some possessed rope works, slaughterhouses, and other supporting businesses. In the VOC's nearly two-century existence, it built nearly 1,600 ships. By the eighteenth century, the annual expenses for timber, fittings, and other shipbuilding materials exceeded 2 million guilders, enough to produce a steady flow of seven to nine very large ships each year and to maintain a fleet of over 100 vessels at any given time.

Closely associated with the VOC's demand for supplies, export commodities, and capital goods was its demand for labor. As late as 1790, the Company's six wharves employed some 2,500 men, while about a thousand more staffed the remaining domestic functions at the auction houses, rope works, and, of course, at the warehouses unloading and sorting Asian commodities and preparing provisions for the long journey to Batavia. The annual payroll for the 3,500 to 3,600 domestic employees in the mid–eighteenth century totaled 1.2 million guilders: 120,000 for the 60 *bewindhebbers*, a similar amount for approximately 150 officials, department heads, accountants, and so on, and about 1 million guilders divided among some 3,400 manual workers.

Much larger, of course, was the number of employees serving on board the ships and in Asia. In 1625, when the VOC's Asian operations were in their infancy, 4,500 employees served at Asian posts, while an additional 3,200 served aboard ships en route. By 1688 the men on board ships numbered 5,900, while the employees stationed in Asia had nearly quadrupled to 16,000. VOC employment abroad reached its peak around the mid–eighteenth century, when nearly 25,000 employees worked in Asia and 11,000 were en route. Then the Company employed nearly 17,000 soldiers, 13,000 sailors, and 6,500 other personnel (craftsmen, officials, merchants, medical personnel, and clergy) for a total of 36,100. Each year the Company paid this vast army of employees (besides room and board) in excess of 4 million guilders, most of which was paid, whether to the employee, his wife, creditors, or survivors, in the Republic rather than in Asia (see Chapter 12, section 12.5.2, for more on this).

The VOC was by far the largest single employer in the Republic – if not in the world – and the unique character of its demand for labor left an indelible impress on the Dutch labor market as a whole. This is described more fully in Chapter 12. Here we can note that employment at the Company's wharves and warehouses was highly prized. The wages were not necessarily higher than those offered by other employers, but the work was steady. Correspondingly, the VOC's stable work force and its steady flow of orders for provisions, supplies, and trade goods made possession of a VOC Chamber a zealously guarded municipal asset. Before 1660, when urban economies flourished and the VOC had not yet assumed its full-blown bureaucratic form, this role was not so apparent. But in the eighteenth century, when Middelburg, Delft, Hoorn, and Enkhuizen had lost much of their earlier economic base, the VOC was the undisputed anchor of their municipal economies.

It remains to consider the VOC's role as a capitalist enterprise. Was the Company a major force in the accumulation of capital? By the conventional form of measuring the profitability of the Company, the answer to this question must be a resounding yes! On the 1602 capitalization of 6.4 million guilders, the VOC paid dividends over its 194-year history totaling 231.8 million guilders, or an annual average return of 18.5 percent. This approach to the issue is certainly relevant to the investor of 1602 with descendants who steadfastly held on to the shares until the end. But at that point, the shares themselves were of no value: The company was bankrupt and saddled with a debt of 120 million guilders. Moreover, the debt assumed this enormous size in part because shareholders continued to receive dividends even after the Company had ceased earning profits.

From a societal perspective, the profitability of the Company appears less impressive.

As we have observed, the Company succeeded in its early decades in amassing substantial profits, most of which it retained to build up its working assets. By 1650 the VOC commanded a stock of working capital in Asia and at home that exceeded the original investment by 37 million guilders. The *Beurs* acknowledged this achievement by valuing the Company's shares at five times par value. [That is, *f.* 37 million + the original investment of *f.* 6.4 million − *f.* 10 million in borrowed funds = *f.* 33 million in shareholders equity; the market valued the *f.* 6.4 million nominal value of VOC shares at five times their par value, or *f.* 32 million.] As of 1650 the accumulated dividends plus the capital gain for an original investor would have totaled over thirteen times the initial investment, or an average annual total return of 27 percent.

After this initial period of phenomenal success, the Company's real profit rate settled in to a much more modest range. The Company's financial success was now related to the commercial acumen of its directors and traders, the physical efficiency of its shipping, and maintenance of a stable political environment in which to do business. Windfalls, spoils of war and conquest, and true monopoly profits receded in importance.

After 1650 the returns to new investors rarely exceeded by much the yield of government bonds, 4.0 to 3.5 percent. The short-term volatility of share prices always attracted speculative trading in VOC shares, but the outlook of the long-term investor seems generally to have dominated the determination of share prices, and that investor had his eye primarily on the expected stream of future dividends. Larry Neal's application of a capital asset pricing model to the VOC's share prices from 1723 to 1793 has confirmed this interpretation. Except for a brief period around 1750, investors did not demand a "risk premium" − a higher return than offered by government bonds − until the Company plunged into irremediable decay after 1780.

The Amsterdam stock market, its reputation among contemporaries for bizarre speculative behavior notwithstanding, appears to have acted rationally in valuing VOC shares. The same cannot be said of the *bewindhebbers'* dividend policy after 1730, and for this reason, the VOC's dividend payout should not be taken as a direct reflection of its profitability.

In sum the VOC was long a profitable enterprise; but the assertions that its profits were fabulous, and that Dutch capital accumulation proceeded chiefly on the broad back of this engine of colonial exploitation, rest on a superficial interpretation of its bookkeeping practices. The profits earned by the Company's *actual* equity were modest after the 1650s, and vanishingly small after 1730.

The new investor of 1730 who (or whose heirs) took the precaution of selling in 1780 before the outbreak of war would have received an average annual dividend yield of 2.9 percent and suffered the loss of half the value of the initial investment, for an annualized total return of 1.9 percent. If the shares had been held to the bitter end, when they were worthless, the annualized total return from 1730 to 1795 would have been 0.9 percent.

The real significance of the VOC in the story of Dutch capital accumulation may well rest, as Immanuel Wallerstein has suggested, in its distributional impact, its tendency to *shift* capital from small to large investors. Not only did the VOC's early dividend policy favor the large merchant-investor, but the very existence of its monopoly privileges excluded newcomers from participation in the Asian trade. The prominent role of Dutch investors in the establishment of rival companies abroad – in Denmark, Sweden, and Oostende – testifies to the frustration generated by the VOC's exclusionary powers.

This tendency to redistribute capital is strikingly apparent after 1730. Then the dividends of the shareholders (numbering in the hundreds) were maintained by borrowing from bondholders (numbering in the thousands) and, ultimately, by borrowing from the state (i.e., the taxpayers, numbering in the hundreds of thousands). Could it be that the "unfairness" in the Company's operations was concentrated in Patria – where it functioned as a privileged monopoly – rather than in Asia – where, in many areas, it functioned as a competitive mercantile firm?

After the mid–seventeenth century, the VOC's importance to the Dutch economy resided chiefly in its enormous size: It paid dividends and interest averaging nearly 2 million guilders per year throughout the period 1660–1780; it paid taxes, chiefly to the Admiralties, averaging 500,000 guilders per year in the eighteenth century; in its banking function, it accepted *assignaties,* pumping steadily rising amounts – 3.6 million annually by the 1770s – into the domestic economy. In the six port cities that hosted the Company's chambers, it employed directly thousands of men and injected annually from 3 to nearly 5 million guilders of wages into their otherwise listless economies, while the 1 to 2 million guilders in orders for supplies employed indirectly many more. It is perhaps not so hard to understand why after 1780 the Republic's government, in its own dying days, stood ready to pour tens of millions of guilders into the bottomless pit of a dysfunctional and mortally wounded enterprise. That enterprise had come to assume a central place in both the Republic's trading system and its domestic economy.

10.4. Trade with the West Indies

10.4.1. 1650S TO 1674–1713

The loss of New Holland (Brazil) snuffed out any hope of developing the WIC into an Atlantic pendant to the VOC. Losses of 3 million guilders per year in Brazil, plus massive defaults on the credit extended to planters to finance the purchase of slaves, plunged the Company hopelessly into debt. Not only was the WIC shorn of its chief colonial possession, it was also stripped of most of its monopoly privileges. Already in 1638 WIC shareholders gained permission to trade privately with Brazil, upon the payment of fees to the Company. In 1648, with decay well advanced, the Brazil trade, and most other New World trades, were thrown open to all Dutch merchants.

In this deregulated setting, Dutch merchants stitched together a new system in which (1) the WIC specialized in the African and slave trades; (2) Dutch merchants and planters encouraged sugar production by extending credit, establishing plantations (many run by Sephardic Jewish planters who had left Brazil), and supplying manufactures to the Caribbean islands controlled by the British, French, and Spanish; (3) food production was encouraged in New Netherlands to sustain Curaçao (the slave entrepôt); and (4) Dutch shipping handled the transport of Caribbean produce to the Netherlands, specifically to the sugar refineries of Amsterdam. In this way the ships, African slave depots, and Amsterdam sugar refineries were kept operating despite the absence of a substantial base of production on Dutch-controlled territory.

This more modest version of a Dutch Atlantic economy, one focused on the trading center at Curaçao, proved to be more robust than the colorful but short-lived Brazilian escapade. But in the hostile environment of mercantilism and colonial empires, this hardy commercialism could survive only by adapting to constraints that became steadily more restrictive.

Dutch investments on Barbados stimulated the transformation of that British possession from a tobacco-farming to a sugar-plantation economy. The English Navigation Acts of 1651 and 1660 were intended, among other things, to exclude the Dutch as suppliers of slaves and manufactures to, and buyers of sugar from, Barbados and other islands. By the mid–1660s, these laws came to be enforced on Barbados, at which point the Dutch turned their attention to the French island of Martinique. French trade ordinances of 1664 and 1673 had much the same intention as the Navigation Acts, of course, and Dutch traders responded by cultivating their longstanding interloper trade with Spanish possessions, especially Cuba and Puerto Rico.

Everywhere, local planters tended to prefer Dutch commercial services to those of national monopolists, a preference reinforced by the Dutch hold over the slave trade. With Elmina (acquired in 1637), Luanda (1641), and some twenty other (formerly Portuguese) African forts under WIC control, the size of the Dutch slave trade was second only to the Portuguese until 1675. In the period 1650–74, the WIC shipped some 57,000 slaves. Most went to Curaçao to await sale to Spanish, French, and British planters. In the 1660s it looked for a time as though the buoyant French and British demand for slaves would revive the fortunes of the WIC, while Dutch private traders would prosper as (illicit) providers of commercial services to the growing plantation economies. WIC shares, practically worthless in 1654, revived to 40 percent of par value by the end of 1664, and sugar shipments to the Republic stood at least at the level achieved during the Brazilian adventure. In 1660 the Republic's 66 sugar refineries, 50 of them in

Amsterdam, supplied more than half of the refined sugar consumed in all of Europe.

But the following years saw the space for the Dutch interloper contract inexorably, as rival colonial powers learned to enforce their monopolist claims with effective economic and military instruments. By 1665, English slave traders could supply their own islands at competitive prices, and the establishment of the French *Compagnie des Indes Occidentales* (1664) and the English Royal African company (1673) marginalized the WIC's market position.[14] English attacks in the Caribbean during the Second and Third Anglo-Dutch Wars reinforced this marginalization, for the several successes of the Dutch fleet operating there under Admiral Abraham Crijnssen could not prevent ultimate British naval mastery of the Caribbean. Nor could this dominance be undone by the last major Dutch show of arms in the region, Admiral de Ruyter's expedition of 1674.

The new restrictions on Dutch trade had an immediate effect on Amsterdam sugar refiners. In 1668 only 34 were in operation; in 1680 only 20. In addition, the combination of commercial losses and military expenditures overwhelmed the fragile finances of the WIC, which declared bankruptcy in 1674. The 1670s were clearly a period of great difficulty for the Dutch economy everywhere: in Europe, Asia, and the Caribbean.

From its founding in 1621, the WIC never earned substantial profits. In order to finance its Brazilian enterprise, it raised 10 million guilders through the issue of new shares, and thereafter it issued bonds, amassing a total debt of 7.5 million guilders by the time of its bankruptcy. The States General immediately chartered a Second WIC, albeit a rather pale reflection of the first. A new capital injection of f. 1.2 million was raised by prevailing upon the holders of the old Company's shares and obligations to pay in cash 4 and 8 percent, respectively, of the face value of the now worthless paper in exchange for the issue of new shares bearing a face value of 15 percent of the old shares and new bonds valued at 30 percent of the old bonds.

The share- and bondholders no doubt wondered whether they were throwing good money after bad. The new WIC had essentially the same restricted monopoly powers as its post–1648 predecessor (the exclusive Dutch right to trade with Africa, including the slave trade). All other New World commerce stood open to all, upon payment of recognition fees intended to cover the WIC's administrative expenses. The Second WIC's monopoly privilege in Africa was removed in 1730 and 1734, and the Company itself was "nationalized" in 1791.

But even in the 1670s, the WIC's monopoly rights were hardly impressive. The French captured the Company's forts at the mouth of the Senegal (Goeree) and the Gambia (Argrim) in 1677, and the West Africa coast soon became crowded with the new forts of slave-trading companies established by Sweden, Denmark, Brandenburg, and even the Duke of Courland. All of these rival firms

---

[14] Charles Wilson, *Profit and Power, A Study of England and the Dutch Wars* (London, 1957), p. 115.

were financed at least in part by Dutch merchants sidestepping the WIC monopoly. All together they ensured the loss of the WIC's position as the leading trader in African gold and slaves.

Ironically, this progressive marginalization of the Dutch position in the Atlantic economy made them the preferred suppliers of slaves and commercial services to the Spanish colonies. The WIC and its Curaçao trade center, its teeth having been drawn by British and French protectionism, prospered in the 1680s and '90s as holder of the Spanish *asiento*, or slave supply contract, and as tolerated purveyor of manufactured goods and shipping services.

This Spanish connection provided a relatively stable setting in which the Second WIC could actually pay a few dividends (ranging between 2 and 8 percent; in 1687, 10 percent of its 4.5-million–guilder capitalization). But it usually paid nothing at all, and in 1713 even the possibility of participating in the Spanish *asiento* was lost as the Peace of Utrecht ending the War of the Spanish Succession awarded it to England's new South Sea Company. The Curaçao slave entrepôt collapsed, and with it the price of the Second WIC's shares. The general expansiveness of the eighteenth-century Atlantic economy was such as to provide Dutch Caribbean trading centers with occasional windfalls, usually the product of warfare among the major powers, but the idea that a second Dutch Atlantic economy based essentially on interloping could be a viable alternative to a colonial economy had been revealed much earlier as mere wishful thinking. Free trade was as little tolerated by the major powers in the Caribbean as it was by the Dutch in Asia.

10.4.2. 1680s–1815

Now the Dutch played their one remaining card in a third attempt to launch an Atlantic economy: the Wild Coast possessions. Plantation agriculture along the Surinam River dates from the mid–seventeenth century, when Sephardic Jewish planters came from Brazil. The Zeeland Chamber of the WIC claimed exclusive rights to Surinam (based on its pre–1621 activities), and the other Wild Coast settlements – Berbice, Essequebo, and Demerary – were similarly encumbered by the territorial claims of prominent Dutch families who enjoyed hereditary leases modeled after the patroonships that the WIC had used in the Hudson River Valley of New Netherlands to encourage settlement and to minimize administrative expenses. A further complication in the development of these tiny, insalubrious settlements was the frequent foreign challenges to Dutch control. England captured Surinam in 1650 and controlled it until 1667, when the Dutch recaptured it. In 1674, to consolidate its hold, the Dutch exchanged New Netherlands (which it had recaptured from the English the previous year) for an English pledge to recognize Dutch rights on the Wild Coast.

Interest in these possessions fluctuated with commodity prices and with the relative attractions of alternative opportunities. In 1682 a basis was laid for investment in the region when the WIC gained title to Surinam from Zeeland and entered into a partnership with the city of Amsterdam and with a Zeeland gentleman, the Heer van Sommelsdyk, to form the *Geoctroyeerde Sociëteit van Suriname* (Chartered Surinam Society). The colony then numbered some 4,300 slaves, 579 Christians, and 232 Jews. As sugar prices began to climb from their low point in 1688, and investment opportunities in Europe became especially limited, capital flowed in the direction of Surinam. The expansion of sugar production received a powerful stimulus when the War of the Spanish Succession (1701–13) effectively blocked French sugar from reaching European markets. Between 1684 and 1713, the slave population of Surinam grew nearly fourfold, and sugar exports rose from approximately 3 million pounds to 15 million pounds.

As the War of the Spanish Succession ended, 171 sugar plantations were active in Surinam, with an additional 20 in Essequebo and Demerary. The planters now faced the full force of French competition from Saint Domingue, it is true, but they hoped to benefit from the WIC's loss of the Spanish *asiento*. They had long complained of inadequate slave shipments from this monopoly supplier, and they now expected to be better served. Shipments did increase, from an average of 800 per year in the period 1685–1715 to nearly 1,400 per year in 1715–38, but this hardly satisfied the planters or their financial backers, the Amsterdam commission houses, who were active in tripling the number of plantations between 1713 and 1740.

In their eyes the WIC's slave-trade monopoly acted to restrict supply and, hence, the rate of expansion of the plantation economy. Just as the plantation interests in Dutch Brazil pushed for liberalization in 1638, so the Surinam interest pushed for further liberalization after 1713. The WIC's continuing financial losses made resistance as difficult as reform. In 1734 the slave trade was opened to free traders, and the last WIC ships sailed in 1738.

During the Second WIC's life as a commercial operation, it had (since 1675) bought 503,000 troy ounces of gold in Africa worth over 20 million guilders in Europe, and it had transported a total of 163,000 slaves from Africa (two-thirds from West Africa, one-third from Angola) to the Caribbean – an average of six slave ships per year carrying an average of 510 slaves each. The WIC sold the 85 percent of these slaves who survived this "middle passage" to the New World for prices that suggest a total revenue in the vicinity of 36 million guilders. When this sum is added to the sales of gold and ivory plus the Company's tax and toll revenues, the Second WIC generated revenues of over 60 million guilders, or an average of 1 million per year. From 1674 to 1734, the WIC equipped and dispatched an average of sixteen ships per year and maintained a payroll of at least 1,000 men – on board its ships and at its African and Caribbean stations. The cost of these operations amost always exceeded the Company's revenues, and at the end of its trading life – the bookkeeping gymnastics of its directors nothwithstanding – the WIC was saddled with a debt of 8 million guilders.

The wonder is why the Second WIC lasted as long as it did – indeed, why it was formed at all. The French had replaced their monopoly company with a free slave trade already in 1672, and the English followed in 1689. During the decades when the Dutch persevered with their monopoly company, their share of the slave trade fell from a strong second place to a weak fourth.

The new free-trade policy was intended to stimulate the expansion of the Dutch plantation economy, and in this it succeeded. Average annual slave shipments to Surinam in 1740–74 stood at 2,900, more than double the rate in the WIC's last decades. Total slave shipments to all destinations reached over 6,200 per year in the 1760s, requiring some twenty sailings per year.

Although the WIC spread its shipping activities by quota among its five chambers, slave trading was always a special interest of the Zeeland ports. When the WIC monopoly fell, private Zeeland merchants quickly emerged to dominate the trade, accounting for 78 percent of all slave sailings after 1734. One Zeeland firm, the *Middelburgsche Commercie Compagnie* (MCC), has left records that offer a rare glimpse into the workings of this notorious trade. In the course of its business life, which stretched from 1720 to 1802, the MCC owned sixty-eight ships. These made a total of 300 sailings, 113 of them as slave traders on the triangular route from Zeeland to Africa to the Caribbean and back to Zeeland. These vessels left Zeeland carrying goods valued at between 25,000 and 50,000 guilders, consisting of textiles (57 percent by value), rifles (9 percent), gunpowder (15 percent), liquor (10 percent), and *snuisterijen*, or trinkets (9 percent).

In Africa the captains traded these goods for slaves, loading an average of 287 per ship. There followed the "middle passage" to Surinam, which took an average of sixty-two days and brought death to 12.3 percent of the boarded slaves (being smaller, the private ships achieved rather lower mortality rates than had WIC vessels). The captains had the slaves sold, preferably at auction, loaded coffee and sugar, and received bills of exchange to transfer their earnings to the Republic. By the end of a typical triangular voyage, lasting 18 months, some 18 percent of the crew members had died.

The profitability of these voyages depended primarily on two factors: slave mortality and slave prices in the West Indies. Table 10.9 displays summary data concerning the Dutch slave trade under both the WIC and the free-trader regimes. The purchase costs and revenues from slave sales are estimates based on good data concerning the number of slaves bought and sold and rather less firm data concerning the purchase and sale prices. It provides us with information comparable to the "gross margins" of the VOC. The key remaining question, then, is how the costs of conducting the slave trade (wages, victuals, and the construction and maintenance of ships) compared to the "surplus" achieved by the trade in slaves.

For the free-trade era, this question is addressed by the records of the MCC, which itself accounted for 13 percent of all activity and appears to have been broadly representative of trade as a whole. The 100 MCC slave voyages carried out between 1740 and 1795 incurred operating costs substantially above the net revenues earned from the slave trade. Their other revenues, chiefly earned in the

Table 10.9. *Quantitative indicators of the Dutch slave trade, 1675–1803.*

Period	Ships	Avg. per year	Avg. slave rev.	Cost of slaves	Surplus	Surplus per ship	Slaves bought	Slaves sold	Survival rate
				West India Company ships					
1675–99	139	5.6	546,000	144,000	402,000	71,786	2,888	2,480	0.86
1700–9	57	5.7	528,000	161,000	367,000	64,386	3,210	2,639	0.82
1710–19	44	4.4	416,000	125,000	291,000	66,136	2,508	2,082	0.83
1720–9	80	8.0	778,000	312,000	466,000	58,250	4,158	3,534	0.85
1730–8	46	4.6	500,000	212,000	288,000	62,609	2,491	1,955	0.78
				Free ships					
1730–9	68	6.8	402,000	163,000	239,000	35,147	1,917	1,606	0.84
1740–9	142	14.2	898,000	381,000	517,000	36,408	4,757	4,082	0.86
1750–9	151	15.1	1,092,000	508,000	584,000	38,675	5,078	4,367	0.86
1760–9	192	19.2	1,618,000	749,000	869,000	45,260	6,241	5,392	0.86
1770–9	179	17.9	1,511,000	950,000	561,000	31,341	5,280	4,578	0.87
1780–1803	87	5.8	620,000	254,000	366,000	63,103	1,409	1,240	0.88

Middelburgsche Commercie Compagnie ships

							Operating cost per ship	Net revenue	Other revenue per ship	Profit (or loss) per ship
1740–9	12	1.2	52,800	24,800	28,000	23,333	45,300	−21,967	20,700	−1,267
1750–9	19	1.9	117,600	52,200	65,400	34,421	49,600	−15,179	23,300	8,121
1760–9	25	2.5	178,600	87,700	90,900	36,360	57,000	−20,640	25,900	5,160
1770–9	35	3.5	324,300	157,100	167,200	47,771	56,500	−8,729	12,400	3,671
1780–95	9	0.6	63,400	26,300	37,100	61,833	95,200	−33,367	25,700	−7,667

Source: Johannes Postma, The Dutch in the Atlantic Slave Trade, 1600–1815 (Cambridge, 1990), pp. 110, 111, 118, 250–1, 264, 268, 295, Appendix 25.

carrying trade on the final leg of the triangular route, prevented the losses from being enormous but did not consistently secure profitability.

Actually, this way of formulating the determinants of profitability is misleading, since the carrying trade was an integral part of the triangular route. It is more relevant to note that if the gross margin (ratio of sale to purchase price) had been 5 percent better than it was (2.55 instead of 2.43), the profits of the MCC would have risen by 116 percent. If slave mortality on the middle passage could have been reduced from 12.5 percent to 10 percent, profits would have risen by 70 percent. As it was, the average annual profit amounted to less than 6,000 guilders, or about 3 percent on the invested capital, and even this modest return was far from predictable: 40 of the 100 voyages ended in loss.

It took more than slaves to expand the scale of the Dutch West Indies trade. Indeed, the purchase of slaves and the expansion of cultivated acreage alike depended on capital investment in the plantations. Little is known about the direct investments of the planters themselves, but nearly all of them established a direct relationship with an Amsterdam banker-commissioner who financed the transport, insurance, and sale of the commodities. The (short-term) credit extended by the bankers in these arrangements averaged about 30,000 guilders per plantation around 1750. Potentially, the 500-plus plantations then operating in Surinam, Essequebo, Demerary, and Berbice may together have had access to 15 million guilders of such credit.

By 1750 the Dutch plantations were sending annually some 18 to 20 million pounds of sugar and 6 million pounds of coffee to the Republic. These West Indian products had a value in Europe of some 6 million guilders, and the entire trade had more than doubled in scope and value since 1713. The sugar imports in particular fell far short of satisfying the demand of the Republic's 145-odd sugar refineries. These refineries, 90 of which were concentrated in Amsterdam, re-exported the bulk of their production and, according to their own statement of 1751, supplemented every pound of colonial sugar with two pounds imported from France. Indeed, in that year the Republic imported 28 million pounds of French raw sugar.

France's mercantilist measures dating from 1664 had denied Dutch traders direct access to French West Indian colonies, but French Atlantic ports from Bordeaux to Nantes remained thick with Dutch ships carrying sugar and other colonial products to Amsterdam for refining and redistribution. In 1751, a new French resolve to reduce its dependence on the Republic's intermediation and to retain more sugar for processing at home placed the Amsterdam refining industry and the entrepôt function in jeopardy.

This situation focused new interest in the Wild Coast settlements. Until then the finances of the plantations had taken the form of short-term credit secured by the traded goods. Credit facilities were vastly expanded beginning in 1753, when the Amsterdam burgemeester and banker Willem Gideon Deutz pioneered the issuance of long-term bonds secured by plantation mortgages. These *planta-*

geleningen attracted capital from private investors (who faced a cessation of new public bond issues after 1750) and made possible the acquisition of slaves and the expansion of cultivated acreage. The bankers were much more generous with the money of private investors than they had been with their own short-term credits.

The French danger quickly faded – in the 1770s the Dutch imported the same proportion of sugar from France as they had in 1751 – but the profit potential suggested by rising sugar prices in the 1750s and then, especially, by rising coffee prices in the 1760s propelled the investment boom for some twenty years. All together, these *plantageleningen* totaled 80 million guilders; about one-half went to Surinam, one-quarter to Berbice, Demerary, and Essequibo, and the remaining one-quarter chiefly to the Danish West Indies, where Dutch economic interests had long dominated.

These credits underwrote a boom in the slave trade, which laid the basis for another doubling of the volume and value of colonial exports – to some 12 million guilders annually – between 1750 and 1770. Curiously, sugar production seems never to have permanently exceeded its mid-century level. In 1775–8 the Republic imported a record 71 million pounds of sugar annually, but only 18 million pounds came from the Dutch plantations. The French connection remained crucial. In contrast, coffee cultivation boomed: By 1775–8 Dutch imports totaled 36 million pounds, six times the level of 1751. Of this, 21 million pounds came from the Dutch plantations, 5 million from the VOC, and 7 million pounds via France. By the 1760s and '70s, Surinam and Guyana sugar and coffee, supplemented by indigo, cotton, and cacao, filled the holds of some eighty ships per year.

Once again this growth, so characteristic of the Atlantic economy, did not readily translate into profitability. A sketch of the trade and payment flows generated by the plantation economies makes this clear. In the decade 1765–74, the plantation economies reached their peak production levels, with some 60,000 slaves working 465 plantations in Surinam alone. Essequibo, Demerary, and Berbice then possessed at least 240 plantations and perhaps 25,000 slaves (in addition, the Carribean islands in 1789 counted some 22,000 slaves plus a free population of 12,000). The chief exports fetched an annual average of 12 million guilders in the Republic. The banking houses tapped some 3.7 million of these earnings in order to reimburse transporters, insurers, and commission agents. Another 2.2 million paid for plantation imports of European goods. The bankers also had to pay bills of exchange generated by the purchase of slaves and the purchase of North American foodstuffs – at least 1.8 million guilders. As Table 10.10 shows, the 12 million guilders annual revenue shrinks quickly to 4.3 million, from which balance taxes, and the hired labor of white supervisors, had to be subtracted. This leaves a balance of under – perhaps substantially under – 3 million guilders. But from 1765 to 1774, the *plantageleningen* contracted by the planters was approaching 50 million guilders, which at 6 percent interest required about 3 million guilders simply to service, and these were by no means the only debts of most planters.

Table 10.10. *Quantitative dimensions of the Dutch West Indies economy.*

A. Dutch West Indies trade, 1765–74: a model	
Value of plantation commodities in the Republic	12.0 million
Value of commodites shipped from St. Eustatius and Curaçao	6.0 million
Total imports from West Indies	18.0 million
Retained imports[a]	6.0
Imports of goods for re-export to West Indies[b]	3.0
Total imports	9.0
Re-exports of West Indies commodities[c]	15.0
Exports to colonies and other W. Indian destinations[b]	6.0
Total exports	21.0
Trade balance [(re)exports - retained imports)	12.0
Total trade turnover	
West Indies imports and exports	24.0
European imports and exports	18.0
Total	42.0

B. Plantation economy, 1765–74: a model	
Sale of plantation commodities in the Republic	12.0 million
Freight, insurance, commission costs	-3.7
Cost of imported goods from the Republic	-2.2
Net imports from North America	-0.2
Slave purchases	-1.6
Colonial taxes	-0.8
Costs of plantation management (minimum)	-0.5
Net revenue	3.0
Interest on plantation loans (50 million at 6% interest)	-3.0

Sources: J. P. van de Voort, *De Westindische plantages van 1720 tot 1795. Financiën en handel* (Eindhoven, 1973); A. van Stipriaan, *Surinaams contrast* (Amsterdam, 1991); C. van der Oudermeulen, "Iets dat tot voordeel der deelgenoten . . .," in G. K. van Hogendorp, *Stukken raakende den tegenwoordigen toestand der Bataafsche bezittingen in Oost-Indië* (The Hague–Delft, 1801).
[a]Assume two-thirds of colonial products are re-exported.
[b]A rough estimate. Exports to the colonies stood at 2.2 million guilders per annum (Van de Voort, pp. 34–5; Stipriaan, p. 274), while the export of European goods via St. Eustatius and Curaçao, which was much more volitile, was estimated by Van der Oudermeulen (1785) at 3 to 4 million per annum. Thus, total exports to the West Indies stood at about 6 million guilders. We assume here that half these exports consisted of home-produced goods and that half were first imported to the Dutch entrepôt.
[c]The 12.0 million guilders of re-exported colonial products included sugar, which was refined in the Republic before exportation, increasing its price by over 50 percent. Other commodities were sorted, packaged, and so on *before* distribution.

Moreover, most of these plantation loans called for the repayment of principal beginning in the tenth year of the loan.[15] Clearly, a crisis was in the making.

Drought in 1769, a sharp fall in coffee prices in 1770, and in 1773 a revolt of the Morranen or "Bosnegers" (runaway slaves who formed independent communities in the interior) plunged the planters into a liquidity crisis. Compounding these problems in the colonies was the financial crisis that broke out in Amsterdam at the end of 1772. As major banking houses suspended payments, the flow of credit dried up, precipitating the bankruptcy of many plantations, the collapse of the Dutch slave trade, and the loss to investors of at least three-quarters of the capital that had been sunk over the years into the plantation loans.

The effect of this debacle on the physical output of the plantations was short-lived, but further expansion was impossible until new profit prospects could again induce new investments. And it is precisely the profitability of production that never revived. The plantations faced sharpened competition and high insurance costs as the political climate worsened. The average wealth of the resident Sephardic community in Surinam, whose members played a key role in the plantation economy, plunged by 60 percent during the 1770s.[16]

Stagnation turned to sharp decline during the Napoleonic period, as contact with the European markets was repeatedly interrupted. By 1813, 83 percent of the 333 remaining Surinam plantations were owned by absentees, often creditors of defaulted planters, who now found themselves in possession of distant properties that they had never aspired to own. In the same year the slave population, which had numbered 45,000 to 50,000 in 1788, stood at 32,489. In 1814 the new Dutch government, under pressure from its British patron, outlawed the slave trade; for all intents and purposes, it had ceased to exist some twenty years earlier. All together, Dutch slave traders had carried over a half million Africans to the New World between 1625 and 1795, half of them in the forty years after 1730.

Never in that long era had antislavery sentiment ever figured as a factor in Dutch society. The playwright Bredero, it is true, found occasion as early as 1615 to denounce slavery in his play *Moortje*: "Onmenschelijck ghebruijck! Godloose schelmery!/ Datmen de menschen vent tot paartsche slavernij!" [Inhuman custom! Godless rascality!/ That people are sold into horse-like slavery!][17] But Bredero may have been motivated more by sentiments of antisemitism than of antislavery; at that early date, slave trading appeared to Hollanders as a specialty of Portuguese Jews. After slavery became an established Dutch practice, nothing could call it into question: neither the toleration of religious minorities at home nor the pressure of slave revolts and escapes in the colonies; neither the economic logic of its

---

[15] J. P. van de Voort, *De Westindische plantages van 1720 tot 1795. Financiën en handel* (Eindhoven, 1973), pp. 110–14.

[16] R. Cohen, *Jews in Another Environment. Surinam in the Second Half of the Eighteenth Century* (Leiden, 1991), pp. 74–6.

[17] G. A. Bredero, *Moortje* (Amsterdam, 1617), lines 233–5. Quoted in J. M. Postma, *Dutch Slave Trade*, p. 11.

capitalism nor the political ideology of the Patriot and French revolutionaries. Perhaps because the white masters in the Dutch slave societies themselves formed such a polyglot community, weakly integrated to the homeland, no debate over slavery ever got off the ground. Indeed, the only notable "exposé" of slavery on the Dutch plantations was written by a foreigner. The Englishman John Gabriel Stedman's *Narrative of a Five Years' Expedition Against the Revolted Negroes of Surinam* (published in 1796), was a salacious best seller. The abolition of slavery came in 1863. After the American emancipation proclamation of that year, only Cuba and Brazil continued longer as New World slave societies.[18]

The Dutch established their plantation economy on a mercantilist footing similar to that of their European rivals. The 1682 charter of the *Geoctroyeerde Sociëteit van Suriname* expressed its aims to be the securing of

> the profit and welfare which, in case of the hoped-for success, will proliferate from this colony: through the growth of commerce and navigation, through the sale [there] of various manufactures and commodities, through the manufacture of the raw materials which will be returned here from there and, having been manufactured, will be traded by others, through the ongoing construction and repair of the ships which will sail there. . . .[19]

In the charter's enumeration of the direct and indirect economic benefits of a plantation economy, one notable item is missing. No word is mentioned concerning the profitable sale of the plantation commodities themselves. This may not have been an accident, for the Dutch plantations always lacked the one thing that their French and British counterparts enjoyed, a protected home market for sugar. The Republic imposed mercantilist restrictions on their New World colonies, requiring them to send their products to, and purchase their manufactures from, the mother country. But the States General did not similarly restrict its citizens at home in the purchase of tropical products. On the contrary, for every pound of raw sugar imported from Dutch colonies, two were imported from France. Consequently, the Wild Coast planters faced the competitive world market price of the Amsterdam entrepôt, while their competitors enjoyed the higher prices of their large, protected domestic markets.

The 200-year history of the Dutch Atlantic economy is one of repeated cycles of hope, frustration, and failure. The empire-building ambitions of the first WIC collapsed in ruin by 1650, causing a loss of capital that surely exceeded 10 million guilders. The innovative commercial system that took the place of these dreams of empire yielded much better results, but it was squeezed step by step into marginality as the mercantilist systems of France and Britain took firmer shape.

---

[18] S. Drescher, "The Long Goodbye: Dutch Capitalism and Antislavery in Comparative Perspective," *American Historical Review* 99 (1994), 44–69.

[19] Quoted in A. Stipriaan, *Surinaams contrast. Roofbouw en overleven in een Caraïbische plantage economie, 1750–1863* (Amsterdam, 1991), p. 25. Authors' translation.

On this basis Dutch participation in the Atlantic economy could long continue – it even grew in absolute size. But in the absence of production centers of its own, the Dutch share of a growing Atlantic economy could only become steadily smaller.

The third initiative took the form of recreating the colonial production centers whose lack was so sorely felt. This, too, was not without its successes: Both the slave trade and the volume of tropical products shipped to the Republic grew substantially. The volume of shipping from all West Indies origins to Zuider Zee ports grew at an average annual rate of nearly 2 percent from the 1710s to the 1770s, while in the same period, the value of Dutch plantation exports grew at an average rate of 2.8 percent per year (see Table 10.11). This was easily the most dynamic sector of Dutch trade in the eighteenth century. Yet the British and French Atlantic economies were not only vastly larger, they also grew faster. The modest Dutch colonial sugar production of the 1680s was good for some 8 percent of total Caribbean region production of 30 to 32 million kilograms. By the 1750s the fabulous growth of Saint Domingue had reduced the share of the Dutch plantations to under 6 percent of total production, and by 1775 the revival of the British plantation islands accounted for a further reduction of the Dutch plantation market share to under 5 percent of a total production of 200 million kg. Even where economic expansion was most rapid, the Dutch suffered a progressive marginalization that made their West Indian economy vulnerable to external shocks, both political and economic. In this context the financial debacle of 1772–3, in which investors lost tens of millions while surviving plantations remained saddled with untenable debt, proved permanent in its effects.

It is instructive to compare the basic features of Dutch colonial trade in the East and West Indies. The VOC succeeded in at least partially controlling supplies of Asian products and acquiring a sufficiently large share of the market to limit competition. This was much more the case in the seventeenth century, when the main traded goods were pepper and spices, than in the eighteenth century, when tea and cotton goods grew in importance. The WIC and private merchants in the New World could never avoid having to face a highly competitive market. This basic difference influenced the contrasting fates of the WIC and VOC – indeed, the contrasting fates of all Atlantic trading companies, of whatever nation, with companies active in Asia.

Still, Dutch trade in east and west also shared some common features. In both areas efforts to expand the volume of colonial trade became intense in the last decades of the seventeenth century and the early eighteenth century. These efforts to compensate for the stagnation of trade within Europe caused both east and west to loom much larger in total Dutch trade by the mid–eighteenth century than had been the case a century earlier. Moreover, despite the very different financial results in Asia and the New World, the scale of the Republic's Atlantic trade compared favorably with that of the Asian trade.

In the 1770s the approximately twenty-four ships returning annually to Patria

Table 10.11. *Indices of Dutch trade with the West Indies (annual averages, indexed to 1710–19 = 100).*

Period	Paalgeld revenue of shipping from W. I. to Zuider Zee		Value of colonial exports to Netherlands		Slaves shipped to New World	
	Revenue[a]	Index	millions of guilders	Index	Slaves	Index
1625–45					721	29
1646–64					713	28
1665–74					4,391	175
1675–99					2,880	115
1688			0.4–0.5	21		
1700–9					3,210	128
1700–4			1.7	80		
1705–9			1.9	90		
1710–19					2,508	100
1710–14	2,767	98	2.4	113		
1715–19	2,906	102	1.8	87		
1720–9					4,158	166
1720–4	2,912	103	2.7	125		
1725–9	3,215	113	2.9	136		
1730–9					4,408	176
1730–4	3,067	108	2.8	130		
1735–9	3,524	124	3.0	142		
1740–9					4,757	190
1740–4	3,566	126	5.2	245		
1745–9	5,023	177	5.9	278		
1750–9					5,078	202
1750–4	4,091	144	5.6	264		
1755–9	9,440	333	7.4	349		
1760–9					6,241	249
1760–4	10,413	367	9.7	458		
1765–9	7,203	254	12.0	566		
1770–9					5,280	211
1770–4	8,106	286	12.0	566		
1775–9	9,766	344	13.1	618		
1780–1794					1,409	56
1780–4			12.8	604		
1785–9			15.3	722		
1790–4			15.9	750		

[a]In this column, periods are 1711–15, 1716–20, etc. The *paalgeld* was a tax (to defray the cost of navigational aids) on ships entering the Zuider Zee. The tax was based on the carrying capacity of the ship.

Sources: WEST INDIES SHIPPING: W. G. Heeres, "Het Paalgeld: Een bijdrage tot de kennis van de Nederlandse handelsstatistiek in het verleden," *Economisch- en sociaal-historich jaarboek* 45 (1982), 1–17. VALUE OF COLONIAL EXPORTS: DATA FOR SURINAM: Alex van Stipriaan, *Surinaams Contrast. Roofbouw en overleven in een Caraïbische plantage economie, 1750–1863* (Amsterdam, 1991), bijlagen 1–3. For the other plantation settlements, output was estimated as a percentage of Surinam, based on the relative number of ships sailing from Berbice, Essequibo, and Demerary; the relative number of plantations in operation; and the relative number of slaves working on those plantations. The share of these settlements rises from 10 to 20 percent of Surinam output in 1700–39 to 50 percent after 1780. SLAVES SHIPPED BY DUTCH SLAVE TRADERS: J. M. Postma, *The Dutch in the Atlantic Slave Trade, 1600–1815* (Cambridge, 1990), p. 110.

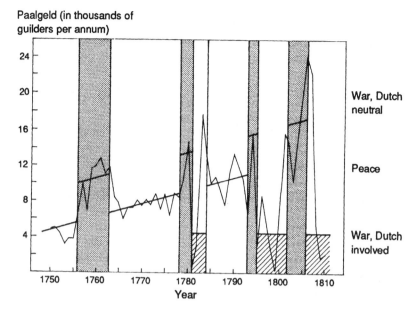

Figure 10.4. West Indies shipping in peace and war. *Paalgeld* revenues from ships entering the Zuider Zee from the Western Hemisphere, 1750–1810. *War, Dutch Neutral:* 1756–63, Seven Years' War; 1778–80, French-English War; 1793–5, French-English War; 1802–6, Peace of Amiens (1802–3) and following period in which Dutch smuggling could flourish. *War, Dutch Involved:* December 1780–4, Fourth Anglo-Dutch War; 1795–1802, French Revolutionary Wars; 1806–13, Continental System applied to Kingdom of Holland, followed by incorporation into Napoleonic Empire. [*Source:* W. G. Heeres, "Het paalgeld: een bijdrage tot de kennis van de Nederlandse handelsstatistiek in het verleden," *Economisch- en sociaal-historisch jaarboek 45* (1982), 1–17.]

from Asia carried goods that sold at auction for over 20 million guilders. In view of the information we have for the Surinam trade alone, we venture to estimate the total value of goods from all Wild Coast plantations at approximately 12 million guilders.

To this, one must add the "interloper" trade carried out from the Antillean islands, Curaçao, and, of increasing importance, St. Eustatius. The transport of sugar from the Danish West Indies and commerce with the Spanish islands formed a relatively stable element in this trade, but political conditions periodically created new opportunities for Dutch neutral shipping. Figure 10.4 displays the vast traffic that fell into Dutch hands whenever it could benefit from its neutral status while England and France were at war. Indeed, the outbreak of the American War of Independence, with its prospect of English embarrassment and the diversion of French commerce to Dutch neutral vessels so delighted the Dutch that the governor of St. Eustatius, temporarily abandoning the circumspect conduct appropriate to his weak military position, offered the first recognition of United States sovereignty with a cannon salute in 1779. (At the same time, John Adams, as American ambassador to the Republic, prowled Amsterdam drawing rooms in search of loans.) Peacetime commerce with these islands seems to have involved each year some 10 to 12 ships from Curaçao and 30 to 40 from St. Eustatius (compared to 58 and 145, respectively, in 1780).[20] They would have added several million guilders of colonial products to the Republic's imports.

To complete this survey, we must estimate the value of sugar and other West Indian products entering the Republic from France for processing and redistribution: about 10 million guilders' worth in 1750, 20 million in 1775–8, and a similar amount in 1789. The dominant position of Saint Domingue in sugar and coffee production gave France a large surplus of colonial products above the needs of her home market. The Republic and Hamburg competed for these supplies to sustain their sugar refining and redistributing functions, both of which were oriented to Northern Europe and the German hinterland.

If we focus attention on two major commodities, sugar and coffee, the dynamic character of trade in colonial goods in the second half of the eighteenth century becomes more plainly visible. Both commodities were shipped to the Republic from both the East and West Indies, although sugar imports from Asia shrank to trifling importance by the mid–eighteenth century. The 35.3 million pounds of sugar and 6.12 million pounds of coffee imported to the Republic in 1753 had a total sale value of about 10 million guilders: 7 million for sugar and 3 million for coffee. By the late 1770s, the volume and value of sugar imports had doubled, while the volume for coffee imports had grown sixfold. Since coffee prices fell, the value of imported coffee rose by fourfold. Together they represented a value of 28 million guilders. From then until the 1790s, the value of imports did not grow further, although the price changes caused coffee to grow in value and sugar to decline. This 28-million–guilder import trade (from all sources) can be compared to the 1640s, when coffee was unknown and sugar imports (at a much higher price per pound) did not exceed 3 or 4 million guilders per year.

In this new economic environment, the Dutch position was not inconsiderable, but it was vulnerable because of the marginal character of her presence in the Caribbean. Under favorable circumstances (i.e., war between England and France), the Hollanders and Zeelanders, activating their Antillean island redoubts, could handle a large volume of tropical produce, as Figure 10.4 shows. But the figure also shows how quickly this business could disappear, reducing the Dutch to the commerce of their own modest possessions. And these could not be defended. When the English attacked St. Eustatius, leveling its settlement in 1781, the "Golden Rock" saw its life as a smuggling center come to an end. When the Dutch state found itself subordinated to French ambition after 1795, it could not prevent the English appropriation of its plantation colonies. Surinam was

---

[20] Van de Voort, *Westindische plantages*, pp. 34–5.

returned in 1815, but the English retained possession of present-day Guyana. Amsterdam's role as a sugar refiner proved more durable. From one source or another, sugar continued to flow in its direction into the nineteenth century. But production levels in 1820 did not exceed those of fifty years before. The Dutch market share fell continually.

10.5. Other growth sectors

The commodities acquired in the East and West Indies came to play a key role in Dutch trade within Europe, compensating for the diminishing importance of grain, woolen and linen textiles, herring and salt, wine and timber. By the mid–eighteenth century, the Republic's entrepôt function clearly rested on the re-export of colonial products more than on the distribution of European commodities. Yet colonial products were not the only growth sectors in Dutch trade. Over the course of the eighteenth century, and particularly in the last two decades, jenever (Dutch gin) became an important export product. The distilleries were concentrated in Schiedam and neighboring towns on the Maas, and they found markets most especially in the Dutch colonies and in England, France, and their colonies. By 1792 the Republic exported 11.5 million liters of jenever, with a declared value of some 1.6 million guilders. In the difficult years after the Fourth Anglo-Dutch War and during the Napoleonic Wars, this was one of the few Dutch industrial exports that managed to hold its own.

Distilling may, with a bit of goodwill, be classified as a form of agricultural processing. As such, the rise of jenever export can be seen as one example of a more general trend in Dutch trade, the growth of agricultural exports. No comprehensive data stand at our disposal for the seventeenth century, but it seems very likely that the value of exported agricultural products – chiefly dairy products – did not approach the value of retained agricultural imports – chiefly breadgrains and industrial raw materials.

As agriculture entered a period of crisis, ushered in by rapidly falling prices in the 1660s and '70s, complaints arose concerning that sector's weak foreign trade posture. A peculiarity of the Republic's levies on foreign trade, the *Convooien*, was that it levied duties of about 20 percent on the chief Dutch agricultural exports, butter and cheese, while imported grain essentially escaped taxation. In response to the agricultural crisis, the States General introduced measures to protect domestic agriculture; they taxed imported livestock in 1671 and severely limited the importation of meat in 1686; and, as we have seen, in 1680 the *Convooien* on the grain trade were reformulated. Such measures may have improved marginally the export position of Dutch agriculture; but probably more important was the rise of labor-intensive, export-oriented crops such as tobacco and madder.

It was only in the late eighteenth century, with the revival of agricultural prices and the growth of the English market for foodstuffs, that the Netherlands became a net exporter of agricultural products. The first reasonably trustworthy statistics date from the years around 1810, when agricultural exports totaled 13 million guilders while imports of foodstuffs totaled 7 million guilders. In addition, the Kingdom of Holland then imported industrial raw materials (oilseeds, hemp, and tobacco) valued at over 5 million guilders, but the overall balance was positive and would grow thereafter to become a durable characteristic of nineteenth- and twentieth-century Dutch trade.

10.6. Dutch trade by region, 1650–1815

The shifting commodity composition of trade in the century after the 1650s directly affected the Dutch commercial position in the various European trading zones. In the Baltic, grain long remained the key commodity, and as we have seen, Dutch merchants continued to dominate that trade until the 1720s. More generally, Dutch ships continued to predominate in the total shipping passing the Danish Sound, but that total was steadily declining in volume and value. In the early 1720s, some 600 to 700 ships sailed annually from the Baltic to the Republic, with goods valued at little more than 12 million guilders. This was perhaps half the volume and value of the Dutch Baltic trade in the mid–seventeenth century. A revival followed in the 1720s, and after a retreat over the next two decades, the expansion became more forceful from 1756 (the outbreak of the Seven Years' War) into the 1770s. At its peak in the 1770s, over 1,000 ships sailed to the Republic annually with goods valued at some 17 million guilders.

But in this era of expansion, Dutch merchants definitively lost their dominant position. The Dutch import trade remained wedded to the commodities in which it had long specialized: grain, of course, plus naval stores and timber. Meanwhile, the volume of goods passing westward through the Sound grew spectacularly, driven by a growing western demand for industrial raw materials such as hemp, flax, and iron. The Republic lost its leading position not so much because of competition (for its control of the grain trade long remained intact) but because of structural changes as reflected in the commodity composition of trade that reduced the value of Amsterdam as a staple market and of the Republic as a final market for Baltic goods.

Dutch exports to the Baltic show more adaptability to structural change, for the staple market was well supplied with the colonial commodities that compensated for the decline of the herring, salt, and woolens that had filled eastbound *fluits* in the seventeenth century. After 1690, Dutch shipments of textiles, while far below the high levels of 1620–50 and the 1680s, stabilized at some 16,000 to 19,000 pieces per year – good for a 40 percent share of the Baltic market into the 1740s. But these textiles were no longer Dutch woolens; they were chiefly Asian cottons, supplied to the Dutch entrepôt by the VOC (and EIC). More dynamic was the re-export of colonial commodities. In the 1660s Dutch ships carried to the Baltic annually some 1.5 million pounds of colonial products (mainly sugar and spices). A century later this figure had risen to 7.2 million pounds per year. But even here, the Dutch market share fell: It supplied two-thirds of the Baltic's demand for colonial products as late as the 1720s, but only one-quarter by the 1770s.

Obscuring the details of Dutch participation in the Baltic trade is the phenomenon of the so-called *voorbijlandvaart*: the practice of Dutch ships sailing directly from the Baltic to their ultimate destination, bypassing the Amsterdam staple market. By comparing shipping records kept in Amsterdam with those kept at the Sound, we gain the impression that this practice involved perhaps 200 ships per year as early as the 1720s and double that number in the second half of the eighteenth century. Dutch trade in the Baltic certainly grew in the course of the eighteenth century, but this growth started from a nadir reached after the sharp contraction of the second half of the seventeenth century, and it failed utterly to incorporate the vigorous expansion of trade in industrial raw materials that propelled the Baltic trade after 1750.

The Republic's dominant position in the Russia trade, achieved soon after the establishment of Archangel as Russia's chief trading port in 1585, held throughout the seventeenth century. Indeed, this far-northern route was busier than ever in the period 1700–19, when the Great Northern War rendered Baltic commerce uncertain. Some sixty Dutch ships per year carried away cargoes valued at over 3 million guilders in these years.

A fruit of that war, the founding of St. Petersburg as Russia's "window to the West," fundamentally altered the Russia trade. Henceforth, the new capital city would be the chief Russian port, and the Dutch role there, represented by some thirty-five to fifty ships per year, never achieved better than a second-best showing behind the British. Moreover, while Dutch ships accounted for a third of all vessels calling at St. Petersburg in the 1720s, their share fell steadily to under 10 percent by the 1780s. The Republic's Russia trade specialists remained attached to Archangel, where an annual fleet of twenty to thirty ships dominated that port's trade into the nineteenth century. This does not much alter the fact that the Russian market as a whole slipped gradually out of the orbit of the Dutch entrepôt.

Trade with Denmark-Norway and the German North Sea coast, which the Dutch called collectively the *Kleine Oost*, largely took the form of an intensive traffic carried out by small coastal vessels. This North Sea littoral formed an important labor recruitment zone for the Republic's merchant marine and ports, while ports such as Emden and Bremen always functioned in the shadow of the Dutch entrepôt. Indeed, the same could be said for Hamburg in the seventeenth century, when easily half of that city's merchants were non-Germans. Between 1600 and 1650, 425 Dutch families entered Hamburg under "stranger's contracts" to form a large portion of its merchant community. (The sudden emergence of "German" ships in periods when the Spaniards imposed embargoes on Dutch shipping is obviously related to this heavy Dutch presence in the German ports.)

But in the eighteenth century, especially after 1750, Hamburg emerged as a major competitor to Amsterdam as an entrepôt for colonial products, sugar refining, and shipping and financial center. In 1633, 994 Dutch ships – mainly small coasting vessels – called at Hamburg, compared to 83 from England and France combined. In 1740, 390 Dutch ships – and in 1765, 453 – entered Hamburg, along with roughly equal numbers of English and French ships. By 1789 the 333 Dutch ships entering Hamburg were less than 20 percent of the total, and Dutch exports to Hamburg accounted for less than 10 percent of the total. The complementarity of these ports in earlier times gave way to a direct competition that diminished the intensity of their mutual trade.

Elsewhere in the *Kleine Oost,* Dutch imports of timber, linen, grain, and livestock, and exports of colonial products, bricks, tile, jenever, and a wide variety of manufactures, remained important but difficult to quantify. An estimate from the 1780s set the number of ships entering the Republic annually from Hamburg at 300, from Bremen at 75, and from the rest of the *Kleine Oost* at 325. But it went on to state that 700 vessels of at least 20 lasts entered and left the Republic via the Wadden Zee, the protected waters giving access to the German and Danish coasts. This was no exaggeration: A careful comparison of the ships entering the Zuider Zee from the open sea at Texel and Vlie in 1778 and the ships paying the *paalgeld* once in its protected waters showed an enormous discrepancy: 104 seagoing vessels from north German ports passed through the inlets; a vast swarm of 1,735 small coasters apparently sailed via the inside passage.[21]

The character of Dutch trade with England changed completely in the 150 years after 1650, under the combined impacts of the Navigation Acts, which restricted Dutch exports in England, and the internal transformation of the British economy, which both increased the variety and volume of British exports to the Republic and changed the composition of Dutch exports to Britain. For the mid–seventeenth century, no comprehensive data stand at our disposal, but it appears that the export of Dutch manufactures and the re-export of goods from continental Europe substantially exceeded Dutch imports, which consisted principally of woolen cloth, much of it unfinished.

By the 1690s, when annual British foreign trade statistics first become available, a fundamental change had taken place: The Republic's exports to Britain were now only one-half to one-third of British exports to the Republic, and the British merchant fleet, which had been perhaps one-quarter the size of the Dutch fleet in 1650, was now approaching parity. This trade gap seems to have widened in the first half of the eighteenth century, before narrowing to a two-to-one ratio in favor of Britain by 1789–92. The peculiarities of the "official values" used in the British trade statistics require caution in drawing conclusions. They probably reflect the volume of trade more faithfully than its value. Still, these data reveal

---

[21] George Welling, "Price-Supply Relations on the Amsterdam Staplemarket, 1778," in W. Heeres et al., eds., *From Dunkirk to Danzig* (Hilversum, 1988), p. 464.

in their long-term stagnation a major decline in Dutch exports of ships, linen, and continental manufactures that was roughly offset by the eighteenth-century growth of Dutch agricultural exports, particularly madder plus jenever. British trade statistics also register the evolution of exports to the Dutch entrepôt. The traditional export of woolen cloth remained by far the most important item into the eighteenth century. Indeed, shipments to Britain's continental armies during the War of the Spanish Succession probably stimulated this trade. After 1715 the swelling export of British grain – especially barley and malt for the jenever distilleries of Schiedam and Rotterdam – enlarged the trade surplus, while after the mid–eighteenth century, coal, textiles, and ironwares emerged as major British exports.

Rotterdam was far and away the most active port in the trade with Britain. The records of ships entering Maas and Goeree (the channels giving access to Rotterdam) show that nearly half of the 800 ships destined for Rotterdam each year in the period 1754–76 came from the British Isles, and that nearly half of these ships departed from a single British port: Sunderland, the port of the Northumbrian coal fields.

The Anglo-Dutch trade shifted quite suddenly, from a positive balance for the Republic to a strongly negative one, over the course of the second half of the seventeenth century. In the first half of the eighteenth century, with the rise of English grain and coal exports, this trade fell substantially into the hands of British merchants (many resident in Rotterdam) and was carried in British ships. Finally, in the second half of the eighteenth century, the commodity composition of this trade changed again; the Netherlands ceased to be a major purveyor of finished manufactured goods and specialized ever more in the exports of foodstuffs and industrial raw materials.

This step-by-step transformation of Anglo-Dutch trade reflects the long-term growth of British industry and commerce. But British emancipation from the Dutch entrepôt was not a simple linear process. Until the middle of the eighteenth century, that entrepôt remained crucial to the functioning of the most rapidly growing segment of British trade, the re-export of colonial goods.

The large British trade surpluses with the Republic that are evident from the 1690s on were substantially the product of rapidly growing re-exports of Virginia tobacco, Indian cotton textiles, and a miscellany of Asian and New World drugs, dyestuffs, beverages, and so forth. The "official values" of these re-exports to the Dutch entrepôt rose from some £200,000–400,000 in 1693–5 and to £900,000–1,100,000 in 1721–50. In the early eighteenth century, nearly half of all British re-exports of colonial goods made their way to the Republic. Prominent among these goods were Indian cotton textiles, the sale of which within Britain was prohibited by laws of 1701 and 1722; up to the 1740s, two-thirds of all the Indian textiles imported into Britain were re-exported to the Republic. Visiting or resident Dutch factors acting for Dutch merchants were conspicuous at the English East India Company's auctions, and their activity secured the Republic's role as the chief European entrepôt for colonial goods. Only after the 1740s did the volume of these re-exports decline, suggesting that the English could then handle the European distribution of their re-exports themselves.

A striking feature of eighteenth-century Anglo-Dutch trade is the intensity of the financial flows between the two countries. Although the Dutch trade balance with Britain was always negative, its income from services and investments was highly positive, apparently sufficiently so to generate a steady net flow of bullion from England to the Republic. In addition, England used Dutch banking services to make payments in Germany and the Baltic. Over the course of the period 1706–80, a total of £59 million, or 650 million guilders, entered the Republic, a sum roughly equal to the total output of Dutch mints in this period. This figure is gross; one must subtract from it the counterflow of coin to England, which regularly bought Dutch coins for use by the EIC in Asia, and which imported gold for domestic use even as it exported silver. Still, it is likely that the eighteenth-century net bullion inflow from England was large and closely connected to the developing financial functions of Amsterdam.

Dutch trade with France, like that with Britain, shifted from one of positive balances around 1650 to negative balances in the eighteenth century. The French trade statistics on which we must depend are not without their ambiguities, but they appear to reveal a substantial decline in the volume and real value of Dutch exports and a rough stability in the real value of French exports to the Republic. The Dutch share of total French foreign trade fell substantially, although it still stood at about 20 percent at the eve of the French Revolution.

The decline in Dutch exports is closely linked to the reduced frequency of French grain purchases in the eighteenth century, and to a growing avoidance of the Amsterdam staple market for Baltic products. Dutch imports of French products – wine, salt, and linen foremost among them – also declined.

In fact, the trade in European products shrank for both countries as Colberts' tariffs and repeated wartime disruptions took their toll. Unlike Dutch trade with England, the commodity composition of French-Dutch trade did not change greatly, and the Republic maintained a trade surplus in this sector throughout the eighteenth century.

When we broaden our gaze to include French re-exports of colonial goods, the picture changes. Eighteenth-century French-Dutch trade revolved increasingly around colonial products. Sugar, coffee, tobacco, indigo, and rice, not of much importance as late as 1700, accounted for half of French exports to the Republic in 1750 and fully 80 percent by 1789.

In Nantes, La Rochelle, and Bordeaux, Dutch merchant colonies, composed of families long resident in France, controlled most trade with northern Europe. As late as 1750, the compiler of the *Dictionnaire Geographique* complained that there were so many Dutch merchants in Nantes that it was difficult to "distinguish the true character of the native population" – echoing, perhaps by habit, the complaint of Jean Eon a century earlier.[22] The specialty of these merchants was intermediation of the slave trade, supplying the French with the goods needed to purchase slaves (textiles, cowries, metal, and petty manufactured goods), and buying the sugar received by the slave traders in payment in the New World.

The Dutch trade balance with France shifted from positive to negative as a consequence of the growth of the colonial trades, specifically French re-exports of Caribbean sugar. After 1750, France sought to free itself of dependence on the Dutch entrepôt for colonial goods, making increasing use of Hamburg as a distribution center. But the sheer volume of the French sugar trade was such that it overwhelmed all other French exports to the Republic. For many purposes French-Dutch trade in the eighteenth century should be seen as a branch of colonial trade rather than of European trade.

Dutch trade with Spain was little affected by the structural changes that we have observed in France, England, and the Baltic. This trade long continued to be characterized by the export of linen and Baltic and Asian commodities, and the import of salt, raw wool, dyestuffs (indigo and cochineal), and, most important of all, precious metals.

Scattered evidence, mainly from consular reports at Cádiz, indicates that the Dutch competed with the French, English, and Genoese for a share of the Spanish-American trade, usually securing between 15 and 20 percent. Ever since the conclusion of peace with Spain in 1648, the Dutch dominated the Spanish wool trade and controlled a large share of Spanish silver exports. The succession of the Bourbons to the throne of Spain in 1701 put a sudden stop to this trade, but after 1713 the trading interests that had yoked these two economies for so long reasserted themselves. In the period 1727–43, an annual average of 300 Dutch ships sailed for Iberia. This trade may have declined in later decades, but from beginning to end, the Dutch maintained a substantial trade surplus with Spain. It probably remained the Republic's chief source of precious metals.

Many of the ships setting sail for Iberia continued on through the Straits of Gibraltar to trade in the Mediterranean. For instance, the French consul in Alicante reported for the period 1664–9 that three convoyed Dutch fleets of fifteen to twenty ships each put into Alicante each year, after having called first at Cádiz and Málaga. They unloaded spices, Dutch and Flemish manufactures, Norwegian lumber, and Swedish iron, accounting all together for about 12 percent of the city's imports. These fleets then set off for Marseilles, Genoa, Livorno, and Smyrna.[23]

In the early eighteenth century, the pattern of Dutch activity must have been similar, for of the 300 Dutch ships per year that sailed to Iberia in the period

[22] Quoted in Pierre Boulle, "Slave Trade, Commercial Organization and Industrial Growth in Eighteenth-Century Nantes," *Review Française d'Histoire d'Outre-Mer 59* (1972), 70–112.

[23] H. Kamen, *Spain in the Later Seventeenth Century, 1665–1700* (London, 1980), pp. 120–2.

1727–43, an average of 70 entered the Mediterranean. Later, in 1778–90, the records of ships entering Amsterdam show some 60 per year with Mediterranean points of departure.

The shipping data reveal long-term stability in the Straits trade, but Dutch participation was always highly sensitive to political factors (after 1689, chiefly determined by relations with France) and to international silk supplies (in the second half of the seventeenth century, the Levant fleet set sail only after the arrival of fleets from Asia and Archangel, bearing news of silk shipments and prices).

In the decades after 1650, the purchase of Turkish mohair and cotton and sale of Leiden *lakens* and Asian spices gave the Dutch a strategic interest in the Levant trade. By 1674 a Venetian agent could report that the Dutch *Leeuwendaalder* had supplanted the Spanish piece of eight as the preferred coin in Levantine markets.[24] But such dominance as the Dutch enjoyed in this region was soon lost to the English and, particularly, the French. By 1715, after more than two decades of French military pressure, the Dutch merchant colonies of Livorno and Smyrna (Izmir) had become but shadows of their former selves, while the colony at Aleppo disappeared altogether. Still, the fading of these Dutch merchant colonies did not necessarily mean the extinction of trade; Levantine merchants established direct contact with the Amsterdam entrepôt, assuming control of most Dutch trade with the region after 1750. These Armenian, Greek, and Jewish merchants were kept out of the English and French trades, but the Dutch reckoned it better to admit them than to risk seeing their trade move to Hamburg or another rival port. This calculated toleration long kept the Amsterdam entrepôt supplied with Levantine goods.

Since many of the goods traded in the Mediterranean were valuable and rather exotic, it is usually thought that the Straits trade represented a large import value in the Republic and generated a major trade deficit, requiring the annual export of millions of guilders in coin to the Levant. But in the 1780s, Italy and the Levant were estimated to be the source of some 7 million guilders of imports to the Republic and to have taken 10 million guilders in exports – a substantial trade surplus. It is safe to say that there is a great deal about the Dutch trade in the Mediterranean that we do not know.

The Republic was not an island, the devout wishes of some of its leaders notwithstanding. Besides a coastline, the Republic possessed borders, across which it traded both by land routes and on the rivers with neighboring German and Southern Netherland states.

Trade contacts with the Southern Netherlands, which had been intense but frequently interrupted in the Republic's early years, may have declined after the conclusion of peace in 1648. The trade occasioned by the presence of a vast Spanish army (and the silver to support it) certainly diminished, but by way of at

---

[24] Archivo di Stato Venezia, Risposte Rep. 157, c. 163. Kindly supplied by Prof. Carlo Cipolla.

least partial compensation, Spanish policy in the Southern Netherlands became pro-Dutch, leading to very low tariffs and few restrictions on trade.

In 1699 this changed when the Brussels government came under the influence of the Count of Bergeyck, Jan van Brouchoren, who pushed through a highly protectionist and pro-French policy. This effort to remove the Southern Netherlands from the Republic's sphere of economic influence failed. Dutch economic and military retaliation quickly forced the revocation of the offending legislation. Nonetheless, the two economies tended to grow apart as the Austrian Netherlands developed the port of Oostende, established its own Asian trading company, and built roads to encourage direct trade with Liège and Germany.

Little is known about the volume of Dutch trade with the Southern Netherlands in the eighteenth century, but nothing suggests significant growth. Trade statistics for 1753 set Dutch exports at 4 million guilders, which was double the value of imports from the South (but these figures exclude the important trade via Zeeland).

The apparent trade stagnation with Flanders and Brabant stands in sharp contrast to the overland and river trade on the river Maas to the Prince-Bishopric of Liège, and on the Rhine to the German states. The flow of trade on these rivers had diminished to a trickle during the Dutch Revolt, and the long era of warfare in the upstream areas that continued to 1648 did nothing to restore the commercial vitality of these routes. The decay of the Dutch river towns in the seventeenth century stood as silent testimony to the powerful forces then reorienting northern Europe's commerce from inland to coastal regions.

Trade with the hinterland revived in the eighteenth century. Much remains unknown about the timing and early character of this revival, but it is clear that both river and overland trade grew with vigor in the second half of the eighteenth century, that the trade balances were heavily in the Republic's favor, and that by the beginning of the nineteenth century, the trade up the Rhine in particular had become (once again) of major importance to the commercial life of the Netherlands.

A modest exchange of German raw materials and linen for Dutch manufactures expanded after the 1680s, first on the strength of massive German timber shipments, and later with the shipment upstream and overland of growing quantities of colonial products. Firms in market towns such as Breda, 's-Hertogenbosch, and Zwolle bought sugar, coffee, tea, and spices through merchant houses in Amsterdam, Rotterdam, and Middelburg. They distributed these colonial goods to the outer provinces of the Republic and on to Flanders, Liège, and Westphalia. The demand for these products grew rapidly, allowing a successful firm such as F. van Lanschot of 's-Hertogenbosch to quadruple its volume between 1750 and 1770, and to quadruple it again in the more difficult period 1770–1814.

This commercial revival generated interest in road and navigation improvements in these areas for the first time in two centuries. On the Rhine the tolls (which did so much to discourage use of the river) allow us to observe a doubling of the number of vessels moving in each direction past points near the Dutch–Prussian border, from about 500 or 600 in the 1740s to 1,000 or 1,200 in 1780–3. This doubling of the traffic is consistent with *Convooien* records available for 1753 and 1790, which also reveal a doubling of the real value of trade (overland as well as riverine) with the German hinterland.

The export of colonial goods was, without question, the dynamic element in this expansion. Spices, sugar, tobacco, tea, and coffee, which accounted for 14 percent of the value of Dutch exports in 1753, accounted for fully 70 percent in 1790. Supplementing these colonial goods were small quantities of manufactured goods, fish, cheese, and salt. In return, Germany sent timber, coal, iron, stone, wine, rags (for paper production), and grain. Later, in 1816–22, the situation was no different. Colonial goods then accounted for at least 70 percent of Dutch exports, while coal, timber, wine, and grain dominated imports from Germany. The value of upstream shipments was easily double the value of the bulky goods moving downstream to the Republic. This was so despite the fact that half the vessels struggling upstream to Germany sailed empty.

10.7. The volume and value of trade, c. 1650–1815

From the mid–seventeenth century until 1780, the Republic's merchant fleet maintained itself at approximately 2,000 merchant vessels with a shipping capacity of around 400,000 to 450,000 tons. This, at any rate, is as much as the scattered and contradictory evidence allows in the way of a summary statement. On this fragile basis, earlier commentators generally concluded that Dutch shipping activity remained roughly stationary in absolute terms, declining only in relative terms. That is, Dutch shipping lost its predominance as the fleet fell under the shadow of the growing English and French merchant fleets, both of which grew rapidly in the course of the eighteenth century. As late as the 1730s, neither rival disposed of a shipping volume greater than the Republic's 400,000 to 450,000 tons; but by the 1780s, the French fleet is said to have reached 700,000 tons and the British fleet to have exceeded 1 million tons.

Two points about the Dutch merchant marine deserve emphasis. The first is that even when overshadowed by its English and French rivals, the merchant fleet remained an enormous presence in the Dutch economy. A fleet of 2,000 ocean-going vessels represented a capital investment of some 40 to 60 million guilders, involved many millions in annual maintenance and replacement costs, and ordinarily offered employment to over 30,000 merchant sailors throughout the century after 1680 (see Table 9.6). Very little is yet known about the economics and the profitability of the shipping business, but it unquestionably remained a major sector of the economy as long as the Republic existed. A late eighteenth-century observer claimed that shipping and related services generated an annual revenue of 30 million guilders. This is probably excessive (it implies 75 guilders of annual revenue per ton of shipping capacity), but the capital and labor involved in this industry could not have been maintained with a great deal less. Shipping always remained a major factor in the Dutch balance of payments, and as trade and shipping came to be less integrated, shipping as a distinct economic sector became more conspicuous.

The second point that needs to be made is that the long-term stability of the size of the merchant fleet does not imply stability in its technical and organizational characteristics. The large fleet of *fluits* sailing to the Baltic, and the specialized timber ships sailing to Norway, declined in number after the late seventeenth century. On the other hand, large vessels of over 150 lasts, usually frigates, gradually became more numerous with the growth of the intercontinental trades and the trade with distant European ports.

By the early eighteenth century, labor productivity had increased beyond the level reached a century earlier. Thanks primarily to the larger average vessel size, each crew member in Baltic and Norwegian shipping handled 12 lasts, compared to 10 lasts in 1636, and about 7 lasts in the mid–sixteenth century. Ships to the Mediterranean now maintained a manning rate of one crew member per 7.7 lasts compared to a rule of thumb of 1:5 in 1636. The issue of shipping productivity growth in the era of sail remains an unsettled one. What we observe seems to be a gradual drift toward greater efficiency and rational exploitation of long-known techniques rather than anything approaching a technical breakthrough. Changing markets, port organization, and military risks weighed heavily in these developments. This is confirmed by the fact that the trend toward larger vessels for some purposes was counterbalanced, especially after 1750, by the growing use, especially in the revived Baltic trade, of small vessels (under 100 tons) such as *koffen*. The many small *rederijen* (shipowning partnerships) of Friesland specialized in the operation of these small vessels, and Amsterdam merchants found them increasingly advantageous as a response to both silted harbors and, after 1780, military dangers.

The average carrying capacity of Dutch vessels sailing to the Baltic declined from 105 lasts in 1700–19 to 96 lasts in 1754–79, to 86 lasts in 1780–99.[25] After 1815, Dutch vessels were smaller still, carrying cargoes that averaged only 65 lasts.

The assumption that changes in the size of the merchant fleet reflect changes in the volume of Dutch trade can only be valid if foreign vessels played no large role in trade with Dutch ports. As late as 1780, this continued to be true; by one account three-quarters of all vessels then calling at Dutch ports were of Dutch registry. After that year matters become more confusing. The outbreak of war with the English induced hundreds of shipowners to place their vessels under neutral flags. Notarial documents survive that record the "sale" of over 500 Dutch vessels for this purpose. Foreign merchants lent their names as *pro forma* owners of Dutch vessels in exchange for a 2 percent commission on the sale price of the ships and an equal commission on freight income. The affairs of the ship contin-

---

[25] J. V. Th. Knoppers, *Dutch Trade with Russia from the time of Peter I to Alexander I* (Montreal, 1976), Vol. I, pp. 281–2.

ued to be managed by the original owner; yet after hostilities ended, few of these vessels were returned formally to Dutch ownership. The separation of trade and shipping permitted the evolution of a remarkably cosmopolitan breed of ship-owners. Based in the Netherlands, they used whatever flag was advantageous and carried goods to whatever port was required. After 1780 we can no longer assume that Dutch ships regularly sailed to Dutch ports for the account of Dutch merchants. The combined pressures of war and attractions of internationalization of shipping untied the remaining connections of shipping to the Dutch entrepôt.

When the dust had settled after the Napoleonic wars, the Dutch merchant fleet was but a shadow of its former self. In 1824 it consisted of about 1,100 vessels. The 900 that had been built in the Netherlands averaged but 100 tons (50 lasts) in capacity while the 200-odd foreign-built ships averaged 250 tons. The 140,000 tons of shipping capacity (one-third of the pre-1780 level) then handled no more than half of the diminished commerce of Dutch ports.

The impression of a merchant marine of roughly constant size until after 1780 is too vague to be of much use as a guide to the volume and value of Dutch foreign trade. For this purpose more sensitive and directly relevant indicators are needed. One such indicator is the record of the number of ships entering Dutch ports year by year (or proxies for such data, such as harbor duties levied per incoming or outgoing ship). The most comprehensive such records, noting the number of ships entering the shipping lanes giving access to the Zuider Zee (Texel and Vlie – see Map 2.2) and to the Maas ports (Maas and Goeree), are available only for the eighteenth century. They can be supplemented by the counts of vessels calling at the harbors of Amsterdam and Rotterdam, which are large subsets of the more comprehensive counts and are available for longer time spans. Together these time series reveal a long-term inflow of some 4,000 vessels per year. There were notable fluctuations in each region. Traffic in the Maas was low around 1710 and in the 1730s and '50s. But in the Zuider Zee, where most ships were bound for Amsterdam, the low points were around 1720 and the 1740s. When taken together the overall fluctuations tend to become more muted until 1780. The Fourth Anglo-Dutch War and the French period struck commerce in both regions in much the same way: Only about 3,400 ships per year entered Holland's ports in the period 1780–4, and under 2,000 per year did so in the period 1795–9. But from 1700 to 1780, the shipping records convey a strong image of stability.

Before then, only the number of ships entering Amsterdam is known (from 1662). Shipping movements were highly variable in the late seventeenth century, but they generally stood at a substantially higher level than after 1700: Except for the crisis years 1672–8 and the years 1688–91, they averaged above 3,000, while thereafter 2,500 was closer to the norm. Before 1662 the receipts from the *veilgeld* – a tax that varied according to the size and point of origin of the ship – give a general idea of Amsterdam's harbor activity. From 1642, when it was introduced, the *veilgeld* rose to an all-time high in 1648–51 – at least 60 percent higher than the 1660s – after which it tended downward, punctuated by war-induced low points until the 1670s.

Trends in the number of ships entering Holland's ports – none of this information sheds light on Zeeland, Friesland, or Groningen – can be summarized as follows: From an historical peak at the mid–seventeenth century, the number of ships tended gently downward, interrupted by the English wars, until the crisis of the 1670s. Thereafter, there was recovery, particularly in the 1690s, after which the trend was again gently downward until the 1740s. After 1750 the number of incoming ships rose, particularly during the Seven Years' War, when the neutral Republic profited from the state of belligerency that hobbled her chief rivals.

The Fourth Anglo-Dutch War, by crippling the Republic's intercontinental trades, can claim the honor of inducing absolute decline in the Republic's shipping volume. This expressed itself not in a gradual diminution of trade but in extreme instability. Caught between great powers no longer willing to tolerate Dutch neutrality, shipping bobbed on turbulent political seas: Brief booms (in 1788–92, stimulated by grain shortages in France, and 1804–5, occasioned by a pause in the wars) were followed by deep depressions, ending in the almost total cessation of trade in 1807–8, and in the years of incorporation in the French Empire, 1811–3.

The general trends are clear enough, as is the timing of major turning points. What remains imperfectly known is the intensity of growth or decline in these various periods. After all, the total number of incoming ships combines indiscriminately the large, richly laden vessels from distant places, and the 50-last coasters from Rouen or Bremen; it weighs equally an East Indiaman and a coal scow from Sunderland.

A frequently invoked indicator of the course of foreign trade is the *Convooien* and *licenten*, the tariffs levied by the Admiralties on imported and exported goods. Since the detailed records of the goods taxed were long ago destroyed, we have for all but a few years nothing more than the total revenue raised by these tariffs. Taken together these revenues give an impression of long-term stability; that is, the usually brief episodes of rise and decline oscillate around a stationary long-term average. The many imperfections of this measure (discussed earlier) have dissuaded us from placing much faith in it.

A superior source, albeit pertaining only to imports to the Zuider Zee ports and available only from 1700 onward, is the *Paalgeld*. This charge on incoming goods, levied for the purpose of maintaining navigational buoys and lighthouses, appears to reflect faithfully changes in the *volume* of imports.

Cargoes entering the Zuider Zee from European ports registered no rising trend in the period of 1711–50, but trade volume rose sharply in the two decades after 1750. From 1765 to 1780, the *paalgeld* receipts from European trades stood 30 percent above the level prevailing before 1750.

This source permits a separate identification of trade with the New World.

This trade – overwhelmingly with the Caribbean region – grew with a special vigor: *Paalgeld* receipts from West Indies ships accounted for 12 to 14 percent of total receipts in the 1710s, 17 percent in the 1750s, and 25 percent by the 1770s (and over 50 percent in the peculiar conditions prevailing between 1805 and 1808).

The *paalgeld* did not register the commercial activity of the trade with Asia. The VOC paid a flat fee per incoming ship. But from the Company's own records, we know that its shipments doubled in volume between the 1680s and 1720s and crept slowly upward until the 1770s. It declined substantially only after 1780.

In summary, the fragmentary records show a decline of European trade led by the decline of the Baltic trade in the second half of the seventeenth century. This persisted until after 1750, when the volume of the Baltic trade grew again. The records reveal more adequately the expansion of the intercontinental trades in the course of the century after 1680. This second complex of trading activities did not compensate fully for the decline of the first until 1750, when a brief but vigorous period of growth re-established the Republic's trade volume at something approaching the mid–seventeenth century level.

The several port cities of the Republic did not participate equally in these trends. The relative importance of the ports changed, reflecting a process that Johan de Vries has labeled "internal contraction." This term refers to the progressive concentration of commercial activity in the strongest of the Republic's trading cities, Amsterdam. By the mid–eighteenth century, little remained of the structure of complementary commercial centers organized around the Amsterdam entrepôt. The *Convooien* receipts, flawed as they are, reveal this process of consolidation. They show that the three small Admiralties representing the ports of Zeeland, North Holland, and the provinces of Friesland and Groningen, declined from 31 percent of all receipts in the 1640s to 16 percent in 1753, and to a mere 8 percent in 1790. Over the same period, the port of Amsterdam's receipts grew from 46 percent in the 1640s to 50 percent in 1753 and 64 percent in 1790. These percentages should not be taken literally (underreporting of Zeeland's trade probably worsened over time), but the basic trend is strongly confirmed by the population trends of the port cities. Amsterdam and Rotterdam (and nearby Schiedam) were the only port cities to maintain and even add to their mid–seventeenth century populations. In contrast, the North Holland and Zeeland ports shrank to nearly half their peak populations. By the late eighteenth century, they were well on their way to becoming the backwaters that would guarantee their appeal to generations of tourists in the twentieth century. It follows from this that the trends of seaborne trade volume sketched earlier – based exclusively on Holland and chiefly on Amsterdam – understate somewhat the extent of decline.

A reconnaissance of evidence concerning the size of the fleet and the volume of foreign trade does not necessarily permit us to draw conclusions about the *value* of Dutch foreign trade. This is particularly true in an era of major change in the structure of trade. We have observed that the decline of trade in voluminous commodities such as grain and timber was compensated for by the rise of trade in much less voluminous colonial commodities. Furthermore, the decline of most secondary ports had as its pendant the revival of river and overland trade through the many inland commercial centers. In this context it is of obvious interest to have independent knowledge of the value of the Republic's imports and exports, including, of course, re-exports.

Theoretically, the *Convooien* enable us to reconstruct the value of imports and exports, but even if they were not badly compromised by underreporting, detailed records survive for only a few isolated years, and only for one or another of the Republic's five Admiralties. The important study of Johan de Vries makes use of surviving 1753 and 1790 *Convooien* for the Admiralties of Amsterdam and the *Maaze* (i.e., Rotterdam) to estimate the value of imports and exports. By his accounting Amsterdam's foreign trade totaled 40.5 million guilders in 1753 and 111.3 million in 1790. Rotterdam's trade stood at 26.0 million in 1753 and 36.8 million in 1790. To this information Johan de Vries adds his guess of the value of the trade of the other ports, of cross-border trade, and of the intercontinental trades (which were exempt from the *Convooien*) to conclude that the total value of the Republic's exports plus imports doubled from 125 million guilders in 1753 to 250 million in 1790. He asserted that the price level doubled in the interval, implying that the real value of foreign trade remained stationary.

Detailed *Convooien* records have also survived for 1667–8 but only for Amsterdam. From this record the French historian Michael Morineau has constructed estimates of exports and imports that, in principle, can be compared to the eighteenth-century estimates of Johan de Vries. Morineau finds Amsterdam's imports to amount to 465,000 tons (of which, 60 percent was grain, 20 percent timber) valued at 53.6 million guilders. Exports by his reckoning were much less voluminous (75,000 tons, 41 percent of which was grain) and were valued at 28.9 million guilders (i.e., only half of imports).

Little can be said about either the accuracy or representativeness of these three point estimates, but when taken at their face value, they lend support to two generalizations: (1) that the total real value of the Republic's foreign trade in the late eighteenth century was of the same order of magnitude as in the 1660s, and (2) that the real value in the mid–eighteenth century was substantially less.

Johan de Vries's claim of stability between 1753 and 1790 is based on a price adjustment that is obviously excessive. A cost of living index (heavily weighted with grain and other foodstuffs, which led the inflation of this period) rose by only 32 percent in the interval 1753–90; Posthumus's wholesale price index, based on twenty-six commodities, rose by only 20 percent, and most colonial commodities, which should weight heavily in any price index intended to adjust foreign trade values, rose very little.

These fragments of information seem consistent with the argument that we have developed in this chapter regarding the *trends* of Dutch foreign trade. But what about the *level* of the value of foreign trade?

The figure of 250 million guilders is broadly consistent with an estimate made in 1784 by VOC director Cornelis van der Oudermeulen in a pamphlet urging reform of the Company. In fact, he offered two independent estimates of the value of Dutch foreign trade. First, he exploited the knowledge that some 4,100-odd ships annually entered Holland's ports, and a like number departed. He supposed that these vessels, on average, carried goods valued in the Republic at about 20,000 guilders. The total value of imports and exports together thus came to 165 million guilders. The small coasting vessels entering Dutch ports via the Wadden Zee, the trade of Zeeland, and the river and overland trades of the Republic accounted for an additional 35 million, by his reckoning. To the European trades valued at 200 million, van der Oudermeulen added the value of the East and West Indies (35 and 28 millions, respectively) to reach a total value of 263 million for a typical year in the 1780s.

Van der Oudermeulen's second, more detailed estimate began with a survey of the Republic's foreign trade on a country-by-country (or region) basis. He was in a position to be well informed about this issue, and later "political arithmeticians" such as W. Keuchenius, R. Metelerkamp, and G. K. van Hogendorp regarded his estimates highly enough to adopt them in their own analyses. The estimates do not always distinguish between exports and imports; he and the other pamphleteers of the time were more interested in the total value of trade and the amount of capital involved in this sector than in the trade balances. But van der Oudermeulen's estimates can be compared to other sources, especially the foreign trade statistics of other countries. In this way we can hope to offer improved estimates of the Republic's imports and exports.

While van der Oudermeulen's chief interest was the total value of foreign trade, our concern is to distinguish imports from exports, and re-exports from the exports of goods produced in the Republic. That is, the trade balance and the entrepôt function are of special interest to us. For this reason we begin by estimating the value of imports and proceed from there to examine the role of re-exports (the entrepôt function), the scope of retained imports, and that of exports of Dutch-produced goods.

Table 10.12 summarizes our estimates for Dutch imports in the 1770s. The value of all imports totaled 143 million guilders; colonial goods accounted for 61 million, or 43 percent of the total: 36 million of this was imported directly from the Dutch colonial system, and the remaining 25 million consisted of French and British re-exports to the Dutch entrepôt.

The greater part of colonial goods, whatever their provenance, did not find its final market in the Republic but was re-exported, sometimes after processing, to a wide variety of European markets. In the case of European goods, redistribution was also of importance, of course, but a higher percentage was retained.

Table 10.12. *Reconstruction of Dutch foreign trade in the 1770s (millions of guilders per year).*

Region	Imports from	Exports to
Southern Netherlands and Germany	10	20
Northern Europe		
Baltic	17	
Other	5	
Total	22	17
Great Britain	20	10
Colonial re-exports	5	
France	5	10
Colonial re-exports	20	
Iberia	16	28
Mediterranean	7	7
Western Hemisphere	18	6
Asia	20	2
Total	143	100

	Imports			Exports		
	Retained	Re-exported	Total	Domestic[a]	Re-exports	Total
European goods	53	27	80	21	27	48
Colonial goods	21	42	63	10	42	52
Total	74	69	143	31	69	100

[a]Includes all value added to re-exported goods.
Source: See page 503.

Following van der Oudermeulen, we set colonial re-exports at 66 percent of imports; European re-exports are set at 35 percent.

It follows from this estimate of re-exports that rather more than half of all imports were retained – 21 million guilders' worth of colonial commodities and 56 million worth of European goods. What might have been the value of Dutch exports, to be added to the 69 million of re-exports? This question can be approached in two ways: by identifying the specific export products and their value, and by estimating the value of exports to their various destinations, region by region. It is clear from several sources that the Republic's trade balance in the late eighteenth century was heavily in deficit. Substantial trade surpluses were maintained only with Spain, Germany, and the Southern Netherlands. Van der Oudermeulen's estimates imply total exports valued at little more than 100 million guilders. If our calculation of re-exports is close to the mark, the export of Dutch products stood at about 31 million guilders. Does this accord with our knowledge of Dutch exports?

In the 1770s the chief Dutch exports by value were jenever, refined sugar, spun tobacco, madder, and dairy products. Exports of paper, linen, soap, herring, and a miscellany of manufactures were individually now of minor importance. When one subtracts from the export value of jenever, sugar, and tobacco the cost of the imported raw materials (which are accounted for under re-exports), the 31-million–guilder figure for Dutch exports is not altogether unreasonable. The trade balance for the 1770s is heavily in deficit, although invisible earnings (from shipping, insurance, banking services) and earnings from foreign investments more than compensated for this, from all we can tell, allowing for a payments surplus from which further investments abroad could be made.

This sketch of the Republic's foreign trade in the late eighteenth century rests on a combination of quantitative data and assumptions checked against our knowledge of domestic production and consumption. It is by no means a precise accounting.

In view of the provisional character of this sketch, it might appear rash indeed to attempt such an exercise for earlier periods, when the insight of van der Oudermeulen is not available to guide us. Still, enough is known to suggest how Dutch foreign trade may have evolved toward its structure in the 1770s. Table 10.13 presents our very approximate estimates of imports, re-exports, and exports for two benchmark periods, the 1650s and 1720s, together with the data for the 1770s. In the 1650s the volume and value of imports were broadly comparable to the 1770s, but the composition and geographical origins of imports differed greatly. Goods from beyond Europe played as yet a modest role: roughly 13 percent of all imports versus over 40 percent in the 1770s. Moreover, half of all exports were of Dutch origin rather than re-exports; by the 1770s only one-third of exports represented domestic production.

In the 1650s the Dutch entrepôt was dominated by grain, timber, salt, and wine plus the products of the domestic economy – woolens, linens, herring, fish,

Table 10.13. *Approximate development of Dutch foreign trade in the 1650s, 1720s, and 1770s (millions of guilders, current values).*[a]

Exports from The Netherlands			
Exports to:	1650s	1720s	1770s
Europe, by sea	105	73	72
Belgium and Germany by land	10	10	20
Extra-European	5	7	8
Total	120	90	100
These exports consisted of			
Re-exports			
European goods	49	26	29
Colonial goods	11	22	40
Domestic exports	60	42	31
Imports to The Netherlands			
Imports from:			
Europe, by sea	120	78	95
Belgium and Germany by land	5	6	10
Extra-European	15	24	38
Total	140	108	143
These imports consisted of			
European goods	124	74	80
Colonial goods	16	34	63
Balance of commodity trade	-20	-18	-43

[a]Invisible earnings (from shipping, insurance, banking services) formed a large positive item, but there is at present little basis on which to estimate it. Eighteenth-century contemporaries felt that 30 million guilders per year was earned in this way. Interest income of foreign investments is known with regard to government bond holdings (see Table 4.8), but returns from direct investments are not. By the 1770s interest on foreign government bonds brought in about 11 million guilders, a figure that continued to rise into the first decade of the nineteenth century. The balance of payments appears to have been positive throughout the period covered here, supporting the capital exports chronicled in Chapter 4.

Source: See page 503.

ships, and pottery products. By the 1720s the classical re-export commodities were in decline, colonial re-exports had grown substantially, and the domestic economy was losing several of its most important export industries (textiles, herring, milled timber), while industries oriented to the re-export sector (tobacco processing, sugar refining, jenever distilling, cotton printing) gained in strength.

Table 10.13 demonstrates that the similarities between the mid–seventeenth and late eighteenth centuries with respect to the volume and value of foreign trade are superficial. The mid–seventeenth century trading complex had the Baltic "mother trade" at its core, importing raw materials for domestic processing and exporting many products of domestic industry. This trading complex, highly integrated with the domestic economy, began to unravel in the 1670s. By the mid–eighteenth century, not much was left of it. But a new trading complex emerged after 1680, reaching maturity after 1750. At its core were the colonial trades, the Republic's new "mother trade." The processing of colonial commodities stimulated important new industries, the *trafieken* of the port cities, but in the eighteenth century, the domestic content of Dutch exports (domestic raw materials and/or value added in processing or manufacturing) fell substantially, giving Dutch trade a much more pronounced re-export character.

This process did not go unnoticed. The Republic's interest in maintaining its entrepôt did not take the form of an ideological attachment to free trade. A pragmatic spirit generally guided tariff policy, and the 1725 tariff revisions introduced a systematic protection of agriculture and domestic manufacturing. Import duties on foodstuffs and manufactures rose while the export duties on these goods disappeared; likewise, import duties on raw materials fell, often to zero, while the export duties on them rose. Protection of domestic production was systematic, but it was not extreme. The 1725 tariff's protectionism was carefully constructed to be consistent with the Republic's entrepôt function, and the overall level of tariffs fell. But they were wholly insufficient to stave off the decline of uncompetitive producers.

This disassociation of trade from domestic production had its pendant in the disarticulation of the trading, shipping, and financing functions of the international merchant. The ownership and operation of ships became increasingly a separate activity from the buying and selling of commodities. In addition, the financing of trade developed into a separate activity. As a consequence the seventeenth-century merchant who integrated all of these activities at the Republic's ports yielded ground to ship-operators *(reders),* many of them located in small Friesian towns, who carried cargoes owned by others. The merchants, in turn, often became commercial agents, selling goods for a fee on behalf of the actual owners. Finally, owners of capital frequently financed trade in which they had no direct commercial interest. Indeed, they stood ready to finance the trade of foreign merchants whose goods did not necessarily flow to or from the Republic. The evolution of the forms of commercial organization is discussed more fully in Chapter 4. Here we simply call attention to the fact that this separation of commercial functions brought about a disintegration of the Republic's trading system. Dutch ships sailed from point of origin to ultimate destination without passing through the Republic's entrepôt (the *Voorbijlandvaart*, or bypass trade); merchants handled the sale of goods without owning them and without assuming the associated risks (the *Commissiehandel*); Dutch capital was invested in the trade of foreigners, liberating them from dependence on the services of Dutch merchants. None of these specialist functions, by themselves, necessarily harmed the Republic's trade, but together they signified a reduction in the relative power of Dutch merchants vis-à-vis the buyers and sellers with whom they dealt.

As grain, timber, salt, and wool and linen yarn imports fell, imports of sugar, coffee, tea, tobacco, and finished cloth rose. Sugar refining, tobacco processing, and jenever distilling grew in the eighteenth century, it is true, but none of these industries added much value to the imported raw materials, nor were they labor-intensive. They could not begin to compensate for the loss of employment occasioned by the decline of shipbuilding and lumber sawing, herring fishing and salting, cooperage, woolen cloth production and finishing, linen bleaching, and beer brewing. The re-export function of the Dutch entrepôt became steadily more pronounced, and even here the effect on domestic employment was probably negative, since the storage and redistribution of colonial products did not require the vast army of workers that had been supported by the grain trade in its heyday.

The eighteenth-century history of the Republic is sometimes described as an effort to preserve the redistributive function of the entrepôt under increasingly adverse circumstances. And yet the entrepôt dimension of Dutch trade became, if anything, more pronounced in the eighteenth century. It was precisely this increased dependence on footloose re-export trades that made Dutch commerce increasingly vulnerable to foreign competition. Moreover, since there were steadily fewer compelling reasons for European trade to focus on the Republic, the disintegration of the shipping, merchant, and financial functions into separate specialties was nothing more than a rational response to a new reality. Each component function made the most of a new environment in which suppliers and customers had more choice and thereby gained leverage over those furnishing commercial services.

Between the mid–seventeenth and late eighteenth centuries, Dutch trade shifted its geographical orientation from the *Oost-* and *Westvaart* axis of the Golden Age – the coastal routes connecting Iberia and France to the North Sea and Baltic – to a new emphasis on the Netherlands' hinterland – accessible overland and by the Rhine and Maas rivers – and to the overseas trading zones in Asia and the Caribbean. The old routes did not lose all importance, but the dynamic elements resided in the new duo of very near and very distant markets that would characterize Dutch foreign trade throughout the nineteenth century as well.

The German hinterland hardly figured in the commercial thoughts of seventeenth-century Dutch merchants, but its growing importance in the eighteenth century became clear around 1750 when the new Stadhouder, Willem IV, and his commercial adviser, the banker Thomas Hope, advocated the introduction of a limited *porto franco*, a free port policy to revive the Republic's entrepôt function. To blunt the competitive challenge that London, Hamburg, and even Oostende and Dunkirk then posed to Amsterdam, the Stadhouder proposed the abolition of all tariffs and the introduction of free transit privileges to all merchants. Tariffs revenues would decline, of course, but the supporters of this *Propositie van 1751* expected this loss to be more than compensated for by the stimulus that it would provide to the entrepôt, to shipping, and to the *trafieken* industries. Opponents doubted whether the abolition of already very low tariffs – the effective rate did not much exceed 1 percent – could act as much of a stimulus to trade. As it happens, the untimely death of Willem IV in 1751 removed such political momentum as the *Propositie* possessed. Moreover, a revival of trade in the 1750s is said to have made merchants complacent and unwilling to innovate, but their unwillingness was reinforced by the gradual realization that the monopoly position the Dutch ports held over the German hinterland was becoming ever more important. Whatever advantages the *porto franco* offered in competition for the flows of coastal trade would seem to be undone by the new possibilities that it offered German merchants to bypass the Dutch and trade directly with the world beyond the Republic's ports. The Netherlands held fast to this prohibition of a free transit trade on the Rhine until 1851.

10.8. Conclusion

Foreign trade rarely acts as the engine of growth of an economy. Even when the foreign trade sector is large relative to the size of the total economy – as it always was in the Netherlands and is to this day – the dynamic role of foreign trade depends on the underlying capacity of the domestic economy to transform and to respond to new possibilities of international specialization and exchange. The strength of the seventeenth-century Dutch economy rested upon just such an interaction of domestic transformation and foreign trade expansion. Together they created an economic complex that allowed Dutch merchants to dominate many markets while producers were encouraged to invest in increasing output.

When these interactions weakened, the whole of the Dutch economy became something less than the sum of its parts. Each of the commercial functions of shipping, trading, and finance became more vulnerable to competition and, thus, riskier and less profitable. The gradual reorientation of trade from the European coastal axis (the *Oost-* and *Westvaart*) to the international-hinterland axis represented an alert response to changing market opportunities. The dynamic eighteenth-century British economy experienced the same reorientation. (In 1720, 80 percent of British exports were destined for continental Europe, and most of them were domestic exports; by the 1780s only 45 percent of exports went to the Continent, and colonial re-exports now dominated. British products went primarily to Ireland and the colonies.) But in the case of the Netherlands, neither its colonial nor its German hinterland markets became great purchasers of *Dutch* manufactures. Correspondingly, the Netherlands did not participate in the booming late eighteenth-century import trades in Norwegian timber or Baltic industrial raw materials. In both cases no amount of commercial sophistication – present in abundance – could overcome the weakness of the linkages to domestic production or, rather, to domestic *industrial* production, for the rural economy did succeed in reorienting itself to the new market opportunities created by rapid British growth. Partially obscured by the heavy hand of warfare, blockades, and the Continental system in the period 1795–1815 was the emergence of the Netherlands as a major exporter of foodstuffs and raw materials.

Sources for Tables 10.12 and 10.13: Cornelis van der Oudermeulen, *Iets dat tot voordeel der deelgenooten van de Oost-Indische Compagnie en tot nut van ieder ingezeten van dit gemeenebest kan strekken* (1785), in G. K. van Hogendorp, *Stukken raakende den tegenwoordigen toestand der Bataafsche bezittingen in Oost-Indië* (The Hague–Delft, 1801). The estimates presented by van der Oudermeulen are adjusted, and distinctions between import and export values made, where necessary, with the use of the following supplementary sources. These sources also guided the estimates of trade volume in the 1650s and 1720s. DUTCH FOREIGN TRADE: W. G. Heres, "Het paalgeld: een bijdrage tot de kennis van de Nederlandse handelsstatistiek in het verledenm," *Economisch- en sociaal-historisch jaarboek* 45 (1982), 1–17; Johan de Vries, *De economische achteruitgang der Republiek in de achttiende eeuw* (second edition, Leiden, 1968), pp. 19–57; H. Brugmans, "Statistiek van den in- en uitvoer van Amsterdam (1 Okt. 1667–30 Sept. 1668)," *Bijdragen en mededelingen van het Historisch Genootschap* 19 (1898), 125–83; J. V. Th. Knoppers, "De vaart in Europa," in J. R. Bruijn et al., eds., *Maritieme geschiedenis der Nederlanden* (Bussum, 1977), pp. 233–43. 1804–07: H. R. C. Wright, *Free Trade and Protection in the Netherlands, 1816–30* (Cambridge, 1955). GERMAN HINTERLAND TRADE: Jurgen Heinz Schawacht, *Schiffahrt und Güterverkehr zwischen den Häfen des Deutschen Niederrheins und Rotterdam vom ende des 18. bis zur mitte des 19. Jahrhunderts (1794–1850/51)* (Cologne, 1973); Marie Scholz-Babisch, *Quellen zur Geschichte des klevischen Rheinzollwesens vom 11. bis 18. Jahrhundert* (Weisbaden, 1971); J. F. E. Bläsing, *Das goldene Delta und sein eisernes Hinterland, 1815–1851* (Leiden, 1973). GERMAN-DANISH COASTAL TRADE *(Kleine Oost)*: E. Baasch, "Hamburg und Holland im 17. und 18. Jahrhundert," *Hansische Geschichtblätter* 35, Band XVI (1910), Bläsing, *Das goldene Delta*, p. 197. RUSSIA: P. de Buck, "De Russische uitvoer uit Archangel naar Amsterdam in het begin van de achttiende eeuw (1703 en 1709)," *Economisch- en sociaal-historisch jaarboek* 51 (1988), 126–93; Jake V. T. Knoppers, *Dutch Trade with Russia from the Time of Peter I to Alexander I. A Quantitative Study of Eighteenth Century Shipping*, 3 vols. (Montreal, 1976); J. van Berkel, "Statistische en andere gegevens betreffende onzen handel en scheepvaart op Rusland gedurende de 18de eeuw," *Bijdragen en mededeelingen van het Historisch Genootschap* 34 (1913), 350–404. BALTIC TRADE: P. de Buck and J. Th. Lindblad, "De scheepvaart en handel uit de Oostzee op Amsterdam en de Republiek, 1722–1780," *Tijdschrift voor geschiedenis* 96 (1983), 536–62; J. A. Faber, "De Sontvaart als spiegel van de structuur-veranderingen in de Europeese economie gedurende de achttiende eeuw," *Tijdschift voor zeegeschiedenis* 1 (1982), 91–101; H. C. Johansen, "Ships and Cargoes in the Traffic between the Baltic and Amsterdam in the late Eighteenth Century," in W. J. Wieringa et al., eds., *The Interactions of Amsterdam and Antwerp with the Baltic Region, 1400–1800* (Leiden, 1983), pp. 161–70; J. A. Faber, "Scheepvaart op Netherland in een woelige periode," *Economisch- en sociaal-historisch jaarboek* 47 (1984), 67–78; Pierre Jeannin, "Preis-, Kosten-, und Gewinnunterschiede im Handel mit Ostseegetriede (1550–1650)," in I. Bog et al., eds., *Wirtschaftliche und sociale Strukturen im saekularen Wandel* (Hanover, 1974), pp. 494–517. ENGLAND: David Ormrod, *English Grain Exports and the Structure of Agrarian Capitalism, 1700–1760* (Hull, 1985); David Ormrod, "English Re-exports and the Dutch Staplemarket in the Eighteenth Century," in D. C. Coleman and Peter Mathias, eds., *Enterprise and History. Essays in Honor of Charles Wilson* (Cambridge, 1984), pp. 89–115; D. W. Jones, *War and Economy in the Age of William III and Marlborough* (Oxford, 1988); D. W. Jones, "Sequel to Revolution: The Economics of England's Emergence as a Great Power, 1688–1712," in J. I. Israel, ed., *The Anglo-Dutch Moment* (Oxford, 1991), pp. 389–406; Charles Wilson, *Profit and Power* (London, 1957); Christopher J. French, "London's Overseas Trade with Europe, 1700–1775," *Journal of European Economic History 23* (1994), 475–501. FRANCE: Michel Morineau, "Le balance du commerce Franco-Neerlandais et le Ressenement economique des Provinces-Unies au XVIIIème siècle," *Economisch- en sociaal-historisch jaarboek 30* (1963–64), 170–235; Michel Morineau, *Pour une histoire économique vraie* (Lille, 1985); John Clark, *La Rochelle and the Atlantic Economy* (Baltimore, 1981), pp. 38–9; Paul Butel, "France, the Antilles, and Europe in the seventeenth and eighteenth centuries: renewals of foreign trade," in James Tracy, ed., *The Rise of the Merchant Empires* (Cambridge, 1990), pp. 153–73. IBERIA: Henry Kamen, *Spain in the Later Seventeenth Century, 1665–1700* (London, 1980), pp. 117–39; John Everaert, *De internationale en koloniale handel der Vlaamse firma's te Cádiz, 1670–1700* (Brugge, 1973), pp. 277–8, 453; Michel Morineau, *Incroyables gazettes et fabuleux métaux* (London and Paris, 1985), pp. 267, 302; Wm. von den Driesch, *Die ausländischen Kaufleute während des 18. Jahrhundert in Spanien und Ihre Beteilingung am Kolonialhandel* (Cologne and Vienna, 1972); Frank Spooner, *Risks at Sea* (Cambridge, 1983), p. 50. MEDITERRANEAN AND LEVANT: Jonathan I. Israel, "The Phases of the Dutch *Straatvaart*, 1590–1713," *Tijdschrift voor geschiedenis 99* (1986), 1–30; G. R. Bosscha Erdbrink, *At the Threshold of Felicity* (Ankara, 1975); Michel Morineau, *Pour une historie economique vraie* (Lille, 1985), pp. 295–326. EAST AND WEST INDIA TRADES: See sources for Tables 10.6, 10.10, and 10.11.

Analysis

Chapter 11
City and country:
The social structure of
a modern economy

11.1. City and country in symbiosis

The preceding chapters have emphasized over and again that Dutch society from the sixteenth century was dominated by its cities. During the sixteenth century, the nobles, and rural society more generally, could still nurture the illusion that they formed a counterweight of significance. But from the final decades of that century, the cities were in fact fully dominant: economically, politically, culturally. The power and influence of the cities in the province of Holland was, of course, proverbial. But in many other provinces, the cities also dominated, as is clear from both the high urbanization rates of these provinces and the constitutional provisions for their influence. Two developments conspired to strengthen the political position of the cities in most provinces in the period that bridges the medieval and early modern eras. The triumph of the Reformation eliminated the clergy as an autonomous center of political power, leaving only the burgers (i.e., the cities) and the nobles to occupy the offices of state. Of these two surviving orders, the nobility had been severely weakened, and in many cases impoverished, by the extended social and internal political conflicts that had filled most of the fifteenth century. The Reformation only exacerbated the problems of this beleaguered order, since it forced its members once again to declare their allegiance, now pro or contra Philip II and the Catholic Church. Many nobles found it impossible, whether for social or spiritual reasons, to renounce their allegiance to the old order and were automatically excluded from the political system when the new Republican order triumphed.

Developments in the province of Zeeland offer a particularly clear example of this process. Before the Revolt the States of Zeeland consisted of three orders –

the abbot of Middelburg, the Zeeland nobility, and the cities – each entitled to a single vote. The Reformation removed the abbot of his franchise. Since most Zeeland nobles had chosen the cause of Philip II, they, too, were stripped of their right to participate in the provincial States. Only the Prince of Orange remained as a qualified representative of the noble order, and three attempts by the other nobles (in 1615, 1616, and 1651) to be restored to their ancient rights were torpedoed by the cities of Zeeland. These cities, indeed, were the great winners of this process. The seven cities with rights to representation in the States no longer shared a single vote, but each now possessed its own voting rights. The Prince of Orange, it is true, also gained a great deal, for he not only possessed the noble vote but dominated, through his acquisition in 1581 of the titles of marquis of Veere and Vlissingen, the votes of those two cities. Of the seven votes in the States of Zeeland, Orange effectively exercised three, and the other four cities (Middelburg, Zierikzee, Goes, and Tholen) one each, giving the cities together a majority. No wonder, then, that they saw little merit in the petitions of the nobles for the restoration of their rights in the provincial assemblies.

In Holland the cities dominated totally. After the Revolt they controlled eighteen votes while the nobility held only one. The political dominance of the cities was not everywhere as strong as in Holland and Zeeland, of course, and especially in Overijssel and Gelderland the nobility always remained an important social force, wielding a political power to be reckoned with. But even there, the cities weighed in more heavily than any other political force. The only real exceptions to the rule of urban dominance existed in Drenthe, a territory with no political influence, and Friesland. The cities of Friesland managed measurably to enhance their political power as a result of the Revolt, but a majority position eluded their grasp. The cities formed one of the Friesian States' four chambers, with the province's three rural "quarters" represented in the three other chambers. In the course of the seventeenth century, the Friesian States even experienced a sort of "refeudalization," as the provincial nobles managed to expand their power in these rural quarters. Yet these Friesian aristocrats hardly constituted a classic example of a hereditary European nobility; most of them were the descendants of rich farmers who fashioned in the course of the late Middle Ages an elite – the so-called *hoofdelingen* – that we here call, by convention, a nobility.

This brief reconnaissance of political relations, which endowed no less than fifty-seven cities with direct political representation in the various provincial states, lets us appreciate once again the pronounced urban character of Republican society. The provinces varied considerably in their constitutional organization, but everywhere the urban preponderance was palpable. And this characteristic was as important for economic life and social relations as it was for politics.

Does this mean that the countryside functioned primarily as a zone of exploitation for the cities? There are moments when this appeared to be the direction in which matters were drifting. We have had several occasions to call attention to the infamous *Order op de buitennering* of 1531, Holland's license to crush the development of rural industry. The urge to follow Holland's cities in this direction existed also in Friesland and Utrecht. But in these provinces, the local nobles were sufficiently strong that without their cooperation, let alone in the face of their active resistance, the efforts to subordinate the countryside to the privileged cities foundered on the shoals of unenforceability. Such measures that prevailed fell into disuse during the Revolt, when political survival required unity and concerted action rather than internal discord.

There is one exception to this rule, and it is a curious one at that. Groningen emerged from the era of the Revolt as the one province where the countryside was permanently subordinated to a dominant city: Groningen. What makes this so strange is that the city of Groningen long remained obstinately loyal to the Catholic camp of Philip II while the rural districts struggled – early and doggedly – against these forces, and thereby against the dominance of the city. The rural districts had good reason to hope that they would finally be released from their medieval subordination to the city when, finally in 1594, the city was restored to Republican obedience. The States General declared that it would establish a new constitutional regime for the province in the following year. It proved to be a moment highly revealing of the natural tendency among the cities, whose political influence in the States General was supreme, to let urban interests always and everywhere prevail: Against all expectations they restored the city of Groningen to her old rights and privileges. These privileges extended to the economic sphere, for Groningen's staple privileges were re-established, requiring the villages to sell their produce exclusively at the city's markets and enforcing the city's monopoly control over rural economic relations in general. In this province, all roads led to the city of Groningen.

Apart from the *curiosum* of Groningen, it cannot be said that animosity characterized the relations between city and country. In most cases the two achieved a sort of symbiosis, or formed an economic continuum. In any event, no deep chasm separated the two. Except perhaps for the more remote areas of Drenthe and the nation's extreme East and South, urban life and culture had so penetrated the rural districts as to diffuse any social contrasts and conflicts of interest. Cities and villages functioned within the context of hierarchical relationships in which one's place sprang not as much from power relations and involuntary dependence as it indicated one's functional role in economic, social, and cultural relations. The high degree of differentiation in this structure of interdependence reflected the early replacement in this region of an autarkic economy with one defined by occupational specialization and market relations. The greater and more differentiated the range of goods available for purchase by rural folk, and the more the city became the source for specialized goods and services, the more citified became the character of rural life and the more self-sufficiency was eroded. Research carried out over the years in North Holland, Friesland, Overijssel, the Veluwe, and Zeeland has repeatedly uncovered a surprising modernity in rural society, as measured by the phenomena of occupational differentiation and density of specialized occupations in rural areas. Put differently, the distances that rural consumers had to travel to be supplied with particular goods and services was often strikingly short. This suggests that rural demand was sufficiently strong to make it attractive for specialists in the rural settlements to offer a substantial variety of goods and services.

Figure 11.1 offers an overview of seven specialized functions that were provided in the villages of North Holland in 1811. These functions are broadly defined, as follows:

Religious: The presence of a church.
Economic: The presence of: (a) storekeepers (retail services), (b) a pawn bank, tavern- or innkeeper (economic services), and (c) clockmaker, silversmith, saddlemaker, wigmaker, or pastry baker (luxury crafts).
Medical: The presence of a doctor or surgeon.
Judicial: The presence of a notary, lawyer, or law court.
Social: The presence of a hospital or orphanage.
Cultural: The presence of a book seller, musician, or sculptor.
Educational: The presence of a Latin School.

Figure 11.1 reveals clearly enough the presence of a continuum of functions distributed among the cities and villages of the region. The region's eight cities stood at the peak of the hierarchy, offering the broadest range of functions. Most comprehensive were the two most important cities, Alkmaar and Hoorn. But Enkhuizen also still managed to offer something in each of the seven categories. In the five smaller cities (Medemblik, Purmerend, Zaandam, Edam, and Monnikendam), no higher-order educational services were available, and one or another of the other functions was also often missing. A second group of thirteen villages possessing a semi-urban character fit neatly under the true cities in North Holland's hierarchy. Places such as Schagen, Beverwijk, Krommenie, and De Rijp generally offered no educational or cultural functions, and sometimes the social or judicial functions were also missing. Then follows a third group of some twenty places that rarely provided the social function but did generally possess judicial officers. These were the larger agricultural villages, such as Assendelft, Graft, Landsmeer, Winkel, Zijpe, and Beemster, which served the needs of farmers in a larger area. Finally came some thirty-six villages that never offered more than three of the seven functions, almost always the religious, economic, and medical. That is, these smallest of settlements possessed a church, a shopkeeper or two, and a surgeon, all serving strictly local needs.

No sharp division separated city from countryside in this example. Differences existed among the cities, as expressed by the point totals that each achieved (based on the completeness with which they carried out each of the indicated functions). These totals ranged from 100 (the maximum score) in Hoorn and Alkmaar down to 60 for Monnikendam. The semi-urban places joined this array to form a nearly seamless declension, one also characteristic within the rural settlements, as the range of functions gradually diminished until the smallest places were reached – the sixteen villages possessing only the "basic equipment" of rural life. Every transition – among the cities, between city and village, among the villages – was a gradual one, forming a continuum in the aggregate.

This example – North Holland in 1811 – might raise doubts as to its typicality: The region was commercialized at an early date, and 1811 is at the very end of our period. Consider, therefore, a comparable analysis of occupational distribution in the Veluwe in 1749. This more remote and thinly populated region may serve as a test of the generalizations just made. Figure 11.2 orders twenty-six occupations by their distribution among twenty-four villages (*kerspels*). None of these places functioned in 1749 without the services of a resident clergyman, schoolmaster/sexton, tavern- and/or innkeeper, and tailor. Only one village lacked a carpenter. Shopkeepers, shoemakers, and millers were missing in only two of the twenty-four villages, a smith in three, and the wagonmaker/wheelwright in five. Thus, nearly every village possessed at least one practitioner of these ten basic occupations. Less common were bakers, brewers, roofers, and weavers, but well over half the villages could avail themselves of these services locally. All the remaining occupations listed in Figure 11.2 show up in less than half the villages. Particularly noteworthy is the scarcity of surgeons; they were present in only ten of the twenty-four villages, while they were ubiquitous in North Holland. Nor does the addition of midwives and apothecaries change matters, for, with but one exception, they were present only in villages with surgeons. Apart from this curious difference between a region of the urbanized West and one in the rural East, the chief conclusion of our comparison must be that by the mid–eighteenth century, both featured a considerable occupational differentiation, and both offered rural dwellers a substantial array of specialized goods and services.

Reinforcing this conclusion is the evidence assembled in Table 11.1, showing the frequency with which selected occupations were encountered per thousand inhabitants in four regions: the Veluwe in 1749, Overijssel in 1795, the islands of Zeeland in 1807, and a portion of North Holland in 1811. The four sources are not altogether consistent in how the data were gathered: In one case only male heads of household are accounted for; in another, women's occupations were included; in a third, only men above age twenty-three (voting age) were surveyed. In addition, the treatment of secondary occupations is not everywhere the same. Still, these blemishes do not generate biases that rob the results of a basic comparative usefulness.

Of the twelve occupations included in the table, four stand out as exceptional. Carpenters, tailors, shoemakers, and tavern-/innkeepers existed everywhere at the minimum rate of two per thousand. That is to say, there was always at least one practitioner of each of these occupations per 500 inhabitants. "At least" is the operative phrase here, for the frequency was usually much higher. In the cases of

Municipality	Points	Religious	Economic	Medical	Judicial	Social	Cultural	Educational
Alkmaar	100	×	×	×	×	×	×	×
Hoorn	100	×	×	×	×	×	×	×
Enkhuizen	85	×	×	×	×	×	×	×
Medemblik	75	×	×	×	×	×	×	—
Purmerend	75	×	×	×	×	×	×	—
Zaandam	70	×	×	×	×	×	×	—
Edam	65	×	×	×	×	×	×	—
Monnikendam	60	×	×	×	×	×	×	—
Schagen	45	×	×	×	×	—	—	—
Beverwijk	40	×	×	×	×	—	×	—
Den Helder	35	×	×	×	×	×	—	—
Krommenie	35	×	×	×	×	×	—	—
Westzaan	35	×	×	×	×	×	—	—
Zaandijk	35	×	×	×	×	×	—	—
Kook a/d Zaan	35	×	×	×	—	—	—	—
Broek in Waterland	30	×	×	×	×	—	—	—
Grootebroek	30	×	×	×	×	×	—	—
Uitgeest	30	×	×	×	×	—	—	—
De Rijp	30	×	×	×	—	×	—	—
Velsen	30	×	×	×	—	×	—	—
Wormerveer	30	×	×	×	—	×	—	—
Assendelft	25	×	×	×	×	×	—	—
Castricum	25	×	×	×	×	—	—	—
Graft	25	×	×	×	×	—	—	—
Ilpendam	25	×	×	×	×	—	—	—
Jisp	25	×	×	×	×	—	—	—
Landsmeer	25	×	×	×	×	—	—	—
Oosthuizen	25	×	×	×	×	—	—	—
Oostzaan	25	×	×	×	×	—	—	—
Venhuizen	25	×	×	×	×	×	—	—
Warmenhuizen	25	×	×	×	×	—	—	—
Winkel	25	×	×	×	×	—	—	—
Wormer	25	×	×	×	×	—	—	—
Zijpe	25	×	×	×	×	—	—	—
Beemster	25	×	×	×	—	—	—	—

Primary level — Secondary level — Tertiary level

Buiksloot	25	x	x	x	—	—	—	—	
Hoogkarspel	25	x	x	x	—	—	x	—	
Scharwoude	25	x	x	x	—	—	—	—	
Blokker	20	x	x	x	x	—	—	—	
Nieuwe Niedorp	20	x	x	x	x	—	—	—	
Schermerhorn	20	x	x	x	x	—	—	—	
Abbekerk	20	x	x	x	—	—	—	—	
Barsingerhorn	20	x	x	x	—	—	—	—	
Beets	20	x	x	x	—	—	—	—	
Bergen	20	x	x	x	—	—	—	—	
Broek op Langedijk	20	x	x	x	—	—	x	—	
Egmond aan Zee	20	x	x	x	—	—	—	—	Local level
Heerhugowaard	20	x	x	x	—	—	—	—	
Hoogwoud	20	x	x	x	—	—	—	—	
Middelie	20	x	x	x	—	—	—	—	
Obdam	20	x	x	x	—	—	—	—	
Oude Niedorp	20	x	x	x	—	—	—	—	
Oudkarspel	20	x	x	x	—	—	—	—	
Ransdorp	20	x	x	x	—	—	—	—	
Twisk	20	x	x	x	—	—	—	—	
Wieringerwaard	20	x	x	x	—	—	—	—	
Wognum	20	x	x	x	—	—	—	—	
Zwaag	20	x	x	x	—	—	—	—	
Andijk	15	x	x	x	—	—	—	—	
Avenhorn	15	x	x	x	—	—	—	—	
Berkhout	15	x	x	x	—	—	—	—	
Bovenkarspel	15	x	x	x	—	—	—	—	
Egmond-Binnen	15	x	x	x	—	—	—	—	
Heemskerk	15	x	x	x	—	—	—	—	
Heiloo	15	x	x	x	—	—	—	—	
Nibbixwoud	15	x	x	x	—	—	—	—	
Nieuwendam	15	x	x	x	—	—	—	—	
Schellinkhout	15	x	x	x	—	—	—	—	
Spanbroek	15	x	x	x	—	—	—	—	
Ursem	15	x	x	x	—	—	—	—	
Akersloot	15	x	x	—	x	—	—	—	
Harenkarspel	15	x	x	—	—	—	—	—	
Sijbekarspel	15	x	x	—	—	—	—	—	
St. Maarten	15	x	x	—	—	—	—	—	
Schoorl	10	x	x	—	—	—	—	—	
Zuidschermer	10	x	—	x	—	—	—	—	
Koedijk	5	x	—	—	—	—	—	—	

Figure 11.1. Service functions of North Holland towns and villages, 1811. The presence of a given function is indicated by an "**x**" and its absence by a "–." The functions are listed in order of the frequency with which they appear in North Holland as a whole. The vertical line, drawn to minimize the number of unfilled spaces, defines the range of functions characteristic of places in each level of the settlement hierarchy. (*Source:* C. Lesger, *Hoorn*, Appendix F.)

	Apeldoorn (2,270) (63%)	Heerde (1,670) (68%)	Epe (1,840) (61%)	Vaassen (930) (53%)	Ede (1,650) (67%)	Barneveld (1,870) (51%)	Scherpenzeel (680) (33%)	Putten (1,870) (77%)	Beckbergen (1,170) (68%)	Lunteren (1,090) (78%)	Oldebroek (1,090) (77%)
Reformed pastor	x	x	x	x	x	x	x	x	x	x	x
Sexton, schoolmaster	x	x	x	—	x	x	x	x	x	x	x
Tavern- or innkeeper	x	x	x	x	x	x	x	x	x	x	x
Tailor	x	x	x	x	x	x	x	x	x	x	x
Carpenter	x	x	x	x	x	x	x	x	x	x	x
Shopkeeper	x	x	x	x	x	x	x	x	x	x	x
Shoemaker, repairer	x	x	x	x	x	x	x	x	x	x	x
Miller	x	x	x	x	x	x	x	x	x	x	x
Smith	x	x	x	x	x	x	x	x	x	x	x
Wheel & wagon maker	x	x	x	x	x	x	x	x	x	x	x
Weaver	x	x	x	x	x	x	x	x	x	x	x
Roofer	x	x	x	x	x	x	x	x	—	x	—
Baker	x	x	x	x	x	x	x	x	x	x	x
Brewer	x	x	x	x	x	x	x	x	x	x	x
Mason	x	x	—	x	x	x	x	—	x	—	—
Surgeon	x	x	—	x	x	x	x	x	—	x	x
Wooden shoe maker	x	x	x	x	x	—	—	—	x	x	x
Spinster	x	x	—	—	x	x	x	x	x	x	—
Cooper	x	x	x	x	x	x	x	x	x	—	x
Painter	x	—	x	x	—	—	—	—	—	—	—
Glassmaker	x	x	x	—	—	—	—	—	—	—	—
Midwife	x	—	—	—	x	—	—	x	—	—	—
Apothecary	—	x	—	—	—	x	—	—	—	—	—
Barber-surgeon	—	—	x	x	—	—	—	—	—	—	—
Clockmaker	—	—	—	x	—	—	x	—	—	—	—
Butcher	—	—	—	—	—	x	x	—	—	—	—

Figure 11.2 (*above and opposite*). Service functions in the church villages (*kerspels*) of the Veluwe, 1749. An "x" indicates the presence of an occupation in a given village. After the name of each village is listed the total population and the percentage of the household heads with occupations who were engaged in agriculture. The villages and occupations are both arranged so as to minimize the number of unfilled spaces. The vertical line defines the occupations that form the "standard equipment" of villages of varying centrality. For details on the village boundaries, see *A. A. G. Bijdragen* 11 (1964), 140–6. [*Source:* H. K. Roessingh, *A. A. G. Bijdragen* 13 (1965), 214–15.]

	Renkum (730) (51%)	Oene (530) (63%)	Loenen (640) (56%)	Bennekom (660) (72%)	Hoevelaken (400) (66%)	Oosterbeek (460) (58%)	Elspeet (350) (69%)	Otterlo (530) (76%)	Garderen (600) (85%)	Voorthuizen (850) (85%)	Veessen (420) (61%)	Vorgten (210) (76%)	Kootwijk (430) (88%)
	x	x	x	x	x	x	x	x	x	x	x	x	x
	x	x	x	x	—	x	x	x	x	x	x	x	x
	x	x	x	x	x	x	x	x	x	x	x	x	x
	x	x	x	x	x	x	x	x	x	x	x	x	x
	x	x	x	x	x	x	x	x	x	x	x	x	—
	x	x	x	x	x	x	x	x	x	x	x	—	—
	x	x	x	x	x	x	x	x	x	x	x	—	—
	x	x	x	x	x	x	x	x	x	x	—	—	x
	x	x	x	x	—	x	x	x	x	x	—	x	x
	x	x	x	x	—	x	x	x	x	x	—	—	—
	x	x	—	x	x	x	x	x	—	—	—	—	—
	—	x	x	x	x	x	—	—	—	—	x	—	—
	x	x	x	x	x	—	—	—	—	—	x	—	—
	x	x	x	—	—	—	x	x	x	—	—	—	—
	x	x	—	—	—	—	—	—	—	—	—	—	—
	—	—	—	—	—	—	—	—	—	—	—	—	—
	—	—	—	—	x	—	x	—	—	—	—	—	—
	—	—	x	x	x	—	x	x	—	x	—	—	x
	—	—	x	—	—	x	—	—	—	x	x	—	—
	—	—	—	—	—	—	—	—	—	—	—	—	—
	—	—	—	—	—	—	—	—	—	—	—	—	—
	—	—	—	—	x	—	—	—	—	—	—	—	—
	—	—	—	—	—	—	—	—	—	—	—	—	—
	—	—	—	—	—	—	—	—	—	x	—	—	—
	—	—	—	—	—	—	—	—	—	—	—	—	—

Table 11.1. *Occupational frequency in four rural districts (practitioners per 1,000 inhabitants).*

	Veluwe 1749	Overijssel 1795	Zeeland islands 1807	Noorderkwartier of North Holland 1811
Carpenter	5.0	5.0	3.7	8.8
Skipper/teamster	1.3 (max.)	6.5	3.3	7.7
Baker	2.6	2.0	1.5	5.4
Tailor	5.4	4.0	3.9	4.1
Shoemaker	4.4	3.6	2.1	2.9
Inn-/tavernkeeper	8.2	2.9	3.5	3.1
Mason	0.6	0.7	ᵃ	2.5
Painter	0.2	0.6	0.5	1.3
Butcher	0.1	0.8	3.2	1.9
Doctor/surgeon	0.6	0.7	1.2	1.8
Smith/locksmith	2.0	1.4	2.0	1.7
Cooper	0.8	0.8	0.7	0.8

ᵃNot listed as a separate occupation.

Sources: Roessingh, "Beroep en bedrijf"; Slicher van Bath, *Samenleving onder spanning*; Harten, "De verzorging van het platteland"; van der Woude, *Het Noorderkwartier.*

the Veluwe and rural Overijssel, there was one carpenter for every 200 inhabitants, and everywhere one could expect to encounter one village tailor for every 200 to 250 inhabitants.

A second occupational group is formed by the bakers and transporters (skippers and teamsters). Each appeared in three of the four regions at a density of at least two per 1,000. The bakers fell below this density only in rural Zeeland, but in the district of North Holland (bounded to the south by the IJ and to the north by a line running from Alkmaar to Hoorn), the frequency reached 5.4. Here there was more than one baker for every 200 inhabitants. Throughout Overijssel and the Veluwe, there was one baker per 400 to 500 inhabitants. There, as in Zeeland, home-breadbaking must still have taken place with some regularity; in Holland nearly everyone must have purchased bread from the baker. Providers of transport services appear frequently everywhere except in the Veluwe. There, rural dwellers who did not transport their own goods had to turn to the cities (mostly little more than market towns) at the fringes of the region, which specialized in this function to the point where one of every fifty town-dwellers – i.e., about one of every twelve male workers – earned his living as a skipper or teamster.

Of the other occupations listed in Table 11.1, only the smiths/lock makers and the coopers exhibit a predictable rural presence. Smiths were found in all four regions at rates between 1.4 and 2.0 per thousand; coopers were present at a steady 0.7 to 0.8 per thousand. The four remaining occupations (doctor/surgeon, mason, painter, and butcher) display highly irregular patterns. We have already noted the sharp difference in the distribution of medical personnel between North Holland and the Veluwe; Table 11.1 confirms this difference, for the Veluwe and rural Overijssel mustered no more than one medical practitioner per 1,400 to 1,700 persons, while the rate in Zeeland was closer to one per 800, and in North Holland, one per 550. As for the other occupations, it appears that only in the maritime zone had economic specialization advanced to the point where many people could earn their livelihood in rural communities as house painters, masons, and butchers. The Veluwe farmers slaughtered their own livestock; in Holland and, even more, in Zeeland, the farmers turned to professionals to slaughter and dress their animals. In Zeeland the concentration of butchers was actually higher in the countryside than in the cities.

We may summarize the foregoing with the claim that from at least the mid–eighteenth century, the Republic's countryside possessed, with certain regional exceptions, an abundant and evenly distributed supply of carpenters, tailors, shoemakers, tavern- and innkeepers, skippers and/or teamsters, bakers, and blacksmiths. These constituted the basic specialist occupations, supplying goods and services in close proximity to the villagers. To these can be added the occupations of cooper and doctor/surgeon. These were somewhat less densely distributed across the countryside, and the medical practitioners were notably scarcer in the eastern provinces, but the average distance to one of these specialists was comparable to that for the seven basic occupations. A more pronounced regional

Table 11.2. *Occupational frequency in three groups of cities (practitioners per 1,000 population).*

	Two Overijssel cities[a] 1795	Six Zeeland cities[b] 1807	Four North Holland cities[c] 1811
Carpenter	4.7	3.0	10.5
Skipper/teamster	4.9	5.2	13.0
Baker	3.4	4.3	7.0
Tailor	6.9	3.8	5.8
Shoemaker	5.9	3.0	6.6
Inn-/tavernkeeper	4.0	8.2	8.2
Mason	3.5	1.6	4.6
Painter	1.4	1.2	4.1
Butcher	1.3	2.2	2.2
Doctor/surgeon	0.9	1.7	2.1
Smith/locksmith	1.5	1.5	2.6
Cooper	1.0	1.3	1.6

[a]Overijssel cities: Zwolle, Deventer
[b]Zeeland cities: Middleburg, Vlissingen, Veere, Goes, Zierikzee, Tholen
[c]North Holland cities: Alkmaar, Edam, Purmerend, Monnikendam
Sources: Roessingh, "Beroep en bedrijf"; Slicher van Bath, *Samenleving onder spanning*; Harten, "De verzorging van het platteland"; van der Woude, *Het Noorderkwartier.*

variation characterized the distribution of masons, painters, and butchers, but in the maritime zone, one could expect to find them in most villages.

Besides the twelve occupations thus far listed, it appears that clergymen, schoolmasters/sextons, and shopkeepers were also reasonably well distributed across the countryside. Thus, most rural dwellers enjoyed direct access to the goods and services of these fifteen occupations without having recourse to the urban economy. To the extent that the rural population did patronize urban suppliers for these things, it must have been incidental to or in combination with the purchase of the more specialized goods and services not available in the countryside. This is suggested by Table 11.2, which shows that the concentration of these basic occupations in the cities (of Overijssel, Zeeland, and North Holland), while generally higher than in the villages, was not of a different order of magnitude. The differences in the number of such specialists in country and city was a matter of degree, which implies that the Dutch countryside was substantially self-sufficient in the provision of a broad range of goods and services.

For most other goods and services, the rural population depended on the Republic's numerous cities (or an occasional large village). Figure 11.1 alerted us to the fact that educational services beyond the most basic sort, cultural activities, and most social and judicial facilities were largely unavailable in the villages. And what was absent in rural North Holland in 1811 would surely have been unavailable in most other regions of the Republic. Moreover, in view of the pronounced stagnation in North Holland's development after the mid–seventeenth century, it is more than likely that the pattern observed for 1811 was substantially in place by the 1670s. Indeed, the villages and smallest cities may then have offered rather more services than in 1811. For example, the village of Wormer possessed a Latin School for a time in the seventeenth century, only to lose it later. The same was true for Purmerend. Book sellers functioned in the third quarter of the seventeenth century in at least six North Holland villages. We hear of them later only in one, Zaandam. Thus, it is by no means obvious that the range of rural services followed a linear path toward ever greater refinement.

For more specialized goods and services, the countryside depended on the cities. The clearest expression of this fact is the number of shopkeepers in the cities and their degree of specialization. In the analysis of Zeeland occupations referred to earlier, we learn that in 1807, the province's cities supported one shopkeeper for every forty inhabitants. The rural areas supported many retailers, but the number in the cities was far larger, and these must have drawn a substantial portion of their custom from the countryside. In the Veluwe countryside in 1749, there were 4.8 shopkeepers per thousand inhabitants; in rural Zeeland in 1807, the ratio reaches 6.4 per thousand. In rural districts more distant from urban centers, the concentration of rural shopkeepers exceeded even these ratios: The Zeeland island of Noord-Beveland, devoid of cities, contained over 10 shopkeepers per 1,000 inhabitants. But even this high ratio pales beside the 25-per-1,000 average of the Zeeland cities. A modest market town such as Goes, with a population of 3,996 in 1809, contained no less than 151 shopkeepers. Yet Goes was, first and foremost, a market town and service center for the rural population of its island, Zuid-Beveland.

The concept of "shopkeeper" should be taken broadly. Besides the true, specialized retailers, the cities also very nearly monopolized a long list of occupations that typically included a retailing dimension, such as: book printer, plumber, cabinet maker, furniture maker, mirror maker, hatter, wig maker, saddler, copper- and tinsmith, tinker, gold- and silversmith, candlemaker, pastry baker, vinegar maker, coffee roaster, watchmaker, wine merchant, surveyor, musician, dance master, painter and sculptor – the list goes on. Every so often one encounters the practitioner of such an occupation in the countryside, but the natural habitat for all these occupations was the city. Together with the shopkeepers, they formed the backbone of the urban economy. The city might acquire other specialties that gave it a particular reputation – as port, textile center, garrison, financial center, government or religious center – but these retailing and service functions formed the economic core of every urban center and secured the continuity of the city even when the more specialized activities disappeared.

The importance of these two groups is readily apparent from the 1807 occupational distribution of Middelburg, the chief city of Zeeland: Shopkeepers numbered 16.7 per 1,000 inhabitants; the conglomeration of specialized services formed an additional 16.6 per thousand. Together, they formed 33.3 per thousand inhabitants. Clearly, this city, whose extraregional commercial functions were plunged into crisis in the Batavian era, was literally preserved from extinction by the stability of this provisioning function.

The rural sector could not avoid dealing with the cities in satisfying its demand for specialized goods and services; and for its part, the urban sector could not maintain itself without its rural markets. The example of Delft will make this point clear. Between 1680 and 1735, this city's population fell by some 9,000, from 24,000 to about 15,000. The employment loss associated with this depopulation may be estimated at roughly 4,500 men, women, and youths. But what were the economic activities from which so many jobs disappeared in this period? The three chief industries of Delft were then tile making, brewing, and textile production. The tile makers experienced their greatest expansion in this period. Far from explaining the decline of employment, the flourishing condition of the ceramics industry only adds to the magnitude of the historical problem. Beer productions declined by some 20 percent between 1685 and 1700, whereafter it remained stable until 1740. Even when associated trades are taken into account, the decline of the breweries could account for no more than a few hundred of the lost jobs. This leaves the textile sector to account for an employment loss of at least 4,000. Delft's production of *lakens* certainly fell in this period (from some 1,500 pieces per year in the early 1680s to 300 pieces by the 1740s), but the production of lesser fabrics such as bays actually rose in partial compensation for this loss. In any event the fate of Delft's textile industry cannot account for more than a small portion of the city's loss of employment.

How then is Delft's population decline of some 9,000 persons between 1680 and 1735 to be explained? From the thirteenth century onward, Delft ranked with Dordrecht and Leiden as one of Holland's chief cities, but by the mid–seventeenth century, two neighboring cities, Rotterdam and The Hague, attained a rough parity with Delft as urban centers. For some 500 years, Delft had been the most important provisioning center for a large part of Holland. But after 1650 it competed on a basis of equality and soon thereafter as an underdog with the ascendant Rotterdam and The Hague. The Hague honored the "law" of governmental centers the world over, growing slowly but steadily. Rotterdam's growth was far less regular, but its commercial advantages eventually pushed up its population far beyond that of Delft. These two ascendant cities found it possible to offer a larger range of crafts and services than could stagnant Delft, which soon found itself geographically squeezed between its two new rivals. Before long, Rotterdam and The Hague had diverted to themselves a large portion of Delft's former rural custom. When the agrarian crisis set in after 1660, reducing the purchasing power of rural consumers, the craft and retailing sectors of the city faced a crisis of doubled intensity: Their hinterland contracted as the purchasing power of their remaining customers fell. Delft's economy slid down the slippery slope. Her diminished service sector encouraged the defection of her remaining customers, while the declining demand forced the further contraction of her service base. This vicious circle continued until the 1730s, when a very gradual recovery of rural purchasing power acted to stabilize Delft's economy, albeit on a much smaller scale than before 1680, and subordinate to its two larger neighbor cities.

It was this process that inflicted on Delft most of its nearly 40 percent loss of population. The provisioning function appears to have been far more important than industry for the maintenance of the city, for when the ceramics and brewing industries both wasted away after 1740, Delft's population remained stable. The reduction of industrial employment was then fully compensated for by the consumer demand of a recovering rural sector.

Delft's experience was far from unique. To be sure, no other Dutch city found itself so overshadowed, even mangled, by its neighbors as did Delft. But every city experienced a decline of rural demand for its goods and services after the 1660s. For Amsterdam, The Hague, and Rotterdam, this factor would have been of only minor consequence. They possessed sufficient extraregional functions to sustain their inhabitants through this difficult period, but cities such as Alkmaar, Hoorn, Gouda, Goes, Dordrecht, Leeuwarden, Groningen, and Utrecht, all must have experienced severe setbacks. The more a city relied on the provisioning of a rural hinterland, the harder it felt these blows.

11.2. Crafts, industries, and occupational structure

The occupational frequencies displayed in Tables 11.1 and 11.2 furnish the means to estimate orders of magnitude – and nothing more exact than that – for the number of persons engaged in the twelve aforementioned occupations. The precision of our estimates obviously is limited by the fact that the four areas from which our data are drawn (Holland's Noorderkwartier, Zeeland, Overijssel, and the Veluwe) possessed just under 20 percent of the Republic's total population (about 350,000 persons) between 1750 and 1810. Even if the data were otherwise without blemish, this limited sample would require caution of the interpreter. Still, even an order of magnitude helps us to think about the character of this economy. Moreover, for eight of the twelve occupations described in the tables, additional information is also available for Friesland, raising to about 25 percent the portion of the total population on which our observations are based.

When account is taken of urban–rural differences in occupational frequencies, the data of the four regions suggest something like the following incidence of the twelve occupations (expressed per thousand population):

Carpenter	4.5	Skipper/teamster	5.5
Baker	2.5	Tailor	5.0
Shoemaker	4.0	Inn-/tavernkeeper	7.0

Mason	2.5	Painter	1.0
Butcher	1.8	Doctor/surgeon	1.0
Smith	1.7	Cooper	1.0

If these estimates of occupational frequency are not too far off the mark, they suggest that some 75,000 persons were active in these trades. A third of this number were active in and around the transport sector (as skippers or innkeepers). One of the occupational categories, that of doctor/surgeon, ranked as a liberal profession. The rest, nearly 50,000 persons, were active in the craft sector.

The Friesian data tend to reinforce these estimated frequencies in the cases of carpenters, smiths, and surgeons (excluding doctors). Coopers (1.6 per 1,000) and bakers (3.7 per 1,000) appeared at a higher frequency in Friesland than our estimates for the nation as a whole would predict, but this is consistent with our knowledge that the number of bakers varied regionally. In the East and South, home-baking held down the number of bakers, while in the large city of Amsterdam, many of the bakers hired apprentices. In 1742 Amsterdam bakers with taxable incomes of at least 600 guilders numbered 472, suggesting hardly more than 2.0 per thousand population; but if the total personnel of these businesses could be counted, the frequency would certainly rise substantially. All things considered, the original estimate of the number of bakers remains plausible.

A larger discrepancy exists between our estimates of the number of shoemakers, tailors, and innkeepers and the Friesian evidence. Relative to other areas, Friesland was full of shoemakers (5.8 per thousand), and their incidence did not vary much between city and country or among the districts of this province. The opposite was the case with tailors, who were implausibly scarce in Friesland: 1.5 per thousand compared with three times this rate in the other areas. Innkeepers were also few and far between in Friesland, which suggests the possibility that the documents on which we rely tended to pass over the poorer practitioners of these occupations.

This comparison of the available Friesian data with that for the other regions reveals several good fits and several deviant cases, but in each case, a plausible argument can be made for the observed results. The occupational frequencies presented at the beginning of this section can be retained as our best estimate, and the single most important message that they convey is that small-scale local services constituted the Republic's largest nonfarm-employment sector by far. In the chapter on industry, and also in our investigations of fishing and ocean shipping, our attention was attracted repeatedly to sectors that gave employment to large numbers of workers. In several cases we found sectors that employed thousands (as in tobacco processing, shipbuilding, lumber sawing, and textiles); in the case of ocean fishing and shipping, we identified a sector employing perhaps 33,000 around 1610 (see Table 9.6). But the attention we lavished on these important industries should not blind us to the fact that the artisanal sector numbered several occupations comparable in employment to the large, attention-grabbing sectors. Among these, carpentry and inland transport each supported some 9,000 to 11,000 men; shoemakers and tailors each numbered some 8,000 to 10,000; smiths and masons, 3,000 to 5,000 each; coopers and painters, some 2,000 each. Their strategic importance to the development of the economy may be doubted; these trades were no "engines of growth." But their ubiquity, penetrating the nation's furthest corners, advanced the process of occupational specialization, which in turn promoted increased labor productivity throughout the economy. The level of economic well-being attained by the Republic depended on this achievement.

The absence of systematic data for earlier periods prevents us from tracing the development of this occupational differentiation. But the substantial growth of labor productivity in agriculture that appears to have been concentrated in the century after 1550 suggests that it is this period that we should search, and especially in the maritime provinces. In fact, rural occupational differentiation may well have retreated somewhat after the mid–seventeenth century. This is hinted at by the disappearance of book sellers from rural North Holland, referred to earlier. Around 1650 it seemed as though the process of occupational differentiation could support even book printers and sellers in rural areas, but after 1670 this proved unsustainable, and these specialists concentrated themselves in the larger cities, and especially in Amsterdam. A similar (over)extension and subsequent retreat characterized the distribution of notaries. Lesger has shown that the number of notaries active in rural North Holland declined after 1650.

These two examples involve occupations for which systematic data are available. There are very probably other, broadly comparable economic specialties that were involved in a process of spreading to rural locations, and that also were halted or forced into retreat by the sharp economic reversals that struck the rural economy with particular force: such occupations as silversmiths, clockmakers, apothecaries, ceramics dealers, and cloth sellers come to mind. Together with many other occupations, these specialties remained largely confined to the cities. And for the acquisition of relative luxuries – such as jewelry, musical and mechanical instruments, tapestries, and refined furniture – one had to visit a major city. When the city of Hoorn prepared to receive Willem III in 1688, the organizers of the festivities found that they had to go to Amsterdam to purchase the desired game and poultry, fine vegetables, candied fruits, and delicatessen items. Even a half-century later, in 1742, Amsterdam did not support more than six *confituriers* and only two poultry specialists. The many still-life paintings that display an abundance of these products offer the viewer a portrait of exclusivity. In most places such items were not normally available at the market or in the shops; they must have been rare indeed on the dinner table.

But for goods and services of a less rarefied sort, the Republic's consumers rarely had to travel far. Most rural communities could supply everyday items themselves, while the broad range of more specialized items – barring the true rarities – were available in the nearest city. This, at any rate, is the image presented by our sources dating from 1749 (Veluwe and Friesland), 1795 (Overijssel), 1807 (Zeeland), and 1811 (Noorderkwartier). By the mid–eighteenth century, this pattern of occupational differentiation was widespread through the Republic. Only the old Generality Lands of the south may have formed a less-developed exception to this statement. About this region little is yet known. The questions we still face are *when* this pattern of occupational differentiation took shape and *how* this should be evaluated in a broader European context.

Neither question admits of a simple answer, for the only information we have is summarized in Table 11.3. The first usable national occupational census dates from 1849, and before 1749 we have nothing apart from fragmentary, local sources. In view of the absence of national-level data for the period of concern to this volume, our first step in placing the Dutch situation in a broader perspective is to use the data of Table 11.3 to estimate the national occupational distribution. Table 11.4 presents our estimates and assumptions. In view of the regionally divergent levels of urbanization, our approach is based on distinguishing the experience of Holland from the rest of the Republic and, in both zones, the cities from the countryside. For each of the four resulting categories, we draw upon data found in Tables 11.1 through 11.3 to calculate the occupational distribution. The weighted average of these distributions yields the following national results:

Agriculture	41%
Industry	32
Trade and transport	16
Other (services)	10
Unknown	1

These results correspond well with the national census of 1849, when the *male* labor force was distributed as follows:

Agriculture	45%
Industry	28
Trade and transport	13
Other (services)	14

Mindful of the inconsistencies in our sources' definitions of the labor force, we can claim for our estimates no great precision, but they are broadly representative of the proportions of the labor force active in each of these large sectors as far back as 1750. Neither structural changes in the economy nor the level of urbanization changed enough in this period to alter substantially the occupational distribution; however, matters may well have been rather different in earlier periods. Since the urbanization level fell from 45 to 38 percent over the period 1675 to 1815, and the estimates of Table 11.4 assume a 40 percent level, the possibility cannot be ruled out that the agricultural labor force of 1675 had been proportionately smaller than a century later. The fact that Holland's population was a

Table 11.3. *Occupational structure by region (in percent of labor force per sector).*

	Year	Agri-culture	Indus-try	Trade and transport	Other occupations	Laborers not assignable
Provincial or regional total						
North Holland	1811	35	38	16	9	2
Friesland	1749	44	27	18	9	2
Veluwe	1749	47	27	17	6	3
Overijssel	1795	46	36	12	5	2
Cities						
North Holland	1811	17	43	25	12	2
Friesland	1749	5	49	27	17	2
Veluwe	1749	7	51	26	13	2
Overijssel	1795	13	49	23	14	1
Rural (excluding industrial zones)						
North Holland	1811	54	25	12	7	2
Friesland	1749	62	19	14	5	—
Clay-pasture district		60	18	16	5	—
Peat-pasture district		49	20	25	5	—
The "Wouden"		66	20	11	4	—
Clay-arable district		69	17	9	5	—
Veluwe	1749	66	22	6	2	3
Overijssel	1795	60	23	11	4	2
Salland		71	18	8	3	0
Vollenhove		34	38	17	5	6
Rural–industrial						
Zaan region	1811	11	65	14	8	2
Twente	1795	44	43	8	3	2

Source: A. M. van der Woude, "A. A. G. Bijdragen and the study of Dutch rural history," in *Journal of European Economic History* 4 (1975), p. 232.

Table 11.4. *Sectoral estimates and weights used in estimating the occupational distribution for the Netherlands at the end of the eighteenth century.*

| | % of the population in 1795 | Share of the population (%) | Labor force in percentages | | | | |
			Agriculture	Industry	Trade & transport	Other occup.	Not allocated
Holland	38.2	Urban 60	5	50	25	17	3
		Rural 40	55	23	15	7	–
Rest of Republic	61.8	Urban 25	7	50	25	15	3
		Rural 75	65	20	10	5	–

larger proportion of the national total in 1675 adds further merit to this possibility. As the population weight of the inland provinces grew after 1675, the role of their dominant economic sector, agriculture, also would have grown. We have every reason to assume that the labor force active in the Republic's agriculture in 1675 was not larger, and was very likely smaller, than at the end of the eighteenth century.

The trade and transport sector was probably larger in 1675 than a century later, since seafaring then drew more heavily on the domestic labor force. The fisheries also employed more labor in 1675 than later, and we have just considered the possibility that artisanal and service employment may have moved in the same direction. All of these considerations taken together reinforce the conclusion that the agricultural sector's share of the labor force as of the late eighteenth century should be seen as an upper bound for the years around 1675. The nonagricultural-employment sectors were probably somewhat larger around 1675 than they later would be. This, at any rate, is the message of local and fragmentary information available for the second half of the seventeenth century, which reveals a degree of occupational differentiation that is not at all inferior to what we have established to be the norm at the end of the eighteenth century.

Through a combination of evidence and inference, we can render plausible the claim that the Republic already by the 1670s had attained an occupational structure and infrastructure of local provisioning that was precociously modern, one where agriculture absorbed no more – and probably less – than 40 percent of the labor force. Industry and crafts, which together accounted for some 32 percent, was not far behind, while the trade and transport sector gave employment to one of every six participants in the labor force. The remaining one-tenth of the labor force found employment in other occupations, which included services and the full range of liberal professions, such as doctors, surgeons, notaries, lawyers, and also clergymen, schoolmasters, government officials, and rentiers. None of these proportions must be taken as exact, but when understood as approximate measurements, and allowing for small adjustments through time, they can be taken as descriptive of an economic structure that persisted for some two centuries, from the mid–seventeenth to the mid–nineteenth centuries.

A simple comparison reveals how exceptional and precocious was the Republic's occupational distribution. Table 11.5 gathers together occupational censuses from a number of European nations. In most cases the first available evidence dates from no earlier than the late nineteenth century. Only in the cases of Great Britain and Germany do we have estimates from around 1800. At that date Great Britain appears just to have succeeded in reducing its agricultural sector below the Republic's level. Unfortunately, earlier English estimates, such as Gregory King's "social table" of 1688, make use of socioeconomic categories that are impossible to transform into the more strictly economic categories used here. England then was almost certainly far more agricultural than the Republic, although perhaps not as much as Germany in 1800. With an agricultural population

Table 11.5. *The occupational structure of several Northwest European countries, circa 1800–80.*

	Republic 1750–1800	Germany 1800	England 1801	Netherlands (men only) 1849	Netherlands (total) 1849	Denmark 1880	Germany 1882	France 1881	Belgium 1880
Agriculture[a]	41	62	36	45	44	50	43	39	30
Industry[b]	32	21	30	28	24	24	33	27	35
Services, other[c]	27	17	34	27	32	26	24	34	35

[a]Agriculture: Agriculture, forestry, and fishing
[b]Industry: Mining, industry, craft production, and construction
[c]Services: Trade, transportation, banking, domestic services, hospitality, recreation, culture, education, medical services, religion, administration, police, and military.

Sources: P. Flora, F. Kraus, and W. Pfenning, *State, Economy, and Society in Western Europe, 1815–1975*, Vol. II; W. Fisher, J. Krengel, and J. Wietog, *Sozialgeschichtliches Arbeitsbuch*, Vol. I; P. Deane and W. A. Cole, *British Economic Growth, 1688–1957*; J. A. de Jonge, *De industrialisatie in Nederland tussen 1840 en 1914*.

approaching two-thirds of the total, Germany represented a situation typical of much of the rest of western and central Europe.

Table 11.5 also includes occupational distributions for several west European lands in the second half of the nineteenth century, including that for the Netherlands in 1849. Here we can check the difference made when the data refer only to male workers as opposed to the total workforce. In the case of agriculture, the impact is nil; more substantial differences emerge in the other sectors, a consequence principally of the large role of women in (domestic) services. Germany seems to attain only after 1880 the occupational structure reached by the Netherlands 100 years earlier – indeed, most likely 200 years earlier. France in 1880 had also attained this early Dutch standard, while Denmark, with half its labor force still in agriculture, still had some way to go. On the European continent around 1880, only Belgium had moved decisively beyond the occupational distribution of the eighteenth-century Republic.

To summarize, the territory of the modern Netherlands possessed in the period 1650–1850 a differentiated occupational structure far in advance of the rest of Europe. By the late eighteenth century, only England had attained (later to surpass) this level, to be followed during the first half of nineteenth century by Belgium.

11.3. The nobility: A group defined by hunting privileges?

When the young Belle van Zuylen, herself descended from the Utrecht noble family Tuyll van Serooskerken, posed the question "What defines nobility?" she could find no more convincing answer than "the right to hunt." Her mid–eighteenth-century characterization of her fellow aristocrats, intended as ridicule, was formally correct (the nobles did possess unrestricted hunting rights) yet misleading in its implication of exclusivity. In her own province, the burgemeesters and sheriffs of Utrecht, Amersfoort, Rhenen, Wijk bij Duurstede, and Montfoort, plus the former burgemeesters and members of the *vroedschap* (town council) of Utrecht, and the president of the provincial high court, *all* enjoyed these same rights and had since at least 1683. In Holland the burgemeesters and *vroedschappen* of all eighteen voting cities – effectively, the entire regent class – secured for themselves this typically aristocratic privilege in 1716. Together they vastly outnumbered the handful of surviving nobles in Holland's sparse hunting grounds. Even in Gelderland, with its numerous petty nobility, the same process of "democratization" had taken place. In short, Belle van Zuylen was misleadingly incomplete.

Her intention, of course, was to stress the societal irrelevance into which her fellow nobles had descended. We should pause for a moment to consider whether in this judgment she was on firmer ground than in the formal accuracy of her answer. Was the nobility a moribund group that contributed nothing of importance to the economic life of the Republic?

To begin with we must be aware of the small size of the nobility as a group. Already at the beginning of the sixteenth century, the old hereditary nobility of Holland did not form as much as half of 1 percent of the population. And even this small share melted away in later decades. This happened in part because of the departure of families that remained Catholic and whose properties lay chiefly in the Southern Netherlands, such as Egmond, Arenberg, and Ligne; but the chief cause was the extinction of lineages in a group that withdrew into itself and to which no new blood and new names were introduced. Nowhere in the Republic did the provincial States exercise their sovereign right to create new nobles. Titles acquired abroad might have possessed social value in the Republic, but they conferred there no formal rights, not even after several generations. In theory, no one could deny that noble titles acquired abroad would, in the fullness of time, give their bearers the status of "old nobility," but in practice this transformation required the passage of centuries.

The dying out of noble families was a phenomenon common to the Republic as a whole. No fewer than 48 noble families of the Veluwe disappeared between 1600 and 1800. Friesland, which possessed 74 old noble families in 1500, saw this number decline steadily in the following 300 years. The disappearance of 9 cannot be documented precisely, but of the other 65, there remained 58 in 1600, 34 in 1700, and only 16 noble families in 1800. In Drenthe a nobility formally vested with political rights was first defined in the early seventeenth century. Of the 24 families with claims to these rights in 1650, only 10 remained in 1797, and of these, only 3 could claim direct descent from the original group. The rest were chiefly nobles who had entered the province in the course of the eighteenth century.

In Groningen, which like Friesland and Zeeland did not afford to the nobility formal representation in the provincial States, the noble families closed themselves off socially after 1650 and faced a slow but certain extinction. Until then a number of urban families had been recognized as noble, but thereafter, no more. Rural Groningen could count 45 noble families in 1600, 33 in 1700, and only 10 in 1800.

Matters seem to have been somewhat less lugubrious in Overijssel, where 185 resident noble families paid the 500th Penny tax of 1675, and in 1758 there were still 172 nobles to pay the wealth tax of that year. Here and in neighboring Gelderland, the nobles were far more numerous than in Holland, but even in these eastern provinces, this order represented but a fraction of 1 percent of the population.

Through the dying out of the male lines of a closed social group, property should have become steadily more concentrated in the hands of the surviving lines, whose average wealth we would expect to rise. The evidence does not conform to this expectation, however, which suggests that as a group, the nobility suffered a long-term loss of assets. This diminution of wealth would have led to the impoverishment of many individual nobles were it not for the compensating effects of wealth concentration in the receding number of surviving families. In order to gain a better understanding of this process, we turn now to an investigation of what little is known about the types of wealth owned by the nobility. Feenstra has examined the wealth holdings of Groningen and Drenthe nobles on the basis of probate inventories, chiefly from the eighteenth century. Then, land and real property more generally dominated the asset profile. Among nobles of rural Groningen, land constituted from 40 to 70 percent of their total fortunes, while their country houses (called *borgs*) and attached manorial rights accounted for (in 18 of 30 cases) between 0 and 20 percent of total wealth. In Drenthe, where these types of real property can rarely be distinguished, their total value was somewhat less important. In 8 of the 16 examined cases, it formed over half of total wealth; in the other 8, it fell somewhat short of 50 percent. Stocks, bonds, and other credit instruments plus cash accounted for nearly all of the remaining noble wealth. Among 27 of 38 Groningen fortunes, bonds did not exceed 20 percent of total value, but this leaves 11 in which it did, and there were 4 cases in which cash on hand was of great importance. In two cases cash accounted for 20 to 30 percent of the total fortune! In Drenthe, proverbial as a rustic backwater, 6 of the 16 examined inventories revealed the presence of bonds and other paper valued at over half the total estate. There were also 6 cases with large cash holdings – up to 20 percent of the total. Why did so many nobles hold such large cash balances? The fact that our documents record wealth directly after a death could distort our picture, of course, but another possible explanation could be a shortage of investment possibilities other than bonds (which they already possessed in abundance).

Seventeenth-century inventories of noble wealth in these provinces were too few for Feenstra to make firm generalizations. The limited available sources suggest that real property was then even more dominant than later, and that cash holdings played as yet no role. But until more documents can be located and studied, even these statements must remain highly tentative.

The primacy of landownership in the wealth composition of nobles elsewhere in the North (Friesland) and East (Overijssel and the Veluwe) cannot as yet be established directly via probate inventories, but it is strongly suggested by what is known about the distribution of landownership itself. In 1520, in the Overijssel district of Salland, the nobles possessed nearly 30 percent of the cultivated land (measured by value), and in 1601 only a little less. In Twente the nobles as a class then possessed a bit more than 30 percent, while on the Veluwe, Roessingh's study of all taxable real property (land, houses, mills) found that nobles owned about 20 percent around 1650. Nearly two centuries later, after the completion of the first cadastral register of all real property, noble ownership had retreated gently to 16 percent. Nobles possessed rather less property here than in Salland, but their holdings were concentrated on the most fertile soils (especially in the pleasant riparian zone between Arnhem and Zutphen).

In Friesland nobles owned much of the land, and there, too, their holdings tended to be concentrated in particular districts, such as the far north and north-

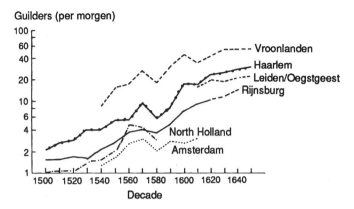

Figure 11.3. Rental price of farmland at various locations, 1500–1650 (guilders per *morgen*). [*Source:* J. Kuys and J. T. Schoenmakers, *Landpachten in Holland 1500–1650* (as drafted in H. F. K. van Nierop, *Van ridders tot regenten*).]

west of the province. It seems to have been generally true that the holdings of large landowners tended to be near their places of residence. On the Veluwe, that was in the aforementioned area between Arnhem and Zutphen; in Overijssel noble estates were strikingly concentrated in central Salland; while in Groningen and Drenthe, noble land tended to be concentrated in and around the jurisdictions where their country houses lay.

The fortunes of Holland's nobility, no less than nobles elsewhere, were dominated by real property, and this made land rents their most important source of income. In the sixteenth and first half of the seventeenth centuries, landowners generally succeeded in adjusting land rents in step with the extraordinarily favorable agricultural conjuncture (see Figures 11.3 through 11.5). At the very least, they maintained the real value of their incomes, and quite a number of nobles managed to increase their land holdings in this period. Many noble incomes in Holland were supplemented by a second source of income: tithe rights. These, too, held their value during the price revolution of the long sixteenth century, so that we have no reason to believe that Holland's handful of nobles faced a structural diminution of their incomes before the mid–seventeenth century.

The great importance of landownership to Holland's nobles does not imply its converse: that nobles were the predominant owners of agricultural land in Holland. Aggregating the available information about property ownership in Holland poses a daunting challenge because of the substantial local variation. But it is hard to avoid the conclusion that in the first half of the sixteenth century, nobles owned something between 5 and 10 percent of Holland's land, ranking them as a group no higher than fourth, after the farmers themselves (with perhaps 40 to 50 percent), the town burgers (20 to 30 percent), and the various religious insti-

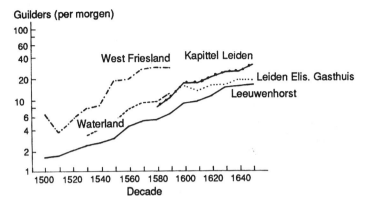

Figure 11.4. Rental price of farmland belonging to various owners, 1500–1650 (guilders per *morgen*). [*Source:* J. Kuys and J. T. Schoenmakers, *Landpachten in Holland 1500–1650* (as drafted in H. F. K. van Nierop, *Van ridders tot regenten*).]

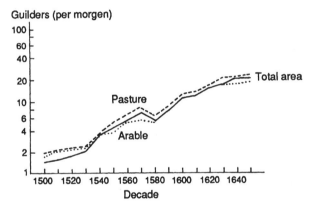

Figure 11.5. Average rental prices for all farmland, for pasture, and for arable, 1500–1650 (guilders per *morgen*). [*Source:* J. Kuys and J. T. Schoenmakers, *Landpachten in Holland 1500–1650* (as drafted in H. F. K. van Nierop, *Van ridders tot regenten*).]

tutions. Individually, many of the 200-odd noble families ranked as important property owners, of course, and their local prominence was reinforced by the tendency of their holdings to be concentrated in villages where they also possessed seigneurial rights.

Inevitably, the changed environment in which the agrarian economy found itself after the mid–seventeenth century also had consequences for the rental income that could be drawn from the land. Figure 11.6 illustrates these consequences with data assembled by Baars and applied to a "model farm" based on the historical experience of the Beijerlanden district of South Holland. Both the

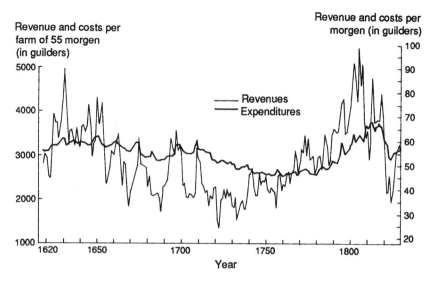

Figure 11.6. Revenues and expenses of a hypothetical 55-*morgen* farm in the Nieuw-Beijerland Polder, 1618–1830 (in guilders). (*Source:* C. Baars, *De geschiedenis van de landbouw in de Beijerlanden,* 199.)

costs and revenues per *morgen* (0.85 hectare) and those for a "model" 55-*morgen* farm can be read from this figure. Between 1655 and 1765, this hypothetical farm almost always generated losses, sometimes very large losses. Of course, agricultural production could never have suffered ongoing losses for over a century and survived. That it did survive can be explained by the model's use of the contractually agreed-upon rents as a farm cost. In reality, landlords frequently reduced rents informally, carried unpaid rents on their books for years, and periodically forgave accumulated arrears. The rents actually paid could fluctuate enormously, but until the mid–eighteenth century, even the good years usually were not good enough to raise the rents to the contractually established levels.

Landowners absorbed these losses, suffering large reductions in their incomes, for to press for full payment would have brought about the ruin of their tenants, in a setting where qualified replacements were scarce. Small wonder, then, that landowners often found it preferable to sell their land, usually at a fraction of its earlier price (see Figure 11.7), in the hope that the (meager) proceeds might be invested with more profit in another sector of the economy. Indeed, so many institutional landowners (which supply the historian with most of the archival records concerning land rents) pursued this policy of divestment that very few long-running time series of land rentals exist for the era of agricultural depression. Only by splicing together short runs of rental data drawn from the pasture districts of North Holland has it been possible to reconstruct the long-run development

Guilders per morgen

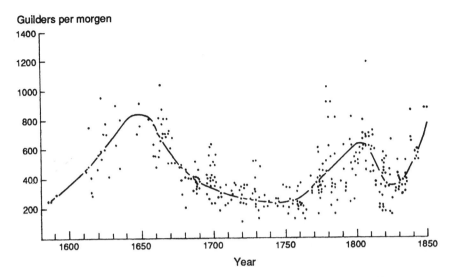

Figure 11.7. Sale prices of farmland in Nieuw-Beijerland, 1590–1850 (in guilders per *morgen*). (*Source:* C. Baars, *De geschiedenis van de landbouw in de Beijerlanden*, 112.)

across the period 1600–1800. These data, displayed in Figure 11.8, show that the rents actually paid between 1650 and 1750 could fall to 30 percent of their initial level. In addition, many farmers were also in arrears with their tax payments and perhaps also with the polder authorities. The situation in Holland was more desperate than in many other provinces, for reasons discussed in Chapter 6, but landowners everywhere suffered sharp reversals of fortune in the century after 1660.

Nobles and other landowners turned their attention increasingly to other sources of income as their rent receipts collapsed. Already around 1600 the historian Everard van Reyd wrote that the Republic was a place where "the land was flooded with money and goods, and all who held offices and governed could become rich, if they so desired."[1] It can hardly surprise us, then, that with the onset of agrarian depression, the interest in public office intensified. Adriannus van der Goes noted the agrarian crisis as early as 1671. "The council of his highness [the Stadhouder] met to lease [certain] properties," he wrote, "but instead of yielding 20, 22, 23 they yielded only 8 or 9 guilders per morgen. . . ." In another letter in the same year he observed: "he who . . . wishes to live here will need to have a large fortune (*capitael*) and hold a good office." "Regents do best [in acquiring such appointments]," he wrote further on, and "land is now-a-day a poor investment (*slegt capitael*)." Access to lucrative government offices

---

[1] "de landen overvloeyden met gelt ende goet ende ale die in officiën ende regiering waren, konden rijck werden, indien zy't sochten."

Index (1640-1646 = 100)

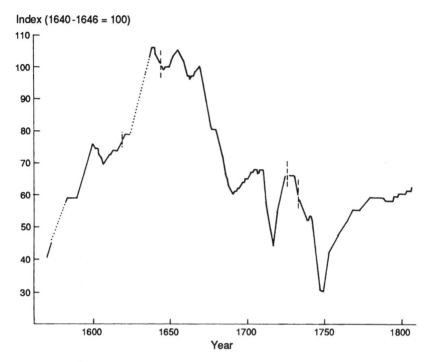

Figure 11.8. Index of the rental price of pasture land in western North Holland, 1600–1800, seven-year moving average (1640–6 = 100). (*Source:* A. M. van der Woude, "The Long-Term Movement of Rent," 179.)

depended on political power, of course, and efforts to reserve such power were more intense than ever by 1671.

In Holland a nobleman's access to financially appealing offices required membership in the *Ridderschap*, the official college of nobles that was regarded as the representative of rural society in the provincial States, where it exercised a single vote. In order to gain admission to the *Ridderschap*, one had to demonstrate noble lineage and be in the possession of historically noble property or seigneurial rights. Additional provisions, such as not being Catholic, further limited access. In 1666 the procedures for admission were reviewed systematically, with the intention of reducing the intake of new members to a minimum. From then on only the eldest son of a member could succeed to the *Ridderschap*, and only when he attained age twenty-five, and only if the sitting members did not vote unanimously against his inclusion. In practice, membership had become hereditary. It was possible for nobles from Holland to be taken in by majority vote, but those from elsewhere, even those in possession of properties in Holland, needed a unanimous vote to be admitted to the *Ridderschap*. In sum, eldest sons could all but demand entry; other Holland nobles could hope to gain admission if their credentials were unimpeachable; and outsiders could be vetoed by a single member. The wagons were being drawn in a tight circle.

This heightened exclusivity is understandable in view of the diminished profitability of landownership, for the *Ridderschap* had lucrative offices to divide among its members. It appointed, among others, the chairman of the *College van Gecommitteerde Raden* (the executive committee) for Holland's southern district, a member to the Council of State, to the Admiralties of Amsterdam and of Rotterdam, to the *Particuliere Gemenelands Rekenkamer* (the general auditor's chamber), and to the College of Curators of Leiden University. It appointed two councilors to the (law) Court of Holland and two directors of the East India Company. In addition, there were the many paid appointments to special missions and committees. All these noble appointees could expect sizable payments for every meeting they attended, and they commanded higher salaries and per diem allowances than did urban burgers appointed to the same functions. Moreover, the fees and perquisites attached to many offices exceeded the official salaries, while many functions included the right to appoint persons to lesser offices, whereby a nobleman could build up a clientele.

In Groningen the provincial States consisted of two voting entities: the city of Groningen and the *Ommelanden* (literally, the surrounding countryside). Governance of the *Ommelanden* was entrusted to the *Landdag*, a body to which were admitted *jonkers*, *hoofdelingen*, *eigenerfden*, and – in those districts with no qualified *eigenerfden* – *volmachten*. The first two categories were a kind of gentry, while the latter two were simply landowning farmers. To qualify as an *eigenerfde*, one had to own at least 30 *grazen* (about 15 hectare) with a minimum value of 1,000 guilders. For decades debate raged as to whether the property qualifying someone as an *eigenerfde* had to be concentrated in a single district (*kerspel*) or not, whether a brick residence needed to be located on this property, and other questions of this nature. In 1649 these issues were resolved, and in a generous and democratic way: The minimum property qualification sufficed, and provision was made to clarify in which district one had the right to participate.

But only ten years later, in 1659, this settlement was undone. A new regulation required that the 30 *grazen* of land be concentrated in a single district and that the *eigenerfde* inhabit a house in the same district. At the same time, the three quarters of the Groningen countryside were each divided into three subquarters and the number of districts set at 133, thereby making it harder for any individual to possess the required amount of land in a single district. In 1663 efforts to further reduce political participation failed, but enough had already been done to strengthen the hand of the *jonkers* in the *Landdag*. The fragmentation of landownership and the large number of districts combined to reduce the number of qualified *eigenerfden* in most districts to a very small number – often enough, to zero. *Jonkers* further strengthened their hold by buying the votes of farmers through lending them money for the purpose of assembling the necessary 30 *grazen* within a single district.

With these votes in their pockets, the small number of *jonkers* in a given subquarter could usually come to terms concerning the division of offices and patronage. Only a struggle for supremacy among two or more families could disturb such an arrangement. In seven of Groningen's nine subquarters, the dominant families usually managed to keep the peace by negotiating so-called "contracts of correspondence," unofficial agreements among the families. In the subquarter of Marnsterdeel, two families, Tjarda van Tarkenborgh and Van In-en Kniphuisen, monopolized political power throughout the first half of the eighteenth century. In the bordering subquarter of Halfamptsteradeel, the houses of Alberda van Menkema and Dijsterhuis disposed of all appointments. This system of monopolization finally collapsed in 1748–9, when a farmers' revolt – Groningen's variant of the *pachtersoproer* (revolt against tax farming) in Holland – forced a revision of rules governing entry to the *Landdag*.

In rural Friesland throughout the Republican era, some 10,000 votes selected the representatives to the three districts which, in turn, cast three of the four votes in the provincial States. Roughly one vote for every ten rural inhabitants makes a rather democratic impression; such a broad franchise was not attained by most western countries until the late nineteenth century. The reality, however, was less impressive, especially after the mid–seventeenth century as noble and regental families began to exert their influence.

Voting rights in Friesland were attached to particular parcels of land and/or houses. The ownership of these properties gave one control of the attendant votes. By comparing the voting rolls of 1640 with those of 1698, Faber has been able to demonstrate that the province's leading families pursued a policy of strategic property purchase, leading to a concentration of votes in their hands. The similarity with events in neighboring Groningen is striking. The objective was to achieve effective political control with a minimum investment in "voting property": by concentrating purchases in villages with few voting properties, and in districts that could be controlled by such villages. In 1640 the regental families held 26 percent of the votes, giving them control of 19 percent of the villages. By 1698 they had expanded their votes to 38 percent of the total, but these were so distributed as to give them control of 53 percent of the villages and 17 of the 30 *grietenijen* (the rural districts).

The Friesian *grietenij* Hemelumer Oldeferd offers a clear example of the oligarchization process at work. In 1640 the farmers and burgers from nearby towns controlled a majority of the votes in each of this district's nine villages. By 1698 one man, Jacobus van de Waeijen, controlled 84 of the *grietenij*'s 604 votes (14 percent). They were concentrated in five small villages where he possessed a majority of all votes, thereby giving him control of the *grietenij*. It can hardly come as a surprise that he had been elected *grietman*, a position that gave him control of local offices and gave access, as representative of his *grietenij* in the States of Friesland, to provincial and even national functions.

An analysis of the Friesian *grietmannen*, the members of the judiciary, and other offices reveals that family control of these functions became much more pronounced in the century after 1650 than before. The controlling families were not all nobles. Urban regents also participated in this process of oligarchization, but the nobles played a leading role.

In Groningen the *jonkers* managed in 1659 to revise the rules governing political participation in a way that concentrated local power in their hands and strengthened their hold over provincial politics. In Holland the core of the noble order managed in 1666 to appropriate for itself all of the resources and influence of the *Ridderschap*. In Friesland the regental families, thick with nobles, managed to push the province's landowning farmers into a marginal political position. In each case a relatively small group, for whom land rents formed a major source of income, focused its economic and political resources on the political system. By garnering a larger number of offices that provided fixed salaries, fees, and perquisites, they hoped to compensate for the declining incomes flowing from the agrarian sector. This strategy seems to have worked rather better in the northern and eastern provinces than in Holland, which may be explained by the fact that land rents fell further in Holland than anywhere else.

To be fair to these scheming nobles, they possessed few alternatives to make good this economic setback. To be recognized as nobles, they were obligated to maintain a certain style of life. One was a nobleman not only because of birth but also because the outside world acknowledged one as such, and this precluded manual work and commerce, activities incompatible with noble status. Members of the noble order were expected to serve the sovereign in military capacities, as well as in governing and administrative positions. In addition, they could serve as patrons of nonnoble institutions (such as local churches, monasteries, poor-relief agencies, chambers of rhetoric, etc.). This last type of office only cost the nobles money, but the others, especially military commissions, could be a rich source of income. To be sure, such an appointment was not easily come by: One needed influence with the provincial States and/or at the Stadhouder's court. But a military career always had great appeal, especially for the younger sons of noble families. The poor province of Drenthe paid little to the financial support of the army and, consequently, had few appointments to distribute, but it still managed to settle no fewer than seventy-three commissions on provincial nobles in the period 1600–1773 – all of them monopolized by eight families. The financial value of these functions is not always known with precision, but it was not trivial. We know that one of these Drenthe noblemen, Jan van Echten, enjoyed a salary of 3,600 guilders per year in 1719.

As for the civil offices laid claim to by the Republic's nobles, we know that they often generated far more income than their official salaries alone. In some cases they were so desirable that grateful appointees made generous gifts to their patrons: 3,000 guilders to a burgemeester of Zutphen for appointment to the high provincial office (the *landschrijversambt*); the fabulous sum of 14,000 guilders to a member of the college of nobles for appointment to the lucrative post of receiver-general of public revenues.

The nobles of Utrecht not only enjoyed access to the normal run of offices and sinecures but also controlled the secularized assets that had supported the prebendiaries of the religious chapters in this pre–Revolt Bishopric. The College of Nobles of Utrecht could sell these offices and divide the proceeds among themselves. These sales normally yielded 7,000 to 8,000 guilders. In 1735, when the nobles of the *Ridderschap* each pocketed 1,000 guilders from the sale of a prebend, one of them averred it would be nice "if only it occurred weekly." As it was, these nobles did quite well: A 1740 estimate claimed that each Utrecht noble with a government function earned on average 5,000 guilders per year.

The noble orders of Utrecht, Holland, and Overijssel also enjoyed the right to draw sums from the secularized church lands for distribution to their unmarried daughters. And those nobles charged with the administration of these lands enjoyed a generous compensation for their efforts. The *jonkers* of the Veluwe took an unusual interest in tax collecting. They acquired the right to assess and collect particular taxes – not by accident, after 1650. It happens that the noble tax collectors could hold back as their fee 6 percent of the tax revenue, good for some 12,000 guilders after expenses. Only the Batavian Revolution of 1795 put an end to these typical *ancien régime* practices.

The nobility devoted much energy to the acquisition of public offices, especially when their agricultural incomes flagged. But were they really averse to all forms of commercial life? This certainly had not always been the case, for nobles had taken a leading role in sixteenth- and early seventeenth-century land reclamation projects. Count Egmond had taken the lead in the sixteenth-century drainage of the Alkmaardermeer and of the Beijerlanden, a vast project to which he gave the name of his wife, Sabina van Beyeren. Shortly thereafter, Hendrik van Brederode launched the drainage of the Bergermeer; Johan van Duvenvoorde, Lord of Warmond, participated in the drainage of the Beemster polder. He was also involved in the reclamation of dune lands: The Keukenduin, once the sand covering was removed and sold, became the Keukenhof. Initiatives of this type were, of course, closely associated with the traditional role of the nobles as landowners and improvers. But after 1650 such investments lost their profitability, and they suddenly stopped.

Much the same can be said of investments in peat-digging enterprises, such as attracted the Van Echten's of Drenthe, among others. These investments diminished markedly in the century after 1650. When after 1750 investments in peat production revived, we see nobles also taking an interest in reforestation projects and in timber harvesting, encouraged by rising lumber prices. All of these activities required large, long-term investments, but it must be added that nobles became involved in drainage, peat digging, and forestry almost entirely because of their status as great landowners. Rarely did they act in a strictly commercial capacity.

Something approaching true entrepreneurship among nobles can be found in the Veluwe region, where the Van Isendoorn à Blois and the Hackfort families possessed the water rights in the villages of Vaassen and Loenen, respectively. Some thirty water mills, mostly for paper making, crowded the banks of the streams, each one paying for the right to use the water power. The nobles took the initiative to augment the natural power supply by digging connecting channels, improving the course of the streams, and placing contractual obligations on the millers intended to make more efficient use of the water. In the second quarter of the eighteenth century, these paper mills suffered from intensified French competition. The two noble families then bought up the mills, even forcing reluctant mill owners to choose between sale and demolition. Once acquired at distress prices, the mills were renovated, and the nobles leased them under carefully controlled terms. The rising lease payments that resulted came at just the time that agricultural prices were reaching their nadir. The mills generated up to 35 percent of the total income of the Van Isendoorns, but after 1750, as their agrarian incomes recovered, these noble families gradually lost interest in investing further in this sector. The inverse relationship between these initiatives and the state of the agricultural economy is once again apparent. But it is also striking that these two noble families, the only ones of the Veluwe region who made such investments, were also the region's only Catholic nobles. As Catholics they were barred from access to lucrative civil (but not military) offices.

Such entrepreneurial activity remained highly exceptional among the nobles of the Republic. Since we now know that income from seigneurial rights was of marginal importance, the conclusion is inescapable that property ownership and tithes constituted their foremost source of income, supplemented with the direct and indirect incomes that flowed from office holding. Another source of income consisted of the interest earned by their invested liquid capital, sometimes in the form of personal loans, but more often held in the form of government bonds, annuities, equities, and the like. In Groningen and Drenthe, the value of this last income source ranged between 10 and 50 percent of the total assets of eighteenth-century noble estates.

The investment patterns of the nobles in these two adjacent provinces reveal substantial differences. The Groningen nobility invested the great majority of their liquid wealth locally: in bonds of the city of Groningen and of the province, and in shares of the West India Company (which had a Groningen chamber). VOC shares, in contrast, were rare. The nobles of remote Drenthe, on the other hand, invested but a minor portion of their liquid wealth within their province. Their investment behavior had a more cosmopolitan flavor, as they bought up often substantial amounts of Swedish, Danish, Prussian, English, French, Russian, and even American bonds.

Nowhere else in the Republic has so systematic an analysis of noble assets been made, but no shortage of individual examples reinforce the conclusion that financial instruments were everywhere of considerable importance. Indeed, several noble families ranked with the greatest international investors of the eighteenth century. Margaretha Bentinck, the widow of Arent van Wassenaar van Duyvenvoorde – as illustrious a noble house as the Republic possessed – left at her death nearly 140,000 guilders in domestic public debt; some 50,000 guilders owed by the Marquisate of Bergen op Zoom, Leerdam, and the Barony of Acquoy; 100,000 *daalders* in Saxon bonds; 10,000 guilders in East Friesian bonds; and shares in the Bank of England and the South Sea Company worth 19,000 pounds sterling.

We must resist the temptation to focus exclusively on the wealth of the richest nobles. The study of the Groningen probate inventories reveals that very few nobles held assets worth in excess of 100,000 guilders. In Drenthe such an estate was even rarer. Moreover, in Overijssel, where a condition for inclusion in the *Ridderschap* was the possession of a suitable residence (a *havezathe*) plus land valued at a minimum of 25,000 guilders, no small number of nobles depended on the intentional overvaluation of their estates to escape dismissal from the noble order. In 1675 the stated wealth of the 83 nobles who possessed no *havezathe* did not quite average 17,000 guilders. The 102 Overijssel nobles who did possess a *havezathe* owned land valued at an average of 80,000 guilders. A century later, in 1758, the first group had grown to 93 fortunes that did not even attain the average value of 9,000 guilders; the second, wealthier group, had shrunk to 75 estates with an average value of under 39,000 guilders. Between 1675 and 1758, the total number of noble households in Overijssel fell from 185 to 172, but the average value of all of these households fell from about 50,000 to little more than 20,000 guilders (Table 11.6).

The regional differences in this province-wide average reinforce our view that the collapse of agricultural prices – and, thus, of agrarian property values – stands behind this contraction of noble wealth. The nobles of the districts of Salland and Twente suffered the sharpest contraction, while those of the Land van Vollenhove, with its peat bogs and commercial activity, and those resident in the cities suffered the least. Where low crop prices, recurring epizootics, and the resultant tenant default gnawed away at noble incomes, the chief compensatory strategy was the acquisition of well-paying public offices and – for younger sons and Catholic families – military commissions.

If we now return to the observation of Belle van Zuylen with which this section was introduced, no other conclusion seems possible than that the nobles of the Republic cannot be included among its economically dynamic social groups. Their economic goals rarely went beyond the protection and maintenance of their ancestral property in order to use the income derived therefrom to maintain a life style deemed (by noble and commoner alike) necessary to validate one's claim to nobility. When the income from property ownership fell substantially,

Table 11.6. *Noble fortunes in Overijssel in 1675 and 1758 (in guilders).*

	>10,000		2,000–10,000		<2,000		Total	
	N	Average	N	Average	N	Average	N	Average
				1675				
Three cities	25	27,580	11	3,955	—	—	36	20,361
Salland	75	60,653	6	3,750	—	—	81	56,438
Twente	37	87,487	11	5,818	1	1,500	49	67,398
Vollenhove	17	55,059	2	2,500	—	—	19	49,520
Overijssel	154	61,114	30	4,500	1	1,500	185	51,011
				1758				
Three cities	18	25,060	17	5,490	6	1,092	41	13,438
Salland	35	36,819	22	4,942	15	992	72	19,615
Twente	28	43,881	10	5,903	4	1,345	42	30,788
Vollenhove	13	35,835	3	4,632	1	1,995	17	28,338
Overijssel	94	36,535	52	5,288	26	1,108	172	21,733

Source: B. H. Slicher van Bath, *Samenleving onder spanning*, p. 645.

the nobles turned to public offices and their often attractive salaries. In practice, it became increasingly difficult to distinguish the nobles from the urban regents. Their field of interest tended to be more rural, to be sure, but even this distinction must not be pushed too far. Nobles took up residence especially in the cities of Overijssel, Gelderland, and Utrecht, where they came to fill many governing offices. Nor were they absent from high office at the provincial and national levels, where they served side by side with urban regents. The nobles stood apart from the urban regents chiefly in one respect: They evinced a pronounced preference for marriage within their own order.

As consumers the nobles cannot be said to have maintained a life style that differed essentially from that of urban patricians. Their way of life was distinct only in their occupancy of a certain type of house – castles and other fortified dwellings called variously *havezathe, borg, stinze* – usually well supplied with family portraits, with which they sought to render visible their chief claim to high status, their genealogy. Otherwise, their carriages, horses, servants, furniture, utensils, and consumption of food and drink did not distinguish them significantly from their rich urban compatriots.

11.4. Rural people

We turn now to a topic, the social stratification and legal status of the agricultural population, that in most European countries stands at the core of their historical development. In Chapters 2, 5, and 6, we have sought to highlight the distinctive character of rural society in the Netherlands, a character that renders inapplicable such conventional historical themes as "the transition from feudalism to capitalism" and "the abolition of serfdom." Our argument is not that rural society was wholly exempt from social inequality, landlords, and even feudal institutions – far from it. Rather, our argument is that the development of rural society in most regions did not follow historical scenarios consistent with the conventional themes of European agrarian history. Here, having examined in the preceding sections of this chapter the social elites and the craft and service sectors of rural society, we propose to examine in greater detail the social world of the farmers, the cotters, and the landless laborers who worked the land.

The past generation of historical research has by no means ignored the agricultural sector of the Dutch economy. Much has been learned, but, as so often is the case, this advance has rendered still more acute the sense that much remains unclear. One reason for this is evident enough: Countrymen were much more anonymous than the noble families and even than persons active in crafts and services. The individual book seller, schoolmaster, clergyman, miller, carpenter, and estate manager is given a much sharper profile by the archival materials than is the farmer, cotter, or day laborer. These last-mentioned groups were, of course, vastly more numerous than the others, but they were also far more diverse. More than any other sector of the economy, agriculture was and is a highly location-specific activity. Regional differences in soil types and ecology caused agricultural practices to vary enormously, even over short distances. And these differences could cause the same external event to give rise to quite distinct responses. Consequently, any generalization based on fragmentary information – whether it concerns farm size, crop choice, the use of family or hired labor, or the incidence of tenancy – runs the risk of distortion and oversimplification.

A good example of the stubborn complexity of rural society is provided in Bieleman's study of Drenthe. There a 1630 document allowed him to establish that 61 percent of the farms in twenty-four villages was owned by the peasants. These twenty-four villages were all located in a region of quite uniform topography, yet, village by village, peasant proprietorships varied from 31 to 97 percent of all farms. Such examples can be multiplied with ease, suggesting that even an army of researchers would not suffice to uncover fully the varied and changing character of agriculture in the past.

Nonetheless, it remains the historian's responsibility to proceed beyond the appreciation of detail and nuance to the exploration, however tentatively, of pattern and process. To abdicate this task, as in the style of many microhistories, is to convert history from a room with a view into a room with a mirror. Thus, with all due caution, we proceed with the task, considering first the patterns of landownership and the distribution of farm size.

We noted in the preceding section that the nobles, while they were often large landowners, did not as a group constitute the primary owners of this factor of production. We saw that in Holland already in the first half of the sixteenth century, the farmers themselves formed the largest landowning class (with about

50 percent). In Friesland matters were very different: This was distinctly a province of tenants and has largely remained so ever since. In 1511 the farmers who owned their own land formed a small minority on the northern clay soils, where arable farming predominated. To the south, where pasture predominated, owner-occupiers were even less common. But farther to the south and east, on the poorer peat and sand soils of the Wouden district, peasant proprietorship was widespread. And even farther south, in the Land of Vollenhove of the neighboring province of Overijssel, peasant proprietorship probably exceeded the 50-percent level estimated for early sixteenth-century Holland. However, when we proceed farther into Overijssel, beyond Zwolle and onto the sand soils, peasant landownership suddenly becomes very uncommon again. In the district of Salland in 1520, neither the number nor the value of parcels in the hands of the land users exceeded 10 percent of the total. Nor do data drawn from a smaller sample of these villages in 1601/2 show much improvement (see Table 11.7). When we turn toward the east of the province and enter Twente, peasant proprietorship once again increases substantially (see Table 11.8), and when we turn north again, to the isolated sandy heaths of Drenthe, the position of the peasants as of 1630 is stronger still. In general, it appears that the ratio of ownership to tenancy varied substantially within the alluvial zone (represented here by Holland and Friesland), and at least as much on the extensive sandy soils of the eastern Netherlands.

We find, thus, a wide variety of local situations, ranging from a preponderance of peasant landownership, via mixed arrangements, to a concentration of most – sometimes nearly all – land in the hands of nonfarmers. But here we must pause to warn against a rushed conclusion that where the cultivators themselves owned little land, rural society was dominated by the conflicting interests of "lords" and "peasants." Tenancy did not necessarily imply subordination and exploitation. On the contrary, many of the most prosperous farmers were tenants, while many of the poorest peasants owned their own land.

In the preceding section, we noted how landowners often absorbed, via rent forgiveness and/or the assumption of tax burdens, the losses inflicted on farm operations by setbacks such as the recurring cattle plagues and the persistence of low prices. The landowners either absorbed a portion of their tenants' losses or faced the prospect of seeing ruined farmers abandon their land. Another method of spreading the risks of farming was sharecropping tenancy, which tended to spread during periods of agrarian malaise and to contract again in better times.

At least as problematic for a lord/peasant dualism was the fact that neither of these "classes" exhibited much uniformity or solidarity. Nonpeasant property was by no means all concentrated in the hands of powerful noble families. Instead, a wide variety of persons and institutions functioned as landowners. Another look at Tables 11.7 and 11.8 shows that even in the Salland district of Overijssel, where peasants themselves owned 10 percent or less of the land in the sixteenth century, the nobles – large and small – only controlled 30 percent. This left 60 percent,

Table 11.7. *Distribution of landed property by social categories in Salland, 1520 and 1601–2.*

	1520		1601–2		
	Number	Value	Number	Value	Area
Noble properties	33.2	32.2	27.0	28.7	29.7
Church properties	17.9	18.3	14.7	18.2	17.5
Peasant proprietors	10.0	7.6	7.2	5.8	7.8
Other owners	38.9	41.9	51.1	47.3	45.0
Total	100.0	100.0	100.0	100.0	100.0

Source: B.H. Slicher van Bath, *Samenleving onder spanning*, p. 624.

Table 11.8. *Distribution of property by social category in Salland and Twente, 1601–2.*

	By number		By value		By area		
	Salland	Twente	Salland	Twente	Salland	Twente	
						Abandoned farms	
						Excluding	Including
Noble properties	27.0	29.2	28.7	32.8	29.7	31.2	30.5
Church properties	14.7	22.3	18.2	26.2	17.5	25.1	25.2
State domains	—	7.6	—	10.5	—	9.5	10.2
Peasant prop.	7.2	21.6	5.8	12.7	7.8	17.2	14.8
Other owners	51.1	19.3	47.3	17.8	45.0	17.0	19.3
Total	100.0	100.0	100.0	100.0	100.0	100.0	100.0

Source: B. H. Slicher van Bath, *Samenleving onder Spanning*, p. 631.

which was divided between two broad categories, the Church and urban interests. Under the first we find the property of monasteries and chapters, of parish churches and clergy, of poor-relief funds, hospitals, other charitable institutions, and small religious communities. The urban landowners consisted of individual burgers, of course, but also all manner of civic institutions. In Salland this last category owned more than any other, and in Holland the urban landowners were second only to the farmers themselves. But the "urban interest" was no more a homogeneous group than any of the others. Not only did the urban institutions vary in size and purpose, but private individuals ranged from rich burgers, some of whom had invested the bulk of their fortunes in agrarian property, to unremarkable individuals who had fallen into the possession of a few loose parcels of land. Rare indeed was the village where land was concentrated in the hands of a single institution or family; not even concentration in the hands of members of the same social class occurred with any frequency. Instead, we find village after village where landownership was distributed across a wide assortment of landlords: several noble gentlemen and religious institutions, various burgers and urban institutions, and, last but by no means necessarily least, the farmers themselves. Nor should we think of farmers as owners only of the land they personally used. On the contrary, for a wide variety of reasons, they were likely to function as landlords to others at the same time that they were tenants on land they used themselves.

In this connection we must recall that in much of the Republic's territory, serfdom had come to an end – if it had ever existed – well before the end of the Middle Ages. By the sixteenth century, it played no role in Holland, nor in Friesland and Groningen. The remains of the feudal system did linger on in the Veluwe and in the eastern parts of Gelderland and Overijssel. In the district of Twente, the last formal feudal obligations were not extinguished until 1811. In the Salland district, they had fallen into disuse much earlier, while in the quarter of Zutphen, these obligations lost any significance after 1700. The reason why the serfs of Twente continued for so long to recognize the rights of their lord is that the feudal lord there was none other than the provincial government. To the bitter end, its officials saw to the strict enforcement of the state's feudal rights, but in the larger scheme of things, this was no more than an oddity: At the beginning of the eighteenth century, servile status attached to no more than 168 persons. Nor were these last Dutch serfs poor or oppressed. Most, in fact, were in possession of substantial farms, and their obligations as serfs were often less than those of commercial tenants. They were not at all eager to see "feudalism" disappear!

The burdens weighing upon the shoulders of the Republic's farmers were not segneurial rights and feudal obligations but rather short-term leases, tithe payments, and mortgages. Few historians have studied the last-mentioned of these obligations. Hoppenbrouwers' study of the Land van Heusden is one of the few that has paid attention to this issue, and he is of the opinion that around 1500, a large portion of the land owned by the farmers had been mortgaged. A century later the same can be said of farms in Twente. Further research may well reveal that mortgage payments weighted heavily on sixteenth-century farmers. This is hinted at by the contemporary observation that participants in North Holland's *Kaas en brood* [Cheese and bread] rebellion of 1491–2 "veel scaden van brieven, quitancien, registeren ende in andere dingen deden" [suffered much from letters (of credit), invoices, registers, and other things]. Was the violence of this peasant uprising directed against the owners of debt instruments? The peasants' creditors must have been townspeople, the very group that most increased its share of landed property ownership in the sixteenth century.

Still, it was not the peasants but the nobles whose property ownership declined in this period. In the Land van Heusden, this is precisely what happened between the end of the fourteenth and the mid–sixteenth centuries. In Salland it was once again the urban residents (referred to as "Other owners" in Table 11.7) who gained most, and the nobles who lost most, in the period 1520 to 1600. Of the three social categories – noble, farmer, and burger – it was this last that appears to have been most active in the acquisition of land, both via investment in drainage projects and via the purchase of secularized church lands, a portion of which the state sold during the Revolt.

When we take the very long view, across the entire period covered by this book, a rather different pattern of landownership reveals itself. Salland's pattern is known for 1751, and when it is compared with the situation of 1520, a striking diminution of the relative position of both the nobles and the Church is revealed. Peasant proprietorship, on the other hand, had doubled. Much of this increased peasant landownership was the product of reclamation of wastes, which formed the nuclei of new farms. To this they added over time the lands of religious institutions, which were periodically put up for sale. Later comparisons are possible for 1888 and 1910. By then the dominance of peasant proprietorship had advanced even further. In all of Overijssel, farmers owned 67 percent of the land. When this is compared to 1520 or 1601, at a time when peasants owned only a small fraction of the land, the nature of the transformation is revealed to be one that got well under way only after the end of the seventeenth century.

In Drenthe the story is no different. We noted earlier that already in 1630, peasant proprietors controlled 61 percent of the cultivated land. When we can once again make a direct comparison, in 1876, their share had risen to over 70 percent.

In Friesland tenancy dominated the rural economy, and we have just noted the post-1650 elite offensive that added additional property to the holdings of nobles and patricians. But here, too, the eighteenth century, the second half especially, brought a major advance in peasant proprietorship. Consider the example of the following *grietenijen*:

Percentage of land owned by farmers

	1711	1757	1805
Barradeel		14	26
Dantumadeel		26	45
Westdongeradeel		20	41
Henaarderadeel		5	13
Rauwerderhem	4	7	13
Schoterland	21	25	30

Thanks to a silver-lined late eighteenth century, Friesland's farmers managed to increase substantially the land under their control.

The farmers of Groningen also experienced a long-term improvement of their control over landed property, but there it was a judicial process rather than a strictly economic one that brought this result about. In the sixteenth century, property leases in Groningen did not differ from those elsewhere: Upon termination of a lease, the landowner was free to change tenants and adjust the rent.

Over the course of time, the owner gradually lost his discretionary power over his property, and the terminable lease became a heritable lease. This occurred because the tenant commonly retained possession of his house and farm buildings, for the simple reason that he built and paid for these himself. As long as these structures remained crude and temporary, this property right did not amount to much, but the development of larger, more permanent brick buildings brought profound change to the relationship between owner and tenant. The nonrenewal of a lease obliged the landowner to compensate the tenant for the fair value of the structures; and as these became more valuable, the owner acquired a stronger interest in renewing the lease while the tenant acquired an incentive to make improvements to the property, the better to secure his tenure. In this way, the right to the use of land became ever more separated from its ownership.

This process was powerfully reinforced by the conduct of the provincial government, which became by far the largest landowner once it had appropriated the Church's extensive (over 25,000 hectare) holdings in the province. It never made use of its right to terminate a lease, and it increased the rent only once, in 1632. The *de facto* position of the tenants became very strong indeed, and when, in 1764 and 1774, the province sold these lands, that which was not bought by the tenants themselves was acquired by investors who immediately faced a long legal battle in attempting to undo the customary rights of the tenants. The tenants emerged the victors in this conflict. In return for a substantial lump-sum payment, they secured legal confirmation of fixed rents and the heritability of their tenures. With full disposition over the land, these tenants were effectively the new owners. Something very similar to this occurred to the remaining servile tenures in the eastern provinces, when these were extinguished by the Batavian regime. In both the northern and eastern provinces, we observe a long-term process of augmented peasant control of the land, which was especially pronounced in the eighteenth century.

For Holland only a few local studies stand at our disposal, but they point in the same direction as the fuller information available for the outer provinces. The most complete study of landownership over a long time period concerns the Beijerlanden, three large polders in South Holland that were drained in 1557 (Oost-Beijerland), 1582 (Nieuw-Beijerland), and 1631 (Zuid-Beijerland). In each of these polders, nobles and urban patricians owned most (80 to 90 percent) of the land at the outset, while burgers and institutions, both religious and secular, held less than 10 percent. These urban and religious landowners gradually increased their share, reaching 15 percent by 1780, whereupon it fell back to 10 percent again by 1810. By then the originally dominant nobles and patricians held no more than a quarter of the cultivable land. Clearly, in the intervening period of over 200 years, the farmers bought up more and more of the land. Beginning with next to nothing, they came to hold some 20 percent of the land by 1620, and after a retreat to 15 percent around 1680, their purchases increased steadily, so that they held about 60 percent by the beginning of the nineteenth century.

Even in the depths of the agrarian depression of the first half of the eighteenth century, the farmers found opportunities to buy land from nobles who were either distressed by bankruptcy or convinced by prudence to rid themselves of properties whose rental incomes did not cover the taxes and other charges with which they were burdened. Later, as agricultural prices rose while land rents remained in the doldrums (see Chapter 6, section 6.5), it was the turn of urban patricians to sell. Once again, more often than not, it was the local farmers who stood ready to buy. Most of the land in these polders changed hands at liquidation prices: In Zuid-Beijerland, land that had cost 1,000 guilders per hectare in 1650 was sold in 1750 for 225 guilders, and as late as 1800 for 450 to 475 (see also Figure 11.7).

The trend revealed by the local example of the Beijerlanden polders is wholly consistent with what we have already established for the northern and eastern provinces, and it is also consistent with the large-scale, eighteenth-century sell-off of farm land by institutional owners convinced that other investments would yield a higher return. In the village of Warmond, for example, we know that institutions owned a quarter of the land in the late Middle Ages and still possessed 22 percent in 1680. By 1832 the just-completed *kadaster* registered only 8 percent of the land as owned by institutions. Furthermore, the village's chief nobleman, the Lord of Warmond, owned 141 hectare in 1680, while his heirs of 1832 could claim only 85 hectare. Therefore, the local farmers must have been the chief gainers, by default.

Much remains to be learned about landownership in Holland, not to mention the entire zone south of the rivers, about which our ignorance compels silence. But the evidence assembled here does justify the conclusion that farmers booked a major advance in landownership. In the course of the agrarian depression, they showed a much greater attachment to landownership than any other group, a predisposition that allowed many of them to buy land at very low prices. This, in turn, established the basis of their prosperity in the late eighteenth century and the Batavian-French period.

The trend toward increased ownership of land by farmers was accompanied by other long-term processes, leading to the related phenomena of increased average farm size and concentration of landownership among fewer persons. The latter development is well documented in Warmond. This village measured 1,349 *morgen* of improved land in 1680; by 1832 the encroaching waters of the Haarlemmermeer had reduced the village to 1,118 *morgen*. During the interval the number of private property owners fell from 352 to 129, while the land owned by these persons fell only from 1,049 to 1,029 *morgen*. The same concentration process occurred in the North Holland village of Uitgeest. In 1690 its land was splintered among no fewer than 784 owners; by 1773 there were only 295, a reduction that proceeded with inexorable force, decade by decade. It was especially nonresident holders of loose parcels who disappeared in this process.

The concentration process can be followed step by step in Egmond-Binnen

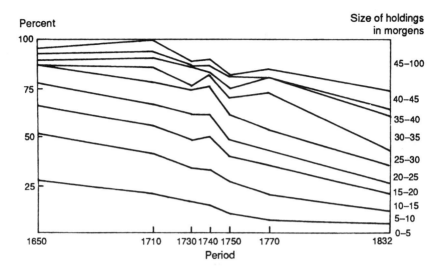

Figure 11.9. Distribution of the improved land in Egmond-Binnen by size of holding, 1650–1832. (*Source:* A. M. van der Woude, "De contractiefase," 377).

with the help of Figure 11.9, which shows the distribution of land by size categories at intervals between 1650 and 1832. In 1650 almost 30 percent of the land was held by persons who possessed no more than 5 *morgen* in the village. In 1750 such owners controlled only 10 percent of the land, and after 1770 no more than 6 percent. The fate of the larger landowners, those with at least 25 *morgen*, was the mirror image of the small fry. The land under their control rose from 15 percent in 1650 to nearly 40 percent in 1750, and 55 percent in 1800. Property-ownership patterns in the village were utterly transformed as outside owners sold to resident farmers, and the larger among these farmers engrossed land at the expense of their smaller neighbors.

If land*ownership* becomes concentrated in the hands of farmers, and especially the larger farmers, then it is likely that land *use* will also become more concentrated – that is, that the average size of farm enterprises will increase. Evidence in support of this view for the seventeenth and eighteenth centuries is not hard to come by. Hoppenbrouwers, in his study of the Land van Heusden, a district of South Holland, has established that small to very small holdings predominated throughout the period 1375–1550. With most farms under 5 *morgen* in size, it seems inevitable that many farmers, owners, and tenants alike sought supplementary sources of income beyond their own holdings. And this is a picture confirmed for Holland as a whole by the *Informacie* of 1514. Even in districts already specialized in animal husbandry, a farmer with ten or more cows was quite exceptional. Four to six head of cattle was closer to the norm for a dairy farmer in early sixteenth-century Holland, and there were many small operators with only three or four. At this time small to tiny farms blanketed Holland's countryside, and large farmers were few.

This pattern was reinforced in many areas, especially in North Holland, by a division of labor within the household that sent men off the homestead to work seasonally in such activities as fishing, seafaring, dike repair, reed cutting, and so on, while the wife took responsibility for the agricultural work. This phenomenon is described more fully in Chapter 6, section 6.1, and its consequences for the labor market are analyzed in Chapter 12, section 12.5.

The small-scale character of early sixteenth-century agriculture dissolved in the course of the next century under a variety of pressures. If rural dwellers were not to lag far behind the growth of urban prosperity in the century after 1580, farm revenues would have to be raised, a goal that then could only be reached through intensification and specialization. This led, in turn, to the gradual transfer of various craft and service functions from the farm household to nonfarm specialists (such as carpenters, masons, weavers, tailors, shoemakers, bakers, teamsters, and bargemen). The time also came when the demand for the labor of farmers in the by-employments mentioned earlier diminished, as shipping, fishing, and construction labor themselves became more specialized. All these processes, underpinned by increases in the capital stock per worker, redirected the labor of farm households inward, toward agricultural production itself. Success in this redeployment of farm labor required capital investment in agriculture (better drainage, larger farm buildings, fertilizer, etc.) and the achievement of an increased scale of operation. It is not impossible that the many large new farms created by the great lake drainage schemes of the early seventeenth century stood as a model for this development. At any rate we witness in district after district small enterprises with their few head of cattle giving way to farms that stalled substantial herds. In the Zeevang, a district north of Edam, farms with 4 to 7 head of cattle were still the norm as late as 1675, but by 1740 the modal herd size ranged between 12 and 16 head. In Spanbroek, only 6 of the 142 farm operations of 1604 possessed over ten "cattle equivalents" (where 2 heifers = 1 cow); in 1670 these larger enterprises had grown to 23 of the 111 farms and by 1707 had grown to 27 of the 83 remaining farms. While the total number of cows grazing in Spanbroek remained stable, the number of farms fell (from 142 to 84), and the average number of cattle-equivalents per farm rose (from 5.1 to 8.6).

The consolidation of a class of large farmers in North Holland represents a particularly dramatic transformation of the social landscape, but the trend toward increased scale of farm operations was general throughout the Netherlands' alluvial zone. In the pasture lands of South Holland as well as the marine clay soils of the Groningen Oldambt, myriad small farms gave way to a smaller number of large production units. In Friesland this process can be followed with data gathered for five *grietenijen* scattered across the province's soil types (Westdongeradeel, Barradeel, Dantumadeel, Baarderadeel, and Rauwerderhem). In these districts as a whole, the number of farms declined between 1711 and 1805, from 1,065 to 992 in 1757 to 944 in 1805. Correspondingly, the average size of these farms rose by 12 percent, from 27.5 to 32.2 hectare. But these averages obscure the redistribution process at work, concentrating land in the largest farms. Between 1511 and 1793, farms with over 30 hectare in Leeuwarderadeel rose from 8 to 27 percent of all farms, in Ferwerderadeel these rose from 9 to 29 percent, in Baarderadeel from 10 to 25 percent, and in Henaarderadeel from 12 to 27 percent. Smaller farms (defined as those under 22 hectare [60 *pondematen*] in 1511 and 20 hectare in 1793) declined from 77 to 25 percent in Wymbritseradeel, and from 69 to 29 percent in Idaarderadeel.

Data sufficient to achieve blanket coverage of the Netherlands' various rural districts are not available, but they are probably not necessary to establish what appears to be very nearly a law of agricultural history in the alluvial zone (i.e., the development toward larger farms and the consolidation of a class of large farmers). Looking back from today, only the period 1880–1950 stands out as an exception to this rule. Then, special factors – including the introduction of chemical fertilizers and very rapid population growth – pushed farms toward a smaller average size. Both before and after this exceptional interlude, the search for a viable agriculture has led toward ever larger scales of operations.

Thus far we have spoken only of the western and northern provinces. Generalizing about farm size in the eastern provinces is more difficult, among other reasons because farmers here typically had access not only to the arable and pasture land that they owned or rented but also to the undivided common lands of the village. But if we look only at the amount of arable land per farm, then the average came to 4.6 hectare per farm in Drenthe in 1650, 3.7 hectare in the arable districts of Salland in 1601, and 3.3 hectare in Twente in the same year. The data for later years suggest a diminution of average farm size rather than the reverse. The available sources are not without their interpretive problems, but this apparent trend toward smaller farms in the East is probably the result of (1) more rapid population growth there after 1650, and (2) the presence throughout the sandy soils of this region of waste lands from which were periodically carved new parcels of arable. As existing farms were partitioned by inheritance, the addition of a reclaimed parcel of waste land may just have sufficed to establish a new cotter holding. Over time the number of farms rose. Continual reclamation of waste increased the cultivated land area, too, but since this did not keep pace with the number of farms, average farm size declined.

This process of splitting off new holdings from established farms was also encouraged by the tendency to reduce the cattle-raising component of mixed husbandry in favor of more intensive crop production. This shift required more labor per hectare of land, giving employment to land-poor cotters. In Drenthe, where this process has been most thoroughly studied, rural society found itself moving farther and farther from what around 1600 it held up as an ideal: communities where a majority of farmers operated "full" homesteads of 32 Groningen *mudden*

Table 11.9. *Farms grouped according to the amount of their arable land, in the sandy-soil region of Drenthe (circa 1650) and Salland and Twente (1601–2) (in percentage of farms per size category).*

Size category (in ha.)	<2.2	2.2–4.3	4.4–6.5	6.6–8.6	>8.7	N
Drenthe	37	18	15	14	16	2,783

Size category	<2.0	2.0–4.9	5.0–9.9	>10.0	N
Salland	15	42	42	1	1,056
Twente	29	49	21	1	1,447

Sources: J. Bieleman, *Boeren op het Drentse zand*, p. 240; B. H. Slicher van Bath, *Samenleving onder spanning*, p. 424.

(8.7 hectare) of arable land. Already in 1650 only 16 percent of the farms in the sandy-soil zones of the province attained this size, while 14 percent were two-thirds of full size, and 15 percent were but half size. Still, the full and two-third size categories together accounted for 30 percent of all farms and laid claim to over 65 percent of all arable land. The large farmers controlled the land – and rural society – but they were substantially outnumbered already in 1650 by the small peasants with no more than 2 hectare of arable land each. Table 11.9 allows us to compare this situation with the Overijssel districts of Salland and Twente. There the very small holdings were not so numerous – or should we say not *yet* so numerous? The fifty-year interval between the observations may well have filled Salland and Twente with the cotters who were latterly so evident in Drenthe.

These early seventeenth-century farm size data cannot be compared with comprehensive information again until 1910, by which time the large-scale reclamation of waste land and the arrival of chemical fertilizers had created a very different agrarian world in the eastern provinces. Still, the fact remains that farms with over 10 hectare of arable land, which made up 1 percent of Salland and Twente farms in 1601, now accounted for nearly 18 percent of all farms. In Drenthe 26 percent of all farms were so large. The conclusion is hard to avoid that the larger farms grew in importance somewhere between 1650 and 1900 – the same trend we have already established for the West and North. The timing of this development in the East is not clear, but van Zanden offers evidence from several localities to suggest that by 1811–12, a consolidation of land into larger farms was already well underway. Here, too, land rents tended to lag well behind rising commodity prices after 1750, creating a situation in which the larger farmers prospered. They acquired the financial means to buy land from impoverished nobles and indebted governments (selling domain lands) and to engage in reclamation of the waste lands.

So far we have described rural society in the eastern provinces as experiencing

Table 11.10. *Social stratification in sixteen Drenthe villages, 1672–1804.*

	Shopkeepers	Farmers	Cotters	Poor[a]	Total
1. Heads of household, absolute numbers					
1672	118	1,061	377	82	1,638
1692	250	1,157	413	89	1,909
1742	391	1,116	697	116	2,320
1774	388	1,099	779	220	2,486
1804	472	1,059	927	144	2,602
2. In percentages of all households					
1672	7	65	23	5	100
1692	13	61	21	5	100
1742	17	48	30	5	100
1774	16	44	31	9	100
1804	18	41	36	5	100
3. Average annual increase/decrease in number of households per category					
1672–92	+6.6	+4.8	+1.8	+0.4	+13.6
1692–1742	+2.8	-0.8	+5.5	+0.5	+8.2
1742–74	-0.1	-0.5	+2.6	+3.3	+5.2
1774–1804	+2.8	-1.3	+4.9	-2.5	+3.9
4. Population in 1804 relative to 1672 (1672 = 100)					
1804	400	100	246	176	159

[a]Poor = households receiving poor relief.
Source: J. Bieleman, *Boeren op het Drentse zand*, p. 132.

rapid population growth, a less rapid extension of cultivated area, and a tendency toward concentration of that land into larger farms. An inevitable consequence of these three processes was heightened social differentiation in rural society. Some portion of the population's natural increase must have been removed by migration to the cities. Of what remained in the countryside, a portion must have found employment in trades and service occupations or in rural industry. But much of the growing population remained within the agrarian sphere, where differentiation became sharper: between large and small farmers, and between farmers, cotters, and farm laborers.

The division between large and small farmers at a moment in time was shown in Table 11.9. Table 11.10 lets us observe the evolution of the major social groups in sixteen Drenthe villages. The increasing social stratification of rural society on the sandy soils of the eastern Netherlands is revealed with exceptional clarity. Over the entire period 1672–1804, the number of "real" farm households in these

Table 11.11. *Cotter households as a percentage of all farmer and cotter households in the arable farming areas of Salland (S) and Drenthe (D).*

Year	Percentage	Year	Percentage
1520	22 (S)	1742	38 (D)
1602	22 (S)	1774	41 (D)
1672	26 (D)	1795	47 (S)
1692	26 (D)	1800	44 (S)
1720	45 (S)	1804	47 (D)

Source: J. Beileman, *Boeren op het Drentse zand*, p. 137.

sixteen villages did not grow at all. Given the growth of population in these villages, the share of all households in farming fell from 65 to 41 percent. The growing "surplus" population found work primarily in the broad category of shopkeepers, craftsmen, and service providers. In 130 years their numbers grew threefold. A slower but still substantial growth of cotters and a small growth of "poor" households accounted for the remaining population growth.

It is particularly instructive to examine the timing of the growth of these rural groups. In the period 1672–92, it was the category of shopkeepers and service providers that grew most rapidly. In 1672 the sixteen villages could count only 118 of them; twenty years later there were 250, more than twice as many. We have already emphasized the early growth of the service occupations in the Republic. The evidence of Table 11.10 shows that in rural Drenthe, the breakthrough of such occupations occurred in the final quarter of the seventeenth century. Together with the southern provinces, remote Drenthe would have been among the last regions of the Republic to experience this elaboration of local services. In this period there was still room for growth in the farm sector; between farmers and service providers, most of the growth of population was accounted for, so that neither the cotters nor the "poor" increased much in number.

After 1692 overall population growth slowed markedly, but now there was no room for more farmers and not much in the service sector. Consequently, the increase in population after 1692 caused the number of cotters to more than double and pushed up the number of charity recipients as well.

Drenthe's experience was not unique. The rise in its cotter population only mirrored developments in the other eastern provinces, as is demonstrated in Table 11.11. There the cotter population is expressed as a percentage of the total agricultural population (farmers plus cotters). The figures for Salland and those for Drenthe fashion a seamless pattern, revealing a sharp increase in the number of cotters around 1700. This was precisely the period in which labor-intensive crop production offered wage work, which made life on the dwarf holdings of the cotters sustainable. When we keep our gaze fixed on the numerous cotter households, the image of self-sufficient production looms large in this region; but when we note how the bulk of the region's farm land was worked – by these selfsame cotters – for commercial purposes, then the image of a classic isolated peasant society quickly dissolves.

The occupational information gathered in Overijssel for the 1795 census reveals the substantial presence of a third agrarian social type. Alongside the farmers and cotters, the landless farm laborers took their place. In 1602 their numbers were vanishingly small, less than 3 percent of the rural adult male labor force. But in 1795 they constituted 15 percent of that labor force, and much more than that wherever commercial grain production was dominant. The rise of this class went hand in hand with the consolidation of large farms, a process for which we have now found evidence in nearly all parts of the country.

A clear example of this process is provided by Figure 11.10, which plots the number of nonfarm houses per farm in seven Friesian *grietenijen* at intervals between 1711 and 1805. Everywhere the ratio rises by about 50 percent. Of course, not all the additional houses were occupied by farm laborers, but there is good reason to believe that most of them were. Note also how the ratio of houses to farms differed systematically from district to district. The highest concentrations of landless laborers were found in the arable farming district, where the demand for labor was greatest; then came that portion of the "Wouden" district where peat digging offered work to the landless. The pasture districts of Friesland made relatively little use of such labor, but still much more than Weststellingwerf, a district whose agrarian structure was similar to – and physically adjacent to – the Drenthe-Overijssel arable farms discussed previously.

Holland was also not without its landless farm laborers. The arable farms of the South Holland islands certainly had a great need for their labor, but they also existed in large numbers in the pasture districts. In the countryside directly north of Amsterdam, the Noorderkwartier, the *registre civique* of 1811 counted 2,158 independent male heads of farm households and 1,274 males who were servants and day laborers. This large group was the proletarianized remnant of a labor market development of the seventeenth century, one that transformed the many (part-time) farmers of the sixteenth century into commercial farmers, craft and service workers, and, at the bottom of the social pyramid, landless farm workers. Much remains to be learned about this silent minority of Holland's countryside.

Now that we have discussed the nobles, the farmers, the cotters, the farm laborers, and the persons engaged in services, we are left with one final group: the rural operatives in proto-industry. Such workers existed in many locations, but as noted in Chapter 8, they formed major concentrations in four districts of the Republic. The Zaan region was the first important zone of rural industry, followed by Twente, the region around Helmond-Eindhoven, and Tilburg and environs.

The Zaan region and the adjacent Schermereiland formed a rural zone dominated by its industrial workers. Unlike the other zones of rural industry, however,

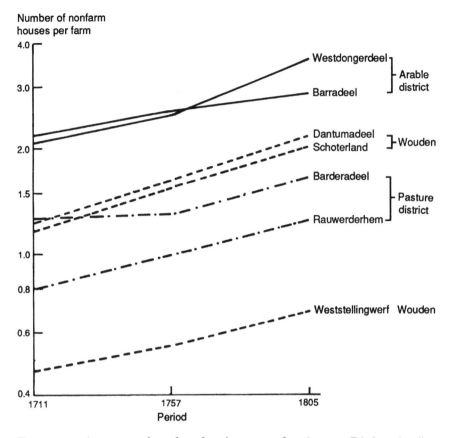

Number of nonfarm
houses per farm

Figure 11.10. Average number of nonfarm houses per farm in seven Friesian *grietenijen*, 1711–1805. (*Source:* J. A. Faber, *Drie eeuwen Friesland*, 491–2.)

few of these workers labored with their family at home. The other centers of rural industry were more characteristic of European proto-industry: All were located at the Republic's periphery and flourished because of their low wages. As we have already noted, they proved especially attractive to the textile industry, which organized rural cottage production to escape the high costs of cities such as Leiden and Haarlem.

Apart from a brief effort to establish bleaching works in Oostzaan, the only significant branch of textile production in the Zaan region was sail-cloth weaving. This activity made use of cottage production, but nearly all other Zaan industries depended on energy generated by windmills or were oriented to the shipbuilding wharves, which drew the workers out of their cottages and into workshops and factories. The Zaan region also distinguished itself from other centers of rural industry in that it was not a zone of low wages. In fact, it paid the highest wages available in the countryside. In this unique center of rural industrial production, workers with industrial occupations dominated local society utterly. Around 1730, at their peak, the Zaan industries employed some 3,600 workers, then some 57 percent of the adult male labor force.

Of the remaining zones of rural industry, we are best informed about Twente. We are dealing here with a classic example of proto-industry. Here lived a population of (by the Republic's standards) poor peasants who sought to supplement their incomes by turning to cottage handicrafts during the slack seasons of the agricultural calendar. These peasants had long grown flax among their other crops and were accustomed to reserving a portion of their output to produce linen for their own use. The decline of grain prices after 1660 encouraged an expansion of this and other industrial crops. At just this time, Twente's population growth began generating signs of overpopulation, as reflected by the growth in the number of cotter holdings. The overabundance of labor in the region encouraged a further expansion of labor-intensive flax cultivation and greater dedication to the spinning and weaving of linen. Following the classic pattern of rural industry, Twente's cotters combined linen production with agriculture and offered their abundant family labor at very low costs.

As linen production emerged to become more than an incidental activity serving local needs, merchants intervened to organize the sale of the final product and, simultaneously, to stimulate the further expansion of production by bringing in supplemental supplies of spun yarn. This brought into existence a class of professional weavers, cottagers divorced from agriculture and wholly dependent on the linen trade for their livelihood. As Twente's rural industry entered this new phase between 1725 and 1750, production tended to drift away from the agricultural hamlets toward the region's larger villages and towns, where the merchants lived and where the cottage weavers could more easily be supplied.

After 1750 the revival of grain prices lessened the attractiveness of flax cultivation. As early as 1755, we encounter reports of raw materials being shipped in from Holland and Zeeland to keep the weavers supplied. But the rise of grain prices also increased the weavers' cost of living, most of whom now had little if any connection to the land. Moreover, the important English market for the region's linens now sat behind high tariff walls (to nurture the new Scottish and Irish linen industries), while in such markets as remained, prices were pressed downward by German and Silesian linen, where costs were even lower than in Twente. On top of all this, the government raised the excise taxes. In short, the rural industry of Twente quickly found itself squeezed between rising production costs on the one hand, and intensified international competition pushing linen prices downward on the other.

The second half of the eighteenth century was a difficult period for Twente's

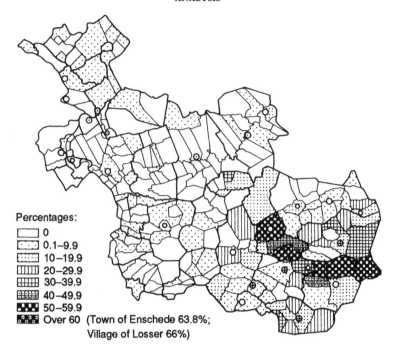

Percentages:
- ☐ 0
- ▦ 0.1–9.9
- ▦ 10–19.9
- ▦ 20–29.9
- ▦ 30–39.9
- ▦ 40–49.9
- ▦ 50–59.9
- ▦ Over 60 (Town of Enschede 63.8%; Village of Losser 66%)

Map. 11.1. Percentage of the adult male labor force active in the textile industry in Overijssel in 1795. (*Source:* Slicher van Bath, *Historische ontwikkeling*, 26.)

rural industry, and the contrasts between rich and poor became sharper. The taxable wealth of the putting-out merchants of Almelo, which had averaged 57,500 guilders in 1694, had more than doubled by 1715. The merchants of Vriezenveen saw their average wealth rise from 37,000 guilders in 1675 to 125,000 in 1711, to 174,000 in 1758. But the households too poor to be taxed (and described as "pauper" or "poor" in the tax registers) grew from 27.5 percent in 1675 and 20.6 percent in 1723 to 34.5 percent in 1764, and even 49.8 percent in 1767. Many of these poor folk were no doubt weavers, which is suggested strongly by the close correspondence between the concentrations of weavers and the seats of poverty. Their large numbers are evident from Map 11.1, which shows how the weavers were distributed among the local jurisdictions of Overijssel in 1795. In several places they exceeded 50 percent of the labor force; in the city of Enschede, 64 percent. But in that textile center in 1753, only 109 of its 225 looms were in operation, and of the town's 142 weaving families, 72 were without work. And in the rural jurisdiction of Enschede, matters were even worse: 214 of the 849 looms were idle; 440 of the 605 weaving families were without work.

Dense rural populations dependent on rural industrial employments proved to be highly vulnerable to distant market forces, and little is yet known about their local adaptive strategies. Their poor housing was proverbial, even then. Little dwellings, no more than 3.5 meters square and with low ceilings, are described; but to what extent was such housing common to poor people everywhere at a time of vigorous population growth? Sod huts, baking sheds, and pig sties served to house people at such a time, both before and after the downturn of the regional linen industry.

This is not to say that material life in rural society did not respond to changes in the economic conditions in the long run. The *verstening* – the reconstruction of homes and farm buildings with brick – which occurred in most regions in the course of the long sixteenth century, is a good example of such a response, as is the finding that rural probate inventories (in this case from Oirschot in North Brabant) listed accumulations of jewelry that grew and contracted in step with the general trend of rising and falling grain prices. A second such study, focusing on the town of Weesp and its rural district, established that during the agrarian depression of the first half of the eighteenth century, the number of farm households leaving utensils of silver and gold fell dramatically. The same was true of other luxury items, such as porcelain, books, mirrors, large tin plates and bowls, and pendulum clocks. These urban goods diffused quickly among seventeenth-century farm households, but the further diffusion of these luxuries and of eighteenth-century novelties such as the reading desk and coffee and tobacco accessories slowed after 1700. Simultaneously, the inventories begin to record the presence of cheaper surrogates for the fashionable items and the retention of objects that had gone out of fashion in the cities (such as coral chains, silver buttons, and spoon display racks). It appears that several decades of persisting agrarian depression set the material culture of farmers onto a separate path, consciously distinct from urban norms. The diffusion of goods from city to country appears to have been faster and more direct in the seventeenth century than it would be again until the twentieth. This brings us to the sort of speculation that calls for far more research into the consumption patterns of early modern social groups, a study that is still in its infancy.

11.5. City people

The rich literature on the many preindustrial cities of the Netherlands has generated what we might call the classic categories of social stratification. In this scheme the lowest rung of the social ladder is occupied by an anonymous underclass – contemporaries called it *het grauw* – of vagabonds, beggars, paupers, and others without steady work and often enough with no fixed address. These people come to our attention chiefly via the records of the law courts. Above this desperate social cellar, but often just barely above, one finds the mass of market sellers, street peddlers, and hawkers. This miscellaneous army of petty traders sold fish, wood, fruit, vegetables, peat, flowers, sand, secondhand wares, patent medicines, and much more. Most were as poor as church mice, borrowing each morning a wheelbarrow and a guilder's worth of goods in the hope that enough could be sold to leave something over at the end of the day, when the barrow and the guilder had to be returned – plus a stuiver or two of interest. Not all of these peddlers were wholly without means, of course. Some kept a servant and tramped the countryside with a substantial inventory of wares. But most lived from hand to mouth, sharing their low station with the unskilled and unregulated mass of porters, haulers, and other casual day laborers. All of these persons together formed the lowest social category, a group representing from 10 to 20 percent of the urban labor force, although this figure could vary from place to place and with the tides of fortune.

Just above this unskilled and insecure mass, we find domestic servants, sailors, soldiers, and numerous unskilled and semiskilled wage workers. This group was certainly the largest in the lower half of urban society, consisting especially of many workers in the textile trades. But each city seems to have had its own characteristic specialty, such as the pipe-makers' assistants of Gouda, the distillery workers of Schiedam, the shipbuilding assistants of Amsterdam, and so on.

All that distinguished this group from the one just below it was a somewhat greater permanence of employment, and it took very little to slip into the desperate lower circle: the ebbing of the business cycle, a war year temporarily bringing trade to a halt, a bout of illness, or an accident bringing physical disability. Besides these personal or transitory phenomena, structural factors could also press members of this broad working-class category down into the misery of the lowest social class. This occurred to large numbers in the late eighteenth century, when the steady rise of food prices systematically undermined purchasing power. In the first half of the seventeenth century, rising prices had also eroded purchasing power at intervals, but in this economically expansive period, unemployment was not the ubiquitous affliction that it would later become. Generally, it was less the level of the wage than the incidence of unemployment that pushed families into poverty and dependence. When after 1750, and with special force after 1780, falling real wages went hand in hand with widespread unemployment, the condition of the urban proletariat spiraled downward, reaching a nadir during the first decade of the nineteenth century when both industry and foreign trade came to a virtual standstill.

With little quantitative information to measure their size, and a porous boundary separating the two groups, much must remain vague about these lower rungs of the urban social ladder. Together they would have claimed close to half of the urban population, and in the long era of wage stability that set in by 1650, the incomes of adult males residing in the cities of the western provinces probably averaged something under 250 guilders per year. Average family incomes could then have stood a bit above 300 guilders. Urban incomes in the eastern and southern provinces certainly were lower than this, since wage rates there varied between 60 to 70 percent of those in the maritime provinces.

Above these two lowest socioeconomic groups, we find what the Dutch called the *burgerij*, a term that corresponds roughly with the usage Americans give to the term "middle class." It was a broad category intended to bring under its umbrella everyone capable of maintaining certain standards of respectability, which in turn permitted participation in the civic culture that sustained the political nation. Only a small top layer of urban society actually exercised political power, but this small "political nation" needed to be responsive, or to show itself to be responsive, to the sentiments that lived among the *burgerij*, and that could be expressed by their guilds and civic militias. Contemporaries often referred to this broad burger category as the *goede gemeente* (good citizens) and referred to the lower groups as the *schamele gemeente* (poor, shabby community).

Just as "middle class" is far too expansive a concept to be used without sub-differentiation, so the *burgerij* tended to be divided into lower, broad middle, and upper subgroups. Ordinary self-employed craftsmen and shopkeepers with a modest turnover formed the most important elements of the lowest level of the burgers. They were joined by the better sort of personnel in shops and businesses, as well as by the lowest ranks of public officeholders, such as weigh-house porters, lift bridge operators, harbor functionaries, and so on. The small self-employed persons and the salaried employees outside the public sector stood at the very cusp of the *burgerij*, always in danger of sliding down the far slope into the ranks of the lower orders. An untimely death of the breadwinner, extended illness, intemperance – indeed, any number of vices or misfortunes – sufficed to bring social degradation to the many families, perhaps a quarter of the urban total, with annual incomes between 350 and 500 guilders.

Just above this group, but sharing the designation of *smalle burgerij* (burgers of slim means), we find households earning between 500 and 600 guilders annually. This included (1) a small number of (well-educated) public-sector employees such as bookkeepers, clerks, schoolmasters, supervisors, and inspectors, and (2) a larger number from the private sector, including publicans, the operators of simple inns, and the run of bakers, smiths, butchers, inland shippers, shoemakers, tailors, plumbers, coopers, corset makers, glaziers, and broom makers. This group was also populated by specialized shopkeepers of all sorts, such as dealers in bedding and linens, cheese, cotton goods, coffee and tea, stockings, ribbons, tobacco, and rope. The operators of coaches for hire, undertakers, obstetricians, certain surgeons, teamsters, and the less prosperous apothecaries also belonged to this group. All in all they numbered some 10 percent of the urban labor force.

This leaves no more than about 20 percent of urban households to account for, the upper reaches of the income pyramid with incomes in excess of 600 guilders per year. The recipients of annual incomes between 600 and 1,000 guilders consisted first of all of the more successful craftsmen, tradesmen, and retailers whose poorer colleagues populated the 500- to 600-guilder category. Many bakers, apothecaries, book sellers, surgeons, grocers, innkeepers, brokers, wig makers, shippers, smiths, carpenters, gold and silver smiths, and the better sort of mercers managed to elevate themselves to this income level. Here we also encounter military officers of the lower ranks and a good number of wine merchants, butchers, and notaries. Senior clerks, bookkeepers, and other municipal officials as well as wholesalers, lesser merchants, and modest rentiers also enjoyed annual incomes between 600 and 1,000 guilders. Characteristic of this income class, comprising some 12 to 14 percent of the urban households, was a certain accumulation of capital. This typically took the form of an inventory of merchandise or raw materials. But house ownership and a cash reserve are also commonly encountered.

This leaves 6 to 8 percent of the urban households with incomes in excess of 1,000 guilders per year. This was the *grote burgerij* from which was drawn the political and commercial leadership of the country. Here we find, first and foremost, the merchants and (in the eighteenth century) most of the rentiers. They were joined by much of the Protestant clergy and the liberal professions, including medical doctors, notaries, solicitors, and some of the barristers. Here, too, we find industrialists and entrepreneurs, such as brewers, soap refiners, distillers, and groats grinders. Finally, of course, this upper group included the senior ranks of the officer corps and high government officials, such as the clerks of court (*griffiers*), municipal secretaries, sheriffs, commissioners, collectors of the land tax, and many more. At the very top of this pyramid, forming a charmed circle within the income elite, was the governing patriciate itself: the burgemeesters, town council members (*vroedschap*), judicial officers (*schepenen*), and counsellors. But individuals moved regularly between these governing positions (with their high salaries and honoraria) and the other high offices. Thus, the life styles of nearly all of the members of the *hoge burgerij* were broadly similar. An exception must be made only for the very rich, with incomes above 5,000 guilders per year. Among them we are more likely to find horses and carriages, pleasure yachts, country homes, art collections, and exotic porcelain.

We can recapitulate the preceding reconnaissance of the socioeconomic landscape of urban Holland with the stylized division of the lower 80 percent of household incomes presented in Table 11.12. We make the assumption that an annual income of 200 guilders formed a practical lower limit to household incomes (i.e., that a family unit could not be maintained in Holland's cities with less than this amount). Given the pyramidal structure of incomes, we set the average income for each income category except the lowest somewhat below the arithmetic average. This model of Holland's urban incomes is based on the stable structure of wages and salaries prevailing in the long period from before 1650 to after 1800, and it yields an average income for the bottom 80 percent of households of 363 guilders per year.

For the remaining 20 percent of the urban population, we are in a position to offer a better-informed description, one based on an income tax levied on nearly all households in Holland with incomes of at least 600 guilders. Introduced in 1742, this *Personeele Quotisatie* was soon withdrawn but not before the provincial government had compiled detailed lists of taxable individuals, their incomes, and their occupations. Such lists for sixteen cities have survived. To facilitate analysis

Table 11.12. *Sketch of assumed household income distribution for incomes under 600 guilders in the cities of Holland.*

Description	Income class (guilders per year)	%	Average income	Total	Average annual income for all households
Lesser Burgerij	500–600	8	540	4,320	
"	400–500	12	440	5,280	
"	350–400	15	370	5,550	
Working class	300–350	30	325	9,750	
"Het Grauw"	200–300	15	275	4,125	
All incomes under 600		80		29,025 / 80 =	362.81

we have grouped them into four categories: Amsterdam; four large cities (Haarlem, Leiden, The Hague, Rotterdam); five middle-sized cities (Delft, Dordrecht, Enkhuizen, Gouda, Hoorn); and six small cities (Gorinchem, Medemblik, Monnikendam, Purmerend, Schiedam, Schoonhoven). Of Holland's eighteen voting cities, we lack data for only three (Alkmaar, Edam, and Den Briel). This gap is not a serious drawback, since the data for the sixteen available cities allow us to estimate the nature of the missing information.

This source does possess other shortcomings, however. To begin with, the law exempted from taxation all foreigners, the *salaries* of professors, clergymen, and most high military officers, and the incomes of all craft journeymen. The professors, clergymen, and officers were only taxed on their nonsalary incomes, an obvious understatement of income, but one, given their finite number, for which we can compensate. The exception for journeymen need not detain us, since very few of them could have enjoyed incomes that crossed the 600-guilder threshold by much. Exempting them was simply a matter of expediency.

As for the accuracy of the income registers themselves, the procedures used to construct them impress us as careful and thorough. In Amsterdam a commission drawn from the town council, assisted by the city's precinct captains (*wijkmeesters*) and tax collectors, labored over an extended period to compile a register of all persons who were likely to fall above the taxable income limit. Then a separate commission from The Hague came to establish just who was and was not taxable. This procedure generated a list of those probably taxable on the basis of external evidence, and a final list of the persons definitely subject to tax.

The Amsterdam records preserve all of this information; by comparing these lists, we can identify the occupations that had many members with incomes near the 600-guilder limit and those whose practitioners were (nearly) all securely above the limit. The commissioners from The Hague (less subject to local pressure than the local committee, whose responsibility was to compile the master list, for which local knowledge was essential) removed from the provisional tax rolls 38 percent of all weigh-house porters. Among the tailors 32 percent were excused for falling under the 600-guilder limit, while this occurred to 28 percent of the wig makers, 22 percent of the shoemakers, 21 percent of the masons, 17 percent of the surgeons, 15 percent of glaziers, shippers, house painters, and tobacco retailers, and 11 percent of saddle makers and tavernkeepers. One gets the impression that for occupations such as these, only a small, high-earning elite proved to be taxable, since the local authorities must already have dismissed most of the practitioners from consideration as obviously below the 600-guilder income limit. At the same time, these occupations that generated incomes breaching the 600-guilder limit raised up many marginal cases that required the scrutiny of the committee from The Hague. Given this procedure, those occupations for which there were few or no persons who failed to meet the income qualification are likely to be ones (nearly) all of whose practitioners were safely above the 600-guilder limit, and which were therefore all but fully represented in the *Personeele*

Quotisatie. Examples are (with the number of nonqualifying persons per hundred taxable in parentheses): apothecaries, butchers, sugar refiners, *schepenen* and *kassiers* (private bankers)(0); jewelers, brokers, millers, and drapers (2).

The procedures followed in compiling the registers of the *Personeele Quotisatie* of 1742 give us confidence in their general accuracy. We have used them to calculate the total incomes of households in the sixteen cities for which these records have been preserved. In making these calculations, shown in Table 11.13, we followed these steps. The sixteen cities were gathered into the four groups introduced earlier, and their populations and average household size set as shown in the table. The documents identify income by categories (such as 600–700, 1,200–1,500, etc.). In each case we use the median income (650, 1,350, etc.).

Our calculations reveal a pattern of average incomes above 600 guilders that places the largest city, Amsterdam, at the top, followed by the other large cities, and then the middle-sized cities. The recipients of incomes above 600 guilders in the small cities formed the smallest share of the total population in their cities, but, perhaps for this very reason, they could boast of an average income slightly above that of the middle-sized cities. As for the incomes of nontaxable residents, we have already estimated (in Table 11.12) an average income of 363 guilders. The pattern of higher incomes among the cities suggests that the average incomes of those under 600 guilders per year also varied by city size. The prospects for steady work and supplements to earned income must have been greater in the larger cities (while nonmonetized support from garden plots, backyard goats, and the like will have weighed more heavily in the smallest towns). Therefore, we distribute the 363-guilder average income as shown in the final column of Table 11.13: highest in Amsterdam and progressively lower in the smaller size categories.

Overall, just over 20 percent of all households in the sixteen cities enjoyed incomes above the tax floor of 600 guilders, but here, too, the larger the city, the larger the percentage of high-income households. In Amsterdam they formed nearly a quarter of the population; in the small cities, just over one-eighth.

Our procedures yield an average household income for Holland's urban population of 654 guilders per year. This requires some upward adjustment for underassessment and exemptions; but taken at face value, Table 11.13 implies that the top 21 percent of income earners received at least 56 percent of total personal income.

Does this represent a highly unequal distribution of income? Answering this question requires comparison. For example, the distribution of income in the Netherlands around 1990 placed 41 percent of total personal income in the top 20 percent of households. But this represents gross income, before adjusting for the redistributional effect of taxes. The net disposable income of the top 20 percent of Dutch households stands at 36 to 37 percent of total income. One can argue that the assessment procedures of 1742 (based on existing tax documents recording taxable property, consumption, and incomes from government bonds) focused on disposable income and thus approximated a modern definition of net

Table 11.13. Reconstruction of personal income in sixteen Holland cities in 1742.

	Amsterdam[a]	Four large cities[b]	Five middle-size cities[c]	Six small cities[d]	Total income in guilders
Taxable	12,655 (23.0%)				23,241,550
Nontaxable (f 385 per household)	42,345				16,302,825
Total	55,000				39,544,375
Taxable		8,026 (21.7%)			13,996,350
Nontaxable (f 360 per household)		28,974			10,430,640
Total		37,000			24,426,990
Taxable			3,172 (16.7%)		4,471,050
Nontaxable (f 335 per household)			15,828		5,302,380
Total			19,000		9,773,430
Taxable				824	1,239,400
Nontaxable (f 310 per household)				5,326	1,651,060
Total				6,150	2,890,460
Personal income in the 16 cities:					
Taxable	24,677 households = 21.2%				42,948,350
Nontaxable	92,473 households = 78.9%				33,686,905
Total					76,635,255

[a] Amsterdam; average household size = 4.00.
[b] Haarlem, Leiden, The Hague, Rotterdam; average household size = 3.78.
[c] Delft, Dordrecht, Enkhuizen, Gouda, Hoorn; average household size = 3.68.
[d] Gorinchem, Medemblik, Monnikendam, Purmerend, Schiedam, Schoonhoven; average household size = 3.74.

income. At any rate the weak progressivity of taxes then and the strong progressivity of modern taxation needs to be kept in mind.

The distribution of income was definitely far less equal in 1742 than in 1990. The top fifth of income earners claimed 56 percent of total personal income then, compared to 37 percent (net) or 43 percent (gross) now. The mid–eighteenth-century Republic certainly was a land of greater social contrasts than the late twentieth-century welfare state, but how did it compare with other preindustrial European societies? Besides various highly impressionistic descriptions, we have quantitative studies only for eighteenth-century England (the work of Peter Lindert and Jeffery Williamson). These do not permit a simple, direct comparison with our estimates for Holland, but they do support the tentative, and intriguing, observation that the top 10 percent of English income recipients (in 1688, 1759, and 1801) enjoyed an even larger share of total income than did their Dutch counterparts, while the second 10 percent did rather better in Holland.

When we turn from the question of income distribution to that of absolute levels of income, our data prove rather more tractable. The average (uncorrected) income of households in the cities of Holland stood at 654 guilders (see Table 11.13), and these cities housed about 60 percent of Holland's population. When the 40 percent resident in the countryside are assigned an average income equal to that of the smallest cities (470 guilders per household), the resulting average income for the province as a whole comes to about 580 guilders. At an average household size of 4.0 persons, per capita income would then stand at 145 guilders per year; at 3.8 persons per household (our preferred estimate), 152 guilders; and at 3.6 persons, 160 guilders. We noted previously that these estimates require some correction for omissions and understatements of the taxed incomes. We return to this task in Chapter 13, section 13.3 (especially Table 13.1). Here we can conclude tentatively that Holland's per capita income in 1742 was at least 150 guilders per year.

No sources yet found permit direct estimates of income for Holland, or for any large portion of the Republic, at an earlier date. Personal income can be thought of as consisting of returns to labor (which dominated incomes below 600 guilders), rents from real property, and profits from capital investment. Thus, any effort to reason how incomes might have evolved before 1742 would need to establish the chief trends of those economic categories.

The course of profits and interest is the most difficult to track. Our account of the commercial economy in Chapters 9 and 10 argues for a fall in the profitability of foreign trade after 1660. Perhaps, then, the incomes of merchants and shipowners were much higher circa 1650 than can be observed in 1742. But working to offset that loss is the growth of interest income flowing from domestic and foreign bonds. This growth is sketched in Chapter 4 and reveals an annual income from investments of many millions of guilders per year that had no mid–seventeenth-century counterpart.

Net income from the ownership of real property, especially of agricultural land, fell sharply after 1660, in some cases to less than zero. This development, charted in Chapter 6, did not begin to right itself until after the 1740s. Any overall account of the course of nonwage incomes in Holland or the Republic will be affected very sensitively by the choice of assumptions concerning the composition of total wealth, and by changes in the structure of assets over time. This is a matter to which we return in Chapter 13.

The course of labor income is often thought to be a simpler matter to track, since wages seemed to be literally frozen for at least 150 years after 1650. This issue is examined with some care in the following chapter, where the Republic's famed wage rigidity is shown to be not quite what it appeared; but of even greater importance for the course of total income was the incidence of unemployment. We have virtually nothing on which to base estimates of unemployment rates. Indeed, the very concept has limited applicability to the Republican period – just as it is becoming less meaningful in our own time. But the evolution of wages and labor-market structure certainly hints at a growing problem of employment, especially for the less skilled workers. Within a general framework of stable wages, it was the wages for the unskilled and the unprotected (by guilds or large employers, for instance) that bore the greatest downward pressure.

The economy's employment problems tended to be shifted toward the underside of the social structure, and it is there that a "great disappearing act" took place. As poor men sought an escape from un- and underemployment by signing up with the VOC, and disappearing from the country (and often from among the living), the resulting sex-ratio imbalance in the cities depressed marriage rates and thereby reduced the number of births. These demographic responses hardly constitute an ideal equilibrating mechanism, but very gradually they tended to adjust the supply of labor to the retreating demand.

This demographic process worked with special force in Holland's cities and in rural North Holland, where a large loss of population occurred between 1670 and 1740. Even if the incidence of unemployment remained utterly stable between these dates, this decline of population in the highest-earning zones of the country would bring about a serious fall in aggregate wage income. But the initiation of this downward spiral would be hard to explain in the absence of a decline in employment opportunities.

A crisis centered in the wage-earning population could not stop there, of course. The resulting income and population decline undermined the viability of a wide variety of service occupations, from notaries to bakers, from booksellers to tavernkeepers. Even incomes above the 600-guilder line must have been affected. The overall effect of this crisis was to reduce aggregate income, but since not all incomes fell proportionately, it probably also led to a growth of the share of total income in the hands of higher-income groups. We say "probably" because the effects of falling rents and commercial profits on the higher incomes remain to be factored in.

We focus here on Holland and its 10-percent fall in population during the period 1670–1740. In the Republic as a whole, this loss was compensated for by growth in the eastern and southern provinces. But the wage and income levels there always remained significantly lower than in Holland and the maritime zone, so that the total income of the Republic as a whole must have experienced a significant downward pressure.

Before the mid–seventeenth century, a large growth of income seems patent, even though we cannot really quantify it. After the mid–eighteenth century, there are again some signs of revival in aggregate income. After the tax riots of 1748, the government made no further attempts to levy income taxes, so we have nothing to compare with the 1742 information. But taxes on wealth were levied often enough, and they point in the direction of a growth of the higher-wealth categories. The rise of prices complicates any assessment of nominal wealth and income data, but it is possible that the (slow) growth of population and rents and the (more rapid) accumulation of financial assets buoyed incomes, especially for the upper classes. These positive trends were mixed with less welcome developments, especially the erosion of real wages; but the fundamental break with a wealth and income structure that had embroidered on a pattern established in the seventeenth century came only with the great shocks at the end of the eighteenth century. They began with the liquidation of the VOC and WIC, were followed by widespread foreign bond defaults, and culminated with the *tiërcering* of the national debt in 1811.

The data provided by the income tax of 1742, which we have already exploited to estimate Holland's per capita income, also provide a rare opportunity to examine the economic structure of the upper reaches of urban society. We have learned already from Table 11.13 that the incidence of households earning over 600 guilders declined with the size of city, ranging from 23 percent of households in Amsterdam to about 13 percent of the households in the small cities. This pattern reflects the generally lower income levels for most occupations in smaller cities, but it is also a product of differences in the occupational structure of cities of different sizes.

These two patterns, one systematic and the other structural, tended to counteract each other. The practitioners of most occupations could expect to earn less the lower their city stood in the urban hierarchy, but in smaller cities a higher percentage of households held high-income occupations and offices. This was not true, of course, for occupations such as book printers, brokers, jewelers, and other luxury retailers. These were typical "big-city" specialties, and they were scarce in Holland's small cities. Nor was it true of occupations such as silversmiths, hardware dealers, and butchers. Such occupations were distributed quite evenly across the population, suggesting both a broad, uniform demand and the absence of scale economies in their operations. But with occupational categories such as notaries, sitting and former burgemeesters, other public officials, brewers, and even groats grinders, the small cities found their advantage. Holders of such functions may have received smaller incomes in small cities than in Amsterdam, but

Table 11.14. *Incomes of persons earning at least 600 guilders per year in sixteen Holland cities in 1742: Ten economic sectors, including all occupations whose practitioners earn over 100,000 guilders in total taxable income.*

Sector	Number taxable	Total income	Average income
1. Government	1,024	4,860,150	4,746
2. Wholesale trade	2,802	8,630,430	3,080
3. Manufacturers	852	1,687,850	1,981
4. Retail trade, shopkeeping	4,084	4,335,550	1,062
5. Medical care	726	990,500	1,364
6. Administration	614	1,019,350	1,660
7. Construction	613	610,550	996
8. Transportation	520	504,500	970
9. Rentiers and occupation unknown	4,336	9,633,050	2,222
10. Miscellaneous	991	1,579,800	1,594
Total	16,556	33,851,730	2,045

there were many more of them per 10,000 population, and this tended to lift the overall average income of small cities. Thus, incomes for any given occupation fell as one descended the urban hierarchy, but the occupational structure of smaller cities offered a partial compensation to this trend in the form of a denser presence of certain high-income occupations.

In order to examine the top of the urban income pyramid more closely (it commanded, after all, well over half of total income), we have pooled the data from all sixteen cities and identified all occupations whose practitioners together accounted for a total income of at least 100,000 guilders. This exercise yielded sixty qualifying occupations and encompassed 67 percent of all taxable households. Together they controlled 33,842,230 guilders of taxable income, or 79 percent of the taxable total. (The hundreds of occupations left out of this investigation were carried out by one-third of the taxable households, but they accounted for only 21 percent of total taxable income. Correspondingly, their average income, 1,120 guilders, was barely half of the 2,045 guilders of the sixty selected occupations.)

In order to get a clear view of the these sixty occupations, we have gathered them into ten sectors, shown in Table 11.14. A glance at this table suffices to make several important points: the large number of high-income persons concentrated in the retailing, commercial and wholesaling, and rentier sectors; the very high average incomes of public officeholders, followed at some distance by the merchants and traders of the wholesaling sector; the surprisingly high income level of persons with administrative functions. The total incomes accruing to each of these ten categories are also highly revealing, with rentiers and persons with unspecified occupations in the first place, followed by merchants, which is no

Table 11.15. *Incomes in sixteen Holland cities in 1742: Persons with incomes over 600 guilders in miscellaneous occupations (Sector 10, Table 11.14).*

Occupation	Total taxable	Total income	Average income
Butcher	223	415,600	1,864
Clergyman	174	344,400	1,979
Miller	158	177,800	1,125
Tailor	145	116,900	806
Schoolmaster	113	101,200	896
Lawyer	94	257,700	2,741
Kassier	84	166,200	1,979
Total	991	1,579,800	1,594

surprise, and government officeholders, which is a surprise. There are enough unexpected results in Table 11.14 to justify a closer look.

This closer look is provided in Tables 11.15 through 11.24, which show details concerning the underlying occupations of the ten categories. We begin with Table 11.15, which assembles the occupations with at least 100,000 guilders of total taxable income that could not be grouped in any of the nine other categories. This miscellany includes butchers, clergymen, grain millers, tailors, schoolmasters, lawyers (barristers), and *kassiers* (private bankers): seven occupations with a total of 991 taxpaying members and a respectable average annual income of nearly 1,600 guilders.

The incomes of schoolmasters and tailors stood far below this average. In fact, what we see here are those fortunate few whose incomes broke through the 600-guilder level. The large majority of their colleagues were not subject to tax, and of those who do appear on the tax rolls, most are found in the lowest income categories. This is especially true of the tailors. We already noted that many tailors initially earmarked for taxation were later found to fall below the 600-guilder level; indeed, if the tailors were as numerous as is suggested by our earlier discussion (see Table 11.2), the 145 taxed individuals were the most fortunate of some 2,200 tailors active in the 16 cities.

If the taxed tailors did not account for more than 8 percent of all tailors, the situation would have been only marginally better for the schoolmasters and millers. They, too, had many colleagues below the 600-guilder income level. After all, the 1742 tax registers list only 79 millers in Amsterdam, while we know that in 1734, the city numbered 122 millers of all sorts.

The butchers enjoyed such a high annual income, 1,864 guilders, that we might assume they were nearly all represented on the tax rolls. But a closer inspection of their distribution across the income categories reveals an interesting peculiarity. In Amsterdam the 107 butchers range across all the income categories from 800 to 4,500 guilders. Only 5 of them fell in the 600- to 700-guilder class. But the 116 butchers of the fifteen other cities fell into a very different distribution. On the one hand were 40 butchers with 600 to 700 guilders, and 15 more with incomes that reached as high as 1,000 guilders. On the other hand were 61 butchers earning 2,500 to 3,000 guilders each. Clearly, we are dealing here with two very different sorts of butchers: retail butchers who, like the millers and schoolmasters, probably represent the top of a distribution that includes many persons earning less than 600 guilders, and large-scale butchers, probably also involved in cattle trading and/or fattening. These two types of meat dealers, so distinct in all other cities, tended to converge in Amsterdam, where the large local market offered opportunities for retail butchers to attain a large scale of operation.

The *kassier*, a type of private banker, was very much an Amsterdam specialty, where we find 64 of the 84 *kassiers* on the tax rolls. Most earned over 1,000 guilders, but 12 stood right at the 600- to 700-guilder limit, suggesting that a few of these financial specialists may have escaped our notice. Among the clergymen we can be certain that a large number have escaped our notice, their average income of nearly 2,000 guilders notwithstanding, for the official salaries of the Reformed Church's *predikanten* were tax exempt. (Since even the pastors of small rural churches earned at least 550 guilders, plus housing and other allowances, just about all of the Republic's 1,550 *predikanten*, and certainly all with urban pulpits, would fall within the income range that we are investigating here.) Through its effort to shelter the clergy from taxation, our source exposes with exceptional clarity the large private incomes enjoyed by many who served the public church. Even less expected is the evidence that so many Catholic priests pulled down very respectable incomes: In Amsterdam most of them earned close to 3,000 guilders; in other cities they averaged well over 1,000 guilders.

The highest average income of any occupation in this miscellaneous category was earned by the lawyers, who were very largely concentrated in The Hague and Amsterdam (41 and 31, respectively, out of a total of 94 taxed lawyers). Despite the very high incomes of most lawyers, there were still 18 who earned no more than 600 to 1,000 guilders. Thus, Holland may have possessed a few more lawyers than the 94 listed on the tax rolls, but they certainly had not yet infested the body politic as, in some countries, they later would.

Table 11.14 already alerted us to the fact that the largest total income of any occupational category accrued to the rentiers and persons for whom no occupation was given. Table 11.16 makes clear that the enormous weight of this category is attributable to the truly astonishing number of rentiers (3,567) as well as to their high average income. At this point we might recall Table 4.8 and its estimates of interest and dividend payments. By the 1740s these annual disbursements amounted to some 24 million guilders. Four million of this was retained by the state as a tax on bond income, and some unknown amount went to persons outside Holland. It does not seem impossible that 16 million guilders then flowed

Table 11.16. *Incomes in sixteen Holland cities in 1742: Persons with incomes over 600 guilders, not actively employed (Sector 9, Table 11.14).*

Occupation	Total taxable	Total income	Average income
Rentier	3,567	8,616,050	2,415
Unknown, none	769	1,017,000	1,323
Total	4,336	9,633,000	2,222

annually into the hands of individuals and institutions in Holland. Just how this money was distributed across the various claimants remains unknown, but when one pauses to note that these payments easily exceeded 10 percent of Holland's total income (see Tables 11.13 and 13.1), then the conclusion is almost unavoidable that they injected even more than 10 percent of total income into the cities. In this light the finding that rentiers controlled nearly 9 million guilders of annual income – 1 out of every 9 guilders of urban income – is not at all implausible. The importance of such individuals to consumer demand in the eighteenth-century cities of Holland must have been enormous. A city lacking appeal to rentiers as a place of residence – Leiden, Gouda, and Schiedam come to mind – found it difficult to support a full range of shops and crafts. Likewise, the enormous concentration of rentiers in The Hague allowed this "overgrown village" to offer a range of goods and services second only to Amsterdam, a metropolis with six to seven times The Hague's population. And even then, it was The Hague, not Amsterdam, where in 1742 one could find two specialized florists, three stores specializing in chocolate, a swordhandle maker, a carriage painter, two bedframe drapers, and – surely the most remarkable of all – no fewer than eight purveyors of East Indian articles. The city of old "Asia hands" described by Louis Couperus 150 years later seems already to have been taking shape! In all these specialties, The Hague was unique, and in specialties such as gold and silver embroidery makers, purveyors of the finest china, engravers, harness makers, ivory turners, and turtleshell decorators, it was about as well supplied as the much larger Amsterdam. All of this gives testimony to the presence of a clientele with enormous purchasing power, and it was a clientele thick with wealthy rentiers.

Yet even "coupon clippers" do not deserve to be stereotyped. They did not all ride about in beautifully lacquered carriages pulled by thoroughbred horses; not all slept in beds that had received the professional attention of bedstead drapers; not all were regular customers of florists and East India shops. In fact, many rentiers were far from rich. Besides Amsterdam's 1,659 taxed rentiers, we know of 71 who were removed from the final tax roll because their income, on closer inspection, failed to reach the 600-guilder limit. Moreover, over a third of the rentiers who were taxable in both Amsterdam and The Hague, and even more in the other cities, received incomes below 1,000 guilders – in Amsterdam nearly

Table 11.17. *Incomes in sixteen Holland cities in 1742: Persons with incomes over 600 guilders active in construction and transportation (Sectors 7 and 8, Table 11.14).*

Occupation	Total taxable	Total income	Average income
Carpenter	457	456,500	999
Mason	156	154,050	988
Construction total	613	610,550	996
Skipper	369	359,450	974
Messenger	151	145,050	961
Tranportation total	520	504,500	970

Table 11.18. *Incomes in sixteen Holland cities in 1742: Persons with incomes over 600 guilders active in administration (Sector 6, Table 11.14).*

Occupation	Total taxable	Total income	Average income
Bookeeper	249	439,700	1,766
Clerk	214	335,150	1,566
Notary	151	244,500	1,619
Total	614	1,019,350	1,600

a quarter were clustered in the 600- to 700-guilder category. All of this suggests the presence of a fair number of "poor" rentiers: the widowed and retired, but also persons who had left failing businesses. Of course, there were also many very rich rentiers – 44 percent of those in The Hague enjoyed over 2,500 guilders per year – but the social category of rentier included many men, and perhaps especially women, situated in the middle ranks of the *burgerij*.

When we turn to the construction and transport sector (Table 11.17), we are dealing even more with occupations that yielded most practitioners under 600 guilders per year. The taxable master carpenters and masons (journeymen fortunate enough to earn over 600 guilders were exempt) achieved an average income of just under 1,000 guilders; this was also the case for the taxable inland shippers and messengers, almost all of whom were employed by municipal governments.

"White collar" employees are found in the category "administration" (Table 11.18). Clerks, like messengers, were almost all public employees. Among the 80 taxed clerks in Amsterdam, only one was recorded as "with a merchant." The employment of 4 was left unspecified, but the remaining 75 worked for the municipal government (treasury, public works, etc.) or for quasi-governmental institutions (e.g., clerks at the VOC warehouse). These employees earned hand-

Table 11.19. *Incomes in sixteen Holland cities in 1742: Persons with incomes over 600 guilders active in medical care (Sector 5, Table 11.14).*

Occupation	Total taxable	Total income	Average income
Surgeon	307	312,750	1,019
Apothecary	239	323,650	1,354
Medical doctor	180	354,100	1,967
Total	726	990,500	1,364

some salaries, supplemented by numerous fees and emoluments. Over half of all the taxable clerks earned over 1,000 guilders. This and their high average income (1,566 guilders) raises a question about public-sector salaries, to which we return later.

Bookkeepers differed from clerks in being less dependent on (quasi-)governmental employment. Of the 188 taxable bookkeepers in Amsterdam, the descriptions for 52 specified employment for the city, VOC, and so on. But these public-sector bookkeepers earned on average 2,880 guilders, nearly twice the income for the remaining bookkeepers. This high average was certainly pulled upward by several extraordinarily well-paid individuals: The chief bookkeeper for the VOC earned 15,000 guilders; the Bank of Amsterdam's four top bookkeepers earned 9,500, 6,500, 5,500, and 3,250 guilders; the Bankruptcy Court's bookkeeper took in 8,500; the chief bookkeeper of the VOC ship wharf, 8,500, and the VOC's payroll master, 6,500. In general, only 8 of 52 public-sector bookkeepers earned under 1,000 guilders, while this was true of fully 68 of the 120 private-sector bookkeepers.

Table 11.19 describes the incomes of medical personnel. Together they took in nearly a million guilders, a sum that piques one's curiosity about the total cost of professional medical care in the sixteen cities. One must add to the incomes of these persons the costs of operating and maintaining the hospitals and asylums. These costs could not have been enormous, nor did the costs of other medical personnel – the low-paid attendants, midwives and their male counterparts, and the surgeons earning under 600 guilders – amount to a large sum. If all of these costs added 1 million guilders to the incomes of surgeons, apothecaries, and doctors listed in Table 11.19, the total labor and operating costs associated with medical care for the sixteen cities covered by our data might have reached 2 million guilders.

To this sum we must add the costs of medicines. Next to nothing is known about this, but if apothecaries' incomes amounted to, say, one-sixth of their turnover (assuming a net profit of 16 percent), then some 2 million guilders would have been spent on medicines. This would imply that every Hollander – urban and rural – spent a bit over 2 guilders per year on medicines. This may not be

Table 11.20. *Incomes in sixteen Holland cities in 1742: Persons with incomes over 600 guilders active in manufacturing (Sector 3, Table 11.14).*

Occupation	Total taxable	Total income	Average income
Groats grinder	159	260,400	1,638
Fabrikeur	146	357,400	2,448
Distiller	123	130,650	1,062
(Sugar) refiner	113	331,650	2,935
Candlemaker	101	105,550	1,045
Brewer	96	280,400	3,116
Sail maker	83	119,450	1,439
Soap maker	31	102,350	3,302
Total	852	1,687,850	1,981

far from the truth: The regents of Amsterdam's *Aalmoezeniers* orphanage purchased medicines at an average of 2.20 guilders annually for each of their poor charges in the period 1730–79. Total medical costs are now approaching 4 million guilders. Since our estimate of total income in the sixteen cities approaches 80 million guilders, it would appear that expenditures on medical care may have reached 5 percent of total urban income. This estimate surprises us by its high level and should, in any event, be lowered to accommodate the fact that some portion of rural medical needs were served by urban practitioners. But even if our estimate were reduced to 3 percent, and it is hard to see how it could be lower than this, the economic importance of medicine to this economy will have become apparent. This is a topic deserving of more detailed study.

We turn now, with Table 11.20, to the owners and operators of what might best be called industrial enterprises. The total income of these "manufacturers" is disappointingly small. When their 1.7 million guilders is placed beside the 13 million earned by wholesale and retail traders, our first thought must be that our source has omitted many industries. And, in fact, this is the case; important industries operated outside the cities (such as paper making), and others are omitted here because they fell below the 100,000-guilder limit. But the inclusion of these smaller industrial activities would not materially change the overall picture, while the impact of rural industrialists can only be guessed at. What does emerge clearly from Table 11.20 is how the richest manufacturers by far were soap makers, sugar refiners, and brewers. Manufacturing families that managed to penetrate the charmed circle of the town patriciate usually based their wealth on these three industries. A fourth category, the groats grinders, loom large primarily because of their large number. Their average incomes were also quite high, which was not the case with the distillers. The latter's 1,062-guilder average income places them in the company of candlemakers and surgeons, which reflects the fact that the distilling of alcohol was a fairly simple process requiring only a modest capital investment.

The category of unspecified *fabrikeurs* (manufacturers) consisted of individuals highly concentrated in three cities: Amsterdam (35, with an average income of 4,250 guilders), Haarlem (35, earning 2,125) and Leiden (41, earning 1,520). Not only did the manufacturers of Amsterdam stand head and shoulders above their colleagues in Haarlem and Leiden, but within the entire group, incomes were spread widely, with 15 in the lowest 600- to 700-guilder category and one industrial prince earning 24,000 to 26,000.

Most of these manufacturers were involved in textile production. This is specified in several instances, but can be inferred for the unspecified manufacturers from our knowledge of the occupational distribution. Leiden and Haarlem were, of course, known as centers of textile production, but Amsterdam, though it possessed a much more diversified economic structure, also lodged a major textile sector. This becomes apparent from a review of the occupations given by grooms in their marriage applications. In view of the limited occupational mobility experienced by workers until very recent times, a man was highly likely to persist in the work he had when he married (typically, at age twenty-five to thirty), and since the occupations of 90 to 95 percent of all seventeenth-century grooms are known (this information ceased to be collected after 1715), our knowledge of Amsterdam's adult male occupational structure is reasonably well founded.

In every quarter of the seventeenth century, occupations best described as "industrial and craft production" dominated the city economy: 1601–25, 61 percent; 1626–50, 49 percent; 1651–75, 53 percent; 1676–1700, 54 percent. A notable stability characterizes the percentage of grooms active in this sector, especially after 1625. And within this large sector, the stability among the various industrial branches was greater still. Textile production always claimed over a quarter of newly married men active in the industrial sector; clothing, woodworking, and construction followed, in competition for second place, and these three were always closely followed by the leather trades. Behind all these we find metalworking and food, drink, and tobacco processing. Far behind all these came shipbuilding. Together, these eight specializations always accounted for 83 to 94 percent of all grooms active in some form of industrial or craft production.

Certainly the most important feature of these marriage data is the striking occupational stability across a century of dynamic change. Only minor shifts are observable: a slight tendency toward decline in textiles and clothing, and a rise, particularly late in the century, of food, drink, and tobacco processing. Construction showed more variability than other sectors, which is only to be expected of this classic cyclical industry. All in all, stability is the dominant message, and it is this feature that emboldens us to take the liberty of assuming that this occupational pattern continued to characterize Amsterdam well into the eighteenth century.

If this assumption can be accepted, then it follows that most of the unspecified manufacturers listed in Table 11.20 were active in the textile sector. The wood,

Table 11.21. *Incomes in sixteen Holland cities in 1742: Persons with incomes over 600 guilders active in retail trade (Sector 4, Table 11.14).*

Occupation	Total taxable	Total income	Average income
Shopkeeper			
Spices/groceries	374	465,350	1,244
Tobacco	266	301,500	1,133
Coffee and tea	257	227,250	884
Books	219	267,700	1,222
Fats, oils, and candles	197	163,500	830
Cotton goods	137	150,750	1,100
Woolen goods	127	189,800	1,494
Dry goods	127	166,850	1,314
Ironwares	117	185,950	1,589
Jewelry	114	238,150	2,089
Linen goods	106	131,350	1,239
Subtotal	2,041	2,488,150	1,219
Artisans with shops			
Baker	885	773,200	874
Pastry baker	167	149,950	898
Silversmith	217	245,850	1,133
Subtotal	1,269	1,169,000	921
Beverage sellers			
Tavernkeepers	774	678,400	876
Total	4,084	4,335,550	1,062

leather, and metalworking sectors plus construction and clothing were dominated by small craftsmen employing perhaps a few assistants. Few manufacturers will be found there. This leaves textile production as the only remaining industry in which manufacturers were active. Standing behind the nearly 150 *fabrikeurs* of Amsterdam, Haarlem, and Leiden in 1742 were several tens of thousands of textile workers. The more fortunate of these workers filled the lowest ranks of the *burgerij*; far more of them fell into the large, still poorly profiled class below.

If we set aside as economically inactive the large class of rentiers, then the 4,084 shopkeepers/retailers formed by far the largest taxable group. Their average income, as shown in Table 11.21, was not especially high (1,062 guilders), nor did the various types of shopkeepers differ much in their average incomes. Only the jewelers (all but four of whom lived in Amsterdam and The Hague) stood clearly above the rest, with incomes averaging over 2,000 guilders. They were followed by the hardware dealers (who, as we noted earlier, were distributed evenly across the urban population). Their 1,589-guilder average income speaks to the importance of iron articles in a society that continued to rely on wood as

Table 11.22. *Distribution of incomes of taxable Amsterdam shopkeepers in 1742.*

Income category	Number	%	Income category	Number	%
ƒ600–800	1,189	38	ƒ3,000–3,500	61	2
800–1,000	584	19	3,500–4,000	8 ⎫	
1,000–1,200	440	14	4,000–4,500	25 ⎪	
1,200–1,500	231	8	4,500–5,000	6 ⎬	2
1,500–2,000	275	9	5,000–6,000	10 ⎪	
2,000–2,500	182	6	6,000–7,000	8 ⎭	
2,500–3,000	81	2	7,000–9,000	4	
			Total	3,104	100

the principal construction material. Just below the hardware dealers, we find dealers in *laken*, the finest woolen cloth. With an average income of nearly 1,500 guilders, they always stood a step ahead of the shopkeepers specializing in cotton and linen. The incomes of specialists in silk exceeded all of these, but they were too few in number to appear in our tables.

Below these relatively high-income shopkeepers, we encounter the very numerous fraternities of beer sellers and bakers (both bread and pastry bakers). They, together with the sellers of fats, candles, and oils and the purveyors of coffee and tea, all eked out average annual incomes under 900 guilders. Here, once again, we can be confident that there were many more such shopkeepers whose low incomes exempted them from taxation. In Amsterdam alone the tax commissioners excused 136 shopkeepers who had initially been suspected as likely prospects for taxation. They must have formed only the tip of an iceberg of lower-income shopkeepers. The size of that submerged mass cannot be known with certainty, but its likely vastness is suggested by Table 11.22. This table presents the income distribution of all taxed Amsterdam shopkeepers and shows how nearly 40 percent of all 3,104 fell within the 600- to 800-guilder range. A total of 4,000 to 5,000 Amsterdam shopkeepers would not seem impossible. This would have resulted in 18 to 23 shopkeepers per 1,000 population, while we noted earlier (Chapter 11, section 11.1) that the cities of Zeeland in 1807 managed to support 25 shopkeepers per 1,000 population. Ratios such as these, when applied to all sixteen cities, would imply the presence of 8,000 to 10,000 shopkeepers, no more than half of whom earned incomes sufficient to appear in Table 11.21. Shopkeepers occupied a central place in the urban economies, where retail trade was the most stable, and certainly most ubiquitous, function.

How surprising can it be, then, that the municipal governments sought to concentrate not only craftsmen but also shopkeepers into guilds, the better to regulate them? A 1688 membership list of thirty-seven of Amsterdam's guilds

ANALYSIS

covered some 11,000 persons. With their dependents, these guild members represented some 40,000 persons, or one-fifth of the city's population. Moreover, several guilds are missing from this list, including the *Groot kramersgilde*, which covered all shopkeepers for whom no specialized guilds existed. Then there were the journeymen and apprentices, who in many cases were barred from guild membership. The guilds represented well over a fifth of the urban workforce – the broad base of the *burgerij*.

The guilds offered the city governments a variety of policy tools with which to intervene in the local economy. Municipalities could shape population policy by easing or restricting settlement in the city. Requiring that new guild members buy citizenship rights (*poorterschap*), setting the price of such rights, establishing or dismantling of guild organization for a particular activity, setting the price of entry to such a guild, differentiating entry costs according to one's natal place and religion, setting standards to be upheld in the evaluation of an aspirant's masterpiece (demonstration of skill), tolerating variations in these standards according to one's parentage and birthplace, establishing numerical limits on a guild's membership – all of these were measures that might be used by the Republic's town governments to intervene in economic life.

In general, the economy's early seventeenth-century "boom" period saw the municipal governments competing with one another to attract craftsmen and traders of all sorts. Thereafter, certainly after mid-century, tighter regulation became the norm. In the eighteenth century, these regulations often amounted to outright protectionism, intended to regulate the local labor market to the advantage of the settled citizenry. The guilds offered their members a degree of protection from the competition of an overstocked trade by granting their children favored access to protected occupations. Guilds also offered some protection from illness, disability, and death by organizing social funds that paid benefits to eligible members. For consumers the guilds were no unalloyed benefit, but the town governments could regulate them to serve consumer interests by fixing prices and demanding quality guarantees. In general, the guilds sought to deflect any economic blows and hardships from their burger members onto nonburgers and nonresidents. It will be evident why the ideal of economic liberalism placed abolition of the guilds high on the agenda of the Batavian regime; but it will be equally evident why this issue met with the determined resistance of the city governments.

In contrast to the retail sector, wholesale trade generally was left as free of restriction as possible. With 2,802 taxpaying representatives, this commercial sector formed, after the rentiers and the retailers, the third largest economic category. But among economically active persons, these merchants and commercial agents controlled by far the largest total income (8.6 million guilders) of any of our categories. Since so much has been said about them in Chapters 9 and 10, we here restrict ourselves to a consideration of their numbers and incomes as of 1742.

Table 11.23 lists six merchant groups that achieved an aggregate income of at least 100,000 guilders. Wine merchants were numerous, but their average income

Table 11.23. *Incomes in sixteen Holland cities in 1742: Persons with incomes over 600 guilders active in commerce and wholesale trade (Sector 2 in Table 11.14).*

Occupation	Total taxable	Total income	Average income
Merchant	1,606	6,375,000	3,969
Wine merchant	694	1,165,530	1,679
Broker	348	732,800	2,106
Timber merchant	72	152,100	2,111
Linen merchant	41	103,550	2,526
Cotton merchant	41	101,450	2,474
Total	2,802	8,630,430	3,080

was at a relatively low 1,679 guilders. Then came brokers, timber merchants, linen merchants, and cotton merchants, all with average incomes between 2,000 and 2,500 guilders. Finally, we come to the unspecified merchants, a very large group with a very high average income of nearly 4,000 guilders. This pattern suggests that we are dealing with three distinctive types of merchant.

In the wine trade – just as in the distribution of brandies and beer – the government had fiscal reasons to maintain a sharp distinction between wholesalers and retailers. What was often conflated in other trades was clearly distinguished in the case of taxed alcoholic beverages. Here, the tavernkeepers (*tappers*) stood at the final step of distribution, selling directly to consumers. Above them stood two levels of trade and distribution, separated by governmental regulations: the merchant-importer and the wine merchant, who acted as a middleman between the importer and the retailer, but who under certain circumstances might also sell directly to consumers. When in 1659 Amsterdam acted to re-establish a wine merchants' guild, its ordinance distinguished clearly between "merchants-importers," who could sell in lots no smaller than 12 hogsheads (2,328 liters), and *tappers*, who sold "*ter consumptie of ter sleet*" (for consumption on or off the premises). Various regulations sought to ensure the maintenance of this distinction. Thus, no *tapper* could also work as the manager of a wine merchant's cellar. No *tapper* could sell both French and Rhine wines at the same time. Amsterdam even forbade *tappers* from living within two houses of a wine merchant in 1634, a regulation softened by 1678 to forbid their both living under the same roof. These merchant categories could not have been watertight (otherwise, why so many regulations?), but we should understand the wine merchants listed in Table 11.23 to have been chiefly middlemen, who bought the product from importers, bottled it, and sold it to *tappers* (the retailers) and to such private individuals prepared to acquire substantial quantities at a time. Their average income of 1,679 guilders, closer to the incomes of the better sort of shopkeeper than of merchants, would seem to confirm this interpretation of their function. It is strengthened by the fact that our documents record several wine merchants who combined this trade with that of grocer, boardinghouse operator, salt wholesaler, and minter. On the other hand, their close association with wine importing is suggested by their concentration in cities known to be centers of that trade (Amsterdam, 394 wine merchants; Rotterdam, 151; Dordrecht, 31; Hoorn, 16). The Hague, with its upscale citizenry but no port, had only 24.

The large number of wine merchants constitutes, in and of itself, an historical puzzle. Seven hundred of them in Holland's cities means one wine merchant per 1,100 men, women, and children. Some of these merchants certainly served clients elsewhere in the Republic, but cities such as Utrecht, Groningen, Zwolle, Arnhem, and Middelburg also housed wine merchants. If the other cities had no more than 100 wine merchants, each would still have served, on average, 2,600 inhabitants of all ages. Given the age structure of the time, this would have yielded perhaps 1,700 potential customers. Yet a wine merchant's turnover must have been substantial if his business was to generate an income equal to the average cited in Table 11.23.

How much wine did Republican Netherlanders drink? Probate inventories hint that they drank quite a bit, for these documents include among the "death debts" the costs incurred at the burial feasts. These "festivities" were by no means rare, and drink weighed heavily in the total costs. The frequent excesses at such events motivated the burgemeesters of Amsterdam in 1696 to act against the ostentatious consumption of wine, a move that led directly to the so-called *aansprekersoproer* (morticians' riot), the most dramatic act of mass violence of the seventeenth century, an event that would be spoken of for decades. Its 1690 predecessor, the "Costerman riot" in Rotterdam, also involved wine. It began as a late-night skirmish between young revelers and a tax farmer who tried to remove from their possession a clandestine vat of wine that they were carrying to a party. No matter what the event – militia banquets, guild feasts, meetings of polder boards, of *trekschuit* commissioners, and so on – the records include substantial wine bills. For people of means, wine drinking was an everyday occurrence and often required the maintenance of a wine cellar. Thus, at the Van Isendoorn's castle in the Veluwe, annual wine expenditures could reach 800 guilders, and in 1719–22 the Generality's Receiver-General Cornelis de Jonge van Ellemeet (one of the Republic's richest men, to be sure) spent an average of 540 guilders per year on wine – good for 1,000 to 1,500 liters of wine of varying quality.

Concerning aggregate wine consumption, we have it on the testimony of Matthias van Geuns that in the period 1753–87, the residents of the city of Utrecht consumed just over, and in 1790–98 just under, 11,000 *anker* of wine per year. This amounted to an annual per capita consumption of somewhere between 11 and 14 liters. For the country as a whole, our first data go back no further than 1831. Then per capita consumption was no higher than 3.2 liters, and even this fell as the nineteenth century progressed: to 2.84 liters in 1877, and 2.01 liters in

1891. There is no denying the riskiness of comparing the experience of a single eighteenth-century city with nineteenth-century national averages; yet it seems highly likely to us that wine consumption in the late Republic far exceeded that of the nineteenth century. (Such a trend would be consistent with British experience, where per capita wine consumption declined from about 5 liters in the sixteenth century to roughly 3 liters in the late seventeenth, to less than 2 liters in the 1840s.) The fact that consumption continued to fall all through that century strengthens us in this opinion. If the Republic's per capita consumption in 1742 stood at 5 liters, and if wine then sold for about ƒ0.40 per liter, the 800-odd wine merchants then operating in the country would have averaged gross receipts of some 5,000 guilders per year. This would seem to be a minimum turnover in order to extract an income averaging 1,700 guilders. There is much we still do not know about this trade, but two things now seem very likely: In the time of the Republic, wine was drunk much more widely than it would later be, and the Republic's wine trade was much more important than is usually assumed.

When we turn to the merchants proper, we confront the occupational group whose large number and high average incomes placed them in a position of economic dominance in the Republic. The tens of thousands of farmers surely earned a total income that exceeded the 6.4 million of the merchants, but the concentration of this income – perhaps 5 percent of Holland's total – in the hands of 1,600 merchants justifies treating commerce and wholesale trade as the "commanding heights" of Holland's economy.

Among these merchants there were, of course, a number who earned truly princely sums, even in 1742: Seven could not deny earning over 30,000 guilders per year, and another twenty earned between 20,000 and 30,000. On the other hand, only 10 percent of the people who assumed the designation *koopman* (merchant) earned under 1,000 guilders. There can have been very few merchants who escape our ken by earning under 600 guilders. We have nearly the entire merchant community before us here, and 40.3 percent earned between 1,000 and 3,000 guilders, while 43.3 percent earned between 3,000 and 10,000. Even setting aside the 101 prodigies earning over 10,000 guilders per year, this was a remarkably and uniformly prosperous group. When we compare them to the highest-income manufacturers (the soap makers, brewers, and sugar refiners), the latter's marginal position in Holland's urban society immediately becomes clear. The handful of these manufacturers with incomes above 3,000 guilders find themselves lost in a sea of 800 merchants earning more than that amount.

The only large group with which the merchants could really compare their incomes – and which, in truth, exceeded them by a substantial margin – was the class of high government officeholders (Table 11.24). These officeholders, such as burgemeester, *schepenen* (judges), and member of the town council, were nearly all recruited from the regental families of the urban patriciate. But these families also supplied most of the persons who filled the myriad other, lesser administrative functions, often by combining more than one position in the same person.

Table 11.24. *Incomes in sixteen Holland cities in 1742: Persons with incomes over 600 guilders active in government service (Sector 1, Table 11.14).*

Occupation	Total taxable	Total income	Average income
Town council member	192	1,019,850	5,312
Schepen (judge)	134	1,035,350	7,726
Burgemeester	123	852,200	6,928
Administrator	123	277,650	2,257
Secretary	97	460,150	4,744
Commissioner	77	181,400	2,356
Tax administrator	60	126,000	2,100
Captain	54	158,800	2,941
Prosecutor	52	151,200	2,908
Military supplier	44	130,350	2,963
Judicial officer	36	260,000	7,222
Tax receiver	32	207,200	6,475
Total	1,042	4,860,150	4,746

Table 11.24 lists high offices that together employed over 1,000 men. But we know, of course, that there were many other governing functions that we neglect in these tables, because the total income of all practitioners did not reach 100,000 guilders. There was obviously only one Grand Pensionary of Holland (income: 29,000 guilders), and other less famous offices can be added to this one. Besides the many specialized functions not included in Table 11.24, the high incomes of the incumbents notwithstanding, there were still other high officeholders outside the sixteen cities covered by our data. There were, in short, many more than 1,000 persons filling the governing ranks of Holland. When one surveys Holland's states and its organs, the magistracies of all eighteen voting cities, the law courts, drainage boards, and other governing colleges, a total of 2,000 persons – representing 1 percent of all households, or nearly 2 percent of all urban households – cannot be dismissed as an exaggerated estimate of Holland's patriciate. How did such a large governing elite emerge, one with incomes (and wealth!) that exceeded that of all other groups, bar none?

The political turmoil that began in the late fifteenth century, and culminated a century later with the Revolt, so transformed the Dutch social elites that few patrician families of 1600 could honestly claim a medieval pedigree. Such old governing families as remained were chiefly to be found in the eastern provinces, where nobles constituted an important part of the urban patriciate. In Holland, Zeeland, Friesland, and Groningen, however, this was not the case: There the political and religious impact of the Revolt brought about an all but complete break in the political leadership of old families.

The need of cities and provinces for persons of sufficient wealth and stature to assume governing functions did not abate, of course. In fact, the vigorous growth of the cities in the maritime provinces gave rise to a major expansion and internal differentiation of public administration. After the Revolt, new governing boards and colleges took shape to deal with everything from fisheries to banking, from marriage certificates to the VOC. All these public bodies needed to be staffed and led, and they all, new and old functions alike, tended to require ever more attention. Participation in the governance of a city became a more time-consuming activity in the century after the Revolt, in many cases a full-time job.

This bureaucratization was pushed forward not only by the internal dynamic of the growing cities. A changed relationship between cities and the provincial and central governments was also at work, as the higher bodies required the cities to exercise a broader range of functions. And as the central government itself became more complex, adding new commissions, councils, and colleges, it called more often on the patrician families to fill the new positions. These positions often required prolonged absences from one's home city.

The familiar inevitability of this public-sector dynamic led, in the peculiarly decentralized context of the Republic's constitution, to the creation of urban patriciates that found (and sought) their chief work in the field of governance. Entry to the patriciate tended more and more to require the abandonment of active involvement in private economic life. Consequently, one could not seriously consider such work, let alone be considered an eligible candidate, without possessing substantial real property and/or financial wealth. Such assets came to form the economic foundation for patrician families, but this foundation was renewed and strengthened by the handsome salaries attached to many of the offices to which they could hope to be appointed. Indeed, as economic conditions worsened after the third quarter of the seventeenth century, these offices with their secure incomes became enviable possessions.

The personal advantages attaching to participation in town governance were not obvious to everyone at first. In the Republic's early years, there seemed to be – and there were – superior routes to the achievement of wealth and influence. One might doubt whether men of talent would have served in the highest councils in sufficient numbers were it not still generally possible to combine public service with an active economic life. Leiden's late sixteenth-century *vroedschap*, for example, contained numerous businessmen, merchants, and even some nobles. By 1600 the nobles had disappeared, but the *vroedschap* still counted among its forty members four brewers, two *laken* merchants, two grain merchants, a notary, a cloth dyer, a shoemaker, a baker, and a surveyor. In 1580 Rotterdam's thirty-two-member *vroedschap* included six merchants, four investors in ocean shipping, four brewers, a doctor, and eight persons active in the textile industry. Nine other members represented various lesser trades. Thirty years later Rotterdam's *vroedschap* had been reduced to twenty-four members, but it still included ten persons active in the ocean shipping sector. However, when we examine the persons appointed to the more time-consuming offices (burgemeester, *schepen*), it is clear that professionalization of office already was underway, and this was also the case with the appointments to the representative bodies of the provincial and central governments.

After 1610 a generation penetrated high office that had not participated personally in the struggle for independence but that was in a position to begin drawing advantage from the Republic's growing prosperity. Prince Maurits' 1618 intervention in the appointment of magistrates brought many new faces to power, but this disruption could delay only briefly the long-term consolidation of the governing elite. Under the stadhoudership of Maurits' successor, Frederik Hendrik (1625–47), it was already customary for urban patricians to groom their scions for public life by sending them to the university, followed often by the culturally refining experience of extended travel through France and Italy – the Grand Tour. Wives and daughters began to dress more opulently, with costlier adornment, and we see the origins of such elite status symbols as the country house with its formal gardens, and the elegant carriage with its team of horses.

In these years the financial and social advantages of participation in town government became fully evident. Just as with the nobles (as described in section 11.3), the economic reversals of the decades after 1660 encouraged the patriciate to tighten its grip on income-generating public offices. By the early eighteenth century, little remained left to chance – or to merit. Elaborate written agreements among the regental families established formulas intended to govern, sometimes for decades, the distribution of offices and the appointment of new members to the *vroedschap*.

Whatever their intention might have been, these oligarchic "contracts of correspondence" did not really succeed in turning the patrician families into a closed group, cut off from other social groups after the manner of Holland's remaining nobles. In Amsterdam and most other large cities, there were always nonregental families with the wealth to support the life style of – and maintain close social contacts with – the regental families. Through marriage and selection into the *vroedschap*, individuals and their families were drawn continually from the high *burgerij* into the patriciate. This capillary process functioned less well in the smaller and economically weakened cities, where a significant income gap opened between the regents and the foremost burgers. In such a situation, the renewal of the patriciate became a difficult matter, usually solved by "importing" regent sons and daughters by marriage from other cities. The situation in Gouda may be offered as an example. In 1625 the 40 members of the *vroedschap* controlled 8 percent of wealth subject to the 100th Penny tax; in 1722 membership had been cut back to 28, but these individuals controlled 19 percent of Gouda's taxable wealth.

The Republic's political structure was such that a small-city regent possessed career possibilities much more lucrative than those open to a small-city merchant. For example, as burgemeester of the rather down-at-the-heels river city of Gorinchem around 1740, Diederik van Bleiswijk received a parsimonious salary of 500 or 600 guilders. But from this position, a capable man could hope to be tapped for higher-level appointment. Van Bleiswijk moved up to the *Gecommitteerde Raden* (the provincial executive body) in The Hague, for which he received 3,000 guilders per year, and he later was appointed to the Admiralty, which yielded him an income, after deducting expenses, of about 1,500 guilders.

The holders of high public office received, on average, the highest incomes of any group in Holland. Against the 4,000-guilder average of the formidable merchant class, standing as a group head and shoulders above the rest of Holland's burgers, we now find arrayed the *schepenen* of the city judiciary, the *raadsheren* of the higher law courts, and the sitting and former burgemeesters, all with average incomes at or above 7,000 guilders. Nor are we dealing here with a handful of people, for together they formed a group nearly 300 men strong. And they were followed by over 300 more – the tax receivers (a highly desirable appointment), the town council members, and the town secretaries – all groups with average incomes between 4,700 and 6,500 guilders per year. Below them stood another small army of court prosecutors, tax inspectors, commissioners and officials, whose incomes averaged between 2,000 and 3,000 guilders.

Clearly, the high incomes of these members of the political elite did not derive entirely from the handsome salaries attached to the offices they held. In order to reach the highest level of the income pyramid – where the burgemeesters and *schepenen* are found – one needed a private fortune. Indeed, to be eligible for appointment to these offices in the first place, a substantial private fortune was, with rare exception, an essential qualification. And, of course, by 1742 the accumulation of private fortunes had been going on for a long time. In 1585, in the Republic's earliest days, it is said that Amsterdam housed only six persons with wealth of over 100,000 guilders. At the very top, with perhaps 150,000 guilders, we already find a burgemeester (and iron merchant), Dirck Jansz. Graaf. By 1631 nearly 100 Amsterdammers admitted to a wealth of at least 100,000 guilders, and the richest then were worth over 400,000. Twenty years later the richest men, Guillielmo Batholotti and Louis de Geer, were genuine millionaires. Altogether exceptional was the fortune of the Amsterdam burgemeester Jeronimus de Haze de Georgio. At his death in 1725, he left 3.3 million guilders.

The great majority of regents did not approach these prodigies in wealth; moreover, the size of their fortunes varied considerably by city. Eighteenth-century Amsterdam, where 2 to 4 percent of *all* testators left estates of over 90,000 guilders, was in no sense typical. In eighteenth-century Gouda, the estates of the members of the *vroedschap* did not average more than 70,000 guilders, and their relations could muster no more than 32,000 on average. Half of Gouda's regents had fortunes of under 50,000 guilders to fall back on. But Gouda's elite was unusually poor; Hoorn was a city of similar size, and in the eighteenth century, its best days were behind it, but the fortunes of her *vroedschap* members averaged over 200,000 guilders. A few very large fortunes lifted this average, but the median regental fortune still stood at 140,000 guilders, and a regent with under 50,000 was a rarity in Hoorn. Of the 20 largest fortunes left in eighteenth-century Hoorn, 14 belonged to regents, as did all of the largest 7.

Of the Leiden *vroedschap* members whose wealth is known to us (38 percent of all eighteenth-century regents), half left estates valued at over 120,000 guilders. This median is not far below that of Hoorn, and in Leiden many nonregental relatives of these people were also very rich, with estates averaging nearly 100,000 guilders. But in Leiden's case, these averages hide a large cluster of poorer regents and their relations, reminiscent of the situation in Gouda.

About the wealth of regents in other cities, especially outside Holland, very little is yet known. Large fortunes may have been concentrated in Holland, but the cities of the other provinces were not without their wealthy families. A wealth tax levied in 1672 uncovered 68 residents of Middelburg with over 60,000 guilders, and 6 with over 300,000; and mid–eighteenth-century Zierikzee seems to have had at least as many of these very large fortunes, including one, that of Pieter Mogge van Renesse, that totaled 1.6 million guilders at his death in 1756. Friesland numbered 26 urban residents with over 100,000 guilders of taxable wealth in 1672 and 12 in 1697 and again in 1743. Overijssel's modest cities yielded 6 persons with over 100,000 in 1675, but only 2 in 1758. In interpreting these data, recall that the definitions of "taxable wealth" differed from place to place and time to time, as did the efficiency of collection.

The size of these fortunes is one thing; their composition is another. Table 11.25 gives an overview of the composite investment portfolios of the wealthy citizens of three eighteenth-century cities in Holland. The data reflect the composition of estates at the time of death. Such a table drawn up for the fortunes of, say, 1620, would certainly have looked very different, for it was only thereafter, and even more after 1689, that the place of public debt instruments came to loom so large. Fortunately, the seventeenth-century composition of regent families' fortunes in one city – Leiden – can be compared to that of their eighteenth-century successors. Table 11.26 reveals unambiguously how the growth of the public debt transformed the top of the Republic's wealth pyramid into creditors of the state. Bonds issued by the Generality, by Holland and the other provinces, and by the various cities, made up less than a quarter of pre-1675 regental portfolios but between half and two-thirds of the wealth of every group listed in Table 11.25. In this way a large portion of all eighteenth-century tax revenues were siphoned via interest payments into the private incomes of the richest Netherlanders, who reinvested no small part of this income, when possible, in new bonds. In a society of limited investment possibilities, especially for the vast sums controlled by the very rich, the elite had a vested, practical interest in the public debt. And since the political elite itself was a major investor in this debt, it acted as a guarantor for the regular payment of interest.

Investment in foreign government bonds was very largely an eighteenth-century phenomenon, one that spread beyond the circle of specialists only when

Table 11.25. *The composition of fortunes at death in three cities of Holland, 1700–80 (in percentage of wealth per type of asset).*

	Members of the *vroedschap*			Relatives of regents			Rich burgers	
	Leiden	Gouda	Hoorn	Leiden	Gouda	Hoorn	Gouda	Hoorn
Houses	4.7	5.6	3.8	5.0	6.4	5.6	3.5	6.7
Farms, land	8.7	9.3	11.7	8.2	7.2	9.7	8.7	6.0
Lordships	0.5	0.3	2.2	0.1	—	0.6	1.4	—
Bonds:								
Generality	2.7	1.8	2.6	2.8	2.5	1.7	3.0	2.9
Holland	50.5	57.6	42.0	54.0	68.1	55.1	52.6	49.1
Cities	2.8	2.3	1.3	1.4	3.5	3.6	0.9	1.6
Other	4.7	1.8	8.4	3.0	2.6	6.8	5.0	3.1
Annuities	1.5	0.6	2.5	0.7	0.5	2.2	0.4	1.3
VOC shares	3.4	3.6	14.8	4.1	1.5	7.7	2.4	1.7
WIC shares	0.2	0.7	0.8	0.0	0.1	0.0	0.0	—
Foreign bonds	11.7	6.5	2.3	15.0	3.9	1.9	10.5	6.5
Private loans	4.5	4.6	1.5	3.2	3.2	2.7	7.9	9.1
Business assets	2.0	4.1	2.4	0.1	0.2	0.5	1.1	5.7
Cash	2.2	1.2	3.7	2.3	0.3	2.0	2.6	6.4
Number of cases	68	65	39	50	56	20	34	39
Average value	ƒ154,159	69,813	208,228	99,777	31,956	43,402	105,370	63,435

Sources: J. J. de Jong, *Met goed fatsoen, De elite in een Hollandse stad. Gouda, 1700–1780;* M. Prak, *Gezeten burgers. De elite in een hollandse stad. Leiden, 1700–1780;* L. Kooijmans, *Onder regenten. De elite in een Hollandse stad. Hoorn, 1700–1780.*

Table 11.26. *The composition of fortunes at death of Leiden regents in two periods: before 1650 to 1674 and 1700–80.*

	<1650–74	1700–80
Houses	43.2	4.7
Land	15.2	9.2
Bonds	24.1	60.7
Annuities	0.7	1.5
VOC – WIC shares	1.3	3.6
Foreign bonds	—	11.7
Private loans	15.5	4.5
Other	—	4.2
Number of cases	33	68

Sources: SEVENTEENTH CENTURY: D. J. Noordam, *Geringde buffels en heren van stand. Het patriciaat van Leiden, 1574–1700* (Hilversum, 1994), p. 91; EIGHTEENTH CENTURY: M. Prak, *Gezeten burgers. De elite in een hollandse stad. Leiden, 1700–1780* (The Hague, 1985), p. 274.

the Republic itself ceased borrowing. Even then, not all investors felt comfortable with the idea, a fact reflected in the uneven but generally small commitment to this type of asset among the wealth holders profiled in Table 11.25.

As the ownership of public bonds rose, the elite's real property holdings diminished to become a rather minor matter. The regents of Holland's cities were not large landowners in the eighteenth century or (to judge from Leiden's regents) before. Landownership (including the possession of seigneurial rights) rarely exceeded 10 percent of the total wealth of the rich families of these three cities. Even adding the houses that they occupied personally, in both city and country, does not lift the value of real property above 15 percent. However, the place of real property in the total wealth of rich urban families had been much more prominent a century earlier, a result of both the higher value of property before 1660 and the smaller size of the public debt before that date. Leiden's seventeenth-century regents had invested over 40 percent of their wealth in urban real property.

And what of investments in productive activities? The ownership of shares in the VOC and WIC did not require direct involvement in Company affairs, of course, but eligibility for appointment to a directorship in the VOC was a motivation for the purchase of shares, which may explain the substantial share ownership of patrician families in Hoorn, home of a Company chamber. The trivial value of West India Company shares, incidentally, should not be misinterpreted.

This does not signify a lack of investment; it reflects the very low value of WIC shares in the eighteenth century. It is not impossible that the seventeenth-century patrician families of, say Gouda, invested as much money in WIC shares as in VOC shares. The latter rose in value; the former became virtually worthless.

Direct investment in productive activities consisted of business capital and private loans to individuals. Here we observe another major change in the behavior of Leiden's regental families between 1675 and 1700 – private lending falls from 15.5 to 4.5 percent of total wealth – and between the eighteenth-century regents in general, who rarely placed more than 4 percent of their assets in these activities, and the rich burgers of Gouda and Hoorn, who actively invested 9 and 15 percent of their wealth, respectively. The difference is there, but one cannot suppress a sense of disappointment in these data. Did the government-oriented regents and commercially based burgers differ only in this, the investment of 2,000 or 3,000 guilders in active commerce? Perhaps not. The "rich burgers" of Leiden are omitted from Table 11.25 since the available data did not allow for a direct comparison with the other cities. But these Leiden merchants and industrialists appear to have been both very rich and very committed to private trade and lending. Their active investments usually exceeded in value their ownership of bonds. Finally, we must remember the potential bias in our data. The approach of death, or simple old age, can encourage disinvestment from active commerce, a phenomenon that may help to explain the many thousands of guilders of cash held in most of these estates.

Clearly, the wealth of a city was concentrated in the hands of persons who themselves formed the government or were closely related to such persons. The converse is also true: Persons of wealth (and persons who aspired to wealth) found it expedient to fashion close ties with the government. Once rich, the chance was very great that a family sooner or later would find itself entangled with the patriciate and, in time, be admitted to its ranks. And once that step was taken, the family's active participation in economic life would inevitably diminish. Governing required not only time but also a style of life that featured the maintenance of intensive contacts with other members of the governing elite, which in turn was the precondition for a successful political career.

In fact, the interest in officeholding spread far beyond the circle of patricians. The highest offices were for them alone, but there were many lesser posts, theirs to dispose of, that were highly prized for their security as well, it would seem, as for their relatively high pay. Table 11.14 established that the "Government" sector accounted for some 14 percent of total taxable income in Holland's cities. But even this underestimates the weight of this sector. Our procedure was to examine only occupational groups that represented at least 100,000 guilders of taxable income, and government work tended to be divided into many small, even unique, functions. In order to correct for this bias, we have identified for two cities *all* persons in government service and compared their taxable income to the total. In the small city of Gorinchem (about 5,000 population, residing in some 1,300 households), only 120 persons enjoyed an income over 600 guilders. Of these, 37 held government offices (including positions at drainage boards and the VOC), and this 31 percent of taxed individuals received 49 percent of total taxed income. In little Gorinchem the taxable public officials stood head and shoulders above their private-sector counterparts, with average incomes of 2,518 versus 1,148 guilders.

Gorinchem was small, and a few exceptional officials may have distorted the results. Let us consider the case of Delft, a city of about 17,000 inhabitants in 1742. Of Delft's 582 taxed citizens, 125 held some type of public office. This 21.5 percent of taxed persons garnered 42 percent of Delft's taxable income. The income gap was even greater than in Gorinchem: 3,042 guilders for the average public official; 1,146 for the average private citizen. We have already noted that salaries formed only part of the income of public officials, and not necessarily the larger part. But we have also established that more than half of their nonsalary income took the form of interest on domestic debt instruments. Indirectly, this was also an income drawn from the public sector.

If "government" officeholders commanded 49 percent of taxable income in the small city of Gorinchem and 42 percent in the larger city of Delft, we might expect the weight of the public sector to decline further in larger cities such as Rotterdam and Leiden. Certainly in Amsterdam, with its host of rich merchants, this must have been the case. But it was precisely in that rich city that the burgemeesters had in their gift the disposition of a truly bewildering multitude of jobs, offices, and sinecures – ranging from simple appointments of charwomen, lock tenders, and porters, to middle-level placements of concierges, clerks, and messengers, to the bestowal of desirable positions as secretaries, tax receivers, and commissioners. All together, some 3,000 positions were theirs to fill in the mid–eighteenth century. We cannot yet be certain of this, but it is not improbable that some 15 percent of all jobs in the cities of Holland were public positions of one sort or another.

Since our analysis of Holland's upper-income urban population has proceeded by occupational group, we will conclude with an attempt to identify the most salient characteristics of this key segment of the Republic's population. Table 11.27 provides an overview of the upper-income occupational structure by listing in order of size the fifteen highest-ranked occupations in each of three ways: by the number of persons so occupied, by the collective income of the occupational group, and by the average income of group members.

In the first ranking, the enormous number of rentiers and merchants is the first thing to attract our attention. With the third and fourth ranked occupations, bakers and tavernkeepers, we must keep in mind that they form only the taxed peaks of much larger occupational groups, most of whose members earned under 600 guilders per year. More unexpected is the presence high in this ranking of specialized occupations such as wine merchant (no. 6!), broker, surgeon, bookkeeper, and apothecary.

Table 11.27. *Top fifteen occupations with total incomes above 100,000 guilders, ranked by total taxable persons, total income, and average income.*

	Largest number		Largest total income		Highest average income	
1.	Rentier	3,567	Rentier	8,616,050	*Schepen*	7,726
2.	Merchant	1,606	Merchant	6,375,000	Judicial officer	7,222
3.	Baker	885	Wine merchant	1,165,530	Burgemeester	6,928
4.	Tavernkeeper	774	*Schepen*	1,035,350	Tax receiver	6,475
5.	Unknown	769	Town councilman	1,019,350	Town councilman	5,312
6.	Wine merchant	694	Unknown	1,017,000	Secretary	4,744
7.	Carpenter	457	Burgemeester	852,200	Merchant	3,969
8.	Grocer	374	Baker	773,000	Soap maker	3,302
9.	Skipper	369	Broker	732,800	Brewer	3,116
10.	Broker	348	Tavernkeeper	678,400	Military supplier	2,963
11.	Surgeon	307	Grocer	465,350	Captain	2,941
12.	Tobacconist	266	Secretary	460,150	Refiner	2,935
13.	Coffee & tea shopkeeper	257	Carpenter	456,500	Prosecutor	2,908
14.	Bookkeeper	249	Bookkeeper	439,700	Lawyer	2,741
15.	Apothecary	239	Butcher	415,600	Linen merchant	2,526

When we turn to the fifteen largest aggregate taxable incomes, the rentiers and the merchants stand, once again, far above the rest of the field. And, once again, the prominent position of the wine merchants (now no. 3 in rank) comes as a surprise. In this ranking we see the emergence of the governing elite, the *schepenen*, the members of the city councils, the burgemeesters, and town secretaries. Their modest total numbers notwithstanding, they penetrate the ranks of the major income concentrations of urban society. The reason for this is clear enough, of course, and is displayed in the third column, where the occupational groups are ranked by average income. Here the first six positions are all occupied by public offices. Further down we find two more, the captains and prosecutors, and if we regard the solicitors (private contractors who supplied and paid military regiments in accordance with strict regulations) as a sort of veiled functionary, then no less than nine of the fifteen occupations with the highest average incomes were located in the public sector. In this important way, the eighteenth-century world differed fundamentally and essentially from our own.

11.6. The economic position of women and children

The place of women and children in the Republic's labor markets might be deferred to the following chapter, which is dedicated to that topic, were it not for the paucity of historical information available even now on female labor force participation rates, relative wages, competition and complementarity of male vs. female and adult vs. child labor, and other issues. Here we approach this essential subject more as a social phenomenon, arranging our data fragments tentatively, asking questions more often than we can propose answers.

Our problem is not that female and child labor was purposefully kept secret in the preindustrial past. On the contrary, the belief that such extrahousehold labor was inherently shameful, exploitative, or degrading was unknown before the nineteenth century. People spoke of it freely, but for other reasons they spoke of it rarely and then, from our perspective, uninformatively. The most natural things in a society are the ones that go unremarked and unrecorded. Thus, the *presence* of female labor is noted often in our sources (here the greater gender-specificity of Dutch than of English occupational titles is of assistance), even though the details of women's employment relations remain unspoken. What we are told bespeaks long-established role patterns that accorded whole domains of work to women. Women carried out the preparation of dairy products, and spinning was always primarily a source of "distaff" income. All sorts of housework (cleaning, child care, tending the sick) was performed overwhelmingly by women, both in the home and in institutions such as the Republic's numerous orphanages, hospitals, and asylums.

None of these examples surprises us, but the contemporary understanding of "women's work" extended further to specific forms of heavy physical outdoor labor. These jobs were not necessarily filled only by women, and even when they were, they worked in close proximity to men. The salt pans provide a good example. The refining of salt required little skill but a great deal of pulling, carrying, and dragging of large quantities of raw salt, peat, and water. Women worked in nearly all of them, as they did at the brickworks, at the breweries, and as stackers and dryers in the peat bogs. One gets the impression that women held a special place in the labor market for a good number of relatively unskilled types of heavy labor.

Indeed, we know of municipal policies actually to reserve such labor for women. Ordinances governing the distribution of peat in the cities specified men as the *carriers* but women as the *fillers* of the peat bags. In Amsterdam the many grain warehouses were served by *zaadverschietsters*, women who turned the grain periodically to prevent overheating. We are not certain that this job was officially reserved for women, but this was the case in eighteenth-century Utrecht, where the city formed a women's guild with the exclusive right to pull passing boats and barges through the city's canals.

Our list of heavy, dirty jobs for women is not yet exhausted. The bleaching fields near Haarlem were filled with women dragging the heavy, acidic linen cloth and yarn, drenched in buttermilk. The hackling of flax and, especially, hemp was another female specialty. In Gouda, a regional center for the working of hemp – so essential to the fisheries and merchant marine – municipal ordinances required that the doors and windows of hemp hackling halls be kept closed to protect passersby from the clouds of particulate generated by this work. The unventilated interiors must have been hellish for the hacklemaids, who actually rose up in revolt in 1655.

These examples of female work lead us to the textile industry, which, as everywhere in Europe, made use of women's labor on a large scale. A striking visual confirmation of the prominent place of women in this industry is found in a series of scenes, painted around 1600 by Isaac van Swanenburgh, depicting the major phases of cloth production such as wool combing, the drawing of warp, weaving, and cloth dyeing. In all of these large canvases, women are prominent. Yet it does not appear that they worked in every phase of production. The city's medieval drapery regulations (applying to the types of cloth produced until the time of the Revolt) make it clear that only two activities were not gender-specific (wool carding and a type of yarn finishing called *ploten*). In all other phases of production, the regulations speak specifically of either men or women. The gender-based division of tasks invariably assigned to women the work requiring the fewest specialized skills (as suggested by the requirements for specific training in the regulations). Women worked as wool combers, spinners, nappers, and *wiedsters* (the removal with knives of imperfections from the weave), while the men concerned themselves primarily with weaving, fulling, dyeing, shearing, and draping. The overall impression left by these regulations is that the core tasks in the production process were intended for men, and that their wives and daughters or hired women would assume the subsidiary tasks. A substantial status difference characterized the work on either side of the gender line, and this was reinforced by the fact that only the work dominated by men was organized into guilds or other organizations.

The importance of Leiden's textile industry makes it logical to begin our examination of women workers there, but the other seats of woolens production, and the other branches of the textile industry, also made ample use of female labor. Unfortunately, less documentation is available to illuminate their work practices. We know that Amsterdam's important cotton-printing industry employed women in large numbers, and they seem to have been especially prominent in the drawing and coloring of patterns. This, at any rate, is suggested by pictures of these work processes (as in the cartoonlike penny prints [*censprenten*] of the time); nowhere can one actually read about this. But information from beyond the Republic's borders confirms the reality of the popular illustrations: In 1805 the French cotton printer Oberkampf employed at his works in Jouy 175 (male) printers and no fewer than 570 (female) colorers. Women were present at many workplaces, but the (written) sources are often silent about their presence. The organization of work focused on the man; behind him women and children stood in a sort of historical shadowland.

An improved understanding of the economic roles of women is important in its own right, but it has a special role to play in the Dutch case because of a prominent feature of its larger cities, described in Chapter 3, section 3.5: These cities experienced highly unbalanced sex ratios, with large surpluses of either adult men or women, especially in the prime working ages between twenty and fifty. What did it mean for the employment opportunities of men and women that Holland's cities attracted surpluses of adult males up to the third quarter of the seventeenth century and that thereafter, under less flourishing economic conditions, those same cities featured substantial female surpluses right into the nineteenth century?

Foreign visitors to the Republic often listed among its "curiosities" the independent spirit of its women. Not only did they appear to outsiders as self-assured and even bossy, but in law and custom they had, by the standards of the time, considerable scope for independent action. Thus, the Republic's orphanages, acting *in loco parentis*, trained the girls in their custody in a variety of textile-related skills with the expectation that they would leave the institution to find work as single women. In southern Europe the orphanages defined their responsibility as settling their girls in marriages. The Dutch orphans were expected to find mates on their own, and while single, women of legal age could act independently in legal proceedings.

Once married, Dutch women – as with women elsewhere in Europe – became the legal equivalent of minors; husbands assumed guardianship over their wives and took control of their property. However, in practice, married women were conceded contractual rights wherever the husband did not actively object, and they could, and often did, secure such rights legally through the negotiation of prenuptial agreements. The substantial contractual autonomy of married women was probably related to their strong position as heirs. Widows ordinarily received half the estate of their deceased husband. The other half went to the children, but widows often controlled this as well until the children, even males, reached their majority. The English ambassador to the Republic, Josiah Child, concluded from all this that men of property and affairs could "hold on [to] their trades to their dying days, knowing the capacity of their wives to get in their estates and carry on their trades after their deaths."[2] The relatively strong position of women in Dutch legal practice is well illustrated by the conflicts that arose over inheritance between the settlers of New Netherlands and their British conquerers, who sought to impose Britain's more patriarchal legal traditions after 1664. In general, the elaboration of civil society in this complex, urban, and heterogeneous country provided a measure of economic and social space for women that was not typical of European societies until much later.

The foreign visitor to the Republic certainly was impressed, or should we say struck, by the prominent presence of women in public places, especially as shopkeepers. Their commercial functions often involved continuing the business of a deceased husband, but not always, as the case of Griete Pietersdochter shows. She was a widow with four illiterate children when she remarried. Her new husband, Jacob Elias (1559–1616), was upwardly mobile after the manner of a Horatio Alger story. Beginning as a salt refiner's assistant, he became in time the owner of salt pans, became a merchant, and finally was admitted to the *vroedschap* of Amsterdam. His wife also rose in stature, which is apparent from the fact that (1) her children from this second marriage received schooling, and (2) at her death in 1602, she left a personal estate of 9,000 guilders. It appears that she earned this fortune from the operation of her own shop.

This woman's example could hardly be typical (and we would know nothing of her achievement had she not married the founder of a powerful Amsterdam lineage), but it illustrates what an entrepreneurial woman with business talent could achieve in the legal context of the Dutch Republic. Microhistorical research exploiting genealogical records might well provide further insights into the "hidden" work of wives and widows.

Not all women's work was hidden, of course. When they functioned as heads of household (as widows usually, but also when single or in lieu of an absent husband), their work comes into full view. In the Veluwe the 1749 occupational census revealed one of every six working heads of household to be a woman, and 30 percent of these female heads of household were shopkeepers or merchants. These women operated shops of every sort imaginable, including groceries, apothecaries, bookshops, dry goods stores, and secondhand shops. We also

---

[2] Josiah Child, *A New Discourse of Trade* (London, 1693), p. 3. This discussion of legal practice is based on David E. Narrett, *Inheritance and Family Life in Colonial New York City* (Ithaca, NY, 1992), pp. 43–51.

encounter them as teachers, innkeepers, bakers, butchers, brewers, shoemakers, millers, weavers, wine merchants, midwives, and seamstresses – and as blacksmiths, lumber merchants, teamsters, and buttonmakers.

The high percentage of female household heads found in the Veluwe should not be generalized to the Republic as a whole. In neighboring Overijssel only 7 percent of households were headed by women in 1795. What we can conclude from these examples is that throughout the Republic, even in its eastern margins, women were an independent presence in economic life.

We return to the more general question raised by the large surplus of women in the cities of the late seventeenth and eighteenth centuries. How did the many single and widowed women, and those effectively alone with husbands abroad or at sea, support themselves? The departure of many men from the urban econo- mies, and the inflow of single women, may be taken as evidence of a relatively favorable economic environment for women. But a bit of further reflection on the matter forces us to reconsider. The men who departed, primarily as recruits with the VOC (see Chapter 3, section 3.5, and Chapter 12, section 12.5.2), were not engaged in upward mobility. Since they left primarily out of necessity, to escape unemployment and poverty, their departure could hardly have served to improve the economic environment for the remaining women.

Where, then, could opportunities for women be found? In any event, not anywhere in the multilayered public sector. The fact that it has not yet proved possible to construct a wage series for any type of work dominated by women speaks directly to this point, for nearly all data on wage payments are drawn from public-sector records. A survey of the 3,000-odd jobs and appointments at the disposition of Amsterdam's mid–eighteenth-century burgemeesters uncovers only 300 that were filled by women. And of these, fully 260 were accounted for by the low-level work of handling peat and filling peat containers. Beyond this small army working the city's peat unloading docks, the burgemeesters appointed a number of midwives, charwomen, market sweepers, and a few scriveners who took notations at the city gates and the weigh house. By far the best-paid female employees of the city were the registrar for the winegaugers (earning 700 guilders per year) and the four auction-house estimators (together dividing 1,350 guilders). The state was, in short, no significant employer of women.

Among the types of work that employed many women outside the household, heavy, unskilled labor in what can broadly be called the industrial sector may have been the most important. We have already mentioned a number of these activities, but the list can be extended. The packing of herring in barrels employed women in all the fishing ports, and the Zaan region paper mills hired women to sort and tear into strips the rags that were their chief raw material. What we do not yet know is how many of these women in industrial employments were married, supplementing a family income, as opposed to widowed, alone, or oth- erwise self-supporting. Nor do we know how the pay for this heavy, unskilled work compared with similarly unskilled male employments. Presumably it was lower, but the only specific evidence known to us shows that female cleaning personnel (hired to clean town halls, Admiralty and VOC buildings, etc.) earned daily wages equal to that of the lowest paid males (such as porters and common laborers).

Women who were young and single had in household service a ready alternative to industrial work, and they appear to have favored it heavily. The ongoing migratory stream of young single women to the cities, even as many of these cities fell into economic decay, stands in testimony to this ongoing attraction. Most of these young women worked as domestic servants, while their peers remaining in the countryside would have worked as farm servants and milkmaids until their marriage. This "life-cycle" employment was hardly a fleeting thing – it could last from about age fifteen to marriage after age twenty-five – but marriage definitely brought such employment to an end. And what of those women who did not marry? Did they remain on as faithful retainers of their employers until their old age? In fact, we hardly ever encounter household servants of mature years in the sources. For whatever reason (low pay, the preferences of employers, a desire for greater freedom?), women left domestic service at some point, probably finding work in the vast, unregulated urban world of taverns and inns, working as barmaids, servers, cooks, chambermaids, and the like. Institutions such as orphanages and hospitals also employed single women; and, of course, a grimmer alternative was the "industrial" work of loading peat, sorting rags, bleaching clothing, and so on.

Less likely, because it was less accessible to an unmarried woman, would have been a transition to the sector where many other women found employment: retail trade. Establishing or acquiring a shop or other retail business required an initial capital. An inheritance or the assistance of relatives could put the necessary sum in a woman's hands. In the case of married women, widowhood often brought the responsibilities of continuing a retail business in which they had assisted. But there were certainly many cases where married women became storekeepers with capital supplied by their husbands, so that the wife could thereby contribute to the family's income. This seventeenth- and eighteenth-century equivalent of the sixteenth-century fisherman or sailor whose wife operated a small farm in his absence appears to have been a widespread household strategy.

The evidence for such household strategies is primarily indirect. Once again, we are presented with information about the (usually male) household head with no specific reference made to the employment of the wife. But in many cases when a dual occupation is mentioned, the second-mentioned occupation is likely to have been the responsibility of the wife. This seems pretty obvious in the case of combinations such as farmer-shopkeeper, farmer-innkeeper, and farmer-tavernkeeper, all of which occur regularly in the occupational censuses. Inn- and tavernkeeping were also combined with carpentry, shoemaking, and tailoring. In these cases the wife's contribution may have weighed heavily in total family income, just as it could in another frequent combination: baker-innkeeper. Unfortunately, the recording of these occupational combinations occurred quite haphazardly. Unless they were volunteered, there was no reason to inquire into the possible economic activity of the wife. But our interpretation of these informational fragments is supported by the Amsterdam registers of the *Personeele Quotisatie* of 1742, which we have already drawn upon at some length.

Of the 13,745 households initially regarded as taxable (including those later removed from the rolls when their incomes were determined to fall below 600 guilders), 14.7 percent were female heads of household. Fully 59 percent of these 2,164 well-to-do women were listed as rentiers, but the second most common occupation was shopkeeper. These women ran shops of every sort: They included specialists in tobacco, every sort of fabric, pork, candles, books, hosiery, pipes, glassware, tea and coffee, combs, kitchenware, beds, knives, shoes, ribbons, whalebones, and on and on. Retail trade even then seemed an inexhaustible fount of specialization.

In Amsterdam perhaps more than in other cities, shopkeeping served as one of the most important economic activities by which married women could contribute to the family's income. Of course, in most cases – it is something we cannot now reconstruct – the wife worked in a business that stood formally under her husband's name. In the case of a shopkeeper's wife, matters were little different than with a farmer's wife: Both worked with their spouse in the family business, without keeping separate books. This assumption is more than pure speculation; how else should we think of the ship captain recorded in Amsterdam's 1742 tax register, who sailed regularly to Surinam but who also stood recorded as the owner of a dry goods store? Or the captain who sailed to the East Indies but ran simultaneously a cotton goods shop? Or the skipper on the regular service to Zwolle who also had a porcelain shop, another who sailed the Harderwijk route who had a grocery, and yet another who sailed to Leiden yet also ran a tobacco shop? These combinations could only have been possible if someone else, and we must think in the first instance of a wife, assumed primary responsibility for the shopkeeping activity.

These examples seem compelling because the primary occupations of the men required their regular, and often extended, absence from home. But many additional examples exist that are not necessarily, but very probably, illustrative of the same phenomenon: A bookseller who also ran a porcelain, cloth, and linens shop; the watchmaker with a coffee outlet; the gauger of the timber stockpiles who also sold stemware; the tailor with a hosiery shop; the ivory carver with a secondhand goods shop; the shoemaker with a spice shop; the many brokers who also kept one or another type of shop. Most if not all of these men must have depended on their wives for the conduct of their second listed occupation. And if the aforementioned case of Griete Pietersdochter (married to Jacob Elias) can serve as an example, such second sources of income could be a far from trivial supplement to the family's total income.

These examples of probable female enterprise are evocative of a larger, dimly lit world of women's work ranging from high-fashion retailing through petty trade to inn, hostel, and barkeeping (see Chapter 4, section 4.3.2, for a remarkable example) and, not to forget, prostitution. Here, too, the large, rich literature on Republican prostitution places emphasis on female ownership and operation. The *besteedster* was a woman who placed domestic servants with employers and, in some cases, also supplied bordellos and whorehouses, which were operated by a *waardin*, the establishment's madam. This woman may have been married, but her husband, the *waard*, almost always played a subordinate role in the operation, serving drink and keeping order while his wife ran the business.

What we do not gain from these many interesting and evocative examples of women's work and enterprise is a sense of what today is called the female labor-force participation rate. How did it compare with that of men, how did the family life cycle shape the nature or incidence of this participation, how did it vary by social rank, how did women's earnings compare with men's? Everywhere in the sources, the women stand obscured, if not completely hidden, behind the men. In nearly every administrative document (but not court proceedings, hence our knowledge of prostitution, thievery, etc.), it was the men who were addressed, since they alone were responsible for family or household. Their legal status as head of household was not changed in the Netherlands until 1970, and this stands as a serious impediment to gaining answers to the sorts of questions that today seem obvious and basic.

The importance of gaining some insight into these quantitative dimensions can be demonstrated by adding the phenomenon of child labor to the discussion, and by inquiring into the relative positions of male, female, and child labor. No precise measurement is possible, of course, but the so-called *Goldberg Enquête* of 1801 does provide information concerning the incidence of each of these three types of labor in the firms that cooperated in the inquiry. The document provides data for 144 businesses in the department of *Oude IJssel* and 361 in the department of *Texel*. (Following the French example, the Batavian government had abolished the historical provinces and introduced departments. *Oude IJssel* comprised the old provinces of Overijssel and Drenthe, plus small adjacent parts of Gelderland and Friesland; *Texel* covered Holland north of Leiden and part of western Utrecht but excluded Amsterdam and its environs.) There were, to be sure, many municipalities that did not respond to the inquiry, and there were many firms that did not cooperate in municipalities that did respond. And not all firms responded in a consistent, informative manner. Despite these typical teething problems of the modern bureaucratic state, the usable results that did come in are sufficient to acquire a fair overview of the incidence of female and child labor in craft and industrial enterprises. They are summarized in Table 11.28.

The striking message of this inquiry of 1801 is that the employment of children was far more widespread than that of women. In the two departments together, no more than 15 percent of the 505 firms claimed to employ women. And even that gives a distorting impression, for nearly *all* textile operations in Twente em-

Table 11.28. *The incidence of female and child labor among firms responding to the* Goldberg *enquête of 1801 in the Departments of Oude IJssel and Texel.*

	Number of firms that responded (at least in part) to the inquiry		Number of firms that mention female employees		Number of firms that mention employing boys, girls, or children	
	N	%	N	%	N	%
Oude IJssel	144	100	36	25	59	41
Texel	361	100	40	11	183	50
Total	505	100	76	15	242	47

ployed women, lifting the incidence of female employment in *Oude IJssel* to 25 percent of all firms. If textiles, and perhaps paper making in the Veluwe, are set aside as atypical, the employment of women in craft and industrial enterprises appears to have been quite exceptional, involving no more than about 10 percent of firms.

Many of the firms that responded to the inquiry still failed to state how many workers were employed. But those that did respond confirmed that (outside of textiles) nearly all the firms were small, rarely employing more than five workers. The number of women working in that small fraction of firms that employed any at all could not often have exceeded one or two. This implies that even where women were employed (once again, excluding textiles), they formed a distinct minority of the work force. If the firms hiring *any* women did not much exceed 12 percent, the percentage of women in this craft and industrial labor force must have been substantially less. Only in the textile districts would matters have been different.

This source yields a much lower incidence of female participation in formal economic life than our earlier impressionistic discussion has prepared us for. We should take note of the possibility that an inquiry of 1801 might be unrepresentative of the preceding centuries. The growth of unemployment in the late eighteenth century may have forced women out of the types of employment represented in these data. It is also possible that the rural and small-town economies that dominated the two departments for which the sources survive are unrepresentative of the larger cities. These reservations notwithstanding, we should treat seriously the hypothesis that the relatively low level of Dutch women's participation in the *wage* labor force in modern times is actually a phenomenon with origins that must be traced far into the past. Any number of possible explanations can be suggested that might render this hypothesis plausible, such as the relatively high standard of living under the old Republic, or the power of social emulation in a society without sharp, formal class barriers. But it may be most fruitful to relate the nondomestic work experience of Dutch women to this society's pioneering role in developing the very concept of middle-class domesticity. In this crucible of *gezelligheid*, standards of domestic comfort rose higher and spread further down the social scale than elsewhere before the nineteenth century. What the Frenchman Jean Nicolas Parival called, in 1661, an "idolâtre excessif" placed claims on the time of women – to scrub the stoop, clean the house, polish the brass, and so forth – that must have constrained their work lives already in the seventeenth century in ways that would be felt elsewhere only in the nineteenth.

No such constraints limited the utilization of children in the paid labor force. Table 11.28 reveals that in 1801 nearly half of all surveyed firms made use of child labor. We remain in the dark about how large this young work force was, but the inquiry was keen to distinguish (1) between the employment of boys and girls, and (2) between these adolescents on the one hand and (younger) children on the other. No definition is provided for this latter distinction, and we can doubt whether any consistent criterion was applied by those who filled in the forms. Firms that made use of all three categories of child labor included paper mills, brickworks, pin makers, and all branches of the textile industry. No specific type of firm hired only girls, but boys and children (and not girls) were hired by ropeworks and hatmakers, while boys alone were preferred by leather tanners and all sorts of industrial windmill operators. On the other hand, only young children were found in the dangerous precincts of the smiths' forges (presumably to work the bellows).

The employment of adolescents, especially of boys, often involved the training of the young person in a skill. The employment of young children, however, typically occurred where some simple task or maneuver had to be performed. In an unmechanized world, there were many such tasks, and the army of child workers was vast. Thus, the pipe makers of Gouda always worked with one or more boys and/or girls (see "Pipe Makers" in Chapter 8, section 8.3.3). At the industry's peak, when over 600 pipe makers were active in the city, there must have been more children, perhaps 1,000, working in this industry alone. In Amsterdam's cotton-printing industry, the operator of every press hired on his own account a child to spread dyestuff across the printing frame. The operators of the Republic's hundreds of passenger barges all hired young jockeys (as young and light as possible) to ride the draught horses along the towpath.

Thousands of children were hired one by one, but the labor of children also attracted the interest of entrepreneurs with bigger plans. In 1690 the Huguenot clergyman Pierre Isard sought to interest the regents of Amsterdam's *Aalmoezeniers* orphanage in delivering to him fifty boys and fifty girls, all between eight and fourteen years of age, with a view to establishing a silk-spinning works after the

French manner. In the mid–eighteenth century, the Haarlem manufacturer Caspar Swertner sought to interest the city government in a mass recruitment of children whose parents received public assistance so he might establish a factory producing damask linen tablecloths. Swertner was preceded in this sort of scheme as early as 1678 by a Johan Joachim Becker, and earlier still, in 1635, the city fathers of Delft tried to breathe new life into the city's moribund textile industry by marshaling the labor of the city's orphans. Later, their Leiden counterparts shipped orphans in their care to rural Brabant, there to work for Leiden entrepreneurs trying to develop a low-cost textile industry. The forced deployment of orphans and the children of the poor was nothing new. Already in 1575 we read of a Gorinchem pin maker, Cornelis Jansz. Houbraken, trying to set up a pin manufactory in Leiden with the assured labor of fifty boys and fifteen or sixteen girls.

Until late in the history of the Republic the labor potential of orphaned, abandoned, or simply very poor children was repeatedly an object of interest to entrepreneurs and schemers. Children eight to fourteen years of age, often in large numbers, were set to work in a variety of (generally unsuccessful) initiatives. When they were a year or two older, the orphan boys often faced a certain pressure to consider seriously signing up as ships' boys with the labor-hungry VOC. The orphanage regents were not always disinterested parties in persuading the boys to sign, a kind of corruption that was taken very much for granted in the hard social world of the seventeenth and eighteenth centuries. But the second half of the eighteenth century introduced a real change to these habits of mind. The workhouses established then to employ the poor and their children (see Chapter 12, section 12.6) sought to secure a genuine marriage of philanthropy and economic revival. By the end of the century, one would be hard pressed to find a single city that had not established, or sought diligently to establish, such a facility. In some cities many hundreds of children were exposed to these efforts at uplift through ethical labor. It was the (still almost wholly ineffectual) beginning of a new attitude toward child labor.

Chapter 12
The standard of living
and the labor market

12.1. Introduction

The modern study of Dutch society in the seventeenth century is very largely inspired by paintings, and the paintings of that era betray a fascination with the material world. The moral messages that the Dutch masters wished to convey form a topic of continuing debate among art historians; but the material context in which those messages were placed remains as an astonishing fact, a fact so fascinating that, for many, it is the chief message of Dutch art. This people "firmly convinced in the substantiality of things" (J. Huizinga) raised up a material culture that constituted a work of art in its own right.

Dutch culture was by no means unique in the attention that it paid to the material dimensions of life, but in other European societies, the focus of attention rarely strayed far from courts and aristocratic life and, hence, from a material culture in which the practical and useful had no respectable place. In the Netherlands the visual arts focused on social classes below the very top and exhibited an unembarrassed concern with everyday objects.

This visual evidence inevitably piques our interest in the material circumstances of ordinary people in Dutch society. How broadly diffused was the comfortable simplicity of middle-class life? Did ordinary working people participate, to some degree, in the economic growth of the seventeenth century, or did their lives, as with those of other ordinary Europeans, continue to be perched at the margins of subsistence, exposed to the full force of the scourges of harvest failure, war, and disease? The answer to this question can aid in the appreciation of Dutch visual culture, but it also goes to the heart of any interpretation of Dutch eco-

607

nomic development. Was this just one more variant of a traditional economy, with all its inherent limitations, or did it establish a material and social basis for more dynamic forms of economic relations?

Our focus in this chapter is on wage earners, their incomes, and the labor markets in which they sought their livelihoods. By no means were all participants in the labor force wage earners. Farmers, shopkeepers, and many inland and ocean shippers, fishermen, and craftsmen were self-employed, their incomes depending in part on their capital and on the market prices of their goods and services. Among the laborers proper, many earned piece rates or received salaries or stipends for the performance of specified tasks. True wage earners were always a minority of the total labor force in our period. But in view of the substantial urbanization and market-oriented character of the rural and urban sectors alike, it is likely that wage earners were by the seventeenth century a large minority, and that their circumstances will be broadly representative of piece-rate and stipend recipients, whose rates of pay in an economy with efficient markets should be influenced strongly by the level of wages.

But with this assertion, we assume something that is disputed: that the pre-industrial labor market was really a market – that economic forces substantially determined what laborers were paid for their time, skill, and effort. A common alternative to this assumption is the belief that "tradition," as enforced by institutions and mental predispositions, governed wage formation to such an extent that custom was far more influential than the market. A variant of this institutional approach to labor-market behavior holds that wages were not really compensation for work done at all, but rather were a form of maintenance, a payment just sufficient for survival that permitted the labor force to reproduce itself. In this approach the wage is not so much fixed by custom and inertia as it is determined by the impotence of labor – whether via political weakness or low productivity – to secure for itself anything more than a subsistence wage.

In the study of the Dutch labor market, the purely institutional approach has not met with much favor. Given its precocious urbanization and market-oriented economy, the Republic's labor markets could hardly have been dominated by customary arrangements reflecting a static social hierarchy. The "subsistence wage" approach, on the other hand, is often invoked to describe the place of wage labor in the Dutch economy. The starting point of such arguments is usually the assumption that the supply of labor was abundant, so that employers could draw upon a vast pool of underemployed rural labor, whether from the Republic or the neighboring countries, without having to increase wages. This belief in a reservoir of underemployed labor has led one scholar to assert that labor in the Republic's cities systematically was paid *below* the reproduction level (since cheap replacement labor was readily available, as on a slave plantation).

This belief in a crude superexploitation of labor in the precociously capitalistic Dutch Republic is consistent with the remarkable passage in *Das Kapital*, where Marx (who was no stranger to the Netherlands – his Dutch mother never really mastered German, and his relatives included the founder of Philips) recites the economic achievements of the Republic around 1648 and asserts that "the total capital of the Republic was probably more important than that of all the rest of Europe put together."[1] He then adds that "by 1648 the people of Holland were more overworked, poorer, and more brutally oppressed than those of all the rest of Europe put together."

The same large-scale migration of labor to the maritime provinces that has convinced "pessimists" that wages must have been driven to – if not below – subsistence, has inspired other historians – the "optimists" – to interpret the Dutch economy as a powerful attractive force, pulling migrants to a zone of relatively high living standards.[2] Both of these interpretations of labor migration hold certain assumptions about the factors determining the supply of labor, and further assumptions about the market power of employers that shapes the demand for labor. In what follows we proceed from the position that wages and other types of labor compensation can be explained as market phenomena. Of course, the workings of supply and demand in labor markets are today no less than in preindustrial society, modified substantially by institutional and behavioral factors. Rather than assuming these factors to take a particular form, we seek to describe them historically in the context of an economic analysis of labor market development.

12.2. Nominal wages

The most comprehensive wage data available to us refer to construction labor: skilled carpenters, masons, stone-cutters, roofers, and so on, and unskilled hod carriers and miscellaneous outdoor laborers. Because of the homogeneity of such labor over time and space, these data offer the advantage of comparability with other historical studies of wages. However, we must be mindful of the possibility that construction wages may not always be representative of wages in other sectors, as the demand for construction labor may follow a different course than that for, say, textile workers or shipwrights. Our comprehensive construction labor data therefore is supplemented by more limited information on wages for other workers and by salary data for a broad range of municipal employees, clergymen, and sailors.

Let us begin with the wages of skilled and unskilled construction labor. Tables 12.1 and 12.2 present the average course of nominal wages for several grades of laborer: masters (carpenters and masons), their journeymen, masons' assistants (hod carriers), unskilled laborers, and sawyers. In each case the time series are based on

[1] Karl Marx, *Capital* (Moscow, 1961), Vol. I, pp. 754.
[2] For a fuller account of optimist and pessimist views, see Jan de Vries, "How Did Pre-industrial Labour Markets Work?" in George Grantham and Mary MacKinnon, eds., *Labour Market Evolution* (London, 1994), pp. 39–63.

Table 12.1. *Average wages: Western Netherlands, 1500–1815 (stuivers per day, summer wages).*

Year	Master	Journeyman	Unskilled	Hod carrier	Sawyer
1500	5.10	4.25	3.50	2.92	4.83
1510	5.50	4.63	4.00	2.92	4.83
1520	5.34	4.50	3.17	3.15	5.25
1530	6.05	1.58	3.50	3.25	5.67
1540	6.39	5.30	4.00	3.50	7.00
1550	7.18	6.21	3.98	3.79	6.33
1555	7.98	6.30	4.15	3.70	6.83
1560	7.93	6.65	5.04	4.08	8.75
1565	9.77	7.69	4.96	5.17	10.90
1570	10.30	7.97	5.63	5.17	10.80
1575	9.57	8.00	5.75	6.43	11.40
1580	13.27	12.10	8.00	7.83	13.75
1585	13.95	12.12	8.80	9.20	15.75
1590	17.00	14.50	9.70	9.50	21.88
1595	18.59	16.70	11.75	11.38	20.63
1600	18.77	17.20	12.83	11.55	21.67
1605	20.25	17.67	12.83	11.55	24.50
1610	20.09	18.03	14.83	13.00	27.00
1615	21.53	18.75	14.38	13.50	26.50
1620	21.08	20.00	14.50	13.50	26.33
1625	21.60	19.88	14.29	13.40	26.67
1630	23.21	20.65	16.20	13.40	26.33
1635	25.29	22.10	19.10	15.16	26.33
1640	24.04	21.48	19.58	16.00	26.67
1645	25.40	22.75	17.40	16.71	28.00
1650	25.55	23.50	19.70	16.07	28.67
1655	25.87	23.47	17.50	16.43	28.00
1660	27.00	24.58	18.90	16.75	30.33
1665	27.57	24.83	19.40	17.00	31.50
1670	27.29	24.58	18.80	17.50	
1675	27.21	24.89	19.07	17.79	
1680	27.41	24.53	19.17	17.79	
1685	27.11	24.03	18.00	17.80	
1690	26.92	24.18	19.25	17.80	
1695	27.58	23.85	17.50	17.80	

1700	27.54	23.77	18.00	18.20
1705	27.54	23.83	18.00	18.20
1710	27.11	23.92	18.00	18.20
1715	27.29	23.92	18.00	18.80
1720	27.65	24.21	18.00	18.80
1725	27.16	24.12	18.00	18.80
1730	27.48	24.29	19.25	18.80
1735	28.34	25.41	19.13	18.80
1740	28.13	24.87	17.33	18.60
1745	27.75	24.33	17.33	18.60
1750	28.35	24.70	18.00	18.60
1755	28.00	24.93	17.33	18.60
1760	28.00	25.08	17.33	19.20
1765	28.25	24.30	17.50	19.20
1770	28.38	24.30	17.50	19.20
1775	28.50	24.90	17.25	19.20
1785	28.70	24.55	17.20	19.20
1790	28.60	25.23	17.20	19.20
1795	28.63	24.63	17.20	19.20
1800	28.63	25.30	17.20	19.20
1805	28.45	25.30	17.67	19.20
1810	28.20	25.45	17.57	19.20
1815	28.50	25.63	18.25	19.20

Sources: ALKMAAR: L. Noordegraaf, *Daglonen in Alkmaar, 1500–1850* (Amsterdam, 1980). MEDEMBLIK: G. A. Medemblik, Oud Archief, Bijdragen tot de Thesauriersrekening, 1591–1813, no. 150. AMSTERDAM: G. A. Amsterdam, Fabrieksambt, no. 2; Part. Arch. 367, Burgerweeshuis archief, no. 446–8; H. P. H. Nusteling, *Arbeid en werkgelegenheid in Amsterdam* (Amsterdam, 1985), 252. SPAARNDAM AND HALFWEG: Hoogheemraadschap van Rijnland, Oud Archief, Bijlagen tot re rekeningen, no. 9530–10086. LEIDEN: Hoogheemraadschap van Rijnland, as above; G. A. Leiden, Oud Archief, Trekvaarten en jaagpaden, no. 60, bijlagen tot de rekeningen. UTRECHT: R. A. Utrecht, Kapittel ten Dom, no. 704; G. A. Utrecht, Acquiten kameraar rekening, no. 1260. GOES: G. A. Goes, Rekeningen van de stad, no. 783–959; rekeningen stadsfabriek, no. 1813–14, 1793–7. THE HAGUE: G. A. Den Haag, Oud Archief, no. 5198, rekeningen van Delftse straatweg, L. Noordegraaf, & J. T. Schoenmakers, *Daglonen in Holland 1450–1600* (Amsterdam, 1984). Dordrecht, Noordegraaf, and Schoenmakers, as above. RURAL NORTH HOLLAND: Hoogheemraadschap van de Uitwaterende Sluizen, Rekeningen van de Rentmeester, no. 74.

Table 12.2. *Average wages: Eastern Netherlands, 1500–1815 (stuivers per day, summer wages).*

Year	Master	Journeyman	Unskilled	Hod carrier	Sawyer
1500	3.20		1.60	1.75	
1510	3.50	4.63	2.00	2.00	
1520	4.10		2.20	2.60	
1530	4.20		2.40	3.00	
1540	4.30		2.40	3.00	
1550	5.25	5.00	2.63	3.00	
1555	5.17	5.04	2.63	3.00	
1560	5.50	5.29	3.67	3.33	
1565	5.67	6.00	3.67	3.83	
1570	5.67	6.22	3.67	3.83	
1575	6.00	6.09	4.33	4.33	
1580	7.09	7.96	5.25	6.00	
1585	9.78	10.04	6.00	6.17	
1590	10.46	10.75	6.33	7.33	
1595	11.96	12.11	8.00	8.17	
1600	12.40	12.08	8.00	8.33	
1605	13.37	12.19	8.00		
1610	13.79	12.26	8.25		
1615	14.33	12.67	9.35		
1620	14.76	13.09	9.40		
1625	16.04	14.40	10.13		
1630	16.70	16.73	11.00	12.00	17.33
1635	18.80	17.54	11.25	13.00	17.20
1640	18.63	17.18	11.70	13.00	
1645	18.84	17.57	11.67	13.00	18.00
1650	18.33	18.30	12.00	13.00	18.66
1655	19.40	17.97	13.00	14.40	
1660	21.09	18.20	12.50	14.67	18.33
1665	20.80	18.20	12.20	14.00	18.66
1670	20.75	18.20	13.20	14.67	19.66
1675	20.67	18.30	13.25	14.70	19.66
1680	20.50	17.55	13.13	14.00	20.33
1685	19.00	17.40	12.25		
1690	19.25	17.40	11.75		
1695	19.25	17.40	11.75		
1700	19.25	18.00	11.75		

1705	19.25	18.00	11.75
1710	20.25	18.40	11.50
1715	20.25	18.40	11.50
1720	20.25	18.40	11.50
1725	19.50	18.40	12.25
1730	19.50	18.40	12.25
1735	20.00	18.40	12.25
1740	20.00	18.40	12.25
1745	20.00	18.80	12.25
1750	20.00	18.80	12.88
1755	20.00	18.80	12.88
1760	20.00	18.80	12.88
1765	20.00	18.40	12.88
1770	20.00	18.80	11.88
1775	20.00	18.80	11.88
1780	20.00	18.80	11.88
1785	20.00	18.80	11.88
1790	20.00	18.40	12.75
1795	20.00	17.50	
1800	20.00		
1805	21.00		
1810	21.00	19.00	12.50
1815	21.00	18.70	12.50

Sources: FRANEKER: G. A. Franeker, no. 725–831, kwitanties en bijlagen tot de rekeningen. GRONINGEN: G. A. Groningen, Oud Archief, no. 332b, Bijlagen tot de stadsrekeningen. KAMPEN: G. A. Kampen, Oud Archief, no. 1977–89, 685; D. van der Vlis, "Daglonen in en rond Kampen van 1526 tot 1810," *Overijsselse Historische Bijdragen* 96 (1981), 77–97. ZUTPHEN: G. A. Zutphen, no. 2010–14; Rekeningen, bijlagen tot rekeningen van timmermeester. ARNHEM: G. A. Arnhem, Secretarie rekeningen en bijlagen, no. 1636–92; Rentmeester rekeningen en bijlagen, no. 1305–1548; Fortificatiën, no. 3388–446. NIJMEGEN: G. A. Nijmegen, Oud Archief, no. 2892–3, 1953–66, 33089; T. L. M. Engelen, "Nijmegen in de 17de eeuw," *Nijmeegse studiën* 7 (1978); P. H. M. G. Offermans, *Arbeid en levensstandaard in Nijmegen omstreeks de Reductie (1550–1600)* (Zutphen, 1972), 147–53. 's-HERTOGENBOSCH: G. A. Den Bosch, stadsrekening, no. 10–3361, bijlagen to stadsrekeningen, no. 1–180; Godshuizen Archief, no. 581–93, 643–55.

wage data for ten locations in the "Western Netherlands" (Holland, Utrecht, and Zeeland) and seven locations in the "Eastern Netherlands" (all other provinces). The available observations are averaged by five-year periods (ten-year periods before 1550). Since observations are not available for all seventeen locations in every period, the minor short-term fluctuations usually carry little meaning, but the longer-term trends are broadly based, representing the experience of labor in cities large and small, as well as several rural locations.

In the mid–sixteenth century, carpenters and masons earned 7 or 8 stuivers per day everywhere in Holland except in and around Haarlem, where wages were higher at 9 or 10 stuivers. As one moved south or east, the wages declined to 6 stuivers at Bergen op Zoom and Utrecht, and further still to 5 stuivers in the cities of Gelderland, Overijssel, and Limburg. Much the same pattern characterized the wages paid to unskilled laborers and hod carriers: 3.5 to 4.5 stuivers throughout Holland (except Amsterdam, where 5 stuivers was paid), 3 stuivers in Utrecht (and little more than that in Brabant and Flanders), and 2.5 to 3 stuivers in the eastern cities.

These 1550 wage levels represented an increase over the wages paid a century earlier. Then (based on a more limited range of observations) unskilled workers in Holland earned about 1 stuiver less, and skilled workers as much as 3 stuivers less. Nominal wages rose during a period of currency instability in the turbulent 1480s and again after 1520. Most wage rates remained fixed for long periods, however, while the adjustments that were made tended to favor the more skilled laborers. The "skill premium" (the fraction by which skilled workers' wages exceeded those of the unskilled) rose from some 50 to 67 percent in 1460 to over 80 percent in the period 1520–50.

After 1550, wage increases became more frequent, and after 1570, in a period of political turmoil, rapid price inflation, and rapid economic expansion, they became more frequent still, especially in 1572–83 and 1592–1616. A drainage board that regularly hired labor at Spaarndam raised wages eight times in these periods.

After the 1610s, money wages stabilized until the 1630s, after which occasional raises lifted wages to a level, usually reached by 1665, that was rarely exceeded thereafter. By the last quarter of the seventeenth century, master craftsmen in the Western Netherlands earned at least 28 stuivers per day, while in the northern and eastern provinces, 20 stuivers was the most common wage rate. Unskilled labor earned at least 18 stuivers in the West, 15 stuivers in intermediate locations such as Utrecht, and 12 stuivers in the eastern towns.

Once this pattern of daily wage rates was attained, further wage adjustments were minor and exceedingly infrequent. Some wage rates remained unchanged for 200 years and were not increased substantially until 1870. Moreover, this wage rigidity extended far beyond the ranks of construction laborers. The official pay rates for most grades of labor employed by the VOC did not change from 1636 to the Company's demise in 1795. The thousands of employees of the great ship wharves of the admiralties and the VOC faced the same pay scales from *at least*

1695 (we cannot determine precisely when these rates went into effect) until *at least* 1780 – and here we know that post-1780 adjustments were very small until 1847.

The available data reveal no substantial wage differentials between urban and rural locations or, for that matter, between large and small cities. Indeed, in various periods the very highest wage quotations are observed at Spaarndam and Woerden (mid–sixteenth-century craftsmen) or in rural North Holland (late seventeenth-century common labor).

The markets for particular grades of labor seem to have been reasonably well integrated, but a substantial east–west wage differential persisted throughout the three centuries of our investigation. A comparison of Tables 12.1 and 12.2 shows that wages in the East rose more rapidly than in Holland-Zeeland up to the eve of the Revolt. By then, eastern wages stood at 70–75 percent of the western level. Thereafter, the explosive growth in the maritime region caused the eastern wages to fall back again. After 1620, eastern craftsmen recovered much of the lost ground, but unskilled laborers rarely were paid more than two-thirds of the average western wage until 1740, after which the eastern wage rose to about 70 percent of the western unskilled wage.

Wage rates were always quoted per day. The workday for manual laborers typically extended from 5 A.M. to 7 P.M. and was divided into four periods of labor (*schoften*) interrupted by rest pauses. These pauses – a half-hour at about 8 A.M. and again at about 4 P.M. plus an hour to 90 minutes at noon – resulted in an 11- to 12-hour working day. With the approach of winter, as the days grew shorter, the workday in most sectors grew shorter as well. In the winter months, work typically began at sunrise and ended at sundown, and this short 7- to 8-hour day was divided into only two work periods. The winter pay rate was almost always less than the summer rate. The pay rates quoted previously are all summer wages. Employers varied considerably in how much they discounted this wage in the winter and in how long they paid the lower winter wage. A common demarcation of the winter pay period, was November 11th (St. Maarten) to February 22nd (St. Peter), as was a 20 to 25 percent winter pay reduction. But the winter wage could be much lower, and the period in which it was paid much longer.

There is little evidence that the length of the working day, as such, was an object of much negotiation, but the length and number of the pauses, and the level and duration of the winter wage, were frequently adjusted, suggesting that they formed the arena in which employers and workers contested the terms of employment. Until 1631, the city of Utrecht paid its manual worker at the winter wage for 11 weeks and the summer wage for the remaining 41. It lengthened the winter wage period by stages, until in 1735 the winter wage was paid for 23 weeks. In Kampen the city did not reduce wages in winter at all until 1644. Thereafter, a combination of lengthened winter wage periods and reduced winter wages lowered the maximal annual earnings of municipal workers after 1715 to

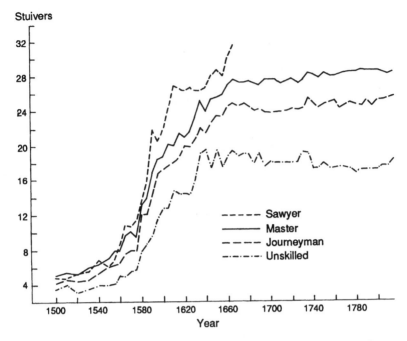

Figure 12.1. Average wages in the Western Netherlands, 1500–1815. Summer day wages, in stuivers per day. (*Source:* See Table 12.1.)

80 percent of the 1644 level. All the while the summer wage remained fixed at 12 stuivers per day. This example is extreme, but many marginal adjustments in winter pay tended to reduce potential earnings in the century after 1650.

Even more consequential for the maximum annual earnings of wage laborers were changes in the length of the work year. Until the mid–sixteenth century, the system of work in the Netherlands shared the pan-European characteristic of frequent interruptions by Christian holidays. The liturgical year and local saints' days removed 40 to 50 days plus the 52 Sundays from the calendar, leaving about 260 to 265 working days. All over Europe there was dissatisfaction with the large number of holidays, an achievement of the fifteenth century when labor was scarce and the demand for leisure high. Protestant and Catholic countries alike began consciously to prune saints' days from the list of observed holidays, but none acted as radically as the Calvinist churches in the Netherlands. In 1574, as soon as Calvinism had gained ascendancy in Holland and Zeeland, the Synod of Dordrecht urged the abolition of all holidays except Sunday. Only after special pleading did Easter Monday, Ascension day, Pentecost Monday, Christmas, and second Christmas day escape this radical step, establishing at the stroke of a pen, as it were, a work year of 307 days. It is hardly credible that practice followed theory instantaneously; equally unlikely is such a sudden jump in the demand for labor. But by the early years of the seventeenth century, pay records show individuals routinely laboring over 300 days per year. By then the adjustment had been made; the work year had been extended by over 15 percent, increasing the potential supply of labor to the economy as well as the maximum annual earnings of the workers – at the cost of considerable leisure. The work year, including the work pauses, amounted to some 3,600 to 3,800 hours; only in the four summer months did workers enjoy any free daylight hours apart from Sundays.

Thus far we have found that all time series of wages bear a strong family resemblance. Some rise more rapidly than others, but they all experience the same basic turning points. This is not the case with the compensation paid to salaried employees. Salaried workers are rarely studied in this context, since the heterogeneity of occupations was great and salary variations among individuals within an occupation were common. Moreover, many salaried functions were not intended to be full-time jobs. Some were sinecures; other salaries were but the tip of an income iceberg: The holder of the position could collect fees for the performance of his duties. It is, in short, easy to misinterpret the meaning of a salary – in the past no less than today.

In view of these daunting problems, we proceed here under the assumption that a single broadly based index will stand the best chance of reflecting the general course of compensation to salaried workers. The index presented in Figure 12.2 incorporates a large number of different occupations spread across the Western Netherlands: Reformed ministers in Amsterdam, smaller cities, and in rural areas; school teachers in Amsterdam, Leiden, and Middelburg; a broad range of municipal employees in Amsterdam, Middelburg, and Goes; orphanage employees in Amsterdam and Utrecht; windmill operators at various rural locations employed by the Hoogheemraadschap van Rijnland. The twelve separate indexes have been combined into a single unweighted index stretching from 1540 to the nineteenth century.

The unusual course of salary compensation is readily apparent when it is related to the course of wages in the building trades (Figure 12.2c). Salaried employees fared poorly during the sixteenth-century price inflation, as few adjustments were made in money earnings until after the 1550s. Thereafter, salaries rose even faster than day wages, more than restoring the relative position of salaried employees by the mid–seventeenth century. After mid-century, as wages begin to assume their notorious rigidity, many salary earners enjoyed further raises. By 1800 the salary index stood 26 percent higher than in 1664. The salary earners were mostly employees of public or semipublic bodies, and most possessed special education or training. Further research will be necessary before we can interpret these findings with confidence.

The nominal wages charted here deserve attention in their own right; after all, this is what employers paid, and this is what directly affected the cost of produc-

Index (1540–1555 = 100)

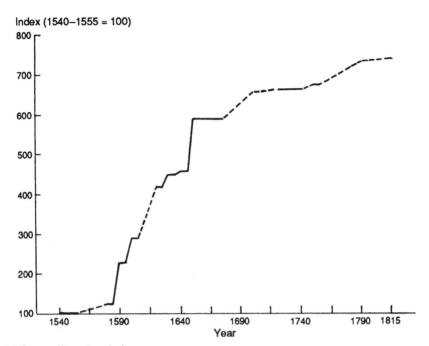

(a) Composite salary index

Index (1540–1555 = 100)

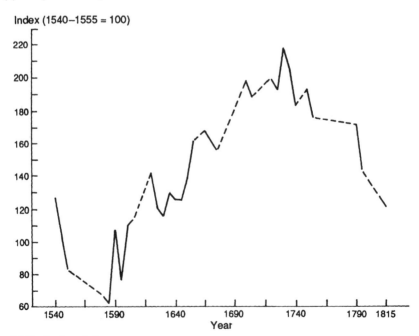

(b) Real salary index

Index (1540–1555 = 100)

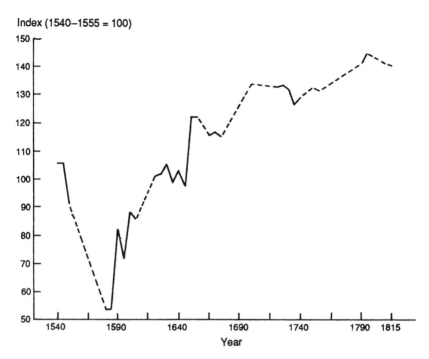

(c) Salaries relative to journeymen's annual earnings

Figure 12.2 (*above and opposite*). Trends in earnings of salaried workers, 1540–1815. (Index, 1540–55 = 100). [*Sources:* G. A. Utrecht, Archief van de financiekamer, no. 1222–3; Burgerweeshuis archief, no. 116–18. G. A. Amsterdam, Archief Thesaurieren Ordinaris, no. 255–347, Rapiamus; no. 725–32, Weddeboeck; Part. Archief 367, Burgerweeshuis, no. 732a, 445, Lonen der Suppoosten. G. A. Goes, Oud Archief, no. 783–959, Rekeningen. MIDDELBURG: H. M. Kesteloo, *De stadsrekeningen van Middelburg* (Middelburg, 1881), 10 vols. LEIDEN: N. W. Posthumus, *De geschiedenis van de Leidse lakenindustrie* (The Hague, 1908–39), 3 vols.; S. M. Coebergh van den Brink, *Meer dan zes eeuwen Leids Gynmasium* (Leiden, 1988), pp. 15, 59; Hoogheemraadschap van Rijnland, Oud Archief, Polderboeken, no. 3184–5, 3769–70.]

tion and the demand for labor. It can be shown that the level of nominal wages in the maritime provinces of the Netherlands was approximately at the level of southern England in the first quarter of the sixteenth century (in both areas, building craftsmen's daily wages translated to about 4.5 grams of silver), rose beyond the English level, but not yet above the Southern Netherlands level in the last two decades of the sixteenth century, and then surpassed that level after 1600 to reign supreme in northern Europe until the end of the eighteenth century, when English wages assumed that position (see Table 12.3).

Table 12.3. *Unweighted mean daily summer wage paid to labor in the building trades in four countries (expressed in current stuivers).*

Place	1582–92	1650–79	1745–54	1790–9
Unskilled Labor				
Holland	9.0	18.7	18.3	17.9
E. Netherlands	6.9	13.6	13.6	13.1
Belgium	9.5	13.8	12.0	11.9
Germany	5.3	9.0	7.9	7.6
England	6.0	12.1	14.2	19.9
Journeymen				
Holland	11.5	25.1	25.2	24.8
E. Netherlands	10.5	18.6	18.9	19.5
Belgium	16.1	25.0	22.5	22.3
Germany	7.5	15.0	12.0	11.4
England	9.0	18.7	20.4	27.9

Wage Rate Index
(100 = highest average wage in each time period)

	1582–92	1650–79	1745–54	1790–9
Unskilled Labor				
W. Netherlands	95	100	100	90
E. Netherlands	73	73	74	66
Belgium	100	74	66	60
Germany	56	48	43	38
England	63	65	78	100
Journeymen				
W. Netherlands	71	100	100	89
E. Netherlands	65	74	75	70
Belgium	100	99	89	80
Germany	47	60	48	41
England	56	75	81	100

Sources: HOLLAND: See Table 12.1. EASTERN NETHERLANDS: See Table 12.2. ENGLAND: E. H. Phelps Brown and Sheila V. Hopkins, "Seven Centuries of Building Wages," *Economica* 22 (1955), 195–206. GERMANY: M. J. Elsas, *Umriss einer Geschichte der Priese und Löhne in Deutschland,* 2 vols. (Leiden, 1936, 1949); Otto Aden, *Entwicklung und Wechsellagen ausgewählter Gewerbe in Ostfriesland* (Aurich, 1964). The German average incorporates data from Augsburg, Emden, Frankfurt am Main, Cologne, Leipzig, Speyer, and Würzburg. BELGIUM: Ch. Verlinden et al., *Dokumenten voor de geschiedenis van prijzen en lonen in Vlaanderen en Brabant (Xve–XVIIIe eeuw),* 4 vols. (Bruges, 1959–73). The Belgian average incorporates data from Bruges, Ghent, Antwerp, Brussels, Aalst, Mechelen, and a rural area near Antwerp.

12.3. The cost of living

Dutch employers paid higher wages than their competitors in neighboring countries, but did the wage earners enjoy higher living standards? In order to answer this question, nominal wages must be converted to real wages. That is, instead of expressing the wage in money terms, it must be expressed as a level of purchasing power. By constructing an index of the cost of living, by means of which nominal wages are deflated to real wages, purchasing power can be compared over time. Besides such a chronological comparison, we would also like to compare real wages diacronically, across regions and countries. This is a task of considerably greater complexity, however, since it requires the construction of separate cost of living indexes for each location, all comparably constructed and adjusted for currency differences. The available price data fall short of what is needed to carry out a full comparative study. We will have to be content here with more limited comparisons of purchasing power.

The first consideration in any study of the cost of living in a preindustrial European society is the price of grain, the largest single item of expenditure for most people. The prices of wheat and rye are fundamental to economic history, and we have already referred to their trends and fluctuations several times. Many studies of real wages simply express the wage as the quantity of rye or wheat that it could buy at prevailing prices, but there are two good reasons to resist this in the Dutch case. First, nearly all urban residents and most rural dwellers in the maritime provinces did not buy grain and bake their own bread; they purchased bread from bakers. The price of bread is the more relevant information, and this was governed in the cities by the *broodzetting*, a municipal regulation of the maximum bread price that incorporates not only the market price of grain but also taxes and the baker's costs of production. Since the two latter elements formed a large and stable element in the total, bread prices fluctuated much less than did the price of grain, as is clear from Figure 12.3.

The second reason is that the Dutch diet, especially in the maritime zone, seems to have depended less exclusively on bread than is often assumed, or than is observed in other countries. This is a subject about which our knowledge remains very limited, especially for the sixteenth century. Institutional records reveal the composition and cost of the diets offered to those in their care, and of these, orphanage records offer what is probably the most useful information. Table 12.4 summarizes the composition of diets in four institutions. The infirmary of the *begijnhof* of Lier (a city in the Southern Netherlands) and the Utrecht *Burgerweeshuis* give an imperfect glimpse into the sixteenth-century diet. Fuller information is provided for two Amsterdam institutions. One, the Amsterdam *Burgerweeshuis*, was well endowed and catered to orphans left by the established "burgers" of the city. The *Aalmoezeniersweeshuis*, on the other hand, depended on subsidies from the city and cared for children ineligible for admission to any of the city's numerous other orphanages.

Index (1660–1780 = 100)

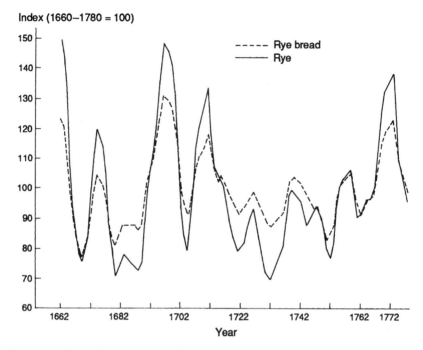

Figure 12.3. Rye prices and rye bread prices compared. Five-year moving averages of rye and rye bread prices. (Index, 1660–1780 = 100.) [*Sources:* RYE PRICES: N. W. Posthumus, *Inquiry into the History of Prices in Holland* (Leiden, 1943), Vol. I, Prussian rye prices at Amsterdam. RYE BREAD PRICES: N. W. Posthumus, *Geschiedenis van de Leidsche lakenindustrie* (The Hague, 1908–39), Vols. II and III, Leiden bread prices.]

In both of these institutions, bread rarely accounted for more than 25 percent of total food costs, and often much less. Meat and fish usually claimed a larger portion of the budget than bread, and dairy products (butter, cheese, buttermilk, and fresh milk) always did.

The general composition of orphanage diets remained remarkably stable until the last days of the Republic. The *Aalmoezeniers* orphanage, whose income depended on a wide variety of fees levied on economic activity plus municipal subsidies, felt the late eighteenth-century crisis immediately. Rising food prices, increased child abandonment, and insufficient income forced austerity on this institution beginning in the 1780s; the elite Burgers' orphanage, protected by its restrictive admission policy and cushioned by its endowment, lived on in relative comfort. But it was not altogether spared; the partial default on government bonds in 1811 forced a massive austerity program. These two institutions fairly reflect how the crisis hit the working- and middle-class segments of society. Ultimately,

Table 12.4. *Distribution of total food expenditures by category in four institutions, 1526–1857.*

Food category	Lier Beguijn-hof Infirmary 1526–75	Utrecht Burger-weeshuis 1593–1609	Amsterdam Burgerweeshuis				Amsterdam Aalmoezeniersweeshuis					Amsterdam Burgerweeshuis	
			1638–49	1650–65	1665–75	1690–1743	1683–1749	1750–79	1780–9	1790–5	1799–1808	1816	1851–7
Bread	44.5	37.5	21.6	29.0	19.6	19.6	18.7	20.0	20.7	25.8	32.5	28.3	32.1
Peas, beans, and vegetables	0.0	2.5	8.9	8.5	8.1	8.3	13.5	13.3	14.4	15.6	20.5	20.3	25.9
Meat and fish	27.4	18.3	23.7	21.0	23.4	23.3	13.5	15.9	14.0	11.1	6.7	14.2	13.5
Butter, cheese, and milk	1.4	32.4	34.4	29.7	34.4 {	32.8	33.9	34.5	35.0	33.7	24.3	31.1	21.0
Beer	19.0	[b]	} 11.4	11.9	14.4	10.4	9.7	7.0	6.0	5.0	4.0	2.0	1.0
Other[a]	7.7	9.3				5.6	10.7	9.3	9.9	8.7	12.0	4.1	6.5

[a] Syrup, sugar, oil, raisins and currants, vinegar, salt, and pepper.
[b] This institution brewed its own beer from grain accounted for under "bread."

Sources: E. Schokkaert and H. van der Wee, "A Quantitative Study of Food Consumption in the Low Countries during the Sixteenth Century," *Journal of European Economic History* 17 (1988), 131–58; H. van der Wee, *The Antwerp Market and the Growth of the European Economy*, Vol. 1 (The Hague, 1963), Appendix 47. G. A. Utrecht, Burgerweeshuis archief, no. 116, Rekening. G. A. Amsterdam, Part. Archief 367, Burgerweeshuis, no. 164–5, Generaal rekening, no. 446–8 Fabriekboek: Part. Archief 343, Aalmoezeniersweehuis, no. 60–3, Boekhouding.

neither could avoid the adoption of a new, austere diet, and this proved to be no temporary measure; the new diet of little meat and little cheese would define orphanage practice throughout the nineteenth century.

The origins of the nutritionally superior "Republican diet" remain uncertain. The evidence presented in Table 12.4 suggests that in the sixteenth century bread, meat, and beer dominated the diet much more than after 1630, when peas, beans, vegetables, and dairy products rose in importance to offer a healthier and more varied diet. But the demise of the "Republican diet" is unambiguous. After the 1780s (for the poor) and 1811 (for the middle class), this paradigm of Republican prosperity had to yield to a diet of fewer calories dominated by bread, potatoes, vegetables, and legumes.

Is it reasonable to regard these institutional diets as broadly representative of the habits of private households? In some respects it is not. Individuals must surely have been more exposed to price and income fluctuations than institutions, and institutions probably were more conservative in their habits; it was part of their task to suppress desires while supplying basic needs. But there are also several reasons to accept the orphanage practices as a useful indication of social reality. First, private householders of modest means *could* have consumed the type of diet provided by the orphanages. Table 12.5 shows the daily costs per orphan of the diet provided by the *Burgerweeshuis* from 1638 to 1675 and the *Aalmoezenierswees-huis*, decade by decade, from 1683 to 1808. This diet answered reasonably well to modern visions of good nutrition and provided about 2,200 to 2,400 calories per day. In this table we calculate the annual cost of feeding such a diet to five persons (11,000 to 12,000 calories per household) and express it as a percentage of the annual household income of a fully employed unskilled laborer or hod carrier. Until the 1750s this diet never exceeded two-thirds of an unskilled work-er's income. After 1770 the orphanage diet began to exceed his reach, but this is partly because the orphanage drifted toward a richer diet. Its retrenchments after 1780 increased the "affordability" of its diet, but this too was only temporary. The high prices around 1800 – which recurred frequently until 1817 – forced the orphanage to cut its diet back to a meager 1,800 calories per person and to slash meat consumption. Even so, the fully employed workman wishing to purchase 11,000 calories of this more austere diet would have found it far beyond his reach.

A second factor arguing in favor of the representativeness of the orphanage diets is the substantial similarity of elite and lower-class institutional diets; the differences are of degree rather than of kind, suggesting that they reflect broadly diffused norms. The burger orphans got more of almost every type of food than did the riff-raff in the care of the Aalmoezeniers, but hardly anything in the diet of the one was not also found in the diet of the other.

Finally, the orphanage diets are broadly consistent with the information that begins to become available at the end of the eighteenth century about the food consumption standards of the broader population. For instance, in 1798 per capita consumption of wheat and rye in Holland totaled 98 kg., and that of meat 27 kg.

Table 12.5. *Cost of an orphanage diet as a percentage of the annual household income of unskilled laborers, 1638–1808.*

Year	Daily household food cost in stuivers[a]	Annual income in guilders[b]	Percentage spent on food[c]	Orphanage[d]
1638–49	9.00	290.02	56.6	BWH
1650–65	10.50	293.92	65.2	BWH
1666–75	10.00	305.66	59.7	BWH
1683–9	8.45	299.64	51.5	AWH
1690–9	10.50	302.78	63.6	AWH
1700–9	9.95	303.00	59.9	AWH
1710–19	11.00	305.51	65.7	AWH
1720–9	10.35	308.03	61.3	AWH
1730–9	9.80	317.96	56.2	AWH
1740–9	11.05	300.73	67.1	AWH
1750–9	12.25	306.05	73.0	AWH
1760–9	12.60	306.47	75.0	AWH
1770–9	14.10	305.71	84.2	AWH
1780–9	11.72	302.99	70.6	AWH
1790–5	11.44	304.67	68.5	AWH
1799–1808	20.50	304.67	122.8	AWH

[a]Food costs: The average daily cost of the orphanage diet (described in Table 12.4) multiplied by five. This expenditure is sufficient to acquire approximately 11,000 calories, except in 1780–95, when the orphanage expenditure must be multiplied by 10 percent, and 1799–1808, when it must be multiplied by 22 percent.

[b]Annual income: The maximum annual earnings of unskilled laborers (see Table 12.1), multiplied by 20 percent to reflect other family income.

[c]Percent spent on food: Daily food costs × 365 days, divided by annual income.

[d]Orphanage: BWH, Burgerweeshuis; AWH, Aalmoezenierweeshuis, both in Amsterdam.

Source: See Table 12.4.

The excise tax on slaughtered livestock suggests a per capita meat consumption of 36 kg. in 1807–8. This average pertains to the entire nation and is easily double the consumption levels then prevailing in Belgium or Germany. Butter consumption could be reconstructed only for one town, Beverwijk, but then over a longer period; in 1760–84, per capita consumption stood at nearly 15 kg. The provincial excise tax levied on butter yielded revenues that correspond to a rather constant consumption level around 10 kg. per capita throughout the period 1650–1800, which, in view of the untaxed rural consumption and the general incentives to avoid payment, should be regarded as an underestimate.

Compare these averages to the orphanage records: Through the eighteenth century, bread consumption stood at approximately 140 kg. (in both orphanages), meat consumption varied between 18 and 22 kg. (38 to 40 kg. at the Burgers' orphanage), and butter consumption between 12 and 15 kg. (15 to 17 kg. at the Burgers' orphanage). The chief difference between institutional and individual consumption patterns is the relative importance of rye. In the cities of Holland, wheat bread cost, pound for pound, 70 to 100 percent more than rye bread. This price difference substantially exceeded the difference in the underlying grain prices; it reflected the higher taxes on wheat bread and the higher profit margin allowed for wheat bread by the municipal *broodzetting* (which often incorporated cross-subsidization of the poor man's staple, rye bread). Despite this, eighteenth-century consumers in Holland ate twice as much wheat as rye, while the institutions usually provided more rye than wheat. For example, in Haarlem the bakers sold nearly three loaves of wheat bread for every loaf of rye bread in 1733–5, and two loaves of wheat per loaf of rye throughout the second half of the eighteenth century. The city's charitable institutions, on the other hand, distributed three to four times as much rye bread as wheat in 1698–9 and 1733–5, and twice as much rye as wheat bread in the latter half of the eighteenth century. Haarlem's consumption ratios correspond with those for Holland as a whole when the latter are first observable at the end of the century. From these data one can conclude that the poorer one was, the more rye bread one ate. But it is noteworthy that even the most hard-pressed institutions never stopped purchasing wheat. The two grains were always provided in combination. This was not the case in the eastern provinces. There rye dominated to the virtual exclusion of wheat, especially among the rural population.

In order to calculate the purchasing power of wages, we have calculated a cost of living index that incorporates the chief elements of the Dutch diet, weighted roughly in accordance with the institutional diets previously discussed. This index is an improvement over a real wage index based only on grain prices, but it is still incomplete. Fuel, clothing, and other industrial products need to be included. Except for peat, the chief fuel, the available price data for nonfoodstuffs leave much to be desired; we rely on the index of industrial prices compiled by N. W. Posthumus in his study of the Leiden textile industry.

Finally, a cost of living index should incorporate the rental cost of housing.

This is the most difficult cost to deal with because housing is a heterogeneous and immobile product. A given dwelling can change its character over time, as depreciation and repairs take place, and the rental value can vary according to local demand. Thus, the average rental value of the cheaper houses in Amsterdam rose by 50 percent between 1630 and 1700, while in Leiden, rents at these two dates were nearly identical. Given the heterogeneity of housing costs and the limited state of our knowledge about them, we have decided not to incorporate this important item in our index.

The resulting cost of living index, more properly a "basket of consumables" index, is displayed in Figure 12.4. (Before 1575, when the full range of price information is unavailable, the index relies on Southern Netherlands commodity prices, which are highly correlated with the limited assortment of available northern prices.) This index reveals price trends that were broadly similar throughout Europe. After a slow buildup in the early decades of the sixteenth century, consumer prices rise irregularly but rapidly until 1600. Then after a brief respite, the inflationary process resumes, reaching its apogee in the 1650s. Thereafter, prices tend to fall, again very irregularly, to the 1730s, whereupon an upward trend is reasserted that becomes sharply inflationary after the French Revolution.

12.4. Real wages

The purchasing power of Dutch labor is calculated here by deflating the maximum annual earnings of each type of labor by the basket of consumables index. The resulting real wage indexes are shown in Figures 12.5a (for master craftsmen) and 12.5b (for hod carriers).

The basic trends can be summarized as follows:

1. Late fifteenth-century real wages fluctuated erratically, so the high real wages around 1500 may not be a fair benchmark, but it is probable that all laborers suffered a decline in purchasing power from the late medieval peaks. This decline continued into the 1550s.
2. The decline was arrested around 1560, after which real wages rose erratically, but with special force after 1580, until 1620.
3. Sharply rising prices caused real wages to plunge in the 1620s, but thereafter recovery set in. The wars against England and France repeatedly interrupted the upward course of real wages, but after each setback, higher levels were reached until purchasing power reached a peak in the 1680s.
4. From the several real wage peaks occurring between the 1680s and 1730s, a new trend of declining real wages set in, reaching its nadir after 1800.

Table 12.6 shows the relationship between wage and price changes in each of these phases. From 1500 to 1560, rising prices substantially outstripped wage increases. In the following sixty years, prices rose as fast as before, but they were

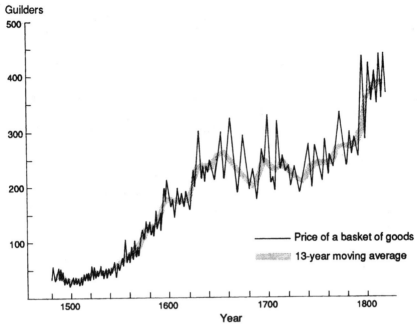

Figure 12.4. Cost of living index, Northern Netherlands, 1480–1819. *Methods:* The cost of living indicator is expressed as the annual guilder cost of a basket of consumables with the following composition: Rye (1,050 kg.), yellow peas (143.5 kg.), beef (100 kg.), cheese (50 kg.), butter (50 kg.), beer (621 liters), peak (100 turf tons), and a composite of industrial products weighted to equal 25 percent of the food subtotal in the period 1575–99. The beer is replaced by coffee, tea, and gin in the period after 1750. This food basket supplies over 14,000 kcalories per day. [*Sources:* 1575–1819: N. W. Posthumus, *Inquiry into the History of Prices in Holland* (Leiden, 1943–64), 2 vols., *Geschiedenis van de Leidsche lakenindustrie* (The Hague, 1908–39), 3 vols. BEFORE 1575: H. van der Wee, "Prices and Wages as Development Variables: A Comparison between England and the Southern Netherlands, 1400–1700," *Acta Historiae Neerlandica 10* (1977), 58–78. These data are presented in full only in the original Dutch version, published in *Album offert à Charles Verlinden à l'occasion de ses trente ans de professorat* (Ghent, 1975), pp. 413–35.]

now substantially outstripped by rising wages. In the brief period from 1615–19 to 1625–9, the rise of wages was brought to a standstill, and real wages deteriorated, but this setback was more than made good in the following fifty-five years. Until the 1660s, wage increases outstripped rising prices; thereafter, falling prices and stable wages sent purchasing power to a new high point. The price-driven character of the real wage movements after the 1660s continues through the later phases; both the fluctuation between 1680 and 1740, and the steady decline of real wages thereafter, were almost entirely the result of price changes.

Index (1451–1475 = 100)

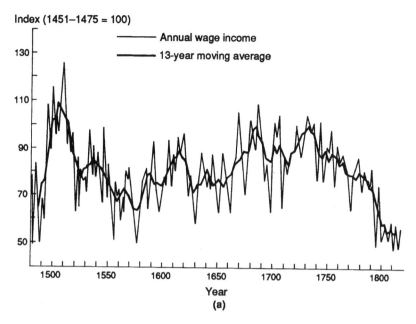

(a)

Index (1451–1475 = 100)

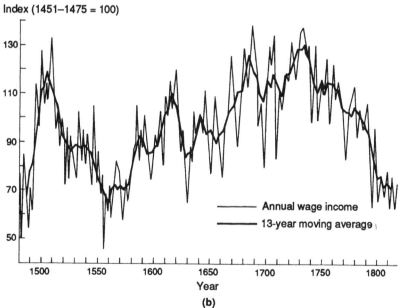

(b)

Figure 12.5a (top). Real wage index for master craftsmen in the Western Netherlands, 1480–1813. (*Source:* See Table 12.1 and Figure 12.4.)

Figure 12.5b. Real wage index for hod carriers in the Western Netherlands, 1480–1813. (*Source:* See Table 12.1 and Figure 12.4.)

Table 12.6. *Change in the cost of living and in nominal wages in selected periods, 1500–1685.*

Period[a]	Cost of living index	Wage index for:			
		Unskilled	Hod carrier	Master	Journeyman
1500/10–1560/4	240	144	140	156	156
1560/4–1575/9	165	122	170	130	130
1575/9–1615/19	165	268	225	241	251
1615/19–1625/9	128	99	99	100	106
1625/9–1640/4	105	137	119	117	112
1640/4–1680/4	90	98	111	108	110

[a]For each period the index is set at 100 for the initial five years. The index numbers shown are for the final five years within each period. Thus, for the period 1560/4 to 1575/9, the cost of living rose from 100 in 1560/4 to 165 in 1575/9, while in the same period, wages for unskilled labor rose from 100 to 122. That is, prices rose by 65 percent while the wages for unskilled labor rose by 22 percent.

These long-run trends are not the whole story, of course. The figures reveal substantial short-run price volatility, and for the large majority of people who could not bridge the intervals of high price with stored provisions or money savings, these crises were very serious matters, however positive the long-term trends might have been. We return to this issue later in this chapter.

The Dutch real wage trends can be placed in a broader context by comparing them to a similarly constructed real wage index for England constructed by E. H. Phelps Brown and S. Hopkins. Their time series is based on the wages for construction labor and is deflated by a basket of consumables price index comparable to our Dutch index.

The English and Dutch series, cast in thirteen-year moving averages, are shown together in Figure 12.6. Since each national series is expressed in its own currency and deflated by its own cost of living index, we cannot be certain that a given index number represents equal purchasing power in the two countries. But the similar construction of the baskets of consumables, the substantial price integration between the two countries, and the nearly equal exchange values (and silver contents) of money wages in the early sixteenth and again in the early nineteenth centuries, all argue in favor of our placing two indexes in the manner shown.

The central feature of Figure 12.6 is the dramatically divergent paths followed by Dutch and English real wages between 1580 and 1620. In both countries labor suffered a decline in purchasing power from the late medieval high points to 1550. After that date the decline was arrested in Holland, and after the 1570s a vigorous growth or restoration of real wages took place. But over the same period, English real wages fell by half. Nor was England alone in suffering this real wage erosion. Studies of the sixteenth-century price revolution have established that plunging real wages characterized most of Europe. The Dutch experience in this

Index (1451–1475 = 100)

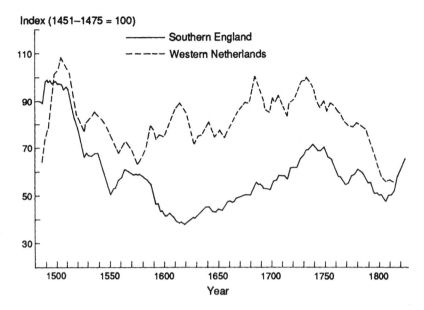

Figure 12.6. Real wages of craftsmen in the Western Netherlands and southern England, 1480–1819. Thirteen-year moving averages. (Index, 1451–75 = 100.) [*Sources:* WESTERN NETHERLANDS: see Table 12.1. SOUTHERN ENGLAND:, E. H. Phelps Brown and Sheila V. Hopkins, "Seven Centuries of Building Wages," *Economica 22* (1955), 196–206 and "Seven Centuries of the Prices of Consumables, Compared with Builders' Wage-rates," *Economica 23* (1956), 196–214. Their time series leaves several short gaps, the most important of which is in the 1620s. Values for these years have been proposed in Jack Goldstone, "Urbanization and Inflation: Lessons from the English Price Revolution of the Sixteenth and Seventeenth Centuries," *American Journal of Sociology 89* (1984), 1122–60.]

era stands out, and what distinguished the Republic from her neighbor was not a deviant price history but larger and more frequent increases in the money wage.

The effect of this relatively brief period of vigorous growth was to open an enormous gap between real wages in the two countries, which lasted well into the eighteenth century. This brings us to the second notable feature of Figure 12.6. After 1730 the Dutch advantage wasted away, to disappear by about 1800. Once again, the price trends in both countries were similar; the gap closed as English money wages rose periodically, while those in the Netherlands remained fixed at their mid–seventeenth-century level.

The available evidence is far from comprehensive but is quite unequivocal in identifying an era of Dutch "exceptionality" from the end of the sixteenth century well into the eighteenth century. In this period nominal wages in the Western Netherlands stood at a higher level than in surrounding countries (Table 12.3), and the purchasing power of those wages broke away from the common European trend after 1580. There is nothing in this evidence to support the belief that the Dutch standard of living broke through all known ceilings to reach hitherto unattainable heights. Rather, it is the avoidance of real wage erosion that appears as the main achievement. But before settling on such a modest conclusion, it is advisable to penetrate behind the veil of wages and prices – the intersections of the supply and demand curves – to observe the workings of the labor market itself.

Three questions call themselves to our attention. First, what happened in the period 1580–1620 to cause wage levels to depart from the earlier (and later) pattern of long-term rigidity? Second, what can account for the wage rigidity of the long period after the mid–seventeenth-century, and specifically, how should the period 1680–1730 be interpreted? Do the very high real wages of that era signal a peak of prosperity? Finally, do our real wage calculations accurately portray conditions in the period 1770–1815? Did purchasing power really plunge so decisively to the low levels touched earlier only – and then but briefly – in the 1550s and 1480s? In all three cases, we need to supplement our knowledge of prices with information concerning the factors affecting the supply and demand for labor, the actual earnings (rather than just the wage rate), and the operations of the labor market more generally.

12.5. The labor market

12.5.1. AN EXPLOSION OF DEMAND – AN EXPLOSION OF SUPPLY

The first matter demanding attention is the supply of labor, a topic that both optimists and pessimists regard as central to understanding the experience of labor in the Republic's numerous urban centers. There can be no doubt that the supply curve of labor shifted sharply to the right in the half-century after the 1570s. This relatively brief period warrants careful attention because in it was concentrated the most intense immigration to the Republic, the most rapid urbanization within the Republic (and, hence, a probable increase in the percentage of the labor force working for wages), and a major increase in the length of the working year (the consequence of the reform of religion). In this period Holland's population nearly doubled, its urban population rose from about 40 to nearly 60 percent, and the maximum length of the work year rose from about 260 to 307 days. Natural increase, immigration, proletarianization, and Reformation all combined to flood the Netherlands with wage labor; the effective supply of nonfarm labor grew by nearly 3 percent per year in the period 1570–1620. If the demand for labor had not also increased, the equilibrium wage would certainly have fallen, as we know that it did in surrounding countries.

The demand for labor grew with sufficient vigor to absorb this supply at rising real wages, and this growing demand was felt especially by unskilled labor. The

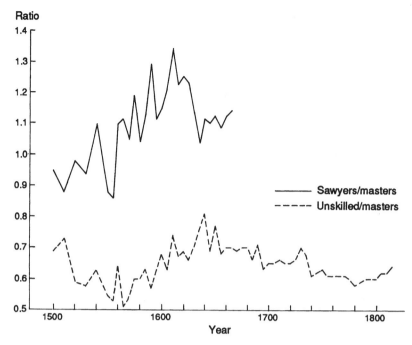

Figure 12.7. Skill premiums in the Western Netherlands, 1500–1815. (*Source:* See Table 12.1.)

wages of unskilled workers had deteriorated relative to skilled workers in the period 1460 to 1550–70 – from 67 to 55 percent of the skilled wage. But as the pre–Revolt malaise in the urban economies dissolved to make way for a vigorous growth, the relative position of the unskilled improved. By 1630–50 (see Figure 12.7), their wages stood at 75 percent of the skilled wage, a graphic demonstration of rapid economic expansion pressing upon the supply of labor.

There is no hint of Malthusianism here. On the contrary, the wage evidence is consistent with an economy in which heavy investment is expanding employment opportunities and increasing productivity. This is illustrated with telling clarity by the wage history of sawyers. The demand for sawyers sensitively reflected investment levels, since urban expansion, farm improvements, and shipbuilding all required sawn lumber. As beneficiaries of the "investment accelerator," sawyers saw their wages rise from some 90 percent of the masters' wages in the first half of the sixteenth century to a peak of 130 percent by 1610 (see Figure 12.7). It should not surprise us to hear that a certain Cornelis Cornelisz. responded to this "bottleneck" in the economy by adapting a windmill to saw timber mechanically in 1596. It took time to perfect the sawing mill and to overcome municipal restrictions on its use, but the relative wages of sawyers fell

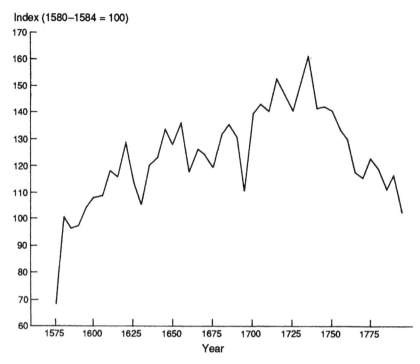

Figure 12.8. Wages relative to industrial prices. An index of skilled and unskilled wages, divided by an index of industrial prices, 1575–1799. (Index, 1580–4 = 100.) [*Sources:* WAGES: see Table 12.1. The index weights journeymen's and unskilled workers' wages equally. INDUSTRIAL PRICES: An index published by N. W. Posthumus, *Leidsche lakenindustrie* (The Hague, 1908–39), 3 vols., pp. I:203, II:1000, 1080. The index is composed of the following items: vegetable oil, soap, writing paper, wrapping paper, candles, woolen cloth (bays and *lakens*), yarn, sole leather, vinegar, and lime.]

after 1610, Amsterdam's sawyers' guild was disbanded in 1627, and after 1665 there are not enough references to their employment to sustain the time series; the sawyers became victims of technological unemployment. As befits a modern economy, the investment process that had driven up sawyers' wages turned to remove that obstacle to continued expansion.

The rise of labor productivity can be inferred from the tendency of nominal wages to rise faster than industrial prices between the 1580s and 1650s. The ratio of wages to industrial prices remained roughly constant in the first three quarters of the sixteenth century, but thereafter the cost of labor regularly outpaced the price of industrial products (see Figure 12.8). By the 1650s, labor productivity would have had to exceed that of 1580–1600 by roughly a third in order to restore the earlier balance of labor costs to industrial product prices – that is, to prevent unit labor costs from rising.

A labor force growing rapidly, attaining higher levels of productivity, and earning higher real wages – this is the appealing picture we have of the Dutch labor market from the Revolt to the mid–seventeenth century, and most intensely to 1620.

The new demand for labor was broadly based, both geographically and by sector; but a conspicious feature of the labor market in these expansive decades was the large role of casual and temporary employment. The herring fishery, Baltic shipping, peat digging, and the many infrastructural projects such as polder drainage, canal construction, and urban expansion all offered employment on a seasonal or highly temporary basis. This was reinforced by the growing specialization in agriculture, whereby more acute seasonal peak labor demands arose for hay making, crop harvesting, and the preparation of labor-intensive commercial crops. Specific conditions varied from place to place, of course, but a remarkable feature of the labor markets in much of Holland was the way in which these varied employments were integrated by a large, flexible labor force, both urban and rural. Rural smallholders took work as fishermen and as construction laborers on polder projects; Enkhuizen herring fishermen also signed on, before and after the season, with merchant skippers sailing for the Baltic. Indeed, the sailing dates for the main Baltic fleets, mid-April and the end of August, seem calculated to avoid the height of the herring fishery, July and August.

We know little about just how these activities were integrated by individual families, but we have many examples in which hundreds, often thousands, of workers suddenly appeared to dig a canal, repair dikes, or work on polder drainage. And we know from contemporaries that the dates of the harvests and sailing of fleets caused their work crews to melt away like butter left out in the summer sun.

There were, of course, other, more permanent forms of employment available in the Golden Age economy, but the highly flexible supply of casual labor was both conspicuous and strategic to the most rapidly growing sectors of the economy.

The temporary and seasonal character of so many employments hardly contributed to the economic security of Dutch laborers, but there is reason to believe that prolonged seasonal and frictional unemployment was not often a major problem in these decades. By sweeping aside dozens of religious holidays in 1574, the basis was laid for a more rational organization of work. This increased labor potential appears to have been realized, exposing, as it were, a second obstacle to effective labor (and other resource) utilization – the idleness enforced upon many activities by the onset of winter. By the 1640s, the campaigns launched by cities throughout the maritime zone to establish scheduled passenger barge services invariably stressed year-round dependability as one of the chief advantages of the proposed venture. The horse-drawn barges would replace the vagaries of wind and tide and the certainties of seasonally impassable roads with comfortable, scheduled services that could be interrupted only by prolonged frost. Even then, the promoters envisioned wagons and sleds gliding over the ice-covered canals to speed travelers to their destinations even in the coldest days of winter.

As the towpath-equipped canals, *trekvaarten*, were built and scheduled services were implemented (see Chapter 2), their use through the seasons of the year proved to be remarkably uniform. In winter the barges carried only marginally fewer passengers than in summer, and when ice-bound waterways idled the barges, the toll receipts of the towpaths rose, revealing an intensified use of wagons and sleds – just as the promoters envisioned (see Figure 12.9).

This unlikely source reveals a vigorously growing economy pressing against the available resources, and seeking to augment those resources by lifting enforced idleness from the winter season. In the preindustrial economy, the winter can be viewed as a sort of "time frontier" where, at a price, new production capacity can be achieved. The construction and use of the new *trekvaarten* (they were introduced, route by route, between 1632 and 1665) suggests that the seventeenth-century Dutch economy strove to maintain operations through the winter months, offering employment to many who in earlier generations would have been idle or engaged in less valuable activities.

Both the direct evidence of rising wages and the indirect evidence of abundant employment lead us to the conclusion that real incomes rose substantially after the 1570s, driven by investment that increased the demand for, and the productivity of, labor over a broad range of sectors.

12.5.2. THE SEGMENTED LABOR MARKET

In the course of the third quarter of the seventeenth century, the Dutch labor market assumed features very different from those of the preceding century, features that were to endure into the nineteenth century. The new labor market structures were, in part, logical outgrowths of the long expansion era that had preceded it and, in part, a response to factors external to the labor market that established the new environment in which it functioned. Among the latter, the most important was the reversal of the long-term price trend. After rising throughout the sixteenth century, and drifting irregularly higher until the 1660s, commodity prices fell sharply over the next twenty-five years. Industrial prices, particularly of textiles, began their downward course even earlier. The contemporaneous exhaustion of population growth is the second essential fact, although one can debate how "exogenous" this was with respect to the labor market. At any rate, the nonagricultural labor supply, after growing at 3 percent per annum in 1570–1620, and by perhaps 1 percent per year over the following forty years, ceased to grow – indeed, probably contracted slightly – through most of the next century.

A third important feature defining the post-1660s economy was the sudden plunge of investment in infrastructure, capital goods, and urban and residential construction. The abandonment of projects and shelving of plans catalogued in

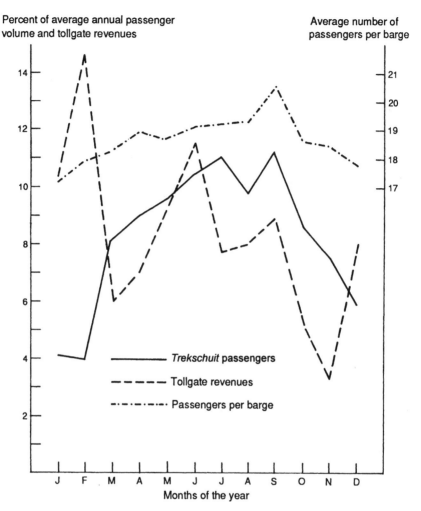

Percent of average annual passenger volume and tollgate revenues

Average number of passengers per barge

Months of the year

Figure 12.9. Monthly distribution of *trekschuit* and road traffic, Amsterdam–Haarlem, 1644–53. (*Source:* G. A. Haarlem, trekvaarten en veerdiensten, nos. 13–27.)

Chapter 2 is reflected in Figure 8.7, which displays the annual revenue of Holland's *grove waren*, an excise tax on building materials.

These features shaped the new labor market environment while the long preceding era of expansion endowed the economy with a broad range of specialized and reasonably secure jobs, secured by a combination of capital investment, institutional consolidation, and political intervention. The drainage projects, in combination with other factors, increased the number of large commercialized farms. There was progressively less space in the rural economy for the smallholder with by-employments but an increased demand for permanent farm servants. The expansion of commerce to other continents increased the demand for sailors prepared to work for years at a time rather than for a voyage of two or three months. New capital-intensive industries such as industrial windmills, refineries, and ship wharves offered relatively steady employment in comparison to textiles. The growing cities created many positions in what we would call the service sector (including the expansion of charitable institutions), and the magistrates tended to encourage guild formation in previously unorganized occupations in order to facilitate the maintenance of an orderly and peaceful urban society. In Amsterdam, for example, the number of guilds doubled in the century after the Revolt, by which time a third of the city's adult male labor force were guild members. Everywhere, domestic freight transportation came to be governed by arrangements where appointed skippers and teamsters were granted exclusive franchises to carry goods between specified points, in exchange for commitments to offer a defined level of service (the *beurtveren* described in Chapter 5). The *trekschuit* services providing intercity passenger transportation were governed by similar regulations.

The great (semi)public enterprises that expanded or assumed a durable institutional form after 1650 – the Admiralty ship wharves, the VOC harbor facilities, the drainage authority maintenance works, the municipal public works departments – offered a large number of desirable, reasonably secure jobs, while the capital-intensive private firms that required trained, permanent employees – the mills, refineries, and ship wharves – added substantially to the number of jobs yielding the manual worker incomes that stood at the peak of what preindustrial Europe had to offer.

The consolidation of this stable sector of specialized employments might be regarded as the fruit of economic growth. Of course, the labor market continued to possess a large sector of casual, seasonal, and labor-intensive jobs. This vast, relatively informal sector of the economy was of strategic importance as the economy grew, but after the mid–seventeenth century, its character changed. The most labor-intensive sector, textile production, was the first to feel the pressure of international competition. High domestic production costs and declining international prices forced adjustments (see Chapter 8) that gradually reduced urban textile employments. This process was inaugurated in 1650 with a substantial reduction of piece rates, which defined the compensation of weavers and most other textile workers. By the late 1660s, investment-related employment contracted as urban expansion, land reclamation, and infrastructural improvements came to a standstill. Hard on the heels of these employment setbacks came the reduction of labor demand in agriculture (as relative price changes stimulated more land-intensive production) and in the herring fisheries, a phenomenon of a probably unrelated, coincidental nature (see Chapter 7, section 7.3). All of these sectors had once offered seasonal employments that fed into a single, flexible labor system.

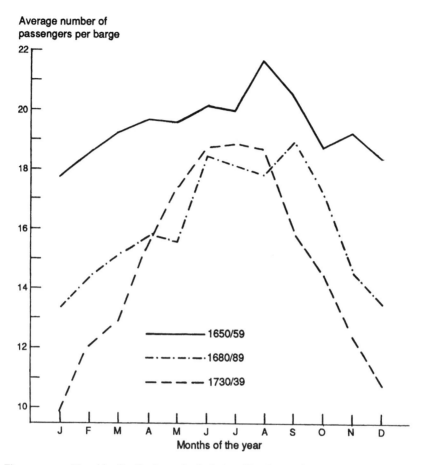

Figure 12.10. Monthly distribution of *trekschuit* traffic, Amsterdam–Haarlem, 1650–1739. (*Source:* G. A. Haarlem, trekvaarten en veerdiensten, nos. 13–27.)

The tendency toward a more pronounced seasonal concentration of economic activity is revealed with special clarity by the evolution of the demand for passenger barge transportation. Figures 12.10 and 11 show across the period 1650–1739 (1) a sharp decline in winter demand, and (2) the disappearance of demand for alternative road transportation during winter canal closures due to ice. Just as we have interpreted the intense mid–seventeenth-century interest in year-round transportation as an effort to exploit a "time frontier" of unexploited resources, so we interpret this growing seasonal concentration as an expression of "temporal contraction." A firm with excess capacity idles its least productive equipment first and, if it can, its least productive workers. In the casually organized sectors of the

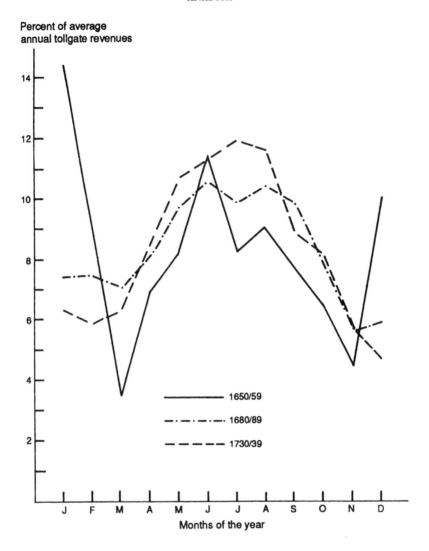

Figure 12.11. Monthly distribution of tollgate revenues on the Amsterdam–Haarlem *trek-vaart* in selected decades, 1650–1739. (*Source:* G. A. Haarlem, trekvaarten en veerdiensten, nos. 13–27.)

preindustrial economy, this contraction did not as much take the form of laying off some workers while the others continued as it shortened the work season (i.e., avoiding work in those periods when productivity was lowest and operating costs were highest).

With the decline of these seasonal and casual employments, it became increasingly difficult for laborers to stitch together something approaching a full year's work. In the sixteenth century, many casual laborers, particularly in rural North Holland, had possessed small farms. Seasonal unemployment then could partly be cushioned by household production. But by the second half of the seventeenth century, both the demand for nonagricultural labor at high wages and changes in the rural economy had reduced considerably the supply of such labor. Then workers of all types, dependent on wages in a high-cost economic environment, found it impossible to live as before on the surviving remnants of the seasonal and casual labor market.

The case of Enkhuizen is instructive in this regard. This Zuider Zee port grew rapidly, on the strength of the herring fishery and merchant shipping, to a population in excess of 20,000 by the mid–seventeenth century. The seasonal character of these industries made it possible for many workers to combine them. But the demand for seamen began to decline already after 1620 as the Baltic trade became ever more concentrated in Amsterdam, and it contracted even more after 1650 as the skippers sought their crew members from small communities in Friesland, the North Sea Islands, and abroad. It has long been thought that this displacement was motivated by the search for lower-cost labor, but a decline in the number of Hollanders offering themselves for this work also may have played a role. In any event, by the early eighteenth century, there were very few seamen in either Enkhuizen or the rural communities in its region.

The decline of employment in the merchant marine had a major impact on the organization of the herring fishery, which began its own decline after 1670. The diminished fishery remained Enkhuizen's major economic activity until the end of the eighteenth century, but, ironically, employers found willing workers increasingly difficult to come by. In the absence of other employments (such as ocean shipping), workers could not survive in Enkhuizen as seasonal herring fishermen. The city's fleet owners turned increasingly to rural communities where other forms of inland and ocean fishing could supplement the seasonal herring activity. But the crisis spread to the countryside as well: The densely populated Schermereiland district of North Holland annually had sent about 1,000 men to work the herring fleet until the 1660s, and thereafter the demand for labor on the whaling ships more than compensated for the decline of the herring fishery. The demand for labor remained strong, but the demise of the local inland and coastal fisheries undermined the ability of local households to participate in either the seasonal herring or the whaling industries. As ever more households turned to the hemp-processing crafts that arose to serve the sail-cloth industry, the local supply of ocean fishing crew members fell from over 1,000 in 1650 to 100 in 1728. Ironically, the declining herring industry found its supply of local labor declining even more rapidly than its demand; wages were increased around 1700, and by 1750 foreign labor was employed (despite laws prohibiting this).

Many seasonal employments remained after the mid–seventeenth century –

hay making, peat digging, and the rapidly growing whaling industry being the most important. But instead of complementing each other, as had been the case while the economy grew, they now tended to compete: All these activities required labor in a brief summer period.

As the demand for casual labor became more seasonally concentrated, the domestic supply diminished, since such work could not often be integrated into a viable complex of employments and other forms of support. This is the context in which the maritime provinces of the Netherlands began to attract large numbers of migrant laborers from the eastern provinces and particularly from Germany, beginning in the third quarter of the seventeenth century.

Precisely because the decline of labor demand took the form of the unraveling of the domestic seasonal employment system, the remaining demand came to be satisfied by workers for whom such work *could* be integrated into a viable seasonal employment system, and these were found among the *heurlingen,* or cotter farmers, of Westphalia, Osnabrück, and Lippe, in northwest Germany. Seasonal work in the peat bogs, hayfields, and workshops of the Republic could be integrated with their small holdings, given the high wages in the west and the low cost of living in their homelands. The makings of a durable migrant labor system – the *Hollandgängerei* – were in place, and from the late seventeenth century until the early nineteenth century, 10,000 *hannekemaaiers* or more, their backpacks crammed with sausages and rye bread, annually crossed the Dutch border on foot, most of them destined for the ferries at Hasselt, which would carry them across the Zuider Zee to Holland. It was precisely in the period 1675–1700 that the number of skippers on the Hasselt–Amsterdam route doubled, from 7 or 8 to 14 or 15, at which level this link in the migrant labor system remained until the beginning of the nineteenth century.

The wrenching changes occurring in the Dutch labor market in the second half of the seventeenth century did not result in chronically high unemployment because of a third and final new element: the expansion of the Dutch East India Company. Although the VOC had grown rapidly from small beginnings after 1602, the doubling of its size between about 1680 and 1740 had an enormous impact on the labor markets of the Dutch port cities and of the hinterlands that supplied them with labor. A job with the VOC on shore was, as noted in Chapter 10, section 10.3.4, greatly prized, but to sign on as a sailor, let alone as a soldier, appealed to few people who had a choice: The pay was low, the dangers high, and the separation from home lasted for years. Over half of those who embarked for Asia aboard a VOC vessel never returned. The lotterylike character of this work must have attracted some adventuresome souls (a survivor who was prudent with his earnings could return with a tidy sum), but in general the crews mustered aboard VOC ships were unskilled and unemployed, in debt, and/or in trouble at home. Even in the early days of the Company, foreign employees had to be recruited in large numbers. Already in the 1630s, 40 percent of those setting sail for Asia were not Dutch, and by the 1660s the foreign share had risen to half. Signing on as a VOC soldier was even less attractive; in the 1660s only 25 percent of them came from the maritime provinces.

But diminished employment opportunities of the later seventeenth century, particularly the crisis in the casual labor sector, generated a new interest in VOC employment: The Dutch share of VOC employees rose from 50 percent around 1660 to 73 percent around 1700. In this same interval, the maritime provinces' share of newly recruited VOC soldiers rose from 25 to 50 percent. Since the Dutch share was growing in a total Company employment that itself was being steadily enlarged, the VOC's overall impact on Dutch labor markets grew enormously (see Figure 12.12). In the first half of the eighteenth century, an average of nearly 20 percent of each cohort of twenty-year-old men who had been born in the province of Holland died abroad while in the service of the VOC. It is hardly an exaggeration to say that the Company swept the city streets of beggars and the unemployed.

The recruitment, year-in, year-out, of thousands of young men did not occur effortlessly. Re-enlistment played a relatively modest role, especially in the lower ranks, since so few experienced hands returned, and impressment, the technique favored by the British, was not legal in the Republic's free labor market. Orphanages steered their charges toward the VOC, it is true, but the great majority of new employees had to be recruited in the open market, and a "service industry" of considerable complexity emerged to cater to the VOC's manpower needs. The identification of likely recruits, and the housing and maintenance of these mainly penniless fellows over the many weeks or months before one of the VOC's three annual fleets set sail, came to be the work of *zielverkopers*, or "soul sellers." A peek into the organization of this minor industry, which functioned in all of the VOC's port cities, reveals a great deal about the underside of Dutch urban life – and of its financial complexity.

Not *all* of the men who signed on with the VOC were poor, footloose, single men. Some were married or otherwise established in the port city. While away they supported their wives and families by means of the periodic transfer of their earnings. The sailor had to arrange for this before his departure, and payment was made to the designated beneficiary only when the VOC bookkeepers had received notice that the salary had, indeed, been earned (i.e., that the employee had not died or deserted). These payments were far from sufficient to support a wife, let alone a family, and in the not unlikely event of death, they ceased. Among the income-supplementing activities of these wives and widows, the operation of lodgings for seamen and the supply of recruits to the VOC figured prominently.

The infamous *zielverkopers* were chiefly women. Together with husbands and other male relations who had contacts in the seafaring world, they attracted and

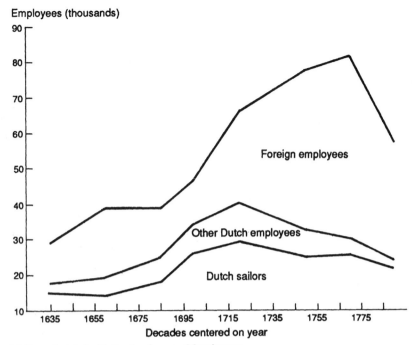

Employees (thousands)

Foreign employees

Other Dutch employees

Dutch sailors

Decades centered on year

(a) Decade totals, Netherlanders and foreigners

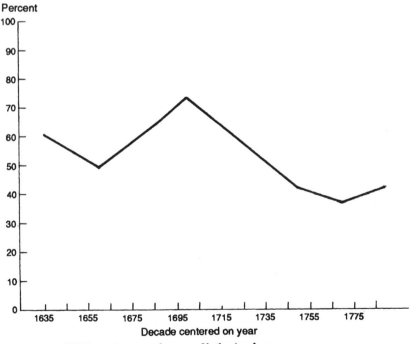

Percent

Decade centered on year

(b) Percent of VOC employees who were Netherlanders

maintained the recruits until the day of enlistment. At that point the recruit received a two-month advance on his salary. This *handgeld*, 18 to 24 guilders for soldiers and common seamen, went to pay the *zielverkoper* for the services she had provided on credit over the preceding weeks. Usually, it was only *partial* payment, for the recruit's expenses ordinarily far exceeded the amount of his advance. It was, after all, the *zielverkoper's* aim to see to it that the recruit (unaccustomed as he was to holding a line of credit) spent freely on food, drink, women, and the contents of his sea chest. To discharge his remaining debt to the *zielverkoper*, the recruit could contract a *transportbrief* with the VOC. This was a promissory note secured by his future earnings (after the first two months, of course). Depending on the size of the debt (in time, common seamen were limited to 150 guilders, able seamen to 200, etc.), the holder of the *transportbrief* could present it to the VOC's bookkeepers for payment once news had reached them that the sum had been earned.

The *zielverkoper*, not usually a person of ample means, now held a debt instrument that would not be paid for years and, should the employee die, might never be paid in full. She turned to a buyer of *transportbreiven*, called a *zielkoper* (a "buyer of souls"), but the Dutch word *ziel* (soul) is close to *ceel*, a corruption of *cedeel*, meaning a sealed document, such as this debt instrument. The *zielkoper* stood ready to buy *transportbrieven* at a discount, thereby financing the labor recruitment enterprises and accepting the risk. These financiers were originally shopkeepers and tradesmen with whom the *zielverkoper* did business. But the more successful of the *zielverkopers* also entered the discounting business, and after 1660 a small number of them – all women – came to dominate it.

The scope of this business grew in the eighteenth century, as the VOC's need for labor and its dependence on raw recruits from abroad grew. Perhaps because of the growing capital requirements of the business, women became less prominent as discounters of *transportbrieven* in the course of the eighteenth century. Former VOC officers and merchants with Company links took over the business. The risks were always considerable, and the post-1740 rise in mortality among Company employees may have been responsible for a spate of bankruptcies among the discounters. When the Amsterdam *zielverkoper* Anthony Carstens, who had taken over much of this business, failed in 1777, the whole labor recruitment system was in danger of collapse. Outside Amsterdam and Rotterdam, the small-fry lodgings operators could no longer find discounters to finance their operations, which forced the VOC chambers to step in as buyers of their own *transportbrieven*. The Zeeland chamber alone bought 3,839 such notes in the period 1783–9, paying 335,500 guilders for notes with a value "at maturity" of nearly 700,000 guilders,

---

Figure 12.12 (*opposite*). VOC employees embarking for Asia (Netherlanders and foreigners), 1630–1795. [*Source:* J. R. Bruijn and J. Lucassen, eds., *Op de Schepen der Oost-Indisch Compagnie* (Groningen, 1980), Appendix 3C.]

which is an indication of the risks involved in this business – and also of the risks facing the fellows who labored on the Company's ships and at its Asian outposts.[3]

We have described a post-1675 labor market composed of three distinct segments: (1) a "core" segment composed of large public and semipublic organizations, guild-organized activities, and capital-intensive enterprises; (2) a casual, seasonal, and labor-intensive employment segment focused on construction, agriculture, peat, whaling, fisheries, and a variety of manufactures; and (3) an "employer of last resort," the VOC. The elements of this segmented labor market were not altogether absent before the mid–seventeenth century, but neither the first nor the third were as large as they would later be, and, more generally, the labor market exhibited greater fluidity and flexibility. The more pronounced labor market segmentation emerged just as the wage data began to reveal the remarkable rigidity and seeming ossification that would persist throughout the eighteenth century and into the nineteenth. Once again, surface stability is revealed to be the product of internal transformation.

The famous post-1650 wage rigidity was chiefly characteristic of the protected employment sector. Here the high nominal wages attained by mid-century continued to be honored despite a diminished demand for labor, and despite falling price levels after the 1660s that increased the purchasing power of those wages to unprecedentedly high levels. Perhaps the "efficiency wage" hypothesis of modern labor economics can help to explain the persistence of these high wages: By honoring the previously attained wage levels, employers could choose the best workers, reduce turnover, and elicit greater effort from their employees. On the other hand, this policy ensures that markets will not clear, that supply will exceed demand. There is little room for doubt that the considerable advantages of employment in this sector created a queuing effect, whereby the unemployed were prepared to engage in extended searches – or waits – for one of the privileged jobs. The knowledge that the patronage of urban regents figured in the disposition of many of these choice jobs is consistent with this scenario.

Workers unable to acquire a permanent job in the high-wage sector could participate in the casual labor market. Wages in this sector were not necessarily lower than in the core sector, although they tended to be more sensitive to immediate supply and demand conditions. We do not know if the 1650 reduction in piece-rate wages paid to Leiden textile workers was experienced more generally, but the gradual deterioration of pay for unskilled workers relative to craftsmen's wages – from at least 70 percent up to 1680 to no more than 61 percent after 1755 – is a signal that the terms of employment among those most exposed to supply and demand forces were not given much protection by custom or inertia. Still, the more serious threat to the well-being of workers in the casual

---

[3] M. A. van Alphen, "De zielverkopers, transportbrieven en transportkopers," in J. Krikke et al., eds., *Amsterdam, haven in de 17de en 18de eeuw* (Amsterdam, 1990). pp. 125–31; J. de Hullu, in J. R. Bruijn and J. Lucassen, eds., *Op de schepen der Oost-Indische Compagnie* (Groningen, 1980), pp. 92–3.

labor market was the intensely seasonal concentration of demand, which sentenced these workers to extended unemployment. Unless nonwage income or charity offered sufficient alternative support, this sector was not viable, and, as we have seen, Dutch labor tended to abandon it to foreign migrant labor – labor that did have access to complementary household resources to secure its reproduction.

This should make clear that the very high real wages registered for most of the period 1680–1740 do not necessarily signify a peak of general prosperity in those decades. On the contrary, these real wage peaks signaled the onset of a major problem for the Dutch economy. The sharply falling price levels after 1670 were not a product of cost-reducing investment and increased production in the Republic. The rising real wages were the product of an exogenous shock in the form of a falling international price level. Under these circumstances the failure to adjust wage rates tended to squeeze profits and force down rents as the wage bill rose. In short order, the withdrawal of capital from profitless endeavors generated unemployment. This, in turn, speeded the construction of the segmented labor market regime that we described earlier, a regime that tended to reinforce the high wage levels by reducing the scope for competition.

Reductions in the nominal wage were as unpopular in the seventeenth century as they are today, and they were almost as rare. The modern techniques of wage reduction – inflation and exchange rate adjustment – were then beyond reach, both technically, given the monetary regime, and politically, in view of the interest of the Republic's merchants, investors, and bankers in monetary stability. Without access to effective policies to restore labor market equilibrium in the short run, all that was left were long-term adjustments in behavior: (1) the demographic responses to unemployment – migration, reduced nuptiality, and fertility, and (2) the social response to uncertainty, the construction of segmented labor markets to provide relative security to the "insiders," those with the permanent, high-wage jobs. The sinister beauty of this system is that it also commands the loyalty of many "outsiders," those who hope, often forlornly, someday to secure one of the attractive jobs.

12.5.3. EXCEPTIONALITY LOST

Thus far we have analyzed the emergence of exceptionally high Dutch wages in the 1570–1650 period and the later maintenance of a high-wage regime for a substantial portion of the labor force through the strengthening of labor market segmentation. In this long high-wage era, living costs also rose – through heavy taxation, high urban rents, and the effects of high wages themselves – but the available evidence on material conditions, the variety of the common diet, and the muted impact of European subsistence crises on the Republic, all offer compelling support to the proposition that a broad segment of the working population enjoyed a standard of living and a relative security unknown elsewhere in Europe. After 1750, and with special force after 1770, this situation of exceptionality was eroded to the point of disappearance. The Netherlands was becoming more "typical" in its standard of living and its exposure to crisis, although its unique labor market and charitable institutions persisted, thereby ensuring that its adjustment to a new economic environment in the nineteenth century would be anything but typical.

The defining characteristic of the new era is a new reversal, in the 1740s, of the secular trend. Thereafter, a pan-European demographic revival was paired with an equally widespread upward trend in commodity prices, led by the prices of basic foodstuffs. In this new environment, real wages tended to decline, just as they had in the sixteenth century and for the same basic reasons. The relative "stickiness" of money wages caused purchasing power to decline substantially from 1750 to 1817 almost everywhere in Europe: in southern England and London, no less than in Sweden, Austria, France, and the Republic. Only the newly industrializing districts of northern England offer a partial exception to this trend, as the Republic itself had formed the exception two centuries earlier.

The measurements summarized in Figure 12.5 probably overstate the deterioration of the real wage in the 1750–1817 period. In the Netherlands, nominal wages in this period continued to stand unchanged at the level that they had reached a century earlier, but there is reason to believe that the actual compensation of labor in this period is not always accurately reflected by the stated wage.

Wage rigidity is not simply explained by "custom" and "tradition." In a world of limited productivity change and no permanent inflationary expectations, wage rigidity is a rational response to the considerable cost and risk of openly adjusting nominal wages. A wage once raised is nearly impossible to lower. Moreover, a selective increase in wages, by changing the pay differentials among various grades of labor, can generate serious unrest. Employers, cognizant of these facts, tended to respond to pressure on wages by altering *effective* compensation through the manipulation of terms of employment *other* than the wage rate itself. This "wage drift" is hard for the historian to detect for the obvious reason that it was not intended that it be generally known.

Before the mid–eighteenth century, effective compensation was sometimes reduced by prolonging the period in which the lower winter wages were paid or by adjusting the beer rations or the "beer money" paid in lieu of the beverage itself. Thereafter, the tendency was to increase effective compensation. Selective labor shortages, particularly those faced by the Admiralties and the VOC, were met by the payment of "signing bonuses" in addition to the unchanged monthly salary. Elsewhere, New Year's "gratifications" and "douceurs" became common. (The Utrecht mint produced *ducatons* specially to meet the demand for New Year's presentation coins in the 1790s.) Both types of bonus could be withdrawn with relative ease when the conditions warranted.

Among day laborers "hidden" wage increases commonly took the form of transforming the "day" for which the daily wage rate was paid from a real to a notional concept. As noted earlier, the workday was divided into work periods, called *schoften*, demarcated by pauses for meals or refreshment. In the summer months, the workday consisted of four *schoften*. The pay records kept by the Rijnland drainage board reveal that its permanent labor force worked about 260 to 270 days per year in the eighteenth century (they were usually laid off in the heart of winter). In 1784 the bookkeepers recorded a sudden jump in the number of days that the crews worked, up to 280, and in the following decade, the days worked rose steadily, so that by 1795 it reached a level in excess of the total number of available days, 313, and by 1799 reached 342. It hovered around 325 for the next twenty years before declining again (see Figure 12.13).

What had happened? In fact, the employees did not labor more than they had before but were being paid for five *schoften* (i.e., 1.25 days' pay) for summer days that had previously been compensated at the rate of four *schoften*. Overall, the drainage board raised the annual earnings of its laborers by 22 percent between 1784 and 1800 without ever changing the posted pay for a day's work.

In distant Groningen the same practice is observed beginning in 1782 among craftsmen in the employ of a village church, while in Amsterdam the Admiralty ropewalk (a rope-making factory) introduced the fifth *schoft* in 1774. In this case an official pay raise in 1796, by abolishing the fictive days, simply acknowledged openly the effective raise made twenty-three years earlier.

It is dangerous to generalize from such limited observations, but it seems likely that Dutch labor markets were not quite as rigid as tradition has it. Numerous accommodations could be made to market forces while the official wage remained fixed.

The late eighteenth-century cost of living index also deserves critical examination. Several changes in consumption habits – probably the combined result of changing relative prices and changing tastes – had the effect of reducing the consumption of grain, whether as bread or in the form of beer, and increasing that of tea, coffee, jenever, and potatoes. The net effect of those changes was to reduce the role of the commodity whose price rose most steeply in the late eighteenth century. If we sidestep the knotty issue of whether these substitutions represented a deterioration of the diet *as perceived by the consumer*, or an improvement of the nutritional quality by some objective measure, we can move to the economic consequence of these substitutions: They reduce the extent to which the cost of living index rises after 1780 (when the diffusion of the potato begins to speed up). The incorporation of those measures that increased effective compensation, and the incorporation of substitutions in consumption that reduce the weight of the commodities rising most rapidly in price, can substantially revise the traditional measures of late eighteenth-century real wage decline. Figure 12.14 shows the consequences of these adjustments in a concrete case: the real wages earned by laborers employed by the Rijnland drainage board in the period 1750–1850. The "fifth *schoft*" and the revision of the cost of living index to include potatoes substantially reduce the measured decline of purchasing power, but they do not eliminate that decline altogether. A sharp reduction of well-being centered on the first decade of the nineteenth century remains. The war-induced inflation of the French period brought unmistakable impoverishment even for those with steady employment.

Days per year

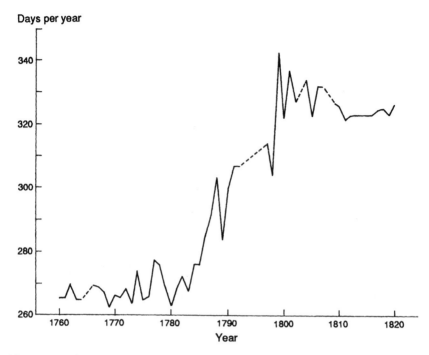

Figure 12.13. Average annual days for which workers at Spaarndam were paid, 1760–1820. (*Source:* Hoogheemraadschap Rijnland, Oud Archief, no. 10905–10920, Werklijsten.)

And however the poor consumer may have perceived the new diet, there is no doubt about the perceptions of observers of a higher station. In 1804 Rutger Metelerkamp claimed that

> the largest part of the laboring class subsists primarily from potatoes, often of poor quality and spoiled, and kettles of tea and coffee, or rather colored, lukewarm water. Many do not eat meat for months at a time, and when grain prices are high many do not even consume bread or grain-dishes. In order to reinvigorate a bit the thus weakened body, strong drink is consumed, and in such quantities that the result is not the strengthening but the further flagging of physical stamina.[4]

---

[4] "Het grootste gedeelte der arbeidende standen bestaat voornamentlijk van aardappelen, die dikwijls slecht en aan bederf onderhevig zijn, en ketels met thee en coffij, of liever gecouleurd laauw water; vleesch eet menig een in maanden niet, en zelfs bij duurte van het koorn, krijgen velen geen brood of meelspijzen te zien. Om echter het verslapte lighaam weder enigzints te verlevendigen, worden sterke dranken gebruikt, en wel in zulk eene hoeveelheid, dat op den duur de verzwakking des lighaams, en niet de versterking ten gevolge hebben." R. Metelerkamp, *De toestand van Nederland* (Rotterdam, 1804), pp. 41–2.

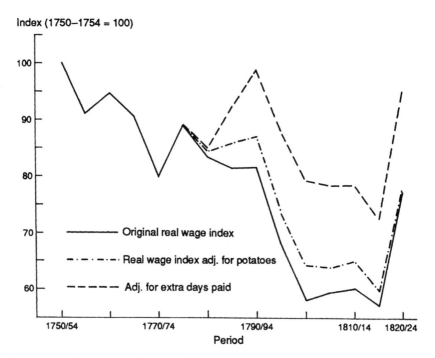

Index (1750–1754 = 100)

Figure 12.14. Real wages of common laborers employed by the Hoogheemraadschap van Rijnland, 1750–1824. (*Sources:* NOMINAL WAGES: Hoogheemraadschap van Rijnland, Oud Archief, no. 10905–10920, Werklijsten. REAL WAGES: See sources cited for Fig.12.4. REAL WAGES ADJUSTED FOR POTATOES: Potato prices from G. A. Alkmaar, Burgerweeshuis Archief, no. 41–55. REAL WAGE ADJUSTED FOR EXTRA DAYS PAID: see Fig. 12.13.

High prices brought misery to much of Revolutionary and Napoleonic Europe. What compounded the economic crisis in the Netherlands, especially in its numerous cities, was the earlier growth of long-term unemployment and – in the case of the many petty retailers, shippers, and craftsmen – underemployment. The anticompetitive devices of the segmented labor market offered less and less protection to the favored workers while the casual labor force expanded, assuming some of the characteristics of a *lumpenproletariat* or, to use the modern term, an *underclass*. It is interesting to note that contemporary observations of growing urban unemployment, poverty, and public begging went hand in hand with a growing reluctance of Dutch workers to sign on as sailors with either the Admiralties or the VOC, the "employer of last resort." Even the traditional merchant marine, which offered better conditions than the VOC, found the domestic supply of seamen drying up in the course of the eighteenth century. The VOC's labor recruitment problems have already been discussed, and the shrinking domestic labor supply is charted in Figure 12.12. By the 1770s, the VOC's demand for labor was at an all-time high, but only 35 percent of the 8,000 men then being sent to Asia each year was domestically supplied. Around 1700, 73 percent of the VOC's recruits had been Dutch born. On board merchant vessels, the situation was apparently no different: Netherlanders formed 76 percent of sampled crew members in 1700–10 but only 42 percent in 1774–5. Nor was the juxtaposition of labor shortage and unemployment confined to the seafaring trades. In Schiedam the "native" population, oriented to the declining fishing industry, proved reluctant to work in the expanding jenever distilleries, where the workers were mostly Germans.

This is but an extreme illustration of a characteristic feature of the urban labor market: its reliance on specific geographical regions for the recruitment of workers with specific skills. Textile workers were drawn from the Southern Netherlands; Amsterdam's bakers were mainly Germans, as were a large number of the bricklayers and stonemasons. The supply of tailors and shoemakers was regularly replenished by migrants from Gelderland, Overijssel, and the directly neighboring German districts. The role of immigrants in the Dutch urban labor market was not as much to fill the bottom rungs of society as to fill specific niches in the occupational structure. A labor market segmentation based on regional circuits of training and migration can give rise to imbalances, where labor shortages and surpluses exist side by side.

But this does not help to explain the shrinking supply of seamen. It was precisely the coastal zones of the Republic that had long been oriented to maritime employment. The explanation for the withdrawal of Dutch labor from the shipping sector in the face of shrinking alternative employment opportunities is not obvious, but the result was growing pauperism.

The Admiralties found recruitment of sufficient men impossible during the War of the Austrian Succession (1740–8). A signing bonus of 25 guilders attracted too few recruits, and the customary remedy of "the sending of someone to Hamburg, Altoona and Bremen and the writing to Denmark [was not found to be a] satisfactory and sufficient means . . . to remedy the shortage of manpower."[5] All that was left was the unappealing choice of raising the bonus to 50 guilders or forbidding the departure of merchant vessels.

An anonymous Admiralty report of 1754 proposed to solve the labor problem of all maritime activities by adopting the English solution: compulsion. The British navy impressed seamen, while England's colonies, merchant skippers, and a wide variety of craftsmen took on indentured servants, who signed away their freedom for many years in exchange for work or instruction in a trade. In the free labor market of the Netherlands, neither practice was legal, nor did the Republic force its convicts to people its colonies.

---

[5] "het zenden van iemand na Hamburgh, Atena en Bremen en het schryven na Denemarken genoegzaam en toereykende middelen . . . om het voorsz. Gebrek van manschappen te kunnen remedieeren." A. R. A. Den Haag, Admiraliteit Colleges, No. 72, Verzameling v.d. Heim, 3 juni 1747.

The 1754 proposal advocated the indenturing to the merchant marine of all youths being raised with the financial support of public or religious charitable institutions. Thereby two problems could be solved simultaneously: (1) the costs imposed by delays to ships and by the need to pay bonuses as a result of labor shortages, and (2) the cycle of poverty in which the unemployed poor existed. The report went on to argue that the cruelty of the proposal to the poor was more than compensated for by the removal of an even greater cruelty now imposed on the citizens, who must support

> a multitude of the poor . . . of which the bulk are lazy idlers and drunkards, who are satisfied to place their fate with the diaconate, and who raise their children to such crafts that, when these reach their majority, most are unable to support themselves, and devolve again to the support of the diaconate as soon as they marry and beget children. In this way diaconal support continues for many from father to children to grandchildren.[6]

The Admiralties rejected this proposal, but its description of an "underclass" is only an early example of a stereotype that flourished throughout the following century. As with most stereotypes, it reduces its subject to a caricature, but there can be little doubt that the late eighteenth century witnessed the growth of a large class of paupers and that this group stood more exposed than before to the ravages of extreme poverty. After 1770 the mortality rate of Amsterdam – the city most severely affected by these developments – began to rise in years of high bread prices (something not observed since the sixteenth century), and the number of abandoned infants grew spectacularly: from 20 per year in the 1760s, to 386 in the 1790s, and 605 in the 1810s. And still – to the puzzlement of contemporaries and historians alike – the deepening poverty did nothing to make volunteers for the navy and VOC more plentiful. During the crisis of 1780–1, the Admiralties found that even the enforced idleness of the entire merchant marine (due to British blockades) did not suffice to direct the unemployed to naval service without the enticement of large signing bonuses. By 1803 the reformer Rutger Metelerkamp felt the need to turn to physiology and morality to account for the otherwise inexplicable character of the economy: the new flaccid diet of the poor and the moral decay brought on by two centuries of comfortable prosperity, he argued, had combined to oppress the Batavian nation with "drowsy indifference, despondency, [and] apathy. . . ."[7] This, to a fervent Patriot, was the embarrassing consequence of riches.

---

[6] "eene meenigte armen . . . waar van de grootste hoop luye lediggangers en dronkaerts zijn, die genoegzaam het alles op de diaconie laaten aankomen, en vervolgens haare kinderen tot zulke handwerken opbrengen, datze tot haare Jaaren gekoomen zijnde, genoegzaam haar onderhoud niet winnen konnen, en wanneer ze dan komen te trouwen en kinderen te verwekken; ten eersten weder aan de diaconie vervallen, waar door verscheide van vader tot kinderen en kindskinderen aan de diaconie verblijven." A. R. A. Den Haag, Admiraliteits Colleges, No. 72, Verzameling v.d. Heim.

[7] "slaperige onverschilligheid, moedeloosheid, [en] *apathie* . . . ." Metelerkamp, *Toestand*, p. 45.

The eighteenth-century Dutch labor market exhibited several strikingly modern features: high wages, probably the highest in Europe, together with substantial unemployment and, at the same time, seasonal labor shortages and a dependence on migrant labor from a neighboring society with a much lower standard of living. These features arose in an institutional setting that lacked the features usually associated with such labor market distortions: unemployment insurance, minimum wage legislation, and union organization. But if we recognize that unemployment occurred in the context of a household economy where trading, public relief, self-provision, and labor – legal and illegal – all played some role, then the provision of poor relief could be very influential, not so much because of its size as because of its strategic place in an economy of makeshifts.

At any rate, contemporary observers did not doubt the importance of poor relief as a factor in determining labor market behavior. As urban unemployment assumed hitherto unknown dimensions, and the rising cost of living exposed ever larger segments of the population to severe deprivation, the belief spread that the labor force and the economy were mismatched; the labor market practices of an earlier era had lived on beyond their time, supporting types of labor for which there was no demand, and failing to train the workers that could participate in a new era of growth.

The Netherlands remained rich long after it had ceased being prosperous. The question that preoccupied reformers was how a rich society should address its poverty in order to restore prosperity. They looked to the poor-relief agencies – where a goodly share of that wealth had been lodged by generations of public-spirited benefactors – as a chief mechanism for the reform (or restoration) of the economy as a whole.

12.6 Income redistribution

In the Netherlands, as everywhere else in pre–Reformation Europe, the relief of poverty was the responsibility of the Church. Under its direction the imperative to practice Christian charity had, over the centuries, channeled considerable resources into the hands of parish churches, abbeys, religious orders, lay brotherhoods, and other bodies. The income from the endowments under their control, supplemented by current gifts, went to the support of indigents and, of course, to the support of the numerous clergy and their religious observances.

A common complaint leveled by contemporaries against this complex of charitable initiatives – again, not only in the Netherlands – was the indiscriminate character of much almsgiving and the haphazard way in which the needs of the poor were addressed. The souls of the givers had a more prominent place in these arrangements than did the needs of the recipients. Thus, the rich Abby of Leeuwenhorst, in Noordwijkerhout, directed much of its giving to distributions of cash, herring, and white bread (all symbols of luxury) each year on White Thursday, the anniversary of the order's founding. Through the fifteenth century, 300 to 500 persons annually made the trip to the abbey to receive these benefits. After 1520 the numbers usually exceeded 1,000 and could reach 4,000. In view of the size of the local population, many of those lining up before the abbey gates must have come from Leiden or Haarlem, both of which were a long day's walk from the abbey. Of what real benefit could this charitable gesture have been to the recipients?

In the economically depressed industrial cities of the early sixteenth-century Habsburg Netherlands, the inability of the numerous charitable agencies to address effectively the distress of the urban population led to proposals to merge all endowments, foundations, and so on into a common fund, and to place this fund under the direction of city magistrates rather than the clergy. The Flemish towns of Ieper and Brugge, followed by Lille, adopted the common fund in the 1520s, and in 1531 Emperor Charles V decreed that the centralization of parochial charity should occur everywhere. With a common fund, the poor could expect more efficient support; in return, they had to be registered with the city and wear an identifying badge. At the same time, begging was to be prohibited and vagabonds barred from entering the cities. These provisions clearly sought to redirect the charitable resources of society to the specific problems of the urban proletariat. Henceforth, charity would be neither indiscriminate nor haphazard. The common fund met with the determined and effective resistance of the Church and was fully implemented nowhere in the Northern Netherlands on the eve of the Revolt.

The leading role of the Church in matters of charity did not remove secular government from this field altogether. If day-to-day almsgiving was a religious prerogative, intervention in times of food shortages was clearly a task for the civil authorities. Throughout the sixteenth century, when food shortages threatened, the cities required their rich citizens to lay up private stores of grain for possible regulated sale during the crisis. They also suspended brewing activities (to conserve grain), prohibited banquets and conspicuous consumption, and authorized religious processions to pray for intercession. Meanwhile, the provincial states and/or the Habsburg government at Brussels acted to regulate the trade in grain by issuing passports (as in 1552) or prohibiting food exports (in 1565 and 1574).

All of these typically medieval food supply measures met with increasing resistance from the trading cities, especially those in Holland, the center of the grain trade. On the eve of the Revolt, neither the charitable practices of the Church nor the trade-restricting provisioning policies of the state answered to the needs of the economy. One did not need to embrace Protestant teaching to be convinced of the case for reform – that case had been made by Catholics and supported by the Emperor – but it remained for the Revolt and the ascendancy of Calvinism actually to bring major changes to poor-relief and food-crisis management.

Beginning in 1574 each province and city that joined the Revolt against Spanish rule expropriated Church property. Following Calvinist practice, each parish was now governed by a consistory (church council) and possessed a board of deacons responsible for poor relief. Monastic and other nonparish assets fell to the provinces and cities, which administered them *ad pios usus* (i.e., for religious, educational, and charitable purposes). The Reformed church proved to be a rather leaner operation than the Roman Catholic church had been, and the funds available for pious purposes other than the maintenance of clergy rose substantially. The first decades after the expropriation in particular witnessed the opening and expansion of schools, orphanages, hospitals, and homes for the elderly.

In this rationalization process, the cities asserted their authority over poor relief, but in practice responsibility for charitable activity lodged, in the first instance, with the church deacons. At first, the Reformed church, as successor to the Roman Catholic church, defined its responsibilities broadly, to entail assistance to nearly all Christians. In many rural areas, this long remained so, but in the course of the first half of the seventeenth century, especially in the cities, a combination of large-scale immigration and the more orthodox self-definition of the Reformed church caused every religious denomination to establish its own diaconate and to support orphanages and homes for the elderly. In the extreme case of Amsterdam, parallel poor-relief agencies existed for the Reformed, Remonstrants, Walloon Reformed, Roman Catholics, Anabaptists, Lutherans, and Sephardi and Ashkenazi Jews. To some extent this structure arose out of fear that the Reformed church would attract converts by virtue of its superior charitable resources. But its longevity – this structure endured into the twentieth century – reflects the widespread belief that each denomination formed a natural affinity group, a "nation" within the state, that had as a primary responsibility the caring for its own.

The activities of the deacons' boards were supported by the income of their invested assets (real property and, increasingly, public bonds), bequests, ongoing collections, and appeals. Obviously, not all church congregations were equally well endowed, nor did the claims made on their support necessarily correspond with their abilities to respond. The deacons' boards did not all provide the same services, but a certain measure of uniformity was secured by their obligation to report to the civil authorities. A change in diaconal policy required the approval of the burgemeesters, and deacons could, when pressed, request supplemental funds from the municipality to discharge their responsibilities. The reluctance of some deacons' boards to acknowledge their subordination to civil authorities did not change the fact that they were fitted into a structure of charity and relief in which the municipalities had ultimate responsibility.

The structure of church poor relief was elaborate, but it was hardly comprehensive, and the cities all established similar public poor-relief institutions to supplement church-based charity. Hospitals, orphanages, and outdoor relief agencies, supported principally by tax revenues and municipal fees, offered support to the more marginal members of society such as recent arrivals and noncommunicant adherents of a church. Other municipal institutions catered to the best-established residents, the burgers. Orphanages restricted to the surviving children of those possessing burger privileges stood at the social pinnacle of the institutions that dispensed charity in the Republic's towns, which came to include hospitals and orphanages, homes for the elderly, workhouses and houses of detention for beggars and criminals, and the outdoor relief provided by the church deacons and the municipal organizations called *aalmoezeniers* and *huiszittenarmen*.

Income transfers to support those without earning power occur in most societies at three levels: the family, the church, and the state. In the Dutch Republic, the family played a more restricted role than in most preindustrial societies because of its nuclear structure, advanced urbanization, and high mobility. All of these factors diminished the role of clanlike support structures and attendant patronage practices. The many privately financed pensioners courts (*hofjes*) and foundations were often intended to assist family retainers and relations, but the characteristic form in which individuals and families sought protection from uncertainty and support in dependency was insurance. Besides the life annuities of the well-to-do (discussed in Chapter 4), there were guild funds (*gildebossen*) for craftsmen and sailors funds (*matrosenbossen* and *zeevarende buidels*) for merchant seamen. These small-group insurance schemes, financed by member contributions, provided unemployment, illness, and widow's benefits to the participants and their survivors. Little is known about the operation of these funds, or about Dutch guilds in general, but fragmentary evidence from Amsterdam guild funds suggests that they may have distributed some 200,000 guilders per year to several thousand members and their survivors in the eighteenth century.

It is precisely the modest scope of informal, family-based income redistribution practices that gave church and public charity its prominent place in Dutch society. Perhaps it also helps to explain the public willingness to finance charitable institutions with bequests and gifts. But this justly celebrated system was notably stronger in its support of persons not active in the labor force – children, the elderly, the sick – than of labor-force participants who suffered unemployment or insufficient income.

This is not surprising; the moral claims of weak and dependent persons were straightforward, the economic resources necessary to their support were relatively predictable, and the danger of abuse of the support offered was minimal since most recipients were institutionalized. The support of labor market participants, on the other hand, was understood to involve moral hazards, the scope of the economic commitment was unpredictable, and the danger of fraud and misuse was ever present. Moreover, providers of charitable support needed to consider not only the moral consequences of their action on the recipients but also the economic consequences for the labor market.

The protection of the poor in times of food scarcity and high prices had a long tradition, of course, and had always been a public responsibility. The chief cities maintained inventories of grain in anticipation of shortage. Amsterdam acquired four warehouses for this purpose, even though the whole city functioned as a giant granary for western Europe. In periods of distress, the cities sold the grain in storage to the bakers at "below-market" prices, and the bakers, in turn, sold bread at correspondingly low prices. The beneficiaries of this policy varied. In the case of Amsterdam, the city-subsidized bread was first available to everyone. The same was true in cities that did not distribute cheap grain but that simply forced down the official bread price (the *broodzetting*) and compensated the bakers directly. By 1623 Amsterdam sought to target its subsidies specifically to those without means. Captains of the civic guard in each ward were instructed to identify those necessitous persons qualifying for the cheap bread. By the crisis of 1662, the city had established a system of *buurtmeesters*, each charged with the oversight of a city ward. They distributed bread coupons to residents deemed eligible. This gave the poor cheap bread, while the bakers got the difference between the market and subsidized price from the city upon presentation of the coupons. This system was used throughout the eighteenth century and worked well as long as the years of extraordinarily high food prices were few and the population requiring assistance not enormous. The problem of large-scale, socially destabilizing dearth did not strike the Dutch Republic with anything like the severity that it affected France and central Europe. The presence of the international grain trade generally dampened the amplitude of grain price fluctuations, while the efficient interregional transportation system reduced the danger of local shortages. In general, the broad-based Dutch diet and the financial means to maintain food inventories enabled the Republic to escape the full force of Europe's recurrent *crises de subsistance*.

The years of pressing scarcity, which had been numerous in the 1565–88 era, occurred only at distant intervals for the next two centuries. Municipal intervention in the price or distribution of bread occurred in many cities in 1597–9, 1623, 1630, 1662, and 1697. In the eighteenth century, the crisis years were 1709, 1714–15, 1740–1, 1757, and 1771–3. Beginning in 1788 the crisis years again became much more frequent, placing new pressures on the Republic's relief arrangements. In this long preceding era of relatively infrequent scarcity, the crisis intervention measures favored in the Netherlands differed from other countries in their generally modest invasiveness (targeting only the poorest consumers, leaving the grain trade free of restrictions) and their decentralized administration.

But the truly striking difference between the relief measures of the Republic and other European countries resided not so much in periodic crisis intervention as in the ongoing support offered by the Republic's deacons' boards and municipal poor-relief agencies to the working poor and the cyclically and seasonally unemployed. The chief focus of poor relief in the Republic was not on the provision of bread in crisis years but on the distribution of bread, peat, and cash to eligible applicants on an ongoing basis. Poor relief played a structural role in the regulation of urban (and some rural) economies and was linked to a prohibition on begging and the maintenance of *tuchthuizen*, punitive workhouses for criminals, including convicted beggars.

Outdoor relief had a strongly seasonal character: In Amsterdam as many as 10 to 12 percent of all households received at least temporary support during the winter months, but in the summer the number supported always fell sharply. This support clearly had the character of an "income supplement"; it was designed to reduce poverty more than to target the problem of unemployment. Through most of the first half of the seventeenth century, it was not difficult to qualify for assistance. As we already noted, the Reformed deacons' boards denied few applicants. In Amsterdam any baptized resident in need could apply, and by 1613 municipal *Aalmoezeniers* stood ready to supplement the work of the deacons. This policy may have reflected a belief that few honest laborers would become permanent charges in a growing economy, while the vigorous prosecution of beggars, thieves, and other truly dangerous folk (for whom in 1595 Amsterdam established its *Rasphuis* for men and *Spinhuis* for women) would weed out the unworthy.

After 1650 the access to poor relief became much more restricted, although the numbers receiving support – in Amsterdam at any rate – do not seem to have declined. In 1652 Amsterdam was divided into wards, each provided with a *buurt-meester*, whose task it was to keep track of the residents in his district. Residents seeking assistance had to apply to the *buurtmeester* first, who assessed the merits of their claim and recommended them to the appropriate church or public agency. In these same years, the church deacons became more restrictive in offering support. In the case of the Reformed diaconate, only professing members of at least two years residence were eligible; by 1701 the residence requirement became four years; later it was lengthened to six. Despite this, the expenditures of the Reformed diaconate rose relentlessly, from 40,000 guilders per year around 1600 to 240,000 in 1645–9, to over 300,000 in the 1670s, and to nearly 500,000 in the 1750s.

Not only the churches but also the municipal authorities lost their enthusiasm for supporting poor migrants. The decisive step came in 1682, when the States of Holland ruled that each city and village was responsible for the support of its poor. The States further provided that communities could refuse admission to migrants who could not provide an "act of indemnity," certifying that the migrant's home community would indemnify the host community if he or she should become a public charge within three years. This new obstacle to migration both confirmed and strengthened the transition from a fluid to a segmented labor market. With the demand for labor less pressing than before, the poor-relief system focused more on taking care of its own. The earlier intolerance of public begging also lessened, perhaps because under the new circumstances, beggars were less likely to be outsiders. In Amsterdam nearly 90 percent of the 320 beggars arrested in an average year before 1700 had been born elsewhere; in the period 1700–60, over half the arrested beggars (averaging 120 per year) had been born in Amsterdam. In the much smaller city of Delft, 20 beggars per year were arrested in the prosperous period 1625–50; in the entire period 1675–1800, the city prosecuted only 17 beggars.

In this newly migrant-resistant environment, Amsterdam stood out as an exception. Alone among Dutch cities, it did not require "acts of indemnity." Just as the VOC functioned as an employer of last resort, so did Amsterdam stand ready to receive migrants of all types. As its church charities restricted their activities to permanent residents, municipal poor relief came to play an increasingly prominent role in Amsterdam, and the city's population came to differ in character from most other cities.

The Republic's charitable and poor-relief institutions assumed a form by the third quarter of the seventeenth century that persisted, with few changes, beyond its demise into the nineteenth century. The numerous church and public agencies hardly formed a coordinated system (2,855 poor-relief agencies and 403 institutions that housed the poor and orphaned were counted in 1829), but one gains the impression that supply and demand were reasonably well balanced and that the outdoor relief provided corresponded to the expectations of both providers and recipients.

How much income was transferred to the poor, unemployed, and dependent persons in the care of these institutions? Given the decentralized nature of the poor-relief system and its multiple sources of financing, no firm answer can be given. The few scraps of evidence we have refer to the late eighteenth and early nineteenth centuries, when demands were greater and means often much reduced from earlier decades. We know that expenditures on poor relief stood at 3.5 million guilders in 1829, while institutional expenditures (for orphanages, workhouses, etc.) amounted to 1.5 million in 1815. But these figures both date from after the government bond default of 1811 (the *tiërcering*). Since the endowments of these charitable bodies are known to have generated 1.3 million guilders in income annually after 1815 (when two-thirds of the bonds remained in default), it is not impossible that the assets under the control of charitable institutions at the end of the old Republic possessed a face value approaching 100 million guilders. All in all, we should think of charitable expenditures before the *tiërcering* as closer to 10 than to 5 million guilders.

Eight to ten million guilders is no trivial sum; it represents 3 to 4 percent of the mid–eighteenth-century national income that we estimate in Chapter 13. Moreover, these expenditures were concentrated in the maritime provinces of the Republic and, even more, in that region's cities. Still, per-household expenditures of 15 to 20 guilders hardly constitute income redistribution in the contemporary sense of that word. No policy of reducing the inequality of income distribution via systematic redistribution existed in the Netherlands, but the multitude of local institutions did provide an early form of "safety net," sufficient to mitigate the most conspicuous forms of need.

The exceptional character of Dutch social policy is not to be found in the size of the payments but in the size of the population deemed eligible for support and in the structural character of care giving. It is the steadiness of charitable expenditure, based on endowments of real property and government bonds plus earmarked taxes and fees, that distinguished Dutch practice from other countries, where most financing was short-term, triggered by emergency conditions. Every year the 10,000 to 15,000 children housed in the Republic's orphanages required the expenditure of well over 1 million guilders; every year the city of Amsterdam spent 400,000 to 500,000 guilders of its tax revenue to support those in need, while private endowments, church collections, and bequests generated as much again. Amsterdam was no typical city (in 1810 it cared for a quarter of all the orphans in the country), but when the expenditures of the other communities are added, it should be clear that charitable institutions functioned as a significant, stabilizing element in the urban economies of the Republic.

After 1770 the balance that had existed between providers and recipients, between supply and demand, was lost. The poorest workers came to face a labor market and a cost of living that the poor-relief system could not satisfactorily ameliorate; meanwhile, among the elites, which had long taken considerable pride in the institutions that testified publicly to their compassion and munificence, some began to question the impact of poor-relief policies on both the moral fiber of the recipients and the working of the labor market.

The poor-relief policies of diaconates and municipalities alike were not so much designed to *support the unemployed* as to *supplement the incomes of those in need* – those without work, of course, but also those with large families, with sick family members, and those headed by widows. The system was designed to deal with regular seasonal fluctuations in demand but not with long-lasting increases or sharp, structural crises. For this the sources of income were far too inelastic.

As problems mounted, the deacons' boards appealed more frequently to the town magistrates for subsidy, and both secular and religious relief bodies resorted with growing regularity to door-to-door solicitations, appealing more insistently to the Christian virtues of charity and brotherly love. But none of this could prevent the emergence of periodic crises that, for the first time since before the 1570s, assumed some of the characteristics long typical of the rest of Europe, where high prices forced a postponement of marriages, pushed death rates up, and sent local craft and industrial production into depression: The *crise de subsistence* reappeared in the Netherlands. The combination of more severe crises, growing structural unemployment, and what contemporaries saw as an autonomous "culture of poverty" spurred critics to propose a redeployment of poor-relief funds from simple material support to interventionist measures designed to lift the poor from their fallen state.

The suspicious eye cast by late eighteenth-century reformers on the poor-relief agencies usually seems mean-spirited to the modern historian. Could the relief offered to able-bodied adult males really have been sufficient to influence their willingness to accept low-wage employment? The benefits given by the chief

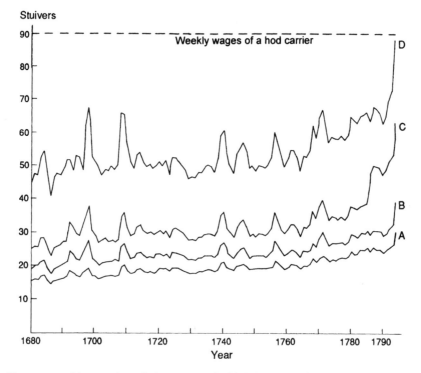

Figure 12.15. Money value of winter poor-relief distributions of the Oudezijds Huiszitten-huis, in stuivers per week, 1681–1795. A, household without children; B, with two children; C, with four children; D, with six children. [*Source:* Marco van Leeuwen, Jan Schoenmakers, and Frans Smits, *Armoede en bedeling in Amsterdam ten tijde van de Republiek* (unpublished report, Historische Seminarium, Universiteit van Amsterdam, 1981.)]

Amsterdam public-relief agencies were mainly in kind; consequently, their monetary value rose in years of high prices. Still, when we compute the total value of winter relief offered to Amsterdam families of varying sizes (see Figure 12.15), insinuations of laziness (or, in the antiseptic terms of economics, a high "reservation wage") seem beyond belief: Until the 1760s a family with four children could rarely expect to receive from poor relief more than one-third of the weekly earnings of an unskilled worker, and that only in the winter months.

But after 1770 the value of relief distributions rose while the purchasing power of wages fell, and it was then when the loudest complaints of "voluntary leisure" were voiced. Moreover, receipt of these payments did not require that all, or any, family members be unemployed; nor did it always preclude the recipients' application to one of the numerous religious charities. As one part of a household survival strategy, these relief payments may have given the recipients an important "degree of freedom" with which to choose which employment to accept, and where.

If the Republic's charitable institutions had come to constitute a moral hazard, reinforcing a culture of poverty, how could their policies be reformed to contribute to economic and social renewal? Perhaps a greater reliance on indoor, institutionalized relief could overcome the drawbacks of outdoor relief. The Republic's penal system had acquired an international reputation in the seventeenth century for its progressive, "therapeutic" approach to punishment. Amsterdam's *Rasphuis*, where male inmates worked at reducing brazilwood to a powdered dyestuff, and its *Spinhuis*, where female inmates spun yarn, were outfitted with visiting galleries to accommodate sightseeing "penal reformers." Besides these penal institutions, there were a few voluntary workhouses (notably, Amsterdam's *Stadszijdewindhuis*, a silk-spinning facility established in 1682 to employ idle young women and to relieve a bottleneck in the silk industry).

After 1770 the interest in workhouses intensified. The decline of labor-intensive industries suggested the desirability of using poor-relief funds to subsidize new ventures that would absorb unemployed labor. The growing claims on poor-relief funds suggested work schemes as a device to reduce the cost of supporting the unemployed, since their productive labor would presumably contribute to their own maintenance. Finally, and most importantly in the eyes of many, the provision of employment would (re)accustom the poor to regular work, teach basic skills, enforce norms of decent behavior, restore dignity, and thereby break the "culture of poverty."

Initiatives to establish work places took shape in at least forty cities, large and small, throughout the Republic. Some were organized directly by the churches or the municipalities, others by entrepreneurs who sought subsidies for their own labor-intensive production plans. The work places concentrated on simple production processes – almost all were concerned with the preparation of fibers for textile production – and although participation was voluntary, their establishment usually was coupled with renewed prohibitions in public begging.

Hardly any of these work-creation schemes achieved their objectives. They generated much less income than their backers envisioned, and the workers exhibited little enthusiasm for the beneficial effects of regular, honest employment. Without either efficient management or productive labor, they lasted as long as the municipal or deacons' subsidies lasted. And since they rarely proved cheaper than direct outdoor relief, most of these "social work places" enjoyed but a brief life span.

Municipal workhouses, such as the enormous structure erected by Amsterdam in 1779–82 to house 800 inmates, the Mendicant Institute of The Hague, and the Rotterdam workhouse, established in 1802 to house 700 inmates (both forced and voluntary) emerged from this era of experimentation as permanent additions to the arsenal of poor-relief institutions; but the naïve initiatives to reform the poor and restore public finances via make-work schemes achieved next to nothing.

These schemes are of interest for what they reveal about the economic thinking of the leading citizens of the post-1770 era. First, industrial production organized in factories had no appeal as a profit-making activity. Indeed, the Leiden textile producer J. van Heukelom expressed his concern in 1780 that via mechanization "the factories will lose their advantageous suitability as a means of providing a multitude of persons with work and bread." Factories were useful as a means of occupying the poor – not as a means of getting rich; they attracted "ethical" capital rather than entrepreneurial capital. Second, the innovative economic thinking of the Netherlands from the 1770s through the first half of the nineteenth century was not focused on the wellsprings of "the wealth of nations"; it focused instead on the problem of poverty and its relief. The writings of L. P. van de Spiegel, J. van der Bosch, and J. de Bosch Kemper reveal the problem of mendicancy as a mark of their society's wealth rather than its poverty. Correspondingly, they had little to say about stimulating economic growth, but much to say about reforming poor relief to restore economic and social health.

Through these decades of economic crisis and enlightened proposals for reform, the poor-relief institutions persevered very largely unchanged. The Batavian revolutionaries envisioned a centralized poor-relief system under state control in their 1801 poor law (reminiscent of Charles V's decree of 1531), but the opposition of the churches and the course of political events stymied its implementation. National supplementary financing sometimes came to the aid of the beleaguered municipalities, but this assistance was more than undone by the effects of the *tiërcering* of 1811, whereby two-thirds of the public debt was effectively repudiated, reducing sharply the incomes of every sort of religious and private charity. Still, most of them muddled through. The orphans got less meat, and the aged, less butter; the poor got potatoes instead of bread. The foundlings were sent to the (cheaper) countryside, and, after 1817, so were many of the urban poor. If the charitable institutions were the dikes intended to hold together the fabric of Dutch society, then one can say, as did Simon Schama in his study of the Batavian and French era, that "by whatever miracle, the dikes did *not* break."[8] Generations of Republican prosperity had ensured that these charitable barriers were sturdy. The crisis of the 1795–1815 period weakened them severely, but they weathered the storm, living on in their old form until 1854. Even the new poor law of that year did not abolish the essentially church-based, municipally organized character of Dutch poor relief. The dikes held, just barely, for the poor. But they also held, just barely, for the privileged. For decades after the fall of the old Republic, its legacy of labor market segmentation, poor-relief practices, and entrenched rentier and commercial economic interests persisted in a symbiotic relationship that posed a formidable obstacle to the new economic initiatives needed to restart modern economic growth in the nineteenth century.

---

[8] Simon Schama, *Patriots and Liberators* (New York, 1977), p. 654.

Chapter 13
The course of the economy:
A macroeconomic analysis

How did the Dutch economy, taken as a whole, function over the period 1500–1815? What were the driving forces behind its spectacular growth? What stood in the way of its later development? Is it possible (and if so, is it sensible) to measure the chief dimensions of this economy's development through the early modern period? Answers to these "big" questions have been implied in the preceding chapters on structural characteristics and sectoral developments, but here we attempt to tie together the various strands of our analysis to address key issues of the overall development of the Dutch economy. We begin with a succinct presentation of salient features of the economy in each of five periods into which we propose to organize Dutch economic history. We turn then to an assessment of the strengths and weaknesses of three alternative approaches to understanding the dynamics that connect these periods, and we conclude with a quantitative portrait of Europe's first modern economy.

13.1. Phases of economic development

13.1.1. BEFORE THE REVOLT

The vitality of Holland's economy in the two centuries preceding the Revolt derived from an historic conjuncture of two forces. Internally, the ecological processes described in Chapter 2 stimulated a transformation of the rural economy that forced thousands of persons from the land and into the towns. At a time in which most of Europe continued to suffer from postplague labor shortages, the maritime zones of the northern Netherlands featured an elastic supply of labor for nonagricultural employments. Externally, the international economy generated new and growing markets in which this region could be a viable competitor. The emergence of Antwerp as a center of northern trade, as well as the demographic revival of Europe, transmitted price and market signals that called for a response. It was in no sense inevitable that the lion's share of these new opportunities in agriculture, trade, and industry would be captured by the Northern Netherlands; the convergence of domestic supply and international demand owed something to the geographic setting of the region and its natural endowments, but it owed much more to a sequence of technological and organizational responses capable of increasing the value of its land and labor.

Holland's "medieval legacy" was not a complex of feudal institutions ensconcing nobles and clerics in positions of perpetual privilege. Its remoteness from the centers of Roman and Carolingian power, as well as its marginal agricultural value and late colonization, provided a setting in which feudal principles were modified or remained unimplemented while new, practical institutional solutions were sought to address the challenges of land drainage and colonization. The imposing problems of deteriorating drainage and increased threats of inundation came to be addressed by institutions in which private, contractual agreements could be formed with relative ease and in which public goods could be provided in a rational manner.

The incentive to invest in public goods (such as new polders, improved drainage, navigable waterways) – to use Holland's institutions for "proactive" rather than only "reactive" purposes – depended on the new opportunities emanating from the Antwerp market and the larger international economy in the century after 1450. As these emerged, the labor that found inadequate support in agriculture quickly responded by shifting to fishing, ocean shipping, and urban industries. And most important, in the region's flexible institutional environment, the Hollanders applied to their new opportunities a sequence of technical improvements that gradually changed the character of the northern European economy. The technique of cleaning and salting herring on board fishing vessels on the open sea revolutionized the international fishing industry; the mastery of the construction and sailing of the fully rigged *carveel* type ship transformed the organization of shipping along the Atlantic and North Sea coasts from Seville to the Baltic; the development of dikes, drainage windmills, and sluices laid the basis for an effective specialization of agriculture in the maritime zones of the Netherlands.

The economic expansion of the century preceding the Revolt cannot adequately be rendered in quantitative terms. The evidence for rising labor productivity in fishing and ocean shipping and for rising land productivity in agriculture is countered by the knowledge that the late fifteenth-century political crisis, the sixteenth-century crisis of urban industry (especially textiles and brewing), and the rapid growth of population, all depressed earnings in many sectors. The growing supply of laborers available for a broad range of seasonal employments met with a declining real wage in the period 1500–75. This the laborers had in common with their counterparts in all European countries. What is less than obvious is how real annual *earnings* evolved over this period. The very high real wages around 1500 may not have translated into correspondingly high earnings for urban workers under the unsettled political conditions of the times. Likewise, we suspect that the commercialized but unspecialized economy of many rural districts suffered from substantial underemployment. By the 1560s, investment in more productive farm capital and the expanding trading sector probably compensated, through reduced underemployment, for the falling purchasing power of daily wages. But in the next decade of political crisis, nothing could compensate for the further deterioration of real wages. Earnings in all sectors plunged.

None of the economy's leading sectors came to international prominence as the result of large domestic concentrations of capital, or of large infusions from outside. Right up to the eve of the Revolt, no individual merchants or industrialists cut much of a figure beside their chief international rivals. The richest Netherlanders remained noble landowners and officeholders (such as the Prince of Orange) who also held important assets outside the region. The richest urban burgers remained the brewers. The economic strength of the Northern Netherlands resided in its broadly based productivity, which lent profitability to a considerable range of activities in many cities and, especially, in the countryside and smaller towns.

The fruitful interaction of domestic supply with international demand is also useful in understanding the economic consequences of the Dutch Revolt against Philip II, the Habsburg Empire, and the Roman Catholic church. This break with the Imperial regime, whose far-flung economic system had buoyed important elements of the Northern Netherlands' economy, was a large and contentious gamble. But the political economy of the Habsburg Empire also imposed important costs and constraints, and by the end of the 1550s, it was no secret that neither the Habsburg fiscal system nor the Antwerp market were functioning with the vitality that they had earlier exhibited. Thus, the Revolt that pushed both of these defining features of Habsburg political economy into crisis contributed to a fateful decentering of the international economy.

Then as now, the international economy had a strong need for a single, dominant center. Today that center is expected to coordinate financial and information flows and be the seat of decision making. In the sixteenth century, it performed these functions in the context of a concrete market where irregular supplies of goods were stockpiled and held in inventories to accommodate the more regular demand for these goods in their final markets. This essential entrepôt, or *stapelmarkt,* function could not, given the prevailing high costs of gathering information and the thin markets for many goods, easily be shared by numerous rival centers. The advantages to consolidation were great. Thus, when her merchant communities scattered from Hamburg to Seville and from London to Frankfurt, Antwerp ceased to perform this role, and a succession struggle among commercial cities was triggered.

The claims of commercial centers in the Northern Netherlands to assume this

667

mantle have not always appeared strong to historians. Correspondingly, the emergence of Amsterdam as Antwerp's successor has usually been explained in political terms. The closing of the Schelde, it is often argued, sealed the fate of Antwerp and "forced" its merchants to move to the North. Once the grand merchants, possessed of ample trading capital and international contacts in the trade of valuable precocities, resettled, they refashioned Amsterdam from a regional seat of routine and prosaic bulk trades into the fabulous emporium of the world.

In our view this approach confuses the chronology of development and fails to recognize the important differences between the character of the old Antwerp and the new Amsterdam entrepôts. Antwerp lost important elements of its trade beginning in the 1550s, and the "closing of the Schelde" in 1585 did not in fact seal the city off from the international economy. Or better put, the added costs to trading with Antwerp after 1585 came as much from the policies of the Spanish Netherlands as they did from the new fees imposed by the Republic. The spectacular events of 1585 tend to blind us to the longer-term factors at work that undermined Antwerp's ability to perform the entrepôt functions in a changing international economy.

That changing international economy, whose growing population and new intercontinental scope greatly increased the volume of trade, was drawn to the Northern Netherlands ports, and ultimately to Amsterdam, by the characteristics that had earlier given those ports command of the bulk trades of the Baltic and North seas: elastic supplies of shipping, low transactions costs, and efficient markets. Once an effective political autonomy had secured the protection of commercial interests, these basic characteristics of northern commerce could be elaborated and institutionalized – indeed, under unrelenting Spanish pressure, *had* to be elaborated with daring and panache – to make the new Republic a suitable haven for merchants from all over Europe. The arrival of grand merchants, rich in capital and special knowledge, added an important dimension to the economic life of the fledgling Republic, but most of them came when things were ready for them, rather like the frosting on a cake.

The "recentering" of the international economy at Amsterdam occurred because its past specialization and its new political autonomy equipped it better than its rivals to meet the changing needs of the market. In a brief "window of opportunity," the institutions, technologies, and specializations that had long marked the Northern Netherlands as peculiar, now came to define its modernity.

13.1.2. THE GOLDEN AGE ECONOMY

In 1578 Amsterdam embraced the rebel cause, and in the following decade the new Republic achieved its *de facto* existence. From then until the third quarter of the seventeenth century, this new state grew quickly in strength, dominated the economy of Europe, and constructed a trading empire that spanned much of the world. This was its Golden Age. At the beginning of his celebrated essay,

"Dutch civilization in the seventeenth century," Johan Huizinga poses the question: "Where else was there a civilization that reached its greatest peak so soon after state and nation came into being?"[1] This question can be asked with equal justice of its economic achievements. By way of answer, we have just emphasized the special character of its pre–Revolt economy and of the unique international opportunities that appeared in the final decades of the sixteenth century. But the manner in which those opportunities were seized remains remarkable. To do them justice, it makes sense to divide this Golden Age into two parts, for the dynamics of the economy's growth differed in important ways between the early decades of creative development and the period that followed.

1580–1621

The explosive growth of Dutch trade described in Chapter 9, which extended the established trade routes connecting Iberia with the Baltic to the Mediterranean, the White Sea, and ultimately to Asia, Africa, and the Western Hemisphere, multiplied and enriched the flows of commodities that reached the ports of Holland and Zeeland. Driving this extension and entrenchment of Dutch trade was a steadily increasing volume of capital invested in the acquisition, stockpiling, and sale of commodities. The growth of the Republic's trading capital surely outpaced the growth of its trade volume, as merchants increasingly (1) offered credit to suppliers in order to secure favored access to raw materials, and (2) financed the sale of commodities with bills of exchange in order to bind customers to the entrepôt.

Explaining the rapid emergence to primacy in international trade of a region not previously known for its capital abundance has long attracted the attention of historians. Where did the capital come from? As Amsterdam gave clearer signals of becoming the entrepôt of European trade, rich merchants from outside the Republic settled there. The diaspora of Antwerp merchants, and those who quickly gathered together their assets after Parma's reconquest in 1585, certainly injected important sums as they drifted toward Amsterdam. Lists of depositors in the Bank of Amsterdam and investors in the VOC are riddled with the names of merchants of southern origin. The early settlement in the Republic of Iberian "new Christians" must also have brought capital to the entrepôt, although these Jewish traders seem to have been more important for their contacts in the Spanish and Portuguese colonies than for their capital per se.

These injections of outside capital – no one has hazarded a guess as to the sums involved – certainly stimulated the rapid early growth of the Dutch trading system, especially by funding some highly risky new ventures. But the chief explanation for the growing amounts of capital committed to inventories of trade goods is the profitability of trade conducted from the Republic. The reinvestment

[1] Johan Huizinga, *Dutch Civilization in the Seventeenth Century* (London, 1968), p. 11.

of major portions of these profits certainly accounted for most of the new funds expanding year by year the trading capital at the disposal of the Republic's merchants. The plausibility of this explanation is supported by the experience of the VOC, which enlarged its net assets from its initial subscription of 6.4 million guilders in 1602 to over 40 million in 1660 entirely through the retention of profits. Even so, it managed in this same period to distribute 62 million guilders in dividends to its shareholders. The growth of Louis Trip's capital, documented by Peter Klein, offers another example of the profit possibilities of the age. Trip invested his initial capital of 46,000 guilders in 1632 in two family businesses, saw his net assets double in fifteen years, and then saw them grow sixfold in the following decade. By the early 1660s, his assets exceeded 600,000 guilders, and they could readily grow further, for he then consumed no more than 10 percent of his enormous annual income. Finally, we should recall the reluctance of wealth holders to invest in government bonds in the years prior to the truce of 1609. By that date Holland's bonds could no longer be regarded as a risky investment, and yet interest rates of 8.3 percent still proved incapable of attracting the capital of economically active persons without guarantees of ready liquidity.

The desired stock of trading capital grew as a result of rising international demand for the goods stockpiled at the Amsterdam entrepôt. But as it grew, the institutions of the commercial economy (the Bank, *Beurs*, notarial system, consular support, money supply) became more efficient; shipping services benefited from the major technological advances represented by the *fluitschip* and mechanized lumber sawing; and merchants became more specialized. Together, these institutional, technological, and organizational improvements reduced transaction costs further than even the bulk trade traditions of the pre–Revolt commercial system had managed to achieve, and this fact drew additional trade and merchants to the Republic.

Besides superior profits, a successful commercial center must offer its merchants the possibility to manage the risks of business. Risk-spreading institutions such as the *partenrederij* and marine insurance helped to manage shipping risks, but limiting exposure to trading losses required the exertion of some measure of control over prices. Peter Klein has argued that the strength of the *stapelmarkt* lay not so much in the efficiency of its competitive markets as in the ability of leading merchants to limit competition, indeed to monopolize supplies of commodities and control prices. Led by the insights of Joseph Schumpeter with respect to entrepreneurial behavior in modern capitalism, Klein reasons that such exercises in market control, far from subverting the *stapelmarkt*, actually strengthened it, since merchants able to limit risk exposure would reinvest more of their monopoly profits in its expansion.

The importance of monopolistic practices among Dutch merchants should not blind us to the fact that the expansion and well-being of the entrepôt also depended on the fleeting nature of most monopolies and benefited from the maintenance of competitive markets for many commodities, especially the important bulk commodities. The merchant community grew sufficiently large that the monopolist practices of some were resisted by others. Even official monopolies such as the VOC and WIC were resisted by Dutch merchants who became prominent investors in rival foreign companies.

The risks of holding inventories in this period were especially great because markets for many goods were thin and volatile. Seeking market control was an understandable impulse. But another risk-reducing feature of the expanding Amsterdam market was the stabilizing influence of the large *domestic* market for many goods. The *stapelmarkt's* primary function, of course, was to import goods and stockpile them for re-export. But the domestic market, either as a final consumer (for grain, timber, raw wool, etc.) or as an intermediate user (raw materials for processing and re-export as finished products) also grew rapidly in this period. The Republic was small, to be sure, but its urban population by 1650 was larger than that of the British Isles and Scandinavia combined, or that of all the German lands. Likewise, the economies of location at the major harbors (for the *trafieken* industries), plus the availability of low-cost fuel for heat-intensive industries, made the Republic a major market in its own right for a wide variety of consumer goods and industrial raw materials. This fact imparted an important measure of stability to the price-forming function of the *stapelmarkt*.

The close connection between the international and domestic markets served by the entrepôt ensured that the explosive growth of the Republic's trading capital after 1580 would lead directly to an increased demand for fixed capital investment. And just as institutional and organizational improvements lowered transaction costs in trade, so technological improvements offered new opportunities for profitable investment in shipbuilding (the aforementioned *fluitschip* and mechanized sawing), in the textile industries (new draperies, mechanized fulling, ribbon frame), and in the *trafieken* (applications of wind power to many industrial processes). The number of technical patents granted by the States General peaked in 1620, at a level never again attained during the life of the Republic (see Figure 8.11).

A credible measurement of the productive capital accumulated in the period 1580–1621 may forever elude us, but its reflection is observable in the rapid growth of the nonagricultural labor force and in its increasing real wages during these four fateful decades. In Chapter 12 we established that natural increase, immigration, urbanization, and the increase in the length of the work year combined to generate a phenomenal 3 percent per annum growth of Holland's effective nonagricultural labor supply over the half-century 1570–1620. In a period when much less rapid rates of population growth sent real wages plummeting all over Europe, the demand for labor in Holland grew even faster, causing nominal wages repeatedly to be increased, so that they outstripped price increases to secure real wages for unskilled laborers 62 percent higher in 1615–19 than in 1575–9. The accelerating demand for capital goods so increased the demand for sawyers' services that their wages rose more rapidly than that of any other manual occupation (until their work was mechanized!), while the general pressure on the labor market allowed unskilled labor to reduce its pay gap with skilled construction labor from 45 percent in the 1560s to 25 percent after 1620.

1621–63

The Golden Age's second phase occurred in a different international environment than had the first. After the commercial crisis of 1618–21, the rate of growth of nearly all European markets decelerated; in many areas it declined absolutely. Moreover, compensation for the stagnation of existing markets by the exploration of new ones offered limited short-term possibilities to the Dutch since their trade routes had already been extended from their core (the "mother trade" between Iberia and the Baltic) to all of maritime Europe and Asia. Only the Western Hemisphere seemed to hold a promise of new markets. In short, the continued growth of Dutch trade now required, more than ever before, direct confrontations with rivals for enlarged market shares in existing markets. The Republic's economy was now swimming against the stream and would, by the 1650s, provoke the active resistance of powerful rivals.

Yet even in this inhospitable environment, the economy achieved significant further growth. The capital accumulated over the period 1580–1621 became an important factor in this phase of economic growth. The steep decline of interest rates (public borrowing rates fell from 8.3 percent as late as 1608 to 4.0 percent in 1655) combined with a growing domestic market to encourage a broad range of domestic investments in infrastructural and agricultural improvements, urban expansion, and further expansions of energy supplies in the form of new peat-producing areas and wind-powered industrial installations. The augmentation of the Republic's trading capital did not cease by any means, but in comparison to the pre-1621 era, this period's growth was pushed forward more by autonomous domestic investments that strengthened the integration of the domestic to the international economy.

The construction of the *trekvaart* network between 1632 and 1667 required an investment of nearly 5 million guilders; the six major polder drainage schemes of North Holland alone absorbed a capital of over 10 million guilders between 1608 and 1640; and the many hundreds of industrial windmills built in this period (at least 400 in the Zaan region alone) represented a commitment of fixed capital that could easily have exceeded 10 million guilders. And we have yet to consider the largest destination for new capital in this period, urban expansion and real property. The total urban population of the Northern Netherlands was nearly doubled in the century after 1580, and most of the major urban expansion and new residential construction to accommodate the nearly 400,000 new urbanites took place after 1610. Until then the cities absorbed the newcomers chiefly by packing them more densely within their old city walls. The new city extensions (Amsterdam's famous "girdle" of canals was begun in 1615; Leiden's successive expansions were begun in 1611, 1644, and 1658), strengthened city fortifications, harbor improvements, and proud new civic structures, all absorbed vast amounts of capital. It was not otherwise in the countryside, where the new, larger farm buildings that spread across the maritime provinces constituted a veritable rebuilding of the rural economy. By the end of the 1640s, the inflow of capital to the real property markets began to assume speculative proportions.

In these two broad phases, the Republican economy achieved by the 1650s a classic harmony among its trading, industrial, agricultural, and fishing sectors, their interrelations cemented by productivity-enhancing investments in each sector. The carrying capacity of the ocean shipping fleet had grown at an average annual rate of 1 percent for a century while its productivity had been enhanced by improved ship designs. The total volume of agricultural output per worker had increased by perhaps 80 percent since the early sixteenth century, as an increased trade orientation had permitted an intensified pursuit of comparative advantage via specialization. No comprehensive measure of industrial growth in this period is yet possible, but the numerous examples of technological improvement, capital investment, and energy intensiveness support the view that output and labor productivity increased substantially. At mid-century the *stapelmarkt* was firmly embedded in a specialized domestic economy equipped with a large stock of capital embodying the most advanced technology of its time. The overall productivity of labor was reflected in the wage level, which was then the highest in Europe. The chief weaknesses of this economy were (1) its incomplete incorporation of the inland provinces, and (2) the limitations to regional trade enforced by the high tariff walls that had arisen between the Northern and Southern Netherlands, as well as by the political crisis of the German lands to the East.

13.1.3. CRISIS AND RESPONSE: 1663–1714

We have had numerous occasions in this volume to call attention to the profound consequences for the Dutch economy of the reversal of the "secular trend" that set in toward the end of the third quarter of the seventeenth century. Historians who doubt the value of such a concept, preferring a history of political events, rarely dispute the seriousness of the crisis itself. The three naval wars with England and, especially, the 1672 French invasion, disrupted Dutch trade profoundly, while the tightening noose of mercantilist restrictions by the Republic's trading partners forced major adjustments in all sectors of the economy. But the enduring impact of these events, in our view, derives from their occurrence in a new economic environment defined by the long-term reversal of prices (hence, the year 1663 marking the onset of this new period) and the related cessation of population growth. In this section it is our task to (1) explain the serious economic problems that brought the Golden Age to a close, and (2) identify the ways in which individuals responded to the crisis. The last quarter of the seventeenth century almost certainly brought absolute decline to the total output of the Dutch economy, but it also witnessed important new initiatives that sought to compensate for those losses and that gave shape to the economy in the eighteenth century.

Crisis

In view of the highly irregular course of prices in the years after 1648, a period peppered with wars and blockades, it might appear that the identification of 1663 as a turning point in long-term prices represents an excessive invocation of the historian's privilege of retrospective analysis. In fact, contemporaries sensed almost immediately that the price decline begun then was no ordinary fluctuation. The new trend touched every commodity, was not caused by harvests and political events, and, for this reason, reasserted itself quickly after temporary reversals. Within two years both urban and agricultural rents, which had tended upward for decades, broke. The sharp decline in land rents, documented in Figure 11.8, continued into the 1690s. The rentals of urban houses are less well documented, but we know that Leiden rents fell by 40 percent between 1660–4 and 1680–4, while in Amsterdam rents on all classes of housing peaked in 1665–6 and then fell from 10 percent (for the cheapest houses) to 25 percent (for the most expensive) by 1681–2 (see Figure 8.9). The enormous investments in real property that had fueled the second phase of the Golden Age economy suddenly lost their profitability, and it would be many decades (at best) before the old rent levels were regained. By 1672 new infrastructural investment had all but ceased, and investors set aside plans for new urban extensions and land reclamations (see Table 2.2). So complete was the cessation of new construction in 1672 that the leaders of Amsterdam's Portuguese Jewish community ordered work of their new synagogue to be halted as well, in order to avoid attracting unfavorable comment. A major source of employment, which had long been buoyed by heavy fixed capital investment, shrank back to a fraction of its Golden Age level, now supported by little more than maintenance and repair work.

The reversal of the secular trend brought an end to rising nominal wage rates, which by 1660 had raised Dutch pay levels to the highest in Europe. Falling prices put downward pressure on wages, of course, and certain piece rates in the textile industry and day wages for unskilled labor were forced down. But the construction of the segmented labor market described in Chapter 12 acted to maintain the structure of wages achieved by 1660.

The remarkably rigid post-1660 nominal wage scale quickly loomed as a key structural problem of the economy. As prices declined the purchasing power of Dutch labor ascended, reaching an unprecedented level by the 1680s that was maintained, with interruptions, until 1740. But this happy result of falling prices came paired with another. Since the price decline was an international phenomenon "imported" to the Republic, and not chiefly the product of local cost-reducing investments, the rigidity of wages had the effect of redistributing revenue away from profits and rent and toward the wage bill; this in turn encouraged a withdrawal of productive factors from the most labor-intensive sectors of the economy. The crisis of the urban textile industries and the flight to labor-saving farming practices are only the most well-documented examples of this trend. But a broad array of products, from salted herring to books and paintings, suffered diminished output in this period.

The scope and volume of the Republic's foreign trade stood at a peak in 1648 from which the first and second Anglo-Dutch wars could not permanently remove it. But the ongoing elaboration of restrictive laws governing foreign trade, especially by England and France, brought the growth of international trade to a standstill and put the Republic – the all-too-conspicuous beneficiary of free trade – under increasing pressure. The Republic's most prominent theorist of political economy, Pieter de la Court, drew the necessary conclusion in the 1669 revision to his *Interest van Holland*:

> for when we consider, that all the trade of our common inhabitants is circumscribed or bounded well nigh within Europe, and that in very many parts of the same, as France, England, Sweden &c. our greatest trade and navigation thither is crampt by the high duties, or by patent companies . . . ; as also how small a part of the world Europe is, and how many merchants dwell in Holland, and must dwell there to support it; we shall have no reason to wonder, if all the beneficial traffick in these small adjacent countries be either worn out, or in a short time be glutted with an over-trade.[2]

The traditional European markets, that is, were both overstocked with merchants and subject to protectionist measures of increasing effectiveness. De la Court was convinced that the future lay in the development of settler colonies and the trade that would emerge on that solid foundation. (He gained a reputation as an early advocate of free trade because he doubted that the monopoly companies abroad, or guilds at home, would act to secure this future, but his vision was of a state-supported and protected empire. In this respect he carried forward the thinking of Coen and Usselinx more than he prefigured the thinking of Adam Smith.)

From this perspective the unfolding crisis was doubly troubling, for the prospects of a New World territorial empire of any size had been dashed with the losses of Brazil and New Netherlands. "Nu zijn wij dit alles quijt [Now all this has been lost to us]," sighed de la Court, with a palpable regret, and the efforts to compensate for this loss by free trade with the plantation colonies of other powers was also beginning to wither in the face of mercantilist restrictions. Moreover, the VOC's trading empire in Asia also faced a crisis, as the newly restrictive policies of Japan and the reckless expansionism of the English EIC brought a halt to the growth of Company trade and placed its profits under severe pressure throughout the 1670s and '80s.

---

[2] Pieter de la Court, *The True Interest and Political Maxims, of the Republic of Holland* (London, 1746; reprinted: New York, 1972), p. 60.

Response

The Republic's economic Golden Age drew to a close in the course of the 1660s and '70s as the growth potential of the investment strategies of the preceding century fell to zero. But this does not mean that there were no new strategies whereby economic growth could be re-achieved. The generations after the 1670s are sometimes viewed as overly cautious defenders of the status quo, lacking in imagination, daring, and energy. They certainly had reason to be cautious; they had a great deal to defend. And yet their search for new strategies to address the new economic environment was nothing less than intense.

In a world of shrinking markets, the striving for consolidation and protection was a natural response, and the post-1670 Republic offers many examples, big and small: from the consolidation of the segmented labor market, the "oligarchization" of political office, and the re-establishment of the WIC in 1674, to the publishing monopoly over all navigational charts acquired by one firm, Johannes van Keulen, in 1685 (a monopoly it held until 1880!). Efforts to limit competition and hold up sagging prices were ubiquitous in this era not only in the Republic but all over Europe.

A problem that struck the maritime zone of the Republic with special force was high production costs, particularly high wage rates. The response took three general forms: changes in product mix, introduction of labor-saving technology, and locational shifts toward lower-wage regions. The first option, by itself, could be no more than defensive, for the flight toward higher-quality production (especially in textiles) necessarily limited Dutch markets further, while the switch of farmers from dairying to livestock fattening reduced the value of total output.

The numerous changes of this sort testify to the market sensitivity of Dutch producers, but if the Republic was to preserve its more labor-intensive industries, investments would be required in technologies to raise labor productivity. These were not altogether lacking; mechanized butter churns and threshing wheels, wind-powered pressing and pulping mills, horse-driven dredging mills and other contraptions, all spread through the economy. But none sufficed to overcome the high unit labor costs, nor was the relative rise of fuel costs satisfactorily addressed in this period.

One reason for this limited technological response may have been the strength of the third option, which was, in fact, a pan-European trend of the time: the integration of low-cost rural labor into commercial production. Chapter 8 describes the transfer of wool and linen weaving to rural Brabant and Twente, while in Chapter 6 we noted the spread of labor-intensive tobacco production through Gelderland. The chief problem facing the Republic in the exploitation of this proto-industrial strategy was the fact that the commercially oriented countryside of the maritime zone did not have low labor costs either, so that the search for cheap labor led putting-out merchants to the eastern and southern borderlands and, quickly enough, beyond the nation's boundaries to Liège and the German states, where the continued orientation of producers to Dutch commercial centers could not be guaranteed.

The tightening mercantilist noose that closed so many markets to the Dutch could also, by its very disruptiveness, create new opportunities. French economic warfare and Dutch retaliatory efforts opened new opportunities for the domestic production of sail cloth (where the Bretons had been strong) and for the Dutch paper industry, which was reinforced by the technical improvements of the wind-powered paper mill (the "Hollander"). Louis XIV's 1685 revocation of the Edict of Nantes sent thousands of Huguenot refugees to the Republic, where they encouraged silk production and several skilled crafts. A bit later, England's restrictions on the importation of Indian cotton cloth gave Amsterdam's cotton-printing industry a larger market than would otherwise have been the case.

In the industrial and agricultural sectors, the Republic's producers maneuvered as best they could in a structure of high costs and limited markets. Lethargy and routine did not characterize their conduct, but neither did decisive cost-reducing investments.

The large capital stock amassed by a century of profitable expansion was the single most potent weapon with which the Republic could respond to new challenges of the late seventeenth century. Little new investment found its way into industry or agriculture, still less into fishing, infrastructure, or European trade. But major new commitments of capital spurred three activities that grew to become the new leading sectors of the eighteenth-century economy. The decisions to double the size of the VOC in the face of new competition from the French and English, to establish a Caribbean plantation economy in the face of large, established producers, and to invest in a new type of whaling enterprise with uncertain prospects, all constituted a massive attempt to break out of the cul-de-sac in which the Republic's economy found itself in the last quarter of the seventeenth century.

Each of these new ventures has been discussed in earlier chapters. Here we wish to call attention to the one key characteristic that unites them: their very high risk.

Dutch whaling dates from the beginning of the seventeenth century, but the industry's character changed after 1660 when the whaling grounds retreated to the far north. The presence of drift ice forced the use of specially constructed ships, where ordinary merchant vessels had been serviceable before. Investors in whaling expeditions now faced higher capital requirements and reduced flexibility. Moreover, the firms had to contend with natural circumstances that caused great volatility in the size of the catch, market forces that caused the price of whale oil to fluctuate greatly (vegetable oils were a close substitute), and international factors that affected the number of competitors and access to foreign markets. The industry was highly speculative, but the Dutch whaling fleet grew from some 75 to 200 ships in the decades after 1660.

The slave trade and sugar production were among the very few growth industries of the late seventeenth century, and nearly every maritime nation sought to participate. After two failed efforts to establish itself in the sugar business (and with most of the Dutch sugar refineries idle by 1680), a new effort was launched in 1682 with the establishment of the *Societeit van Suriname*. From then until 1713, the colony's slave population quadrupled and annual sugar shipments rose from 3 to 15 million pounds. The plantation economy's growth continued for another sixty years, absorbing vast amounts of publicly subscribed capital. Before 1713, when almost all investment was private, little is known about the amounts involved. As we sought to make clear in Chapter 10, these investments enjoyed none of the mercantilist protection offered to English and French planters. The Dutch plantation economy stood fully exposed to the market and political forces emanating from much larger foreign producers.

We turn finally to the Republic's trading enterprise in Asia. In Chapter 10 we recounted how events conspired to rein in the phenomenal growth of the VOC after 1660. In the course of the 1680s, the *Heren XVII* responded with a series of defensive measures – military expenditures to shore up the Company's control over Asian pepper and spices – but also with a commitment to expand the Company's range of imports to the European market. They recognized that capital was available in embarrassing abundance; between 1679 and 1699, they raised over 10 million guilders by issuing long-term bonds, to which they added capital raised in Asia and through the sale of inventories. Their enormous demands for labor now met a more forthcoming response, as Dutchmen proved much more willing than before to consider employment on board VOC ships (see Figure 12.12). In these and other ways, the VOC doubled in size between 1680 and the 1720s, adding to its traditional imports of pepper and spices products with expanding markets such as calicoes, silks, porcelain, coffee, sugar, and tea. In making this bold move, the Company directors recognized that they were shifting from goods over which the VOC had substantial market power to goods traded – in both Asia and Europe – in competitive markets.

All three growth sectors attracted major commitments of capital and labor and succeeded for many decades in increasing the catch of whales, the production of sugar, and the import of Asian commodities. What they rarely succeeded in doing was earning a profit. The sketchy information about the whaling and plantation sectors emphasizes the speculative quality of investments in each; the fuller information about the VOC shows the era of its second great expansion to have been one of profitless growth: Profits were no greater after the Company doubled its size than they had been at the beginning.

In seeking to escape the limited returns offered by the old economic sectors, investors moved out the risk spectrum. However, this risk-taking entrepreneurialism was not rewarded with the expected higher long-term rate of return, because the expansion of each sector entailed increased exposure to international competitive forces uncompensated by the market power of the entrepôt or the resources of the domestic economy.

The Dutch response to the reversal of the secular trend and the political challenges of its rivals was anything but lethargic, self-satisfied, or overly cautious. Nor was it limited to the marginal adjustments of private individuals. The Republic's political leaders quickly recognized the scope of the problem and advocated reforms that would address the problem of high costs that now weighed down upon the economy. The tax burden, with its substantial reliance on excise taxes, had long been heavy, and the extraordinary costs of turning back the French invasion and English blockade of 1672 had forced a sharp increase in the public debt. After the Peace of Nijmegen (1678), most urban regents recognized the necessity of retiring a portion of the debt and reducing taxes, but the deflationary economy brought little relief. In this context we can understand the stubborn opposition, led by Amsterdam, to any and all proposals of Stadhouder Willem III to offer military resistance to Louis XIV, who had embarked on a provocative expansionist campaign along France's northern border. The recovery of the Dutch economy required an extended period of peace and lower taxation in order to reduce the costs of production and trade.

In 1684 Amsterdam's regents presented a detailed analysis of the economic situation to the States of Holland in which they argued that the Republic's commercial capital (what they called the *funds van subsistentie en welvaren*) had diminished by half since 1672, a diminution equal to the fall in value of real property. They reminded those who doubted this that "a decay of commerce and navigation by a quarter reduces profits by half. . . ."[3] Moreover, they argued that the domestic market (the *Commercie van Consumptie*) was also shrinking, further pressing upon the profits of merchants. This was a matter of the utmost gravity, for Holland's public expenditures could be covered only in small part by revenue drawn from her natural resources (the *Gront van Hollandt*); thus, she depended as no other state on the profitability of her commercial capital, something which was *t'eenmael artifcieel* – an inherently artificial source of well-being. They ended in a somber mood: Peace in Europe now allowed "Princes and Potentates to apply themselves especially to the augmentation within their own lands of commerce, navigation, and manufactures."[4] And history taught that "commerce and navigation, and the prosperity that flows therefrom, is transferred from the one

---

[3] "een decadentie van een vierde-part van de Commercie ende Navigatie de helft van de Winsten weghneemt . . ." Algemeen Rijksarchief Den Haag, Financie van Holland, no. 806a. Footnotes 4, 5, and 6, are from the same source.

[4] "Princen en Potentaten haer insonderhiejdt [te] appliceren tot vermeerderingh van Commercie, Navigatie en Manufacurije in haar Landen."

nation to the other, as in all ancient times so during those times closer to our own centuries."[5] One can readily understand then "how carefully one must deal with the aforementioned matters in order to fulfill one's duty as a good regent."[6]

The concern and frustration of Amsterdam's regents are palpable in this document: The economic crisis was not so much one of falling trade volume as one of falling profits. In the current environment, this could be remedied only by reducing costs, and the most conspicuous force driving up costs was taxation. Yet even after several years of peace, no tax reductions had yet been achieved, and the Prince of Orange now advocated a foreign policy that was certain to require vast expenditures.

Amsterdam and its allies in Holland's government long held fast to a policy of peace and fiscal retrenchment. But repeated French provocations – the Revocation of the Edict of Nantes in 1685, French reinstatement in 1687 of the draconian 1667 tariff lists, the confiscation of Dutch ships in French ports in September 1688 – finally convinced even the most dedicated advocates of fiscal austerity that the future well-being of the Republic's economy depended on the destruction of French mercantilism (and, thus, the discouragement of those states that followed her lead). Such a project could only be contemplated in coalition with England, and this left the regents little choice but to provide financial support for Stadhouder Willem III's ambitions to acquire the English crown.

The Stadhouder's invasion of England and the Dutch army's occupation of London (the Glorious Revolution) constitute a spectacular historical event, one that seems inexplicable except in terms of Willem's ambition, James's liabilities, and Louis's calculations. But the momentous and essential decision to commit Dutch resources to this enterprise, and to the war that inevitably would follow, can only be understood as a great gamble, a risky investment to use the one resource that the Republic had in abundance – money – to re-establish an international environment in which the economy could once again prosper. Only in the contractionary and deflationary world that had existed by then for over twenty years could this drastic measure have seemed sensible, even necessary, to the regents.

After the Republic's private investors had ventured millions in risky initiatives to expand overseas trade and whaling, they risked in their public capacity some 200 million guilders (raised in public borrowing between 1690 and 1713) and imposed a major new tax burden on society in order to establish, in alliance with England, a European order in which the Republic and its economy could prosper once again. Together with the high-risk private investments of the era, this public gamble established the basic contours of the eighteenth-century economy of the

---

[5] "de Commercie en Navigatie, en 't welvaren, daer uijt spruijtende, van de eene natie tot de andere is overgebracht, so in al oude tijden, als geduijrende die gene die aen onse Eeuwen naerder zijn."
[6] "hoe sorghvuldigh men omtrent alle 't gene voorsz, is behoort te zijn, om aen de plicht van goede Regenten te voldoen."

Republic; but like those private ventures, it too proved to be a profitless investment.

13.1.4. THE EIGHTEENTH-CENTURY ECONOMY

A recurring theme of preceding chapters has been that the Republic's eighteenth-century economy cannot correctly be understood as simply a worn and hollowed-out version of its Golden Age predecessor. The structural changes set in motion by the late seventeenth-century crisis gave the post-1713 economy its own character and its own possibilities for development. The urban industrial sector suffered a severe loss of labor-intensive production and capital-goods production, which was compensated for only partially by industries requiring proximity to the ports or by large inputs of skilled labor and fixed capital. The agricultural sector moved in two directions, as local conditions dictated: toward less labor-intensive livestock raising and very labor-intensive industrial crop production. In a nutshell, foreign trade shifted from the "mother trade" and related European routes toward the new combination of intercontinental trade and hinterland distribution.

To the twentieth-century observer, all these developments occurred in slow motion; more sudden was the emergence of a new fiscal-financial complex. By 1713 the investment of some 200 million guilders in the public debt over the previous twenty-four years had caused capital to be withdrawn from productive investment and was instrumental in the striking concentration of wealth into fewer hands. The fiscal system that supported this enormous debt ensured that the Republic would remain a high-cost economy, while it poured annually nearly 14 million guilders (after tax) into the hands of the narrowed band of bondholders (see Table 4.8). This fact more than any other gave the eighteenth-century economy its distinctive shape.

The political eclipse of the Republic during its long coalition with England forced it, after 1713, to take refuge in a policy of political neutrality. This and the emergence of effective commercial rivals in London and Hamburg greatly eroded the market power of the Amsterdam entrepôt. The integration of shipping, trading, and production that had been the hallmark of the Golden Age now gave way to the separation of the shipping, trading, financing, insuring, and producing sectors. In each of these sectors, it proved possible to find avenues for expansion, even for the development of wholly new businesses. Earlier chapters have recounted the growth of certain industries, the expansion of specialized, export-oriented agricultural production, and the opportunistic growth of shipping in periods of European war, most notably during the Seven Years' War.

The eighteenth-century economy was not without its bright spots, especially as renewed European demographic growth and the revival of prices after 1750 invigorated foreign markets. The most prominent and dynamic of eighteenth-century growth sectors were finance and trade in colonial goods. But these sectors shared with the others the tendency toward disarticulation of the Republican economy; and the idle resources increasingly characteristic of the industrial towns, plus the marginalized position of Dutch traders in many European markets, detracted significantly from the overall performance of the economy. In our view the per capita gross national income stood at a lower level in the 1740s (when a good portion of national income can be measured) than it had in the 1660s (when it cannot). The diminution of population, deurbanization, decline of labor-intensive industries, and diminished profitability of trade and agriculture, all point in this direction. Thereafter, from the 1740s to 1780, the possibility of a modest rise of national income cannot be dismissed, although it is likely that any improvement was concentrated at the very top of the income scale. In those years the successful marketing of colonial products to the German hinterlands, the expansion of Dutch shipping in European waters, the revival of agricultural profitability, and the growing inflow of foreign investment earnings may well have overcome the effects of continuing deindustrialization.

This puzzling economy appears to have existed in a state of internal disequilibrium throughout the eighteenth century. Its labor market maintained its segmented, high-wage structure into the era of falling prices, thereby increasing the wage bill, depressing profits, and stimulating industrial disinvestment and unemployment. Its fiscal system became hostage to the enormous public debt accumulated during the reign of the Stadhouder-King. After 1713, interest payments absorbed over 70 percent of Holland's tax revenue, vitiating the military and curtailing public investment as the treasury struggled to chip away at the vast overhang of debt. Holland's immense burden also acted as a powerful disincentive to the other provinces to contemplate fiscal reform. For the Republic as a whole, interest payments on the public debt amounted to about 7 percent of mid–eighteenth-century national income (as estimated later in this chapter); in 1995 such interest payments amount to 6.2 percent of Dutch GDP (gross domestic product).

Consider for a moment the following counterfactual historical exercise. If, beginning with the emergency of 1672, Holland had raised an additional 500,000 guilders in taxes, the public borrowing requirements by 1713 would have been 40 percent less than they were in fact, and the enhanced ability to retire debt after 1713 (because of both higher revenue and lower interest payments) would have reduced Holland's public debt to 130 million in 1780 instead of the actual 321 million. Would this additional tax burden (3 percent of Holland's total tax revenue in the 1670s, about 2 percent after 1745) have been the straw that broke the camel's back – an excessive imposition on an economy already undermined by heavy taxation? Much would have depended on the form that this additional tax took (it would have been much less than 3 percent had it been spread across the whole Republic!), but it is certainly likely that the eighteenth-century economy would have enjoyed much greater flexibility, while the state would have enjoyed greater latitude in responding to its post-1780 crisis. This higher rate of taxation would have been consistent with a "tax-smoothing" policy: long-run budget balancing supplemented by short-term borrowing. Clearly, the Republic chose to follow a different course, one in which debt financed a permanent part of the state's revenue needs.

One reason suggested for the regents' preference for public bonds over taxation is the perceived diminution of profitable private investment opportunities in the eighteenth century. But whether they received larger bond redemption payments or larger annual interest payments, the post-1713 problem of bondholders remains essentially the same: how to invest large flows of income in excess of current consumption. The path in fact chosen – to invest abroad in English funds, plantation loans, and foreign government bonds – established Amsterdam as Europe's premier international capital market. By the 1770s, foreigners paid Dutch investors annual interest payments of some 15 million guilders, a figure that would double by 1790.

The growth of international finance was not without its benefits, but together with the domestic fiscal system which fed that growth, it placed the Republic's domestic economy before a stubborn, structural problem. The large public debt, holding the promise of higher future taxes, encouraged a high savings rate among bondholders. Given the flaccidity of domestic demand – public or private – for these savings, they were invested abroad, thereby further reducing aggregate demand at home. Under these conditions the Republic's traditional balance of payments surplus (consisting of a trade deficit more than offset by shipping and investment earnings) tended to grow, bearing two consequences: increased strength of the guilder in foreign exchange markets, which discouraged exports, and increased capacity to import, the propensity toward which was heightened by the increased inequality of income distribution. This, too, reduced the demand for domestic goods.

Finally, this economy, with so few factors expanding domestic demand and with such high costs discouraging industrial production, failed to experience the demographic growth that returned to nearly all other parts of Europe between 1730 and 1750. Thus, incentives for domestic, productive investment of the large capital fund generated by the eighteenth-century Dutch economy (or, rather, by its fiscal system) were all but nonexistent, which only exaggerated the isolated, disconnected quality of such growth sectors as existed.

13.1.5. THE FINAL CRISIS, 1780–1815

The Dutch economy of 1780 was not healthy, and it had not been so for a long time. But it was also not without means to prosper anew. It was, to begin with, extremely rich. Its international banking sector lacked but one critical feature: effective credit-creating institutions to maintain liquidity in times of crisis.

Its merchant fleet was as large as it had ever been. Much of it now simply provided shipping services, and it depended on continued international – or, rather, the British High Court of Admiralty's – recognition of the Dutch doctrine of "free ship, free goods," but the expansion of European trade offered it reasonable prospects for growth.

Relative to its size, the Republic controlled a very large share of the trade in colonial goods, the international demand for which was growing rapidly. The VOC was in pressing need of reform or replacement, and the New World plantation investments had just suffered massive default, but the resources to address these problems were not lacking.

Rapid growth in the Republic's hinterlands, especially in Germany, offered new possibilities for trade, particularly in the distribution of colonial goods and industrial products. Political tensions could disrupt this trade, but the more immediate obstacle to its intensification was poor transportation infrastructure, a factor that also limited the effective integration of the Republic's own eastern provinces to the maritime heartland.

The agricultural economy enjoyed high productivity. And rising prices and growing markets in England offered it substantial opportunities for export-oriented expansion.

Indeed, as late as 1782, Laurens van de Spiegel, who would later become (the Republic's last) Grand Pensionary, sought to convince his countrymen of the economy's favorable prospects in his *Schets tot een vertoog over de intrinsique en relatieve magt van de Republijk* [Outline of an argument concerning the intrinsic and relative power of the Republic]. In comparing the contemporary economy to that of 1648 (the acknowledged high point of the Golden Age), van de Spiegel reviewed the many millions of guilders invested in activities which had come to maturity and prosperity only since that date. He conceded that important sectors had suffered losses and declined in the intervening 134 years, but on balance he believed the intrinsic, or absolute, economic power of the Republic to have grown, even though its position relative to neighboring countries had diminished. Thanks to the careful analysis of the Republic's eighteenth-century economy by Johan de Vries, this assessment, with its emphasis on stability and continuity until at least 1780, remains influential.

Van de Spiegel's argument was not entirely wishful thinking; the economy had indeed developed features that it did not possess in 1648; but the essential point, lost to any analysis that stresses continuity, is that the Republic's economy had passed through a crisis that forced profound mutations in its structure. The entrepôt of the eighteenth century, focused on the regional distribution of colonial goods, was not the broad *stapelmarkt* of the seventeenth century. The chief industries of the eighteenth century, processing mainly imported malt, sugar, and tobacco, employed but a fraction of the domestic labor and raw materials of their seventeenth-century predecessors. The prosperous agriculture of the eighteenth century responded to the growing British market, not that of domestic consumers and industries. And the value of the Republic's vast stock of capital no longer relied upon profitable production and trade, but rather on a fiscal system that sucked resources from a stagnant tax base.

The future well-being of this economy required a recognition of its actual position in Europe and the world and the resolve to equip it with the institutions and infrastructure necessary to stimulate those sectors capable of further growth. That future would be no Golden Age. The very legacy of the golden past (its high wages, high taxes, high-income agriculture, large foreign earnings, and, most important, the "distributional coalitions" that had formed over the decades to defend vested interests, especially fiscal interests) now made the Republic inhospitable to most forms of industrial production. This necessarily limited its possibilities greatly, especially for the sort of technological improvements that would drive nineteenth-century economic growth.

But from 1780 on, a new conjuncture of internal and external forces combined to plunge the Netherlands into a crisis that brought the collapse of the old Republic and bequeathed only the tattered remnants of the old economy to its post-1814 successor. The external forces that mauled the Republic repeatedly in this period are as well known as they are dramatic; it would be easy to ascribe to them the full responsibility for the economy's painful suffocation. The British declaration of war in 1780 ended the protection that neutrality had given to Dutch shipping and mortally wounded the VOC. The ascendancy of revolutionary France over Dutch affairs in 1795 imposed an enormous new tax burden (over the years, 230 million guilders of direct payments to France) that soon overwhelmed the fiscal system, forced the public debt into default, and closed the curtain on Amsterdam's role as a major international capital market. The Revolutionary and Napoleonic wars squeezed Dutch commerce into the illegal interstices of British blockades and the French Continental System. For a time the large Dutch shipping and trading sector managed to sustain itself by using flags of convenience, nurturing connections with the neutral American merchant fleet, and generally living by its wits. But beginning in 1806, this *entrepôt de la contrebande*, as the French contemptuously called it, was systematically shut down. The ultimate incorporation of the Netherlands into the French Empire placed this commercial society in the impossible position of having legal access to no major market, not even to the French Empire of which it was an ostensible part. In the desperate years 1811–13, the ports were bereft of shipping, and the remnants of industry collapsed.

Yet the ability of these external forces to wreak havoc upon the economy was powerfully enhanced by the old Republic's own accumulated and unattended weaknesses. In 1780 the British attacked a VOC crippled by decades of poor leadership and incapable of implementing serious reform even when the only alternative was bankruptcy. The Republic could protect neither its merchant ships nor its borders, because six decades of austerity had hollowed out its defenses without significantly restoring its finances. The Patriot Revolt of 1787 expressed

the Christianized enlightenment views of a squeezed middle class of lesser merchants, manufacturers, and tradesmen, whose productivist vision of a national
economy required a government ready to confront the obsolete particularism that
ensconced the regent elites in their self-satisfied power. Whatever the limitations
of Patriot economic thinking, their defeat at the hands of a Prussian military force
called in to re-establish Willem V (the King of Prussia was Willem's brother-in-
law) to his stadhoudership ensured that the final years of the old Republic would
be mired in inaction. When in the wake of another invading army – that of
revolutionary France – the Patriots did come to power in the first days of 1795,
the political obstacles seemed cleared for a thorough institutional housecleaning
and a vigorous policy in support of domestic industry and agriculture, what they
regarded as the "most natural and certain source of a people's prosperity."[7] But
the Patriots soon found that the obsolete structures of a rich economy are not
easily swept away, especially not when the superficiality of their critiques hobbled
every effort to achieve political consensus. After a decade of their indecisive rule,
it became the turn of the French to rule more directly, first in the form of Louis
Napoleon's Kingdom of Holland, then by incorporating the Dutch provinces into
the French Empire. This rule brought more abrupt breaks with past practice but
in a setting of such turmoil that positive accomplishments remained few. The
restoration of an independent Dutch state in 1814 left a great deal to be done,
and undone.

In this long period of crisis, disinvestment from the commercial and industrial
sectors (in the face of unprofitability, high risks, taxation, and forced lending) and
the destruction of asset value through foreign and domestic default undermined
the remaining international stature of the commercial and financial sectors. Domestically, the disruption of institutions and the irregular access to markets
plunged the once-protected sectors of employment (the public agencies, the
VOC, the guilds) into a crisis that tore at the venerable structure of the labor
market and overwhelmed the Republic's charitable system. This crisis hit hardest
in the cities of Holland and Zeeland, which lost 10 percent of their population
between 1795 and 1815. In the same period, the rural areas plus the provincial
cities grew by 10 percent. Deurbanization, re-agriculturalization, and pauperiza-
tion dominated the final days of this economy – or, to be more accurate, the
not-quite-final days.

The "restored" Dutch state of 1814 proved, in fact, to be a great innovation.
The old Republic was truly dead, and the new United Kingdom of the Netherlands embroidered on Patriot and Napoleonic foundations more than its Or-
angist founders or British patrons could admit. But the Republican economy,
long sclerotic and reeling from a multitude of fresh wounds in this extended
period of crisis, still breathed. Notwithstanding G. K. van Hogendorp's wishful

---

[7] "[De] natuurlijkste en zekerste bronnen van den welvaart der Volkeren." (Pieter Vreede, August
10, 1796).

pronouncement heralding the return to power of the Prince of Orange ("The sea is open, trade revives, . . . the days of old return!"),[8] the old economy lingered on with no real recuperative powers but also without a rival possessed of the strength to administer the final blow. An extended period of transition lasted until the 1850s. Then a final liquidation of the old public debt, and the abolition of the excise taxes on basic commodities, placed the Netherlands in a position to embark on a second epoch of modern economic growth.

13.2. Coming to terms with an advanced preindustrial economy

As we approach the end of this study, we come unavoidably to a question raised in the introduction: With what concepts may we best understand the development of the Netherlands' economy in its international setting? Should the Republic be tied firmly to the conceptual tether that constrains the rest of Europe in the early modern period, or should we stress its exceptionality – its unique experience as a precocious and premature expression of a market economy? Or is there another approach?

13.2.1. THE USES AND LIMITATIONS OF THE MALTHUSIAN MODEL

In the overwhelmingly agrarian world of preindustrial Europe, the demographic insights of Robert Thomas Malthus have long formed an indispensable basis for the analysis of economic life. His axiom, that there exists an inherent potential for human life to multiply faster than its means of support, allowed him to argue that the unequal struggle between these two forces would lead inevitably to mortality crises – positive checks – whereby the growth of population would be reined in by malnutrition, illness, and death. This fate was universal and unavoidable, he argued, *unless* societies cultivated practices to limit the growth of their numbers by prudential behavior – called preventive checks – adequate to reduce fertility to a level consistent with the protection of established living standards. In his view the key to such prudence was restricting access to the institution of marriage.

Malthus's formulations inform many of the most fruitful and influential interpretations of preindustrial European society. The historian E. Le Roy Ladurie saw them at work in France, where "twelve to thirteen generations of peasants were busy reproducing themselves within limits of finite possibilities whose constraints proved inexorable."[9] Many historians have interpreted the secular trend,

---

[8] "de zee is open, de handel herleeft, . . . de oude tijden keren terug!"
[9] E. Le Roy Ladurie, "Motionless History," *Social Science History 1* (1977), 122.

the slow oscillations of population and prices that establish the framework for periodization in the preindustrial economy, as driven by a Malthusian dynamic. And the shorter, more frequent *crises de subsistance* that repeatedly destabilized European societies are frequently held to reveal the positive check at work. The essence of Malthusian interpretations of economic history is the belief that population and economy interact in the form of *negative feedback loops*, such that any impulse toward growth is, in time, reversed – checked – to restore equilibrium. In an economy dominated by Malthusian forces, economic expansion is necessarily limited, episodic, and stunted.

The Northern Netherlands and especially its maritime zones were already at the end of the fifteenth century less overwhelmingly agrarian than most of the rest of Europe. But a Malthusian approach to this economy hardly seems misplaced as it experienced rapid population growth, a growth more concentrated in the countryside than in the cities until the 1570s. This growth, distinguished from the rest of sixteenth-century Europe only by its very high rate, brought with it the pan-European price inflation and its companion, a decline in the purchasing power of labor.

The mid-century famines placed the Netherlands, North and South, very much in the company of the rest of Europe, but by the end of the century, a conventional Malthusian model is no longer adequate to account for the economic and demographic dynamics of the new Republic. As we documented in Chapter 12, the purchasing power of labor began to rise after the 1570s and stood at levels well above that of neighboring countries until deep into the eighteenth century. Neither preventive nor positive checks intervened to reverse the sixteenth-century deterioration of living standards. Indeed, the rate of population growth accelerated, now fueled by massive immigration. The decisive difference was the rapid construction of an economy in which productivity growth successfully could fend off the inherent tendency toward diminishing returns of a growing population. What was needed was a lifting of the food-supply constraint both on the rise of population, in general, and on the redeployment of labor toward higher-productivity uses outside agriculture, more specifically. It had been the fruitful interaction of Holland's Baltic trade and its agricultural sector over the course of many decades that made possible the lifting of this Malthusian constraint, and after the Revolt, its implications for economic restructuring were explored more fully. Strong *positive feedback loops*, where an impulse toward expansion stimulates further growth, now made their appearance in the Dutch economy, significantly weakening the influence of Malthusian forces.

From the end of the sixteenth century on, demographic forces interacted with the economy in ways far more complex than can be comprehended within a Malthusian model. But this does not mean that population movements were of no importance. Far from it. The international grain trade and the rise in real wages broke the power of the positive check, leaving the preventive check (i.e., the regulation of nuptiality) to adjust population size to economic conditions.

But how did this preventive check function in a highly urbanized society with an "open" economy?

In this society international migration fluctuated alongside fertility in response to the changing demands of the labor market. Some 500,000 permanent migrants entered the Republic during its lifetime (see Chapter 3), and an even larger number left it, chiefly as seamen who died abroad. Moreover, taming the positive check did not mean taming mortality in general. Urban mortality was structurally high, just as everywhere in preindustrial Europe, and the long-term deterioration of ground-water quality in the maritime provinces forced rural mortality to high levels as well (see Chapter 2). These factors form an essential backdrop to the two major climacterics of Dutch population.

The first of these turning points, the cessation of population growth after the 1660s – indeed, the absolute decline of population in several regions and many cities – is strongly associated with the crisis that brought the Golden Age economy to an end. The new stagnation of population was clearly responsible for the dramatic collapse of domestic investment. But the Republic shared this demographic reversal with most of the countries of northwestern Europe, which raises the question of causation. The one thing that can now be said is that in the Republic it was not simply that overpopulation or diminishing labor productivity was forcing delays in marriage. After all, real wages were high, and agriculture was becoming less labor intensive. Rather, the population was responding to a "modern" problem of diminished employment and profit possibilities.

The second "turning point" is placed in quotation marks because it is actually the point at which nothing turned. Almost everywhere else in Europe, population growth revived and accelerated after 1730–50. But in the Republic, the upturn was localized, confined chiefly to inland rural districts, and was very modest. At the national level, it is barely measurable. Not until after 1815 did the Netherlands begin to participate in Europe's demographic growth; by then its population, which had been nearly 40 percent of England's in 1670–1700, stood at but 21 percent of the English figure.

How is this "nonevent" to be explained? A high average age at marriage and a rigorously nuclear family structure of probably the smallest households in Europe, which had characterized most of the Republic since the mid–seventeenth century, was not about to be given up. An economy whose growth prospects remained modest may well have strengthened this resolve, of course, but could that be the entire explanation for the maintenance of a very low marital fertility in an environment of high mortality? In a Europe where population change still revolved around some combination of land, food prices, mortality crises, marriage age, and peasant norms, the relevant factors in the Republic had become: jobs, urbanization, migration, marriage age, and modern expectations. Demographic factors are important to the understanding of the Republic's economy, and certain issues are far from being resolved; but those issues will have to be placed in a different context than the Malthusian model.

13.2.2. MERCHANT CAPITALISM AND THE *STAPELMARKT*

The chief alternative to a Malthusian approach, with its almost exclusive focus on domestic economic factors, is the concept of merchant capitalism, which starts from the premise that international economic forces define the character of, and set the limits to, advanced market economies in the preindustrial era. There is no single widely accepted definition of merchant capitalism, but all efforts to develop the concept end up positing the existence of some form of economic dualism, where a precapitalist economy of peasants, lords, and guilds is penetrated by merchant capitalism, nurtured by international markets and political interests.

The interpretation of the *stapelmarkt* as a clearinghouse of Europe's surplus goods, a *literal* marketplace made essential by the primitive technology and limited markets of the time, is consistent with this general approach. The existence of such a glittering center of commerce presupposes the existence of a backward Europe – the two go hand in hand. Moreover, just as Europe's need for a stapling function causes greatness to be thrust on a single, concrete market, so the essentially external factors that favor its location in one place can easily remove it to another. The merchant capitalism of the *stapelmarkt* and its international market network is cosmopolitan, rootless, and ultimately footloose.

The "world-system" concept of Immanuel Wallerstein bears a family resemblance to the *stapelmarkt* idea. He credits more creative power to the economic centers, the core, of the world economy; its trading functions go far beyond service as a warehouse for surplus goods. Rather than serving the larger, more primitive economy with a vital function, Wallerstein sees the core as siphoning profit from the periphery to support a uniquely privileged elite. The "hegemony" of the core establishes the conditions necessary for the large-scale accumulation of capital; and the Republic was, in Wallerstein's account, the first capitalist hegemon. And yet it was a strangely incomplete hegemon. This Marxian interpretation shares the view of the empiricist Violet Barbour, who concluded her *Capitalism in Amsterdam in the Seventeenth Century* with the assessment that "her golden age was rather the climax of a period of transition than the beginning of a new economic age."[10] Wallerstein underscores that transitional character with the claim that until true national economies emerged, "Dutch world trade became a sort of precious vital fluid which kept the machine [i.e., the world economy] going. . . ."[11] This was, in the words of yet another historian, "a greatness *ad interim*."[12]

The dualism inherent in merchant capitalism receives greater emphasis in the interpretation of Eric Hobsbawm, who labeled the advanced commercial life of

[10] Violet Barbour, *Capitalism in Amsterdam in the Seventeenth Century* (Ann Arbor, 1963), p. 142.
[11] Immanuel Wallerstein, *The Modern World-System* (New York, 1973), Vol. 1, p. 214.
[12] E. H. Kossmann, "The Dutch Republic" *New Cambridge Modern History* (Cambridge, 1961), Vol. 5, p. 283.

the Republic as a "feudal business economy." For all its sophistication, this commercial economy drew its sustenance from the "feudal" economies of its trading partners. Its commercial elites had neither the power nor the desire to transform the markets that they penetrated, since their profits depended on the very market imperfections and scarcities enforced by feudal institutions. Thus, the Republic's prosperity and apparent modernity held no promise of things to come, neither for itself nor for the regions it subordinated; rather, it was the fragile product of the privileged economic niche occupied, *ad interim*, by the Republic.

Another approach, one also emphasizing the incapacity of merchant capitalism to transform an economy, locates the source of its weakness in a parasitic relationship to the productive sectors – agriculture and, especially, industry. Jan Luiten van Zanden argues that merchant capitalism can profit from this economy only by drawing the labor force out of its self-sufficient smallholdings and into commercial agriculture and urban industry (dualism again).[13] But the technological stagnation of these sectors, which merchant capitalists cannot or will not address, makes survival in the commercial sector all but impossible for the "premature" proletariat. Hence, the domestic economic expansion stimulated by merchant capitalism is necessarily self-destructive, for a wage-labor force cannot sustain itself.

What all these arguments have in common is a vision of preindustrial market systems as self-limiting and inherently incapable of initiating sustained economic development. The technological means were absent, and more importantly, the self-interest and economic vision of merchant capitalists constrained their investment behavior and their political initiatives. These arguments look back toward the preindustrial era from the vantage point of industrial Europe to assert that the failure of advanced commercial economies to initiate the Industrial Revolution was "no accident": For one reason or another, they all lacked vital ingredients and were crippled at birth by fatal limitations.

The development of merchant capitalism as a category or stage of economic life has so often relied on the putative "lessons" of Dutch economic history that we can hardly pass over it without comment. But the arguments developed in the preceding chapters will have made it clear why we find no need to resort to such a special category. It serves to "ghettoize" preindustrial market economies, explaining away their achievements and failures rather than explaining them.

Still, even though its answers do not satisfy us, the concept of merchant capitalism does call attention to important questions. The entrepôt function clearly was the beating heart of the Dutch economy, and this was a function dominated by merchants. Did the cultivation of this traditional distributional function raise up interests and reinforce mentalities that would later pose obstacles to more balanced economic development? To begin with, we must recall those characteristics of the Amsterdam entrepôt that distinguished it from its Antwerp pre-

[13] Jan Luiten van Zanden, *The Rise and Decline of Holland's Economy* (Manchester, 1993).

decessor. Amsterdam's continuous markets (focused at the *Beurs* rather than at the periodic fairs) and active trade (where Dutch merchants penetrated foreign markets and often controlled production facilities) made it a mustering field not only for the coincidental surplus production of Europe's regional economies but also for information. It developed more fully than its predecessors the decision-making and capital-allocation functions that continue to be an essential element in the organization of the international economy to this very day. Far from an expression of the limitations of *merchant capitalism*, with its need for a stockpile of tangible goods, the Dutch entrepôt matured to become the nerve center of *capitalism*, with its primary need for efficient access to information.

Did the merchant capitalist's preference for investing in the circulating capital of trade limit investment in the fixed capital of production? "Merchant capitalism" as a category is largely predicated on the assumption that it maintained and reinforced imperfections in capital markets that limited investment in the productive assets of industry and agriculture. Yet the seventeenth-century expansion of the Republic's trading capital quickly led to increased investment in every manner of domestic production. We have shown that the trading functions of the Dutch ports did not float disembodied above domestic production. They prospered with the growing integration of the economic sectors and were weakened by their disarticulation.

A final claim made by the merchant capitalism concept is related to this last one: Merchants profiting from exchange, it is argued, expressed little interest in technical or organizational changes that could radically lower costs, broaden markets, or increase competition. Rightly or wrongly, they believed that their profits depended on restriction and monopoly. At home and abroad, their hostility to mercantilism was not so much the expression of support for free trade as an assertion of merchant domination over producers.

The Republic certainly had its share of monopolist practices and market-restricting institutions. Nor have these disappeared with the *ancien régime*. What is more noteworthy is (1) the acute attention to costs in this economy whose commercial core relied on the distribution of bulk goods, and (2) the large number of technological and organizational innovations that propelled the economy forward in the seventeenth century. The conspicuous absence of technical innovation in industry in the eighteenth century was directly related to the structural unviability of most industrial production, not to the dead hand of merchant interests.

Malthusian and merchant capitalist concepts, when applied to the economic history of the Dutch Republic, have one thing in common: They reduce its growth and development to a powerless and self-limiting episode, at best a stage on which others might someday build, and they reduce its crisis and stagnation to an inevitable denouement, part of the natural respiration of a traditional world. Since Malthusian concepts are obviously of limited direct applicability in a highly urbanized, trade-oriented economy, the invocation of a capitalism defined as unique to the preindustrial world has enjoyed broad appeal. But it suffers not only from inconsistency with the facts of the Republic's economic behavior; it is conceptually flawed in its overemphasis of the discontinuity in economic history represented by the British Industrial Revolution. By judging all earlier economies by the norms of the "first industrial nation," it misleads in the same way as do assessments of nineteenth-century European economies that use the British experience as a template of successful development.

The implication of all this for the economic history of the Netherlands is simple: Its successes and failures ought to be assessed in modern terms. The institutional, political, and technological idiosyncrasies of its time require incorporation in any analysis, of course, but there is no justification for positing the existence of a deep chasm separating the traditional from the modern, the preindustrial from the industrial. The economic history of the Netherlands in the sixteenth through eighteenth centuries is a history of modern economic growth.

13.2.3. THE FIRST MODERN ECONOMY

A "modern economy" need not be one with the outward attributes of a twentieth-century industrial economy; rather, it should incorporate the generic features that make those outward signs possible. Foremost among those features are:

- markets, for both commodities and the factors of production (land, labor, and capital), that are reasonably free and pervasive;
- agricultural productivity adequate to support a complex social and occupational structure that makes possible a far-reaching division of labor;
- a state which in its policy making and enforcement is attentive to property rights, to freedom of movement and contract, and at the same time is not indifferent to the material conditions of life of most inhabitants; and
- a level of technology and organization *capable* of sustained development and of supporting a material culture of sufficient variety to sustain market-oriented consumer behavior.

This list of characteristics is not intended to serve as a formal definition of – let alone a prescription for – economic development. Its purpose is to suggest the variety of features necessary (and the lack of necessity that they be present in a specific form or strength) for an historical economy to be analyzed with modern economic concepts and fruitfully compared to other modern economies.

Although certain other European polities may have shared all these features for a time, the United Provinces can lay claim to being the first modern economy by virtue of continuity (it has been a modern economy ever since) and by virtue of its leadership in establishing the conditions for economic modernity over much of Europe. It became not only the commercial entrepôt for Europe; it also achieved Europe's highest overall level of total factor productivity for the better part of the seventeenth and eighteenth centuries. That is, it became the first of what Angus Maddison calls a "lead country," operating nearest to the techno-logical frontier and doing most to define that frontier, until it was dislodged from that position by Great Britain, by his reckoning, toward the end of the eighteenth century. Britain, in turn, ceded this place at the technological frontier to the United States toward the end of the nineteenth century.

Of defining importance to the first modern economy, as to all such economies, was productivity-increasing investment. The amassing of trading capital and strat-egies to assert monopoly power with that capital may have formed the core of the early Republican economy, but the long-term success of this enterprise de-pended on the achievement of higher productivity in agriculture, fishing, industry, and trade. In each of these sectors, investment brought technical and organiza-tional improvements that came to set the standard for low costs (as in shipping), high quality (as in herring fishing and cloth finishing), or labor productivity (as in dairying and industries such as lumber milling, papermaking, and shipbuilding).

These technological and organizational advances were by no means continu-ous, let alone self-sustaining – qualities sometimes deemed essential to the defi-nition of modern economic growth – but they did help to achieve standards of performance that were not quickly superseded by competitors. Although we can-not measure directly the capital stock available per worker, everything we have been able to document concerning the importance of fixed capital in industry, the low labor-to-tonnage ratios in ocean shipping, and the scope of capital in-vestment in agriculture supports the view that the capital/labor ratio rose to un-precedented heights.

In addition, we have noted the large amount of energy available per worker. The Republic's peat deposits provided a uniquely large supply of heat energy – in excess even of England's coal output until well into the eighteenth century – and this was supplemented by industrial windmills, horse-powered mills, imported coal, and the largest per capita endowment of ocean, inland, and fishing vessels in Europe.

Finally, we can note the substantial investment in "human capital" (i.e., in economically valuable skills). The occupational structure of this economy was such that a large fraction of the labor force required formal education and oc-cupational training, both of which required investment, at least in terms of fore-gone income. This fact was not lost on Amsterdam's guardians of the poor (the *Aalmoezeniers*), who advocated establishing an orphanage for their young wards in 1665 in order to ensure, among other things, that they would be adequately educated. The poorest orphans' limited exposure to formal education proved to be very damaging, they argued, for "once they become skilled in their craft they still do not possess the capacity to keep records of that which they make, buy, or sell."[14] The early rise of basic literacy rates (see Chapter 5), the large proportion

---

[14] "In dien se tot perfectie van haer ambacht comen hebbende geen capaciteyt van 't geen datse maken, coopen off vercoopen, notitie te houden." (G. A. Amsterdam, Part. Arch. 343, no. 8).

of the labor force trained in formal apprenticeships, and the large proportion, by the standards of that time, enrolled in universities and illustrious schools, all reflect a substantial investment in human-capital formation.

The most direct evidence that the Dutch permanently raised labor productivity above the levels prevailing in other countries is of two kinds: the fact that already in the mid–seventeenth century an agricultural sector employing under 40 percent of the total labor force could almost be a net food exporter (which it indeed became by 1800), and the fact that nominal wages between about 1600 and 1800 were the highest of Europe. Labor markets were, and are, full of imperfections, but in the Republic's open economy, such a large and long-lasting international wage gap (see Table 12.3) could only have been supported by real and enduring productivity differences.

A steady attention to costs and efficiency characterized this market-oriented economy. As in any society, customs, institutions, and laws evolved to protect powerful interests and to maintain social peace. We have noted the impediments to economic efficiency in the labor market, the herring fishery, and the VOC, among others. But a critic of the notion that a striving for greater efficiency was characteristic of the Dutch economy could choose no better example than the structure and evolution of the state. The independent Republic's resolute determination to preserve the power of the provinces and to enhance that of the cities created a polity in which the monopolistic exploitation of municipal and provincial autonomy, with its myriad impediments to trade, added costs to transactions of every kind. While this market fragmentation was not unusual in the Europe of 1600, by 1750 it had begun to acquire an antique patina. Elsewhere, the pressing needs of state centralization stimulated bureaucratic and centralized administration. To this seemingly inexorable process, the Republic, whose fiscal needs grew as fast as its neighbors', was immune, and this immunity imposed important limitations on private efforts to lower costs.

A second essential characteristic of the modern economy is the continuous accumulation and effective preservation of capital. The episodic character of capitalism in preindustrial Europe – the strong tendency to withdraw capital to the social safety of agricultural property, and to keep commercial capital highly liquid, making commitments for the shortest possible period – reflected the chronic problem of finding productive placements for capital consistent with the owner's level of risk aversion. That is, the challenge of early European capitalism was not so much the initial accumulation of capital as its continuous productive employment.

The Republic built on earlier Italian and Flemish experience to put in place institutions and practices that offered superior access to information, risk-spreading investment forms, and financial intermediation to the investor. The Dutch capitalist had ready access to a broad array of investment options – from the sixteenth-century *partenrederij*, a flexible partnership form applicable to a wide variety of industrial, fishing, and trading enterprises; to the seventeenth-century

Beurs, which reduced the cost and risk of trade in commodities, bonds, and equities; to the eighteenth-century merchant banks, underwriters of bond offerings for foreign states and colonial plantations. This institutional resourcefulness led active merchants to shift to acceptance credit, commission trade, and marine insurance. It led others toward government bonds. We have argued that these shifts were not so much signs of flawed character as they were capital-preserving steps in a changing international environment.

Yet it is undeniable that the financial institutions and practices of this first modern economy left much to be desired. The "irrational" speculative manias – involving tulips, hyacinths, VOC shares, and English funds – hardly qualify as serious indictments. On the contrary, they only underscore the modern character of this economy. The real weaknesses of the Dutch capital markets resided in their eventual overreliance on the government bond market and the absence of a banking institution capable of restoring liquidity in times of crisis. The lack of demand for domestic investment may well have removed any incentive to innovate in the financial sector, but the autarkic structure of merchant banks, financing clients (states) too few in number and too powerful, ultimately proved unable to manage the risks of the late eighteenth-century world.

One might question whether even the most admirable financial institutions could have weathered the political storms of the Revolutionary and Napoleonic era; but the crisis, drawing the curtain on Amsterdam's role as Europe's foremost capital market, certainly was intensified by the overexposure of Dutch capital to government bonds. Her eighteenth-century "accumulation without growth" depended on the health of fiscal systems at home and abroad. The diversification of investment that had characterized the expansive era turned into its opposite in the eighteenth century, and no leadership, public or private, acted to check this tendency.

This brings us to the third hallmark of the economy's modernity: its diversified structure and advanced division of labor. The foundations for this achievement were laid very early. Indeed, the diversified character of this economy was not so much a *consequence* of the explosive growth of its foreign trade after 1580 as it was its *precondition*. Simultaneously exploiting the opportunities of their location and struggling with the limitations of their environment, the fifteenth- and sixteenth-century inhabitants of the Northern Netherlands constructed the rudimentary features of a market-oriented economy well positioned to pursue the benefits of specialization and exchange for which Adam Smith would later become such an effective proponent. This preparation helps to account for the explosive character of the economy's growth after the 1580s. Triggered by the new opportunities in foreign trade, the economy quickly began to expand in industry, fishing, and agriculture.

By the mid–seventeenth century, under 40 percent of the labor force was engaged in agriculture, a broadly diversified industrial complex absorbed perhaps 30 percent of the labor force, and a highly articulated commercial structure spread its intricate net across the country. The numerous cities formed a complex of interdependence, with the lesser ports specializing in functions to serve Amsterdam, Rotterdam, and Middelburg, and the industrial towns cultivating particular branches of production. The countryside, in turn, came to be more highly differentiated by agricultural specialization while the villages evolved into service centers, often of considerable complexity. The legal privileges of the cities notwithstanding, the diffusion of typically urban service functions extended far down the hierarchy of central places, even to modest villages. As demonstrated in Chapter 11, few inhabitants of the Republic were far removed from a basic complement of commercial services.

The integration of specialized agriculture and industry with the growing entrepôt functions of the ports imparted a special dynamism to the Golden Age economy. This integration constitutes the most important reason to question interpretations of this economy that view it as a single city's "empire of trade and credit . . . unsustained by the forces of a modern state."[15]

In the Republic a large number of mutually conflicting economic interests had to be balanced. The privileges always granted in the interests of foreign trade form a durable constant in Dutch economic policy, but this should not blind us to the ongoing struggles among the cities, each defending its parochial interests, that resulted in foreign policy shifts, monetary unification, tariff adjustments (in the 1680s and 1725), and the encouragement of specific industries, such as the herring fisheries, whaling, and silk production. These debates could also result in nothing more than long-term deadlock, as in the improvement of internal waterways and trade policy with the Southern Netherlands.

The improbable political structure of the United Provinces has called into question its basic capacity to identify and assert a coherent national interest. Yet the careful weighing of the various domestic interests and an alert defense of vital interests abroad characterized this decentralized state until a strong national leadership asserted itself, in the form of Willem III, to involve the Republic in an enterprise whose mix of national interest and dynastic ambition seemed, inexorably, to shift toward the latter.

In an age when national interest usually expressed itself in some form of mercantilism, the weakness of such tendencies in Dutch policy have long attracted attention. A proto-liberal, principled adherence to free trade can be adduced from the *Mare Liberum* of Hugo Grotius (1609), which advocated freedom of the seas, and from the hostility to monopolies and privileges expressed in Pieter de la Court's *Interest van Hollandt* (1662). But the Republic's foreign trade policies almost always breathed the spirit of pragmatism. It was not hindered by any principle from protecting domestic production or discriminating against specific trading partners, and it did both when this seemed advantageous. But the Republic found itself in a position in which such measures were rarely advantageous

---

[15] Barbour, p. 13.

to more than a sectional interest. States such as England and France, struggling to integrate and assert control over the economies of their territories and colonial possessions, found protectionism a useful tool. These states were, so to speak, larger than their economies; they stood before the task of asserting some sort of direction over largely autonomous areas. In contrast, the Republic's economic interests spread far beyond the boundaries of the state. Her chief aim had to be maintaining access to the supplies of goods and labor and the markets for her specialized output on which her diversified economy depended.

The limited application of mercantilist policies did not reflect the antiquated political economy of "the last of Europe's city-states"; it expressed instead the characteristic policy constraints of a "lead economy," such as would later be displayed by nineteenth-century Britain and the post–World War II United States.

The reader prepared to concede that the Republic could muster a rational and even effective economic policy in the seventeenth century might still balk at rehabilitating the political reputation of the "Periwig Age," when the regent families, substantially divorced from commercial life and living from the passive income of financial assets, evolved into an oligarchy of perpetual officeholders. We do not propose such a rehabilitation, but it is nevertheless instructive to place the regents and rentiers in a broader context. They were much like the contemporary English aristocracy that dominated that country's government – not so much disdainful of commercial life as satiated and self-satisfied, with portfolios dominated by land and government bonds all locked up in entailed estates. If one elite presided over a powerful economic expansion while the other witnessed a progressive economic marginalization, this probably had less to do with differences in their personal qualities than with deeper structures and macropolitical conditions that were not easily changed. Rarely does one find an *existing* elite purposely initiating major economic renovations of a society.

This brings us to the final misunderstood dimension of the Republic's economic modernity: its decline. On the face of it, this is an inadmissible attribute of a modern economy, since most definitions require that it achieve long-term sustained growth in per capita income driven by continuous technological improvement. From this perspective the failure of Dutch economic growth to continue through the eighteenth century offers the most compelling testimony that it did not constitute a modern economy in the first place.

To suggest that the Republic suffered a "modern decline" must seem perverse, but that is our argument. The economy did not suffer a Malthusian crisis, nor did it revert to some preindustrial norm after a brief, "accidental" boom. In sector after sector, as the preceding chapters have shown, the economy struggled with the modern problems of profits, employment, market access, and costs. The environmental problems accumulating after 1670 were not the product of poverty (such as soil depletion), but the unforeseen consequence of rapid development (such as deteriorating water quality, soil subsidence, and harbor silting). The demographic reversals that also set in after 1670 were no expression of overpopulation or increasingly frequent food shortages, but were most probably related to the high level of urbanization and the high incidence of migration induced by economic growth, and to the checks to nuptiality posed by a changing occupational structure. The agricultural depression was a purely market phenomenon. Indeed, the less commercialized regions suffered least from the fall in commodity prices and the stable or rising production costs, which together pinched severely on the farmers of the maritime zone. The industrial sector was large and varied, but a structural problem of high costs and restricted foreign-market access defined the environment in which a varied pattern of retreat from labor-intensive production and shift to capital- and energy-intensive production took place. The crisis in foreign trade did not so much force a dismantling of the *stapelmarkt* as it stimulated a variety of counterthrusts intended to refashion it. The problems facing the commercial sector did not stem from the crabbed mental horizons of merchant capitalists; they were problems of profits, markets, and political power to which the Republic's merchants responded with at least partial success. Finally, the crisis of the Republic's fiscal system is no tale of royal fecklessness or the hubris of plutocrats; it describes an altogether modern problem, but one which occurred at a time when the modern means of managing excessive public debt (the expansion of the tax base and, failing that, monetary inflation) were not available.

The responses to this multitude of problems were not altogether without success, and the eighteenth-century economy generated new activities with significant growth potential. But the Republic never successfully surmounted the obstacle of high costs that undermined, eventually, nearly all forms of industrial production. Given the key role that industrial technology would play in the nineteenth-century economy, this deindustrialization – itself arguably an outward sign of enviable prosperity – proved to be more than an ordinary weakness. It ensured that the Republic would play no important role in developing those technologies via the "learning-by-doing" processes essential in that empirical age (or, for that matter, any age), and it would of necessity lose its place on the productivity frontier.

13.3. Taking the measure of the first modern economy

One of the chief objectives of the past generation of economic historians has been to achieve reliable estimates of the total output (gross domestic product, or GDP) or, alternatively, the total national income of the chief Western economies as they industrialized in the course of the nineteenth century. Such studies invariably face disheartening gaps in the necessary evidence, and the methodological issues are often arcane and tiresome. Yet to the "new economic historians" who came to the fore beginning in the 1960s, these efforts were critically important: If anecdote and casual empiricism were to give way to rigorous hypothesis testing, a reliable quantitative framework of macroeconomic variables needed to be constructed. If the causes of economic growth were to be uncovered, the available historical record of measured economic performance would have to be extended back beyond the twentieth century to the origins of growth – to the Industrial Revolution.

No similar enthusiasm encouraged the application of the concept of national income accounting to earlier, preindustrial economies. The scarcity of usable historical data stands as a considerable obstacle to the further backward extension of national income estimates, of course; but a more important factor acting to discourage such work was the belief that little could be learned from efforts to measure economies that existed close to subsistence and that were incapable of achieving a growth that was more than episodic and cyclical in character. In an economy where few people actually worked regularly for wages, where unpriced, nonmarketed output was a large part of the total, and where exogenous events such as epidemics, war, and even climatic change rendered all economic output highly unstable, the application of national income accounting has seemed to be an academic exercise drained by its anachronism of any interpretive power.

These arguments are not without force, but there exist two important reasons to explore the possibilities of estimating national income in the seventeenth and eighteenth centuries. The first is derived from the results of such work on the "first industrial nation," Great Britain. Britain's rate of growth of industrial output now appears to have been much slower during the classic Industrial Revolution than had earlier been thought. This casts doubt on the abruptness of the Industrial Revolution; it also recasts the character of the preindustrial British economy, which was richer and more industrial than previously had been believed. Since the late eighteenth century can no longer be thought of as a "ground zero" of economic growth, the character and pattern of economic performance before then warrants closer examination.

The second reason is derived from our interpretation of the Dutch economy during the Republic. If this was the first modern economy, the concept of national income accounting should not be anachronistically misplaced. On the contrary, it should help us to understand that economy's achievements and its place in the larger history of European economic development.

The task of assessing the national income of the Netherlands before the nineteenth century has two component parts: estimating the *level* of national income at one or more benchmark periods, and tracking the *trends* of national income over time. Regrettably, the absence of reliable nineteenth-century Dutch national income data makes it impossible simply to extend trend estimates backward from a nineteenth-century benchmark. For this reason a plausible estimate of the level of national income in the period under investigation here is of special importance.

What resources stand at our disposal to estimate the size of this economy? One has already be n discussed (see Chapter 11, section 11.5): the *Personeele Quotisatie* of 1742. This assessment of the taxable income of (almost) all urban Hollanders with annual incomes above 600 guilders impresses us by the care with which it was compiled. It certainly understates the total income of the households liable for taxation, but its high degree of internal consistency gives confidence that the discrepancies are neither enormous nor uncorrectable.

The *Personeele Quotisatie* is a reliable document, but its coverage is distinctly limited: to Holland's top fifth of income earners. In the first decade of the nineteenth century, French-inspired statistics gathering and the estimates of contemporary political arithmeticians place at our disposal more comprehensive quantitative information, but the price for broad coverage is dubious reliability and probable unrepresentativeness, since the period 1800–10 was one of wild price volatility and boom-and-bust cycles in foreign trade.

Consider first the 1742 estimates of personal income. In Chapter 11 we saw that the taxed income of household heads earning at least 600 guilders per year in sixteen cities of Holland totaled 43 million guilders, or approximately 460 guilders per capita. The pattern of income across cities of different size and other evidence concerning wage earnings of adult males earning less than 600 guilders led us to estimate per capita income in Holland as a whole at about 152 guilders. But we also noted that this figure is certain to be an underestimate. The *Personeele Quotisatie* specifically excluded the salaries of ministers, professors, and military officers; it defined taxable income in terms of disposable income (i.e., excluding direct tax payments and investment); it took no account of the earnings of non-family household members (i.e., servants); and it excluded nonhousehold income such as the retained earnings of firms (notably, the VOC), institutions, and government bodies. Finally, given its fiscal nature, the *Personeele Quotisatie* almost certainly understated the incomes that it did not intend to exclude. It follows that two corrections must be made to our initial estimates: one for the intentionally excluded income, and another for the understatement of taxable income.

Of the intentionally excluded income, only the savings and direct tax payments represent a large sum. The other items cannot represent more than several million guilders in total, but Holland's direct taxes alone exceeded 8 million guilders. No estimate of the missing income can claim great accuracy, but we believe a range of 15 to 25 million guilders is unlikely to exaggerate the intended exclusions. Even less confidence can be attached to any estimate of understated taxable income. Let us, again, be cautious and suggest a 7.5 to 12.5 percent range. Table 13.1 displays the per capita income estimates drawn from Chapter 11 and applies to them the adjustments proposed here to reach a likely range of per capita income for Holland as a whole.

In order to propose a national income estimate for the entire Republic, we need to consider how the incomes of urban and rural Holland might compare to those of the other provinces. Table 13.1 shows our estimates, which reflect the assumptions listed at the bottom of the table. In general, we were guided by the regional wage differentials described in Chapter 12 and the agricultural productivity differentials described in Chapter 6.

How plausible is the resulting estimate of national income for 1742? At current prices – in 1742 the overall price level was close to its nadir – the Republic's

Table 13.1. *Estimate of Dutch national income, 1742.*[a]

	Urban	Rural	Total
Holland			
1. Based on *Personele Quotisatie* per capita income	172	124	152
2. Underreporting factor (7.5–12.5%)	185–94	124	—
3. Excluded income	21–42	16	—
4. Revised per capita income estimates	206–36	140	180–98
5. Total income of Holland, in millions	98.9–113.3	43.4	142.3–56.7
Other maritime provinces (Zeeland, Friesland, Groningen, Utrecht)			
6. Assumed per capita income	145	124	131
7. Total income, in millions	21.8	37.2	59.0
Inland provinces (Drenthe, Overijssel, Gelderland, North Brabant, Limburg)			
8. Assumed per capita income	124	75	87
9. Total income, in millions	22.3	41.3	63.6
Total Republic			
10. Per capita income	177–94	105	134–42
11. National income, in millions	143.0–57.4	121.9	264.9–79.3

[a]Explanations: LINE 1: Estimates from Chapter 11, section 11.5. LINE 2: For underreporting factor, see text. LINE 3: Excluded income factor. The total excluded income is estimated to range between 15 and 25 million guilders. Excluded salaries of clergy, etc., may have totaled 1 million; incomes of non–family members of households (servants) may have totaled 3 million (60,000 servants × annual salary of 50 guilders); direct taxes 8–10 million; undistributed nonhousehold income and savings form imponderables: We can neither estimate them nor, in the case of the latter, be certain how the tax assessors treated such income. LINE 6: Urban income is assumed to be an unweighted average of the unadjusted income in Holland's cities, excluding Amsterdam (from Table 11.14); rural income is assumed to be equal to the unadjusted rural income in Holland. LINE 8: Urban income is assumed to equal the unadjusted income of Holland's smallest cities (from Table 11.14); rural income is set at 60 percent of the unadjusted maritime zone average, as suggested by wage and productivity differentials discussed in Chapters 6 and 12.

national income represented an overall per capita income of 134 to 142 guilders, rather unevenly distributed between country and city and among provinces, as shown in Table 13.1. The total wage bill (the adult male labor force multiplied by the *unskilled* wage for 300 days' work) amounted to some 45 percent of total income. Total interest income from domestic and foreign government bonds (the latter still very small) amounted to about 8 percent of total income, but nearly 15 percent of income in the maritime cities, where bondholders were concentrated. Total provincial and federal tax revenue stood between 12 and 15 percent of national income. Retained imports accounted for about 25 percent. The value of all agricultural output, in the 70- to 80-million-guilder range, accounted for about 25 to 30 percent of total income. These quantitative relationships are reassuring. They suggest that the 40 percent of the labor force engaged in agriculture earned about 25 to 30 percent of total income; that the total tax burden (which excludes municipal and other local taxation) was about equal to that of England at the time; and that Holland, representing 40 percent of the Republic's population, enjoyed 54 to 56 percent of national income and paid over 60 percent of total taxes.

If we turn next to 1800–10, the *Nationaale Balans der Bataafsche Republiek* of W. M. Keuchenius ventured to make an estimate of national income for an unspecified "peacetime year" around 1800. His estimate cannot be accepted at face value, since he obviously misestimated the income of certain sectors and ignored others altogether. Keuchenius held the Physiocratic belief that industry, crafts, services, and transport were of no account (unless they worked for export) since, as he put it "the profit from this passes from one hand to another, without enriching the country or augmenting the stock of money."[16] Fortunately, the observations of his contemporaries (Issac Gogel, Rutger Metelerkamp, and Gijsbert Karl van Hogendorp) plus calculations made from Batavian data by modern historians can assist us in correcting Keuchenius's work. Table 13.2 presents his estimates together with our proposed corrections.

This revision of Keuchenius is compatible with the national income estimates of J. L. van Zanden, which are based on calculations of returns to labor, real property, and capital. The apparent increase in per capita income between 1742 and 1800–10 is only that – apparent. The increase in prices in the intervening sixty years exceeded considerably the 15 to 20 percent increase in per capita income at current prices. Our cost of living index rises by at least 40 percent over this period, but a proper GNP deflator would be somewhat lower, since wages increased little, if at all. It is also important to keep in mind the volatility of the Dutch economy in these years. Keuchenius (and we in correcting him) assumed the favorable conditions of peacetime (such as the short period after the Peace of

---

[16] "dewijl de winst hier van uit de eene in de andere hand gaat, zonder een land te verrijken, of 't geld te vermeerderen." W. M. Keuchenius, *Nationaale Balans der Bataafsche Republiek* (Amsterdam, 1804).

Table 13.2. *Sketch of 1800–10 national income based on the corrected estimates of W. M. Keuchenius (in millions of guilders).*

	Keuchenius		Correction	
Income				
Domestic government debt	30			
Foreign government debt	40	too high	21.5	(see Table 4.8)
Agricultural income	83	too low	110.0[a]	
Foreign trade, shipping, banking	30			
East and West Indies revenues	20			
Exported manufactures	3	too low	15	(see Table 10.12)
Fisheries	15	too low	5	(see Chapter 7)
Missing from Keuchenius:				
Industrial production				
Domestic services			75.5	
Domestic trade and transport				
National income (in millions)	221		307	
Per capita national income	116		162	
Expenditures				
Agricultural products:				
Domestic	73	too low	95	
Imports	10			
Fish	14	too high	4	
East and West Indies products	13	too low	21	(see Table 10.12)
Wine, salt, Mediterranean products	21.5	too high	15	
Imported industrial raw materials	10.5			
Miscellaneous imports	4.0			
Manufactures:				
Domestic	0	missing	[b]	
Imports	20			
Services, transportation	0	missing	[b]	
Savings	0	missing	[b]	
Taxation	55	too high	46.6	(see Table 4.3)
Missing from Keuchenius:				
The *b* items:			81.0	
Total expenditures	221		307	
Per capita	116		162	

[a]The income of the agricultural sector is based on van Zanden, Nederlandse landbouw, p. 125, where he estimates agricultural income for 1810 as consisting of rent, 40 million; wage income, 50 million; and 6.4 million of interest and inventory depreciation. An additional 12 million is attributable to the peat, forest, and horticultural sectors.

[b]The estimate of the items missing from Keuchenius's survey includes the savings of the population. In Table 4.8 we estimated total investment in domestic and foreign government bonds at 50 million per year to 1804 and 22.4 million thereafter. Savings from interest income are thought to have ranged between 15 and 20 million per year.

Compare this estimate with the following estimates of J. L. van Zanden.

1. *De economische ontwikkeling van de Nederlandse landbouw in de negentiende eeuw, 1800–1914* (Wageningen, 1985), Appendix III. Here 1820 national income is estimated, in current guilders, as follows:

Wage bill: labor force 801,000 (35% of population) × f0.75 (average daily wage) × 250 days per year =	150.0 million
Real property income:	
land rental value	44.0 million
house rental value	25.1 million
Capital income: real property is assumed to represent 39% of all capital, hence all other assets yield:	177.0 million
Profits: assumed to range between 10% and 25% of wage and capital income	
Final estimates range between:	
National income	360–409 million
Population	2.289 million
Per capita income	159–79 guilders

GNP deflator for 1815–24 (1910 = 100): 90–110.

2. "Economische groei in Nederland in de negentiende eeuw. Enkele nieuew resultaten," *Economisch- en sociaal-historisch jaarboek 50* (1987), 51–76. The estimate of national income for 1820 is the same as for 1. But a new estimate of Gross National Product is offered for 1805, based on indexes of output by sector linked to the 1910 CBS estimate for GNP. Total GNP is estimated as 17.7% of the 1910 figure, which in per capita terms amounts to 48% of the 1910 level. Since per capita GNP in 1910 equaled 390 guilders, the 1805 level in 1910 guilders was 187 guilders.

To summarize:

National income estimate (1800–10)	f162	current prices
van Zanden national income estimate (1820)	f159–79	current prices
van Zanden GNP estimate (1805)	f187	1910 prices
	f168–206	current prices

Amiens of 1802); the slide into oblivion at the end of the decade, when interest income plummeted, shipping income disappeared, and East and West Indies goods could not approach Dutch ports, is not reflected in this reconstruction of national income.

These two efforts to gauge the *level* of Dutch national income are tentative and subject to revision. The 1742 estimate depends on assumptions about how the incomes of the well-to-do of Holland's cities are related to the rest of the population. The 1800–10 estimate is grounded in evidence relating to interest income, tax revenues, the agricultural sector, and foreign trade; much less secure are the estimates of that large terrain of economic activity about which Keuchenius himself was silent. But if a level of per capita income in the range of 130 to 145 guilders, in 1740s purchasing power, is accepted as likely for the two periods examined here, an instructive comparison can be made with the competing British economy across the North Sea (see Figure 13.1). The research of C. Knick Harley and Nicholas Crafts sets the British gross national product (expressed in 1720–44 prices) at approximately 80 million pounds, or 120 guilders per capita. At constant prices, this per capita income grew by no more than 7.5 percent up to 1800, and by 25 percent by 1830. By then, British per capita income had certainly surpassed the Dutch level, but in 1760 the Republic's income level stood above that of Britain and, most likely, the rest of Europe. Indeed, it is not obvious that this lead had been eliminated by 1800.

What about the century before 1742? Here we must turn to the estimation of *trends* of total output, as revealed by indicators believed to move in sympathy with national income. The preceding chapters have provided no small number of *partial* indicators of these trends. If they all moved in the same direction, our task would be simple, but it is precisely because of the complexity of the structural change in the period 1660–1740 that the various sectors of the economy moved in different directions. The decline of fishing, agriculture, European trade, the textile and brewing industries, and shipbuilding is clear. But the expansion of intercontinental trade, the paper, sugar, tobacco, and distilling industries, and finance is equally clear, and the weighting of all these various developments is no simple task.

One might sidestep this complex problem of measurement and weighting by appealing to certain indicators thought to reflect the overall consequences of these divergent trends. The Republic's gradual deurbanization, from a high point of some 42 percent around 1675 to 38 percent in 1795, appears to be a telling phenomenon. Since urbanization is generally thought to bring higher incomes, higher productivity, and faster technical and organizational change, its opposite might be expected to reflect a reversal of these salutary processes. But the Republic's rural sector was not the seat of rank backwardness that is tacitly assumed in this interpretation, which casts some doubt on the direct association of deurbanization with economic decline.

A more promising general indicator of the overall performance of the economy

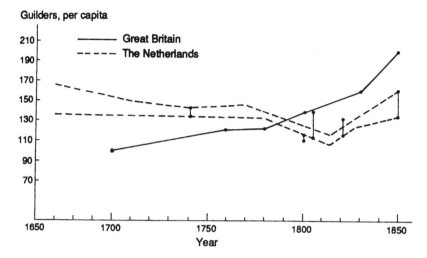

Figure 13.1. Dutch and British per capita national income compared. This graph presents
the general course of national income in Great Britain with a sketch of the likely course
of Dutch national income and several point estimates. All prices have been reduced to
1720–44 price levels. [*Sources:* GREAT BRITAIN: C. Knick Harley, "Reassessing the Industrial
Revolution: A Macro View," in Joel Mokyr, ed., *The British Industrial Revolution. An
Economic Perspective* (Boulder, CO, 1993), pp. 171–226. See also N. F. R. Crafts and C.
Knick Harley, "Output growth and the British Industrial Revolution: A restatement of
the Crafts-Harley view," *Economic History Review* 45 (1992), 703–30. THE NETHERLANDS:
POINT ESTIMATES. 1742: Our estimates, see text (Chapter 11, section 11.5, and Chapter 13,
section 13.3). For additional discussion of national income in 1742, see J. L. van Zanden,
"De economie van Holland in de periode 1650–1805: groei of achteruitgang? Een overzicht
van bronnen, problemen en resultaten," *Bijdragen en mededelingen betreffende de geschiedenis
der Nederlanden 102* (1987), 565–77. CIRCA 1800: Based on revisions of estimates made by
R. Metelerkamp, *De toestand van Nederland in vergelijking gebragt met die van enige andere
landen van Europa* (Rotterdam 1804); and W. M. Keuchenius, *De inkomsten en uitgaven der
Bataafsche Republiek, voorgesteld in eene Nationale Balans* (Amsterdam, 1803). For revisions,
see text. 1805 AND 1820: J. L. van Zanden, "Economische groei in Nederland in de negentiende eeuw," *Economisch- en sociaal-historisch jaarboek 50* (1987), pp. 53, 58; and J. L. van
Zanden, *De economische ontwikkeling van de Nederlandse landbouw in de negentiende eeuw, 1800–
1914* (Wageningen, 1985), pp. 378–83. 1850: There are several estimates, but they vary
considerably, and the proper price deflator is also in doubt. The range shown in the graph
is based on discussions in van Zanden, "Economische groei," p. 69, and Jan de Vries, "The
Decline and Rise of the Dutch Economy, 1675–1900," in Gavin Wright and Gary Saxonhouse, eds., *Technique, Spirit, and Form in the Making of the Modern Economies: Essays in
Honor of William N. Parker* (Greenwich, CT, 1984), pp. 152–3. We accept 215 guilders
(1900–9 guilders) as the most plausible estimate. Deflated, this yields an estimate of 150 to
160 guilders, the upper bound of the 1850 point estimate. TRENDS: The dashed lines indicate
the general direction of change and rough turning points in the course of Dutch national
income. They are based on discussion in this volume and arguments presented in Jan de
Vries, "Decline and Rise." See also J. L. van Zanden, "Economie van Holland."]

Passenger-kilometers (in millions)

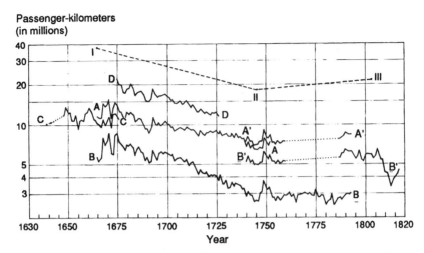

Figure 13.2. Annual volume of passenger barge travel on various aggregations of routes, plus estimated total volume of the entire system at three dates. Aggregate series: **A**, Amsterdam–Haarlem, Haarlem–Leiden, Leiden–The Hague/Delft, Amsterdam–Leiden, Leiden–Utrecht, Groningen–Winschoten. **A'**, all routes in **A**, plus Amsterdam–Monnikendam–Edam–Hoorn. **B**, Leiden–The Hague/Delft, Amsterdam–Leiden, Leiden–Utrecht, Groningen–Winschoten. **B'**, Amsterdam–Haarlem, Haarlem–Leiden, Leiden–Utrecht. **C**, Amsterdam–Haarlem, Leiden–The Hague/Delft, The Hague–Delft, Delft–Maassluis. **D**, all routes in **A'**, plus The Hague–Delft, Amsterdam–Weesp, Amsterdam–Gouda. **I** = 1665, **II** = 1745, and **III** = 1805. [*Source:* Jan de Vries, *Barges and Capitalism. Passenger transportation in the Dutch economy (1632–1839)* (Utrecht, 1981), p. 223.]

is provided by the intercity barge transportation system that connected thirty cities in the Republic's maritime zone. Beginning in 1632, horse-drawn barges, *trekschuiten*, maintained regularly scheduled passenger services on routes that eventually blanketed Holland and stretched across Friesland and Groningen. The demand for these intercity transport services was certainly affected by changing prices, and the populations of the cities connected by the canal system worked their own effect on the flows of traffic. But once these variables are accounted for, the record of passenger travel traces out trends that appear best explained by the changing disposable real incomes of the consumer base – the urban population of the maritime zone. Figure 13.2 shows the overall trend in travel volume, measured in passenger-kilometers. Once the effect of price and population changes is taken into account, a decline in demand of 33 percent remains for the period from the 1660s to the 1740s.[17] Between the 1740s and 1790s, unexplained demand changes are close to zero. Of course, a 33 percent decline in

[17] For a detailed account of these adjustments, see Jan de Vries, *Barges and Capitalism* (Utrecht, 1981), pp. 275–303.

demand for intercity passenger travel does not imply a 33 percent decline in personal income. The income elasticity of demand for this service probably considerably exceeded unity. Thus, a 1 percent decline in income would cause a decline in demand for passenger travel by more than 1 percent. The course of passenger travel revealed in Figure 13.2 seems consistent with a nontrivial decline in income, but we cannot say by exactly how much. Moreover, we must not lose sight of the fact that the passenger barge system served only the maritime provinces. Incomes in the inland provinces are likely to have followed a rather different course.

Another way of tracking the performance of the Dutch economy is to rely on tax revenues. Since so much of Holland's public revenue relied on excise taxes imposed on a wide variety of products and services, an examination of the various levies and the revenues that they generated should permit a reconstruction of trends in production, consumption, and trade. Certain taxes do, indeed, reveal useful information about sectors of the economy. But these taxes tended, for obvious reasons, to fasten on the most stable and transparent elements of economic life, and it should not surprise us that many of the most important and longest-lived excise taxes yielded remarkably stable revenues through the decades. Thus, an interesting study by J. L. van Zanden, which relies heavily on excise tax records to estimate developments in the gross national product of the province of Holland in the period 1650–1805, has produced a picture of rough stability: a 10 percent decline between the 1650s and 1700, restored by the 1760s, only to be lost again by 1800–5.

However, these results prove highly sensitive to the assumed weights of each sector and to the course of development of the least well-founded estimates, those for trade. Our analysis of the changing character of Dutch foreign trade is incompatible with his belief (based on taxes on domestic trade volume) that the trade sector grew, in real terms, by 13 percent between the 1650s and the period 1800–5. If this sector declined by only 5 percent and all van Zanden's other estimates were accepted as accurate, Holland's GNP would show a 15 to 18 percent decline over this 150-year period.

Finally, we can exploit the trends in energy use.[18] Available heat energy derived from peat and coal grew significantly in the century ending around 1660: Holland's output rose while its peat exports to Brabant ceased; the northern provinces emerged from nowhere to supply nearly half of the Republic's peat consumption

---

[18] Coal import estimates are based on R. W. Unger, "Energy Sources for the Dutch Golden Age," *Research in Economic History 9* (1984), 221–53. Peat output in the northern provinces has been reconstructed in M. A. W. Gerding, *Vier eeuwen turfwinning. De verveningen in Groningen, Friesland, Drenthe en Overijssel tussen 1550 en 1950* (Wageningen, 1995, A. A. G. Bijdragen 35). Peat output in Holland-Utrecht is the least certain element, but Gerding and the excise tax on peat consumption in Holland provide clues. These sources suggest a per capita supply of peat and coal equal to approximately 3 million kilocalories in 1650–60 (8–10% coal), 2.5 million kilocalories in 1730–50 (16–18% coal), and 2.8 million kilocalories in 1780–90 (25% coal).

by 1650; small shipments of coal down the Maas from Liège were supplemented by 1650 with English coal supplying especially breweries and refineries. All of these sources together provided a per capita heat energy supply of some 3 million kilocalories, a figure that must be double to triple the 1560 figure. In the century after 1660, peat output fell (see Chapter 2, section 2.3.3). The import of coal rose, accounting for nearly 20 percent of heat energy by 1750, but total per capita energy use may have been 15 to 20 percent below its 1660 level. After 1750 both peat output and coal imports rose again, although it does not appear likely that per capita energy use in 1780–90 equaled that of 1650–60.

The only conclusions that can be drawn from these exercises with partial and imperfect data are (1) that it is very hard to show growth in national income between the 1660s and 1740s; (2) that a real and lasting decline in per capita income in the maritime region remains a strong possibility; and (3) that the second half of the eighteenth century showed some signs of recovery before the crisis at the end of the century. This means that if per capita income stood at 134 to 142 guilders in 1742, its level in years of peace during the 1650s and '60s will not have been lower than this and may have stood somewhat higher (much higher when expressed in the higher price levels of the mid–seventeenth century). Since British national income is now thought to have grown by 20 percent between 1700 and 1760, it follows that the small superiority of Dutch income over British around 1740–60 (10 to 15 percent) must have been greater in the late seventeenth century (perhaps 30 to 40 percent), a conclusion that is reinforced by the real wage trends of the two countries described in Figure 12.6. This means that the Dutch Republic's *total* GNP in the decades when England launched war after war against it was probably 40 to 45 percent the size of the British (i.e., England and Wales plus Scotland). By 1800, when Britain's population had doubled and its per capita income had risen by 30 percent, the Republic's total economy was dwarfed by that of its historic rival, which was now five times its size.

Finally, we come to the Golden Age itself. Can we venture an estimate of the rate of growth of the economy in the century before the 1660s? No, for the most basic information needed to express that growth in quantitative terms is unavailable. But real growth of per capita income there was, of that we are confident. The evidence for it is found (1) in the agricultural sector, where our rough estimates suggest a near doubling of labor productivity between 1510 and 1650; (2) in the substantial augmentation of physical capital and energy sources in industry; (3) in the reduced manning rates per ton of ocean shipping volume; and (4) reflecting these productivity gains, in the increased real wages documented in Chapter 12. The 30 to 40 percent differential between Dutch and English per capita incomes in the second half of the seventeenth century did not reflect some natural condition; it was a human achievement, most of which was put in place in the decades after 1580, as the first modern economy took shape.

Chapter 14
Postlude

In the introduction to this book, we proposed to interpret the Netherlands from the sixteenth through the eighteenth centuries as the site of the "first modern economy." Now, at the end of our labors, we wish to take a few final pages to reflect on the implications of our thesis – implications for the interpretation of Dutch and European history, but also implications for the concepts of modernization, the Industrial Revolution, and modern economic growth.

Our claims for the economic history of the Netherlands stand in tension with a formidable bulwark of historical periodization and social scientific convention: the French (political) and (English) Industrial Revolutions that together establish the dividing line between the traditional and modern, the agrarian-commercial and the industrial worlds. The coupling of a social and political "modernization" with an economic and technological "industrialization" implied by these contemporary revolutions has led many students to the view that the two – modernization and industrialization – were so inextricably intertwined as to be synonymous.

No extended discussion is needed to demonstrate how poorly served was Dutch history by this concept. The Netherlands' early economic advance had to be set aside as a curiosity of another epoch, while the late advent of its factory-based industrialization cast doubt on any claims that its earlier development had, in fact, established a modern society.

The past generation of historical scholarship has placed on the defensive every element of the concept of a traditional/agrarian versus modern/industrial world. The first to go was the notion that modernization and industrialization were intertwined. The establishment of modern political and social institutions came to be seen more as a necessary-but-not-sufficient precondition for successful industrial development – for an industrial revolution. Then, in an increasingly post-industrial world, scholars began to question whether the Industrial Revolution constitutes an inevitable rite of passage of a society entering upon modern economic growth. The dismantling of this structure standing guard over the entryway to the modern world is not uncontested, to be sure, but we regard it as a project whose time has come, not least because it creates new possibilities for the integration of Dutch economic history into that of Europe as a whole. The Netherlands pioneered in the construction of a modern society long before the eighteenth century and embarked on modern economic growth without first passing through an industrial revolution. A corollary to this is that modern economic growth is not what it is commonly held to be.

Consider the problem of industrialization in the Netherlands. The delayed introduction of substantial factory-based industry until the last decades of the nineteenth century is now well established. But does this established fact also imply that Dutch society until the end of the nineteenth century was backward and its economy stagnant? An influential model of the industrialization process seemed to offer no alternative to such a conclusion. Alexander Gerschenkron's analysis of European industrialization, presented in his 1962 essay "Economic Backwardness in Historical Perspective," argued that delayed industrialization was a symptom of backwardness, which in turn signified the absence or imperfection of institutions and ideologies needed to mobilize economic resources effectively. When, at last, industrial growth began in a backward country, it would tend (in comparison to the early industrializers) to be more rapid (taking the form of a "great spurt") and feature a larger scale of enterprise, greater bank direction, and more invasive state involvement.

Although Gerschenkron was a formidable polyglot, he never focused his talents on the Dutch economy. This was understandable given his argument, since the Dutch nineteenth-century economy exhibited only fleetingly some of the features he predicted – under King Willem I's failed program of economic rejuvenation. Much later, when industrialization finally did get underway, it possessed none of the characteristic "late industrializer" attributes predicted by Gerschenkron. The reason for this is not hard to uncover: The Netherlands was not backward. Or, to be more precise, it was not backward in the sense that Gerschenkron, with his eyes fixed on German and Russian experience, had in mind. He supposed that industrialization proceeded from the base of an agrarian society endowed with little capital, human or physical. But what if it was to proceed from an urban, commercial society with a large stock of capital, but invested in obsolete plant, equipment, and skills?

This situation – obsolescence rather than backwardness – could not be incorporated in a model predicated on the core assumptions of the modernization-industrialization complex described earlier. It is, however, a situation familiar enough *within* the industrial era. Already early in this century, Thorstein Veblen introduced the concept of the "penalties of the pioneer" and Jan Romein spoke of the "law of the disadvantaging lead." Both of these iconoclastic thinkers had the Victorian-Edwardian deceleration of the British economy in mind, but if it can be admitted that a modern society existed before the Industrial Revolution, then there is no reason not to apply the insights of Veblen and Romein to the case of the Netherlands in the late eighteenth and early nineteenth centuries. It follows, then, that the nineteenth-century industrial development of the Netherlands was not held back by its backwardness but rather by its very modernity.

Definitions of modernity and modernization cannot detain us here, but one element of most definitions requires our attention, and that is the assumption of rational behavior. The Weberian assertion that modernity is calculating instead of magical, individual instead of communal, and generally demystifying, leads us directly to a key concept of modern economic life: *homo oeconomicus*. Economic man, the rational actor seeking to maximize economic well-being, is no stranger to the pages of this book. Without the assumption of rational behavior, the decision making that stands at the heart of our analysis of behavior and motivation – as it concerns whether to work at a given wage, marry at a given age, or sell at a given price – would fall to the ground.

Of course, the decisions of *homo œconomicus* inevitably occur in a specific context of institutions and technologies. Thus, what is rational in a seventeenth-century context may seem quite puzzling from the perspective of the twentieth century. If economic man were truly a timeless concept, there would be no need for economic historians. But our argument for the modernity of Dutch society does not rest on the claim that its inhabitants acted rationally. Seventeenth-century Dutchmen and seventeenth-century Albanians alike saw to it that five-dollar bills were not left lying on the street unclaimed (to use a favorite image of Chicago School economists).

The claim to modernity is based, to stay with the image of five-dollar bills, on the number of such bank notes that are uncovered from under heavy stones and fresh cowpies. In other words, a modern economy is not simply one where people act consistently within the constraints imposed by their circumstances, but one where their resources and preferences allow them to act to change those circumstances for the better. We are dealing with a dynamic rather than a static concept: A modern economy is one with features that assist in the processes of institutional, organizational, and technological change that improve the efficiency of production and distribution.

The society of the Netherlands distinguished itself not by being filled with rational actors who would not neglect to pick up five-dollar bills from the street, but by its advancement of processes that assisted those rational actors in increasing the efficiency of economic activity. Those modernizing, dynamic processes included urbanization, education, mobility, monetization, and political and legal development.

As we stressed in Chapter 3, the urbanization of the Netherlands attained by the mid–seventeenth century a level found nowhere else in Europe before the nineteenth century, placing information and markets within reach of persons throughout the country. In Chapter 5 we focused attention on the high levels of schooling attained by the population, both at the level of basic literacy and of higher training. The importance of education to industrialization remains unclear and contested, but its importance to the development of a differentiated, complex commercial economy needs no further rehearsal here.

Education and urbanization tend to support mobility, both physical and social, and the role of mobility in enhancing the flexibility and innovation in an economy is central to modern economic growth. The vast scope of physical mobility in the Republic received our attention in Chapter 3, where we charted international and interregional migration, and in Chapter 5, where we described the extensive transportation network of the Republic's maritime zone. There remains much to learn, especially about rural-to-urban and interurban migration within the maritime zone, but the overall picture of extensive physical mobility seems secure. Much less is known about social mobility. Did sons inevitably follow in the footsteps of their fathers, or did urbanization, education, and physical mobility enhance the possibilities for intergenerational social mobility? The increasing occupational differentiation documented in Chapter 11, and the evolving structure of the labor market described in Chapter 12, would seem to have required a substantial social mobility and to have enhanced the circulation of elites until some point in the seventeenth century. Thereafter, social mobility may have been reduced sharply, but much more research is needed to establish the validity of these impressions.

Monetization is clearly a critical factor in the spread of the calculating, rational conduct that we associate with a modern society. In the case of the Netherlands, our discussion in Chapter 4 found that at the earliest date that we can follow this process, payment in kind was of distinctly secondary importance. The life of this society soon came to be enveloped in a swelling stock of money fed by multiple sources of supply. Once again, not until the nineteenth century did Europe raise up an equal in this respect.

Finally, we come to the issue central to all concepts of modernization, the state. The Republic of the United Netherlands has long remained an enigma from the perspective of the modern nation-state. It was at once a precocious forerunner to that state and a stubborn exception to the historical dynamic of modern state formation – an "antistate" in an age of absolutism. But if we concern ourselves less with the ultimate fate of a state apparatus and more with its practical functions, then the unambiguously modern character of this state quickly becomes apparent. The Republic was a well-ordered government long capable of protecting the security of its citizens, nurturing the economic interests of its merchants and fishermen, establishing vigorous institutions to advance its colonial ambitions, and maintaining domestic tranquility. The last of these functions it carried out via the development of a modern fiscal system and a program of poor relief which, by the standards of the time, was remarkably comprehensive. The modernity of the fiscal system resided in its ability to tap a broad tax base with an almost progressive set of levies, and in its long ability to support a public debt in which the population invested with confidence. The modernity of the poor-relief system resided in its capacity to protect the weak not only in times of crisis but on an ongoing basis, as befits the needs of an urban, commercial, and individualistic society. To be sure, both the tax and poor-relief systems fell short of the standards of a twentieth-century welfare state. But both of these Republican achievements represented major advances on the characteristic policies of Europe's *ancien régime* agrarian bureaucracies.

These features of Dutch society in the seventeenth and eighteenth century placed the rational actor, the *homo oeconomicus*, in a dynamic setting conducive to innovation. This is the basis on which we argue for the modern character of the Dutch economy long before the double blows of the French and British revolutions could be felt. But there was much more about the society of the Netherlands in our period that endowed it with an early modernity, including religious toleration (see Chapter 5), a household structure composed primarily of nuclear families with few nonfamily residents (see Chapter 3), a relatively open and complex social structure (see Chapter 11), and a political regime that, while far from open to broad participation, was ideologically anti-absolutist and in practice sensitive to the interests of the citizens. In all of these respects, the Netherlands pursued a sociopolitical path that appeared reactionary to the conventional wisdom of absolutist Europe in order to establish a precocious modernity.

The rigorously decentralized constitution of the Republic did not prevent this hydra-headed polity from taking forceful action, especially when acting in the international arena. As a consequence, expressions of dissatisfaction with the Republic's institutions are barely detectable in the seventeenth century. Then the only important constitutional issue concerned the political position of the House of Orange. The weaknesses of the political system impressed themselves on the public mind only as economic problems and the steadily climbing public debt generated internal tensions. From the time of Van Slingelandt and the failed Great Council of 1716–17 to the era of the Patriots and their failed revolution in 1787, a long succession of reform proposals clamored for the attention of the political nation. The only reform of consequence in this entire period was the replacement of tax farming with direct collection of excise taxes. Vested interests proved too strong to reform a system that by the late eighteenth century appeared to possess a distinctly archaic and obfuscatory character in a Europe of states developing more centralized, well-integrated regimes. But, here again, we must ask ourselves whether this evolving political debility was the result of a species of traditionalism or whether it might not better be understood as a product of the "gridlock" to which regimes that must balance the interests of multiple constituencies are prone. In short, the political crisis of the Netherlands may be understood most fruitfully as an early version of a "distributional coalition" problem common to rich, mature societies.

Thus far, our strategy has been to demonstrate the essential modernity of Dutch society in the time of the Republic in order to render plausible our earlier argument, presented most fully in Chapter 13, that the economic experience analyzed in this book constituted "modern economic growth" and, further, that the Republic raised up the first modern economy. The reader who may be persuaded that important features of social modernity could have emerged well before the changes generally associated with the era of the Enlightenment and French Revolution may still be reluctant to make the parallel concession that modern economic growth could have taken place before the Industrial Revolution. After all, the core claim for the Industrial Revolution, as recently restated by Joel Mokyr, is that "before the Industrial Revolution technological change and economic growth did occur sporadically . . . but were invariably checked by stronger forces. After 1750 the fetters on sustainable economic change were shaken off. . . ."[1] This post-1750 event remains of world historical significance, Mokyr argues, because of its irreversibility. "Even if Britain's relative position in the developed world has declined in recent decades, it has remained an urban, sophisticated society. . . . Britain taught Europe and Europe taught the world how the miracles of technological progress, free enterprise, and efficient management can break the shackles of poverty and want." The message is clear; the economic growth that had invariably been reversed before became irreversible after the British Industrial Revolution, and, as this revolution's name asserts, the critical development making this possible was located in the industrial sector.

Our position can be stated succinctly: The British Industrial Revolution was of enormous importance, but it contributed to the achievement of modern economic growth as part of a larger process. That larger process of economic modernization involved more than industrial production, unfolded in a European zone larger than England, and began well before the late eighteenth century. The British industrial variant of modern economic growth proved to be enormously influential, as Mokyr's statement demonstrates, but today it is clear that many successful examples of economic development did not – and do not – follow that model closely. Since so much of the contemporary developed and developing world cannot plausibly claim the British Industrial Revolution as its linear ancestor, it would seem to be incumbent on the economic historian to develop a more "inclusive" conceptual framework.[2]

This is not the place to develop that larger framework. We have made the case in this book that the economy of the Netherlands played a pioneer role in the larger phenomenon of modern economic growth, and we can demonstrate

---

[1] Joel Mokyr, "Editor's Introduction: The New Economic History and the Industrial Revolution," in Joel Mokyr, ed., *The British Industrial Revolution. An Economic Perspective* (Boulder, CO, 1993), p. 131.

[2] For an introduction to the revisionist literature on the Industrial Revolution, see Jan de Vries, "The Industrial Revolution and the Industrious Revolution," *Journal of Economic History 54* (1994), 249–70.

briefly, using an unlikely source, that the task of developing the more inclusive framework may not be all that difficult. Even now, some forty years after its first enunciation, the *Stages of Economic Growth* of W. W. Rostow remains a classic expression of "high-modernism," where the claims made for the exemplary character of early British industrialization, which Rostow generalized to a universal "take-off" stage, were expressed with a confidence never since replicated. Today, Rostow's five stages no longer impress for their analytical insights, but they linger on as a convenient systematic description – a "straw man" from which to launch more penetrating arguments about the onset of modern growth.

Now, as we have noted, Rostow's great concern was to account for the onset of modern industrialization, but in each of his stages, he sought to relate the specifically economic factors leading to that objective to social and political factors as well. And, if we redirect our concern from industrial growth to economic growth more generally, Rostow's stages tend to follow very faithfully the sixteenth- and seventeenth-century experience of the Netherlands. In his initial presentation of the model, when he still spoke of three rather than five stages, we read: "the sequence of economic development is taken to consist of three periods: a long period (up to a century or, conceivably, more) when the preconditions for take-off are established; the take-off itself, defined within two or three decades; and a long period when growth becomes normal and relatively automatic. These three divisions would, of course, not exclude the possibility of growth giving way to secular stagnation or decline in the long term."[3] This sequence fits the history of the Netherlands remarkably well: a gathering of economic forces in the century after 1480, the explosive take-off between 1585 and 1621, and the extension and consolidation of that creative era in the following fifty or sixty years, whereafter stagnation and decline affected more and more sectors of the economy.

The congruence between Rostow's claim that "[in the] most general case the achievement of preconditions for take-off required major changes in political and social structure and, even, in effective cultural values [p. 27]" and the sixteenth-century experience of the Northern Netherlands is evident to the reader of Chapters 5 and 11. This society established a new state with a new governing elite as it undercut the positions of its nobles and transformed its religious life.

When we proceed to Rostow's take-off stage, matters might seem to get more difficult, since this was so obviously tailored to the expectation of massive industrialization. At the economic heart of this stage is "a necessary but not sufficient condition . . . that the proportion of net investment to national income rises from (say) 5% to over 10%, definitely outstripping the likely population pressure . . . and yielding a distinct rise in real output per capita [p. 30]." Since the testing of this proposition with data drawn from the British Industrial Revolution has long remained mired in controversy, it would be asking too much to expect a decisive quantitative confirmation for the Dutch case. But examples drawn from

---

[3] W. W. Rostow, "The Take-Off into Self-Sustained Growth," *Economic Journal* 66 (1956), p. 27.

every sector of this economy in the late sixteenth and early seventeenth centuries stress the importance of capital investment. It is by no means impossible that Rostow's expectation was satisfied, as capital poured into the fishing, agricultural, industrial, ocean shipping, colonial, and commercial sectors. Rostow's expectations concerning the sources of this capital are also met. "By and large," he wrote, "the loanable funds required to finance the take-off have come from two types of sources: from shifts in the control over income flows, including income-distribution changes and capital imports; and from the plough-back of profits in rapidly expanding particular sectors. . . . One extremely important version of the plow-back process has taken place through foreign trade [pp. 38–40]." It was a major objective of Chapter 9 to demonstrate the key role of shipping and trade in the accumulation of capital in the take-off era, while the substantial redirection of income streams that had been controlled by the pre–Reformation church played an important (but not yet fully researched) role in the financing of education and the state.

Finally, we turn to the post–take-off phase, which Rostow labeled in *The Stages of Economic Growth* as the "drive to maturity." This he defined "as the period when a society has effectively applied the range of (then) modern technology to the bulk of its resources."[4] The Republic never succeeded in applying its "best-practice" technologies uniformly to the entire country; a substantial productivity gap persisted between the maritime and inland zones. But no such gap characterized the urban and rural sectors of the maritime zone. A broad diffusion of human and physical capital among the cities and villages is reflected in the substantial uniformity of wage rates among these locations and the absence of a sharp rural–urban wage differential. The Republic's economic expansion was by no means confined to one or a few privileged locations.

Enough has been said to render plausible our claim that Rostow's model of industrialization serves well – perhaps better than for its intended purpose – as a schematization of the first modern economy. Still, one discordant note remains. Whether we rely on Mokyr or Rostow, the presumption of sustained, even unending, growth adheres to the definitions of modern economic growth, while the economic history of the Republic was clearly one of growth followed by stagnation, something approximating an S-shaped, or logistic, curve. Instead of persisting exponential growth, our study describes a society whose growth eventually moved asymptotically toward a limit, rather as the classical economists predicted.

The adherence of the classical economists to "dismal" scenarios ending in stationary states for the economy, and in positive checks to population growth, can hardly surprise anyone familiar with the basic features of the preindustrial economy. That economy depended on the land, and on the land's solar-based growth processes, not only for the acquisition of vegetable and animal foodstuffs

[4] W. W. Rostow, *The Stages of Economic Growth* (Cambridge, 1960), p. 59.

(grain, meat, dairy products, etc.) but also for its supplies of clothing (wool, hides, and vegetable fibers such as linen and hemp), construction materials (timber, reed, brick), and thermal energy (for heating, food preparation, and industrial processes). The supplies of food, raw materials, and thermal energy all depended directly on the amount of available land and on the solar energy captured by that land. Moreover, all these uses of land stood in competition with each other. Increasing the area devoted to one use (say, meat production) required the contraction of another (for example, vegetable or timber production). Of course, the preindustrial world was quite capable of improving the productivity of these limited assets: Through better crop-rotation systems, heavier fertilization, selective livestock breeding, and so on, more output could be squeezed from a unit of land. Favored localities could push this system to impressive lengths, but ultimately, photosynthesis was decisive.

This age-old regime was altered fundamentally by the technologies of the Industrial Revolution, for these made available for economic application the vast stores of energy and mineral resources accumulated in the earth in the course of geological time. The invention of the steam engine and the discovery of coal-based iron smelting and refining processes caused the supplies of these minerals to influence directly the modern standard of living. Moreover, experience with these technologies led directly to further developments – in chemistry, electricity, and other fields – all of which have sustained a long-term process of economic growth.

The tendency toward firm limits of the old "photosynthesis regime" stands in sharp contrast to the sustained growth potential of the "geological energy regime." The breakthrough to the second of these regimes constitutes an historical discontinuity of the first rank and would seem to raise serious questions about the reasonableness of our argument that the Netherlands had established the first modern economy already *before* this breakthrough, in the sixteenth through eighteenth centuries. In defense of our position, we raise the following considerations.

First, the Republic's economy had gone a great distance to liberate itself from the preindustrial energy ceiling. None of its striking characteristics – the high urbanization and population density, the broad range of craft-industrial activities, the high standard of living – can be explained without noting the large amounts of organic and kinetic energy that it harnessed. Coal was not the chief source of this energy, to be sure. The Republican economy was largely based on peat, and in the eighteenth century, domestic supplies were still far from being exhausted. Indeed, the country produced as much peat in the nineteenth century as in the seventeenth and eighteenth combined. However, these energy supplies were supplemented by substantial amounts of coal. The English coastal coalfields near Newcastle supplied most of the Dutch demand, and this coal could be shipped to the chief maritime towns of the Republic at prices comparable to those paid at London.

Our second point, thus, is that the Republic's growth did not decelerate because of the supply constraints of inelastic energy sources, but because of economic circumstances that limited demand. The Netherlands was, in fact, an early adopter of the seminal industrial invention, the steam engine. Already in the 1780s, drainage boards had acquired them for pumping purposes. However, they remained conspicuously rare in the industrial sector, where the high costs of production could not be undone by the introduction of steam engines alone. This "failed transition" was no small thing; it limited Dutch contact with a long and fruitful sequence of nineteenth-century technological advances that were intimately connected to steam power and its applications. But the transition at issue was not one from a traditional, supply-limiting economy to sustained modern economic growth; it was a demand-delayed transition from a first to a second cycle of modern economic growth.

This formulation harbors an implicit claim about modern economic growth. It is not self-sustained, exponential, and unbounded; and – not to mince words – the Republic's pioneering experience in the sixteenth through eighteenth centuries, including its experience with stagnation, may end up being a fair model for the process begun in most western countries sometime between 1780 and 1850.

The economist whose name is most closely associated with the concept of modern economic growth, Simon Kuznets, pondered the question of whether it had a characteristic "time pattern." "The intriguing question is whether we should expect the rate of growth in per capita income to fall after a while, from whatever high levels it may have reached at the end of the acceleration phase."[5] Writing in the heady years of the post–World War II boom, he could not conceive of "technological or other limitations on the *supply* side . . . as an important factor." Still, he acknowledged that "[it is difficult] to imagine unlimited growth in any social process" and concluded that "the major reason [for deceleration] would therefore lie on the demand side."

Today, supply constraints on long-term economic growth come more readily to mind than they did in the 1950s. The economic exhaustion of energy reserves, the pressure on all types of resources that would result from a universalization of western living standards, the costs of compensatory action to limit environmental deterioration, all are supply-side factors that are taken much more seriously today than in the past.

But even if human ingenuity loosens these constraints in a timely way, there remains a whole other domain of limiting factors that are more social and cultural in character. When Kuznets speculated about a demand-led deceleration of economic growth, he supposed that it would emanate from the increased preference for leisure of a high-income, goods-satiated society. This satiation point remains

---

[5] Simon Kuznets, "The Meaning and Measurement of Economic Growth," in his *Six Lectures on Economic Growth* (Glencoe, IL, 1959), pp. 13–41. See also his *Modern Economic Growth* (New Haven, CT, 1966).

elusive, but other, less sunny scenarios loom on the horizon. To begin with, the very power of modern science and technology is, in combination with our cultural values, leading modern societies toward a low-fertility, low-mortality demographic regime in which the elderly (over age 65) population will grow by the mid–twenty-first century to 25 or 30 percent of the total. As recently as 1900, this age group usually fluctuated between 5 and 7 percent of the total population. The consequences for the dependency ratio (the working population relative to the dependent – young and old – population) will be considerable, but not so severe as the savings requirements to finance an extended and medicalized old age.

The reduced size of youth cohorts might appear to offer some compensation for this heavy expense, but educational and training costs have long shown inexorable upward tendencies. And costs of this sort are driven upward by the changing mix of labor demanded by modern economies, whereby growing proportions of the population are defined as "unemployable" and, hence, become the proper object of educational and therapeutic programs.

These are only the most evident forces imposing high fixed costs on mature, modern economies. Such cost structures undermine the viability of many types of production, reducing the demand for capital and labor in productive activities.

After a decade of economic depression in the 1930s, Joseph Schumpeter wrote a prognosis for capitalism in which he rejected the then-fashionable "stagnationist" view that modern technology had run its course and modern growth had ended. In *Capitalism, Socialism, and Democracy*, he argued that there was no reason to believe the economy in the next fifty years could not grow at the rate of the previous fifty (in fact, it grew much faster).[6] Yet this assessment of the economy's productive powers did not make him optimistic about the survival of capitalism. It would succumb, he argued, not to its technical failure, but to its sociopolitical weakness. An unloved system, unable to hold the loyalty of its beneficiaries, would be undermined by social changes and political challenges that would bring socialism. This specific prediction does not seem especially prescient today, but Schumpeter's more general message may yet be valid. The ability of a society to address its new problems – problems generated by its very success – while remaining true to its values and to the commitments made in the course of its ascendancy, and while suffering the erosion of the social institutions that had undergirded that ascent, goes to the heart of our contemporary predicament. This was also the Republic's predicament.

This brings us back to our argument that modern economic growth is no process of growth without end but rather tends at some point toward deceleration and stagnation. A first cycle of such growth, crisis, and stagnation was pioneered by the Netherlands between the sixteenth century and 1850; a second cycle,

---

[6] Joseph Schumpeter, *Capitalism, Socialism and Democracy* (New York, 1943), especially chapters 11–14.

affecting the whole western world, began between 1780 and 1850. When will it end? This we cannot answer, but the situation in which the old Republic found itself in the early eighteenth century seems in many ways illustrative of the problems of today.

Bibliography

Aalbers, Johan. *De Republiek en de vrede van Europa.* Groningen, 1980.

"Holland's Financial Problems (1713–33) and the Wars against Louis XIV." *Britain and the Neder-lands.* eds. A. C. Duke and C. A. Tamse. The Hague, 1977. 79–93. VI.

Aalbers, Johan, and Maarten Prak, eds. *De bloem der natie. Adel en patriciaat in de Noordelijke Nederlanden.* Meppel, 1987.

Aalbers, P. G. *Het einde van de horigheid in Twente en Oost-Gelderland, 1795–1850.* Zutphen, 1979.

Abel, Wilhelm. *Agrarkrisen und Agrarkonjunktur. Eine Geschichte der Land- und Ernährungswirtschaft Mitteleuropas seit dem hohen Mittelalter,* 3rd ed. Hamburg & Berlin, 1978. (English trans., *Agricultural Fluctuations in Europe from the Thirteenth to the Twentieth Centuries.* London, 1978.)

Abrams, Philip, and E. A. Wrigley, eds. *Towns and Society. Essays in Economic History and Historical Sociology.* Cambridge, 1978.

Accarias de Serionne, Jacques. *La Richesse de la Hollande.* London, 1778.

Achilles, W. "Getreidepreise und Getreidehandelsbeziehungen europäischer Räume im 16. und 17. Jahrhundert." *Zeitschrift für Agrargeschichte und Agrarsoziologie* 7 (1959): 32–55.

Aden, O. *Entwicklung und Wechsellagen ausgewählter Gewerbe in Ostfriesland von der Mitte des 18. bus zum Ausgang des 19. Jahrhunderts.* Aurich, 1964.

Aerts, E., and F. Crouzet, eds. *Economic Effects of the French Revolutionary and Napoleonic Wars.* Proceedings, Tenth International Economic History Congress. Leuven, 1990.

Aerts, E., et al., eds. *Studia Historica Oeconomica. Liber amicorum Herman Van der Wee.* Leuven, 1993.

Akveld, L. M. "Noordzeevisserij." *Maritieme Geschiedenis der Nederlanden, 3* (Bussum, 1977): 318–34.

Album aangeboden aan Charles Verlinden ter gelegenheid van zijn dertigjarig professoraat. Ghent, 1975.

Algemene Geschiedenis der Nederlanden. Bussum: 1979–81. Vols. 4–10.

Allen, Robert C., and Richard W. Unger. "The Depth and Breadth of the Market for Polish Grain, 1500–1800." *Baltic Affairs.* eds. J. Ph. S. Lemmink et al. (Nijmegen, 1990), 1–18.

Alphen, Marc A. van. "Zielverkopers, transportbrieven en transportkopers." *Amsterdam, haven in de 17e en 18e eeuw.* eds. J. Krikke et al. Amsterdam, 1990. 22–7.

Ankum, L. A. "Een bijdrage tot de Zaanse olieslagerij." *Tijdschrift voor geschiedenis* 73 (1960): 39–57, 215–51.

Anonymous. "Bemerkungen über das Niederländische Postwesen." *Archiv der Postwissenschaft* 1 (1830): 17.

723

"Dobbering der graan prijzen hier te lande in de 16e en 17e eeuw." *Tijdschrift voor Staathuishond-kunde en Statistiek 4* (1848): 73–84.

Arntz, W. J. A. "De baksteenindustrie in Friesland." *Klei* (1953): 44–49.

"Export van Nederlandsche baksteen in vroegere eeuwen." *Economisch-historisch jaarboek 23* (1947): 57–133.

Åström, Sven-Erik. "Technology and Timber Exports from the Gulf of Finland, 1661–1740." *Scandinavian Economic History Review 23* (1975): 1–14.

Attman, Artur. "The Bullion Flow from the Netherlands to the Baltic and the Arctic, 1500–1800." *The Interactions of Amsterdam and Antwerp with the Baltic Region, 1400–1800.* eds. W. J. Wieringa et al. Leiden, 1983. 19–22.

Dutch Enterprise in the World Bullion Trade, 1550–1800. Göteborg, 1983.

Aymard, Maurice, ed. *Dutch Capitalism and World Capitalism.* Cambridge and Paris, 1982.

Baars, C. *De geschiedenis van de landbouw in de Beijerlanden.* Wageningen, 1973.

"De geschiedenis van het grondbezit van Gelderse en Utrechtse edelen in de Beijerlanden." *A. A. G. Bijdragen 28* (1986): 109–44.

Baasch, Ernst. "Hamburg und Holland im 17. und 18. Jahrhundert." *Hansische Geschichtsblätter 16* (1910): 45–102.

Holländische Wirtschaftsgeschichte. Jena, 1927.

Baelde, M. *De domeingoederen van de vorst in de Nederlanden omstreeks het midden van de 16e eeuw (1551–1559).* Brussels, 1971.

"Financiële politiek en domaniale evolutie in de Nederlanden onder Karel V en Philips II (1530–1560)." *Tijdschrift voor geschiedenis 76* (1963): 14–33.

Baetens, R. *De nazomer van Antwerpens welvaart: De diaspora en het handelshuis De Groote tijdens de eerste helft der 17e eeuw.* Brussels, 1976.

"The Organization and Effects of Flemish Privateering in the Seventeenth Century." *Acta Historiae Neerlandica 9* (1976): 48–75.

Bakker, J. P. "The Significance of Physical Geography and Pedology for Historical Geography in the Netherlands." *Tijdschrift voor economische- en sociale-geografie 49* (1958): 214–26.

"Zijn de bijzonder hoge vloeden in ons land in vroeg-historische en historische tijden aan bepaalde perioden gebonden?" *Folia Civitatis 8* (1953): no. 22 (March 7), no. 23 (March 14), no. 24 (March 21).

Bang-Andersen, A., et al., eds. *The North Sea. A Highway of Economic and Cultural Exchange.* Stavanger, 1985.

Barbour, Violet. *Capitalism in Amsterdam in the Seventeenth Century.* Baltimore, 1950.

Bardet, Jean-Pierre, et al., eds. *Mesurer et comprendre. Mélanges offerts à Jacques Dupâquier.* Paris, 1993.

Barro, Robert J. "On the Determination of the Public Debt." *Journal of Political Economy 87* (1979): 940–71.

Beaujon, A. *Overzicht der geschiedenis van de Nederlandsche zeevisserij.* Leiden, 1885.

Becht, H. E. *Statistische gegevens betreffende de handelsomzet van de Republiek der Vereenigde Nederlanden gedurende de 17de eeuw, 1579–1715.* The Hague, 1908.

Beenakker, J. J. J. M. *Van Rentersluze tot strijkmolen. De waterstaatsgeschiedenis en landschapsontwikkeling van de Schager- en Niedorperkoggen tot 1653.* Alphen a/d Rijn, 1988.

Beers, J. K., and C. Bakker. *Westfriezen naar de Oost. De kamers der VOC te Hoorn en Enkhuizen en hun recruteringsgebied, 1700–1800.* Hoorn, 1990.

Begheyn s. j., P. J., and E. F. M. Peters. *Gheprint te Nymeghen. Nijmeegse drukkers, uitgevers en boekverkopers, 1479–1794.* Nijmegen, 1990.

Beins, E. "Die Wirtschaftsethik der Calvinistischen Kirche der Niederlande 1565–1650." *Nederlandsch archief voor kerkgeschiedenis 24* (1931): 85–156.

Bel, J. G. van. *De linnenhandel van Amsterdam in de XVIIIe eeuw.* Amsterdam, 1940.

Berg, N. P. van der. *Munt-, crediet- en bankwezen, handel en scheepvaart in Nederlandsch Indie.* The Hague, 1907.

Berkel, K. van. "Enige opmerkingen over de aard van de technische innovatie in de Republiek omstreeks 1600." *Tijdschrift voor de geschiedenis der geneeskunde, wiskunde, natuurkunde en techniek 31* (1980): 131–43.

Berkvens-Stevelinck, C., H. Bots, P. G. Hoftijzer et al., eds. *Le magasin de l'univers. The Dutch Republic as the Centre of the European Book Trade.* Leiden, 1992.

Beylen, J. van. "Zelandiae Descriptio." *Mededelingen van de Marine Academie 10* (1957): 81–114.

Bieleman, Jan. *Boeren op het Drentse zand, 1600–1900.* A. A. G. Bijdragen 29. Wageningen, 1987.

Bijhouwer, J. T. P. *Het Nederlandse landschap.* Amsterdam-Antwerp, 1971.

Bijkerk, J. "De omvang en de samenstelling van de huishoudens in Delft anno 1749." 1972. Landbouwhogeschool Wageningen, unpublished paper.

Bijl, M. van der. *Idee en interest. Voorgeschiedenis, verloop en achtergronden van de politieke twisten in Zeeland . . . tussen 1702 en 1715.* Groningen, 1981.

"Pieter de la Court en de politieke werkelijkheid." *Pieter de la Court en zijn tijd.* eds. H. W. Blom and I. W. Wildenberg. Amsterdam, 1986. 65–91.

Bijlsma, R. "De uittocht der Delfshavensche haringreeders naar Rotterdam in 1638." *Rotterdams jaarboekje* (1913): 160–6.

"Rotterdams scheepvaartverkeer in de 18de eeuw." *Nieuwe Rotterdamsche Courant.* Nov. 25 1905.

Bläsing, J. F. E. *Das goldene Delta und sein eisernes Hinterland 1815–1851.* Leiden, 1973.

Blink, H. *Woeste gronden, ontginning en bebossing in Nederland voormaals en thans.* The Hague, 1929.

Blom, H. W., and I. W. Wildenberg, eds. *Pieter de la Court in zijn tijd. Aspecten van een veelzijdig publicist (1618–1685).* Amsterdam, 1986.

Blondé, B. *De sociale structuren en economische dynamiek van 's-Hertogenbosch, 1500–1550.* Tilburg, 1987.

Blussé, Leonard, and Femme Gaastra, eds. *Companies and Trade. Essays on Overseas Trading Companies during the Ancien Régime.* Leiden, 1981.

Boekel, P. N. *De zuivelexport van Nederland tot 1813.* Utrecht, 1929.

Boekman, E. "De bevolking van Amsterdam in 1795." *Tijdschrift voor geschiedenis 45* (1930): 271–92.

Boelmans Kranenburg, H. A. H. "Visserij in de Noordelijke Nederlanden." *Algemene Geschiedenis der Nederlanden.* 6:129–37; 8:249–61.

"Zierikzee als visserijplaats." *Zeeuws tijdschrift 20* (1970): 77–84.

Boer, D. E. H. de. *Graaf en grafiek. Sociale en economische ontwikkelingen in het middeleeuwse 'Noordholland' tussen 1345 en 1415.* Leiden, 1978.

Boer, D. E. H. de, and J. W. Marsilje, eds. *De Nederlanden in de late Middeleeuwen.* Utrecht, 1987.

Boerdendonk, M. J. *Historische studie over den Zeeuwschen landbouw.* The Hague, 1935.

Boeren, P. C. *Het hart van Brabant. Schets eener economische geschiedenis van Tilburg.* Tilburg, 1942.

Bog, I., and G. Franz, eds. *Wirtschaftliche und soziale Strukturen im säkularen Wandel. Festschrift für Wilhelm Abel zum 70. Geburtstag.* Hannover, 1974.

Bogucka, Maria. "Amsterdam and the Baltic in the First Half of the Seventeenth Century." *Economic History Review 26* (1973): 433–47.

"Dutch Merchants' Activities in Gdansk in the First Half of the 17th Century." *Baltic Affairs.* eds. J. Ph. S. Lemmink et al. (Nijmegen, 1990), 19–32.

Bok, Marten Jan. *Vraag en aanbod op de Nederlandse kunstmarkt, 1580–1700.* Utrecht, 1994.

Bok, Marten Jan, and Gary Schwartz. "Schilderen in opdracht in Holland in de 17e eeuw." *Holland, Regionaal-historisch tijdschrift 23* (1991): 183–95.

Boogaart, E. van den. "De Nederlandse expansie in het Atlantisch gebied 1590–1674." *Algemene Geschiedenis der Nederlanden.* 7:220–54.

Boomgaard, P., L. Noordegraaf, and H. de Vries, eds. *Exercities in het verleden. Twaalf opstellen over de economische en sociale geschiedenis van Nederland en koloniën, 1800–1950.* Assen, 1981.

Boon, L. J. "De grote sodomietenvervolging in het gewest Holland, 1730–1731." *Holland, Regionaalhistorisch tijdschrift 8* (1976): 140–52.

Borger, G. J. *De Veenhoop. Een historisch-geografisch onderzoek naar het verdwijnen van het veendek in een deel van West-Friesland.* Amsterdam, 1975.

"Ontwatering en grondgebruik in de middeleeuwse veenontginning in Nederland." *Geografische tijdschrift* 10 (1976): 343–53.

Bosscha Erdbrink, G. R. *At the Threshold of Felicity. Ottoman-Dutch Relations during the Embassy of Cornelis Calkoen at the Sublime Porte, 1726–1744.* Ankara, 1975.

Boulle, Pierre. "Slave Trade, Commercial Organization and Industrial Growth in Eighteenth-Century Nantes." *Revue Française d'Historie d'Outre-Mer 59* (1972): 70–112.

Boxer, Charles R. *The Dutch in Brazil, 1624–1654.* Oxford, 1957.

The Dutch Seaborne Empire, 1600–1800. New York, 1965.

Braam, A. van. *Bloei en verval van het economisch-sociale level aan de Zaan in de 17de en 18de eeuw.* Wormerveer, 1946.

"Over de omvang van de Zaandamse scheepsbouw in de 17e en 18e eeuw." *Holland, Regionaal-historisch tijdschrift 24* (1992): 33–49.

Brakel, S. van. "Statistische en andere gegevens betreffende onzen handel en scheepvaart op Rusland gedurende de 18de eeuw." *Bijdragen en mededelingen van het Historisch Genootschap 34* (1913): 350–404.

Braudel, Fernand. *Afterthoughts on Capitalism and Material Culture.* Baltimore: Johns Hopkins University Press, 1977.

Civilisation matérielle, économie et capitalisme. XVe-XVIIIe siècle. Paris, 1979. (English trans., *Civilization and Capitalism, 15th–18th Centuries.* New York, 1981–4. 3 vols.)

Bree, P. J., and L. Hacquebord. "Hebben de Nederlanders de Groenlandse walvis in de Noordatlantische wateren uitgeroeid?" *Walvisvaart,* eds. L. Hacquebord and W. Vroom (Amsterdam, 1988), 146–52.

Breen, Joh. C. "Uit de geschiedenis van den Amsterdamschen wijnhandel." *Jaarboek van de Vereeniging van Nederlandsche wijnhandelaars* 1917:131–79; 1918:83–144; 1919:75–122. (Also published in Joh. C. Breen, *Uit Amsterdams verleden.* Amsterdam, 1934. 209–319.)

Bremer, J. T. *Drie eeuwen zoutharingvisserij te Enkhuizen, 1550–1850.* Enkhuizen, 1981.

Brenner, Robert. "The Agrarian Roots of European Capitalism." *Past and Present 97* (1982): 16–113.

Brewer, John. *The Sinews of Power.* New York, 1988.

Briels, J. "De Zuidnederlandse immigratie, 1572–1630." *Tijdschrift voor geschiedenis 100* (1987): 331–55.

Zuid-Nederlanders in de Republiek, 1572–1630. Een demografische en cultuurhistorische studie. Sint Niklaas, 1985.

Brood, P. *Belastingheffing in Drenthe, 1600–1822.* Meppel, 1991.

Brugman, H. "Statistiek van de in- en uitvoer van Amsterdam, 1 Oct. 1667–30 Sept. 1668." *Bijdragen en mededelingen van het Historisch Genootschap 19* (1898): 125–83.

Brugmans, I. J. *Paardenkracht en mensenmacht. Sociaal-economische geschiedenis van Nederland, 1795–1940.* The Hague, 1961.

Welvaart en historie. Tien studien, 2ed ed. The Hague, 1950.

Bruijn, J. R. "De personeelsbehoefte van de VOC overzee en aan boord, bezien in Aziatisch en Nederlands perspectief." *Bijdragen en mededelingen betreffende de geschiedenis der Nederlanden 91* (1976): 218–48.

"De walvisvaart: de ontplooiing van een nieuwe bedrijfstak." *Walvisvaart.* eds. L. Hacquebord and W. Vroom (Amsterdam, 1988), 16–24.

"From Minor to Major Concern: Entrepreneurs in 17th Century Dutch Whaling." *Early European Exploitation of the Northern Atlantic, 800–1700.* Groningen, 1981. 43–53.

"Productivity, Profitability, and Costs of Private and Corporate Dutch Ship Owning in the Seventeenth and Eighteenth Centuries." *The Rise of Merchant Empires.* ed. James D. Tracy. 174–94.

"Scheepvaart in de Noordelijke Nederlanden, 1580–1650." *Algemene Geschiedenis der Nederlanden.* 7:137–55.

"Scheepvaart in de Noordelijke Nederlanden, 1650–1800." *Algemene Geschiedenis der Nederlanden.* 8:209–38.

"The Timber Trade. The Case of Dutch-Norwegian Relations in the Seventeenth Century." *The North Sea.* eds. A. Bang-Andersen et al. 123–35.

"Zeevarenden." *Maritieme Geschiedenis der Nederlanden.* 3:146–90.

Bruijn, J. R., and C. A. Davids. "Jonas vrij. De Nederlandse walvisvaart, in het bijzonder de Amsterdamse in de jaren 1640–1664." *Economisch- en sociaal-historisch jaarboek 38* (1975): 141–78.

Bruijn, J. R., F. S. Gaastra, and I. Schöffer. *Dutch-Asiatic Shipping in the 17th and 18th Centuries.* Rijks Geschiedkundige Publicatien 165. The Hague, 1987.

Bruijn, J. R., and J. Lucassen, eds. *Op de schepen der Oost-Indische Compagnie.* Groningen, 1980.

Bruijn, J. R., and W. F. J. Mörzer Bruyns, eds. *Anglo-Dutch Mercantile Marine Relations 1700–1850.* Amsterdam, 1991.

Brulez, Wilfrid. "The Balance of Trade of the Netherlands in the Middle of the 16th Century." *Acta Historiae Neerlandica 4* (1970): 20–48.

"De diaspora der Vlaamse kooplui op het einde der XVIe eeuw." *Bijdragen voor de geschiedenis der Nederlanden 15* (1960): 279–306.

"De zoutinvoer in de Nederlanden in de 16e eeuw." *Tijdschrift voor geschiedenis 68* (1955): 181–92.

Brünner, E. C. G. *De order op de buitennering van 1531.* Utrecht, 1918.

Brusse, P., and M. Windhorst. " 'Tot welvaren van de stadt ende verbeteringh van de neringhe'. Arbeidsmarktregulering en economische ontwikkeling in de Amersfoortse textiel, 1450–1800." *Textielhistorische bijdragen 30* (1990): 7–19.

Buck, P. de. "De Russische uitvoer uit Archangel naar Amsterdam in het begin van de achttiende eeuw (1703 en 1709)." *Economisch- en sociaal-historisch jaarboek 51* (1988): 126–93.

Buck, P. de, and J. Th. Lindblad "De scheepvaart en handel uit de Oostzee op Amsterdam en de Republiek, 1722–1780." *Tijdschrift voor geschiedenis 96* (1983): 536–62.

"Navigatie en negotie. De galjootsgeldregisters als bron bij het onderzoek naar de geschiedenis van de Oostzeehandel in de achttiende eeuw." *Tijdschrift voor zeegeschiedenis 9* (1990): 27–48.

Buis, J. *Historia Forestis. Nederlands bosgeschiedenis.* A. A. G. Bijdragen 26 and 27. Wageningen, 1985.

Buist, J. T. *De Nederlandsche staatsschuld sedert 1814.* Haarlem, 1857.

Buist, M. G. *At spes non fracta: Hope & Co., 1770–1815. Merchant Bankers and Diplomats at Work.* The Hague, 1974.

"Geld, bankwezen en handel in de Noordelijke Nederlanden, 1792–1844." *Algemene Geschiedenis der Nederlanden.* 10:289–322.

Burema, L. *De voeding in Nederland van de middeleeuwen tot de 20e eeuw.* Assen, 1953.

Burke, Peter. *Venice and Amsterdam: A study of seventeenth-century elites.* London, 1974.

Bussemaker, Th. "Lyst van ambten en officiën ter begeving staande van burgemeesteren van Amsterdam in 1749." *Bijdragen en mededelingen van het Historisch Genootschap 28* (1907): 474–518.

Butel, P. "France, the Antilles, and Europe in the Seventeenth and Eighteenth Centuries: Renewal of Foreign Trade." *The Rise of the Merchant Empires.* ed. James Tracy. 153–73.

Carter, Alice Clare. *Getting, Spending, and Investing in Early Modern Times.* Assen, 1975.

Cate, A. H. ten. "Het Weeshuis der Hervormde gemeente te Zwolle, 1834–1854." *Overijsselse historische bijdragen 96* (1981): 99–122.

Chaudhuri, K. N. *The Trading World of Asia and the English East India Company, 1660–1760.* Cambridge, 1978.

Child, Josiah. *A New Discourse of Trade.* London, 1693.

Christensen, Axel E. *Dutch Trade in the Baltic around 1600.* Copenhagen–The Hague, 1941.

Ciéslak, E. "Amsterdam als Bankier von Gdansk im 18. Jahrhundert." *The Interactions of Amsterdam and Antwerp with the Baltic Region, 1400–1800.* eds. W. J. Wieringa et al. 123–32.

Clark, John G. *La Rochelle and the Atlantic Economy during the Eighteenth Century.* Baltimore, 1981.

Coebergh van den Brink, S. M. *Meer dan zes eeuwen Leids Gymnasium.* Leiden, 1988.

Cohen, Robert. *Jews in Another Environment. Surinam in the Second Half of the Eighteenth Century.* Leiden, 1991.

Coleman, Donald C., and A. H. John, eds. *Trade, Government, and Economy in Pre-industrial England.* London, 1976.

Coleman, Donald C., and Peter Mathias, eds. *Enterprise and History. Essays in Honor of Charles Wilson.* Cambridge, 1984.

Colenbrander, B. W., et al., eds. *Molens in Noord-Holland. Inventarisatie van het Noordhollandse molenbezit.* Amsterdam, 1981.

Colenbrander, S. "Van cocon tot zijden stof." *Ons Amsterdam* 43 (1991): 300–4.

" 'Zo lang de weefkonst bloeijt in't machtig Amsterdam'." *Textielhistorische bijdragen* 32 (1992): 27–44.

Collins, James B. *The Fiscal Limitations of Absolutism. Direct Taxation in Early Seventeenth-Century France.* Berkeley, 1988.

"The Role of Atlantic France in the Baltic Trade: Dutch Traders and Polish Grain at Nantes, 1625–1675." *Journal of European Economic History* 13 (1984): 239–89.

Coolhaas, W. Ph. *Generale missiven van gouverneurs-generaal en raden aan Heren 17 der Verenigde Oost-Indische Compagnie.* Rijks Geschiedkundige Publicatien 112. The Hague, 1964. 2.

Generale missiven van gouverneurs-generaal en raden aan Heren 17 der Verenigde Oost-Indische Compagnie. Rijks Geschiedkundige Publicatien 125. The Hague, 1968. 3.

Cools, R. H. A. *De strijd om den grond in het lage Nederland. Het proces van bedijking, inpoldering en droogmaking sinds de vroegste tijden.* Rotterdam, 1948.

Coumans, G. "Geld en geluk. De familie van de Meulen in gezins-historisch perspectief, 1600–1800." *Jaarboek Oud-Utrecht* (1984): 99–120.

Court, Pieter de la. *Het welvaren van Leiden: Handschrift uit het jaar 1659.* ed. F. Driessen. The Hague, 1911.

Interest van Holland, ofte Gronden van Hollands welvaren. Amsterdam, 1662. (English trans., *The True Interest and Political Maxims of the Republic of Holland.* London, 1746; reprinted New York, 1972.)

Crafts, N. F. R., and C. Knick Harley. "Output Growth and the British Industrial Revolution: A Restatement of the Crafts-Harley View." *Economic History Review* 45 (1992): 703–30.

Dam, J. D. van. "Ontwikkeling in de Delftse aardewerkindustrie, 1580–1660." *De stad Delft.* eds. I. V. T. Spaanders and R. A. Leeuw. 3:135–43.

Dam, Peter van. *Beschryvinge van de Oostindische Compagnie.* eds. F. W. Stapel, and C. W. Th. van Boetzelaar. Rijks Geschiedkundige Publicatien 63, 68, 74, 83, 87, 96. The Hague: 1927–54.

Davids, C. A. "De technische ontwikkeling van Nederland in de vroeg-moderne tijd. Literatuur, problemen en hypothesen." *Jaarboek voor de geschiedenis van bedrijf en techniek* 8 (1991): 8–37.

"On the Diffusion of Nautical Knowledge from the Netherlands to Northeastern Europe, 1550–1850." *From Dunkirk to Danzig.* eds. W. G. Heeres et al. 217–36.

"The Transfer of Windmill Technology from the Netherlands to Northeastern Europe from the 16th to the Early 19th Century." *Baltic Affairs.* eds. J. Ph. S. Lemmink et al. (Nijmegen, 1988), 33–52.

Davids, K., and L. Noordegraaf, eds. *The Dutch Economy in the Golden Age.* Economic and Social History in the Netherlands 4. Amsterdam, 1993.

Davis, Ralph. *A Commercial Revolution: English Overseas Trade in the 17th and 18th Centuries.* London, 1967.

The Rise of the English Shipping Industry in the 17th and 18th Centuries. London, 1962.

Day, John. *The Medieval Market Economy.* Oxford, 1987.

Deelder, C. L., and A. H. Huussen. "Opmerkingen betreffende de kuilvisserij op de voormalige Zuiderzee, voornamelijk in de zestiende eeuw." *Holland, Regionaal-historisch tijdschrift* 5 (1973): 221–42.

Dekker, C. *Zuid Beveland. De historische geografie en de instellingen van een Zeeuws eiland in de middeleeuwen.* Assen, 1971.

Dekker, P. *De laatste bloeiperiode van de Nederlandse Arctische walvis- en robbevangst, 1761–1775.* Zaltbommel, 1970.

Deursen, A. Th. Van. "Bronnen en hun gebruik. Het verpachtingsregister van de visgronden bij de sluis van Westgraftdijk." *De verleiding van de overvloed.* eds. R. Sanders et al. 55–64.

Het kopergeld van de Gouden Eeuw. Assen: 1978–80, 4 vols. (English trans., *Plain Lives in a Golden Age.* Cambridge, 1991.)

"Staat van oorlog en generale petitie in de jonge Republiek." *Bijdragen en mededelingen betreffende de geschiedenis der Nederlanden 91* (1976): 44–55.

Deyon, Pierre, et al., eds. *Les hésitations de la croissance, 1580–1740.* Paris, 1978.

Diederiks, H. *Een stad in verval: Amsterdam omstreeks 1800.* Meppel, 1982.

Diederiks, H. A., C. A. Davids, and D. J. Noordam, eds. *Een stad in achteruitgang. Sociaal-historische studies over Leiden in de achttiende eeuw.* Leiden, 1978.

Diepeveen, W. J. *De vervening in Delfland en Schieland tot het einde der zestiende eeuw.* Leiden, 1950.

Dijk, H. van, and D. J. Roorda. *Het patriciaat in Zierikzee tijdens de Republiek.* n.p., 1979.

"Sociale mobiliteit onder de regenten van de Republiek." *Tijdschrift voor geschiedenis 84* (1971): 304–28.

Dillen, J. G. van, ed. *Bronnen tot de geschiedenis van het bedrijfsleven en het gildewezen van Amsterdam, 1512–1672.* Rijks Geschiedkundige Publicatien 69, 78, 93. The Hague: 1929, 1933, 1951.

ed. *Bronnen tot de geschiedenis der wisselbanken (Amsterdam, Delft, Middelburg, Rotterdam).* Rijks Geschiedkundige Publicatien 59–60. The Hague, 1925.

"De Amsterdamse wisselbank." *Economisch-historish jaarboek 11* (1925): 245–8.

Duurtemaatregelen te Amsterdam in de 17de eeuw. Amsterdam, 1915.

"Eenige stukken aangaande den Amsterdamschen graanhandel in de tweede helft der zeventiende eeuw." *Economisch-historisch jaarboek 9* (1923): 221–30.

"Effectenkoersen aan de Amsterdamse Beurs, 1723–1794." *Economisch-historisch jaarboek 17* (1931): 1–46.

ed. *History of the Principal Public Banks.* The Hague, 1934.

Van rijkdom en regenten. Handboek tot de economische en sociale geschiedenis van Nederland tijdens de Republiek. The Hague, 1970.

Dissel, E. F. van. "Grond in eigendom en in huur in de ambachten van Rijnland omstreeks 1545." *Handelingen en mededelingen van de Maatschappij der Nederlandsche Letterkunde* (1896): 152–4.

Dobbelaar, P. J. *De branderijen in Holland tot het begin der negentiende eeuw.* Rotterdam, 1930.

Döhmann, K., and W. H. Dingeldein. *Singraven. De geschiedenis van een Twentse havezate.* Brussels: 1934.

Dongelmans, B. P. M. *Van Alkmaar tot Zwijndrecht. Alfabet van boekverkopers, drukkers en uitgevers in Noord-Nederland, 1801–1850.* Amsterdam, 1988.

Doorman, G. *Octrooien voor uitvindingen in de Nederlanden uit de 16e-18e eeuw.* The Hague, 1942.

Doorninck, M., and E. Kuijpers. *De geschoolde stad. Onderwijs in Amsterdam in de Gouden Eeuw.* Amsterdam, 1993.

Dormans, E. H. M. *Het tekort. Staatsschuld in de tijd der Republiek.* Amsterdam, 1991.

Dorsman, L. *G. W. Kernkamp. Historicus en Democraat, 1864–1943.* Groningen, 1990.

Dreisch, Wilhelm von den. *Die ausländischen Kaufleute während des 18. Jahrhunderts in Spanien und Ihre Beteiligung am Kolonialhandel.* Cologne-Vienna, 1972.

Drescher, Seymour. "The Long Goodbye: Dutch Capitalism and Antislavery in Comparative Perspective." *American Historical Review 99* (1994): 44–69.

Drimmelen, D. E. van. *Schets van de Nederlandse rivier- en binnenvisserij tot het midden van de 20ste eeuw.* Nieuwegein, 1987.

Druenen, P. G. van. "Gilden, trafieken en de rol van de overheid." *Jaarboek voor de geschiedenis van bedrijf en techniek 5* (1988): 414–26.

Dubois, S. *Belle van Zuylen, 1740–1805. Leven op afstand.* Zaltbommel, 1969.

Dudok van Heel, S. A. C. "Amsterdamse schuil- of huiskerken?" *Holland, Regionaal-historisch tijdschrift* 25 (1993): 1–10.

Duinkerken, J. *Schepenen aan de Zuiderzee. De magistraat van Harderwijk, 1700–1750.* Zutphen, 1990.

DuPlessis, Robert S., and Martha C. Howell. "Reconsidering the Early Modern Urban Economy: The Cases of Leiden and Lille." *Past and Present 94* (1982): 49–84.

Ebeling, Dietrich. *Bürgertum und Pöbel: Wirtschaft und Gesellschaft Kölns im 18. Jahrhundert.* Cologne, 1987.

Der Holländerholzhandel in den Rheinlanden. Stuttgart, 1992.

Edelman, T. *Bijdrage tot de historische geografie van de Nederlandse kuststreek.* The Hague, 1974.

Eeghen, I. H. van. *De gilden. Theorie en praktijk.* Bussum, 1965.

Eerenbeemt, H. J. F. M. *Armoede en arbeidsdwang. Werkinrichtingen voor 'onnutte' Nederlanders in de Republiek, 1760–1795.* The Hague, 1977.

Eiras Roel, A., ed. *Long Distance Migrations (1500–1900).* 17th International Congress of Historical Sciences. Madrid, 1990.

Elerie, J. N. H., and P. C. M. Hoppenbrouwers, eds. *Het Oldambt, Deel 2. Nieuwe visies op geschiedenis en actuele problemen.* Historia Agriculturae 22. Groningen, 1991.

Elias, J. E. *De geschiedenis van een Amsterdamse regentenfamilie. Het geslacht Elias.* The Hague, 1937.

Elsas, M. J. *Umriss einer Geschichte der Preise und Löhne in Deutschland.* Leiden, 1949.

Elzinga, S. *Het voorspel van den oorlog van 1672. De economisch-politieke betrekkingen tusschen Frankrijk en Nederland in de jaren 1660–1672.* Haarlem, 1926.

Emmer, P. C. "De laatste slavenreis van de Middelburgsche Commercie Compagnie." *Economisch- en sociaal-historisch jaarboek 34* (1971): 72–123.

"De slavenhandel van en naar Nieuw Nederland." *Economisch- en sociaal-historisch jaarboek 35* (1972): 94–147.

"The West India Company, 1621–1791. Dutch or Atlantic?" *Companies and Trade.* eds. L. Bussé and F. Gaastra. 71–95.

Engelen, Th. L. M. "Nijmegen in de 17de eeuw." *Nijmeegse Studien 7* (1978): entire.

Engelen, Th. L. M., J. Folkerts, and F. M. M. Hendrickx, eds. *Fabrieken en trafieken in het Departement van de Oude IJssel (1800). De bedrijfsenquête van Johannes Goldberg.* Zwolle, 1990.

Engels, P. H. *De belastingen en de geldmiddelen van den aanvang der Republiek tot op heden.* Utrecht, 1862.

Eon, Jean. *Le Commerce honorable ou considations politiques.* Nantes, 1646.

Everaert, J. *De internationale en koloniale handel der Vlaamse firmas te Cadiz, 1670–1700.* Bruges, 1973.

Faber, J. A. "De Noordelijke Nederlanden van 1480 tot 1780; Structuren in beweging." *Algemene Geschiedenis der Nederlanden.* 5:196–250.

"De Sontvaart als spiegel van de structuurveranderingen in de Europeese economie gedurende de achttiende eeuw." *Tijdschrift voor zeegeschiedenis 1* (1982): 91–101.

"The Decline of the Baltic Grain Trade in the Second Half of the Seventeenth Century." *From Dunkirk to Danzig.* eds. W. G. Heeres et al. 31–51.

Drie eeuwen Friesland. A. A. G. Bijdragen 17. Wageningen, 1972.

Dure tijden en hongersnoden in preindustrieel Nederland. Amsterdam, 1976.

"The Economic Decline of the Dutch Republic in the Second Half of the 18th Century and the International Terms of Trade." *Dunkirk to Danzig.* eds. W. G. Heeres et al. 107–16.

"Heu oder Butter. Anpassung friesischer Bauern an Veränderungen im Preis- und Kostengefüge während des 18. Jahrhunderts." *Wirtschaftliche und soziale Strukturen.* eds. I. Bog et al. 188–98. 1.

"Scheepvaart op Nederland in een woelige periode: 1784–1810." *Economisch- en sociaal-historisch jaarboek 47* (1984): 67–78.

Faber, J. A., H. A. Diederiks, and S. Hart. "Urbanisering, industrialisering en milieu-aantasting in Nederland in de periode van 1500 tot 1800." *A. A. G. Bijdragen 18* (1973): 251–71.

Faber, J. A., H. K. Roessingh, B. H. Slicher van Bath, et al. "Population Changes and Economic Developments in the Netherlands: A Historical Survey." *A. A. G. Bijdragen 12* (1965): 47–133.

Farret, J. P., A. G. Verster, and J. H. van Swinden. *Rapport over de telling van het volk van Amsterdam.* Amsterdam, 1795.

Feenstra, H. *De bloeitijd en het verval van de Ommelander adel (1600–1800).* Groningen, 1981.

Drentse edelen tijdens de Republiek: een onderzoek naar hun economische positie. n.p., 1985.

Feijst, G. van der. *Geschiedenis van Schiedam.* Schiedam, 1975.

Feyter, C. A. de. *Industrial Policy and Shipbuilding. Changing economic structures in the Low Countries, 1600–1800.* Utrecht, 1982.

Filarski, R. *Kanalen van de Koning-koopman. Goederenvervoer, binnenscheepvaart en kanalenbouw in Nederland en België in de eerste helft van de negentiende eeuw.* Amsterdam, 1995.

Fischer, W., J. Krengel, and J. Wietog. *Sozialgeschichtliches Arbeitsbuch. Band I. Materialen zur Statistik des Deutschen Bundes, 1815–1870.* Munich, 1982.

Floud, Roderick, and Donald McCloskey, eds. *The Economic History of Britain since 1700,* 2nd ed. Cambridge, 1994.

Fockema Andreae, S. J. *De Nederlandse staat onder de Republiek.* Amsterdam, 1962.

Het Hoogheemraadschap van Rijnland. Leiden, 1934.

Fockema Andreae, S. J., E. H. ter Kiele, and R. C. Hekker. *Duizend jaar bouwen in Nederland.* Amsterdam: 1948–57.

Formsma, W. J., M. G. Buist, and W. H. R. Koops, eds. *Historie van Groningen.* Groningen, 1976.

Freedberg, David, and Jan de Vries, eds. *Art in History, History in Art: Studies in Seventeenth Century Dutch Culture.* Santa Monica, California, 1991.

French, Christopher J. "London's Overseas Trade with Europe, 1700–1775." *Journal of European Economic History 23* (1994): 475–501.

Friis, Astrid. *Alderman Cockayne's Project and the Cloth Trade.* Copenhagen–London, 1927.

Frijhoff, W. Th. M. *La société Neerlandaise et ses gradues, 1575–1814.* Amsterdam, 1981.

Frijhoff, W. Th. M., et al., eds. *Geschiedenis van Zutphen.* Zutphen, 1989.

"Opleiding en wetenschappelijke belangstelling van het Nederlandse regentenpatriciaat tijdens de Republiek: uitgangspunten, kenmerken, ontwikkelingen." *Bulletin Werkgroep Elites 8* (1987): 6–20.

Fritschy, J. M. F. "De 'generale Beleenbank' en de financiële problemen in de beginjaren van de Bataafse Republiek." *Jaarboek voor de geschiedenis van bedrijf en techniek 3* (1986): 109–34.

De patriotten en de financiën van de Bataafse Republiek. The Hague, 1988.

Fruin R., ed. *Enqueste ende Informatie upt stuck van der reductie ende reformatie van den schiltaelen, voertijts getaxeert ende gestelt geweest over de landen van Hollant ende Vrieslant, gedaen in den jaere MCCCCXCIIII.* Leiden, 1876.

ed. *Informacie up den staet faculteyt ende gelegentheyt van de steden ende dorpen van Hollant ende Vrieslant om daernae te regulieren de nyeuwe schiltaele, gedaen in den jaere MDXIV.* Leiden, 1866.

Tien jaren uit den tachtigjarigen oorlog, 1588–1598. Leiden, 1858.

Fruin, R., and H. T. Colenbrander. *Geschiedenis der staatsinstellingen in Nederland tot den val der Republiek,* 2nd ed. The Hague, 1992.

Fuchs, J. M. *Beurt- en wagenveren.* The Hague, 1946.

Fullerton, Kemper. "Calvinism and Capitalism. An explanation of the Weber thesis." *Protestantism, Capitalism and Social Science.* ed. R. W. Green. 8–31.

Gaastra, Femme. *Bewind en beleid bij de VOC: de financiële en commerciële politiek van de bewindhebbers, 1672–1702.* Zutphen, 1989.

De geschiedenis van de VOC. Haarlem, 1982. (2nd. ed., Zutphen, 1991).

"De VOC in Azië, 1680–1795." *Algemene Geschiedenis der Nederlanden.* 9:427–64.

"The Export of Precious Metals from Europe to Asia by the Dutch East India Company, 1602–1795." *Precious Metals in the Later Medieval and Early Modern Worlds.* ed. J. F. Richards. 447–75.

"Geld tegen goederen: Een structurele verandering in het Nederlands-Aziatisch handelsverkeer." *Bijdragen en mededelingen betreffende de geschiedenis der Nederlanden 91* (1976): 249–72.

731

"The Shifting Balance of Trade of the Dutch East India Company." *Companies and Trade.* eds. L. Blussé and F. Gaastra. 47–69.

Garber, Peter M. "Tulipmania." *Journal of Political Economy 97* (1989): 535–60.

Gelder, H. A. Enno van. "Friesche en Groningse edelen in de tijd van de opstand tegen Spanje." *Historische opstellen opgedragen aan prof. H. Brugmans.* Amsterdam, 1929. 78–94.

Getemperde vrijheid. Groningen, 1972.

Van Beeldenstorm tot pacificatie. Acht opstellen over de Nederlandse revolutie der zestiende eeuw. Amsterdam, 1964.

Gelder, H. E. van. "De 'Draperye' van Den Haag." *Die Haghe, bijdragen en mededelingen* (1907): 229–350.

"Gegevens betreffende de haringvisscherij op het einde der 16e eeuw." *Bijdragen en mededelingen van het Historisch Genootschap 32* (1911): 1–62.

Gelder, H. Enno van. *De Nederlandse Munten.* Utrecht, 1965.

Munthervorming tijdens de Republiek, 1659–1694. Amsterdam, 1949.

Gelder, H. Enno van, and Marcel Hoc. *Les monnaies des Pays-Bas Bourguignons et Espagnols, 1434–1713.* Amsterdam, 1960.

Genabeek, J. van, ed. *Het wonen. Balans en perspectief van de Nederlandse cultuurgeschiedenis.* Amsterdam, 1990.

Gerding, M. A. W. *Vier eeuwen turfwinning.* A. A. G. Bijdragen 35. Wageningen, 1995.

ed. *Geschiedenis van Mappel.* Meppel, 1991.

Geschenkron, Alexander. *Economic Backwardness in Historical Perspective.* Cambridge, MA, 1962.

Geyl, P. *Kernproblemen van onze geschiedenis.* Utrecht, 1937.

Glamann, Kristof. *Dutch-Asiatic Trade, 1620–1740.* Copenhagen-The Hague, 1958.

Glassman, Debra, and Angela Redish. "New Estimates of the Money Stock in France, 1493–1680." *Journal of Economic History 45* (1985): 31–46.

Goedewagen, D. A. "De geschiedenis van de pijpmakerij te Gouda." *De merken en het merkenrecht.* ed. G. C. Helbers. 1–6.

Gogel, I. J. A. *Memoriën en correspondentiën betreffende den staat van 's Rijks geldmiddelen in den jare 1820.* Amsterdam, 1844.

Goldstone, Jack. "Urbanization and Inflation. Lessons from the English Price Revolution of the Sixteenth and Seventeenth Centuries." *American Journal of Sociology 89* (1984): 1122–60.

Goslinga, C. Ch. *The Dutch in the Caribbean and on the Wild Coast, 1580–1680.* Assen, 1971.

The Dutch in the Caribbean and in the Guianas, 1680–1791. Assen, 1985.

Gottschalk, M. K. E. "De ontginning der Stichtse venen ten oosten van de Vecht." *Tijdschrift van het Koninklijk Nederlandse Aardrijkskundig Genootschap 73* (1956): 207–22.

Gouda, Francis. *Poverty and Political Culture. The Rhetoric of Social Welfare in the Netherlands and France, 1815–1854.* Lanham, Maryland, 1994.

Gouw, J. L. van der. "Het ambacht Voorschoten." *Zuid Hollandse Studiën 5* (1956): 1–167.

Govers, F. G. G. *Het geslacht en de firma F. van Lanschot 1737–1901.* Tilburg, 1972.

Grapperhaus, F. H. M. *Alva en de Tiende Penning.* Zutphen, 1982.

Convoyen en licenten. Zutphen, 1986.

Green, R. W., ed. *Protestantism, Capitalism and Social Science. The Weber Thesis Controversy.* Lexington, MA, 1973.

Greup, G. M. *De Rijnverbinding van Amsterdam en haar geschiedenis.* Amsterdam, 1952.

Greup-Roldanus, S. G. *Geschiedenis der Haarlemmer blekerijen.* The Hague, 1936.

Groen, A. "Het Uitgeester verpondingskohier van 1731 bezien in het licht van de sociaal-economische veranderingen binnen dit dorp tijdens de 18e eeuw." *Holland, Regionaal-historisch tijdschrift 18* (1986): 91–108.

Groeneveld, E. J. *De economische crisis van het jaar 1720.* Groningen, 1940.

Groeneveld, S., ed. *Bestuurders en geleerden.* Amsterdam, 1985.

Gruys, J. A., and C. de Wolf. *Thesaurus 1473–1800. Nederlandse boekdrukkers en boekverkopers.* Bibliographica Neerlandica XXVIII. Nieuwkoop, 1989.

Guicciardini, L. *Beschryvinghe van alle de Nederlanden (overgheset in de nederduytsche spraecke door Cornelium Kilianum; Met verscheyden historien ende aenmerckinghen vermeedert ende verciert door Petrum Montanum).* Amsterdam, 1612. (Original Italian title, *Descrittione de Tutti i Paesi-Bassi.* Antwerp, 1567.)

Gutmann, Myron. *War and Rural Life in the Early Modern Low Countries.* Princeton, 1980.

Hacquebord, L., and W. Vroom, eds. *Walvisvaart in de Gouden Eeuw.* Amsterdam, 1988.

Haks, D. *Huwelijk en gezin in Holland in de 17e en 18e eeuw.* Assen, 1982.

Hardenberg, H. *Het Burgerweeshuis voor Nederlands Hervormden te 's-Gravenhage.* The Hague, 1964.

Harkx, W. A. J. M. *De Helmondse textielnijverheid in de loop der eeuwen.* Tilburg, 1967.

Harley, C. Knick. "Reassessing the Industrial Revolution: A Macro View." *The British Industrial Revolution. An economic perspective.* ed. Joel Mokyr. 171–226.

't Hart, Marjolein C. *In Quest for Funds. Warfare and State Formation in the Netherlands, 1620–1650.* Leiden, 1989.

"Intercity Rivalries and the Making of the Dutch State." *Cities and the Rise of States in Europe.* eds. Charles Tilley and Wim P. Blockmans. Boulder, CO, 1994. 196–217.

The Making of a Bourgeois State. War, Politics and Finance during the Dutch Revolt. Manchester, 1993.

"Staatsvorming, sociale relaties en oorlogsfinanciering in de Nederlandse Republiek." *Tijdschrift voor sociale geschiedenis 16* (1990): 61–85.

Hart, Simon. "De Italië-vaart, 1590–1620." *Jaarboek Amstelodamum 70* (1978): 42–60.

Geschrift en getal; Een keuze uit de demografisch-, economisch- en sociaal-historische studiën op grond van Amsterdamse en Zaanse archivalia. Dordrecht, 1976.

Harten, J. D. H. "De verzorging van het plattemand van de Zeeuwse eilanden in de Franse Tijd." *Bulletin Geografisch Instituut Rijksuniversiteit Utrecht 3.1* (1971): 31–73.

"Stedelijke invloeden op het Hollandse landschap in de 16de, 17de en 18de eeuw." *Holland, Regionaal-historisch tijdschrift 10* (1978): 114–34.

Have, O. ten. *De leer van het boekhouden in de Nederlanden tijdens de 17de en 18de eeuw.* Delft, 1933.

Heer, C. de. *Bijdrage tot de financiële geschiedenis der Oost-Indische Companie.* The Hague, 1929.

Heeren, Jac J. M. "Uit de geschiedenis der Helmondsche textielnijverheid." *Economisch-historisch jaarboek 12* (1926): 145–74.

Heeres, J. E. *De wijzigingen in den regeeringsvorm van Stad en Lande in de jaren 1748 en 1749.* Groningen, 1885.

Heeres, W. G. "De heffing van het paalgeld door Kampen en Amsterdam." *Economisch- en sociaal-historisch jaarboek 46* (1983): 128–41.

"Het paalgeld. Een bijdrage tot de kennis van de Nederlandse handelsstatistiek in het verleden." *Economisch- en sociaal-historisch jaarboek 45* (1982): 1–17.

Heeres, W. G., et al., eds. *From Dunkirk to Danzig. Shipping and Trade in the North Sea and the Baltic, 1350–1850.* Hilversum, 1988.

Heeringa, K. *Bronnen tot de geschiedenis van den Levantschen handel.* Rijks Geschiedkundige Publicatien 34. The Hague, 1917.

Bronnen tot de geschiedenis van den Levantschen handel. Rijks Geschiedkundige Publicatien 95. The Hague, 1952.

Heeringa, T. *De Graafschap. Een bijdrage tot de kennis van het cultuurlandschap en van het Scholtenprobleem.* Zutphen, 1934.

Heijer, Henk den. *De geschiedenis van de WIC.* Zutphen, 1994.

Hekker, R. C. "De ontwikkeling van de boerderijvormen in Nederland." *Duizend jaar bouwen in Nederland.* eds. S. J. Fockema Andreae et al. 195–316. 2.

Helbers, G. C., ed. *De merken en het merkenrecht van de pijpmakers te Gouda.* Gouda, 1942.

Henderikx, P. A. *De beneden delta van Rijn en Maas. Landschap en bewoning van de Romeinse tijd tot ca. 1000.* Hollandse Studiën 19. Hilversum, 1987.

Heringa, E. *Tynsen op de Veluwe.* Groningen, 1931.

Heringa, J., D. P. Blok, and M. G. Buist, eds. *Geschiedenis van Drenthe*. Meppel, 1985.

Hobsbawm, Eric J. "The Crisis of the 17th Century." *Past and Present* (1954): 5:33–53; 6:44–65.

Högberg, S. "Baltic Grain-trade in the 18th Century." *Baltic Affairs*. eds. J. Ph. S. Lemmink et al. (Nijmegen, 1988), 121–6.

Hogendorp, G. K. van. *Stukken raakende den tegenwoordingen toestand der Bataafsche bezittingen in Oost-Indië*. The Hague–Delft, 1801.

Holleman, F. A. *Rechtgeschiedenis der heerlijke veren in Holland*. n.p., 1928.

Hollestelle, J. "De Nederlandse steenbakkerij in de zeventiende en achttiende eeuw." *Economisch- en social-historisch jaarboek 44* (1982): 11–21.

Holthuis, Paul. *Frontierstad bij het scheiden van de markt. Deventer: militair, demografisch, economisch; 1578–1648*. Deventer, 1993.

Hoppenbrouwers, P. C. M. *Een middeleeuwse samenleving. Het land van Heusden, ca. 1360–1515*. A. A. G. Bijdragen 32. Wageningen, 1992.

"Grondgebruik en agrarische bedrijfsstructuur in het Oldambt na de vroegste inpolderingen (1630–1720)." *Het Oldambt*. eds. J. N. H. Elerie and P. C. M. Hoppenbrouwers. 73–94. 2.

Houtte, J. A. van. "Anvers aux XVe et XVIe siècles: Expansion et apogée." *Annales: E. S. C. 16* (1961): 248–78.

An Economic History of the Low Countries 800–1800. London, 1977.

Hovy, J. *Het voorstel van 1751 tot instelling van een beperkt vrijhavenstelsel in de Republiek (propositie tot een gelimiteerd porto-franco)*. Groningen, 1966.

Hudig, F. W. *Das Glas*. Vienna-Amsterdam, 1923.

Huizinga, J. *Dutch Civilisation in the Seventeenth Century and other Essays*. London, 1968. (Original Dutch edition, 1941.)

Hullu, J. de. "Op de schepen der Oost-Indische Compagnie." *Op de schepen der Oost-Indische Compagnie*. eds. J. R. Bruijn and J. Lucassen. 50–133.

Ishizaka, Akio. "Die niederländische und englische Akzise im 17. Jahrhundert: Ein Beitrag zur vergleichenden Steuergeschichte der Merkantilistischen Periode." *Wirtschaftskrafte und Wirtschaftswege. Festschrift für Hermann Kellenbenz*. ed. J. Schneider. 509–28. 2.

Israel, Jonathan I. "The Amsterdam Stock Exchange and the English Revolution of 1688." *Tijdschrift voor geschiedenis 103* (1990): 412–40.

ed. *The Anglo-Dutch Moment*. Oxford, 1991.

Dutch Primacy in World Trade, 1585–1740. Oxford, 1989.

The Dutch Republic and the Hispanic World, 1606–1661. Oxford, 1982.

"The Economic Contributions of Dutch Sephardi Jewry to Holland's Golden Age, 1595–1713." *Tijdschrift voor geschiedenis 96* (1983): 505–35.

"Een merkwaardig literair werk en de Amsterdamse effectenmarkt in 1688: Joseph penso de la Vega's 'Confusión de Confusiones'." *Zeventiende eeuw 6* (1990): 159–65.

"The Holland Towns and the Dutch-Spanish Conflict, 1621–1648." *Bijdragen en mededelingen betreffende de geschiedenis der Nederlanden 94* (1979): 41–69.

"The Phases of the Dutch Straatvaart (1590–1713). A Chapter in the Economic History of the Mediterranean." *Tijdschrift voor geschiedenis 99* (1986): 1–30.

Jackson, G. *The British Whaling Trade*. London, 1978.

Janse, K. P. J. "De kopienden als bron voor de economische geschiedenis van het Gooi, 1500–1850." *Economisch- en sociaal-historisch jaarboek 55* (1992): 35–73.

Jansen, P. C. "Het ritme van de dood. Sociale conjunctuur in Amsterdam, 1750–1800." *Ons Amsterdam 25* (1973): 88–91.

"Nijverheid in de Noordelijke Nederlanden 1650–1780." *Algemene Geschiedenis der Nederlanden*. 8: 102–123.

Janssen, G. B. *Baksteenfabricage in Nederland, 1850–1920*. Gelders Historische Reeks XVII. n.p., 1987.

Jeannin, P. "Les Comptes du Sund comme source pour la construction d'indices généraux de l'activité économique en Europe (XVIe–XVIIIe siècle)." *Revue historique 231* (1964): 55–102, 307–40.

"Les Interdépendences économiques dans le champ d'action européen des Hollandais (XVIe–XVIIIe siècle)." *Dutch Capitalism and World Capitalism*. ed. M. Aymard. 147–70.

"Preis-, Kosten- und Gewinnunterschiede im Handel mit Ostseegetreide." *Wirtschaftliche und soziale Strukturen im säkularen Wandel*. eds. I. Bog et al. 494–517.

"The Seaborne and the Overland Trade Route of Northern Europe in the XVIth and XVIIth Centuries." *Journal of European Economic History* 11 (1982): 5–59.

Johansen, H. C. "Ships and Cargoes in the Traffic between the Baltic and Amsterdam in the Late Eighteenth Century." *The Interaction of Amsterdam and Antwerp with the Baltic Region*. eds. W. J. Wieringa et al. 161–70.

John, A. H. "English Agricultural Improvement and Grain Exports, 1660–1765." *Trade, Government and Economy*. eds. Donald C. Coleman and A. H. John. 45–67.

Jones, D. W. "Sequel to Revolution: The Economics of England's Emergence as a Great Power, 1688–1712." *The Anglo-Dutch Moment*. ed. Jonathan I. Israel. 389–406.

War and Economy in the Age of William III and Marlborough. Oxford, 1988.

Jong, C. de. *Geschiedenis van de oude Nederlandse walvisvaart*. Pretoria–Johannesburg, 1978.

"Walvisvaart." *Maritime Geschiedenis der Nederlanden*. 2:309–15; 3:335–52.

Jong, D. J. de, et al. *Hardinxveld en de riviervisserij*. Hardinxveld–Giesendam, 1988.

Jong, J. J. de. *Een deftig bestaan. Het dagelijks leven van regenten in de 17e en 18e eeuw*. Utrecht–Antwerp, 1987.

Met goed fatsoen. De elite in een Hollandse stad. Gouda, 1700–1780. The Hague, 1985.

Jonge, J. A. de. *De industrialisatie in Nederland tussen 1850 en 1914*. Amsterdam, 1968.

Jong-Keesing, E. E. de. *De economische crisis van 1763 te Amsterdam*. Amsterdam, 1939.

Jongste, J. A. F. de. *Onrust aan het Spaarne. Haarlem in de Jaren 1747–1751*. The Hague, 1982.

Jörg, C. J. A. *Porselein als handelswaar. De porseleinhandel als onderdeel van de Chinahandel van de VOC, 1729–1794*. Groningen, 1978.

Kamen, Henry. *Spain in the Later Seventeenth Century, 1665–1700*. London, 1980.

Kampen, S. C. van. "De ontwikkeling van de scheepsbouwnijverheid in Rotterdam en Dordrecht." *Akademiedagen 9* (1956): 70–87.

De Rotterdamse particuliere scheepsbouw in de tijd van der Republiek. Assen, 1953.

Kaplan, Steven L. *Bread, Politics and Political Economy in the Reign of Louis XV*. The Hague, 1976.

Kappelhof, A. C. M. *De belastingheffing in de Meierij van Den Bosch gedurende de Generaliteitsperiode, 1648–1730*. Tilburg, 1986.

"De demografische ontwikkeling van de Meijerij van Den Bosch." *Historisch-geographisch tijdschrift* 4 (1986): 6–12.

Kato, Eiichi. "Unification and Adaptation, the Early Shogunate and Dutch Trade Policies." *Companies and Trade*. eds. L. Blussé and F. S. Gaastra. 207–29.

Kellenbenz, Hermann, ed. *Precious Metals in the Age of Expansion*. Papers of the 14th International Congress of the Historical Sciences, Stuttgart, 1981.

Schwerpunkte der Eisengewinnung und Eisenverarbeitung in Europa, 1500–1650. Cologne-Vienna, 1974.

Kent, H. S. K. "The Anglo-Norwegian Timber Trade in the Eighteenth Century." *Economic History Review* 8 (1955): 62–74.

Kernkamp, J. H. *De handel op den vijand, 1572–1609*. Utrecht: 1931–4. 2 vols.

Kesteloo, H. M. *De stadsrekeningen van Middelburg*. Middelburg, 1881.

Ketner, F. *Handel en scheepvaart van Amsterdam in de vijftiende eeuw*. Leiden, 1946.

Keuchenius, W. M. *De inkomsten en uitgaven der Bataafsche Republiek, voorgesteld in eene Nationale Balans*. Amsterdam, 1803.

Keuning, H. J. *De Groninger veenkoloniën. Een sociaal-geografische studie*. Groningen, 1933.

Het Nederlandse volk en zijn woongebied. The Hague, 1965.

Kaleiduscoop der Nederlandse landschappen. The Hague, 1979.

Kjaerheim, S. "The Norwegian Timber Trade in the Seventeenth Century." *Scandinavian Economic History Review* 2 (1957): 188–201.

Klein, P. W. "De heffing van de 100e en 200e penning van het vermogen te Gouda, 1599–1722." *Economische-historisch jaarboek 31* (1967): 57–62.

De Trippen in de 17de eeuw. Een studie over het ondernemersgedrag op de Hollandse stapelmarkt. Assen, 1965.

Kapitaal en stagnatie tijdens het Hollandse vroegkapitalisme. Rotterdam, 1967.

"Nederlandse glasmakerijen in de zeventiende en achttiende eeuw." *Economisch- en sociaal-historisch jaarboek 44* (1982): 31–42.

Klep, P. M. M. *Bevolking en arbeid in transformatie. Een onderzoek naar de ontwikkelingen in Brabant, 1700–1900.* Nijmegen, 1981.

"Population Estimates of Belgium by Province (1375–1831)." *Historiens et populations. Liber amicorum Etienne Hélin.* Louvain-la-Neuve, 1991. 485–508.

Klep, P. M. M., et al., eds. *Wonen in het verleden, 17e–20e eeuw.* Amsterdam, 1987.

Klerck de Reus, G. C. *Geschichtlicher Ueberblick der administrativen rechtlichen und finanziellen Entwicklung der Niederländischen Ost-Indischen Compagnie.* Verhandelingen van het Bataviaasch Genootschap 47. The Hague, 1894.

Kley, J. van der, ed. *Vaarwegen in Nederland.* Assen, 1967.

Kloek, E. M. *Wie hij zij, man of wijf. Vrouwengeschiedenis en de vroegmoderne tijd: drie Leidse studies.* Hilversum, 1990.

Klompmaker, H. "Handel, geld- en bankwezen in de Noordelijke Nederlanden." *Algemene Geschiedenis der Nederlanden.* 6:58–74.

"Handel, geld- en bankwezen in de Noordelijke Nederlanden 1580–1650." *Algemene Geschiedenis der Nederlanden.* 7:98–127.

Kloot Meyburg, B. W. van der. "Bijdrage tot de geschiedenis van de meekrapcultuur in Nederland." *Economisch-historisch jaarboek 18* (1934): 59–153.

Knaap, G. J. *Kruidnagelen en christenen. De Verenigde Oost-Indische Compagnie en de bevolking van Ambon, 1656–1696.* Dordrecht, 1987.

Knoppers, J. V. Th. "De vaart in Europa." *Maritieme Geschiedenis der Nederlanden.* 3:226–61.

Dutch Trade with Russia from the time of Peter I to Alexander I. A Quantitative Study of Eighteenth-Century Shipping. Montreal, 1976.

Knoppers, J. V. Th., and F. Snapper. "De Nederlandse scheepvaart op de Oostzee vanaf het einde van de 17e eeuw tot het begin van de 19e eeuw." *Economisch- en sociaal-historisch jaarboek 41* (1978): 115–53.

Knotter, A. "Bouwgolven in Amsterdam in de 17e eeuw." *Wonen in het verleden.* eds. P. M. M. Klep et al. 25–37.

"De Amsterdamse scheepvaart en het Noordhollandse platteland in de 16e en 17e eeuw; Het probleem van de arbeidsmarkt." *Holland; Regionaal-historisch tijdschrift 16* (1984): 123–54.

Knotter, A., and J. L. van Zanden. "Immigratie en arbeidsmarkt in Amsterdam in de 17de eeuw." *Tijdschrift voor sociale geschiedenis 13* (1987): 403–31.

Kooijmans, L. *Onder regenten; De elite in een Hollandse stad. Hoorn 1700–1780.* The Hague, 1985.

Koolbergen, H. van. "De materiële cultuur van Weesp en Weesperkarspel in de zeventiende en achttiende eeuw." *Volkskundig bulletin 9* (1983): 3–52.

"Sieraden in de Noordelijke Kempen (1645–1820)." ' . . . die jakken en rokken dragen'. ed. F. Livestro-Nieuwenhuis. 32–38.

Kool-Blokland, J. L. *De elite in Heusden, 1700–1750. Een prosopografische analyse.* Tilburg, 1985.

De zorg gewogen. Zeven eeuwen godshuizen in Middelburg. Middelburg, 1990.

Koopmans, C. V. E. C. *Dordrecht, 1811–1914. Een eeuw demografische en economische geschiedenis.* Hilversum, 1992.

Kooy, T. P. van der. *Hollands stapelmarkt en haar verval.* Amsterdam, 1931.

Korte, J. P. de. *De jaarlijkse financiële verantwoording in de Verenigde Oostindische Compagnie.* Leiden, 1984.

Kossmann, E. H. "The Dutch Republic." *New Cambridge Modern History.* Cambridge, 1961. 5:275–300.

Kranenburg, H. A. H. *De zeevisscherij van Holland in den tijd der Republiek.* Amsterdam, 1946.
"Het afslagwezen van de visserij in het Beneden-Maas gebied, 1400–1600." *Zuid-Hollandse Studiën* 4 (1954): 72–92.
"Het zeevisserijbedrijf van de Zijdenaars in de 15e en 16e eeuw." *Tijdschrift voor geschiedenis 62* (1949): 321–33.
Krantz, F., and P. M. Hohenberg, eds. *Failed Transitions to Modern Industrial Society: Renaissance Italy and Seventeenth-Century Holland.* Montreal, 1975.
Krelage, E. H. *Bloemenspeculatie in Nederland.* Amsterdam, 1942.
Krikke, J., V. Enthoven, and K. Mastenbroek, eds. *Amsterdam, haven in de 17e en 18e eeuw.* Amsterdam, 1990.
Kuiper, Y. M. E. "Uitsterven of uithuwelijken? Een analyse van het demografisch gedrag van de adel in Friesland in de 18e en 19e eeuw." *Tijdschrift voor sociale geschiedenis 12* (1986): 269–99.
Kuppers, W., and R. van Schaïk. "Levensstandaard en stedelijke economie te Zutphen in de 15de en 16de eeuw." *Bijdragen en mededelingen "Gelre" 72* (1981): 1–45.
Kuys, J., and J. T. Schoenmaker. *Landpachten in Holland, 1500–1650.* Amsterdam, 1981.
Kuznets, Simon. "The Meaning and Measurement of Economic Growth." *Six Lectures on Economic Growth.* Glencoe, IL, 1959. 13–41.
Lambert, Audery M. *The Making of the Dutch Landscape. A Historical Geography of the Netherlands.* London, 1971.
Lambooij, H. *Getekend Land. Nieuwe beelden van Hollands Noorderkwartier.* Alkmaar, 1987.
Le Roy Ladurie, E. "L'histoire immobile." *Annales: E. S. C. 29* (1974): 673–82. (English trans., "Motionless History," *Social Science History 1* (1977): 115–36.)
Leaven, A. H. "The Frankfurt and Leipzig Book Fairs and the History of the Dutch Book Trade in the Seventeenth and Eighteenth Centuries." *Le magasin de l'univers.* ed. C. Berkvens-Stevelinck. 185–98.
Leemans, W. F. *De grote Gelderse tollen en hun tollenaars in de 18e en begin 19e eeuw.* Arnhem, 1981.
"Handel en migratie te Zaltbommel." *Bijdragen en mededelingen "Gelre" 70* (1979): 79–95.
Leeuw, R. A. "Ontwikkeling in de Delftse aardewerkindustrie, bloei en verval." *De stad Delft.* eds. I. V. T. Spaanders and R. A. Leeuw. 143–52.
Leeuwen, M. H. D. van. *Bijstand in Amsterdam, ca. 1800–1850. Armenzorg als beheersings- en overlevingsstrategie.* Zwolle, 1992.
Leeuwen, M. H. D. van, and J. E. Oeppen. "Reconstructing the Demographic Regime of Amsterdam, 1681–1920." *Economic and Social History in the Netherlands 5* (1993): 61–102.
Leeuwen, M. H. D. van, J. Schoenmakers, and F. Smits. *Armoede en bedeling in Amsterdam ten tijde van de Republiek.* Unpublished paper, Historisch Seminarium, University of Amsterdam, 1981.
Lemmink, J. Ph. S., and J. S. A. M. van Koningsbrugge, eds. *Baltic Affairs. Relations Between the Netherlands and North-Eastern Europe, 1500–1800.* Nijmegen, 1990.
Leon, Pierre, ed. *Les hesitations de la croissance, 1580–1740.* Paris, 1978.
Lesger, C. M. "Amsterdam, Harlingen and Hoorn. Port Functions in the Zuiderzee Region during the Middle of the Seventeenth Century." *From Dunkirk to Danzig.* eds. W. G. Heeres et al. 331–60.
Hoorn als stedelijk knooppunt; Stedensystemen tijdens de late middeleeuwen en vroegmoderne tijd. Hilversum, 1990.
Huur en conjunctuur; De woningmarkt in Amsterdam, 1550–1850. Amsterdam, 1986.
"Intraregional Trade and the Port System in Holland, 1400–1700." *The Dutch Economy in the Golden Age.* eds. K. Davids and L. Noordegraaf. 186–217.
Lindblad, J. Th. "Evidence of Dutch-Swedish Trade in the 17th Century." *Baltic Affairs.* eds. J. Ph. S. Lemmink et al. 205–28.
Sweden's Trade with the Dutch Republic, 1738–1795. Assen, 1982.
Linden, H. van der. *Recht en territoir. Een rechtshistorisch-sociografische verkenning.* Assen, 1972.

Lindert, Peter H., and Jeffrey G. Williamson. "Revising England's Social Tables, 1688–1812." *Explorations in Economic History 19* (1982): 385–408.

Lis, Catharina, Hugo Soly, and D. van Damme. *Op vrije voeten? Sociale politiek in West-Europa (1450–1914)*. Leuven, 1985.

Livestro-Nieuwenhuis, F., ed. ". . . die jakken en rokken dragen." *Brabantse klederdrachten en streeksieraden*. 's-Hertogenbosch, 1986.

Loenen, J. van. *De Haarlemse brouwindustrie vóór 1600*. Amsterdam, 1950.

Lottin, A., et al., eds. *Etudes sur les villes en Europe occidentale*. Paris, 1983.

Lucassen, J. "Beschouwingen over seizoengebonden trekarbeid." *Tijdschrift voor sociale geschiedenis 8* (1982): 327–58.

"Dutch Migration, 1600–1900." *Long Distance Migrations*. ed. A. Eiras Roel. 19–44.

Naar de kusten van de Noordzee; Trekarbeid in Europees perspektief, 1600–1900. Gouda, 1984.

"Zeevarenden." *Maritieme Geschiedenis der Nederlanden*. 2:126–58.

Luzac, Elias. *Hollands rijkdom, behelzende den oorsprong van den koophandel en van de magt van dezen Staat*. Leiden, 1783. 4 vols.

Maanen, R. J. C. van. "Hollandse vermogensheffingen in de zeventiende en achttiende eeuw." *Nederlands Archievenblad 88* (1984): 61–72.

Maddison, Angus. *Dynamic Forces in Capitalist Development: A Long-run Comparative View*. Oxford, 1991.

Malowist, Marion. *Croissance et régression en Europa XIVe–XVIIIe siècles*. Paris, 1972.

Mansvelt, W. M. F. *Rechtsvorm en geldelijk beheer bij de Oost-Indische Compagnie*. Amsterdam, 1922.

Maritieme Geschiedenis der Nederlanden. Bussum, 1977. 4 vols.

Marshall, S. *The Dutch Gentry, 1500–1650. Family, Faith and Fortune*. New York, 1987.

Martens, P. J. M. *De zalmvissers van de Biesbosch: een onderzoek naar de visserij op het Bergse Veld, 1421–1869*. Tilburg, 1992.

Matthey, I. B. M. *Op fiscaal Kompas. Westeremden, het verleden van een Gronings terpdorp*. Groningen, 1975.

Mayhew, N. J., ed. *Coinage in the Low Countries (880–1500). The Third Oxford Symposium on Coinage and Monetary History*. B. A. R. International Series 54. Oxford, 1979.

"Population, Money Supply, and the Velocity of Circulation in England, 1300–1700." *Economic History Review 48* (1995): 238–57.

McCants, Anne. *The Role of the Charitable Institution in the Early Modern Dutch Economy: The Case of the Amsterdam Burgerweeshuis*. Unpublished doctoral dissertation, University of California at Berkeley, 1991.

McCusker, John J., and James C. Riley. "Money Supply, Economic Growth, and the Quantity Theory of Money: France, 1650–1788." *Explorations in Economic History 20* (1983): 274–93.

Meertens, P. J. "Godefridus Cornelisz. Udemans." *Nederlandsch archief voor kerkgeschiedenis 28* (1936): 65–106.

Meijere-Huizinga, H. M. de. "Een kijkje bij een Leidse regentenfamilie in de 18e eeuw." *Leids jaarboekje* (1970): 107–19.

Mélanges d'histoire offerts à Henri Pirenne. Brussels, 1926.

Menkman, W. R. *De geschiedenis der West-Indische Compagnie*. Amsterdam, 1947.

Merens, A. *De geschiedenis van een Westfriese regentenfamilie. Het geslacht Merens*. The Hague, 1957.

Metelerkamp, R. *De toestand van Nederland in vergelijking gebragt met die van enige andere landen van Europa*. Rotterdam, 1804.

Middelhoven, P. J. "De Amsterdamse veilingen van Noord-Europees naaldhout." *Economisch- en sociaalhistorisch jaarboek 41* (1978): 86–114.

Mitchell, B. R. *British Historical Statistics*. Cambridge, 1988.

Moes, J. K. S., and B. M. A. de Vries, eds. *Stof uit het Leidse verleden. Zeven eeuwen textielnijverheid*. Utrecht, 1991.

Mokyr, Joel, ed. *The British Industrial Revolution. An Economic Perspective*. Boulder, CO, 1993.

"Editor's Introduction: The new Economic History and the Industrial Revolution." *The British Industrial Revolution. An Economic Perspective.*

Industrialization in the Low Countries, 1795–1850. New Haven, CT, 1976.

Mokyr, Joel, and Erik Buyst. "Dutch Manufacturing and Trade during the French Period (1795–1814) in a Long Term Perspective." *Economic Effects of the French Revolutionary Wars.* eds. Erik Aerts and François Crouzet. 64–78.

Molen, S. J. van der. *Turf uit de Wouden: bijdrage tot de geschiedenis van de hoogveengraverij in Oostelijk Friesland tot 1900.* Leeuwarden, 1978.

Montias, J. M. *Artists and Artisans in Delft: A Socio-economic Study of the Seventeenth Century.* Princeton, 1982.

Moorman van Kappen, O., J. Korff, and O. W. A. Baron van Verschuer. *Tieler- en Bommelerwaarden, 1327–1977. Grepen uit de geschiedenis van 650 jaar waterstaatszorg in Tielerwaard en Bommelerwaard.* Tiel-Zaltbommel, 1977.

Morineau, Michel. *Incroyables gazettes et fabuleux métaux.* London–Paris, 1985.

"La balance du commerce franco-néerlandais et le resserrement économique des provinces-unies au XVIIIème siècle." *Economisch- en sociaal-historisch jaarboek 30* (1964): 170–235.

Pour une histoire économique vraie. Lille, 1985.

"Quelques rémarques sur l'abondance monétaire aux Provinces Unies." *Annales: E. S. C.* 29 (1974): 767–76.

Muinck, B. E. de. *Een regentenhuishouding omstreeks 1700. Gegevens uit de privé-boekhouding van Mr. Cornelis de Jonge van Ellemeet, Ontvanger-Generaal der Verenigde Nederlanden (1646–1721).* The Hague, 1965.

Muller Fzn, S. *Geschiedenis der Noordsche Compagnie.* Utrecht, 1874.

Munro, John H. "The Central European Mining Boom, Mint Outputs, and Prices in the Low Countries and England, 1450–1550." *Money, Coins, and Commerce: Essays in the Monetary History of Asia and Europe from Antiquity to Modern Times.* ed. Eddy Van Cauwenberghe. Leuven, 1991. 119–83.

"Monetary Contraction and Industrial Change in the Late-Medieval Low Countries, 1335–1500." *Coinage in the Low Countries.* ed. N. J. Mayhew. 95–161.

Nachold, O. *Die Beziehungen der Niederländischen Ostindischen Kompagnie zu Japan im siebzehnten Jahrhundert.* Leipzig, 1897.

Nagtegaals, P. "Stadsfinanciën en stedelijke economie. Invloed van de conjunctuur op de Leidse stadsfinanciën, 1620–1720." *Economisch- en sociaal-historisch jaarboek 52* (1989): 96–147.

Neal, Larry. *The Rise of Financial Capitalism. International Capital Markets in the Age of Reason.* Cambridge, 1990.

Nederlandsche Jaarboeken; Nieuwe Nederlandsche Jaarboeken. Monthly publication, 1747–65; 1766–98.

Nervrett, David E. *Inheritance and Family Life in Colonial New York City.* Ithaca, NY, 1992.

Nie, W. L. J. *De ontwikkeling der Noord-Nederlandsche textielverwerij.* n.p., 1937.

Nierop, H. F. K. van. *Van ridders tot regenten. De Hollandse adel in de zestiende en eerste helft van de zeventiende eeuw.* Hollandse Historische Reeks 1. n.p., 1984. (English trans., *The Nobility of Holland.* Cambridge, 1993.)

Nierop, L. van. "De handeldrijvende middenstand te Amsterdam in 1942." *Jaarboek Amstelodamum 45* (1953): 193–230.

"De zijdenijverheid van Amsterdam historisch geschetst." *Tijdschrift voor geschiedenis 45* (1930): 18–40, 151–72.

"Het kohier van de personele quotisatie te Amsterdam over het jaar 1742 en de Amsterdamse vrouw." *Jaarboek Amstelodamum 43* (1949): 80–102.

Nieuwenhuisen, A. M. "Het college voor de kleine visscherij te Maassluis." *Tijdschrift voor geschiedenis 46* (1931): 262–75.

Nijman, D. G. "Louis de Geer (1587–1652), vader van de Zweedse industrie?" *Tijdschrift voor geschiedenis 104* (1991): 213–32.

Noordam, D. J. *Geringde buffels en heren van stand. Het patriciaat van Leiden, 1574–1700.* Hilversum, 1994.

Noordegraaf, L. *Daglonen in Alkmaar 1500–1850*. Amsterdam, 1980.

Hollands welvaren? Levensstandaard in Holland 1450–1650. Bergen, 1985.

ed. *Ideën en ideologieën. Studies over economische en sociale geschiedschrijving in Nederland, 1894–1991*. Amsterdam, 1991.

"Levenstandaard en levensmiddelenpolitiek in Alkmaar vanaf het eind van de 16e tot het begin van de 19e eeuw." *Alkmaarse Historische Reeks* 4 (1980): 55–100.

"Nicolaas Wilhelmus Posthumus, 1880–1960. Van gloeiend marxist tot entrepreneur." *Ideën en ideologieën*. ed. L. Noordegraaf. 727–51. 2.

"Nijverheid in de Noordelijke Nederlanden, 1480–1580." *Algemene Geschiedenis der Nederlanden*. 6: 12–26.

"Nijverheid in de Noordelijke Nederlanden, 1580–1650." *Algemene Geschiedenis der Nederlanden*. 7: 66–85.

Noordegraaf, L., and C. J. van Baar. "Werkschuwheid en misbruik van sociale voorzieningen? Het beleid van de Alkmaarse armenzorg, 1750–1815." *Alkmaarse silhouetten*. Alkmaar, 1983. 91–108.

Noordegraaf, L., and J. T. Schoenmakers. *Daglonen in Holland 1450–1600*. Amsterdam, 1984.

Noordegraaf, L., and G. Valk. *De gave gods. De pest in Holland vanaf de late middeleeuwen*. Bergen, 1988.

North, Douglass C., and Robert P. Thomas. *The Rise of the Western World*. Cambridge, 1973.

North, H. "Waldwarenhandel und -Produktion." *The Interactions of Amsterdam and Antwerp with the Baltic Region, 1400–1800*. eds. W. J. Wieringa et al. 73–84.

North, Michael. *Geldumlauf und Wirtschaftskonjuntur im südlichen Ostseeraum an der Wende zur Neuzeit (1440–1570)*. Kieler Historische Studien 35. Sigmaringen, 1990.

"Getreideanbau und Getreidehandel im Königlichen Preussen und im Herzogtum Preussen." *Zeitschrift für Ostforschung 34* (1985): 39–47.

Nusteling, H. P. H. *Welvaart en werkgelegenheid in Amsterdam 1540–1860*. Amsterdam/Diemen, 1985.

O'Brien, Patrick. "European Economic Development: The Contribution of the Periphery." *Economic History Review 35* (1982): 1–18.

O'Brien, Patrick, and Peter Mathias. "Taxation in Britain and France, 1715–1810." *Journal of European Economic History 5* (1976): 601–50.

Offermans, P. H. M. G. *Arbeid en levensstandaard in Nijmegen omstreeks de Reductie (1550–1600)*. Zutphen, 1972.

Oldewelt, W. F. H. "De beroepsstructuur van de bevolking der Hollandse stemhebbende steden volgens de kohieren van de familiegelden van 1674, 1715 en 1742." *Economisch-historisch jaarboek 24–25* (1950–2): 80–161; 167–248.

"De Hollandsche imposten en ons beeld van de conjunctuur." *Jaarboek Amstelodamum 47* (1955): 48–80.

"De scheepvaartstatistiek van Amsterdam in de 17e en 18e eeuw." *Jaarboek Amstelodamum 45* (1953): 114–51.

"Het aantal bedelaars, vondelingen en gevangenen te Amsterdam in tijden van welvaart en crisis." *Jaarboek Amstelodamum 39* (1942): 21–34.

Kohier van de personele quotisatie te Amsterdam over het jaar 1742. Amsterdam, 1945. 2 vols.

Ondernemende geschiedenis. 22 opstellen geschreven bij het afscheid van Mr. H. van Riel. The Hague, 1977.

Oomens, C. A. *De loop der bevolking van Nederland in de negentiende eeuw*. Voorburg, 1989.

Oostindie, Gert. *Roosenburg en Mon Bijou. Twee Surinaamse plantages, 1720–1870*. Dordrecht, 1989.

Ormrod, David. "English Re-exports and the Dutch Staplemarket in the Eighteenth century." *Enterprise and History*. eds. Douglas C. Coleman and Peter Mathias. 89–115.

English Grain Exports and the Structure of Agrarian Capitalism, 1700–1760. Hull, 1985.

Oudermeulen, C. van der. "Iets dat tot voordeel der deelgenoten van de Oost-Indische Compagnie kan strekken (1785)." *Stukken raakende den tegenwoordigen toestand*. ed. G. K. van Hogendoorp.

Oudheidkundige Kring 'Die Goude'. *Gouda zeven eeuwen stad. Hoofdstukken uit de geschiedenis van Gouda*. Gouda, 1972.

Paauw, S. van der. *Verhaal van de middelen tot verversching van het water in de grachten van de stad Leiden.* Leiden, 1828.

Parker, Geoffrey. *The Army of Flanders and the Spanish Road, 1567–1659.* Cambridge, 1971.

Parker, William N., and Eric L. Jones, eds. *European Peasants and Their Markets.* Princeton, 1975.

Pauw, C. "De Spaanse lakenfabrieken te Guadalajara en de Leidse lakenindustrie in het begin der achttiende eeuw." *Economisch-historisch jaarboek 24* (1950): 34–79.

Petrejus, E. W. *De Bomschuit, een verdwenen scheepstype.* Rotterdam, 1954.

Phelps Brown, E. H., and Sheila V. Hopkins. "Seven Centuries of Building Wages." *Economica 22* (1955): 195–206.

"Seven Centuries of the Prices of Consumables, Compared with Builders' Wage-Rates." *Economica 23* (1956): 196–214.

Pinkse, V. C. C. J. "Het Goudse Kuitbier." *Gouda zeven eeuwen stad.* 91–128.

Pinto, Isaac de. *Traité de la circulation et du crédit.* Amsterdam, 1771.

Poederbach, J. J. Th. "Het armenhuis der stad Amsterdam." *Jaarboek Amstelodamum 18* (1920); *19* (1921); *20* (1922).

Poel, J. M. G. van der. "Landbouw in de Noordelijke Nederlanden 1770–1840." *Algemene Geschiedenis der Nederlanden.* 10:159–182.

Pol, A. "Tot grieff van Indië. Goud export door de VOC en de muntproduktie in Nederland, 1720–40." *Jaarboek voor munt- en penningkunde 72* (1985): 65–195.

Pol, Lotte C. van de. "Prostitutie en de Amsterdamse burgerij: Eerbegrippen in een vroegmoderne stedelijke samenleving." *Cultuur en maatschappij in Nederland, 1500–1850.* eds. Peter te Bekhorst, Peter Burke, and Willem Frijhoff. Meppel, 1992. 179–218.

Popkin, Jeremy D. "The Book Trades in Western Europe during the Revolutionary Era." *Papers of the Bibliographical Society of America 78* (1984): 403–45.

Poppel, F. W. A. *Trouwen in Nederland. Een historisch-demografische studie van de negentiende en vroegtwintigste eeuw.* A. A. G. Bijdragen 33. Wageningen, 1992.

Posthumus, N. W. *Bescheiden betreffende de provinciale organisatie der Hollandsche lakenbereiders (de sgn. Droogscheerderssynode).* Amsterdam, 1917.

De geschiedenis van de Leidsche lakenindustrie. The Hague: 1908–39. 3 vols.

"De industriële concurrentie tusschen Noord- en Zuid-Nederlandsche nijverheidscentra in de XVIIe en XVIIIe eeuw." *Mélanges d'histoire offerts à Henre Pirenne.* 369–78.

ed. *De Oosterse handel te Amsterdam. Het oudst bewaarde koopmansboek van een Amsterdamse vennootschap betreffende de handel op de Oostzee, 1485–1490.* Leiden, 1953.

De uitvoer van Amsterdam, 1543–1545. Leiden, 1971.

"Een zestiende-eeuwse enquête naar de buitenneringen rondom de stad Leiden." *Bijdragen en mededelingen van het Historisch Genootschap 33* (1912): 1–95.

An Inquiry into the History of Prices in the Netherlands/Nederlandsche prijsgeschiedenis. Leiden: 1943–64. 2 vols.

"Statistiek van den in- en uitvoer van Amsterdam in 1774." *Bijdragen en mededelingen van het Historisch Genootschap 34* (1913): 516–28.

"Statistiek van den in- en uitvoer van Rotterdam en Dordrecht in het jaar 1680." *Bijdragen en mededelingen van het Historisch Genootschap 34* (1913): 529–37.

"The Tulip Mania in Holland in the Years 1636 and 1637." *Journal of Economic and Business History 1* (1929): 434–55.

Postma, Johannes Menne. *The Dutch in the Atlantic Slave Trade, 1600–1815.* Cambridge, 1990.

"West African Exports and the Dutch West India Company, 1675–1731." *Economisch- en sociaalhistorisch jaarboek 36* (1973): 53–74.

Prak, Maarten. "Aristocratisering." *Spiegel historiael 23* (1988): 226–32.

"Civil Disturbances and Urban Middle Class in the Dutch Republic." *Tijdschrift voor sociale geschiedenis 15* (1989): 165–73.

Gezeten burgers; De elite in een Hollandse stad. Leiden 1700–1780. The Hague, 1985.

"Sociale geschiedschrijving van Nederlands ancien régime." *Tijdschrift voor sociale geschiedenis* 14 (1988): 133–59.

Prakash, Om. *Dutch East India Company and the Economy of Bengal, 1630–1720*. Princeton, 1985.

Priester, P. *De economische ontwikkeling van de landbouw in Groningen, 1800–1910*. A. A. G. Bijdragen 31. Wageningen, 1991.

Pringsheim, O. *Beiträge zur wirtschaftlichen Entwicklungsgeschichte der Vereinigten Niederlande im 17. und 18. Jahrhundert*. Leipzig, 1890.

Prooije, L. A. van. "De invoer van rijns hout per vlot 1650–1795." *Economisch- en social-historisch jaarboek* 53 (1990): 30–79.

Rankin, Hugh F. *The Golden Age of Piracy in the Caribbean, 1620–1680*. New York, 1969.

Rapp, Richard P. "The Unmaking of the Mediterranean Trade Hegemony: International Trade Rivalry and the Commercial Revolution." *Journal of Economic History* 35 (1975): 499–525.

Ravesteyn Jr., W. van. *Onderzoekingen over de economische en sociale ontwikkeling van Amsterdam gedurende de 16e en het eerste kwart der 17e eeuw*. Amsterdam, 1906.

Reekers, S. *Westfalens Bevölkerung, 1818–1955*. Münster, 1956.

Reese, J. J. *De suikerhandel van Amsterdam van het begin der 17e eeuw tot 1813*. Haarlem, 1908.

Renting, Geert. " 'de Heeren van Dordrecht op het werck van Panderen.' Gelderse kaarten in het Dordtse gemeentearchief." *Holland. Regionaal-historisch tijdschrift* 22 (1990): 102–10.

Reyters-Soeters, N. "Die van de heeckelneringhe." *Bijdragen 'Die Goude'* 3 (1941): 130–3.

Richards, J. F., ed. *Precious Metals in the Later Medieval and Early Modern Worlds*. Durham, NC, 1983.

Riemersma, J. C. *Religious Factors in Early Dutch Capitalism, 1550–1650*. The Hague, 1967.

Riley, James C. "The Dutch Economy after 1650: Decline or Growth?" *Journal of European Economic History* 13 (1984): 149–89.

International Government Finance and the Amsterdam Capital Market. Cambridge, 1980.

Rink, Oliver A. *Holland on the Hudson. An Economic and Social History of Dutch New York*. Ithaca, NY, 1986.

Roessingh, H. K. "Beroep en bedrijf op de Veluwe in het midden van de achttiende eeuw." *A. A. G. Bijdragen* 13 (1965): 181–274.

"Het Veluwse inwonertal 1526–1947." *A. A. G. Bijdragen* 11 (1964): 79–150.

Inlandse tabak; Expansie en contractie van een handelsgewas in de 17e en 18e eeuw in Nederland. A. A. G. Bijdragen 20. Wageningen, 1976.

"Landbouw in de Noordelijke Nederlanden, 1650–1815." *Algemene Geschiedenis der Nederlanden*. 8: 16–72.

"Tobacco Growing in Holland in the Seventeenth and Eighteenth Centuries: A Case Study of the Innovative Spirit of Dutch Peasants." *Acta Historiae Neerlandica* 11 (1978): 18–54.

Romein, Jan. "De dialektiek van de vooruitgang. Bijdrage tot het ontwikkelingsbegrip in de geschiedenis." *Het onvoltooid verleden. Kultuurhistorische studies*. Amsterdam, 1937. 9–64.

Rommes, R. "Pest in perspectief. Aspecten van een gevreesde ziekte in vroegmoderne tijd." *Tijdschrift voor sociale geschiedenis* 16 (1990): 244–66.

Rostow, Walt Whitman. *Stages of Economic Growth. A Non-Communist Manifesto*. Cambridge, 1960.

"The Take-off into Self-sustained Growth." *Economic Journal* 66 (1956): 25–47.

Royen, P. C. van. *Zeevarenden op de Koopvaardijvloot omstreeks 1700*. Amsterdam, 1987.

Sanders, R., et al., eds. *De verleiding van de overvloed. Balans en perspectief van de Nederlandse cultuurgeschiedenis*. Amsterdam, 1991.

Sangers, W. J. *De ontwikkeling van de Nederlandse tuinbouw (tot het jaar 1930)*. Zwolle, 1952.

Sannes, H. *Geschiedenis van het Bildt*. Franeker: 1951–6. 3 vols.

Schaars, A. H. G. *De bosbouw van het 'Entel' in de tweede helft van de achttiende eeuw*. Zutphen, 1974.

Schama, Simon. *The Embarrassment of Riches*. New York, 1987.

Patriots and Liberators. Revolution in the Netherlands, 1780–1813. New York, 1977.

Schawacht, Jurgen Heinz. *Schiffahrt und Gütervekehr zwischen den Häfen des deutschen Niederrheins und Rotterdam vom Ende des 18. bis zur Mitte des 19. Jahrhunderts (1794–1850)*. Cologne, 1973.

Schilling, Heinz. "Die Geschichte der nördlichen Niederlande und die Modernisierungstheorie." *Geschichte und Gesellschaft 8* (1982): 475–517.

Schmidt, C. *Om de eer van de familie. Het geslacht Teding van Berkhout 1500–1950; Een sociologische benadering.* Amsterdam, 1986.

Schneeloch, Norbert H. *Actionäre der Westindischen Compagnie von 1674.* Stuttgart, 1982.

"Das Kapitalengagement der Amsterdamer Familie Bartolotti in der Westindischen Compagnie." *Wirtschaftskrafte und Wirtschaftswege.* ed. J. Schneider. II: 171–92.

Schneider, Jürgen, ed. *Wirtschaftskrafte und Wirtschaftswege. Festschrift für Hermann Kellenbenz.* Nuremberg, 1978.

Scholliers, E. *Durée du travail et diminution du temps du travail.* Brussels, 1983.

Scholz-Babisch, Marie. *Quellen zur Geschichte des klevischen Rheinzollwesens vom 11. bis 18. Jahrhundert.* Wiesbaden, 1971.

Schoorl, H. *Zeshonderd jaar water en land. Bijdrage tot de historische geo- en hydrografie van de Kop van Noord Holland.* Groningen, 1973.

Schreiner, J. "Die Niederländer und die norwegische Holzausfuhr im 17. Jahrhundert." *Tijdschrift voor geschiedenis 49* (1934): 303–28.

Nederland og Norge, 1625–1650. Treslastforsel og handelspolitikk. Oslo, 1933.

Schumpeter, Elizabeth Boody. *English Overseas Trade Statistics, 1697–1808.* Oxford, 1960.

Schumpeter, Joseph A. *Capitalism, Socialism and Democracy.* New York, 1943.

Schurink, H. J. A. M., and J. H. van Mosselveld. *Van heidorp tot industriestad.* Tilburg, 1955.

Schutte, G. J. *Een Hollandse dorpssamenleving in de late 18de eeuw. De banne Graft, 1770–1810.* Franeker, 1989.

Het Calvinistisch Nederland. Utrecht, 1988.

Schutten, G. J. *Varen waar geen water is; Reconstructie van een verdwenen wereld. Geschiedenis van de scheepvaart ten oosten van de IJssel van 1300 tot 1930.* Hengelo, 1981.

Schuurman, A. J. "Woonculturen op her Nederlandse platteland." *Het wonen.* ed. J. van Genabeek. 45–64.

Sickenga, Folkert Nicolaas. *Bijdrage tot de geschiedenis der belastingen in Nederland.* Leiden, 1864.

Sigmond, J. P. *Nederlandse zeehavens tussen 1500 en 1800.* Amsterdam, 1989.

Silliman, Benjamin. *Journal of Travels in England, Holland and Scotland.* New Haven, CT, 1820.

Simon Thomas, M. *Onze IJslandvaarders in de 17e en 18e eeuw.* Amsterdam, 1935.

Slicher van Bath, B. H. *An Agrarian History of Western Europe, 500–1850.* London, 1963.

"Een Fries landbouwbedrijf in de tweede helft van de 16e eeuw." *Agronomisch-Historische Bijdragen 4* (1958): 67–188.

Een samenleving onder spanning. Geschiedenis van het platteland van Overijssel. Assen, 1957.

"Historische ontwikkeling van de textielnijverheid in Twente." *Textielhistorische bijdragen 2* (1961): 21–39.

"Theorie en praktijk in de economische en sociale geschiedenis." *A. A. G. Bijdragen 14* (1967): 105–228.

Smit, H. J. "Het Kamper pondtolregister van 1439–1441." *Economisch-historisch jaarboek 5* (1919): 209–96.

Smit, J. G. "De ambtenaren van de centrale overheidsorganen der Republiek." *Tijdschrift voor geschiedenis 90* (1977): 378–90.

Smit, W. J. *De katoendrukkerij in Nederland tot 1813.* Rotterdam, 1928.

Smith, Woodruff D. "The Function of Commercial Centers in the Modernization of European Capitalism; Amsterdam as an Information Exchange in the Seventeenth Century." *Journal of Economic History 44* (1984): 985–1005.

Snapper, F. "Een voorlopige reconstructie van de scheepvaart statistiek van Holland, 1741–1794." *Sociaal- en economisch-historisch jaarboek 48* (1985): 118–29.

Oorlogsinvloeden op de overzeese handel van Holland, 1551–1719. Amsterdam, 1959.

Sneller, Z. W. "De opkomst der Nederlandsche katoenindustrie." *Bijdragen voor vaderlandsche geschiedenis en oudheidkunde* 6th series, 4 (1926): 237–74; 5 (1927): 101–13.

"De tijkweverij te Rotterdam en te Schiedam in de eerste helft der 17e eeuw." *Tijdschrift voor geschiedenis* 45 (1930): 237–66.

Sogner, S. "Women's Position in Migration. The Norwegian case as illustrated by the trek to Holland in the early modern period." *Paper presented to the First European Conference of the International Commission on Historical Demography,* Santiago de Compostela, 1993. 27–42.

"Young in Europe around 1700: Norwegian Sailors and Servant Girls Seeking Employment in Amsterdam." *Mesurer et comprendre.* eds. J. P. Bardet et al. 515–32.

Soltow, Lee. "Income and Wealth Inequality in Amsterdam, 1585–1805." *Economisch- en social-historisch jaarboek 52* (1989): 72–95.

Soly, H., and A. K. L. Thys. "Nijverheid in de Zuidelijke Nederlanden." *Algemene Geschiedenis der Nederlanden* 6: 27–57.

Spaanders, I. V. T., and R. A. Leeuw, eds. *De Stad Delft.* Delft, 1982.

Spading, K. *Holland und die Hanse im 15. Jahrhundert. Zur Problematik des Übergangs vom Feudalismus zum Kapitalismus.* Weimar, 1973.

Spiegel, Laurens van de. *Nadenken van eenen staatsman weegens zijn ministerie in Holland.* n.p., 1800.

Schets tot een vertoog over de intrinsique en relative magt van de Republiek. n.p., 1782.

Spooner, Frank. *The International Economy and Monetary Movements in France, 1493–1725.* Cambridge, 1972.

Risks at Sea. Amsterdam Insurance and Maritime Europe, 1766–1780. Cambridge, 1983.

Spufford, Peter. *Money and Its Uses in Medieval Europe.* Cambridge, 1988.

Steensgaard, Niels. *The Asian Trade Revolution of the Seventeenth Century.* Chicago, 1974.

"The Dutch East India Company as an Institutional Innovation." *Dutch Capitalism and World Capitalism.* ed. Maurice Aymard. 235–57.

Steur, A. G. van der, ed. *Bijdragen tot de geschiedenis van Warmond.* The Hague, 1969.

Steur, J. J. *Herstel of ondergang. Voorstellen tot redres van de VOC, 1740–1795.* Utrecht, 1984.

Stienstra, J., and G. Groenhuis. "De Veenhuizer venen in de Gouden Eeuw: een mislukte Hollandse investering." *Nieuwe Drentse volksalmanak 101* (1984): 69–83.

Stipriaan, A. van. *Surinaams contrast. Roofbouw en overleven in een Caraïbische plantage economie, 1750–1863.* Amsterdam, 1991.

Stokvis, P. R. D. "Het sterftepatroon in preïndustrieel Den Haag (ca. 1700–1855). De mythe van de stedelijke oversterfte en de sterfte naar jaargetijde en doodsoorzaken." *De negentiende eeuw 17* (1993): 206–16.

Stol, T. *De veenkolonie Veenendaal; Turfwinning en waterstaat in het zuiden van de Gelderse Vallei, 1546–1653.* Zutphen, 1992.

Stols, E. *De Spaanse Brabanders, of de handelsbetrekkingen der Zuidelijke Nederlanden.* Brussels, 1971.

Stoppelaer, J. H. de. *Balthasar den Moucheron.* The Hague, 1901.

Stuijvenberg, J. H. van, ed. *De economische geschiedenis van Nederland.* Groningen, 1977.

Temple, Sir William. *Observations upon the United Provinces of the Netherlands.* London, 1673; reprinted Oxford, 1972.

Tijn, Th. van. "Pieter de La Court: zijn leven en zijn economische denkbeelden." *Tijdschrift voor geschiedenis 69* (1956): 304–70.

Timmer, E. M. A. *De Generale Brouwers van Holland. Een bijdrage tot de geschiedenis der brouwnering in Holland in de 17e, 18e en 19e eeuw.* Haarlem, 1918.

Tracy, James D. *A Financial Revolution in the Habsburg Netherlands: 'Renten' and 'Renteniers' in the Country of Holland, 1515–1565.* Berkeley, 1985.

Holland under Habsburg Rule, 1506–1566. Berkeley, 1990.

ed. *The Rise of Merchant Empires. Long-distance Trade in the Early Modern World, 1350–1750.* Cambridge, 1990.

"The Taxation System of the Country of Holland during the Reigns of Charles V and Philip II, 1519–1566." *Economisch- en sociaal-historisch jaarboek 48* (1984): 71–117.

Redeemable Bonds (Losrenten) in the Early Dutch Republic. Unpublished paper, University of Minnesota, 1988.

Trevor Roper, H. R. "Religion, the Reformation and Social Change." *Religion, the Reformation and Social Change, and Other Essays.* London, 1967. 1–45.

Trompetter, C. "Bevolkingsontwikkeling, textielnijverheid en armoede. Een nieuwe visie op de demografische geschiedenis van Twente, 1675–1795." *Economisch- en sociaal-historisch jaarboek 55* (1992): 155–88.

"Ontmoedigend overheidsbeleid als stimulans voor ondernemerschap. De tariefherziening van 1725 en het ontstaan van de bombazijnnijverheid in Twente." *Textielhistorische bijdragen 33* (1993): 43–54.

Unger, Richard W. "Brewing in the Netherlands and the Baltic Grain Trade." *From Dunkirk to Danzig.* eds. W. G. Heeres et al. 429–46.

"Dutch Herring, Technology and International Trade in the Seventeenth Century." *Journal of Economic History 40* (1980): 253–279.

Dutch Shipbuilding before 1800. Assen, 1978.

"Energy Sources for the Dutch Golden Age; Peat, Wind and Coal." *Research in Economic History 9* (1984): 221–53.

"Integration of Baltic and Low Countries Grain Markets, 1400–1800." *The Interactions of Amsterdam and Antwerp with the Baltic Region, 1400–1800.* eds. W. J. Wieringa et al. 1–10.

"Wooden Shipbuilding at Dordrecht." *Mededelingen van de Nederlandse Vereniging voor Zeegeschiedenis 30* (1975): 5–19.

Unger, W. S. "De publikatie der Sonttabellen voltooid." *Tijdschrift voor geschiedenis 71* (1958): 147–205.

"De Sonttabellen." *Tijdschrift voor geschiedenis 41* (1926): 137–155.

"Middleburg als handelsstad, XIIe–XVIe eeuw." *Archief Zeeuws Genootschap* (1935): 1–173.

Uytven, R. van. "Sociaal-economische evoluties in de Nederlanden voor de Revoluties (veertiende-zestiende eeuw)." *Bijdragen en mededelingen betreffende de geschiedenis der Nederlanden 87* (1972): 60–93.

Veblen, Thorstein. *Imperial Germany and the Industrial Revolution.* New York, 1915.

Veluwenkamp, J. W. *Ondernemersgedrag op de Hollandse stapelmarkt in de tijd van de Republiek; De Amsterdamse handelsfirma Jan Isaac de Neufville & Comp., 1730–1764.* Meppel, 1981.

Ven, G. P. van de. *Aan de wieg van Rijkswaterstaat. Woordingsgeschiedenis van het Pannerdenskanaal.* Zutphen, 1976.

Verduin, J. A. *Ontwikkelingen in de Drentse bevolking gedurende de 17e en 18e eeuw.* Drentse Historische Studiën 4. Assen, 1982.

Verhulst, A. *Precis d'histoire rurale de la Belgique.* Brussels, 1990.

Verkade, M. A. *De opkomst van de Zaanstreek.* Utrecht, 1952.

Verlinden, Ch, et al., ed. *Dokumenten voor de geschiedenis van prijzen en lonen in Vlaanderen en Brabant (XVe–XVIIIe eeuw).* Bruges: 1959–73. 4 vols.

Vermaas, J. C. *Geschiedenis van Scheveningen.* The Hague, 1926.

Verstegen, S. W. "De familie van Isendoorn à Blois en de verpachting van de Vaassense watermolens." *Bijdragen en mededelingen 'Gelre' 73* (1982): 41–59.

"De luister van het oude stamhuis. Het beheer der bezittingen en de levenssfeer van een Veluws adellijk geslacht in de achttiende eeuw." *De bloem der natie.* eds. Johan Aalbers and Maarten Prak. 79–92.

Gegoede ingezetenen. Amsterdam, 1989.

Visser, C. *Verkeersindustrieën te Rotterdam in de tweede helft der achttiende eeuw.* Rotterdam, 1927.

Vleggeert, J. C. *Kinderarbeid in Nederland 1500–1874. Van berusting tot beperking.* Assen, 1964.

Vlis, D. van der. "Daglonen in en rond Kampen van 1526 tot 1810." *Overijsselse historische bijdragen 96* (1981): 77–97.

Voer, F. J. de. *Skiednis fan de lege feanterij yn Opsterlan en Smellingerlan.* Leeuwarden, 1954.

Vogel, J. *Een ondernemend echtpaar in de achttiende eeuw, Pieter Merkman jr. en Isabella van Leeuwarden; De Haarlemse garenlintindustrie.* Delft, 1987.

Voorn, H. *De papiermolens in de provincie Zuid-Holland, alsmede in Zeeland, Utrecht, Noord-Brabant, Groningen, Friesland, en Drenthe.* Wormerveer, 1973.

De papiermolens in de provincie Gelderland. Haarlem, 1985.

Voort, J. P. van de. *De Westindische plantages van 1720 tot 1795. Financiën en handel.* Eindhoven, 1973.

"Noordzeevisserij." *Maritieme Geschiedenis der Nederlanden.* 2:289–308.

Voorthuijsen, W. D. *De Republiek der Verenigde Nederlanden en het mercantilisme.* The Hague, 1965.

Vooys, A. C. de. "De sterfte in Nederland in het midden der 19e eeuw." *Tijdschrift van het Koninklijk Nederlandsch Aardrijkskundig Genootschap 68* (1951): 233–71.

Voskuil, J. J. "De verspreiding van koffie en thee in Nederland." *Volkskundig bulletin 14* (1988): 68–93.

"Tussen Twisk en Matenesse. Faseverschillen in de verstening van de huizen." *Volkskundig Bulletin 8* (1982): 1–46.

Van vlechtwerk tot baksteen; Geschiedenis van de wanden van het boerenhuis in Nederland. Arnhem, 1979.

Vrankrijker, A. C. J. de. "De textielindustrie van Naarden." *Tijdschrift voor geschiedenis 51* (1936): 152–64, 264–83.

Vries, Jan de. "Art History, Economic History, and History." *Art in History, History in Art.* eds. David Freedberg and Jan de Vries. 248–82.

Barges and Capitalism; Passenger Transportation in the Dutch Economy (1632–1839). A. A. G. Bijdragen 21. Wageningen, 1978; republished Utrecht, 1981.

"The Decline and Rise of the Dutch Economy, 1675–1900." *Technique, Spirit and Form in the Making of Modern Economies; Essays in Honor of William N. Parker.* eds. G. Saxonhouse and G. Wright. Greenwich, CT, 1984. 149–89.

The Dutch Rural Economy in the Golden Age, 1500–1700. New Haven, CT, 1974.

The Economy of Europe in an Age of Crisis, 1600–1750. Cambridge, 1976.

"Histoire du climat et économie: des faits nouveaux, une interpretation different." *Annales: E. S. C. 32* (1977): 198–226.

"How Did Pre-industrial Labour Markets Function?" *The Evolution of Labour Markets.* eds. George Grantham and Mary MacKinnen. London, 1994. 39–63.

"The Industrial Revolution and the Industrious Revolution." *Journal of Economic History 54* (1994): 249–70.

"Landbouw in de Noordelijke Nederlanden, 1490–1650." *Algemene Geschiedenis der Nederlanden.* 7: 12–43.

"On the Modernity of the Dutch Republic." *Journal of Economic History 33* (1973): 191–202.

"Peasant Demand Patterns and Economic Development; Friesland 1550–1750." *European Peasants and their Markets; Essays in Agrarian Economic History.* eds. William N. Parker and Eric L. Jones. 205–66.

Vries, Johan de. *De economische achteruitgang der Republiek in de achttiende eeuw,* 2nd ed. Leiden, 1968.

"De ontduiking der convooien en licenten in de Republiek tijdens de achttiende eeuw." *Tijdschrift voor geschiedenis 71* (1958): 349–61.

"Van der Spiegel's "Schets tot een vertoog over de intrinsique en relative magt van de Republyk (1782)." *Economisch-historisch jaarboek 27* (1958): 81–100.

Vroom, E. "Het Ensser-geld." *Verslagen en mededelingen von de vereniging tot beoefening van Overijsselsch regt en geschiedenis 63* (1948): 168–81.

Wagenaar, Jan. *Amsterdam in zijne opkomst, aanwas, geschiedenissen . . . .* Amsterdam: 1760–1802. 4 vols.

Wagenvoort Herman. *Tontines, een onderzoek naar de geschiedenis van de lijfrenten by wijze van tontine . . . .* Utrecht, 1961.

Wallerstein, Immanuel. *The Modern World System. Capitalist Agriculture and the Origins of the European World Economy in the Sixteenth Century.* New York, 1974.

Wätjen, H. "Zur Statistik der Holländischen Heringfischerei im 17. und 18. Jahrhundert." *Hansische Geschichtsblätter 16* (1910): 129–85.

Wee, H. van der. "Antwoord op een industriële uitdaging: de Nederlandse steden tijdens de late middeleeuwen en nieuwe tijd." *Tijdschrift voor geschiedenis 100* (1987): 169–84.

"De economie als factor bij het begin van de opstand in de Zuidelijke Nederlanden." *Bijdragen en mededelingen van het Historisch Genootschap 83* (1969): 15–32.

"De industriële ontwikkeling in de Nederlanden tijdens de 17de–18de eeuw. Enkele kritische bemerkinginen naar aanleiding van het debat over de proto-industrie en poging tot aanvulling van het synthese-model." *Academiae Analecta 46* (1984): 59–77.

The Growth of the Antwerp Market and the European Economy (Fourteenth–Sixteenth Centuries). The Hague, 1963. 3 vols.

"Monetary, Credit and Banking Systems." *Cambridge Economic History of Europe.* eds. E. E. Rich and C. H. Wilson. Cambridge, 1977. 290–392. 5.

"Money and Economic Interdependence between the Northern and Southern Netherlands and the Baltic (15th–17th Centuries)." *The Interactions of Amsterdam and Antwerp with the Baltic Region, 1400–1800.* eds. W. J. Wieringa et al. 11–18.

"Prijzen en lonen als ontwikkelingsvariabelen. Een vergelijkend onderzoek tussen Engeland en de Zuidelijke Nederlanden, 1400–1700." *Album offert à Charles Verlinden.* 413–47.

ed. *The Rise and Decline of Urban Industries in Italy and the Low Countries (Late Middle Ages–Early Modern Times).* Leuven, 1988.

"Structural Changes and Specialization in the Industry of the Southern Netherlands, 1100–1600." *Economic History Review 28* (1975): 203–21.

Wee, Herman van der, and Eddy van Cauwenberghe, eds. *Productivity of Land and Agricultural Innovation in the Low Countries.* Leuven, 1978.

Wehler, Hans-Ulrich. *Modernisierungstheorie und Geschichte.* Göttingen, 1975.

Welling, George. "Price-supply Relations in the Amsterdam Staplemarket, 1778." *From Dunkirk to Danzig.* ed. W. Heeres. 457–70.

Westergaard, Waldemar. *The Danish West Indies under Company Rule (1671–1754).* New York, 17.

Westermann, J. C. "Statistische gegevens over de handel van Amsterdam in de zeventiende eeuw." *Tijdschrift voor geschiedenis 61* (1948): 3–15.

Wiel, P. *Wirtschaftsgeschichte des Ruhrgebietes. Tatsachen und Zahlen.* Essen, 1970.

Wieringa, W. J., et al., eds. *The Interaction of Amsterdam and Antwerp with the Baltic Region, 1400–1800.* Leiden, 1983.

Wiese, H. "Der Rinderhandel im nordwesteuropäischen Küstengebiet vom 15. Jahrhundert bis zum Beginn des 19. Jahrhunderts." *Rinderhandel und Rinderhaltung im nordwesteuropäischen Küstengebiet vom 15. bis zum 19. Jahrhundert.* eds. H. Wiese und J. Bölts. Stuttgart, 1966. 1–129.

Wijnroks, E. H. "Anglo-Dutch Rivalry in Russian Trade in the Latter Half of the Sixteenth Century: A Historiographical Essay." *Baltic Affairs.* eds. J. Ph. S. Lemmink et al. (Nijmegen, 1990), 413–32.

'Onsen haen hort Koninck,' De Nederlands-Russische handelsrelaties vanaf het ontstaan der directe handel op Rusland tot aan het gezantschap van Burghen van Veltdrad naar het hof van de Tsaar, 1550–1630. Nijmegen, 1988.

Wijsenbeek-Olthuis, T. *Achter de gevels van Delft; Bezit en bestaan van rijk en arm in een periode van achteruitgang (1700–1800).* Hilversum, 1987.

Willemsen, R. T. H. W. "Dutch Sea Trade with Norway in the Seventeenth Century." *From Dunkirk to Danzig.* eds. W. G. Heeres et al. 471–82.

Enkhuizen tijdens de Republiek; Een economisch-historisch onderzoek naar stad en samenleving van de 16e tot de 19e eeuw. Hilversum, 1988.

Wills, John E., Jr. *Pepper, Guns, and Parleys. The Dutch East India Co. and China, 1662–1681*. Cambridge, MA, 1974.

Wilson, Charles. *Anglo-Dutch Commerce and Finance in the 18th Century*. Cambridge, 1941.

"Cloth Production and International Competition in the Seventeenth Century." *Economic History Review 12* (1960): 209–21.

Profit and Power: A Study of England and the Dutch Wars. London, 1957.

Winsemius, J. P. *De zeven ambachten en het hoogheemraadschap van Delfland*. Delft, 1962.

Winter, J. M., ed. *War and Economic Development. Essays in Memory of David Joslin*. Cambridge, 1975.

Wiskerke, C. "De geschiedenis van het meekrapbedrijf in Nederland." *Economisch-historisch jaarboek 25* (1952): 1–144.

Woltjer, J. J. "Een Hollands bestuurders te Delft." *De Nederlanden in de late middeleeuwen*. eds. D. E. H. de Boer and J. W. Marsilje. 261–79.

Woud, Auke van der. *Het lege land. De ruimtelijke ordre van Nederland, 1798–1848*. Amsterdam: 1987.

Woude, A. M. van der. "Alfabetisering." *Algemene Geschiedenis der Nederlanden*. 7:257–64.

"De consumptie van graan, vlees en boter in Holland op het einde van de achttiende eeuw." *A. A. G. Bijdragen 9* (1963): 127–53.

"De contractiefase van de seculaire trend in het Noorderkwartier nader beschouwd." *Bijdragen en mededelingen betreffende de geschiedenis der Nederlanden 103* (1988): 373–98.

"De Goldberg-enquête in het Departement van Texel, 1801." *A. A. G. Bijdragen 18* (1973): 95–250.

"Demografische ontwikkeling van de Noordelijke Nederlanden, 1500–1800." *Algemene Geschiedenis der Nederlanden*. 5:102–168.

"The Future of West European Agriculture. An exercise in applied history." *Review. Fernand Braudel Center 15* (1992): 243–56.

Het Noorderkwartier; Een regionaal historisch onderzoek in de demografische en economische geschiedenis van westelijk Nederland van de late middeleeuwen tot het begin van de negentiende eeuw. A. A. G. Bijdragen 16. Wageningen, 1972.

"Landbouw en geschiedenis, een prognose van agrarische ontwikkelingen in Europa in het licht van het verleden." *Europa en de landbouw*. eds. P. C. M. Hoppenbrouwers and A. H. G. Schaars. Wageningen, 1990. 73–96.

"Large Estates and Small Holdings. Lords and Peasants in the Netherlands during the Late Middle Ages and Early Modern Times." *Grand domaine et petites exploitations. Seigneur et paysan en Europe au Moyen Age et aux temps modernes*. eds. P. Gunst and T. Hoffman. Eighth International Economic History Congress. Budapest, 1982.

"Les villes néerlandaises." *Etudes sur les villes en Europe occidentale*. eds. A. Lottin et al. 305–85.

"The Long-term Movement of Rent for Pasture Land in North Holland and the Problem of Profitability in Agriculture (1570–1800)." *Productivity of Land*. eds. H. van der Wee and E. van Cauwenberghe. 171–82.

Nederland over de schouder gekeken. Utrecht, 1986.

"Population Developments in the Northern Netherlands (1500–1800) and the Validity of the Urban Graveyard Effect." *Annales de démographie historique* (1982): 55–75.

"Sex Ratio and Female Labour Participation in the Dutch Republic." *Socio-economic Consequences of Sex-ratios in Historical Perspective*. eds. A. Fauve-Chamoux and S. Sogner. Eleventh Economic History Congress. Milan, 1994. 55–68.

"The Volume and Value of Paintings in Holland at the Time of the Dutch Republic." *Art in History, History in Art*. eds. David Freedberg and Jan de Vries. 285–329.

Woude, A. M. van der, J. de Vries, and A. Hayami. "Introduction." *Urbanization in History. A Process of Dynamic Interaction*. Oxford, 1990. 1–19.

Woude, C. C. van der. "Boekenbezit en boekenconsumptie te Gent en omstreken, 1770–1830." Unpublished M. A. thesis, State University of Ghent, 1986.

748

Wright, H. R. C. *Free Trade and Protection in the Netherlands, 1816–1830.* Cambridge, 1955.

Wrigley, E. A. *Continuity, Chance and Change: The Character of the Industrial Revolution in England.* Cambridge, 1988.

"The Process of Modernization and the Industrial Revolution in England." *Journal of Interdisciplinary History 3* (1973): 225–59.

"Two Kinds of Capitalism, Two Kinds of Growth." *London School of Economics Quarterly 2* (1988): 97–121.

Yntema, Richard J. "The Brewing Industry in Holland, 1300–1800." Unpublished Ph.D. thesis, University of Chicago, 1992.

Ypma, Y. N. *Geschiedenis van de Zuiderzeevisserij.* Amsterdam, 1962.

Ysselsteyn, G. T. van. *Geschiedenis der tapijtweverijen in de Noordelijke Nederlanden.* Leiden, 1936.

Zanden, J. L. van. *Arbeid tijdens het handelskapitalisme; Opkomst en neergang van de Hollandse economie, 1350–1850.* Bergen, 1991. (English trans., *The Rise and Decline of Holland's Economy.* Manchester, 1993.)

De economische ontwikkeling van de Nederlandse landbouw in de negentiende eeuw, 1800–1914. A. A. G. Bijdragen 25. Wageningen, 1985.

"De economie van Holland in de periode 1650–1805: groei of achteruitgang?" *Bijdragen en mededelingen betreffende de geschiedenis der Nederlanden 102* (1987): 562–609.

"Economische groei in Nederland in de negentiende eeuw. Enkele nieuwe resultaten." *Economisch- en sociaal-historisch jaarboek 50* (1987): 51–76.

"Holland en de Zuidelijke Nederlanden in de periode 1500–1700: divergerende ontwikkelingen of voortgaande economische integratie?" *Studia Historica Oeconomica.* eds. E. Aerts et al. 357–67.

"Lonen en de kosten van levensonderhoud, 1600–1850." *Tijdschrift voor sociale geschiedenis 11* (1985): 309–24.

Zanden, J. L. van, and D. J. van der Veen. "Boeren, keuters en landarbeiders. De sociale structuur van Salland aan het begin van de negentiende eeuw." *Tijdschrift voor sociale geschiedenis 10* (1984): 155–93.

Zeeuw, J. W. de. "Peat and the Dutch Golden Age; The Historical Meaning of Energy-attainability." *A. A. G. Bijdragen 21* (1978): 3–31.

Zeiler, F. D. "Kampen textielstad." *Textielhistorische bijdragen 32* (1992): 7–26.

Zijlstra, S. *Des lieven geldes isser aan alle oorden gebrek.* Drentse Historische Studiën. Assen, 1982.

Zwitzer, H. L. *'De militie van den staat'; Het leger van de Republiek der Verenigde Nederlanden.* Amsterdam, 1991.

"Het Quotenstelsel onder de Republiek der Verenigde Nederlanden alsmede enkele beschouwingen over de Generale Petitie, de Staat van Oorlog en de Repartitie." *Mededelingen van de sectie militaire geschiedenis Landmachtstaf 5* (1982): 5–58.

Index